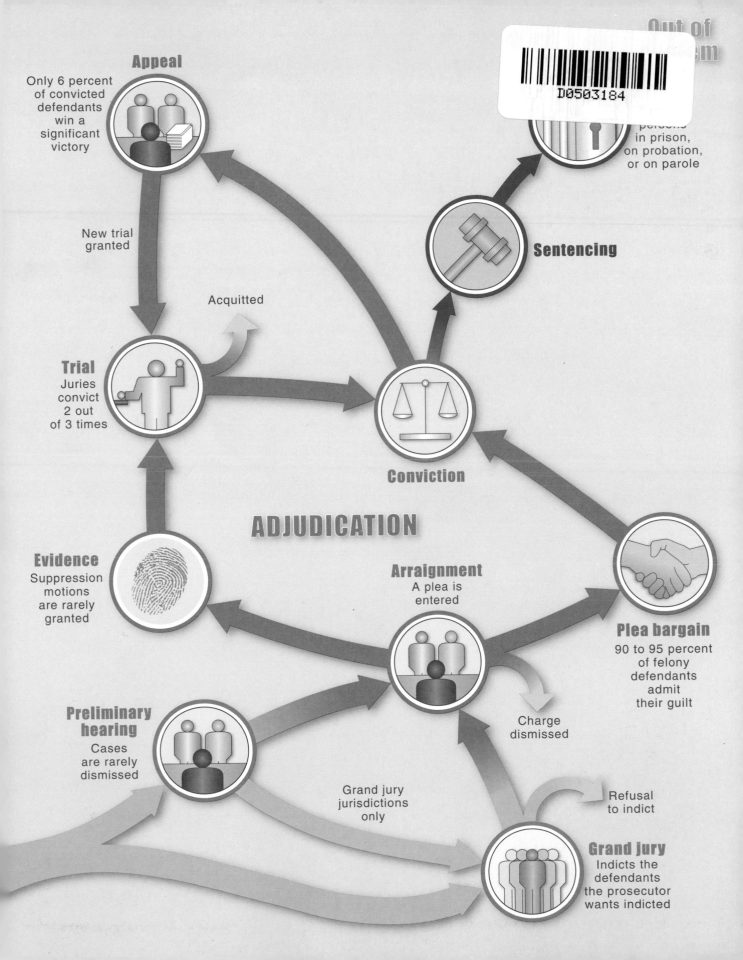

Appeal

Only 6 percent
of convicted
defendants
win a
significant
victory

persons
in prison,
on probation,
or on parole

Sentencing

New trial
granted

Acquitted

Trial
Juries
convict
2 out
of 3 times

Conviction

ADJUDICATION

Evidence
Suppression
motions
are rarely
granted

Arraignment
A plea is
entered

Plea bargain
90 to 95 percent
of felony
defendants
admit
their guilt

Charge
dismissed

**Preliminary
hearing**
Cases
are rarely
dismissed

Grand jury
jurisdictions
only

Refusal
to indict

Grand jury
Indicts the
defendants
the prosecutor
wants indicted

AMERICA'S COURTS

AND THE CRIMINAL JUSTICE SYSTEM

TENTH EDITION

AMERICA'S COURTS

AND THE CRIMINAL JUSTICE SYSTEM

DAVID W. NEUBAUER, PH.D.
UNIVERSITY OF NEW ORLEANS

HENRY F. FRADELLA, J.D., PH.D.
CALIFORNIA STATE UNIVERSITY, LONG BEACH

WADSWORTH
CENGAGE Learning™

Australia • Brazil • Canada • Mexico • Singapore • Spain • United Kingdom • United States

WADSWORTH
CENGAGE Learning™

**America's Courts and the Criminal Justice
System, Tenth Edition**
David W. Neubauer and Henry F. Fradella

Senior Publisher: Linda Schreiber-Ganster

Senior Acquisitions Editor: Carolyn
Henderson Meier

Development Editor: Robert Jucha

Assistant Editor: Megan Power

Editorial Assistant: John Chell

Media Editor: Ting Jian Yap

Senior Marketing Manager: Michelle
Williams

Marketing Assistant: Jillian Myers

Senior Marketing Communications
Manager: Tami Strang

Content Project Manager: Christy Frame

Creative Director: Rob Hugel

Senior Art Director: Maria Epes

Print Buyer: Paula Vang

Rights Acquisitions Account Manager,
Text: Bob Kauser

Rights Acquisitions Account Manager,
Images: Robyn Young

Production Service: Lindsay Burt, MPS
Content Services

Photo Editor: Kelly Franz, Pre-Press PMG

Copy Editor: Debbie Stone

Cover Designer: Riezebos Holzbaur Design
Group

Cover Image: ©Randy Duchaine/CORBIS

Compositor: MPS Content Services

For product information and technology assistance, contact us at
Cengage Learning Customer & Sales Support, 1-800-354-9706.

For permission to use material from this text or product,
submit all requests online at **www.cengage.com/permissions**.
Further permissions questions can be e-mailed to
permissionrequest@cengage.com.

Library of Congress Control Number: 2009929798

ISBN-13: 978-0-495-80990-6

ISBN-10: 0-495-80990-X

Wadsworth
20 Davis Drive
Belmont, CA 94002
USA

Cengage Learning is a leading provider of customized learning solutions
with office locations around the globe, including Singapore, the United
Kingdom, Australia, Mexico, Brazil, and Japan. Locate your local office at
www.cengage.com/global.

Cengage Learning products are represented in Canada by
Nelson Education, Ltd.

To learn more about Wadsworth, visit **www.cengage.com/wadsworth**

Purchase any of our products at your local college store or at our
preferred online store **www.ichapters.com**.

Printed in Canada
2 3 4 5 6 7 13 12 11

FROM DAVID:
TO JEFF, KRISTEN, AND AMY

FROM HANK:
TO THE GREAT MENTORS I HAVE HAD, FOR
THEIR FRIENDSHIP AND GUIDANCE:

HENRY F. DRESSEL, ESQ.
DR. ROBERT L.K. RICHARDSON,
THE HONORABLE STEPHEN M. MCNAMEE,
DR. JOHN R. HEPBURN,
DR. RONALD E. VOGEL, AND
DR. M. SUE STANLEY.

ABOUT THE AUTHORS

DAVID WILLIAM NEUBAUER was born in Chicago. He grew up in Aurora, Illinois, graduating from West Aurora High School in 1962. After receiving a B.A. in political science from Augustana College in Rock Island in 1966, graduating *cum laude* and being elected to Phi Beta Kappa, he began graduate work at the University of Illinois, receiving a Ph.D. in 1971.

Neubauer has previously taught at the University of Florida and Washington University in St. Louis. He is now professor emeritus at the University of New Orleans, where he chaired the political science department from 1982 to 1986.

Neubauer served as a consultant to the Federal Judicial Center on two court management projects, and he worked with the American Judicature Society as principal investigator on a project (funded by the National Institute of Justice) concerning court delay reduction. Over the years he has served on review panels for the National Institute of Justice, the Bureau of Justice Statistics, the National Science Foundation, the National Institute of Mental Health, and the National Center for State Courts. He also served as a consultant to the Metropolitan Crime Commission of New Orleans.

Neubauer is the co-author of *Judicial Process: Law, Courts, and Politics in the United States*, Fifth Edition (2010), co-author of *Battle Supreme: The Confirmation of Chief Justice John Roberts and the Future of the Supreme Court* (2006), and editor of *Debating Crime: Rhetoric and Reality* (2001). All are published by Wadsworth.

HENRY F. FRADELLA was born in New York, NY and grew up in that city and its Monmouth Country, NJ suburbs. After graduating with highest honors from the Searing School in Manhattan in 1986, Fradella earned a B.A. in psychology in 1990 from Clark University, graduating *summa cum laude* and as a member of Phi Beta Kappa. Fradella then earned a masters in Forensic Science and a law degree in 1993 from The George Washington University, and a Ph.D. in interdisciplinary justice studies from Arizona State University in 1997.

Prior to becoming a full-time academic, Fradella worked as an autopsy technician in the Office of the Chief Medical Examiner of Washington, D.C.; practiced law; and worked in the federal courts as a judicial law clerk. He began his career in academia as an assistant professor at The College of New Jersey. After having earned tenure and promotion to the rank of associate and then full professor over 10 years, Fradella resigned from TCNJ in 2007 to become a professor in, and chair of, the Department of Criminal Justice at California State University, Long Beach.

Fradella is the author of over 60 articles, reviews, and scholarly commentaries; three sole-authored books; and three additional books written with co-authors. Four of these six books were published by Wadsworth. Dr. Fradella has guest edited two volumes of the *Journal of Contemporary Criminal Justice*, and served three terms as the legal literature editor for West's *Criminal Law Bulletin*.

Brief Contents

CONTENTS

PART II

LEGAL ACTORS

Chapter 5

The Dynamics of Courthouse Justice 114

Chapter 6

Prosecutors 136

PART IV

SENTENCING THE CONVICTED

Chapter 15

Sentencing Options   370

America's Courts and the Criminal Justice System, Tenth Edition, examines the history, traditions, and philosophy underlying our system of justice as it is played out in the criminal court. In a complex, sometimes contradictory, and often fragmented process, defendants are declared innocent or found guilty, and the guilty are fined, placed on probation, or sentenced to a period of incarceration. This book is about the defendants caught up in the process: the three-time losers, the scared young first offenders, and the business executives who are before the court to answer an indictment. But most of all, this book focuses on the prosecutors, judges, defense attorneys, and jurors who are involved in the daily decisions about guilt or innocence, probation or prison.

The impact of these decisions on crime and criminals is the subject of widespread controversy. Concern over how the courts handle criminal cases has been a staple of American political rhetoric for decades. The nature of this public debate, as well as solutions proposed to correct the problems, are integral parts of this book. To be sure, the last decades have witnessed significant deep-seated changes and readjustments in the criminal justice system—given all the public posturing, one would hardly expect less.

This book is written for undergraduate courses that deal with America's criminal courts. Such courses (or parts of courses) are taught in various departments: criminal justice, criminology, administration of justice, political science, sociology, psychology, and social welfare. This book highlights not only the pivotal role of the criminal courts within the criminal justice system but also the courts' importance and impact on society as a whole.

America's Courts and the Criminal Justice System, Tenth Edition, focuses on the dynamics of the courthouse. Thus, it differs from casebooks, which use appellate court decisions to highlight the history, structure, and philosophy of courts. Although these are important matters, casebooks often project a rather sterile image of courthouse justice and omit what courts do in practice, how they do it, and, most important, why they do it.

This book's emphasis on the dynamics of courthouse justice grows out of our own research. During our professional careers, we have spent considerable time in state and federal courts in all parts of the nation. One of us worked in a federal courthouse; the other has conducted years of field research interviewing numerous judges, jurors, prosecutors, defense attorneys, probation officers, jailers, police officers, and defendants. We have observed these officials in action and discussed with them their problems and their views of possible solutions. By the luck of the draw, one of us has also served on juries in state and federal court, while the other has appeared in court has both a lawyer and as an expert witness. Throughout this book, we have tried to convey to the reader the sense of being in the courthouse.

NEW TO THIS EDITION

Writing the Tenth Edition was gratifying and stimulating. It was gratifying to learn from peer-reviewers that numerous colleagues in the professoriate and their students have found previous editions of the book useful. It was stimulating because it involved closely examining recent changes in both scholarship and public dialogue. The Tenth Edition offers a current perspective on a continually evolving subject: the criminal court process. In this edition, the chapter structure remains the same as in the previous edition, but new topics are included and new special features have been added.

We have made every effort to report the most up-to-date statistics available and to cite current empirical research throughout the Tenth Edition. The Tenth Edition also features a streamlined presentation. The many boxes concerning the murder trial of Shareef Cousin have been eliminated and put on the companion web site for this book. The same is true for all web-related resources, links, and exercises.

TWO CONTINUING FEATURES

The Tenth Edition incorporates two features used in the previous edition.

CASE CLOSE-UP

Each chapter highlights an important court decision that has affected our nation's criminal justice system. Some, like *Miranda* and *Gideon*, are familiar names. Others are less well known. But each highlights the dynamic nature of courts in the United States.

COURTS AND CONTROVERSY

These boxed features provide multiple perspectives on the topics discussed in the chapter. To better focus on the wide-ranging debate surrounding the criminal courts in the United States, these controversies have been given an expanded subhead. Thus, throughout the book, these features will discuss controversies centering on judicial administration, crime reduction, gender equity, racial discrimination, and economic inequality.

A NEW FEATURE

The Tenth Edition incorporates a new feature to illustrate the points raised in each chapter.

LAW AND POPULAR CULTURE

The popular media is filled with stories about America's courts and the people who work in them. The task of thinking critically about how the media both portrays and distorts the justice system is to focus on the contrasting caricatures offered by fictional treatments. Depending on the dramatic needs of the movie or TV show, the police may be portrayed as diligent or brutal, prosecutors pictured as crusaders of justice or preventers of justice determined to convict the easiest suspect, judges presented as insightful masters of the system or politically motivated hacks, defense attorneys projected as crusaders for their clients' interest or corrupters of the justice system, and prison guards presented as understanding human beings or brutal sociopaths. To help students think critically about their media-formed misconceptions about the courts system, each chapter of this book focuses on a film or a television series that relates to one of the chapter's primary themes as depicted on television or in the movies. For a complete list of the television series and movies covered in each chapter's "Law and Popular Culture" box, see pages 5–6.

THREE THEMES

In rewriting the Tenth Edition, we continued with the three themes introduced in the previous editions. Although they have been with the book since the beginning, the new edition's emphasis on the themes of law on the books, law in action, and law in controversy provides a stronger foundation than ever for understanding the court system.

LAW ON THE BOOKS

The starting point of this text is to provide readers with a working knowledge of the major structures and basic legal concepts that underlie the criminal courts. In deciding guilt or innocence and determining the appropriate punishment, the courts apply the criminal law through a complicated process termed *criminal procedure*. The structure of the courts, the nature of the criminal law they apply, and the procedures followed all have important consequences for how the courts dispense justice.

But to understand the legal system, one needs to know more than the formal rules. Also necessary is an understanding of the assumptions underlying these rules, the history of how they evolved, and the goals they seek to achieve. A discussion of the assumptions, history, and goals makes clear that America's criminal justice process is not monolithic but consists of a number of separate and sometimes competing units. It also points out conflicts over the goals the criminal courts are expected to achieve.

Law in Action

Many books leave the false impression that an understanding of the formal law and major structures of the court is all that one needs to know about the criminal courts. This kind of analysis provides only a limited view of how the courts administer justice. The law is not self-executing. It is a dynamic process of applying abstract rules to concrete situations.

In making decisions about charges to be filed, the amount of bail to be required, and the sentence a convicted person will receive, judges, prosecutors, and defense attorneys must make choices for which the formal law provides few precise guidelines. Thus, the second theme of this book is law in action, which emphasizes the dynamics of the criminal court process.

An examination of law in action reveals a gap between how the law is supposed to operate and how it is actually applied. For example, the law in theory suggests that the guilt of defendants should be decided by a jury trial. In practice, however, trials are rare. Most defendants plead guilty without a trial. Asking why there is a gap between the law on the books and the law in action is a big step toward understanding the dynamics of courthouse justice.

Law in Controversy

No treatment of the criminal courts would be complete without a discussion of the problems they are confronting. Are the courts too slow? Are judges too soft in sentencing? Does the criminal court process discriminate against the poor? These are just a few of the questions about the operations of the criminal courts that this book will consider. In turn, many organizations, groups, and individuals have probed the problems facing the criminal courts and proposed reforms. The third theme of this book is to discuss and analyze the controversies surrounding courthouse justice and analyze the reforms that have been suggested for what ails the courts. Not everyone agrees on the types of changes needed. Some argue that certain reforms will produce greater difficulties without solving the original problems. This book examines competing perspectives on the changes and reforms that are being proposed.

Chapter-by-Chapter Changes

Chapter 1—This introductory chapter takes a look at several different public perceptions of the criminal courts on which this text will focus. The new recurring feature for the Tenth Edition, "Law and Popular Culture" is introduced. The "Murder Trial of Shareef Cousin," a recurring feature in each chapter of the previous edition, has been removed from the tenth edition.

Chapter 2—Chapter 2 contains expanded coverage of basic legal issues ranging from presumptions and inferences to the complexities of the different burdens of proof. The summary of the elements of criminal law has been expanded and new examples are provided. The chapter now includes key landmark cases, including *District of Columbia v. Heller* (2008), *Cooper Industries v. Leatherman Tool Group, Inc.* (2001), *Ker v. California* (1963); and *Powell v. Alabama* (1932). The new Law and Popular Culture box features the movie *Chicago* (2000).

Chapter 3—This chapter now includes expanded coverage of the various sub-types of jurisdiction; the most up-to-date information and statistics on the federal judiciary and its caseload (including expanded coverage of federal question jurisdiction, diversity jurisdiction, discrimination and civil rights cases, and the five types of prisoner petitions); more in-depth coverage of the "rule of four" in the certiorari process; recent changes in the processing of enemy combatants; and a broader discussion of the role of the chief justice and the various administrative agencies related to the operation of the federal courts. The Law and Popular Culture box examines the military courts in the film *A Few Good Men* (1992).

Chapter 4—In this chapter, we have judiciously acknowledged the growing importance of specialized courts, especially mental health courts. We also added the most recent research on problem solving courts and updated how the war on drugs continues to affect state court caseloads. The Law and Popular Culture box looks at the hard-hitting movie *Traffic* (2000).

Chapter 5—In this chapter on the courthouse and the individuals who work there, we have included the latest research on court delay and information on the professionalization of court administration. And, the section on variability in courtroom work groups has been revised to incorporate Ostrom et. al's book *Trial Courts as Organizations* (2007). The Law and Popular Culture feature looks at the courtroom workgroup on long running television show *Law and Order*.

Chapter 6—Prosecutors are the focus of this chapter. We include a discussion of the recent high profile Duke lacrosse player rape prosecution. A new Table 6.1 on state court prosecutors' offices is found in the chapter. The Law and Popular Culture box focuses on the conflicts prosecutors experience between the desires of a crime victim and the realities of getting a criminal conviction as illustrated in the 1988 film *The Accused*.

Chapter 7—The chapter on defense counsel now includes expanded and up-to-date coverage on defenders' caseloads and of case law concerning the right to counsel, self-representation, and ineffective assistance of counsel. The new Law and Popular Culture box in this chapter looks at the "win at all costs" persona of the unethical attorneys on the television show, *Boston Legal*, noting the difference over time in media depictions of defense lawyers.

Chapter 8—The chapter on judges examines the diminished role of the ABA in federal judicial appointments; discusses the growing controversy over judicial elections; analyzes recent social scientific literature on the quality of judges and judicial decision-making; and adds both updated and expanded information concerning judicial diversity issues. The chapter also includes a discussion of the Breyer Commission Report (2006) and the 2008 Judicial Conference Rules for Judicial-Conduct and Judicial-Disability Proceedings. Several new cases are cited, including the West Virginia judicial election case (*Caperton v. Massey Coal*, 2009). The effect that the syndicated television show *Judge Judy* has on public perceptions of judges and judicial behavior is the subject of the Law and Popular Culture box.

Chapter 9—The most current research on both victim and perpetrator demographic characteristics is presented in this revised chapter with a focus on gender, age, and race/ethnicity. A new box explores how the growing population of Hispanics in the United States is reshaping the U.S. justice system. Coverage of the delicate balance between the rights of the accused with those of the victim has been updated to include the U.S. Supreme Court's decision in *Carey v. Musladin* (2009). The Law and Popular Culture feature compares and contrasts the realities of sex crime defendants and victims with

their portrayal on *Law and Order: Special Victims Unit* (1999–present).

Chapter 10—This chapter on the processing of criminal cases explores the most current research on the differences in the quality of arrests and the functions of the grand jury. It also offers an expanded discussion of the differences in the procedures at initial appearances compared to preliminary hearings. There is also a thorough update on white collar crime, highlighted by the well-publicized proceedings against financier Bernard Madoff. The Law and Popular Culture feature examines television news coverage of arrests and pretrial processes.

Chapter 11—This chapter includes an expanded discussion of substandard jail conditions in some communities. The chapter presents the latest research on bail and pretrial detention. The popular and controversial television show *Dog the Bounty Hunter* is the subject of the Law and Popular Culture feature, which explores the often shady world of bounty hunters.

Chapter 12—This chapter includes substantial new content, including: a more in-depth analysis of the rules for disclosing exculpatory or impeachment evidence; expanded coverage of the exclusionary rule and the "fruit of the poisonous tree" doctrine; a more detailed exploration of the search warrant process, including information on affidavits, warrant particularity, and limitations on the execution of search warrants; and coverage of key U.S. Supreme Court decisions concerning search and seizure, especially in the area of warrantless searches. Numerous new case citations are presented. The law of search and seizure as depicted in the futuristic science-fiction motion picture *Minority Report* (2002) is featured in the Law and Popular Culture box.

Chapter 13—The most up-to-date research on plea bargaining is integrated into this chapter, with particular attention paid to the varying ways in which judges are involved in plea negotiations. A newer *Boykin* form is presented as a revised exhibit. The section on "placing the plea agreement on the record" has been updated and expanded to include a discussion of the allocution process. The new Law and Popular Culture feature looks at *American Violet* (2008), a film that chronicles the story of a young black woman falsely accused of drug dealing who must choose whether to accept a plea that would keep her out of prison, or risk up to 25 years of incarceration for a crime she did not commit.

Chapter 14—This chapter has been significantly overhauled since the Ninth Edition to include expanded coverage of: the various types of evidence; the *voir dire* process; *Daubert* and the admissibility of expert testimony; the use and misuse of forensic science in the courtroom, focusing on its roles contributing to wrongful convictions and in exonerating the wrongfully convicted; and the psychological literature about jury selection and jury decision making. The Law and Popular Culture feature compares the reality of forensic science with the "forensic science-fiction" depicted on the top-rated television show *CSI: Crime Scene Investigation*.

Chapter 15—The chapter on sentencing options contains expanded coverage of the philosophical justifications for punishment, including an explanation of empirical studies testing deterrence theory and rehabilitative approach; a new discussion of evidence-based corrections; an expanded discussion of the Prison Litigation Reform Act; analysis of the psychological literature on death-qualified juries; and more in-depth coverage of the death penalty, including several new U.S. Supreme Court cases. The debate over capital punishment is explored through the crippling movie *Dead Man Walking* (1995) in the Law and Popular Culture box.

Chapter 16—This chapter presents the latest developments concerning state and federal sentencing, including changes in the interpretation of sentencing guidelines. Also included are the latest studies on race and sentencing. Prison life as depicted in the classic film *The Shawshank Redemption* (1994) is the subject of the Law and Popular Culture box.

Chapter 17—This chapter has been significantly updated to offer a much more in-depth study of the appeals process. The rewrite includes coverage of appellate standards of review; the increasing controversy regarding citing and using "unpublished decisions" as precedent; the impact of the *Apprendi* decision on appellate caseloads; and an expanded discussion of wrongful convictions. Key cases decided by the Roberts Court are also included. A new Exhibit 17.6 on the Distribution of Types of Criminal Appeals in the Federal Appellate Courts is also presented. The film *Reversal of Fortune* (1990) is discussed in the Law and Popular Culture box to illustrate the rarity of criminal defendants winning on appeal.

Chapter 18—This chapter now includes a new controversy box entitled "Do Traffic Fines Improve Safety or Merely Raise Revenue?" Special attention is paid to the growing use of photo radar and its effect on traffic courts. A discussion of Broken Windows Theory and the impact that its implementation has had on the lower courts is presented. Recent information on drunk driving is also included. The lack of media coverage of the lower courts, with the notable exception of the television show *Night Court*, is the focus of the Law and Popular Culture box.

Chapter 19—This chapter looks at new citations and updated statistics on juvenile crime and transferring juveniles to adult court. The former Epilogue on Courts, Crime and Justice has been eliminated. The depiction of juvenile proceedings in the movie *The Client* (1994) is the subject of the Law and Popular Culture box.

PEDAGOGICAL INNOVATIONS

This edition contains an array of pedagogical aids to facilitate student learning. These include:

- Chapter learning objectives open each chapter and are revisited in the Chapter Review to facilitate student mastery of chapter concepts. The learning objectives are also linked to the text's supplements (test bank and website quizzes) to further advance learning.
- End-of-chapter critical thinking questions provide students with an opportunity to practice their skills in this key area.
- End-of-chapter list of key terms with page references serves as a helpful study tool.
- Suggestions for further reading are offered so students can explore chapter concepts further.
- Numerous exhibits and figures amplify text coverage for easier understanding by students.

SUPPLEMENTS

An extensive package of supplemental aids is available for instructor and student use with this edition of *America's Courts and the Criminal Justice System*.

Supplements are available to qualified adopters. Please consult your local sales representative for details.

FOR THE INSTRUCTOR

- **ExamView® Computerized Testing** Create, deliver, and customize tests and study guides, both in print and online, in minutes with this easy-to-use assessment and tutorial system. ExamView offers both a Quick Test Wizard and an Online Test Wizard that guide you step by step through the process of creating tests, while the unique WYSIWYG capability allows you to see the test you are creating on the screen exactly as it will print or display online. You can build tests of up to 250 questions using up to 12 question types. Using ExamView's complete word processing capabilities, you can enter an unlimited number of new questions or edit existing questions. The updated test bank includes the following for each chapter: 25 multiple-choice questions, 20 true–false questions, 20 fill-in-the-blank questions, and 5 essay questions.

- **Instructor's Resource Manual with Test Bank** The updated and revised *Instructor's Resource Manual* for the Tenth Edition, prepared by Laurie Kubicek of California State University and Pauline Brennan of the University of Nebraska Omaha, provides detailed outlines, key terms and concepts, discussion topics and student activities, recommended readings, critical thinking questions, and testing suggestions that will help you more effectively communicate with your students while allowing you to strengthen coverage of course material.

- **PowerLecture DVD** This instructor resource includes Microsoft® PowerPoint® lecture slides with graphics from the text, making it easy for you to assemble, edit, publish, and present custom lectures for your course. The PowerLecture DVD also includes polling and quiz questions that can be used with the JoinIn on TurningPoint personal response system and integrates ExamView testing software for customizing tests of up to 250 items that can be delivered in print or online. Finally, all of your media teaching resources in one place!

eBANK LESSON PLANS

The Lesson Plans, created by Marcy Hehnly of Chattahoochee Technical College, bring accessible, masterful suggestions to every lesson. The Lesson Plans include sample syllabi, learning objectives, lecture notes, discussion topics, in-class activities, a detailed lecture outline, and assignments. Lesson Plans are available on the PowerLecture resource and the instructor website, or by emailing your local representative and asking for a download of the eBank files.

- **JoinIn™ on Turning Point®** Spark discussion and assess your students' comprehension of chapter concepts with interactive classroom quizzes and background polls developed specifically for use with this edition of *America's Courts and the Criminal Justice System*. Also available are polling/quiz questions that were custom selected to accompany this textbook. Wadsworth's exclusive agreement with TurningPoint lets you run tailor-made Microsoft® PowerPoint® slides in conjunction with the "clicker" hardware of your choice. Enhance how your students interact with you, your lecture, and each other.

- **WebTutor™** Jumpstart your course with customizable, rich, text-specific content within your Course Management System. Whether you want to Web-enable your class or put an entire course online, WebTutor™ delivers. WebTutor™ offers a wide array of resources, including media assets, test bank, practice quizzes, and additional study aids. Visit webtutor.cengage.com to learn more.

- **Criminal Justice Media Library** This engaging resource provides students with more than 300 ways to investigate current topics, career choices, and critical concepts.

- **ABC® Videos** Featuring short, high-interest clips from current news events specially developed for courses including Introduction to Criminal Justice, Criminology, Corrections, Terrorism, and White-Collar Crime, these videos are perfect for use as discussion starters or lecture launchers. The brief video clips provide students with a new lens through which to view the past and present, one that will greatly enhance their knowledge and understanding of significant events and open up to them new dimensions in learning. Clips are drawn from such programs as *World News Tonight*, *Good Morning America*, *This Week*, *PrimeTime Live*, *20/20*, and *Nightline*, as well as numerous ABC News specials and material from the Associated Press Television News and British Movietone News collections.

- **Classroom Activities for Criminal Justice** This valuable booklet, available to adopters of any

Wadsworth criminal justice text, offers instructors the best of the best in criminal justice classroom activities. Containing both tried-and-true favorites and exciting new projects, its activities are drawn from across the spectrum of criminal justice subjects, including introduction to criminal justice, criminology, corrections, criminal law, policing, and juvenile justice, and can be customized to fit any course. Novice and seasoned instructors alike will find it a powerful tool to stimulate classroom engagement.

- **The Wadsworth Criminal Justice Resource Center** www.cengage.com/criminaljustice Designed with the instructor in mind, this website features information about Wadsworth's technology and teaching solutions, as well as several features created specifically for today's criminal justice student. Supreme Court updates, timelines, and hot-topic polling can all be used to supplement in-class assignments and discussions. You'll also find a wealth of links to careers and news in criminal justice, book-specific sites, and much more.

FOR THE STUDENT

- **Companion Website www.cengage.com/ criminaljustice/neubauer** The new companion website provides many chapter-specific resources, including chapter outlines, learning objectives, glossary, flash cards, crossword puzzles, and tutorial quizzing.
- *Handbook of Selected Supreme Court Cases,* **Third Edition** This supplementary handbook covers nearly 40 landmark cases, each of which includes a full case citation, an introduction, a summary from WestLaw, excerpts from the case, and the decision. The updated edition includes *Hamdi v. Rumsfeld, Roper v. Simmons, Ring v. Arizona, Atkins v. Virginia, Illinois v. Caballes,* and much more.
- **Careers in Criminal Justice Website** Featuring plenty of self-exploration and profiling activities, the interactive Careers in Criminal Justice website helps students investigate and focus on the criminal justice career choices that are right for them. Includes interest assessment, video testimonials from career professionals, resume and interview tips, and links for reference.
- **CL eBook** CLeBook allows students to access Cengage Learning textbooks in an easy-to-use online format. Highlight, take notes, bookmark,

search your text, and, in some titles, link directly into multimedia: CLeBook combines the best aspects of paper books and ebooks in one package.

ACKNOWLEDGMENTS

Writing the Tenth Edition was made easier by the assistance and encouragement of people who deserve special recognition. First and foremost, we would like to thank the Wadsworth criminal justice team, who provided a fresh perspective on the new edition: Carolyn Henderson Meier (senior acquisitions editor) and Robert Jucha (developmental editor).

We are also grateful to the gifted production team who turned raw manuscript into a polished book and dispensed good cheer along the way, especially Lindsay Burt and Juli Cook. As always, colleagues from a number of schools and institutions offered valuable critiques. They include George Cole (University of Connecticut), Paul Wice (Drew University), Stephan Meinhold (University of North Carolina–Wilmington), and Chris DeLay (University of Louisiana–Lafayette).

As always, David's wife and children deserve a special note of thanks for their love and support. He dedicates the book to his children, in response to their bemusement at the idea that Daddy was busy writing a book.

Hank thanks David for asking him to become a co-author on this most influential of books. Dave, I was honored when you selected me to assist with this project and I enjoyed working with you immensely. Hank's partner Kyle also deserves special thanks for being supportive and putting up with his long hours of work on the book even when it meant feeling neglected.

David W. Neubauer   **Henry F. Fradella**
Slidell, Louisiana   **Irvine, CA**

REVIEWERS OF AMERICA'S COURTS AND THE CRIMINAL JUSTICE SYSTEM

Special thanks are due to the reviewers of this and all previous editions.

Patricia A. Binfa
Westwood College

Mark S. Brown
University of South Carolina

Reynolds N. Cate
St. Mary's University

Vincent R. Jones, Esq.
Governors State University

Linda Robyn
Northern Arizona University

James Alfini
American Judicature Society

Ruben Auger-Marchand
Indiana University; Purdue University

E. Stan Barnhill
University of Nevada–Reno

Barbara Belbot
University of Houston–Downtown

Larry Berkson
American Judicature Society

Anita Blowers
University of North Carolina–Charlotte

Paula M. Broussard
University of Southwestern Louisiana

Frank Butler
Temple University

Elizabeth Callahan
Lincoln University

Kathleen Cameron-Hahn
Arizona State University

Bill Clements
Norwich University

Glenn S. Coffey
University of North Florida

George Cole
University of Connecticut

Beverly Blair Cook
University of Wisconsin–Milwaukee

Mark Dantzker
Loyola University of Chicago

Erika Davis-Frenzel
Indiana University of Pennsylvania

Chris DeLay
University of Louisiana–Lafayette

Max Dery
California State University–Fullerton

Thornton Douglas
University of Illinois–Chicago

Mary Ann Farkas
Marquette University

Roy Flemming
Wayne State University

David O. Friedrichs
University of Scranton

James A. Gazell
San Diego State University

Marc Gertz
Florida State University

Gary S. Green
Minot State University

Pamela L. Griset
University of Central Florida

Joseph Hanrahan
Westfield State University

Peter Haynes
Arizona State University

Michael Hazlett
Western Illinois State University

Edward Heck
University of New Orleans

Ellen Hockstedler
University of Wisconsin–Milwaukee

Lou Holscher
Arizona State University

N. Gary Holten
University of Central Florida

Kimberly Keller
University of Texas–San Antonio

Rodney Kingsnorth
California State University–Sacramento

Karl Kunkel
Southwest Missouri State University

Jim Love
Lamar University

Patricia Loveless
University of Delaware

David O. Lukoff
University of Delaware–Newcastle

James Maddex
Georgia State University

Stephen Meinhold
University of North Carolina–Wilmington

Larry Myers
Sam Houston State University

Elizabeth Pelz
University of Houston–Downtown

Richard Perry
San Jose State University

Eric Rise
University of Delaware

John Paul Ryan
American Judicature Society

Joseph Sanborn
Glassboro State College

Jefferey M. Sellers
University of Southern California

Jose Texidor
Penn State University

David O. Thysens
Saint Martin's College

Frederick Van Dusen
Palm Beach Community College

Donald Walker
Kent State University

Russell Wheeler
Federal Judicial Center

Paul Wice
Drew University

Sheryl Williams
Jersey City State College

Nancy Wolfe
University of South Carolina

1

COURTS, CRIME, AND CONTROVERSY

Rock music producer Phil Spector, center, stands with his attorney Doron Weinberg, left, as the verdict is read at his second-degree murder trial in Los Angeles in 2009. Spector was convicted in the shooting death of film actress Lana Clarkson at his mansion six years earlier. While trials of famous celebrities garner intense media coverage, such celebrated cases are relatively rare. Indeed, law and crime as depicted in both media and popular culture often differ significantly from the realities of day-to-day operations of the criminal justice system.

CHAPTER OUTLINE

LEARNING OBJECTIVES

After reading this chapter you should be able to:

1. Indicate in what ways the case of *House v. Bell* differs from a typical felony prosecution.

2. Describe how the courts are related to the other components of the criminal justice system.

3. Discuss the major types of courts found in the United States.

4. Identify the most important actors in the courthouse.

5. List the steps in a typical felony prosecution.

6. Explain how a law in action perspective complements a law on the books approach to studying the criminal courts.

7. Distinguish between the crime control model of criminal justice and the due process model of criminal justice.

The semen on the panties and nightgown of Carolyn Muncey belong to her husband and not the defendant, argued a lawyer for death row inmate Paul House. The existence of new technology, the lawyer argued—DNA tests that weren't available when House was convicted over 20 years ago—means House deserves a new trial. The DNA evidence is immaterial, countered the lawyer for the State of Tennessee; House doesn't deserve yet another hearing in federal court over his state court conviction because the semen was not an essential part of the evidence presented at his initial trial.

At first glance, arguments like these seem commonplace. After all, lawyers make arguments like these every working day in courthouses across the nation, and actors, playing the role of lawyers, make similar arguments almost every night on television. But this argument was hardly typical, because it was made before the U.S. Supreme Court. For the first time ever, the nation's highest court was considering a case brought by a death row inmate who was trying to use DNA evidence to prove his innocence.

The widespread use of DNA evidence to convict guilty defendants at trial and exonerate the innocent on appeal is just one example of the dynamic nature of the legal system in the United States. Changes in science and technology have had a dramatic impact on evidence introduced during trial. Although courts and law have a long history that provides stability, this does not mean that courts and law are static institutions. On the contrary, changes in society end up in courthouses in a variety of ways. At times, specific events are the catalyst for change. In the aftermath of the terrorist attacks of September 11, 2001, for example, courts have wrestled with questions about the scope of electronic eavesdropping and whether alleged Al-Qaeda terrorists can be held in the U.S. military prison at Guantanamo Bay without trial. At other times, courts have been forced to adapt to changes in other branches of government. Legislatures across the nation, for example, have launched wars on drugs that have flooded the courts with a growing number of cases even as other crime decreases. Likewise, changes in public opinion affect how justice is administered. Concerned about crime rates that are too high, the public has demanded that judges get tough with criminals. Even changes in popular culture affect America's legal institutions. The popularity of crime-themed television shows like *Law & Order* and *CSI*, for example, has prompted jurors to expect sophisticated forensic evidence in even the most mundane cases. (see Law and Popular Culture box).

Courts are independent from the other branches of government, but this does not mean that they are divorced from the society they serve. Rather, societal issues impact the kinds of cases brought to court and how they are handled. Concerns about gender equity have prompted a closer look at how courts handle domestic violence and at district attorneys who too often fail to prosecute sexual assaults. That crime and poverty are so intertwined leads some to question whether legal officials turn their backs on white-collar crimes. The persistence of racial inequalities leads some to question why minorities are underrepresented as judges and overrepresented in the nation's prisons.

How courts adapt to change is important. And while change in society is inevitable, it is also unsettling. Simply stated, change produces controversy. A good deal of this book examines the controversy surrounding courts and crime.

COURTS AND CRIME

Carolyn Muncey disappeared from her rural Tennessee home late one Saturday night. The next afternoon two neighbors found her body dumped in the woods a short way down the bank leading toward the creek. She had a black eye, bloodstains on her wrists, and bruises on her legs and neck. The county medical examiner testified that the cause of death was a severe blow to the left forehead, causing a hemorrhage to the right side of the brain.

LAW AND POPULAR CULTURE

Overview

"The long-running TV drama *Perry Mason* inspired me to become a lawyer," observed Supreme Court Justice Sonia Sotomayor during her Senate confirmation hearing. The even longer running TV drama *Law & Order* has no doubt inspired a younger generation to become lawyers, judges, and/or police officers. But no matter the particular fictional episode or the specific generation, the general point is clear—much of what we learn about law and courts is influenced by what we watch on TV or view at the movies. The opposite also provides true—the activities of judges, prosecutors, and defense attorneys are influenced by jurors' perceptions of law derived from the media.

The media, including TV, radio, newspapers and magazines, provide coverage of sensational crimes and major trials. The media also use horrendous crimes and sensational trials to entertain. Increasingly, the line between fact and fiction is blurred. Richard Sherwin, a former prosecutor, argues in his book *When Law Goes Pop* that the line between law and popular culture is vanishing (2002). What lay citizens see on a fictional TV show like *Law & Order* is what they expect to see when they sit as jurors in factual trials, which means that real life judges, prosecutors, and defense attorneys need to shape their presentations around the activities of fictional judges, prosecutors, and defense attorneys.

From the perspective of a book on *America's Courts and the Criminal Justice System,* the extensive media attention to law has major advantages. Media coverage of real trials and portrayals of fictitious ones provide dramatic illustrations that the outcome is influenced by the law (law on the books), the actions of people (law in action), and the disagreements that result (law in controversy). The same can be said for police drug busts, prosecutors' decisions to seek the death penalty,

defense attorneys cross-examining witnesses, and judges' decisions to admit evidence. But there are disadvantages as well. In trying to dramatize occasionally dull legal proceedings, the media coverage can distort reality. This is especially a concern when jurors expect to be dazzled with the forensic scientific evidence they see on shows like *Forensic Files, Bones, Dr. G.,* and the various iterations of *CSI* (Tyler 2006). Media coverage can provide caricatures, not pictures, of courts and the criminal justice system. Thus, at times, a principal task of a book on courts and the criminal justice system is to encourage readers to "unlearn" what they think they know.

The task of thinking critically about how the media both portrays and distorts the justice system is to focus on the contrasting caricatures offered by fictional treatments. Depending on the dramatic needs of the movie or TV show, the police may be portrayed as diligent or brutal, prosecutors pictured as crusaders of justice or preventers of justice determined to convict the easiest suspect, judges presented as insightful masters of the system or politically motivated hacks, defense attorneys projected as crusaders for their clients' interests or corrupters of the justice system, and prison guards presented as understanding human beings or brutal sociopaths.

To highlight the importance of law and popular culture, each chapter of this book focuses on a film or a television series, that relates to the substance of that chapter, as follows:

Chapter	Law and Popular Culture Box
2	*Chicago* (2002)
3	*A Few Good Men* (1992)
4	*Traffic* (2000)
5	*Law and Order* (1990–present)

CONTINUED

Overview

As you watch these or other TV shows and movies about the legal system, be prepared to answer the following questions:

1) To what extent does the film or TV show stress flaws in the legal system? Who is at fault and why? As you compare various segments, are the flaws similar or different?

2) To what extent does the film or TV show accurately depict the American legal system? To what extent does it distort reality?

3) In the end, is "justice" done and if so, how? Is the "justice" arrived at in this segment similar to or different from the "justice" arrived at in other segments.

The murder of Carolyn Muncey provides a poignant example that crime has been a pressing national concern for decades. Newspapers headline major drug busts. Local television news broadcasts graphic footage of the latest murder scene. Not to be outdone, the national media offer tantalizing details on the latest sensational crime or prominent criminal. Meanwhile, official government statistics document that levels of crime are high (but declining), and unofficial pollsters report that Americans believe crime rates are too high. These concerns prompt governmental response. Candidates for public office promise that, if elected, they will get tough on criminals. Government officials, in turn, announce bold new programs to eradicate street crime, reduce violence, and end the scourge of drugs. In some areas, most notably in New York City and San Diego, such crime control efforts significantly reduced crime (Corman and Mocan 2005; Jacobson 2005). Such efforts, however, have been less effective in other areas of the United States, where street crime remains a volatile, persistent, and intractable issue.

A good deal of the political rhetoric about crime focuses on the criminal courts. Prosecutors are viewed as being too ready to engage in plea bargaining. Judges are accused of imposing unduly lenient sentences. Appellate courts are blamed for allowing obviously guilty defendants to go free on technicalities. Meanwhile, the police complain that Supreme Court decisions handcuff the fight against crime. Victims of crime become frustrated by lengthy trial delays. Witnesses protest wasted trips to the courthouse. Judges and defense attorneys—much more so than police chiefs and prison wardens—are blamed for high crime rates.

The purpose of this chapter is to build on public perceptions of the criminal courts by focusing on a few basic topics. We begin by discussing where the courts fit in the criminal justice system.

Next, attention shifts to the three activities that set the stage for the rest of the book:

- Finding the courthouse
- Identifying the actors in the courthouse
- Following the steps of the process

As we will see shortly, the judicial process is complicated, so throughout this book we will examine the courts from three complementary perspectives:

- Law on the books
- Law in action
- Courts and controversy

The "law on the books" perspective helps us understand the legal foundations of our nation's criminal justice system. The "law in action" perspective helps us understand how discretionary decisions are made within the context of the formal law. Finally, the "courts and controversy" perspective helps us think about policy choices, priorities, potential reforms to the system, and what directions such reforms should take.

THE COURTS AND THE CRIMINAL JUSTICE SYSTEM

The Union County sheriff took the lead in the Muncey murder investigation, aided by the Tennessee Bureau of Investigation. Suspicion quickly focused on Paul House after a family friend reported seeing him near the Muncey house before the body was discovered. During a voluntary interview in the local jail, House didn't help his case by making false statements to the police. Later, two local law enforcement officers drove the evidence overnight to the FBI crime lab in Washington, D.C. These officials also contacted Utah officials because Paul House was on parole following a 5-year sentence for sexual assault in that state. Since his arrest, House had been confined in prison by numerous jail guards and prison wardens. Indeed, the respondent in his case, Ricky Bell, is the warden of the Riverbend Maximum Security Institution, which holds most of the state's death row inmates. And as we will discuss shortly, numerous lawyers and judges in state and federal court also played a role.

The diverse people and agencies involved in the arrest, prosecution, and conviction of Paul House for the murder of Carolyn Muncey provides an insight into the size and complexity of the criminal justice system in the United States. Fighting crime is a major societal activity. Every year, local, state, and federal governments spend $214 billion on the criminal and civil justice system in the United States (Bureau of Justice Statistics 2009). These tax dollars support an enormous assortment of criminal justice agencies, which in turn employ a large (and growing) number of employees; approximately 2.5 million people earn their living working in the criminal justice system. These government officials are quite busy: Every year the police make more than 14 million arrests, and every day correctional personnel supervise 7.3 million people. Yet as large as these figures are, they still underestimate societal activity directed against crime. A substantial number of persons are employed in the private sector in positions either directly (defense attorneys and bail agents) or indirectly (locksmiths and private security) related to dealing with crime (Hakim, Rengert, and Shachmurove 1996; Ribovich and Martino 2007).

The numerous public agencies involved in implementing public policy concerning crime are referred to as the **criminal justice system**. Figure 1.1 depicts the criminal justice system as consisting of three overlapping circles: Police are responsible for apprehending criminals; the courts are responsible for deciding whether those arrested are legally guilty and, if so, determining the sentence; corrections is responsible for carrying out the penalty imposed on the guilty.

The major components of the criminal justice system do not make up a smoothly functioning and internally consistent organization. Rather, the criminal justice system is both interdependent and fragmented.

AN INTERDEPENDENT CRIMINAL JUSTICE SYSTEM

Viewing the various components of criminal justice as a system highlights the fact that these different agencies are interdependent and interrelated. Police, courts, and corrections are separate government institutions with different goals, histories, and

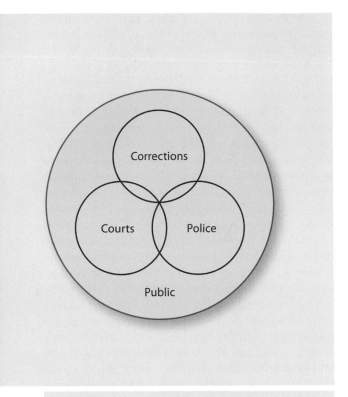

FIGURE 1.1 THE OVERLAPPING CIRCLES OF THE CRIMINAL JUSTICE SYSTEM

operating procedures. Though separate, they are also tied together because they must interact with one another. The courts play a pivotal role within the criminal justice system because many formal actions pertaining to suspects, defendants, and convicts involve the courts. Only the judiciary can hold a suspect in jail prior to trial, find a defendant guilty, and sentence the guilty person to prison. Alternatively, of course, the courts may release the suspect awaiting trial, find the suspect not guilty, or decide to grant probation.

The decisions that courts make have important consequences for other components of the criminal justice system. Judges' bail policies, for example, immediately affect what happens to a person arrested by the police; likewise, corrections personnel are affected because the bail policies of the judges control the size of the local jail population. If the decisions made by the courts have important consequences for police and prisons, the reverse is equally true: The operations of law enforcement and corrections have a major impact on the judiciary. The more felons the police arrest, the greater the workload

of the prosecutors; and the more overcrowded the prisons, the more difficult it is for judges to sentence the guilty.

A FRAGMENTED CRIMINAL JUSTICE NONSYSTEM

The system approach to criminal justice dominates contemporary thinking about criminal justice. But not everyone is convinced of the utility of this conceptualization. Some people point to a nonsystem of criminal justice. Although the work of the police, courts, and corrections must, by necessity, overlap, this does not mean that their activities are coordinated or coherent. From the perspective of the nonsystem, what is most salient is the fragmentation of criminal justice. Fragmentation characterizes each component of the criminal justice system. The police component consists of more than 17,000 law enforcement agencies, with varying traditions of cooperation or antagonism. Likewise, the corrections component includes more than 1,820 state and federal correctional facilities, to say nothing of thousands of local jails. But corrections also encompasses probation, parole, drug treatment, halfway houses, and the like.

The same fragmentation holds true for the courts. In many ways, talking about courts is misleading, because the activities associated with "the court" encompass a wide variety of actors. Many people who work in the courthouse—judges, prosecutors, public defenders, clerks, court reporters, bailiffs—are employed by separate government agencies. Others who work in the courthouse are private citizens, but their actions directly affect what happens in this governmental institution; defense attorneys and bail agents are prime examples. Still others are ordinary citizens who find themselves in the courthouse either because they are compelled to be there (defendants and jurors) or because their activities are essential to the disposition of cases (victims and witnesses).

The fragmentation within the three components of the nonsystem of criminal justice is compounded by the decentralization of government. American government is based on the principle of federalism, which distributes government power between national (usually referred to as federal) and state governments. In turn, state governments create local units of government, such as counties and cities. Each of these levels of government is associated with its own array of police, courts, and corrections.

This decentralization adds tremendously to the complexity of the American criminal justice system. For example, depending on the nature of the law allegedly violated, several different prosecutors may bring charges against a defendant, including the following: city attorney (local), district attorney (county), attorney general (state), U.S. attorney (U.S. district court), and U.S. attorney general (national).

TENSIONS AND CONFLICTS

Criminal justice is best viewed as both a system and a nonsystem. Both interdependence and fragmentation characterize the interrelationships among the agencies involved in apprehending, convicting, and punishing wrongdoers. In turn, these structural arrangements produce tensions and conflicts within each component. For example, the prosecutor may loudly condemn the actions of a judge, or a defense attorney may condemn the jury for an unjust verdict.

Tensions and conflicts occur also among the components of criminal justice. The interrelationships among police, courts, and corrections are often marked by tension and conflict because the work of each component is evaluated by others: The police make arrests, yet the decision to charge is made by the prosecutor; the judge and jury rate the prosecutor's efforts.

Tensions and conflicts also result from multiple and conflicting goals concerning criminal justice. Government officials bring to their work different perspectives on the common task of processing persons accused of breaking the law. Tensions and conflicts among police, courts, and corrections, therefore, are not necessarily undesirable; because they arise from competing goals, they provide important checks on other organizations, guaranteeing that multiple perspectives will be heard.

FINDING THE COURTHOUSE

Because the murder occurred in Union County, Tennessee, the courts in that county first heard the case. After his arrest, Paul House was brought to the County Court of Union County for an initial appearance and was later tried in the Circuit Court of Union County. Later, his conviction would be reviewed by two levels of Tennessee courts and all levels of the federal judiciary. By rough count, over the

next 20 years his case was heard in eight courts with at least 42 judges playing some role. The *House* case is atypical because it is a death penalty case; ordinary felonies rarely involve this many courts or this many judges. Nonetheless, it begins to illustrate the complexity of the court system in the United States.

The criminal justice system, as argued here, is both a system and a nonsystem, tied together by core tasks but also marked by tensions and conflicts. The same holds true for the courts. Judges, prosecutors, and defense attorneys, for example, share the common task of processing cases but at the same time exhibit different perspectives on the proper outcome of the case. Understanding this complexity, in *America's Courts and the Criminal Justice System* we examine the nation's judiciary from three complementary perspectives. Part I is about finding the courthouse, or the basic organization of our court system; Part II concerns identifying the actors in the courthouse; and Part III focuses on following the steps of the process from arrest to appeal.

By rough count, 17,000 courthouses are operating in the United States. Some are imposing turn-of-the-century buildings noted for their elaborate architecture. Others are faceless modern structures marked by a lack of architectural inspiration. A few courts, you might be surprised to learn, are in the front of a funeral parlor or the back of a garage, where justices of the peace preside in rural areas. Buildings aside, courts are governmental organizations created to hear specific types of cases. Figure 1.2 offers a preliminary overview of different types of courts in the United States.

One distinction is between federal and state courts. The term *dual court system* refers to separate state and federal courts (rarely do cases move from one system to the other).

Another important difference between courts relates to function. Most courts are trial courts. As the name implies, this is where trials are held, jurors sworn, and witnesses questioned. Trial courts are noisy places resembling school corridors between classes. Amid the noisy crowd you will find lawyers, judges, police officers, defendants, victims, and witnesses walking through the building during working hours.

Trial courts, in turn, are divided between major and lower. Lower courts initially process felony cases (set bail, for example) but cannot find the defendant innocent or guilty and therefore cannot sentence. Their primary activity involves processing the millions of minor offenses such as public drunkenness, petty theft, and disorderly conduct. Major trial courts, on the other

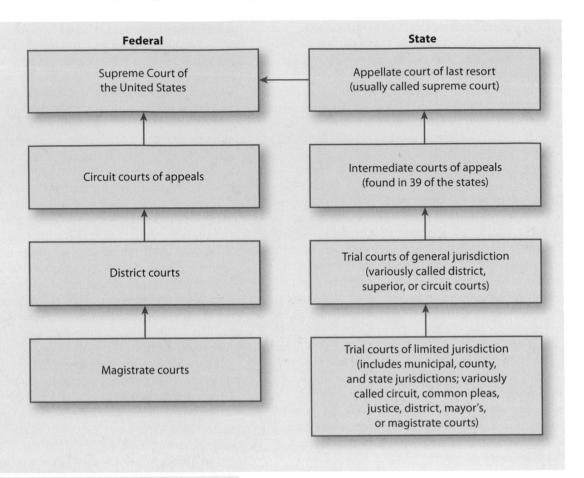

FIGURE 1.2   OVERVIEW OF COURT STRUCTURE IN THE UNITED STATES

hand, are responsible for the final phases of felony prosecutions. In these courts, defendants charged with crimes such as murder, robbery, burglary, and drug dealing enter a plea of guilty (or occasionally go to trial), and the guilty are sentenced.

Other courts (fewer in number) are appeals courts that review decisions made by trial courts (usually only the major trial courts). Appeals courts review decisions made elsewhere, but no trials are held, no jurors employed, no witnesses heard. Rather, appellate courts are places where lawyers argue whether the previous decision correctly or incorrectly followed the law. In many ways, appellate courts are like a monastery, where scholars pore over old books and occasionally engage in polite debates. Given the growing volume of cases, the federal government

and most states have created two levels of appellate courts: intermediate courts, which must hear all cases, and supreme courts, which pick and choose the cases they hear.

Although the U.S. Supreme Court stands atop the organizational ladder, it hears only a handful of the cases filed each year (fewer than 80 per year). Thus, its importance is measured not in terms of the number of cases decided but in the wide-ranging impact these few decisions have on all stages of the process.

IDENTIFYING THE ACTORS IN THE COURTHOUSE

The main courtroom in the Union County courthouse was no doubt full when Paul House was tried for capital murder in 1985. Sitting at one table were the prosecutors; at another, the defendant and his defense attorneys. Immediately in front of these two tables was the judge, sitting high on the bench with several key court staff arrayed below him. On one side was the witness chair, which during the course of the trial was occupied by friends and family of the deceased as well as various law enforcement officers. And on the other side was the jury box, filled with local citizens. The jury found House guilty of murder and sentenced him to death.

All of these persons in the *House* case are important. For this reason, Part II focuses on the actors in the courthouse. Enter a trial courtroom, and you will observe numerous people either busily engaged in doing something or seemingly doing nothing. Some of the actors in the courthouse are easily identifiable by the clothes they wear. The person sitting high above everyone else and wearing the black robes is the judge. The person in handcuffs arrayed in a bright

orange jumpsuit is the defendant. And the men and women dressed in uniforms are law enforcement officers. But the roles being performed by the others in attendance are not readily apparent. It is clear that those sitting in front of the railing are more important than those in back of it. Until court proceedings begin, the observer is never sure whether they are victims, defendants, family, witnesses, reporters, potential jurors, or retired citizens whose hobby is court watching. After the proceedings begin, the roles of those in back of the railing become more apparent.

Some participants are present on a regular basis; others, only occasionally. Many are public employees, but some are private citizens. Using the categories applied to the criminal justice system, Table 1.1 provides a chart of many of the actors one would expect to see in a courthouse on any given day. Some of the titles vary from place to place. Similarly, the participants vary depending on the type of case. In a

TABLE 1.1
ACTORS IN THE COURTHOUSE

	COURTS			PUBLIC	
POLICE	LAWYERS	COURT SUPPORT STAFF	CORRECTIONS OFFICIALS	REGULAR PARTICIPANTS	IRREGULAR PARTICIPANTS
Federal	Prosecutor	Clerk of court	Probation officer	Bail bondsman	Defendant
State	Public defender	Court reporter	Jail	Newspaper reporter	Victim
Sheriff	Private defense attorneys	Pretrial services	Prison		Witness
Local	Judge	Bailiff	Drug rehabilitation program		Juror
Special districts	Law clerk	Court administrator			Victim advocates
Private security		Victim-/witness-assistance program			
		Rape crisis center			

murder case, for example, a scientist from the crime lab may be presenting evidence, but in a child sexual abuse case, the actors will more likely include a social worker or psychiatrist. A brief overview of the main actors will help set the stage.

PROSECUTORS

The organization of prosecutors in the United States is as fragmented as the courts in which they appear. To limit ourselves only to state courts and state prosecutions, in most states you find one prosecutorial office for the lower courts (typically the city attorney), another for the major trial court (typically called the district attorney or the state's attorney), and yet another at the state level (almost uniformly called the attorney general).

Regardless of the level, prosecutors are the most influential of the courthouse actors. Their offices decide which cases to prosecute, which cases to plea-bargain, and which cases to try. They may also be influential in matters such as setting bail and choosing the sentence.

DEFENSE ATTORNEYS

The U.S. Constitution guarantees defendants the right to counsel. But for most defendants this abstract "right" collides with economic reality. Many defendants cannot afford to hire a lawyer, so the government must provide one at government expense, either a court-appointed lawyer or a public defender. Only a handful of defendants hire a private lawyer.

Our notions of defense attorneys have been shaped by fictional characters who are always able to show that their clients are innocent. Reality is strikingly different. Often defense attorneys urge their clients to plead guilty based on the assessment that a jury will find the defendant guilty beyond a reasonable doubt. Even when cases are tried, defense attorneys only occasionally are able to secure a not-guilty verdict for their clients.

JUDGES

Judges in state courts are by and large elected by the voters. Federal judges, on the other hand, are nominated by the president of the United States and confirmed by the U.S. Senate.

Judges are the ultimate authority figures in the courthouse because only judges can set bail, only judges can instruct jurors about the meaning of the law, and only judges can impose sentences. Exercising this authority, though, is limited by the reality of high caseloads. The quickest way to dispose of cases is by a plea of guilty. Thus, judges must be responsive to prosecutors and defense attorneys if they are to achieve their principal goal of disposing of cases.

DEFENDANTS AND THEIR VICTIMS

Defendants are, by and large, young, poor, and uneducated males. A large percentage stand accused of property crimes (theft and burglary) or low-level drug offenses. They are hardly the clever and sophisticated criminals portrayed in fiction. African-Americans and Latinos comprise a disproportionately large percentage of felony defendants, a fact that has placed race and ethnicity at the forefront of the politics of justice (Walker, Spohn, and DeLone 2007).

The victims of crime are playing an increasingly important role in the criminal courts. Once banished to a bit part of testifying, they are increasingly demanding major roles in setting bail, agreeing to pleas of guilty, imposing sentences, and granting release from prison. Groups such as Mothers Against Drunk Driving (MADD) and the National Organization for Victim Assistance (NOVA) have become a potent political force.

FOLLOWING THE STEPS OF THE PROCESS

House v. Bell (2006), the official name of the case we have been following, is atypical for a couple of reasons. For one, a trial was held; most defendants plead guilty rather than go to trial. The *House* case is also atypical because it was successfully appealed to the U.S. Supreme Court; only about 35 criminal cases a year are heard by the nation's highest court. But the fact that it was atypical brings into focus all the steps of the process.

From arrest to appeal, a case passes through numerous stages. Exhibit 1.1 presents the steps of criminal procedure in the order in which they typically occur. These steps are meant to provide only a basic overview. The specifics of criminal procedure vary from state to state, and federal requirements differ from state mandates. Moreover, prosecutions of serious crimes (felonies) are more complicated than prosecutions of less serious offenses (misdemeanors). Rest assured that the remainder of the text will complicate this oversimplification. But for now we will focus on a defendant charged with a

Exhibit 1.1		
STEPS OF CRIMINAL PROCEDURE		
	LAW ON THE BOOKS	**LAW IN ACTION**
Crime	Any violation of the criminal law.	About 12 million serious crimes are reported to the police yearly.
		Property crimes outnumber violent offenses eight to one.
Arrest	The physical taking into custody of a suspected law violator.	About 2.2 million felony arrests are made each year.
Initial appearance	The accused is told of the charges, bail is set, and a date for the preliminary hearing is set.	Occurs soon after arrest, which means the judge and lawyers know little about the case.
Bail	Guarantee that a released defendant will appear at trial.	Every day the nation's jails hold more than 780,000 people.
Preliminary hearing	Pretrial hearing to determine whether probable cause exists to hold the accused.	Cases are rarely dismissed, but the hearing provides the defense attorney a look at the evidence.
Charging decision	Formal criminal charges against the defendant, stating what criminal law was violated.	From arrest to the major trial court, half of cases are dropped.
Grand jury	A group of citizens who decide whether persons accused of crimes should be charged (indicted).	Grand juries indict the defendants the prosecutor wants indicted.
Arraignment	The defendant is informed of the pending charges and is required to enter a plea.	Felony defendant's first appears before a major trial court judge.
Evidence	Formal and informal exchange of information before trial.	Prosecutors turn over evidence of guilt in hopes of obtaining a plea of guilty.
	Defense may seek to have evidence suppressed because it was collected in a way that violates the Constitution.	Suppression motions are rarely granted but are at the heart of a major debate.
Plea negotiations	The defendant pleads guilty with the expectation of receiving some benefit.	About 90 to 95 percent of felony defendants admit their guilt.
Trial	A fact-finding process using the adversarial method before a judge or a jury.	Most likely only in serious cases; defendant is likely to be convicted.

Exhibit 1.1

CONTINUED

	LAW ON THE BOOKS	LAW IN ACTION
Sentencing	Punishment imposed on a defendant found guilty of violating the criminal law.	Seven million persons in prison, on probation, or on parole.
Appeal	Review of the lower-court decision by a higher court.	Only 6 percent of convicted defendants win a significant victory.

noncapital state felony. (The truly unique features of the multiple waves of review of death penalty will be examined in Chapter 17.)

CRIME

The amount of crime in the United States is difficult to quantify precisely, but compared to other industrialized nations it is high. Every year people report about 10.4 million serious crimes to the police (many others are never reported and therefore never make the official statistics). Although the media focus on crimes of violence, the overwhelming majority of crimes involve burglary and theft. Drug offenses, although they are not numerous, are not included in these figures because typically these crimes are not reported to the police.

Legally, crimes fall into three categories: felonies (in most states punishable by 1 year or more in prison); misdemeanors (typically punishable by a sentence in a local jail); and ordinance violations (subject to fine or a short jail term). Felonies are filed in major trial courts, whereas misdemeanor and ordinance violations are typically heard in the lower courts.

ARREST

Every year the police make more than 10.6 million arrests for nontraffic offenses. Most are for minor crimes, but nearly 1.7 million involve serious crimes, such as murder, rape, assault, robbery, burglary, and theft. The police are able to make an arrest in only one out of five crimes known to the police. As a result, only a fraction of the nation's major crimes ever reach the courts.

INITIAL APPEARANCE

An arrested person must be brought before a judge without unnecessary delay. For felony defendants, the initial appearance is largely a formality because no plea may be entered. Instead, defendants are told what crime they are alleged to have committed and perfunctorily advised of their rights, and a date for the preliminary hearing is set. For misdemeanor defendants, the initial appearance is typically the defendant's only courtroom encounter; three out of four plead guilty and are sentenced immediately.

BAIL

The most important event that occurs during the initial appearance is the setting of bail. Because a defendant is considered innocent until proven guilty, the vast majority of defendants have the right to post bail. But this legal right is tied to the defendant's economic status. Many defendants are too poor to scrounge up the cash to pay the bail agent's fee; thus they must remain in jail awaiting trial. The overriding reality, however, is that U.S. jails are overflowing. As a result, pretrial detention is limited largely to defendants who are alleged to have committed serious crimes; judges set a very high bail because they don't want these defendants wandering the streets before trial. For defendants charged with less serious crimes, judges and prosecutors may want to keep them in jail while awaiting trial, but the citizens are not willing to invest the tens of millions of dollars needed to build more jails.

PRELIMINARY HEARING

During the preliminary hearing the prosecutor must prove probable cause to believe the defendant committed the crime. Probable cause involves two elements: proof that a crime was committed and a link between the defendant and that crime. This is not a particularly high or exacting standard of proof, so most of the time the judge finds that probable cause is present and orders the defendant held for further proceedings. In most courthouses, few cases are dismissed at the preliminary hearing for lack of probable cause.

CHARGING DECISION

Sometime after arrest a prosecutor reviews the case, paying particular attention to the strength of the evidence but also keeping in mind office policies on case priorities. Half the time this review results in dismissal. One out of two defendants is lucky indeed; they are released without the filing of criminal charges. But the other half are in deep trouble; their chances of being found not guilty are now slim indeed.

GRAND JURY

Like the preliminary hearing, the grand jury is designed as a check on unwarranted prosecutions. Grand juries are required in all federal felony prosecutions, but only about half the states use them. If the grand jury thinks enough evidence exists to hold the defendant for trial, it returns an indictment (also called a "true bill") charging the defendant with a crime. On rare occasions, grand juries refuse to indict (such refusal is called a "no bill" or a "no true bill"). Legal theory aside, grand juries are dominated by the prosecutor, and they obligingly indict whomever the prosecutor wants indicted.

ARRAIGNMENT

Although the two terms are often used interchangeably, arraignment differs from the initial appearance. During arraignment, the defendant is given a copy of the formal charges, advised of his or her rights (usually more extensively than at the initial appearance), and for the first time is called upon to enter a plea. Not surprisingly, most defendants plead not guilty, but a handful admit their guilt then and there and enter a plea of guilty. Overall, little of importance happens during arraignment; this legal step is somewhat equivalent to taking class attendance.

EVIDENCE

The term *discovery* refers to the exchange of information prior to trial. In some states, but not all, the prosecutor is required to turn over a copy of the police reports to the defense prior to trial. In general, however, the defense is required to provide the prosecutor with little if any information. The formal law aside, many prosecutors voluntarily give defense attorneys they trust extensive information prior to trial, anticipating that the defense attorney will persuade the defendant to enter a plea of guilty.

Motions are simply requests for a judge to make a decision. Many motions are made during trial, but a few may be made beforehand. The most significant pretrial motions relate to how the police gathered evidence. Defense attorneys file motions to suppress evidence—that is, to prevent its being used during trial. Motions to suppress physical evidence contend that the police conducted an illegal search and seizure (*Mapp*). Motions to suppress a confession contend that the police violated the suspect's constitutional rights during questioning (*Miranda*).

PLEA NEGOTIATIONS

Most findings of guilt result not from a verdict at trial but from a voluntary plea by the defendant. Ninety percent of all felony convictions are the product of negotiations between the prosecutor and the defense attorney (and sometimes the judge as well). Although the public thinks of plea bargaining as negotiating a lenient sentence, the reality is that each courthouse has an informal understanding of what a case is worth. Thus, plea bargaining is governed by informal understandings of what sentence is appropriate for a given type of defendant.

TRIAL

Trial by jury is one of the most fundamental rights granted to those accused of violating the criminal law. A defendant can be tried either by a judge sitting alone (called a "bench trial") or by a jury. A jury trial typically begins with the selection of 12 jurors. Each side makes opening statements, indicating what they think the evidence in the case will show. Because the prosecutor has the burden of proving the defendant guilty beyond a reasonable doubt, he or she is the first to call witnesses. After the prosecution has completed its case, the defense has the opportunity to call its own witnesses.

When all the evidence has been introduced, each side makes a closing argument to the jury, and the judge then instructs the jury about the law. The jurors retire to deliberate in secret. Though the details of trial procedure vary from state to state, one factor is constant: The defendant's chances for an acquittal are not good.

SENTENCING

Most of the steps of the criminal process are concerned with determining innocence or guilt. As important as this question is, the members of the courtroom work group spend most of their time deciding what sentence to impose on the guilty. Indeed, defendants themselves are often more concerned about how many years they will have to spend in prison than about the question of guilt.

The principal decision the judge must make is whether to impose a prison sentence or place the defendant on probation. Fines are rarely used in felony cases. The death penalty is hotly debated but in actuality is limited to only some first-degree murder cases. Prison overcrowding is the dominant reality of contemporary sentencing; roughly 1.5 million inmates are incarcerated in state and federal prisons. Only recently has attention begun to focus on the fact that the political rhetoric of "lock them up and throw away the key" has resulted in severe prison overcrowding.

APPEAL

Virtually all defendants found guilty during trial contest their fate, filing an appeal with a higher court in the hope that they will receive a new trial. Contrary to public perceptions, defendants are rarely successful on appeal; fewer than 1 in 10 appellants achieve a significant victory in the appellate courts. Moreover, appeals are filed in only a small proportion of all guilty verdicts; defendants who plead guilty rarely appeal. Appellate court opinions, however, affect future cases because the courts decide policy matters.

LAW ON THE BOOKS

Although the results of DNA testing are routinely introduced into evidence today, DNA testing did not exist when Paul House was convicted of murdering Carolyn Muncey in 1985. Twenty years later, House's lawyers argued that he deserved a new trial not only because the evidence showed that he did not commit the murder but also because the newly discovered evidence proved that her husband was really the guilty party. Although the argument strikes us as pretty straightforward, the legal issues are considerably more complicated. Over the years, House's lawyers had filed petitions in various courts, but along the way, they did not properly present certain constitutional claims in Tennessee court. Legally, this meant that House had defaulted on those claims. Now he could raise these issues in federal court only if he could prove that he was indeed innocent, a much narrower standard than the usual appellate court argument that the defendant deserves a new trial because errors that occurred during the first trial meant that the defendant had not received a fair trial.

Ultimately, the decision in the *House* case involves important aspects of how and when state prison inmates, particularly those on death row, may have their cases reviewed by federal courts. Likewise, court decisions try to specify how the police may legally search, how judges should instruct juries, and what sentences should be imposed on the guilty.

An important first step in understanding how American courts dispense justice is to learn the basic law underlying the process. The structure of the courts, the legal duties of the main actors, and the steps in the criminal process are all basic to understanding how the courts dispense criminal justice. These elements constitute law on the books—the legal and structural components of the judiciary. In essence, the starting point in understanding the legal system is knowing the formal rules.

Law on the books is found in constitutions, laws enacted by legislative bodies, regulations issued by administrative agencies, and cases decided by courts. Little doubt exists that decisions by the U.S. Supreme Court have far-reaching ramifications. To highlight the importance of court decisions, each chapter's Case Close-Up provides an in-depth look at some of the court decisions that have shaped our nation's criminal justice system (see Case Close-Up: Overview).

LAW IN ACTION

Law on the books only partially explains what happened and is happening in the *House* case. Although the formal law was certainly important, it

Overview

Each chapter of this book features a case that has had a major impact on the criminal justice system. Many of these cases are significant U.S. Supreme Court decisions.

Indeed, some of these cases have been absorbed into the English language. *Miranda* and *Mapp,* for example, have almost become household names, and to actors in the system, they are a useful shorthand. Others are less well known but have affected the process in important ways.

Throughout the book, we have tried to stress not only the legal principles involved in the decisions but also the nature of the litigants themselves.

CHAPTER	CASE CLOSE-UP
2	Civil and Criminal Prosecutions of Celebrities
3	Was Zacarias Moussaoui the 20th Hijacker?
4	*Ewing v. California* and Three Strikes Laws
5	*Barker v. Wingo* and the Right to a Speedy Trial
6	*Burns v. Reed* and Prosecutorial Misconduct
7	*Gideon v. Wainwright* and the Right to Counsel

8	*Chisom v. Roemer* and Diversity on the Bench
9	*Payne v. Tennessee* and Victim Impact Statements
10	*County of Riverside v. McLaughlin* and a Prompt Hearing before a Magistrate
11	*U.S. v. Salerno* and Preventive Detention
12	*Miranda v. Arizona* and Limiting Police Interrogations
13	*Santobello v. New York* and Honoring a Plea Agreement
14	*Sheppard v. Maxwell* and Prejudicial Pretrial Publicity
15	*Roper v. Simmons:* Should Juveniles Be Sentenced to Death?
16	*Kimbrough v. United States* and Federal Sentencing Guidelines in Crack Cocaine Cases
17	*House v. Bell* and Federal Court Scrutiny of State Death Row Inmates
18	*North v. Russell* and Nonlawyer Judges
19	*In re Gault* and Due Process in Juvenile Courts

CASE CLOSEUP

cannot totally explain why the jury voted to sentence House to die (other juries in somewhat similar cases vote for life imprisonment). Nor can law on the books explain why some appellate court judges decided that the law meant that House deserved another hearing, but other judges, looking at the same facts and reading the same law, reached the opposite conclusion.

In many ways, law on the books represents an idealized view of law, one that stresses an abstract set of rules that is so theoretical that it fails to incorporate real people. On the one hand, law on the books provides only an imperfect road map of the day-to-day realities of the courthouse. The concept of law in action, on the other hand, focuses on the factors governing the actual application of the law. It stresses that in the criminal courthouses of the United States, few cases ever go to trial. Most defendants plead guilty rather than have their cases tried. Moreover, judges, prosecutors, and defense attorneys devote considerable time to determining the appropriate sentence to impose on the defendant after he or she is found guilty.

COURTS AND CONTROVERSY

Overview

Many of the issues facing other parts of the criminal justice system also confront the courts. Indeed, the courts are often the focus of debates about what the justice system does wrong. Controversy surrounding the courts is widespread and involves a number of issues.

- Controversy over judicial administration centers on issues such as reducing delay and establishing drug courts.
- Controversy over crime reduction involves debates over forcing defendants to take a drug test and abolishing the insanity defense.
- Controversy over gender equity involves debates over gender bias in the courtroom and whether the courts fail to treat domestic violence as a serious offense.
- Controversy over racial discrimination centers on issues such as underrepresentation of minority judges and allegations of discriminatory sentencing.
- Controversy over economic inequality centers on debate over underprosecution of white-collar crimes.

Each chapter of this book examines one or more controversies. To look ahead, here are some of the general controversies facing the courts and some of the specific issues that will be discussed.

CHAPTER	CONTROVERSY
2	Should Asset Forfeiture Be Limited?
3	Should the Double Jeopardy Clause Prohibit Parallel State and Federal Prosecutions? Should State Crimes Also Become Federal Violations?
4	Is It Time to End the War on Drugs?
5	Is Gender Bias a Significant Problem in the Courts?
6	Are Sexual Assaults against Women Underprosecuted?

The law in action perspective stresses the importance of discretion. At virtually every step of the process a choice has to be made whether to move the case to the next step or stop it now. These decisions are made by the legal actors—police, prosecutors, and judges, for example. They are also made by ordinary citizens as well, whether in their role as victims, witnesses, or jurors.

A wide gap exists between legal theory (law on the books) and how that law is applied (law in action). Although some people find this gap shocking, actually it is not; after all, no human institution ever lives up to the high ideals set out for it. If you spend 5 minutes observing a stop sign on a well-traveled street, you will find that not all cars come to a complete stop, and some do not seem to slow down much at all. Yet at the same time, the stop sign (the law on the books in this example) clearly does affect the behavior of drivers (law in action).

In Exhibit 1.1, the law on the books column seems to suggest a streamlined criminal process, with defendants entering at arrest and steadily and methodically moving through the various stages until conviction and sentencing. This is not the reality. The criminal process is filled with numerous detours. At each stage officials decide to advance the defendant's case to the next step, reroute it, or terminate it. The result is that many cases that enter the criminal court process are eliminated during the early stages.

A law in action perspective helps us understand the dynamics of courthouse justice. High caseloads are the reality in courthouses across the nation. As a result, judges are under pressure to move cases lest a backlog develop. Similarly, in most cases the formal rules found in law on the books fail to provide answers to all the questions that arise in a case. As a result, prosecutors must

7	Are We Spending Too Little or Too Much on Indigent Defense?
8	Is Judicial Independence Being Undermined?
9	Should the Victims' Rights Amendment Be Adopted?
10	Are White-Collar Criminals Underprosecuted?
11	Should Defendants Be Forced to Take a Drug Test?
12	Should the Exclusionary Rule Be Abolished?
13	Who Benefits from Plea Bargaining?
14	Should the Insanity Defense Be Abolished? Should Cameras Be Allowed in the Courtroom?

15	Should Restorative Justice Replace Revenge-Based Sentencing? Should a Moratorium on the Death Penalty Be Imposed?
16	Should Federal Penalties for Crack Be Lowered to Remove Racial Disparities? Are "Three Strikes and You're Out" Laws Fair?
17	Should Federal Courthouse Doors Be Closed to State Prisoners? Innocent on Death Row?
18	Should Drunk Driving Prosecutions Be Increased? Do Traffic Fines Improve Safety or Merely Raise Revenue?
19	Should Juveniles Be Tried as Adults?

make discretionary choices about matters such as what sentencing recommendation to make to the judge. Finally, cooperation, rather than conflict during trial, often characterizes the behavior of courthouse actors. As a result, defense attorneys often find that negotiating a plea of guilty, rather than going to trial, is in the best interest of their client.

COURTS AND CONTROVERSY

The *House* case illustrates some of the controversies surrounding courts and crime in the United States. Most immediately, the case involves a long-standing debate over when federal courts should review state court convictions. But in reality this

debate is about the death penalty. Supporters of the death penalty argue that lengthy reviews only undermine the deterrent value of the criminal justice system. Critics of the death penalty counter that extensive reviews are the only way to prevent the execution of an innocent defendant.

At the heart of the public's concern about crime has been a debate over the actions and inactions of the criminal courts. What the courts do (and do not do) and how they do it occupies center stage in the nation's continuing focus on crime. Numerous reforms have been suggested, but no agreement has been reached as to what types of change are in order. Throughout this book, the Courts and Controversy boxes highlight many issues facing the courts that are debated today (see Courts and Controversy: Overview).

In the public dialogue on the issues facing the criminal courts, conservatives square off against liberals, and hard-liners against those said to be soft on crime. This sort of terminology is not very helpful. Such phrases as "soft on crime" attract our attention to questions about the goals of the criminal courts, but they are not useful for systematic inquiry because they are ambiguous and emotional (Neubauer 2001).

More constructive in understanding the controversy over the criminal courts are the crime control and due process models developed by Herbert Packer (1968) and discussed by Samuel Walker (2006). In an unemotional way, these two models highlight competing values concerning the proper role of the criminal courts. The conservative crime control model proposes to reduce crime by increasing the penalties on criminals. The liberal due process model advocates social programs aimed primarily at reducing crime by reducing poverty. Exhibit 1.2 summarizes the two views.

CRIME CONTROL MODEL

The most important value in the **crime control model** is the repression of criminal conduct. Unless crime is controlled, the rights of law-abiding citizens will not be protected, and the security of society will be diminished. Conservatives see crime as the product of a breakdown of individual responsibility and self-control. To reinforce social values of discipline and self-control, and to achieve the goal of repressing crime, the courts must process defendants efficiently. They should rapidly remove defendants against whom inadequate evidence exists and quickly determine guilt according to evidence. The crime control model holds that informal fact-finding—initially by the police and later by the prosecutor—not only is the best way to determine whether the defendant is in fact guilty but also is sufficiently foolproof to prevent the innocent from being falsely convicted. The crime

Exhibit 1.2
COMPETING VALUES IN THE CRIMINAL JUSTICE SYSTEM

	CRIME CONTROL MODEL	DUE PROCESS MODEL
Key value	Repress crime.	Protect rights of citizens.
Causes of crime	Breakdown of individual responsibility.	Root causes are poverty and racial discrimination.
Police fact-finding	Most likely to determine guilt or innocence.	Only formal fact-finding can protect the innocent.
Goal of courts	Process guilty defendants quickly.	Careful consideration of each case.
Rights of defendants	Technicalities let crooks go free.	Price we pay for living in a democracy.
Sentencing	Punishment will deter crime.	Rehabilitation will prevent crime.
Advocacy groups	The National Center for Policy Analysis is an advocacy group often associated with the crime control model of criminal justice. For their views on a variety of criminal justice issues, go to **http://www.ncpa.org/iss/cri.**	The American Civil Liberties Union (ACLU) is often identified with the due process model of criminal justice. For their views on a variety of criminal justice issues, go to **http://www.aclu.org.**

control model, therefore, stresses the necessity of speed and finality in the courts to achieve the priority of crime suppression.

According to the crime control model, the courts have hindered effective law enforcement and therefore have produced inadequate protection of society. Advocates of this model are concerned that criminals "beat the system" and "get off easy." In their view, the cure is to eliminate legal loopholes by curtailing the exclusionary rule, abolishing the insanity defense, allowing for preventive detention of dangerous offenders, and increasing the certainty of punishment.

DUE PROCESS MODEL

In contrast, the **due process model** emphasizes protecting the rights of the individual. Its advocates are concerned about lawbreaking; they see the need to protect the public from predatory criminals. At the same time, however, they believe that granting too much leeway to law enforcement officials will only result in the loss of freedom and civil liberties for all Americans. This alternative diagnosis stresses different causes of crime. Liberals see crime not as a product of individual moral failure but as the result of social influences (Currie 1985). In particular, unemployment, racial discrimination, and government policies that work to the disadvantage of the poor are the root causes of crime; only by changing the social environment will crime be reduced (Currie 1989).

Although adherents of the due process model do not downgrade the need for controlling crime, they believe that single-minded pursuit of such a goal threatens individual rights and poses the threat of a tyrannical government. Thus, the key function of the courts is not the speed and finality projected in the crime control model, but an insistence on careful consideration of each case. The dominant image is one of the courts as an obstacle course. The due process model stresses the possibility of error in the informal fact-finding process and therefore insists on formal fact-finding to protect against mistakes made by the police and prosecutors.

Proponents of the due process model believe that the courts' priority should be to protect the rights of the individual. Any resulting decrease in the efficiency of the courts is the price we must pay

in a democracy based on individual liberties. The due process model emphasizes the need to reform people through rehabilitation. Community-based sentencing alternatives are considered preferable to the extensive use of prison sentences. Advocates of this approach are concerned that the court system is fundamentally unfair to poor and minority defendants; they therefore support the decisions of the Warren Court expanding protections for criminal defendants.

CONCLUSION

Paul House won a victory, but only a narrow one, before the U.S. Supreme Court. By a 5-to-3 margin the Court ruled that he was entitled to a new hearing, but not necessarily a new trial. Later, a federal judge ordered a new trial. Then, in May 2009—1 month before that new trial was to take place—prosecutors dropped the charges against Paul House. The district attorney acknowledged that new DNA evidence raised significant doubt concerning House's involvement in the death of Carolyn Muncey. Accordingly, the new trial was cancelled and House was set free after having spent 22 years on death row. The *House* case represented "a real-life murder mystery, an authentic 'who-done-it' where the wrong man [could have been] executed," according to one of the judges on the U.S. Court of Appeals for the Sixth Circuit who dissented when the intermediate federal court voted to uphold House's conviction without granting him a new trial (*House v. Bell*, 2004, p. 709). Television shows and mystery novels lead us to believe that all or most criminal cases are whodunits. Most are not. Indeed, by the time cases make it as far as the plea stage, the vast majority are slam dunks—all agree the defendant is guilty.

The story line of the murder of Carolyn Muncey is an old one—did the neighbor kill her, or was it her husband? What is new is the role that technology plays in unraveling this plot line. Advanced forensic tests like DNA testing, not available 25 years ago, raise major questions about what seemed certain to the jurors during the original trial—all the evidence pointed to the guilt of House; 22 years later, scientific evidence called that conclusion into doubt. Given rapid advances in science, 25 years from now similar questions may be raised about today's trials.

Courts are often involved in change. In turn, this change can prove unsettling and thus lead to controversy. This book takes a look at many of these controversies, which reflect the conflicting views of the purposes of the criminal justice process as summarized in the crime control versus due process models of justice. The *House* case certainly fits here. Adherents of the crime control model argue that over 20 years of court hearings have eroded the deterrent effect of punishment. It is past time to execute a brutal murderer like Paul House, they argue. Proponents of the due process model stress that it is vitally important to make sure that the defendant is really guilty. Allowing a little more time to make sure that an innocent person is not executed is essential to the notion of justice, they argue.

Ours is a law-drenched age. Voters and elected officials alike see the solution to pressing social problems in terms of passing a law. Somehow we are not serious about an issue unless we have a law regulating it, and we are not really serious unless we have criminal laws. But laws are not self-enforcing. Some people delude themselves by thinking that passing a law solves the problem. This is not necessarily so. Indeed, if the problem persists, frustration sets in. Thus, legislatures mandate that drivers purchase automobile insurance, but accident victims become frustrated when they discover the other party has no insurance. Similarly, judges require defendants to pay restitution, but crime victims discover that impoverished defendants (particularly those in prison) have no ability to pay. In the same vein, conservatives call for preventive detention, but jailers find no jail cells available.

Although most people know something about the law, they also "know" much that is contrary to fact. Some of these public understandings and misunderstandings about law are the product of education. High-school-level American government and history textbooks, for example, offer a simplified, formal picture of law and the courts, lawyers, and trials. Americans also learn about the legal system by going to the movies, watching television, and reading fiction. At times, people who rely on these sources are badly misled. Entertainment programs misrepresent the nature and amount of crime in the United States. Because murder makes a much better show than embezzlement or burglary, entertainment rarely shows street crime other than drug offenses.

Television also offers a number of false or doubtful propositions. It tells us, for example, that criminals are white males between the ages of 20 and 50, that bad guys are usually businesspeople or professional criminals, and that crime is almost always unsuccessful in the end. Television and film also often misrepresent the roles of actors in the legal system. With few exceptions, police are in constant action, chasing crooks in cars, running after them on foot, and capturing them only after exchanging gunfire. Perry Mason set the pattern for atypical portrayals of lawyers by always securing his client's acquittal. In addition, entertainment distorts important issues of civil liberties. As soon as we know who did it and that the guilty crook has been apprehended, the case is solved with no need for the prosecutor to prove the defendant guilty.

These understandings and misunderstandings form the backdrop for this book. The Epilogue will examine in greater depth how and why courts figure so prominently in the public rhetoric over crime.

CHAPTER REVIEW

1. Indicate in what ways the case of *House v. Bell* differs from a typical felony prosecution.

House v. Bell differs from a typical felony prosecution because it was a death penalty case, a jury trial decided guilt, and the appellate process was extensive.

2. Describe how the courts are related to the other components of the criminal justice system.

Law enforcement, courts, and corrections are separate sets of organizations, but they are also interdependent. The courts process cases after suspects are arrested, and corrections handles defendants who are found guilty by the courts.

3. Discuss the major types of courts found in the United States.

In the United States separate systems of federal courts and state courts exist. Within each system one or two levels of trial courts and one or two levels of appellate courts hear cases.

4. Identify the most important actors in the courthouse.

Judges, prosecutors, and defense attorneys are the most important actors in the courthouse. Defendants and victims are also important because they are the source of cases for the courts.

5. List the steps in a typical felony prosecution.

A typical felony prosecution begins with an arrest, followed by an initial appearance, the setting of bail, a preliminary hearing, a charging decision, and grand jury action. If a case survives these hurdles in the lower courts the case is transferred to a major

trial court for arraignment, decisions about evidence, plea negation, and a trial. The guilty are then sentenced, and some guilty parties file an appeal.

6. Explain how a law in action perspective complements a law on the books approach to studying the criminal courts.

The law on the books approach to studying the criminal courts stresses the importance of examining the formal law and how courts interpret that law. The law in action approach is complementary because it stresses the importance of discretion throughout a criminal prosecution.

7. Distinguish between the crime control model of criminal justice and the due process model of criminal justice.

The crime control model emphasizes the need to repress crime and efficiently process the large number of guilty defendants. The due process model of criminal justice emphasizes the importance of protecting the rights of citizens and providing careful consideration for each case.

CRITICAL THINKING QUESTIONS

1. On a sheet of paper, apply the general overview of court structure in the United States (Figure 1.2) to your local community.

2. On a sheet of paper, apply the list of Actors in the Courthouse (Table 1.1) to your local community. If you live in a rural area, how does your list differ from that of someone who lives in a larger community? If you live in a large metropolitan area, how does your list differ from that of someone living in a more rural area?

3. What private, nongovernmental organizations are important to the criminal justice system of your community?

4. Use newspapers, radio, and criminal justice discussion lists or chat groups to monitor discussions concerning the criminal justice system. Do citizens make distinctions among police, courts, and corrections, or do they lump everything under the general rubric of the criminal justice system?

KEY TERMS

crime control model 20   criminal justice system 7   due process model 21

WEB RESOURCES

Go to the America's Courts and the Criminal Justice System companion website at

http://www.cengage.com/criminaljustice/neubauer

where you will find more resources to help you study.
Resources include web exercises, quizzing, and flash cards.

FOR FURTHER READING

Bogira, Steve. *Courtroom 302.* New York: Vintage, 2005.

Dixon, Jo, Aaron Kupchik, and Joachim Savelsberg (eds.). *Criminal Courts.* Surrey, United Kingdom, 2006.

Fox, Richard, Robert Van Sickel, and Thomas Steiger. *Tabloid Justice: Criminal Justice in an Age of Media Frenzy.* 2nd ed. Boulder, CO: Lynne Rienner, 2007.

Garland, David. *The Culture of Control: Crime and Social Order in Contemporary Society.* Chicago: University of Chicago Press, 2002.

Kappeler, Victor, and Gary Potter. *The Mythology of Crime and Justice.* 4th ed. Prospect Heights, IL: Waveland Press, 2005.

Marion, Nancy. *A Primer in the Politics of Criminal Justice.* 2nd ed. Monsey, NY: Criminal Justice Press, 2007.

Neubauer, David. *Debating Crime: Rhetoric and Reality.* Belmont, CA: Wadsworth, 2001.

Neubauer, David, and Stephen Meinhold. *Judicial Process: Law, Courts, and Politics in the United States.* 5th ed. Belmont, CA: Wadsworth, 2010.

Unnever, James, Francis Cullen, and Bonnie Fisher. "'A Liberal Is Someone Who Has Not Been Mugged': Criminal Victimization and Political Beliefs." *Justice Quarterly* 24: 309–334, 2007.

2 LAW AND CRIME

Michael Vick, center, arrives at federal court in Richmond, Virginia, in August of 2007. Vick, a disgraced NFL quarterback, served nearly two years in prison after pleading guilty for his part in financing and operating the "Bad Newz Kennels" as the center of an illegal dog-fighting ring.

CHAPTER OUTLINE

THE BASIS OF LAW

THE COMMON LAW HERITAGE
Judge-Made Law
Precedent
Multiple Sources of Law

THE ADVERSARY SYSTEM
Safeguards
Presumptions and Inferences
Burdens of Proof

CASE CLOSE-UP
Civil and Criminal Prosecutions of Celebrities

THE RIGHTS OF THE ACCUSED
Due Process
Bill of Rights

CIVIL LAW
Basis for Filing a Civil Suit
Remedies
Using Civil Remedies to Fight Crime
Civil Liability of Criminal Justice Officials

COURTS, CONTROVERSY, AND REDUCING CRIME
Should Asset Forfeiture Be Limited?

CRIMINAL LAW

ELEMENTS OF A CRIME
Guilty Act
Guilty Intent
Fusion of Guilty Act and Guilty Intent
Attendant Circumstances
Results

LEGAL DEFENSES

EFFECTS OF THE CRIMINAL LAW ON THE COURTS
Criminal Law and Inconsistencies

LAW AND POPULAR CULTURE
Chicago (2002)
Criminal Law and Plea Bargaining
Criminal Law and Sentencing

CONCLUSION

CHAPTER REVIEW

LEARNING OBJECTIVES

After reading this chapter you should be able to answer the following questions:

1. List the four key elements defining law.

2. Identify the three key characteristics of the common law.

3. Analyze the importance of the adversary system.

4. Name the four amendments of the Bill of Rights that deal specifically with criminal procedure.

5. List the five major areas of civil law.

6. Discuss the five elements (corpus delicti) of a crime.

7. Identify some of the most important legal defenses in American law.

8. Discuss the effects of the criminal law on courts.

The trial of Kobe Bryant was poised to become yet another media event offering the public an insight into the lifestyles of the rich and famous. Bryant, the NBA superstar, stood accused of raping a young woman at an upscale resort in the Colorado Rockies. During pretrial proceedings, the public seemed fascinated by every news leak about who did what. But just as jury selection was about to begin, the prosecutor dropped the charges when the alleged victim decided not to participate. Although the media quickly lost interest, Bryant's legal problems were far from over. Earlier the 20-year-old woman had filed a civil lawsuit seeking unspecified monetary damages, but given Bryant's celebrity status, few doubted that "unspecified" translated into big dollars. The civil and criminal lawsuits against Kobe Bryant drew immediate comparisons to the legal difficulties of other celebrities, like former football star O. J. Simpson and pop superstar Michael Jackson. Like Bryant, they were acquitted of criminal charges but later faced civil lawsuits.

The multiple legal proceedings surrounding celebrities like Kobe Bryant, O. J. Simpson, and Michael Jackson illustrate the complexities of U.S. law. And it is this law that constitutes the basic source of authority for the courts. Thus, before we can assess the type of justice produced by the courts, we need to know something about the law that is applied in reaching those results. Bear in mind that the United States has no uniform set of criminal or civil laws. Instead, each jurisdiction enacts its own set of criminal prohibitions, leading to some important variations from state to state.

This chapter begins by providing a working definition of law, then examines our common law heritage, including the adversary system and the rights of the accused. Next, the discussion shifts from procedure to substance. After looking at differences between civil law and criminal law, we will concentrate on the elements of a crime and legal defenses. The chapter concludes with a discussion of the consequences of criminal law for the criminal court process.

THE BASIS OF LAW

The basis of law can be summarized in two words: human conflict. A controversy over how much money is owed, a quarrel between husband and wife, a collision at an intersection, and the theft of a television set are a few examples of the great number of disputes that arise and threaten to disrupt the normal activities of society. Business and everyday activities depend on mechanisms for mediating inevitable human conflicts. Without such mechanisms, individual parties might seek private, violent means of settlement. The legendary feud between the Hatfields and the McCoys illustrates the disruptiveness of blood feuds motivated by revenge—not only in the lives of the individual parties directly involved but also in the larger society.

Law is an everyday word, but as Law Professor Lawrence Friedman (1984, p. 2) suggests, "It is a word of many meanings, as slippery as glass, as elusive as a soap bubble." Although there are various approaches to defining the term, most scholars define **law** as a body of rules enacted by public officials in a legitimate manner and backed by the force of the state (Neubauer and Meinhold 2010). This definition can be broken into four phrases, and each has important implications for how we think about law.

The first element—law is a body of rules—is self-evident. What is not immediately obvious, however, is the fact that these rules and regulations are found in a variety of sources: statutes, constitutions, court decisions, and administrative regulations.

The second element—law is enacted by public officials—is of critical importance. All organizations of any size or complexity have rules and regulations that govern their members. But these private rules are not law under our definition unless they are recognized by public officials—judges, legislators, and executives in particular.

The third element—law is enacted in a legitimate manner—means that it must be agreed upon ahead of time how the rules will be changed. Thus, legislatures have methods for passing new laws, bureaucrats have procedures for applying those laws, and judges follow a well-known process in interpreting those laws.

The final element—law is backed by the force of the state—says that these rules and regulations would be largely meaningless without sanctions. Thus, what differentiates law from other societal rules is that law has teeth to it. As Daniel Oran's *Law Dictionary for Nonlawyers* (2000) puts it, law is "that which must be obeyed." In most instances, however, it is not necessary to apply legal sanctions, because the threat is enough to keep most people in line most of the time.

It is also important to stress what this working definition of law omits—namely, any mention of justice. In a representative democracy, public perceptions of law embody fundamental notions of justice, fairness, and decency (Walker 2006). It is the potential linking of law and justice (in the form of unjust laws) that also makes law so difficult to define. But law and morality do not necessarily equate. Our working definition of law deliberately excludes any reference to justice because there is no precise legal or scientific meaning to that term. Furthermore, people use justice to support particular political and social goals. In the public arena, *justice* is a catchall term used in several different ways. As discussed in Chapter 1, backers of the crime control model see justice differently than do supporters of the due process model.

THE COMMON LAW HERITAGE

The American legal system traces its origins to England and is therefore referred to as Anglo-Saxon or **Anglo-American law**. Common law is used in English-speaking nations, including England, Australia, New Zealand, Canada, and the United States. (The only exception is the state of Louisiana, which derives its civil law from the Napoleonic Code and the Continental legal heritage; the state's criminal law, however, derives from the common law.)

The common law first appeared in medieval England after the Norman conquest in 1066. The new rulers gradually introduced central government administration, including the establishment of courts of law. Initially, the bulk of the law was local and was administered in local courts. A distinct body of national law began to develop during the reign of Henry II (1154–1189), who was successful in expanding the jurisdiction of the royal courts. The king's courts applied the common customs of the entire realm rather than the parochial traditions of a particular village. Thus, the term **common law** meant general law as opposed to special law; it was the law common to the entire land.

During the development of the common law legal system, a distinctive way of interpreting the law gradually emerged. Three key characteristics of this common law heritage stand out: The law was judge-made, based on precedent, and found in multiple sources.

JUDGE-MADE LAW

One key characteristic of the common law is that it was predominantly **judge-made law** (rather than legislatively enacted). Until the late 19th century, no important body of statutory law existed in either England or the United States. Rather, judges performed the task of organizing social relationships through law. In the field of civil law, for example, the common law courts developed the rights and obligations of citizens in such important areas as property, contracts, and torts. Even today, American law in these areas is predominantly judge-made.

Similarly, in the field of criminal law, by the 1600s the English common law courts had defined felonies such as murder, arson, robbery, larceny, and rape. Moreover, the legal defenses of insanity and self-defense had also entered the common law. These English criminal law concepts were transplanted to America by the colonists. After the Revolution, common law crimes considered applicable to local conditions were retained. Although legislative bodies, not the courts, now define crimes, contemporary statutory definitions often reflect their common law heritage.

PRECEDENT

A second key characteristic of the common law is the use of **precedent**, often referred to as **stare decisis** ("let the decision stand"). The doctrine of precedent requires a judge to decide a case by applying the rule of law found in previous cases, provided the facts in the current case are similar to the facts in the previous cases. By following previous court decisions, the legal system promotes the twin goals of fairness and consistency. Exhibit 2.1 gives an example of the precedent-based citation system used in American law.

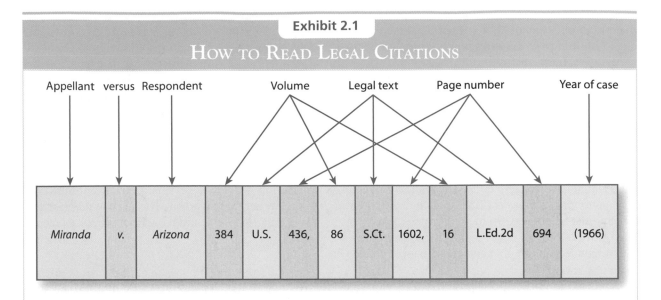

Exhibit 2.1

HOW TO READ LEGAL CITATIONS

Appellant	versus	Respondent	Volume	Legal text	Page number		Year of case
Miranda	*v.*	*Arizona*	384	U.S.	436,	86 S.Ct. 1602, 16 L.Ed.2d 694	(1966)

When first confronted with legal citations, students are often bewildered by the array of numbers. But with a few basics in mind, these citations need not be confusing; they are efficient aids in finding court decisions.

The full citation for *Miranda* is as follows: *Miranda v. Arizona*, 384 U.S. 436, 86 S.Ct. 1602, 16 L.Ed.2d 694 (1966). The lead name in the case usually refers to the party who lost in the lower court and is seeking to overturn that decision. That party is called the "appellant." The second name refers to the party (or parties) who won at the lower level (in this instance, the state of Arizona). The second party is called the "appellee," or more simply, the "respondent." Miranda is the appellant who is seeking to overturn his conviction. The state of Arizona is named as the respondent because criminal prosecutions are brought in the name of the state.

After the names of the parties come three sets of references. All decisions of the U.S. Supreme Court are reported in the *Supreme Court Reports,* which is published by the U.S. Government Printing Office. It is the official reporting system and is abbreviated U.S. In addition, decisions of the Supreme Court are reported in two private reporting systems: the *Supreme Court Reporter,* which is abbreviated S.Ct., and in *Lawyers Supreme Court Reports, Lawyers Edition,* which is abbreviated L.Ed.2d. The numbers preceding the abbreviation for the volume refer to the volume number. Thus, *Miranda* can be found in volume 384 of the *Supreme Court Reports.* The numbers after the abbreviation refer to the page number. Thus, the *Miranda* decision in volume 384 begins on page 436; in volume 86 of the *Supreme Court Reporter,* it is on page 1602. A library usually carries only one of the reporting systems, so the multiple references make it easy to locate the given case, no matter which of the three reporting systems is available. The final number in parentheses is the year of the case.

Decisions of other appellate courts at both the federal and state levels are reported in a similar manner in other volumes.

The common law's reliance on precedent reflects a cautious approach to problem solving. Rather than writing a decision attempting to solve the entire range of a given legal problem, common law courts decide only as much of the case as is necessary to resolve the individual dispute. Broad rules and policy directives emerge only through the accumulation of court decisions over time. Unfortunately, many Americans make the mistake of translating the common law heritage, particularly the doctrine of precedent, into a static view of the courts and the law. The entire history of Anglo-American law emphasizes the importance of common law courts' shaping old law to new demands. In the words of Justice Oliver Wendell Holmes (1920, p. 187):"It is revolting to have no better reason for a rule of law than that it was so laid down in the times of Henry IV. It is still more revolting if the grounds upon which it was laid down have vanished long since, and the rule simply persists from blind imitation of the past."

One way courts achieve flexibility is in adapting old rights to new problems. Another is the ability of courts to distinguish between precedents. Recall that the doctrine of precedent involves previous cases with a similar set of facts. Courts sometimes state that the present facts differ from those on which previous decisions were based and reach a different ruling. Finally, judges will occasionally (but very reluctantly) overturn a previous decision by stating that the previous court opinion was wrong. However, the common law is committed to gradual change to maintain stability; it is often said that the law and the courts are conservative institutions.

MULTIPLE SOURCES OF LAW

The third key characteristic of the common law is that it is found in multiple sources (a concept sometimes expressed as "uncodified"). In deciding the legal meaning of a given crime (murder, for example), it is not sufficient to look only at the legislative act. One must also know how the courts have interpreted the statute. Depending on the issue, the applicable rules of law may be found in constitutions, statutes, administrative regulations, or court decisions.

Within the hierarchy of law, constitutions occupy the top rung. A **constitution** is the first document that establishes the underlying principles and general laws of a nation or state. The U.S. Constitution is the fundamental law of the land. All other laws—federal, state, or local—are secondary. Similarly, each state has a constitution that is the "supreme law of the state." State courts may use the state constitution to invalidate the actions of legislators, governors, or administrators.

Constitutions define the powers that each branch of government may exercise. For example, Article III of the U.S. Constitution creates the federal judiciary (see Chapter 3).

Constitutions also limit government power. Some limitations take the form of prohibitions. Thus, Article I, Section 9, states, "The privilege of the Writ of Habeas Corpus shall not be suspended." Other limitations take the form of specific rights granted to citizens. The clearest example is the first 10 amendments to the U.S. Constitution, known collectively as the Bill of Rights. For example, the First Amendment begins, "Congress shall make no law respecting an establishment of religion, or prohibiting the free exercise thereof." State constitutions also contain bills of rights, many of which are modeled after their national counterpart.

Constitutions also specify how government officials will be selected. The U.S. Constitution provides that federal judges shall be nominated by the president, confirmed by the Senate, and serve during "good behavior." Similarly, state constitutions specify that state judges will be selected by election, appointment, or merit (see Chapter 8).

The second rung of law consists of **statutes**. Laws enacted by federal and state legislatures are usually referred to as "statutory law." A statutory law enacted by a local unit of government is commonly called a **municipal ordinance**.

Until the latter part of the 19th century, American legislatures played a secondary role in the formulation of law. It was not until the 20th century that state legislatures became the principal source of law (Friedman 1984). A fundamental reason for the growing importance of legislatively enacted statutes was that rapidly industrializing society was faced with new types of problems. Questions of how to protect the interests of workers and consumers were much broader in scope than those typically handled by the courts. The common law took decades to develop and refine legal rights and obligations, but the growing needs of an increasingly complex society could not afford the luxury of such a lengthy time frame. Legislators could enact rules of law that were not only much broader in scope than those adopted by judges but also more precise and detailed. Thus, a great deal of law today is statutory.

The third rung of American law consists of **administrative regulations**. Legislative bodies delegate rule-making authority to a host of governmental bureaucracies called by various names, such as agencies, boards, bureaus, commissions, and departments. All levels of government—federal, state, and local—authorize administrative agencies to issue specific rules and regulations consistent with the general principles specified in a statute or municipal ordinance. The Internal Revenue Service, by rule, decides what constitutes a legitimate deduction. State boards, by rule, set standards for nursing homes. Local zoning boards, by rule, decide where restaurants may be built.

Administrative regulations are the newest, fastest-growing, and least understood source of law. The rules and regulations promulgated by government agencies are extensive. The federal bureaucracy alone issues thousands of pages of new rules and policy statements each year. Often administrative rules and regulations are interpreted by courts.

Appellate court decisions also remain an important source of law. According to the common law tradition, courts do not make law, they merely find it. But this myth, convenient as it was for earlier generations, cannot mask the fact that courts do make law. This tradition, though, suggests a basic difference between legislative and judicial bodies. Legislative bodies are free to pass laws boldly and openly. Moreover, their prescription of the rules is general and all-encompassing. Courts make law more timidly, on a piece-by-piece basis, and operate much more narrowly.

Although American law today is primarily statutory and administrative, vestiges of judge-made law persist. The law governing personal injury remains principally judge-made, as do procedural matters such as rules of evidence. The major influence of case law (another term for court decisions), however, is seen in interpreting the law of other sources. The Constitution is a remarkably short document—some 4,300 words—and it is full of generalizations such as "due process of law," "equal protection of the laws," and "unreasonable searches and seizures." The founding fathers left later generations to flesh out the operating details of government. Supreme Court decisions have been primarily responsible for adapting constitutional provisions to changing circumstances. Through an extensive body of case law, the Court has supplied specific meaning to these vague phrases. For this reason, the Court has often been seen as an ongoing constitutional convention (Chapter 17).

Case law is vital in determining the meaning of other sources of law as well. Statutes, for example, address the future in general and flexible language. The interpretations that courts provide can either expand or contract the statute's meaning. No lawyer is comfortable with his or her interpretation of an alleged violation of the criminal law without first checking to see how the courts have interpreted it.

THE ADVERSARY SYSTEM

Law is both substantive and procedural. **Substantive law** creates legal obligations. Tort, contract, and domestic relations are examples of substantive civil law. Murder, robbery, and burglary are examples of substantive criminal law. **Procedural law**, on the other hand, establishes the methods of enforcing these legal obligations. Trials are the best-known aspect of American procedural law, but trials do not exist alone. Before trial there must be orderly ways to start, conduct, and end lawsuits. An important aspect of procedural law centers on the roles lawyers and judges play in the legal process.

In many nations of the world, criminal investigations are conducted by a single government official whose function is to establish a unified version of what happened, seeking out facts that show the defendant's guilt as well as those that indicate that he or she is innocent. The Anglo-American legal system rejects such an approach. Its guiding premise is that a battle between two opposing parties will uncover more of the truth than would a single official, no matter how industrious and well-meaning. Under the **adversary system**, the burden is on the prosecutor to prove the defendant guilty beyond a reasonable doubt, and the defense attorney is responsible for arguing for the client's innocence and asserting legal protections. The judge serves as a neutral arbitrator who stands above the fight as a disinterested party, ensuring that each side battles within the established rules. Finally, the decision is entrusted to the jury (although in some instances a judge alone may decide).

SAFEGUARDS

The guiding assumption of the adversary system is that two parties, approaching the facts from entirely different perspectives, will uncover more of the truth than would a single investigator, no matter how industrious and objective. Through cross-examination, each side has the opportunity to probe for possible biases in witnesses and to test what witnesses actually know, not what they think they know. The right to cross-examination is protected by the Sixth Amendment: "In all criminal prosecutions, the accused shall enjoy the right . . . to be confronted with witnesses against him."

By putting power in the hands of several different parties, the adversary system creates another type of safeguard. Each actor is granted limited powers, and each has limited powers to counteract the others. If the judge is biased or unfair, the jury has the ability to disregard the judge and reach a fair verdict; if the judge believes the jury has acted improperly, he or she may set aside the jury's verdict and order a new trial. This diffusion of powers in the adversary system incorporates a series of checks and balances aimed at curbing political misuse of the criminal courts.

In diffusing power, the adversary system provides a third safeguard: It charges a specific actor—the defense attorney—with asserting the rights of the accused. Defense attorneys search out potential violations of the rights of the accused. They function as perpetual challengers in the criminal court process and are ready at every juncture to challenge the government by insisting that the proper procedures be followed.

PRESUMPTIONS AND INFERENCES

All trials are governed by both rules of procedure and rules of evidence. One of the foundations of evidence law is that the trier-of-fact must have an evidentiary starting place at the outset of a trial. In a criminal trial, that starting place usually involves two presumptions. A **presumption** is a conclusion or deduction that the law requires the trier-of-fact to make in the absence of evidence to the contrary. In contrast, **inferences** are permissive; they are conclusions or deductions the trier-of-fact may reasonably make based on the facts that have been established by the evidence, but the trier-of-fact is not required to do so. Criminal trials start with two presumptions: the presumption of sanity and the presumption of innocence. The **presumption of sanity** requires that all defendants be presumed sane unless sufficient evidence of their insanity is proven, usually by clear and convincing evidence. The **presumption of innocence** requires the trier-of-fact to accept that the defendant is innocent unless the prosecution meets its burden to prove that the defendant is guilty beyond a reasonable doubt—a level of proof explored in greater detail below.

BURDENS OF PROOF

The concept of the "burden of proof" actually encompasses two separate burdens: the burden of production and the burden of persuasion. If a party has the **burden of production** (often referred to as the burden of going forward), he or she must produce evidence to put facts in issue. The **burden of persuasion**, more commonly called the "burden of proof," is the obligation of a party to prove a fact to a certain level, either beyond a reasonable doubt, by a preponderance of the evidence, or by clear and convincing evidence. The various levels of proof used in evaluating if the burden of persuasion has been met are depicted in Table 2.1. The burden of persuasion comes into play after all the evidence is produced, when it is time for the judge to decide the ultimate issue in a bench trial or time to instruct the jury. The prosecution always bears the burden in persuading the trier-of-fact that the defendant committed each and every element of all crimes charged. In some circumstances, however, the defendant in a criminal trial bears the burden of persuasion to prove a certain defense, such as insanity. When the defendant bears the burden of persuasion to prove a defense, it is called an **affirmative defense**.

At the low end of the scale, there is no proof. Just above that, there is what the law calls "mere suspicion"—a hunch or the feeling of intuition. Although intuitively knowing something is undoubtedly a skill that serves law enforcement officers well, mere suspicion is insufficient proof of any fact in a court of law.

The next level up from mere suspicion is **reasonable, articulable suspicion**. This differs from mere suspicion only slightly, but in an important way. Instead of just having a hunch or an intuitive feeling, a person can articulate the reasons why he or she is suspicious. Moreover, the explanations offered as the bases for the suspicion are objectively reasonable—clearly understandable to another person who hears the explanations. This level of proof is necessary for law enforcement personnel to conduct a "stop and frisk." These brief, limited, investigative detentions are also known as "*Terry* stops" as a result of the U.S. Supreme Court's landmark decision in *Terry v. Ohio* (1968).

The next highest level of proof is called **probable cause**. Defining probable cause is no easy task. It is differentiated from reasonable, articulable suspicion by the existence of facts—independently verifiable factual information that supports the conclusion that there is a "fair probability" that a crime occurred or that a particular person was involved in a crime.

In most civil cases, the standard of proof is a **preponderance of the evidence**. It is commonly understood as proof that something is more likely than not. Thus, if the plaintiff is able to show that the probability is more than 50 percent that the defendant did what is claimed, the judgment will be for the plaintiff. It is also the standard of proof used to establish the validity of waivers of constitutional rights, as well as the burden for proving that exceptions to the Exclusionary Rule apply. **Clear and**

TABLE 2.1
LEVELS OF PROOF

	NO PROOF	MERE SUSPICION	ARTICULABLE REASONABLE SUSPICION	PROBABLE CAUSE	PREPONDER- ANCE OF THE EVIDENCE	CLEAR AND CONVINCING EVIDENCE	BEYOND A REASONABLE DOUBT	BEYOND ALL DOUBT
		A "hunch" serves law enforcement officers well, but is insufficient proof in any stage in the judicial process.	Standard established in *Terry v. Ohio* for a "stop and frisk"—a limited investigative detention.	Necessary to arrest a person, conduct a search, or seize evidence.	Plaintiff's burden in most civil cases; burden for establishing "knowing, intelligent, and voluntary" waivers of most constitutional rights; burden for establishing exceptions to the exclusionary rule.	Plaintiff's burden in some civil cases; defendant's burden for proving insanity; government's burden to civilly commit a dangerous person.	Prosecution's burden to prove each element of a criminal offense	Proof to an absolute certainty is not required in any phase of the judicial process in the United States.

SOURCE: John Ferdico, Henry F. Fradella, and Christopher Totten. *Criminal Procedure for the Criminal Justice Professional*. 10th ed. Belmont, CA: Wadsworth, 2008.

convincing evidence is a higher level of proof than the preponderance of the evidence standard, yet it falls short of proof beyond a reasonable doubt. It is the standard of proof in some civil cases. It is also the level of proof to which a defendant in some criminal cases must establish an affirmative defense like insanity. If there is clear and convincing evidence, the trier-of-fact should be reasonably satisfied as to the existence of the fact, yet they may have some doubts.

One of the most fundamental protections recognized in the American criminal justice process is the **presumption of innocence**. The state has the burden of proving all the elements of the crime(s) charged **beyond a reasonable doubt**; defendants are not required to prove themselves innocent. If the prosecution fails to meet this burden of proof on any element of a crime, the defendant must be acquitted (*In re Winship* 1970). A specific definition for the "beyond a reasonable doubt" standard has not been adopted by the U.S. Supreme Court, leading to some confusion among jurists and jurors

alike. In fact, jury instructions explaining reasonable doubt are often the basis for appeal. It is sufficient to say that proof beyond a reasonable doubt requires that the guilt of the defendant be established to a reasonable, but not absolute or mathematical, certainty. Probability of guilt is not enough. In other words, to satisfy the standard of "beyond a reasonable doubt," the jury must be satisfied that the charges against the defendant are almost certainly true. A challenged definition of beyond a reasonable doubt that was upheld by the U.S. Supreme Court reads as follows: "A reasonable doubt is an actual and substantial doubt arising from the evidence, from the facts or circumstances shown by the evidence, or from the lack of evidence" (*Victor v. Nebraska* 1994). Keep in mind that reasonable doubt is an inherently qualitative concept; it cannot be quantified, and any attempt to do so for a jury is likely to result in reversible error (see Chapter 17).

The Case Close-Up: Civil and Criminal Prosecutions of Celebrities illustrates how differing burdens of proof can lead to different verdicts.

Civil and Criminal Prosecutions of Celebrities

The trial of Kobe Bryant held the promise of becoming a major media event, perhaps rivaling the coverage of the O. J. Simpson trials. Although most trials are too mundane to evoke public interest, the legal woes of celebrities often turn into major media events. And this case had all the right ingredients to become a mega–trial event: A charismatic NBA superstar was accused of a tawdry rape at an exclusive resort in the Colorado Rockies. The sense of drama built with pretrial posturing by the defense that sexual conduct was consensual and suggestions (again by the defense) that the DNA tests proved she had had other recent sexual partners. Lawyers for the victim were quick to deny these allegations and became outraged when the victim's name was accidentally released, in apparent violation of Colorado's rape shield law, which seeks to keep the name of the rape victim private. But just as the media attention was reaching its zenith, the case suddenly collapsed. The Eagle, Colorado, prosecutor announced that the sexual assault charge against Kobe Bryant had been dropped because his accuser was reluctant to testify in open court. Lingering in the

background was the understanding that both sides had reached a settlement in the civil case, which left some wondering whether the victim was willing to forgo the criminal prosecution in exchange for a lot of money.

The media coverage of the criminal charges against Kobe Bryant immediately drew comparisons to the trial a decade earlier of another athletic superstar, O. J. Simpson. From the beginning, the case seemed to have it all. The shocking news of the murder of Nicole Brown Simpson seemed like an event from a paperback novel: A beautiful blonde and her male companion brutally murdered near her home. The defendant was well known and well liked—a former star football player who after his playing days enjoyed a wide following as a TV sports personality.

Nor was the trial itself an anticlimax. Prominent lawyers basked in the media attention, while obscure prosecutors quickly became media celebrities, and a good-natured judge appeared, at times, unable to control the "media circus." For 37 weeks, witnesses testified and experts offered their opinions, with lawyer pundits quick to label some "flaky" and others just plain wrong. Throughout, the defense kept the focus on the conduct of the Los Angeles Police Department during the case, alleging, at best, shoddy police work and, at worst, racial bias.

A year after O. J. Simpson was acquitted of criminal charges, the civil trial began. The underlying allegation—that Simpson murdered his ex-wife and Ronald Goldman—remained the same, but the rules in the proceedings were fundamentally different. For one, the nature of the accusations differed. In the criminal trial, Simpson was charged with homicide, but in the civil case the allegations involved wrongful death (a type of tort). Instead of having to prove guilty intent, the plaintiff had only to establish that Simpson was negligent, an allegation that is easier to prove because it is a broader concept. Moreover, because this was a civil action, the plaintiff had to prove its case with only a preponderance of evidence.

Constitutional protections likewise differ in criminal and civil proceedings. In a criminal case, the defendant has the right to remain silent, and during the criminal trial, the defense did not call Simpson to the stand. But in a civil case, the defendant can be forced to testify, and testify Simpson did. Prior to the trial, the plaintiff's attorneys took Simpson's deposition. And during trial they called him to the stand as a plaintiff witness.

Finally, the Simpson cases illustrate important differences in remedies. If Simpson had been found guilty of murder, he most certainly would have gone to prison. In the civil case, the jury awarded compensatory damages of $8.5 million and punitive damages of $25 million. But the plaintiffs are unlikely to recover anything near the $33.5 million jury award because Simpson said he was broke and could not pay.

The outcome of the Kobe Bryant civil lawsuit proved to be very different. Three weeks before the criminal case against Bryant collapsed, the woman filed a civil lawsuit. Months after the criminal case abruptly ended, the Los Angles Lakers star settled the civil lawsuit. As is customary, terms of the settlement were not released. Thus, the public can only speculate that the financial settlement was substantial, but published reports indicate that the woman expected a windfall (Siemaszko 2005).

CASE CLOSEUP

The Rights of the Accused

Procedural law in the United States places a heavy emphasis on protecting the individual rights of each citizen. A key feature of a democracy is the insistence that the prevention and control of crime be accomplished within the framework of law. The criminal process embodies some of society's severest sanctions: detention before trial, confinement in prison after conviction, and, in certain limited situations, execution of the offender. Because the powers of the criminal courts are so great, there is concern that those powers might be abused or misapplied. The Judeo-Christian tradition places a high value on the worth and liberty of each individual citizen.

Restrictions on the use and application of government power take the form of rights granted to the accused. One of the most fundamental protections is the right to remain silent. Another is the right to a trial by jury. These protections exist not to free the guilty but to protect the innocent (see Exhibit 2.2). Basing the criminal justice process on the necessity of protecting individual liberties (of the innocent and guilty alike) obviously reduces the effectiveness of that process in fighting crime. To ensure that innocent persons are not found guilty, Anglo-American criminal law pays the price of freeing some of the guilty.

The primary justification for providing constitutional safeguards for those caught in the net of the criminal process is to ensure that innocent persons are not harassed or wrongly convicted. The American legal system is premised on a distrust of human fact-finding. The possibility of wrongly convicting an innocent person arises when honest mistakes are made by honorable people. But it also arises when dishonorable officials use the criminal justice process for less-than-honorable ends. In countries without built-in checks, the criminal justice process provides a quick and easy way for government officials to dispose of their enemies. For example, a common ploy in a totalitarian government is to

Exhibit 2.2

PROVISIONS OF THE U.S. CONSTITUTION DEALING WITH CRIMINAL PROCEDURE

	CONSTITUTIONAL LANGUAGE
Crime	Article I Section 9.3: No bill of attainder may be passed by the legislature.
	Article I Section 10.1: No state may pass any bill of attainder.
	Article I Section 9.3: The legislature may not pass an ex post facto law.
	Article I Section 10.1: No state may pass an ex post facto law.
Arrest	Amendment IV: Right against unreasonable search and seizures applies to arrest.
Initial appearance	Amendment VI: Right to know charges.
Bail	Amendment VIII: Right against excessive bail.
Preliminary hearing	Amendment VI: Right to assistance of counsel.
Charging	None
Grand jury	Amendment V: Right to a grand jury for a capital or otherwise infamous crime.
Arraignment	Amendment VI: Right to know charges.
Evidence	Amendment IV: Right against unreasonable search and seizures.
	Amendment V: Right against self-incrimination.
Plea bargaining	None
Trial	Amendment V: Right not to be tried twice for the same crime.
	Amendment VI: Right to a speedy trial; right to an impartial jury; right to a public trial; right to be confronted by witnesses against oneself; right to a jury from state or district where crime shall have been committed; right to obtain witnesses in one's favor; right to conduct cross-examination; right to speak at trial.
Sentencing	Amendment VIII: Right against excessive fines; right against cruel and unusual punishment.
	Amendment XIII: Right against involuntary servitude.
Appeal	Article I Section 9.2: Privilege of the writ of habeas corpus shall not be suspended.

charge persons with the ill-defined crime of being an "enemy of the state." The possibility of political misuse of the criminal justice process by a tyrannical government or tyrannical officials is a major concern in the Anglo-American heritage.

Another reason that democracies respect the rights of those accused or suspected of violating the criminal law is the need to maintain the respect and support of the community. Democratic governments derive their powers from the consent of the governed. Such support is undermined if power is applied arbitrarily. Law enforcement practices that are brutal or overzealous are likely to produce fear and cynicism among the people—lawbreakers and law abiders alike. Such practices undermine the legitimacy that law enforcement officials must have in order to enforce the law in a democracy.

DUE PROCESS

The principal legal doctrine for limiting the arbitrariness of officials is due process. Due process of law is mentioned twice in the Constitution:

- "No person shall . . . be deprived of life, liberty or property without due process of law." (Fifth Amendment)
- "No state shall deprive any person of life, liberty or property without due process of law." (Fourteenth Amendment)

The concept of **due process of law** has a broad and somewhat elastic meaning, with definitions varying in detail from situation to situation. The core of the idea of due process is that a person should always be given notice of any charges brought against him or her, that a person should be provided a real chance to present his or her side in a legal dispute, and that no law or government procedure should be arbitrary. The specific requirements of due process vary somewhat, depending on the Supreme Court's latest interpretations of the Bill of Rights.

BILL OF RIGHTS

The major obstacle to the ratification of the Constitution was the absence of specific protections for individual rights. Several of the most prominent leaders of the American Revolution opposed the adoption of the Constitution, fearing that the proposed national government posed as great a threat to the rights of the average American as had the king of England. Therefore, shortly after the adoption

of the Constitution, 10 amendments, collectively known as the **Bill of Rights**, were adopted. Many of these protections—particularly the Fourth, Fifth, Sixth, and Eighth Amendments—deal specifically with criminal procedure.

Originally, the protections of the Bill of Rights restricted only the national government. Through a legal doctrine known as **selective incorporation**, however, the Supreme Court ruled that the due process clause of the Fourteenth Amendment made some provisions of the Bill of Rights applicable to the states as well. Although not all the protections of the Bill of Rights have been incorporated into the Fourteenth Amendment, all of the major protections now apply to the states as well as to the national government (Exhibit 2.3). The major provisions of the Bill of Rights incorporated through the due process clause of the Fourteenth Amendment are protections against unreasonable searches and seizures (Fourth Amendment); protection against self-incrimination (Fifth); the right to counsel and trial by jury (Sixth); and the prohibition against cruel and unusual punishment (Eighth).

CIVIL LAW

Most disputes that come to court involve private parties. Conflicts over failure to pay money owed or injuries suffered in an automobile accident are settled on the basis of the body of rules collectively known as **civil law**. These suits are brought because the courts possess powers that private parties do not; courts can, for example, order a person to pay a business money owed under a contract or award monetary damages suffered for an injury received in an automobile accident.

A civil suit is brought by a private party. But "private parties" are not limited to individual citizens. They may include groups of citizens (advocacy groups and homeowners' associations, for example) as well as businesses and the government. Given these "legal fictions," it is best to view civil law as every lawsuit other than a criminal proceeding.

BASIS FOR FILING A CIVIL SUIT

Civil law is considerably more voluminous than criminal law. Exhibit 2.4 summarizes the major branches of civil law, which form the basis for

---

Exhibit 2.3

CASES INCORPORATING PROVISIONS OF THE BILL OF RIGHTS INTO THE DUE PROCESS CLAUSE OF THE FOURTEENTH AMENDMENT

FIRST AMENDMENT

Establishment of religion: *Everson v. Board of Education* 1947

Free exercise of religion: *Cantwell v. Connecticut* 1940

Freedom of speech: *Gitlow v. New York* 1925

Freedom of the press: *Near v. Minnesota* 1931

Freedom to peaceably assemble: *DeJong v. Oregon* 1937

Freedom to petition government: *Hague v. CIO* 1939

SECOND AMENDMENT

Right of the militia to bear arms: *[Presser v. Illinois, 1886]* NI *District of Columbia v. Heller* 2008*

FOURTH AMENDMENT

Unreasonable search and seizure: *Wolf v. Colorado* 1949

Exclusionary rule: *Mapp v. Ohio* 1961

Warrant requirement: *Ker v. California* (1963)

FIFTH AMENDMENT

Grand jury: *[Hurtado v. California, 1884]* NI

No double jeopardy: *Benton v. Maryland* 1969

No self-incrimination: *Malloy v. Hogan* 1964

Compensation for taking private property: *Chicago, Burlington and Quincy Railroad v. Chicago* 1897

SIXTH AMENDMENT

Speedy trial: *Klopfer v. North Carolina* 1967

Public trial: *In re Oliver* 1948

Impartial jury: *Parker v. Gladden* 1966

Jury trial: *Duncan v. Louisiana* 1968

Venue: [Implied in Due Process] NI

Notice: *Cole v. Arkansas* 1948

Confrontation of witnesses: *Pointer v. Texas* 1965

Compulsory process: *Washington v. Texas* 1967

Assistance of counsel in capital cases: *Powell v. Alabama* 1932

Assistance of counsel in noncapital felony cases: *Gideon v. Wainwright* 1963

Assistance of counsel in most misdemeanor cases: *Argersinger v. Hamlin* 1972

SEVENTH AMENDMENT

Jury trial in civil cases: [*Walker v. Sauvinet,* 1875] NI

EIGHTH AMENDMENT

No excessive bail: [*United States v. Salerno,* 1987] NI

No excessive fines: *Cooper Industries v. Leatherman Tool Group, Inc.* 2001

No cruel and unusual punishment: *Robinson v. California* 1962

NINTH AMENDMENT

Privacy**: *Griswold v. Connecticut* 1965

Heller holds that the Second Amendment protects an individual right to possess a firearm but does not address the issue of incorporation.

**The word *privacy* does not appear in the Ninth Amendment (nor anywhere else in the Constitution), but in *Griswold,* several justices viewed the Ninth Amendment as guaranteeing that right.

NI: Not incorporated

SOURCE: Adapted from John Ferdico, Henry F. Fradella, and Christopher Totten, *Criminal Procedure for the Criminal Justice Professional.* 10th ed. Belmont, CA: West/Wadsworth, 2008.

---

filing suit in court. **Tort** law involves the legal wrong done to another person. Injuries suffered during automobile accidents are a prime example of tort law. When lawyers speak of an injury, however, they do not necessarily mean a physical injury. The term has a broader meaning, including any wrong, hurt, or damage done to a person's rights, body, reputation, or property.

Another type of private law involves **contracts**—agreements between two or more persons involving a promise supported by mutual obligations (termed "consideration"). Money owed on a credit card and bank loans for buying a new car are considered contracts.

Property, which centers on the ownership of things, is another division of private law. Property

Exhibit 2.4

MAJOR AREAS OF CIVIL LAW

	LAW ON THE BOOKS	LAW IN ACTION
Tort	A legal injury (other than contract) resulting from violating a duty.	Examples: negligence, assault, false arrest, trespass.
Contract	An agreement between two or more parties creating a legally enforceable contract.	Money owed is the major source of cases in small claims courts.
Property	Ownership of a thing. *Real property:* Land and things on it. *Personal property:* Everything else.	Lawsuits disputing ownership of property are rarer today than they were 100 years ago.
Domestic relations	Law relating to the home. *Divorce:* The ending of a marriage by court order. *Custody:* Court determination of care and keeping of children after divorce. *Support:* Financial obligation to provide for children after divorce. *Alimony:* Court-ordered payments by a divorced husband (or wife) to the ex-wife (or ex-husband) for ongoing personal support. *Adoption:* Legally taking a child of another (or, in some states, an adult) as one's own, with all the rights and duties there would have been if the child had been one's own originally.	Domestic relations constitutes the single largest category of cases filed in the major trial courts. At times, civil and criminal issues overlap, most obviously in domestic abuse cases (Chapter 9). Formally or informally, some big cities have created family courts, which handle both civil and criminal matters involving juveniles (Chapter 19). Nonpayment of child support by ex-husbands (often called "deadbeat dads") is a growing problem.
Inheritance	Receipt of property from a dead person. *Will:* A document in which a person tells how his or her property should be handed out after death. *Intestate:* Dying without making a will. *Probate:* The process of proving that a will is genuine and giving out the property listed in it.	Courts routinely process probate cases because the will is clear and the amount of money in question is small. On occasion, though, the heirs of the rich and famous have been known to publicly contest distribution of the large sums of money left behind.

law regulates three types of property: "real property"—involving land and real estate; "personal property"—rights concerning tangible, movable items; and "intellectual property"—covering original ideas. Intellectual property has grown to be an increasingly important area of the law in the digital age, as it governs the regulation of patents, trademarks, and copyrights.

Domestic relations constitutes a major and growing area of law. These matters of family law mainly involve divorce and related issues such as child custody, child support, and alimony. Some areas of domestic relations overlap with juvenile law (Chapter 19). Domestic disputes are also a common reason that police may be summoned, and at times criminal conduct may be involved (see Chapter 9 for a discussion of domestic violence).

Property received from a person who has died is governed by laws on **inheritance**. The best-known example is a *will,* a written document telling how a person's property should be distributed after his or her death.

REMEDIES

Individuals, groups, or governments sue because they want something from another party. What they want is termed a **remedy**. A court's official decision about the rights and claims of each side in a lawsuit is known as a **judgment**. Thus, if the plaintiff wins, the judgment also contains a remedy, which is the relief granted by the court. Exhibit 2.5 summarizes the major civil remedies.

Most civil cases involve a request for monetary damages. The **plaintiff** (the person who starts a lawsuit) demands that the **defendant** (the person

---

Exhibit 2.5
MAJOR CIVIL REMEDIES

	LAW ON THE BOOKS	LAW IN ACTION
Declaratory judgment	A court decision declaring the legal rights of the parties.	Principal outcome of divorce cases.
Monetary damages	*Compensatory damages:* Payment for actual losses suffered by a plaintiff.	Principal outcome of tort cases.
	Punitive damages: Money awarded by a court to a person who has been harmed in a malicious or willful way by another person. The purpose is to warn others.	Rarely awarded. Major source of debate over product liability.
Equity	*Temporary restraining order (TRO):* A judge's order to a person to keep from taking certain action before a full hearing can be held on the question.	Can be granted without the other party present. Expires after a few days.
	Preliminary injunction: A judge's order to a person to keep from taking action after a hearing but before the issue is fully tried.	During the hearing, each side presents its case. The plaintiff must be able to show that irreparable damages will occur if the injunction is not issued.
	Permanent injunction: A judge's order to a person to keep from taking certain action after the issue has been fully tried.	As with all injunctions, violations are punishable by contempt of court, which can include not only fines but also jail time.

against whom a lawsuit is brought) pay money to the plaintiff. For example, in a case involving an automobile accident, the injured party may request a sum of money to pay for hospital expenses, doctors' fees, lost wages, and general "pain and suffering." **Monetary damages** are sums of money that a court orders paid to a person who has suffered a legal injury.

Another type of remedy occasionally requested is a **declaratory judgment**, which is a judicial determination of the legal rights of the parties. For example, in prisoner litigation, lawyers seek a declaration that prison conditions violate constitutional standards (see Chapter 15).

A third type of remedy is called an **injunction** (and comes from the type of law found in England termed "equity" or sometimes "chancellory" law). An injunction is a court order that requires a person to take an action or to refrain from taking an action. For example, a court may issue an injunction prohibiting a company from dumping industrial wastes into a river. To qualify for an injunction, the plaintiff must demonstrate to the court that it will suffer irreparable damages. An injunction is a powerful measure that can be enforced by the contempt power of the court. Thus, a person who violates an injunction can be fined or sent to jail.

Using Civil Remedies to Fight Crime

Civil law is having an increasing impact on the criminal justice system (Ross 2002). Victims of crime are increasingly resorting to civil litigation, in addition to victim compensation and restitution, as a means of recovering from the ill effects of crime (National Center for Victims of Crime 2002). Moreover, victims' rights advocates are advocating civil remedies as one way for victims to reassert control (see Chapter 9). In criminal prosecutions the prosecutor essentially makes all decisions, but in civil litigation it is the plaintiff and plaintiff's lawyer who make the decisions. Although parallel civil and criminal proceedings have been brought for years, they are being used today more frequently than ever before, especially in three areas—civil forfeiture cases related to drug offenses; lawsuits brought by victims of sexual assault; and civil remedies to compensate victims of white collar crime (McCampbell 1995; Lininger 2008).

The overlap between civil and criminal law is highlighted by a number of efforts to fight drug use. Legislators at both the state and national levels are passing laws that allow for the eviction of residents from public housing if they are convicted of drug possession and

laws that permit drug testing of employees. Likewise, nuisance-abatement suits have targeted so-called crack houses. These essentially civil laws increase the arsenal of legal weapons that law enforcement officials may use against the sale and use of illegal drugs. But some people now wonder whether the use of civil remedies, particularly asset forfeiture, may have gone too far (see Courts, Controversy, and Reducing Crime: Should Asset Forfeiture Be Limited?).

Rape victims are pursuing justice in the civil courts at a growing rate, seeking damages from almost anyone they can find who may have shared liability for the rape. These lawsuits often proceed on the basis of the legal theory of premises liability. In premises liability cases, the victim alleges that the owner or manager of the property failed to provide adequate security and thereby contributed to the occurrence of the crime. The claims raise issues concerning inadequate security resulting from poorly trained security guards, too few security guards, or environmental design flaws. In short, premises liability lawsuits argue that the crime that occurred was foreseeable and that the defendant had a legal duty to provide adequate security (Gordon and Brill 1996; Kanter 2005).

In recent years, civil justice has become almost as controversial as criminal justice. Perhaps nowhere is this more apparent than in efforts to curb drunk driving. Seemingly every session, legislatures vote in even tougher penalties for driving while intoxicated (see Chapter 18). But at the same time, civil lawsuits filed by persons injured in automobile accidents caused by drunk drivers are viewed with skepticism. Tort reformers often implicitly suggest that such lawsuits unnecessarily drive up the already high cost of automobile insurance.

The principal downside of civil remedies is the obvious: Few criminal defendants have the economic resources to make litigation financially worthwhile. Indeed, in the most prominent civil lawsuits, the plaintiffs' motives have been primarily vindication, with little likelihood of collecting a dime from Bernhard Goetz or anything close to the $33.5 million O. J. Simpson was ordered to pay (see Exhibit 2.6).

Civil Liability of Criminal Justice Officials

In the modern era, it is not just criminal defendants who find themselves hauled into civil court but police officers, prosecutors, and prison guards as well. Increasingly, criminal justice officials find that they must defend themselves against a variety of civil

	Exhibit 2.6	
PROMINENT EXAMPLES OF CIVIL ACTIONS FOLLOWING CRIMINAL PROSECUTIONS		
PERSON	**CRIMINAL PROSECUTION**	**CIVIL ACTION**
Bernhard Goetz	Criminal jury convicted the subway vigilante of illegally having a gun but acquitted him of more serious charges after the 1984 shooting of a youth Goetz claimed was trying to rob him. The shooting had clear racial overtones (Goetz is white; his victim, black).	A 1996 civil jury ordered Goetz to pay $43 million to the man he left paralyzed. It is unlikely that Darrell Cabey, who was paralyzed and suffered brain damage, will be able to collect from the unemployed electrician.
O. J. Simpson	In the televised "trial of the century," the jury acquitted O. J. Simpson of murdering his former wife Nicole Brown Simpson and her friend Ronald Goldman. The verdict divided the nation along racial lines.	A civil jury found Simpson liable for the killings of his ex-wife and her friend. The jury awarded $8.5 million in compensatory damages to Goldman's parents and $25 million in punitive damages. The plaintiff's ability to collect on the judgment is limited because Simpson had placed most of his money in retirement accounts that cannot be seized.
Rodney King	Two Los Angeles police officers were acquitted in state court of beating Rodney King, but they were later convicted in federal court (Chapter 3).	The city of Los Angeles settled the civil lawsuit for $3.8 million.
Randall Weaver	After a months-long standoff, federal agents arrested Randall Weaver at his mountain home in Ruby Ridge, Idaho. During the arrest a firefight broke out, and Weaver's wife and son were killed. A criminal jury acquitted Weaver of a variety of gun charges.	The U.S. Justice Department paid $3.1 million to settle wrongful death claims against federal agents for the 1992 death of Randall Weaver's wife and son.
Amadou Diallo	Four NYPD officers were acquitted of murder. The Justice Department will not file federal charges.	The city of New York settled the case for $3 million.
Kobe Bryant	The prosecutor dropped charges of sexual assault when the victim refused to testify.	Bryant settled out of court for an undisclosed amount of money.
Michael Jackson	The jury acquitted the pop icon of sexually molesting a child at his Neverland ranch.	Media report that Jackson settled out of court at least one earlier case involving improper sexual contact with a minor.

Courts, Controversy, and Reducing Crime

NBC's *Dateline* television series focused on two small Louisiana sheriff's departments accused of targeting innocent motorists on heavily traveled I-10 and seizing their cars for a hefty departmental profit. The law lets police seize property from drivers who they think may be violating drug laws, even if they don't find any drugs. To recover their property, motorists must first post a bond and then wage a long court battle. The local officials blasted the NBC report as "trash journalism designed to boost ratings," but they did acknowledge that their rural jurisdictions collected $19 million a year—37 percent of all asset forfeitures in the state (Wardlaw 1997). This TV report focused national attention on complaints that some law enforcement officials have abused their powers under asset forfeiture.

Asset forfeiture involves government seizure of the personal assets obtained from, or used in, a crime. *Assets* refer to property, businesses, cars, cash, and the like. For example, a car used in the distribution of illegal drugs may be forfeited to the government. Asset forfeiture was part of British common law as early as 1660. More recently, it is identified with the Racketeer Influenced and Corrupt Organizations

Act (RICO for short) enacted by Congress in 1970. Congress was concerned about the infiltration of organized crime into the regular business marketplace and sought to discourage such activities by taking away the profits.

One form of asset forfeiture is criminal: A defendant convicted under the RICO law is subject not only to criminal penalties (fines and imprisonment) but also to forfeiture of property obtained from the profits of the illegal enterprise. Thus, drug dealers who pour their profits into a restaurant can have the restaurant seized by government agents.

But asset forfeiture is not limited to criminal actions. The more potent form of asset forfeiture is civil in nature. The government is proceeding not against a person but against the property in what is termed an **in rem** procedure (a lawsuit brought against a thing rather than against a person). Once the property is seized, the burden of proof is on the property owner to show that the property was not used illegally (Cassella 1996). Through the years, Congress has greatly expanded the scope of asset forfeiture, and all states except one have enacted asset forfeiture laws.

lawsuits. Perhaps the best known are cases filed by prison inmates under 42 U.S.C. § 1983 (often called "Section 1983 cases") alleging that conditions of confinement constitute cruel and unusual punishment in violation of the Eighth Amendment. These lawsuits have reshaped American prisons in recent years (see Chapter 15).

Other civil lawsuits seek monetary damages for misconduct on the part of law enforcement personnel. Most commonly these lawsuits allege that the police used excessive force or were negligent in using deadly force. Conversely, some lawsuits center on the inactions of law enforcement or correctional personnel. Local governments have been found liable for the death of a person in detention when police officers failed to prevent suicide (Kappeler, Vaughn, and Del Carmen 1991). Similarly, prison

officials have been held liable for failure to prevent inmate-against-inmate assaults (Vaughn 1996).

Criminal justice officials also find themselves in civil court as defendants in growing numbers of cases filed by their own employees. Some lawsuits allege discrimination in hiring or promotion. Others argue that the plaintiff was sexually harassed. Chapter 3, on federal courts, will explore how a wide range of federal laws shape the internal operations of law enforcement and corrections.

Criminal Law

Some disputes are viewed as so disruptive to society that they require special treatment because civil law remedies are not enough. There are several important

The major concern over asset forfeiture laws is that they make it too easy for law enforcement officials to seize the assets of innocent persons (Levy 1996). The Supreme Court has begun to rein in the government's forfeiture power. In the case of a South Dakota man who had his mobile home and auto body shop seized after being convicted of selling two grams of cocaine, the Court unanimously ruled that the amount seized (almost $43,000) was disproportionate to the crime (*Austin v. U.S.* 1993; Giffuni 1995). In the next term, the Court held that the same provisions of the Bill of Rights also apply in asset forfeiture (*U.S. v. James Daniel Good Real Property* 1993). But innocent owners can still have their assets seized (*Bennis v. Michigan* 1996; *U.S. v. Ursery* 1996). And after years of debate, Congress passed the Civil Asset Forfeiture Act of 2000, which shifts the burden of proof to the government. The new law also awards lawyers' fees to those who successfully challenge confiscation of property.

Research concludes that there is no clear answer to whether asset forfeiture encourages policing for profit. However, the study found that local law enforcement agencies circumvent restrictive state laws (those placing limits on the proceeds they can receive) by teaming up with federal officials to receive equitable sharing payments (Worrall and Kovandzic 2008).

The debate over asset forfeiture crosses traditional ideological lines. Due process advocates want limits on asset forfeiture because they think that innocent people end up being presumed guilty. Similarly, crime control supporters also want strong restrictions on asset forfeiture because they think it improperly gives the government too much authority over important property rights. The leading interest group is Forfeiture Endangers Americans' Rights (FEAR), which highlights perceived abuses of asset forfeiture at the state and federal levels (http://www.fear.org). On the other side of the debate is the Department of Justice's Asset Forfeiture Program within the U.S. Department of Justice, which stresses that asset forfeiture is a nationwide law enforcement program that continues to be an effective and powerful strategy in the fight against crime (http://www.usdoj.gov/jmd/afp).

What do you think? Should more limits be placed on law enforcement officials' ability to seize assets of suspected wrongdoers? Do large financial incentives like these provide too great a temptation?

differences between civil law and **criminal law** (see Table 2.2). One difference centers on who has been harmed. Whereas a breach of the civil law is considered a private matter involving only the individual parties, violations of the criminal law are considered public wrongs. As such, criminal law relates to actions that are considered so dangerous, or potentially so, that they threaten the welfare of society as a whole.

A second difference involves prosecution. Unlike the civil law, in which private parties file suit in court alleging an infringement of private rights, violations of public wrongs are prosecuted by the state.

The types of penalties imposed on law violators is a third difference. In civil law, the injured party receives compensation. Violators of the criminal law, however, are punished. In setting penalties, American law often makes a distinction between a misdemeanor and a felony. In general, a **misdemeanor** is a criminal offense less serious than a **felony**. Misdemeanors are generally punishable by a fine or up to a year in jail; felonies usually involve prison sentences of more than a year. The stress on punishment derives from the goal of criminal law to prevent and control crime. It is important to recognize that the criminal law is intended to supplement, not supplant, the civil law. Thus, as discussed earlier, a person may be prosecuted criminally and the victim may also seek to recover civil damages for the same act (see Case Close-Up: Civil and Criminal Prosecutions of Celebrities). In automobile accidents involving drinking, for example, the drunk driver may be charged criminally with drunk driving and the injured party may also file a civil suit seeking monetary damages.

TABLE 2.2

DIFFERENCES BETWEEN CIVIL AND CRIMINAL LAW

	CIVIL	CRIMINAL
Moving party	Plaintiff	State
Defending party	Defendant	Defendant
Burden of proof	Preponderance of the evidence	Guilty beyond a reasonable doubt
Jury verdict rules	Less than unanimous (many states)	Unanimous (most states)
Remedy	Monetary damages	Prison or probation
Defendant's testimony	May be forced to testify	Constitutional right to silence
Right to counsel	No constitutional right to counsel	Constitutional right to counsel
Prosecution	Must hire own lawyer	The government through the district attorney
Examples	Tort, contract, property, probate	Assault, theft, burglary

ELEMENTS OF A CRIME

Corpus delicti, a Latin phrase meaning "body of the crime," refers to the essential **elements of a crime.** In defining the elements of a particular offense, criminal laws are based on five general principles. Most behavior cannot be called criminal unless:

- a guilty act is committed, with a
- guilty intent, and
- the guilty act and the guilty intent are related.

In addition, a number of crimes are defined on the basis of:

- attendant circumstances and/or
- specific results.

An understanding of the basic concepts embodied in the statutory definitions of crime is essential for correctly interpreting definitions of crime. In turn, these basic concepts produce numerous categories of criminal activities (murder, voluntary manslaughter, and involuntary manslaughter, for example).

GUILTY ACT

Before there can be a crime, there must be a **guilty act (actus reus).** Thus, criminal liability occurs only after a voluntary act that results in criminal harm. The requirement of a guilty act reflects a fundamental principle of American law: No one should be punished solely for bad thoughts. Depending on the crime, there are different types of guilty acts. Most crimes have a voluntary act as the actus reus. Thus, a person who strikes another while suffering an epileptic seizure would not be guilty of battery, because the act (hitting) was not voluntary. An omission—a failure to act when there is a legal duty to act—can also qualify as an actus reus, such when failing to file income taxes, failing to yield the right-of-way, and failing to provide adequate care for one's children. The act of possession can also qualify as an actus reus, such as the offense of possession of an illegal drug. Differences in the nature of the guilty act account for many gradations of criminal offenses. To choose one obvious example, stealing property is considered separately from damaging property.

An important subdivision of the guilty act is a class of offenses labeled as **attempts** (for example, attempted burglary or attempted murder). The law does not want a person to avoid legal liability merely because someone or something prevented the commission of a crime. Typically, though, the penalties for attempt are less severe than if the act had succeeded. One result is that in some states, defendants often plead guilty in an attempt to reduce the possible severity of the prison sentence.

GUILTY INTENT

Most crimes consist of two elements, the guilty act itself and the accompanying mental state. The rationale is that criminal sanctions are not necessary for those who innocently cause harm. As Justice Holmes (1881, p. 3) once pithily put it, "Even a dog distinguishes between being stumbled over and being kicked." The mental state required for a crime to have been committed is referred to as **guilty intent** or **mens rea** ("guilty mind").

Despite its importance in criminal law, guilty intent is difficult to define because it refers to a subjective condition, a state of mind. Some statutes require only general intent (intent to do something that the law prohibits), but others specify the existence of specific intent (intent to do the exact thing charged). Moreover, legislatively defined crimes have added new concepts of mental state to the traditional ones. Thus, crimes differ with respect to the mental state the prosecution must prove existed in order to secure a criminal conviction. Larceny (termed "theft" in some states), for example, typically requires proof of a very great degree of intent; the prosecutor must prove that the defendant intentionally took property to which he knew he was not entitled, intending to deprive the rightful owner of possession permanently. Negligent homicide, on the other hand, is an example of a crime involving a lesser degree of intent; the prosecution need only show that the defendant negligently caused the death of another. Most crimes require that the defendant knew he or she was doing something wrong. Also, the law assumes that people know the consequences of their acts. Thus, a person cannot avoid legal liability by later saying, "I didn't mean to do it."

FUSION OF GUILTY ACT AND GUILTY INTENT

The criminal law requires that the guilty act and the guilty intent occur together, a concept often referred to as the union of actus reus and mens rea. Here is an example that illustrates this concept of **fusion of the guilty act and guilty intent**: Suppose that you pick-up another student's textbook believing it to be your own. Although you take the book—an act that would constitute the actus reus for theft—you had no criminal intent; you made an honest and reasonable mistake. Thus, without the union of actus reus (the taking of the book) and mens rea (the intent to steal), you would not be liable for theft.

ATTENDANT CIRCUMSTANCES

Some crimes require the presence, or absence, of **attendant (accompanying) circumstances**. Driving at a speed of 150 miles per hour would constitute a crime only if it occurred on a public roadway; it would not be a crime to drive at that speed on a racetrack. The location of the speeding is the attendant circumstance for the crime. Attendant circumstances may also be used to define the level or "degree" of crime. For example, most states differentiate between classes of theft on the basis of the amount stolen. The law might provide that a theft of less than $500 be treated as a misdemeanor and a theft of $500 or more be treated as a felony. The amount stolen is the attendant circumstance.

RESULTS

In a limited number of criminal offenses, the **result** of the illegal act plays a critical part in defining the crime. The difference between homicide and battery, for example, depends on whether the victim died or lived. Similarly, most states distinguish between degrees of battery, depending on how seriously the victim was injured. Note that the concept of results differs from that of intent. In all of the preceding examples, the defendant may have had the same intent. The only difference was how hearty the victim was or perhaps how skillful the defendant was in carrying out his or her intentions.

Based on the five general principles—guilty act, guilty intent, fusion, attendant circumstances, and results—the corpus delicti of each crime (murder, robbery, rape, and burglary, for example) differs (Exhibit 2.7). The elements of a particular crime provide the technical (that is, legal) definitions of a crime. For this reason, criminal statutes must be read closely, because each clause constitutes a critical part of the offense. Before a defendant can be convicted, all the elements of a crime must be proven.

LEGAL DEFENSES

Under the law, individuals may have performed illegal acts but still not be found guilty of a criminal violation because of a legally recognized justification for the actions or because legally they were not

Exhibit 2.7		
CHARACTERISTICS OF THE MOST COMMON SERIOUS CRIMES		
	LAW ON THE BOOKS	**LAW IN ACTION**
Homicide	The killing of one human being by another.	Homicide is the least frequent violent crime. Most often murderers are relatives or acquaintances of the victim.
Rape	A sexual intercourse that occurs without the effective consent of the victim.	Contrary to portrayals of sexual assaults by strangers in many movies and television shows, the overwhelming number of such crimes are "acquaintance rapes," in which the victim knew the assailant.
Robbery	The taking or attempting to take anything of value from the care, custody, or control of a person or persons by force or threat of force or violence and/or by putting the victim in fear.	Half of all robberies involve one offender. Half of all robberies involve the use of a weapon.
Assault	*Aggravated* assault is an unlawful attack by one person upon another for the purpose of inflicting severe or aggravated bodily injury. This type of assault is usually accompanied by the use of a weapon or other means likely to produce death or great bodily harm.	Simple assault occurs more frequently than aggravated assault. Simple assault is the most common type of violent crime.
	Simple assault is an unlawful attack by one person upon another for the purpose of inflicting less than severe bodily injury. This type of assault does not involve the use of a weapon or other means likely to produce death or great bodily harm.	
Burglary	The unlawful entry into a structure to commit a felony or a theft.	Residential property is targeted in two out of three burglaries.
Larceny (theft)	The unlawful taking, carrying, lending, or riding away of property from possession or constructive possession of another.	Pocket picking and purse snatching occur most frequently inside businesses or on street locations.

	LAW ON THE BOOKS	LAW IN ACTION
Motor vehicle theft	The theft or attempted theft of a motor vehicle. A motor vehicle is self-propelled and runs on the surface, not on rails.	Motor vehicle theft is relatively well reported to the police, but the crime has a low rate of being solved.
Arson	Any willful or malicious burning or attempt to burn, with or without intent to defraud, a dwelling house, public building, motor vehicle, aircraft, or personal property of another.	Single-family residences are the most frequent targets of arson.

Exhibit 2.7 CONTINUED

Source: Federal Bureau of Investigation, *Uniform Crime Reports.* Washington, DC: U.S. Department of Justice, 2003; Bureau of Justice Statistics, *Report to the Nation on Crime and Justice.* 2nd ed. Washington, DC: Government Printing Office, 1988.

responsible for their actions. These **legal defenses** derive from the way crime is defined.

Some defenses are predicated on the principle of justification. Self-defense is the classic example of a defense of justification. While intentionally killing someone normally constitutes a serious crime, such a killing would be justified—and, therefore, not criminal—if it occurred as a result of defending oneself against an unlawful attack by another person threatening the imminent use of deadly force.

Other defenses are based on the principle of excuse—the notion that, under certain extraordinary circumstances, one should be excused for committing an act that would usually be criminally punished. For example, the law recognizes the defense of duress—unlawful pressure on a person to do what he or she would not otherwise have done. Duress includes force, threat of violence, and physical restraint. In a defense of duress, the defendant is contending, in essence, that he or she should be treated as a victim rather than as a criminal. Similarly, the law assumes that persons with certain types of mental illness are incapable of forming criminal intent. Indeed, the best-known, and also most controversial, legal defense is insanity. In Chapter 14 we will examine how insanity and other legal defenses are occasionally used at trial.

The requirement of guilty intent gives rise to several other legal defenses. Some types of people are considered legally incapable of forming criminal intent and therefore cannot be held criminally responsible for their actions. Children are prime examples.

Until children reach a certain age (7 in most states), they are presumed not to be responsible for their actions and therefore cannot be criminally prosecuted. After reaching this minimum age, but before becoming an adult, a child's criminal violations are treated as acts of **juvenile delinquency** (Chapter 19). The premise of juvenile delinquency acts is that people under a certain age have less responsibility for their actions than adults do. The exact age at which a person is no longer considered a juvenile, and can thus be prosecuted as an adult, differs from state to state. As more and more youths are committing violent crimes, states are lowering the age for prosecuting a minor as an adult (see Chapter 19).

EFFECTS OF THE CRIMINAL LAW ON THE COURTS

Because the criminal code constitutes the basic source of authority for law enforcement agencies, the way crimes are defined has an important bearing on the entire administration of criminal justice. Chapter 5 will consider in greater detail the relationship between law and discretion. For now we will examine the criminal law and inconsistencies, plea bargaining, and sentencing.

CRIMINAL LAW AND INCONSISTENCIES

Inconsistencies exist within each criminal code (sometimes referred to as the "penal code"). All

LAW AND POPULAR CULTURE

Chicago (2002)

In an effort to remake the image of his client Roxy Hart (played by Renee Zellweger), lawyer Billy Flynn (played by Richard Gere) holds a press conference. He starts by calling on Mary Sunshine, an obviously friendly reporter from a dry newspaper who poses a predictably softball question: "Do you have any advice for young girls seeking to avoid a life of jazz and drink?" "Absolutely," Flynn responds. "Mrs. Hart feels it was the tragic combination of liquor and jazz which led to the downfall." And then he launches into a song called the "Press Conference Rag," intended to influence how his client's story gets told.

The film *Chicago* (2002), based on the musical of the same name, is set during the Roaring Twenties, when jazz, illegal liquor, sin, and the city of Chicago seemed synonymous. What is somewhat unusual is that it focuses on women killing men, a topic not typically portrayed in works of fiction. What is not unusual, however, is how lawyers try to manipulate the press to influence judges and juries. From the nation's beginning, defendants have hired lawyers to improve their public standing, hoping that will translate into favorable treatment by the criminal justice system.

The fictional, media-savvy Billy Flynn uses the press in an effort to complete an extreme makeover of his client Roxy Hart, who suffered from very serious image problems. (She murdered her lover and then tried to have her husband take the fall.) Real-life celebrity lawyers, such as Mark Geragos, employ similar strategies for clients such as Michael Jackson and Scott Peterson, who also need extreme makeovers of their public images. The pop star Michael Jackson was charged with sexually molesting several young boys and then paying their families in a cover-up. Scott Peterson was accused of murdering his pregnant wife and unborn child and then concocting an elaborate cover-up story.

Formal press conferences and informal news leaks played key roles during the prosecutions of Peterson and Jackson. In an earlier era, lawyers often preferred to keep their clients and their legal woes out of the public eye. But, today, many lawyers seem to delight in calling public attention to their clients and their legal peccadilloes. Not surprisingly, high-profile lawyers are accused of playing to the cameras (and reporters) both inside and outside the courtroom. Indeed, an assistant district attorney suggested, "It looks like Geragos is trying to manipulate the media and the jury and he's been pretty good at it" (CBS News 2004). At times, though, such complaints are little more than sour grapes; after all, police and prosecutors regularly use the media to project a negative image of defendants.

Trials are an obvious source of interest for journalists because they represent the classic "whodunit." Thus, it is not surprising that the press follow some trials closely. Most trials are too mundane to evoke much public interest, but the legal woes of Peterson and Jackson proved to be major news events that often displaced more serious material about the war in Iraq and the presidential election. What has changed over time is the advent of cable news channels, which provide extensive coverage of celebrity trials. The challenge for the media is how to cover those trials when a legal team is trying to manipulate the press. In turn, the growth of electronic media has made the reporters as much of the story as the lawyers (and their clients). The O. J. Simpson trial, for example, made legal reporter Greta Van Susteren a household name in the same way the Peterson and Jackson trials contributed to Nancy Grace's rise to fame.

It is unclear whether efforts by celebrity lawyers such as Mark Geragos and Johnny Cochran (O. J. Simpson's lead attorney) ultimately matter to either the jury or the rest of the public. Peterson was convicted of murder and sentenced to death. Jackson, on the other hand, was acquitted (although Geragos had left the Jackson defense team before trial). One thing is clear, though, and that is that the media appear

CONTINUED

Chicago (2002)

more than willing to continue to cover these trials and the actions of the celebrity attorneys. Whether that is good for the legal system or for justice is a question that remains unanswered. As we will discuss in Chapter 14, prejudicial pretrial publicity is a major concern in high-profile cases.

In a highly dramatic fashion, the movie *Chicago* illustrates the tension between law on the books and law in action. Law on the books projects the rules of law as abstract and absolute. Law in action, on the other hand, stresses real people and the subjectivity of facts. From arrest to sentencing, prosecutors, defense attorneys, judges, jurors, and probation officers are required to interpret what facts are most relevant and

what conclusions to draw from those facts. That there may be disagreements in these assessments produces another theme of this book—law in controversy.

1. What do you think? Do the media have an obligation to ignore events concocted by lawyers simply to put a favorable spin on their clients' situations?

2. How could you study whether television coverage of these trials has an influence on the trial or the verdict?

3. In what ways do modern celebrity attorneys such as Mark Geragos resemble the fictionalized Billy Flynn in *Chicago*?

---

too often, criminal statutes resemble a crazy quilt of inconsistent sets of criminal definitions and penalties. Because legislatures change criminal codes piecemeal, the end product is a set of criminal laws with obsolete prohibitions and inconsistent penalties. Typically, such contradictions indicate a lack of agreement in American society about what behavior should be criminalized and what penalties are appropriate.

In practice, judges and prosecutors attempt to rectify these inconsistencies by informally developing a consistent set of penalties. It should be obvious that the courts must apply the law as they find it. The corollary is that the courts often must rectify inconsistencies in that law. Disparities in possible sentences as provided in state statutes require judges, prosecutors, and defense attorneys to arrive at a workable penalty structure. Society would be outraged if serious crimes elicited the same punishment as minor ones, even if the law technically allowed the two categories of offenses to be treated the same way.

CRIMINAL LAW AND PLEA BARGAINING

Variations in the definitions of crimes make the criminal courts fertile ground for plea bargaining. In particular, differences in degrees of seriousness provide the

means for charge bargaining (the defendant pleads guilty to a less serious offense than the one charged). For example, in some states, assault and battery involves five degrees (categories). Although the law must attempt to differentiate between, say, a punch thrown in anger and a deliberate gunshot wound that leaves its victim permanently paralyzed, the existence of many different degrees of seriousness facilitates pleas to less serious offenses. Thus, prosecutors may deliberately overcharge in hopes of inducing the defendant to later plead guilty to a lesser charge (see Chapter 13).

CRIMINAL LAW AND SENTENCING

The most obvious way criminal law affects the operations of the criminal courts is in sentencing. As we will discuss in greater detail in Chapters 15 and 16, the legislature establishes sentencing options from which judges must choose. Because of the public's concern about crime, pressures are strong to increase penalties. As a result, legislatures increase the harshness of sentencing, and the courts mitigate that harshness. According to Rosett and Cressey (1976, p. 95; see also, Champion 2007), such legislative action and courthouse reactions follow a predictable pattern:

- Step I. Laws calling for severe punishments are passed by legislatures on the assumption that fear of great pain will terrorize the citizenry into conformity.
- Step II. Criminal justice personnel soften these severe penalties for most offenders (a) in the interests of justice, (b) in the interests of bureaucracy, and (c) in the interests of gaining acquiescence.
- Step III. The few defendants who then insist on a trial and are found guilty, or who in other ways refuse to cooperate, are punished more severely than those who acquiesce.
- Step IV. Legislatures, noting that most criminals by acquiescing avoid "the punishment prescribed by law," (a) increase the prescribed punishments and (b) try to limit the range of discretionary decision making used to soften the harsh penalties.
- Step V. The more severe punishments introduced in the preceding step are again softened for most offenders, as in Step II, with the result that the defendants who do not acquiesce are punished even more severely than they were at Step III.

This book will return often to the question of whether the legislatures or the courts have adopted the more appropriate stance.

CONCLUSION

The lack of public trials in the legal proceedings involving Kobe Bryant left citizens divided over where justice lay. Was the prosecutor right (or wrong) in dropping the case in the face of a reluctant witness? Was the plaintiff right (or wrong) in accepting an out-of-court settlement rather than forcing a public trial that might produce public accountability for his behavior? Similar questions were raised following the public trials of O. J. Simpson. Was the

criminal jury right (or wrong) in finding the former football star not guilty of two counts of murder? Was the civil jury equally right (or wrong) in finding Simpson liable for the killings of his ex-wife and her friend? Similar questions haunted Michael Jackson until his death in 2009, even though he had been acquitted of allegations concerning the sexual abuse of minors.

The civil and criminal cases involving Kobe Bryant, O. J. Simpson, and Michael Jackson also illustrate the importance of understanding both law on the books and law in action. The law on the books—the elements of crimes such as murder and sexual assault—is abstract. The law in action—what victims, defendants, lawyers, judges, and juries do—is concrete. Ultimately, the meaning of the law is not what the judge instructs to the jury (law on the books) but the decision reached by the jury (law in action). By voting not guilty, the first jury decided that Simpson's conduct was not criminal. By deciding he was liable, another jury decided that his conduct violated community standards. In the Kobe Bryant case, it was the prosecutor's prediction of what the jury would decide that led to dropping the charges. Moreover, it was the anticipation of what a civil jury might decide that led Bryant and his lawyers to accept an out-of-court settlement.

What activities should be labeled criminal is a source of constant political discussion. Actions viewed as bad in the past may no longer be considered bad. As society changes, so do public perceptions of public wrongs, and pressures develop to add more activities to the list of officially proscribed ones. Through all of this change, we must not lose sight of the essential fact that law is an integral part of society. Law is not imposed on society; rather, it reflects the sociology, economy, history, and politics of society. Law was created to help society, not the other way around.

CHAPTER REVIEW

1. List the four key elements defining law.

Law is defined as: (1) a body of rules, (2) enacted by public officers, (3) in a legitimate manner, and (4) backed by the force of the state.

2. Identify the three key characteristics of the common law.

The three key characteristics of the common law are: (1) judge-made law, (2) precedent, and (3) multiple sources of law.

3. Analyze the importance of the adversary system.

The adversary system seeks to protect individual rights by diffusing governmental power in several actors and insisting that the defendant is presumed innocent until proven guilty.

4. Name the four amendments of the Bill of Rights that deal specifically with criminal procedure.

Of the first 10 amendments to the Constitution collectively known as the Bill of Rights, the Fourth, Fifth, Sixth, and Eighth deal specifically with criminal procedure.

5. List the five major areas of civil law.

The five major area of civil law are: tort, contract, property, domestic relations, and inheritance.

6. Discuss the five elements (corpus delicti) of a crime.

No behavior can be called criminal unless: (1) a guilty act is committed, with a (2) guilty intent, and (3) the guilty act and the guilty intent are related. In addition, a number of crimes are defined on the basis of: (4) attendant circumstances, and (5) specific results.

7. Identify some of the most important legal defenses in American law.

Some of the most important legal defenses in American law include duress, juvenile delinquency, and insanity.

8. Discuss the effects of the criminal law on courts.

How the law defines crimes affects the administration of justice in the courts in several important ways, including the need to reconcile inconsistencies in the criminal law, providing the basis for plea bargaining, and the harshness of sentences.

CRITICAL THINKING QUESTIONS

1. Constitutional rights of the accused is, of course, a controversial topic. The crime control model, in particular, decries letting the obviously guilty go free on "technicalities," whereas the due process model emphasizes basic rights. Examining Exhibit 2.2, what common ground do these two approaches share? Where do they disagree most?

2. All non–English-speaking industrial democracies use the inquisitorial system rather than the adversary system. In this system, the judge, not the prosecutor and not the defense attorney, calls witnesses and questions them. Would you prefer being tried under the adversary system or the inquisitorial system? Would you have confidence in the willingness of the judge to search out equally evidence for conviction and evidence for acquittal?

3. One of the biggest societal changes in recent years has been the rapid expansion of computer technology. How have legislatures responded to crimes involving the use of computers? How has the Internet changed the debate over pornography?

KEY TERMS

administrative regulations 31

adversary system 32

Anglo-American law 29

affirmative defense 33

attempt 47

attendant (accompanying) circumstances 47

beyond a reasonable doubt 35

Bill of Rights 38

burden of persuasion 33

burden of production 33

civil law 38

clear and convincing evidence 33

common law 29

constitution 31
contract 39
corpus delicti 46
criminal law 45
declaratory judgment 42
defendant 41
domestic relations 41
due process of law 38
elements of a crime 46
felony 45
fusion of the guilty act
    and guilty intent 47
guilty act (actus reus) 46
guilty intent (mens rea) 47
inference 33

inheritance 41
injunction 42
in rem 44
judge-made law 29
judgment 41
juvenile delinquency 49
law 28
legal defense 49
misdemeanor 45
monetary damage 42
municipal ordinance 31
plaintiff 41
precedent 29
preponderance of the
    evidence 33

presumption 33
presumption of innocence 33
presumption of sanity 33
probable cause 33
procedural law 32
property 39
reasonable, articulable
    suspicion 33
remedy 41
result 47
selective incorporation 38
stare decisis 29
statute 31
substantive law 32
tort 39

WEB RESOURCES

Go to the America's Courts and the Criminal Justice System companion website at

http://www.cengage.com/criminaljustice/neubauer

where you will find more resources to help you study.
Resources include web exercises, quizzing, and flash cards.

FOR FURTHER READING

Brunet, James. "Discouragement of Crime through Civil Remedies: An Application of Reformulated Routine Activities Theory." *Western Criminology Review* 4 (2002): 68–79.

Dombrink, John, and Daniel Hillyard. *Sin No More: From Abortion to Stem Cells, Understanding Crime, Law, and Morality in America.* New York: NYU Press, 2008.

Gardner, Thomas, and Terry Anderson. *Criminal Law.* 10th ed. Belmont, CA: Wadsworth, 2009.

Payne, Dennis. *Police Liability: Lawsuits against the Police.* Durham, NC: Carolina Academic Press, 2002.

Pollock, Joycelyn. *Ethical Dilemmas and Decisions in Criminal Justice.* 6th ed. Belmont, CA: Wadsworth, 2010.

Ross, Darrell. *Civil Liability in Criminal Justice.* Cincinnati: Anderson, 2006.

Samaha, Joel. *Criminal Law.* 9th ed. Belmont, CA: Wadsworth, 2008.

Scheb, John M., and John M. Scheb II. *Criminal Law.* 5th ed. Belmont, CA: Wadsworth, 2009.

Tushnet, Mark. Out of Range: *Why the Constitution Can't End the Battle over Guns.* New York: Oxford University Press, 2007.

3

FEDERAL COURTS

© Hiroko Masuike/Getty Images

Bernard Madoff walks out from federal court in New York City after a bail
hearing in January 2009. Madoff was accused of and eventually pled guilty
to running a $50 billion Ponzi scheme through his investment company.
At his sentencing, the judge called his crime an "extraordinary evil" that
took "a staggering toll" on rich and poor alike. Madoff was sentenced to
the maximum allowable term of 150 years in prison for his fraud, the most
severe sentence ever imposed for a "white collar" offense.

Chapter Outline

LEARNING OBJECTIVES

After reading this chapter you should be able to:

1. Define the four primary types of jurisdiction: geographical, subject matter, personal, and hierarchical.

2. Compare and contrast the tasks of trial and appellate courts.

3. Explain the historical evolution of the federal courts into their present structure and operations.

4. Analyze the different responsibilities and workloads of U.S magistrate judges, district judges, circuit judges, and Supreme Court justices.

5. Analyze the impact the federal courts have on the administration of criminal justice at the state and local levels through their federal question jurisdiction.

6. Differentiate the jurisdiction and functions of Article III courts from Article I courts and other specialized federal courts.

7. Distinguish the various agencies and their hierarchical responsibilities for the administration of the federal court system.

8. Evaluate the major problems facing the federal courts and the strengths and weaknesses of the major solutions that have been proposed to address these problems.

ALFONSO LOPEZ, JR., a 12th-grader at Edison High School in San Antonio, Texas, thought he had found an easy way to make a quick buck. "Gilbert" would pay him $40 to take a .38-caliber pistol to school and deliver it to "Jason," who planned to use it in a "gang war." Based on an anonymous tip, school officials confronted Lopez, who admitted carrying the unloaded weapon (but he did have five bullets on his person). Lopez was charged in federal court with violating the Gun-Free School Zones Act of 1990. After a bench trial, Lopez was found guilty and sentenced to 6 months in prison. The Supreme Court reversed the conviction, however, concluding that the U.S. Congress had no authority to outlaw guns in schools.

The Supreme Court's decision in *United States v. Lopez* first attracts our attention because it deals with gun control—one of the truly hot button issues of American politics. But a closer probing raises other, even more important questions. What should be a federal crime? After all, weapons offenses are usually violations of state law, and indeed Mr. Lopez was initially charged in state court; but these charges were dropped after federal officials stepped in. How is it that five conservative judges, appointed by

Republican presidents and pledged to getting tough on crime, reversed a conviction that was certainly popular with the American public? After all, Republicans have accused liberal federal judges (seemingly those appointed by Democratic presidents) of being soft on crime.

The issues, both direct and indirect, raised in *United States v. Lopez* trace their origins to the early days of the Republic. The founding fathers were deeply divided over which cases federal courts should hear. Indeed, the drafters of the U.S. Constitution were deeply divided over whether there should be any federal courts besides the U.S. Supreme Court. A principal task of this chapter, therefore, is to discuss how the current federal judicial structure—magistrate, district, and appellate courts and the Supreme Court—is a product of more than 200 years of political controversy and compromise about the proper role of the federal judiciary. The remainder of the chapter focuses on the specialized courts and the administrative structure. Most important, we will discuss the contemporary debate over how many cases are too many for the federal courts to handle, thus illustrating that the controversies continue. But first, to establish some common ground about the often confusing topic of court organization, we begin this chapter by examining some basic principles.

Basic Principles of Court Organization

Even lawyers who regularly use the courts sometimes find the details of court organization confusing. Court nomenclature includes many shorthand phrases that mean something to those who work in the courts daily but can be quite confusing to the outsider. Learning the language of courts is like learning any foreign language—some of it can come only from experience. Before studying the specifics of federal and state courts (Chapter 4), it is helpful to understand the basic principles of court organization within the dual court structure that exists in the United States.

Dual Court System

The United States has a **dual court system**: one national court system plus separate court systems in each of the 50 states and the District of Columbia.

The result is more than 51 separate court systems. Exhibit 3.1 illustrates the structure of the dual court system in the United States. The division of responsibilities is not as clear cut as it looks, however. State and federal courts share some judicial powers. Some acts—for example, selling drugs or robbing banks—are crimes under federal law and under the laws of most states, which means the accused could be tried in both federal and state courts. Moreover, litigants in state court may appeal to the U.S. Supreme Court, a federal court, if a federal question is presented, such as a question of federal constitutional law.

One of the most immediate consequences of the dual court system is the complexity it adds to the criminal justice system. In essence, the framers of the U.S. Constitution created two parallel criminal justice systems consisting of their own law enforcement, court structure, and correctional systems. Of all the levels of complexity created by the dual court system, perhaps the most confusing is the application of the constitutional prohibition against double jeopardy (see Courts, Controversy, and the Administration of Justice: Should the Double Jeopardy Clause Prohibit Parallel State and Federal Prosecutions?).

Jurisdiction

Court structure is largely determined by limitations on the types of cases a court may hear and decide. **Jurisdiction** is the power of a court to decide a dispute. A court's jurisdiction can be further classified according to four subcomponents: geographical jurisdiction, hierarchical jurisdiction, subject matter jurisdiction, and personal jurisdiction.

Geographical Jurisdiction and Venue

Courts are authorized to hear and decide disputes arising within a specified **geographical jurisdiction** (sometimes referred to as "territorial jurisdiction"). Geographical jurisdiction in criminal cases is primarily concerned with a sovereign's power to punish conduct that violates its criminal laws. Thus, the courts of California have no jurisdiction to try a person accused of committing a crime in Oregon; Oregon has such power, since the accused is alleged to have violated its criminal law. But which courts within the state of Oregon would hear the case? That is a matter of venue.

Venue is the particular location or area in which a court having geographic jurisdiction may hear a case. Proper venue is based on statutorily defined

Exhibit 3.1

OVERVIEW OF THE DUAL COURT STRUCTURE OF THE UNITED STATES

United States Supreme Court
The High Court of Last Resort in the United States
The most powerful court in the world. It has virtually complete control of the cases it hears by exercising its discretionary appellate jurisdiction over decisions of the U.S. Courts of Appeals and the decisions of the highest courts in the state systems if a question of federal law (including federal constitutional law) is presented. Typically hears fewer than 30 criminal cases each term.

The Federal Courts
Hears cases throughout the U.S.
Decides roughly 70,800 criminal cases each year.

The State Courts
Important variations from state to state.
Decides roughly 6.6 million adult criminal cases each year.

United States Courts of Appeals
Mandatory appellate jurisdiction over the decisions of the U.S. District Courts.
12 Regional Circuits and 1 Federal Circuit that hears appeals from specialized trial courts like the U.S. Court of International Trade, the U.S. Claims Court, and the U.S. Court of Veterans' Appeals.
The last stop for the vast majority of defendants convicted in federal court, very few of which win a significant victory.

State High Courts of Last Resort
Mandatory and discretionary appellate jurisdiction over decisions rendered by lower state courts.
Major policy maker for the state.
Final decider for questions of state law.
Typically decides a handful of criminal appeals each year.

United States District Courts
Trial courts of original jurisdiction over federal cases.
94 federal districts (including territorial ones in the District of Columbia, Puerto Rico, Guam, the U.S. Virgin Islands, and the Northern Mariana Islands).
Mandatory appellate jurisdiction over decisions by non-Article III courts.
Adjudicates all federal crimes like drug smuggling, mail fraud, robbery of FDIC-insured banks. Also adjudicates civil lawsuits like civil right cases, claims of federal civil law (e.g., copyright and trademark infringement), and state civil law claims involving diversity of citizenship, such as torts.

State Intermediate Appellate Courts
(40 out of 50 states)
Mandatory appellate jurisdiction over decisions by the state's major trial courts.
Few criminal appellants win a significant victory.

State Major Trial Courts
Superior Courts/Courts of Common Pleas/District Courts
Trial courts of general jurisdiction that are usually arranged by county or groups of counties to hear felonies (murder, rape, robbery) and civil cases that do not involve small claims (accident cases, contract disputes). Sometimes they have appellate jurisdiction over state's minor trial courts.

Non-Article III Courts
U.S. Bankruptcy Courts, U.S. Tax Court, decisions of U.S. Magistrate Judges, and Administrative Law Judges (ALJ) in various federal agencies like the FCC, Social Security Administration, EEOC, NLRB, FTC, etc.
U.S. Magistrate Judges are responsible for preliminary stages of all federal felony cases. Magistrates also hear many minor criminal cases and assist with the processing of habeas corpus petitions and other civil lawsuits.

State Minor Trial Courts
Municipal Courts/Justice of the Peace Courts/ Magisterial District Courts
Limited original jurisdiction to hear misdemeanor cases (petty theft, public drunkenness, disorderly conduct), civil and criminal traffic violations, local ordinance violations, and small claims of a civil nature.

geographic subdivisions. These subdivisions are often determined by city or county boundaries, although other boundaries can be set that are unrelated to city or county lines. Divisions in the federal system are a good example of this. The state of Washington is a large and populous state. Instead of having one federal district coterminous with the boundaries of the state, there are two federal districts in Washington, the eastern district and the western district. Larger states are subdivided even further; California, for example, has a northern, eastern, central, and southern district. A federal case that arises from an act in Sacramento is properly tried in the northern district of California; the other districts in California would lack proper venue.

A defendant can waive venue in the district or county where a crime was committed by consenting to venue in another district or county. In state courts, venue can generally be transferred only to another district or county within a particular state, since only the courts of that particular state would have geographic jurisdiction over alleged violations of its own criminal law. In contrast, venue can be changed between districts of the federal system since the offense is against the United States—the same sovereign in all federal courts across the country.

Changes of venue in the federal courts are typically granted for one of two reasons. First, venue may be transferred to another location that is much more convenient for the parties and witnesses than the intended place of trial. Second, a change of venue is appropriate when a defendant is unlikely to get a fair and impartial trial in the federal district where the crime is alleged to have taken place. Intense pretrial publicity, for example, may have prejudiced the local jury pool. Since the right to a fair trial is guaranteed by the Sixth Amendment, a federal court should transfer venue to another federal district where the jury pool is less affected by publicity in the district where the crime allegedly occurred. For example, Timothy McVeigh, the defendant in the Oklahoma City bombing case, was tried for his crimes outside Oklahoma, even though that is where he committed the offenses. The extensive pretrial publicity and the intense personal connection to the case of the potential jurors in Oklahoma City made it very likely that the defendant could not get a fair and impartial trial in Oklahoma. The case was therefore transferred to Denver, Colorado, where the jury pool was less personally involved and more likely to meet the constitutional due process guarantees of a fair and impartial jury.

One major complication arising from geographical jurisdiction occurs when a person is arrested in one state for committing a crime in another state. **Extradition** involves the surrender by one state of an individual accused of a crime outside its own territory and within the territorial jurisdiction of the other state. If an American fugitive has fled to a foreign nation, the U.S. Secretary of State will request the return of the accused under the terms of the extradition treaty the United States has with that country (but a few nations of the world do not have such treaties).

Subject Matter Jurisdiction

Court structure is also determined by **subject matter jurisdiction**. Trial courts of *limited or special jurisdiction* are restricted to hearing a limited category of cases, typically misdemeanors and civil suits involving small sums of money. State courts typically have traffic courts or juvenile courts, both of which are examples of subject matter jurisdiction. The federal courts are all courts of limited jurisdiction, since they are limited to adjudicating certain types of cases (to be discussed later in this chapter). In contrast to trial courts of limited/special jurisdiction, trial courts of *general jurisdiction* are empowered to hear all other types of cases within the geographical jurisdiction of the court. In the state court systems (to be discussed in the next chapter), the county trial court fits here.

Personal Jurisdiction

Personal jurisdiction (sometimes called *"in personum* jurisdiction") refers to a court's power over an individual person or corporation. A court gains power over a particular defendant by virtue of the defendant's having done some act within the place where the court is located or having had some contact with the place in which the court is located. In criminal cases, personal jurisdiction refers to a court's authority to try a defendant for violating the state's criminal law. While a bit of an oversimplification, courts obtain personal jurisdiction over a defendant by the defendant having violated the law of the particular sovereign while within the forum state. This is relatively straightforward for traditional crimes against a person such as assault, rape, or murder. In contrast, establishing personal jurisdiction over a criminal defendant accused of fraud or cybercrimes who was not physically present in the forum state at the time the alleged crime occurred can be quite complicated (see Kerr 2008).

Courts, Controversy, and the Administration of Justice

Should the Double Jeopardy Clause Prohibit Parallel State and Federal Prosecutions?

Lemrick Nelson, Jr., who is African-American, was acquitted of state charges of murdering Jewish scholar Yankel Rosenbaum during a 1991 race riot in Brooklyn. Yet he was convicted in 1997 in federal court of violating the victim's civil rights. To some, the federal conviction meant that justice was finally done. But to others, the federal prosecution was itself a miscarriage of justice.

Of all the complexities created by the dual court system, perhaps the most confusing to laypersons and lawyers alike is the application of the constitutional prohibition against double jeopardy. The Fifth Amendment provides, "Nor shall any person be subject for the same offense to be twice put in jeopardy of life or limb." How, then, can a defendant be tried in both state court and federal court for the same crime? The answer is that the double jeopardy clause prevents only trial by the same government for the same offense (*Bartkus v. Illinois* 1958). This justification has been termed the "dual sovereign doctrine," because

two different sovereign governments (state and federal) are prosecuting the defendant for actions that happen to violate their separate criminal laws. Consider a defendant arrested for robbing a bank. The federal government can try the defendant for robbing a federal bank, and the state government may try the same defendant for robbery. Although the event is the same, it violates both federal and state laws.

The Supreme Court justified its decision in terms of federalism; the Court felt that a jurisdiction's interest would be impaired if the jurisdiction (state or federal) were unable to try an individual who had been tried elsewhere facing lesser penalties. Not all agree with this interpretation, however. Critics argue that the dual sovereign exception has no legal or historical basis (Piccarreta and Keenan 1995). The ACLU would bar parallel prosecutions by different governments for the same event, a view shared by sundry defendants who have been acquitted in one court only to be convicted in another.

Hierarchical Jurisdiction

The third subcomponent of jurisdiction is **hierarchical jurisdiction**, which refers to differences in the courts' functions and responsibilities. **Original jurisdiction** means that a court has the authority to try a case and decide it. **Appellate jurisdiction** means that a court has the power to review cases that have already been decided by another court. Trial courts are primarily courts of original jurisdiction, but they occasionally have limited appellate jurisdiction—for example, when a trial court hears appeals from lower trial courts such as mayor's courts or a justice of the peace court. Appellate courts often have a very limited original jurisdiction. The U.S. Supreme Court has original jurisdiction involving disputes between states, and state supreme courts have original jurisdiction in matters involving disbarment of lawyers.

Differentiating Trial and Appellate Courts

Virtually all cases begin in a **trial court** that has original jurisdiction. In a criminal case, the trial court arraigns the defendant, conducts a trial (or takes a guilty plea), and if the defendant is found guilty, imposes sentence. In a civil case, the trial court operates in much the same way, ensuring that each party is properly informed of the complaint and conducting a trial or accepting an out-of-court settlement. Because only trial courts hear disputes over facts, witnesses appear only in trial courts. Trial courts are considered finders of fact, and the decision of a judge (or jury) about a factual dispute is very difficult to challenge on appeal (Chapter 17).

The losing party in the trial court generally has the right to request an appellate court to review the case. The primary function of the **appellate court** is to ensure that the trial court correctly

The application of the double jeopardy clause has, in recent years, engendered considerable controversy in several highly publicized cases, including:

- Two Los Angeles police officers were acquitted of state charges in the 1991 beating of Rodney King but were later convicted in federal court of violating his civil rights.
- Four white New York police officers were acquitted in state court of murdering Amadou Diallo in 2000. The U.S. Justice Department later decided against federal prosecution.

These few cases aside, separate state and federal prosecutions are rare. As a practical matter, policies of the U.S. Department of Justice establish a strong presumption against federal reprosecution of a defendant already prosecuted by a state for the same conduct (Litman and Greenberg 1996).

What is perhaps most striking about the controversy over parallel prosecutions by dual sovereigns is that it cuts across the ideological dimensions that structure so much of our nation's debate concerning crime policy. In the Rodney King case, for example, members of the police union readily accepted the ACLU position. Similarly, some groups that are otherwise noted for conservative positions oppose parallel prosecutions. In short, the crime control and due process models are not particularly helpful in understanding this controversy.

As for Lemrick Nelson, a federal appellate court reversed his conviction, citing irregularities with jury selection. But on retrial, the jury returned a mixed verdict, finding Nelson had violated Mr. Rosenbaum's civil rights but did not cause his death. After years of denials, Nelson admitted during the retrial in federal district court in Brooklyn that he had stabbed Mr. Rosenbaum (Glaberson 2003).

What do you think? Are federal prosecutions after failed state prosecutions a good way to remedy miscarriages of justice, or are the rights of defendants unnecessarily placed in jeopardy?

---

interpreted the law. But appellate courts may also make new law.

Appellate and trial courts operate very differently because their roles are not the same. Appellate courts exercising appellate jurisdiction do not hear testimony from witnesses, conduct trials, or use juries. Those actions occur in a trial court exercising original jurisdiction. Moreover, instead of a single judge deciding, as in trial courts, a group of judges makes appellate court decisions; there may be as few as 3 or as many as 28 judges. (For more details on appellate courts and the appeals process, see Chapter 17.)

HISTORY OF THE FEDERAL COURTS

At first glance, the history of the federal courts appears to be a debate over details of procedure. But a closer look reveals that the political controversies that have shaped the federal judiciary go to the heart of the federal system of government, often involving the allocation of power between the national and state governments. Thus, any discussion of the federal courts in the early 21st century must begin with two 18th-century landmarks—Article III of the U.S. Constitution and the Judiciary Act of 1789. Although there have been important changes since, the decisions made at the beginning of the Republic about the nature of the federal judiciary have had a marked impact on contemporary court structure.

THE CONSTITUTIONAL CONVENTION

One major weakness of the Articles of Confederation was the absence of a national supreme court to enforce federal law and resolve conflicts and disputes between courts of the different states. Thus,

LAW AND POPULAR CULTURE

A Few Good Men (1992)

"You can't handle the truth!" thunders Colonel Nathan Jessup (portrayed by Jack Nicholson), highlighting the fact that "truth" can be a multilayered concept. Jessup is base commander at Guantánamo, Cuba. He is one of the Marines' "few good men" and on the fast track to being promoted to general. His view of truth highlights a clash between the code of the professional solider and the canons of civilian society. His response also shows that, to some, higher principles should prevail over mundane realities. Corporal Dawson (Wolfgang Bodison) and Private Louden Downey (James Marshall) are charged with killing Willie Santiago, a fellow Marine who was not only disgruntled but wanted out of the Marine Corps altogether.

The Judge Advocate General (JAG) appoints Lieutenant Daniel Kaffee (Tom Cruise) to defend the two young Marines. This seems a curious choice, because Kaffee has never tried a case and often boasts that he plea-bargained 44 cases in a row. But this time, two fellow lawyers—Lieutenant Commander JoAnne Galloway (Demi Moore) and Lieutenant Weinberg (Kevin Pollack)—goad Kaffee to probe behind the obvious.

The dramatic action hinges on whether the two young Marines were acting on their own or whether their superiors ordered a Code Red (Marine lingo for severe hazing as a punishment for failure to perform duties). As the investigation proceeds, it becomes obvious that lies (like truth) are multilayered. With but one exception, the top brass is lying. Documents have been forged. And a key witness disappears, only to mysteriously reappear just when the defense seems to have hit rock bottom.

How closely the movie matches reality is impossible to tell, because trials in military court are closed to the public. But it does point to a key tension between military law and broader notions of justice.

After World War II, a number of top German officials, military officers included, were tried for war crimes. The Nuremberg War Trials established the principle that soldiers cannot rely on illegal orders as a defense against wrongdoing. (See the movie *Judgment at Nuremberg* [1961].) Thus, the attempt by the defense to show that Corporal Dawson and Private Downey should be acquitted because they were merely following orders is not legally recognized. If the orders were illegal, they had a duty to refuse to follow them. In the real world, however, low-ranking soldiers like Downey and Dawson are unlikely to be schooled in such legal niceties. In the end, they stand by their principles as proud Marines, whereas those higher up seem to be ethically challenged. The movie is also rife with unethical activity by the lawyers.

After you watch this movie, be prepared to answer the following questions:

1. What image does this movie project about plea bargaining (discussed in Chapter 9)? The case goes to trial, but would the defendants have been served if they had pled guilty?
2. Defense attorney Daniel Kaffee rejects the plea bargain offered by the prosecutor. Was Kaffee representing the best interests of his clients or only flattering his own ego?
3. What image does this movie project about judicial independence? Would a civilian judge act the same way as the military judge?
4. How does this military court trial differ from a similar trial in a civilian court? How does this trial differ from trials in other movies?
5. Would the outcome of this trial have been different in a civilian court than in a military court? If so, how and why?
6. What image does this movie project about female lawyers?
7. What image does this movie project about legal ethics?

when the delegates gathered at the Constitutional Convention in Philadelphia in 1787, a resolution was unanimously adopted that "a national judiciary be established." There was considerable disagreement, however, on the specific form that the national judiciary should take. Article III was one of the most hotly debated sections of the Constitution.

The dominant question of whether there should be a federal court system separate from the state systems produced two schools of thought. Advocates of states' rights (later called "Anti-Federalists") feared that a strong national government would weaken individual liberties. More specifically, they saw the creation of separate federal courts as a threat to the power of state courts. As a result, the Anti-Federalists believed that federal law should be adjudicated first by the state courts; the U.S. Supreme Court should be limited to hearing appeals only from state courts. On the other hand, the Nationalists (who later called themselves "Federalists" because they favored ratification of the Constitution) distrusted the provincial prejudices of the states and favored a strong national government that could provide economic and political unity for the struggling new nation. As part of this approach, the Nationalists viewed state courts as incapable of developing a uniform body of federal law that would allow businesses to flourish. For these reasons, they backed the creation of lower federal courts.

The conflict between Federalists and Anti-Federalists was resolved by one of the many compromises that characterized the Constitutional Convention. **Article III** is brief and sketchy, providing only an outline of a federal judiciary: "The judicial Power of the United States, shall be vested in one Supreme Court, and in such inferior Courts as the Congress may from time to time ordain and establish." The brevity of this provision left Congress with the task of filling in much of the substance of the new judicial system.

THE JUDICIARY ACT OF 1789

Once the Constitution was ratified, action on the federal judiciary came quickly. Indeed, the first bill introduced in the Senate dealt with the unresolved issue of inferior federal courts. The congressional debate included many of the same participants, who repeated all the arguments involved in the judiciary debates at the Constitutional Convention. After extensive debate, Congress passed the Judiciary Act of 1789, which laid the foundation for our current national judicial system. The Judiciary Act of 1789 represented a major victory for the Federalists; they were successful in creating separate federal district courts. At the same time, the act was a compromise that allayed some of the Anti-Federalists' fears. The organization of the federal judiciary supported state interests in three ways (LaCroix 2007; Richardson and Vines 1970).

First, the boundaries of the district courts were drawn along state lines; no district encompassed more than one state. Thus, from the outset, the federal judiciary was "state-contained." Even though district courts enforced national law, they were organized along local lines, with each district court responsible for its own work under minimal supervision.

Second, by custom the selection process ensured that federal district judges would be residents of their districts. Although nominated by the president, district judges were to be (and are today) local residents, presiding in their home area, and therefore subject to the continuing influence of the local social and political environment (see Chapter 8).

Third, the act gave the lower federal courts only limited jurisdiction. The Federalists wanted the full range of federal jurisdiction granted by the Constitution to be given to district and circuit courts. However, to achieve a lower federal court system, they were forced to reduce this demand greatly. But this issue would reappear repeatedly over the next 100 years.

1789–1891

The Judiciary Act of 1789 provided only a temporary compromise on the underlying disagreements between Federalists and Anti-Federalists. The Federalists immediately pushed for expanded powers for the federal judiciary. These efforts culminated in the passage of the Judiciary Act of 1801, which created many new judgeships and greatly extended the jurisdiction of the lower courts. The Federalist victory was short-lived, however. With the election of Thomas Jefferson as president, the Anti-Federalists in Congress quickly repealed the act and returned the federal judiciary to the basic outlines of the previous court system. The 1801 law is best remembered for the resulting lawsuit of *Marbury v. Madison* (1803), in which Chief Justice John Marshall created the power of judicial review (the Court can strike down as unconstitutional an act of Congress) (Neubauer and Meinhold 2010).

Between 1789 and 1891 there was general agreement on the inadequacy of the federal judicial system, but the underlying dispute persisted. Congress passed numerous minor bills modifying the system in a piecemeal fashion. Dissatisfaction centered on two principal areas: circuit riding and the appellate court workload.

One of the most pronounced weaknesses of the 1789 judicial structure was circuit riding. The Supreme Court justices, many of them old and ill, faced days of difficult and often impossible travel. In 1838, for example, the nine justices traveled an average of 2,975 miles. There were numerous complaints from the justices about the intolerable conditions that circuit-riding duties imposed on them.

Beyond the personal discomforts some justices encountered, the federal judiciary confronted a more systemic problem—mounting caseloads. Initially, the federal judges of the newly created trial courts had relatively little to do because their jurisdictions were very limited. The Supreme Court likewise had few cases to decide. But the initially sparse workload began to expand as the growth of federal activity, the increase in corporate business, and the expansion of federal jurisdiction by court interpretation created litigation for a court system that was ill equipped to handle it. From the end of the Civil War until 1891, it was not uncommon for an appeal to wait 2 or 3 years before it was argued before the Supreme Court. The essential cause was that the high court had to decide every case appealed to it.

COURT OF APPEALS ACT OF 1891

At first glance, the creation of the court of appeals in 1891 appears to have been an automatic response to increased federal litigation resulting from a rapidly expanding population and the growth of business following the Civil War. A closer look indicates that it was the culmination of "one of the most enduring struggles in American political history" (Richardson and Vines 1970, p. 26). There was no debate over the difficulties facing the federal court system. All parties to the controversy agreed that the federal judiciary needed relief; what was in dispute was the nature of the relief.

To solve the burden of mounting litigation in the federal courts, the supporters of states' rights wanted to return cases to the state level by reducing the jurisdiction of federal courts. The supporters of national power, on the other hand, argued for expanding the jurisdiction of federal courts by creating a system of federal appellate courts that would take

a great deal of the burden off the high court and also allow the trial courts to function as true trial courts.

The landmark Court of Appeals Act of 1891 represented the climactic victory of the nationalist interests. The law created new courts known as circuit courts of appeals. Under this new arrangement, most appeals of trial decisions went to a circuit court of appeals. In short, the creation of the circuit courts of appeals released the high court from hearing many types of petty cases. The high court now had much greater control over its workload and could concentrate on deciding major cases and controversies.

FEDERAL COURTS TODAY

In 1925, Congress passed the Judges Bill, which among other things gave the Supreme Court much greater control over its docket. In 1988 Congress eliminated even more mandatory appeals to the high court. Exhibit 3.2 summarizes other key developments in the federal judiciary.

The current structure of federal courts is best understood in terms of four layers of courts: magistrate, district, appellate, and Supreme Court. In addition, the federal judiciary includes specialized courts and administrative structures.

U.S. MAGISTRATE JUDGES

U.S. magistrate judges are the federal equivalent of state trial court judges of limited jurisdiction. Although they are officially a subcomponent of the district courts, their duties and workload merit separate discussion. Congress created **U.S. magistrate judges** in 1968 to replace the former position of U.S. commissioners. The purpose was to provide a new type of judicial officer in the federal judicial system to alleviate the increased workload of the U.S. district courts (Anderson 2007).

Magistrate judges perform quasi-judicial tasks and work within the judicial branch of government. They are not, however, Article III judges. Magistrate judges are selected by district court judges. Full-time magistrate judges are appointed for 8-year terms, and part-time magistrate judges for 4 years. They may, however, be removed for "good cause." Except in special circumstances, all must be lawyers. According to the Administrative Office of the U.S. Courts, there are 505 full-time magistrate judges and 46 part-time magistrate judges.

	Exhibit 3.2	

KEY DEVELOPMENTS IN THE FEDERAL JUDICIARY

U.S. Constitution	1787	Article III creates U.S. Supreme Court and authorizes lower federal courts.
Judiciary Act of 1789	1789	Congress establishes lower federal courts.
Marbury v. Madison	1803	The Court has the authority to declare an act of Congress unconstitutional.
Courts of Appeals Act	1891	Modern appellate structure is created.
Judges Bill	1925	Supreme Court is given control over its docket.
Court Packing Plan	1937	FDR's attempt to pack the Court is defeated.
Administrative Office Act	1939	Current administrative structure is created, including judicial conference and judicial councils.
Federal Judicial Center	1967	Research and training unit is created.
Federal Magistrate Act	1968	Commissioners are replaced by U.S. magistrates (later the name is changed to "magistrate judges").
Multidistrict Litigation Act	1968	Created the Judicial Panel on Multidistrict Litigation and gave it the power to transfer to a single district court the pretrial proceedings for civil cases involving common questions of fact, such as litigation regarding airplane crashes, products liability, patent infringements, and securities fraud.
Bankruptcy Reform Act	1978	Conferred original bankruptcy jurisdiction on the U.S. district courts and established a bankruptcy court in each judicial district to exercise bankruptcy jurisdiction.
Foreign Intelligence Surveillance Act	1978	Authorized the chief justice of the United States to designate seven federal district court judges to review applications for warrants related to national security investigations on a special court named the "Foreign Intelligence Surveillance Court." The Act also created the U.S. Foreign Intelligence Surveillance Court of Review, a special appellate court whose only function is to review denials by the Foreign Intelligence Surveillance Court of applications for electronic surveillance warrants.

Exhibit 3.2
CONTINUED

Federal Courts Improvement Act	1982	Congress combined the jurisdictions of the U.S. Court of Customs and Patent Appeals and the U.S. Court of Claims into one court, the U.S. Court of Appeals for the Federal Circuit.
Sentencing Commission	1984	Commission is charged with developing sentencing guidelines.
Congressional Act of 1988	1988	Some mandatory appeals to the Supreme Court are eliminated.
Antiterrorism and Effective Death Penalty Act (AEDPA)	1996	Right of state prisoners to file habeas corpus petitions in federal court is severely limited.
USA Patriot Act	2001	The government's ability to gather domestic antiterrorism intelligence is expanded, allowing for less court scrutiny and closing some court proceedings to the public.
Military Trials for Enemy Combatants Act	2006	The president was empowered to identify enemy combatants and detain them indefinitely without their being able to obtain federal court review of their detentions through habeas corpus proceedings, a right traditionally afforded to prisoners.
House v. Bell	2006	Creates a narrow exception to the AEDPA by allowing prisoners with evidence of actual innocence to obtain habeas corpus review if a "miscarriage of justice" would occur with the court's review.
Boumediene v. Bush and *Al Odah v. United States*	2008	The Supreme Court invalidated the provision of the Military Trials for Enemy Combatants Act that deprived the detainees of their constitutional right to habeas corpus review in the federal courts.

Magistrate judges are authorized to perform a wide variety of duties. In felony cases, they are responsible for preliminary proceedings, including holding initial appearances, conducting preliminary hearings, appointing counsel for indigents, setting bail, and issuing search warrants. In misdemeanor and petty offense cases, the jurisdiction of magistrate judges is more extensive; they may preside over trials, accept pleas of guilty, and also impose sentences. On the civil side, they supervise discovery, review Social Security disability benefit appeals, and even conduct full civil trials with the consent of the litigants. In short, under specified conditions and controls, magistrate judges may perform virtually all tasks carried out by district court judges, except trying and sentencing felony defendants (*Gonzales v. United States* 2008).

CASELOAD OF U.S. MAGISTRATE JUDGES

Magistrate judges play an increasingly important role in helping district court judges dispose of their growing caseloads. In a typical year, for example, magistrate judges handle approximately 950,000 matters for the federal courts, including being involved in some way in roughly 539,000 felony matters. In addition, they dispose of approximately 100,000 misdemeanor and petty offenses and 23,000 prisoner litigation cases. Magistrate judges are also involved in assisting with nearly 275,000 civil matters, although they preside over only about 5 percent of all civil trials in federal courts.

U.S. DISTRICT COURTS

Congress has created 94 **U.S. district courts**, of which 89 are located within the 50 states. There is also a district court in the District of Columbia and four territorial district courts located in Guam, Puerto Rico, the Virgin Islands, and the Northern Mariana Islands.

There is at least one district court in each state; moreover, based on the compromise that produced the Judiciary Act of 1789, no district court crosses state lines. Some states have more than one district court: California, New York, and Texas, for instance, each have four. Because district courts often encompass large geographical areas, some hold court in various locations, or divisions. Some districts have only one division, while others have several.

Congress has created 678 district court judgeships for the 94 districts. The president nominates district judges, who must then be confirmed by the Senate (see Chapter 8). Once they take the oath of office, they serve during "good behavior," which for practical purposes means for life. The number of judgeships in each district depends on the amount of judicial work as well as the political clout of the state's congressional delegation; the number ranges from 3 in sparsely populated Wyoming to 44 in densely inhabited Manhattan (officially called the U.S. District Court for the Southern District of New York).

Judges are assisted by an elaborate supporting cast of clerks, secretaries, law clerks, court reporters, probation officers, pretrial services officers, and U.S. marshals. The larger districts also have a federal public defender. Another important actor at the district-court level is the U.S. attorney. There is one U.S. attorney (see Chapter 6) in each district, nominated by the president and confirmed by the Senate, but unlike the judges, he or she serves at the pleasure of the president.

The work of the district judges is significantly assisted by 352 **bankruptcy judges**. Although bankruptcy judges are adjuncts of the district courts, they are appointed for 14-year terms by the court of appeals in which the district is located. In 2005, bankruptcy filings reached an astonishing level with more than 1.78 million petitions filed. The vast majority of these bankruptcy filings were non–business-related, typically involving consumers who cannot pay their bills; the others were filed by businesses big and small. That same year, however, Congress passed the Bankruptcy Abuse Prevention and Consumer Protection Act of 2005. The law made it more difficult for consumers to discharge debts that they were having trouble paying. As a result, the number of bankruptcy petitions filed since the Act was passed has dropped to around 800,000 per year.

CASELOAD OF U.S. DISTRICT COURTS

In the federal system, the U.S. district courts are the federal trial courts of original jurisdiction. Figure 3.1 provides an overview of case volume in the federal courts. The volume of cases is large and growing in complexity. Each year, around 335,000 civil and criminal cases are filed in the U.S. district courts (not including bankruptcy, misdemeanors, and the like). These numbers represent a dramatic increase in workload over the past several decades.

The district courts are the trial courts for all major violations of federal criminal law (magistrate judges hear minor violations). Each year, U.S. attorneys file approximately 60,000 criminal cases, primarily for drug violations, embezzlement, and fraud. For many years, federal prosecutions remained fairly constant (roughly 30,000 per year), only to shoot up beginning in 1980. A major part of this upsurge has been due to a dramatic increase in drug prosecutions. Today, drug prosecutions account for 27 percent of all federal criminal cases. Moreover, trials of criminal cases are now more frequent (and also longer) than in years past. Thus, although civil, not criminal, cases account for most of the work of the district courts, in some districts criminal filings are limiting the ability of these courts to decide civil cases.

Civil lawsuits consume considerably more of the federal courts' time than criminal cases do. Although only a small number of all civil cases are filed in federal courts as compared with state courts, federal civil cases typically involve considerably larger sums of money than the cases filed in state court. This is due, in part, to the types of cases over which the federal courts have jurisdiction. Federal courts are permitted to hear only civil cases involving diversity of citizenship and several types of cases that involve questions of federal law, including prisoner petitions.

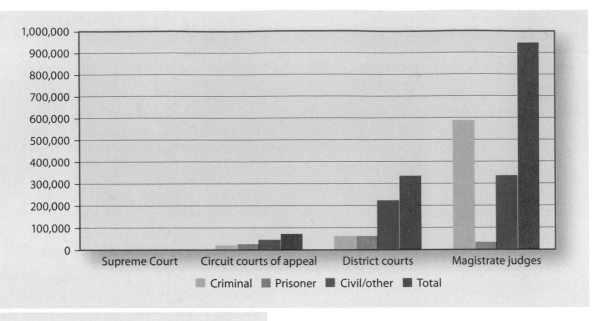

FIGURE 3.1   CASE FILINGS IN THE U.S. COURTS

DIVERSITY JURISDICTION

Diversity of citizenship cases involve suits between citizens of different states or between a U.S. citizen and a foreign country or citizen. For example, a citizen from California claims to be injured in an automobile accident in Chicago with an Illinois driver and sues in federal court in Illinois because the parties to the suit are of "diverse citizenship." Pursuant to the Supreme Court's decision in *Erie Railroad Co. v. Tompkins* (1938), federal courts apply state—not federal—law when adjudicating state claims in federal court under their diversity of citizenship jurisdiction.

From the 1980s through mid-1990s, diversity cases constituted approximately 25 percent of the civil docket of the district courts, thus making a significant contribution to the workload of the district courts. In an effort to restrict the types of minor disputes that may be filed in federal court, Congress in 1996 raised the amount-in-controversy to $75,000 (28 U.S.C. § 1332(a)). At first, this change in jurisdictional amount decreased the number of diversity cases filed in federal courts each year such that diversity cases were reduced to 18.7 percent of the federal civil caseload in 2000. However, the effects of the change in the amount-in-controversy were short-lived. Since 2005, diversity filings have constituted between 25 and 30 percent of the federal civil case load. Given the burdensome workload that diversity jurisdiction brings to the federal courts, combined with the fact that the exercise of diversity jurisdiction requires the federal courts to apply state law—a task that is arguably better performed in state courts—both judges and legal scholars have called for the abolition of diversity of citizenship jurisdiction in the federal courts. If that were to occur, the federal courts would be able to focus on federal questions. However, Congress has not heeded such calls. Rather, Congress may have decided to maintain the status quo because it agreed with the overwhelming sentiment of lawyers in private practice that state courts are biased against out-of-state defendants (Underwood 2006). Alternatively, Congress may simply have opted to continue using the federal courts to resolve interstate disputes.

FEDERAL QUESTIONS

Article III provides that federal courts may be given jurisdiction over "Cases, in Law and Equity, arising under this Constitution, the Laws of the United States, and Treaties made, or which shall be made under their authority." Cases that fall under this type of jurisdiction are generally referred to as involving a **federal question**. Although some federal question cases present issues concerning the interpretation or application of the U.S. Constitution,

Exhibit 3.3
FEDERAL QUESTION JURISDICTION CASES

- Suits between states—Cases in which two or more states are parties.
- Cases involving ambassadors and other high-ranking public figures—Cases arising between foreign ambassadors and other high-ranking public officials.
- Federal crimes—Crimes defined by or mentioned in the U.S. Constitution or those defined and/or punished by federal statute. Such crimes include treason against the United States, piracy, counterfeiting, crimes against the law of nations, and crimes relating to the federal government's authority to regulate interstate commerce. However, most crimes are state matters.
- Bankruptcy—The statutory procedure, usually triggered by insolvency, by which a person is relieved of most debts and undergoes a judicially supervised reorganization or liquidation for the benefit of the person's creditors.
- Patent, copyright, and trademark cases—

  (1) Patent—The exclusive right to make, use, or sell an invention for a specified period (usually 17 years), granted by the federal government to the inventor if the device or process is novel, useful, and non-obvious.

  (2) Copyright—The body of law relating to a property right in an original work of authorship (such as a literary, musical, artistic, photographic, or film work) fixed in any tangible medium of expression, giving the holder the exclusive right to reproduce, adapt, distribute, perform, and display the work.

  (3) Trademark—A word, phrase, logo, or other graphic symbol used by a manufacturer or seller to distinguish its product or products from those of others.

- Admiralty—The system of jurisprudence that has grown out of the practice of admiralty courts: courts that exercise jurisdiction over all maritime contracts, torts, injuries, and offenses.
- Antitrust—The body of law designed to protect trade and commerce from restraining monopolies, price fixing, and price discrimination.
- Securities and banking regulation—The body of law protecting the public by regulating the registration, offering, and trading of securities and the regulation of banking practices.
- Other cases specified by federal statute—Any other cases specified by an applicable federal statute, such as of civil rights, labor relations, environmental cases, and cases arising under the Americans with Disabilities Act.

SOURCE: "Understanding Federal and State Courts." Available online at http://www.uscourts.gov/outreach/resources/fedstate_lessonplan.htm

most federal question cases concern the application or interpretation of a statute enacted by Congress as illustrated in Exhibit 3.3. Some of these laws—and the decisions of the federal courts interpreting them—significantly affect the operation of the criminal justice system.

The Constitutionalization of Criminal Procedure

Under Chief Justice Earl Warren, the U.S. Supreme Court sparked a due process revolution (Chapter 17), giving defendants the right to counsel (Chapter 7), broadening notions of a fair trial (Chapter 14), and expanding the right to appeal (Chapter 17). The federal courts have also set standards regulating how local and state law enforcement officers gather evidence and interrogate suspects (Chapter 12). And the federal courts continue to impact greatly the sentencing and punishment of criminal offenders (Chapters 15 and 16). Violations of these constitutional rights as interpreted in relevant federal court precedent can lead to a conviction being overturned either on direct appeal or collaterally in a habeas corpus case (Chapter 17).

Discrimination Laws and Civil Rights Cases

Federal laws prohibit discrimination on the basis of race, religion, sex, age, or national origin in domains such as employment, welfare, housing, and voting. For example, except in rare instances, employers are required to ignore gender when hiring or promoting, provide equal pay to all employees, and treat pregnancy like any other temporary disability (Kruger 2007). Bona fide occupational qualifications, however, are exempt. Thus, valid job-related requirements necessary to normal business operations are allowed. Criminal justice agencies, though, should avoid height and weight requirements that are not legitimately related to job performance.

Similarly, the roughly 43 million people with disabilities in the United States are protected against discrimination in employment and in their use of public facilities and services under the Americans with Disabilities Act. These protections affect the design and functionality of police departments, courthouses, and correctional facilities to accommodate the special needs of the disabled. In *Yeskey v. Pennsylvania Department of Corrections* (1998), the U.S. Supreme Court held that the Americans with Disabilities Act applies to the ways in which police officers and correctional officials interact with people with disabilities. As a result, police may be civilly liable for arresting someone because they confuse the effects of a disability with criminally aggressive behavior activity, or because they fail to accommodate a person's disability during investigation, interrogation, or arrest (Osborn 2008). Similarly, the Court held in *United States v. Georgia* (2006) that states and municipalities can be held civilly liable for failing to maintain correctional facilities that accommodate the special needs of disabled prisoners.

Prisoner Petitions

In spite of a criminal conviction, inmates in local, state, and federal custody all retain certain constitutional rights The Supreme Court emphasized this point in *Wolff v. McDonnell* (1974), when it said, "There is no iron curtain drawn between the Constitution and the prisons of this country" (pp. 555–556). To enforce their rights, prisoners are permitted to file several types of civil lawsuits that are collectively referred to as **prisoner petitions**.

There are five main types of prisoner petitions that are filed in federal court. The first is a **habeas corpus petition**. With approximately 22,400 cases filed annually in the federal courts, habeas actions account for 42 percent of the annual prisoner petition filings and roughly 8.7 percent of the total federal civil caseload. Typically filed under 28 U.S.C. § 2254, habeas corpus cases are those in which inmates may collaterally challenge their convictions (after exhausting all available state remedies to do so) by arguing that their trial was constitutionally defective. Habeas cases are explored in more detail in Chapter 17.

The second common form of prisoner filing are **motions to vacate sentences** by persons in federal custody. These motions allow a federal prisoner to try to get a sentence set aside or corrected because the sentence was imposed contrary to law. Such motions might allege that the court lacked jurisdiction to impose a criminal sentence, or that the sentence was in excess of that allowed under the law (Chapters 15 and 16). Only about 1,100 of these motions were filed each year prior to 1995. Three U.S. Supreme Court cases affecting criminal sentencing—*Bailey v. United States* in 1995, *Apprendi v. New Jersey* in 2000, and *United States v. Booker* in 2005—all resulted in increases in these filings (see Chapter 16). The *Booker* decision declaring the Federal Sentencing Guidelines unconstitutional caused a record 10,361 of these motions being filed in 2005. Today, approximately 6,000 such motions are filed each year. They account for 11 percent of the annual prisoner petition filings and roughly 2.3 percent of the total federal civil caseload.

The third type of prisoner action is called a **mandamus petition**. While rare (only around 855 such petitions filed each year), mandamus petitions (derived from the Latin for "we command") seek court orders that compel a public entity or official to do something that is owed to the plaintiff as a matter of constitutional or statutory right.

The fourth and most common type of prisoner petitions are those filed under 42 U.S.C. § 1983, commonly referred to as **Section 1983** civil rights actions. Section 1983 allows individual persons to sue those who act under color of state law—state actors like police officers and correctional officers—to redress alleged deprivations of constitutional rights via the Due Process Clause of the Fourteenth Amendment. With approximately 23,500 prisoner civil rights cases filed annually in the federal courts, Section 1983 cases account for 43 percent of the annual prisoner petition filings and roughly 9.1 percent of the total federal civil caseload.

Section 1983 was originally passed by Congress in 1871 as part of post–Civil War efforts to provide a mechanism for private persons to enforce the rights secured by the Fourteenth Amendment (Schwartz 2008). Section 1983's applicability to criminal justice began with the Supreme Court's decision in *Ex Parte Hull* (1941), which held that some constitutional protections stayed with people following criminal conviction and followed them into prison. Twenty years later, in *Monroe v. Pape* (1961), the Court permitted the plaintiff to sue under Section 1983 after the police allegedly conducted an illegal search of his home in violation of the Fourth Amendment. A few years later, in *Cooper v. Pate* (1967), a federal circuit court of appeals allowed prisoners to challenge the conditions of their confinement under the Eighth Amendment's Cruel and Unusual Clause to alleged beatings and racial intolerance using Section 1983. As a result of this line of cases, Section 1983 is routinely used to sue police officers for a range of alleged constitutional rights deprivations, such as claims of excessive force, claims of illegal searches and seizures, and claims of interference with Fifth or Sixth Amendment rights (or both) to counsel during interrogations (Chapter 12). Similarly, correctional officials are routinely sued for alleged denials of First Amendment rights, interference with the Sixth Amendment right to access the courts, and violations of the Eighth Amendment's guarantee against cruel and unusual punishment based on claims of excessive force, lack of medical care, or inhumane conditions of confinement (Schwartz 2008). Moreover, since the 1978 decision in *Monell v. Department of Social Services*, it is clear that governmental municipalities, and not just the individual, can be held liable for damages under Section 1983. It is important to note that Section 1983 applies only to state actors; it cannot be used to sue federal officials. Cases against federal actors must be brought under the final type of prisoner petition cases.

The fifth type of prisoner petition cases are those brought under *Bivens v. Six Unknown Agents of the Federal Bureau of Narcotics* (1971). **Bivens actions**, as they are termed, are the federal counterparts to cases brought under Section 1983 against state actors. Under *Bivens*, private persons are permitted to sue those who act under color of federal authority (e.g., federal law enforcement or correctional

officers) for alleged deprivations of constitutional rights via the Due Process Clause of the Fifth Amendment. Approximately 1250 *Bivens* cases are filed annually in the federal courts. They account for 2 percent of the annual prisoner petition filings and less than one-half of 1 percent of the total federal civil caseload.

Discrimination and Civil Rights Caseload in the Federal Courts

According to the U.S. Department of Justice's Bureau of Justice Statistics (2008), nonprisoner civil rights filings doubled in U.S. district courts from 1990 (18,922 filings) to 1997 (43,278 filings). This increase in the civil rights caseload of the federal courts was due, in large part, to the major expansion of federal civil rights by various acts of Congress, most especially the passage of the Americans for Disabilities Act of 1990 and the Civil Rights Act of 1991, which amended several older employment discrimination laws, including, among others, Title VII of the Civil Rights Act of 1964 and the Age Discrimination in Employment Act of 1973. In the early 2000s, civil rights filings stabilized at around 40,500 cases per year. Since then, however, they have declined to around 32,000 filings, thereby accounting for approximately 12.5% of all civil cases filed in the federal courts. The median award for successful plaintiffs was $154,500 (Bureau of Justice Statistics 2008).

Prisoner petitions have steadily grown to account for a considerable portion of the workload of the federal courts. Collectively, civil rights cases from state and federal inmates have increased significantly, from about 3,500 filings in 1960 to a record high of more than 68,235 cases in 1996. These numbers were driven, in large part, by the sharp increase in the prison population over the corresponding period. The following year, prisoner petitions began to decrease as a result of Congress enacting the Prison Litigation Reform Act (PLRA) of 1996. The PLRA made it more difficult for prisoners to file Section 1983 cases by requiring them to exhaust administrative remedies before filing a federal case; by making them pay certain fees from which they had previously been exempt; and by barring them from filing subsequent cases if they had prior Section 1983 cases dismissed for being frivolous or malicious.

Today, about 54,000 prisoner petitions are filed each year in federal court. They collectively constitute about 21 percent of the total civil caseload of the

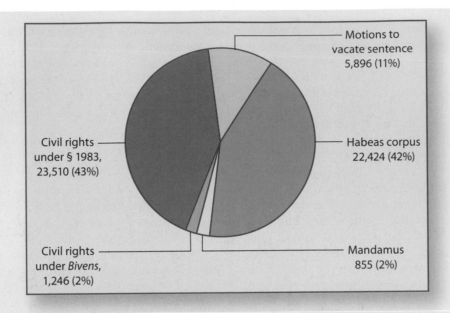

FIGURE 3.2   PRISONER PETITION FILINGS IN FEDERAL COURT

Source: James C. Duff. "Judicial Business of the United States Courts: 2007 Annual Report of the Director." Washington, DC: Administrative Office of the U.S. Courts.

federal courts. As illustrated by Figure 3.2, Section 1983 cases and habeas corpus petitions account for the vast majority of the prisoner petitions.

U.S. magistrate judges greatly assist federal district judges with habeas petitions and prisoner civil rights. But, because they are not Article III judges, magistrates generally write a report to the U.S. district judge to whom the case is formally assigned. The report concludes with a recommendation for how to rule in the case. The report and recommendation is usually adopted by the district judge who ultimately orders the final judgment in the case.

U.S. COURTS OF APPEALS

As mentioned previously, Congress created the **courts of appeals** in 1891 to relieve the Supreme Court from hearing the growing number of appeals. The courts of appeals are the intermediate appellate courts of the federal system. Originally called "circuit courts of appeal," they were renamed and are each now officially known as the U.S. Court of Appeals for the _____ Circuit. Each circuit hears appeals from specific district courts. At present, there are 14 circuits: 11 numbered circuits (each containing at least three states); a Circuit Court of Appeals for the District of Columbia; the Court of Appeals for the Federal Circuit; and the Court of Appeals for the Armed Forces.

As illustrated in Figure 3.3, the numbered circuits and the Circuit Court of Appeals for the District of Columbia are geographically arranged. All 12 of these circuit courts are empowered to review all final decisions of U.S. district courts, as well as certain interlocutory decisions of district courts (see Chapter 17). They also have the power to review and enforce orders of many federal administrative bodies. In contrast, the Federal Circuit is the only civilian judicial circuit whose jurisdiction is based on subject matter rather than geographical boundaries. It was created by an act of Congress in 1982 and granted nationwide jurisdiction to hear specialized appeals concerning certain types of government contracts, patents,

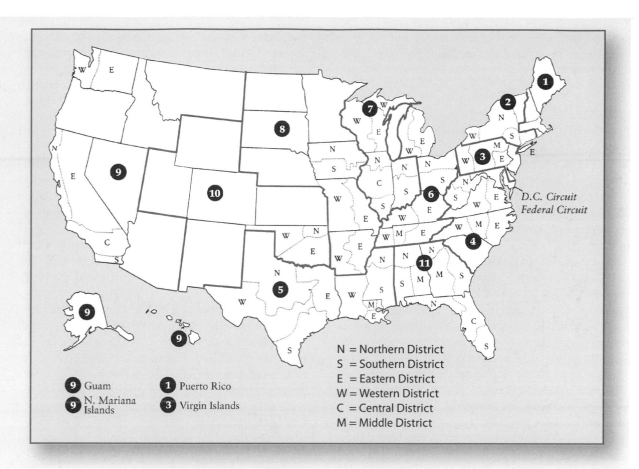

FIGURE 3.3 GEOGRAPHIC BOUNDARIES
OF THE FEDERAL COURTS

Source: Russell Wheeler and Cynthia Harrison.
Creating the Federal Judicial System. 2nd ed.
Washington, DC: Federal Judicial Center, 1994, p. 26.

trademarks, certain non-tort money claims against the U.S. government, federal personnel, and veterans' benefits. Finally, the Court of Appeals for the Armed Forces hears appeals only from cases decided in military courts and tribunals concerning members of the U.S. armed forces on active duty and other persons subject to the Uniform Code of Military Justice.

The courts of appeals are staffed by 179 judges nominated by the president and confirmed by the Senate. As with the district courts, the number of judges in each circuit varies, from 6 (the First Circuit) to 29 (the Ninth Circuit), depending on the

volume and complexity of the caseload. Each circuit has a chief judge who performs administrative duties in addition to hearing cases. As a rule, the judge who has served on the court the longest and who is under 65 years of age is designated as the chief judge. Several staff positions aid the judges in conducting the work of the courts of appeals. A circuit executive assists the chief judge in administering the circuit. The clerk's office maintains the records. Each judge is also allowed to hire three law clerks. In addition, each circuit has a central legal staff that screens appeals and drafts memorandum opinions.

In deciding cases, the courts of appeals normally use rotating three-judge panels. Along with active judges in the circuit, these panels often include visiting judges (primarily district judges from the same circuit) and senior judges. By majority vote, all the judges in the circuit may sit together to decide a case or rehear a case already decided by a panel. Such **en banc** hearings are relatively rare, however; in a typical year fewer than 100 are held throughout the entire nation.

CASELOAD OF U.S. COURTS OF APPEALS

Over the past four decades, the caseload of the courts of appeals has skyrocketed. This dramatic increase in caseload has not been matched by an equivalent increase in judgeships, however. In 1960 there were 68 judgeships whose workload involved hearing 172 cases per three-judge panel. Today, there are 179 circuit court judges who hear 1,049 cases per three-judge panel.

The number of appeals filed annually in the federal courts has varied between 54,679 in 2000 to a high of 68,473 in 2005. That number has fallen slightly, as 58,410 appeals were filed in 2007, the most recent year for which statistics are available. Appeals from criminal convictions in the U.S. district courts constitute about 22.5 percent of the workload of the courts of appeals. Appeals from decisions in prisoner petition cases comprise 26.5 percent of the federal appellate caseload. Thus, criminal and prisoner petitions account for roughly half of the appeals filed each year, while civil appeals, including bankruptcy appeals and appeals from administrative agencies, account for the other half of the federal court of appeals' caseload.

A decision by the court of appeals exhausts the litigant's right to one appeal. The losing party may request that the Supreme Court hear the case, but such petitions are rarely granted. As a result, the courts of appeals are the "courts of last resort" for virtually all federal litigation. Their decisions end the case; only a tiny percentage will be heard by the nation's highest court.

U.S. SUPREME COURT

The United States **Supreme Court** is the court of last resort in the federal court system, meaning that it is a court from which no appeal is possible. The Supreme Court has one chief justice and such number of associate justices as may be fixed by Congress. By act of Congress in 1948, the number of associate justices is eight. Power to nominate the justices is vested in the president of the United States, and appointments are made with the advice and consent of the Senate. Once confirmed to the Supreme Court, there is no mandatory retirement age for Supreme Court justices; so as long as they maintain "good behavior," the justices may remain on the court until their death or until they voluntarily choose to retire.

The Constitution grants the Supreme Court original jurisdiction in a limited number of cases. In other words, the Supreme Court acts as a trial court in certain types of cases, such as controversies between the United States and a state, between two states, or between foreign ministers or ambassadors. Such cases are quite rare; so in the overwhelming majority of cases, the Supreme Court exercises its appellate jurisdiction, reviewing the decisions of the lower federal courts and the highest state courts.

With a few limited exceptions, the appellate jurisdiction of the Supreme Court is not mandatory, but rather discretionary. In other words, the Court has great discretion with regard to the appeals it elects to hear and decide. The Supreme Court exercises this discretion through the granting of a **writ of certiorari**, which means that the Court, upon petition of a party, agrees to review a case decided by one of the circuit courts of appeals or the highest court of a state. The writ of certiorari is an order issued by the Supreme Court to a lower court to send the case records so that the Supreme Court can determine whether the law has been correctly applied.

GRANTING CERT: THE RULE OF FOUR

A vote of four Supreme Court justices is required to grant certiorari to review a case. This is often referred to as the **rule of four**. The rule of four is not contained in any law or formal rule of the Court; rather, it is a custom that has been observed since the Supreme Court gained the ability to control its own docket with the creation of the circuit courts of appeal in 1891 (Fang, Johnson, and Roberts 2007). The rule of four is remarkable in that it is a device through which "a minority of the Court can impose on the majority a question that the majority does not think it appropriate to address" (Kurland and Hutchinson 1983, p. 645). This power of a minority of justices appears to make a difference in about 25 percent of the Court's cases; for the other three-quarters of their caseload, a majority of justices agree that a case presents an issue that the Court should address through plenary review (Fang, Johnson, and Roberts 2007).

Whether certiorari is granted by four or more justices, the Court's discretion is always guided by whether a case presents questions that have some general "importance beyond the facts and parties involved" (*Boag v. MacDougall* 1982, p. 368) (Rehnquist, J., dissenting). For example, the Court may grant certiorari in cases involving important and unsettled questions of federal law; or in situations involving a conflict among state high courts or the federal circuits concerning the interpretation of federal law, most especially one ruling on a question of interpretation of the U.S. Constitution. Note that failure to grant certiorari is not an affirmation in disguise of the lower court's decision. It simply means that the petitioner failed to persuade four of the nine justices to hear the appeal.

CASELOAD OF U.S. SUPREME COURT

Only a small percentage of the requests for a writ of certiorari (or *cert,* as it is often called) is granted. In particular, the legal issue must involve a "substantial federal question." This means state court interpretations of state law can be appealed to the Supreme Court only if there is an alleged violation of either federal law or the U.S. Constitution. For example, a suit contending that a state supreme court has misinterpreted the state's divorce law would not be heard because it involves an interpretation of state law and does not raise a federal question. The same is true for decisions of state high courts recognizing controversial rights, such as the right for same-sex couples to marry, when the decisions are based entirely on their state constitutions. As a result of this limitation that cases raise a substantial federal question, the vast majority of state cases are never reviewed by the Supreme Court.

By statute, the Supreme Court begins its annual term on the first Monday in October and it continues for 8 or 9 months, ending in June or early July. Each term is comprised of rotating intervals of sittings and recesses, each of which lasts approximately 2 weeks. During *sittings*, the justices hear cases and deliver opinions. During *recesses*, they study the cases on their docket and work on researching and writing their opinions. In addition, each week, the justices evaluate roughly 130 petitions for writs of certiorari.

Through its discretionary powers to hear appeals, the Supreme Court limits itself to deciding about 80 cases a year. With the exception of capital cases, the Court does not really act as an error-correction court. Rather, the Court marshals its time and energy to decide the most important policy questions of the day (see Chapter 17).

CIRCUIT JUSTICES

Each justice on the Supreme Court is assigned to serve as a **circuit justice**. While the function of circuit justices has varied over time, their role today is concerned primarily with addressing certain requests for extension of time and ruling on requests for stays in cases coming from the circuit (or circuits) to which the justice is assigned. A **stay** is a court order that temporarily suspends activity in a case. If the circuit justice thinks that there is merit in a case such that the full Supreme Court should have an opportunity to decide whether to hear the case, the circuit justice may grant the stay. This is particularly important in capital cases in which a stay of execution can keep a death-row prisoner alive until the full Court can review the case.

SPECIALIZED COURTS

The magistrate, district, appeals courts, and Supreme Court handle the bulk of federal litigation and therefore are a principal focus of this book. To round out our discussion of the federal judicial system, however, we also need to discuss briefly several additional courts that Congress has periodically created. These courts are called specialized federal courts because they are authorized to hear only a limited range of cases—taxes or patents, for example. They are created for the express purpose of helping administer a specific congressional statute.

Exhibit 3.4 gives an overview of the specialized federal courts and highlights two important distinctions. First, most specialized courts have permanent, full-time judges appointed specifically to that court. A few specialized courts, however, temporarily borrow judges from federal district courts or courts of appeals as specific cases arise.

The second distinction relates to the specialized courts' constitutional status. Judicial bodies established by Congress under Article III are known as **constitutional courts**. The Supreme Court, courts of appeals, and district courts are, of course, constitutional courts. Judicial bodies established by Congress under **Article I** are known as **legislative courts**. Courts presided over by bankruptcy judges and U.S. magistrate judges are examples

Exhibit 3.4
SPECIALIZED FEDERAL COURTS

COURT	LEVEL		JURISDICTION
Courts with Permanent Judges			
Tax Court	Article I	Trial	Tax disputes
Court of Federal Claims	Article I	Trial	Monetary claims against the federal government
Court of Veterans Appeal	Article I	Trial	Federal veterans' benefits
Court of International Trade	Article I	Trial	Imports of foreign goods
U.S. Court of Appeals of the Armed Forces	Article III	Appellate	Uniform Code of Military Justice
Court of Appeals for the Federal Circuit	Article I	Appellate	Trademarks, patents, foreign trade, claims against the federal government
Courts with Judges Borrowed from Other Federal Courts			
Alien Terrorist Removal Court	Article III	Trial	Decides whether an alien should be removed from the United States on the grounds of being an alien terrorist
		Trial	Electronic surveillance of foreign intelligence agents
Foreign Intelligence Surveillance Court of Review		Appellate	Electronic surveillance of foreign intelligence agents

SOURCE: Adapted from Lawrence Baum, *American Courts: Process and Policy.* 2nd ed. Boston: Houghton Mifflin, 1990, p. 37; Lawrence Baum, "Specializing the Federal Courts: Neutral Reforms or Efforts to Shape Judicial Policy?" *Judicature* 74: 217–224, 1991.

of legislative courts. The constitutional status of federal courts has important implications for judicial independence. Article III (constitutional court) judges serve for a period that amounts to a lifetime appointment, but Article I (legislative court) judges are appointed for a specific term of office. Moreover, Article III judges are protected against salary reductions while in office. Article I judges enjoy no such constitutional protection. In short, constitutional courts have a greater degree of independence from the other two branches of government than do the legislative courts. The specialized federal courts are overwhelmingly civil in their orientation, handling such matters as patents and tariffs on imported goods. But two specialized courts bear directly on criminal matters, the military courts and the Foreign Intelligence Surveillance Act Court. In addition, a murky legal area has arisen because of the capture of those who are called "military noncombatants"; it is not clear in which courts they will be tried.

MILITARY JUSTICE

Congress adopted the Uniform Code of Military Justice in 1950, extending significant new due process rights in courts-martial. Congress also created the U.S. Court of Appeals for the Armed Forces, composed of five civilian judges appointed by the president for 15-year terms. The intent was clearly to extend civilian influence to military law. The Military Justice Act of 1968 contributed to the further civilianization of courts-martial. The code covers criminal acts but can also punish acts that are not criminal for civilians (for example, disrespect of an officer). Moreover, on a military base, military justice applies not only to members of the armed services but also to civilian employees, and it covers acts committed by military personnel on and off a military base (Fidell, Hillman, and Sullivan 2007).

As with other systems of criminal law, the objective of military justice is to provide a forum for determining guilt or innocence. But in addition, courts-martial serve the purpose of enforcing order and discipline in the military. In the words of the U.S. Military (U.S. Joint Service Committee on Military Service 2008, p. I-1): "The purpose of military law is to promote efficiency and effectiveness in the military establishment, and thereby to strengthen the national security of the United States." Thus, although military justice is not exempt from the Constitution, it is certainly distinctive. Military justice differs from state and federal justice in the following ways:

- Proceedings are open to military society.
- The burden of proof is less demanding.
- Three- and five-person juries are used.
- The jurors are military personnel.
- A two-thirds majority is sufficient to convict.
- Convictions are automatically appealed to a higher military court.

The principal concern with military courts is that jurors may be unduly influenced by military commanders.

In recent years, a few high-profile cases have thrust military justice into the news. Some of the more prominent cases include these:

- Seven Marines and a Navy corpsman were charged with premeditated murder of an innocent civilian in the Iraqi town of Haditha. Charges against several of these military personnel were ultimately dropped, but at least one has been convicted so far.
- Several Army personnel were found guilty of abusing inmates in Iraq's notorious Abu Ghraib prison.
- Seven U.S. soldiers from an elite Airborne division were charged with knowingly engaging in sex for money on a public website.

ENEMY COMBATANTS

In response to September 11, the United States invaded Afghanistan, capturing hundreds of persons suspected of being members of the al Qaeda terrorist organization. The military decided that those captured did not qualify as prisoners of war (and therefore subject to the Geneva Convention) but instead would be considered *enemy combatants*. Hundreds were held at the Navy base in Guantánamo Bay, Cuba, because they were not subject to the jurisdiction of the U.S. federal courts. (One of the alleged hijackers, though, was tried in federal court. See Case Close-Up: Was Zacarias Moussaoui the 20th Hijacker?)

By 2003 the Bush administration decided that these enemy combatants would be tried in military courts, where the proceedings would be secret and the potential punishments could include the death penalty. Pending trials have created an international furor, with critics arguing that the United States is not living up to its tradition of respecting the rule of law. Closer to home, the American Bar Association condemned the decision that those tried would not be able to talk to their lawyers in private. The Supreme Court rejected the Bush administration's argument that the president, as commander-in-chief of the military, had the authority to create such military commissions (*Hamdan v. Rumsfeld* 2006).

In 2006 Congress passed the Military Trials for Enemy Combatants Act, which allows the president to identify enemies, imprison them indefinitely, and interrogate them beyond the reach of the full court reviews traditionally afforded criminal defendants and ordinary prisoners. The Supreme Court declared these processes unconstitutional in *Boumediene v.*

Bush (2008). As a result, a number of enemy combatants have been released by order of courts reviewing their detention in Guantánamo Bay. During the first year of President Obama's administration, the government has continued to struggle with what to do with the Guantánamo facility and its prisoners. Although President Obama issued an executive order directing that the Guantánamo Prison be closed by January 2010, Congress voted to deny funding for the closure (Taylor 2009). What will happen to the roughly 240 detainees who remain in Guantánamo as of this writing remains to be seen.

FOREIGN INTELLIGENCE SURVEILLANCE COURT

The Foreign Intelligence Surveillance Court has authority over electronic surveillance of foreign intelligence agents. Because it was created by the Foreign Intelligence Surveillance Act (FISA), it is popularly referred to as the FISA Court. This court has no permanent judges; rather, the chief justice appoints 11 justices who hear requests for warrants as needed. The courtroom is inside the U.S. Department of Justice, and only the judge is allowed to review the requests submitted by the Justice Department. By statute, the judge is authorized to sign a search warrant for electronic eavesdropping based on "clear and convincing evidence," a legal standard that is less stringent than that required for a normal search warrant. The differences in standards means that any evidence gathered by a FISA warrant may not be used in a criminal prosecution (see Chapter 12).

For years, the FISA Court labored in obscurity. Indeed, the only visible public role came in year-end reports, which invariably indicated that the court had approved all warrant requests. This lack of public attention changed greatly with the revelation in late 2005 that the National Security Agency was conducting warrantless surveillance of domestic phone conversations of suspected foreign terrorist groups like al Qaeda. The Bush administration contended that the president had inherent war powers under the Constitution to order eavesdropping without warrants even though some in Congress disputed this interpretation. In the wake of controversy, a republican-controlled Congress enacted the Protect America Act of 2007. The law mandated that telecommunications providers assist the government in intercepting international phone calls and e-mails for national security purposes. The law was upheld in 2008 over a Fourth Amendment challenge (see Chapter 12) by a decision of the Foreign Intelligence Surveillance Court of Review, although the decision was not made public until early 2009. That court has appellate review over decisions of the Foreign Intelligence

Was Zacarias Moussaoui the 20th Hijacker

Holding back tears, NYPD officer Jim Smith tried to explain to the jurors how the death of his wife Moira still affects Patricia, their 6-year-old daughter. Moira Smith, also an NYPD officer, was one of the first to respond when a passenger jet ripped into the World Trade Center's north tower on September 11, 2001. She was trying to save a woman suffering from an asthma attack when the south tower collapsed. "The loss to Patricia, I can't begin to explain," Smith said. "I tell her, her mom was a hero, and she died trying to save others" (Hirschkorn 2006).

Smith's tearful testimony was one of the five heart-wrenching victim-impact statements presented during the trial of Zacarias Moussaoui. After lengthy and sometimes bizarre legal proceedings, Moussaoui is the only person who has been convicted in connection with the September 11 terrorist attacks.

Three weeks before September 11, 2001, Zacarias Moussaoui, a French national of Moroccan descent, was taking flying lessons when he was arrested on immigration charges. The government's theory is that Moussaoui was to be the 20th hijacker on that fateful day. The prosecution also argued that Moussaoui should be put to death because he lied to the FBI, thus withholding evidence that would have prevented the terrorist attack.

Throughout the proceedings, Moussaoui seemed more intent on clashing with Judge Leonie Brinkema and his own defense attorneys than seeking to save himself. Some of his statements were so outlandish that he gave every appearance that he wanted to be a martyr. He often ranted against the judge and refused to cooperate with his court-appointed lawyers. Initially, Judge Brinkema reluctantly let Moussaoui act as his own lawyer (Chapter 7), but she ended his self-representation because of inflammatory and unprofessional briefs. In the end, his lawyers tried to spare his life, while he insisted on a sentence of death.

The proceedings were also marked by accusations of governmental misconduct. At one point Judge Brinkema ruled that the federal prosecutors could not seek the death penalty because they refused to grant Moussaoui's lawyers access to certain government evidence (but the Fourth Circuit Court of Appeals sided with the prosecutors and the Bush administration). During the sentencing phase, she showed anger with allegations of witness tampering by government officials.

Moussaoui tried to plead guilty (on July 18, 2002), but Judge Brinkema ruled that he did not appear to understand what he was doing and gave him a week to consider his plea (Chapter 13). On July 25, he attempted again to plead guilty but ultimately withdrew his guilty plea the same day. Three years later (April 20, 2005), the defendant sent the judge a letter saying he wanted to plead guilty, and over the objections of his lawyer, he did so.

The guilt phase of the death penalty case (Chapter 15) began with jury selection in February 2006. In an unusual move, the guilt phase was itself split into two parts. First, the jury had to determine whether this was a death-eligible case. Testifying against his lawyers' advice, Moussaoui stated he was supposed to hijack a fifth jetliner on September 11. The jury found that Moussaoui's crime was death-eligible, and the trial shifted to deciding whether he should be sentenced to death.

In addition to the victim-impact statements, the jury heard the cockpit voice recording of one of the doomed airliners. Moussaoui again testified against his lawyers' advice, stating that he had "no regret, no remorse" about the attacks. Trying to undermine their own client, the defense called a psychologist to the stand who testified that the defendant was a paranoid schizophrenic with delusions. Several survivors also testified that he should not die (Lewis 2006).

In what many considered a surprising move, the federal jury rejected the death penalty for Moussaoui, concluding that he played only a minor role in the September 11, 2001, terrorist attacks (Lewis 2006).

Defiant to the end, Moussaoui boasted "America, you lost . . . I won." But when Moussaoui was formally sentenced, the judge had the last word. "You came here to be a martyr and to die in a great bang of glory. But . . . instead you will die with a whimper. The rest of your life you will spend in prison" (Serrano 2006). A few days later, before dawn, U.S. marshals flew Moussaoui, now prisoner 51427-054, to the Supermax federal prison in Colorado. He will spend 23 hours a day in his cell with little or no contact with the other notorious criminals imprisoned there.

In many ways, the trial of Zacarias Moussaoui lacked a compelling sense of public drama partly because it dragged on for almost 4 years and partly because there was no live television coverage—federal courts do not allow cameras in the courtroom (Chapter 14). But ultimately the trial lacked real drama because the outcome (as to guilt) was never really in doubt. After all, the defendant repeatedly made clear that he wanted to be found guilty and wanted to be executed, thus ensuring that (in his mind at least) he was a martyr to an important cause. Thus, the only real tension in the case came to center on the question of whether he should die or not, and as the trial progressed, that question increasingly became linked to who was Zacarias Moussaoui the person, not what role he would have played in the tragic events of September 11. Indeed, in the end, the trial failed to provide closure to the important question of whether Zacarias Moussaoui was indeed the 20th hijacker. Some of his statements were so outlandish, and so contradictory, that some close observers of the case came to believe that his claims were simply not believable. Overall, the trial seems to represent only a macabre footnote to a national tragedy. The federal courts have been hearing cases debating the permissible scope of the government's War on Terrorism, but the Moussaoui trial was devoid of any major legal issues. Thus, the trial will be remembered only for the bizarre behavior of the defendant, not for any enduring addition to our nation's legal history.

CASE CLOSEUP

Surveillance Court. The court reasoned that requiring the government to obtain a warrant would impair its ability to gather time-sensitive information, thereby potentially putting national security interests at risk. The opinion concluded by saying that as long as the executive branch has "several layers of serviceable safeguards to protect individuals against unwarranted harms and to minimize incidental intrusions, its efforts to protect national security should not be frustrated by the courts" (*In re Directives Pursuant to Section 105B of the Foreign Intelligence Surveillance Act* 2008, p. 29).

FEDERAL JUDICIAL ADMINISTRATION

The Administrative Office Act of 1939, which largely created the current administrative structure of the federal judiciary, illustrates the interplay between judicial administration and politics. During the mid-1930s, the conservative majority on the Supreme Court declared many pieces of New Deal legislation unconstitutional. After his reelection in 1936, President Franklin Delano Roosevelt put forth his Court-packing plan: The Court would be expanded from 9 to 15 justices, thus allowing FDR to pack the Court with justices more sympathetic to his policies. There was no legal barrier to such an action because the Constitution fails to specify how many justices shall serve on the Court. But the political obstacles proved insurmountable; many of Roosevelt's backers felt that tampering with the Court was a bad idea. The Court-packing plan never passed, but it did call attention to the president's complaints that the administration of federal courts was inefficient. At the same time, some judges were dissatisfied with the old system of court management because it was located in the Department of Justice, an executive agency. Thus, a movement arose among federal judges and national court reformers to clean their own house. The result was a compromise plan—the Administrative Office Act of 1939. The act expanded the responsibilities of the Judicial Conference, created the Administrative Office of the U.S. Courts, and established the judicial councils. These agencies, along with the office of the chief justice, the Federal Judicial Center, and the more recently created U.S. Sentencing Commission, are the main units involved in administering the federal courts.

A summary of their functions, composition, and hierarchical structure is presented in Exhibit 3.5

CHIEF JUSTICE

The chief justice is the presiding officer of the Supreme Court and has supervisory authority over the entire federal judicial system. In fulfilling these duties, the chief justice is allotted an extra law clerk and an administrative assistant to help with the administrative tasks for the Court and for the judicial system as a whole.

At the Supreme Court itself, the chief justice presides over all courtroom proceedings as well as the private conferences in which the justices discuss and vote on cases. As a matter of tradition, the chief justice normally speaks either first or last in these conferences, thereby having significant influence on the discussion. The chief justice assigns associate justices (and himself) to serve as the circuit justice for the various federal circuits. While the chief justice's vote in a case carries no more or less weight that the vote of any of the associate justices, the most senior justice always decides who will write the opinion of the Court in a given case. Since the chief justice is the most senior position on the court (regardless of the number of years the chief justice has actually served on the Court), that means that the when the chief justice votes with the majority of justices in a given case, he possesses the important power to assign the authorship of the majority opinion. This includes the ability to keep important constitutional cases for himself.

Other administrative tasks at the Supreme Court for the chief justice include regulating attorney admissions to the Supreme Court bar; formally opening and closing each court term; supervising and working with the Court's clerk, librarians, and reporter of decisions; budgeting; advocating for the courts before Congress; and serving as a spokesperson not only for the Supreme Court, but also for all of the federal courts. For example, former Chief Justice William Rehnquist often spoke about the need for Congress to increase the number of federal judges, increase the salaries of judges to be competitive with the private practice of law, reduce the workload of the courts, and protect judicial independence. Chief Justice John Roberts has continued to echo all of these sentiments. For example, in the *Annual Report* he prepared as of the date of publication of this book, Chief Justice Roberts pointed out that the entire judicial system of the United States received

Exhibit 3.5

ORGANIZATION OF FEDERAL JUDICIAL ADMINISTRATION

Executive Branch
Participates in legislative process. Transmits appropriations requests. Provides buildings and security. Is represented on rules committees.

Congress
Appropriates funds. Enacts legislation on court organization and jurisdiction. Reviews procedural rule amendments.

Supreme Court
Approves rule amendments.

Chief Justice of the United States

Administrative Office of the U.S. Courts
The chief justice appoints the director and deputy director after consultation with Judicial Conference.
Functions: Provides, under Conference supervision, administrative support to courts (including budget, personnel, space and facilities), staff to Judicial Conference and its committees, legislative coordination, other functions.

Judicial Conference of the United States
Members: Chief justice (chair); chief judge and district judge from the twelve regional circuits; chief judge, Court of Appeals for the Federal Circuit; chief judge, Court of International Trade.
Functions: Sets national administrative policy for the federal judiciary; approves appropriations requests for submission to Congress; recommends changes in rules of procedure to the Supreme Court for submission to Congress; other statutory functions.

Committees of the Judicial Conference
Members: Judges, practicing lawyers, and legal scholars appointed by the chief justice, and ex officio government officials.
Functions: Make recommendations to the Conference and, in a few cases, exercise statutory responsibilities.

Federal Judicial Center
Board: Chief justice (chair); seven judges elected by the Judicial Conference; Administrative Office director. Board appoints Center director and deputy director.
Functions: Provides orientation and continuing education to judges and personnel of courts, research support to courts and Judicial Conference committees.

Chief Judges of the Circuits

U.S. Sentencing Commission
Members: Seven voting members appointed by the president (no more than three of whom may be federal judges) and two nonvoting ex officio members.
Functions: Promulgates sentencing guidelines and otherwise establishes federal sentencing policies as directed by the 1984 Sentencing Reform Act.

Judicial Conferences of the Circuits
Optional circuit-wide meetings, called no more than once a year by the chief circuit judge, about various topics related to the administration of justice. All federal judges may attend, and each court of appeals must adopt rules to provide for participation by members of the bar.

Judicial Councils of the Circuits
Members: Chief judge (chair); circuit and district judges in equal numbers; council size determined by majority vote of all active circuit and district judges.
Functions: (1) Make necessary orders for administration of justice within the circuit (all judges and employees of the circuit are statutorily directed to give effect to council orders); (2) consider complaints of judicial misconduct or disability under if referred by the chief circuit judge; (3) review district court plans in various administrative areas, as required by statute or Judicial Conference.

Courts of Appeals, District Courts, and Bankruptcy Courts
Courts, each with a chief judge and clerk of court, also develop and implement administrative policy in numerous areas within the framework depicted above.

SOURCE: Russell Wheeler. *A New Judge's Introduction to Federal Judicial Administration*. Washington, DC: Federal Judicial Center, 2003.

only two-tenths of 1 percent of the total federal budget, a figure that causes the courts to "continuously look . . . for ways to do more with less" (2008, p. 4). This chronic underfunding of the courts has led to federal judges' pay being steadily eroded, since they have not been provided with cost-of-living increases for several years even though Congress has given such increases to all other federal employees (including all members of Congress).

Outside the walls of the Supreme Court, the chief justice has many other ceremonial and administrative responsibilities. By mandate of Article I, Section 3 of the U.S. Constitution, the chief justice presides over impeachment trials of the president of the United States in the U.S. Senate. The chief justice normally administers the oath of office to the president and vice president at inaugurations. He supervises the acquisitions of the law department at the Library of Congress. The chief justice also possesses the significant authority to appoint judges to special tribunals and courts, such the U.S. Foreign Intelligence Surveillance Court and the Judicial Panel on Multidistrict Litigation (a group of seven federal judges who select the venue for the district that coordinates all pretrial proceedings for multiple cases across the country concerning the same basic cause of action with common questions of face, such as mass tort actions resulting from a plane crash or a product-liability case). And, the chief justice serves on the boards of three cultural institutions: The Smithsonian (often serving as its Chancellor), the Hirshhorn Museum, and the National Gallery of Art.

In the role of leader of the federal courts system, the chief justice serves as the chairperson the Judicial Conference of the United States, supervises the Administrative Office of the U.S. Courts, and serves as the chairperson of the Federal Judicial Center. All three of these organizations are discussed in greater detail below.

JUDICIAL CONFERENCE OF THE UNITED STATES

The Judicial Conference of the United States is the administrative policymaking organization of the federal judicial system. It is comprised of 26 members that include the chief justice, the chief judges of each of the courts of appeals, one district judge from each circuit, and the chief judge of the Court of International Trade. The conference meets semiannually for 2-day sessions. Because these short meetings are not sufficient to accomplish a great deal, most of the work is done by about 25 committees. The chief

justice of the United States has the power to appointment members to the committees, all of which contain not only members of the Judicial Conference itself, but also other judges, law professors, and practicing attorneys selected by the chief justice.

One of the most important responsibilities of the Judicial Conference is drafting proposed amendments to the rules that govern proceedings in the federal courts. These include the Federal Rules of Civil Procedure, Federal Rules of Criminal Procedure, Federal Rules of Bankruptcy Procedure, Federal Rules of Appellate Procedure, and the Federal Rules of Evidence. Other committees of the Judicial Conference oversee judicial codes of conduct, information technology in the federal courts, and court administration and case management.

The Judicial Conference directs the Administrative Office of the U.S. Courts in administering the judiciary budget and makes recommendations to Congress concerning the creation of new judgeships, increases in judicial salaries, and budgets for court operations. The Judicial Conference also plays a major role in discipline (including impeachment) of federal judges (a topic discussed in greater depth in Chapter 8). In short, the Judicial Conference is a vehicle through which federal judges play a major role in developing policy for the federal judiciary.

ADMINISTRATIVE OFFICE OF THE U.S. COURTS

Since its establishment in 1939, the Administrative Office (AO) of the U.S. Courts has been responsible for implementing the policies established by the Judicial Conference by handling the day-to-day administrative tasks of the federal courts. The director of the AO is appointed by the chief justice and reports to the Judicial Conference. Acting as the Judicial Conference's official representative in Congress, the AO's lobbying and liaison responsibilities include presenting the annual budget requests for the federal judiciary, arguing for the need for additional judgeships, and transmitting proposed changes in court rules. The AO also serves as the housekeeping agency of the judiciary responsible for allotting authorized funds and supervising expenditures. Throughout the year, local federal court staff send the AO a vast array of statistical data on the operations of the federal courts, ranging from the number of filings to the speed of the disposition of cases. The data are published in three separate volumes. The heftiest is the *Annual Report,* which runs hundreds of pages long and is now available on the Internet.

FEDERAL JUDICIAL CENTER

The Federal Judicial Center is the research and training arm of the federal judiciary. Its activities are managed by a director appointed by the board, which consists of the chief justice, the director of the Administrative Office, and judges from the U.S. district court, courts of appeals, and bankruptcy court. One of the principal activities of the Federal Judicial Center is education and training of federal judicial personnel, including judges, probation officers, clerks of court, and pretrial service officers. The center also conducts research on a wide range of topics, including the work of the magistrate judges, ways of measuring the workload of the courts, and causes of delay.

JUDICIAL COUNCILS

The judicial council (sometimes referred to as the "circuit council") is the basic administrative unit of a circuit. The membership consists of both district and appellate judges of the circuit. A judicial council is given sweeping authority to "make all necessary and appropriate orders for the effective and expeditious administration of justice within its circuit." Working within this broad mandate, the councils monitor district court caseloads and judicial assignments. Although the law specifies that "all judicial officers and employees of the circuit shall promptly carry into effect all orders of the judicial council," the actual enforcement powers are limited. The major weapons at the councils' disposal are persuasion, peer group pressure, and publicity directed at the judge or judges who are reluctant to comply with circuit policy. At times, for example, circuit councils have ordered that a district judge receive no new cases until his or her docket has been brought up to date. Judicial councils are also authorized to investigate complaints of judicial disability or misconduct (a topic probed in greater detail in Chapter 8).

U.S. SENTENCING COMMISSION

The U.S. Sentencing Commission is an independent agency in the judicial branch of government. It consists of seven members—a chairperson, three vice chairs, and three commissioners appointed by the president of the United States. The Sentencing Commission was created by the Sentencing Reform Act of 1984. Its original purpose was to develop federal sentencing guidelines. Today, the Commission is also charged with evaluating the effects of the sentencing guidelines on the criminal justice system, recommending to Congress appropriate modifications of substantive criminal law and sentencing procedures, establishing a research and development program on sentencing issues, and monitoring the performance of federal probation officers with respect to their roles in recommending sentences to federal judges (see Chapter 16).

CASELOADS IN THE FEDERAL COURTS

The onset of the Industrial Revolution increased the caseload of the federal courts, a trend that was later accelerated by Prohibition, then the New Deal, and even further by federal lawmaking often associated with President Lyndon Johnson's "Great Society" programs. Growing caseloads, in turn, prompted changes and additions to the federal judiciary; appellate courts have been added and specialized courts created.

What is new is the pace of that expansion. For most of our nation's history, the growth in federal cases was gradual. No longer. Over the past 50 years, district court filings have increased more than 6-fold, and court of appeals cases have increased more than 10-fold. According to the Administrative Office of the U.S. Courts, federal judges today are faced with unprecedented levels of work. By and large, federal judges across the country face a greater number of cases each year and, in some instances, are encountering record levels of work.

The caseload problem is particularly acute in some metropolitan jurisdictions, where federal judges must postpone civil trials for months and even years to accommodate criminal trial schedules (particularly of major drug dealers) in accordance with the Speedy Trial Act (see Chapter 5). The solutions most often suggested for the problem of rising federal court caseloads are increasing the number of federal judges and reducing federal jurisdiction.

INCREASE THE NUMBER OF FEDERAL JUDGES?

Through the years, increases in the number of cases filed in federal court have been followed by an increase in the number of federal judgeships. More recently, however, the dramatic increases in federal court cases have not been accompanied by a corresponding increase in the number of federal

COURTS, CONTROVERSY, AND REDUCING CRIME

Should State Crimes Also Become Federal Violations?

Walk into federal court for the first time, and you probably won't expect to see defendants like Alfonso Lopez. We associate federal courts with big cases and important issues. Bank embezzlers and big-time drug dealers are what we expect to see. Street criminals like Lopez are more likely to be found in state courts. But increasingly, the dockets of federal courts are being crammed with such criminals.

Deciding what should be a federal offense and what should be a state crime reflects both issues of law and political disagreements. Under federalism, one of the powers reserved to the states is the power to regulate persons and property in order to promote the public welfare (commonly referred to as *police powers*). Based on these police powers, state governments and their local subdivisions pass laws to promote the public health, welfare, and safety. Thus, most crimes are defined by the states (see Chapter 2).

Congressional Expansion

Over the years Congress has extended federal criminal jurisdiction beyond the basics centering on federal property and interstate commerce. The underlying motivation has been public concerns (some would say public hysteria) about public morality (Meier 1994). Thus, the Mann Act of 1910 prohibited the interstate transportation of prostitutes, the Harrison Act of 1914 outlawed drugs associated with deviants, and the Volstead Act ushered in Prohibition in 1919.

Contemporary demands to expand federal criminal jurisdiction typically reflect contrasting partisan and ideological positions. Conservatives generally favor reducing federal court caseloads but have called for increasing federal criminal jurisdiction to include carjacking and transferring numerous gun cases from state to federal courts. These efforts, if successful, would potentially result in numerous

judgeships. Particularly at the appellate level, the creation of new judgeships has lagged far behind the increase in filings.

It is unlikely that in the short term the number of federal judgeships will be increased. Only Congress can authorize additional judgeships, and Congress has been locked in a decades-long partisan battle over the federal judiciary. Chapter 8 will explore ongoing political battles between Republicans and Democrats over who should fill existing vacancies on the federal bench. Given this partisan divide, it is unlikely that additional judgeships will be created until one party controls a filibuster-proof majority of the United States (and the president is a member of that party) because new judgeships would become political spoils for the party in control at that time.

REDUCE FEDERAL JURISDICTION?

To cope with rising caseloads, federal judges have proposed not only creating more judgeships but also reducing the types of cases that can be filed in federal court. According to the *Report of the Federal*

Courts Study Committee (1990), Congress created most of these problems by unwisely expanding federal court jurisdiction, and therefore Congress should act immediately to pass remedial legislation. Alas, having been labeled as the culprit, it is hardly surprising that Congress gave the report a chilly reception (Biskupic 1993; Underwood 2006). In short, the nation's top elected lawmakers have been at odds with the nation's top appointed law interpreters for most of the past century, and this disagreement is not likely to be resolved.

Arguments based on numbers of cases stress issues of efficiency but typically need to be understood within a broader framework of political winners and losers. Thus, some disagreements reflect divisions along the lines of the due process versus crime control models of justice. But other disagreements reflect institutional differences: The views of federal judges (whether appointed by Republican or Democratic presidents) contrast with the views of federal lawmakers. Part of the political battle over federal court jurisdiction involves the scope of federal criminal law. See Courts, Controversy, and Reducing Crime: Should State Crimes Also Become

violent offenders who were armed with a weapon being prosecuted in federal, not state, court.

Democrats oppose such efforts but tend to support expansion of federal criminal law to cover citizens with limited political power. Thus, they favor expanding federal criminal legislation to cover hate crimes, stalking, and violence against women. And most of all they back gun control as the best strategy for controlling crime. Republicans oppose such efforts.

The *Lopez* and *Morrison* Decisions

Federal judges, whether appointed by Republican or Democratic presidents, almost uniformly oppose the federalization of state crimes (Schwarzer and Wheeler 1994). Former Chief Justice Rehnquist (1993) decried what he called the near transformation of some federal courts into national narcotics courts. Thus, the *Lopez* case is ultimately significant

not because it involves guns but because the Court sets limits on what crimes Congress may federalize.

Chief Justice William Rehnquist's majority opinion stressed that in passing the Gun-Free School Zones Act in 1990, Congress "did not issue any findings showing a relationship between gun possession on school property and commerce." More recently, a bare conservative majority of the Court declared part of the Violence Against Women Act of 1994 unconstitutional (*United States v. Morrison* 2000). In particular, victims of rape and other violent felonies "motivated by gender" can no longer sue their attackers in federal court (although state remedies are still available).

These decisions have sparked intense debate. To some, overexpansion of federal jurisdiction is a genuine concern in matters like this. But to others, the concern over caseload appears to be a façade masking conservative antipathy toward gun control and protecting the rights of vulnerable members of society.

Federal Violations? to explore why this topic cuts across typical ideological perspectives.

CONSEQUENCES OF FEDERAL INVOLVEMENT IN THE CRIMINAL JUSTICE SYSTEM

Crime has been a pressing national concern for decades. As a result, national elected officials, whether members of Congress or the president, have often made crime a key campaign issue. In turn, the crime policies of nonelected officials, whether bureaucrats or judges, have been closely scrutinized. Despite all this clamor at the national level, the role of the federal government in the criminal justice system is limited. Crime remains primarily the responsibility of state and local governments. This imbalance between federal officials' need to be seen as doing something about the crime problem and their limited jurisdiction to do anything explains a good deal of the political dynamics surrounding the role of the

federal government (and the federal judiciary) in the criminal justice system.

FORUM FOR SYMBOLIC POLITICS

In spite of the limited scope of its involvement in crime, the federal government remains the focal point of the national debate. Crime is a powerful issue and, therefore, has attracted a variety of interest groups. Some focus on crime issues directly—for example, the National Association of Chiefs of Police and Mothers Against Drunk Driving (MADD). Other interest groups, such as the American Civil Liberties Union (ACLU) and the National Organization for Women (NOW), find that crime and crime issues are related to other concerns.

Interest groups have a major impact on public policy. Most directly, they lobby on behalf of their members for favorable government policies. They can also mount campaigns encouraging their members to write federal officials in favor of (or in opposition to) specific proposals. Some organizations likewise make campaign contributions to selected officials.

The National Rifle Association (NRA), for instance, contributes to officials who are dubious about gun control, whereas the Brady Campaign to Prevent Gun Violence supports candidates who favor gun control.

FEDERAL DOLLARS

A basic rule of American politics is that citizens' demands for services exceed the willingness of voters to raise taxes to pay for those services. Those who one day vocally demand a tax reduction are quick to demand expanded government services the next day. Funding the criminal justice system illustrates this rule. Citizens demand that courts "get tough with criminals" but are unwilling to raise taxes to build new prison cells. Likewise, pleas for more cops on the beat are seldom followed by requests for increased taxes to pay for such increased people power. Faced with these limitations, local and state officials often turn to Washington as a source of "free" money (with *free* defined as "no local taxes"). In turn, federal officials find that appropriating federal money is one way of assuring voters that they take the crime problem seriously.

Congress has authorized spending for a variety of anticrime programs. Some are general in nature—for example, block grants for local projects that reduce crime and improve public safety. Similarly, 60 percent of the research budget of the National Institute of Justice—the principal federal agency involved in the war on crime—is spent on developing new technology for law enforcement and the criminal justice system. Other spending programs are targeted toward specific concerns—for example, domestic violence and victim assistance programs (see Chapter 9).

Overall, though, the amount of federal dollars is small compared to what local and state governments spend. Moreover, federal money is often limited to a short period of time (typically 3 years). After federal funding ends, state or local units of government are expected to take over funding, but often these agencies are strapped for cash, meaning that successful programs are canceled.

CONCLUSION

Offenders like Alfonso Lopez were no doubt on Justice Scalia's mind when he condemned what he called the deterioration of the federal courts. In the 1960s, the federal courts had few judges and small caseloads, but the cases they did hear were "by and large…cases of major importance." In contrast, Justice Scalia argued that while the federal courts now have more judges and larger caseloads, many of these cases are "minor" and "routine," concerning "mundane" matters of less import or even "overwhelming triviality" (quoted in Galanter 1988). Thus, to one of the Court's leading conservatives, the federal courts should be returned to their rightful role of deciding major controversies; lesser ones would be banished to state courts.

In the more than two decades since Justice Scalia made those comments, other judges, scholars, and commentators with diverse political viewpoints have echoed his sentiments that the federal courts handle too many routine cases that ought to be handled in state court so that the federal courts could focus on more important federal questions (Bradley 2004; Federal Courts Study Committee 1990). Such concerns are most evident with regard to the seemingly ever-expanding federalization of crimes—most especially drug cases (Husak 2008; Luna 2005). But in an era when crime remains a major political issue, rolling back federal jurisdiction to the "good old days" (whenever that might have been) is unlikely to happen. What we learn ultimately is that the jurisdiction of federal courts is determined in no small measure by decisions of elected officials in Congress. In an earlier era, federal officials decided that federal law should cover matters such as prostitution, consumption of alcoholic beverages, gambling, and organized crime. Today they focus more on drug dealers, crooks who use guns, and intimate-partner-violence offenders.

Federal prosecutions often grab the headlines because the crimes are large or audacious or because the accused are people of prominence. In turn, the public by and large identifies the judiciary with federal courts. But we should not be misled. The federal courts are a relatively small part of the nation's judicial system. A major city such as Chicago or Los Angeles prosecutes more felons in a year than the entire federal judiciary. The nature of the crimes brought to federal court differs strikingly from those appearing in state judiciaries, though. State courts handle primarily street crimes that require immediate action—burglary, armed robbery, and murder, for example. By contrast, with the exception of drug-related offenses, federal crimes largely concern immigration offenses, fraud cases, firearms violations, and money laundering. It is to the more common state courts that we turn our attention in the next chapter.

CHAPTER REVIEW

1. Define the four primary types of jurisdiction: geographical, subject matter, personal, and hierarchical.

Geographical jurisdiction limits the power of courts to adjudicate disputes arising within certain geographic boundaries. Subject matter jurisdiction concerns the types of cases a court may hear and decide. Personal jurisdiction refers to a court's power over a specific person or legal entity (such as a partnership or corporation). Hierarchical jurisdiction concerns whether the court has the power to originally decide a case or review it on appeal.

2. Compare and contrast the tasks of trial and appellate courts.

Trial courts are primarily concerned with considering evidence to resolve factual decisions within the bounds of the law. Appellate courts primarily review the legal decisions made by trial courts. In doing so, they serve dual purposes: error correction and policy formation (see Chapter 17).

3. Explain the historical evolution of the federal courts into their present structure and operations.

Article III of the U.S. Constitution established the U.S. Supreme Court and gave Congress the power to create lower courts. Congress has exercised its authority under Article III to create inferior courts at different times in U.S. history. Today, the trial courts that primarily exercise original jurisdiction in the federal system are the U.S. District Courts, whereas most appeals are resolved by the U.S. Courts of Appeals.

4. Analyze the different responsibilities and workloads of U.S magistrate judges, district judges, circuit judges, and Supreme Court justices.

U.S. magistrate judges assist U.S. district judges by conducting pretrial criminal matters, supervising discovery in civil cases, and making reports and recommendations concerning the disposition of motions and prisoner petitions. District court judges preside over trials and write opinions adjudicating many types of civil disputes. Typically sitting in panels of three, circuit judges review the records in cases appealed from district courts and write opinions ruling on the merits of legal arguments raised in those appeals.

5. Analyze the impact the federal courts have on the administration of criminal justice at the state and local levels through their federal question jurisdiction.

By interpreting the requirements of federal law—especially the U.S. Constitution—the federal courts set the parameters for the operation of the criminal justice system so that police, prosecutors, defense attorneys, and judges honor the individual rights and liberties guaranteed in Constitution.

6. Differentiate the jurisdiction and functions of Article III courts from Article I courts and other specialized federal courts.

Article III courts are empowered to adjudicate "cases and controversies" arising under the U.S. Constitution, federal law, and certain cases between citizens of different states or different counties. Article I courts are tribunals created by Congress to handle specialized types of cases, especially those that arise under the regulatory law of federal agencies. The decisions of Article I courts are generally reviewable in Article III courts. Article III judges are nominated by the president and confirmed to office by the U.S. Senate. Article I judges are not; they are appointed for fixed terms. Article I judges enjoy two protections to foster their independence: life-tenure (unless impeached) and a guarantee that their salaries can never be decreased. Article I judges do not have these protections.

7. Distinguish the various agencies and their hierarchical responsibilities for the administration of the federal court system.

The Judicial Conference of the United States sets national administrative policy for the federal judiciary. Under the supervision of the Judicial Conference, the Administrative Office of the U.S. Courts provides administrative support to courts (including budget, personnel, space, and facilities). The Federal Judicial Center provides orientation and continuing education to judges and personnel of courts, as well as research support for courts and Judicial Conference committees. The U.S. Sentencing Commission promulgates sentencing guidelines and otherwise establishes federal sentencing policies as directed by the 1984 Sentencing Reform Act.

8. **Evaluate the major problems facing the federal courts and the strengths and weaknesses of the major solutions that have been proposed to address these problems.**

Heavy caseloads are the major problem facing the federal courts. Not only does the heavy workload burden those who work in the courts, but also it affects litigants whose cases may be delayed because of backlog. Adding more staff, especially more federal judges, could help, but is cost prohibitive. Reducing the jurisdiction of the federal courts, especially by eliminating diversity of citizenship jurisdiction, could also help, but has not gained sufficient political support for Congress to have acted on the proposal.

CRITICAL THINKING QUESTIONS

1. To what extent are contemporary debates over the role of the federal government similar to, but also different from, the debates in the late 18th century?

2. How would the criminal justice system be different today if the founding fathers had decided not to create a separate system of federal courts and instead allowed federal laws to be enforced in state courts?

3. How would you reduce the federal court caseload? In considering where you would reduce federal court jurisdiction, also consider where you might increase it. What do your choices reflect about your political values?

4. To what extent does the debate over federalization of state crimes cut across traditional ideological values as represented in the due process model and the crime control model?

5. Federal law enforcement is limited in scope but subject to considerable public attention. Why?

KEY TERMS

appellate court 62

appellate jurisdiction 62

Article I 77

Article III 65

bankruptcy judge 69

Bivens actions 73

constitutional courts 77

courts of appeals 74

circuit justice 77

diversity of citizenship 70

dual court system 59

en banc 76

extradition 61

federal question 70

geographical jurisdiction 59

habeas corpus petitions 72

hierarchical jurisdiction 62

jurisdiction 59

legislative courts 77

mandamus petitions 72

motions to vacate
    sentences 72

original jurisdiction 62

personal jurisdiction 61

prisoner petitions 72

rule of four 76

Section 1983 72

subject matter
    jurisdiction 61

Supreme Court 76

stay 77

trial court 62

U.S. district courts 69

U.S. magistrate judges 66

venue 59

writ of certiorari 76

WEB RESOURCES

Go to the America's Courts and the Criminal Justice System companion website at

http://www.cengage.com/criminaljustice/neubauer

where you will find more resources to help you study.

Resources include web exercises, quizzing, and flash cards.

FOR FURTHER READING

Banks, Christopher. *Judicial Politics in the D.C. Circuit Court*. Baltimore: Johns Hopkins University Press, 1999.

Brody, David. "The Misuse of Magistrate Judges in Federal Criminal Proceedings: A Look at the Non-Ministerial Nature of Sentencings." *Justice System Journal* 23: 259–262, 2002.

Carp, Robert, and Ronald Stidham. *The Federal Courts.* 4th ed. Washington, DC: CQ Press, 2001.

Chutkow, Dawn. "Jurisdiction Stripping: Litigation, Ideology, and Congressional Control of the Courts." *Journal of Politics* 70: 1053–1064, 2008.

Collins, Paul, Daniel Norton, Kenneth Manning, and Robert Carp. "International Conflicts and Decision Making on the Federal District Courts." *Justice System Journal* 29: 121–144, 2008.

Frederick, David. *Rugged Justice: The Ninth Circuit Court of Appeals and the American West, 1891–1941.* Berkeley: University of California Press, 1994.

Fritz, Christian. *Federal Justice in California: The Court of Ogden Hoffman, 1851–1891.* Lincoln: University of Nebraska Press, 1991.

Hall, Kermit, and Eric Rise. *From Local Courts to National Tribunals: The Federal Courts of Florida, 1821–1990.* Brooklyn, NY: Carlson, 1991.

Luna, Erik. 2005. "The Overcriminalization Phenomenon." *American University Law Review* 54: 703–746.

Lurie, Jonathan. *Military Justice in America: The U.S. Courts of Appeals for the Armed Forces, 1775–1980.* Lawrence: University of Kansas Press, 2001.

"Native Americans in the Criminal Justice System: Issues of Self-Determination." *Journal of Contemporary Criminal Justice* 14: 1-86, 1998.

Sayer, John William. *Ghost Dancing the Law: The Wounded Knee Trials.* Cambridge, MA: Harvard University Press, 1997.

Smith, Christopher. *Judicial Self-Interest: Federal Judges and Court Administration.* Westport, CT: Praeger, 1995.

Spitzer, Robert. *The Politics of Gun Control.* Chatham, NJ: Chatham, 1994.

Wilkins, David. *American Indian Sovereignty and the U.S. Supreme Court: The Masking of Justice.* Austin: University of Texas Press, 1997.

Zelden, Charles. *Justice Lies in the District: The U.S. District Court, Southern District of Texas, 1902–1960.* College Station: Texas A&M University Press, 1993.

Zimring, Franklin, and Gordon Hawkins. "Toward a Principled Basis for Federal Criminal Legislation." *Annals of American Academy of Political and Social Science* 543: 14–26, 1996.

4

STATE COURTS

© Oswaldo Paez/AP Photo

Suspected drug traffickers, arrested and handcuffed by the police, walk past packages containing cocaine in Cali, 185 miles southwest of Bogota, Colombia. The cocaine, destined for the United States, was found in brick form, wrapped in brown paper, and hidden in a Cali apartment. While this arrest occurred in Colombia, the world's leading cocaine exporter, similar "drug busts" occur in the United States, especially in cities and towns along the United States–Mexican border.

CHAPTER OUTLINE

LEARNING OBJECTIVES

After reading this chapter you should be able to:

1. Outline the four layers of a typical state court system.

2. Describe the types of criminal cases handled by the trial courts of limited jurisdiction.

3. Identify the types of civil and criminal cases filed in trial courts of general jurisdiction.

4. Explain briefly the differences between a state supreme court in states with and without intermediate courts of appeals.

5. List the key components of court unification.

6. Identify how problem-solving courts using therapeutic jurisprudence handle cases.

7. Discuss the consequences of court organization.

After attending several judicial conferences around the nation, two judges had little trouble identifying the major problem facing the Los Angeles County municipal courts: Soaring drug prosecutions were further crowding jails that were already full. Implementing a solution, however, proved a more troublesome and time-consuming process. To establish a drug court, the judges needed the active cooperation of other judges, the district attorney, the public defender, treatment providers, and the sheriff. To ensure that these agencies had a voice in the process, a coordinating council was formally established. Finally, after months of meeting and planning, two drug courts were created (Torres and Deschenes 1997).

Discussions of state courts usually contain references to major cases such as armed robberies and automobile accidents. But this is only part of their workload. State judges must also adjudicate cases involving wives who want divorces from unfaithful husbands and husbands who physically abuse their wives; juveniles who rob liquor stores and juveniles who simply drink liquor. The contemporary realities reflect an increase in the number of cases placed on the dockets of state courts and rising societal expectations about the administration of justice—while staffing levels remain constant. Thus, although an earlier generation viewed court reform in terms of a neater organizational chart, contemporary discussions are more likely to focus on topics such as finding a better way to handle drug cases.

This chapter examines the structure and functions of state courts. We begin with a discussion of the development of American courts and then divide the somewhat confusing array of state courts into four levels: trial courts of limited jurisdiction, trial courts of general jurisdiction, intermediate courts of appeals, and courts of last resort. (Chapter 18 examines the lower courts in depth, and we will discuss juvenile courts in Chapter 19.) We will examine the efforts of court reformers to reorganize state court structure as well as the consequences of court organization for the administration of justice.

HISTORY OF STATE COURTS

Just as American law borrowed heavily from English common law, the organization of American courts reflects their English heritage. But the colonists and later the citizens of the fledgling new nation that called itself the United States of America adapted this English heritage to the realities of the emerging nation. Issues such as the clash of opposing economic interests, the debate over state versus national power, and outright partisanship have shaped America's 50 diverse state court systems.

COLONIAL COURTS

Early colonial courts were rather simple institutions whose structure replicated English courts in form but not in substance. The numerous, complex, and highly specialized English courts were ill suited to the needs of a small group of colonists trying to survive on the edge of the wilderness, so the colonists greatly simplified the English procedures. As towns and villages became larger, however, new courts were created so that people would not have to travel long distances to have their cases heard. Moreover, a notion of separation of governmental powers began to emerge. In the early days, the same governmental body often held executive, legislative, and judicial powers. The county courts, for example, stood at the heart of American colonial government. In addition to adjudicating cases, they performed important administrative functions (Friedman 2005). Gradually, different institutions began to perform these tasks.

Diversity was the hallmark of the colonies, with each colony modifying its court system according to variations in local customs, different religious practices, and patterns of commercial trade. Some of these early variations in legal rulings and court structures have persisted and contribute to the great variety of U.S. court systems today (Friedman 2005; Glick and Vines 1973).

In the northern colonies, biblical codes were often adopted. In the South, laws governing slavery were enacted. Overall, public punishments like the pillory and the stock were commonly used, but the death penalty was used less often than in England.

EARLY AMERICAN COURTS

After the American Revolution, the functions of state courts changed markedly. Their governing powers were drastically reduced and taken over by the legislative bodies. The former colonists distrusted lawyers and harbored misgivings about English common law. They were not anxious to see the development of a large, independent judiciary. Thus, state legislatures often responded to unpopular court decisions by removing some judges or abolishing specific courts all together.

A major source of political conflict between legislatures and courts centered on the issue of free money. Legislators were more responsive to policies that favored debtors, usually small farmers. Courts, on the other hand, reflected the views of creditors, often merchants. Out of this conflict over legislative and judicial power, the courts gradually emerged as an independent political institution.

In the northern states, European immigration generated cultural and religious tensions between new arrivals and native residents. In the South, the justice system focused on tracking down escaped slaves. Meanwhile, the nation was steadily moving west, and a unique form of frontier justice emerged.

COURTS IN A MODERNIZING SOCIETY

Rapid industrialization following the Civil War produced fundamental changes in the structure of the American judiciary. Increases in population led to a higher volume of litigation. Just as important, the growing concentration of people in the cities (many of whom were immigrants) meant the courts were faced with a new set of problems. Thus, by the end of the 19th century, the nation had to respond to a new type of social problem—crimes committed by juveniles (see Chapter 19).

The American courts, still reflecting the rural agrarian society of the early 19th century, were inadequate in the face of rising demands for services (Colburn 2006; Jacob 1984). States and localities responded to societal changes in a number of ways. City courts were created to deal with new types of cases in the urban areas, including public drunkenness, gambling, and prostitution. Specialized courts were formed to handle specific classes of cases (for example, small claims courts and family relations courts). Additional courts were created, often by specifying the court's jurisdiction in terms of a geographic boundary within the city.

The development of courts in Chicago illustrates the confusion, complexity, and administrative problems that resulted from this sporadic and unplanned growth. In 1931, Chicago had 556 independent courts; the majority were justice of the peace courts, which handled only minor offenses (Glick and Vines 1973). The jurisdiction of these courts was not exclusive; that is, a case could be brought before a variety of courts, depending on the legal and political advantages that each offered. Moreover, each court was a separate entity; each had a judge and a staff. Such an organizational structure meant that cases could not be shifted from an overloaded court to one with little to do. Each court also produced patronage jobs for the city's political machines.

The sporadic and unplanned expansion of the American court system has resulted in an often confusing structure. Each state system is different. Although some states have adopted a unified court structure, others still have numerous local courts with overlapping jurisdictions. To reduce confusion, we will examine state courts at four levels: trial courts of limited jurisdiction, trial courts of general jurisdiction, intermediate appellate courts, and courts of last resort. Table 4.1 summarizes the tremendous volume of cases decided each year by state courts.

TRIAL COURTS OF LIMITED JURISDICTION: LOWER COURTS

At the first level of state courts are **trial courts of limited jurisdiction**, sometimes referred to as *inferior courts*, or more simply, *lower courts*. The United States has more than 13,500 trial courts of limited jurisdiction, staffed by about 18,500 judicial officers (LaFountain et al. 2008). The lower courts constitute 85 percent of all judicial bodies in the United States. The number of trial courts of limited jurisdiction varies from none in Idaho, Illinois, Iowa, Massachusetts, Minnesota, South Dakota, and the District of Columbia (where their functions have been absorbed by the major trial courts) to more than 2,900 in New York and 2,500 in Texas.

Variously called district, justice, justice of the peace, city, magistrate's, or municipal courts, the lower courts decide a restricted range of cases. Most of these courts are created by city or county governments and therefore are not part of the state judiciary. Thus, lower courts are typically controlled only

TABLE 4.1

CASE FILINGS IN STATE TRIAL COURTS (IN MILLIONS)

	TRAFFIC	CIVIL	CRIMINAL	DOMESTIC	JUVENILE	TOTAL
General jurisdiction[a]	14.1	7.6	6.6	4.2	1.4	33.9
Limited jurisdiction	41.5	9.7	15.0	1.6	.7	68.5
Total	55.6	17.3	21.6	5.8	2.1	102.4

[a] Includes unified, general, and unified/general jurisdiction courts.

SOURCE: LaFountain, Robert, Richard Schauffler, Shauna Strickland, William Raftery, Chantal Bromage, Cynthia Lee, and Sarah Gibson. 2008. *Examining the Work of State Courts, 2007*. Williamsburg, VA: National Center for State Courts.

by the local governmental bodies that create them and fund them.

The caseload of the lower courts is staggering—more than 61 million matters a year, the overwhelming number of which are traffic cases (more than 41 million in any given year—see Table 4.1). The caseload indicates that these are the courts with which the average citizen is most likely to come into contact. For this reason, Chapter 18 will examine the lower courts in more depth, highlighting their role in conducting the preliminary stages of felony cases and deciding misdemeanor, traffic, and small claims cases.

TRIAL COURTS OF GENERAL JURISDICTION: MAJOR TRIAL COURTS

At the second level of state courts are the **trial courts of general jurisdiction**, usually referred to as *major trial courts*. An estimated 2,000 major trial courts in the 50 states and the District of Columbia are staffed by more than 11,000 judges (LaFountain et al. 2008). The term *general jurisdiction* means that these courts have the legal authority to decide all matters not specifically delegated to lower courts. The specific division of jurisdiction between the lower courts and the major trial courts is specified by law—statutory, constitutional, or both. The most common names for these courts are district, circuit, and superior. The specific names used in all states are listed in Table 4.2.

TABLE 4.2

MAJOR TRIAL COURTS IN DIFFERENT STATES

Circuit Court

Alabama, Arkansas,[a] Florida, Hawaii, Illinois, Indiana,[b] Kentucky, Maryland, Michigan, Mississippi,[a] Missouri, Oregon, South Carolina, South Dakota, Tennessee,[a] Virginia, West Virginia, Wisconsin

Court of Common Pleas

Ohio, Pennsylvania

District Court

Colorado, Idaho, Iowa, Kansas, Louisiana, Minnesota, Montana, Nebraska, Nevada, New Mexico, North Dakota, Oklahoma, Texas, Utah, Wyoming

Superior Court

Alaska, Arizona, California, Connecticut, Delaware,[a] District of Columbia, Georgia, Maine, Massachusetts, New Hampshire, New Jersey, North Carolina, Rhode Island, Vermont,[c] Washington

Supreme Court

New York[d]

[a] Arkansas, Delaware, Mississippi, and Tennessee have separate chancery courts with equity jurisdiction.

[b] Indiana uses superior and circuit courts.

[c] Vermont also uses district courts.

[d] New York also uses county courts.

SOURCE: Richard Schauffler, Robert LaFountain, Neal Kauder, and Shauna Strickland, eds., *Examining the Work of State Courts, 2004: A National Perspective from the Court Statistics Project*. Williamsburg, VA: National Center for State Courts, 2005.

The geographical jurisdictions of the major trial courts are defined along existing political boundaries, primarily counties. Each court has its own support staff consisting of a clerk of court, a sheriff, and others. In most states, the trial courts of general jurisdiction are also grouped into judicial districts or circuits. In rural areas these districts or circuits encompass several adjoining counties. Here the trial court judges are true generalists who hear a wide variety of cases as they literally ride circuit, holding court in different counties on a fixed schedule. More populated counties have only one circuit or district for the area. Here, judges are often specialists assigned to hear only certain types of cases, such as criminal, family, juvenile, or civil. Refer to Table 4.1 for some basic workload data on the major trial courts.

As discussed in Chapter 3, the lion's share of the nation's judicial business takes place at the state, not the federal, level. About 31 million cases are filed each year in the nation's state trial courts, more than 80 times the number of similar filings in the federal district courts. Moreover, the types of cases filed in the state courts differ greatly from those filed in the federal courts. Litigants in federal courts are most often big businesses and governmental bodies. In sharp contrast, litigants in state courts are typically individuals and small businesses.

CRIMINAL CASES

Whereas federal courts hear a high percentage of cases dealing with white-collar crimes and major drug distribution, state courts decide primarily street crimes. The more serious criminal violations are heard in the trial courts of general jurisdiction. The public associates felonies with crimes of violence, such as murder, robbery, and rape, but as Chapter 10 will show, 90 percent of criminal violations involve nonviolent crimes, such as burglary and theft. State courts must also process a rising volume of drug-related offenses, ranging from simple possession of small amounts of illicit drugs to the sale of large quantities of cocaine and heroin. Over the past decade and a half, criminal cases filed in general jurisdiction courts (primarily felonies) increased 25 percent. Most criminal cases do not go to trial. Thus, the dominant issue in the trial courts of general jurisdiction is not guilt or innocence, but what penalty to apply to the guilty.

CIVIL CASES

The focus on criminal cases in the media might lead one to believe that criminal cases account for the majority of court business. In reality, civil cases dominate the dockets of major trial courts. Press attention also suggests that personal injury lawsuits dominate civil filings. In reality, tort cases make up a relatively small percentage of the docket.

Domestic relations constitutes the single largest category of cases filed in the major trial courts. These matters of family law involve mainly divorce and related issues such as determining child custody, setting levels of child support, allocating economic resources (homes, cars, and savings accounts), and in some states, providing for spousal support (alimony and the like). Domestic relations cases account for a full one-third of case filings. Moreover, domestic relations cases constitute the fastest-growing part of the civil caseload.

Estate cases (often referred to as "probate") are the second most common type of case filed in the states' major trial courts. For those who made a will prior to their death, the courts supervise the distribution of assets according to the terms of the will. For those who failed to make a will before dying, the courts determine which heirs will inherit the estate. Most estate matters present the judge with little if any controversy.

Personal injury cases constitute the third most common type of case filings in state trial courts of general jurisdiction. Tort law covers a wide range of legal injuries. Most involve a physical injury, which can vary from a sprained ankle to wrongful death. Although tort cases may involve a wide range of activities, most stem from accidents involving motor vehicles. Tort cases constitute only about 8 percent of all filings in trial courts of general jurisdiction, but they are the most likely to go to trial. Only the handful that involve large sums of money are likely to be covered in the press. Contrary to popular belief, there has been no "litigation explosion" (Neubauer and Meinhold 2010); tort case filings have decreased 21 percent during the past decade (LaFountain et al. 2008).

A variety of other types of civil cases are also filed in state trial courts of general jurisdiction. **Contract** cases arise when one party claims that the other party has failed to live up to the terms of a contract and asks for monetary damages as compensation. Other cases allege violations of property rights, which typically involve mortgage foreclosures. Thus, most of the other cases are commercial matters, involving businesses in one form or another. Most commercial cases involve debt collection in one form or another.

LAW AND POPULAR CULTURE

Traffic (2000)

"You have a daughter. Why is it important to get a handle on this drug problem?" queries the anonymous female reporter. "Because it is an issue that affects all families," responds Robert Wakefield, a justice of the Ohio Supreme Court and soon to be the nation's next drug czar. But, while Wakefield is busy being briefed by high-level officials about how to wage the War on Drugs, his teenage daughter Caroline is secretly being educated by a group of underachievers about how to become addicted to drugs.

"I'm not sure I made the slightest difference," confides the nation's drug czar to his heir apparent. The movie *Traffic* makes it crystal clear that the general was being removed not for lack of zeal, but for his failure to master the political dimensions of the War on Drugs. Publicly elected officials treat the War on Drugs like a third rail—touch it and you die. Privately, however, many government officials (some even in law enforcement) have serious doubts that this war is winnable.

Few films do anything like spark a national debate, but the Academy Award–winning movie *Traffic* did just that. In *Traffic*, director Steven Soderbergh presents the complexity of America's War on Drugs through three divergent narratives that only occasionally overlap.

The first narrative is set in the morally hazy world of Tijuana, Mexico. The central figure is Rodriguez (Benicio Del Toro), an honest police officer who earns $316 a month. His efforts to curtail one of the two major drug cartels in the area run afoul of the ambitions of General Arturo Salazar (Tomas Milian). General Salazar is one of Mexico's toughest anticrime figures, but his reasons for asking Rodriguez and his partner, Manolo Sanchez (Jacob Vargas), to join his efforts are not immediately clear. However, Rodriguez knows that if he doesn't join General Salazar, his life will be in jeopardy.

The second narrative is set in the political ambiguity of Washington, D.C. The main figure is Robert Wakefield (Michael Douglas), a justice of the Ohio Supreme Court who has been selected to be the nation's drug czar. Before taking the job he is briefed about the political expectations of the job. His predecessor, for example, was removed because he lacked the capability to perform the "political component" of the job. But, as he tries to understand the official perspectives of the War on Drugs, a more personal view develops: His teenage daughter Caroline (Erika Christensen) is doing more than experimenting with drugs—she is becoming addicted. She escapes a drug treatment program and ends up in the inner city, where she is forced to prostitute herself to support her drug habit.

The third narrative is set in the socially snobby country clubs of La Jolla, California. The dominant person is Helena Ayala (Catherine Zeta-Jones), whose rich husband allows her to live the good life. But the Drug Enforcement Administration (DEA) has turned a mid-level drug dealer who fingers Helena's husband, Carl, as the area's major supplier. Suddenly, her husband is whisked away by the DEA, and she soon learns the truth about her husband's source of wealth. She also learns that her husband owes millions and, unless she can deliver the money, her children will be killed. Facing financial ruin, she soon takes command of the operation and devises a way to make the government's key witnesses "unavailable to testify."

The movie *Traffic* puts a face on the complex issues in the War on Drugs and raises many issues about how our society and, ultimately, our courts deal with the drug issue. The War on Drugs has led to rapidly increasing court dockets across the United States. In an effort to cope with rising case volume, many courts have created drug courts that respond in a therapeutic way to drug offenders and, at the same time, seek to reduce prison populations. Although the film and the subsequent commentary did not focus specifically on the issue of drug courts, such agenda

CONTINUED

Traffic (2000)

setting by the media can lead to change in society that ultimately affects the courts.

Traffic depicts drug dealers very differently than did the 1971 movie *The French Connection*. In that movie, Gene Hackman starred as a New York detective trying to break up an organized crime gang smuggling heroin from Turkey through the French port of Marseilles. *The French Connection* presents no moral or policy ambiguities; it is an action movie about a good cop arresting bad guys. Thus, simply busting big-time drug dealers is the end in and of itself.

After watching *Traffic*, be prepared to answer the following questions:

1. How would a change in the legalization of drugs affect court dockets?
2. How does *Traffic*'s promotion of a more "therapeutic culture" contrast with the legal system's increasing use of drug courts?
3. The film displays the inherent discretion built into law enforcement. In what ways does such discretion contribute to the difficulty of running the drug war and, ultimately, managing drug courts?

INTERMEDIATE COURTS OF APPEALS

A century ago, state court systems included only a single appellate body—the state court of last resort. Like their federal counterparts, however, state courts have experienced a significant growth in appellate cases that threatens to overwhelm the state supreme court. State officials in 39 states have responded by creating **intermediate courts of appeals (ICAs)** (Exhibit 4.1). The only states that have not followed suit are sparsely populated ones with a low volume of appeals. The ICAs must hear all properly filed appeals. Subsequent appeals are at the discretion of the higher court. Thus, a decision by the state's intermediate appellate court is the final one for most cases.

The structure of the ICAs varies in several ways. Twenty-four states organize their ICAs on a statewide basis, and the rest on a regional basis. In most states these bodies hear both civil and criminal appeals. Alabama and Tennessee, however, have separate courts of appeals for civil and criminal cases. The number of judges in the intermediate courts of appeals ranges from 3 to the 105 in the California Court of Appeal. Like their federal counterparts, these courts typically use rotating three-judge panels for deciding cases.

The ICAs handle the bulk of the caseload in the appellate system, and their workload has increased dramatically in the past decade. States have created these courts and given them additional judgeships in hopes of relieving the state supreme courts of crushing caseloads, only to find that the ICAs experience the same problems.

ICAs will be covered in more detail in Chapter 17, but in general, intermediate courts of appeals engage primarily in error correction; they review trials to make sure that the law was followed. The overall standard is one of fairness—the defendant is entitled to a fair trial but not a perfect one. As a result, defendants find that appellate courts are markedly unsympathetic to their legal arguments; only 1 of 16 achieves a major (even if temporary) victory. Although the public perceives that appellate courts are prone to release defendants on technicalities, the opposite is true. Moreover, the handful of defendants who win the right to a new trial are often convicted during that second trial.

As we will shortly see, the intermediate courts of appeals represent the final stage of the process for most litigants. Very few cases make it to the appellate court in the first place, and of those cases, only a handful will be heard by the state's highest appellate court.

COURTS OF LAST RESORT: STATE SUPREME COURTS

The court of last resort is generally referred to as the **state supreme court**. The specific names vary from state to state, and to further complicate the

Exhibit 4.1

INTERMEDIATE COURTS OF APPEALS (NUMBER OF JUDGES IN DIFFERENT STATES)

APPEALS COURT
Massachusetts (25)

APPELLATE COURT
Connecticut (9), Illinois (52)

APPELLATE DIVISION OF SUPERIOR COURT
New Jersey (34)

APPELLATE DIVISIONS OF SUPREME COURT
New York (55)

APPELLATE TERMS OF SUPREME COURT
New York (15)

COMMONWEALTH COURT
Pennsylvania (9)

COURT OF APPEALS
Alaska (3), Arizona (22), Arkansas (12), Colorado (16), Georgia (12), Idaho (3), Indiana[a] (15), Iowa (9), Kansas (14), Kentucky (14), Michigan (28), Minnesota (16), Mississippi (10), Missouri (32), Nebraska (6), New Mexico (10), North Carolina (15), Oregon (10), South Carolina (9), Tennessee[b] (12), Utah (7), Virginia (11), Washington (22), Wisconsin (16)

COURTS OF APPEAL
California (105), Louisiana (53), Ohio (68)

COURTS OF APPEALS
Texas (80)

COURT OF CIVIL APPEALS
Alabama (5), Oklahoma (12)

COURT OF CRIMINAL APPEALS
Alabama (5), Tennessee (12)

COURT OF SPECIAL APPEALS
Maryland (13)

DISTRICT COURT OF APPEALS
Florida (62)

INTERMEDIATE COURT OF APPEALS
Hawaii (4)

SUPERIOR COURT
Pennsylvania (15)

NONE
Delaware, District of Columbia, Maine, Montana, Nevada, New Hampshire, North Dakota, Rhode Island, South Dakota, Vermont, West Virginia, Wyoming

[a] Temporary
[b] Civil only

SOURCE: Bureau of Justice Statistics. 2007. *State Court Organization, 1987-2004.* Washington, DC: U.S. Department of Justice.

picture, Texas and Oklahoma have two courts of last resort—one for civil appeals and another for criminal appeals. The number of supreme court judges varies from a low of five to as many as nine (see Exhibit 4.2). Unlike the intermediate appellate courts, these courts do not use panels in making decisions; rather, the entire court participates in deciding each case. All state supreme courts have a limited amount of *original jurisdiction* in dealing with matters such as disciplining lawyers and judges.

In states without an intermediate court of appeals, however, the supreme court has no power to choose which cases will be placed on its docket, and in most other states the high court has a purely *discretionary docket*. As with the U.S. Supreme Court,

the state supreme courts select only a few cases to hear, but these cases tend to have broad legal and political significance. The ability of most state supreme courts to choose which cases to hear and which cases not to hear makes them important policymaking bodies. Whereas intermediate appellate courts review thousands of cases each year, looking for errors, state supreme courts handle a hundred or so cases that present the most challenging legal issues arising in that state.

Nowhere is the policymaking role of state supreme courts more apparent than in deciding death penalty cases. In most states with death penalty laws, if the judge imposes the death penalty, then the case is automatically appealed to the state's highest

Exhibit 4.2	

COURTS OF LAST RESORT IN DIFFERENT STATES (NUMBER OF JUDGES)

SUPREME COURT
Alabama (9), Alaska (5), Arizona (5), Arkansas (7), California (7), Colorado (7), Connecticut (7), Delaware (5), Florida (7), Georgia (7), Hawaii (5), Idaho (5), Illinois (7), Indiana (5), Iowa (8), Kansas (7), Kentucky (7), Louisiana (7), Michigan (7), Minnesota (7), Mississippi (9), Missouri (7), Montana (7), Nebraska (7), Nevada (7), New Hampshire (5), New Jersey (7), New Mexico (5), North Carolina (7), North Dakota (5), Ohio (7), Oklahoma[a] (9), Oregon (7), Pennsylvania (7), Rhode Island (5), South Carolina (5), South Dakota (5), Tennessee (5), Texas[a] (9), Utah (5), Vermont (5), Virginia (7), Washington (9), Wisconsin (7), Wyoming (5)

COURT OF APPEALS
District of Columbia (9), Maryland (7), New York (7)

SUPREME JUDICIAL COURT
Maine (7), Massachusetts (7)

COURT OF CRIMINAL APPEALS
Oklahoma[a] (5), Texas[a] (9)

SUPREME COURT OF APPEALS
West Virginia (5)

[a] Two courts of last resort in these states.

SOURCE: Bureau of Justice Statistics. 2007. *State Court Organization, 1987-2004*. Washington, DC: U.S. Department of Justice.

court, thus bypassing the intermediate courts of appeals. Because of the high stakes, state supreme courts expend considerable time and energy in reviewing these cases. The outcomes of these reviews, though, vary greatly from state to state; some state supreme courts rarely overturn a death penalty decision, but others are very prone to reverse it.

The state supreme courts are the ultimate review board for matters involving interpretation of state law. The only other avenue of appeal for a disgruntled litigant is the U.S. Supreme Court, but successful applications are few and must involve important questions of federal law. Chapter 17 will probe why many state supreme courts have in recent years emerged as significant governmental bodies. In state after state, the supreme courts are deciding issues that have a major impact on the law and government of their jurisdiction.

COURT UNIFICATION

Historically, court reform focused on organizational structure. To court reformers, the multiplicity of courts is inefficient (because judges cannot be shifted to meet the caseload needs of other courts) and also inequitable (because the administration of

justice is not uniform). Thus, traditional court reform has most often identified with implementing a unified court system. Figure 4.1 provides a diagram of a state (Florida) with a unified court system; Figure 4.2 offers a contrasting diagram of a state (Texas) with limited unification.

KEY COMPONENTS

The principal objective of a **unified court system** is to shift judicial administration from local control to centralized management. The loose network of independent judges and courts is replaced by a coherent hierarchy with authority concentrated in the state capital. Although court reformers differ about the exact details of a unified court system, their efforts reflect five general principles: a simplified court structure; centralized administration, rule making, and budgeting; and statewide financing (Berkson and Carbon 1978).

Court reformers stress the need for a **simplified court structure** with a simple, uniform court structure for the entire state. In particular, the multiplicity of minor and specialized courts, which often have overlapping jurisdiction, would be consolidated in one county-level court. This would mean that variations between counties would be eliminated and replaced by a similar court structure throughout the

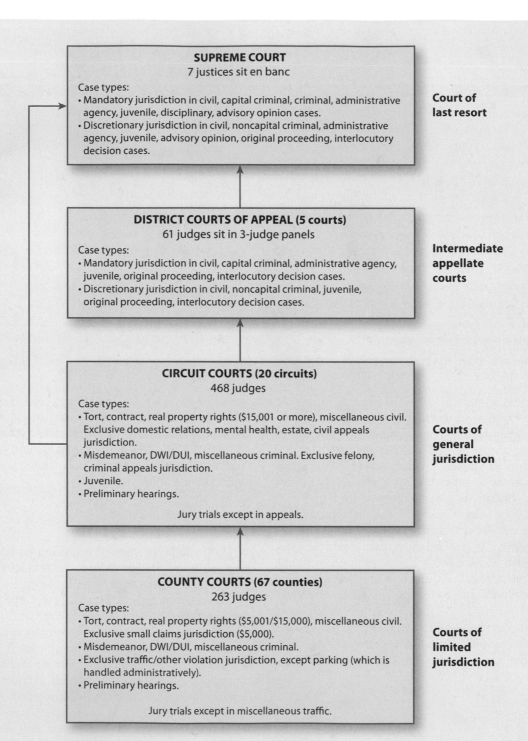

SUPREME COURT
7 justices sit en banc
Case types:
• Mandatory jurisdiction in civil, capital criminal, criminal, administrative agency, juvenile, disciplinary, advisory opinion cases.
• Discretionary jurisdiction in civil, noncapital criminal, administrative agency, juvenile, advisory opinion, original proceeding, interlocutory decision cases.

Court of last resort

DISTRICT COURTS OF APPEAL (5 courts)
61 judges sit in 3-judge panels
Case types:
• Mandatory jurisdiction in civil, capital criminal, administrative agency, juvenile, original proceeding, interlocutory decision cases.
• Discretionary jurisdiction in civil, noncapital criminal, juvenile, original proceeding, interlocutory decision cases.

Intermediate appellate courts

CIRCUIT COURTS (20 circuits)
468 judges
Case types:
• Tort, contract, real property rights ($15,001 or more), miscellaneous civil. Exclusive domestic relations, mental health, estate, civil appeals jurisdiction.
• Misdemeanor, DWI/DUI, miscellaneous criminal. Exclusive felony, criminal appeals jurisdiction.
• Juvenile.
• Preliminary hearings.

Jury trials except in appeals.

Courts of general jurisdiction

COUNTY COURTS (67 counties)
263 judges
Case types:
• Tort, contract, real property rights ($5,001/$15,000), miscellaneous civil. Exclusive small claims jurisdiction ($5,000).
• Misdemeanor, DWI/DUI, miscellaneous criminal.
• Exclusive traffic/other violation jurisdiction, except parking (which is handled administratively).
• Preliminary hearings.

Jury trials except in miscellaneous traffic.

Courts of limited jurisdiction

FIGURE 4.1 EXAMPLE OF A STATE WITH A UNIFIED COURT STRUCTURE: FLORIDA COURT STRUCTURE

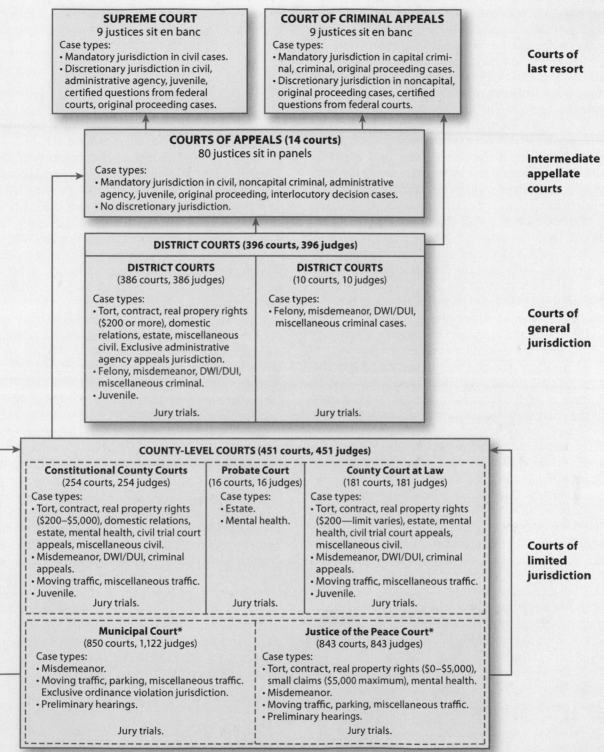

SUPREME COURT
9 justices sit en banc
Case types:
• Mandatory jurisdiction in civil cases.
• Discretionary jurisdiction in civil, administrative agency, juvenile, certified questions from federal courts, original proceeding cases.

COURT OF CRIMINAL APPEALS
9 justices sit en banc
Case types:
• Mandatory jurisdiction in capital criminal, criminal, original proceeding cases.
• Discretionary jurisdiction in noncapital, original proceeding cases, certified questions from federal courts.

Courts of last resort

COURTS OF APPEALS (14 courts)
80 justices sit in panels
Case types:
• Mandatory jurisdiction in civil, noncapital criminal, administrative agency, juvenile, original proceeding, interlocutory decision cases.
• No discretionary jurisdiction.

Intermediate appellate courts

DISTRICT COURTS (396 courts, 396 judges)

DISTRICT COURTS
(386 courts, 386 judges)

Case types:
• Tort, contract, real propery rights ($200 or more), domestic relations, estate, miscellaneous civil. Exclusive administrative agency appeals jurisdiction.
• Felony, misdemeanor, DWI/DUI, miscellaneous criminal.
• Juvenile.

Jury trials.

DISTRICT COURTS
(10 courts, 10 judges)

Case types:
• Felony, misdemeanor, DWI/DUI, miscellaneous criminal cases.

Jury trials.

Courts of general jurisdiction

COUNTY-LEVEL COURTS (451 courts, 451 judges)

Constitutional County Courts
(254 courts, 254 judges)
Case types:
• Tort, contract, real property rights ($200–$5,000), domestic relations, estate, mental health, civil trial court appeals, miscellaneous civil.
• Misdemeanor, DWI/DUI, criminal appeals.
• Moving traffic, miscellaneous traffic.
• Juvenile.

Jury trials.

Probate Court
(16 courts, 16 judges)
Case types:
• Estate.
• Mental health.

Jury trials.

County Court at Law
(181 courts, 181 judges)
Case types:
• Tort, contract, real property rights ($200—limit varies), estate, mental health, civil trial court appeals, miscellaneous civil.
• Misdemeanor, DWI/DUI, criminal appeals.
• Moving traffic, miscellaneous traffic.
• Juvenile.

Jury trials.

Municipal Court*
(850 courts, 1,122 judges)
Case types:
• Misdemeanor.
• Moving traffic, parking, miscellaneous traffic. Exclusive ordinance violation jurisdiction.
• Preliminary hearings.

Jury trials.

Justice of the Peace Court*
(843 courts, 843 judges)
Case types:
• Tort, contract, real property rights ($0–$5,000), small claims ($5,000 maximum), mental health.
• Misdemeanor.
• Moving traffic, parking, miscellaneous traffic.
• Preliminary hearings.

Jury trials.

Courts of limited jurisdiction

* Some municipal and justice of the peace courts may appeal to the district court.

FIGURE 4.2 EXAMPLE OF A STATE WITH LIMITED COURT UNIFICATION: TEXAS COURT STRUCTURE

state. Overall, the court reformers envision a three-tier system: a state supreme court at the top, intermediate courts of appeal where the volume of cases makes it necessary, and a single trial court.

Reformers envision **centralized administration**, with the state supreme court, working through court administrators, providing leadership for the state court system. The state court system would embody a genuine hierarchy of authority, in which local court administrators would be required to follow the policy directives of the central office and would in turn be held accountable by the state supreme court. Thus, a centralized state office would supervise the work of judicial and nonjudicial personnel.

Reformers argue that the state supreme court should have the power to adopt uniform rules to be followed by all courts in the state. Examples of **centralized rule making** include procedures for disciplining errant attorneys and time standards for disposing of cases. In addition, judges could be temporarily assigned to other courts to alleviate backlogs and reduce delay. Centralized rule making would shift control from the legislature to judges and lawyers.

Centralized judicial budgeting would give the state judicial administrator (who reports to the state supreme court) the authority to prepare a single budget for the entire state judiciary and send it directly to the legislature. The governor's power to recommend a judicial budget would be eliminated. Likewise, lower courts would be dependent on the supreme court for their monetary needs and unable to lobby local representatives directly. Thus, decisions about allocating funds would be made at the state and not the local level.

Along with centralized judicial budgeting, reformers argue for the adoption of **statewide financing** of the judiciary. Although courts are mandated by state law, they are often financed in whole or in part by local governments. Given that courts are often not a high priority for local government, they end up with less-than-adequate local financing. State government, in contrast, has more money and could better support necessary court services.

With the recent economic downturn across the nation, the issue of how to fund the courts has taken on new significance. Faced with mounting deficits, many states are cutting funding for the courts, with potentially serious consequences. In the words of the American Bar Association (2009), judicial independence is "a value that is indispensable to our democratic republic. A large part of that independence lies in courts having consistent, adequate funding to deliver justice." Yet at the same time public demands for court services are increasing. Faced with these realities, court leaders are being encouraged to examine zero-cost or very-low-cost innovations (Broccolina and Zorza 2008).

ANALYSIS

The assumptions and philosophy of traditional notions of court reform have been called into serious question. Some scholars believe that the old principles of court reorganization hamper creative thinking about the direction court reform should take (Flango 1994; Lamber and Luskin 1992). One concern is that the concept of a unified court system does not allow for a desirable diversity. The standard blueprint of court organization fails to consider, for example, important differences in the working environment of courts in densely populated cities as opposed to those in sparsely inhabited rural areas.

Critics have also charged that traditional concepts of court reform stress abstract ideals of court organization (law on the books) to the neglect of the realities of the courthouse (law in action) (Baar 1980). As a result, court reformers suffer from elite bias. Their perceptions of the problems of the courthouse extend only to cases with policy significance involving major community actors and rarely extend to ordinary cases affecting average citizens. In the biting words of Laura Nader (1992), court reformers talk about ridding the courts of "garbage cases," which include domestic violence, substance abuse, and neglected children. The solutions proposed by lawyer elites seem unresponsive to the realities of ordinary cases heard in the nation's trial courts. A judiciary with a clearly delineated organizational structure staffed by judges selected on the basis of merit (see Chapter 8) will face the same problems of large caseloads and types of cases—juvenile delinquency, for example—that are difficult to decide. Moreover, courts, no matter how well organized, must cope with public sentiments demanding getting tough with crime (see Case Close-Up: *Ewing v. California* and Three Strikes Laws).

PROBLEM-SOLVING COURTS

Contemporary court reform concentrates more on improving the quality of justice meted out by American courts and less on providing a neat

Ewing v. California and Three Strikes Laws

Forty-year-old Gary Ewing was caught moments after he attempted to steal three golf clubs hidden in his pants leg. Under normal circumstances Ewing would have been prosecuted for a misdemeanor violation. But his background of several previous convictions marked the case as unusual. Thus, the Los Angeles District Attorney decided to prosecute Ewing under California's "three strikes and you're out" law; as a result, he was sentenced to 25 years in prison without parole.

Three strikes laws have become an increasingly popular reaction to citizen frustrations over crime. As discussed further in Chapter 16, these laws systematically increase potential prison sentences for defendants who have been convicted of violent offenses. In California, however, only one of the convictions must be for a violent crime, thus adding to the controversy in the nation's most populous state. Critics argue that such laws are fundamentally unfair because the sentence is disproportionate to the actual crime committed. However, in *Ewing v. California*, a majority of the U.S. Supreme Court rejected this argument, holding that the sentence was not disproportionate and hence not a violation of the Eighth Amendment prohibition against cruel and unusual punishment.

Justice O'Connor's opinion for the majority stressed that in enacting three strikes laws, the California legislature had made a deliberate policy choice that individuals who repeatedly engage in serious or violent criminal behavior have not been deterred by conventional punishments, and therefore society can protect itself by isolating the defendant. Justice Stevens and three other justices dissented, arguing that a 25-year sentence for such a petty offense was "grossly disproportionate" and therefore constituted cruel and unusual punishment.

Legislatively mandated get-tough-on-criminal policies like "three strikes and you're out" laws most immediately impact corrections. Across the nation, the prison population has risen steadily (see Chapter 15). But these policies also impact the judiciary in several ways.

These laws increase the volume of criminal prosecutions. Note that Ewing would normally have been tried in a misdemeanor court, where costs are low and trials are few. Instead, he was prosecuted in a more costly felony court, where trials are more likely and also more time-consuming. In Los Angeles, for example, only 4 percent of felonies go to trial, compared with 25 percent of three strikes cases (Schultz 2000).

Get-tough policies affect the judiciary because of uneven application of the laws. Some prosecutors choose to apply the laws, but others do not. Thus, critics contend that three strikes laws distort the justice process. In the words of law professor Charles Weisselberg, an innocent person facing a third-strike offense runs the risk of going to trial. Because of the previous convictions, the prosecutor has an enormous advantage in forcing a plea bargain (Ryan 2002).

In deferring to the state legislature, the Court's decision in *Ewing* is strikingly different from the *Lopez* decision discussed in Chapter 3. Recall that in *Lopez*, the Supreme Court struck down a federal law that threatened to add to the growing caseloads of federal courts; but in Ewing, the Court seemed unconcerned that state legislatures were greatly adding to the docket of state courts.

CASE CLOSEUP

organizational chart. The modern agenda of court reform includes topics such as reducing trial court delay (Chapter 5), improving the efficiency of the appellate courts (Chapter 17), creating alternative dispute resolution (Chapter 18), and establishing community courts (Chapter 18).

Contemporary court reform is often identified with problem-solving courts. Although problem-solving courts vary considerably from place to place, they all emphasize addressing the underlying issue of the individual appearing in court. Moreover, these judicial bodies actively collaborate with service providers (Casey and Rottman 2004). Conceptually, problem-solving courts are based on therapeutic jurisprudence.

Contemporary court reform involves the creation of specialized courts to deal with specific types of cases. Initially, these were called "designer courts" or "boutique courts," indicating their specialized nature. Common examples include drug court, domestic violence court, juvenile drug court, gun court, drunk driving court, elder court, mental health court, and reentry court (which deals with prisoners reentering the community). More recently, these specialized courts have been said to rely on **therapeutic jurisprudence** (Rosenthal 2002; Wexler and Winick 1996). Such courts have five essential elements:

1. Immediate intervention
2. Nonadversarial adjudication
3. Hands-on judicial involvement
4. Treatment programs with clear rules and structured goals
5. A team approach that brings together the judge, prosecutors, defense counsel, treatment provider, and correctional staff (Rottman and Casey 1999)

Drug courts, domestic violence courts, and mental health courts are prime examples of courts based on the concept of therapeutic jurisprudence.

Drug Courts

The emergence of **drug courts** illustrates how the judiciary is responding both to increases in caseload and changes in the types of cases being brought to court. In the mid-1980s, drug case-loads increased dramatically in courts throughout the country. As a centerpiece of the so-called war on drugs, elected officials across the nation backed efforts to arrest, prosecute, and imprison persons possessing or selling illegal drugs. As a result, arrests for drug-abuse violations represent the largest single category of police activity—more than 1.5 million per year. Particularly in the nation's major urban areas, drug arrests have become the single most dominant police activity.

Faced with a rapidly increasing caseload of types of cases that did not seem to fit the traditional criminal court model, courts began to experiment with new ways of processing cases by creating drug courts. Rather than viewing these defendants as criminals, they saw them as persons with an addiction problem. Drug courts emphasize treatment. The assumption is that treatment will reduce the likelihood that convicted drug offenders will be rearrested.

Dade County (Miami) Circuit Court is an example of a treatment approach to drug offenders. It has received extensive national publicity because it was the first in the nation. To be eligible, defendants must have no prior felony convictions, must be charged with possession only (not sale), and

must admit their drug problem and request treatment. These offenders are diverted into treatment. The sentencing judge, rather than a probation officer, monitors offenders' progress. Participants must periodically report to the drug court judge, who assesses their progress and moves them through the phases of the program.

Initial evaluations gave favorable rates of success. For example, compared to defendants not in the program, offenders in the Miami drug court treatment program had lower incarceration rates, less frequent rearrests, and longer times to rearrest (Goldkamp and Weiland 1993). More sophisticated evaluations, however, have highlighted the complex impact of drug courts. In Washington, D.C., participation in a drug court treatment program has been relatively poor—only 41 percent of those eligible chose to participate. Moreover, completion of the program took much longer than anticipated; cases were open an average of 11 months as opposed to the 6 months estimated (Harrell, Cavanagh, and Roman 2000). Overall, there is sufficient evidence to conclude that drug courts have a positive impact; participants in drug courts are less likely to be rearrested for drug offenses and more likely to hold a job (Banks and Gottfredson 2004; Gottfredson, Najaka, and Kearley 2003). But the impact of drug courts varies by time, manner, and place (Goldkamp 2002). Moreover, the drug court model appears to be relatively ineffective when applied to drunk drivers (Bouffard, Richardson, and Franklin [in press]; Bouffard and Richardson 2007).

Within a decade, drug courts have moved from experimental innovation to well-established programs. Nearly 2,000 are now operational in all 50 states (National Drug Court Institute 2009). But the future is clouded by financial problems. Sustaining drug courts in the face of a hodgepodge of budgeting is challenging (Douglas and Hartley 2004).

Domestic Violence Courts

Domestic violence courts comprise another type of problem-solving court being created in a growing number of communities across the nation. Domestic violence was once considered a private family matter but is now viewed as a significant social problem (Chapter 9). Changes in how police and prosecutors respond to domestic violence cases have produced changes in how courts respond as well.

In domestic violence courts, the emphasis is on integration. These courts respond to a historical problem in the court system, which required domestic violence victims and their families to appear in different courts before multiple judges, often located in different courthouses in different parts of the county. As a result, a single family could be involved in several courts before several different judges and face the possibility of conflicting court orders. Today, common practices of domestic violence courts typically include the following:

- Assigning a judge and staff to hearing domestic violence cases
- Providing early access to advocacy for victims
- Coordinating with community partners who provide services for victims of domestic abuse
- Consolidating related cases (Casey and Rottman 2004).

Operating within this general framework, more than 300 specialized domestic violence courts have been created across the nation (Center for Court Innovation 2009). Some are more specialized than others (Stop Violence Against Women 2009). One example is Manhattan's Specialized Domestic Violence Court. By removing domestic violence cases from mixed-docket courts, this specialized court seeks to increase defendant accountability, promote victim safety, and better coordinate the activities of governmental agencies that respond to domestic violence. Also called "integrated domestic violence courts," they are dedicated to the one-family–one-judge concept. Thus, a single judge handles multiple criminal, family court, and divorce cases involving the same defendant (Peterson 2004).

Since domestic violence courts are a recent innovation, it is hard to draw firm conclusions about their effectiveness. An evaluation of Manhattan's Specialized Domestic Violence Court showed mixed results: Conviction rates did not increase, cases were disposed of more quickly, defendants were more likely to be placed in a batterer-intervention program, and rearrests increased (Peterson 2004). Overall, the evidence indicates that these courts enhance victims' and defendants' satisfaction with the court process and deliver more services to victims and their families (Casey and Rottman 2004).

Mental Health Courts

Mental health courts are a third type of problem-solving court using the concept of therapeutic jurisprudence. Over the past several years there has been a growing awareness that the mentally ill are overrepresented in the criminal justice system. It is estimated that anywhere from 7 to 16 percent of those in jail suffer from serious mental illness, a rate that is four times that of the general adult population. Indeed, Los Angeles County Jail and New York's Rikers Island held more people with mental illness than the largest psychiatric hospital inpatient facilities in the United States (Council of State Governments Justice Center 2008a). Not only do mentally ill defendants present special security risks in courts and jails, but they are also more likely to repeatedly recycle through the criminal justice system.

A growing number of courts across the nation are establishing mental health courts that are remarkably diverse. Nonetheless, these courts exhibit several key features:

- A specialized court docket is created.
- Mentally ill defendants are processed on the basis of therapeutic jurisprudence rather than the adversary style of justice.
- Judges supervise a community-based treatment plan for each defendant involving a team of court staff and mental health professionals.
- The judge periodically reviews the progress of each defendant.
- Criteria define a participant's completion (sometimes called "graduation form") of the program (Council of State Governments 2008b).

Judge Matthew D'Emic (2009) of the Brooklyn Mental Health Court writes that in the 7 years of that court's operation, over 275 persons have successfully graduated. But he is quick to point out that public policy should not be driven by anecdotes of individual successes but rather by research that systematically evaluates the effectiveness of the growing number of mental health courts. Such evaluations must take into account the difficult population that these courts work with as well as the difficulty of coordinating efforts not just within the criminal justice system but also in the mental health community.

Consequences of Court Organization

What activities legislatures define as illegal has a major impact on the courts (see Courts, Controversy, and Reducing Crime: Is It Time to End the War on Drugs?). In turn, how the courts are organized and administered has a profound effect on the way cases are processed and on the type of justice that results.

Courts, Controversy, And Reducing Crime

The association of drugs with social problems begins to explain why the war on drugs enjoys considerable public support. There is no doubt that drug addiction produces untold human suffering in the United States. And there is little doubt that drugs are also associated with crime; indeed, two out of three people arrested by the police show evidence of recent use of illegal drugs (crack, methamphetamines, and marijuana, for example) and/or legal drugs (primarily alcohol).

Public support for the war on drugs is also fueled by its link to controlling marginal groups. Historians suggest that medical or scientific knowledge about the harm of drugs has never played a significant role in formulating U.S. drug policy. Rather, U.S. policy has been driven by the desire to control groups considered threats to the existing social order. Thus, the Harrison Narcotics Act of 1914 targeted opium (used by Chinese in California), marijuana (smoked by Mexican Americans in the Southwest), and cocaine (allegedly being used by African Americans in the South).

One reason that the war on drugs is difficult to wage is because the focus of the debate is always changing. Some wondered whether President George Bush was fighting the wrong war on drugs. The Bush administration made marijuana the major focus of its antidrug efforts partly, it says, because pot is a "gateway" drug—kids try it and then move on to even more serious drugs. To law enforcement officials around the nation, though, *meth* (methamphetamine) is America's most dangerous drug (Jefferson 2005). Indeed after four decades of presidents waging various wars on drugs, these efforts are being pushed out of the public limelight by the "war on terror." Even though the war on drugs is less visible, arrests and convictions for drugs remain the main reason for the swelling prison population.

Beneath the broad consensus supporting the war on drugs, however, is a growing disquiet. Off the record, some criminal justice officials guardedly express reservations about the war on drugs. In public, some scholars are now voicing the urgent need to rethink the war on drugs. In *Drug War Politics: The Price of Denial*, Eva Bertram and her colleagues (1996) argue that despite spending billions of dollars on reducing the supply of drugs and punitive approaches to those who use illegal drugs,

Decentralization and Choice of Courts

Although people often talk about the American legal system, no such entity exists. Instead, America has 51 legal systems—the federal courts and separate courts in each of the 50 states. Chapter 2 stressed the significant differences in the law among these separate systems. As a result, lawyers sometimes try to maneuver cases so that they are heard in courts that are perceived to be favorable to their clients. For example, some criminal offenses violate both state and federal laws. As a general rule, federal officials prosecute major violations, leaving more minor prosecutions to state officials.

The prosecution of the DC-area snipers illustrates the importance of the choice of courts. During a 3-week shooting spree, John Muhammad and Lee Malvo engaged in 13 shootings, killing 10 people and wounding 3. The U.S. attorney general decided to transfer the defendants to Virginia because that state's law makes the death penalty more likely than in the other jurisdictions where murders occurred—Maryland and the District of Columbia. After both were convicted, Muhammad was sentenced to death, but Malvo (because he was young) was sentenced to life imprisonment.

Local Control and Local Corruption

The 50 state court systems are in actuality often structured on a local basis. The officials who staff these courts—judges and lawyers, prosecutors and defense attorneys—are recruited from the local community they serve and thus reflect the sentiments of that community. As a result, the U.S. system of justice has

the war on drugs is a failure. Failure, however, only convinces the advocates of the war on drugs that greater efforts need to be made. In short, in the war on drugs, nothing succeeds like failure.

It is not just the failure to reduce drug supply (or demand) that concerns critics, but also the social impact of these efforts. In *Reckoning: Drugs, the Cities, and the American Future*, sociologist Elliott Currie (1993) condemns current drug policy for destroying inner-city communities by swelling prison populations with the unemployable minority poor. In *Unequal under Law: Race in the War on Drugs*, political scientist Doris Marie Provine (2007) argues that the race-neutral language of the law merely hides racial meanings.

The public support for and private disquiet over the war on drugs reflect the differences between the crime control and due process models of criminal justice. Three points—focusing on causes, equality, and punishment—are at issue.

- The crime control model begins with the judgment that drug abuse is caused by a breakdown of individual responsibility. The due process model views substance abuse as a disease that needs to be treated.
- According to the crime control model, the solution is punishment. Arrest and conviction will serve as a lesson to the violator and will also deter others. The due process model replies that filling the prisons is costly and ineffective. It is therefore more effective and also less costly to emphasize rehabilitation programs.
- The due process model is very concerned that current drug policies fall unequally on racial minorities. The crime control model counters with seemingly banal indifference: "You do the crime, you serve the time."

What do you think? Does the nation need to change its drug policies to place more emphasis on treatment and prevention, and less on arrest, conviction, and imprisonment? To continue the debate over the war on drugs, visit the Opposing Viewpoints Resource Center at **www.galegroup.com/opposingviewpoints** and use the search term "narcotics, control of" to find articles that express opposing viewpoints on this topic.

close ties to local communities and the application of "state" law often has a local flavor. Jurors in rural areas, for example, often have markedly different attitudes toward guns than jurors in suburban areas.

Local control of justice has the obvious advantage of closely linking courts to the people they serve. But local control has also been an incubator of corruption and injustice. Every state invariably has a town or two where gambling and prostitution flourish because the city fathers agree to look the other way. Not surprisingly, they often receive monetary benefits for being so nearsighted. Increasingly, though, such activities attract the attention of state police, state attorneys general, and federal prosecutors.

The locally administered criminal justice system has also been marked by pockets of injustice. At times, the police and the courts have been the handmaidens of the local economic elite. In the South, historically, the police and the courts hindered efforts to exercise civil rights by arresting or harassing those who sought to register to vote, eat at whites-only lunch counters, or simply speak up to protest segregation. The dual court system has provided a safety valve for checking the most flagrant abuses of local justice. Often, it is federal—not state or local—officials who prosecute corrupt local officials.

CONCLUSION

The implementation of drug courts in Dade County in Florida and in Washington, D.C. (as well as numerous other areas across the nation) illustrates a major shift in thinking about court reform in the United States. Whereas traditional court reform emphasized consolidating various judicial bodies, the emerging agenda encourages the creation of specialized courts. Modern court reform also actively encourages working with members of the community, whereas the older tradition stressed notions of professionalism that disdained popular input. Likewise, court reform in the contemporary context stresses the importance of working with other agencies rather than viewing the judge as a lone authority figure. The next chapter focuses on these other agencies, elaborating on the concept of the courtroom work group.

What is perhaps most striking is that the ideas that have dominated discussion of court reform for most of this century are now being quietly buried. Instead of stressing organizational charts and other abstract notions, most efforts to reform the judiciary now focus on more specific matters— reducing court delay and targeting drug cases for special treatment, for example. Thus, today's court reform is marked by tremendous experimentation at the local level. Judges and other court actors identify a problem and seek solutions, adapting local resources and local understandings in the process. This adaptation to change has always been the hallmark of the American judiciary. Perhaps the only differences today are the rapid pace of change and the public attention paid to these ongoing efforts at judicial reform.

CHAPTER REVIEW

1. Outline the four layers of a typical state court system.

A typical state court system includes lower courts (trial courts of limited jurisdiction), major trial courts (trial courts of general jurisdiction), intermediate appellate courts, and a court of last resort (often called the "state supreme court").

2. Describe the types of criminal cases handled by the trial courts of limited jurisdiction.

The lower courts handle the preliminary stages of felony cases and also decide a large number of misdemeanor, traffic, and small claims cases.

3. Identify the types of civil and criminal cases filed in trial courts of general jurisdiction.

The major trial courts decide felony cases and civil cases including domestic relations, estate, personal injury, and contract cases.

4. Explain briefly the differences between a state supreme court in states with and without intermediate courts of appeals.

In states without intermediate appellate courts, state courts of last resort must hear all criminal appeals. In states without intermediate courts of appeals, state courts of last resort have discretion to hear only the cases they decide are the most important.

5. List the key components of court unification.

The key components of court unification include simplified court structure, centralized administration, centralized rule making, centralized judicial budgeting, and statewide financing.

6. Identify how problem-solving courts using therapeutic jurisprudence handle cases.

Courts using therapeutic jurisprudence have five essential elements: (1) immediate intervention, (2) nonadversarial adjudication, (3) hands-on judicial involvement, (4) treatment programs with clear rules, and (5) a team approach to treatment.

7. Discuss the consequences of court organization.

The organization of courts in the United States impacts the processing of cases in several ways, including the decentralization of justice, which at times can mean that there is a choice of courts and that local control has at times resulted in local corruption.

CRITICAL THINKING QUESTIONS

1. Although we typically talk of state courts (as opposed to federal courts), would it be better to talk about local courts? To what extent are there major variations within your state?

2. Compare your state's court structure to those in Figures 4.1 and 4.2. How unified is your state court structure?

3. Have there been discussions in your state of court reorganization? What major interest groups are urging court reform, and what advantages do they suggest? What interest groups are opposing

court reform, and what disadvantages do they cite?

4. Why do crime control advocates often oppose drug courts, and why do due process proponents support drug courts?

5. Make a list of state and local politicians who have been tried in federal court. Were there parallel state investigations or prosecutions? To what extent would corrupt local officials be better off if federal court jurisdiction were limited?

KEY TERMS

centralized administration   104

centralized judicial budgeting   104

centralized rule making   104

contract   97

domestic relations   97

drug courts   106

estate   97

intermediate courts of appeals (ICAs)   99

personal injury   97

simplified court structure   101

state supreme court   99

statewide financing   104

therapeutic jurisprudence   106

trial court of general jurisdiction   96

trial court of limited jurisdiction   95

unified court system   101

WEB RESOURCES

Go to the America's Courts and the Criminal Justice System companion website at

http://www.cengage.com/criminaljustice/neubauer

where you will find more resources to help you study.

Resources include web exercises, quizzing, and flash cards.

FOR FURTHER READING

Abadinsky, Howard. *Drug Use and Abuse: A Comprehensive Introduction*. 6th ed. Belmont, CA: Wadsworth, 2008.

American Judicature Society. "The Cost of Justice: Funding State Courts." *Judicature* 88: 158–169, 2005.

Beckett, Katherine, Kris Nyrop, and Lori Pfinst. "Race, Drugs, and Policing: Understanding Disparities in Drug Delivery Arrests." *Criminology* 44: 105, 2006.

Champagne, Anthony. "Judicial Reform in Texas: A Look Back after Two Decades," *Court Review* 43 (2): 68, 2006.

Gerber, Rudolph. *Legalizing Marijuana: Drug Policy Reform and Prohibition Politics*. Westport, CT: Praeger, 2004.

Hartley, Roger, and James Douglas. "Budgeting for State Courts." *Justice System Journal* 24: 251–264, 2003.

Lightcap, Tracy. "Issue Environments and Institutionalization: Structural Changes in U.S. State Judicial Institutions, 1975–1995." *Justice System Journal* 24: 183–204, 2003.

Nafisi, Terry. "One Hundred Years since Pound: Has Court Reform Mattered?" *Justice System Journal* 27: 223–236, 2006.

Nolan, James. *Reinventing Justice: The American Drug Court Movement*. Princeton, NJ: Princeton and Oxford University Press, 2001.

Slate, Risdon, and W. Wesley Johnson. *The Criminalization of Mental Illness: Crisis and Opportunity for the Justice System*. Durham, NC: Carolina Academic Press, 2008.

Solomon, Freda. "New York City's Gun Court Initiative: A Pilot Program Study." CJA Research Brief No. 11. New York: New York City Criminal Justice Agency, 2006.

Stojkovic, Stan, John Klofas, and David Kalinich. *The Administration and Management of Criminal Justice Organizations: A Book of Readings*. 4th ed. Long Grove, IL: Waveland Press, 2004.

Willrich, Michael. *City of Courts: Socializing Justice in Progressive Era Chicago*. New York: Cambridge University Press, 2003.

Winick, Bruce, and David Wexler, eds. *Judging in a Therapeutic Key: Therapeutic Jurisprudence and the Courts*. Durham, NC: Carolina Academic Press, 2003.

Winkle, John III, and Robert Oswald. "The Role of Trial Judges in State Court Reform: The Case of Mississippi." *Judicature* 91: 288-297, 2008.

5

THE DYNAMICS OF COURTHOUSE JUSTICE

A judge watches as a sheriff's deputy checks his notes before answering a question posed to him by a lawyer. While such a scene is typical, the courtroom work group is composed of many people who rarely are depicted in news photos or on television. Rather, the courtroom work group work together "behind-the-scenes" out of shared norms and their mutual interdependence on each other.

CHAPTER OUTLINE

LEARNING OBJECTIVES

After reading this chapter, you should be able to:

1. Have a general sense of who works where in the courthouse.

2. Analyze the importance of assembly-line justice.

3. Describe why discretion is found in the criminal courts.

4. Identify the principal actors in the courtroom workgroup.

5. Indicate why ethics is important to the American legal system.

6. Contrast differing understandings of why delay is a problem in the courts.

7. Discuss the strengths and weaknesses of speedy-trial laws.

8. Explain why law in action approaches to court delay are more effective than law on the books approaches.

Sixteen times Willie Barker's murder case was set for trial, and sixteen times it was continued. At first the defense readily agreed, gambling that Barker's codefendant would be found not guilty. Thus, some of the continuances were caused by the six separate trials before the codefendant was finally convicted. Other continuances were granted because of the illness of the police investigator. It was not until 5 years after arrest that Barker was convicted of murder. To Barker's lawyer, this lengthy delay clearly violated the Sixth Amendment's right to a speedy trial. The Kentucky prosecutor replied that the delay did not jeopardize Barker's right to a fair trial.

Barker v. Wingo underscores three key points about criminal-case processing in contemporary courts. First, courts deal with lots of cases. From the perspective of victims and defendants, criminal cases are discrete life events, but from the vantage point of judges, prosecutors, and defense attorneys, the docket consists of numerous cases, each demanding the court's time. The pressure to move cases, often referred to as assembly-line justice, is the first concept discussed in this chapter.

Second, the problems in prosecuting and convicting Barker indicate that discretion is often needed in interpreting the law. After all, the meaning of "speedy trial" is not self-evident. As we shall see, the concept of discretion begins to grapple with the day-to-day realities of courthouse dynamics.

Third, the *Barker* case shows that case dispositions involve far more than the isolated actions of individual judges. From arrest through trial and sentencing, case dispositions require mutual activity on the part of prosecutors and defense attorneys, to say nothing of police officers and probation officers, bail agents and bailiffs. This chapter uses the concept of the courtroom work group to analyze the complexities of interaction among courthouse regulars.

This chapter examines the dynamics of courthouse justice by analyzing three major explanations for the great difference between textbook images of criminal procedure and the realities of the courtroom. We will then apply these concepts to one of the most often mentioned problems of American justice—delay. As in the *Barker* case, though, we will see that deciding how long is too long is a knotty question. But first let us begin with a tour of a typical U.S. courthouse.

THE COURTHOUSE AND THE PEOPLE WHO WORK THERE

Court jurisdiction and court structure are admittedly intangible concepts. Courthouses, on the other hand, are concrete. From the outside, courthouses appear to be imposing government buildings, but on the inside they are beehives of activity. Most immediately, courthouses are places where you find lawyers arguing before juries, talking to their clients, and conversing with one another. But courthouses also employ numerous nonlawyers who perform vital roles; without clerks and probation officers, bail agents and bailiffs, courthouses could not function. Not to be overlooked, ordinary citizens (whether victims or defendants, witnesses or jurors) also perform important roles in the courthouse.

In trying to understand how lawyers and nonlawyers, regular participants and occasional ones, dispense courthouse justice on a daily basis, it is helpful to start with a walking tour of a courthouse. What goes on inside a courthouse, of course, varies in important ways. In the courthouses of small towns, for example, one finds only a few courthouse regulars who handle many different types of matters. By contrast, in the courthouses of major cities you will find numerous courthouse regulars who specialize in specific duties. Moreover, in some courthouses, civil and criminal cases are heard in the same courtroom at the same time; in other jurisdictions, civil and criminal cases are separated in time and place. These variations aside, the following provides an overview of a typical day in a medium-sized courthouse in the United States.

THE COURTHOUSE

Early-American courthouses were simple structures with "plain furnishings and finishes" (Sahoo 2006, p. 9). But by the mid-1800s, major courthouses were designed to be "imposing, grandiose" structures that incorporated "formal architectural elements such as columns, domes, clock towers, and grand entrances" (Sahoo 2006, p. 9). Today, courthouses in the United States "come in a myriad of designs, from centuries-old stone fortresses to modern-day, multifloor monolithic towers, from the one-room council chambers to the abstract designs of the creative architect" (Zaruba 2007, p. 46).

The locations of courthouses vary dramatically as well. In some cities, courthouses are landmarks in the center of downtown areas. Such courthouses have served as anchors "for many commercial and community activities" (Sahoo 2006, p. 9). In sharp contrast, criminal courts of other cities were purposefully constructed near pretrial detention facilities in isolated and inconvenient locations for security reasons. Clustered nearby are older buildings, occupied by bail agents and defense attorneys. Garish neon signs proclaiming "Bail Bonds, 24-Hour Service" compete with unpainted wooden structures to provide a general sense of urban decay. The courthouse building likewise often has a haggard and unkempt look about it. Beneath the veneer of decades of grime, though, one sees a once grand building built during an era when citizens took great pride in their public buildings. Although criminal court buildings are constructed in a variety of architectural styles, they nevertheless all seem to present an image of stolidity and unyielding strength.

In the modern era, court security concerns drive courthouse design, renovation, and function. Entrance is usually gained by climbing an excessive number of steps that lead to a single set of doors through which all people must enter.

> Visitors or employees entering the courthouse are met by CSOs [Court Security Officers] and screened as they pass through a metal detector. Persons setting off a metal detector are scanned by a CSO using a handheld detector. Briefcases, packages, and other items in which dangerous or prohibited items might be stored are X-rayed. The CSOs also hand-check any item deemed suspicious or problematic. Policies regarding the use, or even the presence, of cellular and digital phones, personal digital assistants, or other electronic devices are set by each individual courthouse. (Novak, 2003, p. 24)

In older courthouses, prisoners used the same entrances and circulation paths as judges, jurors, and members of the public. Modern courthouses, however, are designed to transfer prisoners securely from holding facilities into courthouses using different entrances and restricted internal routes so that they are kept separated from the public and courthouse personnel (Novak 2003; Zaruba 2007).

Once inside a courthouse, visitors may find themselves in an austere, small area or in a massive lobby with an impressively high arched ceiling. Either way, the lobby and hallways typically resound with animated conversations among lawyers, bail agents, bailiffs, defendants, family members, witnesses, and a variety of other interested parties. Indeed, for many bail agents and private criminal lawyers these hallways are their daytime offices.

© Don Smetzer/PhotoEdit

© Library of Congress

THE COURTROOM

After some difficulty, most first-time visitors manage to locate the specific courtroom of interest, entering through a double set of heavy doors, which suggests that this is not an ordinary public building. This initial impression of orderliness under law quickly gives way to a sense of social anarchy. One is immediately confronted with a visual and audio reality far different from that portrayed on television or in the movies. What is happening inside the courtroom is best viewed in terms of sets of actors who congregate in different locations.

In the front is an imposing bench, which dominates the courtroom, literally elevating the black-robed judge on a pedestal. Court begins by the customary call of the crier: "All rise, the court for _____ County is now in session, the Honorable _____ _____ presiding." On cue, the judge strides mindfully from behind a hidden door, law book or case folder tucked under one arm. Just below the bench sits the clerk of court (sometimes called the "calendar clerk"), who controls the scheduling of cases and keeps the judge apprised of the relevant details of the case. To one side of the bench sits the court stenographer, whose machine mysteriously makes a shorthand record of the proceedings. Also in attendance is a bailiff, who tries to maintain order in the courtroom. The judge's staff also may include a law clerk and a secretary (who jealously guards access to the judge when he or she is not presiding in the courtroom).

About 10 to 20 feet from the front of the bench are two tables reserved for the defense and prosecution, respectively. The district attorney's (DA) table is piled high with case folders needed for the day's activities. Somehow, no matter how high the pile of case folders, a file or part of a file is invariably missing, resulting in last-minute scurrying by frantic assistant DAs trying to rectify the periodic lapses of the prosecutorial bureaucracy. The mountain of files on the public defender's table nearly matches that of the prosecutor's. The public defender (PD) likewise finds that files are missing or incomplete, resulting in scurrying around looking for missing pieces of paper. When a case involving a private criminal lawyer is called, the PD temporarily gives up the seat at the defense table, but the files remain, an indication that it is really the PD who dominates. Between the bench and the lawyers' table stands a battered wooden podium, which is typically used only for ceremonial occasions—most notably, when the defendant enters a plea of guilty, or the lawyers argue before a jury. Otherwise, lawyers typically argue while sitting behind the table.

To the side of the bench is the jury box. On trial day, jurors occupy these seats; when no jury trial is being conducted, a variety of folks can be found in and around the jury box, waiting, socializing, and occasionally conducting business. Often the easiest to identify are police officers in court to provide testimony. Also in attendance are probation officers, substance-abuse counselors, and pretrial services representatives. Bail agents also often drop in to make sure that the persons they have posted bail for have indeed arrived as scheduled.

Often sitting in the jury box, too, are defendants who have been detained before trial. Defendants out on bail sit in the public sector, but those in jail sit in brightly colored uniforms with the name of the county jail readily displayed. Often they are manacled together and are temporarily unchained when their cases are called. Surrounding the defendants, hovering like brooding hens, are the sheriff's deputies. The number of deputies in court provides a pretty good indication of the perceived threat of the defendants; the higher the ratio of guards to prisoners, the more serious the crime and the criminal.

A railing separates the courthouse regulars from the occasional participants. The first row or two are reserved for lawyers waiting for their cases to be called. Sitting in the remaining rows are the defendants (those who have been freed on bond or released on their own recognizance), family members, and perhaps a variety of other observers—for example, senior citizens, who enjoy rooting for the prosecutor. Increasingly in contemporary courthouses, one will also find victim advocates affiliated with organizations such as victim/witness-assistance programs, Mothers Against Drunk Driving, child advocates, and rape crisis centers. Like senior citizens, these people make known their desire for harsh punishments. Table 5.1 summarizes the courthouse actors and their main activities.

What is disconcerting to the newcomer to the courtroom is that these actors seem in constant motion. Small groups form and re-form as cases are called and defendants summoned before the bench. In one corner, an assistant DA can be seen conversing with an assistant PD, while in the back of the room a private defense attorney is engaged in whispered conversations with the defendant and his mother. Moreover, the cast of characters is ever changing. Many actors are in court for a specific case, and when that case has finished, they leave, often walking to another courtroom where they have other cases to attend. Most exasperating of all, the courtroom alternates between bursts of energy and periods of lethargy. Cases are called, only to be put on hold because one of the needed participants is temporarily busy elsewhere in the courthouse.

BEHIND THE SCENES

Outside the great hall of the courthouse and behind the individual courtrooms are areas where visitors

TABLE 5.1
COURTHOUSE ACTORS

	MAIN ACTIVITIES
Law Enforcement	
Court security staff	Provide security throughout the courthouse
Sheriff's deputy	Transports prisoners to and from jail
Bailiff	Maintains order in the courtrooms
Courts	
Lawyers	
Prosecutor	Government official who conducts criminal proceedings
Public defender	Government attorney who represents indigent defendants
Private defense attorney	Lawyer paid by defendant for representation
Judge	Officer who presides in a court of law
Law clerk	Performs legal research for the judge
Court Support Staff	
Clerk of court	Record keeper, often responsible for jury selection
Court reporter	Makes verbatim transcript of proceedings
Secretary	Handles routine work of judge's office
Translator	Renders another language into English and vice versa
Court administrator	Supervises and performs administrative tasks for the court
Corrections	
Probation officer	Recommends defendants for probation and monitors their activities
Pretrial service representative	Handles release of qualified pretrial detainees
Drug rehabilitation program representative	Recommends defendants for drug rehabilitation and monitors progress
Public	
Bail agent	Secures pretrial release of defendants for a fee
Newspaper reporter	Provides media coverage of key events
Defendant	Person accused of violating the law
Victim	Person who has suffered a loss due to crime
Witness	Anyone who will testify in court
Jurors	Citizens who will decide guilt or innocence
Rape crisis center representative	Provides counseling to rape victims
Child advocate	Person who speaks up for child's best interest
Court watchers	Reporters, researchers, students, retirees, and others who go to court to observe proceedings
Victim/witness assistance	Public or private agency seeking to improve treatment program of victims and witnesses

seldom venture. What is immediately obvious is that the steady march of people and the accompanying din are absent. Behind the scenes work the actors who provide essential support for courtroom activities.

Courts are paperwork bureaucracies. Even the simplest case requires sheets and sheets of paper: the initial charge, and later, the indictment, bail release forms, pretrial motions, notice of appearance of counsel, and so on. Most of the behind-the-scenes people process this paperwork. Their actions are almost never visible, but their inaction can make headlines.

Other behind-the-scenes actors are managers. A constant complaint is that the courts are mismanaged. Alas, trying to define management in a court setting proves to be elusive. Part of the difficulty is that in many jurisdictions, three distinct sets of court managers—clerks of court, chief judges, and court administrators—are often in competition. Just as important, it is difficult to define what the managers should be doing. A fundamental conflict exists between management (standardized work processes and standard outputs) and the profession of law (individual attention to cases that are fundamentally different). Thus, at the heart of the problem of managing the courthouse is the tension between the rationality of bureaucracy and the antibureaucratic philosophies of judges (DuPont-Morales, Hooper, and Schmidt 2000; Saari 1982).

The **clerk of court**, variously referred to as *prothonotary, register of probate,* and *clerk,* is pivotal in the administration of local judiciaries. They are responsible for docketing cases, collecting fees, overseeing jury selection, and maintaining court records. These local officials have enormous power. Since they are elected officials in all but six states, they can operate semiautonomously from the judge. Thus, they have traditionally competed with judges for control over judicial administration (Aikman 2006; Mays and Taggart 1986).

Judges are responsible for court administration, but they have most often been ineffective managers. This is primarily due to the unique environment in which the courts operate. Judges may be held responsible, but they seldom have the necessary authority (Aikman 2006; Jacob 1997). Moreover, they are not trained in management. The end result is that the lawyers who become judges are not accustomed to analyzing patterns of case dispositions or managing large dockets—the essential skills a manager needs. These problems are reflected in the position of chief judge. Although the chief judge has gen-

eral administrative responsibilities, the position is really one of "first among equals." Particularly when the chief judge assumes the position by seniority, as many do, there is no guarantee that the person will be interested in management or will be effective at it.

One of the most innovative approaches to court problems has been the creation of a professional group of trained administrators to assist judges in their administrative duties. In short, management—like law—is a profession; therefore, well-trained managers can give the courts what they have often lacked—managerial skill and bureaucratic knowledge. The development of the professional position of court administrator has been sporadic (Flanders 1991; Lawson and Howard 1991). However, by the 1980s, every state had established a statewide court administrator. In the years since then, court administration has become increasingly professionalized (Aikman 2006). Moreover, the profession has expanded significantly; today, most courts (even at the trial court level) routinely employ professional court administrators (Aikman 2006). The primary duties of these officials are preparing annual reports, summarizing caseload data, preparing budgets, and troubleshooting. Usually, they report to the state supreme court or the chief justice of the state supreme court.

Tension between judges and the court administrator may arise. Some judges are reluctant to delegate responsibility over important aspects of the court's work, such as case scheduling (Aikman 2006; Mays and Taggart 1986). In practice, the distinction between administration and adjudication is not clear cut. A court administrator's proposal to streamline court procedures may be viewed by the judges as an intrusion on their role in deciding cases. For example, it is not easy to determine whether transferring a judge from one assignment to another is a judicial or nonjudicial responsibility (Aikman 2006; Hoffman 1991; Stott 1982).

DYNAMICS OF COURTHOUSE JUSTICE

The brief tour of the courthouse indicates that justice is very unlike the dramatizations one sees on TV or in the movies. First-time observers find scant relationship between the dynamics of courthouse justice (law in action) and widely held cultural images (law on the books).

LAW AND POPULAR CULTURE

Law & Order

Law & Order is the longest-running drama series on network television. First aired in 1990, the show has proven so popular that the producers have spun off shows such as *Law & Order: Special Victims Unit* and *Law & Order: Criminal Intent*. The shows are also aired regularly on cable television. Indeed, it has been estimated that a viewer can watch a full 20 hours of these shows each week.

Part of the popularity of *Law & Order* stems from its "ripped-from-the-headlines" style. Each episode is self-contained. The stripped-down quality means that plot is everything. And the stories often have a twist—the most obvious suspect is not necessarily the one who committed the murder. Although there are continuing characters, there is little effort at character development (Dempsey 2003). The entrapping sense of reality is reinforced by the video—outdoor scenes are shot on the streets of New York City, and indoor scenes are shot on a soundstage on the Hudson River.

At its best, *Law & Order* (and its numerous spinoffs) is willing to confront social issues, such as sexually transmitted diseases and promiscuous sex, that typically go unmentioned on prime-time television. Unlike stereotypical crime stories in which most characters live stereotypical lives, the episode characters on *Law & Order* are more likely to experience issues associated with interracial dating and illegal immigration. Overall, the series seems best when its plots highlight the complexities of emotionally charged issues such as child molestation and child custody battles.

But how real is *Law & Order*? To scholars, the sense of realism projects a number of dubious images about policing and prosecution. *Law & Order* often distorts policing and prosecution beyond recognition. Investigation techniques are often bad, as, for example, in the episode in which the police searched the car of the murder victim on the street instead of impounding the vehicle inside a weather-free building.

Interrogation techniques are equally faulty. Suspects are interrupted as they make statements instead of being allowed to tell their version before facing more probing questions. Plea bargaining sessions also represent major distortions of reality. Typically on *Law & Order*, the defendant is in the same room as the prosecutor and the defense attorney. Overall, the program gives the impression that the law (particularly the part related to the constitutional rights of all citizens) is a nuisance. Indeed, disrespect for the law extends to police actions—some episodes show police brutality (minor but often unnecessary force in arresting a suspect).

Television shows such as *Law & Order* have had a major impact on the American legal system. Professors teaching courses like violent crime scene analysis find that they must first help students unlearn what they had learned incorrectly from watching television (Lacks 2007). Similarly, juries now demand forensic evidence. Moreover, jurors have to be instructed that *Law & Order* is fiction, not fact. Chapter 14 focuses on a closely related show, *CSI: Crime Scene Investigations*. Defense lawyers love the "*CSI* shows because they have caused juries to demand DNA analysis in nearly every two-bit 7-Eleven holdup. Prosecutors, meanwhile, feel hampered by the fact that 10 eyewitnesses are not enough to satisfy *CSI*-watching jurors who crave the supposedly conclusive proof of hair follicles on a knife" (Goehner, Lofaro, and Novack 2004).

Concerns that fiction might dictate fact are not hypothetical. The Texas Appellate Court reversed the conviction of Andrea Yates (the Houston woman who drowned her children in a bathtub) because the prosecution psychiatrist falsely testified that he had consulted on a *Law & Order* episode with a similar theme (Liptak 2005). Frequent viewers of television crime dramas significantly increase concerns about crime (Holbrook and Hill 2005).

CONTINUED

Law & Order

1. Watch a few episodes of *Law & Order*. Compare and contrast the dynamics of the courtroom workgroup on the show with the material presented in this chapter.

2. How would you characterize the relationship between the police officers and the prosecutors on *Law & Order*? How realistically do you think those relationships are portrayed? Why?

3. As stated above, investigations, interrogations, and plea bargain negotiations are often distorted on *Law & Order*. What do you think the show does well in its portrayal of the criminal justice system? Explain your answer.

- Expecting to see individual trials, they instead witness a parade of defendants and their cases. In particular, newcomers to the courthouse are often struck by the sheer volume of cases.
- Expecting the law to provide guidance, they instead find that decisions are not necessarily clear-cut and that some leeway is available. How else can one explain disagreements over lengths of prison sentences and terms of probation?
- Expecting to observe the conflict (and perhaps even hostility) projected by the adversarial model, courthouse watchers discover cooperation among judges, prosecutors, and defense attorneys. At times conversations become animated, but by and large the verbal exchanges reflect a good amount of badinage.

In exploring these differences, practitioners and scholars have used three concepts—assembly-line justice, discretion, and the courtroom work group (see Exhibit 5.1).

- Assembly-line justice explains why few cases receive individual treatment.
- Discretion emphasizes that decisions, although guided by law, are not totally determined by rules found in statutes or court decisions.
- The courtroom work group concept stresses the importance of the patterned interactions of judges, prosecutors, and defense attorneys.

As we shall see, each of these explanations is useful in understanding the dynamics of courthouse justice.

ASSEMBLY-LINE JUSTICE

The most commonly advanced reason that criminal courts do not administer justice according to the textbook image is **assembly-line justice**. This explanation was put forth by the President's Commission on Law Enforcement and Administration of Justice (1967, p. 31):"The crux of the problem is that there is a great disparity between the number of cases and the number of judges." Not only judges but also prosecutors, defense attorneys, and probation officers are in short supply. The deluge of cases is reflected in every aspect of the courts' work, from overcrowded corridors and courtrooms to the long calendars that judges, prosecutors, and defense attorneys face each day. Although written more than 40 years ago, sadly, these facts have not changed, as the court system remains grossly underfunded and understaffed today (Broccolina and Zorza 2008).

STRENGTHS OF THE EXPLANATION

The assembly-line justice explanation highlights some important features of the contemporary courthouse. No one disputes that the volume of cases is large and growing (see Chapter 10). Every year approximately 14 million persons are arrested—3 million for felonies and the rest for misdemeanors. Because of the large volume, overworked officials are

---

	Exhibit 5.1	
THREE CONCEPTS EXPLAINING THE DYNAMICS OF COURTHOUSE JUSTICE		
CONCEPT	**DEFINITION**	**EXAMPLES**
Assembly-line justice	The operation of any segment of the criminal justice system with such speed and impersonality that defendants are treated as objects to be processed rather than as individuals.	War on drugs has greatly increased case volume. Judges feel pressure to move cases.
Discretion	The authority to make decisions without reference to specific rules or facts.	Prosecutors decide whether to file criminal charges. Judges choose between prison or probation.
Courtroom work group	The regular participants in the day-to-day activities of a particular courtroom; judge, prosecutor, and defense attorney interacting on the basis of shared norms.	Cooperation more than conflict governs working relationship of courtroom actors. Case disposition requires joint actions of judge, prosecutor, and defense attorney. Rules of thumb guide bail release and sentencing.

often more interested in moving the steady stream of cases than in individually weighing each case on the scales of justice. Particularly in large cities, tremendous pressures exist to move cases and keep the docket current lest the backlog becomes worse and delays increase. In short, law on the books suggests a justice process with unlimited resources, whereas law in action stresses an administrative process geared toward disposing of a large volume of cases.

To cope with large caseloads, prosecutors, defense attorneys, and judges often apply several mass-production techniques. Thus, actors often specialize in specific tasks. In big-city public defender's offices, for example, one assistant will conduct the initial interview with the defendant, another will represent him or her at the initial appearance, and still another will negotiate the plea. Another mass-production technique is group processing. During the initial appearance, felony defendants are often advised of their rights in one large group rather than individually. Moreover, in the lower courts, sentences are often fixed on the basis of the defendant's membership in a given class rather than detailed consideration of the individual case (see Chapter 18).

WEAKNESSES OF THE EXPLANATION

Although the assembly-line justice explanation draws our attention to some important aspects of the criminal courts, it also obscures many important considerations. First of all, this orthodox explanation stresses that excessive caseloads are a modern problem. Repeated references are made to the "rise" of plea bargaining and the "decline" of the trial. However, these vivid metaphors distort history. American courts have been faced with caseload pressures for more than a century. Even more important, plea bargaining predates any of the "modern" problems of the courthouse. Indeed, plea bargaining "began to appear during the early or mid-nineteenth century and became institutionalized as a standard feature of American urban criminal courts in the last of the nineteenth century" (Haller 1979, p. 273; see also Fisher 2003). In short, the historical evidence must be ignored if one tries to explain how justice is administered in the courthouse simply in terms of too many cases resulting from the growth of big cities.

Emphasizing excessive caseloads also fails to consider the types of cases trial courts must decide. Most trial court cases, criminal or civil, present no disputed questions of law or fact. Rather, most case dispositions reflect **routine administration**: "A matter is routine when a court has no disputed question of law or fact to decide. Routine administration means the processing or approving of undisputed matters" (Friedman and Percival 1976, p. 267). Most cases, therefore, end with a plea of guilty (rather than a trial), not because the courthouse has too many cases, but because the courts are confronted with a steady stream of routine cases in which the only major question is the sentence to be imposed. This has led some commentators to conclude that the emphasis on due process procedures that "dominated the era between the 1930s and the 1970s, [has been] supplanted by a model . . . in which the focus (both in criminal and civil cases) is on how to achieve resolution without or with little adjudication" (Resnik 2006, p. 1140).

Although heavy caseloads are part of the conventional wisdom surrounding the operations of criminal courts, several studies cast serious doubt on this proposition. A 1979 study in Connecticut compared two courts—one with a heavy caseload, another with a light one. It would be logical to expect major differences in how cases were processed and in the substance of justice handed out, but the results indicated that the courts were remarkably similar. Neither court had many trials. In neither did the defense attorneys engage in pitched battle with the prosecution. Both courts set bail in approximately the same amounts and imposed roughly similar sentences. Each court spent the same amount of time per case, moving through its business "rapidly and mechanically." The only difference was that the busier court was in session longer than the court with fewer cases (Feeley 1979). This and other studies clearly suggest that the criminal court process cannot be understood solely on the basis of excessive caseloads, because such an explanation omits too many important considerations—most especially organizational relationships and local legal culture (Heumann 1975; Lynch 1994; Nardulli 1979; Roach-Anleu 2000).

DISCRETION

Law on the books projects an image of a legal system that seemingly runs by itself—a mechanical process of merely applying rules of law to given cases. Law in action, however, emphasizes a legal system in which the legal actors exercise discretion because choices must be made.

Discretion lies at the heart of the criminal justice process. From the time a crime is committed until after a sentence is imposed, discretion is exercised every time key decisions are made. After arrest, the prosecutor may decide not to prosecute. Once charges have been filed, a lower-court judge must set the amount of bail and decide whether sufficient probable cause exists to hold the defendant for the grand jury. In turn, grand juries have discretion over indictments; trial juries, over conviction; and the judge, over sentencing.

Discretion is best defined as the lawful ability of an agent of government to exercise choice in making a decision. Viewed from this perspective, discretion has three major subcomponents: legal judgments, policy priorities, and personal philosophies (Cole 1970; Stith 2008).

Many discretionary decisions in the criminal court process are made on the basis of legal judgments. An example would be a prosecutor who refuses to file a criminal charge because in her legal judgment the evidence is insufficient to prove all the elements of the offense. Some legal judgments stem from a prediction about the likely outcome of a case at a later stage in the proceedings. The prosecutor, for example, may believe that the defendant did violate the law but that no jury would convict.

Other discretionary decisions reflect policy priorities. Because criminal laws are so broad and general, they must be selectively enforced. The number of crimes that could be charged is virtually unlimited, but the resources devoted to detecting wrongdoers and processing them through the courts (and later incarcerating them) are limited. Thus, discretionary decisions are often made on the basis of policy priorities. Through policy priorities, court officials try to devote more resources to prosecuting serious crimes, such as murder, rape, and armed robbery, rather than minor offenses.

Other discretionary decisions reflect the decision makers' personal values and attitudes—their personal philosophies. Judges and prosecutors have varying views of what offenses are serious and deserving of a high priority. Differences among judges in the same courthouse are readily apparent. Some differences center on the purpose of the criminal law. Those who believe that the courts can deter crime (through heavy sentences, for example) behave differently from those who discount the role the courts can play in deterrence. Stated another way, the same differences of opinion about crime that characterize society as a whole likewise divide courthouse actors.

The Courtroom Work Group

Every day, the same group of courthouse regulars assembles in the same courtroom, sits or stands in the same places, and performs the same tasks as the day before. The types of defendants and the nature of the crimes they are accused of also remain constant. Only the names of the victims and defendants are different. Whereas defendants come and go, the judges, prosecutors, defense attorneys, clerks, and probation officers remain the same. To even the most casual observer, the courthouse regulars occupy a special status. They freely issue instructions to the temporary visitors to the courthouse (don't smoke, don't talk, don't read the newspaper), although they smoke, talk, and read the newspaper themselves. The ordinary citizens sit on hard benches in the rear of the courtroom and may approach the bench only when specifically requested. The courthouse regulars, on the other hand, enjoy easy access to the front part of the courtroom.

The activities of the courthouse regulars represent a complex network of ongoing social relationships (Blumberg 1970; Flemming, Nardulli, and Eisenstein 1992; Guzik 2007; Neubauer 1974b; Sarat and Felstiner 1995). These relationships are as important as they are complex. James Eisenstein and Herbert Jacob (1977) have proposed that the best way to analyze the network of ongoing relationships among the courthouse actors is through the concept of the **courtroom work group**.

Judges, prosecutors, and defense attorneys are representatives from separate, independent sponsoring institutions. They are drawn together by a common task: Each must do something about a given case. As a result, courthouse regulars work together cooperatively on a daily basis in ways not envisioned by the formal adversary model (Jacob 1991; Lichtenstein 1984; Lynch and Evans 2002). Indeed, in problem-solving courts (especially those subscribing to a therapeutic jurisprudence model), such cooperation forms the philosophical backbone for the courts' existence (Worrall & Nugent-Borakove 2008). To understand the extent as well as the limits of this cooperation, we need to examine

why courtroom work groups form in the first place and their impact on the administration of justice.

Mutual Interdependence

The criminal courthouse is not a single organization but rather a collection of separate institutions that gather in a common workplace. Whereas most large organizations consist of distinct divisions operating under a central leadership, the criminal courthouse consists of separate institutions without a hierarchical system of control. A judge cannot reward a prosecutor or a public defender who performs well. Rather, each of the courthouse regulars is a representative of a sponsoring institution, which hires and fires them, monitors their activities, and rewards their performance.

None of these actors can perform his or her tasks independently; they must work together. These interactions are critical because none of the courthouse regulars can make decisions independently; each must consider the reactions of others. This is most readily seen in the work of the defense attorney. In representing his or her client, the defense attorney must consider the type of plea agreement the prosecutor may offer, the sentencing tendencies of the judge, and the likelihood of a jury verdict of guilty. Prosecutors and judges are interdependent in similar ways.

Each member of the work group can achieve individual goals and accomplish separate tasks only through work-group participation. The actors come to share common interests in disposing of cases. Hence, cooperation—mutual interdependence—within the work group is viewed as leading to mutual benefits. Assistant prosecutors, for example, are judged by their superiors not so much on how many cases they win but on how few they lose. Thus, to secure their primary goal of gaining convictions, they must depend on defense attorneys to sell their clients on the advantages of the bargain offered and also on judges to impose the agreed-upon settlement.

Shared Decision Making

Courtroom work groups reflect shared decision making. Judges retain the legal authority to make the major decisions, such as setting bail and imposing sentences, but they often rely on others. They routinely follow the bail recommendations of the prosecutor and accept guilty-plea agreements reached by the defense and prosecution. This does not mean that the judge is without power; the other actors must be sensitive to what the judge might do. Prosecutors (and defense attorneys) know the amount of bail a particular judge has set in past situations, so that is what they recommend in the current case.

This shared decision making is highly functional because it diffuses responsibility. Judges, prosecutors, defense attorneys, and others are aware that the decisions they make could turn out to be wrong. Since such dire results cannot be predicted, the members of the courtroom work group share a sense that when one of their members looks bad, they all look bad. Decisions, therefore, are made jointly. If something later goes wrong, work group members have protected themselves: Everyone thought it was a good idea at the time (Clynch and Neubauer 1981).

The hallmark of work groups is regularity of behavior. This regularity is the product of shared norms about how each member should behave and what decisions are desirable. Courthouse workers can make their common worksite a fractious and unpredictable place for carrying out assigned tasks or, through cooperation, a predictable place to work. The greater the certainty, the less time and resources they need to spend on each case. Newcomers learn these important informal norms of cooperation through a process referred to as *socialization*.

SOCIALIZATION

A problem common to all organizations, courts included, is the need to break in new members, a process known as "socialization." Through socialization, newcomers are taught not only the formal requirements of the job (how motions are filed and so on), but also informal rules of behavior. In other words, veteran members of the courtroom workgroup have to "break in" new members so that they understand the ways things are done (Haynes, Ruback, and Cusick 2008; Wiseman 1970).

Thus, newcomers learn not only from their peers but also from other members of the social network. One of the most important things they learn is the importance of shared norms. It is the shared norms that provide structure to what otherwise would appear to be an unstructured, almost chaotic, process. These shared norms are referred to as *normal crimes*.

NORMAL CRIMES

As discussed earlier, most of the matters before the courts are routine. Although each case is unique, most fall into a limited number of categories. Based on similarities among cases, members of the work group develop certain ideas about types of crimes and criminals. A landmark study in 1965 by Sudnow aptly labeled this phenomenon the **normal crime**, a term still used today. The legal actors categorize crimes on the basis of the typical manner in which they are committed, the typical social characteristics of the defendants, and the types of victims. Once a case has been placed into one of these categories, it is usually disposed of on the basis of a set pattern. In essence, normal crimes represent a group sense of justice.

REWARDS AND SANCTIONS

Actors who violate these rules of personal and professional conduct can expect sanctions from the other members of the work group. A variety of rewards (carrots) are available as benefits to those who follow the rules. For example, defense attorneys who do not unnecessarily disrupt routines are able to negotiate a sentence that is slightly less severe than normal. In turn, some sanctions (sticks) may be applied to those who do not cooperate. Judges can sanction uncooperative private defense attorneys, for instance, by making them wait for their case to be called. By far the more effective approach is the carrot, because it operates indirectly and is less disruptive. The imposition of sanctions can lead to countersanctions, with the result that the network is disrupted even further.

VARIABILITY IN COURTROOM WORK GROUPS

Virtually all criminal courts studied to date exemplify the patterns just discussed of how courtroom work groups operate, but some important variations need to be considered. For example, the stability of the work groups varies—low turnover in some courts promotes stability in the work group, while high turnover in others produces ongoing disruptions of the relationships in the courthouse.

Mavericks can be found in most courthouses. Some defense attorneys engage in hostile relations with prosecutors and exhibit many "Perry Mason" attributes of adversarial behavior. They do so at a price, however: They are seldom able to negotiate effectively for good deals (Covey 2007).

The content of the policy norms varies from community to community. Property crimes are viewed as more threatening in rural areas than in urban ones, so the appropriate penalty for a defendant convicted of burglary in a rural area is more severe than that for a defendant convicted in a big city. In recent years, one set of major concerns about the policy norms relates to gender equity (see Courts, Controversy, and Gender Equity: Is Gender Bias a Significant Problem in the Courts?).

To the general public, perhaps the most visible variation between work groups concerns delay. Each courthouse has, over time, evolved a set of expectations about the proper pacing of case dispositions. Some courthouses process cases in a timely fashion, others less so.

THE PROBLEM OF DELAY

A commonly mentioned problem affecting many of the nation's courts is that too many cases take too long to reach disposition. The magnitude of the backlog and the length of the delay vary greatly, however, depending on the court involved . Clearly, degrees of delay exist. The 17 courts listed in Table 5.2 fall into three relatively distinct clusters. Seattle and Cincinnati are examples of faster courts—with a median time of 100 days or less from arrest to disposition. Moderately fast courts—Tucson and Omaha, for example—have disposition times ranging from 100 to 150 days. In slower courts such as Austin and Baltimore City, the median time is greater than 150 days (Ostrom and Hanson 2000). Some research suggests that determinate sentencing laws (see Chapter 15) increased court delay, particularly in California, Connecticut, New Mexico, North Carolina, and Virginia (Marvell and Moody 2000). Stated another way, delay appears to be a problem in some jurisdictions, but a number of American trial courts handle their cases very expeditiously.

In a general sense, the term **delay** suggests abnormal or unacceptable time lapses in the processing of cases (Neubauer et al. 1981). The inherent subjectivity of the term becomes apparent when we try to define unnecessary delay (Neubauer 1983; Steelman 1997). No consensus has been reached about how long is too long. Past commissions have provided yardsticks ranging from 6 months to 2 years (American Bar Association 1968; National Advisory Commission 1973; President's Commission 1967). The most commonly used benchmark is the recommendation of the American Bar Association that all felony cases reach disposition within 1 year of filing.

TABLE 5.2

FELONY CASE DISPOSITION TIME IN SELECTED CITIES (DAYS FROM ARREST TO DISPOSITION)

CITY	MEDIAN DAYS FROM ARREST TO DISPOSITION
Faster courts	
Seattle, WA	59
Cincinnati, OH	79
Portland, OR	85
Santa Clara, CA	86
Des Moines, IA	100
Moderate courts	
Grand Rapids, MI	104
St. Petersburg, FL	105
Tucson, AZ	113
Omaha, NE	115
Baltimore County, MD	135
Oakland, CA	143
Slower courts	
Baltimore City, MD	162
Austin, TX	193
Fort Worth, TX	195
Sacramento, CA	224
Birmingham, AL	304
Hackensack, NJ	314
All courts combined	126

SOURCE: Brian Ostrom and Neal Kauder, *Examining the Work of State Courts, 1998*. Williamsburg, VA: National Center for State Courts, 1999.

CONSEQUENCES OF DELAY

Concern that "justice delayed is justice denied" is as old as the common law itself. In the 13th century, the nobles forced King John to sign the Magna Carta and promise not to "deny or delay right or justice."

COURTS, CONTROVERSY, AND GENDER EQUITY

Is Gender Bias a Significant Problem in the Courts?

The past several decades have witnessed a monumental change in the gender composition of the American workforce. Not only are a higher percentage of women working outside the home, but women are also increasingly working in what were once considered male professions. Law most certainly is a case in point. Today, women constitute anywhere from one third to one half of all law students and make up more than 10 percent of the nation's judges.

One of the areas of most concern to the women's rights movement is gender bias. Thirty-six states have created task forces to investigate gender bias in the legal system. Some state task forces define gender bias as making decisions based on stereotypes about men and women; others stress insensitivity toward certain aspects of men's and women's lives; still others emphasize intentional bias and ill will. Regardless of the precise definition, a team of researchers at Boise State University found these reports to be remarkably consistent. The state task forces consistently found gender bias in four areas of the legal system: domestic violence, sexual assault, divorce, and behavior toward female workers and domestic violence (Chapter 9) (Hemmens, Strom, and Schlegel 1997).

Sexual assault is one area in which women experience gender bias. Sexual assault is underreported because women believe they will not be believed and will themselves be blamed. Moreover, women perceive that reporting sexual assault will result in a revictimization, with the past sexual history of the female (more so than the male) thrown open to scrutiny.

Divorce cases are another area in which the possibility of gender bias looms. The state task force reports unanimously found that women suffer from gender bias in terms of awarding alimony, division of property, and child support. The courts, on the other hand, appear to be biased against fathers in child custody awards.

Finally, all the state task force reports found gender bias against female lawyers and court employees. Of principal concern were offensive and intolerable actions toward female participants in the legal system. The most common form of gender bias mentioned was the practice of judges' and attorneys' addressing female lawyers in a demeaning manner. Female lawyers, more so than their male counterparts, were addressed by their first names. Moreover, terms like "sweetie," "little lady lawyer," "pretty eyes," and "dear" were used.

In the 19th century, the novelist Charles Dickens condemned the tortuous process of litigation in the English courts. Today, judicial reformers and critics argue that case delay undermines the values and guarantees associated with the legal system. The three most often cited negative consequences of delays in the courthouse center on defendant, society, and citizen.

Historically, court delay was considered a problem because it jeopardized the defendant's right to a speedy trial. The Sixth Amendment provides that "in all criminal prosecutions, the accused shall enjoy the right to a speedy and public trial...." Defendants may languish in jail for a number of months before guilt or innocence is determined. A

number of states have enacted speedy-trial laws premised on the need to protect the defendant's rights.

More recently, delay has been viewed as hampering society's need for a speedy conviction. This view stresses harm done to the prosecution's case. As the case becomes older and witnesses' memories diminish, the defendant's chances of acquittal increase. In short, the state is also viewed as possessing the right to a speedy trial. Thus, in recent years some jurisdictions have enacted speedy-trial laws to try to increase conviction rates.

Regardless of the costs or benefits to either the defense or the prosecution, a third perspective emphasizes that delay erodes public confidence in the judicial process. Citizens lose confidence in

Another common form of gender bias suffered by female attorneys (and judges) is sexist remarks or jokes. Gender bias also affects hiring and promotion. Female lawyers perceive that it is harder to get hired, and once hired they are paid less and have fewer opportunities for promotion.

It is important to underscore that these findings are based on reports of specific events ("Have you ever had remarks made about your looks?") as well as perceptions of gender bias or problems. Women consistently reported problem areas at higher levels than men. Answers to questions like those asked in surveys, of course, can be understood in different ways. Perhaps women are oversensitive to these issues (or alternatively, males are oblivious). Another stumbling block is the difficulty in estimating the true extent of the gender bias problem. Perceptions of bias could be the product of an isolated few who have contact with many female lawyers and judges, or they could be the result of persistent practices by numerous male lawyers and judges.

Perceptions of gender bias are a serious matter because they affect litigants' perceptions of the fairness of justice. If litigants and/or their lawyers perceive that they are treated differently, they have less confidence in the process of justice, irrespective of the outcome of the case. It is also important to underscore that the gender bias issues investigated must be taken seriously because they directly affect the lives of many women and their children as well. Moreover, the issues are some of the most explosive facing the justice system and have become, in a relatively few years, important public issues.

Gender bias is not a problem created by the court system but a reflection of prevailing attitudes in society. Although "current laws and affirmative action plans have furthered women's equality, they cannot by themselves change the attitudes of individuals. It is the individual attitudes that require change if gender bias is to be eradicated" (Hemmens, Strom, and Schlegel 1997, p. 31).

What do you think? Is gender bias a serious problem in the nation's courthouses? Have you seen or experienced biased behavior by lawyers, judges, or other court personnel? If you are troubled by using individual reports to make the case for gender bias, what alternative methods would you use to study the problem?

the swiftness or certainty of punishment. In addition, victims and witnesses may be forced to make repeated, needless trips to the courthouse. Such appearances can cost citizens time and money and ultimately discourage them from prosecution. Overall, delay in disposing of cases strains the resources of the criminal justice system.

ASSESSING THE COSTS OF DELAY

Assertions about the costs of delay require careful scrutiny. A general consensus has emerged that delay is a problem facing the courts, with no agreement about the particulars. The three perspectives just described stress varying reasons that delay is a problem. Some perceive that lengthy pretrial incarceration forces defendants to enter into detrimental plea bargains. Others, however, portray caseload pressures as forcing prosecutors into offering unduly lenient negotiated agreements.

In 1978, The National Center for State Courts sponsored a landmark study on the problem of delay in criminal cases (Church and McConnell 1978). The report noted that few of the assertions about the social costs of delay have been subjected to empirical examination. While there was some evidence to indicate that jail overcrowding and defendants' skipping court appearances (Chapter 11) were related to case delay, the report did not find support for the assertions that case delay causes deterioration of cases or pressures prosecutors to offer lenient plea bargains. Over the decades since then, we have learned more about the problems of court delays. While improved case-flow management implemented in the 1980s and 1990s clearly shortened the median time from arrest to disposition, as illustrated in Table 5.2, it is clear that such techniques "can probably never be viewed as a full and final solution to court delay" (Steelman 1997, p. 158).

LAW ON THE BOOKS APPROACH TO COURT DELAY

The law on the books approach to court delay focuses on resources and procedures. It is an article of faith among many commentators that the problem of delay results from an imbalance between available resources and mounting caseloads (Church and McConnell 1978). A common response is to supplement resources—add judges, prosecutors, clerks, and so on. Beyond adding more resources, traditional court reformers emphasize streamlining procedures. They view procedural stages such as preliminary hearing, grand jury indictment, and pretrial motions as sources of delay.

This conventional wisdom about court delay has been called into serious question (Church 1982; Gallas 1976). In *Justice Delayed* (Church et al. 1978), the National Center for State Courts studied 21 courts across the nation and found that the level of court resources was not associated with court delay. The relative size of court caseloads, for example, bore little relationship to case-processing time. Similarly, court procedures were poor predictors of delay. Courts that emphasized plea bargaining (as opposed to trying cases) were as fast (or as slow) as their opposite numbers (see also Steelman 1997).

These findings explain why the law on the books approach—issuing more and more rules and regulations—is often ineffective in speeding up case dispositions and reducing excessive caseloads. Speedy-trial laws are a case in point.

SPEEDY-TRIAL LAWS

Besides the provisions of the U.S. Constitution, 35 state constitutions have speedy-trial guarantees, but these provisions apply only when the delay has been "extensive." What constitutes unnecessary delay, however, is difficult to pinpoint (see Case Close-Up:

Barker v. Wingo and the Right to a Speedy Trial). Given the vagueness of these constitutional standards, legislatures have shown considerable interest in putting some teeth into the guarantee of a speedy trial. The best-known such effort is the Speedy Trial Act of 1974 (amended in 1979), which specifies time standards for the two primary stages in the federal court process. A span of 30 days is allowed from arrest to indictment, and 70 days from indictment to trial. Certain time periods, such as those associated with hearings on pretrial motions and the mental competency of the defendant, are considered excludable time.

Speedy-trial statutes exist in all 50 states (Herman and Chemerinsky 2006), but they have a different orientation from their federal counterpart. Most state laws are defendant-centered; that is, they are designed to protect defendants from suffering extensive delay, particularly if they are incarcerated prior to trial. By contrast, the federal law is designed to protect the interests of society; that is, a speedy trial is viewed as an important objective irrespective of whether the defendant's interests are in jeopardy.

LIMITS OF SPEEDY-TRIAL LAWS

Efforts to mandate speedy trials are striking in their lack of specifics. These laws are not based on an analysis of why delay occurs. Moreover, they do not provide for any additional resources (more judges or prosecutors) to aid the courts in complying. This can produce unforeseen consequences. In a number of federal courts, compliance has come at the price of delaying civil cases. Potential difficulties also arise because not all cases fit easily into the mandated time frames. A major murder case or a large drug-smuggling case takes longer to prepare than an ordinary burglary prosecution.

Researchers approach speedy-trial laws with considerable skepticism. Various studies find that such laws have had limited impact in speeding up the flow of cases through the state criminal court process (Church et al. 1978; Mahoney et al. 1988; Nimmer 1978). The primary reason is that most state laws fail to provide the court with adequate and effective enforcement mechanisms. As a result, the time limits specified by speedy-trial laws are seldom a guide to actual practice. One study found that North Carolina's speedy-trial law did indeed speed up the criminal docket, but Connecticut's law did not (Marvell and Luskin 1991). The federal speedy-trial law has proven effective. The average criminal case filed in the federal courts in the early 1970s

Barker v. Wingo and the Right to a Speedy Trial

The police arrested two suspects—Willie Barker and Silas Manning—for beating an elderly couple to death with a tire iron in Christian County, Kentucky. The district attorney had a stronger case against Manning and believed that Barker could not be convicted unless Manning testified against him. Thus, the DA first sought a conviction against Manning. The court-appointed lawyer initially had no objection to continuing the trial; after all, an acquittal could only help Barker.

The Commonwealth of Kentucky, however, encountered more than a few difficulties in its prosecution of Manning. Altogether, six trials were conducted. Two ended in hung juries, and two others in convictions that were reversed on appeal. Finally, Manning was convicted of murdering one victim, and a sixth trial resulted in a conviction for the other murder.

During these legal maneuverings, Barker was in jail for 10 months, which largely explains why it was not until the 12th continuance was requested that the defense filed a motion to dismiss the charges. By the time the Commonwealth was ready to try Barker (after two more continuances), another problem arose: The chief investigator on the case was ill, resulting in two additional continuances. Eventually, the judge

announced that the case would be dismissed if it were not tried at the next scheduled date. The trial finally commenced, with Manning as the chief prosecution witness; Barker was convicted and given a life sentence.

In assessing these lengthy delays, the opinion of the Court notes that "the right to speedy trial is a more vague concept than other procedure rights. It is, for example, impossible to determine with precision when the right has been denied. We can not definitely say how long is too long in a system where justice is supposed to be swift but deliberate" (p. 522). In essence, the right to a speedy trial is relative, not absolute. The test would be a balancing test, in which the conduct of both the prosecution and the defendant are weighted. Calling the delay "extraordinary," the Court nonetheless ruled that Barker was not seriously prejudiced by the more than 5-year delay.

Only in extraordinary circumstances has the Court ordered criminal charges dismissed for lack of timely trial. One such situation involved an 8-year gap between indictment and arrest. The government was negligent in making any effort to track down the defendant, and the defendant was entitled to go free without a trial (*Doggett v. U.S.* 1992).

CASE CLOSEUP

took 7 months to reach a disposition. By the early 1980s, the average case was disposed of in less than 3 months. Thus, the federal approach of court planning followed by fixed standards works to reduce delay (Garner 1987). Overall, researchers stress that law in action approaches to reducing court delay are ultimately more effective.

LAW IN ACTION APPROACH TO COURT DELAY

Law on the books approaches to reducing court delay are ineffective because they ignore the dynamics of courthouse justice. All too often, the impression conveyed is that case-flow management is somehow

removed from other issues in the criminal court process. Delay is related not to how many cases a court must process but to the choices that the actors make in how they process these cases. Defense attorneys, for example, may seek continuances to avoid harsh judges, to obtain more time to prepare a defense, or even to pressure the client to pay the agreed-upon fee. Prosecutors may use delay to increase the stakes of plea bargaining or to postpone weak cases they are likely to lose. Judges acquiesce to requests for continuances so as not to disrupt the dispositional process (Flemming, Nardulli, and Eisenstein 1987).

For these reasons, lawyers and judges are generally content with the existing pace of litigation in their courts. Practitioners were asked to provide appropriate case-processing times for typical cases. Within the four courts studied—the Bronx, Detroit,

Miami, and Pittsburgh—there was little systematic disagreement among judges, defense counsel, and prosecutors on the appropriate pace of case dispositions (Church et al. 1978). More recent studies have similarly concluded that "pervasive local legal culture that transcends court jurisdiction, court size, judicial resources, court rules, or calendaring systems as the explanation of differences in the pace of litigation in fast and slow courts" (Gallas 2006, p. 23). Findings like these show why law in action approaches to court delay seek to alter practitioners' attitudes regarding proper case disposition times. Improving case scheduling and trying to achieve better coordination among courtroom work group members are two such approaches.

CASE SCHEDULING

Waiting is one activity that people in the courthouse inevitably engage in. A busy courtroom can grind to a halt because an important witness fails to show up or a lawyer is detained in another courtroom. From an administrative perspective, the courts are extremely complex institutions. The disposition of a case often requires the presence of the following individuals: judge, clerk, court reporter, bailiff, defendant, prosecutor, defense attorney, police officer, victim, and witness. Depending on the procedural stage, jurors, a probation officer, a pretrial services representative, and an interpreter may also need to appear.

Many of these people have several different courts to appear in during a single day. For example, defense attorneys, prosecutors, and probation officers may have several cases set for the same time. There can be administrative problems, too. Because of an illegible address, the defendant never receives a notice. Or the jailer may forget to include the needed defendant on the day's list. If just one person is late, the others must wait, and if one person never shows up at all, the hearing must be rescheduled.

EFFORTS AT COORDINATION

As we have noted previously, the court is actually a collection of agents from separate and independent organizations: judge, police officer, prosecutor, sheriff, clerk, and probation officer. Most of these organizations are headed by elected officials or, like the police, report to elected officials. They have their own bases of power, their own separate legal mandates, and their own scheduling problems. Judges and court administrators, therefore, have only limited control over coordinating interagency schedules

and cooperative efforts (although they are often held responsible when something goes wrong).

VARIABILITY IN COURTROOM WORK GROUPS REVISITED

The variability in courtroom workgroups (discussed earlier in this chapter) has major consequences for how long it takes courts to dispose of cases. A team of researchers associated with the National Center for State Courts studied a blend of urban and rural courts in California, Florida, and Minnesota. In each courthouse, they interviewed the wide range of officials discussed in this chapter. They focused on how cases were managed and how court actors interacted and found four distinctive ways of doing things. Two (of the four) courthouse cultures illustrate the key findings.

Some courts were characterized as hierarchical because there was a clear chain of command among judges, administrative staff, and courtroom staff. Courts with a hierarchical culture processed felony cases significantly faster than other courts. Other courts were characterized as communal because they valued communication, cooperation, and compromise. Courts with a communal culture processed felony cases slower than other courts The authors caution that no cultural type is necessarily good or bad. Rather, variations in courtroom workgroups reflect responses to multiple goals as well as differing ways of managing relations between a diverse set of courthouse actors (Ostrom et al. 2007).

LEGAL ETHICS

Lawyers suffer from a negative public image, which is one reason the legal profession places considerable emphasis on **legal ethics**. *Ethics* refers to the study and analysis of what constitutes good or bad conduct (Pollock 2007). Legal ethics represents a specific type of ethics. First, it is an example of applied ethics, in which ethical principles are applied to specific issues. Legal ethics is also an example of professional ethics, because it involves the behavior of a profession, in this case the legal profession. All ethical systems, legal ethics included, have a moral component. But morality and ethics are different. Whereas morality emphasizes a set of moral absolutes, legal ethics involves the difficult task of helping lawyers sort out the best option when perhaps no good options exist.

Legal ethics is of critical importance because the American legal system is based on the adversarial system, which stresses verbal combat. At its basis, this system represents a fight between opposing viewpoints, and the use of legal ethics is one way to regulate this verbal combat to ensure, in essence, a fair fight. At heart, legal ethics emphasizes protecting clients by ensuring that they have competent attorneys to forcefully present their cases. Legal ethics also seeks to promote public respect for the legal system. Thus, lawyers are not allowed to mislead the court, nor can they knowingly allow witnesses for their side to perjure themselves.

Regulation of the legal profession begins with codes of legal ethics and professional responsibilities. The American Bar Association (ABA) adopted the *Model Rules of Professional Conduct* in 1983, which it updates periodically. These rules serve as models for the ethics rules of most states. But, consistent with federalism (see Chapter 3), each state has adopted its own code. Thus, state bar associations, not the national association of lawyers, enforce these codes. Law students are required to take a course in legal ethics, and before they can be admitted to the bar, they must pass a separate test on legal ethics.

The codes of legal ethics promulgated by the legal profession are increasingly supplemented by statutes and court decisions. Most important, the Supreme Court has made significant rulings on when prosecutors must disclose exculpatory information to the defense (Chapter 12) and when prosecutors may not use race as a factor in jury selection (Chapter 14).

The primary responsibility for establishing and enforcing professional standards of conduct for the legal profession rests with the highest court of each state. In turn, state courts of last resort have delegated enforcement to the state bar association, which establishes a specific committee to enforce the provisions. Disciplinary proceedings typically begin with the filing of a complaint by a disgruntled client, although judges, other lawyers, or the committee itself can initiate action. Complaints about attorney misconduct are typically investigated in secret, although a few states mandate a more public process. Most complaints are dismissed because of insufficient evidence. But when evidence of an ethical violation exists, the committee files charges and conducts a private hearing. If the charges are proved, the committee recommends disciplinary actions, which can range from a reprimand (either private or public) to a suspension of the license to practice law for a given period of time to restitution to the client. The most severe sanction is disbarment, which permanently revokes a lawyer's right to practice law. These recommendations may be appealed to the state supreme court, which, after a public hearing, may accept, modify, or reject them. Bar association sanctions against lawyers are relatively rare, however.

The typical remedy for legal mistakes made during the trial is an appellate court reversal (Chapter 17). Legal ethics is enforced in other ways, as well, including sanctions meted out by judges (Chapter 8) and civil lawsuits for legal malpractice (Chapter 7). Typically though, lawyers working in the criminal justice system enjoy legal immunity, which is to say you cannot sue a prosecutor, defense attorney, or a judge just because you lost your case.

The ethical issues surrounding the three types of lawyers who appear in court vary greatly depending on the role they play. In the next chapters, we will examine some of the legal issues facing prosecutors, defense attorneys, and judges.

CONCLUSION

Discussions of court delay and its consequences all too often are conducted in abstract terms. *Barker v. Wingo,* however, forces one to deal with some of the realities. The Court's opinion is clearly mindful of the fact that to interpret the right to a speedy trial in a manner understood by the drafters of the Constitution would, in all likelihood, result in a brutal murderers being set free.

Barker v. Wingo and our discussion of the problem of delay show that the actual operations of the criminal courts differ greatly from official expectations. Three concepts—excessive caseloads, discretion, and the courtroom work group—have been used to explain this gap between the law in action and the law on the books. Although courts are burdened with too many cases, an excess of cases is at best only a partial explanation for the behavior of the criminal courts. More important is the role discretion plays in the court system, shaping the dictates of formal law to the actual cases and defendants that come to the criminal courts. The courtroom work group concept emphasizes the interactions among the key actors in court. The next three chapters will examine in greater depth how prosecutors, defense attorneys, and judges work within the courtroom work group, and why.

Chapter Review

1. **Have a general sense of who works where in the courthouse.**

Bail bondsmen have their offices outside courthouses. Judges, lawyers, clerks, court stenographers, law clerks, and bailiffs work inside the courtroom. Clerks of court and court administrators work behind the scenes.

2. **Analyze the importance of assembly-line justice.**

The concept of assembly-line justice stresses the high volume of cases in courthouses and the emphasis on moving the docket.

3. **Describe why discretion is found in the criminal courts.**

At every key stage of the criminal court process, humans must apply the law. Choices are made on the basis of legal judgments, policy priorities, and values and attitudes of the actors.

4. **Identify the principal actors in the courtroom workgroup.**

The *courtroom workgroup* refers to the regular participants like judges, prosecutors, and defense attorneys who interact on a daily basis.

5. **Indicate why ethics is important to the American legal system.**

Legal ethics are important because they provide necessary boundaries on conflict represented by the adversary system and also seek to ensure clients that their lawyer is working in their best interests.

6. **Contrast differing understandings of why delay is a problem in the courts.**

Some see delay as a problem because it works to the disadvantage of the prosecutor, others see delay as a problem because it jeopardizes the rights of defendants, and still others see delay as a problem because it reflects a wasting of resources.

7. **Discuss the strengths and weaknesses of speedy-trial laws.**

Speedy-trial laws reflect a law on the books approach to problem solving. Although these laws have the advantage of calling attention to delay as a problem, they are limited because they provide no mechanisms to deal with discretion.

8. **Explain why law in action approaches to court delay are more effective than law on the books approaches.**

Law in action approaches to solving the problem of delay can prove effective because they focus on coordinating the activities of the key actors in the courthouse. Without such coordination, the local legal culture is unlikely to be changed.

CRITICAL THINKING QUESTIONS

1. Take a tour of your local courthouse. How does your perception of it match the description at the beginning of this chapter? Compare notes with other classmates; perhaps they focused on features that you did not.

2. Place yourself in the position of a felony court prosecutor. In what ways does the cooperation of other members of the courtroom work group work to your benefit? How would your answer be different if you approached the question from the vantage point of the judge or the defense attorney?

3. Of the several consequences of delay, which one do you think is the most important? Which one is the least important?

4. In *Barker v. Wingo*, the Court stressed the legitimate reasons for the 16 trial continuances. But is there a danger that prosecutors might illegitimately seek continuances?

KEY TERMS

assembly-line justice 122

clerk of court 120

courtroom work group 125

delay 127

discretion 124

legal ethics 132

normal crime 126

routine administration 124

WEB RESOURCES

Go to the America's Courts and the Criminal Justice System companion website at

http://www.cengage.com/criminaljustice/neubauer

where you will find more resources to help you study.
Resources include web exercises, quizzing, and flash cards.

FOR FURTHER READING

Braswell, Michael, Belinda McCarthy, and Bernard McCarthy. *Justice, Crime and Ethics.* 5th ed. Cincinnati: Anderson, 2005.

Church, Thomas, and Milton Heumann. *Speedy Disposition: Monetary Incentives and Policy Reform in Criminal Courts.* Albany: State University of New York Press, 1992.

Harris, John, and Paul Jesilow. "It's Not the Old Ball Game: Three Strikes and the Courtroom Workgroup." *Justice Quarterly* 17: 185–204, 2000.

Lipetz, Marcia. "Routines and Deviations: The Strength of the Courtroom Workgroup in a Misdemeanor Court." *International Journal of the Sociology of Law* 8: 47–60, 1980.

Martin, John. *Strategic Planning in the Courts: Implementation Guide.* Denver: Center for Public Policy Studies, 1995.

Zaffarano, Mark. "Team Leadership: Using Self-Directed Work Teams in the Courts." *Justice System Journal* 17: 357–372, 1995.

6

PROSECUTORS

© HARRY LYNCH/MCT/Landov

Former District Attorney Mike Nifong, left, speaks while Duke lacrosse player Reade Seligmann, right, listens in the courtroom at a Durham County, NC, court building in 2006. Instead of trying to find the truth about what happened on March 13, 2006, Nifong set out to prove that three Duke University lacrosse players had raped an exotic dancer. Nifong's conduct led to his being disbarred from the practice of law by the State Bar of North Carolina. But the result of the disciplinary action against Nifong may never be able to erase the stain left by a case that went wrong from the start for Duke lacrosse players Dave Evans, Collin Finnerty, and Reade Seligmann.

CHAPTER OUTLINE

ROLE OF THE PROSECUTOR

Broad Discretion

Decentralization

CASE CLOSE-UP

Burns v. Reed and Prosecutorial Misconduct

PROSECUTION IN FEDERAL COURTS

Solicitor General

Criminal Division of the Justice Department

U.S. Attorneys

PROSECUTION IN STATE COURTS

State Attorney General

Chief Prosecutor

Local Prosecutor

THE PROSECUTOR'S OFFICE AT WORK

Assistant District Attorneys

Learning the Job

Promotions and Office Structure

Supervision

Attempts at Greater Supervision

PROSECUTORIAL ETHICS

PROSECUTORS AND COURTROOM WORK GROUPS

Conflicting Goals and Contrasting Work Groups

Political Styles and Contrasting Work Groups

LAW AND POPULAR CULTURE
The Accused (1988)

THE EXPANDING DOMAIN OF THE PROSECUTOR

Improving Police–Prosecutor Relationships

Community Prosecution

COURTS, CONTROVERSY, AND GENDER EQUITY

Are Sexual Assaults against Women Underprosecuted?

CONCLUSION

CHAPTER REVIEW

LEARNING OBJECTIVES

After reading this chapter you should be able to:

1. Discuss the two major characteristics of prosecutors in the United States.

2. Describe the three most important entities in federal prosecution.

3. Identify the three somewhat overlapping agencies involved in prosecution in state courts.

4. Explain the major factors affecting the work life of assistant district attorneys.

5. Analyze the principal factors affecting prosecutorial ethics.

6. Outline two major examples of the expanding domain of the prosecutor.

"I WOULDN'T ALLOW DURHAM to become known for 'a bunch of lacrosse players from Duke raping a black girl'," proclaimed Mike Nifong, candidate for district attorney. After a 30-year career as an assistant prosecutor in Durham County, North Carolina, Nifong was running for election as district attorney in his own right, and his comments fanned the fires quickly of what quickly became a sensational national case. Following a party thrown by the Duke lacrosse team, three team members were accused of sexually assaulting a women who had been hired as a stripper. Nifong would win the election, but the charges would eventually be dismissed for lack of evidence, and Nifong himself would be disbarred.

Although the Duke lacrosse sexual assault case was highly unusual, it illustrates the influential role prosecutors play in the criminal justice system. More so than judges and defense attorneys, the prosecutor is the most powerful official in the criminal courts. From initial arrest to final disposition, how the prosecutor chooses to exercise discretion determines to a large extent which defendants are prosecuted, the type of bargains that are struck, and the severity of the sentence imposed.

This chapter discusses several factors involved in the work of the prosecutor. We begin by examining the prosecutor's role in the criminal justice system and then consider separately the structure of federal and state prosecutors' offices. Our focus then shifts to actual courtroom behavior, looking at prosecutors at work. But prosecutors do not work in isolation. Thus, the later parts of this chapter look at prosecutors within the context of the courtroom work group and their expanding domain in the criminal justice system.

ROLE OF THE PROSECUTOR

The prosecutor is of critical importance because of the office's central position in the criminal justice system. Whereas police, defense attorneys, judges, and probation officers specialize in specific phases of the criminal justice process, the duties of the prosecutor bridge all of these areas. This means that on a daily basis, the prosecutor is the only official who works with all actors of the criminal justice system. As Justice Robert Jackson once remarked,

"The prosecutor has more control over life, liberty, and reputation than any other person in America."

Prosecutors stand squarely in the middle of the fragmented nonsystem of criminal justice discussed in Chapter 1. Naturally, the various actors have conflicting views about how prosecutorial discretion should be used—the police push for harsher penalties; defense attorneys, for giving their clients a break; and judges, to clear the docket. Thus, prosecutors occupy a uniquely powerful and highly visible position in a complex and conflict-filled environment. Amid the diffusion of responsibility that characterizes the criminal justice system, power has increasingly been concentrated in the hands of the prosecutor (Misner 1996; Worrall and Borakove 2008).

BROAD DISCRETION

A key characteristic of the American **prosecutor** is broad discretion. Although the prosecutor works in the courthouse, the office of prosecutor is part of the executive branch of government. This independence from the judiciary is vital for the proper functioning of the adversary system, since prosecutors at times challenge judicial decisions. The breadth of prosecutorial power stems from numerous court cases since 1833. Typical is *People v. Wabash, St. Louis and Pacific Railway,* an 1882 decision in which the Illinois Court of Appeals stated that the district attorney (DA) "is charged by law with large discretion in prosecuting offenders against the law. He may commence public prosecutions . . . and may discontinue them when, in his judgment the ends of justice are satisfied." In decisions like this one, appellate courts have allowed the modern prosecuting attorney to exercise virtually unfettered discretion relating to initiating, conducting, and terminating prosecutions (Albonetti 1987; Jacoby 1980; Sarat and Clarke 2008). Exhibit 6.1 provides an overview of the role of the prosecutor throughout the criminal justice process.

It is only during the trial itself that appellate courts have placed restrictions on the exercise of prosecutorial power. In the context of the adversary system, the prosecutor is expected to advocate the guilt of the defendant vigorously. But the prosecutor is also a lawyer and is therefore an **officer of the court**; that is, he or she has a duty to see that justice is done. Violations of the law must be prosecuted, but in a way that guarantees that the defendant's rights are respected and protected. In 1935, the Supreme Court spelled out the limitations imposed on prosecutors by their obligation as officers of the court: "He may prosecute with earnestness and vigor—indeed, he should do so. But while he may strike hard blows, he is not at liberty to strike foul

ones. It is as much his duty to refrain from improper methods calculated to produce a wrongful conviction as it is to use every legitimate means to bring about a just one" (*Berger v. United States* 1935, 88).

In recent years, the Supreme Court has expressed repeated concern about prosecutorial misconduct. Convictions have been reversed because prosecutors were too zealous in their advocacy. But at the same time, the nation's highest tribunal has also decided that prosecutors enjoy absolute immunity from civil lawsuits when acting as courtroom advocates. However, under other conditions, prosecutors may be sued civilly (see Case Close-Up: *Burns v. Reed* and Prosecutorial Misconduct).

DECENTRALIZATION

Another characteristic of the office of prosecutor is decentralized organization. Although the American prosecutor represents the state in the prosecution

Exhibit 6.1
ROLE OF THE PROSECUTOR IN STEPS OF CRIMINAL PROCEDURE

	LAW ON THE BOOKS	LAW IN ACTION
Crime	Must enforce all laws to the fullest.	The impossible legal mandate means that priorities must be established.
Arrest	Little involvement.	In major crimes, may advise the police whether sufficient evidence of probable cause exists to arrest.
Initial appearance	Represents the government.	Manages the chaos in the lower court, where there are many cases and little is known about the crime or the defendant.
Bail	Can make a bail recommendation to the judge.	Typically recommends a high bail amount to the judge.
Charging	Exclusive domain of the prosecutor.	Often decides which defendants will be charged with what crime.

Exhibit 6.1

CONTINUED

	LAW ON THE BOOKS	LAW IN ACTION
Preliminary hearing	Dominates this step because of the authority to call witnesses.	Highly successful in having defendants bound over for further proceedings.
Grand jury	Acts as legal adviser to the grand jury.	The prosecutor largely decides which cases will be heard; the grand jury tends to "rubber stamp" prosecutorial requests for indictments.
Arraignment	Formally presents the charges against the defendant in open court.	By taking the case this far, the prosecutor has indicated his or her willingness to move forward on a case.
Evidence		
Discovery	Important variations in state law regarding how much information must be disclosed prior to trial.	Informally provides trusted defense attorneys with information to induce a plea of guilty.
Suppression motions	Argues that police acted legally in searching and/or interrogating the suspect.	Argues that police acted legally in searching for evidence to be admitted.
Plea bargaining	District attorneys have considerable discretion in plea bargaining.	Based on normal penalties, dictates the terms under which defendant pleads guilty.
Trial	Presents witnesses proving defendant guilty and urges jury to return a verdict of guilty.	Very successful in gaining convictions.
Sentencing	In many jurisdictions, the district attorneys can make a sentencing recommendation to the judge.	Judge is more likely to follow the district attorney's sentencing recommendation than the defense attorney's.
Appeal	Argues before the appellate court why the lower court conviction should stand, and often wins.	Wins a significant victory in most appeals.

of criminal cases, the office is not centralized, as it is in England and most of Europe (Flemming 1990; Jehle and Wade 2006). Instead, prosecution is highly decentralized, with more than 8,000 federal, state, county, municipal, and township prosecution agencies.

Commensurate with the nation's often confusing dual court system, separate prosecutors are found in federal and state courts. The structure, however, is not parallel with court structure; that is, each court does not have attached to it a specific prosecutor. DAs, for example, often conduct the trial in the trial court of general jurisdiction and then appeal through both layers of state courts and, on rare occasions, even to the U.S. Supreme Court (a federal judicial body). Moreover, different prosecutors' offices may handle the same case; sometimes, the city attorney conducts the preliminary stages of a felony case in the lower courts, and the district attorney prosecutes in the trial court of general jurisdiction.

Exhibit 6.2 provides a rough overview of typical state and federal prosecutorial structure. Be aware, however, that the apparent hierarchy of prosecutorial structure is an illusion. In the federal courts, the U.S. attorneys enjoy considerable autonomy from the U.S. Justice Department, and in the states, local district attorneys are totally separate from state attorneys general. We will begin with prosecution in federal courts and then turn to the more complex realities of state prosecutions.

Burns v. Reed and Prosecutorial Misconduct

Even though it might result in some "incompetent, lousy prosecutors getting off," prosecutors should be immune from civil lawsuits, argued an assistant solicitor general in the first Bush administration. Granting total immunity to prosecutors will only result in "shredding the Constitution to tiny bits," countered the lawyer for Cathy Burns. At issue was the conduct of Chief Deputy Prosecutor Rick Reed of Muncie, Indiana, who had given poor legal advice to the police. As a result, Cathy Burns had been held on attempted murder charges (later dropped), partly because the prosecutor deliberately misled the trial court judge (Campbell 1990).

On the evening of September 2, 1982, Cathy Burns called the Muncie, Indiana, police and reported that an unknown assailant had entered her house, knocked her unconscious, and shot her two sons while they slept. The police came to view Burns as their primary suspect, even though they had no physical evidence to support their conclusion. Speculating that Burns had multiple personality disorder, the officers decided to interview her under hypnosis, but they were concerned that hypnosis might be an unacceptable investigative technique. They therefore sought the advice of Rick Reed, chief deputy prosecutor, Delaware County, Indiana, who told the officers they could proceed with the hypnosis. Under hypnosis, Burns allegedly confessed, but neither the police nor the district attorney (DA) informed the judge that the "confession" was obtained under hypnosis (and therefore inadmissible).

Cathy Burns spent 4 months in the psychiatric ward of a state hospital. During this time, she was fired from her job as a dispatcher with the Muncie Police Department and the state obtained temporary custody of her sons. Medical experts concluded that she did not have multiple personalities, and she was released. The criminal charges against her were later dropped when the judge ruled that the evidence obtained under hypnosis was not admissible.

Cathy Burns filed a civil rights suit (section 1983, discussed in Chapter 2) in the U.S. District Court for the Southern District of Indiana. Before trial, the Muncie Police Department settled for $250,000 (Campbell 1991). But the court dismissed Burns's suit against the DA, holding that Reed enjoyed absolute immunity, a position upheld by the U.S. Court of Appeals for the Seventh Circuit (894 F.2d 949, 1990).

In situations like this, should the DA be immune from a civil lawsuit? Yes, said the Supreme Court, arguing that without this type of legal protection, prosecutors would hesitate to provide legal advice for fear of being harassed by civil lawsuits. Prosecutors enjoy immunity for their actions during trial and pretrial court proceedings. Therefore, Reed could not be sued for his actions in supporting the application for a search warrant and presenting evidence at the probable cause hearing. But there are limits, the Court decided: Advising police during the investigative phase of criminal cases was not intimately associated with the judicial phase of the criminal process. Therefore,

Reed was potentially liable for the legal advice he provided the police.

The Court revisited the issue 2 years later and laid down a slightly more discernible line of permissible and impermissible conduct. The Court restated that prosecutors have absolute immunity from civil damage suits for actions in connection with the traditional role of courtroom advocacy. But DAs enjoy only "qualified immunity" for other actions. The Court unanimously held that statements made in a news conference were not protected by absolute immunity. But the justices split 5–4 on whether investigative actions by the DA were subject to suit. The bare majority held, "There is a difference between the advocate's role in evaluating evidence, and interviewing witnesses as he prepares for trial … and the detective's role in searching for the clues and corroboration that might give him probable cause to recommend that a suspect be arrested" (*Buckley v. Fitzsimmons* 1993).

Carol Burns, the plaintiff in *Burns v. Reed*, was last reported working as a supervisor in a discount department store in Muncie, richer from her civil settlement with the police (minus lawyers' fees). As for Rick Reed, the aftermath has been more promising: He is now the District Attorney for Delaware County, Indiana, the voters evidently not convinced that his behavior was out of line.

Whether *Burns v. Reed* applies to Mike Nifong in the Duke lacrosse case is unclear. The players sued the former North Carolina prosecutor but the federal judge ruled that they would have to prove that Nifong "willfully and maliciously prosecuted the players," a high legal hurdle (McDonough 2008). But the issue may be moot. Nifong has filed for bankruptcy and even if he were to be found liable in a civil judgment, its unlikely the plaintiffs would ever recover any monetary damages (Chapter 2).

CASE CLOSEUP

PROSECUTION IN FEDERAL COURT

Prosecutions in federal courts are conducted by the U.S. Department of Justice. Billed as the world's largest law firm, the Department of Justice represents the U.S. government in all legal matters not specifically delegated to other agencies. The department is headed by the **U.S. attorney general**, who is a member of the president's cabinet. Top-level officials are presidential appointees who reflect the views of the administration on important policy issues. Day-to-day activities are carried out by a large cadre of career lawyers, who enjoy civil service protection and have, over the years, developed invaluable expertise in particular areas of law (Landsberg 1993; Sisk et al. 2006).

The Department of Justice has grown tremendously in recent years. The Department of Justice is a sprawling series of bureaucracies including investigatory and law enforcement offices such as the Federal Bureau of Investigation, the Drug Enforcement Administration, the U.S. Marshals Service, and the Federal Bureau of Prisons. Also in the Department of Justice is the Office of Justice Programs, which oversees the Bureau of Justice Assistance and other entities.

In terms of prosecution, three entities—solicitor general, criminal division, and U.S. attorneys—are particularly important. We will examine them from the top down, although, as we shall see, there is no hierarchy and considerable autonomy.

SOLICITOR GENERAL

The **solicitor general** is the third-ranking official in the Justice Department. The solicitor general's principal task is to represent the executive branch before the Supreme Court. But at the same time, the justices depend on the solicitor general to look beyond the government's narrow interest. Because of the solicitor general's dual responsibility to the judicial and executive branches, the officeholder is sometimes called the Tenth Justice, an informal title that underlines the special relationship with the Supreme Court (Aberbach and Peterson 2006; Caplan 1988; Meinhold and Shull 1993).

The office of the solicitor general is in essence a small, elite, very influential law firm whose client is the U.S. government. The staff consists of 23 of the most able attorneys found anywhere. As the representative

Exhibit 6.2

OVERVIEW OF PROSECUTORS IN THE DUAL COURT SYSTEM

FEDERAL	STATE
Solicitor general Represents the U.S. government before the U.S. Supreme Court in all appeals of federal criminal cases. Often appears as amicus in appeals involving state criminal convictions.	**Attorney general** Chief legal officer of the state. Civil duties more extensive than criminal duties. Has limited authority in criminal prosecutions.
Criminal division Prosecutes a few nationally significant criminal cases. Exercises nominal supervision over U.S. attorneys.	**Chief prosecutor** Has great autonomy in prosecuting felony cases. Typically argues cases on appeal.
U.S. attorney Prosecutes the vast majority of criminal cases in federal courts. Enjoys great autonomy in actions.	**Local prosecutor** Handles preliminary stages of felony cases. Prosecutes the large volume of cases in the lower court.

NOTE: To learn more about the vast bureaucracies included in the U.S. Department of Justice, go to **http://www.usdoj.gov**

of the United States in litigation before the Supreme Court, the solicitor general's office argues all government cases before the Court. For example, the assistant solicitor general argued the major issues in *Burns v. Reed.* But the influence of the office extends further.

Roughly half the work of the solicitor general's office involves coordinating appeals by the federal government. With few exceptions, all government agencies must first receive authorization from the solicitor general to appeal an adverse lower court ruling to the Supreme Court. The office requests Supreme Court review only in cases with a high degree of policy significance and in which the government has a reasonable legal argument. In turn, the solicitor general has a high rate of success in petitioning the Supreme Court and in winning cases argued on their merits.

CRIMINAL DIVISION OF THE JUSTICE DEPARTMENT

The criminal division formulates criminal law enforcement policies over all federal criminal cases, except those specifically assigned to other divisions. The criminal division, with the U.S. attorneys, has the responsibility for overseeing criminal matters under

more than 900 statutes, as well as certain civil litigation. The criminal division is organized into a number of units that handle matters such as fraud, organized crime, and public integrity. Several of the units deal with international matters and have become more visible with U.S. efforts to fight terrorism.

Criminal division attorneys prosecute many nationally significant cases—for example, the Unabomber and the Oklahoma City bombing cases. In the wake of 9/11, the criminal division has directed prosecutions of several alleged terrorists and overseen the detainment of enemy noncombatants on federal military bases. Through the years, the criminal division has also received extensive press coverage for cases involving corrupt government officials, alleged members of organized crime, and major drug-dealing enterprises.

U.S. ATTORNEYS

The **U.S. attorneys** serve as the nation's principal litigators under the direction of the attorney general. Ninety-three U.S. attorneys are stationed throughout the United States, Puerto Rico, the Virgin Islands, Guam, and the Northern Mariana Islands.

U.S. attorneys are appointed by, and serve at the discretion of, the president, with the advice and consent of the Senate. One U.S. attorney is assigned to each of the judicial districts, with the exception of Guam and the Northern Mariana Islands, where one serves both districts. Each U.S. attorney is the chief federal law enforcement officer of the United States within his or her particular jurisdiction. The 93 U.S. attorneys are assisted by 4,700 assistant U.S. attorneys, who increasingly have become career employees (Lochner 2002).

U.S. attorneys represent the federal government in court in many matters. They have three statutory responsibilities:

- Prosecution of criminal cases brought by the federal government
- Initiation and defense of civil cases in which the United States is a party
- Collection of certain debts owed the federal government

The volume of litigation varies considerably among the districts. U.S. attorneys along the Mexican border, for example, initiate a large number of drug prosecutions. Nonetheless, each district handles a mixture of simple and complex litigation. U.S. attorneys exercise wide discretion in the use of their resources to further the priorities of local jurisdictions and the needs of their communities. According to the U.S. Department of Justice website, "United States Attorneys have been delegated, and will continue to be delegated, full authority and control in the areas of personnel management, financial management, and procurement." Although the criminal division supervises all federal prosecutions, in practice U.S. attorneys enjoy considerable autonomy. This is partly because of remoteness from Washington, D.C.—the 93 U.S. attorneys are widely dispersed geographically. The selection process also plays a role. Many U.S. attorneys owe their appointments primarily to persons other than the attorney general or, in some cases, even the president (Bell 1993). Thus, in the vast majority of cases, the decisions are made by U.S. attorneys scattered across the nation rather than by the central office based in Washington, D.C.

PROSECUTION IN STATE COURTS

Decentralization and local autonomy characterize prosecution in state courts. The result is divided responsibility, with state prosecution authority typically found in three separate offices: state, county (or district), and local. At times, the relationship among these separate agencies is marked by competition; various prosecutors jockey to be the first to prosecute a notorious defendant. We will examine the three major state prosecutors from the top down, but bear in mind that each office is separate and not necessarily subject to the dictates of the office above it.

STATE ATTORNEY GENERAL

The position of attorney general, the state's chief legal officer, is typically spelled out in the state's constitution. Among the most important duties are providing legal advice to other state agencies and representing the state in court when state actions are challenged. In recent years, attorneys general have focused on their civil responsibilities by emphasizing their role in protecting consumers from various forms of fraud. Thus, the typical home page of the attorney general of a state proclaims how many individual consumer complaints (many of which involve motor vehicles and home repair fraud) are handled annually. Many state attorneys general have also been visible in filing consumer lawsuits against major U.S. businesses. The biggest of all involves the suits by more than 30 states against the tobacco industry.

State attorneys general have chosen to emphasize their civil responsibilities because they typically have limited authority over criminal matters. Local autonomy is a key characteristic of the office of prosecutor. In general, state officials do not monitor the activities of local prosecutors. Although the **state attorney general** is the state's chief law enforcement official, his or her authority over local criminal procedures is quite limited. Indeed, in a handful of states, the attorney general has no legal authority to initiate or intervene in local prosecutions. In other states, this authority is limited to extreme situations.

Thus, the state attorney general exercises virtually no control or supervision over chief prosecutors at the county level. This lack of supervisory power, coupled with the decentralization of the office, means that local prosecutors enjoy almost total autonomy. Only the local voters have the power to evaluate the prosecutor's performance, by means of their votes.

CHIEF PROSECUTOR

The American prosecutor has few direct parallels elsewhere in the world (Flemming 1990; Jehle and

Wade 2006). Compared to their counterparts in England and Europe, American prosecutors enjoy unmatched independence and discretionary powers (Albonetti 1987).

Variously called the "district attorney," "county attorney," or "prosecuting attorney" (see Exhibit 6.3), the prosecutor is the chief law enforcement official of the community. Altogether 2,344 chief prosecutors are employed across the nation, with a staff of almost 80,000. Structure and workload differ according to the size of the population. The typical office serves a population of 36,000 people, with 250 adult felony cases in the district, a staff of 9, and a budget of $355,000. But deviations are readily apparent (Perry 2006). The great majority of the nation's prosecutors' offices are small ones (see Table 6.1). Frequently, rural prosecutors are part-time officials who also engage in private law practices.

Elections are a key characteristic of the office of prosecutor, as 95 percent of chief prosecutors are locally elected officials who typically serve 4-year terms. The exceptions are Alaska, Connecticut, Delaware,

Exhibit 6.3	
CHIEF PROSECUTORS WHO HANDLE FELONY CASES IN STATE COURTS	
TITLE	**STATES**
District attorney	Alabama, California, Colorado, Georgia, Kansas,[a] Louisiana, Maine, Massachusetts, Mississippi, Nevada, New Mexico, New York, North Carolina, Oklahoma, Oregon, Pennsylvania, Texas,[a] Wisconsin, Wyoming[a]
County attorney	Arizona, Iowa, Kansas,[a] Minnesota, Montana, Nebraska, New Hampshire, Texas,[a] Utah
State's attorney	Connecticut, Florida, Illinois, Maryland, North Dakota, South Dakota, Vermont
Prosecuting attorney	Arkansas, Hawaii, Idaho, Indiana, Michigan, Missouri,[a] Ohio, Washington, West Virginia
Commonwealth attorney	Kentucky, Virginia
County prosecutor	New Jersey
District attorney general	Tennessee
County and prosecuting attorney	Wyoming[a]
Solicitor	South Carolina
Circuit attorney	Missouri[a] (City of St. Louis)
No local prosecutor	Alaska, Delaware, Rhode Island

[a] Kansas, Missouri, Texas, and Wyoming use varying names depending on the jurisdiction.

SOURCE: Steven Perry, Prosecutors in State Courts, 2005. Washington, DC: Bureau of Justice Statistics, National Institute of Justice.

TABLE 6.1
STATE COURT PROSECUTORS' OFFICES, 2005

| | ALL OFFICES | Full-Time Offices (Population Served) | | | PART-TIME OFFICES |
		1,000,000 OR MORE	250,000 TO 999,999	UNDER 250,000	
Number of offices	2,344	42	213	1,515	574
Median					
2004 Population served	36,515	1,475,488	449,685	42,263	12,764
Total staff size	9	419	105	10	3
Salary of chief prosecutor	$85,000	$149,000	$125,000	$95,000	$42,000
Budget for prosecution	$354,755	$33,231,705	$6,034,575	$388,544	$132,586

SOURCE: Bureau of Justice Statistics, "Prosecution Statistics" http://www.ojp.usdoj.gov/bjs/pros.htm

the District of Columbia, New Jersey, and Rhode Island, where chief prosecutors are either appointed or are members of the state attorney general's office.

Because of elections, the work of the American prosecutor is deeply set within the larger political process. For a lawyer interested in a political career, the prosecutor's office offers a launching pad. Indeed, prosecutors "virtually own the politically potent symbols of 'law and order' politics" (Flemming, Nardulli, and Eisenstein 1992, p. 23).

Numerous government officials—governors, judges, and legislators—have begun their careers as crusading prosecutors. Many prosecutors, however, do not plan to enter politics. Studies in Wisconsin and Kentucky, for example, indicated that more than half of the prosecutors had no further political ambitions. They viewed the office as useful for gaining visibility before establishing a private law practice (Engstrom 1971; Jacob 1966). Thus, after serving one or two terms in office, former DAs typically practice private law or assume other positions in the public sector—primarily judge (Jones 1994).

The tremendous power of the prosecutor means that political parties are very interested in controlling the office. The chief prosecutor has numerous

opportunities for patronage. In some communities, partisan considerations play a large role in the hiring of assistant district attorneys (Eisenstein, Flemming, and Nardulli 1988). Political parties may also want one of their own serving as district attorney to guarantee that their affairs will not be closely scrutinized and to act as a vehicle for harassing the opposition.

LOCAL PROSECUTOR

Little is known about the activities of local prosecutors—variously called "city attorneys," "solicitors," or the like—although recent estimates place their numbers at about 5,700. In some jurisdictions, local prosecutors are responsible for the preliminary stages of felony cases as they are processed in the lower courts. In these jurisdictions, it is the **local prosecutor** (not the chief prosecutor) who represents the government at the initial appearance, argues bond amounts, and conducts the preliminary hearing. These decisions may have important consequences for later stages of the felony prosecution, but the chief prosecutor's office has no direct control over these matters.

Local prosecutors, however, are primarily responsible for processing the large volume of minor criminal offenses disposed of in the lower courts. Public drunkenness, petty theft, disorderly conduct, and minor assaults are the staple of these judicial bodies (see Chapter 18).

THE PROSECUTOR'S OFFICE AT WORK

In the courtroom, one's attention normally gravitates toward the individual lawyers as they call witnesses, ask questions, and cross-examine the opponent's witnesses. These individual activities, however, must be understood within the larger context in which they occur. The day-to-day work of the prosecutor's office is executed by more than 78,000 attorneys, investigators, and support staff. How these persons are hired, trained, and supervised has a major bearing on the exercise of prosecutorial discretion.

ASSISTANT DISTRICT ATTORNEYS

Most assistant district attorneys (sometimes called "deputy district attorneys") are hired immediately after graduation from law school or after a short time in private practice. Usually, they have attended local law schools rather than the nation's most prestigious law schools (whose graduates prefer higher-status, better-paying jobs in civil practice).

In the past, many prosecutors hired assistants on the basis of party affiliation and the recommendations of elected officials. Increasingly, however, greater stress is being placed on merit selection, a trend exemplified by the Los Angeles prosecutor's office—the nation's largest, with more than 1,000 lawyers—where hiring is done on a civil service basis.

The turnover rate among assistant DAs is high. Most serve an average of 3 to 6 years before leaving prosecution to enter private practice, politics, business, or another field. Indeed, 35 percent of all prosecutors' offices nationwide report significant problems retaining assistant DAs, with low salaries cited as the leading reason for the high turnover (Perry 2006). Indeed, low salaries were "the primary obstacle cited by prosecutors' offices with recruitment problems (83%) and offices with retention problems (71%)," especially when compared to the higher salaries lawyers earn in private law practice—a disparity that seems to grow over time (Perry 2006, p. 3).

Turnover is also a product of assistants' growing tired of the job. With its never-ending stream of society's losers, the criminal courthouse can become a depressing place to work. Moreover, regular trial work creates numerous physical and psychological pressures. In the words of a former New Orleans prosecutor, "The average trial assistant leaves work every day with a huge stack of papers under his arm. The grind can really wear you down. There's just too much work" (Perlstein 1990). In *Bronx D.A.*, Sarena Straus (2006) discussed the day she reached her breaking point. She was a felony prosecutor in the Domestic Violence and Sex Crimes Unit. She had just interviewed a 6-year-old autistic boy who watched his sister get stabbed to death that morning. "When I finished the interview, I went back to my office. It was 7 p.m. Everyone else had gone home for the evening. I sat in my office and cried." Realizing she could no longer separate herself from her work, she left the office.

Although many assistants view their job as a brief way station toward a more lucrative and more varied private practice, some see it as a permanent career position. In Wisconsin, the average tenure is about 6 years, and perhaps just as important, some assistants advance to become the elected DA in their county, run for the position in a neighboring county, or make other lateral moves (Jones 1994). Across the nation, a marked trend toward a prosecutorial "civil service" has become obvious, with assistants moving from office to office (Jones 2001).

LEARNING THE JOB

Law schools provide an overview of law on the books—criminal law, criminal procedure, evidence, and constitutional law, to name just a few. But they give their students very little exposure to law in action. Thus, the typical assistant DA comes to the job having little familiarity with the day-to-day realities of the profession. Here is how one lawyer described his first days on the job:

> For the first week or two, I went to court with guys who had been here. Just sat there and watched. What struck me was the amount of things he [the prosecutor] has to do in the courtroom. The prosecutor runs the courtroom. Although the judge is theoretically in charge, we're standing there plea-bargaining and calling the cases at the same time and chewing gum and telling the people to quiet down and setting bonds, and that's what amazed me. I never thought I would learn all the terms. What bothered me also was the paperwork.

Not the Supreme Court decisions, not the *mens rea* or any of this other stuff, but the amount of junk that's in those files that you have to know. We never heard about this crap in law school (Heumann 1978, p. 94).

For decades, training in prosecutors' offices was almost exclusively on the job; it was not unusual for recent law school graduates with no experience to be sent into court on their first day on the job. One assistant summed up the office tradition as follows: "They have a very unique way of breaking people in. They say, 'Here's a file. There's the jury. Go try it'" (Flemming, Nardulli, and Eisenstein 1992). More recently, large prosecutors' offices have begun to train new employees more systematically. After a week of general orientation to the different divisions of the office, new assistants are allowed to watch various proceedings and observe veteran trial attorneys at work.

An important part of learning law in action involves working with the office clientele. Here is how journalist Gary Delsohn (2003, p. 13) described the reality of the prosecutor's office in Sacramento, California:

In an urban prosecutor's office, witnesses you build a case around are often just a shade less unsavory than the defendants you're trying to put away. It's blue-collar law. To succeed, a prosecutor has to be willing and able to deal with all kinds of people.

Young lawyers looking for civility and intellectual challenges are best advised to work for the attorney general or the U.S. Attorney's office.

New assistants quickly learn to ask questions of more experienced prosecutors, court clerks, and veteran police officers. Through this socialization process, assistants learn important unwritten rules about legal practice relating to what types of violations should be punished and the appropriate penalties to be applied to such violations. Assistants also learn that their performance (and chances for promotion) are measured by how promptly and efficiently they dispose of cases. They become sensitive to hints—for example, if a judge complains that a backlog is developing because prosecutors are bringing too many minor cases, the new assistant usually gets the message that his or her plea-bargaining demands are too high.

Promotions are also related to the candidate's reputation as a trial attorney. Assistants are invariably judged by the number of convictions they obtain. In the courthouse environment, however, not losing a case has a higher value than winning. Thus, assistants learn that if the guilt of the defendant is doubtful or the offender is not dangerous, it is better to negotiate a plea than to disrupt the courtroom routine by attempting to gain a jury conviction.

PROMOTIONS AND OFFICE STRUCTURE

As assistants gain experience and settle into the courthouse routine, they are promoted to more demanding and also more interesting tasks. Promotions are related to office structure (Flemming, Nardulli, and Eisenstein 1992). Small prosecutors' offices usually use vertical prosecution, in which one prosecutor is assigned responsibility for a case from intake to appeal (Nugent and McEwen 1988). In these offices, assistants are promoted by being assigned more serious cases. However, such an assignment system is administratively burdensome in large courthouses; assistants would spend much of their time moving from one courtroom to another and waiting for their one or two cases to be called. Therefore, most big-city prosecutors' offices use horizontal prosecution, in which prosecutors are assigned to specific functions, such as initial appearance, charging, preliminary hearing, grand jury, trial, or appeal. On a regular basis, one or two attorneys are systematically assigned to one courtroom with a given judge. Through time, prosecutors come to know the judge's views on sentencing and the like. Under horizontal prosecution, assistants spend a year or more handling misdemeanor offenses before they are promoted by being assigned to courtrooms with felonies.

Over the past decades, specialization has become increasingly common in chief prosecutors' offices, particularly in densely populated jurisdictions. Often it is the most experienced trial attorneys who staff these positions. Specialized units dealing with murder, sexual assault, armed robbery, and major drug crimes are the most prestigious, mainly because trial work is both plentiful and challenging.

SUPERVISION

Assistant district attorneys are supervised by a section head, who is supposed to ensure that they follow policies of the office. However, for several reasons, assistant DAs enjoy fairly broad freedom.

Office policies are often general and somewhat vague. In small offices, they are seldom even put in writing. Official and unofficial policies are simply part of what the assistant learns informally; for this reason, it is hard for the bureau chief to enforce them. In large offices, decentralized work assignments mean that supervisors can exert only limited control over specific cases or individual assistants. Assistant DAs spend most of their time not in the central office but in the courtroom. Indeed, in crowded courthouses, trial assistants often have offices adjoining the judge's chambers and only rarely appear in the prosecutor's office at all. It is therefore difficult for supervisors to observe and monitor the assistant district attorney's activities. Each assistant has dozens of cases that require individual decisions on the basis of specific facts, unique witness problems, and so on. A supervisor has no way to monitor such situations except on the basis of what the assistant orally reports or writes in the file. Here, as elsewhere, information is power. Assistants can control their supervisors by selectively telling them what they think they should know (Neubauer 1974b).

ATTEMPTS AT GREATER SUPERVISION

The traditional form of prosecutorial management is centered on autonomy; each individual assistant DA is granted a great deal of freedom to make his or her own decisions. The Erie, Pennsylvania, DA's office is typical; it "promulgated few formal written policies, gave most of its assistants fairly wide latitude to dispose of cases in ways consistent with the general aim of the office, and relied on informal supervision" (Eisenstein, Flemming, and Nardulli 1988, p. 215).

Concerned that autonomy allows too much unchecked discretion, some prosecutors have attempted to exert greater supervision by adopting a rigid system of office policies. Some forbid any charge reductions whatsoever for some types of defendants (habitual offenders) and for serious charges such as violent offenses and major drug dealing (Eisenstein, Flemming, and Nardulli 1988). To ensure compliance with these detailed office policies, formal, detailed, bureaucratic enforcement mechanisms are imposed. Typical is DuPage County, Illinois, where the DA's office "was highly centralized, rigidly enforcing the 'bottom-line' pleas established by the indictment committee. The DA's office relied on a formally structured hierarchy to administer its policies" (Eisenstein, Flemming, and Nardulli 1988, p. 215). Chief prosecutors believe that these management systems

monitor prosecutorial discretion, minimize differences among individual assistants, and concentrate scarce crime-fighting resources (Jacoby 1980).

Attempts by supervisors to control the work of the assistants tend to erode the morale of the office, as the following account from the Sacramento, California, DA's office illustrates. According to one of the top supervisors in the office, second-guessing is rarely worth the trouble, because the deputies tend to "stay pissed" forever. Indeed, one assistant is still furious 7 years after his boss refused to allow him to participate in a meeting involving his case (Delsohn 2003). Overall, office review of all case files (to ensure that policies have been followed) makes some assistants uncomfortable because they think that they are not completely trusted. Reductions in individual discretion increase the general level of tension in the office. One trial assistant related how a colleague was summarily fired on the same day he violated office policy on plea bargaining. All the assistants resented and feared the administrator who fired him (Eisenstein, Flemming, and Nardulli 1988, p. 215).

PROSECUTORIAL ETHICS

The Duke lacrosse case has become the poster child for prosecutorial misconduct. But this was a truly exceptional case and needs to be analyzed within an array of legal issues that limited prosecutorial power.

Ethical issues facing prosecutors are very different from those confronting defense attorneys because prosecutors do not represent individual clients. Prosecutors often define their jobs as representing victims of crime (Chapter 9) and the police (Chapter 10), but these are not typically considered to fit under the attorney–client relationship. Rather, the client of the prosecutor is the government, and for this reason prosecutors are given special responsibilities. In the words of the Standards: "The duty of the prosecutor is to seek justice, not merely to convict" (Standard 3-1.2c, American Bar Association 2006).

Because prosecutors represent the government, they enjoy a great deal of legal immunity (see Exhibit 6.4). As stressed in this chapter, citizens can sue prosecutors civilly only in the narrowest of circumstances. For example, a defendant whose conviction is overturned on appeal (and is later found not guilty) cannot sue the prosecutor for malpractice. The appellate court reversal is viewed as a sufficient remedy.

Exhibit 6.4
KEY DEVELOPMENTS CONCERNING THE PROSECUTOR

Berger v. United States	1935	The prosecutor's primary interest is in doing justice, not simply winning cases.
Imbler v. Pachtman	1976	Prosecutors enjoy absolute immunity from civil liability when initiating and pursuing a criminal prosecution.
Morrison v. Olson	1988	Independent counsel law is constitutional.
Burns v. Reed	1991	Prosecutors enjoy only qualified immunity from lawsuits concerning advice given to the police.
Buckley v. Fitzsimmons	1993	Prosecutors enjoy only qualified immunity from civil lawsuits for actions during criminal investigations and statements made during news conferences.
Kalina v. Fletcher	1997	A prosecutor may be sued for making false statements of fact in an affidavit in support of an arrest warrant.

Disclosure of evidence is the dominant legal ethics issue confronting prosecutors. Chapter 12 discusses a series of Supreme Court cases that require the prosecutor to hand over to the defense exculpatory evidence (evidence that tends to show the innocence of the defendant). But this can be a vague mandate that leads some prosecutors to hand over as little evidence as possible. One result is that appellate courts find that prosecutors sometimes improperly withhold evidence from the defense, and therefore the guilty verdict is reversed and a new trial ordered. Note that this is the typical remedy—appellate reversal—and does not sanction the erring prosecutor. Only on rare occasions do prosecutors face sanctions from the bar association for failure to disclose evidence to the defense.

Conflict of interest is another ethical issue facing prosecutors (and defense attorneys as well). Prosecutors employed part-time, for example, may confront a host of ethical issues. In private practice, a lawyer may represent an individual, but if that person runs afoul of the law, then the prosecutor must recuse himself. Conflicts of interest may also arise when the prosecutor leaves the office for private practice. As a general rule, the now-private lawyer may not represent anyone who was prosecuted while he or she was working for the prosecutor's office. Even if the lawyer had no contact with the case, the lawyer may not represent that individual defendant.

Prosecutors exercise a tremendous amount of discretion and several ethical standards relate to how this discretion should be used. One set of issues relates to charging. The standard is that a prosecutor should not institute criminal charges not supported by probable cause. Chapter 10 explores the ambiguity of the legal standard of probable cause. This, in turn, may lead to criticism that prosecutors unfairly failed to prosecute a case. Conversely, prosecutors may be criticized for unfairly prosecuting a defendant based on political motives.

The ethical issues surrounding prosecutors' discretion to seek the death penalty are often debated. Only a small subset of homicides are considered to be eligible for the death sentence (Chapter 15). Prosecutors often must make a series of close calls in deciding which defendants should face capital punishment. To ensure that these decisions are made in an even-handed manner, many big-city prosecutors' offices have a special review process. Moreover, the courts have imposed a proportionality requirement—that is, they seek information that the decision to seek the death penalty in a specific case is proportional to the decision in other cases. Although ethical issues like this one are at the forefront of the debate over capital punishment, appellate courts rarely find that prosecutors abused their discretion.

→ How much information to release to the public presents another ethical issue for prosecutors (Pollock 2010). In the modern era, both the prosecution and the defense often try their cases in the press before a jury is picked. For this reason, judges often impose a gag order on high-profile cases (Chapter 14), prohibiting either side from releasing information to the press. In ordinary cases, only on rare occasions have judges found that prosecutors went too far in seeking to convince the public (meaning potential jurors) of the overwhelming guilt of the defendant.

PROSECUTORS AND COURTROOM WORK GROUPS

Prosecutors spend most of their time working directly with other members of the courtroom work group. Even when interviewing witnesses or conducting legal research, the prosecutor is anticipating the reactions of judges and defense attorneys. Thus, the activities of prosecutors can be understood only within the setting of the courtroom work group (Worden 1990).

The prosecutor is the most important member of the work group. Prosecutors set the agenda for judges and defense attorneys by exercising discretion over the types of cases filed, the nature of acceptable plea agreements, and the sentences to be handed out. Prosecutors also control the flow of information about cases by providing access to police arrest reports, laboratory tests, and defendants' criminal histories. By stressing certain information or withholding facts, prosecutors can influence the decisions of judges and defense attorneys.

As the dominant force in the courtroom work group, prosecutors clearly set the tone for plea bargaining. This is how one veteran explained his perspective:

I get so damned pissed off and tired of these guys who come in and cry, "My guy's got a job" or "My guy's about to join the army," when he's got a rap sheet as long as your arm. His guy's a loser, and he's wailing on my desk about what a fine man he is. What really wins me is the guy who comes in and says, "O.K., what are we going to

do with my criminal today? I know he has no redeeming social value. He's been a bad son of a bitch all his life, so just let me know your position. But frankly, you know, my feeling is that this is just not the case to nail him on. We all know if he does something serious, he's going." And before long the guy who approaches it this way has you wrapped around his little finger (Carter 1974, p. 87).

Prosecutors' actions, in turn, are influenced by other members of the courtroom work group.

Through the socialization process, assistant district attorneys internalize the accepted ways of doing things in the courthouse, learning to plead cases out on the basis of normal crimes (discussed in Chapter 5). Prosecutors who stray too far from the shared norms of the courtroom work group can expect sanctions. The judge may informally indicate that the state is pushing too hard for a harsh sentence or may publicly chastise a district attorney in open court, thus threatening the attorney's status among peers. The defense attorney may not agree to a prosecutor's request for a continuance or may use delaying tactics to impair the state's efforts to schedule cases, thus further disrupting the prosecutor's efforts to move cases. (The prosecutor, of course, is not without countersanctions. These will be discussed in the next two chapters.)

Operating within the constraints of the courtroom work group, effective assistant DAs are those who make tactical decisions that maximize their objectives. Experienced prosecutors, for example, know which defense attorneys can be trusted, granting these people greater access to information about the case and listening to them more when the case involves unusual circumstances. Prosecutors also quickly learn the tendencies of the judge. No experienced prosecutor can afford to ignore how the judge wishes the courtroom to be run.

Although the prosecutor is generally the most important member of the courtroom work group, work groups show considerable variability. Differences between one community and the next abound, and in big-city courthouses, these differences often exist from courtroom to courtroom. Conflicting goals and varying political styles are two factors that account for contrasting work groups.

CONFLICTING GOALS AND CONTRASTING WORK GROUPS

On the surface, the goals of prosecutors seem the model of simplicity: Their job is to convict the guilty.

But a closer examination shows that the goals are not as clear cut as they first appear. Prosecutors define their main job in different ways. Some stress working closely with law enforcement agencies. Thus, they serve as police advocates in court and stress punishing the guilty. Others emphasize their role as court-based officials. Thus, they define their job as impartially administering justice and emphasize securing convictions (Delsohn 2003; Eisenstein 1978; LaFave 1965). The uncertainties about which goals should come first have historically produced marked diversity among prosecutors, with some prosecutors' offices focusing on the administration of justice, and others focusing on an adversarial model (McDonald 1979; Utz 1979). Such differences in philosophies still exist today (Baker 1999; Delsohn 2003), although media attention has often focused on prosecutors whose "win at all costs" mentality has eroded public confidence in those who are supposed to advocate for justice (Roberts and Stratton 2008).

POLITICAL STYLES AND CONTRASTING WORK GROUPS

The prosecutor's role within the courtroom work group also needs to be understood within the broader political context in which the office functions. This was the conclusion of Roy Flemming's (1990) study of nine prosecutors' offices in three states. Because they exercise broad discretion (in the context of decentralization and local autonomy), elected prosecutors choose political styles. This choice is both personal and strategic. It depends first on the prosecutor's satisfaction or dissatisfaction with the office's status within the courthouse community. It also depends on the prosecutor's perception of the value of conflict as a means of changing the office's status.

Prosecutors satisfied with the status of the office adopt an "office conservator" style. Office conservators accept the status quo. Continuity is often a key consideration; former assistants are elected with the blessings of the previous officeholder and the support of the local political establishment. Once in office, conservators do not deliberately step on toes; if they push for change, it generally comes as a response to the requests of others. Montgomery County, Pennsylvania, provides an example. The newly elected DA retained the preexisting staff intact. He did fashion some guidelines regarding guilty pleas, but they were flexible, symbolic gestures—signals

that a changing of the guard had taken place, not a revolution. Most important, however, the DA tolerated the judges' traditional dominance of the courthouse community.

Prosecutors who are less content with the status of their offices face a more complicated set of choices. They must decide whether conflict is an effective tool for them to use. These "courthouse insurgents" are very dissatisfied with the status quo and are prepared to do battle to change it. They do not shy away from open conflict, nor do they hesitate to challenge the courthouse community in pursuit of their goals. DuPage County, Illinois, is an example. The state's attorney was an outsider to the county who won the office by narrowly defeating the Republican party's favored candidate in a bitterly fought, mudslinging primary. Perceiving that the office failed to stand up to defense attorneys, the new state's attorney turned the office inside out. Immediately after election, he eliminated the part-time staff, hired aggressive assistants, and instituted policies severely restricting plea bargaining. Moreover, the insurgent DA minced no words in publicly criticizing judges and defense attorneys.

"Policy reformers" are also dissatisfied with the status quo, but unlike courthouse insurgents, they are cautious, often conciliatory, in their approach. Upon taking office, they gradually move to tighten their offices' guilty-plea policies, encourage more assertive attitudes among their assistants, and try to develop innovative approaches to prosecutorial work. They do not shrink from trying to alter their relationships with judges. Erie, Pennsylvania, provides a case in point. Embittered by the decline of the office when he left as an assistant to enter private practice, the new Erie prosecutor bucked the political establishment and decisively trounced the incumbent in the Democratic party primary to win the office. However, his plans to restore the respect of the office clashed with the docket policies of the court. Rather than fighting openly, the Erie DA mounted an indirect campaign to wrest control of the docket from the judges.

Flemming's study highlights two aspects of prosecutorial behavior that are not immediately obvious. First, differences in political styles cross party lines; these are not Republican or Democratic styles. Second, differences in political styles are not necessarily constant through time. In several communities, a district attorney was initially elected as an insurgent or a policy reformer but through the years came to adopt a conservator style.

LAW AND POPULAR CULTURE

The Accused (1988)

Sarah Tobias is one of the few victims who got to tell her story. In *The Accused* (1988) Sarah Tobias (Jodie Foster) is raped by three men in a bar while several bystanders cheer on the assailants. Sarah's sexual assault complaint is handled by Kathryn Murphy (Kelly McGillis), an assistant district attorney who sees showing compassion to crime victims as an impediment to her principal task of winning at all costs in the courtroom.

Winning this case appears extremely difficult. Sarah had been drinking and smoking marijuana the night of the assault, her live-in boyfriend was a drug dealer, and she had flirted with one of her assailants before the assault. Because her questionable behavior and character severely weakens the prospects of victory, Kathryn plea-bargains the case down to reckless endangerment.

Later, Sarah is seriously hurt in a demolition derby-style encounter in a record store parking lot with one of the bystanders from the night of the assault. Kathryn visits Sarah in the hospital and has a change of heart. Realizing that her plea bargain cheated Sarah out of seeing justice done in a public courthouse, she decides to prosecute the bystanders for criminal solicitation, which is defined as behavior that "commands, induces, entreats or otherwise attempts to persuade another person to commit a felony." The head district attorney is so convinced his assistant will lose such a case he says, "Drop it, you've got more important things to do." But Kathryn forges ahead and, this time, the case goes to trial.

The bystanders are convicted—but was justice done? The process portrays Sarah as victimized twice—by the rapists the first time and the legal system the second. Such complaints are heard frequently about our legal system, especially in sexual assault cases. And what are the possible effects of such treatment? One possibility is that crimes go unreported. Many rapes, just like numerous other crimes, may never be prosecuted (Chapter 9). The non-reporting of crimes represents the beginning of the criminal justice system's funneling process (Chapter 10). *The Accused* illustrates the importance of this metaphor as it shows the complexity of the decisions that victims, police, witnesses, district attorneys, lawyers, judges, and the jury face. Sarah's decisions—from her choice to report the crime to her choice of dress and lifestyle—are all coldly scrutinized, as shown by the way she is treated by the nurses at the hospital, and the way her personal life becomes a factor in the case. The district attorney's decision to offer a plea to the assailants (Chapter 13) appears to be based on her own beliefs about Sarah's character and her uncertainty about winning a trial. Only after Sarah is victimized again does Kathryn experience a change of heart and decides to prosecute the bystanders.

The film uses the gritty and dark images of violent sexual assault and it accurately illustrates the often-unpleasant preliminary stages of the criminal justice process that may actually discourage crime reporting. Unlike many victims, Sarah spoke out and ultimately got her day in court. She got to tell "her story."

After watching this movie, be prepared to answer the following questions:

1. How do the characters in *The Accused* deal with the discretion that is inherent in their jobs?

2. How can you use Jody Foster's character as a vehicle for illustrating the reasons why victims are often frustrated when they learn about the funneling process?

3. If more victims were "given their day in court," how would the criminal justice system change?

4. The Accused is actually based on a real case that took place in Massachusetts. But decades have past since that time. How has the criminal justice system changed in that time, especially with regard to the way sexual assaults are handled?

THE EXPANDING DOMAIN OF THE PROSECUTOR

The domain of the prosecutor has been expanding throughout the past century, and pressures to place greater authority in the hands of the prosecutor are likely to continue (Davis 2007; Worrall and Borakove 2008). Within the fragmented, sometimes nonsystem of criminal justice, the prosecutor is in the best position to provide coordination. Moreover, with crime as a dominant issue in elections, the prosecutor is uniquely able to capitalize on his or her role as the community's chief law enforcement official and to promise the voters to expand crime-fighting efforts.

We will examine two types of programs that exemplify the contemporary expansion of the domain of the prosecutor: improving police–prosecutor relationships and community prosecution.

IMPROVING POLICE–PROSECUTOR RELATIONSHIPS

Police and prosecutors are commonly viewed as members of the same crime-fighting team, but a closer look reveals a more complex reality. Police and prosecutors have differing perspectives on the law. To the police, the case is closed when the suspect is arrested, but prosecutors stress that they often need additional information to win in court (Stanko 1981).

Inadequate police reports present a classic illustration of noncoordination within the criminal justice system. The thoroughness of police investigations and the quality of their arrests directly affect the likelihood of the prosecutor's obtaining a conviction. In a survey of 225 (mostly big-city) prosecutors, 66 percent cited inadequate police preparation of crime reports as a major problem in their offices (Nugent and McEwen 1988). Commonly mentioned problems were that names and addresses of victims and witnesses were lacking, full details of how the crime was committed were missing, and vital laboratory reports were not forwarded on time. Faced with incomplete or inaccurate police reports, the prosecutor may be forced to drop charges (see Chapter 10).

Police and prosecutors in several jurisdictions have adopted strategies to improve coordination and communication among themselves (Buchanan 1989). In Indianapolis, for example, the prosecutor has funded a computer message system that enables attorneys in the office to transmit notes, case dispositions, and subpoenas directly to police officers at their work locations. In Alameda County, California, and Montgomery County, Maryland, "street jump" narcotics officers and prosecutors consult frequently, both in person and over the telephone, to build cases that meet the requirements of the search-and-seizure law.

A few agencies have gone further, institutionalizing teamwork and making communication between investigators and prosecutors a top priority. In Multnomah County, Oregon, the Organized Crime/Narcotics Task Force has brought together 12 investigators from several area agencies and two prosecutors from the district attorney's office, instituting daily informal contact about the progress of pending cases. Moreover, prosecutors act as consultants to the police during the investigative phase. Thus, investigators can get answers to difficult legal questions in a few minutes, just by walking down the hall.

Programs like these indicate that, despite a long history of difficulties, some agencies apparently are bridging the gap. But a word of caution is in order. No research to date has systematically evaluated these programs to indicate their overall effectiveness. Until such research is conducted, no predictions can be made about which programs are likely to be effective in other communities.

COMMUNITY PROSECUTION

The historic image of the district attorney stresses case processing: The DA files charges and doggedly pursues a conviction. But this traditional image is becoming blurred as locally elected prosecutors respond to a wide variety of social problems such as domestic violence (Chapter 9), drug abuse (Chapter 10), disorder on city streets (Chapter 18), and growing numbers of juvenile offenders (Chapter 19). In responding to these types of social problems, which often reflect disintegrating neighborhoods, prosecutors today are more likely to stress problem-oriented approaches ("Community Prosecution" 2008). At times, the specifics are hard to pin down because the approaches are truly shaped to local needs rather than to national program guides (Coles and Earle 1996). But these new approaches have three elements in common (Jacoby 1995):

- Crime prevention is recognized as a legitimate prosecutorial goal.
- The most effective results are obtained within small, manageable geographic areas.
- Change is more likely to occur through cooperative efforts or partnerships, rather than prosecutorial dictates.

COURTS, CONTROVERSY, AND GENDER EQUITY

Are Sexual Assaults against Women Underprosecuted?

In *The Accused* (1988), Sarah Tobias (Jodie Foster) is raped by three men in a bar while several bystanders cheer on the assailants. Her sexual assault complaint is handled by Kathryn Murphy (Kelly McGillis), an assistant district attorney who sees showing compassion to crime victims as an impediment to her principal task of winning at all costs in the arena of the courtroom. Winning this case will be extremely difficult. Sarah had been drinking the night of the assault, her live-in boyfriend is a drug dealer, and she had flirted with one of her assailants before the assault. Because her questionable moral character severely weakens the prospects of victory, the district attorney plea-bargains the case down to "aggravated assault."

To some, this fictional account of a sexual assault comes too close to reality. The movie portrays Sarah as victimized twice—assaulted by the rapist the first time and the legal system the second. On the other hand, the Duke lacrosse player sexual assault prosecution serves as a cautionary tale, because in these types of cases, stories of victims can change and the physical evidence does not always corroborate the victim's version of the truth.

Sexual assault is one of the most visible gender equity controversies in the criminal justice system. Along with domestic violence (see Chapter 9) and gender bias in the courtroom (Chapter 5), it is the topic that feminists have most identified as involving systematic bias throughout the criminal justice system.

A report of the U.S. Senate Judiciary Committee—The Response to Rape: Detours on the Road to Equal Justice (1993)—forcefully concludes that the justice system creates serious barriers to women who are sexually assaulted. For one, many of the 876,000 sexual assaults occurring every year are not prosecuted (Bureau of Justice Statistics 1995). According to this line of thinking, prosecutors and police are prone to view allegations of rape skeptically. A widespread belief exists that many allegations of rape are false, even though the FBI reports that false allegations occur in only 2 percent of all reported cases.

But not all are convinced that the evidence supports the allegation that sexual assaults are underprosecuted. Skeptics counter that over the past decade for which data are available, sexual assault rates have declined by more than 35 percent (Bureau of Justice Statistics 2006). Nor is there evidence that the "moral character" of the victim plays a significant role. A study in Detroit assessed the influence of blame and responsibility factors in decisions of police and prosecutor to go to court. The authors concluded that little evidence existed that victim characteristics affected case outcomes. Rather, the presence of evidence—the victim's ability to identify her assailant, for example—was the dominant reason for cases being prosecuted or not (Horney and Spohn 1996).

What do you think? Are sexual assaults underprosecuted? If so, is the reason because criminal justice officials fail to adequately consider the plight of the victim or because these cases are more likely to have evidence problems?

The Neighborhood District Attorney approach in Multnomah County (Portland, Oregon) provides a case in point. Business leaders in Lloyd District (an inner-city neighborhood) called for more police protection as well as the assignment of a special prosecutor to the district (for which they provided 1 year's funding). Citizen demands were invariably expressed in traditional law enforcement terms— more police, more arrests, and more convictions, particularly of repeat offenders. The Lloyd District special prosecutor, however, quickly saw that people's concerns were more immediate than he had imagined. "They wanted something done about prostitution, public drinking, drug use, vandalism, [minor] assaults, littering garbage, and 'car prowls' (thefts from cars)" (Boland 1996, p. 36). Although none of these problems (except thefts from cars) fit traditional notions of serious crime, they nonetheless raise serious concern among citizens. (This approach clearly emphasizes the activities of the local courts, discussed in Chapter 18.)

As the program developed, several distinctive features became apparent. For one, the assistant DA used the laws in new ways, including using civil remedies to fight crime (see Chapter 2). Perhaps most important, the program was problem-oriented: Rather than focusing on individual arrestees, the Neighborhood District Attorney addressed problems from a larger perspective, with long-term goals in mind. Ultimately, what emerged was an approach, not a program. Rather than being guided by clearcut procedures, Portland has adopted a highly flexible organization that can meet the different needs of different neighborhoods (Boland 1996).

Overall, community prosecution stresses a proactive approach: Rather than reacting to crime through prosecution, these programs stress crime prevention (Coles and Kelling 1999). And often the crimes stressed are minor ones that are nonetheless serious irritants to local residents (Goldkamp, Irons-Guynn, and Weiland 2002).

CONCLUSION

Prosecutors in the United States are powerful, but, as with all other governmental officials, there are limits. In the Duke lacrosse case, the state's attorney general took over the case and eventually dismissed all charges because of a lack of evidence. Moreover, the North Carolina Bar Association charged Nifong with lying to the judge, withholding key DNA evidence from the defense, and making inflammatory statements to the public. The North Carolina Supreme Court agreed and disbarred him.

The Duke lacrosse case and the Supreme Court decision in *Burns v. Reed* are examples of prosecutorial misconduct and efforts to control prosecutorial abuse. But these examples must be assessed within the broader context. For years, courts have granted prosecutors wide-ranging discretionary powers. The exercise of this discretion shapes the dynamics of the courthouse. In effect, all others involved in the criminal courts—judges, defense attorneys, probation officers, juries, witnesses, and so on—must react to the decisions made by the prosecutor. But the law imposes few formal restrictions on the use of these discretionary powers. Prosecutors' offices are decentralized, autonomous, and headed by locally elected officials.

This does not mean that prosecutorial discretion is uncontrolled; rather, it is influenced by other members of the courtroom work group. Through the socialization process and the occasional application of sanctions, new prosecutors are educated in the norms of the courtroom work group.

CHAPTER REVIEW

1. **Discuss the two major characteristics of prosecutors in the United States.**

The role of the prosecutor involves broad discretion and decentralization.

2. **Describe the three most important entities in federal prosecution.**

The three most important entities in federal prosecution are the U.S. Solicitor General, the Criminal Division of the U.S. Department of Justice, and the offices of 94 U.S. Attorneys.

3. **Identify the three somewhat overlapping agencies involved in prosecution in state courts.**

The three major agencies involved in prosecution in state courts are the state attorney general, the chief prosecutor and the local prosecutor.

4. **Explain the major factors affecting the work life of assistant district attorneys.**

Assistant district attorneys are typically young lawyers who must learn how law in action is practiced, seek promotions to prosecuting more serious crimes, and are often loosely supervised.

5. Analyze the principal factors affecting prosecutorial ethics.

As governmental officials, prosecutors are largely immune from civil lawsuits and if an error is made, an appellate court reversal is the typical remedy.

6. Outline two major examples of the expanding domain of the prosecutor.

Programs aimed at improving police–prosecutor relationships and community prosecution are two contemporary examples of the expanding domain of the prosecutor.

CRITICAL THINKING QUESTIONS

1. Robert Misner (1996) argued that given the fragmented nature of the criminal justice system (see Chapter 1), over the past 30 years responsibility has increasingly been centralized in the hands of the district attorney. What factors support this assessment?

2. Should state attorneys general be given authority to supervise locally elected district attorneys? How would such increased authority alter the criminal justice system?

3. How much authority should assistant district attorneys be given? As licensed attorneys, should they be given a large amount of discretion to dispose of cases according to their best judgment, or should they have more limited authority so that the office has a uniform policy?

4. Of the three political styles—office conservator, courthouse insurgent, and policy reformer—which best describes your local prosecutor?

5. Community prosecution stresses the need for the prosecutor to reach out to the community, but what does "community" mean? Is this reform based on a naive assumption that all members of the same geographic entity share similar views? How might different communities within the same city (or perhaps county) stress different law enforcement priorities?

KEY TERMS

local prosecutor   146

officer of the court   139

prosecutor   138

solicitor general   142

state attorney general   144

U.S. attorney general   142

U.S. attorneys   143

WEB RESOURCES

Go to the America's Courts and the Criminal Justice System companion website at

http://www.cengage.com/criminaljustice/neubauer

where you will find more resources to help you study.

Resources include web exercises, quizzing, and flash cards.

FOR FURTHER READING

Baker, Mark. *D.A.: Prosecutors in Their Own Words*. New York: Simon & Schuster, 1999.

Banks, Cyndi. *Criminal Justice Ethics: Theory and Practice*. Thousand Oaks, CA: Sage, 2008.

Davis, Angela. *Arbitrary Justice: The Power of the American Prosecutor*. New York: Oxford University Press, 2007.

Delsohn, Gary 2003. *The Prosecutors: Kidnap, Rape, Murder, Justice: One Year behind the Scenes in a Big-City DA's Office*. New York: Plume.

Delsohn, Gary. 2003b. *The Prosecutors: A Year in the Life a District Attorney's Office*. New York: Dutton/Penguin.

Forst, Brian. "Prosecutors Discover the Community." *Judicature* 84: 135–141, 2000.

Frohman, Lisa. *Prosecutors and Prosecution*. Burlington, VT: Ashgate, 2008.

Markovits, Daniel. *A Modern Legal Ethics: Adversary Advocacy in a Democratic Age*. Princeton, NJ: Princeton University Press, 2008.

Sanders, Andrew, ed. *Prosecution in Common Law Jurisdictions*. Brookfield, VT: Dartmouth, 1996.

Straus, Sarena. 2006. *Bronx D.A.: True Stories from the Sex Crimes and Domestic Violence Unit*. Fort Lee, NJ: Barricade Books.

Suthers, John. *No Higher Calling, No Greater Responsibility: A Prosecutor Makes His Case*. Goldon, CO: Fulcrum, 2008.

Worrall, John, and M. Elaine Nugent-Borakove (eds.). *The Changing Role of the American Prosecutor*. Albany, NY: SUNY Press, 2008.

7

DEFENSE ATTORNEYS

Defense attorney Alan Konop addresses the jury with his hand on the shoulder of the Reverend Gerald Robinson, who was accused of killing a nun in a hospital chapel 26 years before his trial date. He was convicted at the age of 68 and sentenced to 15 years to life in prison. His conviction was affirmed by an Ohio appeals court.

Chapter Outline

Learning Objectives

After reading the chapter, you should be able to:

1. Interpret the four major legal issues surrounding the right to counsel.

2. Discuss how the courtroom work group affects how defense attorneys represent their clients.

3. Explain why most lawyers do not represent criminal defendants.

4. Compare and contrast the three systems of providing indigents with court-appointed attorneys.

5. Recognize possible tensions between lawyers and clients.

6. Analyze the importance of legal ethics to the defense of criminal defendants.

Clarence Earl Gideon had been in and out of prison since the age of 14. His brushes with the law had been minor—public drunkenness and petty theft primarily—but now he faced a much more serious charge: burglarizing a poolroom in Bay Harbor. As he stood before the judge, he appeared to be a shipwreck of a man; his wrinkled face and trembling hands suggested a person much older than 51. Yet "a flame still burned inside Clarence Earl Gideon . . . he had a fierce feeling that the State of Florida had treated him wrongly" (Lewis 1972, p. 6).

He demanded that the court appoint a lawyer to defend him. The trial judge flatly refused; unrepresented by counsel, Gideon was found guilty. But on appeal he was luckier. The Supreme Court plucked this obscure case from the bowels of the criminal justice system to issue a landmark decision: All indigent defendants were entitled to court-appointed counsel in felony trials. *Gideon v. Wainwright* (1963) was not only a victory for Clarence Earl Gideon but, more important, sent shock waves through the criminal justice system.

The Court's decision in *Gideon* underscores the importance of lawyers in the criminal justice system. But what role do defense attorneys play in representing their clients? Some view defense attorneys as fighting to free falsely accused clients. Others, though, often contrast this favorable image with a less complimentary one of defense attorney as a conniver who uses legal technicalities to free the guilty.

This chapter assesses these conflicting images in terms of the daily realities of the small proportion of the legal profession who represent defendants accused of violating the criminal law. The picture is a complicated one. Some defense attorneys suffer from the shortcomings mentioned by their critics; others do not. But all face day-to-day problems and challenges not usually encountered by the bulk of American lawyers who represent higher-status clients. The key topics of this chapter are the factors influencing the type of legal assistance available to those who appear in criminal courts: the legal right to counsel, the tasks defense attorneys perform, their relationship with courtroom work groups, the nature of the criminal bar, the relationship between lawyer and client, and, finally, the various systems for providing legal assistance to the poor.

Gideon v. Wainwright and the Right to Counsel

From his prison cell, Clarence Earl Gideon drafted a petition that, despite the garbled prose of a man with no real education, nonetheless raised a major legal principle:

> When at the time of the petitioners trial he ask the lower court for the aid of counsel, the court refused this aid. Petitioner told the court that this [Supreme] Court made decision to the effect that all citizens tried for a felony crime should have aid of counsel. The lower court ignored this plea. (Lewis 1972)

Every year thousands of pauper petitions like this are sent to the Supreme Court; few are ever heard. But this petition struck a responsive chord. The Court signaled the importance of the issue when it appointed Abe Fortas, one of the best-known lawyers in Washington, D.C., to represent Gideon. (Fortas would later be appointed to the Court.)

In what became officially known as *Gideon v. Wainwright*, the Court forcefully noted that "in our adversary system of criminal justice, any person, hauled into court, who is too poor to hire a lawyer, cannot be assured a fair trial unless counsel is provided for him. This seems to us to be an obvious truth. ..."

The Sixth Amendment states that "in all criminal prosecutions, the accused shall enjoy the right ... to have the assistance of counsel for his defence." As written by the framers more than 200 years ago, this constitutionally protected right to counsel meant only that the judge could not prevent a defendant from bringing a lawyer to court. (In England, defendants had been convicted despite requests to have their lawyers present.) Thus, the Sixth Amendment affected only those who could afford to hire their own lawyers.

Beginning in the 1930s, the Supreme Court took a more expansive view of the right to counsel. Criminal defendants in federal cases were entitled to a court-appointed lawyer if they were too poor to hire their own. But a different rule prevailed in the state courts. Only defendants accused of a capital offense were entitled to court-appointed counsel; indigent defendants charged with ordinary felonies or misdemeanors were not (*Betts v. Brady* 1942). Thus, a significant number of defendants in state courts had to face the legal maze of criminal proceedings by themselves.

Gideon v. Wainwright (1963) significantly expanded the legal meaning of the right to counsel. As occasionally happens, the Court reversed its earlier precedent in *Betts*.

That the government hires lawyers to prosecute and defendants who have the money hire lawyers to defend are the strongest indications of the widespread belief that lawyers in criminal courts are necessities, not luxuries. The right of one charged with crime to counsel may not be deemed fundamental and essential for fair trials in some countries, but it is in ours.

Now, all indigent defendants charged with a felony were entitled to the services of a lawyer paid by the government, irrespective of whether they were on trial in state or federal court.

Gideon proved to be a major transforming event in the American criminal justice system. It was the first major decision of the Warren Court's revolution in criminal justice. But unlike other decisions, it proved not to be controversial. The Court's rationale, focusing on basic fairness and the importance of lawyers, gave it widespread legitimacy. Moreover, *Gideon* focused on the need for a lawyer at the trial itself. Later decisions—*Miranda* in particular—restricted police gathering of evidence and proved to be highly contentious.

CASE CLOSEUP

THE RIGHT TO COUNSEL

Like many other provisions of the Constitution, the Sixth Amendment has a different meaning today than it did when it was first ratified. In a landmark decision, the U.S. Supreme Court held that, based on the Sixth Amendment's provision of **right to counsel**, indigent defendants charged with a felony are entitled to the services of a lawyer paid for by the government (see Case Close-Up: *Gideon v. Wainwright* and the Right to Counsel). Later, the Sixth Amendment right to counsel was extended to juvenile court proceedings as well (*In re Gault* 1967). But as so often happens, answering one question raised several new ones. In the wake of the *Gideon* decision, the Court wrestled with issues involving the right to counsel with regard to: (1) nonfelony criminal prosecutions, (2) stages of the criminal process, (3) ineffective as-

sistance of counsel, and (4) self-representation. Exhibit 7.1 summarizes key developments in the right to counsel.

NONFELONY CRIMINAL PROSECUTIONS

The *Gideon* ruling was limited to state felony prosecutions. In *Argersinger v. Hamlin* (1972), the Court refused to extend the newly discovered constitutional right to court-appointed counsel to those accused of minor violations (misdemeanor or ordinance violations), holding that "absent a knowing and intelligent waiver, no person may be imprisoned for any offense, whether classified as petty, misdemeanor, or felony, unless he was represented by counsel." Later, the justices narrowed the *Argersinger* decision, ruling that a defendant is guaranteed the right to legal counsel, paid by the state if necessary, only in cases that actually lead to imprisonment, not in all cases in which imprisonment is a potential penalty (*Scott v. Illinois* 1979). The net effect of the *Scott* case was to limit the right to counsel in nonfelony prosecutions, particularly if the guilty faced only paying a fine (see Chapter 18).

STAGES OF THE CRIMINAL PROCESS

The *Gideon* ruling spawned another important question: When in the criminal process does the right to counsel begin (and end)? Note that the Sixth Amendment provides for the right to counsel in "all criminal prosecutions," so it is not limited to the trial itself. The Supreme Court adopted a "critical stages" test, under which a defendant is entitled to legal representation at every stage of prosecution "where substantial rights of the accused may be affected," requiring the "guiding hand of counsel" (*Mempa v. Rhay* 1967). As Exhibit 7.2 summarizes, indigent defendants have a right to court-appointed counsel from the time they first appear before a judge until sentence is pronounced and the first appeal concluded. (The only exception is the grand jury, whose peculiar practices will be examined in Chapter 10.) As a general rule, defendants have a Sixth Amendment right to the assistance of counsel once any adversarial proceedings have begun (*Brewer v. Williams* 1977; *Rothgery v. Gillespie County* 2008).

The right to counsel in the pretrial stage is much more limited, however. Applying the critical-stages test, subsequent decisions held that defendants have the right to court-appointed counsel during custodial interrogations (*Miranda v. Arizona*) and police lineups (*Kirby v. Illinois* 1972; *U.S. v. Wade* 1967). However, merely being detained by the police is not sufficient grounds to guarantee a right to counsel (*U.S. v. Gouveia* 1984). (The controversy surrounding the extension of the right to counsel in the police station will be examined in Chapter 12.)

The right to counsel also extends to certain posttrial proceedings, but as in pretrial proceedings, the right to counsel is more limited. Working on the assumption that a person's right to an appeal can be effective only if counsel is available, the Court held that indigents have the right to court-appointed counsel for the appeal (*Douglas v. California* 1963), as well as free trial transcripts (*Griffin v. Illinois* 1956). The Burger Court, however, rejected attempts to extend the *Douglas* ruling beyond the first appeal. Thus, in discretionary appeals and appeals to the Supreme Court, indigent defendants have no right to court-appointed counsel (*Ross v. Moffitt* 1974). One consequence of the *Ross* decision is that defendants sentenced to death must rely on voluntary counsel in pursuing postconviction remedies.

Exhibit 7.1

KEY DEVELOPMENTS IN THE RIGHT TO COUNSEL

Sixth Amendment	1791	"In all criminal prosecutions the accused shall enjoy the right … to have the assistance of counsel for his defence."
Powell v. Alabama	1932	Indigent defendants in a capital case in state court have a right to court-appointed counsel.
Johnson v. Zerbst	1938	Indigent defendants in federal court are entitled to court-appointed counsel.
Betts v. Brady	1942	Indigent defendants in a noncapital case in state court have no right to appointed counsel.
Gideon v. Wainwright	1963	Indigents in state court have the right to appointed counsel (*Betts* overruled).
Douglas v. California	1963	Indigents have a right to court-appointed counsel during the first appeal.

Exhibit 7.1

CONTINUED

In re Gault	1967	Juveniles are covered by the Sixth Amendment's right to counsel.
Argersinger v. Hamlin	1972	Limited the right of nonfelony defendants to have court-appointed counsel.
Faretta v. California	1975	Defendants have the right to self-representation.
Strickland v. Washington	1984	Defense attorney is ineffective only if proceedings were unfair and the outcome would have been different.
Martinez v. Court of Appeal of California	2000	Defendants have no Sixth Amendment right to represent themselves on appeal.
Roe v. Flores-Ortega	2000	A lawyer's failure to file an appeal does not necessarily constitute ineffective assistance of counsel.
Alabama v. Shelton	2002	Indigent entitled to a court-appointed attorney even if facing only a suspended jail term for a minor charge.
Wiggins v. Smith	2003	The failure of an inexperienced defense attorney to conduct a reasonable investigation of the defendant's troubled personal background constituted ineffective assistance of counsel.
Florida v. Nixon	2004	Conceding to the jury the defendant's guilt in a capital trial, with the defendant's consent, does not constitute ineffective assistance of counsel.
Rompilla v. Beard	2005	Death sentence was overturned because the defense attorney failed to search the record for evidence that could have persuaded the jury to spare the defendant's life.
Halbert v. Michigan	2005	Indigent defendants who plead guilt are entitled to state-paid legal help on appeal.
Schriro v. Landrigan	2007	During the penalty phase of a death penalty trial, the defendant refused to allow his attorney to present mitigating evidence about organic brain damage. The defendant was not denied effective assistance of counsel under Strickland.
Indiana v. Edwards	2008	A mentally ill defendant who is nonetheless competent to stand trial is not necessarily competent to dispense with a lawyer and represent himself.

Exhibit 7.2

RIGHT TO COUNSEL DURING STEPS OF FELONY CRIME PROCEDURE

	EXTENT OF RIGHT	SUPREME COURT CASE
Crime	No lawyer required	
Arrest	No lawyer required	
Initial appearance	Lawyer required if critical stage	*Rothgery v. Gillespie County* (2008)
Bail	Lawyer required if critical stage	*Coleman v. Alabama* (1970)
Charging	No lawyer required	
Preliminary hearing	Lawyer required	*Coleman v. Alabama* (1970)
Grand jury	No lawyer allowed	
Arraignment	Lawyer required	*Hamilton v. Alabama* (1961)
Evidence		
Interrogation (preindictment)	Lawyer on request	*Miranda v. Arizona* (1966)
Interrogation (postindictment)	Lawyer required	*Massiah v. U.S.* (1964)
Lineup (preindictment)	No lawyer required	*Kirby v. Illinois* (1972)
Lineup (postindictment)	Lawyer required	*U.S. v. Wade* (1967)
Plea bargaining	Lawyer required	*Brady v. U.S.* (1970)
		Tollett v. Henderson (1973)
Trial	Lawyer required	*Gideon v. Wainwright* (1963)
Sentencing	Lawyer required	*Mempa v. Rhay* (1967)
Probation revocation	Lawyer in court's discretion	*Gagnon v. Scarpelli* (1973)
Parole revocation	Lawyer in board's discretion	*Morrissey v. Brewer* (1972)
Appeal		
First appeal	Lawyer required	*Douglas v. California* (1963)
Discretionary appeal	No lawyer required	*Ross v. Moffitt* (1974)

Some state supreme courts, however, have gone considerably further in mandating counsel for situations in which the Supreme Court has not required counsel under the Sixth Amendment (Bureau of Justice Statistics 1988a).

INEFFECTIVE ASSISTANCE OF COUNSEL

But is it enough to have a lawyer? Must the lawyer also be competent and effective? The Supreme Court has recognized the effective assistance of counsel as essential to the Sixth Amendment guarantee (*McMann v. Richardson* 1970). The Court's most significant holding came in 1984 in *Strickland v. Washington*, in which an "objective standard of reasonableness" was set forth as the proper criterion to be applied in making a determination of the ineffectiveness of counsel. Speaking for the Court, former Justice Sandra Day O'Connor emphasized that the "benchmark for judging any claim of ineffectiveness must be whether counsel's conduct so undermined the proper functioning of the adversarial process that the trial cannot be relied on as having produced a just result." It is important to note that an attorney's decisions regarding trial strategy and tactics—such as the order of presentation of evidence; whether to cross-examine an adverse witness; whether to make an objection—all carry a strong presumption of competent performance. Indeed, the Supreme Court has said, "Strategic choices made after thorough investigation of law and facts relevant to plausible options are virtually unchallengeable" (*Knowles v. Mirzayance* 2009). In short, appellate courts must reverse only if the proceedings were fundamentally unfair and the outcome would have been different if counsel had not been ineffective.

This standard places a heavy burden on the claimant; few appellate courts reverse decisions on these grounds. Indeed, the Court held that a lawyer's failure to file an appeal did not necessarily constitute ineffective assistance of counsel (*Roe v. Flores-Ortega* 2000). However, the Court appears to have a higher *Strickland* threshold in death penalty cases. The Court ordered a new sentencing hearing in a death penalty case because the inexperienced defense attorney failed to conduct a reasonable investigation of the defendant's troubled personal background (*Wiggins v. Smith* 2003). Similarly, the Court overturned a Pennsylvania death sentence because the defense attorney failed to search the record for evidence that could

have persuaded the jury to spare the defendant's life (*Rompilla v. Beard* 2005). But not all appeals on these grounds are successful. During the penalty phase of a death penalty trial, the defendant refused to allow his attorney to present mitigating evidence about organic brain damage. The Court held that the defendant was not denied effective assistance of counsel under *Strickland* (*Schriro v. Landrigan* 2007).

SELF-REPRESENTATION

Can defendants represent themselves if they wish? An important qualification was added to *Gideon* when the Supreme Court ruled that defendants have a constitutional right to self-representation. This means that criminal defendants have the right to proceed **pro se** (Latin for "on his or her own behalf").

The Court, however, did establish limits. Defendants who wish to represent themselves must show the trial judge that they have the ability to conduct the trial. The defendant need not have the skills and experience of a lawyer, and the judge may not deny self-representation simply because the defendant does not have expert knowledge of criminal law and procedure (*Faretta v. California* 1975). This decision has been qualified by the Court's recognition that the trial judge may appoint standby counsel when defendants choose to represent themselves (*McKaskle v. Wiggins* 1984). Standby counsel is available during the trial to consult with the defendant, but it is the defendant, not the standby lawyer, who makes the decisions.

Although self-representation occurs rarely, these cases have the potential to become media spectacles. Perhaps the oddest case of self-representation was that of Colin Ferguson. Ferguson fired into a crowded Long Island Railroad commuter train, killing 6 passengers and wounding 19 others. Ferguson claimed that he acted out of a sense of "black rage;" his lawyer argued he was insane. Ferguson then dismissed his court-appointed lawyer, who objected that the trial would become a complete circus because "a crazy man cannot represent himself." The prediction proved accurate. During his opening statement Ferguson said there were "93 counts in the indictment, only because it matches the year 1993" (McQuiston 1995). Broadcast nationwide on CourtTV, the trial, with its inevitable guilty verdict, was perceived as not a trial but a spectacle and underscored the limits of self-representation. More recently, Dr. Jack Kevorkian represented himself in an assisted suicide case in Michigan, and Zacarias Moussaoui represented himself against charges that he was the 20th participant in the terrorist attack of September 11 (Chapter 3).

A recent case proved that the Court appears ready to limit self-representation in bizarre situations. The Court held that a **mentally ill defendant who is nonetheless competent to stand trial is not necessarily competent to dispense with a lawyer and represent himself** (*Indiana v. Edwards* 2008).

DEFENSE ATTORNEYS AND COURTROOM WORK GROUPS

Lawyers are expected to be advocates for their clients' cases, arguing for legal innocence. As one defense counsel phrased it, "If the attorney does not appear to be taking the side of the defendant, then no one will" (Neubauer 1974b, p. 73). But the zealous advocacy of a client's case is not the same thing as winning at all costs. As a member of the legal profession, a lawyer's advocacy of a client's case is limited by professional obligations. Like prosecutors, defense attorneys are officers of the court, who must fulfill their responsibilities within the framework established by legal ethics. They cannot deliberately mislead the court by providing false information. Nor can they knowingly allow the use of perjurious testimony.

Assessing how well lawyers represent their clients is difficult because of different ways of assessing the work performed. How do we define winning? Our popular culture suggests that winning means an acquittal. But experienced lawyers reject such simplistic notions. A veteran Los Angeles public defender explained:

> What is our job as a criminal lawyer in most instances? Number one is…no kidding, we know the man's done it, or we feel he's done it, he may deny it, but the question is: Can they prove it? The next thing is: Can we mitigate it? Of course you can always find something good to say about the guy—to mitigate it. Those are the two things that are important, and that's what you do. (Mather 1974b, p. 278)

Thus, many defense attorneys define winning in terms of securing probation, or accepting a plea to a misdemeanor. One attorney put it this way: "Given the situation, what is the best that can be done for my client?" (Neubauer 1974b, p. 74). At virtually all stages of the criminal justice process, defendants may have the guiding hand of counsel (see Exhibit 7.3).

How defense attorneys seek to reach the best solution possible for their client is directly related to their relationship with other members of the courtroom work group. Usually, assistant public defenders are permanently assigned to a single courtroom and work every day with the same judge, the same prosecutor(s), the same court reporter, and the same clerk of court. Similarly, private defense attorneys—although they practice before several judges—are a permanent fixture in the criminal courts, for a handful of lawyers dominate the representation of fee-paying criminal defendants in any city. This daily interaction of the criminal bar with the court community shapes the type and quality of legal representation received by those accused of violating the law. Whereas the adversary system stresses the combative role of the defense attorney, the day-to-day activities of the courtroom work group stress cooperation.

The legal system, civil and criminal, is based on controversy. Norms of cooperation work to channel such controversy into constructive avenues. All too often, advocacy is falsely equated with antagonism. Although defense attorneys exchange pleasantries with judges and prosecutors, their personal contacts with these officials outside the courtroom are limited (Mather 1974b).

Another qualification to bear in mind is that cooperative attorneys do not bargain every case; they also take cases to trial. If the defense attorney thinks the prosecutor is driving too hard a bargain or that the state cannot prove its case to the jury, a trial will be recommended. Furthermore, no evidence shows that cooperative attorneys do not argue the case to the best of their abilities during a trial.

REWARDS AND SANCTIONS

Defense attorneys who maintain a cooperative stance toward judges, prosecutors, and clerks can expect to reap some rewards. Defense attorneys have limited (in some instances, nonexistent) investigative resources. Prosecutors can provide cooperative defense attorneys with information about the cases by letting them examine the police reports, revealing the names of witnesses, and so on.

The court community can also apply sanctions to defense attorneys who violate the norms. Some sanctions work indirectly, by reducing a lawyer's income-generating ability. The clerk may refuse to provide beneficial case scheduling, or the judge may drag out a trial by continuously interrupting it for other business. Other sanctions are more direct. A judge can criticize a lawyer in front of his or her client (thus scaring away potential clients in the courtroom) or refuse to appoint certain attorneys to represent indigents—a significant source of income for some lawyers (Nardulli 1978). A final category of sanctions involves the prosecutor's adopting a tougher stance during bargaining by not reducing charges or by recommending a prison sentence that is longer than normal.

Sanctions against defense attorneys are seldom invoked, but when they are, they can have far-reaching effects. Every court community can point to an attorney who has suffered sanctions, with the result that the attorney either no longer practices criminal law in the area or has mended his or her ways.

VARIATIONS IN COOPERATION

Defense attorneys are the least powerful members of the courtroom work group. Because of the numerous sanctions that can be applied to defense attorneys, they are forced into a reactive posture.

Prosecutors assess a defense attorney in terms of "reasonableness"—that is, the ability to "discern a generous offer of settlement and to be willing to encourage his client to accept such an offer" (Skolnick 1967, p. 58). Based on this criterion, Skolnick put attorneys into three categories. One category consisted of defense attorneys who handled few criminal cases. One might suppose that prosecutors would prefer dealing with such inexperienced attorneys, but they did not. Because these attorneys did not know the ropes, they were too unpredictable and often caused administrative problems. In another category were attorneys who had active criminal practices and maintained a hostile relationship with the prosecutor's office. Known as "gamblers," these attorneys exemplified the aggressive, fighting advocate, but because they either won big or lost big, they also served to show the other attorneys the disadvantage of this posture. The final category of attorneys consisted of public defenders and private attorneys who represented large numbers of defendants. These attorneys worked within the system.

Exhibit 7.3		
ROLE OF DEFENSE ATTORNEY IN A TYPICAL FELONY CASE		
	LAW ON THE BOOKS	**LAW IN ACTION**
Crime		Counsels the client about the crime charged.
Arrest		Rarely present.
Initial appearance	Allowed to be present.	Typically advises client to say nothing during the court proceedings.
Bail	Argues for client's release on bail	Judge more likely to listen to the district attorney's (DA's) recommended bail.
Charging		May urge the prosecutor to charge the client with a less serious offense.
Preliminary hearing	Allowed to be present but typically cannot call witnesses.	Good opportunity to find out what really happened in the case.

	Exhibit 7.3 CONTINUED	
	LAW ON THE BOOKS	**LAW IN ACTION**
Grand jury	Only in some states may defense attorney be present.	Grand jury transcripts may be useful for discovery.
Arraign- ment	Allowed to be present.	Chance to talk to the client; may suggest entering a plea of guilty.
Evidence	Requests discovery information from the prosecutor; files motions to suppress confession and/or search and seizure.	Cooperative defense attorneys receive greater discovery information from the DA. Rarely successful in winning suppression motions.
Plea bargaining	Often a direct participant in plea discussions.	Negotiates for most beneficial deal possible.
Trial	Advocate for defendant's rights.	Typically stresses that the prosecutor has not proved the defendant "guilty beyond a reasonable doubt."
Sentencing	Makes a sentencing recommendation to the judge.	Argues for sentence at the low end of the normal penalty scale.
Appeal	Files notice of appeal and writes appellate brief.	Rarely successful on appeal.

AN ASSESSMENT

Are criminal defense attorneys, especially public defenders and regular private attorneys, the co-opted agents of a court bureaucracy or simply calculating realists? This question has been a preoccupation of research on defense attorneys for decades (Flemming 1986b).

Some studies argue that defense attorneys' ties to the court community mean that defendants' best interests are not represented. David Sudnow (1965) argued that public defenders became co-opted when public defenders and prosecutors shared common conceptions of what Sudnow called "normal crimes." Public defenders were more interested that a given case fit into a sociological cubbyhole than in determining whether the event met the proper penal code provisions. As a result, the public defenders seldom geared their work to securing acquittals for their clients. Thus, from the beginning, the presumption of guilt permeated the public defenders' assessment of cases. Similarly, Abraham Blumberg (1967b) concluded that all defense attorney regulars were double agents, working for both their client and the prosecutor. His study of a large New York court likened the practice of law to a confidence game, in which both the defendant and the defense attorney must have larceny at heart; a con game can be successful only if the "mark" is trying to get something for nothing. Judges and prosecutors depended on the defense attorneys to pressure defendants to plead guilty. In short, both Sudnow and Blumberg portray defense attorneys as ideological and as economic captives of the court rather than aggressive advocates.

However, other studies have concluded that defendants' best interests are not eroded when their attorneys adopt a cooperative posture within the courtroom community. Indeed, Jerome Skolnick (1967) suggested that the clients do better as a result of a cooperative posture. Working within the system benefits the client because the prosecutor will be more amenable to disclosing information helpful to the defense, the bargains struck will be more favorable, and the defendant will not be penalized for the hostility of the defense attorney. Furthermore, attorneys identified as agitators may harm their clients' causes because prosecutors and judges will hand out longer sentences. Neubauer's (1974a) study of Prairie City, Illinois, also found that attorneys who remained on good terms with other members of the courtroom work group functioned better as counselors, because they were better able to predict the reactions of the court community to individual cases. In short, the studies by Skolnick (1967), Neubauer (1974a), and Mather (1974b) concluded that attorneys who work within the system are better able to develop a realistic approach to their work, based on experience and knowledge of how their clients will fare.

Little evidence exists, then, that defense lawyers have been co-opted by the criminal justice system. Indeed, a study of what motivates pubic defenders reaches the opposite conclusion. Based on a study of 48 public defenders in three offices, Weiss (2005) concluded that public defenders are cynical about police, prosecutors, and judges. In the end, a skepticism that justice is being done motivates public defenders to vigorously defend their clients.

THE CRIMINAL BAR

Law offices of solo practitioners are a permanent feature of urban architecture. They can be found huddled around the stone edifice of the criminal courts and near the neon lights proclaiming "Harry's 24-Hour Bail Bonds." In Detroit, they are called "the Clinton Street Bar," and in Washington, D.C., "the Fifth Streeters"—titles that are not meant to be complimentary. These lawyers spend little time in their offices; they are most often at the courthouse, socializing with other members of the courtroom work group. Their proximity to the criminal courts and the sparseness of the law books in their offices are good indicators that the law practiced from these offices bears little resemblance to images of defense attorneys presented on television. A number of factors account for the low economic and professional status of the criminal bar.

DIVERSITY AND STRATIFICATION OF THE LEGAL PROFESSION

Law is a diverse profession based partially on the law school attended and the place of work. An interdisciplinary team, law professor John Heinz and sociologist Edward Laumann, conducted a comprehensive study of the diverse tasks that characterize the social role of lawyers. Based on extensive interviews with practicing attorneys, Heinz and Laumann (1982), in *Chicago Lawyers: The Social Structure of the Bar*, reported dramatic differences among several sorts of lawyers.

The most important differentiation within the legal profession involved which clients were served. Some lawyers represent large organizations (corporations, labor unions, or government). Others represent mainly individuals. By and large, lawyers operate in one of these two hemispheres of the profession; seldom, if ever, do they cross the line separating these very different types of legal work. The corporate client sector involves large corporate, regulatory, general corporate, and political lawyers. The personal client sector is divided into personal business and personal plight lawyers (divorce, tort, and so on).

Most of the attorneys who appear in criminal court are drawn from the personal-client sector. They are often referred to as "solo practitioners," because they practice alone or share an office with another attorney. For this group of courtroom regulars, criminal cases constitute a dominant part of their economic livelihood. Thus, studies of private attorneys in different cities report that the bulk of nonindigent defendants are represented by a handful of attorneys (Nardulli 1986; Neubauer 1974a).

ENVIRONMENT OF PRACTICE

It is no accident that in many large cities a distinct criminal bar exists. Low status, difficulty in securing clients, and low fees are three factors that affect the availability of lawyers to represent those accused of violating the law.

Most lawyers view criminal cases as unsavory. Representing criminal defendants also produces few chances for victory; most defendants either plead guilty or are found guilty by a judge or jury. Moreover, many lawyers who represent middle-class clients do not want accused drug peddlers brushing shoulders in the waiting room with their regular clients. Also, despite the legal presumption of innocence, once defendants are arrested, the public assumes they are

---

Exhibit 7.4

THINKING ABOUT GOING TO LAW SCHOOL?

If you are thinking about going to law school, here are some simple steps for using the Internet to help you decide if law school is really for you, and if so, how to get admitted.

Searching for Advice

Advice is plentiful on the Internet and also free. The American Bar Association, for example, offers a set of guidelines for preparing for law school, available online at http://www.abanet.org/legaled/prelaw. In addition, prelaw handbooks are available, including The University of Richmond's Prelaw Handbook at http://oncampus.richmond.edu/academics/as/polisci/prelaw/. Louisiana State University's Prelaw website offers good prelaw advice at http://www.artsci.lsu.edu/poli/prelaw.html.

Taking the LSAT

Information about when and where the Law School Admissions Test (LSAT) is offered is available at the website of the Law School Admission Council (LSAC): http://www.lsac.org. Even better, the LSAC offers a sample test for free. If you think you need help in preparing to sit for the exam, several commercial options are available, including Test-Master LSAT Preparation, http://www.testmasters180.com/; PowerScore Law School Preparation, http://www.powerscore.com/lsat/help/links_school.htm; and the Princeton Review, http://www.princetonreview.com/law/default.asp.

Choosing Which Law School to Attend

In deciding where to go to law school, a useful first stop is http://dir.yahoo.com/Government/Law/Law_Schools/, which provides links to hundreds of law schools. To find out which ones are accredited, make sure you look at The Official Guide to ABA Approved Law Schools, searchable by tuition, region, LSAT scores, and other variables at http://www.abanet.org/legaled/publications/officialguide.html. As for the debate over which law schools are the best, U.S. News and World Report publishes its annual rankings of law schools, readily available at http://www.usnews.com/usnews/edu/grad/rankings/law/lawindex_brief.php.

Applying to Law School

In applying to law school, it is a good idea to apply to several. The application forms are available from the website of the law school. In addition, the LSAC publishes a CD-ROM that includes the applications for many law schools (http://www.lsac.org). If you are interested in financial aid, make sure you visit The Access Group at http://www.accessgroup.org/. If you wonder what they teach in law school, check out this website of law school course outlines: http://www.ilrg.com/students/outlines/.

---

guilty. As a result, the general public perceives attorneys as freeing known robbers and rapists to return to the streets. "Realistically, a lawyer who defends notoriously unpopular clients becomes identified in the public's mind, and not infrequently in the mind of his own profession, with his client" (Kaplan 1973).

To earn a living, lawyers first need clients. Attorneys working in the personal-client sector of the legal profession seldom have a regular clientele. Accordingly, a part of their time is spent securing clients. The criminal lawyer's most important commodity in securing clients is his or her reputation, which often develops on the basis of the lawyer's handling of a specific case. A lawyer's reputation is important in several ways. First, defendants want a

specific attorney to represent them, not a firm of lawyers. Second, attorneys who do not practice criminal law often refer clients to a specific lawyer who does. Finally, a repeat offender may seek out the previous attorney, if he or she felt the lawyer provided good representation in the past. In securing clients, some defense attorneys rely on police officers, bail agents, and court clerks to give their names to defendants who need counsel (Wice 1978).

Obtaining clients is only half the problem facing private attorneys who represent criminal clients. The second half is getting paid. "Criminal lawyers are more concerned than other lawyers with collection of the fee—after all, their clients are mostly criminals" (Lushing 1992, p. 514). The lawyer's fee in a criminal case is generally a flat fee paid in advance. The three most important considerations in setting the fee are the seriousness of the offense, the amount of time it will take the lawyer to deal with the case, and the client's ability to pay. Well-known criminal lawyers, for example, often charge their prosperous clients considerable fees. In the words of a prominent New York City defense attorney, "Reasonable doubt begins with the payment of a reasonable fee" (Gourevitch 2001). The myth that criminal lawyers receive fabulous salaries is mostly untrue; although a few have become quite wealthy, most earn a modest middle-class living (Wice 1978). Of course, many defendants are so impoverished that they cannot afford to hire a private attorney at all.

Providing Indigents with Attorneys

Indigents are defendants who are too poor to pay a lawyer and therefore are entitled to a lawyer for free. Three quarters of state prison inmates had court-appointed lawyers to represent them for the offense for which they were serving time. In urban courthouses, the indigency rate is a little higher: 80 percent of felony defendants are too poor to hire their own lawyer (Smith and DeFrances 1996). Obviously, the Supreme Court's decision in *Gideon*, requiring the state to provide attorneys for indigents, applies to a substantial number of criminal defendants.

Although the Supreme Court has essentially mandated the development of indigent-defense systems, it has left the financing and type of delivery system up to states and counties, which have considerable discretion in adopting programs (Worden and Worden 1989). As with other aspects of the American dual court system, the characteristics of defense systems for the indigent vary considerably, with some state governments funding virtually all indigent criminal defense services, other state government sharing the financial costs of providing counsel with counties, and still others jurisdictions in which county funds are used exclusively (DeFrances 2001).

How best to provide legal representation for the poor has been a long-standing vital issue for the courts and the legal profession. In the United States, the three primary methods are assigned counsel (attorneys appointed by the judge on a case-by-case basis), contract systems (attorneys hired to provide services for a specified dollar amount), and public

defender (a salaried public official representing all indigent defendants). The ongoing debate over the advantages and disadvantages of these three systems highlights some important issues about the quality of legal representation provided the poor.

Assigned Counsel

The assigned counsel system reflects the way professions such as law and medicine traditionally respond to charity cases: Individual practitioners provide services on a case-by-case basis. **Assigned counsel systems** involve the appointment by the court of private attorneys from a list of available attorneys. The list may consist of all practicing attorneys in the jurisdiction or, more commonly, the attorneys who volunteer. The assigned counsel system is used in half of all U.S. counties but serves less than one third of the nation's population. It predominates in small counties, those with fewer than 50,000 residents, where an insufficient volume of cases exists to support the costs of a public defender system.

Critics contend that the assigned counsel system results in the least-qualified lawyers being appointed to defend indigents. In most counties, the only attorneys who volunteer are either young ones seeking courtroom experience or those who seek numerous appointments to make a living. Even where appointments are rotated among all members of the practicing bar (as in New Jersey and in Houston, Texas), no guarantee exists that the lawyer selected is qualified to handle the increasing complexity of the criminal law; the appointee may be a skilled real estate attorney or a good probate attorney, but these skills are not readily transferable to the dynamics of a criminal trial.

The availability of lawyers willing to serve as assigned counsel is directly related to financial compensation. In the past, a number of jurisdictions expected attorneys to represent indigents as part of their professional responsibility, without being paid (**pro bono**). Today, however, the majority of assigned counsel are paid. Most commonly, lawyers are compensated for such defense work on the basis of separate hourly rates for out-of-court and in-court work. However, hourly fees for in-court felony work usually range far below the fees charged in private practice. Critics contend that inadequate compensation pressures attorneys to dispose of such cases quickly in order to devote time to fee-paying clients.

The widely held assumption that rates of compensation are directly related to the quality of criminal defense representation has been challenged

Courts, Controversy, and Economic Inequality

Are We Spending Too Little or Too Much on Indigent Defense?

"No more. We can't ethically handle this many cases" argues David Carrol of the National Legal Aid and Defender Association. At issue are rising caseloads of public defenders coupled with shrinking governmental budgets caused by the economic downturn beginning in 2008. Typical is Florida's Miami–Dade County, where the public defender's office has refused to accept any new lesser-felony cases so they can concentrate on defending current clients (Eckhom 2008). These lawsuits are hardly new. To mark the 40th anniversary of *Gideon v. Wainwright*, Quitman County, an impoverished area of the Mississippi Delta, filed an unusual lawsuit contending that the county was too poor to provide indigent defendants with anything more than assembly-line justice. At issue was who should pay for public defenders. To the county board, it is the state's responsibility to pay these expenses. But officials of the state countered that its budget was in dire straits, and therefore it was unable to afford such services (Liptak 2003). What is new, though, is that the number of such lawsuits is growing. Moreover, some jurisdictions are curtailing death penalty prosecutions because local governments cannot afford the rising cost of an adequate defense in death-penalty cases (Dewan and Goodman 2007).

Lawsuits over funding indigent defense illustrate important ideological differences over court-appointed counsel. Although all camps agree that basic notions of equity and fairness require that indigents have counsel during trial, the scope of this right is disputed. Crime control advocates are concerned that the government spends too much money on providing the poor with lawyers, whereas due process proponents are worried that the government is spending too little.

Crime Control Perspective: We Spend Too Much

Crime control proponents are concerned that the government is paying too much for indigent defense. Indeed, in 1999, the last year for which figures are available, the 100 most populous counties in the nation spent an estimated $1.2 billion to provide indigent criminal defense. Over the years, the cost of providing defense services for the indigent has increased dramatically, tripling between 1982 and 1999 (DeFrances 2001). Hardest hit by the expansion of legal rights and the consequent increase in costs have been local governments and, secondarily, state governments. Indeed, the burden is highest in communities with the greatest needs and fewest resources—those with high crime rates and large populations of the poor.

As expenditures for defense services for the indigent have risen dramatically, there has been a noticeable trend toward containing the costs. One technique is the adoption of stringent indigency standards. Traditionally, big-city judges rarely inquired into the financial capabilities of

by one study. The extent of effort of lawyers in Michigan who handled appellate representation did not vary significantly in relation to the rate of compensation. Overall, professional role expectations of lawyers may be of greater influence on their work than financial considerations (Priehs 1999).

Contract Systems

Contract systems are a relatively new way to provide defense services. A **contract system** involves bidding by private attorneys to represent all criminal defendants found indigent during the term of the contract, in return for a fixed payment (Worden 1991; 1993). Contract systems are most often found in counties with populations of fewer than 50,000, where the key feature is that they place an absolute budget limit on defense services for the indigent.

The primary advantage of contract systems is that they limit the costs government must pay for indigent defense. Critics counter with two types of concerns. The first is that contract programs will

defendants to determine whether they satisfy the court's definition of indigency. However, a report funded by the National Institute of Justice stresses that courts should screen applications "to ensure that only the truly indigent are provided representation at public expense" (Spangenberg et al. 1986, p. 69).

Another way of containing government expenses is cost recovery. In screening applications for defense services for the indigent, many courts now distinguish between defendants so poor that they are exempt from paying any costs of their defense and a new category of "partially indigent" defendants who may be able to pay a portion of the costs (Lee 1992). Thus, some jurisdictions try to collect contributions from the partially indigent prior to disposition of the case. "From a practical standpoint, defendants appear to be more willing to voluntarily contribute to their costs of representation before disposition than being requested to pay after entering a plea or having been found guilty" (Spangenberg et al. 1986, p. 70).

Due Process Perspective: We Spend Too Little

Due process advocates, on the other hand, are concerned that the government is spending too little on indigent defense. Typical is a *Chicago Tribune* editorial, headlined "Paying for Justice" (2000), which argued that it "is not too much to say that many poor people are in prison who would be free

if they had the legal representation that many affluent people do—and vice versa."

From the perspective of the due process model, oppressive caseloads are the single greatest obstacle to effective representation (Gershman 1993). Underfunding indigent defense produces high caseloads. The National Advisory Commission on Criminal Justice Standards and Goals recommends that a maximum effective felony caseload per attorney per year be 150 cases. Yet in many jurisdictions it is typically much higher, sometimes approaching 1,000 clients per year (Cauchon 1999). Such high caseloads undermine the ability of lawyers to even meet their clients in a timely fashion.

Forty years after *Gideon*, the American Bar Association (2004) concluded that indigent defense in the United States remains in a state of crisis, resulting in a system that lacks fundamental fairness and places poor persons at constant risk of wrongful conviction. The lack of attorneys available to defend death row inmates is a major point of contention regarding the death penalty (see Chapters 15 and 17). Overall, the issue of funding indigent defense has become a pressing problem in many states. In the wake of the economic downturn of the early 21st century, state after state has often been forced to reduce funding for indigent defense.

What do you think? Should government be spending less money or more money on court-appointed counsel for the indigent?

inevitably lead to a lower standard of representation through the bidding system, which emphasizes cost over quality. The second is that the private bar will no longer play an important role in indigent defense (Spangenberg Group 2000).

The contract system was held unconstitutional in Arizona when the Arizona Supreme Court held that the Mohave County contract system, which assigned defense representation of the indigent to the lowest bidder, violated the Fifth and Sixth Amendments because the system: (1) did not take into account the time

the attorney is expected to spend on a case, (2) did not provide for support staff costs, (3) failed to take into account the competence of the attorney, and (4) did not consider the complexity of the case (*Smith v. State* 1984). Likewise, courts in several other states have found legal defects in contract systems that result in inadequate funding levels (Spangenberg Group 2000). Skepticism that contract systems actually save money is growing. Several jurisdictions have been frustrated by contract firms submitting increasingly higher budgets after their initial low bids (Wice 2005).

PUBLIC DEFENDER

The **public defender** is a 20th-century response to the problem of providing legal representation for the indigent. Public defender programs are public or private nonprofit organizations with full- or part-time salaried staff who represent indigents in criminal cases in a jurisdiction.

Started in Los Angeles County in 1914, public defender offices spread slowly. By 1965, the National Legal Aid and Defender Association—the national organization that promotes better legal representation for indigents in civil as well as criminal cases—reported programs in only 117 counties. Since 1965, public defender programs have spread rapidly because of Supreme Court decisions (*Gideon* and later *Argersinger*), as well as increased concern for more-adequate representation of indigents. Today, the public defender system represents approximately 70 percent of all indigents nationwide. It predominates in most big cities and has also been adopted in numerous medium-sized jurisdictions. Seventeen states have established statewide, state-funded programs. The remaining public defender programs are funded by local units of government and operate autonomously, with no central administration (DeFrances and Litras 2000).

Proponents of the public defender system cite several arguments in favor of its adoption. One is that a lawyer paid to represent indigents on a continuous basis will devote more attention to cases than a court-appointed attorney who receives only minimal compensation. Moreover, many members of the practicing bar like the idea that they no longer have to take time away from fee-paying cases to meet their professional obligations.

A second advantage often claimed for the public defender system is that it provides more experienced, competent counsel. Because public defenders concentrate on criminal cases, they can keep abreast of changes in the law, and the day-to-day courtroom work keeps their trial skills sharp. The public defender is also likely to be more knowledgeable about informal norms and is therefore in a better position to counsel defendants and negotiate the best possible deal.

Finally, a public defender system ensures continuity and consistency in the defense of the poor (Silverstein 1965). Public defenders are usually able to provide early representation, entering the case at the initial appearance. Moreover, issues that transcend individual cases—criteria for pretrial release, police practices, and so forth—are more likely to be considered by a permanent, ongoing organization than under appointment systems.

ASSESSING THE MERITS OF PUBLIC DEFENDERS

Critics contend that public defenders—as paid employees of the state—will not provide a vigorous defense because they are tied too closely to the courtroom work group. Several studies have investigated this concern by comparing the adequacy of representation provided by assigned counsel to that of public defenders' offices. The dominant conclusion is that there is not much difference (Flemming 1989; Wice 1985; Eisenstein, Flemming, and Nardulli 1988). The National Center for State Courts drew the following conclusions from the nine jurisdictions it studied: (1) Attorneys for indigent defendants resolved their cases more expeditiously than did privately retained counsel. (2) Defense attorneys for the indigent gained as many favorable outcomes (acquittals, charge reductions, and short prison sentences) for their clients as privately retained attorneys did for their clients. (3) Indigent defense attorneys and prosecuting attorneys were equally experienced (Hanson, Hewitt, and Ostrom 1992). Likewise, the outcomes of criminal appeals do not vary between public defenders and privately retained counsel (Williams 1995).

The Public Defender: The Practice of Law in the Shadows of Repute offers a radically different view of public defense attorneys. In this book, Lisa McIntyre (1987) demonstrated that public defense lawyers are indeed free to defend their clients zealously. She found that in the courts of Cook County, Illinois, public defenders are adversarial and even combative opponents of the state's prosecutorial apparatus. McIntyre argues, in fact, that the office of the public defender survives because its effective advocacy for its clients bolsters the legitimacy of the court system.

Why, then, does the public defender's image not reflect this? The freedom to defend against the state cannot include the freedom to embarrass it. Hence, the complexity of the public defender's institutional role requires that the office not advertise its successes. McIntyre shows that the public defender's office deliberately retains its image of incompetency in order to guarantee its continued existence. Public defenders may practice good law, but they must do it in the darker shadows of repute.

The long-standing debate over the adequacy of court-appointed counsel is beginning to give way to a new reality—large governmental expenses. Images and myths play a central role in the debate over funding levels for court-appointed lawyers (see Courts, Controversy, and Economic Inequality: Are We Spending Too Little or Too Much on Indigent Defense?).

The vast majority of public defender agencies attempt to survive from one crisis to the next amid a perpetual flux of inexperienced lawyers. In response to the perpetual problems of the traditional agencies, some reform defender agencies have emerged. *Public Defenders and the American Justice System* by Paul Wice (2005) focuses on one reform defender system—Essex County (Newark), New Jersey. These reform agencies strive to maintain a group of experienced lawyers by emphasizing their independence from any political or judicial influence. One of their hallmarks is stressing the importance of one-on-one representation for each client.

LAWYERS AND CLIENTS

One of the most important tasks of defense attorneys is counseling. As advocates, defense attorneys are expected to champion their clients' cases. But as counselors, they must advise their clients about the possible legal consequences involved. Lawyers must fully and dispassionately evaluate the strengths and weaknesses of the prosecutor's case, assess the probable success of various legal defenses, and—most important—weigh the likelihood of conviction or acquittal. In appraising risks and outlining options, lawyers interpret the law to their clients, who are often unversed in what the law considers important and what the law demands.

To be an effective advocate and counselor, the lawyer must know all the facts of a case. For this reason, the American legal system surrounds the attorney–client relationship with special protections. Statements made by a client to his or her attorney are considered **privileged communication**, which the law protects from forced disclosure without the client's consent. The attorney–client privilege extends not only to statements made by the client but also to any work product developed in representing the client.

Based on trust and a full exchange of information, the attorney assumes the difficult task of advocating a client's case. In civil litigation, the relationship between lawyer and client is often (but not always) characterized by trust and full disclosure (Cox 1993).

In criminal cases, however, the relationship is more likely to be marked by distrust and hostility. Indeed, more than half of defendants are described by their attorneys as passive participants in the overall defense, and 10 percent are described by their attorneys as recalcitrant—that is, rarely or never accepting the attorney's advice (Bonnie et al. 1996).

In the modern era, high caseloads clearly complicate the ability of lawyers, particularly those appointed by the court to represent indigents, to find time to talk with clients. In the book *Indefensible: One Lawyer's Journey into the Inferno of American Justice*, David Feige reflected on days in court when he was unable to make court appearances because he was busy elsewhere. Given a caseload ranging from 75 to 120 active cases, "the simple matter of where to be when becomes one of the most complicated and taxing puzzles we face. It's not unusual to have six, eight, or even ten different courtrooms to go to in a single day" (Feige 2006, p. 87). And on some days, an unexpectedly lengthy appearance in one courtroom means that a lawyer will be unable to meet with a client in another courtroom. In short, becoming a good client manager is something that every public defender has to learn.

LAWYERS' VIEWS ON THEIR CLIENTS

Getting along with clients is one of the most difficult tasks of public defenders. One veteran New York City public defender recounts the lecture he received from his boss early on. "If you're working this job looking for appreciation, you're never gonna last," she said. Instead it has to come from inside "even though we lose and lose, and we get creamed every day…you have to wake up the next morning and fight your heart out, looking for those few times we can stop it" (Feige 2006, p. 33). Nonetheless, client disrespect irritates attorneys and sours their associations with clients. As one public defender complained, "It is frustrating to have to constantly sell yourself" to clients. "The standard joke around this county is, 'Do you want a public defender or a real attorney?'" (Flemming 1986a, pp. 257–258). Many eventually leave the job because of the difficulty of dealing with their clients (Platt and Pollock 1974).

Refusal to cooperate, deception, and dishonesty are serious problems public attorneys face in dealing with their clients (Flemming 1986a). At times, defendants tell their attorneys implausible stories, invent alibis, or withhold key information. A veteran public defender observed that in drug cases, the clients all had the same defense—they left home to buy milk or Pampers for the baby. In the end, "when you've heard every defense a thousand times, true or not, they can all start to sound like bullshit" (Feige 2006, p. 228). The defendant's lack of candor greatly complicates the job of the attorney in representing him or her. Evasions and deceptions can affect tactical and strategic decisions.

Lynn Mather (1974b) described a case in which a public defender went to trial at the request of a client who claimed she had no prior record. To the attorney's surprise, the defendant's presentence report revealed that she had a 5-year history of similar crimes. She was sentenced to prison. The public defender said that his client "fooled everyone." The lack of trust in the attorney–client relationship may stem from the necessity for the lawyer to prepare the client for less than total victory. The defense attorney may at some point have to inform the defendant that imprisonment is a likely result, given the crime, prior record, facts of the case, and so forth. Since defendants involved in the criminal process often do not look beyond the present, postponing bad news from day to day, such statements are not to their liking. Preparing the client for the possibility of conviction clashes with traditional notions that the attorney should always win.

Ultimately, it is the defendant's choice whether to accept the attorney's advice to plead guilty or to go to trial. Lawyers differ in their ability to influence their clients. Private attorneys find their advice accepted more readily than court-appointed lawyers do. This difference in part reflects the type of commitment the defendant has made. The indigent defendant has no choice in receiving the services of a public defender or assigned counsel, whereas defendants with private attorneys have a choice and have shown their commitment by paying a fee.

DEFENDANTS' VIEWS ON THEIR LAWYERS

Public clients are skeptical about the skills of their lawyers and are worried about whose side the lawyers are on. Thus, many defendants view their lawyers, whether public or private, with suspicion, if not bitterness. This is particularly the case with court-appointed attorneys, whom many defendants consider the same as any other government-paid attorney. Some defendants think that public defenders will not work hard on their cases because they are paid whether or not they win. To others, the defense attorney has ambitions to become a judge or prosecutor and therefore does not want to antagonize the court system by fighting too hard. Overall, then, many defendants view the public defender as no different from the prosecutor. In prison, PD stands not for "public defender" but for "prison deliverer." In what has become a classic statement, a Connecticut prisoner responded to Jonathan Casper's (1972) question as to whether he had a lawyer when he went to court with the barbed comment, "No, I had a public defender."

A partial explanation for a breakdown of trust between the client and public defender involves the absence of one-to-one contact. Most public defenders' offices are organized on a zone basis. Attorneys are assigned to various courtrooms and/or responsibilities—initial appearance, preliminary hearing, trial sections, and so on. Each defendant sees several public defenders, all of whom are supposed to be working for him or her. This segmented approach to representation for indigents decreases the likelihood that a bond of trust will develop between attorney and client. It also increases the probability that some defendants will be overlooked—that no attorney will work on their cases or talk to them. One can certainly understand the frustration of this 33-year-old accused murderer with no previous record:

> "I figured that with he being my defense attorney, that as soon as that grand jury was over—because he's not allowed in the hearing—that he would call me and then want to find out what went on. After that grand jury I never saw him for two months." "You stayed in jail?" "Yeah." (Casper 1972, p. 8)

Clearly, not all defendants' criticisms of their attorneys are valid. But valid or not, defendants' lack of trust and confidence in their lawyers is a major force in shaping the dynamics of courthouse justice. Defendants try to con their attorneys, and the lawyers respond by exhibiting disbelief when defendants state unrealistic expectations or invent implausible alibis. For an attorney, failure to gain "client control" can lead to a bad reputation in the courthouse and jeopardize his or her own position within the courtroom work group (Eisenstein, Flemming, and Nardulli 1988).

DEFENSE ATTORNEY ETHICS

Lawyers occupy an ambiguous position in American society. They are admired and respected because of their wealth and influence and at the same time

LAW AND POPULAR CULTURE

Boston Legal (ABC Television, 2004—2008)

Welcome to the law firm of Crane, Poole, & Schmidt, the fictional firm at the heart of *Boston Legal*. While the plots of many episodes differ, most of the story lines center around Alan Shore (played by James Spader), an ethically challenged attorney who, with the help of Denny Crane (played by William Shatner), a senior partner in the firm, gains recognition as an attorney of last resort—the guy who can win cases that no other attorney in private practice would ever want to take. Crane, however, possesses an eccentric personality and engages in bizarre conduct as a function of being in early stages of Alzheimer's. Shirley Schmidt (played by Candice Bergen) is the firm's star litigator and managing partner. In that latter role, she not only has to make major decisions for the firm, but also has to supervise the questionable behaviors of the arrogant and narcissistic team of Shore and Crane.

Crane's own outrageous behavior helps to mentor Shore in his unethical ways. Indeed, it becomes clear that Shore's knack for winning is a function of his highly questionable methods. Shore will not "let trivial things like honesty and integrity get in the way of winning a case" (Smitts 2004). For example, in one episode, he had an unlicensed physician remove a potentially life-threatening bullet from a client who had refused to seek medical treatment in a hospital for fear that the evidence gathered through traditional medical channels would lead to his being criminally convicted.

Television portrayals of fictional lawyers like Alan Shore and Denny Crane create unreasonable expectations in viewers who may need to hire a lawyer. After all, who would not want to be represented by an attorney-gladiator ready to "fight the battle for them" (Slocum 2009, p. 516)? But such expectations are not realistic. In real life, attorneys who practiced law the way Alan Shore and Denny Crane did on *Boston Legal* would find themselves in a lot a trouble with judges and their state bar association. Lawyers are bound by codes of professional responsibility and the rules of court to behave in ways that conform to a set of legal ethics.

Despite the media portrayal of lawyers as angry, avenging gladiators, such a role is less common than most clients think…. But in real life, lawyers like the ones we see on TV and in the movies often end up costing their clients money—that kind of "litigation-as-war" mentality usually ratchets up the attacks and counter-attacks, with the clients becoming even angrier and more frustrated as the litigation escalates into all-out war. And the end result is not only that the lawsuit ends up costing both parties a lot of money in legal fees, but also that clients often end up pretty unhappy with the whole legal process, even if they end up getting much of what they wanted in terms of a financial outcome. Far from getting the justice they wanted and believe they deserve, they end up feeling that the legal system let them down (Slocum 2009, p. 517).

After watching one or more episodes of *Boston Legal*, be prepared to discuss the following questions:

1. Do you think that depictions of the lawyers on *Boston Legal* contribute to the image of unethical criminal defense attorneys? Explain your reasoning.

2. Alan Shore and Denny Crane are just two examples of the media depicting the "win at all costs" defense attorney. Sebastian Stark on *Shark* is another. What other examples of unethical defense attorneys can you find in popular culture?

3. The fictional defense attorneys of yesterday, like Perry Mason, Matlock, or Atticus Finch in *To Kill a Mockingbird* were consistently depicted as highly ethical attorneys who won cases not by ignoring the rules of professional responsibility, but rather by exercising their superior lawyering skills with uncompromised integrity. Why do you think that media portrayals of fictional defense attorneys have changed so much in a generation or two? What, if anything, does this say about the legal profession?

distrusted for the very same reasons. These contradictory assessments are reflected in myths about lawyers as either heroes or villains (Wolfram 1986). Popular culture often portrays lawyers as heroes who valiantly protect clients falsely accused or depicts attorneys as villains for going too far in defending the obviously guilty. Discussions of good lawyers and bad lawyers invariably focus on legal ethics. But this focus often reflects considerable misunderstanding about what lawyers do and what legal ethics is all about.

Years ago I was in an Illinois courtroom talking with a top police official. When asked what was wrong with the criminal justice system, he singled out a specific defense attorney. "We arrest the guilty, but he gets them off on a technicality," he opined. Less than a week later, a police officer in his department was accused of manslaughter for shooting an unarmed youth. The police association immediately hired that same lawyer to defend the indicted officer. This saga illustrates the duality of viewpoints about attorneys and perceived ethical problems. More so than the other lawyers in the criminal justice process, defense attorneys are most often identified as having ethical issues.

Defending unpopular clients is the basis for a great deal of criticism of lawyers. People often ask, "How can you defend a person like that?"—a question that implies that the lawyers' actions are an offense to morality. But at the core of legal ethics is the notion that every party is entitled to legal representation, even unpopular defendants who have committed heinous crimes or defendants whose guilt is overwhelming. The American Civil Liberties Union is unpopular with the public because it is typically at the forefront of representing unpopular groups like the American Nazi Party or the Ku Klux Klan.

Zealous advocacy is another bedrock of legal ethics. Lawyers are expected to be diligent in asserting valid defenses for their clients. However, this ethical standard does not mean that the lawyers must always do what their clients say. Lawyers are professionals bound by ethical rules of the profession. Within this parameter, people often support the zealous advocacy of their own lawyers, while objecting that the advocacy of opposing counsel goes too far. Conversely, defendants often complain that they lacked competent counsel, which typically translates into a complaint that the jury found me guilty.

Confidentiality is another key component of legal ethics. Based on the attorney–client privilege, the lawyer may not voluntarily disclose what the client confided. Nor may judges, prosecutors, or other officers of the court typically force such disclosure. Holding to this principle may expose the lawyer to charges of obstruction of justice. Consider the case of a client who provided his lawyer a diagram of where he buried the kidnapped baby: The lawyer was severely criticized for failing to show the police where the body was buried. (Eventually, a Texas judge ruled that the facts of the case constituted a valid exception to attorney–client privilege.) (Dzienkowski and Burton 2006)

Use of perjurious or misleading testimony is another ethical issue facing defense attorneys (and sometimes prosecutors as well). On the one hand, a lawyer may be reluctant to refuse clients' efforts to present their defense, but on the other hand, as officers of the court, lawyers may not knowingly allow the use of perjured testimony. If lawyers cannot talk their clients out of taking the stand (particularly if the lawyer thinks that the client is now making the situation worse because the jury will not believe the testimony), lawyers have been known to tell the judge in chambers about the situation and let the client testify without the lawyer's help.

Potential conflict of interest is a key ethical issue facing lawyers. Attorneys are prohibited from engaging in representation that would compromise their loyalty to their clients. The most common problem found in the day-to-day practice of law in the criminal courts involves representing two clients who have opposing interests. In a murder case involving more than one defendant, for example, a lawyer may represent only one defendant because the defense might seek to lay the blame solely on another defendant. On the civil side, a lawyer who has represented a couple in various legal matters may be ethically prohibited from representing either party in a divorce proceeding because the lawyer may have learned important details of the couples' finances or other confidential matters.

Lawyers who fail to properly represent their clients may be sued for civil damages (Chapter 2). For this reason, lawyers carry legal malpractice insurance. It is important to stress, though, that lawyers are liable only in very limited situations. Just because a lawyer loses a case does not mean that the lawyer is incompetent.

CONCLUSION

From the bleak perspective of his prison cell, Clarence Gideon had no way of knowing that his petition to the Supreme Court would have the impact it did. Overnight, Gideon went from defending himself to having Abe Fortas—one of the nation's most prestigious lawyers—represent him. Following the Supreme Court reversal of his conviction, Clarence Earl Gideon was given a new trial. His court-appointed lawyer discovered evidence suggesting that the man who had accused Gideon of burglarizing the poolroom had himself committed the crime. Moreover, as a result of the *Gideon* decision, thousands of other prison inmates in Florida and elsewhere were freed.

Nor could Gideon have realized that his name would become associated with a landmark Supreme Court decision. He achieved no small degree of legal immortality. His case was chronicled by *New York Times* reporter Anthony Lewis (1972)

in the book *Gideon's Trumpet*. *Gideon v. Wainwright* transformed the law, signaling a due process revolution in the rights of criminal defendants. Gideon himself was not transformed, however. He avoided any more major brushes with the law, but he died penniless on January 18, 1972, in Ft. Lauderdale, Florida.

The travails of Clarence Earl Gideon illustrate the importance of legal access to the justice system. Perhaps nowhere else is there a greater contrast between the images and the realities of the criminal court process than in the activities of the defense attorney. Unlike fictional defense attorneys, who always defend innocent clients successfully, most defense attorneys deal with a steady stream of defendants who are in fact guilty, and their representation focuses on plea bargaining.

CHAPTER REVIEW

1. Interpret the four major legal issues surrounding the right to counsel.

After *Gideon v. Wainwright* established a right to counsel for indigent felony defendants, courts have wrestled with four areas: (1) right to counsel in nonfelony prosecutions, (2) stages of the criminal process, (3) ineffective assistance of counsel, and (4) self-representation.

2. Discuss how the courtroom work group affects how defense attorneys represent their clients.

Lawyers who work within the parameters of the courtroom work group receive benefits for their clients, including more case information from prosecutors and perhaps better plea bargains. Lawyers who are less cooperative find that they do not get favorable case scheduling considerations and less favorable plea bargains.

3. Explain why most lawyers do not represent criminal defendants.

Most lawyers practice civil law because it is more lucrative, they have higher prestige, and have fewer problems dealing with clients.

4. Compare and contrast the three systems of providing indigents with court-appointed attorneys.

The three major ways of providing indigents with court appointed attorneys are: (1) assigned counsel, (2) contract systems, and (3) public defender. Studies find no major differences between these three systems in results achieved.

5. Recognize possible tensions between lawyers and clients.

Lawyers sometimes view their clients as not telling them the whole truth about a case and at times seeking to manipulate their lawyers. Defendants may view their attorneys as not fighting hard enough for them and seeking to accommodate the judge and prosecutor.

6. Analyze the importance of legal ethics to the defense of criminal defendants.

Legal ethics seek to ensure that lawyers will zealously advocate for their client. Lawyers must assert valid defense and ensure confidentially. But legal ethics places professional limits on how far that advocacy may go, including not using perjured or misleading testimony.

CRITICAL THINKING QUESTIONS

1. The public generally views defense attorneys as too zealous in their advocacy of obviously guilty clients, while many scholars portray an image of defense attorneys, particularly public defenders, as too willing to plead their clients guilty. What do you think? What evidence would you cite for either position?

2. In what ways have contemporary decisions by the U.S. Supreme Court modified the original meaning of the Sixth Amendment? Is the original intent of the Sixth Amendment relevant in today's world?

3. What factors hinder a defense attorney in his or her attempt to protect the rights of the defendant? Think of both system factors and individual ones.

4. What are the major contrasts in the workaday world of private defense attorneys and court-appointed lawyers?

5. Should all attorneys be required to provide pro bono defense for indigents? Would such activities improve the image of the bar? Would such activities be in the best interests of the defendants?

6. If you were arrested, which would you rather have, a private lawyer or a public defender?

KEY TERMS

assigned counsel system 173	privileged communication 177	right to counsel 163
contract system 174	public defender 176	
indigents 173	pro se 167	

WEB RESOURCES

Go to the America's Courts and the Criminal Justice System companion website at

www.cengage.com/criminaljustice/neubauer

where you will find more resources to help you study.

Resources include web exercises, quizzing, and flash cards.

FOR FURTHER READING

Clarke, Cait, and Christopher Stone. *Bolder Management for Public Defense: Leadership in Three Dimensions*. Boston: Harvard University, John F. Kennedy School of Government, Bulletin #1, 2001.

Davis, Kevin. *Defending the Damned: Inside Chicago's Cook County Public Defender's Office*. New York: Atria, 2007.

Etienne, Margareth. "The Ethics of Cause Lawyering: An Empirical Examination of Criminal Defense Lawyers as Cause Lawyers." *Journal of Criminal Law and Criminology* 95: 1195, 2005.

Gould, Jon. "Indigent Defense—A Poor Measure of Justice." *Judicature* 92: 131, 2008.

Klebanow, Diana, and Franklin Jonas. *People's Lawyers: Crusaders for Justice in American History*. Armonk, NY: M. E. Sharpe, 2003.

Schrager, Sam. *The Trial Lawyer's Art*. Philadelphia: Temple University Press, 1999.

Seron, Carroll. *The Business of Practicing Law: The Work Lives of Solo and Small-Firm Attorneys*. Philadelphia: Temple University Press, 1996.

The Spangenberg Group. *Keeping Defender Workloads Manageable*. Washington, DC: Bureau of Justice Statistics, 2001.

Williams, Marian. "A Comparison of Sentencing Outcomes for Defendants with Public Defenders versus Retained Counsel in 'Florida Circuit Court.'" *Justice System Journal* 23: 249–258, 2002.

8

JUDGES

Texas judge Belinda Hill listens to lawyers representing Andrea Yates in her retrial on homicide charges for drowning her five children in a bathtub. Yates was found not guilty by reason of insanity and committed to the maximum-security North Texas State Hospital in Vernon, Texas. Verdicts in high-profile cases like this one often lead to a debate over the role of a judge, including whether judges should be elected or appointed. Although the public often holds judges responsible for all that happens in a courtroom, in reality, judges are often limited by the actions (and inactions) of the other members of the courtroom work group.

Chapter Outline

The Position of Judge
Powers of the Judge
Benefits of the Job
Frustrations of the Job
Law and Popular Culture
Judge Judy

Judges within the Courtroom Work Group

Varying Roads to a Judgeship
Executive Appointments
Election of Judges
Merit Selection

Consequences of Judicial Selection
Which System Is Best?
Similarities in Judges' Backgrounds
Diversity and the Judiciary
Case Close-Up
Chisom v. Roemer and Diversity on the Bench
Courts, Controversy, and the Administration of Justice
Is Judicial Independence Being Undermined?

Judging the Judges
Judicial Independence
Judicial Misconduct

State Judicial Conduct Commissions
Federal Conduct and Disability Act

Judicial Ethics

Conclusion

Chapter Review

Learning Objectives

After reading this chapter, you should be able to:

1. Discuss the role of the judge within the courtroom work group.

2. Name the three major ways that judges are selected in the United States.

3. Analyze the consequences of different methods of judicial selection.

4. Recognize major changes in the composition of the bench over the past several decades.

5. Describe the activities of state judicial conduct commissions.

6. Explain the difference between the impeachment and the removal of a federal judge.

Fact or Fiction?

- Facing a $50 million verdict for fraudulent business practices, a coal executive spends $3 million to support a candidate for a seat on the West Virginia Supreme Court; the candidate wins and then casts the deciding vote to overturn the verdict.

- Facing a multimillion-dollar verdict in a toxic waste case, a large chemical company secretly finances a candidate for the Mississippi Supreme Court who is likely to rule in its favor.

One of these cases is based on a recent U.S. Supreme Court decision; the other on the plot of *The Appeal* by popular fiction writer John Grisham (2008), who is also a lawyer. And Grisham admits that his novel is at least partially inspired by the real case. This blending of fact and fiction, life imitating art, offers a very public example of the long-standing debate in the United States over how best to select judges. Should judges be elected directly by the voters, appointed by an elected official (president or governor), or selected by a hybrid system that gives lawyers a direct role in the process?

The debate over how to select judges underscores the important role of the judge in the American legal system. The purpose of this chapter is to untangle the conflicting notions about what judges do and how they do it. The chapter begins by examining the position of judge and how various pressures (the large number of cases, for example) have eroded the ideal image of a judge's power. Next, the judge will be considered as a member of the courtroom community. A judge's actions are shaped and influenced by the actions of prosecutors and defense attorneys, among others. At the same time, the type of justice handed out varies from one judge to another. A persistent concern is whether judges are as qualified as they should be. Therefore, two suggestions for improving the quality of the judiciary will be examined: merit selection and mechanisms for removing unfit judges. The role of judicial ethics will also be examined.

THE POSITION OF JUDGE

For most Americans, the judge is the symbol of justice. Of all the actors in the criminal justice process, the public holds the judge most responsible for ensuring that the system operates fairly and impartially. And most certainly the trappings of office—the flowing black robes, the gavel, and the command "All rise!" when the judge enters the courtroom—reinforce this mystique. As important as these symbols are, they sometimes raise obstacles to understanding what judges actually do and how they influence the criminal justice process.

The vast array of legal powers often causes us to overestimate the actual influence of the judge by ignoring the importance of the other actors in the courtroom work group. At the same time, the mystique of the office often results in an underestimation of the role of the judge. Judges are not merely impartial black-robed umpires who hand down decisions according to clear and unwavering rules. "This view of the judge as an invisible interpreter of the law, as a part of the courtroom with no more individual personality than a witness chair or a jury box, is a fiction that judges themselves have done much to perpetuate" (Jackson 1974, p. vii).

POWERS OF THE JUDGE

The formal powers of judges extend throughout the criminal court process. From arrest to final disposition, the accused face judges whenever decisions affecting their futures are made (Exhibit 8.1). Judges set bail and revoke it; they determine whether sufficient probable cause exists to hold defendants; they rule on pretrial motions to exclude evidence; they accept pleas of guilty; if a trial takes place, they preside; and after conviction, they set punishment.

Although we tend to think of judges primarily in terms of presiding at trials, their work is much more varied. In the course of their workday, they conduct hearings, accept guilty pleas, impose sentences, or

Exhibit 8.1

ROLE OF JUDGES IN THE STEPS OF CRIMINAL PROCEDURE (TYPICAL FELONY CASE)

	LOWER COURT	MAJOR TRIAL COURT	APPELLATE COURT
Crime			Appellate court opinions are the final word on interpreting criminal laws passed by the legislature.
Arrest	Occasionally signs arrest warrants.		Wrestles with legality of police arrest in context of question of illegal search and seizure.
Initial appearance	Informs defendant of pending charges; appoints counsel for indigents.		
Bail	Sets initial bail amount.	May alter bail amount.	Rarely decides that bail is excessive.
Charging		No authority to intervene.	
Preliminary hearing	Presides over preliminary hearing.		
Grand jury		Chief judge has nominal supervision over the grand jury.	
Arraignment		Informs defendant of pending charges and enters defendant's plea.	
Evidence	Signs search warrants.	Rules on suppression motions involving illegal search and seizure and custodial interrogation.	Rulings establish boundaries for search and seizure and custodial interrogation.
Plea bargaining	Judges rely on pleas to dispose of large dockets.	Some judges actively participate, whereas others are passive.	Rarely rules that plea of guilty was not voluntary.
Trial	Rarely held.	Presides at trial. Rules on admissibility of evidence. Instructs jury as to law applicable to the case.	Decides whether evidence was properly admitted. Decides whether trial judge properly instructed jury as to the law.

Exhibit 8.1
CONTINUED

	LOWER COURT	MAJOR TRIAL COURT	APPELLATE COURT
Sentencing	Typically imposes "normal penalties."	Increasingly difficult and controversial task.	In some jurisdictions, must interpret sentencing guidelines.
Appeal	Rare except in some drunk-driving convictions.	Notice of appeal filed in trial court.	Rarely reverses trial judge.

work in their offices (called **chambers**). In carrying out the responsibilities of the office, judges mainly react to the work of prosecutors and defense attorneys.

BENEFITS OF THE JOB

In discharging their duties, judges enjoy some distinct benefits of the office. Traditionally, they have been given a high level of prestige and respect. Lawyers address the judge as "your honor," and everyone rises when the judge enters or leaves the courtroom. Judges also enjoy other trappings of the office. Federal judges enjoy life terms, as do judges in a handful of states. More commonly, terms of office for state judges range from 6 to 10 years, considerably longer than those of other public officeholders—a reflection of the independence of the American judiciary.

For many lawyers, a judgeship is the capstone to a successful career. Judicial salaries are not the highest incomes in the legal profession, but they are higher than the average of other criminal justice personnel. Annual salaries of general jurisdiction trial judges range from $99,000 to $178,000 (National Center for State Courts 2008). The average is about $133,000. For some lawyers, a judicial salary represents an increase over that received in private practice, and it is certainly more secure. For the majority of lawyers, however, a judgeship represents a significant decrease in earning power. For example, it is not at all unusual to find lawyers in federal court who are paid more than the judges.

Many judgeships carry with them considerable patronage powers. Court positions—bailiffs, clerks, court reporters, probation officers, and secretaries—must be filled. Because these positions are usually not covered by civil service, judges can award jobs to friends, relatives, campaign workers, and party leaders. In some cities, judicial staff positions are significant sources of party patronage.

FRUSTRATIONS OF THE JOB

Because of the pressures of today's criminal justice system, the ideals surrounding the judge are not always borne out by the reality. One of the most frustrating aspects of being a judge is the heavy caseload and corresponding administrative problems (Rosen 1987). Thus, instead of having time to reflect on challenging legal questions or to consider the proper sentence for a convicted felon, trial judges must move cases, acting more like administrators in a bureaucracy than as judicial sages. As a New York judge put it:

> It is clear that the "grand tradition" judge, the aloof brooding charismatic figure in the Old Testament tradition, is hardly a real figure. The reality is the working judge who must be politician, administrator, bureaucrat, and lawyer in order to cope with a crushing calendar of cases. A Metropolitan Court Judge might well ask, "Did John Marshall or Oliver Wendell Holmes ever have to clear a calendar like mine?" (Blumberg 1967a, p. 120)

Although this quote is more than 40 years old, the same judicial frustrations affect judges today (Mayer 2007).

Moreover, the judge's actions are limited by the system—lawyers are late, court documents get lost, jails are crowded. Added to these general constraints is the overall low prestige of criminal court judges, who occupy the lowest rung within the judicial system. Like the other actors in the criminal justice system, the judge becomes tainted by close association with defendants who are perceived as society's outcasts.

LAW AND POPULAR CULTURE

Judge Judy: Justice with an Attitude or Just Plain Nonsense?

Straight-talking Judge Judy (aka Judy Sheindlin) stormed onto the television screen on September 16, 1996, and quickly became the boss of syndicated courtroom television show ratings. Her show is regularly among the top syndicated shows in the country, and you've probably seen it. Before starting her own show, Judge Judy served as a judge in New York, hearing more than 20,000 cases. She is the author of three books for a general audience—*Don't Pee on My Leg and Tell Me It's Raining* (1996); *Beauty Fades, Dumb Is Forever* (1999); *Keep It Simple, Stupid: You're Smarter Than You Look* (2000); and two children's books, *Win or Lose by How You Choose* (2000) and *You Can't Judge a Book by Its Cover: Cool Rules for School* (2001). On the bench, she was known for her outspoken behavior and for being one of New York's toughest judges—attributes she brings to her "syndicourt" (syndicated courtroom) television show with sayings such as "I'm the BOSS, Applesauce."

Some observers see *Judge Judy* and other law-related television shows as beneficial because they reveal to viewers information about how the legal system works. Others disagree and see Judge Judy's behavior and that of her fellow syndicourt show judges as unrepresentative of the real-world job of judging, describing it as "sarcastic, accusatory, and opinionated" (Podlas 2002, p. 41).

A fair question might be, "What difference does it make who's right? If people enjoy the entertainment, what damage could these shows possibly do?" Kimberlianne Podlas (2002) suggests four troubling implications of these shows: (1) They may reduce respect for the bench; (2) they may lead to general misinterpretation of judicial behavior and temperament; (3) they may alter expectations about the legal system; and (4) they may lead participants in real cases to adopt inappropriate models of behavior.

To test whether any of those negative consequences of watching too much syndicourt TV exist, Podlas conducted a survey of 241 potential jurors in three jurisdictions in the northeastern United States. She asked them about their syndicourt viewing behavior and about their views of judges. Her findings reveal that frequent viewers of syndicourt programs, when compared with nonviewers, are far more likely to believe that "judges should have an opinion regarding the verdict, judges should make their opinion clear, judges should ask questions during trial, judges should be aggressive with litigants or express displeasure with their testimony," and perhaps most shockingly, "a judge's silence indicates belief in a litigant" (Podlas 2002, p. 41). Moreover, prior court service or experience did nothing to diminish the impact of watching these programs on attitudes about the judiciary.

Judge Judy may have an admirable goal, for she says on her website, "For 24 years, I tried to change the way families deal with problems on a very small scale, one case at a time. Now I can use the skills I have developed and take my message to more people every day." But it may also be the case that in taking her message—which is inconsistent with the normal behavior of judges and the actual day-to-day operations of America's courts—that she is doing more harm than good to the credibility and legitimacy of the judiciary. After all, Judge Judy is hardly a model for judicial temperament (Bisceglia 2007) so in the end, what you get is social condemnation with your justice (Cohen 2005).

After watching one or more episodes of *Judge Judy,* be prepared to discuss the following questions:

1. Compare the behavior of Judge Judy with that normally expected of judges as described in this chapter.

2. Write down three things you think you know about the legal system based on your own experience watching law-related shows such as *Judge Judy*, and then discuss whether your observations are indeed true.

3. In what way might the popularity of *Judge Judy* be related to the public desire to be able to see actual courtroom proceedings?

Thus, the frustrations of the criminal trial court judge are many. Some judges prefer the relative peace of civil court, where dockets are less crowded, courtrooms quieter, legal issues more intriguing, and witnesses more honest than in the criminal court atmosphere of too many cases, too much noise, too many routine (and often dull) cases, and too many fabricated stories (Rothwax 1996). Other judges, however, like the camaraderie of the criminal court.

JUDGES WITHIN THE COURTROOM WORK GROUP

The public believes that judges are the principal decision makers in courts. Often they are not. Instead, they are constrained by the actions of other members of the courtroom work group—prosecutors, defense attorneys, and probation officers. Thus, judges often accept bail recommendations offered by prosecutors, plea agreements negotiated by defense attorneys, and sentences recommended by the probation officer. In short, although judges still retain the formal legal powers of their office, they often informally share these powers with other members of the courtroom work group.

Sanctions can be applied against judges who deviate from the consensus of the courtroom work group. Defense attorneys and prosecutors can foul up judges' scheduling of cases by requesting continuances or failing to have witnesses present when required. Particularly in big-city courts, judges who fall too far behind in disposing of the docket feel pressure from other judges, especially the chief judge. Judges who fail to move their docket may be transferred to less desirable duties (for example, traffic court or juvenile court).

By no means are judges totally controlled by the courtroom work group. As the most prestigious members of the group, they can bring numerous pressures to bear on prosecutors, defense attorneys, and others. A verbal rebuke to a defense attorney in open court or an informal comment to the head prosecutor that the assistant is not performing satisfactorily are examples of judicial actions that can go a long way toward shaping how the courtroom work group disposes of cases.

The amount of influence judges actually exert on the other members of the courtroom work group varies. Some judges are active leaders of the courtroom work group; they run "tight ships," pressuring attorneys to be in court on time, for example. These judges participate fully in courthouse dynamics. On the other hand, some judges have a laissez-faire attitude, allowing the attorneys as many continuances as they request.

In large courts, "judge shopping" is a common practice. Through the strategic use of motions for continuances and motions for a change of judge, defense attorneys maneuver to have their clients' cases heard by the judge they perceive as most favorable. Such judge shopping is the most direct evidence of variations among judges. Although organizational pressures work to provide a certain degree of consistency among judges, any examination of a multi-judge court immediately shows that judges differ in terms of the sentences they hand out, the way they run their courtroom, and the number of cases they have pending. Knowledge of these judicial differences is often as necessary for the practicing attorney as mastery of the law and rules of procedure.

VARYING ROADS TO A JUDGESHIP

Which lawyers are selected to be judges is determined by both formal selection methods and informal procedures. Exhibit 8.2 presents the major formal selection methods used in the states, including partisan elections, nonpartisan elections, merit selection (usually referred to as the *Missouri Bar Plan*), and appointment. Note, though, that some states use different selection procedures for different levels of the judiciary.

However, formal selection methods (law on the books) are far less important than informal methods (law in action) in determining which lawyers reach the bench. How selection is conducted establishes the formal routes to who becomes a judge; however, when a judicial vacancy occurs, interim selection methods are needed. And while appointment by governors and merit selection predominate in filling temporary vacancies, who is ultimately selected to serve on an interim basis significantly affects the final outcome for filling a vacancy permanently (Holmes and Emrey 2006). We will examine the three major methods of judicial selection—executive

Exhibit 8.2

JUDICIAL SELECTION IN THE STATES

MERIT SELECTION[1]	GUBERNATORIAL (G) OR LEGISLATIVE (L) APPOINTMENT	PARTISAN ELECTION	NON-PARTISAN ELECTION	COMBINED MERIT SELECTION AND OTHER METHODS
Alaska	California (G)	Alabama	Arkansas	Arizona
Colorado	Maine (G)	Illinois	Georgia	Florida
Connecticut	New Jersey (G)	Louisiana	Idaho	Indiana
Delaware	Virginia (L)	Ohio	Kentucky	Kansas
District of Columbia	South Carolina (L)	Pennsylvania	Michigan	Missouri
Hawaii		Texas	Minnesota	New York
Iowa		West Virginia	Mississippi	Oklahoma
Maryland			Montana	South Dakota
Massachusetts			Nevada	Tennessee
Nebraska			North Carolina	
New Hampshire			North Dakota	
New Mexico			Oregon	
Rhode Island			Washington	
Utah			Wisconsin	
Vermont				
Wyoming				

[1] The following eight states use merit plans only to fill midterm vacancies on some or all levels of court: Alabama, Georgia, Idaho, Kentucky, Minnesota, Montana, Nevada, and North Dakota.

SOURCE: American Judicature Society. *Judicial Selection in the States: Appellate and General Jurisdiction Courts* (Des Moines, IA: American Judicature Society, 2008).

appointment, popular election, and merit selection—and explore the influence of both formal and informal selection practices.

EXECUTIVE APPOINTMENTS

In the early years of the Republic, judges were selected by executive appointment or elected by the legislature. Today, these methods of judicial selection are used in only a handful of jurisdictions.

Three states use election by the legislature, and a few others still use appointment by the governor. All Article III federal judges are selected by executive appointment. A number of studies have examined the political dynamics involved in the selection of federal judges (Goldman 1997; Holmes and Savchak 2003).

The U.S. Constitution specifies that the president has the power to nominate judges with the advice and consent of the Senate. Based on this constitutional authorization, both the president and the Senate have a voice in the selection process. When a judgeship becomes vacant, the deputy attorney general of the U.S. Department of Justice (the executive official authorized by the president to handle judicial nominees) searches for qualified lawyers by consulting party leaders of the state in which the vacancy has occurred, campaign supporters, U.S. senators, and prominent members of the bar. This initial private screening has been known to take a year or longer in the presence of conflicts within the president's party over who should be selected.

After the president has submitted his nomination for the vacant judicial post, the process shifts to the Senate. Most nominations are routine. After a hearing by the Senate Judiciary Committee, the full Senate usually confirms, most often without a negative vote being cast. If the nomination is controversial, the committee hearings and Senate vote become the focus of great political activity. Over the past decade, major partisan wrangling has surrounded nominations to the federal bench. Although most of President George W. Bush's nominees to the federal bench were confirmed, Democrats filibustered some nominations to the Courts of Appeals, thus preventing confirmation (Neubauer and Meinhold 2010).

Senators also influence federal judicial selections through the informal power of senatorial courtesy. Senators expect to be consulted before the president nominates a person for a judicial vacancy from their state if the president belongs to the same party.

A senator who is not consulted may declare the nominee personally unacceptable, and senators from other states—finding strength in numbers—will follow their colleague's preferences and not approve the presidential nomination. Through this process, senators can recommend persons they think are qualified (former campaign managers come to mind) or exercise a direct veto over persons they find unacceptable (political enemies, for example). But the influence of senators in general over judicial nominations has been declining (Binder and Maltzman 2004).

Overall the selection process produces federal judges with two defining attributes: They belong to the president's party, and they have often been active in politics.

Although the **American Bar Association (ABA)**, the national lawyers' association, enjoys no formal role in the screening of nominees for the federal bench, it has historically played an influential role through its Standing Committee on Federal Judiciary. The committee traditionally investigated potential judicial nominees by consulting with members of the legal profession and law professors. It then ranked the candidates as "exceptionally well qualified," "well qualified," "qualified," or "unqualified." Although the president has the sole power to nominate, most presidents did not wish to name someone who would later be declared unqualified. Therefore, the deputy attorney general usually sought the ABA's recommendations prior to nomination, and some potential nominees were eliminated in this way. However, the role of the ABA has diminished over the past decade or so in light of alleged political biases in the ABA's ratings of candidates, as well as criticisms against its "special access" in the nomination process in light of the ABA's positions on controversial issues:

> In 1997, Senator Hatch ended the ABA's "quasi-official" role in the Committee process, though ABA representatives continued to testify in confirmation hearings. In 2001, President George W. Bush ended the process of giving the ABA special access to proposed nominees' names in advance of nomination or awaiting its evaluation before making nominations. Although it may be more difficult to elicit candid comments once a nominee is announced, the ABA continues to provide evaluations of whether nominees are professionally qualified, and at least some members of the Senate Judiciary Committee continue to consider the ABA evaluation. (*Georgetown Law Journal*, 2007, pp. 1037–1038)

In recent years, the role of the ABA has been eclipsed by other interest groups (Scherer, Bartels, and Steigerwalt 2008). The Federalist Society, Common Cause, NAACP, and the National Women's Political Caucus are examples of interest groups that seek to influence who is selected and confirmed for a federal judgeship. Interest groups from both sides of the ideological spectrum appear to have decided that federal judgeships are critical to their policy agenda and have begun pulling out all the stops to try to influence who is nominated and who is confirmed. (Bell 2002; Scherer 2005). Despite the rancorous debate, President Bush was generally successful, as were his predecessors, in securing the confirmation of his nominees to the federal bench. Indeed, his two nominations to the U.S. Supreme Court were confirmed after threats of filibusters dissipated (Chapter 17). Likewise President Obama is expected to be successful in securing the confirmation of his nominees to the federal bench because the Democrats enjoy a strong majority in the Senate.

State appointive systems resemble the presidential system for selecting federal judges, except that with **gubernatorial appointments** no equivalent of senatorial courtesy exists at the state level. As with federal appointees, governors tend to nominate those who have been active in their campaigns. At times, governors have been known to make appointments to strengthen their position within a geographical area or with a specific group of voters. In recent years, some governors have allowed bar associations to examine the qualifications of potential nominees. State bar associations are gaining influence, much like the ABA influence on federal judicial appointees. However, governors have greater independence to ignore bar association advice.

ELECTION OF JUDGES

None of the original U.S. states elected its judges (Phillips 2009). Today, however, approximately 30 states use some sort of election mechanism to select at least some of their judges (see Exhibit 8.2). The concept of an elected judiciary is a uniquely American invention at democratizing the political process, one that arose during Andrew Jackson's presidency. It is based on the notion that an elitist judiciary does not square with the ideology of a government controlled by the people (Dubois 1980; Streb 2007). According to this philosophy, there should be no special qualifications for public office; the voters (not the elites) should decide who is most qualified.

In a few states, judges are selected using partisan elections (the nominee's political party is listed on the ballot). Historically, this approach enabled party bosses to use judicial posts as patronage to reward the party faithful. The Supreme Court ruled that party control is constitutional (*New York v. López Torres* 2008). But in the majority of states that elect their judges, nonpartisan elections (no party affiliations are listed on the ballot) are used. Nevertheless, even where nonpartisan elections are used, partisan influences are often present (law in action); judicial candidates are endorsed or nominated by parties, receive party support during campaigns, and are readily identified with party labels.

Traditionally, campaigns for American judgeships have been low-key, low-visibility affairs marked by the absence of controversy and low voter turnout (Streb 2007). Judicial candidates often stressed general themes in their campaigns, such as doing justice and being tough on criminals, thus providing voters few guides to possible differences between the candidates. The general lack of information and the low levels of voter interest give incumbent judges important advantages in running for reelection. The prestigious title "Judge" is often listed on the ballot in front of the judge's name. For this reason, few local lawyers wish to challenge a sitting judge. Once a judge is selected, either through an election or an appointment to fill a midterm vacancy, the chances of being voted out of office are small. Few sitting judges are even opposed for reelection; of those challenged, few are ever voted out of office (Dubois 1984; Streb, Frederick, and Lafrance 2007).

Times are changing, however. In recent years, some **judicial elections** have become nastier, noisier, and costlier (Barnes 2007; Bonneau 2007; Schotland 1998). Mudslinging and attack advertising have become common in some states. Interest groups backed by business or plaintiff lawyers are spending millions to back their candidates (Goldberg, Homan, and Sanchez 2002). Thus, today's races, particularly at the state supreme court level, are hard-fought affairs (Bonneau and Hall 2003; Peters 2008). Moreover, the U.S. Supreme Court ruled that candidates for judicial office are free to announce their views on key issues (*Republican Party v. White* 2002). One consequence is that incumbent judges are now being defeated for reelection at a higher rate than in the past (although at the trial level, incumbents still often win).

MERIT SELECTION

"Remove the courts from politics" has been the long-standing cry of judicial reformers, who oppose popular election of judges because voters have no way to know which lawyers would make good judges. Moreover, election suggests the appearance of impropriety because it provides an incentive for judges to decide cases in a popular manner. To cure these ills, legal reformers advocate merit selection, also known as the **Missouri Bar Plan** because that state was the first to adopt it in 1940.

Merit plans are actually hybrid systems incorporating elements from other judicial selection methods: gubernatorial appointment, popular election, citizen involvement, and—most important—a formalized role for the legal profession. Merit selection involves the establishment of a judicial nominating commission composed of lawyers and laypersons, who suggest a list of qualified nominees (usually three) to the governor. The state's chief executive makes the final selection but is limited to choosing from those nominated by the commission.

After a fixed period of service on the bench, the new judge stands uncontested before the voters in a retention election. The length of the initial, probationary appointment varies greatly from state to state, from 1 year in some states to 10 or 12 years in others (American Judicature Society 2009). The sole question in such a retention election is, "Should Judge X be retained in office?" If the incumbent judge wins a majority of affirmative votes, he or she earns a full term of office (usually 6, 8, or 10 years). Each subsequent term is secured through another uncontested retention ballot. Most judges are returned to the bench by a healthy margin, often receiving 70 percent of the vote. Only a handful of judges have been removed from office. Over a 30-year period, for example, 50 court judges from trial and appellate courts were defeated in 3,912 retention elections in 10 states (i.e., only 1.3% were not retained); 28 of these defeats occurred in Illinois, which requires a judge to receive a minimum of 60 percent of the popular vote to remain on the bench (Aspin et al. 2000; see also, Brody 2008).

Although backers of the Missouri Bar Plan contend that it will significantly improve the judges selected and remove the courts from politics, studies of the merit selection system in operation have reached different conclusions. The politics of judicial selection have been altered but not removed; in fact, removing politics does not seem possible. What the reformers presumably mean is the removal of "partisan" politics. In operation, the Missouri Bar Plan has reduced the influence of political parties while at the same time greatly increased the power of the legal profession (Taylor 2009; Watson and Downing 1969).

Merit selection has won increasing acceptance. A majority of states use the merit system, at least at some level of their state court system (see Exhibit 8.2). In addition, a number of other states have actively considered adopting merit selection. As evidence of the growing importance of merit selection, all states that have altered judicial selection techniques in recent years have adopted some form of the Missouri Bar Plan. Even in states that have not formally adopted merit selection, governors often use "voluntary merit plans" to fill temporary vacancies (Dubois 1980; Holmes and Emrey 2006).

CONSEQUENCES OF JUDICIAL SELECTION

The debate over the best method for selecting state judges has raged for decades. Partisan and nonpartisan elections, used in a majority of states, are supported by those who believe elections are the most appropriate method for guaranteeing the popular accountability of state judicial policymakers. Critics, on the other hand, assert that elections are fundamentally inconsistent with the principle of judicial independence, which is vital for neutral and impartial judicial decision making. Less philosophically, these competing perspectives find expression in tension between the legal profession and political parties over influencing judicial selections. The different methods of judicial selection heighten or diminish the influence of the bar or the influence of political parties. This debate indicates that methods of judicial selection are perceived to have important consequences. Three topics stand out. One centers on which system is "best." The second relates to similarities in judges' backgrounds. The third involves efforts to produce a more diverse judiciary.

WHICH SYSTEM IS BEST?

In evaluating which selection system is best, a key criterion is whether one system produces better judges than another. Judicial folklore has long held that particular systems may produce superior judges. Several studies have systematically analyzed this folklore. Because it is impossible to evaluate a normative concept such as "best," it is necessary to rephrase the question empirically. That is, do judges selected by one method differ from those selected by others? Researchers use measurable judicial credentials, such as education and prior legal experience, as indicators of judicial quality. These studies point to two different types of conclusions.

From the standpoint of individuals who wish to become judges, methods of judicial selection make a difference, but not much. When legislators appoint judges, it is quite clear that former legislators are more likely to be selected than in other systems. Similarly, when the governor appoints, the system benefits those who have held state office (such as legislators). By contrast, elective systems elevate to the bench a higher proportion of persons who have held local political office—which typically means the district attorney (DA). Under the Missouri Bar Plan and elective systems, former DAs are more often selected as judges. When the executive or legislature makes the selection, fewer DAs become judges. From a broader perspective, methods of judicial selection have only a marginal influence on the types of lawyers who become judges. Whether elected by the voters, appointed by the governor, or selected through merit plans, state judges are more alike than different. In terms of personal background characteristics such as prior political experience, ties to the local community, political party affiliation, and quality of legal education, the systems of judicial selection do not appear to produce very different types of judges (Flango and Ducat 1979; Goldschmidt, Olson, and Eckman 2009; Hurwitz and Lanier 2003).

But what of the quality of judging? Does one method of judicial selection produce higher-quality judges than another? Scholars are divided on this question. Some maintain that no systematic evidence proves that one selection system produces better judges than another (Choi, Gulati, and Posner 2008; Emmert and Glick 1987). Others argue that "judicial quality is lower in states that utilize elections to select their judges" (Sobel and Hall 2007). But putting aside the issue of "quality" in light of its subjective nature, it is important to note the evidence that judges selected in partisan elections react to public opinion with an eye toward their own reelections, whereas those appointed to office are free of this constraint (Brooks and Raphael 2003; Pinello 1995). This difference may play a critical role in whether judges are willing to overturn capital convictions (Brace and Boyea 2007). Evidence also exists that judicial-selection methods may influence case outcomes in particular types of cases. For example, Gryski, Main, and Dixon (1986) reported that decisions upholding the sex-discrimination claims occurred far more frequently in states with appointive systems than those with election systems. Pinello (1995) found that appointed judges reversed criminal convictions for constitutional violations at a significantly higher rate than did elected judges (see also Epstein, Knight, and Shvetsova 2002). And Helland and Tabarrok (2002),

using a large sample from cases across the country, found that tort awards for in-state plaintiffs against out-of-state defendants were larger in jurisdictions in which judges were elected. Thus, it does appear that the method of judicial selection matters. Which is "best," however, is a matter of interpretation.

SIMILARITIES IN JUDGES' BACKGROUNDS

Although the United States uses a variety of methods for selecting judges, it is important to note that judges share some important similarities, which may be of even greater importance than the differences. In general, judges are men from the upper middle class, and their backgrounds reflect the attributes of that class: They are more often white and Protestant, and they are better educated than the average American. Increasingly, though, judges are beginning to more closely resemble the American electorate. State supreme court justices, for example, are increasingly women and less likely to be high-status Protestants (Bonneau 2001).

Another similarity among judges is that most were born in the community in which they serve. Trial court judges are usually appointed from particular districts; the persons appointed were often born in that area and attended local or state colleges before going on to a law school within the state.

Finally, judges are seldom newcomers to political life. Almost three out of four state supreme court judges have held a nonjudicial political office. Trial court judges also have held prior office—most often district attorney or state legislator. Eighty percent of federal judges had prior government experience. Before becoming judges, they had some familiarity with the range of public issues that government as well as courts must address. Because of these factors, few political mavericks survive the series of screens that precede becoming a judge. The process tends to eliminate those who hold views and exhibit behavior widely different from the mainstream of local community sentiment.

DIVERSITY AND THE JUDICIARY

The United States is experiencing a revolutionary change in the composition of the bench. The dominant profile of judges as white males has begun to change. Since the presidency of Jimmy Carter, an increasing number of federal court vacancies have been filled with female jurists, a pattern evident during both Republican and Democratic administrations (Goldman and Saronson 1994; Goldman and Slotnick 1999; Goldman et al. 2007). Eighteen percent of President Clinton's nominations to the federal bench were women (Spill and

Bratton 2001). Republican President George W. Bush was also particularly vocal about his goal of diversity (Solberg 2005). And Democrat Barack Obama demonstrated his commitment to judicial diversity early in his presidency by nominating the first Latina to the U.S. Supreme Court, Sonia Sotomayor. Today, the Federal Judicial Center (2009) reports that of the 1298 sitting federal judges, 248 (19.1 percent) are women, 109 (8.4 percent) are African-American, 72 (5.5 percent) are Hispanic, and 11 (0.9 percent) are Asian American. Only 1 federal judge is of Native-American decent and only 1 is openly gay, a lesbian in the Southern District of New York. Thus, while roughly 34 percent of federal judges can be considered "nontraditional," two thirds of the federal judiciary is comprised of white men, all of whom are presumably heterosexual.

The picture with regard to state judges is significantly more complicated. Until the 20th century, the number of women judges in America was so small that they could be counted on the fingers of one hand. The 20th century began witnessing changes, though not very quickly. By 1950, women had achieved at least token representation on the bench (Carbon 1984). Today, the National Association of Women Judges (2009) reports that of the roughly 16,950 state court judges in the United States, 4,325 (25.5 percent) are women. As the number of women serving on the state and federal benches has risen, there has been an understandable interest in probing the "difference" women may bring to the bench (Martin 1993). Speculation by affirmative action activists has suggested that female judges are likely to be more liberal than male jurists. Some studies report gender differences (but often the differences are at best small). For example:

- Research on appellate courts finds that female judges tend to be stronger supporters of women's rights claims, regardless of their ideology (Palmer 2001).
- In Pennsylvania, female judges are somewhat harsher in sentencing criminal defendants. Notably, they are particularly hard on repeat minority offenders (Steffensmeier and Hebert 1999).

Coontz (2000) found significant gender differences in: the ways judges decided claims of self-defense by women in homicide cases; the amount of damages awarded in personal injury cases, especially those involving simple assaults; whether to award alimony; and the length of sentences for people convicted of simple assault.

But other studies find no gender differences among judges. For example:

- A study of Justice Sandra Day O'Connor, the first woman to serve on the U.S. Supreme Court, concludes, "Overall, the findings presented here do very little to support the assertion that O'Connor's decision making is distinct by virtue of her gender" (Davis 1993, p. 139). Justice O'Connor herself (2003) rejected the notion that her sex guided her decision making, a sentiment echoed by Justice Ruth Bader Ginsburg (1993). But Justice Ginsburg may have had a change of heart in 2009. As the only woman on the U.S. Supreme Court during the 2008–2009 term, she viewed a case involving the strip-search of a 13-year-old girl differently than her male colleagues. "They have never been a 13-year-old girl.... It's a very sensitive age for a girl.... I didn't think that my colleagues, some of them, quite understood" (Lewis 2009, p. A16).
- Analysis of more than 2,100 written opinions from 1992 to 1995 indicated that male and female federal district court judges were not significantly different when it came to their decisions (Stidham and Carp 1997).

And still other studies find differences in the ways in which men and women engage in the legal reasoning process, but nonetheless conclude that they reach similar legal conclusions (Miller and Maier 2008). Perhaps the best summary is that drawing conclusions about the difference women make on the bench is still problematical.

In 1973, slightly more than 1 percent of state judges were African-American; by the mid-1980s, the percentage had increased to 3.8 percent (Graham 1990). Today, that figure stands at roughly 5.9 percent (American Bar Association 2009). The underrepresentation of African-Americans on the bench is partially a reflection of the paucity of African-American attorneys. But underrepresentation is also a product of how judges are selected. African-American judges are more likely to be found in states using appointment by either the governor or the legislature; they are less likely to be selected in states using elections (Graham 1990; American Judicature Society 2009). In 1991 the Supreme Court held that the Voting Rights Act of 1965, as amended in 1982, applies to judicial elections (*Chisom v. Roemer* and *Houston Lawyers' Association v. Attorney General of Texas*). These rulings pave the way for major changes in the 41 states, particularly in the South, that use elections for at least some of their judges (Smith and Garmel 1992) (see Case Close-Up: *Chisom v. Roemer* and Diversity on the Bench).

Chisom v. Roemer and Diversity on the Bench

Janice Clark had always wanted to be a judge. As a practicing lawyer, she seemed to possess the education and experience necessary to don the black robes, but she still faced an insurmountable barrier. The problem was not gender—after all, women are being elected to the bench on a regular basis all over the United States. Rather, the insurmountable barrier was race. White voters rarely vote for African-American candidates; indeed, as an African-American candidate for a judgeship, Clark received only 3.2 percent of the white vote. So, as lawyers often do, she filed suit in the U.S. District Court for the Middle District of Louisiana. Joined by African-American voters and lawyers throughout Louisiana, her class action lawsuit alleged that electing judges from multimember districts diluted African-American voting strength in violation of the Voting Rights Act.

The lawsuit was joined by local civil rights groups, as well as several national organizations, including the Voter Information Project and the Lawyer's Committee for Civil Rights Under Law. The nominal defendant was the governor of the state and all other government officials connected with judicial elections. Also appearing for the defendants were attorneys representing the Louisiana District Judges Association and the Orleans Trial Judges Association (*Clark et al. v. Edwin Edwards et al.* 725 F. Supp. 285, M.D. La. 1988).

U.S. District Judge John Parker's opinion stressed that of the 156 district court judgeships in Louisiana, only 2 were held by African-Americans. The reason was that judgeships were elected from the entire judicial district, which had the effect of "diluting black voting strength," a violation of the Voting Rights Act.

This case was one of several filed in the federal courts, and the underlying legal issue was eventually settled at the appellate level in *Chisom v. Roemer* (1991) and *Houston Lawyers' Association v. Attorney General of Texas* (1991). The basic legal issue hinged on an interpretation of the Voting Rights Act of 1965 as amended in 1982. The Voting Rights Act covers representatives. Clearly, legislators are considered representatives, but what of judges? The Fifth Circuit said no, but *Chisom* held otherwise, finding that judges were indeed covered by the Voting Rights Act.

Crossing this important threshold means that, in drawing election districts (either for legislatures or judges), the lines may not dilute minority voting. This conclusion was based on repeated findings of the existence of racially polarized voting, which in an election contest pitting an African-American candidate against a white one, white voters were very unlikely to cast their ballot for the African-American candidate (Engstrom 1989). But the future of this line of decisions is cloudy. In a 5-to-4 decision, the Supreme Court ruled that race is an impermissible consideration in drawing congressional voting districts (*Miller v. Johnson*). Nonetheless, challenges to judicial election and selection procedures under the Voting Rights Act have been mounted in 15 states (Scruggs, Mazzola, and Zaug 1995).

Janice Clark's legal argument eventually became the law of the land. The series of Supreme Court cases firmly established the principle that judges cannot be elected in ways that place minority candidates at an unfair disadvantage. But the eventual impact is far from certain. Each of the states with a significant minority population differs somewhat in tradition and method of judicial selection, factors that shape the emerging systems of judicial selection. But for Janice Clark, the outcome was both immediate and positive. She ran again for the major trial court bench in Baton Rouge and won, taking the oath of office on January 1, 1993. She continues to generate headlines. When a high-ranking state police official publicly complained about one of her decisions, she took to the bench and scolded the official, explaining that the problem was not her interpretation of the law, but how poorly the legislature had written the state's gaming law in the first place. Her unusual candor aside, it will be many years before we know whether minority judges have a long-term impact on the type of justice meted out in courthouses across America.

CASE CLOSEUP

COURTS, CONTROVERSY, AND THE ADMINISTRATION OF JUSTICE

Is Judicial Independence Being Undermined?

To U.S. District Judge Paul Cassell, the recommended sentence (30 to 37 months in prison) for an ex-felon's selling a sawed-off shotgun to a pawnshop was too severe. After all, the defendant, Paul VanLeer, had never committed a violent crime. So Cassell imposed 18 months in prison. To U.S. Attorney General John Ashcroft, this type of lenient sentencing (termed "downward departures" under federal sentencing guidelines) was all too typical of federal judges. So he ordered federal prosecutors across the nation to report every case to the Justice Department. To some, Ashcroft's actions were justified, because federal judges have been imposing lenient sentences in 18 percent of federal cases (U.S. Sentencing Commission 2003). Thus, his new policy would ensure that federal judges would be held accountable for their actions. But to others, the attorney general's actions were just the latest example of judge bashing, because federal prosecutors had found only 19 downward deviations objectionable. Thus, this new policy would serve only to erode judicial independence.

Former Attorney General Ashcroft's criticism of federal judges who sentence "too leniently" is but one example of attacks on judges and the decisions they render. In an adversary system, a judge's decision often fails to find favor with the losing party. But some worry that in the modern era, attacks on judges seriously undermine judicial independence. In recent years, both state and federal judges have been the subject of attack (Raftery 2006).

- Justice Penny White of the Tennessee Supreme Court was voted off the bench in a retention election because she voted in a death penalty case to allow the defendant to put on mitigation evidence (Bright 1997).
- Justice David Lanphier of the Nebraska Supreme Court lost a retention election when a cluster of special interest groups campaigned for his removal over displeasure with selected decisions (Reid 1999).
- H. Lee Sarokin, U.S. Court of Appeals for the Third Circuit (based in Philadelphia), resigned. An appointee of Democratic presidents, he had been criticized by Republican presidential hopeful Robert Dole. According to Judge Sarokin, "The constant politicization of my tenure has made 'my' lifetime dream impossible" (Mauro 1996).
- Jay Bybee, U.S. Court of Appeals for the Ninth Circuit, has been targeted by some for impeachment because of the legal opinions he wrote while head of President Bush's Office of Legal Counsel about harsh treatment of terrorist suspects (Justice at Stake 2009 ["Bybee Invited to Testify"]).

Attacks on the federal judiciary are hardly new. President Jefferson tried to remove Justice Samuel Chase as part of a campaign to "reform" the federal judiciary. In the 1960s, a nationwide campaign was launched by the ultraconservative John Birch Society to impeach Chief Justice Earl Warren. Not surprisingly, attacks on federal judges most often occur during election years (Segal 2000). Thus,

JUDGING THE JUDGES

Judicial-selection techniques attempt to recruit Solomon-like figures to the bench. Judicial education programs help beginning judges learn their new roles and keep veteran judges abreast of changes in the law. The troublesome problem remains,

however: What should be done about unfit judges? Despite the lack of clarity in what attributes a good judge should possess, one central conclusion stands out: A few judges do not fulfill minimal standards. A few are senile, prejudiced, vindictive, tyrannical, lazy, and sometimes corrupt. Proper judicial conduct is indispensable to people's confidence in their judiciary, confidence that itself is indispensable to the rule of law. In recent years such confidence has

during the 1968 presidential election, candidate Richard Nixon attacked the Supreme Court, promising to remake the high court in his own image (see Chapter 17). But almost invariably, challenges to judicial independence fail (Friedman 1998).

Attacks on the judiciary, though somewhat predictable, can still exert a chilling effect on judicial independence. Former Chief Justice William Rehnquist voiced concern along these lines: "There is a wrong way and right way to go about putting a popular imprint on the judiciary" (Carelli 1996). In the same vein, Law Professor Stephen Burbank (1987) reminded us that judicial independence is a means to an end rather than an end in itself. Criticism is one thing; undermining judicial independence is another. "Courts are not independent when state judges are voted off the bench because of unpopular decisions by their courts, and when federal judges reverse decisions or resign from the bench after a barrage of criticism" (Bright 1997, p. 167). Judges are concerned that the increasing tendency to verbally attack judges appears to be related to increasing physical threats against judges. According to the U.S. Marshals Service, threats and harassments against federal judges increased 89 percent in just 5 years (Coyle 2009).

Concerned that recent attacks on judges threaten to alter the delicate balance between judicial independence and judicial accountability, the American Judicature Society has created the Center for Judicial Independence to respond to unwarranted attacks on the judiciary and to sponsor public education programs on relevant issues ("Issues in Judicial Independence and Accountability" 2004). Similarly, Justice at Stake (**http://www.justiceatstake.org**) has launched a campaign to protect fair and impartial courts from outside political pressures. Some attacks on judges appear to be ideological in nature. Retired Justice Sandra Day O'Connor wrote, "What worries me is the manner in which politically motivated interest groups are attempting to interfere with justice" ("After Death Threats" 2009).

It is ironic that Judge Paul Cassell would be criticized for imposing lenient sentences. As a law professor, he was the leading critic of the *Miranda* decision on police interrogations (see Chapter 12) and was confirmed only after Democrats in the Senate expressed skepticism about his ability to be fair and impartial as a judge. Moreover, it has been conservative justices of the Supreme Court like Chief Justice Rehnquist who have defended fellow judges against charges of undue leniency. Thus, this debate illustrates that not all criticisms of judges are ideologically based. Rather, some reflect conflicts with other branches of government. At the federal level, legislators and executives are often displeased with judicial decisions. At the state and local level, prosecutors often publicly express their displeasure when a judge suppresses evidence or imposes a "lenient" sentence. As for Judge Cassell, he has made it clear that he will not let criticism affect his decisions—in short, he will remain independent (Willing 2003).

What do you think? Where do you draw the line between fair criticism of judges and intimidation?

been eroded by questions of judicial misconduct in a variety of states, including California, Illinois, Florida, Louisiana, New York, Oklahoma, Rhode Island, Pennsylvania, and New Hampshire.

JUDICIAL INDEPENDENCE

A critical issue in judging the judges is how to devise a system for removing unfit judges while at the same time guaranteeing **judicial independence**. At times critics attempt to remove a judge from office not because of his or her misconduct, but solely because of displeasure with the substance of the judge's decisions. Clearly, protections against unpopular court rulings constitute the hallmark of an independent judiciary. Yet judicial independence is not an end in itself. As University of Chicago Law Professor Philip Kurland has put it,

"The provisions for securing the independence of the judiciary were not created for the benefit of the judges, but for the benefit of the judged" (quoted in Byrd 1976, p. 267). Courts, Controversy, and the Administration of Justice: Is Judicial Independence Being Undermined? explores this topic in a contemporary setting.

Judicial Misconduct

Systems for removing or disciplining unfit judges must not only strike a balance between judicial accountability and judicial independence, but they must also grapple with the wide range of misbehavior encompassed by the phrase "**judicial misconduct**" (Begue and Goldstein 1987). Most directly, judicial misconduct involves corruption. In recent years judges in big cities such as Chicago, New York, and Philadelphia have been accused of (and sometimes convicted of) criminal offenses such as taking bribes and fixing traffic tickets. But not all judicial misconduct is so venal; sometimes it involves improper or bizarre behavior on the bench (Goldschmidt, Olson, and Ekman 2009; Wice 1991). Exhibit 8.3 summarizes some recent cases that illustrate the range of behavior.

One of the most difficult situations involves judges of advanced years whose mental capacity has become impaired. After years of dedicated service, with exemplary conduct on the bench and no hint of scandal, a judge might become senile. Accordingly, a growing number of states impose mandatory retirement ages for judges. The Supreme Court has ruled that state laws requiring judges to retire at age 70 do not violate the federal Age Discrimination in Employment Act (*Gregory v. Ashcroft* 1991). In another widely followed case, the nation's highest court upheld the prison sentence of David Lanier, a state judge from Dyersburg, Tennessee. Judge Lanier had been convicted in federal court of sexually attacking five women in his courthouse. He had not been prosecuted in state court, nor had the state's conduct commission taken action—many said because the judge was politically well connected and his brother was the county prosecutor. The decision strengthened federal civil rights laws (Chapter 3), but the opinion stopped short of

---

Exhibit 8.3

Examples of Errant State Judges

David Bradfield of the 36th District announced his retirement, effective immediately, in the face of an indefinite suspension following a spat with a Detroit deputy mayor over a parking place (Schmitt 2006).

Rosemarie Williams, the presiding judge of New Jersey's Somerset County's General Equity Part, was reassigned to another county after her conviction for drunk driving (Toutant 2006).

Shannon Jones, a part-time judge in the Tennessee General Sessions Court, was disciplined for accepting a client for his private law practice who also had legal matters before his court ("Publically Censured" 2003).

Rudy Montoya, a Mora County magistrate in New Mexico, agreed to a 90-day suspension without pay while contesting allegations that "he lacks fundamental integrity and honesty... and has intentionally disregarded the law" (Propp 2003).

Gerald Garson, a judge in Brooklyn's Supreme Court (New York's equivalent of the trial court of general jurisdiction), was indicted for taking bribes in divorce and child custody cases (Newman 2003).

Judge Alan Green of Louisiana's 24th judicial district was sentenced to 51 months in prison after being convicted of taking $10,000 in cash from a local bail bondsman (Krupa 2006).

Philadelphia Traffic Court Judge Willie Singletary was charged with misconduct after a YouTube video showed him soliciting campaign funds (Elliott-Engel 2008).

Chief Judge Sharon Keller of the Texas Court of Criminal Appeals was charged with incompetence, violating her duties, and casting public discredit on the judiciary for refusing to delay the closing of the clerk's office for an emergency appeal for a man facing the death penalty. The man was executed several hours later (Kovach 2009).

Exhibit 8.4

KEY DEVELOPMENTS CONCERNING JUDGES

Judicial conduct commission	1960	California creates first judicial conduct commission.
Judicial Conduct and Disability Act	1980	Federal conduct law passed.
Gregory v. Ashcroft	1991	State laws requiring judges to retire at 70 do not violate the federal Age Discrimination in Employment Act.
Chisom v. Roemer; Houston Lawyers' Association v. Attorney General of Texas	1991	Judges are covered by the Voting Rights Act.
U.S. v. Lanier	1997	The trial court improperly ruled that state judges are not covered by federal civil rights laws.
Republican Party v. White	2002	In campaigning for a judgeship, a candidate may discuss issues.
Rules for Judicial Conduct and Judicial Disability Proceedings	2008	Implemented the recommendations of the Breyer Commission to "provide mandatory and nationally uniform provisions" that govern how judicial misconduct proceedings are conducted in the federal circuits.
New York v. López Torres	2008	It is not unconstitutional for the state of New York to allow political parties to use a judicial convention system to pick the party's judicial candidates.
Caperton v. Massey Coal	2009	Judges must recuse themselves from cases when large campaign contributions from interested parties create the appearance of bias.

recognizing a federal right not to be raped by a state official (*U.S. v. Lanier* 1997). Exhibit 8.4 summarizes the Supreme Court cases affecting judges.

Formal methods for removing unfit judges—recall elections and impeachment proceedings—are generally so cumbersome that they have seldom been used. Moreover, these techniques are better directed at corrupt judges than at those whose behavior is improper or whose advanced age has caught up with them. A more workable method for dealing with judicial misconduct is the judicial conduct commission.

STATE JUDICIAL CONDUCT COMMISSIONS

In 1960 California became the first state to adopt a modern and practical system for disciplining its judges. In response to the mounting public clamor for accountability on the part of government officials, every state has followed California's pioneering lead (Brooks 1985). Under the California model, a **judicial conduct commission** is created as an arm of the state's highest court. The commission, made up of judges, lawyers, and prominent laypersons, investigates allegations of judicial misconduct and, when appropriate, hears testimony.

If the commission finds in favor of the judge, the investigation is closed and the matter is permanently concluded (Miller 1991). Confidentiality is essential, lest a judge's reputation be tarnished by a crank complaint. Many complaints are issued by disgruntled litigants, whose charges amount to simple displeasure that the judge did not rule in their favor. If the complaint has merit, the commission may recommend a sanction of private admonishment, public censure, retirement, or removal. The state supreme court retains the final power to discipline errant judges (Gardiner 1986).

Although commissions are armed with the potent weapon of a public recommendation, they prefer to act more informally. If the information gathered suggests judicial misconduct, the commission holds a confidential conference and discusses the matter with the judge, who has an opportunity to rebut the charges. The commission may try to correct the matter; a judge with a substance abuse problem, for example, is encouraged to enroll in a treatment program. If the problems are serious, continuous, or not immediately solvable, the commission usually seeks to force the judge's voluntary retirement. The informal pressures and the threat of bringing public proceedings are often powerful enough to force the judge in question off the bench. The complaints and investigations remain confidential unless the commission finds it necessary to seek a reprimand or removal before the state supreme court.

FEDERAL CONDUCT AND DISABILITY ACT

In 1980 Congress passed the Judicial Councils Reform and Judicial Conduct and Disability Act, which lays out a precise mechanism for acting on complaints against federal judges. Complaints are initially heard by the judicial councils (the administrative arm of each U.S. court of appeals). Most result in either a finding of no misconduct or the imposition of nonpublic sanctions. However, if substantial evidence of serious misconduct exists, the judicial council sends a written report to the Judicial Conference, which may recommend that the U.S. House of Representatives begin impeachment procedures.

Article II of the Constitution provides for the removal of the president, vice president, or civil officers of the United States—including federal judges—for crimes of "treason, bribery, or other high crimes and misdemeanors." The House must first vote articles of impeachment specifying the specific charges. **Impeachment** does not mean conviction, but rather allegations of wrongdoing—roughly equivalent to a grand jury indictment. The trial on the articles of impeachment is conducted before the Senate. Conviction requires a two-thirds vote of the senators present and carries with it **removal** from office and disqualification from holding any future office. Historically, in functioning as both judge and jury in impeachment trials, all senators observed the testimony and cross-examination of

witnesses. But in the modern era, the press of legislative business makes this time-consuming process unworkable. Therefore, in 1986 the Senate made the historic decision to establish a 12-person Impeachment Committee to receive evidence and take testimony prior to the trial on the Senate floor (Heflin 1987).

An unprecedented series of allegations of misconduct against federal judges since 1981 highlights the interlocking relationships among criminal prosecutions, impeachment, and the new statutory scheme (Exhibit 8.5). The impeachment proceedings against U.S. District Judge Alcee Hastings raised the most difficult questions: Unlike Claiborne and Nixon, he was never convicted of a criminal offense. Hastings, the first African-American federal judge ever appointed in Florida, was indicted for soliciting a $150,000 bribe from two convicted racketeers, but the jury acquitted. Hastings argued that racial motivations lay behind the impeachment proceedings. In 1989, the Senate removed Hastings from his judicial office, but in a strange twist Hastings was later elected to the U.S. House of Representatives.

These cases are truly exceptional. Prior to the 1980s, only four federal judges had been removed, the most recent in 1936. But these statistics obscure the fact that many misconduct and disability problems of federal judges are resolved informally by the judiciary itself. Whether the federal courts effectively police themselves, however, is open to debate.

In 2003, an attorney filed an ethical complaint under the Judicial Conduct and Disability Act against U.S. District Judge Manuel Real. The way in which the initial complaint and subsequent complaints against the judge were handled by the Ninth Circuit Court of Appeals caused the case to get the attention of the press, the Judicial Conference, and, ultimately, of Congress (Bazelon 2009). The attention paid to the handling of the allegations against Judge Real, coupled with other instances of ineffective oversight of alleged judicial misconduct, led to the formation of a commission to investigate how the Judicial Conduct and Disability Act of 1980 had been implemented. Because the commission was led by U.S. Supreme Court Justice Stephen Breyer, it came to be known as the Breyer Commission. After 2 years of study, which included details of the botched handling of the complaints against Judge Real, the Breyer Commission issued a 180-page report (2006). While concluding that circuit judges and judicial councils were "doing a very good overall job in handling complaints" (p. 206), the Breyer Commission found that the federal judiciary mismanaged approximately 35 percent of "high-profile complaints… filed by attorneys,

Exhibit 8.5

FEDERAL JUDGES WHO HAVE FACED DISCIPLINARY ACTION

U.S. District Judge Harry Claiborne (District of Nevada) The jury acquitted on the charge of accepting a bribe in a criminal case over which he was presiding but convicted him of income tax evasion. While he was serving a 2-year sentence in federal prison, the Senate found Claiborne guilty on three of four impeachment articles by the required two-thirds vote and removed him from the bench (1986).

Chief Judge Walter Nixon (Southern District of Mississippi) The jury convicted him of perjury for falsely denying before a federal grand jury that he had intervened in a state narcotics case involving the son of a friend. While he was serving his sentence at Eglin Air Force Base in Florida, the Senate removed Nixon from the federal bench (1989).

U.S. District Judge Alcee Hastings (Southern District of Florida) The jury acquitted him of the charge of soliciting a $150,000 bribe from two convicted racketeers. The Eleventh Circuit and the Judicial Conference concluded that Hastings was not only guilty but had also fabricated his defense. The Senate ousted Hastings from office in 1989, but in a strange twist, Hastings was then elected to Congress.

U.S. District Judge Robert Aguilar (Northern District of California) A jury convicted him of obstruction of justice for telling a friend about a government wiretap in a racketeering investigation. The Ninth Circuit reversed, but the Supreme Court reinstated the wiretap conviction (*U.S. v. Aguilar 1995*). After another conviction and yet another appellate reversal, Aguilar resigned from the bench, apparently in exchange for criminal charges being dropped.

U.S. District Judge Robert Collins (Eastern District of Louisiana) A jury convicted him of taking a $100,000 bribe from a drug smuggler. While serving a 7-year prison sentence and facing impeachment proceedings, Collins resigned from the bench before formal Senate action was taken.

U.S. District Judge Brian Duff (Northern District of Illinois) Noted for his temper and for having the highest rate of reversal in the Chicago courthouse, he stepped down amid reports of a Justice Department complaint filed with the Judicial Counsel for the Seventh Circuit. Judge Duff cited medical problems (Robinson 1996).

U.S. District Judge Edward Nottingham (Colorado) Resigned from the bench amid allegations that he viewed an adult website on his government computer and spent $3,000 in a Denver strip club.

U.S. District Judge Samuel Kent (Southern District of Texas) Kent pled guilty to obstruction of justice for lying to judges who investigated sexual misconduct complaints. Sentenced to 33 months in federal prison, he will continue to draw his salary unless Congress removes him from office.

U.S. District Judge Thomas Porteous (Eastern District of Louisiana) Facing allegations that he took cash from lawyers with cases in his court and repeatedly lied under oath, Porteous continues to draw his salary but hears no cases. The Judicial Conference has recommend impeachment proceedings.

---

court personnel, or public officials," such as the ones against Judge Real (Bazelon 2009, p. 469). Ultimately, Judge Real was found guilty of misconduct and publicly reprimanded for having made "inaccurate and misleading" comments during the investigation of the complaints filed against him. More significantly, though, most of the recommendations of the Breyer Commission were adopted by the Judicial Conference of the United State in 2008. These changes included 29 new mandatory rules for improving the "consistency and rigor" disciplinary processes implemented under the Judicial Conduct and Disability Act of 1980 (Bazelon 2009, p. 474).

In turn, these informal methods have been greatly strengthened by the enactment of the federal judicial discipline statute (Fitzpatrick 1988).

JUDICIAL ETHICS

Because of the special role that judges occupy in the adversary system, they are subject to additional ethical constraints beyond those imposed on lawyers. The American Bar Association developed a Model Canons of Judicial Ethics, similar to the codes of legal ethics, but each state has adopted its own canons of judicial ethics. The purpose of these codes of judicial conduct is to preserve the integrity of the judicial system and to foster public confidence in the system (Gray 2003).

A study of State Judicial Discipline Sanctions by the Center for Judicial Ethics of the American Judicature Society found that the baseline cases for sanctions involve judges who drive while intoxicated or are unduly slow in issuing decisions (Gray 2003). Overall, the study concluded that public assumptions about levels of judicial misconduct are not borne out by the evidence. But state supreme courts can do more to tackle this cynicism by providing thorough, well-reasoned opinions in judicial misconduct cases and making them readily accessible to the public. Interestingly, a failure of the judge to cooperate with the state's judicial conduct commission was a contributing factor to a judge's removal (Gray 2003).

Accusations of improper conduct by judges often reflect a lack of understanding of the role of judges in the adversary system. Judges face public criticism for reaching decisions that the public finds unpopular. A major obstacle facing judges who are the focus of negative public comments is the judicial conduct standard prohibiting judges from commenting on cases. But some judges find ways to offer appropriate, but nonprejudicial, defenses. A case in point is Judge Arthur Hunter of New Orleans. The district attorney harshly criticized him for threatening to release defendants because the DA's office could not bring them to trial in a timely manner following Hurricane Katrina. Stressing his credentials as a former police officer, the judge wrote, "Many people have a gross misconception of the role of judges in the criminal justice system.... Judges are like referees in a basketball game. They do not favor either side, but make sure the police, district attorney, and defense attorneys follow all the rules. Judges are not teammates with the district attorney, cheerleaders for the police, or coaches for the defense attorney" (Hunter 2006).

Prohibition on conduct that brings the judicial office into disrepute is another requirement of canons of judicial ethics. Typically, this applies to situations in which the judge is having an extramarital affair or the like. But occasionally it involves not personal conduct but judicial conduct. The best-known example is that of Roy Moore, who was elected chief justice of the Alabama Supreme Court. Consistent with his campaign promises, he installed a large granite monument of the Ten Commandments in the courthouse. When a federal court ordered its removal because it violated the First Amendment of the Constitution, the judge refused to comply. His refusal to obey a lawful court order was deemed to bring the judicial office into disrepute, and so he was removed from the bench (Clark 2005).

The tension between electing judges and appearances of impropriety is emerging as a major issue in judicial ethics. In *Republican Party v. White* (2002) the Supreme Court allowed candidates for judicial office to discuss issues that might come before the court and to criticize past court decisions. The result has been a new dynamic in judicial elections, with some races featuring negative political ads and contentious campaigns (Fortune and White 2008). Some are concerned that elections erode public perceptions of an impartial judiciary. In the words of Justice at Stake (**http://www. justiceatstake.org**): "Can two sides in a lawsuit receive equal justice when one side has spent $3 million to elect the judge deciding the case?" This issue was at the heart of *Caperton v. Massey Coal* (Justice at Stake 2009) in which the Supreme Court held that judges must recuse themselves from cases when large campaign contributions from interested parties create the appearance of bias.

Judges play a key role in enforcing legal ethics. During the course of a lawsuit, a judge may be called on to enforce rules of professional conduct. At times, hearings or trials can become heated. The judge may find that a lawyer went too far in his or her argument or was unduly nasty to opposing counsel. In such cases, the judge may find the lawyer in contempt of court and impose a small fine or a brief jail term. On the civil side, a lawyer may accuse opposing counsel of an ethical violation such as failing to respond in a timely fashion or unnecessarily causing additional work for the lawyer. If the judge agrees, the judge may impose attorney's fees, that is, require the lawyer who caused the misconduct to financially reimburse opposing counsel.

CONCLUSION

Fact or Fiction?

In deciding *Caperton v. Massey Coal Company* the U.S. Supreme Court stressed that the decision addressed an "extraordinary situation": the Court stressed that the owner of Massey Coal spent over $3 million to elect his preferred candidate to the West Virginia Supreme Court, an amount three times more than any of the other supporters. By emphasizing these facts, the justices of the nation's highest court were apparently trying to separate the case from the fictional basis of the novel *The Appeal*. But where fact ends and fiction begins is always hard to tell. John Grisham is a fiction writer who excels in emphasizing extraordinary situations that, while fictional, could still be based on fact. This blending of fact and fiction, life imitating art, provides another chapter in the ongoing national debate over judicial selection.

In the modern era, displeasure with judges has led to renewed interest in how judges are selected. But no matter how we select our judges and who they are, the workaday world of the trial judge bears little resemblance to the high expectations we have about the role of the judge. The trial judge is expected to dispose of a large caseload but is often frustrated by the attorneys' lack of preparation, missing defendants, misplaced files, little time to reflect, and probably most important, insufficient control over many vital aspects of the case. For these and other reasons, judges depend on other members of the courtroom work group. Some depend heavily on the prosecutors, defense attorneys, and probation officers, feeling content to let them make the difficult decisions. Others are much more active participants and are truly leaders of the courtroom work group.

CHAPTER REVIEW

1. Discuss the role of the judge within the courtroom work group.

Judges are the most prestigious members of the courtroom work group, but they are expected to be reasonably responsive to lawyers and are also under pressure to move the docket.

2. Name the three major ways that judges are selected in the United States.

Judges are appointed by executives (like governors and the president), elected by the voters, or appointed through a merit selection process.

3. Analyze the consequences of different methods of judicial selection.

The various selection systems produce judges with very similar backgrounds, including local ties and past political involvement. No evidence exists that one selection system systematically produces "better" or "worse" judges than another, although research does reveal some differences in judicial approaches to decision making.

4. Recognize major changes in the composition of the bench over that past several decades.

Over the past several decades, the composition of the bench has become more diverse, with the selection of a significant number of women and some racial minorities to the nation's courts.

5. Describe the activities of state judicial conduct commissions.

If the state judicial conduct commissions find merit to the complaint about a judge they often work informally to correct the problem. But if the problem is a serious one, the commission may recommend to the state supreme court that the judge be removed from office.

6. Explain the difference between the impeachment and the removal of a federal judge.

If the House of Representatives vote articles of impeachment charging a federal judge with serious misconduct, the Senate conducts a trial and may remove the judge from the bench.

CRITICAL THINKING QUESTIONS

1. Which method of judicial selection (election, appointment, or merit selection) do you think is best? What does your choice reveal about your personal attitudes? Stated another way, do you think the legal profession should have more say in judicial selection (merit) or less influence (elections)?

2. For your state, examine judicial selection in terms of both law on the books (formal method of judicial selection) and law in action (actual practices).

3. At what point are efforts to remove "unfit" judges really efforts to remove judges because of decisions they have made?

4. American society has high expectations for judges, yet the actions of judges are constrained by other members of the courtroom work group. To what extent is criticism of judges, whether local or national, really criticism of the actions and inactions of prosecutors and defense attorneys?

5. Does underrepresentation of women on the bench hurt justice? Would citizens' views of the fairness of courts improve if more nontraditional persons became judges?

KEY TERMS

American Bar
    Association (ABA) 192
chambers 188
gubernatorial appointment 193

impeachment 202
judicial conduct
    commission 201
judicial election 193

judicial independence 199
Missouri Bar Plan 194
removal 202

WEB RESOURCES

Go to the America's Courts and the Criminal Justice System companion website at

www.cengage.com/criminaljustice/neubauer

where you will find more resources to help you study.
Resources include web exercises, quizzing, and flash cards.

FOR FURTHER READING

Baum, Lawrence. *Judges and Their Audiences: A Perspective on Judicial Behavior*. Princeton: Princeton University Press, 2007.

Bonneau. Chris. "Vacancies on the Bench: Open-Seat Elections for State Supreme Courts." *Justice System Journal* 27: 143–160, 2006.

Brody, David. "Judicial Campaign Speech Restricts after *White*: New York Weighs In." *Justice System Journal* 25: 107–114, 2004.

Gray, Cynthia. *Ethical Standards for Judges*. Des Moines, IA: American Judicature Society. 2009.

Peters, C. Scott. "Canons, Cost, and Competition in State Supreme Court Elections." *Judicature* 91: 27–35, 2007.

Salokar, Rebecca, D. Jason Berggren, and Kathryn DePalo. "The New Politics of Judicial Selection in Florida: Merit Selection Redefined." *Justice System Journal* 27: 123–142, 2006.

Sheldon, Charles, and Linda Maule. *Choosing Justice: The Recruitment of State and Federal Judges*. Pullman, WA: Washington State University Press, 1997.

Streb, Matthew (ed.) *Running for Judge: The Rising Political, Financial, and Legal Stakes of Judicial Elections*. New York: NYU Press, 2007.

Songer, Donald, Susan Johnson, and Ronald Stidham. "Presidential Success through Appointments to the United States District Courts." *Justice System Journal* 24: 283–300, 2003.

Van Tassel, Emily Field, and Paul Finkelman, eds. *Impeachable Offenses: A Documentary History from 1878 to the Present*. Washington, DC: Congressional Quarterly, 1999.

9

DEFENDANTS AND VICTIMS

Sarah Ballard tries to control her emotions as she delivers a victim impact statement in which she described how her life was changed by her mother's death in a nightclub fire in Rhode Island that was caused when indoor fireworks ignited soundproofing foam that had been installed in the club. The owners of the club pled "no contest" to 100 counts of involuntary manslaughter. One was sentenced to four years in prison and the other was spared any period of incarceration when he received a suspended sentence and 500 hours of community service. Families of those who died in the fire expressed outrage at the plea bargained sentence. Stories like this call into question how the criminal justice system treats victims.

Chapter Outline

Learning Objectives

After reading this chapter, you should be able to:

1. List the three characteristics of defendants.

2. Describe how victims and witnesses view the court process.

3. Describe how court actors view victims and witnesses.

4. Discuss the prior relationships between defendants and victims and why this is important in domestic violence cases.

5. Identify three types of programs that are designed to aid victims and witnesses in coping with the criminal justice process.

6. Explain why some view victim programs as aiding victims whereas others view these programs as manipulating victims.

The first officer on the scene described Pervis Tyrone Payne as looking like "he was sweating blood." The officer's partner followed the trail of blood into the kitchen, where he found Charissee Christopher and her 2-year-old daughter Lacie butchered to death. After returning a verdict of guilty on two counts of first-degree murder, the trial proceeded to the penalty phase of a capital murder prosecution. The defense called four witnesses, who testified that Payne was a very caring person but had such a low score on an IQ test that he was mentally handicapped. The prosecutor countered by calling the victim's grandmother to the stand, who testified that 3-year-old Nicholas (the lone survivor) kept asking why his mother didn't come home, and he cried for his sister.

During closing arguments, the prosecutor made maximum use of this emotional testimony, imploring the jury to make sure that Nicholas would know later in life that justice had been done in his mother's brutal slaying. The Memphis, Tennessee, jury imposed the death penalty.

The difficulty with the grandmother's testimony in this case is that, just a couple of years before, the Supreme Court had ruled that such emotional statements are inadmissible because they tend to mislead jurors. But in the interim, the membership of the Court had changed with the addition of two conservatives appointed by Republican presidents. By agreeing to hear the case, the Court was signaling that it might be willing to reverse itself and allow victim impact statements during sentencing.

Payne v. Tennessee directs our attention to both defendants and their victims. All too often, when we think about the criminal courts, our minds immediately focus on the members of the courtroom work group: prosecutors, defense attorneys, and judges. We are less likely to think about the other participants: victims, witnesses, or even defendants. Yet these other actors are also important.

Victims greatly influence workload. Courts are passive institutions. They do not seek out cases to decide; rather, they depend on others to bring matters to their attention. How many cases are filed, as well as what kinds of cases are brought to court, is determined by the decisions of others—police, victims, and those who violate the law in the first place. Thus, the courtroom work group has very little control over its workload. Second, victims, witnesses, and defendants are the consumers of the court process. Democratic governments are expected to be responsive to the wishes and demands of their citizens; victims and witnesses often complain about how the courts handle their cases. Victims and defendants are both subjects and objects of the criminal justice process. Their importance for how the courtroom work group administers justice on a day-to-day basis is the subject of this chapter.

CHARACTERISTICS OF DEFENDANTS

In some ways, those accused of violating the criminal law are a diverse lot. Although many defendants are economically impoverished, their numbers also include high-ranking government officials, businesspeople, and prominent local citizens. An indicator of the diversity of defendants centers on how often they are involved with the criminal justice system. At one end of the spectrum are those who are arrested once and are never involved again. At the other end are a small group of career offenders who are responsible for a disproportionate share of offenses (Wolfgang, Figlio, and Sellin 1972; Tracy, Wolfgang, and Figlio 1990). In fact, it is estimated that over 70 percent of all serious criminal offenses are committed by roughly 7 percent of offenders, a group commonly referred to as **career criminals** (DeLisi 2005; Vaughn and DeLisi 2008). To complicate matters further, a generational effect seems to be indicated. Violent offenders are much more likely to have experienced neglect, abuse, or violence in their families (Farrington 2006; Harlow 1999). Moreover, conviction of a parent is correlated with the

Exhibit 9.1	
PROFILE OF STATE PRISON INMATES	
Prior conviction	81%
Racial or ethnic minorities	64%
35 or younger	57%
High school diploma or equivalent	57%
Prior adult incarceration	55%
Violent offense conviction	49%
Raised primarily in single-parent home	43%
Prior incarceration of immediate family member	36%
Drug conviction	21%
Property offense conviction	20%
Married	18%
Women	7%

SOURCE: U.S. Department of Justice, Bureau of Justice Statistics, *Criminal Offenders Statistics*. Available online at http://www.ojp.usdoj.gov/bjs/crimoff.htm#findings. Accessed June 5, 2009.

likelihood of a child offending and being convicted (Farrington 2006; Rowe and Farrington 1997). Whether it is possible to predict who will become a career criminal, however, is subject to extensive debate.

Aside from certain aspects of diversity, the majority of violators conform to a definite profile. Compared to the average citizen, felony defendants are significantly younger, overwhelmingly male, disproportionately members of racial minorities, more likely to come from broken homes, less educated, more likely to be unemployed, and less likely to be married. By the time the court sorting process has ended, those sentenced to prison consist of an even higher proportion of poor, young, illiterate, minority males (Exhibit 9.1). Three characteristics of defendants—gender, poverty, and race—figure prominently in discussions of crime and crime policy and therefore deserve expanded treatment.

OVERWHELMINGLY MALE

Defendants are overwhelmingly male. In fact, women account for only 22.4 percent of all arrests for violent crimes and 32 percent of all crimes (Federal Bureau of Investigation 2008). Although these percentages represent a significant increase over the past few decades, it is unclear whether women are actually committing more crimes or whether changes in the criminal justice system itself have occurred. For example, decreases in sexist and paternalistic thought processes might now lead police to arrest and prosecutors to charge female offenders at higher rates than in the past (Pollock and Davis 2005). Whatever the causes, it is clear that rates of female involvement in the justice system have been increasing in recent years, but their absolute numbers still fall well below those of males.

Courts, Controversy and Racial Discrimination

Can Latinos Get Equal Justice under the Law?

The nomination of Sonia Sotomayor and a recent report of the U.S Census Bureau (2009) have focused attention on race, ethnicity, and the justice system. More than one third of our nation's population belongs to a minority group. Sotomayor is the first Hispanic, an ethnic group that constitutes the fastest-growing segment of the U.S. population, to serve on the U.S. Supreme Court. The U.S. Census Bureau reports that Hispanics now constitute nearly one in six residents, or 46.9 million people. Even more telling for the future: 44 percent of children younger than 18 and 47 percent of children younger than the age of 5 are now from minority families.

Hispanics (the identification adopted by the government) or Latinos (a term some in this group prefer) are diverse in terms of country of origin. Some, like Sonia Sotomayor, are from Puerto Rico, a U.S. territory. Others are Cuban, many of whose parents fled the dictatorship of Fidel Castro. Others are from Mexico, the world's 12th most populous country, with over 111 million people. Others are from other central and South American countries. While united by the Spanish language, the Latino population is suspicious of those from other countries.

Most importantly for American politics, Hispanics are also diverse in terms of their immigration status. No accurate counts of how many illegal immigrants are in the country exist, but many estimate about 11 million. (Some advocacy groups place the number higher.) Immigration has become a major political issue in the United States, dividing both the American population and the nation's two major political parties. Part of this debate focuses on the role of the criminal justice system.

Hispanics share many of the same social disadvantages as blacks (Demuth 2003), including poverty, unemployment, living in neighborhoods with high crime rates and a history of discrimination. But in addition they face some unique problems surrounding language and cultural heritage. Some Latino victims/defendants speak little if any English, which makes it hard for them to understand what is happening during investigations, arrests, court appearances, and the like. Besides lacking language skills, Latino victims/defendants also often lack a basic understanding of the American justice system. Their heritage is European law, which places less emphasis on the rights of criminal defendants. Moreover, in some of their native countries, the justice system has a history of suppression, which makes them particularly fearful of governmental officials.

The social disadvantages faced by Latinos have several important consequences for the criminal justice system. For one, Latinos are less likely to report crimes to the police. In crimes of violence such as assaults, robberies, and rapes, for example, Hispanic women report the crime to authorities just 35 percent of the time, as compared with 51 percent for white women, and 63 percent for black women

Mostly Underclass

Typical felony defendants possess few of the skills needed to compete successfully in an increasingly technological society. They are drawn from what sociologists call the urban underclass (Jencks and Peterson 1991). The association of crime with poverty helps to explain, in part, why the overwhelming number of crimes—primarily burglary, theft, and drug sale—are committed for economic motives. Although crimes of violence dominate the headlines, most defendants are not dangerous; they are charged with property or drug offenses. As for violent crimes, competing theories offer varying explanations for the fact that the "ghetto poor" are disproportionately involved in violent crime. Anderson (1999, p. 33) argued that the "street code" in such economically depressed areas leads to a subculture with norms that are "conspicuously opposed to those of mainstream society" insofar as they endorse violence as an appropriate response to disrespect (see also Bourgois 2003).

(Karmen 2010). The lack of trust in governmental authorities coupled with a fear of being deported is a major reason Latinos often do not report crimes to the police. In turn, Latinos may be targeted because they are less likely to report the crime.

It is also harder for police and prosecutors to deal with crimes in which Latinos are victims or defendants. Traditionally, the Hispanic population was concentrated in states sharing a border with Mexico and a few big cities. Today the population has spread across the nation, meaning that many police departments have few if any officers who can take an accurate police report from a Spanish speaker. The same barriers face prosecutors, public defenders, and judges, with justice sometimes lost in the translation. For example, following the slaying of a Hispanic migrant worker, six Spanish-speaking witnesses were held for months in jail as material witnesses, but they had no court-appointed lawyer because no one in the public defender's office could read the letters they wrote (Alexander-Bloch 2007).

How well or how poorly Latinos fare in the criminal justice system is hard to tell. An extensive body of research has compared white defendants with black defendants, but relatively little is known about Latino defendants (Martinez 2007). But we do know that after arrest Hispanics are more likely to be detained in jail than blacks or whites (Demuth 2003).

The growing Hispanic population and the issues surrounding immigration have strained the U.S. justice system in several important ways (Hsu 2009). When an immigrant, whether in this country legally or illegally, is arrested, he or she is more likely to be detained in jail because Immigration and Customs Enforcement (ICE) puts a hold on that person for possible deportation. As a result, jail populations increase and local officials demand that the U.S. government pay for the additional costs (Bowes 2009). Yet ironically, many illegal immigrants convicted of a minor crime are not deported because the U.S. immigration system is overwhelmed and therefore chooses to deport only those convicted of the most serious offenses (Carroll 2008).

The growing number of immigrants has also placed the United States at odds with the international legal community. The Vienna Convention on Consular Relations gives foreign nationals who are accused of a crime the right to talk with the consulate of their home country. The International Court of Justice found that Texas violated the treaty by not informing Jose Medellin, a Texas death row inmate, of these rights. But the Supreme Court refused to follow the decision of the world court, holding that the treaty was not binding on the United States and that rulings of the International Court of Justice are not binding when they contradict states' criminal procedures (*Medellin v. Texas* 2008). It is also worth noting that the Mexican constitution prohibits that nation from deporting one of its citizens in death penalty cases.

RACIAL MINORITIES OVERREPRESENTED

Race remains a divisive issue in American politics, and nowhere is this more evident than in the area of crime. African-Americans, Hispanics, and Native Americans are arrested, convicted, and imprisoned at significantly higher rates per capita than whites. At the same time, it is important to stress that historically whites constituted the majority of those in prison, a fact conveniently ignored on some radio and TV discussions.

Why minorities are overrepresented in the criminal justice system is a topic of considerable importance (and therefore addressed in several later chapters). To some it is an indication that minorities are more likely to be poor and, therefore, more likely to commit crimes for economic advancement (Haynie, Weiss and Piquero 2008). Others counter that discrimination is the reason; minorities are more likely to be targeted by criminal justice officials and also more likely to receive a harsh sentence (Keen and Jacobs 2009). Whatever the cause, the impact is enormous. An estimated 16.6 percent of African-American males will serve time in state or federal prison in their life-times, as compared with 7.7 percent of Latino males and 2.6 percent of white males (Bureau of Justice Statistic 2007). But no matter the cause, in terms of attitudes about the racial gap in the criminal justice system, whites and African-Americans are worlds far apart (Unnever 2008).

Altogether. one out of three Americans is a minority, with Hispanics having recently become the largest minority (see Courts, Controversy and Racial Discrimination: Can Latinos Get Equal Justice under the Law?).

DEFENDANTS IN COURT

The **defendant** is supposed to stand at the center of the criminal court drama. Yet typical felony defendants are largely powerless to control their fates; they are more objects to be acted upon than keys to what happens. Because most defendants are poor and uneducated, they are ill equipped to deal with the technical abstractions of the criminal court process. Many are incapable of understanding even the simplest instructions about the right to bail or the presumption of innocence. Many are too inarticulate to aid their attorneys in preparing a defense. Many hold unfavorable attitudes toward the law and the criminal justice system and thus regard the judge and all other court personnel, including their defense attorneys, with hostility and distrust.

The nature of the clientele makes criminal courts a depressing place to work. Judges, prosecutors, and defense attorneys seldom come away from their day's activities with a sense of accomplishment, for many of the criminal cases involve social problems—drug addiction, marital problems, lack of education, and mental illness—over which the court personnel have no control. Many cases stem from disputes between people who know one another.

Court personnel have little empathy with or understanding of the types of defendants whose fates they must decide. Members of the courtroom work group are essentially middle class. Little in their backgrounds or training has equipped them to deal with violations of the law committed by the poor.

COURTS THROUGH THE EYES OF VICTIMS AND WITNESSES

Traditionally, victims and witnesses have been the forgotten participants in the criminal justice system. Fictional and nonfictional treatments of the court process direct attention to the criminal as victim rather than to the victim as victim (Elias 1986). More recently, however, a growing number of studies have focused on the victim (Karmen 2010). These studies have identified ways in which the courts, along with the rest of the criminal justice community, have ignored the interests of victims and witnesses.

FRUSTRATIONS IN COPING WITH THE PROCESS

Crime victims once played a prominent role in the criminal process. Before the American Revolution, victims were the central figures in the criminal justice drama. Criminals' fates were closely tied to their victims' wishes. When crime became viewed as an offense against the state, the victim was assigned a subordinate role. As prosecutorial dominance increased, the power of the victim declined (see Chapter 6). Victims lost control over their cases, and their role was reduced to initiating investigations by complaining to the police and testifying for the prosecution as just another piece of evidence in the state's presentation of damning facts against the accused (Karmen 2010).

Several studies have documented the hardships victims and witnesses face while participating in the criminal court process (Cannavale and Falcon 1976; Connick and Davis 1983; McDonald 1976). Although some are minor inconveniences, such as getting to the courthouse and finding a parking place, other hardships are more significant:

- Trial delays, which result in frequent travel and wasted time
- Long waits in uncomfortable surroundings
- Wages lost for time spent going to court
- Fear of the defendant or retaliation from the defendant's associates
- A sense that criminal justice personnel are indifferent to their plight

TRAVAILS OF TESTIFYING

Victims and witnesses also face major problems while testifying in court. Because few people are accustomed to testifying, lawyers must coach their witnesses ahead of time to answer only the question asked, to speak forcefully (but not belligerently), and not to become rattled by cross-examination. Even after such preparation, many witnesses are uncomfortable during cross-examination, as the defense attorney tests their memory, challenges their veracity, or even suggests that they were somehow responsible for their own victimization. After enduring cross-examination, some victims report feeling as though they, and not the offender, have been portrayed as the criminal.

Most of what we know about the ordeal of testifying in court comes from studies of rape victims (Resick 1984). The dominant conclusion is that the victim, rather than the defendant, is put on trial. Testifying in court provokes anxiety for several months, exacerbating psychological distress (Steketee and Austin 1989). Holmstrom and Burgess (1983), both of whom counsel rape victims at Boston City Hospital, followed the cases of 14 women who testified in court during a rape trial. They concluded that the trauma is often significant, because the victim must publicly repeat in detail how the rape occurred. The type of defense used by the defense attorney also has an impact on the victim's adjustment to the crime. A defense claim that the woman consented to sex is injurious, because it puts the victim on trial and calls into question her discouragement of the perpetrator (Steketee and Austin 1989). Moreover, the defense often seeks to blame the victim by suggesting that she consented, did not resist, was provocatively dressed, and so on. It can take little to discredit the victim. Following the Holmstrom and Burgess study, most states have passed legislation limiting inquiry into a rape victim's past sexual conduct (Caringella 2008).

SURPRISING SUPPORT FOR THE SYSTEM

Somewhat surprisingly, despite the problems and frustrations experienced, victims and witnesses still express overall support for the court process (Hagan 1983). A 1976 study conducted in Milwaukee found that victims and witnesses were satisfied or very satisfied with the handling of their cases by the police (81 percent), district attorney (75 percent), and judge (66 percent). Less than 15 percent said that they were dissatisfied (Knudten et al. 1976). Favorable judgments were independent of whether a victim was satisfied with the eventual outcome of the case. Since that time, courts have grown more responsive to the needs of victims and witnesses.

Research suggests that increased levels of victim input into the handling of criminal cases moderately increase victims' satisfaction with the judicial system (Erez and Roberts 2007). Such findings, however, are contingent upon a variety of factors, such as whether victims even know about their rights to participate in various processes, whether the victim was treated with dignity and respect, and whether there was an admission of guilt or an apology from the perpetrator.

VICTIMS AND WITNESSES THROUGH THE EYES OF THE COURT

The criminal courts confront a double bind with regard to victims. On the one hand, victims are valued for the cases they bring to the system; their misfortunes become the raw material of the court process (Exhibit 9.2). On the other hand, individual victims represent a potential source of irrationality in the process. The personal and often emotional involvement of victims in the crime experience can generate particular demands for case outcomes that have little to do with the public interest. Thus, at times members of the courtroom work group perceive that the victim's demands for public justice actually mask a desire for private vengeance (Hagan 1983). Members of the courtroom workgroup also know that particularly in violent and gang-related crime, the same individual may, at difference times be a victim, a witnesses, and an offender (Dedel 2006).

LACK OF COOPERATION

Many victims and witnesses are reluctant to become involved in the criminal justice process. More than half of all major crimes are never reported to the police; even when they are reported, not all victims wish to prosecute (Chapter 10). Particularly in low-income, high-crime neighborhoods of the nation's largest cities, victims and witnesses may fail to cooperate with the police. In the words of Captain Sheilah Coley of Newark, New Jersey: "I don't know what frustrates me more. Those knuckleheads killing each other, or the residents who won't cooperate with my officers." (quoted in Jacobs 2007). When her officers respond to reports of gun fire, potential witnesses respond with blank looks. This lack of cooperation is fueled by hip-hop culture's "stop snitching" mantra.

	Exhibit 9.2	
MAJOR ACTIVITIES OF VICTIMS IN THE STEPS OF THE COURT PROCESS		
	LAW ON THE BOOKS	**LAW IN ACTION**
Crime	No general requirement to report crimes to the police.	Thirty-eight percent of personal and household crimes are reported to the police.
Arrest	A citizen's arrest is the taking of a person into physical custody by a person other than a law enforcement officer for the purpose of delivering the person to the custody of a law enforcement officer.	The vast majority of arrests are made by law enforcement officers. Citizen's arrests may result in injury to the victim and may also result in civil lawsuits.
Initial appearance	Open to the public.	Very unlikely for victim to be present because unlikely to know timing of the event.
Bail	VRA* provides that victims have a right to be heard if present and to submit a statement "to determine a release from custody."	Victims are very rarely present.
Charging	Victim has no role, and the VRA states that "nothing in this article shall provide grounds for the victim to challenge the charging decision."	Reluctance or refusal of victims to cooperate is a key reason for case dismissal.
Preliminary hearing	Besides the right to notice and to be present, the VRA is silent on the role of victims during this stage.	Victims rarely testify because hearsay evidence is admissible.
Grand jury	Grand jury can subpoena victim to testify.	In grand jury states, victim is likely to be subpoenaed to testify.
Arraignment	VRA provides that victims of crimes have the right to notice of proceedings like this.	Victims are rarely present.
Evidence	In some jurisdictions, the defense is entitled to see a copy of the victim's statement to the police.	Even if not required, some district attorneys disclose the victim's statement in hopes of inducing a guilty plea.
Plea bargaining	VRA provides that victims may be heard and may submit a statement during an acceptance of a negotiated plea.	Some jurisdictions allow victims to be heard with regard to the plea bargain, but few actually appear.

Exhibit 9.2

CONTINUED

	LAW ON THE BOOKS	LAW IN ACTION
Trial	If they are to testify, victims generally cannot view the trial (wording in the VRA concerning public proceedings might change this law).	Victim's testimony is a key part of the trial.
Sentencing	VRA provides that victims may be heard and may submit a statement during sentencing.	Victims are unlikely to appear.
Appeal	Like other court proceedings, appellate argument is open to the public.	Victims are very unlikely to be present.

*VRA = Proposed Victims' Rights Amendment to the U.S. Constitution

Some specific witness-related problems include giving the police incorrect addresses, failing to show up in court, and offering testimony that is confused, garbled, or contradicted by other facts. Witness-related problems result in a significant number of cases in which the prosecutor refuses to file charges or the case is later dismissed (Boland et al. 1982). But when victims cooperate with the prosecution, the odds that a case will be prosecuted increase dramatically (Dawson and Dinovitzer 2001).

Not all uncooperative behavior can be blamed on victims and witnesses, however; the court process can be equally at fault. In Washington, D.C., a study focusing on what it called "noncooperative" witnesses reported that 41 percent were never told that they should contact the prosecutor; 62 percent were never notified of court appearances; and 43 percent stated that the police, prosecutor, and judge all failed to explain the witnesses' rights and duties. Other reports have found that the longer the case is delayed, the more likely it is that witnesses will not appear when summoned (Cannavale and Falcon 1976).

WITNESS INTIMIDATION

One form of noncooperation involves witness intimidation. Persons who have been victims of crime, or witnessed a crime, may be pressured not to testify. Witness intimidation may take the form of threats of violence or actual violence itself against the person in question or his or her friends and family members. Property damage may also be involved. Such pressures may be made by the defendant, members of the defendant's family, or other associates (sometimes other gang members) (Dedel 2006). Witness intimidation is often a specific focus of victim/witness assistance programs, discussed later in this chapter.

CHARACTERISTICS OF VICTIMS

How a case is handled is determined by the identity of the victim as well as that of the offender. Prosecutors allocate their limited resources to the cases they believe constitute the most "trouble" (Hagan 1983). Not surprisingly, such judgments correlate with the desire for high conviction rates. Prosecutors assume that judges and juries will find the claims of certain kinds of victims credible and acceptable, but not the claims of others (Stanko 1981–1982). The troubles of older, white, male, employed victims are considered more worthy of public processing (Myers and Hagan 1979), but most victims of violent crime tend to be young, nonwhite, male, divorced or never married, low income, and unemployed (Bureau of Justice Statistics 1988c; Elias 1986). For example, legal outcomes in murder cases were related to the race, gender, and conduct of victims at the time of the incident (Baumer, Messner, and Felson 2000).

PRIOR RELATIONSHIPS BETWEEN DEFENDANTS AND VICTIMS

Perhaps the most important victim characteristic that influences case processing is the prior relationship between defendants and victims. The following case is illustrative.

> An auxiliary police officer watched a woman approach a man as he emerged from a liquor store. It was dark. The officer thought he saw a knife flash in her hand, and the man seemed to hand her some money. She fled, and the officer went to the aid of the victim, taking him to the hospital for treatment.
>
> The officer saw the woman on the street a few days later and arrested her for first-degree robbery on the victim's sworn complaint. It was presumably a "high-quality" arrest—identification of the perpetrator by an eyewitness, not from mugshots or a lineup, but in a crowd. Yet, shortly thereafter, this apparently airtight case was dismissed on the prosecutor's motion.
>
> What the victim had not explained to the police was that the defendant, an alcoholic, had been his girlfriend for the past 5 years; that they had been drinking together the night of the incident; that she had taken some money from him and got angry when he took it back; that she had flown into a fury when he then gave her only a dollar outside the liquor store; and that she had slashed at him with a pen knife in anger and run off. He had been sufficiently annoyed to have her charged with robbery, but, as the judge who dismissed the case said, "He wasn't really injured. Before it got into court they had kissed and made up." In fact, the victim actually approached the defense attorney before the hearing and asked him to prevail upon the judge and the assistant district attorney (ADA) to dismiss the charges against his girlfriend. (Vera Institute of Justice 1981, p. xxii)

This case is one of many cited by the Vera Institute that show the importance of the prior relationship between defendants and victims.

Prior relationships between defendants and victims are more common than generally assumed. In half of all felony arrests in New York, the victim had a prior relationship with the defendant. Prior relationships were frequent in cases of homicide and assault, in which they were expected, but they were also frequent in cases of robbery, in which they were not. Other studies reach a similar conclusion. Nationwide, roughly half of all violent crimes (rape, assault, and robbery) are committed by relatives, friends, or acquaintances of the victim (Bureau of Justice Statistics 2002). Homicides, in particular, are usually committed not by strangers but by someone the victim knows by sight; in fact, the victim and the perpetrator are strangers in only 14 percent of all murders (Fox and Zawitz 2007). Criminal court officials often regard crimes involving people who know one another as not very serious, viewing them as private disputes rather than offenses against the entire community.

DOMESTIC VIOLENCE

The prior relationship between victims and defendants is most apparent in crimes against women. Women are much more likely than men to experience violence committed by an intimate partner, such as a current or former spouse, lover, or boyfriends or girlfriends, including same-sex relationships. Measuring violence between intimate partners is difficult because it often occurs in private and victims are often reluctant to report incidents to anyone because of shame or fear of reprisal. Rates of intimate violence have been declining over the past two decades but still remain a significant issue in American society (Bureau of Justice Statistics 2003a; Catalano 2009).

There has been a growing awareness during the past 40 years that domestic violence is a serious social problem. Advocacy groups for battered women and victims have worked vigorously for policy changes designed to make the criminal justice system treat domestic violence as a serious offense. Jeffrey Fagan (1996) gave this movement a name in his aptly titled book, *The Criminalization of Domestic Violence*. As a result, there have been significant changes in how the criminal justice system responds to domestic violence. The question of what constitutes the most effective criminal justice response, however, has stirred considerable controversy (Maxwell, Garner, and Fagan 2002). The prior relationship between victim and offender causes particular problems for law enforcement officials in the area of domestic violence (Buzawa and Buzawa 1996).

Historically, police officers made an arrest only as a last resort—if taking the suspect into custody seemed the only way to ensure no more violence that night. The police have been urged to make more arrests, and prosecutors to file charges, no matter what the wishes of the victim. Mandatory-arrest policies clearly produce higher arrest rates (Hirschel et al. 2007). Whether these mandatory arrest policies are effective in reducing intimate-partner violence has been questioned, however (Hirschel et al. 1992). Researchers report that arrest reduces domestic violence in some cities but increases it in others (Schmidt and Sherman 1993). Although some exceptions exist, most studies to date indicate that criminal justice interventions deter intimate-partner violence or improve victim safety (Spohn 2008).

Arrests, however, do not always lead to prosecutions. Many women call the police to stop the violence but later have a change of heart and refuse to sign a complaint. In *Bronx D.A.*, Sarena Straus (2006, p. 31) expressed her frustration as a prosecutor in the sex crimes and domestic violence unit:

> I found that a large percentage of the abused women who came into the Complaint Room refused to press charges, and most of them would return time and time again. Many of these women were known to their local precincts as they were constantly calling 911 for help.... The story was often the same. They loved the guy. They knew he wouldn't do it again. He said he was sorry. He bought them flowers. It was their fault because they provoked him.

At times, the district attorneys would pressure the woman to file charges, but often they simply accepted defeat.

The criminalization of domestic violence has also greatly increased the workload of the courts. Between 1989 and 1998, for example, domestic relations cases in state courts across the nation grew by 178 percent (Ostrom and Kauder 1999) with about a 10 percent increase in the following decade (LaFountain et al. 2008). In response to the growing awareness of domestic violence as a serious social problem, many courts in the United States have created domestic violence courts that emphasize a problem-solving approach (see Chapter 4). An evaluation of one such court found significantly lower rates of re-arrests among defendants processed through the domestic violence court (Gover, MacDonald, and Alpert 2003).

LAW AND POPULAR CULTURE

Law and Order: Special Victims Unit (NBC, 1999–present)

This long-running television show tells the stories of an elite squad of police detectives who are assigned to a Special Victims Unit ("SVU") in New York City which investigates sexually-related offenses like rape and child molestation. The show, while fictional, often bases its storylines on real cases. Sometimes, the show gets it right; most of the time, however, its depictions of defendants and victims are inaccurate. Britto et al. (2007) conducted a content analysis of the fifth season of *SVU*. Here are the highlights of their findings.

What they get right:

- As in reality, *SVU* depicts police officers and prosecutors struggling with the difficult subject matter of sexual victimization.
- As in real life, the majority of *SVU* cases do not involve strangers, but rather involve individuals who know each other.

- "The majority of the victims portrayed on *SVU* were shown as innocent or blameless and it appeared that the show actively tried to counter the common myth that victims cause sexual assault" (p. 51).

What they get wrong:

- Clearance Rates—Sex crimes pose significant problems for the criminal justice system. In Manhattan, "just less than one half of all murder and rape reports are cleared by arrest, and of those cleared by arrest only 51% result in a conviction" (p. 49). In contrast, 100% of suspects on *SVU* were caught and 92% of them were convicted in court.
- Types of Rape—Most of the rapes that occur on *SVU* are not spousal or date-rapes; in reality, these two types of rape account for the overwhelming majority of rapes.

CONTINUED

Law and Order: Special Victims Unit (NBC, 1999–present)

- Nature of Harm—While sexual assaults are clearly violent crimes that inflict a tremendous amount of psychological harm, "victims generally survive and in the majority of cases do not require hospitalization for their physical injuries" (p. 45). On *SVU*, however, the crimes are usually extremely violent, resulting in the physical brutalization of victims. Indeed, nearly 60 percent of the victims on the show are dead by the end of an episode.

- Victim Age—Nearly half of all *SVU* victims are under the age of 18. According to the National Crime Victimization Survey, "the actual figure is closer to one-quarter of all victims" (p. 46).

- Victim Gender—Roughly 40 percent of the victims on *SVU* are male whereas "only 12 percent of all victims of sexual assault and murder are male" according to the NCVS victimization rates adjusted for the population of Manhattan (p. 46).

- Victim Race—Almost two-thirds of the victims on *SVU* are white, while the majority of sex crime victims in Manhattan are members of racial and ethnic minority groups.

- Offender and Gender Issues—Females commit approximately 5 percent of the sexual assaults and murders in Manhattan. On *SVU*, however, females commit more than one-third of these offenses. In contrast, males commit 95 percent of the rapes, murders, and manslaughters in Manhattan, but only 63 percent of the crimes on *SVU*. Moreover, female offenders on the show are often portrayed "as being particularly manipulative and cruel in their planning and execution of violent crimes" (p. 48). This is especially true for female juvenile offenders who are depicted as "brutal, vindictive," and "petty"; in contrast, "juvenile male offenders were shown as victims of their circumstances" (p. 48). Finally, male offenders were significantly more likely to plea bargain a reduced sentence, whereas female offenders were more likely to go to trial, be convicted, and receive a harsh suggested sentence.

After watching one or more episodes of *Law and Order: SVU,* be prepared to discuss the following questions:

1. Britto et al. found that although most victims on SVU were portrayed sympathetically, female victims were more likely than men to appear to contribute to their victimization by associating with the wrong crowd, talking to strangers, or using drugs and alcohol" (p. 45). What are the societal implications of this?

2. Do you think that the over-representation of female offenders and male victims on SVU tends to de-gender sex crimes? Why or why not? Because the storylines often illicit sympathy for victims, do you think that these over-representations mask issues of gender inequality, patriarchy, and male socialization? Explain your position.

3. Britto et al. argued that because SVU consistently depicts extremely violent rapes that cause severe injuries or death, the show perpetuates the "myth of the sadistic, psychologically disturbed rapist who preys on innocent victims for 'sick' enjoyment" (p. 51). What effect do you think this has on jurors who sit in judgment of real sexual assault cases that lack the extreme brutality that is often portrayed on the show? Why?

A growing number of courts rely on batterer programs as the mandate of choice. Researchers, however, report that batterer programs standing alone do not appear to reduce recidivism (Labriola, Rempel, and Davis 2008). However, programs involving a coordinated response that involve courts and justice agencies appear to be more effective (Visher et al. 2008).

Legal sanctions against domestic violence are not limited to criminal law. Victims of domestic violence may request a **civil protection order**. Recent legislative changes in most jurisdictions now make these court orders easier to obtain. They are no longer limited to women who have filed for divorce, and they may be issued on an emergency basis without the other party present. However, civil protection orders are not self-enforcing; there is even a danger that a civil protection order may induce a false sense of security among some women who are at risk of continued battery from a former intimate. Conversely, some are concerned that protection orders can be abused. In the words of public defender David Feige (2006, p. 182), "Though a fine idea in principle, orders of protection are constantly abused. It is not at all uncommon for vindictive, angry partners to use orders of protection to wreak havoc on each other—using them as substitutes for eviction orders or citing them to justify ignoring child custody agreements."

Aiding Victims and Witnesses

For decades, reformers have urged that victims and witnesses be accorded better treatment.

- In 1931 the National Commission on Law Observance and Enforcement concluded that effective administration of public justice required willing witnesses, but testifying in court imposed unreasonable burdens on citizens.
- A 1938 American Bar Association report found that witness fees were deplorably low, courthouse accommodations uncomfortable, and witnesses were frequently summoned to court numerous times only to have the case continued.

But it was not until the 1960s that attention was seriously devoted to the problems faced by victims and witnesses in court and to ways of improving the situation (Karmen 2010).

- In 1967 the President's Commission on Law Enforcement and Administration of Justice highlighted a "growing concern that the average citizen identifies himself less and less with the criminal process and its officials."

A few years later, concern for victims and witnesses of crime rose to a crescendo. Crime victims received special attention from the White House.

- In 1982, the President's Task Force on Victims of Crime stressed the need for achieving a balance between the needs and rights of the victim and those of the defendant.

Public and governmental concern over the plight of victims has prompted numerous pieces of legislation (Exhibit 9.3). The Victim and Witness Protection Act, a federal law passed in 1982, required greater protection of victims and witnesses and also mandated guidelines for the fair treatment of victims and witnesses in federal criminal cases. The Victims of Crime Act of 1984 authorized federal funds for state victim programs. Spurred by these concerns, every state has passed comprehensive legislation protecting the interests of victims. In short, a wide variety of programs have been adopted in recent years to improve the treatment crime victims receive from the criminal justice system. The three most common

Exhibit 9.3

Key Developments in Law Relating to Victims

National Crime Victims' Week	1980	Annual event focusing on the plight of crime victims.
Victim and Witness Protection Act	1982	Enhance and protect the necessary role of crime victims and witnesses in the criminal justice process.
Victims' Rights Amendments	1982	California is first state to adopt.

Exhibit 9.3

CONTINUED

Victim of Crimes Act	1984	Established Crime Victim Fund from fines, penalties, and bond forfeitures of convicted federal criminals.
Booth v. Maryland	1987	In capital cases, victim impact statements are unconstitutional because they introduce the risk of imposing the death penalty in an arbitrary and capricious manner.
South Carolina v. Gathers	1989	Characteristics of the victim are irrelevant during death-penalty deliberations.
Payne v. Tennessee	1991	The Eighth Amendment creates no bar to the introduction of victim impact statements during sentencing.
Simon & Schuster v. New York State Crime Victims Board	1991	Declared unconstitutional New York's "Son of Sam" law, which sought to prevent criminals from profiting from their crimes.
Violence Against Women Act	1994	Comprehensive law creating a variety of programs to strengthen law enforcement, prosecution, and victim services in cases involving crimes against women.
The Antiterrorism and Effective Death Penalty Act	1996	A federal court must impose mandatory restitution, without consideration of the defendant's ability to pay.
Victims' Rights Amendment (VRA)	1996	VRA proposed in the U.S. Congress.
	2000	VRA withdrawn in face of virtually certain defeat.
Crime Victims' Rights Act	2004	Federal legislation protecting victims in federal court that parallels the former Victims' Rights Amendment.
Town of Castle Rock, Colorado v. Gonzales	2005	A victim of domestic violence does not have the right to sue the local police department for failing to enforce a restraining order against her husband, who subsequently murdered her three children.
Carey v. Musladin	2009	A federal appeals court overstepped its authority when it granted a new trial to a murder defendant whose victim's relatives sat at the trial, in the view of the jury, wearing buttons with the victim's picture on them.

types of initiatives are: (1) victim/witness assistance programs, (2) victim compensation programs, and (3) a victim's bill of rights.

VICTIM/WITNESS ASSISTANCE PROGRAMS

Victim/witness assistance programs encourage cooperation in the conviction of criminals by reducing the inconvenience citizens face when appearing in court (Finn and Lee 1988). Typical activities include providing comfortable and secure waiting areas, assisting with the prompt return of stolen property that has been recovered, and providing crisis intervention. These programs also provide victims and witnesses with a clearer understanding of the court process by distributing brochures, explaining court procedures, and notifying witnesses of upcoming court dates (Webster 1988). Of particular concern is victim and witness intimidation. Intimidation can be either case-specific—threats or violence intended to dissuade a witness from testifying in a specific case— or communitywide—acts of gangs or drug-selling groups intended to foster a general atmosphere of fear and noncooperation within a neighborhood or community (Healey 1995).

Today, virtually all jurisdictions of any size have established programs aimed at helping crime victims cope with the hardships of victimization and deal with the often-troublesome demands of the criminal justice system. Most are based in criminal justice agencies (prosecutors', police, and sheriffs' offices). Often the program title is Victim Services. Overall, few victims use these programs, and older victims of violent crimes are more likely to use victim services than are younger victims of nonviolent crimes (Sims, Yost, and Abbott 2005).

Evaluations of victim/witness assistance programs have yielded mixed results. In some communities, a victim's willingness to cooperate in the future was positively associated with considerate treatment by criminal justice personnel (National Institute of Justice 1982; Norton 1983). Thus, victims and witnesses receiving help were more likely to appear when summoned than those who had not been aided. But no such impact was found in other communities (Davis 1983; Skogan and Wycoff 1987). Those helped by the program appeared at the same rate as those who were not aided, and there was no change in the rate of case dismissals.

Andrew Karmen (2010) suggests that one explanation for these research findings is that expectations of significant improvements in case outcomes were based on faulty assumptions. The presumption is that the adjudication process is characterized by an adversarial model. The reality is that the courtroom work group has a mutual interest in processing large numbers of cases expeditiously. Thus, whereas victims see their situations as unique events that deserve careful and individual consideration, judges, prosecutors, and defense attorneys see them as routine occurrences, to be disposed of based on "going rates."

VICTIM COMPENSATION PROGRAMS

The criminal justice system in the United States is offender-oriented, focusing on the apprehension, prosecution, and punishment of wrongdoers. While emphasizing the rehabilitation of offenders, the system has done little to help victims recover from the financial and emotional problems that they suffer.

Civil lawsuits are of little relevance, because most criminal defendants have no money to pay monetary damages for personal injuries or damage to property. An increasingly common technique is restitution, in which the court orders the defendant to pay the victim for the losses suffered (see Chapter 15). But a major shortcoming of restitution is that in many crimes no offender is convicted. Even if convicted, many defendants have little or no ability to provide adequate compensation to a victim. And once restitution is ordered, the victim's likelihood of collecting is not good (Davis, Smith, and Hillenbrand 1992).

When restitution by the offender is inadequate or impractical, compensation by a third party (an insurance company, for example) is the only alternative. But many victims, because they are poor, do not have insurance covering medical expenses or property losses. The government is another sort of third party. Victim compensation programs rest on the premise that the government should counterbalance losses suffered by victims of criminal acts. The first compensation program in the United States began in California in 1965. Similar programs quickly emerged in a few other states.

In 1984 Congress passed the Victims of Crime Act, which established a Crime Victims Fund administered by the Office for Victims of Crimes within the U.S. Department of Justice. The fund is financed primarily from fines paid by defendants in federal court (Parent, Auerbach, and Carlson 1992).

The federal backing has now spurred all states to enact legislation providing compensation for at least certain classes of crime victims. The staffs are small, however, and relatively few claims are filed—fewer than 100,000 during a typical year. Most programs provide for recovery of medical expenses and some lost earnings; none reimburses the victim for lost or damaged property. The maximum amount that can be paid in damages ranges from $1,000 to $50,000.

Victim compensation programs appear to provide clear benefits to victims of crime, but the actual results of such programs require careful scrutiny. Preliminary evaluations of compensation programs have yielded findings that are disappointing for administrators (Karmen 2010). Cumbersome administrative procedures lead to added frustrations and increased alienation. Moreover, few victims of violent crimes apply for benefits, and even fewer claimants receive any money (Elias 1986). Eligibility requirements are strict. Most states require that the victim assist in the prosecution of the offender, effectively excluding many domestic violence, child abuse, and sexual assault victims (McCormack 1991). Similarly, most states also have a "family exclusion" clause, which makes victims living in the same household as the offender ineligible. Crime victims must also

be "innocent" victims (those to whom no contributory fault can be ascribed). Indeed, in eight states, all persons with a felony conviction are ineligible for aid, even if their current problem has nothing to do with their past illegal activity (Mitchell 2008). Overall, these programs are designed to spread the limited funds around, rather than to concentrate on a few badly injured victims.

VICTIMS' BILL OF RIGHTS

Nowhere is the awakened concern about victims of crime more readily apparent than in proposals for a victims' bill of rights (Exhibit 9.4). Apart from sharing the title, however, these proposals vary markedly, reflecting different philosophies. In 1982, the President's Task Force on Victims of Crime submitted 68 separate recommendations aimed at achieving a balance between the needs and rights of the victim and those of the defendant. Also in 1982, California voters approved Proposition 8 by a 2-to-1 margin. Known as the Victims' Bill of Rights, it added 12 controversial provisions to the state constitution and the

---

Exhibit 9.4

TEXT OF PROPOSED VICTIMS' RIGHTS AMENDMENT

108th CONGRESS
1st Session
S. J. RES. 1
Proposing an amendment to the Constitution of the United States to protect the rights of crime victims.
In the Senate of the United States
January 7, 2003
Mr. KYL (for himself and Mrs. FEINSTEIN) introduced the following joint resolution; which was read twice and referred to the Committee on the Judiciary

Joint Resolution

Proposing an amendment to the Constitution of the United States to protect the rights of crime victims.

Resolved by the Senate and House of Representatives of the United States of America in Congress assembled, (two-thirds of each House concurring therein), That the following article is proposed as

Exhibit 9.4

CONTINUED

an amendment to the Constitution of the United States:

Article--

SECTION 1.

The rights of victims of violent crime, being capable of protection without denying the constitutional rights of those accused of victimizing them, are hereby established and shall not be denied by any State or the United States and may be restricted only as provided in this article.

SECTION 2.

A victim of violent crime shall have the right to reasonable and timely notice of any public proceeding involving the crime and of any release or escape of the accused; the rights not to be excluded from such public proceeding and reasonably to be heard at public release, plea, sentencing, reprieve, and pardon proceedings; and the right to adjudicative decisions that duly consider the victim's safety, interest in avoiding unreasonable delay, and just and timely claims to restitution from the offender. These rights shall not be restricted except when and to the degree dictated by a substantial interest in public safety or the administration of criminal justice, or by compelling necessity.

SECTION 3.

Nothing in this article shall be construed to provide grounds for a new trial or to authorize any claim for damages. Only the victim or the victim's lawful representative may assert the rights established by this article, and no person accused of the crime may obtain any form of relief hereunder.

SECTION 4.

Congress shall have power to enforce by appropriate legislation the provisions of this article. Nothing in this article shall affect the President's authority to grant reprieves or pardons.

SECTION 5.

This article shall be inoperative unless it has been ratified as an amendment to the Constitution by the legislatures of three-fourths of the several States within 7 years from the date of its submission to the States by the Congress. This article shall take effect on the 180th day after the date of its ratification.

criminal code. More recently, in 2008 California voters approved Proposition 9, which granted additional rights to the victim at the expense of the defendant (Karmen 2010). These versions of the victims' bill of rights reflect the rallying cry of the law-and-order movement, which accuses the courts of protecting the rights of defendants rather than those of victims. Premised on the notion that defendants escape too easily from the court process, these proposals stress substantive changes in the law, such as abolishing the exclusionary rule, limiting bail, restricting plea bargaining, and imposing stiffer sentences.

Other proposed victims' bills of rights are less ideological, emphasizing improvements in court procedures to better the lot of victims and witnesses. For example, the National Conference of the Judiciary on the Rights of Victims of Crime adopted a Statement of Recommended Judicial Practices, suggesting: (1) fair treatment of victims and witnesses through better information about court procedures; (2) victim participation and input through all stages of judicial proceedings; and (3) better protection of victims and witnesses from harassment, threats, intimidation, and harm.

COURTS, CONTROVERSY, AND REDUCING CRIME

Should the Victims' Rights Amendment Be Adopted?

Efforts to protect the rights of victims began with the passage in most jurisdictions of victims' rights legislation. These activities soon expanded to include a demand that these protections be given even greater force of law by placing them in state constitutions, and the public has responded with overwhelming support. Thirty-two states have passed victims' rights amendments to their state constitutions, and others are considering adding similar amendments (National Center for Victims of Crime 2009). Having achieved considerable success at the state level, victims' rights groups began pressing for an amendment to the U.S. Constitution (see Exhibit 9.4).

Proposals to amend the U.S. Constitution are frequently offered but rarely adopted. Amending the Constitution is a difficult and complicated task. Beginning in 1997, both the Senate and House judiciary committees held hearings on the resolution, but in 2000, Senate backers withdrew the legislation rather than see it defeated.

Senator Dianne Feinstein (D-California) was a cosponsor of the proposed amendment, arguing that the Constitution protects the rights of criminal defendants but "crime victims, families, survivors have no rights at all, according to the Constitution of the United States" (Cannon 1996). If the victims' rights amendment were adopted, victims of violent crimes would have the following rights:

- Allowed to be present at major stages of a criminal case
- Permitted to make views known during a plea of guilty and sentencing
- Spared delays in defendants' trials
- Notified of any release or escape of the offender
- Guaranteed full restitution by the offender

The most fundamental concern expressed about the proposed victims' rights amendment is that

Most recently, discussions of the victims' bill of rights have shifted from the state to the national level (see Courts, Controversy, and Reducing Crime: Should the Victims' Rights Amendment Be Adopted?).

AIDING OR MANIPULATING VICTIMS?

After a long period of neglect, aiding victims has become good politics. These efforts are backed by a national movement for the rights of crime victims.

THE VICTIMS' RIGHTS MOVEMENT

Organizing crime victims is a difficult task. Aside from having been harmed by criminals, victims as a group have very little in common (Karmen 2010). Despite these obstacles, victim advocacy groups have become a powerful political voice.

The emergence of the victims' rights movement reflects several parallel trends. One is the law-and-order rhetoric of the 1960s, which emphasized the

its guiding assumption—that victims are being excluded from the judicial process—is patently false. Unlike many nations of the world, in the United States all steps of the criminal process (except grand jury proceedings) are mandated to be open to the public. Victims are excluded from trial only when they will be witnesses, and this is happening more often because of another facet of the victims' rights movement—victim impact statements. More substantively, critics make the following points:

- The high volume of cases processed each year means that local courts will face enormous increases in costs.
- District attorneys' offices face significant unfunded burdens on their limited budgets in the form of additional staff and more mailings and more phone contacts (Davis, Henderson, and Rabbitt 2002).

- Most states have already adopted similar provisions, so a federal constitutional amendment is not needed.
- Endless litigation will ensue, and appellate courts will face difficult issues in resolving potential conflicts between the rights of the accused and the rights of crime victims.
- Victims will experience more, not less, frustration because judges are not likely to impose the harsh sentence demanded by victims.

What do you think? Would adopting a victims' rights amendment to the U.S. Constitution genuinely improve the plight of crime victims, or is it another example of manipulating the plight of victims for political ends? Is this an area in which states should have great freedom to act but the national government only a limited role? In the end, would a victims' rights amendment be effective or just window dressing?

harm criminals do to victims. Another is the women's rights movement, which came to take a special interest in crimes involving women. A key feature of the feminist movement is its emphasis on grassroots activism. Thus, a logical extension of the women's movement was to form local programs to aid women who had been victims of rape or spousal abuse (Weed 1995).

The victims' rights movement involves people striking back to turn tragedy into action and rage into reform (Office for Victims of Crime 1998). The best known of these organizations is Mothers Against Drunk Driving (MADD). Founded by Candy Lightner, whose daughter was killed by a drunk driver, MADD has become the nation's largest victim advocacy group (see Chapter 18). A check of the Internet reveals numerous other groups. Many of these groups are local, emphasizing various types of victims ranging from those harmed by drunk drivers to battered women. These grassroots operations function loosely under the national umbrella organization, the National Organization of Victim Assistance, which provides a larger focus for their specialized concerns.

Today, the victims' rights movement involves a loose coalition of local, state, and national organizations with wide-ranging interests. Their activities constitute a full-blown social movement that seeks to place the interests of crime victims into the mainstream of American political discourse. Although diverse in origins, the victims' rights movement shares a common ideology, seeking to demonstrate the triumph of good over evil. Thus, the movement resonates with a moral view of crime held by many average citizens (Weed 1995).

DIFFERING GOALS

The victims' rights movement reflects the mutual interests of a strange set of political bedfellows, which explains why, beneath the rhetoric about aiding victims of crimes, important disagreements over goals and priorities exist (Viano 1987) (see Case Close-Up: *Payne v. Tennessee* and Victim Impact Statements). A study of a victims' rights organization in Alabama found that the membership was disproportionately white and female, with African-Americans excluded from potential membership. These results suggest that the victims' rights movement is becoming polarized, with some quite concerned about secondary victimization and others more focused on punishment of defendants (Smith and Huff 1992).

Similarly, a study in the state of Washington found that groups supporting the Community Protection Act reflected a punitive orientation toward defendants more than an effort to aid victims of sexual assault (Scheingold, Olson, and Pershing 1994). These differing goals explain why victims' rights laws and constitutional amendments are so contradictory.

DO VICTIMS BENEFIT?

Everyone agrees that victims and witnesses should be treated better during the court process. But political rhetoric should not be allowed to obscure some important issues. Although enthusiasm for helping victims is clearly growing, the willingness to pay for the necessary services is not always present. Overall, legislators and other government officials find voting for victim-oriented legislation politically advantageous, but when it comes to voting money for another "welfare program," they are much more hesitant.

Moreover, it is unclear how much aid victims and witnesses receive from these programs. Once enacted, programs do not always work as intended. Elias (1993) concluded that victim compensation laws were exercises in symbolic politics. Few claimants ever received compensation; the laws provided "political placebos," with few tangible benefits for victims (see also, Erez and Roberts 2007).

Victim/witness assistance programs appear to be important first steps in providing better services to citizens who find themselves thrust into the criminal court process, but not all agree that these programs actually benefit the victim. Sociologist William McDonald (1976, p. 35) charged that "some projects that are billed as 'assisting victims' are more accurately described as assisting the criminal justice system and extending government control over victims. Whether the victims so controlled would regard the project as 'assisting' them is problematic." Some victims do not wish to become involved.

An important question is, at whose expense should victims be compensated? Some versions emphasize protecting the rights of victims by denying privileges and benefits to suspects, defendants, and prisoners. This type of victim's bill of rights is the most recent example of the conflict between the due process model and the crime control model (highlighted in Chapter 1). Other versions emphasize improving the welfare of victims at the expense of the privileges and options enjoyed by members of the courtroom work group (Karmen 2010).

Payne v. Tennessee and Victim Impact Statements

After hearing a "blood-curdling scream," a neighbor called the police, who arrived just as Pervis Tyrone Payne, covered in blood, was leaving the apartment. Inside, they encountered a horrifying scene. Blood covered the walls and floor throughout the unit. Charissee and her daughter were lying dead on the kitchen floor, stabbed numerous times with a butcher knife. Miraculously, Nicholas survived, despite deep knife wounds.

Payne was convicted of two counts of first-degree murder and one count of first-degree assault. During the sentencing phase of the trial, the defense called Payne's parents, his girlfriend, and a clinical psychologist, each of whom testified as to various mitigating aspects of his background and character, including a low IQ that marked him as mentally handicapped.

The state countered with the testimony of Charissee's mother. She testified that the surviving child "cries for his mom. He doesn't seem to understand why she doesn't come home. And he cries for his sister."

During closing arguments, the prosecutor made maximum use of this emotional testimony. She acknowledged there was nothing the jury could do to ease the pain of the families involved in this case. Nor could they do anything about the victims—Charissee and her dead daughter:

> But there is something you can do for Nicholas. Somewhere down the road Nicholas is . . . going to want to know what type of justice was done. He is going to want to know what happened. With your verdict you will provide the answer.

The jury unanimously sentenced Payne to death.

Moving beyond the grisly facts of the case, the legal issue was: Should victim impact statements be admissible during the sentencing phase of capital murder trials? In two recent decisions (*Booth v. Maryland* 1987 and *South Carolina v. Gathers* 1989) the Supreme Court, by a 5-to-4 vote, held that victim impact statements are unconstitutional because they create an unacceptable risk that a jury may impose the death penalty in an arbitrary and capricious manner. Chief Justice Rehnquist swept aside these objections. The Court held that the Eighth Amendment does not prohibit the sentencing jury in a capital case from considering victim impact statements relating to the victim's personal characteristics and the emotional impact of the murder on the victim's family. Justice Thurgood Marshall thundered back in a biting dissent: "Power, not reason, is the new currency of this Court's decision making."

But are victim impact statements sound criminal justice policy? The National Victim Center and other victims' groups support giving victims a voice in the process, rather than reducing them to being a mere statistic. By venting their anger and frustrations, they are better able, proponents contend, to get on with their lives. But critics fear that the venting of frustrations can demean the judicial process. As a certain death sentence was about to be pronounced against Richard Allen Davis for sexually molesting and then killing Polly Klaas (discussed in Chapter 16), Davis told the court that Polly's father had sexually molested her, a charge that crime-victim advocates labeled outrageous and sickening.

This debate aside, research finds that victim participation has had little impact on sentence outcomes, although it has a significant impact on parole hearing outcomes (Morgan and Smith 2005).

Incidents like this one lead critics to wonder whether victim impact statements help victims; perhaps the possibility of speaking in court at a much later date unnecessarily prolongs their grieving process. Victims are not encouraged to reach a sense of closure until they testify (or in some cases, until the defendant is actually executed).

CASE CLOSEUP

CONCLUSION

The future of both Pervis Tyrone Payne and his victim are difficult to predict. Payne is on Tennessee's death row. Having lost on appeal to the Supreme Court, his lawyers hope to set aside the death penalty during further rounds of habeas corpus review. Meanwhile, he sits in his cell, wondering whether he will die. Predicting Nicholas's future is even more difficult. At his young age, his mind might be able to block out the memories of seeing his mother and younger sister murdered in his presence. But the chance of flashbacks and antisocial behavior—which psychologists label posttraumatic stress disorder—is good. It is possible that as he grows up, Nicholas will himself shift from victim to defendant. As we learned in this chapter, many defendants arrested for violent crimes were themselves the victims of violent acts as children.

The perhaps troubling future of Nicholas highlights some of the contradictions still apparent in how society reacts to victims. Today, blaming victims (particularly rape victims) for causing their own misfortune is more unusual than in the past. Instead, numerous groups are ready to step forward and call for helping victims. Yet some of these same voices who are quick to champion the cause of victims are just as quick to denounce what has become popularly called the "abuse excuse."

Victims and witnesses provide the raw material for the court process. The complaints they bring, the credibility of their stories, and their willingness to participate directly affect the courtroom work group's activities. But members of the courtroom work group do not respond uncritically to the demands for their services. They find some stories more believable than others and some claims more worthy than others.

The clientele shapes the criminal court process in a less obvious way. Most defendants are young, male, illiterate, impoverished members of minority groups. Many victims share similar traits. They are also poor, unversed in the ways of the courts, and disproportionately members of minority groups. As a result, in the criminal courts, victims and witnesses often exert little influence over the disposition of the cases in which they are involved.

CHAPTER REVIEW

1. List the three characteristics of defendants.

Defendants are overwhelmingly male and mostly economically underclass, and racial minorities are overrepresented.

2. Describe how victims and witnesses view the court process.

Victims and witnesses face frustrations in coping with the process (long waits and uncomfortable surroundings), experience travails in testifying, but overall exhibit surprising support for the system.

3. Describe how court actors view victims and witnesses.

Members of the courtroom work group become frustrated when victims and witnesses do not cooperate and are intimidated by the defendant or the defendant's friends and family.

4. Discuss the prior relationships between defendants and victims and why this is important in domestic violence cases.

In roughly half of the crimes of violence the defendant and the victim had a prior relationship.

Prior relationships are most notable in domestic violence cases, in which the battered women is not always interested in criminal prosecution.

5. Identify three types of programs that are designed to aid victims and witnesses in coping with the criminal justice process.

Victim/witness assistance programs are designed to help better navigate the court process. Victim compensation seeks to provide economic assistance for victims of crime. And the Victims' Bill of Rights seeks to provide rights for victims because defendants already have rights.

6. Explain why some view victim programs as aiding victims whereas others view these programs as manipulating victims.

Some see the victims' movement as providing much needed support for victims of crime. Others view the victims' movement as manipulating victims by providing symbols but no substance.

CRITICAL THINKING QUESTIONS

1. In what ways are victims and defendants similar? In what ways are they different? Is there any difference in the characteristics of victims and defendants when the victim is male as opposed to when the victim is female?

2. Many discussions of crime suggest that smart defendants are able to beat the rap by pleading insanity (see Chapter 14), slanting their testimony at the urging of the defense counsel (see Chapter 7), and exploiting legal loopholes such as the exclusionary rule (see Chapter 12). Given the profile of the typical criminal defendant, how realistic are these assumptions of a smart crook?

3. To some, the victims' rights movement is more an exercise in symbolic politics than a substantive program. Thus, some critics argue that many of these programs are really more interested in severe punishment of the defendant than in helping victims adjust socially, economically, or psychologically to their new role as victim. Which dimensions of helping victims reflect the crime control model? Which dimensions reflect the due process model?

4. Would your views on victim impact statements be different if the U.S. Supreme Court had chosen a less emotional case to consider in deciding their constitutionality? Overall, do you think victim impact statements correctly allow victims a voice in the process or just add unnecessary emotionalism?

KEY TERMS

career criminals   210   civil protection order   221   defendant   214

WEB RESOURCES

Go to the America's Courts and the Criminal Justice System companion website at

http://www.cengage.com/criminaljustice/neubauer

where you will find more resources to help you study.
Resources include web exercises, quizzing, and flash cards.

FOR FURTHER READING

Gender

Belknap, Joanne. *The Invisible Woman: Gender, Crime and Justice.* 3rd ed. Belmont, CA: Wadsworth, 2007.

Bloom, Barbara, Barbara Owne, and Stephanie Covington. "Women Offenders and the Gendered Effects of Public Policy." *Review of Policy Research* 21: 31–48, 2004.

Klein, Andrew. *The Criminal Justice Response to Domestic Violence.* Belmont: Wadsworth, 2004.

Kruttschnitt, Candace, and Kristin Carbone-Lopez. "Moving beyond the Stereotypes: Women's Subjective Accounts of Their Violent Crime." *Criminology* 44: 321–352, 2006.

Lauritsen, Janet, and Robin Schaum. "The Social Ecology of Violence against Women." *Criminology* 42: 323–356, 2004.

Guzik, Keith. "The Forces of Conviction: The Power and Practice of Mandatory Prosecution upon Misdemeanor Domestic Battery Suspects." *Law and Social Inquiry* 32: 41–74, 2007.

Proctor, Janice. "The Impact Imprisonment has on Women's Health and Health Care from the Perspective of Female Inmates in Kansas." *Women and Criminal Justice* 19: 1–36, 2009.

Renzetti, Claire, Lynne Goodstein, and Susan Miller. *Rethinking Gender, Crime and Justice.* New York: Oxford University Press, 2006.

Poverty

Backstrand, John, Don Gibbons, and Joseph Jones. "Who Is in Jail? An Examination of the Rabble Hypothesis." *Crime and Delinquency* 38: 219–229, 1992.

Dunaway, R. Gregory, Francis Cullen, Velmer Burton, and T. David Evans. "The Myth of Social Class and Crime Revisited: An Examination of Class and Adult Criminality." *Criminology* 38: 589–613, 2000.

Vogel, Mary (ed.). *Crime, Inequality and the State.* New York: Routledge, 2007.

Race

Cao, Liqun, Anthony Adams, and Vickie Jensen. "A Test of the Black Subculture of Violence Thesis: A Research Note." *Criminology* 34: 367–379, 1997.

Free, Marvin. *African Americans and the Criminal Justice System.* New York: Garland, 1997.

Krivo, Lauren, and Ruth Peterson (eds.). "Race, Crime, and Justice: Contexts and Complexities." *Annals of the American Academy of Political and Social Science* 623, 2009.

Mann, Coramae, Marjorie Zatz, and Nancy Rodriguez. *Images of Color, Images of Crime.* 3rd ed. Los Angeles: Roxbury, 2006.

Mincy, Ronald. *Black Males Left Behind.* Washington, DC: Urban Institute Press, 2006.

Reese, Renford. *American Paradox: Young Black Men.* Durham, NC: Carolina Academic Press, 2004.

Ridgway, Delissa (ed.). "The Unique Challenges of Cross-Cultural Justice. *Judicature* 92: 190–242, 2009.

Reisig, Michael, William Bales, Carter Hay, and Zia Wang. "The Effect of Racial Inequality on Black Male Recidivism." *Justice Quarterly* 24: 407–434, 2007.

Russell-Brown, Katheryn (ed.). "Special Issue: Race and Policing." *Criminology and Public Policy* 6: 1–181, 2007.

Walker, Samuel, Cassia Spohn, and Miriam DeLone. *The Color of Justice.* 4th ed. Belmont, CA: Wadsworth, 2007.

Victims

Carr, Patrick, Laura Napolitano, and Jessica Keating. "We Never Call the Cops and Here is Why: A Qualitative Examination of Legal Cynicism in Three Philadelphia Neighborhoods." *Criminology* 45: 445, 2007.

Davis, Robert, Arthur Lurgio, and Susan Harmon (eds.). *Victims of Crime.* 2nd ed. Thousand Oaks, CA: Sage, 2007.

Hickey, Eric. *Serial Murderers and Their Victims.* 5th ed. Belmont, CA: Wadsworth, 2010.

Feder, Lynette, and Laura Dugan. "A Test of the Efficacy of Court-Mandated Counseling for Domestic Violence Offenders: The Broward Experiment." *Justice Quarterly* 19: 343–375, 2002.

Jacques, Scott, and Richard Wright. "The Victimization-Termination Link." *Criminology* 46: 1009–1038, 2008.

Karmen, Andrew. *Crime Victims: An Introduction to Victimology.* 7th ed. Belmont, CA: Wadsworth, 2010.

Schreck, Christopher, Eric Stewart, and D. Wayne Osgood. "A Reappraisal of the Overlap of Violent Offenders and Victims." *Criminology* 46: 871–906, 2008.

ARREST TO ARRAIGNMENT

Neil Entwistle, accused of murdering his wife and nine-month-old daughter, leaves the courthouse after his arraignment in Framingham, Massachusetts. After he was convicted at trial, Entwistle was sentenced to life in prison without the possibility of parole. Violent crimes like Entwistle's are most likely to be covered by the news media even though violent offenses comprise only a small percentage of the crimes committed each year. From the perspective of the criminal justice wedding cake model, this is a celebrated case, partly because Entwistle fled the country to his native England shortly after the killings, requiring international cooperation to bring him to justice.

CHAPTER OUTLINE

LEARNING OBJECTIVES

After reading this chapter you should be able to:

1. Define the two methods of estimating the amount of crime in the United States.

2. Discuss how arrests made by the police impact the criminal court process.

3. List the four ways that criminals are formally charged in court and the major actors in each of these important documents.

4. Contrast how the law on the books approach to criminal justice and the law in action perspective offer contrasting views of the preliminary hearing.

5. Explain why some jurisdictions use grand juries extensively and others do not.

6. Delineate the three major reasons for case attrition.

7. Describe the four layers of the criminal justice wedding cake.

Like thousands of others arrested on Friday, Donald Lee McLaughlin had to wait in jail 3 to 5 days before a judge was available to conduct a probable cause hearing. The U.S. Constitution requires a more prompt hearing, argued the public defender for the County of Riverside, California. Not practical, countered the lawyer for the county, stressing the realities of the contemporary criminal justice system in large urban areas—thousands of arrests, overcrowded jails, and lack of availability of judges, to say nothing of defense attorneys and prosecutors. It is in this context that the high Court had to decide whether a "prompt hearing" meant 24 hours or 36 hours or 48 hours.

County of Riverside v. McLaughlin highlights the importance of the early stages of a felony prosecution. At first glance, the numerous preliminary stages of a prosecution seem to be of only procedural interest, with cases moving automatically from arrest to charging through preliminary hearing and grand jury before arriving at the major trial court. But a closer look indicates that at numerous stages during these early proceedings, prosecutors, judges, police officers, and victims have the option of advancing a case to the next step, seeking an alternative disposition, or dropping the case altogether. These screening decisions result in significant case attrition, with half of all felony arrests being dropped at some point after arrest and before arraignment.

This chapter examines the early stages of a criminal case, focusing on when and why case attrition occurs. The discussion begins with crime and the arrests that sometimes follow. Our attention then shifts to events in the courthouse, including initial appearance, charging, preliminary hearing, grand jury, and (for some cases) arraignment in the trial court of general jurisdiction.

CRIME

Beginning in the early 1960s, the United States experienced a dramatic increase in crime. For almost two decades, the number of crimes known to the police increased much faster than the growth in population. In the early 1980s, the crime rate reached a plateau, and since the early 1990s it has decreased considerably. The peaks and valleys of the official crime figures, however, are largely irrelevant to the general public. Rather, the public continues to perceive (no matter what the official figures say) that crime is on the increase. These fears are reinforced by extensive media coverage, particularly of violent crime.

The most publicized measure of crime is the Federal Bureau of Investigation's (FBI) yearly publication *Uniform Crime Reports*, which divides criminal offenses into two categories. **Type I offenses** consist of eight crimes, referred to as **index crimes**. These crimes produce headlines about rising crime rates. Note that some serious street crimes (such as drug selling) are not included. White-collar crimes committed primarily by the upper class—fraud and stock manipulations, for instance—are also excluded, even though their economic costs are greater than the costs of crimes committed by the poor. Contrary to public perceptions, most felony crimes are for nonviolent offenses involving burglary and larceny; property crimes outnumber violent offenses by a ratio of 8 to 1 (Federal Bureau of Investigation 2008). Type II offenses are the less serious, but more numerous, crimes ranging from theft to simple assault. Drug crimes are counted as Type II offenses.

A major weakness of the *Uniform Crime Reports* is that they are based only on crimes known to the police. But only a fraction of the number of crimes committed are actually reported to the police. Of the personal and household offenses measured in the National Crime Victimization Survey's yearly sample of households, only half of the violent crimes and almost two thirds of the property crimes were not reported to the police (Rand 2008). What this means is that the official FBI crime statistics actually underestimate the total amount of crime in the United States.

ARREST

The term *arrest* is difficult to define because it is used in different ways. In its narrow sense (sometimes called a "formal or technical arrest") **arrest** is defined as the taking of a person into custody for the commission of an offense as the prelude to prosecuting him for that offense. In its broader sense, *arrest* means any seizure of a person significant enough that it becomes the functional equivalent of a formal arrest in that the person seized would reasonably not feel free to terminate the encounter (*United States v. Drayton* 2002).

Of the crimes brought to the attention of the police, 20 percent result in an arrest. The police clearance rate by arrest varies greatly by the type of crime involved. The clearance rate for violent crimes is 45 percent, compared to 17 percent for property crimes (Federal Bureau of Investigation 2008).

Every year the police make an estimated 14 million arrests for nontraffic offenses—mostly minor ones such as simple assault, public drunkenness, disorderly conduct, petty theft, and possession of small amounts of illegal drugs. However, 2.2 million of these arrests are for the serious crimes of homicide, rape, arson, aggravated assault, robbery, burglary, auto theft, and larceny. Figure 10.1 displays recent arrest data by major categories of relevance to the major trial courts.

These arrests are the overwhelming source of criminal cases filed in the courts; only a handful of prosecutions begin with an indictment, for example. Exhibit 10.1 summarizes the steps of criminal procedure.

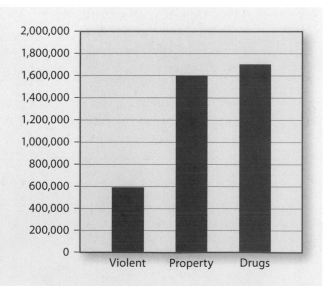

FIGURE 10.1 FELONY ARRESTS

Source: Federal Bureau of Investigation, *Uniform Crime Reports for the United States—2007*. Washington, DC: U.S. Government Printing Office, 2008.

QUALITY OF ARRESTS

The police have a lot to do with what happens in court after arrest. The strength of the evidence police provide to prosecutors is one the most important factors influencing whether prosecutors file criminal charges (Holleran, Beichner, and Spohn 2009). Thus, when police are able to secure tangible evidence and cooperative witnesses for the prosecution (while honoring suspects' constitutional rights), the prosecutor is not only more likely to file charges, but also more likely to win a conviction (Albonetti 1987; Forst, Lucianovic, and Cox 1977; Worrall, Ross, and McCord 2006). Conversely, when police conduct incomplete investigations (missing important evidence or witnesses), or improperly seize, mark, or store the items they do gather, prosecutors find themselves without sufficient evidence to prosecute a case successfully, a situation that often puts stress on the relationship between police and prosecutors (Dantzker 2005). Of course, the quality of law enforcement investigations varies greatly. Not only do individual police officers differ in particular investigatory skills, but also, some police departments, as units, function better than others when conducting investigations because of differences in management, training, resources, procedures, and analytical processes (Keel, Jarvis, and Muirhead 2009).

SWELLING CRIMINAL DOCKETS

Even though serious crime has decreased significantly during the past decade, court dockets keep growing. As stressed in Chapters 3 and 4, the workload of the criminal courts is large and growing.

- In the federal courts, the number of suspects prosecuted by U.S. attorneys has doubled since 1980 (see Chapter 3).
- Over the past decade, criminal cases filed in general jurisdiction courts have increased 33 percent (LaFountain, et al. 2008).

A good deal of the growth in felony caseloads has been drug-related. Police now arrest more than 1.8 million persons a year for drug-related offenses, a 300 percent increase since 1980. The massive increase in law enforcement efforts directed against drug use is clearly overloading the criminal courts. State prosecutors in large urban areas see the enormous effort against drugs as sapping resources, overloading the system, and making it difficult to respond adequately to other types of crime. The major response by courts has been the creation of drug courts (see Chapter 4).

Exhibit 10.1

STEPS OF CRIMINAL PROCEDURE

	LAW ON THE BOOKS	LAW IN ACTION
Crime	Any violation of the criminal law. *Felony:* The more serious of the two types of offense, bearing a possible penalty of 1 year or more in prison. *Misdemeanor:* Lesser of the two basic types of crime, usually bearing a possible penalty of no more than 1 year in jail.	Property crimes outnumber violent types of criminal behavior by about 7 to 1 among Type I offenses. The most common misdemeanors include public drunkenness, disorderly conduct, assault, and theft.
Arrest	The physical taking into custody of a suspected law violator.	2.2 million felony arrests yearly. 12 million misdemeanor arrests yearly.
Initial appearance	The accused is told of the charges advised of rights, bail is set, and a date for the preliminary hearing is set.	Occurs in lower courts. Many misdemeanor defendants plead guilty.
Charging	Formal criminal charges against defendant, stating which criminal law was violated. *Information:* Formal accusation of a crime made by the prosecutor. *Complaint:* Formal accusation of a crime supported by oath or affirmation of the victim. *Arrest warrant:* An official document, signed by a judge, accusing an individual of a crime and authorizing law enforcement personnel to take the person into custody. Prosecutor is supposed to prosecute all known criminal conduct. Prosecutor controls charging decision.	From arrest to arraignment, half of felony arrests are terminated, downgraded, or diverted in some manner. Defendant's chances of getting off are better during these private sessions in the prosecutor's office than during public trials in the courthouse. Complaints very rarely used in felony prosecutions. Prosecutor exercises discretion in deciding which charges should be filed. Some prosecutors allow police input into the charging decision.
Preliminary hearing	A pretrial hearing to determine whether probable cause exists to hold the accused for further proceedings.	In many jurisdictions the preliminary hearing is brief, with a strong probability that the case will proceed.
Grand jury	Required for felony prosecutions in 19 states and the federal courts. Grand juries have extensive powers, not possessed by law enforcement, to investigate crimes.	Typically not a major decision maker. Prosecutor dominates grand jury proceedings, deciding which cases will be presented and which charges filed.

Exhibit 10.1

CONTINUED

	LAW ON THE BOOKS	LAW IN ACTION
Grand jury	*Indictment:* Formal accusation of a crime, made against a person by a grand jury, upon the request of the prosecutor. *Subpoena:* Court order requiring a person to appear before the grand jury and/or produce documents.	The investigatory powers of the grand jury are most likely to be used in cases involving major drug rings, governmental corruption, and significant white-collar crime.
Arraignment	Stage of the criminal process in which defendant is formally informed of the charges pending and must enter a plea.	A significant milestone because it indicates that the evidence against the defendant is strong and a conviction is likely.

INITIAL APPEARANCE

As a general rule, the Supreme Court expects an initial appearance to occur within 48 hours of a warrantless arrest (*County of Riverside v. McLaughlin* 1991). Note that in indictment jurisdictions, if a grand jury has already returned an indictment, an initial appearance is not mandated under *Gerstein v. Pugh*, although some states require an initial appearance for all arrests. The details of this procedure are discussed in Chapter 6.

After a person has been arrested, a law enforcement officer make take the arrested person before a magistrate for an **initial appearance** (sometimes called a *Gerstein* hearing after the case that held a prompt judicial determination of probable cause is required when someone is arrested without an arrest warrant, *Gerstein v. Pugh* 1975). Statutes in different jurisdictions require that this be done promptly, using terms such as "immediately," "without unnecessary delay," "forthwith," or other similar statutory language. These statutes confer a substantial right on the arrestee and create a corresponding duty on law enforcement officers.

The reasons for requiring an initial appearance without unnecessary delay are:

- To verify that the person arrested is the person named in the complaint
- To advise arrested persons of the charges, so that they may begin to prepare a defense
- To advise arrested persons of their rights, such as the right to counsel, the right to remain silent, and the right to either a preliminary hearing or a grand jury indictment
- To protect arrested persons from being abandoned in jail and forgotten by, or otherwise cut off from contact with, people who can help them
- To prevent secret and extended interrogation of arrested persons by law enforcement officers
- To give arrested persons an early opportunity to secure release on bail while awaiting the final outcome of the proceedings. If the person has been bailed earlier, the magistrate simply reviews that bail. Release on personal recognizance may also be granted at the initial appearance.
- To give arrested persons an opportunity to speedily conclude proceedings on charges of minor offenses by pleading guilty to the charges, paying fines, and carrying on with their lives
- To obtain a prompt, neutral "judicial determination of probable cause as a prerequisite to extended restraint of liberty following arrest." (Ferdico, Fradella, and Totten, 2008, pp. 346–347)

Not all states, however, provide for a judicial determination of probable cause at the initial appearance before a magistrate. Some states make a probable cause determination at bail hearings while other states use preliminary hearings for this purpose. Whatever procedure may be used to satisfy the requirements of

Courts, Controversy, and Economic inequality

Are White-Collar Criminals Underprosecuted?

Normally Martha Stewart was at ease before television cameras as she demonstrated the latest in decorating and entertainment ideas, but she was noticeably harried as cameras caught her quick entry into the New York federal courthouse. Martha Stewart became the most recognizable person to be caught up in recent high-profile white-collar crime prosecutions. But the scope of her crime (relatively small) was soon eclipsed by Bernard Madoff, who defrauded investors (some of whom were personal friends) of $50 billion, in the largest Ponzi scheme in American history. Ponzi schemes are named after Charles Ponzi, who in 1919 and 1920 cheated investors out of $10 million. A Ponzi scheme, or pyramid scheme, is a scam in which people are persuaded to invest in a fraudulent operation that promises unusually high returns. The early investors are paid their returns out of money put in by later investors (Lavoie 2008).

Other prominent persons who have been prosecuted for white-collar crimes are:

- Sam Waksal, founder of ImClone, was sentenced to 7 years in prison for selling stock in his company the day before a negative ruling from the Food and Drug Administration.
- Ken Lay and Jeffrey Skilling, top executives of Enron, were found guilty of numerous charges of cooking the books, leading to the nation's biggest corporate collapse. (Lay died shortly thereafter, thus erasing his criminal conviction

and making it more difficult for former employees to pursue restitution in civil court.) Skilling was sentenced to 24 years in prison.

- Bernie Ebbers, the former top executive at Worldcom, was found guilty of criminal activity after that company was forced into bankruptcy because of massive accounting irregularities.
- L. Dennis Kozlowski and Mark Swartz, the former heads of Tyco International, were found guilty of stealing from the company when jurors concluded they lied on the witness stand.

The term *white-collar* is used because it suggests crimes committed by persons of higher economic status, as opposed to the typical street crimes most often associated with the social underclass. As such, the term encompasses a broad range of matters, ranging from crimes against consumers and the environment to securities fraud and governmental corruption (Rosoff, Pontell, and Tillman 2007). The public, though, remains relatively indifferent to white-collar crimes. One reason is that white-collar crimes lack the drama associated with murders and bank robberies. Another is that the defendants are respectable—they don't look like criminals (whatever that might mean). In the words of David Friedrichs (2009), they are Trusted Criminals. Society's contradictory assessments of white-collar criminals are most noticeable when it comes to sentencing: although the crime has

---

Gerstein, County of Riverside v. McLaughlin (1991) held that a jurisdiction that chooses to combine probable cause determinations with other pretrial proceedings must do so as soon as reasonably feasible, but not later than 48 hours after arrest.

Most misdemeanor defendants enter a plea of guilty at their initial appearance and are sentenced immediately (see Chapter 18). For those arrested on a felony, however, a plea is not possible because the initial appearance occurs in a trial court of limited jurisdiction, which has no authority to accept a plea. Thus, the initial appearance is typically a brief affair, as little is known about the crime or the alleged criminal. At times suspects insist on telling their side of the story, but the judge

typically cautions that anything said can be used against the defendant. Lawyers provide the same advice.

Charging

The criminal court process begins with the filing of a formal written accusation alleging that a specified person or persons committed a specific offense or offenses. The **charging document** includes a brief description of the date and location of the offense. All the essential elements (*corpus delicti*) of the crime must be specified. These accusations satisfy the Sixth Amendment

negatively affected some individuals, the offenders do not present a physical threat to society. To some, draconian sentences (often amounting to effective life imprisonment) are excessive (Podgor 2007).

Allegations that white-collar crimes are under-prosecuted, however, require close scrutiny. After all, a number of major prosecutions and convictions have occurred over the years. In addition, since the Enron scandal, public attention to white-collar crimes has clearly increased, and Congress passed the Sarbanes–Oxley Act, which, among other things, sharply increased penalties for various forms of fraud ("Go Directly to Jail" 2009). At the federal level, the Justice Department and other federal regulatory agencies such as the Securities and Exchange Commission have large staffs devoted to these matters. At the local level, though, district attorneys' offices have only small staff devoted to fraud and similar crimes because the office is overwhelmed by the sheer volume of day-to-day street crimes like murder, robbery, and drug offenses. Moreover, convincing a jury to return a guilty verdict in a white-collar crime presents a difficult task to prosecutors. For one, jurors often find it difficult to follow the detailed testimony from accountants. For another, a "smoking gun" seldom points convincingly to guilty intent (Glater and Belson 2005). But juries are increasingly returning guilty verdicts, particularly in cases like Tyco, where jurors said they did not find the defendants' stories on the witness stand to be credible (Maremont and Bray 2005). Nor are juries any longer impressed with the "dummy defense," whereby chief executives testify that they were paid millions every year but knew nothing about the details of their company (Norris 2005).

As for Martha Stewart, a federal jury in New York City found her guilty of lying to investigators about selling stock that plunged in value soon after her trade. She protested her innocence and appealed (unsuccessfully). But in a surprise move, she agreed to serve her 5-month sentence while her case was on appeal. She emerged from her prison cell calling her time behind bars "life-altering and life-affirming" (Geller 2005). She resumed her career, something that almost never happens to others found guilty of white-collar offenses. In turn, some suggest that celebrities like Martha Stewart have been singled out not so much because of their alleged criminal activity but simply because they are in the public eye (Iwata 2003). Madoff, though, failed to generate any favorable publicity and he pled guilty, receiving a sentence of 150 years that guarantees he will spend the rest of his life in jail.

What do you think? Are white-collar crimes underprosecuted? Would white-collar crimes be better deterred by more prosecutions or more government regulations?

provision that a defendant be given information on which to prepare a defense. Applicable state and federal laws govern technical wording, procedures for making minor amendments, and similar matters.

The four types of charging documents are: complaint, information, arrest warrant, and indictment (which will be discussed later). Which one is used depends on the severity of the offense, applicable state law, and local customs.

A **complaint** must be supported by oath or affirmation of either the victim or the arresting officer. It is most commonly used in prosecuting misdemeanor offenses or city ordinance violations. An **information** is virtually identical in form to the complaint, except that it is signed by the prosecutor. It is required in felony prosecutions in most states that do not use the grand jury. In grand jury states, an information is used for initiating felony charges pending grand jury action. An **arrest warrant** is issued by a judicial officer—usually a lower-court judge. On rare occasions, the warrant is issued prior to arrest, but for most street crimes, the police arrest the suspect and then apply for an arrest warrant. Some states require that the prosecutor approve the request in writing before an arrest warrant can be issued. An ongoing controversy is whether police and prosecutors devote sufficient attention to white-collar crimes (see Courts, Controversy, and Economic Inequality: Are White-Collar Criminals Underprosecuted?).

LAW ON THE BOOKS: PROSECUTORIAL CONTROL

Through the charging decision, the prosecutor controls the doors to the courthouse. He or she can decide whether charges should be filed and what the proper charge should be. Although the law demands prosecution for "all known criminal conduct," the courts have traditionally granted prosecutors wide discretion in deciding whether to file charges. For example, no legislative or judicial standards govern which cases merit prosecution and which should be declined. Moreover, if a prosecutor refuses to file charges, no review of this decision is possible; courts have consistently refused to order a prosecutor to proceed with a case.

LAW IN ACTION: POLICE INFLUENCE

Although the prosecutor has the legal authority to dominate the charging process, the police often influence the prosecutor's decision. Police and prosecutors regularly discuss cases before charges are filed. Sometimes, the police exercise considerable influence by pressuring prosecutors to overcharge defendants or to file charges even though the evidence is weak (Cole 1970; Skolnick 1993). Prosecutors, however, rarely need external pressure to overcharge defendants; they do so because it gives them leverage in the plea-bargaining process (see Chapter 13). But in a large number of cases, prosecutors decline to file charges against those arrested by police. In most jurisdictions, the number of police arrests that result in no criminal charges being filed varies between 20 and 50 percent (Boland, Mahanna, and Sones 1992; Collins 2007; Neubauer 1974a; O'Neill 2003).

LAW IN CONTROVERSY: SHOULD PROSECUTORS SET HIGH STANDARDS FOR CHARGING?

Police departments sometimes object when prosecutors set high standards for charging because they see case rejections as an implicit criticism of the arresting officer for making a "wrong" arrest. Prosecutorial screening can have consequences at the polls. In one jurisdiction where a district attorney refused to file charges in a significant number of arrests, the Fraternal Order of the Police forced the incumbent not to seek reelection (Flemming, Nardulli, and Eisenstein 1992).

PRELIMINARY HEARING

In most states, any person who has been arrested for a felony and has not been indicted by a grand jury (and, therefore, has been charged via an information or complaint or similar document filed by a prosecutor), has the right to a preliminary hearing. At the **preliminary hearing** (also called the "preliminary examination"), the magistrate must determine whether **probable cause** exists to believe that a felony was committed and that the defendant committed it. In this context, *probable cause* means a fair probability, under the totality of the facts and circumstances known, that the person arrested committed the crime(s) charged. Usually held before a lower-court judge, the preliminary hearing is designed "to prevent hasty, malicious, improvident, and oppressive prosecutions, to protect the person charged from open and public accusations of crime, to avoid both for the defendant and the public the expense of a public trial, to save the defendant from the humiliation and anxiety involved in public prosecution, and to discover whether or not there are substantial grounds upon which a prosecution may be based" (*Thies v. State* 1922, p. 541).

As stated above, the initial appearance before a magistrate may or may not include a probable cause hearing. If not, then a separate preliminary hearing is required unless: (1) the defendant is charged with a petty offense or misdemeanor; (2) the defendant waives the hearing; or (3) a grand jury has already determined that probable cause exists for the defendant to stand felony trial. Rule 5 of the Federal Rules of Criminal Procedure provides that, when the preliminary hearing is required, "[t]he magistrate judge must hold the preliminary hearing within a reasonable time, but no later than 10 days after the initial appearance if the defendant is in custody and no later than 20 days if not in custody."

LAW ON THE BOOKS: WEIGHING PROBABLE CAUSE

The preliminary hearing is a formal adversarial proceeding conducted in open court; normally, a transcript of the proceedings is recorded. During a preliminary hearing, the state does not have to prove the defendant guilty beyond a reasonable doubt, as would be required during a trial. Rather, the prosecutor needs only to establish probable cause that a crime has been committed and that the defendant committed it. If the magistrate finds probable cause to believe that the defendant committed the offense, the magistrate **binds over** the defendant to the trial court for adjudication of the felony charges. The magistrate may admit the defendant to bail at the

County of Riverside v. McLaughlin and a Prompt Hearing before a Magistrate

Beyond the bare fact that he was arrested in Riverside County, California, little is known about Donald Lee McLaughlin. Who he was, why he was arrested, and whatever happened to his case quickly became irrelevant. For whatever reason, the public defender's office decided that the facts of his case made him an ideal candidate to be used as a plaintiff in a suit filed in federal court. The office was prepared to challenge countywide practices; a plaintiff was needed and, at the last minute, McLaughlin's name was inserted. Thus, McLaughlin's name went first in a class action lawsuit filed on behalf of McLaughlin and all other individuals in the same situation.

McLaughlin v. County of Riverside raised the difficult question of how prompt is prompt. California law mandated a probable cause hearing for all those arrested without a warrant within 48 hours of arrest, weekends and holidays excluded. Thus, an individual arrested late in the week might in some cases be held for as long as 5 days before appearing before a neutral judicial official; over the Thanksgiving holiday, a seven-day delay was possible. The U.S. district court agreed with part of McLaughlin's plight and ordered a probable cause hearing within 36 hours of arrest. Having lost in the trial court, the county appealed (hence the names changed place, with the county now listed as the moving party). The Ninth Circuit affirmed the district court's decision, and the county appealed to the U.S. Supreme Court, which granted cert.

Although *County of Riverside v. McLaughlin* appears to be a minor quibble over a few hours, the underlying issues are much more fundamental, centering on where to strike the balance between an individual's right to liberty and society's need for effective law enforcement. The Supreme Court has allowed police officers to make arrests, based on their own assessment of probable cause, without first obtaining a warrant. To counterbalance this privilege, the Court established that

an individual arrested without a warrant is entitled to a prompt judicial determination of probable cause afterward. In *Gerstein v. Pugh*, they wrestled with this issue and held that the defendant was entitled to a timely determination. The Court ruled that the 30-day wait in Florida was too long, but failed to be much more specific. As a result, Gerstein "created a nationwide divergence in postarrest and pretrial procedures and subjected some individuals to what numerous courts and commentators believed to be unjustifiably prolonged restraints of liberty following their arrests" (Perkins and Jamieson 1995, p. 535).

Justice Sandra Day O'Connor, the most centrist justice on the Supreme Court (see Chapter 17), wrote the opinion of the Court, and her opinion reflects the ability to strike a compromise. The earlier decision in *Gerstein*, she wrote, provided flexibility to law enforcement but not a blank check. She recognized that the standard of "prompt" has proved to be vague and therefore has not provided sufficient guidance. In the future, *prompt* shall be defined in most circumstances as 48 hours—a time period she labeled as a "practical compromise between the rights of individuals and the realities of law enforcement." A 24-hour rule would compel local governments across the nation to speed up their criminal justice mechanisms substantially, presumably by allotting local tax dollars to hire additional police officers and magistrates. What is perhaps most striking is how forthright the opinion is in recognizing that law on the books must take into account law in action.

What is most interesting about the four dissenters is their ideological mix. The three moderates agreed with the lower courts that the 36-hour standard was best. But Justice Antonin Scalia, one of the Court's most conservative members, would fix the time at 24 hours, a standard he says existed in the common law from the early 1800s.

CASE CLOSEUP

preliminary hearing or may continue, increase, or decrease the original bail. (Bail is discussed in further detail in Chapter 11.) If the magistrate does not find probable cause, the magistrate dismisses the complaint and releases the defendant. A dismissal at this stage does not invoke the constitutional safeguard

against double jeopardy. This means that the prosecution may recharge the defendant and submit new evidence at a later preliminary hearing. Nor does a dismissal prevent the prosecution from going to the grand jury and obtaining an indictment in states that have both grand jury and preliminary hearing

Exhibit 10.2

DIFFERENCES IN PRETRIAL PROCEDURES TO DETERMINE WHETHER PROBABLE CAUSE EXISTS TO MAKE A DEFENDANT STAND TRIAL IN FELONY CASES

GRAND JURY PROCEEDINGS	PRELIMINARY HEARING
Primary function is to determine whether probable cause exists to believe that the defendant committed the crime or crimes charged.	Primary function is to determine whether probable cause exists to believe that the defendant committed the crime or crimes charged.
If probable cause is found, the grand jury returns an indictment/"true bill" against the defendant that is signed both by the prosecutor and by the foreperson of the grand jury.	If probable cause is found, the judge binds over the defendant for the trial court for adjudication by signing an information.
Held in the grand jury room in a closed session (i.e., secret proceedings not open to the public).	Held in open court (i.e., open to the public).
Informal proceeding in which no judicial officer presides.	Formal judicial proceeding presided over by a judge or magistrate.
Nonadversarial proceeding in which the grand jury hears only evidence presented by the prosecution.	Adversarial proceeding in which both the prosecution and the defense may present evidence to the presiding judicial officer.
Defendant has no right to be present or to offer evidence.	Defendant has the right to be present, to offer evidence, and to cross-examine adverse witnesses.
Defendant has no Sixth Amendment right to counsel.	Defendant has a right to the effective assistance of counsel under the Sixth Amendment.
Grand jury has the power to investigate crimes on its own initiative.	No power to investigate crime.
Grand jury has the power to subpoena witnesses and evidence.	No subpoena power.
Grand jury has the power to grant immunity.	No power to grant immunity.

SOURCE: John Ferdico, Henry F. Fradella, and Christopher Totten. *Criminal Procedure for the Criminal Justice Professional.* 10th ed. Belmont, CA: Wadsworth, 2008.

procedures. Exhibit 10.2 compares the preliminary hearing with grand jury proceedings.

LAW IN ACTION: VARIATIONS IN USING THE PRELIMINARY HEARING

Defense attorneys weigh several factors in deciding whether to demand a preliminary hearing or waive it

(Flemming 1986b; Prosser 2006). Practices of the local prosecutor are one important consideration. If the district attorney's files are open and plea-bargaining policies are well known, it is viewed as time-consuming and redundant to hold a preliminary hearing. Second, strategic and tactical considerations are involved. Waiving the preliminary hearing may reflect an assessment that the information to be gained from holding a preliminary hearing does not outweigh the potential damage to the defendant's case (for example, the publicity that may surround a rape case). A third factor is client control. Defense attorneys sometimes insist on a preliminary hearing to impress on their client the gravity of the situation. Finally, the preliminary hearing gives the defense attorney an overview of the evidence against the client and provides the opportunity for discovery (see Chapter 12).

The tactical decision of holding or waiving the preliminary hearing highlights the complexity of the preliminary hearing from the law in action perspective. Although the legal purpose of the preliminary hearing is simple, the actual conduct of these hearings is quite complex. In some courts, they may last an hour or more; in others, they consume only a few minutes. In some jurisdictions, preliminary hearings are an important stage in the proceedings; in others, they are a perfunctory step, in which probable cause is found to exist in virtually every case.

This variability makes it difficult to generalize about the importance of the preliminary hearing, but studies do reveal four major patterns. In some jurisdictions, preliminary hearings are almost never held. In many, they are short and routine, lasting but a few minutes with the defendant almost always bound over to the grand jury (Neubauer 1974b). In most jurisdictions, the preliminary hearing is largely ceremonial, resulting in few cases being screened out of the criminal process; but in a few courts, it is quite significant (McIntyre and Lippman 1970; Washburn 2008).

GRAND JURY

Grand juries make accusations; trial juries decide guilt or innocence. The **grand jury** emerged in English law in 1176, during a political struggle among King Henry II, the church, and noblemen. At first, criminal accusations originated with members of the grand jury themselves, but gradually this body came to consider accusations from outsiders as well.

After the American Revolution, the grand jury was included in the Fifth Amendment to the Constitution, which provides that "no person shall be held to answer for a capital, or otherwise infamous crime, unless on a presentment or indictment of a grand jury." The archaic phrase "otherwise infamous crime" has been interpreted to mean felonies. This provision, however, applies only to federal prosecutions. In *Hurtado v. California* (1884), the Supreme Court

held that states have the option of using either an indictment or an information. In 19 states, the grand jury is the exclusive means of initiating prosecution for all felonies. In a few, it is required only for capital offenses. In the remainder, the grand jury is an optional investigative body (Exhibit 10.3).

Grand juries are impaneled (formally created) for a set period of time—usually 3 months. During that time, the jurors periodically consider the cases brought to them by the prosecutor and conduct other investigations. If a grand jury is conducting a major and complex investigation, its time may be extended by the court. The size of grand juries varies greatly, from as few as 6 jurors to as many as 23, with an average size of 17. Grand jurors are normally selected randomly, in a manner similar to the selection of trial jurors. In a handful of states, however, judges, county boards, jury commissioners, or sheriffs are allowed to exercise discretion in choosing who will serve on the grand jury.

LAW ON THE BOOKS: SHIELD AND SWORD

The two primary functions of grand juries have been aptly summarized in the phrase "shield and sword" (Zalman and Siegel 1997). *Shield* refers to the protections the grand jury offers, serving as a buffer between the state and its citizens and preventing the government from using the criminal process against its enemies. *Sword* refers to the investigatory powers of this body (Alpert and Petersen 1985). If the grand jury believes grounds for holding the suspect for trial are present, they return an **indictment**, also termed a **true bill**, meaning that they find the charges to be true. Conversely, if they find the charges insufficient to justify trial, they return a no bill, or **no true bill**.

Many legal protections found elsewhere in the criminal court process are not applicable at the grand jury stage. One unique aspect of the grand jury is secrecy. Because the grand jury may find insufficient evidence to indict, it works in secret to shield those merely under investigation from adverse publicity. By contrast, the rest of the criminal court process is required to be public. Another unique aspect is that indictments are returned by a plurality vote; in most states, half to two-thirds of the votes are sufficient to hand up an indictment. Trial juries can convict only if the jurors are unanimous (or, in four states, nearly unanimous). Finally, witnesses before the grand jury have no right to representation by an attorney, whereas defendants are entitled to have a

Exhibit 10.3
GRAND JURY REQUIREMENTS

GRAND JURY INDICTMENT REQUIRED	GRAND JURY INDICTMENT OPTIONAL	GRAND JURY LACKS AUTHORITY TO INDICT
All crimes	Arizona	Connecticut
New Jersey	Arkansas	Pennsylvania
South Carolina	California	
Tennessee	Colorado	
Virginia	Georgia	
	Hawaii	
All felonies	Idaho	
Alabama	Illinois	
Alaska	Indiana	
Delaware	Iowa	
District of Columbia	Kansas	
Maine	Kentucky	
Massachusetts	Maryland	
Mississippi	Michigan	
Missouri	Montana	
New Hampshire	Nebraska	
New York	Nevada	
North Carolina	New Mexico	
Ohio	North Dakota	
Texas	Oklahoma	
West Virginia	Oregon	
	South Dakota	
Capital crimes only	Utah	
Florida	Vermont	
Louisiana	Washington	
Minnesota	Wisconsin[a]	
Rhode Island	Wyoming	

[a] Wisconsin has not convened a grand jury in more than 30 years.

SOURCE: David B. Rottman and Shauna M. Strickland. 2006. *State Court Organization, 2004.* Washington, DC: Department of Justice, Office of Justice Programs, Bureau of Justice Statistics.

lawyer present at all vital stages of a criminal prosecution. Nor do suspects have the right to go before the grand jury to protest their innocence or even to present their version of the facts.

In furtherance of their investigative powers, grand juries have the authority to grant **immunity** from prosecution. The Fifth Amendment protects a person against self-incrimination. In 1893 Congress passed a statute that permitted the granting of **transactional immunity**. In exchange for a witness's testimony, the prosecutor agrees not to prosecute the witness for any crimes admitted—a practice often referred to as "turning state's evidence." The Organized Crime Control Act of 1970 added a new and more limited form of immunity. Under **use immunity**, the government may not use a witness's grand jury testimony to prosecute that person. However, if the state acquires evidence of a crime independently of that testimony, the witness may be prosecuted. The Supreme Court has held that use immunity does not violate the Fifth Amendment's prohibition against self-incrimination (*Kastigar v. United States* 1972). Use immunity gives witnesses less protection than does transactional immunity. A witness may not refuse the government's offer of immunity, and failure to testify may result in a jail term for contempt of court.

The investigative powers of the grand jury to gather evidence are also seen in its **subpoena power**. Under the court's authority, the grand jury may issue a subpoena requiring an individual to appear before the grand jury to testify and/or bring papers and other evidence for its consideration. Failure to comply with a subpoena (or offer of immunity) is punishable as **contempt**. A person found in contempt of the grand jury faces a fine or being jailed until he or she complies with the grand jury request. Thus, contempt of the grand jury is potentially open ended—as long as the grand jury is in existence and as long as the person refuses to comply, the person can sit in jail. Critics contend that some prosecutors call political dissidents to testify to find out information unrelated to criminal activity.

The contempt power can also be used for punishment. A prosecutor may call a witness, knowing that he or she will refuse to testify, and then have the witness jailed. In this way, a person can be imprisoned without a trial. This has happened mainly to newspaper reporters. In *Branzburg v. Hayes* (1972), the Supreme Court ruled that journalists must testify before a grand jury. Some journalists have gone to jail rather than reveal their confidential sources, because they believe that to do so would erode the freedom of the press protected by the First Amendment.

LAW IN ACTION: PROSECUTORIAL DOMINATION

The work of the grand jury is shaped by its unique relationship with the prosecutor. In theory at least, the prosecutor functions only as a legal adviser to the grand jury, but in practice, the prosecutor dominates. Grand jurors hear only the witnesses summoned by the prosecutor, and, as laypeople, they are heavily influenced by the legal advice of the prosecutor. Indeed, the high court has ruled that the government is under no obligation to disclose to the grand jury evidence that would tend to clear the defendant (*U.S. v. Williams* 1992). (This is one of a number of significant developments in the way criminal procedure has been shaped by the courts; see Exhibit 10.4.)

The net result is that grand juries often function as a rubber stamp for the prosecutor. One study found that the average time spent per case was only 5 minutes; in 80 percent of the cases, there was no discussion by members of the grand jury; rarely did members voice a dissent; and finally, the grand jury approved virtually all of the prosecutor's recommendations (Carp 1975). Similarly, federal grand juries rarely return no true bills. In short, grand juries generally indict whomever the prosecutor wants indicted (Gilboy 1984; Neubauer 1974b; Washburn 2008).

LAW IN CONTROVERSY: REFORM THE GRAND JURY?

The grand jury system has been the object of various criticisms. In theory, the grand jury serves as a watchdog on the prosecutor, but some portray the grand jury as "the prosecutor's darling," a "puppet," or a "rubber stamp." To William Campbell (1973), U.S. District Court judge for the Northern District of Illinois, "The grand jury is the total captive of the prosecutor who, if he is candid, will concede that he can indict anybody at any time, for almost anything, before any grand jury" (p. 174). These concerns have prompted a call for abolition of the grand jury. Early in the 20th century, judicial reformers succeeded in abolishing grand juries in some states. More recently, such abolition efforts have not been successful, however, because they require a constitutional amendment.

Today, critics call for reforming the grand jury (Brenner 1998; Washburn 2008). Often these calls are based on concerns that grand jury proceedings have been misused to serve partisan political ends, harassing and punishing those who criticize the government. The leading advocate for federal grand jury reform is the National Association of Criminal Defense Lawyers (2000). This organization advocates a Citizens' Grand Jury Bill of Rights, which among other things would grant witnesses the right to counsel during testimony, require prosecutors to disclose evidence that might exonerate the target, and allow targets of investigations to testify (Lefcourt 1998).

ARRAIGNMENT

Arraignment occurs in the trial court of general jurisdiction. During the arraignment, the defendant is formally accused of a crime (either by an information

Exhibit 10.4

KEY DEVELOPMENTS CONCERNING CRIMINAL PROCEDURE

Crime		
Lanzetta v. New Jersey	1939	A law is unconstitutional if it forbids an act in terms so vague that "men of common intelligence must necessarily guess at its meaning."
U.S. v. Lopez	1995	U.S. Congress does not have the authority under the commerce clause to prohibit guns in schools.
Arrest		
Chimel v. California	1969	During a search incident to arrest, the police may search only the person and the area within the immediate vicinity.
Payton v. New York	1980	Unless the suspect gives consent or an emergency exists, an arrest warrant is necessary if an arrest requires entry into a suspect's private residence.
Initial appearance		
Sixth Amendment	1791	"In all criminal prosecutions, the accused shall enjoy the right… to be informed of the nature and cause of the accusation."
Coleman v. Alabama	1970	Defendant has a right to counsel if the initial appearance is a "critical stage" in the proceedings.
Charging		
Sixth Amendment	1791	"In all criminal prosecutions, the accused shall enjoy the right… to be informed of the nature and cause of the accusation."
People v. Wabash, St. Louis and Pacific Railway	1882	Prosecutor has discretion in beginning prosecutions and may terminate them when, in his (or her) judgment, the ends of justice are satisfied.
Burns v. Reed	1991	Prosecutor enjoys absolute immunity to civil lawsuit for all actions involving the adversarial process.
Preliminary hearing		
Gerstein v. Pugh	1975	Arrested persons are entitled to a "prompt" hearing, and 30 days is too long.
County of Riverside v. McLaughlin	1991	A jurisdiction that provides judicial determinations of probable cause within 48 hours of arrest will, as a general matter, comply with the promptness requirement.
Press Enterprises v. Superior Court	1986	The preliminary hearing must be open to the public.
Grand jury		
Fifth Amendment	1791	"No person shall be held to answer for a capital, or otherwise infamous crime, unless on a presentment or indictment of a grand jury."
Hurtado v. California	1884	States are not required to use a grand jury in charging felonies.

Exhibit 10.4		
CONTINUED		
U.S. Congress	1893	Prosecutors may grant a witness transactional immunity for testimony before the grand jury.
Organized Crime Control Act	1970	Prosecutors may grant a witness use immunity for testimony before the grand jury.
Kastigar v. U.S.	1972	Use immunity does not violate the Fifth Amendment protection against self-incrimination.
Branzburg v. Hayes	1972	Journalists have no constitutional right to maintain the confidentiality of their news sources when subpoenaed before grand juries, and are compelled to give testimony.
U.S. v. Williams	1992	Prosecutors are under no obligation to present exculpatory evidence to the grand jury.
Campbell v. Louisiana	1998	A white criminal defendant may challenge his conviction on grounds that African-Americans were discriminated against in the selection of grand jurors.
Arraignment Sixth Amendment	1791	"In all criminal prosecutions, the accused shall enjoy the right... to be informed of the nature and cause of the accusation."
Hamilton v. Alabama	1961	Defendant has the right to court-appointed counsel if indigent.

or indictment) and is called upon to enter a plea. Thus, initial appearance and arraignment are similar in that the defendant must be informed with some specificity about the alleged criminal actions. The major difference is that felony defendants are not allowed to enter a plea (either innocent or guilty) in a lower court because that court lacks jurisdiction to take a plea and to sentence.

Procedurally, the arraignment provides the court the opportunity to ensure that the case is on track for disposition. The judge summons the defendant, verifying his or her name and address, and the lawyer provides formal notification to the court that he or she represents the defendant in this matter. Most important, the arraignment means that the defendant must enter a plea. Typically, defendants plead not guilty and a trial date is established. In some jurisdictions, however, a significant proportion enter a plea of guilty (Neubauer 1996).

The arraignment is rarely a major decision-making stage in the process. Rather, its real importance is measured more indirectly. The arraignment is important because it signifies to all members of the courtroom work group that the defendant is in all probability guilty and that the likelihood of being found not guilty is now slim. Thus, from the perspective of law in action, the arraignment says something very important about case attrition.

LAW IN ACTION PERSPECTIVE: CASE ATTRITION

The law on the books perspective suggests a mechanical process—cases move almost automatically from one pretrial stage to the next. In sharp

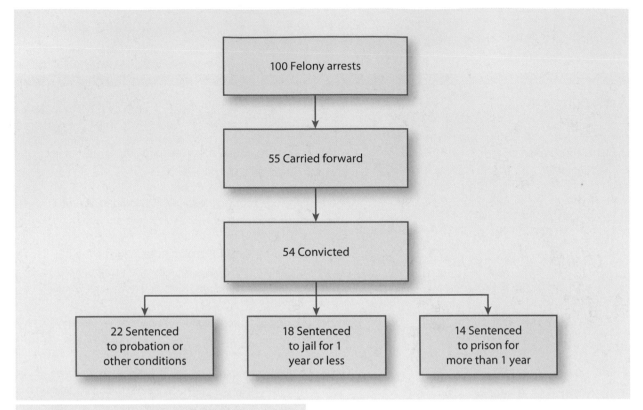

FIGURE 10.2   CASE ATTRITION OF FELONY ARRESTS IN 28 URBAN PROSECUTORS' OFFICES.

Source: Barbara Boland, Paul Mahanna, and Ronald Sones, *The Prosecution of Felony Arrests*, 1988. Washington, DC: U.S. Department of Justice, Bureau of Justice Statistics, 1992.

contrast, the law in action perspective emphasizes a dynamic process—cases are likely to be eliminated during these early stages.

A detailed picture of case attrition emerges in the research summarized in Figure 10.2. For every 100 arrests, 24 are rejected, diverted, or referred to other jurisdictions during prosecutorial screening. Of those that survive the initial hurdle, 21 are later dismissed by the prosecutor through a **nolle prosequi** (no prosecution). When this happens, the case is said to be "nolled," "nollied," or "nol. prossed." Overall, only 55 of the 100 arrests are carried forward to the trial stage.

The high attrition rate of felony cases early in the process contrasts sharply with the small percentage of acquittals during the trial phase. Once cases reach the felony court, relatively few are dismissed. Most end in either a plea or a trial (Boland, Mahanna, and Sones 1992). These statistics underscore the fact that decisions made during early steps of felony prosecutions are much more important in terminating cases than the later activities of judges and juries. However, important variations arise among courts in the stage at which case attrition occurs. These variations reflect differences in state law, the structure of courts, and local traditions. Thus, a critical stage for case screening and case attrition in one court may be of little importance in another jurisdiction.

WHY ATTRITION OCCURS

Case attrition is the product of a complex set of factors, including the relationships among the major actors in the criminal justice system, the patterns of informal authority within the courtroom work group, the backlog of cases on the court's docket, and community standards defining serious criminal activity. We can best examine why attrition occurs by using the three facets of discretion discussed in Chapter 5: legal judgments, policy priorities, and personal standards of justice. As with other attempts to understand discretion, these categories are not mutually exclusive—some screening decisions are based on more than one criterion.

LEGAL JUDGMENTS

Legal judgments are the most important reason that cases drop by the wayside after arrest and before arraignment. Prosecutors, judges, and grand jurors begin with a basic question: Is there sufficient evidence to prove the elements of the offense? (Cole 1970; Feeney, Dill, and Weir 1983). One assistant district attorney phrased it this way: "When I examine the police report I have to feel that I could go to trial with the case tomorrow. All the elements of prosecution must be present before I file charges" (Neubauer 1974b, p. 118).

The legal-evidentiary strength of the case is the reason cited most often for prosecutors declining to prosecute cases (Albonetti 1987; Holleran, Beichner, and Spohn 2009; Jacoby et al. 1982; Miller and Wright 2008). Such problems include noncooperation by victims and witnesses; insufficient evidence to prove the elements of charged crimes; problems with the strength or credibility of witnesses' testimony; and, on rare occasion, problems with the ways in which law enforcement obtained evidence. Lack of cooperation from victims and witnesses poses a particular problem in some urban areas (DeFrances, Smith, and van der Does 1996; Miller and Wright 2008).

Focusing on the strength of the state's case introduces an important change in evaluative standards. From an initial concern with *probable cause*, the emphasis shifts to whether it is a *prosecutable case*. At the preliminary hearing, the judge determines whether probable cause exists—that a crime has been committed and that grounds to believe that the suspect committed it are present. From the prosecutor's perspective, however, probable cause is too gross a yardstick; even though probable cause exists, a case may still be legally weak. Thus, a prosecutable case is not merely one that satisfies the probable-cause standard required of police in making an arrest and used by the judge at the preliminary hearing. Rather, it is a case that meets the standards of proof necessary to convict.

POLICY PRIORITIES

Case attrition also results from general prosecutorial policies about priority of cases. Prosecutors devote greater resources to more serious offenses (Gilboy 1984; Jacoby et al. 1982). At times, these case priorities are reflected in office structure; district attorneys around the nation have established priority prosecution programs that focus on major narcotics dealers, organized crime, sex offenders, and the like. Just as important, prosecutors use informal criteria that govern allocation of scarce resources. For example, some U.S. attorneys will not prosecute bank tellers who embezzle small amounts of money, get caught, and lose their jobs. The stigma of being caught and losing the job is viewed as punishment enough. Similarly, numerous local and state prosecutors have virtually decriminalized possession of small amounts of marijuana by refusing to file charges. Based on informal office policies, district attorneys are reluctant to prosecute neighborhood squabbles and noncommercial gambling. And, of course, politics also plays a role, as district attorneys are much more likely to prosecute property and drug crimes in election years than at other times (Dyke 2007).

PERSONAL STANDARDS OF JUSTICE

Personal standards of justice—attitudes of members of the courtroom work group about what actions should not be punished—constitute the third category of criteria that explain case attrition. Thus, some cases are dropped or reduced for reasons other than failure to establish guilt (McIntyre 1968; Miller and Wright 2008). Even if the evidence is strong, defendants might not be prosecuted if their conduct and background indicate that they are not a genuine threat to society. In Detroit, among other places, a different phrase is used—but the thought is the same. Across the nation, these reasons for rejection are referred to as "Prosecution would serve no useful purpose" or "interests of justice" (Boland, Mahanna, and Sones 1992). Often, personal standards of justice are based on a subjective assessment on the part of the prosecutor that the case is not as serious as the legal charge suggests. In most courthouses, officials refer to some cases as "cheap" or "garbage" cases (Rosett and Cressey 1976). Decisions not to file charges in cheap cases reflect the effort of court officials to produce substantive justice.

THE CRIMINAL JUSTICE WEDDING CAKE

The tyranny of criminal justice statistics is that they treat all cases in the same way. A homicide counts the same as a $75 theft, which under state law is petty larceny but is reported as a major felony in the *Uniform Crime Reports* (adopted in the 1930s). Merely counting the number of criminal events gets in the way of understanding how and why court officials treat cases of murder differently from those of petty theft. To understand case attrition, Samuel Walker (2006) suggested that it is useful to view criminal justice as a wedding cake (see Figure 10.3).

The wedding cake model is based on the observation that criminal justice officials handle different kinds of cases very differently. The cases in each layer have a high degree of consistency; the greatest disparities are found between cases in different layers. An examination of these layers illuminates the paradox of American criminal justice:"The problem is not that our system is too lenient, or too severe; sadly, it is both"(Zimring, O'Malley, and Eigen 1976).

CELEBRATED CASES

The top layer of the criminal justice wedding cake consists of a few celebrated cases. O. J. Simpson is clearly the most celebrated of the modern celebrated cases. But every year, a few cases dominate media attention because of the number of persons killed, the bizarre nature of the crime, or the prominence

of the defendant. Likewise, local communities may have a few celebrated cases, either because a local notable has been charged with a serious crime or because the crime itself was particularly heinous.

From the moment these cases begin, criminal justice officials treat them as exceptional, making sure that every last detail of the judicial process is followed. The cases are also extraordinary because they frequently involve the rarest of criminal court events—the full jury trial. To the fascination of the viewing and reading public, controversial matters are aired in public. As in morality plays of old and soap operas of today, public attention is focused on the battle between good and evil, although who is playing which role is not always obvious.

These celebrity cases are most likely to be broadcast on television, with some cable stations offering instant analysis and critique. Because of the publicity surrounding them, celebrated cases have a tremendous impact on public perceptions of criminal justice. On one level, these cases reinforce the textbook notion that defendants will receive their day in court, complete with a Perry Mason–type defense counsel and an attentive jury. But on another

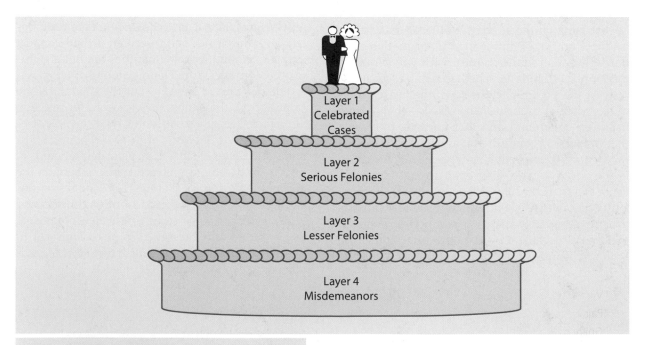

FIGURE 10.3 THE CRIMINAL JUSTICE WEDDING CAKE

Source: Samuel Walker, *Sense and Nonsense about Crime and Drugs: A Policy Guide.* 6th ed. Belmont, CA: Wadsworth, 2006.

level, celebrated cases highlight the public's worst fears—the rich often get off scot-free because they can afford an expensive attorney. All too many seem to beat the rap. People assume that the court process ordinarily functions this way, but in fact it does not. Celebrated cases are atypical; they do not reflect how the courts operate on a day-to-day basis.

SERIOUS FELONIES

The second layer of the wedding cake consists of serious felonies. The courtroom work group distinguishes between this level and the next on the basis of three main criteria: the seriousness of the crime, the criminal record of the suspect, and the relationship between the victim and the offender. The guiding question is, How much is the case worth? Serious cases end up in the second layer; the "not-so-serious" ones in the third. Murders, armed robberies, and most rapes are treated by all members of the courtroom work group as serious felonies, resulting in less likelihood that the suspect will be released on bail (see Chapter 11). In addition, at this level, more pretrial maneuvering (Chapter 12) means less chance that the sides can reach a plea agreement (Chapter 13) and a strong likelihood of trial (Chapter 14) and eventually an appeal (Chapter 17).

LESSER FELONIES

Of course, no automatic formula dictates sorting cases into serious and not-so-serious felonies; the key is a commonsense judgment about the facts of the case. What first appears to be a serious offense might be downgraded because the victim and the offender knew one another. For example, what starts out as an armed robbery might later be viewed as essentially a private disagreement over money owed, with the criminal act a means of seeking redress outside accepted channels. On the other hand, a suspect's long criminal record might transform an otherwise ordinary felony into a serious one, at least in the eyes of the prosecuting attorney.

Analysis of the true seriousness of a case is part of the everyday language of the courthouse actors. Serious cases are routinely referred to as "heavy" cases or "real" crimes, and the less serious ones as "garbage," "bullshit," or simply not real crimes. The practical consequences are that second-layer felonies are given considerable attention, whereas third-layer crimes receive less attention and are treated in a routine and lenient manner.

THE LOWER DEPTHS

The bottom layer of the criminal justice wedding cake is a world unto itself, consisting of a staggering volume of misdemeanor cases, far exceeding the number of felony cases. About half are "public order" offenses—disorderly conduct, public drunkenness, disturbing the peace, and the like. Only about a third involve crimes against property or persons, many of which are petty thefts or physical disagreements between "friends" or acquaintances. Rarely do these defendants have any social standing. In the eyes of the courtroom work group, few of these cases are worth much, and relatively little time is devoted to their processing. They are usually handled by a different court from the one that handles felony cases and processed in a strikingly different way. Dispositions are arrived at in a routine manner. Defendants are arraigned en masse. Guilt is rarely contested. Even more rarely are the punishments harsh. For these reasons, the lower courts will be treated separately in Chapter 18.

LAW AND POPULAR CULTURE

The Nightly News

"Violent Weekend in the City"
"Pair Arrested in Deadly Home invasion"
"Guilty on All Counts"

The local nightly news often leads with headlines like these because they attract viewers. In case fictional shows have not provided viewers with their daily fill of cops, crimes, criminals, and courts, the local nightly news provides even more coverage. Indeed, at times it is hard to distinguish the entertainment value of fictional crime shows from the media attention to real crimes. We need to think critically about these matters because how the local nightly news covers crime stories has a major impact on how ordinary citizens view the criminal justice system (Surette 2007).

Nightly news provides a lot of crime-related stories because they attract viewers. Local television stations generate considerable revenue from locally produced news shows and the higher the ratings, the higher the

CONTINUED

The Nightly News

advertising revenues. The central goal of generating high ratings leads to the mantra of news directions: "If it doesn't bleed, it doesn't lead." As a result, crime coverage features as much blood and violence as possible. Footage of crimes scenes and police investigations are supplemented by interviews with victims, family members, and neighbors with an emphasis on emotion and cries for vengeance. Conversely, nonviolent crimes merit attention only if the dollar amount is large or a newsworthy person is implicated.

Local TV news devotes a fair amount of time to crimes, but offers less coverage of arrests because arrests by real law enforcement officers are often less dramatic than arrests by fictional cops. Viewers are accustomed to watching TV shows that feature chase scenes and daring arrests. But news cameras are seldom able to capture such action, so TV news often settles for the next best thing—the "perp walk" (perp being short for perpetrator). Police accommodate the media by walking the suspect to jail in front of waiting cameras. TV reporters are quick to ask suspects why they committed such a dastardly crime and suspects are just as quick to respond with a scowl or a profanity-laced diatribe. No matter, the drama has been enhanced. For the police, the perp walk is highly functional because it offers compelling visual evidence that they have done their job—an arrest has been made. For prosecutors, the perp walk is highly valued because the circus-like atmosphere undermines the presumption of innocence—the suspect clearly looks guilty. And, for the media, the perp walk provides dramatic footage.

The TV coverage of the arrest often reinforces the image from TV cop shows that the case is now closed, the suspect has been arrested and is in jail awaiting trial. These notions are reinforced because there is considerably less coverage of later court proceedings in the case. Unless the crime was very dramatic, or the case has achieved celebrity status, TV is interested in little more than a brief report on the outcome of the trial. The lack of attention to trials is partly a function

of the lack of expertise of reporters who are seldom trained in the intricacies of legal proceedings, but also a reflection of what viewers want to see. Television viewers who are accustomed to seeing dramatic moments in fictional trials have less patience for watching actual trials that often proceed at a ponderous pace. If it takes *Law and Order* only an hour to solve the crime, arrest the suspect, and convict him, why does a local municipality or city take days, weeks, months, or even years to accomplish the same thing?

How the local nightly news covers crime, cops, criminals, and courts has several positive features. For one, television provides coverage of one of our nation's most pressing social problems. And in doing so, they put faces on the stories, capturing the emotions of victims, defendants, and their family members. Following a jury verdict, the cameras sometimes capture the joy of victory (a conviction or an acquittal depending on who won) or the agony of defeat (a conviction or an acquittal depending on who lost).

How the local nightly news covers crimes, cops, criminals, and courts also distorts the process in fundamental ways, however. All this news coverage of course reinforces public concern that crime is a serious social problem and out of control. And by concentrating on crimes of violence, the false impression conveyed is that most criminals commit violent offenses. And in the end, all the time local television stations devote to these matters seems to suggest that after the crime footage has been run and the suspect arrested, the case is over. By the time that the defendant pleads guilty or goes to trial, there is a sense that the outcome was foreordained. Trials, rather than being forums for assessing innocence or guilt within the framework of law, are reduced to rubber stamps. Not-guilty verdicts in turn are often portrayed as a defect in the system caused by shifty defense attorneys, soft-hearted judges, or dishonorable witnesses. The end result can be a citizenry even more cynical than before.

CONCLUSION

One could hardly label Donald Lee McLaughlin a bit player in the case that bears his name. He was more of a prop, no more than a convenient arrest, at least from the perspective of the public defender's office in Riverside, California. A live body was needed to challenge systematic practices; he was chosen and then promptly vanished from public awareness.

The debate among the nine justices over 24 versus 36 versus 48 hours seems at best arcane. But this debate illustrates the overriding reality of the modern age: At times, the rights of individuals must be considered not just on their own merits but also in the context in which they are raised. Individually providing each defendant a probable cause hearing within 24 hours would cause no disruption to the system. But providing potentially hundreds of suspects a day such a right runs smack into logistical problems—transporting prisoners from distant jails, hiring more magistrates, making sure that police reports are available quickly, and many other issues.

What is ultimately important about *County of Riverside v. McLaughlin* is that it focuses attention on what is otherwise an invisible time period in the history of a felony prosecution. The specific steps of criminal procedure are important because they help to ensure fairness in the process. But equally important is the substance of the decisions made. In statistical profile, the process resembles a funnel—wide at the top, narrow at the end. Fewer than half of all crimes are ever reported to the police. Only one in five of the crimes known to the police results in an arrest. Thus, most crimes never reach the courts. Of the small subset of criminal events referred to court officials, half are dropped after prosecutorial screening, preliminary hearings, or grand jury deliberations. Prosecutors and judges decline to prosecute or later dismiss charges that have been filed because the case lacks sufficient evidence, falls too low on the priority list, or is viewed as a "cheap" case. The wedding cake model highlights this sorting process. Considerable resources are devoted to serious felonies. Lesser felonies receive less attention; they are more likely to be filtered out of the system.

The decisions made at these early points set the tone of cases moving through the criminal court process. Quantitatively, the volume of cases is directly related to screening decisions. In many areas, it is common for roughly half the defendants to have their charges dismissed during these early stages. Qualitatively, screening decisions greatly influence later stages in the proceedings. Most directly, plea bargaining reflects how cases were initially screened. For instance, it is a long-standing practice in many courts for prosecutors to overcharge a defendant by filing accusations more serious than the evidence indicates, in order to give themselves leverage for later offering the defendant the opportunity to plead to a less serious charge. Thus, the important decisions about innocence or guilt are made early in the process by judges and prosecutors—not, as the adversary system projects, late in the process by lay jurors.

Chapter Review

1. Define the two methods of estimating the amount of crime in the United States.

In the United States the two methods of estimating the amount of crime are the *Uniform Crime Reports*, based on crimes reported to the police, and the National Crime Victimization Survey, based on self-reports from households.

2. Discuss how arrests made by the police impact the criminal court process.

Arrests made by the police impact the criminal court process in two ways: (1) if the police fail to gather enough evidence, it will be difficult for the police to gain a conviction and (2) the increase in the number of arrests has swollen the dockets of the courts.

3. List the four ways that criminals are formally charged in court and the major actors in each of these important documents.

Defendants are formally charged in court with a violation of the criminal law by: (1) a complaint signed by the victim, (2) a bill of information filed by the prosecutor, (3) an arrest warrant prepared by the police, or (4) a true bill issued by a grand jury.

4. Contrast how the law on the books approach to criminal justice and the law in action perspective offer contrasting views of the preliminary hearing.

The law on the books approach to criminal justice emphasizes that during the preliminary hearing the judge decides whether there is probable cause to hold the defendant, while the law in action perspective emphasizes that in most jurisdictions there is a strong probability that the case will proceed.

5. Explain why some jurisdictions use grand juries extensively and others do not.

Grand juries are used extensively in jurisdictions where the constitution requires a grand jury indictment in all felonies. In jurisdictions that do not have this constitutional requirement, grand jury indictments are required in only select offenses.

6. Delineate the three major reasons for case attrition.

The three major reasons for case attrition are: (1) legal judgments (lack of evidence), (2) policy priorities (some cases are considered too minor to be prosecuted), and (3) personal standards of justice (attitudes of the courtroom work group about what actions should or should not be punished).

7. Describe the four layers of the criminal justice wedding cake.

From the top to the bottom, the four layers of the criminal justice cake are: (1) celebrated cases (which are very atypical), (2) serious felonies (which are treated as meriting major attention), (3) lesser felonies (which are treated as of less importance), and (4) the lower depths (which comprise the large volume of misdemeanor arrests).

CRITICAL THINKING QUESTIONS

1. How long can an arrested person be held before being brought before a neutral judicial official? Do you think it was proper for the Court to take into account law in action factors such as case volume in deciding *County of Riverside*?

2. In your community, at what stage does case attrition occur? Do you detect any public displeasure with how the process currently operates?

3. If you were the prosecutor, what arguments would you make to the police chief(s) regarding a policy of careful screening of cases soon after arrest? Conversely, what arguments do you think law enforcement officials would make?

4. To what extent do the issues of weeding out weak cases cut across ideological dimensions? In particular, the crime control model may offer contradictory advice. On the one hand, it suggests prosecution of all wrongdoers to the fullest extent of the law; on the other hand, it values efficiency, emphasizing the early elimination of weak cases so that scarce resources can be concentrated on the strong prosecutions.

5. Do you know of any local crimes that fit the celebrated cases category of the criminal justice wedding cake? Why did these cases receive such attention? Are they similar to or different from cases that receive extensive coverage in the media?

WEB RESOURCES

Go to the America's Courts and the Criminal Justice System companion website at

www.cengage.com/criminaljustice/neubauer

where you will find more resources to help you study.
Resources include web exercises, quizzing, and flash cards.

KEY TERMS

arraignment 247

arrest 236

arrest warrant 241

bind over 242

charging document 240

complaint 241

contempt (of court) 247

grand jury 245

immunity 246

index crimes 236

indictment 245

information 241

initial appearance 239

nolle prosequi 250

no true bill 245

preliminary hearing 242

probable cause 242

subpoena (power) 247

transactional immunity 246

true bill 245

Type I offenses 236

use immunity 246

FOR FURTHER READING

Felson, Richard, Steven Messner, Anthony Hoskin, and Glenn Deane. "Reasons for Reporting and Not Reporting Domestic Violence to the Police." *Criminology* 40: 617–648, 2002.

Friedrichs, David. *Trusted Criminals: While Collar Crime in Contemporary Society*. Belmont, CA: Wadsworth, 2009.

Kingsnorth, Rodney, Randall MacIntosh, and Sandra Sutherland. "Criminal Charge or Probation Violation? Prosecutorial Discretion and Implications for Research in Criminal Court Processing." *Criminology* 40: 554–578, 2002.

Meier, Robert, and Gilbert Geis. *Victimless Crimes? Prostitution, Drugs, Homosexuality, Abortion*. Los Angeles: Roxbury, 1997.

Messner, Steven, and Richard Rosenfeld. *Crime and the American Dream*. 4th ed. Belmont, CA: Wadsworth, 2007.

O'Neill, Michael. "Understanding Federal Prosecutorial Declinations: An Empirical Analysis of Predictive Factors." *American Criminal Law Review* 41: 1439, 2004.

Piquero, Nicole Lepper, and Alex Piquero. "Control Balance and Exploitative Corporate Crime." *Criminology* 44: 397–430, 2006.

Shover, Neal, and Francis Cullen. "Studying and Teaching White-Collar Crime: Populist and Patrician Perspectives." *Journal of Criminal Justice Education*. 19: 155–174, 2008.

Siegel, Larry. *Criminology: Theories, Patterns, and Typologies*. 10th ed. Belmont, CA: Wadsworth, 2010.

Terry, Karen. *Sexual Offenses and Offenders: Theory, Practice, and Policy*. Belmont, CA: Wadsworth, 2006.

11

BAIL

O.J. Simpson leaves the Clark County Detention Center after he posted $125,000 bail in connection with the armed robbery of sports memorabilia at a Las Vegas hotel. Simpson had been acquitted of killing his ex-wife and her friend in a highly publicized trial in 1995. In 2008, however, Simpson was convicted on numerous felonies related to the Las Vegas hotel break-in and was sentenced to at least nine years in prison. Unlike Simpson, many defendants accused of serious felonies are either denied bail or cannot afford to post the bail amount set for their release. Crime control advocates stress the possibility of pretrial crimes, while due process supporters focus on innocent defendants spending time in jail for crimes they did not commit. In reality, most jails are so overcrowded that justice officials often have to release defendants pending trial in order to keep the most dangerous offenders incarcerated until their cases are adjudicated.

Chapter Outline

Law on the Books: The Monetary Bail System

Bail Procedures

Forms of Bail

Conflicting Theories of Bail

Law in Action: The Context of Bail Setting

Uncertainty

Risk

Jail Overcrowding

The Process of Bail Setting

Seriousness of the Crime

Prior Criminal Record

Situational Justice

Bail Agents and Bounty Hunters

The Business Setting

Bail Bondsmen and the Courtroom Work Group

Law and Popular Culture

Dog: The Bounty Hunter (A&E Televisions, 1999–present)

Effects of the Bail System

Jail Conditions

Race and Ethnicity

Failure to Appear

Case Disposition

Bail Reform Based on the Due Process Model

Ten Percent Bail Deposit

Pretrial Service Programs

Bail Reform Based on the Crime Control Model

Pretrial Crimes

Preventive Detention

Courts, Controversy, and Reducing Crime

Should Defendants Be Forced to Take a Drug Test?

Case Close-Up

U.S. v. Salerno and Preventive Detention

Conclusion

Chapter Review

Learning Objectives

After reading this chapter, you should be able to:

1. List the four most common ways that defendants secure pretrial release..

2. Discuss how law in action affects bail setting.

3. Recognize the most important factors in the process of bail setting.

4. Interpret the business setting of the bail agent (bail bondsman).

5. Identify the effect of the bail system on the processing of criminal defendants.

6. Distinguish between bail reform based on the due process model of justice and the crime control model of justice.

Anthony Salerno, organized crime boss, was indicted on 29 counts of racketeering, extortion, and conspiracy to murder. Based on past practices, there is little doubt that Salerno would have been held in jail in an indirect manner until his trial—bond would have been set so high that he would not have been able to post the necessary cash. But Rudolph Giuliani, then U.S. attorney, sought to detain Salerno directly. A recently passed federal law allowed a judge to refuse to set bail if the defendant might harm others while out on bail. The judge found that Salerno met the criteria and ordered him held in jail until trial.

The decision in Salerno represents one of the few times that the Supreme Court has wrestled with the Eighth Amendment's clause that "excessive bail shall not be required." To crime control model advocates, the historical right to bail needs to be modified in the face of pretrial releases of defendants who commit new crimes while out on bail. To due process model supporters, the original understanding that defendants merely charged with a crime should not have to pay a penalty is as applicable today as it was when the Bill of Rights was adopted. But does this debate about law on the books really matter? From the perspective of law in action, jails are so full today that laws allowing judges to detain certain defendants prior to trial are merely toothless tigers.

The *Salerno* case underscores the importance of pretrial detention decisions. Bail represents a defendant's first major encounter with the courts. For various fees, depending on the crime, the accused can purchase freedom and return to home and family. But defendants who cannot post bond must await trial in jail, suffering many of the same penalties normally reserved only for those who have been found guilty. This chapter examines how the American system of pretrial release works, the factors that shape its operation, and the consequences of decisions about bail. Some of the key areas discussed include concerns that bail discriminates against the poor and fears that bail exposes the public to risks of being victimized.

LAW ON THE BOOKS: THE MONETARY BAIL SYSTEM

Bail is a guarantee. In return for being released from jail, the accused promises to return to court as needed. This promise is guaranteed by posting money or property with the court. If the defendant appears in court when requested, the security is returned. If he or she fails to appear, the security can be forfeited. The practice of allowing defendants to be released from jail pending trial originated centuries ago in England, largely as a convenience to local sheriffs. The colonists brought the concept of bail with them across the Atlantic. It eventually became embedded in the Eighth Amendment, which provides that "excessive bail shall not be required."

The Eighth Amendment does not specifically provide that all citizens have a right to bail, but rather that bail, when granted, must not be excessive. A right to bail has, however, been recognized in common law and in statutes since 1789 for all those accused of committing noncapital crimes (*Stack v. Boyle* 1951).

BAIL PROCEDURES

Shortly after arrest, a defendant is brought before a lower-court judge, who sets the conditions of release. Bail procedures vary according to the seriousness of the crime. Those arrested for minor misdemeanors can be released fairly quickly by posting bail at the police station. In most communities, the lower-court judges have adopted a fixed bail schedule (also known as an "emergency bail schedule"), which specifies an exact amount for each offense.

Bail procedures for felony or serious misdemeanor cases are considerably more complex. The arrestee must appear before a lower-court judge for the setting of bail, so those accused of serious crimes remain in police custody for a number of hours before they have the opportunity to make bail.

FORMS OF BAIL

Once bail has been set, a defendant can gain pretrial release in four basic ways. First, the accused may post the full amount with the court in the form of a **cash bond**. All of this money will be returned when all court appearances are satisfied. Because it requires a large amount of cash, this form of bail is seldom used. If, for example, bail is set in the amount of $10,000, most persons cannot raise that much money easily and quickly.

The second method for securing pretrial release is a **property bond**. Most states allow a defendant (or friends or relatives) to use a piece of property as collateral. If the defendant fails to appear in court, the property is forfeited. Property bonds are also rare, because courts generally require that the equity in the property must be double the amount of the bond. Thus, a $10,000 bond requires equity of at least $20,000.

A third alternative for making bail is **release on recognizance (ROR)**. Judges release a defendant from jail without monetary bail if they believe the person is not likely to flee. Such personal bonds are used most often for defendants accused of minor crimes and for those with substantial ties to the community.

Because many of those arrested lack ready cash, do not own property, or lack the needed social clout, the first three options for making bail are only abstractions. Many of those released prior to trial use the fourth method: They hire a **bail agent** (often called a **bail bondsman**), who posts the amount required and charges a fee for services rendered, usually 10 percent of the amount of the bond. Thus, a bail agent would normally collect $1,000 for writing a $10,000 bond. None of that money is refundable.

In the American system of monetary bail, those who are rich enough can buy their freedom and await trial on the streets. But the poor await trial in jail. On any given day, there are more than 785,000 persons in jail (not prison), nearly 63 percent of whom have not been convicted of any crime (Minton and Sabol 2009). Such average daily population figures greatly underestimate the high volume of transactions that occur. Unlike prisons, where the annual turnover of the population is relatively small, large numbers of individuals pass through the revolving door of the jail, "moving into, out of, and back into, the facility during any given year" (Backstrand, Gibbons, and Jones 1992). In a typical year, there are more than 14 million entries and exits.

CONFLICTING THEORIES OF BAIL

Administration of bail has been greatly influenced by a long-standing disagreement over the purposes of bail. Adherents of the due process model stress that the only purpose of bail is to ensure that the defendant appears in court for trial. The basis of this view is the premise of the adversarial system that a person is innocent until proven guilty and therefore should not suffer any hardships, such as a stay in jail, while awaiting trial. According to this view, a judge should calculate bail solely on the basis of what amount will guarantee the availability of the accused for court hearings.

Supporters of the crime control model stress that bail should be used to protect society. They focus on defendants who are likely to commit additional crimes while out on bail. This perspective is reflected in law in action: Informally, judges deliberately set bail so high that defendants perceived to be dangerous will be unable to post bail and therefore await trial in jail. More recently, preventive detention has been formally authorized in some jurisdictions. Exhibit 11.1 summarizes key developments in the laws regarding bail. The competing perspectives of ensuring appearance at trial and protecting society affect the daily realities of bail setting in ways that will be explored throughout this chapter.

LAW IN ACTION: THE CONTEXT OF BAIL SETTING

Deciding whom to release and whom to detain pending trial poses critical problems for American courts. The realities of the bail system in the United States reflect an attempt to strike a balance between the legally recognized purpose of setting bail to ensure reappearance for trial and the working perception that some defendants should not be allowed out of jail until their trial. As Roy Flemming (1982) argued, one can imagine two improbable extremes. On the one hand, the courts could release all defendants prior to trial. On the other, they could hold every suspect. But neither of these extremes is possible. Freeing all those accused of violent offenses is not politically feasible, no matter what the chances are of their later appearing in court. Similarly, jailing them all is not possible, because jails are simply not large enough. Thus, court officials must make decisions every day that balance these competing demands.

Legal protections such as bail are meaningful only in the context of the policies that execute those protections. Only rarely do judges directly decide that a defendant should remain in jail pending trial. Rather, this important decision is made indirectly,

Exhibit 11.1		
KEY DEVELOPMENTS REGARDING BAIL AND PREVENTIVE DETENTION		
Eighth Amendment	1791	Excessive bail shall not be required.
Stack v. Boyle	1951	Bail set at a figure higher than an amount reasonably calculated to ensure the defendant's presence at trial is excessive.
Bail Reform Act	1966	Creates a presumption favoring pretrial release of federal arrestees.
Schilb v. Kuebel	1971	The bail deposit system in Illinois is constitutional.
Bail Reform Act	1984	In setting bail, the judge may consider danger to the community.
U.S. v. Salerno	1987	Federal preventive detention law does not violate the Eighth Amendment.
U.S. v. Montalvo-Murillo	1990	Defendant has no "right" to freedom when a detention hearing was not held at the time of his first appearance; this failure was a minor statutory violation.
Kansas v. Henricks	1997	Upholds the Sexually Violent Predator Act in Kansas, which permits the state to keep sexual offenders in a mental institution after they complete a criminal sentence.

when the amount of bail is fixed. The higher the bail, the less likely it is that the accused will be able to post the required bond. As the amount of bail increases, fewer defendants are able to secure pretrial release (Karnow 2008; Zeisel 1979).

Trial-court judges have a great deal of discretion in fixing bail. Statutory law provides few specifics about how much money should be required, and appellate courts have likewise spent little time deciding what criteria should be used. Although the Eighth Amendment prohibits excessive bail, appellate courts will reduce a trial judge's bail amount only in the rare event that flagrant abuse can be proved. In practice, then, trial court judges have virtually unlimited legal discretion in determining the amount of bail.

The range of choices available to court officials is referred to as the context of "bail setting." Uncertainty, risk, and jail overcrowding are the primary political and institutional factors that shape pretrial release policy in any given court.

UNCERTAINTY

Uncertainty is a major problem facing court officials in making bail decisions. A few short hours after arrest, the defendant appears in court for bail setting. Because of this short time span, only a limited amount of information is available. The details of the alleged crime—the who, what, when, where, and especially the why—are troublingly vague. Thus, the judge must set bail based on little information about the strength of the evidence against the accused (Nagel 1983; Karnow 2008).

Compounding the information void is the lack of adequate facts about the defendant's criminal history. In many courts, police "rap sheets" (lists of prior arrests) are available but typically contain information only about the prior arrests, not about how the case was eventually disposed of—dismissal, plea, or imprisonment, for example. Faced with limited information, court officials must nonetheless make a number of decisions. Is this specific defendant likely to appear in court? Is he or she dangerous to the community? In the context of the crime and the defendant, what is "reasonable" bail? Because of the scarcity of knowledge, defendants may be classified incorrectly as good or bad candidates for release.

RISK

The uncertainty court officials face during bail setting is aggravated by the risks involved. Potentially, any defendant released on bail may commit another crime. Judges fear negative publicity if they release a defendant on ROR who later injures or kills a victim. Police groups, district attorneys, and the local newspapers may criticize a judge severely for granting pretrial release to defendants. In New York City, for example, a judge was nicknamed "Turn 'Em Loose Bruce" by the Patrolman's Benevolent Association. The judge was later reassigned to civil court after a series of public controversies about his setting low bail for defendants accused of violent crimes.

It is important to recognize that in setting bail, judges and other court officials may make two types of mistakes. Type 1 errors involve releasing a defendant who later commits another crime or fails to appear in court. Type 2 errors involve detaining a suspect who should have been released. These two types of errors are inversely related; that is, the more Type 2 errors a judge makes, the fewer Type 1 errors he or she will make. However, Type 2 errors are largely hidden; they appear only if a major tragedy occurs, such as a suicide in jail. Type 1 errors, on the other hand, form the stuff of which newspaper headlines are made. In short, judges face public criticism mainly for Type 1 errors. In assessing risk factors, court officials tend to err on the conservative side, preferring to make Type 2 rather than Type 1 errors.

JAIL OVERCROWDING

The context of bail setting involves not only uncertainty and risk but also available resources. The principal limiting factor is the size of the local jail. Simply stated, jails are filled to capacity. In the decade from 1980 to 1990, the jail population doubled, and from 1990 to 2000, it doubled again. Today, there are approximately 785,000 inmates in local jails (Figure 11.1). Although construction

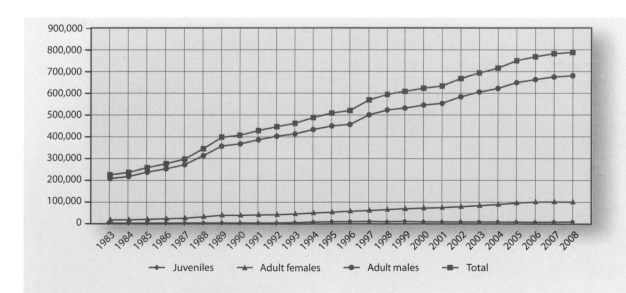

FIGURE 11.1 GROWTH IN U.S. JAIL POPULATION

Source: William Sabol, and Todd Minton. *Jail Inmates at Midyear 2008* (Washington, DC: Bureau of Justice Statistics, 2009). Available online at http://www.ojp.usdoj.gov/bjs/jails.htm

has added thousands of new beds over the years, in some areas, jails systematically operate at over-capacity, meaning that there is little ability to put more arrestees in jail without releasing others (Bureau of Justice Statistics 2009a). Thus, like prisons (discussed in Chapter 15), jails face serious overcrowding problems. Indeed, prison overcrowding is a principal cause of jail overcrowding. With prisons filled to overflowing, recently sentenced defendants must often spend time in local jails awaiting a vacant cell in the state prison.

Jails filled to overcapacity force court officials to make uncomfortable decisions. Although they may believe that the defendant should be held in jail awaiting trial, they may realize that arrestees who have committed more serious offenses have already filled the jail. Thus, as jails become overcrowded or threaten to exceed their capacity, bail-setting practices become more lenient (Flemming 1982; Roth and Wice 1980).

The Process of Bail Setting

Court officials respond to the context of bail setting (uncertainty, risk, and limited jail capacity) through general guidelines concerning the proper amount of bail (shared norms in terms of the courtroom work group concept developed in Chapter 5). Exhibit 11.2 summarizes bail and pretrial release practices as seen by law on the books and law in action.

Judges do not ponder each case as an isolated event; rather, bail guidelines provide cues for evaluating specific cases. In essence, bail setting "involves a search by officials to establish whether or not they should follow custom" (Flemming 1982, p. 29; see also, Karnow 2008). In some communities, these normal bail amounts are specified in written guidelines. In most communities, they operate informally but have a major impact nonetheless. Two factors are particularly important in shaping bail guidelines: the seriousness of the crime and the prior criminal record of the defendant. As will become apparent, situational justice also comes into play.

Seriousness of the Crime

By far, the most important consideration in establishing bail tariffs is the seriousness of the crime: the more serious the crime, the higher the amount of bail. The underlying assumption is that the more serious the crime, the greater will be the defendant's inclination to forfeit bail, and therefore the greater the financial costs should be for such flight (Karnow 2008; Wice 1974). This proposition is confirmed by a Bureau of Justice Statistics report on pretrial release of felony defendants in state courts. About 7 in 10 defendants secured release when bail was set at less than $5,000 but this proportion dropped to 1 in 10 when bail was set at $100,000 or more (Cohen and Reaves 2007). As a result, defendants charged with murder were the least likely to be granted pretrial release (8 percent), whereas those accused of burglary were released 49 percent of the time. Stated another way, the severity of the charge is inversely related to bail release (Cohen and Reaves 2006).

Prior Criminal Record

A second criterion used in setting the amount of bond is the defendant's prior criminal record. Defendants with prior criminal records typically have bond set higher than normal for the offense charged (Karnow 2008; Wice 1974). Nationwide, defendants with an active criminal justice status were almost twice as likely as those without such a status to be detained until case disposition (Cohen and Reaves 2006).

Situational Justice

The use of bail tariffs enables the courts to set bail rather rapidly for most defendants. After consideration of the charge and the prior record, the judge announces the bail amount or grants a recognizance bond. However, not all bail settings are automatic. Judges often seek situational justice, in which they weigh the individual facets of the case and the defendant. Because they have so little information, judges may construct honesty tests such as the following.

> "Have you ever been arrested anywhere in the world since the day you were born to this day?" The defendant replied that he was arrested two or three years ago.
> "What for?"
> "I forget," the defendant answers.

	LAW ON THE BOOKS	LAW IN ACTION
	Exhibit 11.2 **BAIL AND PRETRIAL RELEASE**	
Right to bail	No general right to bail under the Eighth Amendment, but commonly guaranteed as a statutory right.	The average daily jail population is approximately 750,000; more than 14 million admissions to local jails each year. Jails house about a third of all persons incarcerated in the United States.
Capital cases	Defendants awaiting trial on a murder charge that carries the death penalty have no right to bail.	
Methods of release	*Cash:* Defendant may post the full amount of the bond with clerk of court. *Property:* A piece of property with equity of twice the amount of bail posted with the clerk.	Most often used in minor offenses processed in the lower courts. Used on rare occasions.
	Release on recognizance (ROR): Released without posting collateral. *Bail bondsmen (agents):* Post bond with the court for a fee (typically 10 percent of the bond).	Used in lesser felonies. Lower-court defendants typically plead guilty at first appearance. Prefer clients accused of less serious, nonviolent crimes.
Preventive detention	Two out of three jurisdictions allow the court to refuse to set bail if the defendant might flee, might be a risk to others, or both.	Jail overcrowding is the norm, so in many jurisdictions preventive detention is never formally used. Historically, judges set high bail amounts to accomplish the same goal.
Jails	Typically funded by local governments, jails hold suspects awaiting trial, house inmates awaiting transfer to state prisons, and confine those serving short sentences.	The United States has 3,365 jails. Nearly fifty jails are privately owned or operated. Annual cost per inmate is $15,000+.

"Weren't you arrested this year? In April? Weren't you in the Wayne County jail for a day or so? On the 26th?" The judge asks the questions without giving the defendant a chance to reply. After pausing a moment, the judge informs the defendant he has a "pretty bad memory" and adds, "Have to have a bondsman for people with bad memories." (Flemming 1982, p. 57)

The use of honesty tests is but one illustration of the fact that the demeanor of the defendant influences bail setting. Cooperative defendants are more likely to gain pretrial release (Snyder 1989). But a defendant's demeanor in court is only one part of situational justice. Judges, even if unconsciously, often rely on:

> attributions linked to the defendant's gender, race, social class, or other social positions. On the basis of these attributions, judges may project behavioral expectations about the likelihood of a defendant's rehabilitation, the potential danger to the community a defendant represents, the blameworthiness of the defendant, or the likelihood that the defendant will either re-offend or fail to appear at trial and thus adversely affect the judges' career advancement. If judges attach negative attributions to particular groups, there will be an increased likelihood that they will categorize defendants who are members of these groups in disadvantageous ways and that, as a result, these defendants will receive detrimental criminal justice decisions. (Schlesinger 2005, p. 172)

Perhaps because of some of the stereotypes and assumptions that judges attribute to certain defendants based on demographic characteristics, it is not surprising that racial, ethnic, gender, and sexual orientation disparities routinely manifest themselves in bail decisions (Demuth 2003; Katz and Spohn 1995; Schlesinger 2005; Spohn 2008).

BAIL AGENTS AND BOUNTY HUNTERS

Clustered around urban courthouses are the bright neon lights of the bail agent. Boldly proclaiming "Bail Bonds, 24-Hour Service," they are a constant reminder that freedom is available, for a price. Bail agents are as important to America's monetary bail system as they are controversial. To reformers, they are parasites who prey on human misery. Critics point out that because bail agents and bounty hunters are private actors, they are generally not bound by the same constitutional constraints placed on law enforcement officers, who act under governmental authority when they seek, apprehend, detain, and transport bail jumpers. Their behavior often goes unchecked. The exercise of such broad power has often led to corruption, "excessive use of force, false imprisonment, destruction of property, and arrest of innocent citizens" (Baker, Vaughn and Topalli 2008,

p. 125). As a result, organizations like the American Bar Association and the National District Attorneys Association have recommended the abolition of commercial bail, but they have succeeded in only four states (Kentucky, Oregon, Wisconsin, and Illinois) that do not allow commercial bail. Also, the District of Columbia, Maine, and Nebraska have little commercial bail activity (Cohen and Reaves 2007). Despite frequent criticisms and efforts to abolish bail agents, they continue to play an important role in the pretrial processing of defendants in most jurisdictions. An estimated 14,000 commercial bail agencies nationwide secure the release of more than 2 million defendants annually (Cohen and Reaves 2007). But things are slowly changing. Today, largely as a result of state statutory and case law changes,

> bail bond agents and bounty hunters have jurisdictional constraints placed on their actions, and they must follow the law or be subject to criminal prosecution.... For the most part, arbitrary, capricious, and discriminatory actions committed by bail bond agents and bounty hunters are subject to criminal prosecution, although some continue to use their extra-legal authority to flaunt the rule of law.... Partly as a result of the threat of criminal prosecution, many states have bail bond societies and associations that are working to professionalize the industry. More jails, and the Sheriff's Offices that run them, require bail bond agents and bounty hunters to be licensed, are using technology to establish early warning systems to monitor potential misbehavior, and require criminal background checks to detect potential wrong-doing within the industry before it spirals out of control into a major scandal. (Baker, Vaughn and Topalli 2008, p. 129)

To understand the roles of bail agents and bounty hunters in the criminal justice system, one must examine two aspects of their existence: the business setting and the court setting.

THE BUSINESS SETTING

Bail agents are businesspeople, but their business is unique. By allowing commercial intermediaries to post bond, the state has created a business operation within the criminal courts. In essence, the bondsman is a private government subcontractor; key decisions on pretrial release have been transferred from public officials to private parties, who represent neither the interests of the courts nor those of the defendant.

Bail bondsmen make money by providing a specialized form of insurance. For a nonrefundable fee, they post a bond with the court. If the defendant does not appear for trial, the bondsman is responsible for the full amount of the bond. For assuming this risk, he or she is permitted to charge a fee, usually 10 percent of the face amount of the bond.

Rarely, however, do bail bondsmen post a cash surety directly with the court. Instead, they purchase a surety bond from a major insurance company, which charges 30 percent of the bondsman's fee. Thus, if the total amount of the bail is $1,000, the bondsman receives $100 from the client and keeps $70 of it. Because the profit margin in each case is seldom large, bondsmen need to find plenty of clients willing to purchase their services, while simultaneously accepting only those who present a minimal risk of fleeing.

Competition among local bondsmen to gain "good" clients is stiff. Indeed in recent years some bail agents have been known to discount their fees (Nolan 2009). Bondsmen use several techniques to ensure a steady supply of clients. Defendants with prior court experience know how to contact bondsmen who have provided reliable service in the past. Third parties are also a frequent (and sometimes controversial) source of referrals. Defense attorneys sometimes refer a client to a bondsman (often expecting future favors in return). Likewise, police officers, court clerks, or bailiffs may steer defendants toward bondsmen. Such referrals are sometimes an attempt to be helpful, but more often there is an expectation that the person making the referral will be compensated in some way.

Once contact has been made, bondsmen must decide whether to take the arrestee as a client. They consider the following types of defendants bad risks: first offenders (because they are likely to panic); recidivists whose new crime is more serious than previous ones; and violent defendants (they may harm the bondsman). In assessing which defendants are financially reliable, bondsmen use the very criteria ignored by the court: employment history, family situation, and roots in the community. Contrary to popular belief, bondsmen do not accept just anyone as a client. They prefer to write bonds when the bail is low, because their risks are then also low. For example, bondsmen refer to domestic violence suspects as "the bread and butter" of their

livelihood because bonds are high, and these defendants are more likely than other defendants to have the charges against them dropped (Lasley 2003). Thus, many bondsmen make a living by posting bond for numerous defendants accused of minor crimes and an occasional large bond when repayment is ensured. In recent years, budget cuts and the cost of maintaining overcrowded jails have led sheriffs across the nation to release inmates accused of lesser crimes without bond, thus decreasing the profitability of some bail agents (Associated Press 2009).

As a condition of posting bail, the bondsman requires the client to sign a contract waiving any protections against extradition and allowing the bondsman to retrieve the defendant from wherever he or she may have fled. These powers exceed any possessed by law enforcement officials. For example, a bondsman can retrieve a fugitive much more easily than the police can.

BAIL BONDSMEN AND THE COURTROOM WORK GROUP

Experienced bail bondsmen are on a first-name basis with court personnel such as sheriffs, bailiffs, and clerks, who represent a vital part of their business. Each of these officials can help or hinder the bondsman. As one bondsman noted, "The court clerk is probably one of the most important people I have to deal with. He moves cases, he can get information to the judge, and he has control over various calendar matters. When he's not willing to help you out, he can make life very difficult. He knows he's important, and he acts like it" (Dill 1975, p. 658). Bondsmen often contribute financially to judges' reelection campaigns. The relationships between bail bondsmen and the courts are reciprocal.

One way in which bondsmen help the courts is by managing the population of arrested persons. Without bail bondsmen, the courts would be faced with an intolerably large jail population. For decades, bail bondsmen have been the easiest way out of this dilemma. At the same time, bondsmen may also help the court prevent some defendants from being released. When court officials desire that a particular defendant not be released, the bondsmen usually cooperate by refusing to post bond (Dill 1975).

The major financial risk facing bondsmen is that clients will jump bail and fail to appear in court,

LAW AND POPULAR CULTURE

Dog: The Bounty Hunter (A&E Television, 1999–present)

In popular fiction, bounty hunters have often been portrayed as cynical loners, such as Randolf Scott's character in *The Bounty Hunter* (1954) and Steve McQueen's role as John Randal in *Wanted: Dead or Alive* (1958–1961). But the *Star Wars* saga emphasized the notion of the rogue bounty hunter through the characters Boba Fett and Jango Fett. These science-fiction bounty hunters-for-hire did not capture criminal fugitives, but rather sought out the people the "bad guys" wanted.

But today, the most widely known bounty hunger is Hawaii-based Duane "Dog" Chapman. According to his website, Dog Chapman is "considered the greatest bounty hunter in the world," having captured over 6,000 fugitives in his nearly 30-year career. Indeed, the Hawaii State Legislature passed a resolution honoring Dog and his wife, Beth, for their work catching fugitives from justice. While seemingly on the side of justice today, Chapman's past is quite checkered. After he dropped out of school in the seventh grade, he was arrested 18 times for armed robbery and, in 1997, was convicted and sentenced to prison for his role in a murder. While incarcerated in Texas, Chapman claims to have "found God" (indeed, his nickname is God spelled backwards) and changed his perspective on life. He was released on parole after serving just two years in prison. However, he owed back child support to the mother of his first child. The judge presiding over the child support case offered to pay Chapman money if he caught a fugitive. And that is how his career as a bounty hunter was born. Whether Chapman is on the right side of the law, however, is a matter of interpretation.

While bounty hunting is legal in the United States, nearly all foreign countries do not sanction this activity. Indeed, other than in the Philippines and the United States, the private capture of a fugitive by a bounty hunter is considered a criminal kidnapping in most countries. In fact, Dog Chapman was arrested for capturing the millionaire rapist Andrew Luster, heir to the Max Factor make-up empire, in Mexico in 2003. They eventually released him on bail and, ironically, he then fled back to the United States, thereby becoming a fugitive from Mexican justice. He was subsequently arrested by U.S. Marshals and rereleased on bail. Early attempts to fight his extradition to Mexico to stand trial failed. In July 2007, a Mexican judge ruled that authorities had waited too long to file charges against Chapman and two members of his bounty-hunting team, including his son. Based on that ruling, a U.S. magistrate judge in Hawaii dismissed the extradition proceedings, even though the Mexican government had appealed the dismissal of the case by the Mexican trial court judge. In January 2008, a three-judge appellate panel in Mexico unanimously upheld the trial court's decision that the criminal charges against Chapman had to be dismissed. While these rulings effectively ended Dog Chapman's international legal problems, his show was cancelled in November 2007 in the wake of his having used a racial epithet. That cancellation, however, was short-lived. His show resumed production in February 2008 and, as of the writing of this book, still airs on A&E's cable television channel. But his continued success in popular culture may have contributed to his being in trouble with the IRS. The agency filed two liens against his property for back-taxes—one for $2 million and the other for $1.8 million (Petrello 2009). While Chapman disputes that he owes any money to the U.S. government, it appears that his legal troubles are not over.

After watching one or more episodes of *Dog: The Bounty Hunter*, be prepared to discuss the following questions:

1. Penny Harding, the executive director of the California Bail Agents Association criticized Chapman, saying, "He represents all of the things that bail agents are trying to get away from—the cowboy image, the renegade, bring 'em home dead or alive'" (Jablon 2003, para. 2). What do you think of Duane "Dog" Chapman? Why?

2. In light of Chapman's felony convictions, do you think it is appropriate for him to be a bounty hunter? Why or why not?

3. Since bounty hunting is not legal in Mexico, do you think Chapman should have stood trial in Mexico for having crossed the border to Mexico to apprehend Andrew Luster? Explain your reasoning.

4. If you see a few episodes of *Dog: The Bounty Hunter*, you might witness him using some rough tactics to apprehend fugitives. Do you think that bounty hunters, like Dog Chapman, should be able to use tactics to apprehend fugitives that law enforcement officers would generally be prohibited from using? Why?

in which case the entire amount of the bond will have to be made good. Yet in many cities, forfeited bonds regularly go uncollected. Part of this practice is legitimate. To encourage bondsmen to seek out and find those who have fled, courts allow a grace period before bonds are forfeited. But the key reason that many bonds go uncollected is the discretionary power of judges to relieve bondsmen from outstanding bonds. In many cities, bondsmen will not have to pay a bond forfeiture if they can convince the judge that they have made every effort to find the missing client (Wice 1974). But these considerations cannot fully explain all the uncollected bonds that judges are deliberately not trying to collect. Given the help the bondsmen offer the courts, the major way the courts can reciprocate is by not trying to collect bond forfeitures.

EFFECTS OF THE BAIL SYSTEM

The process of setting bail is not neutral. Defendants who have some access to money are much more likely than poor defendants to be bailed out of jail. The fact that some defendants remain in jail awaiting trial (or plea) has direct and perhaps indirect effects.

Most directly, defendants who cannot make bail face a variety of hardships. Even though defendants detained before trial are presumed innocent until proven guilty, they suffer many of the same disadvantages as those incarcerated after

conviction. Economically, they often lose their jobs. Psychologically, they are subjected to stress, anxiety, and isolation. Physically, they are held in a violence-prone atmosphere. Indeed, some defendants spend time in jail during pretrial detention and are later not convicted.

More indirectly, defendants who cannot make bail may be at a disadvantage during the criminal justice process. Conversely, those who have been released may not appear in court as required. The effects of bail have been an active area of concern for the public, policymakers, and researchers alike. The topics that have received the greatest attention are jail conditions, race and ethnicity, failure to appear, and case disposition.

JAIL CONDITIONS

In an influential 1965 book *Ransom: A Critique of the American Bail System*, Ronald Goldfarb described the conditions of jails in the United States as "the ultimate ghetto." Over the Past decades, jail conditions have improved greatly; conditions of conferment lawsuits filed in federal courts (discussed in Chapter 15) have played a role in these improvements. Nonetheless some jails are reported to be substandard:

- In Kentucky, inmates sleep on floors at night and spend their days in crowded, smelly, and noisy cells (Editorial 2008).
- In Cook County, Illinois, the U.S. Attorney's office discovered unnecessary deaths and amputations, grossly inadequate medical care and systematic prisoner beatings (Korecki 2008).

Efforts to improve jail conditions are typically low on the priority list of local officials, who are reluctant to spend taxpayers' dollars and do not want to appear to be coddling criminals.

RACE AND ETHNICITY

Because the American legal system is premised on the ideal of equal justice under the law, there has been an active interest in whether the court processes discriminate unfairly against racial and ethnic minorities (Chapter 16). Considerable research has focused on the sentences imposed on the guilty, but some researchers have also examined bail decisions.

Some studies have found clear differences between the defendants who await trial in jail and those who are released. Hispanics are the group most likely to be detained in jail, whites are the least likely to be detained, and African-Americans are in the middle. These differences are partially the product of variation in economic status. African-American defendants are more likely to receive pretrial detention not because of racially differential decision making but because of their inability to pay bail. Hispanics face a "triple disadvantage" during the bail-setting process—as a group they are least likely to qualify for ROR, have the highest bail amounts set, and are the least able to pay bail (Demuth 2003; Schlesinger 2005). Higher pretrial detention rates for Hispanics may be the product of immigration holds filed by the U.S. Immigration and Customs Enforcement to detain those illegally in the country (Cohen and Reaves 2007).

FAILURE TO APPEAR

Defendants who have gained pretrial release do not always appear in court when required. Skipping bail has several consequences. First, bail is forfeited. Second, a warrant is issued for the suspect's arrest. This warrant, termed a **bench warrant** or a **capias**, authorizes the police to take the person into custody. The person must be delivered to the judge issuing the warrant and cannot be released on bail. Finally, failure to appear often subjects the defendant to a separate criminal charge of bond jumping.

How often bailed defendants fail to appear in court is subject to considerable debate. A study of felony defendants in large urban counties reports that 22 percent of the released defendants missed one or more court dates (Cohen and Reaves 2007). This estimate defined *nonappearance* as missing a single court date, but the problem of people absconding from bail to become fugitives from the law is real. Some studies estimate that 6 percent of released defendants were still fugitives at the end of a year, whereas other studies have reported that up to 30 percent of felony absconders will remain fugitives for a least a full year (Helland and Tabarok 2004).

Defendants who fail to appear do not always intend to miss their court dates. Failure-to-appear rates are closely related to practices within the court. A number of defendants do not show up because they were not given clear notice of the next appearance date. Another way in which courts themselves contribute to nonappearances is by lengthy delay in disposing of cases. As the time from arrest to trial increases, the rate of nonappearances rises even faster.

CASE DISPOSITION

Pretrial detention has a great impact on the legal processing of defendants:

> Viewed from the perspective of maintaining the pleabargaining system, pretrial detention and demoralizing conditions in jails are highly functional. They discourage the defendant from bargaining too hard; they place a high price upon filing motions or demanding a trial.... This is not to argue that those in authority consciously plan rotten jails; clearly most are concerned about jail conditions. But it is to suggest that such conditions are functional, do serve the needs of the production ethic that dominates our criminal justice system. (Casper 1972, p. 67)

The discriminatory impact of bail has been the subject of considerable research. There is widespread agreement in the literature that jailed defendants are more likely to be convicted and (once convicted) more likely to be sentenced to prison than those who have obtained pretrial release (Ares, Rankin, and Sturz 1963; Cohen and Reaves 2007; Phillips 2007, 2008; Reaves 2001). What is in dispute is the interpretation of these findings. Do these disparities result because the lack of pretrial release imposes additional burdens on the defendants? Or are these disparities a statistical artifact of a preselection process? Given that bail tariffs increase with the severity of the crime and the length of the prior record, one might reasonably expect that these defendants would end up disadvantaged, but for good reason.

John Goldkamp (1980) attempted to answer this difficult question through a sophisticated analysis of more than 8,000 criminal cases in Philadelphia. Goldkamp found that jailed defendants did not differ from their bailed counterparts in terms of findings of guilt. At all the significant stages—dismissal, diversion, and trial—jailed defendants were as likely as bailed ones to receive a favorable disposition of their cases. When it came to sentencing, however, jailed defendants were more likely to be sentenced to prison, although the length of the sentence was not related to bail status. Another study (Eisenstein and Jacob 1977) found no uniform impact of bail status on findings of guilt or on sentencing. Does bail status negatively affect the defendant's case? Perhaps the best response is provided by Goldkamp: "It depends." More recently, research in New York City found that in felony (Phillips 2008) and nonfelony cases (Phillips 2007) pretrial detention had a small, but statistically significant effect on the likelihood of conviction and also slightly longer sentences.

BAIL REFORM BASED ON THE DUE PROCESS MODEL

The American system of monetary bail has been the subject of extensive debate for decades. The fairness and effectiveness of pretrial release and detention have been questioned from two conflicting perspectives. The bail reform movement of the 1960s and 1970s was largely concerned with correcting inequities. Requiring suspects to buy their freedom was viewed as unfairly discriminating against the poor. Bail reform based on the values of the due process model is reflected in the Bail Reform Act of 1966, which created a presumption favoring pretrial release. To make bail fairer, reformers advocated adopting a 10 percent bail deposit and institutionalizing pretrial service programs. These programs offered new ways to accomplish the purpose of bail: to guarantee appearance for trial.

TEN PERCENT BAIL DEPOSIT

Bail agents charge a nonrefundable 10 percent fee for posting bond. Since they seem to perform few services for their fee and have often been linked with corruption, bail reformers have attempted to legislate an economic end run around these third-party operators. In a handful of jurisdictions, defendants may gain pretrial release by posting 10 percent of the face amount of the bond with the court. At this point, there is no difference between what the bail agent charges and what the court requires. But when the defendant makes all scheduled court appearances, the court will refund 90 percent of the amount posted. (The remaining 10 percent covers the administrative costs of the program.) The 10 percent bail deposit program directly threatens the bail bond industry. In Illinois, the first state to adopt this program, bail agents have virtually disappeared. In other states, however, agents have been successful in defeating such proposals in the legislature.

PRETRIAL SERVICE PROGRAMS

Bail reformers have been critical of traditional methods of bail setting because the court does not directly focus on whether the defendant is likely to appear in court. What were first called "bail reform projects" but are now termed "pretrial service programs" seek to remedy this deficiency by determining which defendants are good risks. First developed and tested by the Vera Institute of Justice in New York City, the program works as follows. A program worker interviews the defendant shortly after arrest about family ties, employment history, length of time in the community, prior criminal record, and (in a growing number of areas) results of postarrest drug tests. Persons deemed good risks are recommended for release on recognizance. Not all defendants are eligible for the program, however; those arrested for serious charges such as murder, armed robbery, or drug selling are usually excluded. After release, the pretrial service agency makes followup contacts to ensure that the defendant knows when the court appearance is scheduled and will show up.

The guiding assumption of the Vera Project is that defendants with ties to the community are not likely to flee. By providing information about these ties (which normally is not available when

COURTS, CONTROVERSY, AND REDUCING CRIME

Should Defendants Be Forced to Take a Drug Test?

The dual concerns of failure to appear and committing additional crimes while out on bail have become focused on pretrial drug-testing programs.

There is little doubt that drug use among those arrested is high; in a typical year, the percentage of male arrestees testing positive for recent illegal drug use is about 64 percent. This estimate is based on data gathered by the Arrestee Drug Abuse Monitoring (ADAM) program, which conducts urine tests on arrestees in 35 cities (Arrestee Drug Abuse Monitoring 2003). Moreover, one fourth to one half of all adult male arrestees are at risk for dependence on drugs. Likewise, more recent data on 10 cities found that between 49 and 87 percent of those arrested tested positive for at least one substance (Office of National Drug Control Policy 2009).

Pretrial drug-testing programs are based on the following assumptions: First, knowledge of a defendant's drug use at the time of arrest—obtained through a drug test—provides an important predictor of pretrial misconduct. Second, monitoring drug use during the pretrial periods, coupled with sanctions, will reduce the risk of pretrial misconduct (Henry and Clark 1999).

The District of Columbia Pretrial Services Agency was the first to implement pretrial drug testing as part of the bail process. Other jurisdictions have created somewhat similar programs (Pretrial Services Resource Center 1999), and the federal courts implemented Operation Drug TEST (Testing Effective Sanctions and Treatments) in some jurisdictions.

Requiring pretrial drug testing seems commonsensical enough and therefore has become a widely used practice. But are these programs effective? Several studies find that at best they have limited success.

bail is set), the program provides a more workable way to make sure that the wrong people are not detained prior to trial. Research has confirmed the operating assumption (Siddiqi 2004). Where pretrial service programs have been tried, the rate of nonappearance for those released on recognizance has been lower than for those released through bail agents (Wice 1974). Supporters also argue that such programs save money. Because more people are being released, costs for holding defendants in jail are significantly reduced. More recently, pretrial service programs have been adopted as a means for relieving jail overcrowding. Hundreds of such programs now operate throughout the nation. According to the Pretrial Services Resource Center, pretrial programs are being established in smaller jurisdictions at higher rates than ever before. Moreover, pretrial services programs are addressing the challenges raised by two special populations of defendants that are being seen with increasing frequency in the criminal justice system: those suffering from mental illness and those charged with domestic violence offenses (Clark and Henry 2003).

BAIL REFORM BASED ON THE CRIME CONTROL MODEL

By the 1980s, bail reform shifted from a focus on the inequities in the process to concern about the link between bail and crime. To a great extent, the demand for preventive detention was a consequence of a backlash against the bail reform movement of the 1960s. Bail reform based on the values of the crime control model are reflected in the 1984 Bail Reform Act, which made wholesale revisions in the earlier law (Wiseman 2009). Whereas release of the defendant was the primary intent of the earlier law, detention plays a prominent role in the new one. In setting bail, a federal judge may now consider danger to the community and may deny bail altogether when the accused is found to be a "grave

Requiring defendants to participate in drug testing does not reduce failure-to-appear rates (Goldkamp and Jones 1992; Visher 1992). "The lack of predictive power is not surprising from a statistical perspective because drug use is very common among arrestees and pretrial misconduct a relatively rare event" (Belenko, Mara-Drita, and McElroy 1992, p. 577). Nor do pretrial drug-testing programs help predict which defendants will be rearrested while out on bail. Surprisingly, first-time arrestees who tested positive for any illicit substance were better risks for release than repeat offenders who did not test positive for recent drug use (Rhodes, Hyatt, and Scheiman 1996).

But the evidence is not all negative. Drug testing appears to be successful if used as one component of coordinated earlier intervention efforts for adult offenders (Harrell et al. 2002).

Given that evaluations have called pretrial drug-testing programs into question, it is important that policymakers accurately assess the costs of these programs. They are expensive. Just as important, throughout the United States, programs to treat those addicted to alcohol, illicit drugs, or both are plentiful for those covered by medical insurance but sparse for those without coverage (including most of those involved in the criminal justice system). Overall, treatment options for drug-dependent arrestees are limited.

What do you think? Are pretrial drug-testing programs effective in reducing failure-to-appear rates and pretrial crimes? Or are pretrial drug-testing programs ineffective because they are based on faulty assumptions?

danger to others." Bail reform based on the crime control model focuses on two topics: pretrial crimes and preventive detention.

PRETRIAL CRIMES

Most of the attention in the contemporary discussion of bail focuses on defendants who commit additional crimes while on pretrial release. Individual occurrences are easy to find, and adherents of the crime control model are quick to highlight them in their arguments for preventive detention. But how common are such events?

Numerous studies of pretrial crime have been conducted. The dominant conclusion is that arrests of pretrial releasees for serious crimes are relatively infrequent, and convictions for such crimes are even less frequent (Jackson 1987; Walker 1989). At first glance, this does not appear to be the case. Two older studies reported that about 15 percent of those released were rearrested while on pretrial conditional release (Reaves and Perez 1994;

Toborg 1983). More recently, the Bureau of Justice Statistics reported that in large urban areas 21 percent of released felony defendants were rearrested (Kyckelhahn and Cohen 2008). But a simple measure of rearrest distorts the true picture. Many of those rearrested were initially arrested for a misdemeanor and later arrested for another minor offense. A better measure is the percentage of all persons arrested for a felony, released on bail, and later arrested for another felony. Depending on the study, the pretrial crime rate ranges from 5 to 7 percent (Gottfredson 1974; Toborg 1983). Indeed, a study in New York City found that 7 percent of released defendants were rearrested for a felony offense (Siddiqi 2005). The relative infrequency of serious pretrial crime makes its prediction especially difficult (Jackson 1987), not to say suspect. Nonetheless, as a tool in predicting risk, many jurisdictions are now adopting mandatory pretrial drug testing. (See Courts, Controversy, and Reducing Crime: Should Defendants Be Forced to Take a Drug Test?)

PREVENTIVE DETENTION

Should defendants be held in jail awaiting trial with no right to bail? Adherents of the crime control model assume that current bail practices do not successfully restrain dangerous defendants. They point to defendants who commit crimes while out of jail on pretrial release. The suggested alternative is **preventive detention**, which allows judges to hold suspects without bail if they are accused of committing a dangerous or violent crime and locking them up is deemed necessary for community safety. The overwhelming majority of U.S. states have enacted laws that allow courts to consider public safety, danger to the community, jeopardy to others, or similar general reasons in setting conditions of release or in denying release altogether.

The best-known example of preventive detention is the Bail Reform Act of 1984, which authorizes preventive detention for federal defendants accused of serious crimes. After a detention hearing, the defendant may be held in jail without bail for up to 90 days pending trial if the judge finds "clear and convincing evidence" that: (1) there is a serious risk that the person will flee; (2) the person may obstruct justice or threaten, injure, or intimidate a prospective witness or juror; or (3) the offense is one of violence or one punishable by life imprisonment or death. The law also creates a presumption against pretrial release for major drug dealers (Berg 1985). The Supreme Court has upheld the Bail Reform Act, ruling that Congress enacted preventive detention not as a punishment for dangerous individuals but as a potential solution to the pressing social problem of crimes committed by persons on bail (see Case Close-Up: *U.S. v. Salerno* and Preventive Detention).

Are preventive-detention laws merely exercises in symbolic politics, or do they have substantive impact? Early studies suggested the former, as some jurisdictions failed to implement preventive-detention statutes (Toborg and Bellassai 1986) while in other jurisdictions, detention hearings were requested so infrequently that fewer than 2 out of every 1,000 felony defendants were formally detained (Thomas 1976). But more recent data suggests that preventive detention has been implemented on a substantial scale. Detention hearings are being held and defendants detained without bail being set. Roughly 38 percent of felony defendants in U.S. states are detained prior to the disposition of their case. Of these detainees, one in six had been denied bail and the other five "had bail set with financial conditions required for release that were not met" (Cohen and Reaves 2007, p. 1). Thus, approximately 6 percent of all felony defendants are

---

U.S. v. Salerno and Preventive Detention

The 88-page federal grand jury indictment charged that Anthony Salerno, the alleged "boss of the Genovese Crime Family of La Cosa Nostra," and 14 other members described as "associates" violated 29 federal laws ranging from Racketeer Influenced and Corrupt Organizations Act (RICO) violations, mail fraud, wire fraud, and extortion to gambling and conspiracy to commit murder. The front-page article in the *New York Times* was quick to note that the indictments followed an earlier *New York Times* series detailing how the mob had infiltrated concrete companies to control construction of high-rise buildings in Manhattan, including Trump Plaza (Lubasch 1986).

In previous cases like this, bond had typically been set in the millions, with the amount calculated to virtually ensure that the defendant would be unable to raise the necessary funds and would therefore await trial in jail. But in this case, Rudolph Giuliani, U.S. Attorney for the Southern District of New York (primarily Manhattan), chose to seek preventive detention. The Bail Reform Act of 1984 allows a federal court to detain an arrestee pending trial if the government demonstrates by clear and convincing evidence that no release condition "will reasonably assure … the safety of any other person and the community." During the detention hearing, the U.S. attorney introduced evidence gathered through court-ordered wiretaps and also two potential trial witnesses, who asserted that Salerno had personally participated in two murder conspiracies. The district court granted the government's detention motion.

Salerno appealed, and the Second Circuit struck down the law as unconstitutional. Other circuits, though, had reached a different conclusion. An indication that the Court was anxious to hear a case like this one could be seen in the speed of the appellate process; the Court heard oral argument just 10 months after Salerno's arrest.

That the majority of the Court adheres to the crime control model on this issue is made abundantly clear in the opening paragraph of the opinion (after the statement of the facts). Written by Chief Justice William Rehnquist, the majority opinion begins by stressing the reasonableness of the statute: Responding to "the alarming problem of crimes committed by persons on release…," Congress passed the Bail Reform Act of 1984 as the solution to a "bail crisis in the federal courts." As for the Eighth Amendment, the opinion stresses, "Nothing in the text of the Bail Clause limits permissible government considerations solely to questions of flight." Thus, Congress was justified in allowing the courts to deny bail not only if there is a danger of flight but also if the person poses a danger to others.

The three dissenting justices clearly expressed values of the due process model. In Thurgood Marshall's biting words, the Bail Reform Act of 1984 represents the first time Congress "declares that a person innocent of any crime may be jailed indefinitely, pending the trial of allegations which are legally presumed to be untrue." Such practices are "consistent with the usages of tyranny and excesses of bitter experience teaches us to call the police state." Likewise in dissent, John Paul Stevens argued that depriving persons of vital rights on the basis of predictions of future dangerousness is unconstitutional.

Beneath the debate over how best to reduce crime runs an important issue of how to interpret the Constitution (see Chapter 17). One theory, usually associated with conservatives, is strict constructionism: The document should be interpreted on the basis of the original intent of the framers. Another theory, usually identified with liberals, is adaptationist: The meaning of the document should be adjusted to changing conditions of society. The *Salerno* opinion dramatically illustrates that when it comes to the rights of criminal defendants, these positions are reversed. Conservatives stress the need to adapt the Constitution to the pressing current problem of crime, whereas liberals emphasize that the framers were indeed correct in suspecting that the government is capable of tyranny.

CASE CLOSEUP

denied bail and held in pretrial detention, a figure that has remained remarkably consistent since the Bail Reform Act of 1984 and its state law counterparts went into effect.

CONCLUSION

U.S. v. Salerno marked a turning point in the lives of both participants. *Fortune* magazine once described Anthony "Fat Tony" Salerno as the richest and most powerful mobster in America. But at the age of 74, he was sentenced to 100 years in prison. The future for U.S. Attorney Rudolph Giuliani was strikingly different. He resigned his office several years later to run successfully for mayor of New York, with crime as his lead issue. In 1997 he was overwhelmingly reelected, and in 2001 he gained international recognition as the city coped with the disaster of September 11.

Bail serves several purposes in the American court system, some legally sanctioned, others definitely extra-legal. Bail is used to guarantee a defendant's appearance at trial, to protect society by holding those perceived to be dangerous, to punish those accused (but not yet convicted) of violating the law, and to lubricate the system by softening defendants up to enter a plea of guilty. These varying purposes are partially the result of the tension among conflicting principles. Although the law recognizes that the only legal purpose of bail is to guarantee a suspect's future appearance at trial, court officials perceive a need to protect society. Out of these conflicting principles arise compromises.

CHAPTER REVIEW

1. List the four most common ways that defendants secure pretrial release.

The four most common ways defendants secure pretrial release are: (1) cash bond, (2) property bond, (3) release on recognizance (ROR), and (4) bail agent (also called a "bail bondsman").

2. Discuss how law in action affects bail setting.

Law in action affects bail setting in terms of uncertainly, risk, and jail overcrowding.

3. Recognize the most important factors in the process of bail setting.

The most important factors in the process of bail setting are the seriousness of the crime, the prior criminal record of the defendant, and situational justice.

4. Interpret the business setting of the bail agent (bail bondsman).

The bail agent (bail bondsman) provides a specialized form of insurance and makes a profit by focusing on low-risk offenders accused of less serious crimes.

5. Identify the effect of the bail system on the processing of criminal defendants.

Bail affects the processing of criminal defendants in terms of jail conditions, the greater impact on racial and ethnic minorities, the failure of some defendants to appear in court as promised, and case disposition.

6. Distinguish between bail reform based on the due process model of justice and the crime control model of justice.

Bail reform based on the due process model of justice seeks to make the process fairer for defendants by providing 10 percent bail deposit and pretrial service programs. By contrast, bail reform based on the crime control model of criminal justice is concerned with pretrial crimes and stresses the need for preventive detention.

CRITICAL THINKING QUESTIONS

1. How do bail and bail setting illustrate the differences between law on the books and law in action?
2. In what ways do crime control model advocates approach bail differently than do backers of due process model values?
3. Examine the local papers. Have there been reports of defendants' committing crimes while out on bail? Have there been reports of poor conditions in the local jail? How might these reports affect bail setting?
4. Talk with judges, prosecutors, and defense attorneys about the relationship between pretrial release and the following two factors: jail capacity and length of time between arrest and disposition. (You may wish to review Chapter 5.)
5. Are preventive-detention laws effective, or are they exercises in symbolic politics?

KEY TERMS

bail 260
bail agent (bail bondsman) 261
bench warrant (capias) 269
cash bond 260
preventive detention 274
property bond 261
release on recognizance (ROR) 261

WEB RESOURCES

Go to the America's Courts and the Criminal Justice System companion website at

www.cengage.com/criminaljustice/neubauer

where you will find more resources to help you study.

Resources include web exercises, quizzing, and flash cards.

FOR FURTHER READING

Cushman, Robert. *Preventing Jail Crowding: A Practical Guide.* Washington, DC: National Institute of Corrections, 2002.

Goldkamp, John, and Michael White. "Restoring Accountability in Pretrial Release: The Philadelphia Pretrial Release Supervision Experiments." *Journal of Experimental Criminology* 2: 143–181, 2006.

Haapanen, Rudy, and Lee Britton. "Drug Testing for Youthful Offenders on Parole: An Experimental Evaluation." *Criminology and Public Policy* 1: 217–244, 2002.

Holleran, David, and Cassia Spohn. "On the Use of the Total Incarceration Variable in Sentencing Research." *Criminology* 42: 211–240, 2004.

Kerle, Kenneth. *Exploring Jail Operations.* Hagerstown, MD: American Jail Association, 2003.

Phillips, Mary. "Prosecutors' Bail Requests and the CJA Release Recommendations: What Do They Tell the Judge?" *Research Brief Number 9.* New York: New York City Criminal Justice Agency, 2005.

Robertson, James. *Jail Planning and Expansion: Local Officials and Their Roles.* Washington, DC: U.S. Department of Justice, National Institute of Corrections, 2003.

Rose, Kenneth. "Pretrial Justice: Principles and Practice (NIC Update). *Corrections Today* 69: 72, 2007.

12 DISCLOSING AND SUPPRESSING EVIDENCE

© Michael Newman/PhotoEdit

A police officer reads a suspect his Miranda rights after arrest. Miranda is the best-known example of the U.S. Supreme Court's "due process revolution" that greatly changes how crimes are prosecuted. To liberals, due process limits on police power are necessary to protect the rights of all citizens, especially those who are wrongfully accused. Conservatives, however, often argue that the myriad of rights enjoyed by the criminally accused often allow the guilty to go free. This philosophical debate aside, in reality, judges rarely suppress evidence in criminal cases.

CHAPTER OUTLINE

LEARNING OBJECTIVES

After reading this chapter, you should be able to:

1. Explain the reasons why the process of discovery exists in both civil and criminal cases, but is significantly curtailed in the latter.

2. Differentiate formal and informal discovery and the reasons why both are used in criminal cases.

3. Identify the types of evidence subject to mandatory criminal discovery.

4. Compare and contrast the exclusionary rule and the fruit of the poisonous tree doctrine.

5. Summarize how the decision in *Miranda v. Arizona* regulates the process of police interrogations of suspects.

6. Explain the requirements governing the application for search warrants, the issuance of search warrants, and the execution of search warrants.

7. Identify the major exceptions to the Fourth Amendment's warrant requirement.

8. Analyze the effect of the exclusionary rule on the operations of the courtroom work group.

9. Evaluate whether the exclusionary rule should be abolished.

Just before midnight, 18-year-old Lois Ann Jameson (not her real name) left the downtown theater where she worked and walked the two blocks to her normal bus stop. A half-hour later, she arrived in her neighborhood for her usual short walk home. The only unusual event was a strange car, which suddenly veered in front of her. A young Hispanic man got out, grabbed her with one hand, and placed the other over her mouth while dragging her into the parked car. He drove 20 minutes into the desert, where he tore off her clothes and raped her. In a strange twist of circumstances, the assailant drove Lois Ann Jameson back to her neighborhood.

Once she was home, she immediately called the police. To Detective Carroll Cooley, Jameson's story was not only somewhat contradictory but also offered few leads. Jameson couldn't provide a very good description of her attacker. The only lead was her detailed description of the car—an old model, light green, clean on the outside, and dirty brown upholstery on the inside. Moreover, in the backseat of the car was a loop of rope designed to help rear-seat passengers in pulling themselves up. This description eventually led Detective Cooley to a house on the west side of town, where he found a car exactly as described. The subsequent interrogation and conviction of Ernesto Miranda was to change the landscape of American criminal justice.

The *Miranda* warnings are the most controversial part of the Supreme Court's revolution in criminal justice. Responding to criticisms that police procedures were unfair and that the police were not adhering to the procedural requirements of the law, the Supreme Court imposed additional restrictions on police investigative techniques, such as searches, interrogations, and lineups. The Court's decisions produced extensive national controversy. Subsequent Courts, dominated by appointees of Republican presidents, have significantly curtailed (but not eliminated) these earlier decisions.

This chapter examines some of the diverse activities that may occur between arraignment and final disposition (either a guilty plea or a trial). The first topic will be the gathering of evidence, which is termed "discovery." Next will be a discussion of how and why some evidence is excluded from trial.

DISCOVERY

The informal and formal exchange of information between prosecution and defense is referred to as **discovery**. Laboratory reports, statements of witnesses, defendants' confessions, and police reports are examples of information that prosecutors often gather and defense attorneys want to know about before trial.

Discovery seeks to ensure that the adversary system does not give one side an unfair advantage over the other. The guiding assumption of the adversary system is that truth will emerge after a struggle at trial. But as Justice William Brennan (1963) asked, should this struggle at trial be a sporting event or a quest for the truth? Historically, civil trials were largely sporting events, in which the outcome depended heavily on the technical skills of the lawyers. In an effort to eliminate the worst aspects of such contests, the Federal Rules of Civil Procedure were adopted in 1938, and most states have since followed the federal example. By these rules, prior to trial, every party in a civil action is entitled to the disclosure of all relevant information in the possession of any person, unless that information is privileged (Friedenthal, Kane, and Miller 2005). These discovery rules are intended to make a trial "less a game of blind man's bluff and more a fair contest with the basic issues and facts disclosed to the fullest practicable extent" (*U.S. v. Procter and Gamble Co.* 1958, p. 682). A longstanding debate, however, has been fought over the extent of pretrial discovery in criminal cases.

LAW ON THE BOOKS: RULES REQUIRING DISCLOSURE

Although there is a very broad power of discovery in civil proceedings, "there is no general constitutional right to discovery in a criminal case" (*Weatherford v. Bursey* 1977, 559). However, a series of court decisions, statutes, and court rules provide the framework for the criminal discovery process. Courts have expressed concern that requiring too much prosecutorial disclosure might result in the defendant's taking undue advantage (*State v. Tune* 1953). For example, the defendant, knowing of the state's case, might procure perjured testimony or might intimidate witnesses who are likely to testify (Mosteller 2002).

Discovery in federal cases is governed primarily by sections of Rules 12, 16, and 26 of the Federal Rules of Criminal Procedure. Collectively, these rules provide a defendant, upon motion, rights to discovery concerning tangible objects; tape recordings; books, papers and documents (including written or recorded statements made by the defendants or witnesses) that are relevant to the case; the defendant's prior criminal record, if any; the results or reports of physical examinations, scientific tests, experiments, and forensic comparisons; and summaries of any expert testimony that the government intends to offer in its case-in-chief. These materials may total only a few items and pages, or they may fill many boxes. The rules often afford the government similar reciprocal discovery upon its compliance with the request of the defendant.

In state courts, the type of information that is discoverable varies considerably from state to state. Some jurisdictions allow only limited discovery: The trial court has the discretion to order the prosecutor to disclose the defendant's confession and other physical documents, but that is all. Other jurisdictions take a middle ground: Discovery of confessions and physical evidence is a matter of right, but discovery of other items (witnesses' statements, for example) is more difficult. Finally, a few states have adopted liberal discovery rules: A presumption strongly in favor of prosecutorial disclosure exists, with only certain narrow exceptions. Exhibit 12.1 summarizes significant developments in criminal discovery law.

Exhibit 12.1
KEY DEVELOPMENTS IN CRIMINAL DISCOVERY LAW

Jencks v. U.S.	1957	Prior inconsistent statements of a witness must be made available to defense counsel.
Brady v. Maryland	1963	Due process of law is violated when prosecutors conceal evidence that might be favorable to the defense.
Williams v. Florida	1970	Requiring defense to disclose an alibi defense prior to trial does not violate the defendant's privilege against self-incrimination.
U.S. v. Agurs	1976	Under *Brady*, the prosecutor must disclose evidence only if such evidence would have been persuasive and produced reasonable doubt about guilt.
Weatherford v. Bursey	1977	No general constitutional right to discovery in criminal cases.
Kyles v. Whitley	1995	Materiality of evidence not disclosed is determined by looking at the effect of all the evidence, not simply one item.

Exhibit 12.1

CONTINUED

Wood v. Bartholomew	1995	Failure of prosecutor to turn over inadmissible polygraph evidence was not a *Brady* violation.
Strickler v. Greene	1999	Even though petitioner was not given exculpatory evidence, there was no *Brady* violation because there was no prejudice.
Youngblood v. West Virginia	2006	*Brady* violations extend to impeachment evidence as well as exculpatory evidence. It is the duty of the prosecutor to determine whether the police possess evidence favorable to the defense.

Discovery of Exculpatory Evidence

Because of growing discontent with the discovery system, American courts have cautiously expanded mandatory disclosure by the prosecutor, especially with respect to disclosures of exculpatory evidence and impeachment material. **Exculpatory evidence** is any evidence that may be favorable to the defendant at trial either by tending to cast doubt on the defendant's guilt or by tending to mitigate the defendant's culpability, thereby potentially reducing the defendant's sentence. In *Brady v. Maryland* (1963, p. 87), the U.S. Supreme Court held that "the suppression by the prosecution of evidence favorable to an accused upon request violates due process where the evidence is material either to guilt or punishment, *irrespective of the good faith or bad faith of the prosecution*" (italics added). This is commonly referred to as the *Brady* rule.

The *Brady* rule is limited to admissible evidence. Thus, the prosecution has no obligation to provide the defense potentially exculpatory information that would not be admissible in court. For example, in *Wood v. Bartholomew*, 516 U.S. 1 (1995), the U.S. Supreme Court held that there is no requirement to turn over the results of a polygraph examination of a witness because polygraph results are inadmissible.

The *Brady* rule applies only to exculpatory evidence that is *material*. Exculpatory evidence is material "only if there is a 'reasonable probability' that, had the evidence been disclosed to the defense, the result of the proceeding would have been different. A 'reasonable probability' is a probability sufficient to undermine confidence in the outcome" (*United States v. Bagley* 1985, p. 682). Needless to say, this standard requires a judgment call on the part of prosecutors, and in recent years the Court has ruled that prosecutors have been too narrow in their interpretation.

In *Kyles v. Whitley* (1995), the prosecutor failed to disclose the statements of two of four witnesses and other evidence relating to Kyles's car. In a 5-to-4 decision, Justice David Souter wrote that the test was a cumulative one, looking at all the evidence that was not disclosed, not just isolated pieces. Moreover, to gain a new trial, the defense need only show a reasonable probability of a different result (not a preponderance of the evidence). "The question is not whether the defendant would more likely than not have received a different verdict with the evidence, but whether in its absence he received a fair trial, understood as a trial resulting in a verdict worthy of confidence" (p. 434). Applying this test, the Court ruled that the *Brady* rule had been violated in the case. What made the case particularly challenging, though, was that the prosecution did not know about the exculpatory evidence in the case because the police had not revealed the two witness statements to the prosecutor. According to the Court, though, prosecutors are responsible for ensuring that police communicate relevant evidence to the prosecutor's office. It is worthy to note that on retrial, three juries declined to convict Kyles, and charges were eventually dropped.

Brady does not require the prosecution to make its files available to the defendant for an open-ended "fishing expedition." Nor does *Brady* require the disclosure of inculpatory, neutral, or speculative evidence. However, prosecutors' obligations under *Brady* are not limited to situations in which the defendant specifically requests the evidence. As the "attorney for the sovereign," the prosecutor "must always be faithful to his client's overriding interest that 'justice shall be done'" (*United States v. Agurs* 1976, pp. 110–111).

Discovery of Impeachment Evidence

In *Jencks v. United States* (1957), the Supreme Court ruled that the government must disclose any prior inconsistent statements of prosecutorial witnesses so that the defense could conduct a meaningful cross-examination of such witnesses. Congress both expanded and limited the holding in *Jencks* when it enacted the Jencks Act. That law requires the prosecutor to disclose, after direct examination of a government witness and on the defendant's motion, any statement of a witness in the government's possession that relates to the subject matter of the witness' testimony. Thus, the Jencks Act requires disclosure of all prior statements of witnesses, even if the prior statements are not inconsistent with any subsequent statement by the witnesses, expanding the holding of *Jencks*. Yet, Congress placed the burden on defense counsel to ask for the information (unlike *Brady* material, which the prosecutor has an ethical obligation to disclose even if not asked). Congress also limited the time frame for such disclose such that it need not take place until after the direct examination of a governmental witness by the prosecution.

In *Giglio v. United States* (1972), the Supreme Court clarified that all impeachment evidence, even if not a prior statement by a witness, also falls within the *Brady* rule. Thus, *Giglio* mandated that the prosecution disclose any and all information that may be used to impeach the credibility of prosecution witnesses, including law enforcement officers. Impeachment information under *Giglio* includes information such as the prior criminal records or other acts of misconduct of prosecution witnesses, or such information as promises of leniency or immunity offered to prosecution witnesses. As with *Brady* material,

the mandates of *Jencks* and *Giglio* do not require the prosecution to make its files available to the defendant for an open-ended fishing expedition.

LAW IN ACTION: INFORMAL PROSECUTORIAL DISCLOSURE

Discovery rules are vitally important to defense attorneys. In states that grant defense considerable discovery rights, the lawyer can go straight to the prosecutor's files and obtain the essentials of the state's case against the defendant. By learning the facts of the prosecutor's case, the defense attorney need not face the difficult task of trying to force his client to voluntarily disclose this information. Across the nation, "nearly all lawyers interviewed felt that clients' veracity is questionable and in need of thorough verification. This forces the attorney to devote extra hours, frequently wasted, verifying a client's version of the facts, which also puts a strain on their relationship—especially when the attorney is forced to confront the defendant with his prevarications" (Wice 1978, p. 45; see also Sternlight and Robbennolt 2008).

In jurisdictions that grant limited discovery rights to the defense, defense attorneys must be more resourceful in determining what actually happened. To that end, a variety of proceedings not directly designed for discovery purposes can be used. At the preliminary hearing, intended to test the sufficiency of the evidence for holding the defendant, the defense hears at least part of the story of some critical witnesses. Similarly, during a hearing on a pretrial motion to suppress evidence, the testimony of key government witnesses may yield important new facts relevant to a trial defense. But eventually, defense attorneys may be forced to confront their clients about inconsistencies (or worse) in their statements, a confrontation that can strain lawyer–client relationships (see Chapter 7).

Some prosecutors have an office policy prohibiting assistant prosecutors from disclosing any information not required by law. But it is more usual that assistant DAs voluntarily disclose certain aspects of the state's case to defense attorneys. Such informal discovery operates within the norms of cooperation of courtroom work groups. Defense attorneys who maintain good relationships with prosecutors and are viewed as trustworthy receive selected information about the case. Conversely, defense attorneys who maintain hostile relationships with the prosecutor, who represent clients who are viewed as troublemakers, or both (the two frequently go to-gether) find the prosecutors holding the cards as tightly to the vest as the law allows.

Informal prosecutorial disclosure does not stem from sympathy for the defendant, but rather from a long-held courthouse theory that an advance glimpse at the prosecutor's case encourages a plea of guilty. From the perspective of the prosecutor, de-fendants often tell their lawyers only part of what happened. Therefore, the defense attorney who learns what evidence the prosecutor possesses can use it to show the defendant that contesting the matter may be hopeless. At times, though, defense attorneys are often frustrated by the prosecution's control over the discovery process, especially when the prosecution fails to disclose important informa-tion until the last possible minute—by which point it has minimal value (Wice 2005).

Informal prosecutorial discovery greatly encour-ages pleas of guilty, at least when the prosecution has a strong case. In their classic studies, Milton Heumann (1978) and Paul Wice (1978) reported that in courthouses where prosecutors emphasize closed discovery, there is often a failure to plea-bargain, and a large number of cases go to trial, frequently without a jury. In contrast, they found that in court-houses where prosecutors have adopted open dis-covery policies, pleas of guilty are entered sooner, resulting in a significantly smaller backlog than is found in most cities with closed discovery. More than three decades later, their findings remain the conventional wisdom subject to the limitation that the prosecution has a strong case. If, on the other hand, the prosecution's case is weak, then open dis-covery may serve to embolden a defendant to take his or her chances at trial (Covey 2007).

LAW AND CONTROVERSY: REQUIRING RECIPROCAL DISCLOSURE

Ordinarily, to obtain discoverable information, a party must make a timely motion before the court; must show that the specific items sought are mate-rial to the preparation of its case; and that its request is reasonable. Some jurisdictions, however, provide for automatic discovery for certain types of evidence, without the necessity for motions and court orders. Who must disclose what to whom, however, var-ies significantly, causing controversy in the criminal justice system.

Defense attorneys understandably press for broader discovery laws. But to what extent should

the defense be required to disclose relevant materials in its possession to the prosecution? After all, the Constitution limits reciprocal discovery in criminal cases, unlike in civil proceedings, because criminal defendants enjoy the privilege against self-incrimination (see Chapter 2). Thus, requirements that the defense turn over to the prosecutor state-ments from expert witnesses that it does not intend to call at trial would probably be unconstitutional. If, however, the defendant intends to call an expert witness at trial, rules such as Federal Rule of Crimi-nal Procedure 16(b) typically require the defense to disclose the expert's identity, qualifications, conclu-sions, and the bases for having reached them.

A few states allow the defendant access to discov-erable information in the prosecution's possession without the defense having a duty to disclose any information to the prosecution. Even in such juris-dictions, however, the defense would have an obliga-tion to disclose certain evidence in support of select affirmative defenses. For example, an **alibi defense** means that the defendant claims the crime was com-mitted while the defendant was somewhere else, and thus could not have been the perpetrator. The de-fense would have to disclose a list of witnesses to be called to support the alibi [Federal Rule of Criminal Procedure 12.1(a)(2); *Williams v. Florida* 1970]. Such pretrial notice enables the prosecutor to investigate the backgrounds of these witnesses and thus be pre-pared to undermine the defendant's contention that he or she was somewhere else when the crime was committed. In the same vein, some states mandate that the defense must disclose to the prosecution pri-or to trial that an insanity plea will be entered or that expert witnesses will be called.

In contrast to jurisdictions with only limited dis-closure requirements for the defense, in some states "a defendant who issues a discovery request to the prosecutor thereby automatically incurs the duty to disclose information to the prosecutor. In still others, a defense discovery request gives the prosecutor the right—presumably almost certain to be exercised—to demand discovery from the defendant" (Easton and Bridges 2008, p. 6). The state of the law govern-ing discovery is constantly changing, but the trend appears to be in favor of broadening the right of discovery for both the defense and the prosecution. The guiding light, as articulated by prosecutors and law-and-order advocates, is that the trial should be a level playing field for all parties; both sides should be prevented from attempting to conduct a trial by ambush.

SUPPRESSING EVIDENCE

The most controversial of the Supreme Court's criminal justice decisions have concerned how the police gather evidence. For example, the rape conviction of Ernesto Miranda in 1966 was overturned because the police had not advised him of his constitutional right to remain silent before he confessed. In 1961, Dollree Mapp's pornography conviction was reversed because the police had illegally searched her house. In both cases, otherwise valid and trustworthy evidence was excluded from trial. These cases are applications of the exclusionary rule.

THE EXCLUSIONARY RULE

The **exclusionary rule** prohibits the prosecutor from using illegally obtained evidence during a trial. This rule is not constitutionally mandated, but rather was judicially created relatively recently in the development of the U.S. legal system. Under the common law, the seizure of evidence by illegal means did not affect its admissibility in court. Any evidence, however obtained, was admitted as long as it satisfied other evidentiary criteria for admissibility, such as relevance and trustworthiness. That changed when the exclusionary rule was first developed in 1914 in the case of *Weeks v. United States*. *Weeks*, however, was limited to a prohibition on the use of evidence illegally obtained by federal law enforcement officers. Not until 1949, in the case of *Wolf v. Colorado*, did the U.S. Supreme Court take the first step toward applying the exclusionary rule to the states by ruling that the Fourth Amendment was applicable to the states through the Due Process Clause of the Fourteenth Amendment. *Wolf*, however, left enforcement of Fourth Amendment rights to the discretion of the individual states; it did not specifically require application of the exclusionary rule. That mandate did not come until 1961, in the landmark decision of *Mapp v. Ohio*. With *Mapp*, the exclusionary rule became the principle method to deter Fourth Amendment violations by law enforcement officials. The rule was also supported by a normative argument: A court of law should not participate in or condone illegal conduct.

The exclusionary rule is commonly associated with the search and seizure of physical evidence under the Fourth Amendment. But the exclusionary rule also applies to the pretrial **confrontations** between witnesses and suspects (show-ups lineups, or photo arrays) that were either unreliable (therefore violating due process) or that occurred in violation of the accused's Sixth Amendment right to counsel. Thus, for example, if a police lineup is improperly conducted, the identification of the suspect may be excluded from evidence during trial pursuant to the exclusionary rule. The exclusionary rule is also applicable to interrogations and confessions that violate either the Fifth Amendment privilege against self-incrimination or the Sixth Amendment right to counsel. However, the rule applies differently depending on the type and severity of the underlying constitutional violation. As the U.S. Supreme Court stated in *Dickerson v. United States* (2000), "unreasonable searches under the Fourth Amendment are different from unwarned interrogation under the Fifth Amendment." Thus, for example, a failure to give *Miranda* warnings before a suspect's confession may not trigger the exclusionary rule to other, future incriminating statements by that same suspect.

FRUIT OF THE POISONOUS TREE

The exclusionary rule is not limited to evidence that is the direct product of illegal police behavior, such as coerced confessions, unnecessarily suggestive lineups, or seizures of items during an unconstitutional search. The rule also requires exclusion of evidence indirectly obtained as a result of a constitutional violation (this type of evidence is sometimes called **derivative evidence**). The exclusionary rule operates to exclude derivative evidence because it is considered to be **fruit of the poisonous tree**. Under this doctrine's metaphors, the poisonous tree is evidence directly obtained as a result of a constitutional violation; the fruit is the derivative evidence obtained because of knowledge gained from the first illegal search, arrest, confrontation, or interrogation. For example, assume that police illegally arrest someone without probable cause and then interrogate the suspect without first administering *Miranda* warnings. During the interrogation, the suspect confesses to a murder and tells the police the location of the body. The exclusionary rule would prevent the confession from being admitted into evidence at trial since it was obtained as a result of two constitutional violations: an illegal arrest and Fifth Amendment self-incrimination violation. If the police then discovered the body where the suspect told them to look, the body and any evidence on it would also be inadmissible at trial since the police found the body as a result of their illegal interrogation of the suspect. The body itself would be considered fruit of the poisonous tree.

As you might imagine, judges loathe excluding derivative evidence under the exclusionary rule or the fruit of the poisonous tree doctrine. Accordingly, the courts have developed several doctrines that mitigate the harsh effects of preventing the use of both illegally obtained evidence and the fruits derived from the illegality. For example, evidence obtained from a source independent of the constitutional violation, such as from a private citizen, is admissible (*Segura v. United States* 1984). Similarly, illegally obtained evidence is admissible if it would have inevitably been discovered by lawful means (*Murray v. United States* 1988). And, if police make a good-faith mistake such that there was no police misconduct to be deterred by excluding evidence, then the evidence may be used at trial (*United States v. Leon* 1984).

CONFESSIONS

For over 70 years, the Supreme Court has struggled to place limits on how police interrogate suspects

(see Exhibit 12.2). The traditional rule was that only confessions that were "free and voluntary" would be admitted at trial. Confessions obtained by physical coercion (beatings or torture, for example) were not allowed into evidence because they were not trustworthy; someone in fear of a beating is likely to say what his or her antagonists want to hear. In the 1930s, the Court rejected confessions based on physical coercion, and subsequently such practices largely ceased (*Brown v. Mississippi* 1936). The Court was then confronted with the slightly different issue of confessions obtained as a result of lengthy interrogations, psychological ploys, and the like. For example, in *Ashcraft v. Tennessee* (1944), the suspect was interrogated for 36 hours with virtually no break, thereby depriving him of any rest. The Court invalidated the confession as involuntary, reasoning that confessions based on psychological coercion should be rejected just as if they were based on physical coercion, because such statements were not likely to be free and voluntary. But it is not easy to define what constitutes psychological coercion. In numerous cases, the Court sought to spell out what factors the trial court should use in deciding what constitutes psychological coercion, but the standards announced were far from precise.

Exhibit 12.2		
KEY DEVELOPMENTS IN INTERROGATION LAW		
Fifth Amendment	1791	"No person...shall be compelled in any criminal case to be a witness against himself...."
English common law	19th century	Involuntary confessions are not admissible in court.
Brown v. Mississippi	1936	Use of physical coercion to obtain confessions violates the due process clause of the Fourteenth Amendment.
Ashcraft v. Tennessee	1944	Psychologically coerced confessions are not voluntary and therefore not admissible in court.
Griffin v. California	1965	If a defendant exercises his or her right to silence, the prosecutor may not ask the jury to draw an inference of guilt from the defendant's refusal to testify in his own defense.
Miranda v. Arizona	1966	Suspect's due process rights were violated because he had not first been advised of his right to remain silent and to have an attorney present during a custodial interrogation.

Exhibit 12.2

CONTINUED

Harris v. New York	1971	Voluntary statements made by the defendants who had not been properly warned of their constitutional rights could be used during trial to impeach their credibility when they took the witness stand in their own defense and contradicted the earlier statements.
Rhode Island v. Innis	1980	A "spontaneous" statement made by a suspect in custody before being Mirandized is admissible so long as the statements were not given in response to police questioning or other conduct by the police likely to illicit an incriminating response.
New York v. Quarles	1984	Overriding considerations of public safety justified a police officer's failure to provide *Miranda* warnings before asking questions about the location of a weapon apparently abandoned just before arrest.
Duckworth v. Eagan	1989	Altered warnings have been upheld. Advising a suspect that counsel could be appointed only "if and when you go to court" does not render *Miranda* warnings inadequate.
Illinois v. Perkins	1990	A law enforcement officer can pose as a prison inmate and elicit a confession from an actual inmate, even though the officer gives no *Miranda* warnings about the inmate's constitutional rights.
Minnick v. Mississippi	1990	Once a suspect has invoked his or her right to counsel, police may not resume interrogation without the suspect's having his or her attorney present.
Pennsylvania v. Muniz	1990	Police officers may ask suspected drunken drivers routine questions and videotape their answers without warning them of their rights.
Arizona v. Fulminate	1991	A coerced confession does not automatically overturn a conviction.
Davis v. U.S.	1994	Police do not need to stop questioning a suspect who makes an ambiguous statement about wanting an attorney.
Dickerson v. U.S.	2000	*Miranda* has become embedded in police practices, and the Court will not overrule it.

	Exhibit 12.2	
	CONTINUED	

Texas v. Cobb	2001	Defendant's confession to murder could be used at trial even though his lawyer in another case was not present when he confessed.
Chavez v. Martinez	2003	The failure of a police officer to give a suspect his *Miranda* rights may not be used in a civil case against the officer alleging police brutality.
Yarborough v. Alvarado	2004	The Court has never ruled that the police must make special concessions to younger suspects as part of *Miranda*, but some justices thought that there may be cases in which age is a factor.
Illinois v. Patane	2004	Physical evidence derived from statements by suspects who were not told of their *Miranda* right to remain silent may be admitted as evidence.
Missouri v. Seibert	2004	Deliberately questioning a suspect twice, the first time without reading the *Miranda* warnings, is usually improper.

THE WARREN COURT CHANGES THE RULES

In an attempt at greater precision, the Supreme Court under the leadership of Chief Justice Earl Warren adopted specific procedures for custodial police interrogations. In the path-breaking decision *Miranda v. Arizona* (1966), the Court imposed what are widely known as *Miranda* warnings.

Before a suspect in custody may be lawfully interrogated, the police are required to tell the suspect:

- You have the right to remain silent.
- Anything you say can and will be used against you in a court of law.
- You have the right to talk to a lawyer and have him or her present with you while you are being questioned.
- If you cannot afford to hire a lawyer, one will be appointed to represent you before any questioning, if you wish.

In addition, the Court shifted the burden of proof from the defense, which previously had to prove that

a confession was not "free and voluntary," to the police and prosecutor, who now must prove that they advised the defendant of his or her constitutional rights and then knowingly and voluntarily waived those rights (see Case Close-Up: *Miranda v. Arizona* and Limiting Police Interrogations).

Even in the liberal Warren Court era, *Miranda* applied only to custodial interrogations. If someone was not "in custody" (they were talking to the police voluntarily and were free to terminate the discussion at any time), *Miranda* warnings were not necessary. Similarly, even if a suspect were in custody, if the police were not engaged in conduct designed to illicit an incriminating response, then *Miranda* was similarly inapplicable. This remains the law to this day.

Another limitation of the *Miranda* rule is that it applies only to "evidence of a testimonial or communicative nature" *Schmerber v. California* (1966, p. 761). Thus, *Miranda* warnings do not need to be given before law enforcement offers obtain nontestimonial

Miranda v. Arizona and Limiting Police Interrogations

By the age of 23, Ernesto Miranda had compiled a long police record. He dropped out of Queen of Peace Grammar School in Mesa, Arizona, after the eighth grade, and shortly thereafter was arrested for car theft. By age 18, his police blotter showed six arrests and four prison sentences. A stint in the military to turn his life around quickly degenerated into his problems in civilian life; after going AWOL, he was given an undesirable discharge. But at 23, he appeared to have turned the corner. His boss at the produce company described him as "one of the best workers I ever had." Indeed, on Wednesday he worked from 8:00 P.M. to 8:00 A.M. and had barely slept an hour when the police knocked on the front door.

Stating that they didn't want to talk in front of his common-law wife, the police took him to a Phoenix, Arizona, police station. A lineup of three other Hispanics from the city jail was quickly assembled. Lois Ann Jameson viewed the four men but could only state that Miranda's build and features were similar to those of her assailant. In the interrogation room, Miranda asked how he did, and Detective Cooley replied, "You flunked." After 2 hours of questioning, he signed a written confession admitting guilt. His subsequent trial was short and perfunctory. The only prosecution exhibit was the signed confession. Needless to say, the jury quickly returned guilty verdicts for kidnapping and rape.

The interrogation of Ernesto Miranda was in most ways unremarkable. It most certainly lacked the blatant duress at the center of earlier Supreme Court decisions on the limits of police interrogation. What was missing, however, was any advice to Ernesto about his rights under the Constitution. Indeed, the police testified that they never told Miranda that he didn't have to talk to the police, nor did they advise him of

his right to consult with an attorney. These facts highlighted the giant chasm between the principles of the Constitution and the realities of police stations in America.

By 1966 the Supreme Court had been grappling with the issue of confessions for three decades. Despite numerous cases, the standards for interrogating suspects were still far from clear. Chief Justice Earl Warren's opinion in *Miranda* expressed concern over the "police-dominated" atmosphere of interrogation rooms and held that warnings were required to counteract the inherently coercive nature of station-house questioning. But in reality, *Miranda* created no new rights. Under American law, suspects have never been required to talk to the police, and the right to counsel extends to the police station as well as the courthouse. In essence, the Court held that the Fifth Amendment privilege against self-incrimination was as applicable to interrogation by the police before trial as it was to questioning by the prosecutor during trial.

Miranda v. Arizona is the Warren Court's best known and, arguably, most controversial decision extending constitutional rights to those accused of violating the criminal law. The four dissenting justices criticized the ruling on both constitutional and practical grounds. To Justice Byron White, the *Miranda* rule was "a deliberate calculus to prevent interrogation, to reduce the incidence of confessions, and to increase the number of trials." Police, prosecutors, and public officials likewise criticized the ruling, and it became a key plank in Richard Nixon's law-and-order campaign in 1968 (see Chapter 17). With four Nixon-appointed justices, the Burger Court began narrowing *Miranda*, but the holding itself has not been overturned. Indeed, *Miranda* has now become settled law, deeply imbedded in the constitutional fabric of our nation.

CASE CLOSEUP

evidence, such as breath or blood samples, handwriting exemplars, lineup participation, or fingerprints.

THE BURGER AND REHNQUIST COURTS LIMIT *MIRANDA*

The Court under the leadership of Chief Justice Warren Burger limited *Miranda*'s application by

carving out exceptions. Here are the three prominent examples:

- Statements taken in violation of *Miranda* requirements are inadmissible in court only as substantive evidence in the prosecution's case-in-chief to prove the defendant's guilt. However, voluntary statements made by defendants who had not been properly warned of their *Miranda* rights may be used during trial to impeach their credibility if they take the witness stand in their own defense and contradict the earlier statements (*Harris v. New York* 1971).

- Overriding considerations of public safety justified a police officer's failure to provide *Miranda* warnings before asking questions about the location of a weapon apparently abandoned just before arrest (*New York v. Quarles* 1984).

- When a suspect subject to custodial interrogation makes incriminating statements without having been Mirandized, but subsequently repeats those incriminating statements after having been read *Miranda* rights, defendants cannot argue that the fruit of the poisonous tree doctrine bars the admissibility of their second admission or confession as being tainted by the first if the initial statements were knowingly and voluntarily given (*Oregon v. Elstad* 1985).

The Rehnquist Court likewise moved to narrow the application of *Miranda* protections, as the following cases illustrate:

- Police do not need to stop questioning a suspect who makes an ambiguous statement about wanting an attorney (*Davis v. U.S.* 1994).

- Police may question a defendant in a murder case without his lawyer in another case being present (*Texas v. Cobb* 2001).

- In *Chavez v. Martinez* (2003), the Court ruled that suspects who are interrogated in violation of the requirements of *Miranda* may not sue police for damages under 42 U.S.C. § 1983 (see Chapter 3) for violations of their Fifth Amendment rights.

- The fruit of the poisonous tree doctrine does not apply to physical evidence derived from statements made in violation of *Miranda*. In *United States v. Patane* (2004), statements made by a suspect in response to police questions that were designed to elicit an incriminating response were suppressed because the defendant had not been read his *Miranda* rights. In response to being asked whether he had any firearms, the defendant told police he had a handgun in his bedroom. The gun had originally been suppressed as fruit of the poisonous tree because it was discovered as a result of the defendant's unwarned statements. The U.S. Supreme Court reversed, holding that the failure to properly advise a suspect of *Miranda* rights does not trigger the fruit of the poisonous

tree doctrine as long as the suspect's unwarned statements were voluntary.

However, the Rehnquist Court was not always unsympathetic to the plight of criminal defendants. One 6-to-2 decision seemed to take *Miranda* protections a step further. The Court overturned a capital murder conviction, holding that once a suspect has invoked his or her right to counsel, police may not resume interrogation without the suspect having his or her attorney present (*Minnick v. Mississippi* 1990). The Rehnquist Court also declined to overrule *Miranda*. Writing for seven justices, Chief Justice Rehnquist opined, "Whether or not this court would agree with *Miranda*'s reasoning and its rule in the first instance, *stare decisis* weighs heavily against overruling it now." Moreover, "*Miranda* has become embedded in routine police practice to the point where the warnings have become part of our national culture" (*Dickerson v. U.S.* 2000).

THE ROBERTS COURT AND *MIRANDA*

As of this writing, the U.S. Supreme Court has not decided any major cases concerning the Fifth Amendment's Self-Incrimination Clause since John G. Roberts became the Chief Justice in 2005. In light of the fact that the Roberts Court has consistently leaned to the right with regard to the rights of the criminally accused, little evidence at present indicates that the Court will do anything other than continue the tradition of the Burger and Rehnquist Courts of giving *Miranda* a narrow reading.

SEARCH AND SEIZURE

The Fourth Amendment provides that "the right of the people to be secure in their persons, houses, papers, and effects against unreasonable searches and seizures, shall not be violated." But what constitutes an **unreasonable search and seizure**?

Historically, the gathering of physical evidence was governed by the common-law rule that "if the constable blunders, the crook should not go free." This meant that if the police conducted an **illegal search and seizure** (search without probable cause), the evidence obtained could still be used. Evidence was admitted in court if it was reliable, trustworthy, and relevant. How the police obtained the evidence was considered a separate issue. Thus, there were no effective controls on search and seizure; law enforcement officials who searched illegally faced no sanctions. But the Supreme Court modified the common law tradition when it adopted the exclusionary rule

for the Fourth Amendment violations in *Weeks v. U.S.* (1914) and subsequently extended its application to the states in *Mapp v. Ohio* (1961). Exhibit 12.3 describes the key developments in search-and-seizure law.

Exhibit 12.3		
KEY DEVELOPMENTS IN SEARCH-AND-SEIZURE LAW		
Fourth Amendment	1791	"The right of the people to be secure in their persons, houses, paper, and effects against unreasonable searches and seizures, shall not be violated, and no Warrants shall issue, but upon probable cause, supported by Oath or affirmation, and particularly describing the place to be searched, and the persons or things to be seized."
Weeks v. U.S.	1914	The exclusionary rule established for federal prosecutions.
Carroll v. United States	1925	So long as probable cause exists, police may search a motor vehicle without a warrant.
Wolf v. Colorado	1949	The exclusionary rule applies to the states as well as the federal government, but states are not required to adopt the exclusionary rule to sanction noncompliance.
Mapp v. Ohio	1961	The exclusionary rule applies to the states as well as the federal government (overturning *Weeks* and *Wolf*).
Katz v. U.S.	1967	For Fourth Amendment purposes, a "search" takes place when police infringe upon a person's actual, subjective expectation of privacy and that expectation of privacy is objectively reasonable by societal standards.
Terry v. Ohio	1968	Police officers may briefly stop someone they observe engaging in conduct that reasonably suggests "that criminal activity may be afoot." Moreover, if they have reason to suspect the suspect is armed, police may frisk of the suspect's outer clothing for their own safety.
Chimel v. California	1969	When making a lawful arrest, police are permitted to make a search incident to the arrest of the arrestee's person and of the surrounding area under the arrestee's immediate control (within the suspect's "wingspan").

Exhibit 12.3

CONTINUED

Rakas v. Illinois	1978	A defendant has standing to object to the admission of unconstitutionally seized evidence only if such seizure violated his own Fourth Amendment rights; a defendant may not assert another person's rights.
Payton v. New York	1980	Absent some exigent circumstances (an emergency), police may not make a warrantless entry into a suspect's home to make an arrest.
United States v. Mendenhall	1980	A person is "seized" within the meaning of the Fourth Amendment when his/her freedom of movement is restrained by means of physical force or show of authority, and under the circumstances, a reasonable person would believe that he was not free to leave or otherwise terminate the encounter.
Illinois v. Gates	1983	Whether probable cause exists must be examined under the "totality of the circumstances."
U.S. v. Leon	1984	Creates a limited "good faith exception."
New Jersey v. T. L. O.	1985	Searches of students by school officials in public schools do not require warrants or probable cause; all that is needed are reasonable grounds to believe that the search will reveal contraband or evidence of criminal activity.
Tennessee v. Garner	1985	The Fourth Amendment prohibits the use of deadly force to apprehend a fleeing suspect unless the pursuing officer has probable cause to believe that the suspect poses a significant threat of death or serious physical injury to the officer or others.
Whren et al. v. United States	1986	Police officers may stop a vehicle for any violation of traffic law even if the underlying traffic offense is only a pretext to investigate other criminal activity.
Illinois v. Krull	1987	The good-faith exception applies to warrantless searches, even when the state statute authorizing a warrantless search was later found to violate the Fourth Amendment.
California v. Greenwood	1988	The Fourth Amendment does not prohibit the warrantless search and seizure of garbage left for collection outside a home since it is abandoned property.

Exhibit 12.3

CONTINUED

Florida v. Riley	1989	Police do not need a warrant to conduct aerial surveillance of a suspect's property from an aircraft in public airspace.
Illinois v. Rodriguez	1990	Police officers were acting in good faith when the victim allowed entry into her apartment even though she no longer resided with the defendant.
Arizona v. Evans	1995	Traffic stop that led to the seizure of drugs was legal, even though the arrest warrant, which was the basis of the search, was improper because it was based on a computer error.
Knowles v. Iowa	1998	Issuing a speeding ticket does not give police authority to search the car.
Illinois v. Wardlow	2000	Fleeing from the sight of police (running away) constitutes reasonable suspicion justifying the police stopping the runner to investigate whether criminal activity is afoot.
Bond v. U.S	2000	Bus and train passengers have an expectation of privacy when they put their luggage into an overhead rack.
Florida v. J. L.	2000	Police cannot stop and search someone solely because they have received an anonymous tip.
Kyllo v. U.S.	2001	Police cannot use a thermal imaging device to scan a building to detect the presence of high-intensity lamps used to grow marijuana.
Hiibel v. Sixth Judicial District Court of Nevada	2004	States may enact laws requiring suspects to identify themselves during police investigations without violating either the Fourth or Fifth Amendments.
United States v. Flores-Montano	2004	Random searches without any level of suspicion may be conducted at U.S. borders or international airports without a warrant or probable cause.
Illinois v. Caballes	2005	In making a routine traffic stop, the police can permit a trained dog to sniff the car for drugs.

Exhibit 12.3		
CONTINUED		

Georgia v. Randolph	2006	The police must have a warrant to look for evidence in a couple's home unless both partners present agree to let them in.
Hudson v. Michigan	2006	While police armed with a search warrant are supposed to knock-and-announce their presence before they can lawfully enter homes to search for and seize evidence, a violation of the knock-and-announce rule will not give rise to the application of the exclusionary rule.
Brendlin v. California	2007	When a police officer makes a traffic stop, both the driver of the car and his/her passengers are all "seized" within the meaning of the Fourth Amendment. Thus, a passenger may challenge the constitutionality of the stop.
Scott v. Harris	2007	A police officer who terminated a high-speed chase of a suspect by applying his push bumper to the rear of the suspect's vehicle, causing it to leave the road and crash and rendering the suspect a quadriplegic, did not act wunreasonably in using such force and, therefore did not violate motorist's Fourth Amendment right against unreasonable seizure.
Virginia v. Moore	2008	A police officer does not violate the Fourth Amendment by making an arrest supported by probable cause for a traffic violation even though arrest is not authorized under state law for such an offense; therefore, evidence seized incident to the arrest is admissible.
United States v. Herring	2009	The Fourth Amendment does not require the suppression of evidence seized following a search that occurred incident to an illegal arrest when the arrest was based on erroneous information negligently provided by another law enforcement agency, as long as the arresting police officer relied on the erroneous information in good faith.

The conservative majorities of both the Burger and Rehnquist Courts have limited the application of the exclusionary rule by creating numerous exceptions.

- A person running at the sight of a police officer could justify the police conducting a stop-and-frisk search (*Illinois v. Wardlow* 2000).
- Police officers do not have to advise suspects that they have a right to refuse consent to a search if asked (*U.S. v. Drayton* 2002).

On rare occasions, though, the Rehnquist Court did place limits on the ability of the police to search.

- Police cannot use a thermal imagining device to scan a building to detect the presence of high-intensity lamps used to grow marijuana (*Kyllo v. U.S.* 2001).
- Police cannot stop and search a person for a gun solely on the basis of an anonymous tip (*Florida v. J. L.* 2000).

During its first term, the Roberts Court (see Chapter 17) decided an important case that may indicate changes to come. The Court left uncertain the 13th-century rule that the police must "knock-and-announce" their presence before entering the premises to conduct a search. By a 5-to-4 decision—with the newest justice, Samuel Alito, casting the deciding vote—the Court held that evidence can be used if found by police officers who entered a home to execute a search warrant and did not first knock-and-announce (*Hudson v. Michigan* 2006). In less than 3 years, the Roberts Court dealt another blow to the exclusionary rule in *Herring v. United States* (2009). The police in that case arrested a suspect on an outstanding warrant. While searching him incident to his arrest, they found drugs and a gun. The warrant had been quashed months earlier, but the county police had been negligent in updating their records. Thus, his arrest and the search of the suspect incident to that arrest were both illegal. However, because the police in the case engaged in no wrongdoing (they relied in good faith on a warrant that turned out to be invalid because of the negligence of police other than the arresting officers), the exclusionary rule was held not to apply.

Nonetheless, over four decades later, the exclusionary rule requirements remain highly controversial (see Courts, Controversy, and Reducing Crime: Should the Exclusionary Rule Be Abolished?). Critics and supporters of the exclusionary rule agree on one central point: The grounds for a lawful search are complex and highly technical. Search and seizure is one of the most difficult areas of Supreme Court decision making, and few think that the system works particularly well (Bradley 1993). Searches fall into two broad categories: searches based on a warrant and warrantless searches.

SEARCH WARRANTS

A **search warrant** is a written document, signed by a judge or magistrate, authorizing a law enforcement officer to conduct a search. The Fourth Amendment specifies that "no Warrants shall issue, but upon probable cause, supported by Oath or affirmation, and particularly describing the place to be searched and the Persons or things to be seized." In light of the plain language of the Fourth Amendment, search warrants issued by a neutral judicial officer (usually a magistrate or judge) are the preferred mechanism for authorizing and conducting searches and seizures in the United States.

Applying for Search Warrants

Once a police officer decides that a search warrant is necessary, the officer usually goes back to the station house to prepare the application, affidavit, and warrant. Three alternative procedures are used. In a few jurisdictions, search-warrant applications are prepared by a deputy prosecutor on the basis of information provided by the officer. In other localities and in the federal system, the law enforcement officer prepares all the documentation and then submits them to a prosecutor, who systematically reviews them before they are presented to the magistrate. Regardless of who actually prepares the documentation, the application must provide sufficient information to a neutral judicial officer to determine that there is "a fair probability that contraband or evidence of a crime will be found in a particular place" (*Illinois v. Gates*, 1983, p. 238). This information is usually provided in an **affidavit**, a sworn written statement of facts sworn to before the magistrate. Several jurisdictions permit issuance of search warrants over the telephone or by e-mail or facsimile (fax), but still require that the information provided by the police to the magistrate be taken under oath and recorded. Law enforcement officers must be careful to include all the relevant information on which probable cause may be based in their written affidavits so that a complete record exists for courts to evaluate the magistrate's decision if the warrant is challenged.

COURTS, CONTROVERSY, AND REDUCING CRIME

Should the Exclusionary Rule Be Abolished?

The exclusionary rule was controversial when it was adopted in 1961 and remains so four decades later. In a 1981 speech, President Reagan's strong words expressed the views of the crime control model in opposition to the exclusionary rule:

> The exclusionary rule rests on the absurd proposition that a law enforcement error, no matter how technical, can be used to justify throwing an entire case out of court, no matter how guilty the defendant or how heinous the crime. The plain consequence of treating the wrongs equally is a grievous miscarriage of justice: The criminal goes free; the officer receives no effective reprimand; and the only ones who really suffer are the people of the community.

But to law professor Yale Kamisar (1978), illegal conduct by the police cannot so easily be ignored. Here is how he states the due process model case for the exclusionary rule: "A court which admits [illegally seized evidence]...manifests a willingness to tolerate the unconstitutional conduct which produced it."

How can the police and the citizenry be expected to "believe that the government truly meant to forbid the conduct in the first place"? A court that admits the evidence in a case involving a "run of the mill" Fourth Amendment violation demonstrates an insufficient commitment to the guarantee against unreasonable search and seizure.

While the *Mapp* decision remains controversial, the nature of the debate has changed. Initially, critics called for abolition of the exclusionary rule (Oaks 1970; Wilkey 1978); now, they just suggest modifications. This shift in thinking is reflected in the Reagan administration's Attorney General's Task Force on Violent Crime (1981). Although composed largely of long-standing critics of the exclusionary rule, the final report called only for its modification, not its abolition.

Issuing Search Warrants

Only judicial officers who have been specifically authorized to do so may issue search warrants. Most jurisdictions give this authority to judicial officers, such as clerks of court, magistrates, complaint justices, justices of the peace, and judges. The vesting of warrant-issuing power in a neutral and detached judicial officer stems from the Supreme Court's mandate that warrants can be issued only by people who are not involved in the "activities of law enforcement" (*Shadwick v. City of Tampa* 1972, 350). A study by the National Center for State Courts provides considerable insight into how search warrants are obtained (Van Duizend, Sutton, and Carter 1984).

Next, the applicant must contact a neutral judicial officer to approve the warrant based on the application and the affidavit detailing the facts that establish probable cause. This is traditionally done in person at a courthouse. However, if court is not in session, it may occur at the home of a judge or even by telephone. The review seldom takes long. In fact, all of the few empirical studies of the search-warrant process found that the process typically takes only a few minutes (Benner and Samarkos 2000; Slobogin 1998; Van Duizend et al. 1984). Moreover, outright rejection is rare. A study by the National Center for State Courts reported that most police officers interviewed by the researchers could not remember having a search-warrant application denied (Van Duizend et al. 1984). The authors concluded that the warrant-review process did not operate as it was intended. Research has suggested two reasons for this. Van Duizend et al. concluded that the review process was largely perfunctory, as some judicial officers regarded themselves more as allies of law enforcement than as independent reviewers of evidence. And Benner and Samarkos (2000, p. 266) reported that computers have also contributed to the rubber-stamping of search-warrant applications by allowing police to prepare applications by cutting-and-pasting"

Among the alternatives proposed, former Chief Justice Warren Burger urged an "egregious violation standard" (*Brewer v. Williams* 1977). Others have proposed an exception for reasonable mistakes by the police (Fyfe 1982). To critics, modifications along these lines would reduce the number of arrests lost because of illegal searches, and the sanction would be more proportional to the seriousness of the Fourth Amendment violation. The Supreme Court, however, has recognized an "honest mistake" or a "good-faith" exception to the exclusionary rule only in extremely narrow and limited circumstances (*U.S. v. Leon* 1984; *Illinois v. Krull* 1987).

The high court is increasingly leaning in this direction, but only on a limited basis (*Arizona v. Evans* 1995). When the Republican party gained control of both houses of Congress in 1995, conservatives increased their efforts to modify the exclusionary rule (*Congressional Quarterly* 1996). These efforts to overturn Supreme Court decisions proved unsuccessful.

The Rehnquist Court included six justices who have publicly criticized *Mapp*. Yet this working majority was unable to agree among themselves as to how to replace *Mapp* while prohibiting truly bad-faith searches by the police. It is too early to predict whether the two newest justices to the Court, John Roberts and Samuel Alito, will vote in different ways from their predecessors. They did, however, vote to extend the good-faith exception to cover negligent errors by police (as opposed to intentional violations of the Fourth Amendment) in *Herring v. U.S.* (2009). As a result, predicting the future of *Mapp* is problematic at best.

What do you think? Should the exclusionary rule be abolished outright, given "good-faith" exceptions, or kept in its present form? If one admits that there are problems in its current application, what realistic alternatives might restrain law enforcement from potentially conducting blatant and flagrant searches in violation of the Fourth Amendment?

pre-packaged, boiler-plated affidavits [that] are produced by merely filling in a few blanks."

The Requirement of Particularity

As the text of the Fourth Amendment makes clear, warrants must describe with particularity "the place to be searched and the persons or things to be seized." This requirement means that warrants should be as detailed as possible. Thus, warrants to search premises should use specific addresses when addresses are known. Warrants to search motor vehicles should include information such as the make, body style, color, year, location, license plate number, and owner or operator of the vehicle (to the extent such information is known). Warrants to search particular people should include the person's name or, alternatively, a detailed description of a person whose name is unknown that includes the person's weight, height, age, race, clothing, address, aliases, etc. Finally, items to be seized must be described with sufficient particularity so that the officers executing the warrant: (1) can identify the items with reasonable certainty, and (2) are left with no discretion as to which property is to be taken.

Executing Search Warrants

The final step is the execution of the warrant. The officer serves the warrant, conducts the search, and seizes evidence. Officers mainly search private residences and impound vehicles for drugs or stolen goods. Regardless of the area or persons to be searched, a few general rules must be followed during the execution of a search warrant.

First, search warrants must be executed in a timely manner to prevent the information that established probable cause from going stale. Second, the scope of law enforcement activities during the execution of the warrant must be strictly limited to achieving the objectives that are set forth with particularity in the warrant. If officers exceed the scope of the authorized invasion under the terms of the warrant, the evidence seized will usually be deemed inadmissible.

Third, search warrants must be executed at a reasonable time of day. This normally means that warrants must be executed during the daytime; however, courts may authorize a nighttime search if the affidavit in support of the warrant sets forth specific facts showing some need to execute the warrant at night.

Fourth, law enforcement officers are generally required to *knock-and-announce* their presence, authority, and purpose before entering premises to execute a search warrant (*Wilson v. Arkansas* 1995). Courts usually require police officers to wait at least 10 to 20 seconds after announcing their presence before entering premises. However, police do not need to knock-and-announce their presence "if circumstances present a threat of physical violence, or if there is reason to believe that evidence would likely be destroyed if advance notice were given, or if knocking and announcing would be futile" (*Hudson v. Michigan* 2006, pp. 589–590). In fact, if such circumstances are known in advance, many states allow for courts to issue "no knock warrants." While violations of the knock-and-announce rule may subject offending officers to civil damages in a lawsuit brought under 42 U.S.C. § 1983 (Chapter 3), *Hudson* held that knock-and-announce violations will not result in application of the exclusionary rule to the evidence seized.

Fifth, in light of the Fourth Amendment's command of reasonableness, courts are also concerned with the amount of time it takes law enforcement personnel to perform a search once it is initiated pursuant to a valid warrant. The police may remain on premises only for as long as it is reasonably necessary to conduct the search. After all the objects described in a warrant have been found and seized, the authority of the warrant expires and police must leave the premises.

Sixth, also because of the Fourth Amendment's reasonableness requirement, officers executing a search warrant must be careful to use only a reasonable amount of force when conducting a search, such a breaking down a door. An otherwise reasonable search may be invalidated if excessive force is used.

Finally, after a search is completed, statutory law generally requires that the officer file a "return" in court, indicating what items were seized, if any.

Courts generally hold that these post-search duties are ministerial acts. Thus, a failure to perform them will usually not result in suppression of any evidence.

WARRANTLESS SEARCHES

Pursuant to the mandates of the plain text of the Constitution, the Supreme Court held in *Katz v. United States* (1967, p. 357), that **warrantless searches** "are per se unreasonable under the Fourth Amendment subject only to a few specifically established and well-delineated exceptions." Accordingly, warrants play a very important role in criminal procedure. It might therefore come as a surprise to many people that the majority of searches are conducted without a warrant under 1 of approximately 10 recognized exceptions to the warrant requirement.

The most common form of warrantless searches are called **consent searches**. This occurs when police ask for permission to search and someone with authority to grant consent agrees to give such permission. Unlike with *Miranda* warnings, though, the police do not need to advise someone of the right to refuse consent. All that is necessary is for the person to voluntarily agree to the search. When asked, the overwhelming number of people—between 88 and 96 percent according to some studies—grant such permission (Taslitz 2007). As one city detective explained, you just make an offer that cannot be refused:

> [You] tell the guy, "Let me come in and take a look at your house." And he says, "No, I don't want to." And then you tell him, "Then I'm going to leave Sam here, and he's going to live with you until we come back [with a search warrant]. Now we can do it either way." And very rarely do the people say, "Go get your search warrant then." (Van Duizend et al. 1984)

Another very common type of warrantless search is called a **search incident to arrest**. Police routinely search every person they arrest "to remove any weapons that the latter might seek to use in order to resist arrest or effect his escape" and to prevent the concealment or destruction of evidence (*Chimel v. California* 1969, p. 763). As long as the arrest was lawful, all items found on an arrested person or within the area immediately under his or her control will be admissible in court.

The **plain view** doctrine is another warrant exception that is commonly used by police. Under this doctrine, when a law enforcement officer is legally in a place in which he or she sees contraband or other evidence that provides probable cause to believe criminal activity is afoot, the evidence may be seized without a warrant (*Washington v. Chrisman* 1982). Plain view is not necessarily limited to what can be seen with the naked eye; flashlights, binoculars, or telescopes can be used to achieve plain view, but high-tech equipment like thermal imaging devices may not (*United States v. Kyllo* 2001). Moreover, plain view may be achieved from the air, as long as surveillance occurs from a reasonable distance, something commonly referred to as an **aerial search** (*Florida v. Riley* 1989). The plain-view doctrine has been expanded to cover other senses, such as "plain smell," even if the "officer" doing the smelling is a trained dog.

A number of warrant exceptions apply based on the location of the search. Searches at airports or international borders do not require warrants (*United States v. Ramsey* 1977). Searches of students in school do not require warrants (*New Jersey v. T.L.O.* 1985). Warrantless searches of public employees and their workspaces are allowed as part of investigations of work-related misconduct (*Skinner v. Railway Labor Executives' Assoc.* 1989). Because one cannot have a reasonable expectation of privacy in open areas, **open fields** may be searched without a warrant (*Cady v. Dombrowski* 1973). And, finally, given the mobile nature of cars, boats, motor homes, and the like, warrants are not required for police to conduct **motor vehicle searches** so long as they have probable cause to believe that the vehicle contains contraband (*Carroll v. United States* 1925).

The grounds for a warrantless search vary, depending on what is being searched. Border searches, for example, do not require any suspicion. In contrast, searches of students in school require reasonable suspicion, while motor vehicle searches require probable cause. Defining the precise limits of reasonable suspicion or probable cause, however, remains elusive. Regardless of the particular level of proof required, however, all searches—whether conducted with or without a warrant—must always be executed in a reasonable manner to comply with the requirements of the Fourth Amendment. Exhibit 12.4 presents an overview of the issues surrounding disclosure and suppression of evidence discussed so far.

Exhibit 12.4

DISCLOSING AND SUPPRESSING EVIDENCE

	LAW ON THE BOOKS	LAW IN ACTION
Discovery	Pretrial procedure in which parties to a lawsuit ask for and receive information such as witnesses' statements, expert witnesses' reports, and lab reports.	In a number of jurisdictions, informal prosecutorial disclosure means that defense attorneys who maintain a cooperative stance toward the district attorney will be able to view most or all of the state's case prior to trial.
Brady material	Prosecutor must turn over exculpatory evidence to the defense prior to trial.	Some defense attorneys assert that some prosecutors do not always live up to their constitutional obligation.
Rules of evidence	In jurisdictions with more open discovery, defense is entitled to see witnesses' statements and lab reports before trial.	Prosecutors who maintain an open discovery policy experience quicker pleas of guilty and less case backlog.
Reciprocal discovery	Requirement that the defense disclose various materials to the prosecutor prior to trial.	In era of "get tough with criminals," an increasingly popular response by legislatures.

	Exhibit 12.4
	CONTINUED

	LAW ON THE BOOKS	**LAW IN ACTION**
Lineups	A lineup must represent the description given by the witness. In addition, after a suspect's Sixth Amendment right to counsel has attached, the suspect has the right to have his/her attorney present during the lineup.	The police routinely take a picture of the persons in the lineup, which is typically sufficient to prove to the court that the lineup was indeed representative.
Interrogations	Method of acquiring evidence in the form of information or confessions from suspects by police.	Suspects who provide incriminating statements are more likely to be charged with a crime, more likely to be convicted, and more likely to be punished severely.
Physical coercion	Statements made to the police obtained by the use of physical force or the threatened use of physical force are not admissible because they are untrustworthy.	Historically, there is every reason to believe that physically coerced confessions were common. In contemporary practice, believable reports of physical coercion are extremely rare.
Psychological coercion	Fifth Amendment protection against self-incrimination means that any statement elicited by the police cannot be used in court if the statement is not "free and voluntary."	During the 1940s and 1950s, the Supreme Court found that a number of confessions were inadmissible because of psychological coercion. Difficulty of applying this standard on a case-by-case basis led the Court to announce *Miranda* warnings.
Miranda warnings	Prior to interrogation, the police must warn a suspect that: (1) you have the right to remain silent; (2) anything you say can and will be used against you in a court of law; (3) you have the right to talk to a lawyer and have him or her present with you while you are being questioned; and (4) if you cannot afford to hire a lawyer, one will be appointed to represent you before any questioning, if you wish.	Three out of four suspects waive their *Miranda* rights (Leo 1996a). Police use advising of *Miranda* rights to gain the confidence of the suspect.

Exhibit 12.4

CONTINUED

	LAW ON THE BOOKS	LAW IN ACTION
Search and seizure	Legal term found in the Fourth Amendment referring to the searching for and carrying away of evidence by police during a criminal investigation.	In street crimes, police officers must make quick decisions about searching a person or a car for contraband. Most often occurs in drug and weapons offenses.
Search warrant	A written order, issued by judicial authority, directing a law enforcement officer to search for property and, if found, to bring it before the court.	Judges or magistrates rarely scrutinize them closely. Police are often successful in obtaining suspect's consent for a voluntary search.
Consent search	Law enforcement officials are under no requirement to tell suspects that they have the right to refuse consent to a search.	Suspects are surprisingly willing to consent to a search of person or car.
Search incident to a valid arrest	After a valid arrest, police officers may search to protect themselves and to prevent the destruction of contraband.	Some officers have been known to search and then fabricate probable cause for arrest.
Plain view	Law enforcement officers may search and seize any contraband or illegal substances or items if they are in the immediate vision of the officers.	Some law enforcement officers allegedly search in hidden areas but later testify the material was in plain view.
Motor vehicle searches	Because motor vehicles are, by their nature, mobile, they may be searched without a warrant as long as probable cause exists to believe they contain contraband or evidence of a crime.	Police investigating a crime may follow a suspect and pull over a car for a minor traffic violation as a pretext for getting a look into the car and talking with the suspect.
Border searches	Random, suspicionless, warrantless searches may be conducted at U.S. borders and their functional equivalents, such as international airports.	The open-ended ability to stop and search anyone sometimes results in racial or ethnic profiling.

LAW AND POPULAR CULTURE

Minority Report (2002)

When this 2002 Stephen Spielberg film was released, its tagline read: "What would you do if you were accused of a murder you had not committed... yet?" The film takes place in Washington, D.C. in the year 2054. Crime in the city is practically nonexistent because the "Pre-Crime Unit" of the police force apprehends criminals *before* they actually commit any crimes. John Anderton (played by Tom Cruise) and his fellow pre-crime police officers are able to do so thanks to the information provided to them from three "precogs"—genetically mutated humans who have the ability to see the future. Their visions occur in dreamlike states, complete with the "disjunctions and distortions of regular dreams" (Capers 2009, p. 798). The precogs project their visions onto a screen so that police can try to make sense of how the crime will unfold, thereby allowing them to make a preemptive arrest. Anderton believes the system to be flawless until the precogs predict that he will commit murder. Thus, the chief of the Pre-Crime Unit becomes a fugitive for a crime he has yet to commit. At the end of the movie, Anderton arrests the person whom the precogs predicted he would kill. Notably, he reads the suspect *Miranda* warnings when making the arrest.

While the fast-paced action film raises a number of philosophical points, it clearly implicates some Fourth Amendment concerns. For one thing, the Washington D.C. of the future has become a surveillance state.

Individuals are tracked via eye scans as they move about the city. Public spaces are surveillance spaces. But then again the same could be said of many cities today. We currently permit such surveillance on the theory that individuals do not have a reasonable expectation of privacy, the sine qua non of a Fourth Amendment right, in information that they knowingly expose to the public and also on the theory of consent. Thus, the expectation of privacy we theoretically enjoy behind closed doors, we lose in public spaces, at least in terms of items exposed to public view. In this respect, the surveillance state that exists in *Minority Report* is the surveillance state that current Fourth Amendment law already sanctions. But *Minority Report*, in a scene in which the police use thermal imaging to ascertain the number of individuals in a building and then release mechanical spiders to conduct retinal scans of those individuals in a search for John Anderton, does serve as a cautionary tale of sorts, exposing the steep declivity of a slippery slope. The scene recalls *Kyllo v. United States*, in which the Supreme Court held that thermal imaging directed at a private residence amounted to a search and thus required a warrant supported by probable cause. Except here, the technology seems to have been refined to survive constitutional scrutiny. In *United States v. Jacobsen*, the Court read the Fourth Amendment as protecting only legitimate activity and thus excluding from its ambit government conduct that could only reveal illegitimate activity. In *United States v. Place*, the Court assumed canine sniffs disclose "only the presence or absence of narcotics, a contraband item" and thus fell within this category. Followed to the extreme, these cases would permit the very mechanical spiders that are used to such effect in *Minority Report*, assuming such spiders are only capable of "seeing" the eyes of, say, a fugitive (Capers, p. 800–801).

1. Recall from this chapter that a lawful arrest must be supported by probable cause. What do you think of the idea of preemptive arrests? Do you think that "visions" of the future from a consistently reliable source, such as the fictional precogs, should be sufficient to establish probable cause for an arrest? Does the fact that the precogs were wrong in Anderton's case affect your view?

CONTINUED

Minority Report (2002)

2. What do you make of Professor Capers' argument that the surveillance depicted in the movie *Minority Report* is of the same qualitative type that is permitted today? Do you think we should reasonably expect any privacy when we are out in public?

3. Professor Capers points out that the thermal imaging scan in *Minority Report* would not be permissible today under the Supreme Court's ruling in *Kyllo v. United States*. However, he cites two additional pieces of precedent which could be interpreted as allowing mechanical spiders to conduct retinal scans. Do you think that type of technology would be an invasion of privacy if used out in public? What about if such devices were used to perform retinal scans of people inside private residences?

4. As stated above, *Miranda* warnings are alive and well in 2054. Why do you think that television shows and movies have embraced *Miranda*? Do you think it is good or bad that these warnings are so engrained in our national psyche that they work their way into science-fiction scripts that depict the future? Why?

THE EXCLUSIONARY RULE AND THE COURTROOM WORK GROUP

The police must often make immediate decisions about searching or interrogating a suspect. In street arrests, officers do not have time to consult an attorney about the complex and constantly evolving law governing these areas. These on-the-spot decisions may later be challenged in court as violations of suspects' constitutional rights. Even though the exclusionary rule is directed at the police, its actual enforcement occurs in the courts, particularly the trial courts.

PRETRIAL MOTIONS

A defense attorney who believes that his or her client was identified in a defective police lineup, gave a confession because of improper police activity, or was subjected to an illegal search can file a motion to suppress the evidence. Most states require that **suppression motions** be made prior to trial.

During the hearing on these pretrial motions, the defense attorney usually bears the burden of proving that the search was illegal or that the confession was coerced. The only exception involves an allegation that the *Miranda* warnings were not given, in which case the state has the burden of proof. The judge's ruling in the pretrial hearing is binding on the later trial.

Pretrial hearings on a motion to suppress evidence are best characterized as "swearing matches." As one defense attorney phrased it, "The real question in Supreme Court cases is what's going on at the police station" (Neubauer 1974b, p. 167). Seldom is there unbiased, independent evidence of what happened. The only witnesses are the participants—police and defendant—and, not surprisingly, they give different versions. This dispute over the facts structures and apportions the roles that the police, defense attorneys, judges, and prosecutors play. Because they must search out the issues, defense attorneys are forced into a catalytic role. By virtue of their power as fact finders at hearings, judges become the supreme umpires that legal theory indicates they should be. Prosecutors, in contrast, play a relatively passive role. Although pretrial motions place prosecutors in a defensive posture, they are not at a major disadvantage, because the police are usually able to provide information indicating compliance.

DEFENSE ATTORNEY AS PRIME MOVER

Because defense attorneys have the responsibility of protecting the constitutional rights of their clients, they are the prime movers in suppression matters. Unless the defense objects, it is assumed that law enforcement officials have behaved properly. Filing a pretrial motion to suppress evidence may produce benefits for the defense. If the motion is granted, the defense wins, because the prosecutor will usually dismiss the case for lack of evidence. Even if the motion is denied, the defense may be able to discover information that may later prove valuable at trial. Moreover, filing a pretrial motion keeps options open; plea bargaining remains a possible course of action.

Despite these apparent advantages, defense attorneys face major barriers in raising objections. Possible violations of *Miranda* or the Fourth Amendment do not come into the lawyer's office prepackaged, just awaiting a court hearing. Defense attorneys must frame the issue and determine whether enough facts exist to support the contention. According to many defense attorneys, the police follow proper procedures most of the time. Thus, the task of the lawyer is to separate the out-of-the-ordinary situation from the more numerous ones in which the police have not violated Supreme Court rulings.

In deciding whether to make a motion to suppress evidence, defense attorneys are influenced by the informal norms of the courtroom work group. Pretrial motions require extra work, not only for the defense attorney but also for the judge and prosecutor. Defense attorneys who file too many frivolous motions or use them to harass the judge, the prosecutor, or both can be given a variety of sanctions. The prosecutor may refuse to plea-bargain in a given case or may insist on a sentence harsher than normal.

The Defensive Posture of the Prosecutor

Suppression motions represent only liabilities for prosecutors. At a minimum, they must do extra work. At worst, they may lose the case entirely. Even if they win the suppression motion, they may have to expend extra effort defending that decision on appeal, where they may lose.

Despite these drawbacks, prosecutors maintain the upper hand. For once, they need only defend, because the defense attorney bears the burden of proof. Because the police control the information involved, prosecutors are generally in a favorable position to argue against excluding evidence. For example, the police are usually able to obtain the defendant's signature on the *Miranda* warning form, which indicates compliance with Supreme Court requirements (see Exhibit 12.5). Similarly, in a search-and-seizure case, the officers are familiar enough with the law to know how to testify in order to avoid suppression of evidence. Of course, the district attorney can dismiss a case that presents potential problems, thus avoiding a public hearing on the matter.

Trial Judges as Decision Makers

The decision to suppress evidence rests with the trial judge. After hearing the witnesses and viewing the physical evidence (if any), the judge makes a ruling based on appellate court decisions. Thus, trial-court judges are key policymakers in applying and implementing Supreme Court decisions concerning confessions and search and seizure.

As noted earlier, a pretrial motion is essentially a clash over the facts. The trial-court judge possesses virtually unfettered discretion in making findings of fact. Judges' backgrounds predispose them to be skeptical of defense motions to suppress. As noted in Chapter 6, many judges were once prosecutors, whose courtroom arguments supported the police. These inclinations are reinforced by the selection process. Judges are, by and large, either appointed by governors or presidents—who are often critical of appellate-court restrictions on gathering of evidence by the police, or elected by the public in campaigns that stress crime reduction. For these reasons, trial judges do not regularly grant defense motions to suppress evidence.

On appeal, higher courts examine whether the law was correctly applied by the trial judge, but they rarely scrutinize the facts to which the law was applied. Such deference is based on the trial judge's proximity to the event. Only trial judges have the opportunity to observe directly how witnesses testify—their responsiveness to questions or their attempts at concealment. Such nuances are not reflected in the trial-court transcript.

Police Testimony

At the center of court hearings on police practices and defendants' rights are events that happened out in the field or in the police station. Although some jurisdictions now require police to tape interrogations, many do not (Leo 1996b; Rosen 2006). What is known in court, therefore, is largely the product of police testimony.

Richard Leo (1996a) observed 122 interrogations in a major urban police department and reported the following. Detectives begin by cultivating the suspect, getting him or her to make eye contact and engage in conversation. The *Miranda* warnings are useful for this purpose because they induce suspects to respond to questions. Thus, three out of four suspects waive their *Miranda* rights. Next, the detective states that his or her job is to discover the truth and typically shares with the suspect some of the

Exhibit 12.5

SAMPLE CUSTODIAL INTERROGATION FORM

KENNER POLICE DEPARTMENT   A   47408

ADVICE OF RIGHTS   KENNER, LA.

DAY_____ DATE _____ TIME _____ COMPLAINT NO. _____

LOCATION_____

NAME _____

BIRTH DATE _____ RACE _____ SEX_____ AGE_____

ADDRESS_____ CITY_____ STATE _____

HIGHEST GRADE COMPLETED SCHOOL _____

ABILITY TO READ: ☐ YES   ☐ NO
ABILITY TO WRITE: ☐ YES   ☐ NO

☐ I am investigating -- or --
☐ You are under arrest for alleged -- Violation of _____

_____ Relative to_____

_____

According to provisions in the Constitution of the United States and of the State of Louisiana it is my duty to inform you that:

1. You have the right to remain silent.
2. Anything you say may be used against you in court.
3. You have a right to consult with and obtain the advice of an attorney before answering any questions.
4. If you cannot afford an attorney, the court will appoint an attorney to represent and advise you.
5. You have a right to have your attorney present at the time of any questioning or giving of any statement.
6. If you decide to answer questions now without an attorney present, you will still have the right to stop answering at any time until you talk to an attorney.

DO YOU UNDERSTAND WHAT I HAVE JUST READ TO YOU?   ☐ YES ☐ NO

   NOTE: IF THE PERSON DOES NOT FULLY UNDERSTAND AND INTELLIGENTLY AND VOLUNTARILY WAIVE THE RIGHT OF COUNSEL, HE CANNOT BE QUESTIONED. IF THE PERSON AT ANY TIME DURING THE QUESTIONING ASKS NOT TO BE QUESTIONED FURTHER OR INDICATES IN ANY MANNER THAT HE DOES NOT WISH TO BE QUESTIONED, THEN THE QUESTIONING MUST CEASE.

ARE YOU WILLING TO ANSWER QUESTIONS AT THIS TIME WITHOUT A LAWYER?   ☐ YES ☐ NO

HAVE ANY THREATS OR PROMISES BEEN MADE TO YOU OR HAS PRESSURE OF ANY KIND BEEN APPLIED TO INDUCE YOU TO ANSWER QUESTIONS OR TO GIVE UP ANY OF YOUR RIGHTS?   ☐ YES ☐ NO

WITH FULL KNOWLEDGE OF MY RIGHTS I WISH TO WAIVE ALL PRIVILEGES AGAINST SELF INCRIMINATION AND MAKE A STATEMENT ABOUT MY KNOWLEDGE OF THIS CRIME.   ☐ YES ☐ NO

_____
                                        Signature of Person Receiving Rights

I have read and explained the RIGHTS OF AN ARRESTEE OR SUSPECT to the person named above, and he . . .
☐ SIGNED, WAIVING HIS RIGHTS
☐ SIGNED AS UNDERSTANDING, NOT WAIVING RIGHTS
☐ REFUSED TO SIGN
☐ WAS UNDECIDED, CONSEQUENTLY WAS ADVISED NOT TO SIGN
☐ PREFERS TO SPEAK WITH ATTORNEY BEFORE MAKING DECISION
☐ OTHER - (EXPLAIN IN REMARKS)

CONCLUDED: DAY_____ DATE _____ TIME _____

RIGHTS READ BY_____

WITNESS_____

WITNESS_____

REMARKS_____

_____

KPD-122

evidence in the case. A two-pronged approach is being used. One is the use of negative incentives, tactics that suggest the suspect should confess because no other plausible course of action exists. The other is the use of positive incentives, tactics that suggest the suspect will in some way feel better or benefit if he or she confesses. The results were as follows:

- No incriminating statement (36 percent)
- Incriminating statement (23 percent)
- Partial admission (18 percent)
- Full confession (24 percent)

A suspect's decision to provide detectives with incriminating information was fateful. Those who incriminated themselves were more likely to be charged with a crime, more likely to enter a plea of guilty, more likely to be convicted, and likely to receive more punishment than their counterparts who did not provide incriminating statements.

Police, prosecutors, and defense attorneys often become embroiled in disputes about what occurred during interrogation. These disputes can be ended by using audio and/or video equipment to record everything that occurs during custodial interviews. Although many law enforcement agencies continue to resist such practices, a growing number of jurisdictions are now making these practices a requirement (Rosen 2006; Sullivan 2004).

LAW AND CONTROVERSY: COSTS OF THE EXCLUSIONARY RULE

A key issue in the ongoing debate over the exclusionary rule centers on its costs. In a widely cited statement, Chief Justice Burger summed up the critics' position as follows: "Some clear demonstration of the benefits and effectiveness of the exclusionary rule is required to justify it in view of the high price it exacts from society—the release of countless guilty criminals" (*Bivens v. Six Unknown Federal Narcotics Agents* 1971, p. 416).

One study of police searches in a major American city concluded that 30 percent of the searches failed to pass constitutional muster. Even though the patrol officers knew they were being observed, they conducted illegal searches nonetheless. But only a handful of these events were documented in official records because so few resulted in arrest or citation (Gould and Mastrofski 2004). The lack of official action, therefore, makes it difficult to truly calculate the cost of the exclusionary rule at subsequent stages of the process.

Assessing the number of convictions lost because of the exclusionary rule is difficult, for reasons discussed in Chapter 10. Case attrition occurs at numerous stages of the proceedings and for various reasons. Several studies shed considerable light on the topic.

Exclusionary rules can lead to the freeing of apparently guilty defendants during prosecutorial screening. Prosecutors may refuse to file charges because of a search-and-seizure problem, a tainted confession, or a defective police lineup. However, this occurs very infrequently. The Comptroller General of the United States (1979) examined case rejections by U.S. attorneys and found that search and seizure was cited as the primary reason 0.4 percent of the time. Similarly, a study of seven communities reports that an average of 2 percent of the rejections were for *Mapp* or *Miranda* reasons (Boland et al. 1982). A more controversial study analyzed 86,033 felony cases rejected for prosecution in California. The National Institute of Justice (NIJ) report found that 4.8 percent were rejected for search-and-seizure reasons. The NIJ conclusion that these figures indicated a "major impact of the exclusionary rule" has been challenged as misleading and exaggerated (Davies 1983). Indeed, compared to lack of evidence and witness problems, *Mapp* and *Miranda* are minor sources of case attrition.

After charges are filed, case attrition can also occur when judges grant pretrial motions to suppress, but in actuality few pretrial motions to suppress evidence are actually filed. Nardulli (1983) reported that motions to suppress evidence were filed in fewer than 8 percent of the cases. Once filed, pretrial motions are rarely successful, although the success rate has varied significantly in the research from a low of 0.3 percent (Davies 1983) to a high of 1.5 percent (Uchida and Bynum 1991).

Piecing together the various stages of the criminal court process leads to the conclusion that the exclusionary rule has a marginal effect on the criminal court system (Nardulli 1983). Examining case-attrition data from California, Davies (1983) calculated that 0.8 percent of arrests (8 out of 1,000) were rejected because of *Mapp* and *Miranda*. As for cases filed, Nardulli calculated that 0.57 percent of convictions (fewer than 6 of 1,000) were lost because of exclusionary rules. Moreover, of the lost convictions, only 20 percent were for serious crimes. Weapons cases and drug cases are those most likely to involve questions about police conduct.

A special panel of the American Bar Association (1988) likewise concluded that constitutional protections of the rights of criminal defendants do not significantly handicap police and prosecutors in their efforts to arrest, prosecute, and obtain convictions for the most serious crimes. Although many people blame the failures of the criminal justice system on judges' concern for defendants' rights, the blame is misplaced. The main problem is that the criminal justice system is stretched too thin, the Association concluded.

CONCLUSION

In many ways Ernesto Miranda fit the pattern of those arrested by the police—a young minority male with little education and few job prospects. But the eventual outcome of his case was hardly typical. His case was heard by the nation's highest court, and he not only won the right to a new trial but also established a new law in the process. Unlike most defendants, whose cases are quickly forgotten, his name became a code word for the rights of criminal defendants.

If *Miranda* the legal principle was to endure, Miranda the man was less fortunate. Initially, his chances of gaining an acquittal during retrial looked promising indeed. After all, the state's only evidence—the signed confession—had been ruled to be inadmissible evidence. It turned out, however, that while in jail Ernesto Miranda had admitted details of the crime to his common-law wife, who by now had grown afraid of him. She testified for the state, and after an hour and a half of deliberations, the jury found Miranda guilty of rape and kidnapping a second time. After serving his prison term, Ernesto Miranda was living in Phoenix when he became involved in a barroom quarrel over small change in a poker game. A large knife normally used to harvest lettuce ended his life. It is no small irony that the Phoenix police read Miranda's killer his *Miranda* rights when they arrested him.

This chapter has examined several important aspects of what occurs while cases are being prepared for trial. One is discovery, the formal or informal exchange of information between prosecution and defense. What information is subject to discovery varies greatly. As a rule, defense attorneys who are cooperative members of the courtroom work group receive more information than others. Another important aspect of preparing for trial centers on suppression of evidence. Confessions and physical evidence that have been illegally obtained cannot be used at trial. If the defense believes that there have been illegal actions by the police, it files a pretrial motion to suppress the evidence. Prosecutors are usually in a favorable position to show that the evidence was obtained legally.

CHAPTER REVIEW

1. Explain the reasons why the process of discovery exists in both civil and criminal cases, but is significantly curtailed in the latter.

Discovery is designed to give both parties to a legal dispute a good idea about the evidence that will be presented at trial. Not only does this exchange of information prevent surprises, but also, it facilitates resolutions without trial, such as the settlement of a civil case or a plea bargain in a criminal case. Discovery, however, is limited in criminal cases, since the prosecution bears the burden of persuasion to prove a defendant guilty beyond a reasonable doubt and the defendant is protected against being forced to incriminate himself/herself. If the defense had to disclose evidence to the prosecution, the privilege against self-incrimination would be rendered meaningless.

2. Differentiate formal and informal discovery and the reasons why both are used in criminal cases.

Formal discovery in criminal cases concerns the exchange of information mandated either by the rules of procedure or applicable law. The crux of mandatory discovery in criminal cases concerns prosecutorial disclosure of exculpatory evidence to the defense. Informal discovery concerns the disclosure of information not mandated by law. It occurs frequently because it often facilitates a prompt resolution of a dispute without the need for trial (i.e., either the prosecutor drops the charges in light of exculpatory evidence disclosed to it by the defense, or the defendant pleads guilty once the strength of the prosecution's case becomes evident).

3. Identify the types of evidence subject to mandatory criminal discovery.

All potentially exculpatory evidence must be disclosed to the defense. This includes any prior inconsistent statements of prosecutorial witnesses, as well as all impeachment evidence that might cast doubt on a witness's credibility.

4. Compare and contrast the exclusionary rule and the fruit of the poisonous tree doctrine.

The exclusionary rule bars evidence from being used in the prosecution's case-in-chief if it was obtained in violation of a defendant's constitutional rights. The fruit of the poisonous tree doctrine bars derivative evidence found as a result the violation of a defendant's constitutional right from being used in the prosecution's case-in-chief unless the evidence is so far attenuated from the constitutional violation that its use would not offend due process.

5. Summarize how the decision in *Miranda v. Arizona* regulates the process of police interrogations of suspects.

Before a suspect in police custody is interrogated, the suspect must be informed of his/her rights under the Fifth Amendment's Self-Incrimination Clause, namely that the suspect has the right to remain silent and the right to have counsel present during an interrogation. Moreover, the suspect must be told that the consequence of voluntarily waving these rights will result in the prosecution being able to use anything the suspect says at trial. If the suspect invokes his/her *Miranda* rights, questioning must stop.

6. Explain the requirements governing the application for search warrants, the issuance of search warrants, and the execution of search warrants.

When law enforcement officers want to conduct a search for evidence, the Fourth Amendment generally requires them to seek a warrant. They apply for a warrant by swearing to the facts they know, usually in an affidavit. A magistrate then considers those facts to determine whether there is probable cause to authorize the search of a particular place or person for particular evidence connected to a specific crime. If such a warrant is issued, the police must execute the warrant quickly and in a reasonable manner.

7. Identify the major exceptions to the Fourth Amendment's warrant requirement.

Police may conduct warrantless searches when granted consent to search by someone with actual or apparent authority to grant such consent; when incident to a lawful arrest; when items are in plain view or in open fields; when probable cause exists to search a motor vehicle; or when emergency situations make it impracticable for police to seek and obtain a warrant first.

8. Analyze the effect of the exclusionary rule on the operations of the courtroom work group.

Because pretrial motions to suppress evidence are relatively rare, the exclusionary rule does not generally impact the operations of the courtroom work group in most cases. However, when questions about the constitutionality of a search or seizure arise, the defense attorney takes charge of the situation by filing a motion to suppress. In somewhat of a role reversal, these motions have the effect of putting the prosecution on the defensive. Moreover, they ultimately cause a judge to have to rule on the credibility of testimony offered by law enforcement officers. Depending on whom the judge believes, the relationships within the courtroom work group can be significantly strained.

9. Evaluate whether the exclusionary rule should be abolished.

Supporters of the exclusionary rule argue that the rule is the only effective deterrent against police misconduct. Thus, they assert that the rule must be preserved in order to guarantee that our constitutional rights are honored. In contrast, those who want to see the exclusionary rule abolished argue that the threat of civil lawsuits should be enough to deter police misconduct. Moreover, they assert that the rule "costs" too much, in that it operates to prevent juries from considering highly relevant evidence, which, in turn, sometimes operates to allow the guilty to go free.

CRITICAL THINKING QUESTIONS

1. In civil cases, each party is entitled to all the information in the possession of the other side (unless that information is privileged). Why are discovery rules in criminal cases different?

2. To what extent do prosecutorial policies that restrict the sharing of information with defense attorneys other than what is legally required represent a contradiction in the crime control model?

3. When the Court announced its decision in *Miranda v. Arizona* in 1966, the decision sparked massive controversy and was a major issue in the 1968 presidential campaign. Yet, over time it has become much more accepted than the Court's decision in *Mapp v. Ohio* regarding search and seizure. What factors might explain this apparent shift in assessments?

4. A number of conservatives call for eliminating or restricting the exclusionary rule in street crimes. Yet some conservatives also call for a stricter rule in white-collar crimes, suggesting that the financial records of a person or a business should be given special protections under the Fourth Amendment. Are these arguments consistent or simply a case of whose ox is being gored? How would these arguments play out if a substantial citizen in the community (whose financial records are being requested) were under investigation for major drug dealings?

5. To what extent is the continuing controversy over search-and-seizure law really a debate over the war on drugs? Recall the controversy in Chapter 8 centering on judicial independence, in which a federal judge in New York suppressed a goodly amount of illegal drugs.

KEY TERMS

aerial search 299

affidavit 295

alibi defense 284

consent search 298

confrontation 285

derivative evidence 285

discovery 280

exclusionary rule 285

exculpatory evidence 282

fruit of the poisonous tree 285

illegal search and seizure 290

motor vehicle searches 299

open fields 299

plain view 298

search incident to arrest 298

search warrant 295

suppression motions 303

unreasonable search and seizure 290

warrantless search 298

WEB RESOURCES

Go to the America's Courts and the Criminal Justice System companion website at

http://www.cengage.com/criminaljustice/neubauer

where you will find more resources to help you study.
Resources include web exercises, quizzing, and flash cards.

FOR FURTHER READING

Brooks, Peter. *Troubling Confessions: Speaking Guilt in Law and Literature*. Chicago: University of Chicago Press, 2000.

Hilton, Alicia M. "Alternatives to the Exclusionary Rule after *Hudson v. Michigan*: Preventing and Remedying Police Misconduct." *Villanova Law Review* 53: 47–82, 2008.

Horne, Jed. *Desire Street: A True Story of Death and Deliverance in New Orleans*. New York: Farrar, Straus, and Giroux, 2005.

Leo, Richard. "*Miranda*'s Revenge: Police Interrogation as a Confidence Game." *Law and Society Review* 30: 259–288, 1996.

Leo, Richard, and George Thomas. *The Miranda Debate: Law, Justice, and Policing*. Boston: Northeastern University Press, 2000.

Levy, Leonard W. "Origins of the Fourth Amendment." *Political Science Quarterly* 114: 79–101, 1999.

Mialon, Hugo M., and Sue H. Mialon. "The Effects of the Fourth Amendment: An Economic Analysis." *Journal of Law, Economics, and Organization* 24: 22–44, 2008.

Sklansky, David Alan. "Is the Exclusionary Rule Obsolete?" *Ohio State Journal of Criminal Law* 5: 567–584, 2008.

13

NEGOTIATED JUSTICE AND THE PLEA OF GUILTY

© Corbis

With his lawyers at his side, Gary Leon Ridgway looks over papers he is signing in which he pleads guilty to 48 counts of aggravated first degree murder in the Green River killing cases. Ridgway pleaded guilty as part of a plea bargain with prosecutors in which his life would be spared. To the public, such a plea bargain may appear to be unduly lenient. In reality, though, such agreements are a part of the normal processing of crimes. Without such pleas, prosecutors risk the possibility of offenders like Ridgway being acquitted at trial. Moreover, if trials were the norm, rather than plea bargains, the system would collapse since it lacks both the time and resources to conduct trials in most criminal cases.

CHAPTER OUTLINE

LEARNING OBJECTIVES

After reading this chapter, you should be able to:

1. Distinguish between the three most common types of plea agreements.

2. Discuss the three major factors influencing bargaining and discretion.

3. Recognize the importance of *Boykin v. Alabama.*

4. List the major reason each of the members of the courtroom work group engage in plea bargaining.

5. Indicate why a few cases go to trial but most defendants plead guilty.

6. Explain why adherents of the crime control model of criminal justice oppose plea bargaining for different reasons from those of adherents of the due process model of criminal justice.

Charged with two counts of felony gambling, Rudolph Santobello pled guilty to one count of a misdemeanor charge of possessing gambling records. Just as important, the prosecutor agreed to make no recommendation as to the sentence. But Santobello's sentencing hearing was delayed for several months, and in the interim the initial judge retired, and another prosecutor replaced the one who had negotiated the plea of guilty. Apparently ignorant of his colleague's commitment, the new

district attorney demanded the maximum sentence, and the new judge agreed, imposing a 1-year jail term. The justices of the U.S. Supreme Court were concerned about the failure of the prosecutor's office to honor the commitment it had made in inducing the guilty plea. Others were no doubt concerned about whether Santobello, who had a long and serious criminal record, should have been allowed to plead guilty with such a light sentence in the first place.

Santobello v. New York highlights the importance of guilty pleas. Although the average American equates criminal justice with trials, only a handful of defendants are ever tried. Instead, most convictions result not from a guilty verdict following a contested trial but rather from a voluntary plea by the accused. Views about this common practice differ. To some, it erodes the cornerstones of the adversary system: the presumption of innocence and the right to trial. To others, it enables the guilty to escape with a light penalty. To still others, it is a modern-day necessity if the courts are to dispose of their large caseloads. All agree, however, that it is the most important stage of the criminal court process.

LAW ON THE BOOKS: TYPES OF PLEA AGREEMENTS

Guilty pleas are the bread and butter of the American criminal courts. Between 85 and 95 percent of all state and federal felony convictions are obtained by a defendant entering a negotiated plea of guilt (Covey 2008; Hashimoto 2008). The data in Figure 13.1 demonstrate the pervasiveness of guilty pleas for specific types of offenses. **Plea bargaining** can best be defined as the process through which a defendant pleads guilty to a criminal charge with the expectation of receiving some consideration from the state.

Plea bargaining is hardly new. Considerable evidence shows that it became a common practice in state courts sometime after the Civil War (Alschuler 1979; Friedman 1979; Sanborn 1986). In Middlesex County, Massachusetts, for example, plea bargaining

had become firmly "normalized" by the 20th century (Fisher 2003). In federal courts, the massive number of liquor cases stemming from Prohibition led to the institutionalization of plea bargaining in the first third of the 20th century (Padgett 1990). What is new is the amount of attention plea negotiations now receive. In an earlier era the issue was discussed only sporadically. The crime surveys of the 1920s reported the dominance of plea bargaining (Moley 1928), but

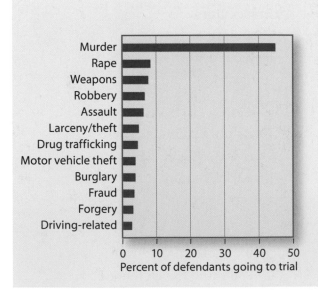

FIGURE 13.1 TRIAL RATES FOR TYPICAL FELONIES BY MOST SERIOUS ARREST CHARGE

Source: Thomas Cohen and Brian Reaves. *Felony Defendants in Large Urban Counties, 2002.* Washington, DC: Bureau of Justice Statistics, 2006.

Exhibit 13.1		
FORMS OF PLEA BARGAINING		
	LAW ON THE BOOKS	**LAW IN ACTION**
Plea bargaining	The process by which a defendant pleads guilty to a criminal charge with the expectation of receiving some benefit from the state.	The majority of findings of guilt occur because of plea bargaining. The proportion of pleas (as opposed to trials) varies among jurisdictions.
Charge bargaining	The defendant pleads guilty to a less serious charge than the one originally filed. Pleading to a less serious charge reduces the potential sentence the defendant faces.	Courthouse norms control allowable reductions. Some prosecutors deliberately over charge so it appears that the defendant is getting a break.
Count bargaining	The defendant pleads guilty to some, but not all, of the counts contained in the charging document. Pleading guilty to fewer counts reduces the potential sentence the defendant faces.	Some prosecutors deliberately file additional charges so they can dismiss some later on, making it appear the defendant got a good deal. In multiple-count charges, sentences are typically served concurrently (not consecutively), so the "sentence reduction" the defendant receives is largely illusionary.
Sentence bargaining	The defendant pleads guilty, knowing the sentence that will be imposed. The sentence in the sentence bargain is less than the maximum.	Sentences are based on normal penalties. Because the normal penalty for an offense is less than the maximum, defendants appear to get off lightly.

most courts persistently denied its existence. It was not until the 1960s that plea bargaining emerged as a controversial national issue. Today, however, although specific aspects of plea bargaining may give rise to periodic controversy, the process itself is so widely accepted that it "dominates the modern American criminal process" (Covey 2008, p. 1238).

Plea bargaining is a general term that encompasses a wide range of practices. Indeed, court officials disagree about what is meant by plea bargaining. Some prosecutors refuse to admit that they engage in bargaining; they simply call it something else (Miller, McDonald, and Cramer 1978). Thus, any discussion of negotiated justice must start with the recognition that important variations exist both in the types of plea agreements negotiated and the process by which such agreements are reached. Typically, plea agreements take one or more of the following three forms: charge bargaining, count bargaining, and sentence bargaining. Exhibit 13.1 summarizes the different types of plea bargaining.

CHARGE BARGAINING

One type of plea agreement is termed **charge bargaining**. In return for the defendant's plea of guilty, the prosecutor allows the defendant to plead guilty to a less serious charge than the one originally filed. For example, the defendant pleads guilty to robbery rather than the original charge of armed robbery. Or the defendant enters a plea of guilty to misdemeanor theft rather than the initial accusation of felony theft. The principal effect of a plea to a less serious charge is to reduce the potential sentence.

Some offenses carry a stiff maximum sentence. A plea to a lesser charge therefore greatly reduces the possible prison term the defendant will have to serve. Bargains for reduced charges are most commonly found in jurisdictions where the state's criminal code is rigid or where prosecutors routinely overcharge to begin with. Thus, some charge reductions reflect the probability that the prosecutor would not be able to prove the original charge in a trial.

COUNT BARGAINING

Another common type of plea agreement is called **count bargaining.** In return for the defendant's plea of guilty to one or more counts in the indictment or information, the prosecutor dismisses the remaining charges. For instance, a defendant accused of three separate burglaries pleads guilty to one burglary count, and the two remaining criminal charges are dismissed.

Like a charge reduction agreement, a count bargain reduces the defendant's potential sentence, but in a very different way. A person charged with multiple counts theoretically can receive a maximum sentence of something like 135 years, a figure arrived at by multiplying the number of charges by the maximum jail term for each charge and assuming that the judge will sentence the defendant to serve the sentences consecutively (one after another). Such figures are often unrealistic, because sentences are typically imposed concurrently (to run at the same time). In practice, the defendant will often receive the same penalty no matter how few (or how many) charges are involved.

SENTENCE BARGAINING

The third common form of plea agreement is called **sentence bargaining.** A plea of guilty is entered in exchange for a promise of leniency in sentencing. There may be a promise that the defendant will be placed on probation or that the prison term will be no more than a given figure—say, 5 years. In a sentence bargain, the defendant typically pleads to the original charge (often termed a **plea on the nose**). In some jurisdictions, however, sentence bargaining operates in conjunction with count bargaining and charge reduction bargaining.

In sentence bargaining, the defendant invariably receives less than the maximum penalty. To some, this is an indication that defendants get off too easily, but in fact, only defendants with long criminal records who have committed particularly heinous crimes would receive the maximum sentence anyway. In practice, courts impose sentences on the basis of normal penalties for specific crimes involving common types of defendants. In sentence bargaining, the sentence agreed to is the one typically imposed in similar cases.

LAW IN ACTION: BARGAINING AND CASELOADS

The common explanation for plea bargaining is that the courts have too many cases. Plea bargaining is usually portrayed as a regrettable but necessary expedient for disposing of cases. In Chapter 5, it was argued that although this explanation contains some truth, it obscures too many important facets of what the courts do and why they do it. Certainly, the press of cases and lack of adequate resources shape the criminal court process, plea bargaining included (Worden 1990). Certainly, because prosecutors need to move cases, they agree to more lenient pleas than they might prefer.

But the caseload hypothesis cannot explain why plea bargaining is as prevalent in courts with relatively few cases as it is in courts with heavy caseloads (Eisenstein and Jacob 1977; Covey 2009). A comparison of plea rates in a number of courthouses across the nation found high plea rates in suburban counties with low crimes rates and below-average caseloads. The vast differences among jurisdictions in the ratio of pleas to trials primarily reflect differences in the prosecution and the police or differences in courtroom work-group culture, not in disparities concerning crime rates or court resources (Boland and Forst 1985; Emmelman 2002).

A similar conclusion emerges from a study that presented the members of the courtroom work group with several hypothetical cases and asked, "Assuming that prosecution, defense, and the court have adequate resources to deal with their caseloads in a fair and expeditious manner, how do you believe this case should be resolved?" (Church 1985, p. 474). The responses indicated that relatively few of the cases would be disposed of by a trial. Furthermore, there was little support for the notion that practitioners considered negotiated guilty pleas a necessary but illegitimate response to inadequate court system resources (see also Warden 2008).

LAW IN ACTION: BARGAINING AND DISCRETION

The principal weakness of the excessive caseload hypothesis is that it assumes a purely mechanical process, ignoring the underlying dynamics. It seems to suggest that if only there were more judges, more prosecutors, more defense attorneys, and more courtrooms, there would be many more trials, and the penalties imposed on the guilty would also increase. Such a view ignores the discretion inherent in the criminal justice process. Plea bargaining is a response to some fundamental issues, the first of which centers on the question of guilt.

PRESUMPTION OF FACTUAL GUILT

The process of negotiated justice does not operate in isolation from the other stages of the criminal court process. What has gone before—for example, the setting of bail, the return of a grand jury indictment, and the prosecutor's evaluation of the strengths of a case—significantly affects how courts dispose of cases on a plea. The opposite is equally true. Throughout the history of a case, decisions on bail, indictment, and screening have been premised on the knowledge that the majority of defendants end up pleading guilty (Wright and Miller 2002).

Recall from Chapter 10 that the bulk of legally innocent defendants are removed from the criminal court process during the screening process through the preliminary hearing, grand jury, or the prosecutor's charging decision. By the time a case reaches the trial stage, the courtroom work group presumes that the defendant is probably guilty. Survival through the prior processing means that prosecutors, defense attorneys, and judges alike perceive that trial defendants are in serious trouble.

One study estimated that about 50 percent of the cases in the major trial court were "hopeless" or devoid of triable issues of law (Schulhofer 1984). These cases are what some court officials term a "dead bang" or a "slam dunk" case, with very strong evidence against the defendant, who has no credible explanation indicating innocence (Mather 1974a). One district attorney summarized the strong evidence of guilt in such cases: "The pervasiveness of the facts should indicate to any competent attorney that the element of prosecution is present and a successful prosecution is forthcoming" (Neubauer 1974b, p. 200).

No two cases are ever the same, of course. Many discussions of plea bargains leave the false impression that the attorneys haggle only over the sentence. In fact, courtroom work groups spend a lot of time discussing and analyzing how the crime was committed, the nature of the victim, the types of witnesses, and the character of the defendant (Maynard 1988; Emmelman 2002). In many cases, the likelihood that the defendant will be acquitted outright is small; however, the possibility exists that he or she might be convicted of a less serious offense. The question of what charge the facts will support is an important part of plea bargaining.

COSTS AND RISKS OF TRIAL

The possibility of trial greatly influences negotiations. Trials are a costly and time-consuming means of establishing guilt. For example, to try a simple burglary case would take from 1 to 4 days (depending on the jurisdiction) and require the presence of the judge, bailiff, clerk, defense attorney, prosecutor, and court reporter. During this period, none of them could devote much time to the numerous other cases requiring disposition. Also, each would be forced to spend time preparing for this trial. A trial would also require the presence of numerous noncourt personnel: police officers, witnesses, victims, and jurors. For each of these people, a trial represents an unwanted intrusion into their daily lives.

Based on these considerations, all members of the courtroom work group have a common interest in disposing of cases and avoiding unnecessary trials. Their reasons may differ. Judges and prosecutors want high disposition rates in order to prevent case backlogs and to present a public impression that the process is running smoothly. Public defenders prefer quick dispositions because they lack the personnel to handle the caseload. Private defense attorneys depend on a high case turnover to earn a living, because most of their clients can afford only a modest fee. In short, all members of the courtroom work group have more cases to try than the time or resources to try them.

To a large extent, then, a trial is a mutual penalty that all parties seek to avoid through plea bargaining. To be sure, not all trials are avoided. But through plea bargaining, scarce trial resources can be applied to the cases that need to be tried.

What to Do with the Guilty

The adversary proceedings of trial are designed to resolve conflict over guilt or innocence. In practice, however, it is not the issue of legal guilt that is most often in dispute, but rather what sentence to impose on the guilty. Sentencing decisions involve more than the verdict of guilt or innocence presented at trial; they incorporate difficult issues of judgment about the type of crime and the nature of the defendant. Moreover, because of the standards of evidence, information relevant to sentencing is not easily introduced at trial. Unlike a trial, plea bargaining does focus on what to do with an offender—particularly, how much leniency is appropriate.

Criminal statutes are broad; the courtroom work group is called upon to apply these broad prohibitions to specific and variable cases. The participants are concerned with adjusting the penalties to the specifics of the crime and the defendant. In the interest of fairness, they seek to individualize justice.

Consider a case with two codefendants of unequal culpability: an armed robbery involving an experienced robber who employed a youthful accomplice as a driver. Technically, both are equally guilty, but in the interest of fairness and substantive justice, the prosecutor may legitimately decide to make a concession to the young accomplice but none to the prime mover. In short, members of the courtroom work group seek to individualize justice.

Bargaining and the Courtroom Work Group

Plea bargaining is a contest involving the prosecutor, defendant, defense counsel, and at times, the judge. Each party has its own objectives. Each attempts to structure the situation to its own advantage by using tactics to improve its bargaining position. Each defines success in terms of its own objectives. Among the conflicting objectives, accommodations are possible, because each side can achieve its objectives only by making concessions on other matters. Plea bargaining is typical of "most bargaining situations which ultimately involve some range of possible outcomes within which each party would rather make a concession than fail to reach agreement at all" (Schelling 1960, p. 70; see also Emmelman 2002).

Plea bargaining typically begins informally, according to two veteran federal prosecutors. When discussing the matter with opposing counsel, prosecutors want to be reassured that the defendant is genuinely interested in pleading guilty and that a reasonable chance exists of reaching an agreement before they invest the time and effort of preparing a formal plea agreement. Consistent with our earlier discussion of the courtroom work group (Chapter 5), trust is a critical component of these discussions. "If the prosecutor and the defense counsel have negotiated plea agreements with each other in the past, expect to do so in the future, and from their past dealings, respect and trust each other, these preliminary, informal discussions are likely to be candid and efficient and may quickly lead to an informal proposed agreement" (Brown and Bunnell 2006).

Bargaining is possible because each of the legal actors understands the realities of law in action: the presumption of guilt, the costs and uncertainties of trial, and the concern with arriving at an appropriate sentence. All these factors influence bargaining positions.

Prosecutors

To the prosecutor, a plea bargain represents the certainty of conviction without the risks of trial. Recall that prosecutors emphasize convictions. Because they value the deterrent objectives of law enforcement, they prefer that a guilty person be convicted of some charge rather than escape with no conviction at all.

The certainty and finality of a defendant's pleading guilty contrast sharply with the potential risks involved in a trial (Covey 2008; Worden 1990). During trial, a number of unexpected events can occur, most of which work to the detriment of the prosecutor. The victim may refuse to cooperate. Witnesses' testimony may differ significantly from earlier statements made in investigative reports. A mistrial—the judge ending the trial without a verdict because of a major defect in the proceedings—could be declared. Even after a jury verdict of guilty, the appellate courts may reverse, meaning that the whole process must be repeated.

In seeking a conviction through a guilty plea, the prosecutor is in a unique position to control the negotiating process (Hashimoto 2008; Holmes, Daudistel, and Taggart 1992). To begin with, the prosecutor proceeds from a position of strength: In most cases, the state has sufficient evidence for conviction. If, however, the case is weak, the prosecutor can avoid the embarrassment of losing a case at trial by either dismissing it altogether or offering such a good deal that the defendant cannot refuse.

To improve their bargaining position, some prosecutors deliberately overcharge. "Sure, it's a lever," said one San Francisco prosecutor, referring to his office's practice of charging every nonautomobile homicide as murder. With unusual candor, he added, "And we charge theft, burglary, and the possession of burglar's tools, because we know that if we charged only burglary there would be a trial" (Alschuler 1968, p. 90; see also Davis 2007).

Prosecutors, of course, control several of the forms of plea bargaining. They are in a position to offer a charge reduction or a count bargain. They can threaten to throw the book at a defendant who does not plead, or they may refuse to bargain at all. If the crime is a serious one and the defendant is viewed as very dangerous, the prosecutor may force the defendant either to plead on the nose, with no sentencing concessions, or to run the risk of trial and a harsher sentence for not having cooperated.

DEFENDANTS

If pleas give prosecutors what they want (convictions), why do defendants plead guilty? To understand plea bargaining, it is important to recognize that it is often in the defendant's best interest to give up the right to be presumed innocent at a trial. The primary benefit of a plea is the possibility of a lenient sentence.

Around the courthouse, it is a common perception that defendants who refuse to plead guilty receive harsher sentences. For example, a judge may impose a stiffer sentence because the defendant compounded the crime by lying on the witness stand or getting some friends to perjure themselves. Or a prosecutor may agree not to invoke state "career criminal" provisions, which impose higher penalties for those with a prior felony conviction. Moreover, for defendants who are unable to post bail, a guilty plea can mean an immediate release (either on probation or for time served).

Ultimately, defendants must decide whether to go along with the plea bargain or to take their chances at trial. Few defendants are in a position to make a reasoned choice between the advantages of a plea and those of a trial; most are poor, inarticulate, and have little formal education. For these defendants, the experience in the courts is like their life on the streets: They learn to go along. Often softened up by the experience in jail awaiting trial, many defendants find that entering a plea is the best way to go along and avoid the possibility of even harsher penalties.

DEFENSE ATTORNEYS

If the prosecutor enters negotiations from a position of strength, the opposite is true of defense attorneys, who have few bargaining chips. If the chances of winning at trial are not high—and they rarely are—defense attorneys must consider the strong possibility that after a trial conviction the defendant may be penalized with a higher prison sentence.

The decision-making process for defense attorneys involves three phases. First, the defense attorney must assess the offer for a guilty plea, weighing the potential costs of delay against the likely outcome of a trial. Second, the defense attorney negotiates the terms of a plea bargain; if the initial offer is better than average, negotiations are less intense than if it is below average. Third, the defense attorney counsels the defendant, who may or may not accept the offer (Emmelman 1996, 2002).

The lawyer's main resource in negotiating a plea agreement is his or her knowledge of the courtroom work group—the types of pleas the prosecutor usually enters, the length of sentence the judge normally imposes in similar cases, and so on. Defense attorneys act as classic negotiators, trying to get the best deal possible for their clients while explaining to the clients the realistic alternatives. As noted in Chapter 7, these two roles can conflict. A defense attorney may negotiate what he or she considers the best deal under the circumstances, only to have the client refuse to go along.

Convincing clients to accept the plea is not always easy. Veteran public defender David Feige (2006, p. 119) recalls a lawyer and his client screaming at each other in the jail holding cell. Although other lawyers and clients are present, "No one interferes, no one tried to calm them down, and lawyer and client go on yelling at each for another four or five minutes." Such interactions are constant. "Overworked, underappreciated lawyers and desperate clients are a potent mix. Many lawyers see intimate client relationships as superfluous." As stressed in Chapter 7, some lawyers try to protect their clients from making bad decisions, but lawyers also have to deal with pressures from judges to move the docket.

JUDGES

Several factors limit a judge's ability to control or supervise plea bargaining. Given the division of powers in the adversary system, judges are reluctant to intrude on prosecutorial discretion. Many of the key bargaining mechanisms—specifically, the charges filed and the charges the defendant is allowed to plead to—are controlled by the prosecutor. Thus, when a prosecutor, defense attorney, and defendant have agreed either to a count bargain or a charge reduction bargain, the judge has no legal authority to refuse to accept the plea.

Even more fundamentally, the judge knows relatively little about each case. Only the prosecutor, defendant, and defense attorney know the evidence for and against the defendant. Without knowledge of why the parties agreed to plea bargain, it is obviously difficult for a judge to reject a plea agreement. In short, the judge is dependent on the prosecutor and, to a lesser extent, the defense attorney.

Within these constraints, judges have some ability to shape the plea-bargaining process. Judicial involvement in the plea-bargaining process can have important consequences. In Essex, New Jersey, for example, trials are rare, and judges spend a great amount of time dealing with the plea-bargaining process. Indeed, "every defender interviewed recalled being coerced into returning to his client and convincing him or her of the judge's strong desire to resolve the case quickly with a plea" (Wice 2005, p. 125).

In the federal court system, judges are prohibited from being involved in plea negotiations (Borenstein and Anderson 2009). The extent to which judges are involved in the process in state courts varies greatly. A survey of state trial court judges (Ryan and Alfini 1979) revealed four basic patterns.

- A few judges are actively involved in plea negotiations, offering recommendations about case disposition.
- Some judges are indirectly involved, reviewing the recommendations made by defense and prosecutor.
- A small percentage of judges attend plea discussions but do not participate.
- The majority of judges do not attend plea-negotiating sessions. Thus, their role is limited to ratifying agreements reached by others.

A review of the rules of criminal procedure across the United States reveals that these four approaches continue, although a clear preference exists for judges not to participate in the plea-bargaining process other than to ratify or reject plea agreements reached independently by the prosecution and the defense (Borenstein and Anderson 2009). But even when judicial participation is limited to ratifying plea negotiations, judges can have an important impact on the process. Regular members of the courtroom work group know the sentence the judge is likely to impose. Therefore, they negotiate case dispositions that incorporate these sentencing expectations. On rare occasions, judges may reject a plea agreement. Such rejections serve to set a baseline for future negotiations.

DYNAMICS OF BARGAINING

Negotiating is a group activity, typically conducted in busy, noisy, public courtrooms. In such a courtroom, the initial impression is of constant talking and endless movement. While the judge is hearing a pretrial motion in one case, a prosecutor and defense attorney are engaged in an animated conversation about a charge reduction in another. Meanwhile, in more hushed tones, a public defender is briefing his client about why a continuance will be requested, and nearby a mother is talking to her son who is being held in jail. These numerous conversations occur while other participants continually move in and out. Police officers leave after testifying in a motion to suppress, bail agents arrive to check on their clients, clerks bring in new files, and lawyers search for the prosecutor assigned to their case. Occasionally, the noise becomes so loud that the judge or bailiff demands silence—a request that usually produces only a temporary reduction in the decibel level.

On the surface, courtrooms appear disorganized. In fact, there is an underlying order to the diverse activities. For example, when the judge calls a case, the other participants involved in that matter are immediately expected to drop all other business and proceed to the front of the court. Decision-making norms govern the substance of the negotiations. In particular, patterns exist as to why some cases go to trial and about understandings regarding penalties for those who do go to trial.

DECISION-MAKING NORMS

Through working together on a daily basis, the members of the courtroom work group come to understand the problems and demands of the others. They develop shared conceptions of how certain types of cases and defendants should be treated. Everyone except the outsider or the novice knows these customs of the courthouse.

As we have seen, plea bargaining is a complex process, but studies in different courts reveal important similarities in shared norms. The most important consideration is the seriousness of the offense. The more serious the crime charged, the harder the prosecutor bargains (Mather 1979; Nardulli, Flemming, and Eisenstein 1984; Piehl and Bushway 2007). The next most important factor is the defendant's criminal record. Those with prior convictions receive fewer concessions during bargaining (Alschuler 1979; Nardulli 1978; Piehl and Bushway 2007; Springer 1983; Smith 1986). Another key consideration is the strength of the prosecutor's case. The stronger the evidence against the defendant, the fewer concessions are offered (Adams 1983; Smith 1986).

These shared norms structure plea negotiations. In each courtroom work group, the set of allowable reductions is well understood. Based on the way the crime was committed and the background of the defendant, nighttime burglary will be reduced to daytime burglary, drunkenness to disturbing the peace, and so on. Thus, contrary to many popular fears, defendants are not allowed to plead to just any charge (Feeley 1979; Emmelman 2002). If a defendant has been charged with armed robbery, the defense attorney knows that the credibility of her bargaining position will be destroyed if she suggests a plea to disturbing the peace. Such a plea would be out of line with how things are normally done.

Courtroom work groups have similar shared norms about sentencing. On the basis of these shared norms, all parties know what is open for bargaining and what is not. The shared norms provide a baseline for disposing of specific cases. Upward or downward adjustments are made, depending on the circumstances of the individual case.

WHY CASES GO TO TRIAL

Although most cases are disposed of by a guilty plea, an important 2 percent to 10 percent of defendants are tried. Cases go to trial when the parties cannot settle a case through negotiation. In large measure, the factors that shape plea bargaining—the strength of the prosecutor's case and the severity of the penalty—are the same ones that enter into the decision to go to trial. Defense attorneys recommend a trial when the risks of trial are low and the possible gains are high.

This broad calculation leads to two very different types of trial cases. In one, the possible gains for the defendant are high because of the chance of an acquittal. There may be reasonable doubt that the defendant committed any crime, or two sets of witnesses may tell conflicting versions of what happened (Neubauer 1974b). A second category of cases going to trial involves situations in which the prison sentence will be high. Even though a judge or jury is not likely to return a verdict of not guilty, the defendant may still decide that the slim possibility of an acquittal is worth the risk of the trial penalty.

However, not all trial cases are the result of such rational calculations. Some defendants insist on a trial, no matter what. Judges, prosecutors, and defense attorneys label as irrational defendants who refuse to recognize the realities of the criminal justice system and insist on a trial even when the state has a strong case (Neubauer 1974b; Bibas 2004). The net effect of these considerations is that some types of cases are more likely to go to trial than others. Property offenses (burglary and larceny) are much less likely to go to trial than homicide, sexual assault, or robbery. Mather (1974a) suggests that property crimes are least likely to go to trial because the state is apt to have a strong case (usually buttressed by the presence of indisputable physical evidence) and the prison sentence will not be long (see also, Bibas 2004). Serious crimes such as murder, rape, and robbery are much more likely to be tried. In some crimes of violence, reasonable doubt may exist because the victim may have provoked the attack. Moreover, a convicted defendant is likely to serve a long prison term and is therefore more disposed to take a chance on an outright acquittal.

JURY TRIAL PENALTY

Although most defendants plead guilty, a significant minority of cases do go to trial. As previously indicated, it is a common assumption in courthouses around the nation that defendants who do not enter a plea of guilty can expect to receive harsher sentences. Typically called the "jury trial penalty," the notion reflects the philosophy, "He takes some of my time, I take some of his." Here, *time* refers to the hours spent hearing evidence presented to a jury (Heumann 1978; King et al. 2005; Uhlman and Walker 1980).

Several studies provide empirical documentation for these courthouse perceptions (Brereton and Casper 1981–1982). In a major Eastern city, "the cost of a jury trial for convicted defendants in Metro City

LAW AND POPULAR CULTURE

American Violet (2008)

Dee Roberts (played by Nicole Beharie), is a 24-year-old African American woman who lives in the housing projects of a small Texas town with her mother, Alma (played by Alfre Woodard), and her four children. At the start of the movie, police conduct one of many military-style, racially motivated drug raids of their housing complex that have been occurring for many years.

Shortly thereafter, Dee is arrested and roughly dragged by the police from the diner where she works as a waitress. She thought she was being taken into custody for not having paid hundreds of dollars in parking tickets. Much to her surprise, however, she is charged with distributing cocaine in a school zone, a serious felony. But Dee has no drug record. She was not carrying any drugs on her at the time of her arrest, nor were any drugs found in her home during the police raid. Yet, she is arrested and prosecuted as a drug dealer on the basis of false information provided by a confidential informant. The local and seemingly racist district attorney, Calvin Beckett (played by Michael O'Keffe), pushes ahead with the prosecution against Dee as part of his self-driven mission to round up "black druggies and hauling them off to jail—by any means necessary" (Ragland 2009, para. 8).

Dee is faced with a difficult choice. If she agrees to plead guilty, she will not have to go to prison. Rather, in exchange for her plea, she would receive a 10-year suspended sentence with a small fine, allowing her to stay at home and raise her children. If, however, Dee rejects the plea offer, she risks a 16- to 25-year prison term and losing custody of her four kids.

Dee's court-appointed lawyer and her mother urge her to take the plea bargain. But Dee refuses to plead guilty to a crime she did not commit. Unlike most people in her situation, Dee eventually receives help from an American Civil Liberties Union lawyer who ultimately is able to get the cocaine distribution charges dropped.

This movie is based on actual events that occurred in Hearne, Texas to Ms. Regina Kelly (the person on whom the character of Dee Roberts is based) in 2000. Ms. Kelly's high-profile case eventually resulted in Texas changing its criminal law so that "cases can no longer

be prosecuted based solely on the claims of a single confidential informant" (Barnes 2009, para. 3).

After you watch this movie, be prepared to answer the following questions:

1. In *American Violet*, the district attorney tells Dee, "If you don't take the plea, we will prosecute you to the fullest extent of the law." Should prosecutors be able to use their power in this way? Is threatening a defendant with the most severe punishment possible if the defendant does not accept a plea a type of extortion? Explain your answer.

2. Dee is pressured by her lawyer and her family to enter a plea bargain even though she is not guilty. Although she fears the "jury trial penalty" that could land her in prison for up to 25 years, she refuses to cave into the pressure to plea. How often do you think wrongfully accused defendants who lack the resources to mount a solid legal defense accept a plea, even though they are not guilty, in order to avoid incarceration? Why do you think people would do this? Would you?

3. The drug raids in Hearne, Texas had been going on for years. Regina Kelly's case brought them to national attention. Using what you learned in Chapter 12 about constitutional criminal procedure, critique the use of military-style drug sweeps of housing projects inhabited by the poor. Why do you think such raids occur? What are the effects on the justice system as a whole when local law enforcement officials conduct such raids?

4. In the real raids in Hearne, Texas, seven other defendants accepted the plea bargains that were offered to them. While the charges were dropped against Regina Kelly, the charges were never dismissed against those who pled guilty to avoid the risk of spending many years in prison (Watkins 2009). What do you think about this? Why?

is high: sentences are substantially more severe than for other defendants" (Uhlman and Walker 1980, p. 337). Although a couple of studies have challenged these conclusions (Eisenstein and Jacob 1977; Rhodes 1978) more recent research finds that the magnitude of the jury trial penalty is stunningly high. In serious cases, the sentence imposed on a defendant who is found guilty after trial will often be more than five times more severe than the expected sentence for the same offense for a guilty plea (King et al. 2005; McCoy 2003; Ulmer and Bradley 2006).

The U.S. Supreme Court has clearly sanctioned the jury trial penalty. A Kentucky defendant accused of forging an $88 check was offered a 5-year prison sentence if he entered a plea of guilty. But the prosecutor indicated that if the defendant rejected the offer, the state would seek to impose life imprisonment because of the defendant's previous two felony convictions. Such stepped-up sentences for habitual criminals were allowed at that time by Kentucky law. The defendant rejected the plea, went to trial, was convicted, and was eventually sentenced to life imprisonment.

In *Bordenkircher v. Hayes* (1978), the high court held, "The course of conduct engaged in by the prosecutor in this case, which no more than openly presented the defendant with the unpleasant alternative of forgoing trial or facing charges on which he was plainly subject to prosecution" did not violate constitutional protections. In dissent, however, Justice Powell noted that the offer of 5 years in prison "hardly could be characterized as a generous offer." He was clearly troubled that "persons convicted of rape and murder often are not punished so severely" as this check forger. See Exhibit 13.2 for other key legal developments involving plea bargaining.

Copping a Plea

"Your honor, my client wishes at this time to withdraw his previous plea of not guilty and wishes at this time to enter a plea of guilty." In phrases similar to this one, defense attorneys indicate that the case is about to end; the defendant is ready to plead. A plea of guilty is more than an admission of conduct; it is a conviction that also involves a defendant's waiver of the most vital rights of the court process: presumption of innocence, jury trial, and confrontation of witnesses (*Boykin v. Alabama* 1969).

In an earlier era, the process of entering a plea of guilty was usually brief and informal. Because the courts and the legal process as a whole were reluctant to recognize the existence of plea bargaining, little law guided the process. Under the leadership of Chief Justice Warren Burger, however, the U.S. Supreme Court sought to set standards for the plea-bargaining process (see Case Close-Up: *Santobello v. New York* and Honoring a Plea Agreement).

Following *Santobello* the plea process has become more formalized. For example, in the U.S. Attorney's Office in the District of Columbia, an initial plea agreement between opposing counsel must first be approved by a senior supervisor. Next, a plea agreement is drafted. "Over the years, written plea agreements have grown longer and more complex as successive generations of prosecutors, defense counsel and judges … have noticed or exploited ambiguities of the parties' rights and obligations. As a result, federal plea agreements in D.C. now often run ten single-spaced pages or more" (Brown and Bunnell 2006). Once a plea agreement has been struck, the next step is the courtroom.

QUESTIONING THE DEFENDANT

In limited circumstances, a defendant will enter a plea of **nolo contendere**—Latin for "I will not contest it." Although a plea of nolo contendere has the same results in criminal proceedings as a plea of guilty, it cannot be used in a subsequent civil proceeding as a defendant's admission of guilt. Thus, this plea is usually entered when civil proceedings and liabilities may result. Most defendants plead guilty to one or more charges listed in the charging document. Before a defendant's plea of guilty can be accepted, the judge must question the defendant. This was not always the case; judges once merely accepted the attorney's statement that the defendant wanted to plead guilty. But in *Boykin v. Alabama*, the Supreme Court ruled: "It was error, for the trial judge to accept petitioner's guilty plea without an affirmative showing that it was intelligent and voluntary" (1969, p. 241).

The judge inquires whether the defendant understands the nature of the charge and the possible penalty upon conviction, whether any threats were made, whether the defendant is satisfied with the services of defense counsel, and whether the defendant realizes that a plea waives the right to a jury trial; a typical *Boykin* form is shown in Figure 13.2. Such questioning serves to ensure that the guilty plea reflects the defendant's own choice, is made with a general

Exhibit 13.2
KEY DEVELOPMENTS INVOLVING PLEA BARGAINING

Boykin v. Alabama	1969	When a defendant enters a plea of guilty, the judge must determine if the plea is knowingly entered and completely voluntary.
Brady v. U.S.	1970	Even though the defendant pled guilty to avoid the possibility of a death penalty, the plea was voluntary and intelligently made and therefore not coerced.
Alford v. North Carolina	1971	Given the defendant's desire to avoid the death penalty and the existence of substantial evidence of guilt, the plea of guilty was valid even though the defendant denied guilt.
Santobello v. New York	1971	When a plea rests in any significant degree on a promise or agreement of the prosecutor, so that it can be said to be a part of the inducement or consideration, such promise must be fulfilled.
Bordenkircher v. Hayes	1978	It is not a violation of due process for a prosecutor to threaten defendants with other criminal prosecutions so long as the prosecutor has probable cause to believe that the accused has committed the offense.
Ricketts v. Adamson	1987	Prosecutor allowed defendant to plead guilty to second-degree murder, contingent upon his testimony against the codefendant. When defendant refused to so testify, the DA prosecuted him for first-degree murder. The defendant was not protected by double jeopardy because he breached the plea agreement.
Alabama v. Smith	1989	Defendant was successful in having his original guilty plea vacated. After trial conviction, the judge imposed a substantially more severe sentence than under the plea agreement. Court held that the enhanced sentence was not vindictiveness because the trial judge had more information available as a result of the trial.
U.S. v. Mezzanatto	1995	Federal prosecutors may use statements made by a defendant during plea bargaining to cross-examine the defendant at trial.
U.S. v. Ruiz	2002	Prior to a plea of guilty, the prosecutor does not have to disclose to the defense as much evidence as before a trial.

understanding of the charges and consequences of conviction, and has not been improperly influenced by the prosecution, law enforcement officials, or the defendant's own attorney. Such questioning also provides an official court record, which prevents defendants from later contending they were forced to plead guilty.

ACCEPTING A PLEA

Judges have discretion in deciding whether to accept the defendant's plea of guilty. In one capital murder case, the defendant protested his innocence but entered a plea of guilty anyway, saying, "I

Santobello v. New York and Honoring a Plea Agreement

Rudolph Santobello was indicted on two counts: promoting gambling in the first degree and possession of gambling records in the first degree, both felonies under New York law. After negotiations with the prosecutor's office in the Bronx, Santobello entered a plea to the lesser included offense of possession of gambling records in the second degree, and the prosecutor also agreed to make no recommendation as to the sentence.

Months lapsed, though, before sentencing. A new defense attorney was hired, and he moved to suppress the evidence on grounds of an illegal search and seizure. The trial judge retired. Another assistant DA assumed control over the case (it is unclear whether his predecessor was promoted or resigned to take a job in private practice). Months later, when Santobello appeared for sentencing, the new prosecutor recommended the maximum 1-year sentence. The judge quickly imposed this sentence, leaving no doubt of his thoughts about the defendant. Reading the probation report, he said: "I have here a history of a long, long serious criminal record.... He is unamenable to supervision in the community. He is a professional criminal." The judge concluded by regretting that a 1-year sentence was all he was allowed to impose.

Chief Justice Warren Burger was beginning his second term on the court. Despite being a product of the law-and-order movement, his decision begins by noting the sloppiness apparent in the DA's office. "This record represents another example of an unfortunate lapse in orderly prosecutorial procedures, in part, no doubt, because of the enormous increase in the workload of the often understaffed prosecutor's office." But, most notably, he continues the theme of workload by coming out strongly in favor of guilty pleas:

> The disposition of criminal charges by agreement between the prosecutor and the accused, sometimes loosely called "plea bargaining," is an essential component of the administration of justice. Disposition of charges after plea discussions is not only an essential part of the process but a highly desirable part.

The Burger Court decision in *Santobello* in essence brought plea bargaining out of the closet. This is the Court's first look at a state non–capital punishment plea. As for the specific issue, "When a plea rests in any significant degree on a promise or agreement of the prosecutor, so that it can be said to be part of the inducement or consideration, such promise must be fulfilled." The net effect was to suggest that state pleas proceed under Rule 11 of the Federal Rules of Criminal Procedure, which requires the parties to disclose in open court the nature of the plea agreement.

In hindsight, what is perhaps most notable is that a justice appointed by President Nixon as representative of his law-and-order philosophy readily embraced plea bargaining. Within just 2 years, Nixon's crime commission denounced the practice and called for its abolition within 5 years—a call that was doomed to failure from the beginning.

CASE CLOSEUP

pleaded guilty on second-degree murder because they said there is too much evidence, but I ain't shot no man.... I just pleaded guilty because they said if I didn't they would gas me for it.... I'm not guilty but I pleaded guilty." The Supreme Court held that given the defendant's desire to avoid the death penalty and the existence of substantial evidence of guilt, the plea of guilty was valid (*Alford v. North Carolina* 1971).

Some judges accept *Alford* pleas, in which the defendant pleads guilty while claiming innocence. They are viewed as a way of speeding up the clogged judicial process. Superficially, the defendant "saves face," but for all practical purposes the *Alford* plea has the same effect as a conventional guilty plea and results in roughly the same punishment. Other judges refuse to accept a plea of guilty unless the defendant fully admits guilt. According to Superior Court Judge Martin McKeever of Connecticut, *Alford* pleas fly "in the face of what crime and punishment should be all about." Thus he does not accept pleas "in cases where culpability is so obvious that the public has a right to know about it" (quoted in Steinberger 1985). Moreover, *Alford* pleas rob "the victim of the opportunity to hear the defendant

STATE OF WISCONSIN, CIRCUIT COURT, _____ COUNTY	For Official Use

State of Wisconsin, Plaintiff
-vs-

_____
Name

**Plea Questionnaire/
Waiver of Rights**

Case No. _____

I am the defendant and intend to plea as follows:

Charge/Statute	Plea	Charge/Statute	Plea
	☐ Guilty ☐ No Contest		☐ Guilty ☐ No Contest
	☐ Guilty ☐ No Contest		☐ Guilty ☐ No Contest

☐ See attached sheet for additional charges.

I am _____ years old. I have completed _____ years of schooling.

I	☐ do	☐ do not	have a high school diploma, GED, of HSED.
I	☐ do	☐ do not	understand the English language.
I	☐ do	☐ do not	understand the charge(s) to which I am pleading.
I	☐ am not	☐ am	currently receiving treatment for a mental illness or disorder.
I	☐ have not	☐ have	had any alcohol, medications, or drugs within the last 24 hours.

Constitutional Rights
I understand that by entering this plea. I give up the following constitutional rights:

☐ I give up my right to a trial.
☐ I give up my right to remain silent and I understand that my silence could not be used against me at trial.
☐ I give up my right to testify and present evidence at trial.
☐ I give up my right to use subpoenas to require witnesses to come to court and testify for me at trial.
☐ I give up my right to a jury trial, where all 12 jurors would have to agree that I am either guilty or not guilty.
☐ I give up my right to confront in court the people who testify against me and cross-examine them.
☐ I give up my right to make the State prove me guilty beyond a reasonable doubt.
I understand the rights that have been checked and give them up of my own free will.

Understandings
- I understand that the crime(s) to which I am pleading has/have elements that the State would have to prove beyond a reasonable doubt if I had a trial. These elements have been explained to me by my attorney or are as follows: ☐ See Attached sheet.
_____

- I understand that the judge is not bound by any plea agreement or recommendations and may impose the maximum penalty. The maximum penalty I face upon conviction is: _____
_____

- I understand that the judge must impose the mandatory minimum penalty. If any. The mandatory minimum penalty I face upon conviction is:_____
_____

- I understand that the presumptive minimum penalty, if any. I face upon conviction is: _____
_____

The judge can impose a lesser sentence if the judge states appropriate reasons.

CR-277, 11/99 Plea Questionnaire/Waiver of Rights   §971.08, Wisconsin Statutes.
This form shall not be modified. It may be supplemented with additional material.
Page 1 of 2

FIGURE 13.2   A TYPICAL BOYKIN FORM

acknowledge and accept responsibility" for his or her crimes, a deprivation that can impair the psychological recovery of victims (Molesworth 2008, p. 914).

PLACING THE PLEA AGREEMENT ON THE RECORD

For years, plea negotiations were officially considered taboo. As a result, the taking of a plea was often a sham. The defendant was expected to lie and deny that a deal had been made (Casper 1972). To prevent the possibility of covering up plea bargaining, many courts now require that a plea agreement be placed on the record. Either a law enforcement officer or the prosecutor states that if a trial were held the evidence would show the defendant to be guilty and then proceeds to summarize the evidence sufficient to prove each of the elements of the offense. The defendant then has the opportunity to offer any corrections or additions, but must **allocute**—provide a factual basis

Plea Questionnaire/Waiver of Rights   Page 2 of 2   Case No. _____

Understandings
- I understand that if I am placed on probation and my probation is revoked:
  - if sentence is withheld, the judge could sentence me to the maximum penalty, or
  - if sentence is imposed and stayed, I will be required to serve that sentence.

- I understand that if I am not a citizen of the United States, my plea could result in deportation, the exclusion of admission to this country, or the denial of naturalization under federal law.

- I understand that if I am convicted of any felony, it is unlawful for me to possess a firearm.

- I understand that if I am convicted of a serious child sex offense, I cannot engage in an occupation or participate in a volunteer position that requires me to work or interact primarily and directly with children under the age of 16.

- I understand that if any charges are read-in as part of a plea agreement they have the following effects:
  - Sentencing – although the judge may consider read-in charges when imposing sentence, the maximum penalty will not be increased.
  - Restitution – I may be required to pay restitution on any read-in charges.
  - Future prosecution – the State may not prosecute me for any read-in charges.

- I understand that if the judge accepts my plea, the judge will find me guilty of the crime(s) to which I am pleading based upon the facts in the criminal complaint and/or the preliminary examination and/or as stated in court.

Voluntary Plea
I have decided to enter this plea of my own free will. I have not been threatened or forced to enter this plea. No promises have been made to me other than those contained in the plea agreement. The plea agreement will be stated in court or is as follows: ☐ See Attached.

Defendant's Statement
I have reviewed and understand this entire document and any attachments. I have reviewed it with my attorney (if represented). I have answered all questions truthfully and either I or my attorney have checked the boxes. I am asking the court to accept my plea and find me guilty.

_____   _____
Signature of Defendant   Date

Attorney's Statement
I am the attorney for the defendant. I have discussed this document and any attachments with the defendant. I believe the defendant understands it and the plea agreement. The defendant is making this plea freely, voluntarily, and intelligently. I saw the defendant sign and date this document.

_____   _____
Signature of Attorney   Date

CR-277, 11/99 Plea Questionnaire/Waiver of Rights   §971.08, Wisconsin Statutes.
This form shall not be modified. It may be supplemented with additional material.
Page 2 of 2

FIGURE 13.2   CONTINUED

for the plea—to each charge; in other words, the defendant, in open court, must admit to the conduct central to the criminality of crimes charged unless permission has been granted for the defendant to enter an *Alford* plea. In some jurisdictions, this hearing is therefore called an **allocution hearing**. This public disclosure allows defendants and attorneys to correct any misunderstandings.

Indeed, the Federal Rules of Criminal Procedure make this practice mandatory in federal courts.

To ensure fairness in negotiations between defense and prosecution, the law now gives defendants a limited right to withdraw a guilty plea. In *Santobello v. New York* (1971), Chief Justice Warren Burger wrote, "When a plea rests in any significant degree on a promise or agreement of the prosecutor, so that it can be said to be a part of the inducement or consideration, such promise must be fulfilled." Subsequent decisions likewise held that defendants must live up to their end of the plea agreement (*Ricketts v. Adamson* 1987).

COURTS, CONTROVERSY, AND THE ADMINISTRATION OF JUSTICE

Who Benefits from Plea Bargaining?

Some people within the court system are concerned that plea bargaining reduces the courthouse to a place where guilt or innocence is negotiated in the same way as one might haggle over the price of copper jugs at a Turkish bazaar (Rubin 1976). Primarily, though, opposition to plea bargaining reflects different ideological preferences. What is particularly interesting is that civil libertarians as well as spokespersons for law and order see plea bargaining as a danger, but often for different reasons.

Does Plea Bargaining Sacrifice Defendants' Rights?

Supporters of the values of the due process model are concerned that plea bargaining undercuts the protections afforded individuals, may lead to the conviction of innocent defendants, and produces few tangible benefits for defendants. This view is aptly expressed by the leading academic critic of plea bargaining, law professor Albert Alschuler:

"Today's guilty plea system leads even able, conscientious, and highly motivated attorneys to make decisions that are not really in their clients' interests" (1975, p. 1180).

A prime concern of due process adherents is that a criminal court process geared to produce guilty pleas negates the fundamental protection of the adversary system—a public trial in which the defendant is presumed innocent—because plea bargaining discourages trials by imposing a penalty on those who may lose at trial. They therefore advocate abolishing bargaining and increasing the number of trials. However, such a position ignores the reality of criminal courts: In most cases, the participants do not substantially disagree over the facts. Moreover, civil libertarian critics look to the jury as the proper forum for separating guilt from innocence. Yet, experienced trial attorneys often have grave doubts about such an approach. In the words of a Los Angeles public defender: "If you've got an

---

LAW IN CONTROVERSY: ABOLISHING PLEA BARGAINING

Chief Justice Burger's opinion in *Santobello* supports plea bargaining because it contributes to the efficiency of the criminal justice processes. But some people find justifying plea bargaining merely on the basis of expediency to be unconvincing. What of justice? some legitimately ask. (See Courts, Controversy, and the Administration of Justice: Who Benefits from Plea Bargaining?)

Doubts about plea bargaining have resulted in attempts in some jurisdictions to abolish or reform the practice. Such efforts conform to one of the most controversial recommendations of the National Advisory Commission on Criminal Justice Standards and Goals (1973)—abolishing plea bargaining altogether. This recommendation was prompted by the commission's view that plea bargaining produces undue leniency. The main weakness of the commission's recommendation

to abolish plea bargaining is that it failed to recognize the importance of law in action. The commission seemed preoccupied with an idealized criminal law that is clear and precise and that does not have to accommodate messy disagreements.

Faced with mounting public criticism and professional concern, prosecutors and judges in a number of American communities have altered traditional plea-bargaining practices. Claims that plea bargaining has been abolished or that major reforms have been instituted require critical analysis. As a result of a growing number of studies of such efforts, some important areas of interest can be highlighted.

ARE THE CHANGES IMPLEMENTED?

In analyzing the impact of changes in plea-bargaining practices, a basic question is whether the changes were indeed implemented. Written policy changes do not always alter the behavior of court actors. For example, some efforts to reform plea

exceptional case—one which is weak and there's a good chance that the defendant may be innocent—then you don't want to take it before a jury because you never know what they'll do" (Mather 1974a, p. 202).

Do the Guilty Benefit?

If advocates of due process are worried that plea bargaining jeopardizes the rights of the individual, the backers of the crime control model express the opposite concern. They believe that plea bargaining allows defendants to avoid conviction for crimes they actually committed, results in lenient sentences, and in general gives criminal wrongdoers the impression that the courts and the law are easily manipulated. In the words of the Pima County, Arizona, prosecutor, "Plea bargains send the wrong message. When criminal offenders are permitted to plead guilty to lesser charges with lesser penalties, the credibility of the entire system is corrupted" (LaWall 2001).

It is not a difficult task to single out individual cases in which these law enforcement criticisms of plea bargaining have merit. But the argument obscures too much. In particular, it confuses cause with effect. A bargained agreement on reduced charges, for example, may be the product of initial overcharging, of evidence problems that surface later, or both. Moreover, such criticisms suggest that in plea bargaining, anything goes—the prosecutor and judge will make any deal to dispose of a case. In reality, each court uses a more or less consistent approach to what charge or count reductions are customary, plus a set of sentencing rules of thumb.

Many of the law enforcement criticisms of plea bargaining may be reduced to an overall displeasure with the leniency of the courts. Whether sentences are too harsh or too lenient should be a separate issue from the vehicle for reaching these sentencing dispositions.

What do you think? Does plea bargaining sacrifice the rights of the defendant, or do the guilty benefit?

bargaining met with resistance from defense attorneys and others. As a result, the programs did not have their intended impact and were later dropped (Covey 2008; Nimmer and Krauthaus 1977). A similar pattern was observed in a northern California county. After the grand jury publicly criticized plea bargaining for undue leniency, the prosecutor responded by trying to eliminate plea bargaining. The defense attorneys then began to take more cases to trial. After the state lost 12 out of 16 jury verdicts, the prosecutor quietly returned to the old policies (Carter 1974). Of course, not all efforts at reform are short-lived. In some jurisdictions, efforts at reforming plea bargaining have been successfully implemented (Covey 2008; Heumann and Loftin 1979; Nimmer and Krauthaus 1977).

IS DISCRETION ELIMINATED OR JUST MOVED ELSEWHERE?

Even when programs are successfully implemented, they may not have the impact intended. Discretion in the criminal justice system (see Chapter 5) has been likened to a hydraulic process. Efforts to control discretion at one stage typically result in its displacement to another part of the process. Thus, the result of "abolishing" or "reforming" plea bargaining is often that the activity simply moves elsewhere. Such a hydraulic process occurred in California after the voters approved Proposition 8 in 1982. One of the key provisions of this victim's bill of rights (see Chapter 9) prohibits plea bargaining for 25 of the most serious crimes. The ban applied only to the major trial court, however. Proposition 8 did not abolish plea bargaining but rather relocated it to the lower court, where the proportion of bargained cases increased (McCoy 1984). Indeed, the overall level of plea bargaining increased. Far from helping the victims of crime, the acceleration of plea bargaining prevented both victims and defendants from understanding the reasons for convictions and sentences (McCoy 1993).

Alaska provides another clear example. In that state, the attorney general forbade assistant prosecutors from engaging in plea bargaining or from making sentencing recommendations to the judge. Judges complained that their responsibilities increased dramatically, meaning they had very little opportunity to give sentencing thorough consideration (Rubenstein and White 1979, p. 277). The hydraulic process seems to explain why a later reevaluation of Alaska's plea-bargaining ban found clear evidence of both evolution and decay in the policy. For example, charge bargaining had reemerged in most of the state (Carns and Kruse 1992).

DO OFFSETTING CHANGES OCCUR?

Efforts to abolish or change plea-bargaining practices may produce offsetting changes. This was the conclusion of an excellent in-depth study of a Michigan county (Church 1976). After a law-and-order antidrug campaign, the newly elected prosecuting attorney instituted a strict policy forbidding charge-reduction plea bargaining in drug-selling cases. One result was an increased demand for trials, although it was not as great as some judges feared. But at the same time, outright dismissals because of insufficient evidence increased. Moreover, a much greater percentage of defendants were sentenced as juveniles rather than adults so that they would not have a felony record. Most important, plea bargaining involving defense attorneys and judges continued in drug cases, and the assistant prosecutor's ability to control the disposition of the cases weakened.

Efforts to increase sentence severity by abolishing or constraining plea bargaining are not always successful. When the Coast Guard effectively eliminated plea bargains in special courts-martial, there was no increase in sentence severity (Call, England, and Talarico 1983). In short, attempts to abolish plea bargaining often produce a number of offsetting changes because overall policies fail to consider the reasons for negotiations.

CONCLUSION

Most of the Supreme Court decisions highlighted in this book deal with serious crimes and punishments—quite often murder and the death penalty. Perhaps the Court decided to rule on *Santobello* because the underlying charge was a minor one. After all, establishing new rules for plea bargaining would prove less controversial if the crime was not a violent one. Nonetheless, it is still curious that Burger's opinion states so many negatives about *Santobello*, leaving little doubt that this small-time alleged member of one of New York's crime families was hardly a model citizen. As for Santobello, the man, little else is known. In covering the case, the *New York Times* discussed only the legal issues, not the local man whose name is now enshrined in a major Supreme Court pronouncement.

Plea bargaining vividly illustrates the difference between law on the books and law in action. The rules of criminal procedure, decisions of appellate courts, and theories of the adversary system suggest that the trial is the principal activity of the criminal courts. Instead, plea bargaining is the predominant activity. Bargaining is best understood not as a response to the press of cases but as an adaptation to the realities of the types of cases requiring court disposition. In most cases, little question about the defendant's legal guilt exists. A trial is a costly and sometimes risky method of establishing that guilt, and it cannot wrestle with the most pressing issue: what sentence to impose on the guilty. Finally, through plea bargaining, courthouse officials are able to individualize justice. In short, it is neither necessary nor desirable that every defendant have a trial.

CHAPTER REVIEW

1. Distinguish between the three most common types of plea agreements.

The three most common types of plea agreements are charge bargaining, count bargaining and sentence bargaining. In a charge bargain, the defendant pleads guilty to a less serious charge than the one originally specified. In a count bargain, the defendant pleads guilty to a few of the charges in the indictment or bill or information. In a sentence bargain, the defendant pleads guilty in anticipation of leniency in sentencing.

2. Discuss the three major factors influencing bargaining and discretion.

The three major factors influencing bargaining and discretion are the presumption of factual guilt, the costs and risks of trial to all parties, and the question of what sentence to impose upon the guilty.

3. Recognize the importance of *Boykin v. Alabama*.

In *Boykin*, the Court held that a plea of guilty was more than an admission of guilt and also involved the waiver of important constitutional rights. As a result, a defendant must knowingly waive his or her constitutional rights before a plea of guilty is accepted.

4. List the major reason each of the members of the courtroom work group engage in plea bargaining.

Prosecutors engage in plea bargaining because they want to gain convictions, defense attorneys seek leniency for their clients, and judges feel pressures to move cases.

5. Indicate why a few cases go to trial but most defendants plead guilty.

Defendants and their lawyers will opt for a trial if they think the case factually presents a reasonable doubt or if the prison sentence will be high.

6. Explain why adherents of the crime control model of criminal justice oppose plea bargaining for different reasons from those of adherents of the due process model of criminal justice.

Adherents of the crime control model of criminal justice oppose plea bargaining because they believe defendants get off too lightly. On the other hand, adherents of the due process model of criminal justice oppose plea bargaining because they believe that innocent defendants might be forced to plead guilty to a crime they did not commit.

CRITICAL THINKING QUESTIONS

1 Should a defendant be allowed to plead guilty without fully admitting guilt? Would you limit *Alford* pleas to situations in which the defendant wishes to avoid the death penalty? Would you allow white-collar defendants to enter *Alford* pleas? Some federal judges will not because they perceive that high-ranking corporate officials want to end the criminal cases without accepting full responsibility for their actions.

2 What types of plea agreements were involved in *Santobello*—charge, count, or sentence? Was the nature of the agreement implicit or explicit? How would you characterize the working relationship between defense and prosecution in *Santobello*?

3 Do defendants benefit from plea bargaining in terms of lower sentences, or is plea bargaining largely a shell game in which defendants are manipulated to think they are getting a good deal?

KEY TERMS

allocute/allocution hearing 326	charge bargaining 315	plea bargaining 314
Boykin form 323	count bargaining 316	plea on the nose 316
	nolo contendere 323	sentence bargaining 316

WEB RESOURCES

Go to the America's Courts and the Criminal Justice System companion website at

www.cengage.com/criminaljustice/neubauer

where you will find more resources to help you study.
Resources include web exercises, quizzing, and flash cards.

FOR FURTHER READING

Brown, Mary, and Stevan E. Bunnell. "Negotiating Justice: Prosecutorial Perspectives on Federal Plea Bargaining in the District of Columbia." *American Criminal Law Review* 43: 1063–1094, 2006.

Fisher, George. *Plea Bargaining's Triumph: A History of Plea Bargaining in America*. Stanford, CA: Stanford University Press, 2003.

McCoy, Candace. *Politics and Plea Bargaining: Victim's Rights in California*. Philadelphia: University of Pennsylvania Press, 1993.

Nardulli, Peter, James Eisenstein, and Roy Flemming. *The Tenor of Justice: Criminal Courts and the Guilty Plea Process*. Champaign: University of Illinois Press, 1988.

Nasheri, Hedieh. *Betrayal of Due Process: A Comparative Assessment of Plea Bargaining in the United States and Canada*. Lanham, MD: University Press of America, 1998.

Vogel, Mary. *Coercion to Compromise: Plea Bargaining, the Courts, and the Making of Political Authority*. New York: Oxford University Press, 2006.

Wright, Ronald, and Marc Miller. "The Screening/Bargaining Tradeoff." *Stanford Law Review* 55: 29–118, 2002.

14

TRIALS AND JURIES

© Lou Dematteis/Reuters/CORBIS

Jurors hold a press conference in the Redwood City, California, courtroom, where they found Scott Peterson guilty of murdering his pregnant, 27-year-old wife and their unborn son. How jurors reach decisions has fascinated lawyers for years, and here, the jury provides some insight into their thought process. After 12 hours of deliberations, they unanimously sentenced Peterson to death, ending one of the most sensational trials in recent memory.

CHAPTER OUTLINE

LEARNING OBJECTIVES

After reading this chapter, you should be able to:

1. Trace the history of trials by jury.

2. **Analyze the scope of the right to a trial by jury in a criminal case.**

3. Evaluate the impact of differences in jury size and unanimity requirements.

4. **Explain how a jury is summoned and selected, including the constitutional limitations on these processes.**

5. Discuss the function of jury consultants in the process of scientific jury selection.

6. **Distinguish between the presumptions that apply at the start of trials and the burdens of proof applicable to overcoming them.**

7. Summarize the basic rules of evidence concerning trustworthiness and relevance of evidence.

8. **Analyze how special limitations on expert witnesses affect the litigation of criminal cases, especially with regard to leading types of forensic evidence.**

9. Identify the steps in a criminal trial.

10. **Describe the effects and implications of pretrial publicity and the solutions that courts use to prevent those effects from influencing a criminal trial.**

"Why Isn't Sam Sheppard in Jail?" screamed the headline of a front-page editorial in a prominent Cleveland newspaper. For weeks, vivid headlines like these made it clear that the press thought the police were not pressing hard enough in arresting Dr. Samuel Sheppard—a socially prominent physician—for the brutal murder of his wife. After conviction, Sheppard served 12 years in prison before the Supreme Court reversed the conviction, likening the trial to a "Roman holiday." In holding that prejudicial pretrial publicity denied Sheppard the right to a fair and impartial trial, the Court set off a long and often heated battle over where freedom of the press ends and the right to a fair trial begins.

Trials attract more attention than any other step of the judicial process. The national media provide detailed accounts of the trials of celebrities like Sam Sheppard and Scott Peterson. The local media offer extensive coverage of the trials of local notables, brazen murderers, and the like. Books, movies, and television use courtroom encounters to entertain. The importance of trials, however, extends far beyond the considerable public attention lavished on them. They are central to the entire scheme of Anglo-American law. Trials provide the ultimate forum for vindicating the innocence of the accused or the liability of the defendant. For this reason, the right to be tried by a jury of one's peers is guaranteed in several places in the Constitution.

Given the marked public interest in trials, as well as their centrality to American law, we would expect trials to be the prime ingredient in the criminal court process. They are not. Trials are relatively rare events. As Chapter 13 established, roughly 95 percent of all felony convictions result from guilty pleas. In a fundamental sense, then, a trial represents a deviant case. But at the same time, the few cases that are tried have a major impact on the operations of the entire criminal justice system. Trials are the balance wheel of the process, determining how members of the courtroom work group bargain cases.

History of Trial by Jury

The primary purpose of the jury is to prevent oppression by the government and provide the accused a "safeguard against the corrupt or overzealous prosecutor and against the compliant, biased, or eccentric judge" (*Williams v. Florida* 1970). Ideally, juries are made up of fair-minded citizens who represent a cross section of the local community. Once selected, their role is to judge the facts of the case. During trial, the judge rules on questions of law, but the jury decides the weight of the evidence and the credibility to give to the testimony of witnesses.

Trial juries are also called **petit juries**, to differentiate them from grand juries. The jury system represents a commitment to the role of laypeople in the administration of justice. The views and actions of judges and lawyers are constrained by a group of average citizens who are amateurs in the ways of the law (Jonakait 2006; Kalven and Zeisel 1966).

ENGLISH ROOTS

The trial by jury has roots deep in Western history. Used in Athens five or six centuries before the birth of Christ, juries were later used by the Romans. They reappeared in France during the 9th century and were transferred to England from there. The concept of the jury functioning as an impartial fact-finding body was first formalized in the Magna Carta of 1215, when English noblemen forced the king to recognize limits on the power of the Crown.

> No Freeman shall be taken or imprisoned, or be disseized of his Freehold, or Liberties, or free Customs, or be outlawed, or exiled or otherwise destroyed, nor will we pass upon him nor condemn him but by lawful judgment of his peers or by Law of the Land.

This protection applied only to nobility ("Freeman"). Its extension to the average citizen occurred several centuries later. Thus, in the centuries after the Magna Carta, the legal status of the jury continued to evolve. Early English juries often functioned more like modern-day grand juries. Only later did they become impartial bodies, selected from citizens who knew nothing of the alleged event.

COLONIAL DEVELOPMENTS

By the time the U.S. Constitution was written, jury trials in criminal cases had been in existence in England for several centuries. This legal principle was transferred to the American colonies and later written into the Constitution. The pivotal role that the right to trial by jury plays in American law is underscored by the number of times it is mentioned in the Constitution.

Article III, Section 2, provides that "the trial of all crimes, except cases of impeachment shall be by jury and such trial shall be held in the state where the said crimes shall have been committed." This section not only guarantees the right to a trial by jury to persons accused by the national government of a crime but also specifies that such trials shall be held near the place of the offense. This prevents the government from harassing defendants by trying them far from home.

The Sixth Amendment guarantees that "in all criminal prosecutions, the accused shall enjoy the right to a speedy and public trial, by an impartial jury." The requirement of a public trial prohibits secret trials, a device commonly used by dictators to silence their opponents.

The Seventh Amendment provides: "In suits at common law … the right to trial by jury shall be preserved." This provision is a historical testament to the fact that the framers of the Constitution greatly distrusted the judges of the day.

Law on the Books: The Constitution and Trial by Jury

Throughout most of our nation's history, the three broad constitutional provisions dealing with trial by jury had little applicability in state courts. The

U.S. Constitution applied only to trials in federal courts. These practices changed dramatically, however, when the Supreme Court ruled that the jury provisions of the Sixth Amendment applied to state as well as federal courts (*Duncan v. Louisiana* 1968). (Technically, the Sixth Amendment was incorporated into the due process clause of the Fourteenth Amendment, which restricts state power.) Subsequent decisions grappled with the problem of defining the precise meaning of the right to trial by jury. (Exhibit 14.1 summarizes key decisions.) The most important issues concerned the scope of the right to a jury trial, the size of the jury, and unanimous versus nonunanimous verdicts.

Scope of the Right to a Trial by Jury

Although juries are considered "fundamental to the American scheme of justice" (*Duncan v. Louisiana* 1968), not all persons accused of violating the

Exhibit 14.1
KEY DEVELOPMENTS CONCERNING THE RIGHT TO TRIAL BY JURY

Magna Carta	1215	English noblemen have the right to a trial by a jury of peers.
U.S. Constitution Article III, Section 2	1789	The trial of all crimes shall be by jury and shall be held in the state where the crime was allegedly committed.
Sixth Amendment	1791	"In all criminal prosecutions, the accused shall enjoy the right to a speedy and public trial, by an impartial jury."
Seventh Amendment	1791	Right to a trial by a jury in civil suits under common law.
Griffin v. California	1965	The privilege against self-incrimination prohibits the prosecutor from commenting on the defendant's failure to testify during trial.
Sheppard v. Maxwell	1966	The defendant was denied a fair trial because of prejudicial pretrial publicity.
Duncan v. Louisiana	1968	The due process clause of the Fourteenth Amendment incorporates the Sixth Amendment's right to a jury trial.
Baldwin v. New York	1970	Defendants accused of petty offenses do not have the right to be tried by a jury of their peers.
Williams v. Florida	1970	State juries are not required by the U.S. Constitution to consist of 12 members.

Exhibit 14.1

CONTINUED

Johnson v. Louisiana	1972	Federal criminal juries must be unanimous.
Apodaca v. Oregon	1972	There is no federal requirement that state juries must be unanimous.
Taylor v. Louisiana	1975	Women cannot be excluded from juries.
Ballew v. Georgia	1978	Six is the minimum number for a jury.
Burch v. Louisiana	1979	Six-member criminal juries must be unanimous.
Chandler v. Florida	1981	The right to a fair trial is not violated by electronic media and still photographic coverage of public judicial proceedings.
Batson v. Kentucky	1986	If a prosecutor uses peremptory challenges to exclude potential jurors solely on account of their race, the prosecutor must explain his or her actions.
Powers v. Ohio	1991	A criminal defendant may object to race-based exclusions of jurors through peremptory challenges whether or not the defendant and the excluded jurors share the same race.
Georgia v. McCollum	1992	The defense is prohibited from excluding jurors based on race.
Daubert v. Merrell Dow	1993	The trial judge must ensure that any and all scientific evidence is not only relevant but reliable.
J.E.B. Petitioner v. Alabama	1994	Lawyers may not exclude potential jurors from a trial because of their gender.
Victor v. Nebraska	1994	"Substantial doubt" is not an overstatement of reasonable doubt.
United States v. Scheffer	1998	Doubts about the accuracy of lie detector tests justifies banning their use in court.
Kumho Tire v. Carmichael	1999	*Daubert* standards for scientific testimony apply to nonscientific testimony as well.
Apprendi v. New Jersey	2000	Any fact that increases the penalty for a crime beyond the prescribed statutory maximum must be submitted to a jury.
Portuondo v. Agard	2000	Prosecutors can tell jurors that the defendant's presence during trial helps them tailor their testimony to fit the evidence.
Ring v. Arizona	2002	It is unconstitutional to have a judge, rather than a jury, decide the critical sentencing issues in death penalty cases.

Exhibit 14.1		
CONTINUED		
Blakely v. Washington	2004	Under the Sixth Amendment, juries, not judges, have the power to make a finding of guilty beyond a reasonable doubt for facts used in state sentencing guidelines.
U.S. v. Booker	2005	The first part of the opinion struck down federal sentencing guidelines as unconstitutional for the reasons expressed in *Blakely v. Washington*. The second part of the opinion allows federal judges to continue to use federal sentencing guidelines as advisory.
Snyder v. Louisiana	2009	Murder conviction in a death penalty case was overturned because judge sat idly by as prosecutors dismissed all the blacks in the jury pool.

criminal law are entitled to a trial by jury. Youths prosecuted as juvenile offenders have no right to have their cases heard by a jury (*McKeiver v. Pennsylvania* 1971). Similarly, adult offenders charged with **petty offenses** enjoy no right to be tried by a jury of their peers. The Sixth Amendment covers only adults charged with serious offenses. In this context, "no offense can be deemed 'petty' for the purposes of the right to trial by jury where imprisonment for more than six months is authorized" (*Baldwin v. New York* 1970). Some state constitutions, however, guarantee a jury trial to anyone facing any criminal charge whatsoever, including traffic offenses.

Some cases are tried without a jury, termed a **bench trial**. State laws vary considerably on when the prosecution and/or defense may waive a trial by jury.

JURY SIZE

During the 14th century, the size of English juries became fixed at 12. Although some colonies experimented with smaller juries in less important trials, the number 12 was universally accepted by the time of the American Revolution. However, in *Williams v. Florida* (1970), the Supreme Court declared that the number 12 was a "historical accident, wholly without significance except to mystics," and therefore not required by the Constitution. The Court concluded that the six-person jury used in Florida in noncapital cases was large enough to promote group deliberations and to provide a fair possibility of obtaining a representative cross section of the community. Attempts to use juries with fewer than six members were struck down by *Ballew v. Georgia* (1978). The defendant's misdemeanor conviction by a five-member jury was reversed because "the purpose and functioning of the jury in a criminal trial is seriously impaired, and to a constitutional degree, by a reduction in size to below six members."

As Exhibit 14.2, illustrates, many states have specifically authorized juries of fewer than 12 jurors, but most allow these smaller juries only in misdemeanor cases. In federal courts, defendants are entitled to a 12-person jury unless the parties agree in writing to a smaller jury, but 6-member juries in federal civil cases are quite common. There has been a good deal of debate over whether small juries provide the defendant with a fair trial (Landsman 2005; McCord 2005; Saks 1996). The debate stems from the fact that social science has produced inconsistent findings on the differences in the conduct of deliberations between 6- and 12-person juries. Some studies have found very few differences (Pabst 1973; Roper 1979), while others have reported significant differences (Hastie, Penrod, and Pennington 1983; Saks and Marti 1997). In a review of the empirical literature on juries, Smith and Saks (2008) reported that:

Exhibit 14.2

STATE PROVISIONS ON THE SIZE OF CRIMINAL JURIES

12-Member Juries Required in Felony Cases	Alabama, Arkansas,[a] California, Colorado, Delaware, District of Columbia, Georgia, Hawaii, Idaho, Illinois, Iowa, Kansas, Kentucky, Maine, Michigan, Minnesota, Mississippi, Missouri, Montana, Nebraska, Nevada, New Hampshire, New Jersey,[a] New Mexico, New York, North Carolina, North Dakota, Ohio, Oklahoma, Oregon, Puerto Rico, Rhode Island, South Carolina, South Dakota, Tennessee, Texas, Vermont, Virginia, West Virginia, Wisconsin, Wyoming.
12-Member Juries Required in Misdemeanor Cases	Alabama, Arkansas,[a] California,[a] Delaware, District of Columbia, Hawaii,[a] Illinois, Maine, New Jersey,[a] Pennsylvania, Puerto Rico, Rhode Island, South Dakota, Tennessee, Vermont
Juries Fewer than 12 Authorized for Felony Cases	Arizona, Connecticut,[b] Florida,[c] Indiana, Louisiana,[c] Massachusetts, Missouri, North Carolina, Pennsylvania,[a] Utah,[c] Washington,[a]
Juries Fewer than 12 Authorized for Misdemeanor Cases	Alaska, Arizona, Colorado, Florida, Georgia, Idaho, Indiana, Iowa, Kansas, Kentucky, Louisiana, Massachusetts, Michigan, Minnesota, Mississippi, Montana, Nebraska, Nevada, New Hampshire, New Mexico, New York, North Dakota, Ohio, Oklahoma, Utah, Oregon, Pennsylvania,[a] South Carolina, Texas, Virginia, Washington, West Virginia, Wisconsin, Wyoming.

[a]The parties may stipulate to a jury that consists of fewer than 12 jurors.
[b]12-person juries are used in death penalty cases unless the defendant elects to use a smaller jury.
[c]12-person juries must be used in death-penalty cases.

ADAPTED FROM: David B. Rottman and Shauna M. Strickland. 2006. *State Court Organization, 2004* (Table 42). Washington, DC: Bureau of Justice Statistics. Available online at http://www.ojp.usdoj.gov/bjs/pub/pdf/sco04.pdf

- racial, ethnic, religious, and sexual minorities are represented in a smaller percentage of 6-person as compared to 12-person juries
- larger juries deliberate longer than smaller juries
- talking time is more evenly divided among members of smaller juries, allowing for less domination by a strong voice or two as compared with larger juries
- members of larger juries more accurately recall evidence both during deliberation and in individual recall afterward
- 12-person juries recall more probative information and rely less than 6-person juries on evaluative statements and nonprobative evidence
- in the civil context, 6-person juries show more variability in their awards and, on average, give larger awards than 12-person juries
- jurors report more satisfaction in the deliberation process with 12-person juries than with smaller ones

In light of these findings, it is not surprising to learn that hung juries—juries unable to reach a unanimous verdict—occur more frequently with 12-person juries than 6-person juries (Hannaford-Agor et al. 2002; Kalven and Zeisel 1966). However, many other factors affect whether a jury hangs: "weak evidence; police credibility problems…; juror concerns about fairness; case complexity; and a dysfunctional deliberation process—a catch-all phrase indicating poor interpersonal interactions among the jurors (Hannaford-Agor et al. 2002, p. 85). Yet, the quest to reduce hung juries has resulted in some jurisdictions authorizing a controversial change in the way juries have historically functioned: nonunanimous verdicts.

UNANIMITY

The requirement that a jury reach a unanimous decision became a firm rule in England during the 14th century. An agreement by all of the jurors seemed to legitimize the verdict, giving the community a sense that the conclusion must be correct. However, the Supreme Court altered this assumption in a pair of 1972 decisions. It held that verdicts in federal criminal trials must be unanimous, but it affirmed state courts' findings of guilty by votes of 9 to 3 and 10 to 2 (*Johnson v. Louisiana* 1972; *Apodaca v. Oregon* 1972). Most state constitutions specifically require unanimous verdicts in criminal trials; only five states (Louisiana, Montana, Oregon, Oklahoma, and Texas) permit nonunanimous criminal verdicts. Of these, only Louisiana and Oregon permit non-unanimous verdicts in serious felony cases. In any case, six-member juries must be unanimous (*Burch v. Louisiana* 1979).

Opponents of nonunanimous verdicts argue that the Burger Court misread the history of the jury, with the result that a basic constitutional right is being sacrificed. They point out that proof beyond a reasonable doubt has not been shown if only some of the jurors vote to convict. These concerns receive some empirical support (Zeisel 1982). A carefully controlled experiment compared unanimous with nonunanimous juries and found that nonunanimous juries tend to be hung less often, deliberate less thoroughly, and result in less satisfied jurors (Hastie, Penrod, and Pennington 1983; see also, Smith and Saks 2008). These findings may be explained by the fact that the deliberation process appears to differ significantly depending on whether a unanimous or majority verdict is permitted.

When juries were not required to be unanimous, they tended to be more verdict driven. That is, they were more likely to take the first formal ballot during the first ten minutes of deliberation and to vote often until they produced a verdict. In contrast, juries that heard the same case but were required to reach a unanimous verdict tended to delay their first vote and discussed the evidence more thoroughly. These evidence-driven juries rated their deliberations as more serious and thorough. (Diamond, Rose, and Murphy 2006, p. 208).

LAW ON THE BOOKS: SELECTING A FAIR AND UNBIASED JURY

Before the first word of testimony, trials pass through the critical stage of jury selection. Many lawyers believe that trials are won or lost on the basis of which jurors are selected. Juries are chosen in a process that combines random selection with deliberate choice.

Jury selection occurs in three stages: compiling a master list, summoning the *venire*, and conducting *voir dire*. Whether these processes actually produce fair and impartial juries has been the subject of much concern.

MASTER JURY LIST

Juries are supposed to be made up of fair-minded laypeople, representatives of the community in which the defendant allegedly committed the crime. Therefore, the first step in jury selection is the development of procedures that will produce a representative cross section of the community. These sentiments are reflected in the Federal Jury Selection and Service Act of 1968, which was designed to ensure that "no citizen shall be excluded from service as a grand or petit juror in the district courts of the United States on account of race, color, religion, sex, national origin, or economic status." This act was prompted by evidence that selection of federal juries was systematically biased. Similar concerns have been expressed about jury selection at the state level (Fukurai, Butler, and Krooth 1991; Re 2007).

The first step in jury selection is the compilation of a **master jury list**. Voter registration lists are the most frequently used source for assembling this list (sometimes called a "jury wheel" or "master wheel"). Voter lists have major advantages: They are readily available, frequently updated, and collected in districts within judicial boundaries. However, basing the master jury list on voter registration tends to exclude the poor, the young, racial minorities, and the less educated (Kairys, Kadane, and Lehorsky 1977; Re 2007). Because of these limitations, many jurisdictions use other sources—telephone directories, utility customer lists, or driver's license lists—in drawing up the master list. The use of multiple sources achieves a better cross section of the community on jury panels, although it sometimes creates problems for jury administrators, who have to deal with a high number of duplicates when multiple sources are merged (Randall and Woods 2008).

Jury panels can be challenged if master jury roles from which the venire was called fail to include racial or other minorities. The Supreme Court has ruled that master jury lists must reflect a representative and impartial cross section of the community (*Duren v. Missouri* 1979). This does not mean, however, that either the venire or the actual petit jury must be "a perfect mirror of the community or accurately reflected the proportionate strength of every identifiable group" (*Swain v. Alabama* 1965, p. 208). Rather, the requirement of a representative cross section of the community applies only to jury pools (*Holland v. Illinois* 1990).

VENIRE

The second step in jury selection is the drawing of the **venire** (or jury pool). Periodically, the clerk of court or jury commissioner determines how many jurors are needed for a given time. A sufficient number of names is then randomly selected from the master jury list and a **summons** is issued—a court order commanding these citizens to appear at the courthouse for jury duty. Even though people who fail to obey a jury summons can be fined or imprisoned, estimates place the nonresponse rate to jury summonses between 20 percent in some jurisdictions to as high as 66 percent in others (Randal and Woods 2008; Schwartz, Behrens, and Silverman 2003).

Not all those summoned will actually serve on the venire. Virtually all states have laws that require jurors to be citizens of the United States, residents of the locality, of a certain minimum age, and able to understand English. Most states also disqualify people who, as a result of mental illness, are not competent to adjudicate a case. Thirty-one states also disqualify convicted felons, although that practice has been increasingly criticized as a type of disenfranchisement that disproportionately affects racial and ethnic minorities (Binnall 2008; Kalt 2003; Wheelock 2005). Persons who fail to meet these requirements are eliminated from the venire. Others will be excused because of **statutory exemptions**. The identities of those

exempted from jury duty by statute vary greatly. Historically, those statutorily excluded included government officials (especially police and firefighters); medical personnel (including paramedics, physicians, nurses, and others); ministers/clergy; educators; lawyers; and full-time students. Today, however, jurisdictions have increasingly been eliminating statutory exemptions for people other than police, firefighters, and emergency medical personnel (Mushlin 2007).

The people who show up when summoned to court and are eligible to serve on a jury usually check in with a jury administrator (or other clerk of the court staff person) who then directs them to a specific courtroom. The petit jury for a particular trial will be selected from this pool of people. The people in this jury pool, however, may be excused from serving on a jury if they convince the judge that jury duty would entail an undue hardship. People try to get excused quite frequently. As van Dyke observed in 1977, although serving on a jury is "a right and privilege of citizenship, most people consider it a nuisance" and request to be excused (p. 111). The sentiment persists today (Losh and Boatright 2002; Sinclair, Behrens, and Silverman 2003).

VOIR DIRE

The final step in jury selection is the **voir dire** (French legal term for "to speak the truth"), which involves the preliminary examination of a prospective juror in order to determine his or her qualifications to serve as a juror. The prospective jurors are questioned by the attorneys, the judge, or both about their backgrounds, familiarity with persons involved in the case (defendant, witness, or lawyer), attitudes about certain facts that may arise during trial, and any other matters that may reflect on their willingness and ability to judge the case fairly and impartially.

The Accuracy of Voir Dire

For hundreds of years, the law has considered voir dire to be an inexpensive and efficient way to select a fair and impartial jury. The process, however, may not be a particularly accurate way to detect bias. Although the venire is sworn under oath to answer truthfully, they do not always do so. Sometimes potential jurors refuse to admit to facts or thoughts they find embarrassing to share, such as prior criminal victimization (Hannaford 2001).

Other reasons may be less personal, but still not be something that potential jurors want to admit in court under oath, such as a predisposition to believe the accused is guilty. Even when venirepersons are not deliberately concealing information, they may unconsciously conceal personal biases or prejudices during voir dire in an attempt to please the court and the attorneys by being "good" jurors (Borgida and Fiske 2008).

Excusing Jurors through Voir Dire

If a potential juror's responses during questioning (whether honest or not) suggests that the person cannot fairly judge the case, the juror may be **challenged for cause** by either the defense or the prosecution. Both sides have an unlimited number of challenges for cause. The presiding judge rules on challenge and, if it is sustained, the juror is excused. Strikes for cause generally fall into one of two categories: principal challenges and fact-partial challenges. *Principal challenges* involve strikes of potential jurors because they have some relationship to one of the "principals" or participants in the case. They are presumed to be partial on account of this relationship. *Fact-partial challenges* involve strikes of potential jurors because the subject matter of the dispute presents issues on which the potential juror is biased, prejudiced, or predisposed to a particular outcome because of their belief system or experiences.

Peremptory challenges are the second method used by the prosecution and the defense in influencing who will sit on the jury. Each side has a limited number of peremptory challenges that can be used to exclude a juror. Originally, these challenges were designed and used for a curative purpose—to correct the mistake of a judge for failing to strike a juror for cause. While they are still used in that manner today, they are primarily used to exclude people that the lawyers believe will be hostile to their side of the case. In other words, based on hunches, prejudice, knowledge of psychology, or pseudoscience, attorneys use peremptory strikes to eliminate the jurors they feel might not vote for their side without having to give a reason.

Attorneys traditionally enjoyed unrestricted freedom to exercise peremptory challenges. But in *Batson v. Kentucky* (1986), the Court restricted the ability of prosecutors who used peremptory challenges to keep African-Americans off the jury in any case involving an African-American

defendant. If a prosecutor uses peremptory challenges to exclude potential jurors solely on account of their race, the prosecutor must explain his or her actions and may be ordered to change tactics. And in a move backed by prosecutors, the Court held that the defense is also prohibited from excluding jurors based on race (*Georgia v. McCollum* 1992). Most recently, the Supreme Court has ordered new trials for several death row inmates because of racial bias during jury selection (*Miller-El v. Dretke* 2005; *Johnson v. California* 2005; *Snyder v. Louisiana* 2008).

The Court extended *Batson* to cover gender jury bias, holding that lawyers may not exclude potential jurors from a trial because of their sex (*J.E.B. Petitioner v. Alabama* 1994). The principle of nondiscrimination at the core of *Batson* and *J.E.B.* has not yet been extended by the Supreme Court to other categories, such as ethnicity, religion, or sexual orientation. But some lower federal courts have done so on their own. For example, the U.S. Court of Appeals of the Second Circuit upheld the application of *Batson* to strikes against Italian-Americans (*United States v. Biaggi* 1988). In addition, some states have enacted statutes to limit peremptory challenges on such bases.

SERVING ON A JURY

Every year, thousands of Americans are called to serve as jurors. Unfortunately, many jurors experience great frustration in the process. They are made to wait hours in barren courthouse rooms; the compensation is minimal, and not all employers pay for the time lost from work; and some potential jurors are apprehensive about criminals and courthouses.

In spite of these hardships, most citizens who actually serve on a jury express overall satisfaction with their jury service, viewing their experience as a precious opportunity of citizenship that generally bolstered their confidence in fellow citizens and public institutions (Gastil et al. 2008; Pabst 1973). Just as important, there is every indication that jurors take their job seriously.

Considerable attention is being devoted to reducing the inconvenience of jury duty. Courts in all states use a juror call-in system. In these jurisdictions, jurors can dial a number to learn whether their attendance is needed on a particular day during their term of service. In addition, an increasing number of courts are reducing the number of days a person remains in the jury pool. Traditionally, jurors were asked to serve for a full 30 days. Although only a few jurors were needed for a particular day, the entire pool had to be present in the courthouse each and every working day. Increasingly, however, jurors are asked to serve for only a few days. An approach known as the one-day/one-trial jury system requires each juror to serve either for one day or for the duration of one trial. The person is then exempt from jury duty for a year or more The one-day/one-trial jury system is much more efficient than older practices not only because it spares many citizens the inconvenience of waiting in courthouses with no trials to hear, but also because it reduces constraints on judicial resources (Litras and Golmant 2006; Sinclair, Behrens, and Silverman 2003).

LAW IN ACTION: CHOOSING A JURY BIASED IN YOUR FAVOR

The National Advisory Commission (1973) has succinctly summarized the official—that is to say, the law on the books—purpose of jury selection as follows: "A defendant is entitled to an unbiased jury; he is not entitled to a jury biased in his favor" (p. 99). Members of the courtroom work group are reluctant to formally question this pious wisdom, but informally their actions are strikingly different. Particularly through selective use of peremptory challenges, lawyers for both prosecution and defense seek jurors predisposed to their side. This is the major reason why in some areas the voir dire has become a time-consuming process. Through educating jurors, trial lawyers seek decision makers who are comfortable with their approach. Through hiring jury consultants, trial lawyers aggressively seek to identify jurors who will be biased in their favor.

EDUCATING JURORS

Attorneys use voir dire for purposes other than eliminating bias. They use the questioning of jurors to establish credibility and rapport with the panel, to educate and sell prospective jurors on their respective theories of the case, and to either highlight or neutralize potential problem areas in the case (Voss 2005). This, in turn, gives lawyers the opportunity to influence jurors' attitudes and perhaps later their vote.

JURY CONSULTANTS

In recent years, jury selection has taken a scientific turn. Rather than relying on personal hunch, attorneys in a few highly publicized cases have employed social scientists to aid them in a more intelligent, systematic use of the voir dire that has come to be called "scientific jury selection."

As described in great detail by Lieberman and Sales (2006), **scientific jury selection** typically involves a small group of experts from a variety of disciplinary backgrounds, including marketing, communications, sociology, and, most especially, psychology. Teams of such **jury consultants** conduct public opinion polls and employ laypeople to participate in focus groups or mock trials. With polls and focus groups, they test which pieces of evidence, witnesses, and arguments might be most effective in convincing people to vote a particular way. With mock trials, they test their whole case and then debrief the mock jurors on why they voted as they did. These processes allow jury consultants to identify the issues in a case that are most relevant to the case outcome, as well as to formulate profiles of the juror characteristics that are likely to affect the trial outcome. Using the information they gather, the jury consultants then design questionnaires to be administered to the potential jurors in an actual case. Once these questionnaires are compiled, the jury consultants are able to advise the lawyers in a case about which potential jurors they should want on the jury, and those whom they should seek to avoid.

Trial consultants are hired most often by defense attorneys, as opposed to the prosecutors. In reality, the consultants try to deselect jurors who are likely to be adverse to their client. Whether this process actually functions any better than attorneys doing traditional jury selection using "pop psychology" and their gut instincts is still being debated both in the empirical literature and by practitioners. Two things, however, seem clear. First, jury consultants can help attorneys develop trial presentations that are clear and convincing. Second, jury consultants appear to be here to stay.

OVERVIEW OF A TRIAL

Once the jury has been selected and sworn, the trial begins (see Exhibit 14.3). It is a common practice in

Exhibit 14.3

STEPS OF THE PROCESS: TRIALS

	LAW ON THE BOOKS	LAW IN ACTION
Trial	The adversarial process of deciding a case through the presentation of evidence and arguments about the evidence.	Only a handful of felonies and even fewer misdemeanors are decided by trial.
Bench trial	Trial before a judge without a jury.	Defense prefers when the issues are either highly technical or very emotional.
Jury trial	A group of average citizens selected by law and sworn in to look at certain facts and determine the truth.	Introduces public standards of justice into the decision-making process.
Jury selection	Process of selecting a fair and impartial jury.	Each side seeks to select jurors who are biased in its favor.
Master jury list	Potential jurors are selected by chance from a list of potential jurors. The list should reflect a representative cross section of the community.	Selecting only from registered voters means that the poor, the young, and minorities are less likely to be called.
Venire	A group of citizens from which jury members are chosen (jury pool).	Judges vary in their willingness to excuse potential jurors because of hardship.
Voir dire	The process by which prospective jurors are questioned to determine whether there is cause to excuse them from the jury.	Lawyers use questioning to predispose jurors in their favor.
Peremptory challenge	Each side may exclude a set number of jurors without stating a reason.	Both sides use peremptory challenges to select a jury favorable to their side.
Challenge for cause	A judge may dismiss a potential juror if the person cannot be fair and objective.	Rarely granted.
Opening statements	Lawyers discuss what the evidence will show.	Lawyers use to lead the jury to a favorable verdict.
Prosecutor's case-in-chief	The main evidence offered to prove the defendant guilty beyond a reasonable doubt.	Defense suggests that the prosecution has not met its burden of proof.

Exhibit 14.3

CONTINUED

	LAW ON THE BOOKS	LAW IN ACTION
Witness	A person who makes a statement under oath about the events in question.	Through cross-examination, defense undermines the credibility of the witness.
Expert witness	A person possessing special knowledge or experience who is allowed to testify not only about facts but also about the opinions he or she has drawn from a review of the facts.	Some expert witnesses testify only for one side or the other.
Defense's case-in-chief	Evidence that defense may present. Because the defendant is innocent until proven guilty, the defense is not required to present evidence.	Defense may rest without calling witnesses, but jurors expect to hear reasons why they should not convict.
Defendant as witness	The defendant may waive his or her privilege against self-incrimination and testify.	Defense attorneys are reluctant to call the defendant to the stand, particularly if there is a prior conviction.
Rebuttal	Evidence that refutes or contradicts evidence given by the opposing party.	Prosecutor will call witnesses to undermine a defendant's alibi.
Closing arguments	After all the evidence has been presented, each side sums up the evidence and attempts to convince the jury why their side should win.	Many trial attorneys believe that a good closing argument will win the case. Each side attempts to convince the jury why their side should win.
Prosecution	Because the prosecution bears the burden of proof, the prosecutor goes first and last.	The district attorney's first closing argument provides an orderly summary of the evidence.
Defense	Closing argument of the defense highlights the evidence leading to a not-guilty verdict.	Typically stresses that the prosecutor has failed to prove the defendant guilty beyond a reasonable doubt.
Prosecution's rebuttal	Rebuts defense allegations.	Impassioned statement, calling upon jurors to do their duty and convict the guilty.

Exhibit 14.3

CONTINUED

	LAW ON THE BOOKS	LAW IN ACTION
Jury instructions	Explanations by the judge informing the jury of the law applicable to the case.	Legal language difficult for average citizens to follow.
Jury deliberations	Jurors are repeatedly instructed not to talk about the case.	Jurors routinely talk with other jurors about the case.
	Jurors deliberate in private. Jurors select a foreperson and discuss the case.	Higher-status individuals participate more. The first vote is usually decisive.
	Jurors may request further instructions from the judge.	Such requests produce great anxiety among lawyers.
	Jurors take an oath to follow the law as instructed by the judge.	Some juries introduce popular law into the decision-making process.
Verdict	Decision that the defendant is either guilty or not guilty (acquittal).	Juries convict three out of four times. Jury verdicts often reflect a compromise.
Hung jury	Jury is unable to reach a verdict.	Defense attorneys consider a hung jury an important victory.
Postverdict motions	Motions filed by the defense after conviction and before sentencing.	Judge must accept a verdict of not guilty.
Motion for acquittal	Defense argues that the jury could not have reasonably convicted the defendant based on the evidence presented.	Trial judges are very reluctant to second-guess jury verdicts and almost never grant this motion.
Motion for a new trial	Defense argues that the trial judge made mistakes and therefore a new trial should be held.	On very rare occasions, trial judges admit that an error occurred and set aside a jury verdict of guilty.

many courts to select several **alternate jurors**, who will serve if one of the regular jurors must withdraw during the trial.

The trial begins with **opening statements** by both sides, outlining what they believe the evidence in the case will prove. The purpose of an opening statement is to advise the jury of what the attorney intends to prove. Opening statements are not evidence; the attorneys offer the jurors "road maps" to guide them through the case. It is important to note that these road maps must be limited to statements of what the attorneys actually believe will be presented as the trial progresses (*United States v. Dinitz* 1976); an opening statement, therefore, must be rooted in some degree of fact. A detailed and well-organized opening statement presents the jury with a *schema*—a thematic framework through which to view the trial. If done well, opening statements may be case-determinative. Research has repeatedly demonstrated that even though jurors are admonished not to make up their minds until the conclusion of trial after having given fair and impartial consideration to all the evidence, many jurors make a preliminary decision with regard to the outcome of the case after hearing opening statements (Kalven and Zeisel 1966; Spiecker and Worthington 2003).

After opening statements, the prosecutor presents the state's *case-in-chief*, calling witnesses and introducing physical evidence and the like to bolster the prosecution's allegation that the defendant is guilty. Once the prosecutor rests, the defense may choose to present its side of the case to the jury. At times, defense attorneys present a classic defense—self-defense, entrapment, insanity, alibi, frame-up, mistake, and so on. But more often than not, the defense instead seeks to undermine whether the prosecutor did indeed prove the defendant guilty *beyond a reasonable doubt.*

When the defense rests, the prosecution is given a final opportunity to present evidence to rebut claims made by the defense. After the prosecutor presents rebuttal evidence (or elects not to), both lawyers move on to their closing arguments, in which each side tries to persuade the jury to return with a desirable verdict. The judge then instructs the jury on the meaning of the law, and then the jurors deliberate. After the jury reaches a verdict, they return to court, and the jury foreperson reads the verdict pronouncing the defendant guilty or not guilty.

Now that we have provided an overview of the trial process, the remainder of this chapter will walk you through each of the trial phases we introduced here.

THE PROSECUTION PRESENTS ITS CASE

After the opening statements, the prosecution presents its main evidence. How the prosecutor proceeds is affected by three important aspects of the law: legal presumptions, the burdens of proof, and the rules of evidence.

STARTING PRESUMPTIONS

The trier-of-fact must have an evidentiary starting place at the outset of a trial. In a criminal trial, that starting place usually involves two presumptions. A *presumption* is a conclusion or deduction that the law requires the trier-of-fact to make in the absence of evidence to the contrary. Criminal trials start with two presumptions: the presumption of sanity and the presumption of innocence. The **presumption of sanity** requires that all defendants be presumed sane unless sufficient evidence of their insanity is proven. The **presumption of innocence** requires the trier-of-fact to accept that the defendant is innocent unless the prosecution meets its burden to prove that the defendant is guilty beyond a reasonable doubt. This means that the state must prove all elements of the alleged crime(s); the defendant is not required to prove himself or herself innocent. This difference is a fundamental one. A moment's reflection will give an idea of how hard it would be to prove that something did not happen or that a person did not commit an alleged criminal act, for it is very difficult to rule out all possibilities. Therefore, a defendant is cloaked with the legal shield of innocence throughout all pretrial and trial processes.

BURDENS OF PROOF

The concept of **burden of proof** actually encompasses two separate burdens, the burden of production and the burden of persuasion. If a party has the **burden of production** (often referred to as the "burden of going forward"), they must produce some evidence to put facts in issue. The **burden of persuasion** is the obligation of a party to prove a fact (or facts) to a certain level, either beyond a reasonable doubt, by clear and convincing evidence, or by a preponderance of the evidence.

In meeting its burden of persuasion in a criminal case, the prosecution is required to prove the defendant guilty beyond a reasonable doubt. **Reasonable doubt** is a legal yardstick measuring the sufficiency of the evidence. Proof beyond a reasonable doubt is proof that leaves a juror firmly convinced of the defendant's guilt. This burden of proof does not require that the state establish absolute certainty by eliminating all doubt—just reasonable doubt. *Reasonable doubt* is an amorphous term that judges have difficulty fully defining (*Victor v. Nebraska* 1994). In attempting to show the defendant guilty beyond a reasonable doubt, the prosecutor calls witnesses and introduces physical evidence based on the rules of evidence.

EVIDENCE

The state tries to convince the jury to return a guilty verdict by presenting evidence. **Evidence** consists of physical objects, testimony, or other things offered to prove or disprove the existence of a fact. There are several types of evidence that may be direct or circumstantial evidence depending on how the evidence is used at trial.

Differentiating Direct and Circumstantial Evidence

Direct evidence is first-hand evidence that does not require any inferences to be drawn in order to establish a proposition of fact. The best example of direct evidence is eyewitness testimony. One need not draw any inference from a witness's testimony that she saw something. Note, however, that direct evidence does not necessarily establish truth. Witnesses can be mistaken or misleading (Chapter 17).

Circumstantial evidence is indirect evidence. To reach a conclusion, the trier-of-fact would have to reason through the circumstantial evidence and infer the existence of some fact in dispute, such as inferring the defendant killed the victim because the defendant's fingerprints were found on the murder weapon.

Types of Evidence

Evidence can be classified as testimonial evidence, real or physical evidence, scientific evidence, and demonstrative evidence. **Testimonial evidence** is oral testimony given under oath. **Real evidence** (also referred to as "physical evidence") consists of tangible objects such as documents, drug paraphernalia, clothing, and weapons. The scientific examination of real evidence, in a laboratory, for example, yields scientific evidence—the formal results of forensic investigatory and scientific techniques. **Demonstrative evidence** has no evidential value by itself. Rather, it serves as a visual or auditory aid to assist the fact-finder in understanding the evidence. Charts, maps, videos, and courtroom demonstrations are forms of demonstrative evidence.

Rules of Evidence

The presentation of evidence during trial is governed by principles called **rules of evidence**. A trial is an adversarial proceeding in which the rules of evidence resemble the rules of a game, with the judge acting as an impartial umpire. Although they may seem to be a fixed set of legal rules, they are not. Like all other legal principles, they are general propositions that courts must apply to specific instances to advance the trustworthiness and reliability of the evidence used at trial. During such applications, judges use a balancing test, carefully weighing whether the trial would be fairer with or without the piece of evidence in question. Some basics of the rules of evidence are summarized in Exhibit 14.4.

Expert Witnesses

In contrast to lay witnesses, expert witnesses are permitted to give opinions on matters about which they have no personal knowledge. In order to do so, however, they first must be qualified as an expert witness based on their knowledge, skill, experience, training, or education. But even the opinions of properly qualified experts are not admissible unless they meet other standards for admissibility.

For much of the 20th century, the *Frye* test governed the admissibility of scientific testimony. In *Frye v. United States* (1923), a federal appeals court refused to allow an expert to testify about the results of a lie-detector test because the instrument had not gained general acceptance in the scientific community. The purpose behind the *Frye* test was to prevent unfounded scientific principles or conclusions based on such principles from being used at trial. Shortcomings of the *Frye* test, however, caused the drafters of the federal rules of evidence to replace *Frye* with rules that the U.S. Supreme Court fleshed out in *Daubert v. Merrill-Dow Pharmaceuticals, Inc.* (1993).

Daubert established that trial court judges are supposed to act as gatekeepers who have a special obligation to ensure the reliability of scientific evidence. *Daubert* suggested several factors (that are neither exhaustive nor applicable to every case) that might be used in evaluating whether a particular scientific theory, study, or test is both valid and reliable, including whether it:

- is empirically testable and capable of replication
- has been published and/or subjected to peer review

Exhibit 14.4
SUMMARY OF SELECT RULES OF EVIDENCE

Best-evidence rule	The **best-evidence rule** means that to prove the content of a writing, recording, or photograph, the original is generally required since a copy is too easily altered.
Competency to testify	A witness must have personal knowledge of the matter about which he or she is testifying; must be capable of understanding the duty to tell the truth—something he or she is required to do by an oath or affirmation; must be capable of expressing himself or herself so as to be understood by the jury either directly or through an interpreter. People who cannot differentiate between truth and nontruth, such as young children and those who are affected by certain types of serious mental illnesses, generally are not competent to be witnesses in court.
Hearsay	**Hearsay** is secondhand evidence. It is testimony that is not based on personal knowledge, but rather is a repetition of what another person has said: "My brother Bob told me he saw Jones enter the store that evening." The general rule is that hearsay evidence is not admissible because it is impossible to test its truthfulness; there is no way to cross-examine as to the truth of the matter. There are numerous exceptions to this rule, however, ranging from dying declarations and ancient writings to statements showing the speaker's state of mind.
Relevancy	Evidence is relevant if it shows the existence of any fact that is of consequence to the determination of the action by making that fact more probable or less probable than it would be without the evidence. Evidence that does not tend to prove or disprove any material fact in dispute is **irrelevant** and inadmissible. Evidence regarding the accused's motive, intent, ability, and opportunity to commit a crime would all be relevant. In contrast, information about the defendant's character, prior convictions, or a reputation would not normally be relevant and is, therefore, inadmissible.
Cumulative or unduly prejudicial evidence	Even relevant evidence may be inadmissible if its use would be a waste of time because it is cumulative (duplicative of other evidence), or if it could unfairly prejudice, confuse, or mislead the jury.
Privilege	Privileged communications protect confidential discussions in certain relationships in which we want to foster open, honest communications. The law usually recognizes privileges that include communications between attorney and client; clergy-member and penitent; physician and patient; psychotherapist and patient; and husband and wife.
Lay opinions	Since opinions are subjective beliefs, most witnesses are not permitted to give their opinions other than general opinions that are rationally based on their own common perceptions, such as whether someone acted drunk, smelled like alcohol, appeared upset, or looked tired.

- has a known or potential rate of error that is acceptably low
- is logical, avoids bias, and has construct validity (how well data fits into preexisting theory)
- adheres to recognized research methods and, if applicable, to proper sampling and statistical procedures for data analysis
- is generally accepted in the relevant scientific community (making *Frye* a part of *Daubert's* test, but not the dispositive factor)

Initially, *Daubert* applied only to scientific evidence. But in *Kumho Tire Co. v. Carmichael* (1999), the Supreme Court held that all expert testimony that involves scientific, technical, or other specialized knowledge must meet the *Daubert* test for admissibility.

Scientific Evidence in the Age of Daubert

Scientific evidence analyzing materials such as blood, firearms, and fingerprints has been routinely admitted into evidence for years if it met the traditional yardsticks of the rules of evidence—trustworthiness and relevance. But when the technologies for gathering and measuring these forms of evidence first emerged, their use as evidence was far from routine. Moreover, as the *Frye* case illustrated by disallowing polygraph results, not all evidence based on "science" was necessarily admissible. Results from hypnosis have similarly been excluded from evidence. But separating science from pseudoscience has never been an easy task.

Even under *Daubert*, just when a scientific principle or discovery crosses the line between the experimental and reliably demonstrable stages is difficult to define. *Daubert* has been reasonably effective at keeping "junk science" (unreliable findings, often by persons with questionable credentials) out of evidence, especially in civil cases seeking monetary compensation based on scientifically questionable claims (Buchman 2004). *Daubert's* impact on forensic science in criminal cases, however, has been surprisingly less dramatic (Fisher 2008; Neufeld 2005). Indeed, forensic scientific evidence either caused or contributed to wrongful convictions in roughly 57 percent of the Innocence Project's DNA exoneration cases (Garrett 2008). Troublingly, in more than a quarter of such exonerations, false or misleading testimony by forensic experts contributed to the wrongful convictions (Giannelli 2007).

> Many forensic techniques, such as hair and fiber analysis, toolmark comparisons, and fingerprint analysis, rely upon a simple "match game," whereby a forensic analyst compares a known sample to a questioned sample and makes the highly subjective determination that the two samples originated from the same source. Although lacking a true scientific foundation, this "Sesame Street Science" plays a prominent role in many cases because of the easy availability of trace evidence, which is easy to leave and easy to find at a crime scene. Other forensic fields, including comparative bullet lead analysis and arson investigation, rely on assumptions that are "under-researched and oversold." (Gabel and Wilkinson 2008, p. 1002)

Exhibit 14.5 summarizes some of the problems with forensic scientific evidence that has been routinely used in criminal trials in the United States.

Note that DNA (deoxyribonucleic acid) evidence is not listed in Exhibit 14.5 as a potentially questionable forensic technique. That is because although judges and lawyers initially debated whether such evidence was admissible, those legal battles have now been resolved. DNA is now considered to be the gold standard of forensic science. As a result, prisoners and their representatives are demanding that old cases be reopened so that DNA tests (not available at the time of the original trial) be performed. These requests are most often identified with the issue of innocents on death row (see Chapter 17). However, in *District Attorney's Office v. Osborne* (2009), the Supreme Court ruled that prisoners have no constitutional right to postconviction DNA testing that might prove their innocence.

There are two limitations to DNA evidence that should be highlighted. First, biological evidence that can be subjected to DNA testing is available in only about 10 percent of criminal cases (Garrett 2008). Second, even when evidence is available, that evidence may have been contaminated or otherwise rendered unreliable because of mistakes by police or crime lab personnel, including mix-up of samples, deficiencies in lab-proficiency testing, and problems with or miscalculations of matching criteria—something that jurors often do not understand (Lieberman et al. 2008).

Exhibit 14.5

PROBLEMS WITH FORENSIC SCIENTIFIC EVIDENCE UNDER *DAUBERT*

Hair microscopy	Used since the 19th century, this technique uses a microscope to compare hair samples using characteristics like color, pigment distributions, and texture. The technique has rarely been subjected to rigorous peer review or proficiency testing. Moreover, the few tests that have been performed revealed that error rates are quite high. In an FBI scientific paper entitled "Correlation of Microscopic and Mitochondrial DNA Hair Comparisons," the authors found that even the most competent hair examiners make significant errors. In 11 percent of the cases in which the hair examiners declared two hairs to be "similar," DNA testing revealed that the hairs did not match. In some jurisdictions, hair microscopy is being phased out and replaced by the more sensitive and discriminating mitochondrial DNA typing test. Yet, many local prosecutors continue to rely on the microscope because mitochondrial DNA typing remains relatively expensive and is offered in only a few laboratories. A study of Innocence Project prisoners found nearly 22 percent of prisoners exonerated by DNA evidence had been wrongly convicted based, in large part, on hair comparisons. Yet, results of this technique are routinely used in court.
Serology	Serology is a branch of biochemistry that tests serums found in the human body (in blood, semen, and other bodily fluids). It can be reliable, yet in 40 percent of the DNA exoneration cases, conventional serology had been used by the prosecutor to secure a conviction. The case transcripts reveal that in the vast majority of these cases, the crime lab serologist misrepresented the data to the advantage of the prosecution.
Fingerprinting	This process compares the impressions of prints from fingers or palms left at a crime scene to known impressions. Empirical studies are just starting to reveal that thousands of misidentification errors are made each year, especially because "non-mate prints can sometimes appear more similar than mate print pairs" to the FBI's automated fingerprint identification system (Cole et al. 2008). Wrongful convictions have also resulted from the misapplication of fingerprint identification. For example, Stephen Cowans was convicted and served 6 years in prison for shooting a Boston police officer. Two fingerprint experts told a jury during the trial that a thumbprint left by the perpetrator was "unique and identical" to Cowans's print because it matched at 16 points. Post-conviction DNA testing excluded Cowans as the perpetrator.
Compositional analysis of bullet lead	This technique compares the quantity of various elements that comprise a lead slug recovered from a crime scene with the composition of the lead found in unused bullets seized from a suspect. In criminal cases, to say that two samples are similar can be very misleading. In fact, the National Research Council of the National Academy of Sciences (2004) concluded that variations in the manufacturing process rendered this technique "unreliable and potentially misleading." The FBI has discontinued the use of this technique accordingly, but hundreds, if not thousands, of criminal defendants may have been convicted based, in part, on this faulty pseudo-science.

Exhibit 14.5

CONTINUED

Firearm, tool-mark, bitemark, and forensic document comparisons	Like examinations of hair samples, these types of forensic analyses rely on an examiner to make comparisons between a crime scene sample and a known exemplar. Thus, they are subject to the same human errors based on subjective judgments as these other techniques. The reliability of these techniques is questionable in light of either unestablished or unacceptably high error rates. For example, a classic study (Risinger, Denbeaux, and Saks 1989) reported that forensic-document examiners were correct between 36 percent and 45 percent of the time, that they erred partially or completely 36 percent to 42 percent of the time, and were unable to draw a conclusion in 19 percent to 22 percent of cases. Experts have recently noted that there is little empirical evidence to support the uniqueness of teeth marks, shoeprints, or weapon markings (Moriarty 2007). Saks and Koehler (2005) reported error rates as high as 64 percent for bite-mark comparison, a 40 percent error rate for handwriting comparison, and a 12 percent error rate for microscopic hair comparison.

SOURCES: Gabel, Jessica D., and Margaret D. Wilkinson. 2008. "'Good' Science Gone Bad: How the Criminal Justice System Can Redress the Impact of Flawed Forensics." *Hastings Law Journal* 59: 1001–1030; Neufeld, Peter J. 2005. "The (Near) Irrelevance of *Daubert* to Criminal Justice and Some Suggestions for Reform." *American Journal of Public Health* 95: S107–S111.

LAW AND POPULAR CULTURE

CSI: Crime Scene Investigation (CBS, 2000–present)

This fictional crime drama is set in Las Vegas, Nevada (although two spin-offs are set in other cities, one in Miami and one in New York). The original *CSI* series chronicles a team of forensic scientists who work for the Las Vegas Police Department. The series was originally set in Las Vegas because the city's actual crime lab is one of the busiest in the United States. Although the television show has been wildly popular, it is widely criticized by law enforcement, forensic scientists, lawyers, and criminologists alike because it lacks any basis in reality. Consider these discrepancies between forensic fact and fiction.

- In reality, crime scene investigators certainly process crime scenes as the team on *CSI* does, but forensic experts do not engage in police activities like pursuing suspects, conducting interrogations, staging sting operations, conducting raids, and so on. "The actors playing forensic personnel portrayed on television, for instance, are an amalgam of police officer/detective/forensic scientist—this job description does not exist in the real world. Law enforcement, investigations and forensic science are each sufficiently complex that they demand their own education, training and methods" (Houck 2006, para. 11).

- The crime laboratories on television have a dazzling array of forensic equipment and technology at their disposal. But some of the technologies that are depicted on *CSI*—upwards of 40 percent according to some experts—do not really exist (Houck). Real crime labs, on the other hand, are often understaffed and lack all of the scientific equipment they need. Moreover, very few crime laboratories can perform all types of forensic analyses,

CONTINUED

CSI: Crime Scene Investigation (CBS, 2000–present)

"whether because of cost, insufficient resources, or rare demand" (Houck, para. 12).

- On *CSI*, a handful of forensic personnel possess an incredible range of scientific expertise. In real crime labs, however, different types of forensic examinations are performed by specialists in the given forensic subfield.

- The *CSI* investigators are seemingly able to lift fingerprints off of almost anything. In reality, prints can be lifted off of only certain surfaces under certain conditions. Moreover, on *CSI*, the prints are uploaded into a computer database and a screen nearly instantly appears with a photo of the person to whom the fingerprint belongs. In reality, many latent fingerprints lifted from crime scenes are not good enough to use for identification purposes. But even when a set of prints can be run through IAFIS (the FBI's integrated Automatic Fingerprint Identification System), the computerized database provides a list of potential matches. This process is not instantaneous; it typically takes up to two hours (FBI 2008). And while IAFIS has the capacity to store and distribute photos, it does not provide pop-up photographic identifications when a set of fingerprints is potentially matched. A human trained in fingerprint comparison must then compare the latent prints with a set of known exemplars.

- On *CSI*, crime-scene evidence is tested immediately, resulting in cases being solved quickly and efficiently. Real crime labs across the United States are seriously backlogged, contributing to between 400 to 1,000 cases going unsolved in each U.S. jurisdiction.

- DNA solves many cases on *CSI*. But evidence on which DNA tests can be run is recovered in only about 10 percent of criminal cases (Garrett 2008). And even when there is evidence to test, the results take several days

at best (often several weeks), not the mere minutes in which genetic tests are run on *CSI*. Most importantly, DNA is not infallible even though *CSI* presents DNA results as 100 percent foolproof.

- CSI routinely overstates the probative value of forensic evidence. "In one episode, for example, investigators perform a remarkable 'reverse algorithm and enhancement' of an audiotaped ransom demand. Using a spectrograph to match the sound waves from the ransom recording to those from a different voice recording, they are able to conclusively identify the kidnapper" (Tyler 2006, p. 1070). While this makes for great fiction, the shortcomings of voice identification are legion, as current technology simply cannot "conclusively identify" a voice to the exclusion of others.

1. Recall from the text of this chapter that several common forensic techniques may be unreliable or prone to either high or unknown error rates. Why do you think that *CSI* presents its storylines in terms of scientific fact rather than exploring the indeterminate nature of several forensic techniques?

2. Were you aware of all of the above differences between forensic fact and forensic science-fiction? If so, how did you learn of the reality? If not, what is your opinion of the show now that you know more about the truth?

3. As you know from reading this chapter, *CSI* and other shows like it, such as *Bones*, *Crossing Jordan*, and *Cold Case*, may have affected jurors' expectations in real criminal trials, a phenomenon referred to as the "CSI Effect." What effect do you think forensically based shows like *CSI* have on criminals? Do you think these shows have influenced how they commit some crimes? Why or why not?

Challenging Scientific Evidence

Most prominently, the O. J. Simpson defense team stressed the mishandling of evidence, suggesting that any subsequent analysis, no matter how precise, was not believable. This case thrust crime labs under the microscope, and the results were not always flattering. Significant errors in laboratory testing have been documented not only at the FBI crime lab, but also in numerous state and local crime labs, especially in Texas, Virginia, and West Virginia (Giannelli 2007; Moriarty 2007). Part of the problem lies with workload, as crime labs have become victims of their own success with requests for scientific tests growing faster than their budgets. But negligence or outright misconduct in crime labs is clearly also to blame (Giannelli 2007; Thompson 2006). As a result, some cases have been dismissed, and some convictions reversed, because testimony concerning scientific evidence proved unreliable. The Supreme Court has made challenging scientific evidence easier, holding that crime laboratory reports may not be introduced as evidence unless the person responsible for creating them gives testimony and is subject to cross-examination (*Melendez-Diaz v. Massachusetts* 2009).

Objections to the Admission of Evidence

During trial, attorneys must always be alert, ready to make timely **objections** to the admission of evidence. After a question is asked but before the witness answers, the attorney may object if the evidence is irrelevant or hearsay. The court then rules on the objection, admitting or barring the evidence. The judge may rule immediately or may request the lawyers to argue the legal point out of the hearing of the jury (this is termed a "sidebar conference").

Occasionally, inadmissible evidence will inadvertently be heard by the jury. For example, in answering a valid question, a witness may overelaborate. When this occurs and the attorney objects, the judge will instruct the jury to disregard the evidence. If the erroneous evidence is deemed so prejudicial that a warning to disregard is not sufficient, the judge may declare a mistrial.

THE DEFENSE PRESENTS ITS CASE

In deciding on the strategy at trial, the defense must carefully consider the strengths and weaknesses of the state's case, the character of the defendant, and how credible the defense witnesses may be. The defense must also weigh reasonable doubt, calling the defendant as a witness, alibi defenses, affirmative defenses, and challenging scientific evidence.

REASONABLE DOUBT

Because the defendant is presumed innocent, the defense does not have to call any witnesses or introduce any evidence. Through cross-examination, the attorney can try to undermine the state's case and create in the jury's mind a reasonable doubt as to whether the defendant committed the crime. The key to such a strategy is the skillful use of the right to confront witnesses, one of the criminal court procedures enumerated in the Sixth Amendment: "In all criminal prosecutions, the accused shall enjoy the right … to be confronted with witnesses against him." One meaning of this provision is that the defendant must be present during trial—that is, the state cannot try defendants who are absent. The right to be confronted with witnesses guarantees the right to **cross-examination**. A fundamental tenet of the adversary system is the need to test evidence for truthfulness, and the primary means of testing the truthfulness of witnesses is cross-examination.

If a defendant has no valid defense but will not plead guilty, the defense attorney's only choice is to force the state to prove its case and hope to create a reasonable doubt in the minds of the jury. But many experienced defense attorneys consider this to be the weakest kind of defense. They believe that to gain an acquittal, the defense must give the jury something to "hang their hat on." Thus, they must consider whether to let the defendant testify.

THE DEFENDANT AS WITNESS

The most important part of defense strategy is the decision about whether the defendant will testify. The Fifth Amendment protection against **self-incrimination** means that the defendant cannot be compelled to be a witness against himself or herself. If the defendant chooses not to testify, no comment or inference may be drawn from this fact. The prosecutor cannot argue before the jury, "If he is innocent, why doesn't he take the stand and say so?" (*Griffin v. California* 1965). Nonetheless, jurors are curious about the defendant's version of what happened. They expect the defendant to protest innocence; in the secrecy of the jury room, they may ponder why the defendant refused to testify.

Defendants may, of course, waive the privilege against self-incrimination and take the stand in their own defense. In deciding whether the defendant should testify, the defense attorney must consider whether the story is believable. If it is not, the jury will probably dismiss it, thus doing more harm to the defendant's case than if he or she had not testified at all.

Like any other witness, a defendant who takes the stand is subject to cross-examination. Cross-examination usually ensures that the defendant cannot tell only a part of the story and conceal the rest. Once the defendant chooses to testify, the state can bring out all the facts surrounding the events to which the defendant testifies. Just as important, once the defendant has taken the stand, the state can **impeach** the defendant's credibility by introducing into evidence any prior felony convictions and, in some circumstances, other prior misconduct. The defense attorney must make the difficult decision about whether to arouse the jury's suspicion by not letting the accused testify or letting the defendant testify and be subjected to possibly damaging cross-examination.

"Damned if they do, damned if they don't" is the conclusion of a research project that interviewed jurors in capital murder trials. In general, jurors wanted the defendants to testify during trial and were confused when they did not. But when defendants chose to testify, jurors concluded that they were lying and showed no remorse (Antonio and Arone 2005).

ALIBI DEFENSE

In an **alibi defense**, defendants argue that they were somewhere else at the time the crime was committed. Witnesses may be called to testify that during the time in question the defendant was drinking beer at a local bar or shopping downtown with some friends. Most states and the federal system require that defendants provide a notice of an alibi defense prior to trial, along with a list of witnesses to be called to support this assertion. A notice of alibi defense gives the prosecution the opportunity to investigate the witnesses' stories before trial. Prosecutors who suspect that witnesses have carefully rehearsed their alibi

testimony can use clever cross-examination to ask questions out of sequence, hoping to catch each witness in a series of contradictions. Prosecutors can also call rebuttal witnesses to suggest that the witnesses are longtime friends of the defendant, who are likely to lie.

AFFIRMATIVE DEFENSES

An **affirmative defense** goes beyond denying the facts of the prosecutor's case; it sets out new facts and arguments that might win for the defendant. In essence, affirmative defenses are legal excuses that should result in a finding of not guilty. Under an affirmative defense, the defense bears the burden of production—the burden of going forward with the evidence. From the defendant's perspective, an affirmative defense is tricky, for it often means that the defendant admits the prosecutor's case. Moreover, juries often view such a defense strategy as an attempt by the defendant to wiggle out of a guilty verdict.

There are several types of affirmative defenses. One is **self-defense**, which is the right of a person to use force on another person in order to protect himself or herself. Another affirmative defense is **duress**, which means a person is compelled to do something he or she does not want to do. Yet another is **entrapment**, which is the act of a law enforcement agent inducing a person to commit a crime that the person was not otherwise disposed to commit. By far, the best-known and also most controversial affirmative defense is the insanity defense. (See Courts, Controversy, and Reducing Crime: Should the Insanity Defense Be Abolished?)

REBUTTAL

After the defense rests its case, the prosecution may call rebuttal witnesses, whose purpose is either to discredit the testimony of a previous witness or to discredit the witness. The prosecutor may call a **rebuttal** witness to show that the previous witness could not have observed what she said she did because she was somewhere else at the time. Or the prosecutor may call witnesses or otherwise present evidence to show that the previous witnesses have dishonorable reputations. The rules of evidence regarding rebuttal witnesses are complex. In general, evidence may be presented in rebuttal that could not have been used during the prosecution's main case. For example, the prosecution may legitimately

Courts, Controversy, and Reducing crime

Should the Insanity Defense Be Abolished?

The insanity defense, one of the most hotly debated topics in criminal law, is rooted in a fundamental concept of Anglo-American law: that a person should not be punished for what he or she cannot help doing. Thus, under the concept of mens rea, an insane person is not criminally responsible for his or her acts, because he or she is incapable of having criminal intent (see Chapter 2).

But what degree of insanity, mental illness, or mental disease makes a person blameless for otherwise criminal acts? This question has been debated for centuries. At the heart of contemporary discussions are marked philosophical divergences within American society concerning an individual's responsibility for his or her own acts. The lack of agreement is reflected in major differences among states concerning the extent to which a person's mental faculties must be impaired before he or she is considered insane. The standards for insanity vary in the United States, but most jurisdictions follow the modern federal formulation of the insanity defense (Fradella 2007). That version of the defense excuses criminal conduct if, as a result of a severe "mental disease or defect" at the time of the commission of the offense, the defendant was unable to substantially appreciate the wrongfulness of his or her conduct. The burden of proof is on the prosecution to prove that the defendant committed the crime in question, but the defense bears the burden of proof as to the defendant's insanity.

The insanity defense has sparked considerable controversy. The public perceives the insanity defense as a dodge used by tricky lawyers trying to gain sympathy for their guilty clients, who avoid punishment by pretending they are insane. When the jury acquitted would-be presidential assassin John Hinckley, Jr., as "not guilty by reason of insanity," there was a heated outcry against the verdict, even though Hinckley was then confined to a mental institution. Public and professional displeasure produced a rush to reform the insanity defense (Fradella 2007). For example, some states have greatly altered the traditional insanity defense and made available the verdict "guilty but mentally ill" or "guilty but insane."

This debate resurfaces during trials of defendants charged with bizarre crimes. For example,

inform the jury of the previous convictions of defendants who take the stand, in an attempt to impeach their credibility.

Closing Arguments

After the prosecution and defense have rested (that is, completed the introduction of evidence), each side has the opportunity to make a closing argument to the jury. **Closing arguments** allow each side to sum up the facts in its favor and indicate why it believes a verdict of guilty or not guilty is in order.

In most jurisdictions, the prosecutor goes first, carefully summing up the facts of the case and tying together into a coherent pattern what appeared during the trial to be isolated or unimportant matters. The prosecutor calls upon the jurors to do their duty and punish the defendant, who has committed the crime. The defense attorney goes next, highlighting the evidence favorable to the defendant, criticizing the witnesses for the state, and showing why they should not be believed. The defense also calls upon the jurors to do their sworn duty and return a not guilty verdict. Because the prosecutor bears the burden of proof, he or she has the opportunity to make one last statement to the jury, refuting the defense arguments.

Closing arguments are often the most dramatic parts of the trial. However, there is a fine line between persuasiveness and unnecessary emotionalism. Jury verdicts have been reversed on appeal because the prosecutor interjected prejudicial statements into the closing argument.

Theodore Kaczynski, the alleged Unabomber, refused to allow his lawyer to plead not guilty by reason of insanity, and he was subsequently convicted. Likewise, the trial of Andrea Yates for killing her children triggered a clash between psychiatrists and prosecutors. During her second murder trial, the jury found her innocent by reason of insanity. She is committed to a Texas mental hospital until a court decides she is no longer deemed a threat.

The Supreme Court has upheld state efforts to restrict the insanity defense. During a bench trial, Eric Clark, a paranoid schizophrenic, argued that he was being pursued by space aliens when he killed an Arizona police officer. Under Arizona's narrow definition of insanity, however, his bizarre behavior did not qualify as a legal defense. Moreover, that state largely prohibits the use of psychiatric testimony to prove insanity. Nonetheless, the Court held that the law does not violate due process protections (*Clark v. Arizona* 2006). In addition, the government may involuntarily administer drugs to render mentally ill defendants competent to stand trial on serious criminal charges (*Sell v. United States* 2003). The Court, though, has held that mentally retarded defendants may not be executed (Chapter 16).

The heated debate over the insanity defense is largely symbolic, however. Insanity is pled in less than one-half of 1 percent of all felony cases and, even when pled, it is unsuccessful three-quarters of the time (Fradella 2007). Moreover, several states make incarceration in a mental institution mandatory if the defendant is found not guilty by reason of insanity. Indeed, such defendants are usually held in a mental institution for a longer period of time than they might have been held in prison had they been found guilty of the crime they were charged with. For these reasons, combined with the great expense of litigating an insanity defense, lawyers consider insanity a defense of last resort.

What do you think? Should the insanity defense be abolished, restricted, or kept the way it is? In particular, do you think that defendants fake insanity, or are defendants really insane and therefore not responsible for their actions? If you were a juror, what types of evidence would convince you to return a verdict of not guilty by reason of insanity?

JURY INSTRUCTIONS

Although in jury trials the jury is the sole judge of the facts of the case, the judge alone determines the law. Therefore, the court instructs the jury as to the meaning of the law applicable to the facts of the case. These **jury instructions** begin with discussions of general legal principles (innocent until proven guilty, guilty beyond a reasonable doubt, and so forth). They follow with specific instructions on the elements of the crime in the case and what specific actions the government must prove before there can be a conviction. If the defendant has raised a defense such as insanity or duress, the judge instructs the jury as to the meaning of the defense according to the law in that jurisdiction. Finally, the judge instructs the jury on possible verdicts in the case and provides a written form for each verdict of guilty and not guilty. Often juries have the option of choosing alternative forms of guilty verdicts, called "lesser included offenses." In a murder case, for example, the jury may find the defendant guilty of murder in the first degree, murder in the second degree, or manslaughter—or they may acquit on all charges.

The judge and the trial attorneys prepare the jury instructions during a special **charging conference** that precedes jury deliberations. Each side drafts suggested instructions, and the judge chooses the most appropriate ones. If the judge rejects a given instruction, the lawyer enters an objection on the record, thus preserving the issue for later appeal. The instructions are written out, signed by the judge, and then read to the jury. Some judges allow the jurors to take a copy of the instructions into the jury room as a guide.

Jury instructions represent a formal, detailed lecture on the law. Because faulty jury instructions are a principal basis for appellate court reversal, judges are careful in their wordings. However, given the complexity of the law, juror comprehension of jury instructions is pitifully low (Ogloff and Rose 2007). For example, given jury instructions stressing that a defendant is presumed innocent until proven guilty by the evidence beyond any reasonable doubt, only 50 percent of the jurors understood that the defendant did not have to present any evidence of innocence, and 10 percent were still uncertain what the presumption of innocence was (Strawn and Buchanan 1976; see also, Frank and Broschard 2006). The major difficulty in improving jury comprehension is the complexity of the law itself; it is difficult to translate into plain English the subtleties of meaning of certain legal terms and the intentional vagueness of the law ("reasonable person" and "preponderance of the evidence" come quickly to mind) (Ogloff and Rose 2007; Steele and Thornburg 1991).

JURY DELIBERATIONS

How juries decide has long fascinated lawyers and laypeople alike. There is a great deal of curiosity about what goes on behind the locked jury room door. During the trial, jurors are passive observers who are not allowed to ask questions and are usually prohibited from taking notes. But after the judge reads the jury instructions, the lawyers, judges, and defendants must wait passively, often in tense anticipation, for the jury to reach a verdict. The only hints of what is happening during **jury deliberations** occur on the rare occasions when the jurors request further instructions from the judge about the applicable law or ask to have portions of the testimony read in open court.

If the jury becomes *deadlocked* (they cannot reach a verdict), the trial ends with a **hung jury**. The prosecutor then has the option of trying the defendant again. Despite recent concerns, the rate of hung juries is low and has been stable for years (Hannaford, Hans, and Munsterman 1999). Nationwide, juries are unable to reach a decision only 6 percent of the time (National Center for State Courts 2003).

ARE JURIES BIASED?

The answer to the question of whether juries are biased depends on what is meant by "biased." For example, on the whole, most jurors are biased toward certain types of evidence. "Empirical research indicates that jurors routinely undervalue circumstantial evidence (DNA, fingerprints, and the like) and overvalue direct evidence (eyewitness identifications and confessions) when making verdict choices, even though false-conviction statistics indicate that the former is normally more probative and more reliable than the latter" (Heller 2006, p. 241). Given the limitations of voir dire, some jurors may be biased such that they are inclined to credit or disregard testimony by police (Dorfman 1999). But whether juries based their decisions on biases concerning extralegal factors such as race, ethnicity, gender, and similar characteristics that ought to be irrelevant is a more difficult question to answer.

Most research suggests that modern juries in the United States appear to perform remarkably well on the whole, deciding cases primarily on the basis of legal factors rather than extralegal ones (Ford 1986; Garvey et al. 2004; Mills and Bohannon 1980). Even in trials involving emotional issues like sexual assault, evidence is the primary factor in decision making. Jurors were influenced by extralegal factors, but these effects were largely limited to weak cases in which the state presented little hard evidence (Reskin and Visher 1986). This is not to say that racism, sexism (including gender stereotypes), homophobia, and the like do not enter into juror decision making; they do. However, the effects of these biases appear to be minimal because they are significantly moderated by legal factors—especially the strength of the evidence (Diamond 2006; Garvey et al. 2004; Mitchell et al. 2005).

THE VERDICT

Once the jury informs the judge that a decision has been reached, the lawyers and the defendant gather in the courtroom. Typically, the foreperson announces the **verdict**. How often do juries convict? Given that the vast majority of cases have already been dismissed or disposed of by a plea of guilty, one might expect that the defendant's chances of winning at trial are roughly 50–50, but the real odds against acquittal are significantly higher. In federal courts, juries convict 82 percent of the time in nondrug cases. Data from the National Center for State Courts

(Ostrom, Kauder, and LaFountain 2002) point in the same direction; juries convict about three-quarters of the time in state criminal cases.

Do juries view cases differently from judges? Harry Kalven and Hans Zeisel (1966) found that judges and juries agree more than three out of four times. When judge and jury disagree, the judge is more likely to convict and the jury to acquit. Subsequent studies have replicated these findings (Eisenberg et al. 2004). But this pattern is tied to several factors, including the severity of the charge, whether the defendant takes the stand to testify in his or her own defense and a jury learns that the defendant has no prior conviction, and whether the defense merely challenges the sufficiency of the state's case or presents its own witnesses to disprove the prosecution's version of the case (Eisenberg et al. 2004; Givelber and Farrell 2008; Levine 1983).

POSTVERDICT MOTIONS

A trial verdict of **acquittal** (not guilty) ends the case; the defendant can leave the courthouse a free person. A verdict of guilty, however, means that further proceedings will occur; the defendant must be sentenced (see Chapters 15 and 16) and in all likelihood will appeal (see Chapter 17).

If the jury returns a verdict of guilty, the defendant still has certain legal options remaining. A guilty defendant may file **postverdict motions**, which are heard prior to sentencing. These motions give the defense attorney the opportunity to reargue alleged mistakes made at trial. The trial judge may have a change of mind and become convinced that some ruling made against the defendant was erroneous. The most common postverdict motion is a *motion for a new trial*. It asserts that serious errors were made at trial (either by the trial judge or by the prosecutor), so the guilty verdict should be set aside and a new trial granted. Postverdict motions are largely a formality; few are ever granted.

LAW IN ACTION: TRIALS AS BALANCING WHEELS

Trials exert a major influence on the operation of the entire criminal court process. This process resembles a balance. A balance wheel regulates or stabilizes the

motion of a mechanism. Although only a handful of cases go to trial, the possibility of trial operates as a balancing wheel on all other cases. Most important, the likelihood of conviction determines the negotiating position of lawyers during plea bargaining. Thus, jury trials must be measured not only in terms of their impact on specific cases but also on how the decisions reached affect similar cases in the future.

POPULAR STANDARDS OF JUSTICE

Juries introduce the community's commonsense judgments into judicial decisions. The University of Chicago jury project (Broeder 1959) found that popular standards of justice are by far the major reason for disagreement between judge and jury. The result is jury legislation—a jury's deliberate modification of the law to make it conform to community views of what the law ought to be (Kalven and Zeisel 1966).

One example of how juries introduce popular standards into the criminal court process involves prosecutions for hunting violations. Rural juries are dubious about laws that restrict hunting privileges. Thus, federal defendants accused of shooting too many birds (and the like) have a good chance of finding friendly juries ready to come to their rescue (Levine 1983).

In recent years, the importance of juries' introducing popular standards into the justice system has been associated with the concept of **jury nullification**—the right of juries to nullify or refuse to apply law in criminal cases despite facts that leave no reasonable doubt that the law was violated. Some advocates of jury nullification base their ideas on a perceived need to reduce government intrusion into citizens' lives; others are motivated by concern over racial injustice (Brooks 2004; Brown 1997; Butler 1995). Judges are quick to denounce jury nullification because they feel that the rule of law is undermined. But others counter that juries have been refusing to follow the law for centuries, and they have every right to send a message by not following a law they find, for whatever reason, to be flawed. Contemporary discussions focus on whether juries should be told they have the right to disregard the judge's jury instructions and substitute their own views and, if so, what the effects of doing so may be (Diamond 2007; Dunn 2007; Galiber et al. 1993; Horowitz et al. 2006).

UNCERTAINTY

Jury trials also affect the criminal court system by introducing uncertainty into the process. Stories about irrational juries form part of the folklore of any courthouse. Here are two examples. During jury deliberations in a drug case, two jurors announced that "only God can judge" and hung the jury by refusing to vote. After an acquittal in a burglary case, a juror put her arm around the defendant and said, "Bob, we were sure happy to find you not guilty, but don't do it again" (Neubauer 1974b, p. 228). Legal professionals resent such intrusions into their otherwise ordered world; they seek to reduce such uncertainties by developing the norms of cooperation discussed throughout this book. Viewed in this light, plea bargaining serves to shield the system from a great deal of the uncertainty that results when lay citizens are involved in deciding important legal matters.

PREJUDICIAL PRETRIAL PUBLICITY

The conviction of Dr. Sam Sheppard for bludgeoning his wife to death in her bedroom and the later reversal by the Supreme Court (see Case Close-Up: *Sheppard v. Maxwell* and Prejudicial Pretrial Publicity) raised the issue of **prejudicial pretrial publicity**. The Court, in holding that Sheppard had been denied a fair and impartial trial, set off a long and heated battle over fair trial versus freedom of the press. Defendants have a right to a fair and impartial trial, but at the same time, press coverage of the crime and the trial are protected by the First Amendment of the Constitution (*Times-Picayune v. Schulingkamp* 1975). Similar concerns have led some courts to ban cameras in the courthouse (see Courts, Controversy, and the Administration of Justice: Should Cameras Be Allowed in the Courtroom?).

Pretrial publicity does affect juries. In a classic study, a team of researchers provided one set of "jurors" with prejudicial news coverage of a case and a control group with "nonprejudicial" information. After listening to an identical trial involving a case in which the guilt of the defendant was greatly in doubt, the study found that the "prejudiced jurors" were more likely to convict than the "nonprejudiced jurors" (Padawer-Singer and Barton 1975). These results have been replicated many times such that it is now widely accepted that even modest pretrial publicity can prejudice potential jurors against a defendant (Moran and Cutler 1991; Studebaker and Penrod 2007).

Historically, very few criminal trials involved prejudicial pretrial publicity; news reports seldom extended beyond police-blotter coverage. But with the advent of 24-hour cable news channels and the ease of information access through the Internet, pretrial publicity affects more cases today than ever before. When there is extensive pretrial publicity, the jury-selection process is greatly strained. Voir dire is geared to ferreting out ordinary instances of unfairness or prejudice, not to correcting the possibility of a systematic pattern of bias. For example, if an attorney excuses all jurors who have heard something about the case at hand, he or she runs the risk of selecting a jury solely from the least attentive, least literate members of the general public. On the other hand, if an attorney accepts jurors who assert that they will judge the case solely on the basis of testimony in open court, he or she is still not certain that the juror—no matter how well-intentioned—can hear the case with a truly open mind.

In trying to reconcile conflicting principles of a fair trial and freedom of the press, trial courts use (singly or in combination) three techniques: limited gag orders, change of venue, and sequestering of the jury. Each of these methods suffers from admitted drawbacks.

LIMITED GAG ORDERS

The First Amendment forbids the court from censoring what the press writes about a criminal case, but it says nothing about restricting the flow of information to the media. Thus, in notorious cases in which it seems likely that selecting a jury may be difficult, judges now routinely issue a limited **gag order** forbidding those involved in the case—police, prosecutor, defense attorney, and defendant—from talking to the press. Violations are punishable as **contempt of court** (disobeying a judge's order). Since these people know the most about the case (and often have the most to gain from pretrial publicity), the net effect is to dry up news leaks. However, consistent with the First Amendment, the press is free to publish any information it discovers. The greatest difficulty is that one of the people involved in the case may secretly provide information, in violation of the judge's order. The judge can then subpoena the reporter and order disclosure of the source. Reporters believe that identifying their sources will dry up the flow of information, so they refuse to testify. They are cited for contempt and go to jail. Thus, the court may infringe on freedom of the press when its intent is simply to guarantee another Bill of Rights protection—the right to a fair trial.

Sheppard v. Maxwell and Prejudicial Pretrial Publicity

On July 4, 1954, Marilyn Sheppard—the pregnant wife of Dr. Samuel Sheppard—was bludgeoned to death in the upstairs bedroom of the couple's home in a fashionable Cleveland suburb. The case produced some of the most sensational press coverage the country had witnessed. Sheppard told the police that he was asleep on a sofa when he was awakened by his wife's screams. Rushing upstairs, he grappled with the intruder, only to be struck unconscious by a blow to the head. From the outset, officials focused suspicion on Sheppard.

The official investigation was prodded by extensive media coverage, which was critical of how the police handled the case. Day after day, vivid headlines called for the arrest of Dr. Sheppard and implied that the police were going easy because he and his family were socially prominent.

To add fuel to the fire, the paper published a front-page editorial headlined "Why Don't Police Quiz Top Suspect," claiming somebody "was getting away with murder." At the coroner's inquest, Dr. Sheppard's attorney was present but not allowed to participate. Live radio broadcast the 6-hour questioning of Sheppard about his activities the night of the murder and about his lovers before that night. Six weeks after the murder, Sheppard was indicted.

The case came to trial 2 weeks before a general election in which the judge was seeking reelection and the prosecutor was running for municipal court judge. The names and addresses of potential jurors were published in the paper, resulting in letters and phone calls concerning the trial. The courtroom was so packed that reporters were allowed to sit behind the defense table, meaning that Sheppard could not converse privately with his lawyer. Every day, newspapers printed trial testimony verbatim; no effort was made to prevent the jury from reading these accounts,

even when evidence was ruled inadmissible. Not surprisingly, after a 9-week trial in which jurors were free to return home every night, Sheppard was convicted of second-degree murder.

Sheppard spent 12 years in prison. Several appeals and habeas corpus petitions were denied. Eventually, the family hired a young Boston lawyer, F. Lee Bailey, who would go on to become one of the most famous and controversial lawyers in the United States. Indeed, Bailey figured prominently in a trial that later received extensive media coverage—the murder trial of former football star and TV commentator O. J. Simpson. Bailey convinced the high court to hear the Sheppard case and won a stunning victory.

Justice Tom Clark held that prejudicial pretrial publicity denied Sheppard the right to a fair and impartial trial (*Sheppard v. Maxwell* 1966). But finding that pretrial publicity can be prejudicial is a far easier task than deciding how to control it. The essential problem underlying the issue of prejudicial pretrial publicity is that two key protections of the Bill of Rights are on a collision course. The Sixth Amendment guarantees defendants the right to a trial before an impartial jury; decisions about guilt or innocence must be based on what jurors hear during the trial, not what they have heard or read outside the courtroom. At the same time, the First Amendment protects freedom of the press; what reporters print, say on radio, or broadcast on television is not subject to prior censorship. Without the First Amendment, there would be no problem; courts could simply forbid the press from reporting anything but the bare essentials of a crime. Although this is the practice in England, such prior restraints are not allowed in the United States.

To the Supreme Court, the answer to this dilemma lay in controlling the flow of information.

CASE CLOSEUP

CHANGE OF VENUE

Recall from Chapter 3 that **venue** refers to the place where a case is tried. If the court is convinced that a case has received such extensive publicity that picking an impartial jury is impossible, the trial may be shifted to another part of the state. If a case has received

statewide coverage, however, such a change is of limited use. Defense attorneys face a difficult tactical decision in deciding whether to request a **change of venue**. They must weigh the effects of prejudicial publicity against the disadvantages of having a trial in a more rural and conservative area, where citizens are hostile to big-city defendants (particularly if they are

COURTS, CONTROVERSY, AND THE ADMINISTRATION OF JUSTICE

Should Cameras Be Allowed in the Courtroom?

The rise of electronic media has added a new dimension to the defendant's right to a fair trial. Trials, of course, are open to the public, and journalists are free to observe and report on courtroom proceedings. However, since the sensational Lindbergh trial of the 1930s, radio and television coverage of the judicial process has been limited. In that case, German immigrant Bruno Hauptman was accused of kidnapping and murdering the son of the famous aviator Charles Lindbergh. Because it was perceived that the daily press coverage of the trial was excessive, rules of court came to forbid cameras or recording devices in the courthouse.

Restrictions on cameras in the courtroom are changing, however. The Supreme Court unanimously held that electronic media and still photographic coverage of public judicial proceedings do not violate a defendant's right to a fair trial; states are therefore free to set their own guidelines (*Chandler et al. v. Florida* 1981). Since then, the barriers against cameras in the courtroom have fallen in state after state. The U.S. Judicial Conference adopted a resolution allowing each court

of appeals to decide whether cameras should be allowed (but only a few circuits have acted favorably). Just as important, only two states still prohibit all forms of electronic coverage of criminal court proceedings. Most states allow electronic coverage of criminal trials (Alexander 1996). State rules and guidelines include many specific restrictions designed to prevent disruptions of the proceedings—limiting the number of cameras in the courtroom and prohibiting camera operators from moving around the courtroom while the trial is in session. The scope of permissible coverage varies greatly, though. In some states, the consent of the parties is required, meaning either side can veto coverage of the proceedings. In others, the news media need only receive permission from the trial judge to broadcast the proceedings.

Some people complain that televising trials distorts the process by encouraging the participants to play to the camera (Thaler 1994). They also argue that by covering only sensational trials and presenting only the most dramatic moments of hours of testimony, television stations fail to portray the trial

---

African-American). Prosecutors generally oppose such moves because they believe that the chances of conviction are greater in the local community. To justify this position, prosecutors cite the expense of moving witnesses, documents, and staff to a distant city for a long trial.

SEQUESTERING THE JURY

A prime defect in the trial of Dr. Sheppard was the failure to shield the jury from press coverage of the ongoing trial. Indeed, jurors read newspaper stories of the trial, which included inadmissible evidence. One remedy that is common in trials involving extensive media coverage is to **sequester** the jury. The jurors live in a hotel, take their meals together, and participate in weekend recreation together. Sheriff deputies censor newspapers and shut off television news. The possibility of being in virtual quarantine for a number of

weeks makes many citizens reluctant to serve. When sequestering is probable, the jury selected runs the risk of including only citizens who are willing to be separated for long periods of time from friends and family, who can afford to be off work, or who look forward to a Spartan existence. At a minimum, sequestration is a trying experience for the jurors.

CONCLUSION

After 12 years in prison, Sheppard was retried. The prosecution put on essentially the same case, but they now faced one of the top defense attorneys in the nation. F. Lee Bailey tore into the prosecutor's witnesses and in his closing argument likened the prosecution's case to "ten pounds of hogwash in a five-pound bag."

process accurately. Others argue that cameras in the courtroom have a valuable educational role, providing the public with a firsthand view of how court proceedings operate.

Law professor Donna Demac argued that televising court proceedings ultimately leads to greater trust in government: "Many people suspect that the legal system dispenses a different standard of justice for the wealthy," but the more the people see the system firsthand, the greater the chance that the system will be fair (quoted in Scardino 1989). Indeed, two separate studies found that viewers of a television trial of moderate interest became more knowledgeable about the judicial process (Alexander 1991; Raymond 1992). As to the possibility of the camera's disrupting judicial proceedings, a detailed study in Florida, where the guidelines are the most liberal of any state allowing camera coverage, concluded: "Broadcast journalists who follow state guidelines present coverage which, upon close examination by presiding judges, participating attorneys and jurors, is perceived as undistorted" (Alexander 1991).

Cases involving celebrities present challenging questions about how much information should be available to the public and what should be withheld. The widely televised trial of O. J. Simpson clearly caused some rethinking about cameras in the courtroom. Perceptions that lawyers were playing to the cameras apparently had an impact in several highly publicized cases that followed. Thus, some trial judges have refused to allow broadcasts of their trials. Similarly, journalists complained that in the Michael Jackson child molestation case, the California judge sealed almost all of the records in the case (Deutsch 2004). In the rape trial of NBA star Kobe Bryant, the Colorado judge restricted inquiries into the alleged victim's prior sex life (Savage and Dolan 2004). In short, celebrity justice cases force judges and the media to walk a fine line between full reporting and turning the case into a spectacle (Hubler 2005).

What do you think? Should cameras be allowed in the courtroom, or should the nation return to its former ban on electronic media in the courthouse? Does the educational role of watching real trials outweigh the possibility that lawyers will play to the cameras?

After deliberating for less than 12 hours, the jury returned a verdict of not guilty. But for Sam Sheppard, liberty proved short-lived. He died in 1970, probably sent to an early grave by journalistic excess.

The Sheppard murder trial has been called the "first trial of the century," second in celebrity status only to the trial of O. J. Simpson. The legacy of the *Sheppard* case lived on not only in the important Supreme Court decision that it spawned but also in fiction—the TV series and later movie *The Fugitive*. More recently, the family has again sought to clear Dr. Sheppard's name. They blame the murder on a former gardener and argue that DNA evidence conclusively proves that an innocent man was convicted amid a media spectacle. However, in 2000 a Cleveland jury refused to find Sam Sheppard innocent, thus dealing a fatal legal blow to his son's efforts to clear his father's name.

In many ways, highly publicized jury trials for defendants—whether well known like Sam Sheppard and O. J. Simpson or hardly known at all—are the high point of the judicial process. Indeed, along with Lady Justice, jury trials stand as the primary symbol of justice. In turn, many Supreme Court decisions emphasize the importance of adversarial procedures at trial. Yet in examining the realities of trial, we are presented with two contradictory perspectives: Full-fledged trials are relatively rare, yet trials are an important dimension of the court process. Every year, 2 million jurors serve in some 200,000 civil and criminal cases. Although only a relative smattering of cases is ever tried, the possibility of trial shapes the entire process. Thus, long after trials have declined to minimal importance in other Western nations, the institution of the jury trial remains a vital part of the American judicial process.

CHAPTER REVIEW

1.   Trace the history of trials by jury.

The right to a trial by jury can be traced to the Magna Carta in 1215. This right was incorporated into Article III, Section 2, of the U.S. Constitution with respect to the federal government, and in the Sixth Amendment, with respect to the states.

2.   Analyze the scope of the right to a trial by jury in a criminal case.

The right to a trial by jury applies to all nonpetty criminal offenses, usually interpreted as offenses punishable by a term of imprisonment of 6 months or more. The right may be waived by a defendant, who may opt for a bench trial in lieu of a jury trial.

3.   Evaluate the impact of differences in jury size and unanimity requirements.

Common law juries have consisted of 12 people since the 14th century. The Supreme Court, however, authorized smaller juries in noncapital cases, but juries with less than six members are not permitted in criminal cases. Since that ruling, many states have specifically authorized juries of fewer than 12 jurors, but most allow these smaller juries only in misdemeanor cases. Some studies have found very few differences between 6- and 12-person juries, while others have reported significant differences.

4.   Explain how a jury is summoned and selected, including the constitutional limitations on these processes.

Potential jurors are summoned to court using master jury lists. The people who are summoned, called the "venire," come to court to participate in voir dire, a process designed to select a fair and impartial petit jury by asking members of the venire about potential biases concerning the case. Those who cannot serve as fair and impartial jurors are excused for cause. A few other members of the venire may be excused by either party using peremptory challenges so long as these challenges are not used in a discriminatory manner that violates the constitutional guarantee of equal protection.

5.   Discuss the function of jury consultants in the process of scientific jury selection.

Jury consultants use social scientific research methods to profile jurors in an attempt to help attorneys select members of the venire for petit jury service who are likely to be predisposed to their side of the case.

6.   Distinguish between the presumptions that apply at the start of trials and the burdens of proof applicable to overcoming them.

The two presumptions that apply to every criminal trial are the presumption of innocence and the presumption of sanity. It is the responsibility of the prosecution to introduce sufficient evidence over the course of a trial to overcome or rebut the presumption of innocence by proving a defendant's guilt beyond a reasonable doubt. In insanity defense cases, the defense usually must prove that the defendant was insane at the time of the commission of a crime by clear and convincing evidence.

7.   Summarize the basic rules of evidence concerning trustworthiness and relevance of evidence.

Only relevant evidence is admitted at trial—evidence that tends to prove or disprove a fact in dispute. Relevance, however, is not enough. Evidence must also be reliable. Thus, hearsay evidence, lay opinion, speculative testimony, and copies of documents (when originals are available) are generally all inadmissible.

8.   Analyze how special limitations on expert witnesses affect the litigation of criminal cases, especially with regard to leading types of forensic evidence.

Historically, and in some jurisdictions even today, expert testimony had to be based on scientific facts that were generally accepted in the relevant scientific community. However, under the *Daubert* standard, reliability is the linchpin to admissibility. Because the reliability of a number of forensic techniques is unknown, the continued use of these techniques has been called into question.

9.   Identify the steps in a criminal trial.

After a jury is selected through the voir dire process, the prosecution and, then the defense, usually deliver their respective opening statements. The prosecution then calls witnesses and conducts direct examination of its witnesses, some of whom will introduce real or scientific evidence. The defense has the opportunity to cross-examine each of the prosecution's witnesses. When the prosecution rests, the defense may call its witnesses and introduce its evidence. The prosecution, then, has the opportunity to cross-examine the defense witnesses. At the conclusion of the trial, both parties make closing arguments. The judge instructs the jury with regard to the applicable law and then the jury deliberates until it reaches a verdict.

10. Describe the effects and implications of pretrial publicity and the solutions that courts use to prevent those effects from influencing a criminal trial.

Pretrial publicity can taint the potential jury pool by exposing them to information that is inaccurate or inadmissible as evidence. When that occurs, the defendant may be deprived of his or her Sixth Amendment right to a fair and impartial jury. To reduce the chances of the media tainting potential jurors, judges may issue limited gag orders forbidding those involved in the case—police, prosecutor, defense attorney, and defendant—from talking to the press. But even still, venire members may have heard media reports that could have influenced their views on a case. The voir dire process is supposed to screen out potential jurors who have already been tainted. In high-profile cases, a change of venue might be necessary to find a pool of potential jurors who could render a fair and impartial verdict, free from the taint of pretrial publicity. During a trial, however, courts routinely instruct jurors not to read newspapers, magazines, or watch television news shows that may report on the trial. Sometimes, to shield jurors from such media influence, the jury may be sequestered.

CRITICAL THINKING QUESTIONS

1. What impact does the jury system have on the rest of the criminal justice system? How would criminal justice function differently if defendants had no right to a trial by a jury of their peers, which is the situation in virtually all of the non–common law nations of the world?

2. If you are in a federal courthouse and observe a six-member jury, what type of case is being tried? Why?

3. Compare two recent trials in your community. What were the similarities and differences in terms of jury selection, the prosecutor's case-in-main, the defense strategy, and the verdict? If possible, compare a murder trial with one involving another major felony. In what ways are murder trials different from, say, a trial for armed robbery or rape?

4. In the wake of the O. J. Simpson verdict of not guilty, many commentators spoke about the collapse of the jury system. Were these sentiments driven by the one verdict, or were there other reasons?

5. Why are some jury verdicts popular and others not? To what extent do differences of opinion over the fairness of a jury verdict reinforce notions that equate justice with winning (see Chapter 2)?

KEY TERMS

acquittal 361	challenge for cause 344	duress 357
affirmative defense 357	change of venue 363	entrapment 357
alibi defense 357	charging conference 359	evidence 350
alternate jurors 348	circumstantial evidence 350	gag order 362
bench trial 340	closing argument 358	hearsay 351
best-evidence rule 351	contempt of court 362	hung jury 360
burden of persuasion 349	cross-examination 356	impeach 357
burden of proof 349	demonstrative evidence 350	irrelevant 351
burden of production 349	direct evidence 350	jury consultants 345

WEB RESOURCES

Go to the America's Courts and the Criminal Justice System companion website at

www.cengage.com/criminaljustice/neubauer

where you will find more resources to help you study.
Resources include web exercises, quizzing, and flash cards.

FOR FURTHER READING

American Bar Association. *Principles for Juries and Jury Trials*. Chicago: Author, 2004. Available online at http://www.abanet.org/juryprojectstandards/principles.pdf

Brewer, Neil, and Kipling D. Williams. *Psychology and Law: An Empirical Perspective*. New York: The Guildford Press, 2007.

Gardner, Thomas, and Terry Anderson. *Criminal Evidence: Principles and Cases*. 7th ed. Belmont, CA: Wadsworth, 2010.

Giles, Robert, and Robert Snyder, eds. *Covering the Courts: Free Press, Fair Trials and Journalistic Performance*. New Brunswick, NJ: Transaction, 1999.

Jonakait, Randolph N. *The American Jury System*. New Haven: Yale University Press, 2006.

Levine, James, and Steen Zeidman. "The Miracle of Jury Reform in New York." *Judicature* 88: 178–184, 2005.

National Institute of Justice. *Eyewitness Evidence: A Guide for Law Enforcement*. Washington, DC: U.S. Department of Justice, 1999.

Robinson, Paul. *Would You Convict? Seventeen Cases That Challenged the Law*. New York: New York University Press, 1999.

Rutledge, Devallis. *Courtroom Survival: The Officer's Guide to Better Testimony*. Belmont, CA: Wadsworth, 2000.

Smith, Alisa, and Michael J. Saks. "The Case for Overturning *Williams v. Florida* and The Six-Person Jury: History, Law, and Empirical Evidence." *Florida Law Review* 60: 441–470, 2008.

Vidmar, Neil, and Valerie Hans. *American Juries: The Verdict*. New York: Prometheus Books, 2007.

Insanity and Other Affirmative Defenses

Caplan, Lincoln. *The Insanity Defense and the Trial of John W. Hinckley, Jr.* Boston: D. R. Godine, 1984.

Fradella, Henry F. *Mental Illness and Criminal Defenses of Excuse in Contemporary American Law*. Bethesda, MD: Academica Press, 2007.

Greenberg, Stuart, Daniel Shuman, and Robert Meyer. "Forensic Psychiatric Diagnosis Unmasked." *Judicature* 88: 210–214, 2005.

Scientific Evidence and DNA

Borgida, Eugene, and Susan T. Fiske. *Beyond Common Sense: Psychological Science in the Courtroom*. Malden, MA: Blackwell, 2008.

Champagne, Anthony, Danny Easterling, Daniel Shuman, Alan Tomkins, and Elizabeth Whitaker. "Are Court-Appointed Experts the Solution to the Problems of Expert Testimony?" *Judicature* 84: 178, 2001.

Cherry, Michael, and Edward Imwinkelried. "Questions about the Accuracy of Fingerprint Evidence." *Judicature* 92: 158–159, 2009.

Clarke, George (Woody), and Janet Reno. *Justice and Science: Trials and Triumphs of DNA Evidence.* New Brunswick, NJ: Rutgers University Press, 2008.

Fisher, Jim. *Forensics Under Fire: Are Bad Science and Dueling Experts Corrupting Criminal Justice?* New Brunswick, NJ: Rutgers University Press, 2008.

Foster, Kenneth, and Peter Huber. *Judging Science: Scientific Knowledge and the Federal Courts.* Cambridge, MA: MIT Press, 1999.

Freeman, Michael, and Helen Reece, eds. *Science in Court.* Brookfield, VT: Ashgate, 1998.

Moriarty, Jane Campbell. "'Misconvictions,' Science, and the Ministers of Justice." *Nebraska Law Review* 86: 1–42, 2007.

Kiely, Terrence F. *Forensic Evidence: Science and the Criminal Law.* Boca Raton, FL: CRC Press, 2006.

15

SENTENCING OPTIONS

A man stands behind the bars of a prison cell. Prison populations are at an all-time high in the United States, with nearly 2.2 million inmates in state and federal custody. Many state prisons are so overcrowded that inmates have won significant victories in federal courts, which have ordered states to improve the conditions of confinement on Eighth Amendment grounds. As a result, many states face major financial challenges in trying to house the growing number of prisoners at a time when the cost of doing so continues to rise. Should this have an effect on sentencing options?

CHAPTER OUTLINE

LEARNING OBJECTIVES

After reading this chapter, you should be able to:

1. Distinguish between the four major sentencing philosophies.

2. **Describe how the three branches of government are involved in sentencing.**

3. List three major issues related to imprisonment as a sentence in the United States.

4. **Identify the three major alternatives to imprisonment.**

5. Outline the Supreme Court rulings on capital punishment that led to the bifurcated process for death penalty sentencing.

6. **Indicate how the Court has narrowed the list of death-eligible cases.**

7. Discuss the major differences between the due process model of criminal justice and the crime control model of justice with regard to the death penalty.

When he was 17 years old, Christopher Simmons and a 15-year-old friend broke into a neighbor's house, hogtied her with duct tape, and then shoved her over a railroad trestle into the Meramec River near St. Louis, Missouri. After the jury convicted Simmons of first-degree murder, they imposed the death penalty. The Supreme Court had earlier ruled that 17-year-olds could be put to death (*Stanford v. Kentucky* 1989), but the rationale for that decision had more recently been undermined when the Court declared that the mentally retarded could not be executed (*Atkins v. Virginia* 2002). But the justices waited almost 3 years to address for a second time the issue of the juvenile death penalty.

In 1972, by the slimmest of margins, the Court declared all existing death penalty laws unconstitutional, and in the process irrevocably altered the debate over what punishments are appropriate for those who violate the criminal law. Since then, the nation's highest court, like the rest of the nation, has been wrestling with the moral issue of who deserves to die at the hands of the state, and like the rest of the nation, it is deeply divided over the matter.

The debate over the death penalty is the most obvious example of the unprecedented attention the nation has devoted to crime over the past few decades. In large measure, the public holds judges, from the Supreme Court on down, responsible for high rates of crime and points to decisions such as *Roper* as examples. Understanding the dissatisfaction with sentencing and the sentencing reforms that have resulted requires an understanding of the legal basis of sentencing. This chapter focuses on the why, the who, and the what of sentencing. Punishments are shaped by philosophical and moral considerations. Asking *why* we sentence focuses attention on the competing justifications for sentencing. Probing *who* should make these choices reveals the complex sentencing structure in the United States. Although the public associates the judge with sentencing, closer scrutiny indicates that other branches of government share sentencing responsibility as well. Finally, examining the *what* of sentencing shows that a variety of sentences may be imposed on the guilty, including prison, probation, intermediate sanctions, fines, and restitution. And most controversial of all, a penalty of death may be imposed on a select number of defendants found guilty at trial.

WHY DO WE SENTENCE?

"An eye for an eye, a tooth for a tooth." "Lock them up and throw away the key." "Let this sentence be a warning to others." "Sentencing should rehabilitate the offender." These statements—variously drawn from the Bible, newspaper headlines, casual conversations, and statements by court officials—demonstrate that no consensus exists on how the courts should punish the guilty. Retribution, incapacitation, deterrence, and rehabilitation are the four principal justifications offered.

These sentencing philosophies differ in important ways. Some focus on past behavior, whereas others are future-oriented. Some stress that the punishment should fit the crime, whereas others emphasize that punishment should fit the criminal. These issues influence contemporary thinking about sentencing.

RETRIBUTION

The idea that offenders deserve punishment lies at the heart of **retribution**. This philosophy toward criminal punishment can be traced back to ancient Babylonia in the Code of Hammurabi, one of the oldest written codifications of laws ever discovered. The code relied heavily on the principle of *lex talionis*—"an eye for an eye, a tooth for a tooth." This revenge-based conceptualization of retributive punishment was also adopted by the Hebrews. Indeed, the Old Testament says, "eye for eye, tooth for tooth, hand for hand, foot for foot, burn for burn, wound for wound, bruise for bruise" (Exodus 21:22-25). In context, though, this old philosophy for justifying punishment has limits:

When one man strikes another and kills him, he shall be put to death. Whoever strikes a beast and kills it shall make restitution, life for life. When one man injures and disfigures his fellow countryman, it shall be done to him as he has done; fracture for fracture, eye for eye, tooth for tooth; the injury and disfigurement that he has inflicted upon another shall in turn be inflicted upon him. (Leviticus 24:17–22).

What is most distinctive about retribution is its focus on past behavior; the severity of the punishment is directly tied to the seriousness of the crime. This concept is based on strongly held moral principles: Individuals are held responsible for their own actions. Because they have disregarded the rights of others, criminals are wicked people and therefore deserve to be punished. Punishing wrongdoers also reflects a basic human emotion, the desire for revenge: Because the victim has suffered, the criminal should suffer as well.

The concept of retribution clearly stands for punitive sentencing, but a closer probing reveals important subtleties involving limits on sentencing. Because society as a whole is punishing the criminal, individuals are not justified in taking the law into their own hands. Moreover, in applying sanctions, the severity of the punishment is limited to the severity of the injury to the victim.

From biblical times through the 18th century, retribution vis-à-vis revenge provided the dominant justification for punishment. Beginning with the Enlightenment, however, revenge lost much of its influence as a justification for criminal punishment. In fact, criminal penalties based on revenge came to be viewed as barbaric. A new, more humane view of retribution evolved that focused on deserved punishment, or **just deserts**. It embodied two distinct but interrelated principles. First, the offender justly deserves to be punished for having wronged another person in violation of the law. Second, society has not only the right, but also the obligation to punish proportionally all transgressions of the criminal law because such acts should be viewed as offenses against society as a whole (e.g., Kant 1790). The just deserts approach to retributive punishment is alive and well in modern times. "Someone who infringes the rights of others…does wrong and deserves blame for his conduct. It is because he deserves blame that the sanctioning authority is entitled to choose a response

that expresses moral disapproval; namely punishment" (von Hirsch 1986, p. 49). The just deserts approach to retributive punishment is predicated on the notion of proportionality. While "offenders are punished simply because they deserve to be," "the severity of their punishment should be no more and no less than they deserve" (Frase 2005, p. 73). In short, the severity of the sanction should be proportionate to the gravity of the defendant's criminal conduct (Banks 2009; Carlsmith, Darley, and Robinson 2002).

Saint Augustine (c. 426) and, later, Saint Thomas Aquinas (c. 1273) and other theologians posited a third conceptualization of retribution based on **expiation**—atonement for sin through deserved suffering. In their opinion, retributive punishment should cause offenders to suffer, but not to achieve revenge or to balance the scales of justice for wrongs committed against individual victims or even society as a whole. Rather, through such suffering, offenders would come to see the errors of their ways, repent, and, ultimately, be forgiven for their sins (see also, Olson 2006–2007).

As a sentencing philosophy, retribution suffers from several limitations. Its focus on crimes of violence offers little apparent guidance for sentencing the far more numerous defendants who have committed property violations. Its moralistic emphasis on individual responsibility does not fit well with modern explanations of human behavior based on social, physical, and psychological factors. Its emphasis on vengeance does not easily square with constitutional limits on government power (individual rights) that are fundamental to a representative democracy. Most important, though, it emphasizes the past behavior of the defendant and exhibits no concern for future criminal activity. Indeed, extended periods of custody may actually have unintended criminogenic effects, thereby increasing the likelihood that inmates might commit future criminal acts rather than be deterred by the sentence they received (see Austin and Hardyman 2004). Thus, sentencing on the basis of retribution may prove to be contrary to the goal of crime reduction.

INCAPACITATION

"Lock them up and throw away the key." Average citizens, outraged by a recent, shocking crime, often express sentiments like this. The assumption of **incapacitation** is that crime can be prevented if criminals are physically restrained. The theory of isolating current or potential criminals differs from the theory of retribution in two important ways. First, it is future-oriented; the goal is to prevent future crimes, not punish past ones. Second, it focuses on the personal characteristics of the offender; the type of person committing the crime is more important than the crime committed. Unlike rehabilitation, however, incapacitation has no intention of reforming the offender.

Since ancient times, societies have banished persons who have disobeyed the rules. England transported criminals to penal colonies, such as Georgia and Australia. Russia exiled dissidents to cold, distant Siberia, where they could not threaten the government. More commonly, nations have used prisons to isolate guilty offenders, preventing them from committing additional crimes in the community. Some people likewise justify the death penalty on the basis that it prevents future crimes.

Incapacitation is probably the most straightforward justification offered for punishing wrongdoers. As a sentencing philosophy, however, it suffers from important limitations. It cannot provide any standards about how long a sentence should be. Indeed, the goal of crime prevention may be used to justify severe sanctions for both trivial and serious offenses. Moreover, isolation without efforts directed toward rehabilitation may produce more severe criminal behavior once the offender is released. Prisons protect the community, but that protection is only temporary. Applying the incapacitation theory to the fullest would require the building of many more prisons, at great expense.

The incapacitation theory of sentencing has never been well articulated. Its assumptions about crime and criminals are simplistic. But in recent years a more focused variant, **selective incapacitation**, has received considerable attention (Goodman-Delahunty, ForsterLee, and ForsterLee 2007). Research has shown that a relatively small number of criminals are responsible for a large number of crimes (DeLisi 2005; Haapanen 1989). These findings have led to an interest in targeting dangerous offenders (Chaiken and Chaiken 1990). Some studies estimate that sending serious offenders to prison for longer periods of time will result in a significant reduction in crime (Shinnar and Shinnar 1975; Spelman 2000). Not all researchers agree, however, that selective incapacitation will greatly reduce crime because predictions of who

will commit crimes in the future are very unreliable (Auerhahn 2006; Cunningham, Reidy, and Sorensen 2008). "Offenders commit crimes at different rates and individuals' offending rates evolve over their life course. Therefore, estimating how many crimes are averted…must depend crucially on when in individuals' lives and at what point in their criminal careers the incarceration occurs (Bhati 2007, p. 357). Moreover, critics argue that even though some offenders may be incapacitated through imprisonment, other people on the verge of criminality are ready to take their places (Auerhahn 1999; Visher 1987). And still other critics argue that the costs of imprisonment typically exceed the benefits gained from preventing certain criminals from recidivating by keeping them incapacitated (Blokland and Nieuwbeerta 2007).

DETERRENCE

"Let this sentence be a warning to others." Phrases like this reflect one of the more modern and also most widely held justifications for punishment. According to **deterrence theory**, the purpose of punishment is the prevention of future crimes. Deterrence is not content to punish the given wrongdoer; rather, it seeks to prevent other potential offenders from committing crimes. Deterrence, however, does not propose to change offenders—just deter them. Much like rehabilitation, deterrence argues that the punishment should fit the criminal. Note that this is a different concern from that of retribution theory, in which the punishment should fit the crime.

Building on the work of 18th-century criminologist Cesare Beccaria (1764), Jeremy Bentham, 19th-century British lawyer, reformer, and criminologist, articulated a coherent theory of deterrence (1830) that still influences us today. To Bentham, punishment based on retribution was pointless and counterproductive. Instead, he argued that sanctions should be used to further society's goal of preventing crime. Bentham believed that human behavior is governed by individual calculation: People seek to maximize pleasure and minimize pain—a principle he referred to as the **hedonistic calculus**. Under this utilitarian theory, the basic objective of punishment is to discourage crime by making it painful. Because people seek to minimize pain, they will refrain from activities, such as crimes, that result in painful sanctions.

Deterrence theory suggests that the criminal justice system can effectuate two types of deterrence: general and specific. The **general deterrent** goal of criminal punishment presumes that the threat of punishment will prevent the general population from engaging in the proscribed conduct. The **specific deterrent** goal of criminal punishment postulates that those for whom the general deterrent of law was insufficient to prevent them from having engaged in the proscribed conduct should be subjected to punishment so that they will be personally discouraged from engaging in the proscribed conduct again.

Both Beccaria and Bentham in their classical deterrence models argued for the existence of several factors that will influence the effectiveness of punishment as a general deterrent. Much scholarly research has demonstrated that the effectiveness of law as a deterrent is dependent on three primary factors: severity, certainty, and celerity (i.e., swiftness). **Severity of punishment** is concerned with how severe the punishment is. The theory postulates that the more severe the punishment, the less likely the actor is to engage in the proscribed conduct. The second factor, **certainty of punishment**, is concerned with how likely the actor is to get away with the crime as opposed to being caught. According to deterrence theory, the more likely it is that the actor is going to be caught, the less likely he or she is to engage in the conduct. Finally, **celerity of punishment** is the factor that looks at the swiftness of punishment. The theory suggests that the faster the punishment is inflicted after the offense, the less likely the person is to engage in the proscribed conduct. Conversely, the later or further off the punishment, the less likely is the person to be deterred.

Notions of deterrence form the core of contemporary discussions about sentencing. In a general sense, many people refrain from committing illegal acts because they fear the consequences of being convicted. After a party, for example, an intoxicated guest may take a taxi home rather than run the risk of being arrested and disgraced by a drunken driving conviction. In this situation, one can easily argue that the threat of punishment does deter. However, what of the person who drinks and drives? Perhaps such an actor has weighed the costs and benefits and decided that the low likelihood of being caught makes the behavior worth the risk. Alternatively, one could argue that drinking and driving is, in itself, an irrational behavior since it puts the lives of the driver and others on the road in jeopardy. This reveals one of the most significant shortcomings of deterrence theory: the threat of severe, certain, and swift punishment is likely to deter only those who are thinking rationally. Irrational thinkers (whether due to mental illness, disability, the effects of drugs or alcohol, or

other reasons) are unlikely to be deterred because their abilities to engage in the hedonistic calculus is impaired. This is particularly true for many crimes of violence that are committed on the spur of the moment or during the "heat of passion."

An extensive literature examines deterrence but reaches no firm conclusions. Some studies find a deterrent effect, and others do not (Levitt 2006; Nagin 1998; Webster, Doob, and Zimring 2006). Although discussions of deterrence are usually coupled with calls for increasing the severity of sentences, some research suggests that the perceived certainty of punishment is more of a deterrent than the perceived severity of punishment (Cullen, Wright, and Blevins 2006; Wilson 1983). Moreover, because deterrence rests on the assumption of rational, calculating behavior, and this precondition is absent in many crimes (as described above), many observers question whether court sentences—particularly severe ones—do indeed deter.

REHABILITATION

One of the more appealing modern justifications for imposing punishment is to restore a convicted offender to a constructive place in society through vocational, educational, or therapeutic treatment. The idea of **rehabilitation** assumes that criminal behavior is the result of social or psychological disorders, and that the treatment of such disorders should be the primary goal of corrections. Success means assessing the needs of the individual and providing a program to meet those needs. Ultimately, then, offenders are not being punished but treated, not only for their own good but also for the benefit of society. Under rehabilitation, sentences should fit the offender rather than the offense.

The concept of rehabilitation dominated thinking about sentencing throughout much of the 20th century, providing the intellectual linchpin for important developments such as probation and parole. Most court personnel and correctional officials have strongly favored rehabilitation. It has also enjoyed widespread public support; almost three out of four persons favor the idea that the main emphasis in prisons should be to help the offender become a productive citizen.

The rehabilitative ideal has been challenged on both normative and empirical grounds. Some commentators have voiced concern that the rehabilitative ideal grants too much discretion to judges and parole boards. As a result of this discretion, the humanitarian goal of rehabilitation can serve to

COURTS, CONTROVERSY, AND REDUCING CRIME

Should Restorative Justice Replace Revenge-Based Sentencing?

After imposing a prison sentence on a rapist, Justice John Kelly observed that the victim was no less distraught than she had been throughout the court proceedings. So before he called the next case, he asked the victim to approach the bench. Speaking briefly and quietly, he concluded with these words: "You understand that what I have done here demonstrates conclusively that *what happened was not your fault.*" Hearing these words, she began to weep and ran from the courtroom. Several days later, the Australian judge called the family and learned that his words had been words of vindication for the woman; they marked the beginning of her psychological healing. Her tears had been tears of healing. In *Restoring Justice*, Daniel Van Ness and Karen Strong (2006) used this example to emphasize their central theme—that sentencing should promote healing. The restorative justice movement seeks to replace retribution with restoration. In essence, the failures of the contemporary criminal justice system are traced to the historical emphasis on vengeance.

Restorative justice is based on three distinct elements (Galaway and Hudson 1996):

● Crime is primarily a conflict between individuals, which results in injuries (physical and/or psychological) to victims, the community, and the offender as well. Therefore, crime is only secondarily a violation of governmental laws.
● The principal aim of the criminal justice system should be to repair these injuries. Therefore, promoting peace and reconciling parties is much more important than punishing the guilty.
● The criminal justice system should facilitate involvement of victims, offenders, and the community. Therefore, lay citizens should play a central role in the criminal justice system, and professionals (police, prosecutors, and probation officers, for example) should play less of a role.

Clearly, proponents of restorative justice reject the crime control model's emphasis on punishment. In their view, vengeance is counterproductive. But at

mask punishment. But such normative concerns appear to be taking a back seat to the empirical data concerning rehabilitation.

Starting in the mid-1970s, evidence revealed that rehabilitative programs did not substantially reduce the later criminality of their clients (Blumstein et al. 1983; Martinson 1974). California, for example, where the rehabilitative model had been most completely incorporated, was also marked by high rates of recidivism (repeat criminal behavior). To some, the key weakness of rehabilitation is that people cannot be coerced to change. Some prisoners participate in prison rehabilitation programs, such as counseling, job training, and religious services, in order to gain an early release—not because they wish to change their behavior.

More recently, though, empirical studies have found that rehabilitation can indeed be effective (see Cullen 2005). Much of the research supporting the rehabilitative model comes from studies that have

evaluated the effectiveness of different correctional interventions. An ever-growing number of modern correctional policies are being crafted in light of the empirical evidence produced by these evaluation studies, a movement called **evidence-based corrections** (MacKenzie 2006; Robinson 2008). As a result, resources are being put into interventions that research has demonstrated to be effective, such as "using behavioral and cognitive approaches, occurring in the offenders' natural environment, being multi-modal and intensive enough to be effective, encompassing rewards for pro-social behavior, targeting high-risk and high-criminogenic need individuals, and matching the learning styles and abilities of the offender" (Listwan, Cullen, and Latessa 2006, p. 20). In contrast, rehabilitative strategies that have proven to be largely ineffective, such as psychodynamic therapies, boot camps, "scared straight" programs, and shock incarceration

the same time, they view the due process model as not going far enough. The rehabilitative model targets offenders but provides no healing for victims and fails to address the trauma they have experienced.

Skeptics voice concern that restorative justice means considerably different things to different people. Indeed, by stressing abstract concepts rather than pointing to specific programs, proponents make it somewhat difficult to discuss restorative justice because many of the examples singled out as demonstrating successful implementation are drawn from other countries.

If skeptics seem somewhat receptive to this new idea, critics express open hostility about subjecting a victim to another, possibly equally damaging, encounter with the defendant. Typical was the person on an Internet discussion list who wanted to know why victims should be forced to bargain with a person who has caused them harm. Perhaps victims do not want to go through the process because of legitimate concerns (unnecessarily revisiting the original trauma) or out of shortsightedness (holding onto the role of victim is comfortable). Overall,

it is clear that the restorative justice understanding of victims is far different from those views that stress punishment and not forgiveness (discussed in Chapter 9).

Restorative justice programs have become increasingly common in the justice system, but relatively little is known about their effectiveness. Some of the early studies have been characterized as using weak research designs. A rigorous study of the Indianapolis Restorative Justice Experiment is important, therefore, because the results were largely positive. Youths who were assigned to family group conferences (as opposed to a control group) were less likely to be rearrested (McGarrell and Hipple 2008).

What do you think? Should our current criminal justice system, which is often characterized as a revenge-based system, be replaced by restorative justice? What types of victims might be most amenable to conferencing? What types of defendants are most likely to express remorse? What elements of the community would be most supportive of restorative justice?

programs are slowly being abandoned (Cullen, Blevins, and Trager 2005; MacKenzie 2006).

The reemergence of rehabilitation as a viable basis for criminal punishment has also been fueled, in part, by the severe economic downturn in the later part of the 21st century's first decade. The extremely high costs of incarcerating so many people—especially nonviolent drug offenders—caused many commentators to question the sustainability of the punitive, "get tough" policies of the 1980s and 1990s (Steen and Bandy 2007). In other words, from a cost–benefit standpoint, the harsh economic reality of the prison–industrial complex has led to a renewed focus on rehabilitative strategies (Robinson 2008).

COMPETING SENTENCING PHILOSOPHIES

Justifications for punishing wrongdoers are based on religious and moral views of right and wrong as well

as empirical perceptions of human behavior (see Exhibit 15.1). Of the four philosophies—retribution, incapacitation, deterrence, and rehabilitation—none alone is adequate; the various goals must be balanced. Therefore, elements of each of these four philosophies have been incorporated into society's efforts to control crime. As a result, sentencing decisions reflect ambivalent expectations about the causes of crime, the nature of criminals, and the role of the courts in reducing crime. The limitations of historical sentencing philosophies have led a small band of adherents to pioneer a new way of thinking about criminals and their victims (see Courts, Controversy, and Reducing Crime: Should Restorative Justice Replace Revenge-Based Sentencing?).

Since the late 1970s, the reasons for sentencing have been the subject of intense debate. After three quarters of a century, the intellectual dominance of the rehabilitative ideal began to crumble and then

---

Exhibit 15.1

CONTRASTING SENTENCING PHILOSOPHIES

	LAW ON THE BOOKS	LAW IN ACTION
Retribution	Punishment inflicted on a person who has infringed on the rights of others and so deserves to be penalized to a degree commensurate with the crime.	Focuses on the crime committed (not on the defendant). Limits punishment to the harm done by the offender.
Incapacitation	Deprives a convicted person of the capacity to commit crimes against society by detention in prison.	Focuses on defendant's history. Can lead to very unequal sentences because minor offenses can be punished more severely than major ones.
Deterrence	Punishment of criminals to prevent future crimes.	Based on Bentham's utilitarian theory. General deterrence (directed toward the general populace) differs from special deterrence (the specific defendant).
Rehabilitation	The process of restoring a convicted offender to a constructive place in society through some form of vocational, educational, or therapeutic treatment.	Focuses on the defendant rather than on the crime committed. Dominant sentencing philosophy for most of the 20th century. Under what conditions defendants can be rehabilitated is subject to extensive debate.

---

collapse. This resulted in widespread sentencing reforms, many of which focus on who should have the authority to impose a sentence and what limits should be placed on that authority.

WHO SHOULD DECIDE THE SENTENCE?

From the inside looking out, sentencing is a judicial function. With a few exceptions, only the judge has the legal authority to send the guilty to prison or to grant probation. From the outside looking in, however, sentencing responsibility involves all three branches of government—legislative, executive, and judicial. The result is a varied and complex sentencing structure that has changed greatly since the mid-1970s.

Throughout most of the 20th century, sentencing was exercised within broad limits set by the legislature, which prescribed maximum sentences. The judicial branch of government had primary authority over who went to prison, and an executive agency—**parole boards**—controlled the length of the prison term. Since the mid-1970s, dramatic changes have been made in the laws under which offenders are sent to prison and in the mechanisms that control how long they stay there. Legislatures have increased their control over the sentencing process, and the judiciary and the parole boards have taken steps to formalize and regularize their exercise of discretion in applying sanctions. The result has been a significant narrowing of sentencing discretion in most states (see Exhibit 15.2).

LEGISLATIVE SENTENCING RESPONSIBILITY

Legislatures are initially responsible for creating sentencing options. Recall from Chapter 2 that there can be no crime and no punishment without law.

Exhibit 15.2

CHANGING SENTENCING STRUCTURES IN THE UNITED STATES

	MOST OF 20TH CENTURY	SINCE THE MID-1970S
Legislative responsibility	Legislators provided wide parameters for possible sentences; little guidance provided about who should be placed on probation; little guidance offered on how long a prison sentence should be.	Perceiving judges as unduly lenient, legislatures have adopted sentencing guidelines, mandatory minimums, and three-strikes laws (see Chapter 16).
Judicial responsibility	Judges had wide discretion in deciding on a specific sentence. Actual sentences imposed could vary significantly from judge to judge.	Judges' sentencing discretion has been greatly curtailed. Judges complain that they are unable to shape sentences to real crimes committed by real criminals.
Executive responsibility	Correction officials enjoyed wide discretion in rewarding good time and deciding when to place a convict on parole.	Good time and parole have been abolished or greatly restricted in most jurisdictions. Prison overcrowding has resulted in even wider discretion for correction officials.

Legislative sentencing responsibility is expressed in the criminal codes enacted by legislative bodies. Legislatures specify terms of imprisonment in two different ways. Consistent with the goal of rehabilitation, which dominated correctional thinking through most of the 20th century, state legislatures adopted **indeterminate sentences** (often called "indefinite sentences"), based on the idea that correctional personnel must have discretion to release an offender when treatment has been successful. States with indeterminate sentences stipulate a minimum and maximum amount of time to be served in prison—1 to 5 years, 3 to 10 years, 20 years to life, and so on. At the time of sentencing, the offender knows the range of the sentence and knows that parole is a possibility after the minimum sentence, minus good time, has been served. How long the person actually remains in prison is determined by the parole authority, based on its assessment of the offender's progress toward rehabilitation.

Because of the growing disillusionment with the rehabilitative model in the 1970s, along with evidence that indeterminate sentences often produced disparate sentencing outcomes for similar crimes, determinate sentences grew in popularity. **Determinate**

sentences (sometimes called "fixed sentences") consist of a specified number of years rather than a range of years. For example, the judge must sentence the defendant to imprisonment for 5 years, or 10 years, or whatever the legislature specifies for a particular offense.

In waging the wars on crime and drugs, legislative bodies have adopted the deterrent theory of sentencing, opting to mandate harsher sentences for criminal violations. In furtherance of this goal, numerous legislative bodies have enacted major changes in sentencing laws, aiming to reduce the amount of discretion exercised by actors in the other branches of government. Several states have restricted the carte blanche authority historically granted judges and have also limited (and in some cases abolished) the discretion of executive agencies as well. Chapter 16 will explore in more detail issues related to mandatory minimums, sentencing guidelines, and the like.

JUDICIAL SENTENCING RESPONSIBILITY

Only judges have the authority to choose among the sentencing options provided by the legislature. Other members of the work group may recommend, but only the judge can decide. Of course, some minor exceptions to this general proposition exist, but these minor exceptions aside, American judges traditionally have enjoyed virtually unlimited judicial sentencing responsibility.

Wide judicial discretion in sentencing reflected the rehabilitative model, which stressed that the punishment should fit the criminal. No two crimes or criminals are exactly alike; sentences should therefore be individualized, with judges taking these differences into account. But no agreement has been reached on what factors should increase the penalty or reduce it. By the mid-1970s, wide judicial discretion had come under attack from both ends of the political spectrum. Advocates of the due process model of criminal justice expressed concern that judicial sentencing discretion was too broad, resulting in inequities such as racial discrimination. Conversely, proponents of the crime control model expressed concern that too much judicial discretion led to unduly lenient sentences. These two political movements, although contradictory, led legislatures to greatly reduce judicial sentencing discretion. Thus, an increasing number of jurisdictions are narrowing judicial discretion over sentencing in some manner.

EXECUTIVE SENTENCING RESPONSIBILITY

Sentences imposed by judges are typically carried out by officials of the executive branch. Of particular importance is the impact of executive officials on prison populations. How long an offender will be imprisoned depends not only on the length of the sentence imposed by the judge but also on the decisions made by governors, parole boards, and departments of corrections. Few prisoners serve their maximum terms of imprisonment. Each year, more than 530,000 inmates are released from prison to serve the remainder of their sentences in the community (Bureau of Justice Statistics 2009). The most common forms of early release are parole, good time, and (to a much lesser extent) executive clemency.

Parole is the conditional release of an inmate from incarceration, under supervision, after a portion of the prison sentence has been served. A parole officer supervises the conditions of release, and any rule violations or new crimes can result in a return to prison for the balance of the unexpired term. Parole boards, which are usually appointed by the governor, vary greatly in their discretion-

ary authority. Approximately 800,000 persons are currently on parole in the United States (Bureau of Justice Statistics 2008).

Another way in which decisions made by the executive branch affect how long an inmate must stay in prison is **good time**; in many states, prisoners are awarded days off their minimum or maximum terms as a reward for good behavior or for participation in various vocational, educational, and treatment programs. The amount of good time that can be earned varies from 5 days a month to 45 days a month in some states. Correctional officials find these sentence-reduction provisions necessary for the maintenance of institutional order and as a mechanism to reduce overcrowding. They usually have discretion in awarding good time.

State governors, as well as the president of the United States, have the power to pardon any prisoner in their respective jurisdictions, reduce sentences, or make prisoners eligible for parole (Moore 1989; Ruckman 1997). **Pardons** are not a common method of prisoner release, however; only a small group of inmates receive executive clemency each year.

The early release of prisoners through the use of parole and good time has come under heavy political attack in recent years. The result has been significant changes in some jurisdictions. Sixteen states and the federal government have abolished parole board authority to release offenders, and another four have abolished parole board authority for releasing violent offenders. Similarly, legislatures in many states have reduced or eliminated good time for certain types of prisoners. Despite efforts to reduce the use of parole and curb the awarding of good time, burgeoning prison populations increasingly force correctional officials to use parole as a backdoor solution to prison overcrowding.

The failure rate for ex-prisoners, whether released on parole or after the expiration of their sentence, is dishearteningly high (Wallman 2005). Each year more than two thirds of the over 630,000 inmates who return to their communities are likely to be rearrested within 3 years (Mears et al. 2008). Considerable attention is now being paid to prisoner reentry (MacKenzie 2006; National Governors Association 2009; Travis 2005). Whether high failure rates are the result of bad behavior on the part of the ex-prisoners or bad public policy is an open question (Wilson 2005).

What Sentence Should Be Imposed?

What types of sentences should be imposed upon the guilty? Today, answers center on prison and probation, with a hot debate over the death penalty. But throughout history, sentences were very different. Flogging, the stocks, exile, chopping off a hand, and branding are just a few examples of punishments historically inflicted on the guilty. Today, such sanctions are viewed as violating the Constitution's prohibition against **cruel and unusual punishment**. In their place, we use imprisonment, probation, intermediate sanctions, fines, and restitution. Many states also make formal provisions for capital punishment, but the death penalty is rarely used. In essence, these forms of punishment are tools created under the sentencing structure to advance society's theories of punishment. They are the options from which the sentencing judge must choose (see Exhibit 15.3).

One can approach the question of which penalty should be imposed upon the guilty from either a micro or a macro perspective. The micro perspective focuses on a specific defendant convicted of a crime. It is from this perspective that victims often view sentencing, and from this vantage point they are often critical of the judge's (or sometimes the legislature's) choice, arguing that the sentence is too lenient. It is vitally important, however, to assess such criticisms from a macro perspective. From this vantage point, prisons are already overcrowded, the caseloads of probation officers overwhelming. It is for this reason that judges occasionally address crime victims and explain the painfully obvious—to send this defendant to prison will require correctional officials to release someone who is possibly an even greater threat to the community.

Exhibit 15.3

SENTENCING OPTIONS

	LAW ON THE BOOKS	LAW IN ACTION
Prison	A correctional facility for housing adults convicted of felony offenses, usually under the control of state government.	Almost 1.5 million U.S. adults are in prison. Seven percent of inmates are female. Forty-five percent of prison inmates are African-American.
Parole	Adults conditionally released to community supervision after serving part of a prison term. The parolee is subject to being returned to prison for rule violations or other offenses.	More than 765,000 are on parole from state or federal prison. Twelve percent of parolees are women. Forty percent of parolees are white.
Probation	Punishment for a crime that allows the offender to remain in the community without incarceration but subject to certain conditions.	More than 4 million adults are under federal, state, or local jurisdiction on probation. Half of all offenders on probation are on probation for a felony.
Intermediate sanctions	A variety of punishments that are more restrictive than traditional probation but less stringent than incarceration.	Much less costly than imprisonment. Community service requires offender to perform public service such as street cleaning or hospital volunteer work.

Exhibit 15.3

CONTINUED

	LAW ON THE BOOKS	LAW IN ACTION
Fines	A sum of money to be paid to the government by a convicted person as punishment for an offense.	Often used in misdemeanors. Recent research shows that it can be effectively used in select felonies.
Restitution	Requirement that the offender pay to the victim a sum of money to make good the loss.	Most defendants are so poor that they cannot reasonably be expected to make restitution.
Capital punishment	The use of the death penalty (execution) as the punishment for the commission of a particular crime.	More than 3,200 prisoners are on death row. Thirty-seven executions were carried out during 2008; 5 fewer than in 2007 and 23 fewer than in 2005. Fifty-six percent of death row inmates are white.

The next chapter will examine how the courtroom work group decides on the specific penalty for a convict. For now, we will examine the various options available, beginning with that most distinctly American institution, the prison.

IMPRISONMENT

Although it has been used from time to time throughout history, **imprisonment** (incarceration) has become the dominant form of punishment only during the past two centuries. The United States imprisons a larger share of its population than any other nation. More than 2.3 million inmates are currently housed in prisons and jails (Bureau of Justice Statistics 2009).

The high rate of imprisonment (which has been termed "penal harm") is not without its critics (Listwan et al. 2008). In *Big Prisons, Big Dreams* Michael Lynch (2007) argues that the dramatic growth in our prison population has not reduced crime because we are not targeting the worst offenders. Prison populations are comprised of the poor, and many are incarcerated for nonviolent drug offenses or for relatively

minor offenses. In *Imprisoning Communities: How Mass Incarceration Makes Disadvantaged Neighborhoods Worse* Todd Clear (2007) adds that high rates of incarceration contribute to the very social problems it is intended to solve: It breaks up families and erodes economic and social networks in economically disadvantaged communities.

One reason for this high rate of imprisonment is the length of sentences. Prison sentences in the United States are quite long compared with those imposed in Europe, where it is rare for a defendant to be sentenced to more than 5 years.

PRISON OVERCROWDING

The political rhetoric of getting tough on criminals (see Chapter 1) clearly has had an impact—prisons are filled to overflowing. Prison overcrowding has become the dominant reality of criminal justice policy. Figure 15.1 shows how the size of the prison population has skyrocketed in recent years, more than tripling from the 1970s to today. The trend is starting to change: Record high numbers of prisoners are still reported every year, but the rate of increase has begun to slow. A few years ago the increases were

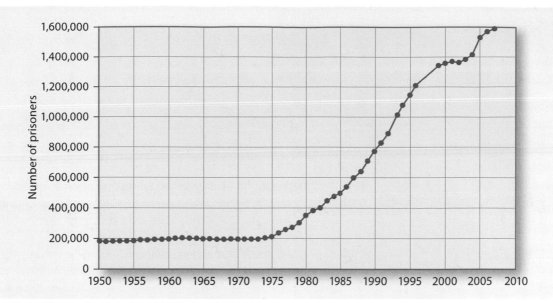

FIGURE 15.1 GROWING PRISON POPULATION

Source: Heather West and William Sabol. *Prisoners in 2007*. Washington, DC: U.S. Department of Justice, Bureau of Justice Statistics, 2008.

averaging from 8 percent to 12 percent per year, but since 2000, the growth of the prison population has slowed to 2 percent each year (West and Sabol 2008). It is worth noting that skyrocketing prison populations occurred during a period when crime rates (see Chapter 10) were largely constant, and now the crime rates are falling.

CONDITIONS OF CONFINEMENT LAWSUITS

The numbers of prisoners provide only part of the picture. Rapid increases in the size of the prison population occurred during the same time that federal courts began to demand improvements in prison conditions, which have often been described as substandard.

Traditionally, courts followed a hands-off policy regarding prisons, choosing not to interfere in their internal administration. But this policy began to change in 1964 (*Cooper v. Pate*). By the 1970s, the federal courts began to scrutinize the operations of correctional institutions to ensure compliance with the Eighth Amendment's protection against cruel

and unusual punishment (DiIulio 1990). Prisoners have sued, in what are often termed **conditions of confinement lawsuits**, contending that state officials have deprived them of their constitutional rights, such as adequate medical treatment and protection against excessive force by correctional officers and violence by other inmates (Hanson and Daley 1995). Unfortunately, though, inmates have also abused their rights to access the courts to redress legitimate grievance by suing over frivolous matters as a means of harassing correctional staff, taking revenge on the courts, or passing the time while incarcerated (Fradella 1999). The volume of meritless suits led Congress to restrict inmates' ability to sue in 1996, when it enacted the Prison Litigation Reform Act. The law was effective in significantly reducing the number of civil rights cases filed by prisoners. Critics, however, point out that in limiting the number of frivolous lawsuits that can clog the courts, Congress may have also made it more difficult for prisoners to file and win meritorious suits (Schlanger 2003). Exhibit 15.4 summarizes key developments in the law concerning imprisonment.

The entire prison systems of at least nine states were declared unconstitutional, and individual prisons were found constitutionally defective in many others. The net effect was that for many years most

Exhibit 15.4
KEY DEVELOPMENTS CONCERNING IMPRISONMENT

Eighth Amendment	1791	Excessive bail shall not be required, nor excessive fines imposed, nor cruel and unusual punishments inflicted.
Cooper v. Pate	1964	Prisoners can sue prison officials in federal court.
Estelle v. Gamble	1976	Deliberate indifference to serious medical needs of prisoners constitutes the unnecessary and wanton infliction of pain, and thus violates the Eighth Amendment.
Ruiz v. Estelle	1980	U.S. District Court declares that conditions of confinement in the Texas prison system are unconstitutional.
Rhodes v. Chapman	1981	Double-celling and crowding do not necessarily constitute cruel and unusual punishment.
Whitley v. Albers	1986	A prisoner shot in the leg during a riot does not suffer cruel and unusual punishment if the action was taken in good faith to maintain discipline rather than for the mere purpose of causing harm.
Mistretta v. U.S.	1989	Federal sentencing guidelines are legal.
Wilson v. Seiter	1991	Prisoners contesting conditions of confinement in federal court must show that prison officials acted with "deliberate indifference" to prisoner needs and living conditions.
Prison Litigation Reform Act	1996	Congress limits the authority of federal courts to supervise the operations of correctional institutions and limits the ability of inmates to file civil rights actions.
Miller v. French	2000	Upheld the Prison Litigation Reform Act, saying Congress could lawfully impose a 90-day time limit to rule on prison condition lawsuits.

states operated all or part of their correctional systems under a federal court order. Federal judges in virtually all states ordered state governments to alter dramatically the way in which they operated their prisons and jails. These court orders specified a maximum prison population, required physical conditions to be upgraded, increased the number of prison guards, and mandated minimal medical facilities (Chilton 1991; Crouch and Marquart 1990; Taggart 1989). These federal court orders have had a significant effect in transforming prison conditions, particularly in the South (Feeley and Rubin 1998).

It is now harder to challenge prison conditions in federal court, however. The Rehnquist Court created a new standard under the Eighth Amendment, holding that the prisoner must show "deliberate indifference" on the part of prison officials (*Wilson v. Seiter* 1991). Overall, the nation's highest court has limited the conditions under which federal courts will recognize violations of a prisoner's rights (Mushlin and Galtz 2009). And the Prison Litigation Reform Act of 1996 significantly limited the federal courts' supervisory powers over state prisons. Nonetheless, state correctional officials are aware that slipping back to old practices will result in future litigation.

High Costs

Getting tough on criminals is popular, yet public opinion polls show that spending money for more prisons is not a high priority for the general public. Prisons are costly to build and even more costly to maintain (Spelman 2009). Estimates of the costs of constructing a single cell exceeds $100,000 (Clear, Cole, and Reisig 2009). The costs of incarcerating a prisoner (clothes, food, and guards, primarily) depend on the level of confinement and also vary from state to state, ranging from $20,000 to $30,000 per prisoner per year. Figure 15.2 shows the total cost of building

Figure 15.2 Financial Projections over 30 Years for Building a New 500-Cell Prison

and maintaining a 500-cell prison over 30 years as $425 million.

Faced with swelling prison populations and federal court orders over conditions of confinement, state legislatures have been faced with spending enormous sums of money to build new prisons and upgrade existing ones. Prison construction during the 1990s was a growth industry, with 213 state and federal prisons built during the first 5 years, at an estimated cost of $30 billion ("In '90s, Prison" 1997). Despite large expenditures, no state has been able to build prisons fast enough to keep ahead of surging prison admissions. Across the nation, prisons were operating at 113% of capacity during the last year for which data are available (West and Sabol 2008).

Some states have declared an emergency situation, thus triggering the early release of certain types of prisoners. States that fail to take such action face sanctions from federal judges. Contempt of court, hefty fines, and judicially mandated release of prisoners are some of the remedies federal judges have imposed on state and local officials who have failed to take action to solve prison overcrowding (Clear, Cole, and Reisig 2009).

The long-standing political debate over sentencing has now given way to the overriding reality of a severe shortage of prison cells. State after state is discovering that the political rhetoric of the late 20th century to get tough on criminals by sending more people to prison for longer periods must give way to the fiscal realities of the 21st century—adjusting sentencing policies to fit prison capacity. The economic recession that began in December 2007 has greatly reduced state tax revenues, forcing states to reexamine how much they can spend on prisons when other important governmental services, such as education, face major budget reductions. Almost out of desperation, states are now turning to alternative penalty programs that resemble ideas that were tried and largely discarded a decade ago.

Probation

Probation is the principal alternative to imprisonment. It is also the most commonly used sanction in the United States; indeed, more than three times as many adults are on probation as are housed in state and federal prisons (Auerhahn 2007).

LAW AND POPULAR CULTURE

Dead Man Walking (1995)

"Dead Man Walking" announces the guard as Matthew Poncelet (played by Sean Penn), is marched to his execution. Sister Helen Prejean (played by Susan Sarandon) accompanies him as his spiritual advisor. The phrase "Dead Man Walking" is used by the people on death row to refer to the prisoners before execution and becomes the apt title of this disturbing and compelling movie.

Sister Helen Prejean, a nun who works as a teacher in a New Orleans housing project, receives a letter from Matthew Poncelet, a convicted murderer awaiting execution at the Louisiana State Prison at Angola. Having exhausted appellate court reviews, his only hope to avoid execution is clemency from the governor, and he requests Sister Prejean's help in filing a petition before the state pardon board.

Poncelet was convicted of raping a teenage girl and leaving her and her boyfriend to die in the woods. As Sister Prejean meets with Poncelet in prison, it becomes clear that he is his own worst enemy. He is racist and sexist. Moreover, he cannot seem to get beyond his pride. He admits his involvement, but insists he did not actually do the killing. All he says about his behavior is that he was high on drugs and alcohol and had not slept in two days. Sister Prejean prods Poncelet to accept responsibility. "You blame everyone else," she says, but "where are you in the picture?" He is forced to admit that "I am not a victim." But is he repentant?

Sister Prejean also reaches out to the families of the victims and experiences firsthand the raw emotions of parents experiencing an unbearable loss. The father of the dead son is a walking zombie devoid of emotion. He knows he must put the past behind him, but his wife cannot do it, and she files for divorce. In the end he reaches out to Sister Prejean to try and find a way out of the hate. By contrast, the parents of the slain daughter talk to Sister Helen, but become outraged when they discover that she is still the spiritual advisor to Poncelet. "How can you sit with that swine," they yell and throw her out of the house. For them, closure can seemingly only come with his execution. But whether their hate was expiated by the execution is unknown.

Dead Man Walking probes the fairness of who lives and who dies in America's capital punishment system. "Ain't nobody with money on death row," notes Poncelet. His volunteer lawyers make a similar argument before the pardon board, arguing that Poncelet was defended by a tax lawyer with no previous experience with a capital case. And now that his one appeal of right has been exhausted, he is totally dependent upon a few volunteer lawyers to fight his battles in court. And what weighs on the mind of Poncelet is the fact that his co-defendant (who he considers more culpable) was sentenced to life imprisonment.

The movie is based on the book of the same title written by real-life Sister Helen Prejean (1993) (although the names of the defendants and victim have been fictionalized). Her experiences in this case transformed her into a crusader against the death penalty. Although now in her 70s, she remains active, having written several additional books on the death penalty and making 120 presentations each year in the United States and Europe (Prejean 2009).

After watching the movie *Dead Man Walking*, be prepared to answer the following questions:

1. Do you think the movie is even handed in presenting the arguments for and against the death penalty?

CONTINUED

Dead Man Walking (1995)

2. How are your views about the death penalty affected by the character of Matthew Poncelet? If he had been more sympathetic, would that influence your views?
3. How do the four major sentencing philosophies—retribution, incapacitation, deterrence, and rehabilitation—apply in this case?
4. Based on watching this movie, what arguments would supporters of victim impact statements

make about why jurors should hear this type of information? What arguments could critics of victim impact statements make about how the sentencing phase of the trial would be better if this type of information were not allowed?

Altogether, about 4 million adults are on probation, a number that represents a doubling in less than two decades. The increasing use of probation is a direct reflection of the serious problem of prison overcrowding. Ironically, it has resulted in a significant amount of "probation crowding" (overload of the probation system equivalent to prison overcrowding) (Byrne, Lurigio, and Baird 1989). Figure 15.3 shows that probation crowding is rising almost as dramatically as prison overcrowding. As a result, probation officers often must handle excessive caseloads.

Unlike incarceration, **probation** is designed as a means of maintaining control over offenders while permitting them to live in the community (under supervision). The major justification for probation is that prisons are inappropriate places for some defendants and that limited supervision is a better way to rehabilitate criminals. Youthful or first-time offenders may only become embittered if mixed in prison with hardened criminals; they may end up learning more sophisticated criminal techniques. But most important, probation is significantly less expensive than imprisonment.

State and federal laws grant judges wide discretion in deciding whether to place a defendant on probation. Generally, statutes allow probation when it appears that

1. The defendant is not likely to commit another offense.
2. The public interest does not require that the defendant receive the penalty provided for the offense.
3. The rehabilitation of the defendant does not require that he or she receive the penalty provided for the offense.

Legislative provisions regarding who may be placed on probation vary considerably from state to state. Some states have statutes prohibiting certain types of offenders—typically violent offenders—from receiving probation.

Offenders placed on probation must agree to abide by certain rules and regulations prescribed by the sentencing judge. Termed "conditions of probation," these rules typically include keeping a job, supporting the family, avoiding places where alcoholic beverages are sold, reporting periodically to the probation officer, and not violating any law. Because probation is a judicial act, the judge can revoke probation and send the defendant to prison if the conditions of probation are violated. Chapter 16 will discuss in greater detail the key role probation officers play in managing the probation population (Lurigio, Olson, and Snowden 2009).

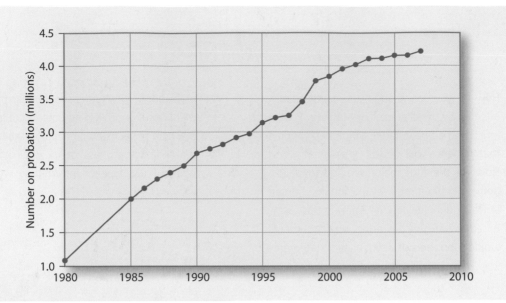

FIGURE 15.3   GROWTH IN PROBATION POPULATION

Source: Lauren Glaze and Thomas Bonczar. *Probation and Parole in the United States, 2007.* Washington, DC: U.S. Department of Justice, Bureau of Justice Statistics, 2008.

FINES

The imposition of a **fine** is one of the oldest and also one of the most widely used forms of punishment. Fines are used extensively for traffic offenses and minor ordinance violations, generating well over $1 billion annually for local governments (Clear, Cole, and Reisig 2009). Judges in the lower courts impose a fine alone or in combination with other sanctions in about 86 percent of their cases. But the imposition of fines is not confined to the lower courts. In the major trial courts, a fine, either alone or together with other sanctions, is imposed in almost 45 percent of the cases. First offenders with a known ability to pay are most likely to be sentenced in this way (Cole et al. 1988).

The limited use of fines as punishment in felony cases contrasts sharply with practices in some Western European countries (Shoham, Beck, and Kett

2007). Some countries have adopted sentencing policies that explicitly make fines the sentence of choice for many offenses, including some crimes of violence that would result in jail sentences in many American courts. In Germany, for example, a major legislative goal is to minimize the imposition of jail terms of less than 6 months. Instead, German courts make extensive use of "day fines," which enable judges to set fines at amounts reflecting the gravity of the offense but also taking into account the financial means of the offender (Hillsman and Mahoney 1988). In the United States, the day fine concept has been relabeled "structured fines" and is being recommended as a less costly sentencing option than imprisonment (Bureau of Justice Statistics 1996). In some respects structured fines reflect a "Robin Hood" approach to criminal justice—the rich pay more (DeLisi and Conis 2010).

American judges frequently cite the poverty of offenders as an obstacle to the broader use of fines as sanctions (Gillespie 1988–1989). Nonetheless, some courts regularly impose fines on persons whose financial resources are extremely limited and are successful in collecting those fines. Some research suggests that fines can be collected. Performance can be improved substantially if administrators systematically apply collection and enforcement techniques that already exist and have been proven effective (Cole 1992; Turner and Greene 1999).

RESTITUTION

Restitution is the requirement that the offender provide reparation to the victim for the harm caused by the criminal offense. Requiring defendants to compensate victims (giving something back) for their losses was customary in ancient civilizations, particularly for the people in the time of the Old Testament. But as the government replaced the victim as the principal party in criminal prosecution, restitution fell into decline; offenders paid fines to the government rather than restitution to the victim (Tobolowsky 1993). Beginning in the mid-1960s, the idea of restitution became the focus of renewed interest and became touted as one of the criminal justice system's more creative responses to crime. Nearly all states have enacted laws providing for the collection and distribution of restitution funds.

Restitution efforts generally take one of two forms—direct or symbolic (Galaway 1988). In **direct restitution**, the offender is required, as a condition of probation, to make monetary payments to the victim. As a criminal sanction, it is largely restricted to property crimes, since it has little relevance if violence figured in the commission of the offense. As we saw in Chapter 9, the 1996 Congressional Act requires the federal court to impose mandatory restitution, without consideration of the defendant's ability to pay. Thus, court-imposed restitution may only increase victim dissatisfaction when the offender fails to pay (Davis and Bannister 1995). A study of the Government Accountability Office of five major white-collar cases in federal court found that only 7 percent of court-ordered payments were ever collected (Schwartz 2007).

In **symbolic restitution**, the offender makes reparation for the harm done in the form of good works benefiting the entire community rather than the particular individual harmed. Such work is often called "community service." This sanction is most often used when there is no direct victim of the offense—for example, in convictions for drunk driving. Community service will be discussed more fully in the "Intermediate Sanctions" section.

INTERMEDIATE SANCTIONS

Concern is growing that the United States relies much too heavily on imprisonment and probation. Prison is viewed as too harsh (as well as unavailable) for many defendants, whereas probation is really unsupervised. Alternative sentences that lie somewhere between prison and probation are often referred to as **intermediate sanctions**. In their influential book, *Between Prison and Probation: Intermediate Punishments in a Rational Sentencing System*, Norval Morris and Michael Tonry (1990) put it this way: "Prison is used excessively; probation is used even more excessively; between the two is a near vacuum of purpose and enforced punishments." This is particularly true of nonviolent offenders who commit one or more minor crimes—the expensive option of prison seems best reserved for more serious offenders, but minor penalties like probation have not worked well in the past.

Intermediate sanctions are based on the concept of continuum of sanctions—the range of punishments vary from low control to high control (see Figure 15.4). At one end of the continuum are fines and community service, which reflect low control over the activities of the guilty person; at the other end are punishments like intensive supervision

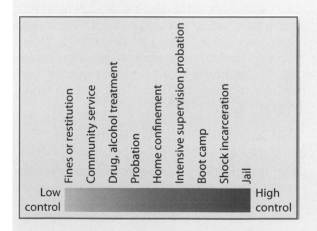

FIGURE 15.4   CONTINUUM OF SANCTIONS
Source: Adapted from Todd Clear, George Cole, and Michael Reisig, *American Corrections.* 7th ed. Belmont, CA: Wadsworth, 2006.

probation and so-called boot camps, which reflect high control just short of the maximum level of control—jail or prison (Clear, Cole, and Reisig 2009). The importance of drug and alcohol treatment has already been stressed in Chapter 4 in the discussion of drug courts. To round out the discussion of intermediate sanctions, we will examine community service, intensive supervision probation, and boot camps.

COMMUNITY SERVICE

Community service is based on the theory of symbolic restitution—the offender has injured the community and therefore should compensate the community for that injury. Thus, a person sentenced to **community service** is required to provide a specified number of hours of free labor in some public service, such as street cleaning, repairing substandard housing, or volunteering in a hospital. Community service is often a key component of community courts (see Chapter 18). In the eyes of the general public, community service is most visible when it is imposed on celebrities like actors and athletes.

The effectiveness of community service is mixed. It does not appear to reach its major goal of reducing prison populations because virtually all of those sentenced to community service would have received probation (not a prison sentence). Nor does community service appear to be particularly effective in reducing criminal behavior—those who participate have higher failure rates than those who receive regular supervision (Allen and Treger 1994). Nonetheless, one study suggests that overall offenders given community service have lower re-arrest rates than would be expected if they had been sentenced differently (Caputo 1999).

INTENSIVE SUPERVISION PROBATION

Given the high number of persons on probation, the amount of offender's contact with a probation officer is typically very limited—perhaps a brief meeting once a month. **Intensive supervision probation** (ISP) involves strict reporting, with the offender required to meet with a probation officer briefly every day. ISP targets offenders who are most likely to be facing imprisonment for their next violation.

Early evaluation of ISP programs found that intensive supervision did reduce re-arrest rates. But at the same time, these offenders were more likely to

be found in violation of their conditions of probation largely because they were being more closely supervised. As a result, even minor violations like arrests for disorderly conduct could result in the offender being in violation of his or her probation and sent to prison. In short, ISP might not be achieving its goal of sending fewer people to prison but instead might actually lead to a larger prison population. Despite questions about its effectiveness, the ISP approach remains popular with judges, prosecutors, corrections officials, and the public (Clear, Cole, and Reisig 2009).

BOOT CAMP

To some, the deterrent effect of incarceration loses its impact after a short time, which leads some to advocate **shock incarceration**—the offender is sentenced to a brief jail or prison sentence (typically 30 to 90 days) and then released on probation. The assumption is that the offender will find the experience so unpleasant that he or she will be motivated to "stay clean."

The best-known example of shock incarceration is the **boot camp**, in which offenders serve a short sentence including a rigorous, paramilitary regimen designed to develop discipline and respect for authority. Proponents of boot camps argue that many young offenders are involved in crime because they have little discipline in their disordered lives. Thus, a relatively brief, quasi-military experience is designed to send the offender off in more productive directions. Critics, however, argue that the military-style physical training and the harshness of the program do little to overcome the problems facing inner-city youths in trouble with the law. Evaluations of boot camp graduates show that they do no better than other offenders after release (Cullen, Blevins, and Trager 2005; Parent 2003). To be effective, boot camp programs must be carefully designed, target the right types of offenders, and provide rehabilitative services (Kurlychek and Kempinen 2006). Findings like these, coupled with the high costs, have led some state and local officials to close their boot camps.

THE DEATH PENALTY

Of all the forms of punishment, the **death penalty** is by far the most controversial, but it is also the least used; only a handful of offenders potentially face the ultimate sanction society can impose on the guilty.

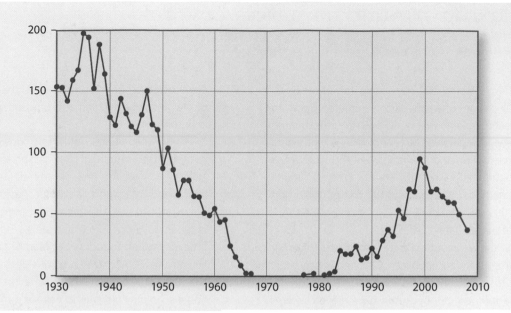

FIGURE 15.5 PERSONS EXECUTED IN THE
UNITED STATES, 1930–2008

Source: Bureau of Justice Statistics. "Capital
Punishment Statistics" http://www.ojp.usdoj.gov/
bjs/cp.htm

Since the Supreme Court ushered in the modern era of the death penalty in 1976, approximately 1,100 executions have been carried out in the United States.

Capital punishment was once almost the only penalty applied to convicted felons. By the time of the American Revolution, the English courts had defined more than 200 felonies, all of which were **capital offenses**. However, many death penalties were not carried out; instead, offenders were pardoned or banished to penal colonies. Over time, courts and legislatures began to recognize other forms of punishment, such as imprisonment and probation.

From the 1930s to the 1970s, the number of executions in the United States fell steadily (see Figure 15.5). During the peak years of 1935 and 1936, nearly 200 executions occurred each year, but executions declined substantially thereafter. From 1967 to 1972, an unofficial moratorium on executions existed. Since 1976, the numbers have steadily increased once again, reaching a peak of 98 in 1998.

Abolition of the death penalty has been a hot political issue. Opponents contend that it is mor-

ally wrong for the state to take a life; it has no deterrent value and is inherently discriminatory. These arguments have led all Western democracies except the United States to abolish the death penalty. Supporters counter that retribution justifies the taking of a life and that the death penalty does deter; they are generally unconcerned or unconvinced about allegations of discriminatory impact. (See Courts, Controversy, and Judicial Administration: Should a Moratorium on the Death Penalty Be Imposed?) In the United States, a series of Supreme Court opinions interpreting the Eight Amendment ushered in the modern era of death penalty jurisprudence.

EIGHTH AMENDMENT STANDARDS

Is capital punishment consistent with the Eighth Amendment's prohibition against cruel and unusual punishment? The Supreme Court first addressed this question in its 1972 landmark decision in *Furman v. Georgia*, which invalidated all 37 state death penalty statutes. The Court was deeply divided, however, with every justice writing a separate opinion.

Furman v. Georgia raised more questions than it answered, and state legislatures attempted to write new capital punishment laws consistent with the Eighth Amendment. By 1976, a total of 37 states had enacted new legislation designed

Courts, Controversy, and Judicial Administration

Should a Moratorium on the Death Penalty Be Imposed?

Anthony Porter was 2 days away from dying by lethal injection when the Illinois Supreme Court intervened, holding that his IQ of 51 dictated that his mental competency be examined. Northwestern University Professor David Protess and his journalism students delved into Porter's case and found that he had not committed the pair of 1982 murders he was convicted for (McCormick 1999). Another suspect later confessed.

In the wake of the Porter case, Illinois Governor George Ryan, a Republican, declared a temporary halt to executions in his state, saying "I now favor a moratorium, because I have grave concerns about our state's shameful record of convicting innocent people and putting them on death row." The thoroughgoing review of the death penalty in Illinois would result in some death row prisoners' being freed altogether because DNA evidence, witnesses who recanted, or independent investigations showed their innocence. Moreover, according to the *Chicago Tribune,* 33 death row inmates were defended by attorneys who were later disbarred or suspended, and 46 convictions were obtained through questionable testimony of jailhouse informants (Stern 2000). Just days before stepping

down as governor, Ryan commuted the sentences of the remaining 167 inmates on death row to life imprisonment.

Over the years, different groups—most notably, the American Bar Association—have called for moratoriums on the death penalty. Illinois and Maryland, however, have been the only states to actually implement a moratorium. Indeed, governors in other states have shown little inclination to follow the lead of the Land of Lincoln. In 2007, however, New Jersey became the first state since 1965 to vote for abolition. Some scholars continue to call for a moratorium (Acker 2007) as do groups like the Death Penalty Information Center. Occasionally, these efforts attract new supporters, such as long-time conservative Richard Viguerie (Death Penalty Information Center 2009).

The focus on innocents on death row represents the latest round in a long-running debate over the death penalty. Not surprisingly, profound ideological differences exist on the three central issues in the death penalty debate: morality, deterrence, and fairness (see Chapter 17). To advocates of the due process model of criminal justice, the death

to avoid the arbitrary application of capital punishment. These laws took two forms. Some states passed mandatory death penalty laws, which removed all discretion from the process by requiring that anyone convicted of a capital offense be sentenced to death. Other states enacted guided discretion statutes, which required judges and juries to weigh various aggravating and mitigating circumstances in deciding whether or not a particular defendant should receive the death penalty (Blankenship et al. 1997).

These new laws were tested in five companion cases, collectively known as the death penalty cases (*Gregg v. Georgia* 1976). Again, the Court was badly divided, but a seven-justice majority agreed that the death penalty did not constitute cruel and

unusual punishment under all circumstances. Next, the Court considered under what circumstances the death penalty was unconstitutional. Mandatory death penalty laws in 21 states were struck down because they failed to focus on the circumstances of the case. Guided discretion death penalty laws, on the other hand, were upheld: "The concerns expressed in *Furman* that the penalty of death not be imposed in an arbitrary or capricious manner can be met by a carefully drafted statute that ensures that the sentencing authority is given adequate information and guidance."

For a death penalty law to be constitutional, the high court ruled, it must provide for a bifurcated process. During the first, or guilt, phase of the trial, the jury considers only the issue of guilt or innocence. If

penalty is immoral because the state should not take a life. To proponents of the crime control model, the death penalty is moral because the defendant has already taken a life.

To advocates of the due process model, the death penalty is not a deterrent, because many of those who commit murder are incapable of rational calculation. To proponents of the crime control model, the death penalty is a deterrent, because some who might murder refrain from doing so because they know they might themselves die.

To advocates of the due process model, the death penalty is unfairly administered. They stress that members of racial minorities are more likely than whites to be executed (see Chapter 16). They also believe that in too many cases, people on death row are innocent or their trials involved procedural irregularities (see Chapter 17). To this, the proponents of the crime control model respond that the fairness of the death penalty is unimportant or unproven. They believe that African-Americans are no more likely to be executed than whites. They also argue that the review process works because appeals have freed the few innocents who were wrongfully convicted.

These issues form the background for the debate by the justices of the Supreme Court over how death penalty cases should be decided (*Kansas v. Marsh* 2006). At the end of its 2005–2006 term, the four liberal justices stopped short of calling for an end to capital punishment, but they pointed to studies finding that dozens of people condemned to death were later exonerated (see Chapter 17). Justice David Souter stressed that we are in a period of new empirical argument about how capital punishment is different. Justice Antonin Scalia responded that these studies were not proven. "Those ideologically driven to ferret out and proclaim a mistaken modern execution have not a single verifiable case to point to, whereas it is easy as pie to identify plainly guilty murderers who have been set free."

What do you think? Of the three main issues in the death penalty debate—morality, deterrence, and fairness—which provides the best argument for abolishing the death penalty? Which one offers the best grounds for keeping the death penalty? Do you think that the issue of innocents on death row justifies a moratorium on the death penalty?

---

the jury unanimously convicts for a crime carrying the death penalty, then the jury reconvenes. During the second, or penalty, phase of the trial, the jury considers aggravating and mitigating circumstances and then decides whether to impose the death penalty. If the death penalty is not imposed, the defendant is usually sentenced to life imprisonment (see Exhibit 15.5).

Contemporary Death Penalty Laws

Many state legislatures, citing public opinion polls showing that a majority of citizens favor the death penalty for murder, quickly revised their laws to conform with those upheld in the death penalty

cases. Today, 37 states and the federal government (covering roughly 90 percent of the nation's population) have death penalty laws on the books. In 2007, New Jersey abolished the death penalty. Before that, the last states to ban the death penalty were West Virginia and Iowa in 1965. Thirteen states and the District of Columbia do not have capital punishment statutes (Figure 15.6).

State death penalty laws differ in terms of which homicides are defined as death-eligible. In a few jurisdictions, a relatively wide range of first-degree murder cases are defined as death-eligible. In others, only a very narrow range of crimes can be considered capital offenses. Important variations also exist in how often states use their death penalty laws. Three capital punishment states have

Exhibit 15.5

KEY DEVELOPMENTS CONCERNING CAPITAL PUNISHMENT

Eighth Amendment	1791	Excessive bail shall not be required, nor excessive fines imposed, nor cruel and unusual punishments inflicted.
Witherspoon v. Illinois	1968	Prospective jurors cannot be excluded because they oppose the death penalty.
Furman v. Georgia	1972	All existing death penalty laws invalidated; five-judge majority expresses different reasons for this action.
Gregg v. Georgia	1976	Death penalty laws do not constitute cruel and unusual punishment under all circumstances. Mandatory death penalty laws struck down.
Coker v. Georgia	1977	Rape is not a grave enough offense to justify the imposition of the death penalty.
Pulley v. Harris	1984	The Eighth Amendment does not require states to assess whether a sentence of death is compared with other cases to determine whether the sentence is proportional.
Lockhart v. McCree	1986	Potential jurors may be excluded if they oppose the death penalty. Thus, a death-qualified jury was upheld (overturning *Witherspoon v. Illinois*).
McClesky v. Kemp	1987	Statistical studies do not show that the application of the death penalty in Georgia is "wanton and freakish."
Thompson v. Oklahoma	1988	Defendants who were 15 or younger at the time they committed murder may not be executed.
Stanford v. Kentucky	1989	It is not unconstitutional to apply the death penalty to persons who were convicted of murder when they were 17.
Penry v. Lynaugh	1989	It is constitutional to execute mentally retarded persons.
Simmons v. South Carolina	1994	Defense may tell jurors that the only alternative to a death sentence is life without parole.
Harris v. Alabama	1995	States may give judges the power to sentence a capital defendant to death even if the jury votes not to impose the death penalty.
Ramdass v. Angelone	2000	Upheld sentence of death even though jurors were not told that defendant would not be eligible for parole if sentenced to life in prison.

Exhibit 15.5

CONTINUED

Williams v. Taylor	2000	Upheld a section of the Antiterrorism and Effective Death Penalty Act intended to shorten time between sentencing and execution.
Atkins v. Virginia	2002	Convicted defendants with an IQ of 70 or less may not be executed (*Penry* overturned).
Roper v. Simmons	2005	The Eighth Amendment forbids the imposition of the death penalty on offenders who were under age 18 when their crimes were committed (reversing *Thompson v. Oklahoma*).
Hill v. McDonough	2006	Challenges to the method of execution are properly filed in federal court under 42 U.S.C. § 1983, not in habeas corpus proceedings.
Kansas v. Marsh	2006	Upheld Kansas law requiring that when juries find that the arguments for and against capital punishment carry equal weight, the automatic sentence must be death.
Uttecht v. Brown	2007	The juror in the capital murder trial was properly excused for cause because a reading of the transcript of the voir dire indicates he expressed reservations about the death penalty.
Baze v. Rees	2008	Because the lethal injection process is not intended to cause unnecessary pain and suffering, it does not create an "objectively intolerable risk of harm" that qualifies as cruel and unusual punishment under the Eighth Amendment.
Kennedy v. Louisiana	2008	The death penalty is unconstitutional as a punishment for the rape of a child.

no one on death row, and a few others have only a very few. On the other hand, a few jurisdictions, particularly in the South and West, regularly use capital punishment (Figure 15.7).

State death penalty laws have been challenged in state and federal courts on a variety of grounds. Over the years state and or federal courts have found parts of these laws unconstitutional, and legislatures have then passed amended statutes. Some of the major challenges to post-*Gregg* death penalty laws have focused on which types of crimes and

criminals are death-eligible. Thus, in the years since the death penalty was reinstated, death penalty laws have been changing on a regular basis as the Supreme Court struggles to come up with consistent standards for capital punishment (Hurwitz 2008).

NARROWING DEATH-ELIGIBLE CASES

Part of the national debate over capital punishment has focused on what crimes deserve the ultimate punishment. The term **death-eligible** refers to

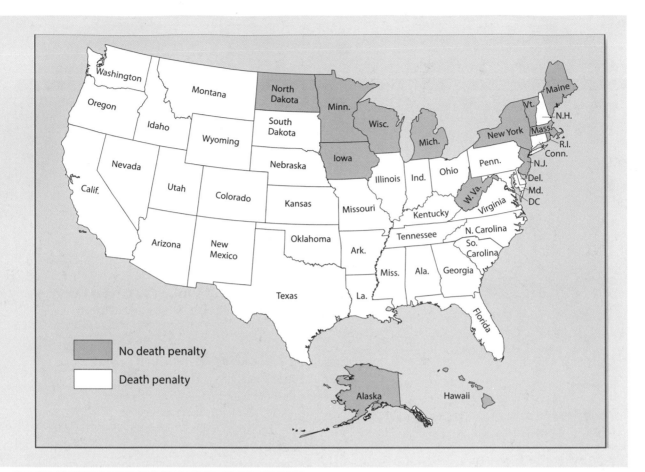

FIGURE 15.6   JURISDICTIONS WITHOUT A DEATH PENALTY

Sources: Tracy Snell. "Capital Punishment, 2007, Statistical Tables." Washington, D.C.: U.S. Department of Justice, Bureau of Justice Statistics, 2008. Available online at: http://www.ojp.usdoj.gov/bjs/pub/html/cp/2007/cp07st.htm. Evans, Brian. 2009. "U.S. Homicide Rates and the Death Penalty." Amnesty International USA: Human Rights Now. Available online at http://blog.amnestyusa.org/deathpenalty/us-homicide-rates-and-the-death-penalty/

crimes that are punishable by death. Today, very few crimes are considered death-eligible but this was not always the case. Over the years, persons were executed for committing a wide variety of crimes besides murder, including rape, robbery, and stealing horses. Legislators have played a major role in narrowing the scope of death-eligible offenses. Today, the focus is on the U.S. Supreme Court. In the wake

of *Gregg v. Georgia* the Supreme Court has placed two important limits on types of crimes that are death-eligible.

State efforts to make non-homicide cases death eligible have been rejected. According to the Supreme Court, rape is not a grave enough offense to justify the imposition of the death penalty (*Coker v. Georgia* 1977). More recently, the Court ruled that the death penalty is unconstitutional as the punishment for the rape of a child (*Kennedy v. Louisiana* 2008). Whether the Court would uphold the death penalty for treason is unclear. Under federal law, treason is also a death-eligible offense, but since no one has been sentenced to death for espionage since the 1950s, the status of this penalty has not been determined.

The Supreme Court has also placed important limits on the minimum age at which the death penalty may be imposed. The minimum age varied from 12 to 18, with a few states not specifying a minimum

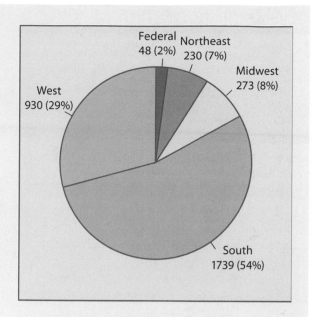

FIGURE 15.7 PRISONERS UNDER SENTENCE OF DEATH, BY REGION

Source: Tracy Snell. "Capital Punishment, 2007, Statistical Tables." Washington, D.C.: U.S. Department of Justice, Bureau of Justice Statistics, 2008. Available online at http://www.ojp.usdoj.gov/bjs/pub/html/cp/2007/cp07st.htm

age. Initially, the Supreme Court ruled that defendants who were 15 or younger at the time they committed murder may not be executed (*Thompson v. Oklahoma* 1988). Later, the Court refused to set aside the death penalty for defendants who were 17 at the time of the crime (*Stanford v. Kentucky* 1989). Most recently, though, the death penalty for juveniles has been outlawed. (See Case Close-Up: *Roper v. Simmons:* Should Juveniles Be Sentenced to Death?)

Besides questions of which cases should be death-eligible, the Supreme Court has also addressed myriad other issues relating to the death penalty.

EVOLVING STANDARDS

The Supreme Court has become America's life-and-death tribunal. No other Supreme Court in history has been as preoccupied with the questions of when life begins and when a state may snuff one out. In the years following *Gregg*, the Court has grappled with numerous issues that have a special relevance in capital cases. Some of these issues have been

discussed in other chapters, including: ineffective assistance of counsel (Chapter 7); an indigent's right to counsel extends only to the first appeal (Chapter 7); the duty of prosecutors to turn over exculpatory evidence to the defense (Chapter 12); prohibition against using race to exclude jurors (Chapter 14); challenges to how DNA evidence has been collected and tested (Chapter 14); juries, not judges, must decide whether death is the appropriate penalty (Chapter 14); limits on when prisoners have a right to DNA evidence to prove their innocence (Chapter 17); and restriction on how many habeas corpus petitions may be filed in federal court (Chapter 17). The following three issues illustrate other questions the Court has faced in the aftermath of *Gregg*.

One long-standing issue has been the exclusion of persons opposed to the death penalty from juries in capital cases. The Warren Court rejected the classic "hanging jury," holding in *Witherspoon v. Illinois* (1968) that states cannot exclude from juries in capital cases any persons who voice general objections to the death penalty or express religious scruples against its imposition. However, the more conservative Rehnquist Court limited *Witherspoon* in *Wainwright v. Witt* (1985), ruling that the Constitution does not prohibit the removal for cause of prospective jurors whose opposition to the death penalty is so strong that it would prevent or substantially impair the performance of their duties as jurors at the sentencing phase of the trial (*Lockhart v. McCree* 1986). More recently, the Roberts Court held that a juror in a capital murder trial was properly excused for cause because a reading of the transcript of the voir dire indicates he expressed reservations about the death penalty (*Uttecht v. Brown* 2007). Decisions like this make it easier for prosecutors to weed out jurors who have concerns about the death penalty, meaning that juries will be more prone to convict (Butler and Moran 2007a, 2007b; Haney 1984, 2005; Moran and Comfort 2006). In fact, a wealth of social scientific data support the notion that so-called **death-qualified juries** differ from regular juries in several important ways:

First, death-qualified jurors are demographically unique. When compared with excludables, they are more likely to be male, Caucasian, moderately well educated, politically conservative, Catholic or Protestant, and middle-class. Second, death-qualified jurors are dispositionally unique. When compared with excludables, they are more likely to have a high belief in a just world (i.e., feel the world is a fair and

Roper v. Simmons: Should Juveniles Be Sentenced to Death?

The jurors in *Roper v. Simmons* wrestled with a truly difficult question: Did Christopher Simmons deserve to live or die? No doubt, his crime was heinous—he and his friend deliberately drowned a neighbor girl who had befriended them. But at 17, was he too young to truly understand the dreadful crime that he had committed? Over the years, other American juries have wrestled with these and similar questions. And in turn, appellate courts have then been asked to provide their opinions (Blecker 2006).

In *Roper v. Simmons,* the Court held that the Eighth Amendment forbids the imposition of the death penalty on offenders who were under the age of 18 when their crimes were committed. The Court's decision affected 72 inmates on death row in 20 states. It also impacted untold numerous current and future murder prosecutions.

Writing for the five-judge majority, Justice Kennedy (a Reagan appointee) argued that capital punishment must be limited to those offenders who commit "a narrow category of the most serious crimes" and whose extreme culpability makes them "the most deserving of execution." Those under 18 cannot with reliability be classified among the worst offenders. Citing factors like juveniles' susceptibility to immature and irresponsible behavior, the Court concluded: "The differences between juvenile and adult offenders are too marked and well understood to risk allowing a youthful person to receive the death penalty." In finding a national consensus opposing the execution of juveniles, the Court set the age of 18 on the basis of state legislative determinations of the age one is old enough to vote, marry, and serve on a jury (Bradley 2006).

The decision in *Roper v. Simmons* highlights major differences of opinion over how the Constitution should be interpreted. Six of the justices believe that the Eighth Amendment to the Constitution (and other critically important parts of the Bill of Rights) should be interpreted on the basis of "evolving standards of decency in a maturing society" (*Trop v. Dulles* 1958). In short, the meaning of the Bill of Rights was not frozen when it was originally drafted but should be interpreted in a common law manner. To Scalia, Rehnquist, and Thomas, the interpretation of the Bill of Rights and

other provisions of the Constitution should be based on their original meaning. Doctrines like evolving standards make interpretation too subjective, they argue.

In a fiery dissent, Justice Scalia (joined by Rehnquist and Thomas) blasted the majority opinion, arguing that it made a mockery of the vision of the federal judiciary set forth by the Founding Fathers and also that it ignored state legislatures. In short, the majority was off base by proclaiming itself the sole arbiter of our nation's moral standards. The finding of a national consensus was based on the flimsiest of grounds, the dissent argued.

The decision in *Roper v. Simmons* also highlights major differences of opinion over the role of international law in interpreting the Constitution. The court's opinion observed that only seven other countries—Iran, Pakistan, China, Saudi Arabia, Yemen, Nigeria, and Congo—allow the execution of juveniles. They concluded that "the overwhelming weight of international opinion against the juvenile death penalty is not controlling here, but provided respected and significant confirmation of the Court's determination that the penalty is disproportionate punishment for offenders under 18." This position provoked strong condemnation from the Court's three most conservative members, who thought that the basic premise of the Court's argument—that American law should conform to the laws of the rest of the world—ought to be rejected out of hand.

Deep divisions among the nine justices over the fairness of the death penalty in America surfaced a year later. At issue was a Kansas law mandating that juries impose the death penalty when they find that the arguments for and against carry equal weight (*Kansas v. Marsh* 2006). Justice Clarence Thomas, writing for the conservative majority, upheld the Kansas law because states enjoy a range of discretion in imposing the death penalty. But Justice David Souter, writing for the court's liberals, argued that the law was obtuse to moral concerns, particularly in the light of studies documenting innocents on death row. In many ways the Court's opinion reflected divisions of opinion over whether a moratorium on the death penalty should be imposed (see Courts, Controversy, and Judicial Administration). Although the Kansas law has only a limited impact—the state has only eight death row inmates—it is significant because Justice Samuel Alito cast the deciding vote. To Kent

Scheidegger, of the pro–death penalty Criminal Justice Legal Foundation, the vote of the newest justices indicates that for the time being, a majority of the court is "not going to engage in further tinkering" (quoted in Holland 2006).

CASE CLOSEUP

just place), espouse legal authoritarian beliefs (i.e., believe the rights of the government should supercede the rights of the individual), exhibit an internal locus of control (i.e., feel that internal factors control the events in their lives), and have a low need for cognition (i.e., lack the tendency to engage in and enjoy effortful cognitive activity). Third, death-qualified jurors are attitudinally unique. When compared with excludables, they are more likely to weigh aggravating circumstances (i.e., arguments for death) more heavily than mitigating circumstances (i.e., arguments for life), evaluate ambiguous expert scientific testimony more favorably, be skeptical of defenses involving mental illness (including the insanity defense), and are more susceptible to the pretrial publicity that inevitably surrounds capital cases. [And], death-qualified jurors are more likely to believe in the infallibility of the criminal justice process and less likely to agree that even the worst criminals should be considered for mercy. Fourth, death-qualified jurors are behaviorally unique with respect to their decision-making processes. When compared with excludables, they are more likely to find capital defendants guilty as well as sentence them to death. [And fifth], death-qualified venirepersons exhibited . . . higher levels of homophobia, modern racism, and modern sexism. (Butler 2007, pp. 857, 858–859)

Yet, in spite of these many differences, constitutional challenges to the composition of death-qualified juries have been rejected by the federal courts for more than 40 years (*Witherspoon v. Illinois* 1968; *Lockhart v. McCree* 1986).

A second issue relates to Eighth Amendment concerns about the execution of the mentally retarded. The Court provided conflicting answers in an opinion written by Justice Sandra Day O'Connor (who was the swing vote in many death penalty

cases). The Court initially concluded that mentally retarded people convicted of capital murder can be executed (*Penry v. Lynaugh* 1989). In 2001, however, the Court reversed *Penry*, holding that the Eighth Amendment bars persons with an IQ of 70 or lower from being executed (*Atkins v. Virginia* 2002). State and federal courts, though, continue to struggle to apply this principle in practice, mainly because the decision in *Atkins* did not provide a functional definition of mental retardation. Rather, *Atkins*

> left each state on its own to solve the problems presented by the holding—from formulating a definition of mental retardation to determining the applicable burden of proof and upon whom that burden falls. As a result, amongst the states there is neither a uniform definition of mental retardation nor a uniform procedure for determining whether a defendant is mentally retarded, and some state legislatures have declined to act on this issue at all. (Hagstrom 2009, p. 242)

Relying on the definition of mental retardation provided by the American Psychiatric Association and the American Association on Intellectual and Developmental Disabilities, some states automatically prohibit the execution of someone with an IQ of less than 70 (Covarrubias 2009). Other states set the bar lower; for example, Arizona bars execution of those with IQs of 65 or lower (Gottsfield and Alcorn 2009). And other jurisdictions consider factors in addition to IQ to determine whether a nexus exists between a capital defendant's IQ and the causation of his or her crime (*Tennard v. Dretke* 2004). Although mental retardation should not be diagnosed solely on the basis of IQ in light of variations in test results across time, the examination of a person's adaptive functioning leaves much subjectivity in diagnosing mental retardation—especially for people with borderline IQ scores (Fabian 2006; Hagstrom 2009). The Supreme Court has also opened the door to constitutional challenges to lethal injection. At issue is whether the chemicals used in lethal injections are too painful and therefore constitute an Eighth Amendment violation of cruel and unusual punishment (*Hill v. McDonough* 2006). In the aftermath of *Hill*, many states halted executions and sought to change their practices. In Missouri, for example, a federal judge barred executions in that state amid resistance from the medical profession over whether doctors should be involved at all in meting out lethal injections (Davey 2006). Two years, later, however, the Court addressed the issue in a different manner. In *Baze v. Rees* (2008), the Court held that because the lethal injection process is not intended to cause unnecessary pain and suffering, it does not create an "objectively intolerable risk of harm" that qualifies as cruel and unusual punishment (p. 1531). But few think that the issue of method of execution has been settled because many questions of state law remain (Fulkerson and Suttmoeller 2008).

DEATH ROW INMATES

As a result of post-*Gregg* statutes, more than 3,200 prisoners are under a sentence of death. Significantly, the number of persons on death row has been decreasing for several years. Death row inmates are predominantly male (a scant 1.7 percent are female) and disproportionately nonwhite (42 percent); most have never completed high school (51 percent) and have a prior felony conviction (65 percent). The median age is 27 at the time of arrest. Figure 15.7 highlights the regional pattern of the use of the death penalty, with the highest percentage of those awaiting execution in the South.

On January 16, 1977, convicted murderer Gary Gilmore's execution by a Utah firing squad attracted considerable national and international attention, not only because he was the first person executed in the United States since the unofficial moratorium began in 1967, but also because Gilmore had opposed all attempts to delay the execution. From the time the Supreme Court reinstated the death penalty in 1976 through the end of 2007, a total of 1,099 persons were executed.

A sentence of death does not necessarily mean that the offender will be executed. From 1976, when the death penalty was upheld, through the end of 2007, a total of 7,547 prisoners were under a sentence of death. Of those, 15 percent were executed. An additional 43 percent had their death sentences vacated on appeal or commuted by the governor, or else they died in prison. The others

remain on death row pending the outcome of their appeals (Snell 2008).

LENGTHY APPEALS

"Death is different"wrote Justice Thurgood Marshall about death penalty cases in general and death penalty appeals in particular (*Ford v. Wainwright* 1986). One way to assess how death penalty cases are different is to examine case-processing time.

Like all defendants found guilty, those sentenced to death are entitled to appellate court review. In death penalty cases, however, special provisions govern appeal. In all except two states, convictions for capital cases are automatically reviewed by the state's highest appellate court (Hurwitz 2008). In the other two, the intermediate appellate courts first hear the appeals. If the conviction is upheld, the next step is filing a writ of certiorari with the U.S. Supreme Court. Even though the chances of four justices voting to hear the case are not high, they are much higher than for ordinary criminal appeals. Having exhausted these appellate remedies, defendants sentenced to death often file numerous writs of habeas corpus in state and federal courts, although this practice changed greatly in 1996 (see Chapter 17).

The review process in death penalty cases is quite lengthy, mainly because of the numerous issues that federal and state courts have dealt with since *Gregg*. Among prisoners executed since 1977, the average time from imposition of sentence to execution was more than 12 years (Snell 2008). This time is nearly double what it was two decades ago.

At the state level, the initial appeal in capital cases averages 2½ years, but with significant geographical differences. In Virginia, for example, the median time for a capital appeal was 295 days, as compared with 1,331 days in Ohio. How long cases took for the initial appeal also varied in terms of the type of cases. More complex cases, a reversal of the trial court verdict, and the presence of dissenting opinions all increased case-processing time (Cauthen and Latzer 2008). After appellants have exhausted this initial appeal, they can turn to federal court. Federal court capital habeas petitions now take twice as long to complete as they did a decade ago. However, the time these cases take show important geographical differences. The U.S. District courts in Texas, for example are speedier in their reviews than their counterpart in California (Gould 2008). Conservatives have objected to allowing condemned prisoners repeated opportunities to file challenges in appellate courts. Congress has responded by limiting federal appellate review (Chapter 17).

COST CONCERNS

After decades of debate over the morality, fairness, and effectiveness of the death penalty, a major new concern has been voiced—cost. In the words of retired California Judge Donald McCartin, who was known as "The Hanging Judge of Orange County" because he sentenced nine men to death row, "It's 10 times more expensive to kill them than to keep them alive" (quoted in Hastings 2009). While some might disagree with McCartin's precise cost estimates, few doubt that death penalty prosecutions and appeals are more expensive than noncapital felony prosecutions because they often require extra lawyers, and the appellate process takes years to complete. High costs of defending capital cases has strained public defender budgets (Chapter 7) and the courts as well.

To assess how cost concerns might affect the death penalty, researchers interviewed prosecutors in South Carolina, where economic issues are particularly important because local governments, not the state, pay for prosecutions. While local prosecutors recognized that cost might be a concern, they claimed that money issues do not influence their decisions regarding whether to file capital charges. An analysis of statistical data, however, showed a different pattern—the wealthier the county, the greater the death penalty caseloads (Douglas and Stockstill 2008).

CONCLUSION

In *Furman v. Georgia* the Supreme Court set in motion a national debate over the death penalty when it struck down all existing state death penalty laws because they violated the Eighth Amendment prohibition against "cruel and unusual punishment." Thirty-five years later the debate continues. Most recently, the Court has held that those under 18 cannot be put to death and that the method of execution can also be challenged in federal courts. No one doubts that in the coming years the Court will write new chapters to this debate.

Although public support for the death penalty has increased, we as a nation execute very few people. Often unrecognized is the fact that murder (the only crime for which the death penalty is allowed) constitutes only a tiny percentage of crime. The public's demands that something be done about "rising" crime rates has directly and indirectly affected the why, who, and what of sentencing.

During the past three decades, there has been an unprecedented public debate over *why* we sentence. The previously dominant goal of rehabilitation has come under sharp attack, and many voices urge that punishment should instead be based on the principle of just deserts. After 40 years of stability, the indeterminate sentencing system has been rejected in state after state.

Intense interest in crime has also produced major alterations in *who* has the authority to sentence. The mix of sentencing responsibilities has changed in major ways. Legislators have inserted themselves more directly in the sentencing process, reducing the sentencing discretion of judges in many jurisdictions. Legislatures have also restricted parole board authority over early release in some jurisdictions and abolished parole altogether in a few areas.

The *what* of punishment has likewise come under intense scrutiny. Prison overcrowding has become the dominant issue. Probation overcrowding is an equally pressing, if less visible, problem. Perhaps more pressing than the debate over capital punishment is the lack of a national debate over prison overcrowding. Our nation's emphasis on getting tough on criminals is apparently a policy without costs, until we total the bill for building and maintaining prisons. Although citizens and public officials want to send even more offenders to prison, they are unwilling to expend large sums of tax dollars to build the needed facilities. Thus, sentencing is likely to remain an important public policy issue for the foreseeable future.

CHAPTER REVIEW

1. Distinguish between the four major sentencing philosophies.

The four major sentencing philosophies are retribution, which seeks to punish wrongdoers; incapacitation, which is aimed at removing offenders from the community; deterrence, whose goal is to prevent the commission of future crimes; and rehabilitation, which emphasizes restoring the offender to a constructive place in society.

2. Describe how the three branches of government are involved in sentencing.

The legislative branch of government defines the range of possible punishment for a given crime. The judicial branch of government has discretion in choosing the specific sentence for the individual criminal. The executive branch of government is responsible for carrying out the actual sentence, including running prisons, pardons, and parole.

3. List three major issues related to imprisonment as a sentence in the United States.

The three issues most directly related to the use of imprisonment as a sentence in the United states are prison overcrowding, which limits how many guilty defendants may be sentenced to prison; conditions of confinement law suits, which ensure minimal living conditions in prison; and the high costs of incarcerating prisoners.

4. Identify the three major alternatives to imprisonment.

The three major alternatives to imprisonment include probation, which is often used in felonies; fines, which are rarely used in felonies; and restitution, which is increasingly imposed after a misdemeanor and or felony conviction.

5. Outline the Supreme Court rulings on capital punishment that led to the bifurcated process for death penalty sentencing.

In 1972 (*Furman v. Georgia*) the Court declared that all death penalty laws were unconstitutional. In 1976 (*Gregg v. Georgia*) the Court upheld death penalty laws that specified aggravating and mitigating circumstances for when the death penalty may be applied and also provided for separate phases of the trial, one to determine guilt and the other to decide on the penalty.

6. Indicate how the Court has narrowed the list of death-eligible cases.

The Court has narrowed the list of death-eligible cases by deciding that only homicide cases may be considered death-eligible and striking down death penalty provisions for rape and the rape of a child. The Court has also narrowed the list of death-eligible cases by declaring that no one under 18 at the time of the crime may be executed.

7. Discuss the major differences between the due process model of criminal justice and the crime control model of justice with regard to the death penalty.

The due process model of criminal justice believes the death penalty should be abolished because it is morally wrong for the state to take a life, the death penalty is not a deterrent to crime, and the death penalty is unfairly administered. The crime control model of criminal justice believes that the death penalty should be retained because it is morally acceptable to take the life of a person who has already taken another person's life, the death penalty is a deterrent, and issues of fairness are either unimportant or unproven.

CRITICAL THINKING QUESTIONS

1. In what ways is restorative justice similar to the four dominant sentencing philosophies of retribution, incapacitation, deterrence, and rehabilitation? In what ways is restorative justice different from these four sentencing philosophies?

2. Should the punishment fit the crime, or should the punishment fit the criminal? In what ways do the four sentencing philosophies provide different answers to this question?

3. What is the mix of legislative, judicial, and executive sentencing responsibilities in your state? What changes, if any, have occurred over the past decade in the balance of sentencing responsibilities?

4. Public criticism of lenient sentencing tends to occur in a select number of violent crimes or highly unusual circumstances. In what ways do such discussions deflect attention from the question of what the appropriate sentence should be for the bulk of defendants convicted of nonviolent crimes (burglary and theft, for example) and drug-related crimes?

KEY TERMS

boot camp 390
capital offense 391
capital punishment 391
celerity of punishment 375
certainty of punishment 375
community service 389
conditions of confinement lawsuit 383
cruel and unusual punishment 381
death-eligible 395
death penalty 390
death-qualified juries 397
determinate sentence 379
deterrence theory 374

direct restitution 389
evidence-based corrections 376
expiation 373
fine 388
Furman v. Georgia 391
general deterrence 374
good time 380
Gregg v. Georgia 392
hedonistic calculus 374
imprisonment 382
incapacitation 374
indeterminate sentence 379
intensive supervision probation 390
intermediate sanctions 389

just deserts 373
lex talionis 372
pardon 380
parole 380
parole board 378
probation 387
rehabilitation 375
restitution 389
retribution 372
selective incapacitation 374
severity of punishment 375
shock incarceration 390
specific deterrent 375
symbolic restitution 389

WEB RESOURCES

Go to the America's Courts and the Criminal Justice System companion website at

www.cengage.com/criminaljustice/neubauer

where you will find more resources to help you study.
Resources include web exercises, quizzing, and flash cards.

FOR FURTHER READING

Abbott, Geoffrey. *Lords of the Scaffold: A History of the Executioner*. New York: St. Martin's Press, 1991.

Bazemore, Gordon. "Whom and How Do We Reintegrate? Finding Community in Restorative Justice." *Criminology and Public Policy* 4: 131–148, 2005.

Bedau, Hugo Adam, and Paul Cassell. *Debating the Death Penalty: Should America Have Capital Punishment? The Experts on Both Sides Make Their Case*. New York: Oxford University Press, 2005.

Bureau of Justice Assistance. "Building an Offender Reentry Program: A Guide for Law Enforcement." Washington, D.C. U.S. Department of Justice. 2006.

Clear, Todd. *Imprisoning Communities: How Mass Incarceration Makes Disadvantaged Neighborhoods Worse*. New York: Oxford University Press, 2007.

Clear, Todd, George Cole, and Michael Reisig. *American Corrections*. 8th ed. Belmont, CA: Wadsworth 2009.

Ewald, Alec, and Marnie Smith. "Collateral Consequences of Criminal Convictions in American Courts: The View from the State Bench." *Justice System Journal* 29: 145–164, 2008.

Gainey, Randy, Sara Steen, and Rodney Engen. "Exercising Options: An Assessment of the Use of Alternative Sanctions for Drug Offenders." *Justice Quarterly* 22: 488–520, 2005.

Gottschalk, Marie. *The Prison and the Gallows: The Politics of Mass Incarceration in America*. New York: Cambridge University Press, 2006.

Haney, Craig. *Capital Punishment as a Social Psychological System*. New York Oxford University Press, 2005.

Huebner, Beth, and Timothy Bynum. "An Analysis of Parole Decision Making Using a Sample of Sex Offenders: A Focal Concerns Perspective." *Criminology* 44: 961–991, 2006.

Johnstone, Gerry, and Daniel Van Ness (eds.). *Handbook of Restorative Justice*. Devon, United Kingdom: Willan, 2006.

Lanier, Charles, William Bowers, and James Acker (eds.). *The Future of America's Death Penalty: An Agenda for the Next Generation of Capital Punishment Research*. Durham, NC: Carolina Academic Press, 2009.

Latzer, Barry. *Death Penalty Cases*. 2nd ed. Boston: Butterworth-Heineman, 2002.

Lin, Ann Chih. *Reform in the Making: The Implementation of Social Policy in Prison*. Princeton, NJ: Princeton University Press, 2000.

Lynch, Michael. *Big Prisons, Big Dreams: Crime and the Failure of America's Penal System*. Piscataway, NJ: Rutgers University Press, 2007.

Mays, G. Larry, and L. Thomas Winfree. *Essentials of Corrections*. 4th ed. Belmont, CA: Wadsworth. 2009.

McCord, David (symposium editor). "The Effects of Capital Punishment on the Administration of Justice." *Judicature* 8: 248–305, 2006.

Paternoster, Raymond, Robert Brame, and Sarah Bacon. *The Death Penalty: America's Experience with Capital Punishment*. New York: Oxford University Press, 2007.

Petersilla, Joan. *When Prisoners Come Home: Parole and Prisoner Reentry*. New York: Oxford University Press, 2003.

Rice, Stephen, Danielle Dirks, and Julie Exline. "Of Guilt, and Repentance: Evidence from the Texas Death Chamber." *Justice Quarterly* 26: 295–326, 2009.

Santos, Michael. *Inside: Life Behind Bars in America*. New York: St. Martin's Press, 2006.

Shepherd, Joanna. "The Imprisonment Puzzle: Understanding How Prison Growth Affects Crime." *Criminology and Public Policy* 5: 285–298, 2006.

Simon, Jonathan. *Poor Discipline: Parole and the Social Control of the Underclass, 1890–1990*. Chicago: University of Chicago Press, 1994.

Travis, Jeremy, and Christy Visher (eds.). *Prisoner Reentry and Crime in America*. New York: Cambridge University Press, 2005.

Unnever, James, Francis Cullen, and John Bartkowski. "Image of God and Public Support for Capital Punishment: Does a Close Relationship with a Loving God Matter?" *Criminology* 44: 835–866, 2006.

Wasby, Stephen, and Robert Howard (eds.). "Special Issue: Court-Related Aspects of Capital Punishment. *Justice System Journal* 29: 243–440, 2008.

White, Welsh. *Litigating in the Shadow of Death: Defense Attorneys in Capital Cases*. Ann Arbor: University of Michigan Press, 2006.

Winfree, L. Thomas, and Howard Abadinsky. *Understanding Crime: Essentials of Criminological Theory*. 3rd ed. Belmont, CA: Wadsworth, 2010.

16

SENTENCING DECISIONS

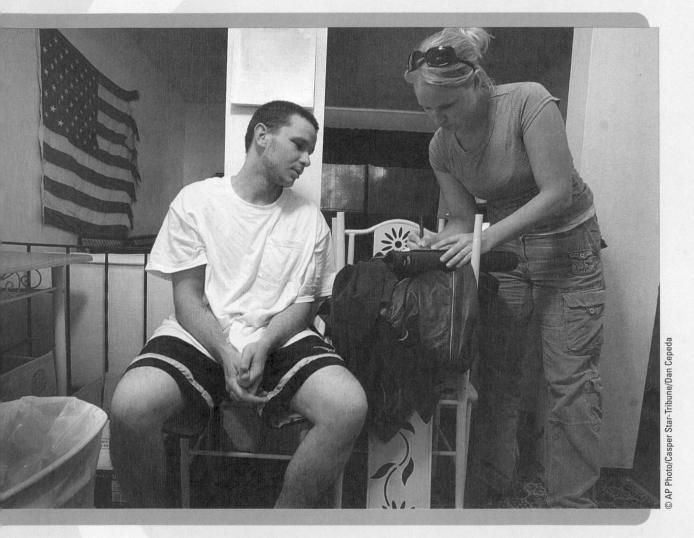

© AP Photo/Casper Star-Tribune/Dan Cepeda

Amid growing concern that the nation relies too heavily on imprisonment, intermediate sanctions are growing in popularity. One example is intensive supervised probation. In this photo, probation officer Bridget Wiggins fills out her report as her probationer looks on. He had been in the Intensive Supervised Probation program in Casper, Wyoming, for six months at the time.

CHAPTER OUTLINE

LEARNING OBJECTIVES

After reading this chapter, you should be able to:

1. Define the concept of normal crimes and indicate the two most important factors in determining normal penalties.

2. **Distinguish between the concepts of discrimination and disparity.**

3. Describe the three competing explanations of why women are sentenced more leniently than men and indicate which one has the most support in the literature.

4. **Explain how scholars approach the issue of racial discrimination differently than the general public and the implications these differing approaches have for the conclusions reached.**

5. Indicate why the offender–victim dyad is important in studies of racial discrimination in capital punishment.

6. **List the two major factors related to disparities and sentencing.**

7. Recognize the main objective of changes in sentencing structure beginning in the late 1960s and the major consequences of these changes.

8. **Outline how the U.S. Supreme Court has limited state sentencing guidelines.**

9. Identify the most recent changes in how the U.S. Supreme Court has responded to federal sentencing guidelines.

10. **Explain the law in action perspective on researching the impact of mandatory minimum sentences.**

Twelve-year-old Polly Klaas was kidnapped from a slumber party in her home while her mother and little sister slept in the next room. Her two friends were found a short time later, bound and gagged, and were able to provide a general description of the bearded intruder. For 9 weeks, hundreds of law enforcement officers and thousands of volunteers attempted to find the girl, but to no avail. Just before Christmas, the bad news came: Polly had been killed shortly after her abduction.

The police arrest of parolee Richard Allen Davis did little to calm an angry public. The kidnapping and murder of Polly Klaas was blamed on a badly flawed criminal justice system that failed to keep a dangerous person like Davis behind bars. The murder of Polly Klaas, and the extensive national media coverage that surrounded it, sparked another round of get-tough-with-crooks legislation. Whereas earlier laws resulted in mandatory minimums, abolition of parole, and sentencing guidelines, the focus now shifted to "three strikes and you're out" laws.

While public attention focuses on the sentences handed out in the handful of sensational cases such as the Polly Klaas murder (refer to the wedding cake analogy used in Chapter 10), judges must wrestle with the sentence to impose on the over 1 million felons convicted each year. The problems members of the courtroom work group face in reaching these sentencing decisions are captured by the powerful symbol of Lady Justice. Held high in her right hand are the scales of justice, symbolizing fairness in the administration of justice. Draped across her eyes is a blindfold, suggesting that all who come before her will receive impartial justice. Grasped low in her left hand is a sword, standing for the power and might of law. Replicas of Lady Justice adorn the exteriors of many American courthouses, but whether the sentencing process inside the courtrooms lives up to those high ideals is open to question.

The scales of justice are the starting point in examining sentencing. This chapter begins by focusing on who is and who is not sentenced to prison, granted probation, or executed. First, we need to know what factors judges and other members of the courtroom work group weigh in deciding between prison and probation. Normal penalties are the most important consideration in sentencing. Based on the seriousness of the offense and the defendant's prior record, courthouses have developed going rates, which are used as parameters in fine-tuning a sentence for a given offender.

The blindfold is the next major topic. Sentences imposed on the guilty are expected to be fair and just. Many observers argue that they are not; disparities and discrimination in sentencing are major topics of concern. Numerous studies probe the extent to which economic status, age, gender, and race improperly pierce the judicial blindfold when sentences are imposed.

The sword of justice will also be discussed. Whereas some worry that the scales of justice are tipped, others are concerned that the sword of justice

is sheathed. Frustration over rising crime rates has given rise to charges that judges are too lenient. Demands that sentences be more certain as well as more severe have become a staple of American politics. Legislators have responded by increasing the severity of some punishments and altering sentencing structures in hopes of producing greater predictability in sentencing. Sentencing guidelines are now the centerpiece in discussions of increasing the predictability of sentencing as well as increasing the severity of penalties.

COURTROOM WORK GROUPS AND SENTENCING DECISIONS

Sentencing is a joint decision-making process. Although only judges possess the legal authority to impose a sentence, other members of the courtroom work group are also influential (Exhibit 16.1).

The extent of this influence varies from jurisdiction to jurisdiction and from judge to judge. Where sentence bargaining predominates, for example, the judge almost invariably imposes the sentence that the prosecutor and defense attorney have already agreed upon. Where count and charge bargaining are used, the actors reach agreements based on past sentencing patterns of the judge. The most significant actors in sentencing are probation officers, prosecutors, defense attorneys, and (of course) judges.

PROBATION OFFICERS

Probation officers perform two major functions in the sentencing process. One is the supervision of offenders after a sentence of probation has been imposed. The other is investigation prior to sentencing (Lurigio, Olson, and Snowden 2009).

The primary purpose of a **pre-sentence investigation (PSI)** is to help the judge select an appropriate sentence by providing information about the crime and the criminal. Most often, the PSI is ordered by the court following the defendant's conviction. A date is set for sentencing the offender, and meanwhile the probation officer conducts the investigation. The pre-sentence report is designed to give the judge, who must select the proper sentence, an appropriate database. This is particularly important when the defendant has entered a plea of guilty, because in these cases the judge knows little about

Exhibit 16.1
THE COURTROOM WORK GROUP AND SENTENCING

	LAW ON THE BOOKS	**LAW IN ACTION**
Probation officer	Conducts pre-sentence investigation (PSI).	Judges most often follow the recommendation in PSI. Studies disagree about whether the sentencing decision is guided by PSI or provides a paper rationale for an already agreed-upon sentence.
Prosecutor	In most jurisdictions, the district attorney (DA) makes a sentencing recommendation to the judge.	Judges are more likely to impose the sentence recommended by the DA than that recommended by the defense attorney.
Defense attorney	During the sentencing hearing, the defense attorney argues for the court to show leniency to the defendant.	Pleas for leniency are viewed as efforts to impress the client and the client's family and therefore are often ignored. Defense attorneys with good working relationships with the other members of the courtroom work group are influential in achieving lenient sentences in selected instances.
Judge	By law, the judge is the only person who can impose a sentence. Mandatory sentences and sentencing guidelines restrict judges' discretion in a growing number of jurisdictions.	Judges most often sentence within the normal penalty structure. Judges often criticize legislatures for restricting judicial sentencing discretion.

the particulars of the crime or the background of the offender.

Historically, the pre-sentence report has been based on police reports, prosecutor's records, an interview with the offender, and perhaps a talk with the defendant's family as well. Using the information gathered from these sources, probation officers typically prepare a pre-sentence report containing a description of the offense, the defendant's version of the crime, the person's prior criminal record and social history, and a psychological evaluation (if needed). But as sentencing systems have become more determinate (Chapter 15), these reports:

have become more succinct, including less offender information. Now, in many jurisdictions, the primary role of the PSI is merely to determine the applicable mitigating and aggravating circumstances. In some states PSIs are no longer required at all, having been replaced by worksheets that calculate prescribed sentences under statutory or administrative guidelines. (Warren 2009, p. 608)

Beyond providing background information, many pre-sentence reports also include a recommendation of an appropriate sentence. However, some judges will not allow a recommendation, claiming that this is the prerogative solely of the court. Even without explicit recommendation, most PSIs leave little room for doubt about what the probation officer thinks the sentence should be. If probation is recommended, the report usually includes a suggested level of supervision (ranging from intensive through regular to minimal), a listing of special conditions of probation, a plan for treatment, and an assessment of community resources available to facilitate rehabilitation.

Probation officers clearly play a significant role in the sentencing process. Judges are very likely to impose the sentence recommended in the PSI. Indeed, one study found a 95 percent rate of agreement between the judge and the probation report when probation was recommended and an 88 percent rate of agreement when the report opposed probation (Carter and Wilkins 1967). Studies have replicated these results with respect to first-time offenders, but found that probation officers recommended incarceration for recidivists almost twice as often as judges imposed it (Campbell, McCoy, and Osigweh 1990; Hagan 1977). Thus, although sentencing judges are not required to follow such recommendations, they usually do.

However, considerable disagreement exists over the actual influence of probation officers in the sentencing process. Some studies suggest that judges seriously consider the recommendations and use them to guide their decisions—that judges lean heavily on the professional advice of probation officers (David 1980; Walsh 1985). Others report that judges skim these reports and read only the sections they deem most important (Norman and Wadman 2000; Rush and Robertson 1987). And still other researchers argue that probation officers have little real influence on the sentencing process—that probation recommendations have been supplanted by plea bargaining. Prosecutors and defense attorneys usually talk to the probation officer before the PSI is submitted to the court. The conversation indicates what information should be stressed to justify the sentence already agreed upon (Kingsnorth and Rizzo 1979). The probation report then provides a rationale after the fact. Overall, the probation officer's role in sentencing is largely ceremonial (Hagan, Hewitt, and Alwin 1979). By and large, recommendations by probation officers "do not influence judicial sentencing significantly but serve to maintain the myth that criminal courts dispense individual justice" (Rosencrance 2004). This, however, may be changing because of the evidence-based corrections movement.

Recall from Chapter 15 that, drawing on similar movements in medicine and the mental health professions, the criminal justice system has slowly been examining "what works" through a scientific lens. *Evidence-based corrections* refers to the correctional practices and interventions "that are supported by the best research evidence…derived from clinically relevant research…based on systematic reviews, reasonable effect sizes, statistical and clinical significance, and a body of supporting evidence" (Warren 2009, p. 597). Evidence-based sentencing makes use of such data by using risk assessment instruments that have been validated by empirical research to help determine whether a particular defendant would be a suitable candidate for a particular correctional rehabilitation or treatment program. A few states, notably Virginia and Arizona, pioneered incorporating such risk assessment into their pre-sentence investigation processes (Warren 2009). A few other states have followed their lead, successfully reducing incarceration rates, recidivism, and correctional expenditures through sentencing offenders to interventions tailored to meet their rehabilitative needs (Aos, Miller, and Drake 2006; Kimora 2008; Warren 2009).

PROSECUTORS

Prosecutors can influence the sentencing decision in several important ways. By agreeing to a count or charge bargain, prosecutors limit the maximum penalty the judge may impose. During the sentencing hearing, prosecutors can bring to the court's attention factors that are likely to increase the penalty—for example, that the victim was particularly vulnerable or that the defendant inflicted great harm on the victim. Alternatively, prosecutors can bring out factors that would lessen the penalty—for example, the defendant's cooperation with the police.

Finally, prosecutors may make a specific sentencing recommendation. If, for example, there has been a sentence bargain, the prosecutor will indicate the penalty agreed on, and the judge will usually adopt that recommendation as the sentence. When such prosecutorial recommendations are based on office policy, they can have the positive effect of muting sentencing disparities among the different judges. In some courts, however, prosecutors are not allowed to make sentencing recommendations, because sentencing is viewed solely as a judicial responsibility.

DEFENSE ATTORNEYS

The defense attorney's role in sentencing begins early in the history of a case. The decision whether to go to trial or to enter a guilty plea is partially based on the attorney's assessment of the sentence likely to be imposed. Based on the knowledge of what sentences have been handed out to past defendants accused of similar crimes and with similar backgrounds, the attorney must advise the client as to the probable sentence.

At the same time, the defense attorney seeks to obtain the lightest sentence possible. One way to accomplish this goal is to maneuver the case before a judge with a lenient sentencing record. Another way is to discuss the case with the prosecutor in hopes that he or she will agree to (or at least not oppose) a recommendation of probation in the pre-sentence investigation. Defense attorneys also try to emphasize certain circumstances that make the defendant look better in the eyes of the judge, prosecutor, and probation officer. They may try to downplay the severity of the offense by stressing the defendant's minor role in the crime or the fact that the victim was not without blame; or they may have friends or employers testify about the defendant's general good character and regular employment.

Overall, though, defense attorneys are less influential than prosecutors. Judges and prosecutors typically view defense attorneys' arguments for leniency as efforts to impress their clients with the fact that they tried as hard as they could.

JUDGES

Courtroom work groups impose informal limits on how judges exercise their formal legal authority to impose sentences. Judges are well aware that the disposition of cases is related to plea bargaining, which in turn depends on being able to anticipate the sentencing tendencies of judges. Judges share in a framework of understandings, expectations, and agreements that are relied on to dispose of most criminal cases. If a judge strays too far from expectations by imposing a sentence substantially more lenient or more severe than the one agreed on by the defendant, defense lawyer, and prosecutor, it becomes more difficult for the prosecutor and defense counsel to negotiate future agreements.

In working within the limits established by the consensus of the courtroom work group, judges are also constrained because the other members of the work group have more thorough knowledge about the details of the defendant and the nature of the crime. In particular, a judge's sentencing decision is restricted by the bargains struck between prosecution and defense. Indeed, judges who enjoy stable relationships with the prosecutors who practice before them are more likely to defer to those prosecutors' sentencing recommendations.

Judges, though, are not without influence. They are the most experienced members of the courtroom team, so their views carry more weight than those of relatively inexperienced prosecutors or defense attorneys. The particular judge's attitudes on sentencing are reflected in the courtroom work group's common understanding of what sentences are appropriate.

NORMAL PENALTIES AND SENTENCING DECISIONS

Sentencing involves a two-stage decision-making process. After conviction, the first decision is whether to grant probation or to incarcerate the defendant. If incarceration is chosen, the second decision is determining how long the sentence should be. Table 16.1 indicates that of the more than 1 million adults found guilty of a felony in state courts every year, 70 percent are incarcerated (either in prison or jail), with the remaining 28 percent sentenced to probation. Thus, for every 100 felons sentenced, 30 are granted probation and 70 are incarcerated (40 in prison and 30 in jail) (Durose 2007).

Making these sentencing decisions is not an easy task; many judges say that sentencing is the most difficult part of their job. The frustrations of sentencing stem in part from the need to weigh the possibility of rehabilitation, the need to protect the public, popular demands for retribution, and any potential deterrent value in the sentence (see Chapter 15). Of course, courtroom work groups do not consider these competing perspectives in the abstract. They must sentence real defendants found guilty of actual crimes. Each defendant and crime is somewhat different. Sentences are expected to be individualized—to fit the penalty to the crime and the defendant.

In seeking individualized sentences, courtroom work groups use **normal penalties** (Spohn 2008; Sudnow 1965). Based on the usual manner in which crimes are committed and the typical backgrounds of

TABLE 16.1

TYPES OF SENTENCES IMPOSED, BY CONVICTION OFFENSE

	PERCENT SENTENCED TO:		
	PRISON	JAIL	PROBATION
All offenses	40	30	28
Violent offenses	54	24	20
Murder	89	3	7
Sexual assault	61	20	17
Robbery	72	15	12
Aggravated assault	43	30	26
Property offenses	37	31	30
Burglary	49	26	24
Larceny	34	35	28
Drug offenses	37	30	30
Weapons offenses	44	28	27

SOURCE: Matthew Durose, *State Court Sentencing of Convicted Felons,* 2004. Washington, DC: U.S. Department of Justice, Bureau of Justice Statistics, 2007. Available online at http://www.ojp.usdoj.gov/bjs/pub/html/scscf04/tables/scs04102tab.htm

the defendants who commit them, courtroom work groups develop norms of what penalties are appropriate for given categories. The normal sentences are not used mechanically; rather, they guide sentencing. It is within the context of these normal penalties that individualization occurs. Upward and downward adjustments are made. Normal penalties governing appropriate sentences for defendants take into account the seriousness of the crime, the prior criminal record, and any aggravating or mitigating circumstances.

SERIOUSNESS OF THE OFFENSE

The most important factor in setting normal penalties is the seriousness of the offense (Spohn 2009; Spohn and DeLone 2000; Steffensmeier, Ulmer, and Kramer 1998). The more serious the offense, the less likely the defendant will be granted probation (see Table 16.1). Also, the more serious the offense, the

longer the prison sentence. These conclusions are hardly surprising. Society expects that convicted murderers will be punished more severely than defendants found guilty of theft. What is important is how courtroom work groups go about the task of deciding what offenses are serious.

When weighing the seriousness of the offense, courtroom work groups examine the harm or loss suffered by the crime victim in what they perceive to be the "real offense" (what really happened, not the official charge). For example, by examining the prior relationship between the defendant and the victim, the courtroom work group may perceive that the underlying crime is a squabble among friends and therefore less serious than the official charge indicates (Vera Institute of Justice 1977; Wilmot and Spohn 2004).

Sentencing on the basis of seriousness is one of the principal ways courts attempt to arrive at consistent sentences. Most courts use a rank ordering that incorporates the full range of offenses—from the most serious crimes of armed robbery and rape, through middle-level crimes of domestic violence, to the lowest level of forgery, theft, and burglary. One reason that sentences appear to critics to be lenient is that most cases are distributed at the lowest level of this ranking.

PRIOR RECORD

After the seriousness of the offense, the next most important factor in sentencing is the defendant's prior record (Albonetti 1997; Spohn 2009; Ulmer 1997). As the prior record increases, so does the sentence. In choosing between probation and imprisonment, the courtroom work group carefully considers the defendant's previous criminal involvement. If the decision has been made to sentence the offender to prison, the prior record also plays a role in setting the length of incarceration. In general, a previous incarceration increases the length of the sentence (Crow 2008; DeLisi 2001; Welch and Spohn 1986).

How courts assess prior records varies. Some consider only previous convictions, whereas others look at arrests as well. In addition, courtroom work groups often consider the length of time between the current offense and the previous one. If there has been a significant gap, the defendant will often receive a sentence more lenient than normal. On the other hand, if the previous conviction is a recent one, this is often taken as an indication that the defendant is a "bad actor," and the severity of the punishment will increase. Finally, the prior record is assessed within the context of the severity of the crime itself. When the crime is perceived as being less serious, individual factors such as prior record seem to be given relatively more weight than when the crime is more serious.

AGGRAVATING OR MITIGATING CIRCUMSTANCES

In passing sentence, judges and other members of the courtroom work group consider not only the formal charge but also the way the crime was committed. Prosecutors and defense counsel engage in a careful calculation of moral turpitude, examining the nature of the crime and the role of the victim. Some of the aggravating circumstances that lead to a higher penalty are the use of a weapon and personal injury to the victim.

Mitigating factors include youth of the defendant, lack of mental capacity, and role (principal or secondary actor) in the crime. One of the most important mitigating factors is the perceived social stability of the defendant. Marital status, relationship with the family, length of employment, and prior alcohol or drug abuse are considered to be indicators of social stability or instability. Social stability is a particularly important predictor of judges' sentencing, especially when probation is under consideration.

LAW IN CONTROVERSY: UNCERTAINTY AND PUBLIC OPINION

Sentencing is more art than science. Judges, prosecutors, probation officers, and defense attorneys are well aware that they will make mistakes in considering the seriousness of the offense, the prior record of the defendant, aggravating or mitigating circumstances, and the stability of the defendant. Uncertainty is ingrained in the process. They may send someone to prison who should not be there or impose a prison sentence that is longer than necessary. Or they may err in the opposite direction: A defendant recently granted probation may commit a serious and well-publicized crime. Note that only the second type of error will reach public attention; mistakes of the first kind may appear, but only well after the fact.

The uncertainties inherent in sentencing are particularly important at a time when public opinion is critical of the courts and sentencing. The majority of Americans feel that sentences are too lenient. In response, courts are sentencing a higher proportion of defendants to prison. Prisons are overcrowded, adding further complexity to the difficult task of arriving at a fair and appropriate sentence.

DISCRIMINATION AND SENTENCING

The ideal of equal justice under the law means that all persons convicted of the same offense should receive identical sentences. But not all deviations from equality are unwarranted. The law also strives for individualized dispositions, sometimes reflecting varying degrees of seriousness of the offense, sometimes reflecting varying characteristics of the offender.

What one person may perceive as unfairness, another may see as justifiable variation. Discussions about unwarranted variation in sentencing involve two widely used terms: *discrimination* and *disparity*. Although widely used, these terms are rarely defined consistently. Moreover, the concepts overlap somewhat. Nonetheless, for our purposes they should be treated as involving distinct phenomena.

Disparity, discussed in more detail later in the chapter, refers to inconsistencies in sentencing; the decision-making process is the principal topic of interest. **Discrimination**, on the other hand, refers to illegitimate influences on the sentencing process; defendants' attributes are the primary focus. Legal factors such as the seriousness of the offense and the prior criminal record of the defendant are considered legitimate factors. Sentencing discrimination exists when some illegitimate attribute is associated with sentence outcomes after all other relevant variables are adequately controlled. These objectionable influences are referred to as "extralegal variables" (Walker, Spohn, and DeLone 2007).

IMBALANCE VERSUS DISCRIMINATION

No one doubts that the criminal justice system reflects an imbalance in terms of the types of people caught in its web. Whether we examine arrests, prosecutions, convictions, or sentences, the statistical profile highlights the same imbalance—poor, young minority males are disproportionately represented.

Evidence of imbalance in outcomes, however, is not proof of discrimination. Imbalance could be the result of legally relevant factors discussed earlier in this chapter (such as seriousness of the offense and prior record). In making claims about discrimination, researchers want to make sure they are comparing cases that are truly similar. By way of illustration, consider two defendants of different races who have received different sentences. One of the defendants is a first offender who pled guilty to burglary and received 1 year of probation. The other has two prior felony convictions and was convicted by a jury of simple robbery and sentenced to 3 years in prison. Irrespective of which offender was white or African-American, we would not conclude solely on this evidence that the sentences were discriminatory. Rather, we would want to compare a number of cases involving similar crimes and defendants with similar backgrounds.

In trying to ensure that like cases are being compared, researchers use statistical controls. A variety of statistical procedures allows researchers to compare first offenders to other first offenders, and burglars to other burglars. Only after legally relevant variables have been held constant can claims about the existence (or absence) of discrimination be made. Earlier studies often failed to incorporate appropriate statistical controls. They considered only the single variables of race and sentencing, for example, and found racial discrimination in the sentencing. When these studies were reanalyzed, Hagan (1974) found that claims of racial discrimination were not supported by the data.

CONFLICTING FINDINGS

Numerous studies have probed the extent to which a defendant's attributes, such as economic status, gender, and race, pierce the judicial blindfold when sentences are imposed. The results are provocative, not only because they raise important issues of equality before the law, but also because they frequently appear to contradict one another.

Some studies find patterns of discrimination, and others do not. Clearly, sentencing discrimination involves complex issues, and researchers disagree over how best to study it. The discussion that follows examines the research concerning discrimination under the headings of economic status, gender, race in sentencing, and race in capital punishment.

DISCRIMINATION AND ECONOMIC STATUS

The courts are a sorting process. At several stages during the process, it is obvious that access to economic resources makes a difference, with the poor receiving less-preferential treatment. For example, the poor are less likely to be released on bail prior to trial and also are less likely to be able to hire a private attorney. These differences during processing carry over to sentencing: Defendants who are not released on bail or are represented by a court-appointed attorney are granted probation less often and are given longer prison sentences.

Outcome differences based on economic status are, therefore, readily apparent in sentencing. The provocative title of a book by Jeffrey Reiman (2007), *The Rich Get Richer and the Poor Get Prison*, reflects this fact. Prisons are indeed the modern equivalent of the poorhouse. Do these patterns indicate that courts discriminate against the poor in sentencing, or are they the product of other, legally permissible, factors? A number of studies yield conflicting and complex answers.

Some studies conclude that unemployment affects sentencing decisions (Chiricos and Bales 1991; Walsh 1987). For example, judges may assess unemployed persons as being at higher risk for reoffending (Spohn and Holleran 2000). In contrast, other studies find that unemployment has no significant influence on sentencing (Clarke and Koch 1976; Myers and Talarico 1986a).

A comprehensive study comparing two cities highlights the complexity of the relationship between economic status and sentencing. In Kansas City, unemployment had a direct effect on the decision to grant probation but none on the length of imprisonment. In Chicago, on the other hand, unemployment had no effect on the decision to grant probation but directly affected sentence length. Perhaps most important, unemployment interacted with race and ethnicity. If the offender was white, unemployment status had no effect. For African-American or Hispanic young males, though, unemployment was related to harsher sentencing. Nobiling, Spohn, and DeLone (1998) concluded that certain types of unemployed offenders are perceived as "social dynamite." The term social dynamite is used to characterize the segment of the deviant population seen as particularly threatening and dangerous. Viewed from this perspective, economic status appears to be a dimension of social stability considered by the courtroom work group during sentencing (see also LaFrenz and Spohn 2006).

DISCRIMINATION AND GENDER

Crime, as Chapter 9 emphasized, is predominantly (but not exclusively) a male enterprise. Of all adults convicted each year, only 18 percent are women (Durose 2007), and the prison population is only 7 percent women. The marked imbalance between male and female defendants complicates efforts to examine gender-based differences in sentencing outcomes. Researchers, nonetheless, focus on two key questions: Why are women increasingly being sentenced to prison, and why are women sentenced more leniently than men? The results of research on gender and sentencing reveal a complex sentencing process.

WHY ARE WOMEN INCREASINGLY BEING SENTENCED TO PRISON?

In recent years the number of women incarcerated in state and federal prisons has increased dramatically. The more than 115,000 women under the jurisdiction of state and federal authorities stands in sharp contrast to the 23,000-plus held in 1985 (Bureau of Justice Statistics 2009). This increase of 500 percent in the number of female prisoners outpaces the increase in male inmates.

Much of this growth in the number (and rate) of women imprisoned is attributed to the war on drugs (Lucas 2008). The number of women incarcerated for drug offenses increased 432 percent from 1986 to 1991 (Bureau of Justice Statistics 1997). Citing evidence like this, Chesney-Lind and Pasko (2004) concluded that the war on drugs has translated into a war on women. In other words, women have been the silent targets of punitive responses against drug use, coupled with get-tough sentencing policies such as sentencing guidelines, mandatory minimums, and three-strikes laws. As a result, the criminal justice system now seems more willing to incarcerate women. Although this claim is indirectly supported by the documented increases in the incarceration rate of women, empirical research suggests that women are less likely to be incarcerated in jail or prison than men and, when they are incarcerated, women receive shorter sentences than men even when sentencing guidelines are in effect that should reduce such gender disparities (Blackwell, Holleran, and Finn 2008).

ARE WOMEN SENTENCED MORE LENIENTLY THAN MEN?

A variety of studies document the more lenient sentencing of women as compared with men—women are more likely to be granted probation and also more likely to receive shorter prison sentences. In *The Invisible Woman*, Joanne Belknap (2007) aptly summarized the three competing hypotheses concerning the treatment of women by the criminal justice system: (1) chivalry or paternalistic treatment, (2) the evil woman, and (3) equal treatment.

The chivalry/paternalism hypothesis stresses that "women are awarded leniency in sentencing as a result of their inherent biological weaknesses and consequently, their need to be protected and coddled both as offenders and as victims" (Franklin and Fearn 2008, p. 279). Paternalism emphasizes the notion that women are childlike, and therefore "women are incapable of achieving, nor are they in fact held to, the same standards of personal responsibility as are men" (Rapaport 1991, p. 368). In essence, gender stereotypes lead predominantly male criminal justice officials to treat women in a protective manner.

The evil woman hypothesis focuses on traditional sex-role expectations. This hypothesis emphasizes that women lose the advantages normally provided by chivalry and paternalism when they are convicted of "manly" crimes such as robbery or assault. This evil woman view argues that women might actually be treated more harshly than men when they deviate from stereotypical sex-role expectations (Griffin and Wooldredge 2006; Weisheit and Mahan 1988).

The third hypothesis is that men and women are actually treated equally during sentencing. Pennsylvania sentencing data indicate that "when men and women appear in (contemporary) criminal court in similar circumstances and are charged with similar offenses, they receive similar treatment" (Steffensmeier, Kramer, and Streifel 1993). Studies in other jurisdictions likewise report no significant gender-based differences (Crew 1991; Spohn and Spears 1997), although an Ohio study finds that after sentencing guidelines were implemented in that state, women were sentenced more leniently than males (but convicted at the same rates) (Griffin and Wooldredge 2006). Boritch (1992, p. 293) wrote that "some of the less severe treatment of women is attributable to the fact that women usually are less serious offenders than men," and therefore studies using appropriate statistical controls for legally relevant variables find less evidence of differential leniency in the severity of sanctions.

In *Gender, Crime, and Punishment*, Kathleen Daly (1994) fleshed out this argument. She selected 40 male–female pairs of apparently similar crimes and then analyzed transcripts of the court proceedings. She concluded that women were involved in less serious crimes, and this factor (not gender) explained "lenient" treatment.

Most contemporary researchers now explicitly reject the evil woman explanation. The continued viability of the chivalry/paternalism hypothesis, however, is still being debated. The hypothesis continues to find empirical support insofar as male offenders who target female victims continue to receive the most severe sanctions as compared with any of the other offender–victim gender dyads (Franklin and Fearn 2008). Regardless of the theoretical explanations,

concern remains that different criteria influence the legal processing of male and female offenders. Some studies report that gender role expectations and stereotypes guide parole decision making (Erez 1992), and that a form of gender bias exists in capital punishment laws (Rapaport 1991).

DISCRIMINATION AND RACE

Critics of the criminal justice system view the high rates of arrest and imprisonment for African-Americans and other minorities as evidence of racial discrimination. Although the law contains no racial bias, these critics claim that, because criminal justice officials exercise discretion, discrimination can and often does occur. (See Courts, Controversy, and Equal Justice: Should Federal Penalties for Crack Be Lowered to Remove Racial Disparities?)

More studies have been done of racial discrimination at the sentencing stage than at any other decision point in the criminal justice system. Studies conducted from the 1930s through the 1960s often reported that extralegal factors such as race were responsible for differences in sanctions. These original findings, however, have not stood up to further analysis, because they failed to use appropriate statistical techniques. When Hagan (1974) reexamined the data from early studies, he found that the relationship between the race of the offender and the sentence handed out was not statistically significant.

Contemporary research using appropriate statistical techniques has produced conflicting findings. Some researchers conclude that African-Americans are sentenced more harshly than whites; others, that no differences exist; and still others, that African-Americans are sentenced more leniently (Walker, Spohn, and DeLone 2007).

One group of studies reported that African-Americans are sentenced more harshly than whites (Spohn and Holleran 2000; Steffensmeier, Ulmer, and Kramer 1998; Zatz 1984). A prominent example of this type of conclusion was based on a study of six American cities. In three Southern cities, African-Americans were sentenced to prison more often than whites. No such differences were found in Northern jurisdictions (Welch, Spohn, and Gruhl 1985). Overall, these studies report modest levels of racial discrimination (Spohn and Cederblom 1991).

COURTS, CONTROVERSY, AND EQUAL JUSTICE

Should Federal Penalties for Crack Be Lowered to Remove Racial Disparities?

Crack is a cheap, smokable form of cocaine that provides a quick high and carries a long federal prison term. Powder cocaine, on the other hand, carries a significantly lesser sentence. Under federal law, 5 grams of crack triggers the same mandatory 5-year prison term for first offenders as does 500 grams of powder cocaine. (Most state codes make no such distinction.)

The difficulty is that the sentences are based on the weight of the drug and not the weight of the active ingredient in the drug. Through the years, sentencing disparities like this have been common but have rarely entered public discussion. In this case, the debate centers on who uses these drugs. Crack cocaine is more likely to be used by African-Americans, and powder by whites. The undeniable result is a racial imbalance—88 percent of people prosecuted in federal courts for trafficking in crack cocaine are African-American.

Some in law enforcement believe that such sentencing disparities are justified because crack use is a more serious problem than the use of powder cocaine. Crack is more often sold by gangs and used by poor people who, in their desperation to repeat the quick high that crack affords, commit robbery or worse to get the money to buy more. Indeed, law enforcement officials often insist that crack is behind a large percentage of the crime they see (Hodges 1997).

When faced with crime issues, Congress typically asks the U.S. Sentencing Commission to study the matter, and study they did. The Sentencing Commission concluded that crack is somewhat more addictive and more closely associated with other crime than is powder cocaine. But the analysis of federal sentencing decisions also documented racial imbalance. The Commission therefore recommended narrowing the sentencing disparity significantly, arguing that a 2-to-1 disparity would be more fitting. But Congress failed to act. The U.S. Supreme Court likewise showed no enthusiasm for tackling this divisive issue. The justices rejected, without comment, the argument that federal sentencing laws are racially discriminatory in treating crack cocaine dealers more severely than traffickers of powder cocaine. As for the executive branch, President Clinton moved cautiously, and later, President Bush opposed any changes.

Over the years the nature of the debate changed with less emphasis on race and more attention

A second group of studies failed to find a link between race and sentencing (D'Alessio and Stolzenberg 2009; Klein, Petersilia, and Turner 1990; Kramer and Steffensmeier 1993; Myers and Talarico 1986a). Research in diverse geographical locations reported the absence of consistent evidence of systematic racial discrimination in sentencing. Perhaps typical is a study of sentencing in federal courts, which found that from 1986 to 1988 "white, black, and Hispanic offenders received similar sentences, on average, in Federal district courts." After sentencing guidelines were imposed in 1989, Hispanic and African American offenders were slightly more likely than white offenders to be sentenced to prison, but these apparent racial differences were directly attributable to

characteristics of offenses and offenders (McDonald and Carlson 1993).

Finally, a few studies concluded that African-Americans were sentenced more leniently than whites (Bernstein, Kelly, and Doyle 1977). For example, research in Atlanta found that African-American defendants received the same sentences as whites after taking into account seriousness of the offense, prior record, and so on. In analyzing sentences handed down by individual judges, however, a more complex pattern emerged. Some judges were clearly antiblack, others problack, and some nondiscriminatory (Gibson 1978).

A meta-analysis of 71 studies that examined the effects of race on criminal sentencing concluded that

directed to the long (and costly) sentences involved. And some leading conservatives began to call for change. In the words of Senator Jeff Sessions (R-AL) "I believe that as a matter of law enforcement and good public policy that crack cocaine sentences are too heavy and can't be justified. People don't want us to be soft on crime, but I think we ought to make the law more rational (quoted in Leinwand 2007).

After years of quiet discussion, the debate over penalties for crack cocaine took several major turns in late 2007. First, the U.S. Sentencing Commission adopted new guidelines that made modest changes: the average sentence for possessing crack cocaine was reduced from 10 years 1 month to 8 years 10 months (Stout 2007). A month later the Supreme Court ruled in *Kimbrough* that District judges could impose shorter prison sentences in crack cocaine cases. The opinion discusses the long-standing debate in this area, noting that "a major supplier of powder cocaine may receive a shorter sentence than a low-level dealer who buys powder from the supplier but then converts it to crack." In turn, the U.S. Sentencing Commission voted to apply the new guidelines retroactively, an action that affected approximately 20,000 federal inmates.

The battle has now shifted to federal courtrooms across the nation. Defense attorneys say that the rules are helping fix systematic sentencing problems that have plagued the federal courts for years. Prosecutors maintain that crack offenders are dangers to society and should be kept incarcerated under the regulations. To date more than 12,000 inmates have had their crack cocaine sentences reduced by an average of 2 years (United Press International 2009).

What do you think? Are the differences in cocaine sentencing fair? Should the apparent racial discrepancy in sentencing drug offenders be a matter of concern? Is crack cocaine more addictive than powder cocaine, and therefore more likely to be linked with crime? If you favor reducing the disparity in sentencing between crack and powder cocaine, would you do so by reducing the penalty for crack cocaine or raising the sanction for powder cocaine? Overall, do you think Congress is justified in imposing a mandatory minimum for drug crimes, or do mandatory minimums end up producing an irrational sentencing structure, with minor offenders being punished more severely than major ones?

even when legal factors (such as criminal history and severity of the offense), were statistically controlled, "on average African-Americans were sentenced more harshly than whites," although racial differences were generally small (Mitchell 2005, p. 462; see also, Crow and Johnson 2008). More recent studies have also found racial disparities in sentencing outcomes for Hispanic offenders, especially in drug-related cases (Brennan and Spohn 2008).

At first blush, the findings on the studies of racial and ethnic effects on sentencing outcomes may appear to be inconsistent, making it difficult to draw firm conclusions. But the results of the most recent and methodologically sophisticated studies evidence that the contemporary sentencing process, while not characterized by "a widespread systematic pattern of discrimination" (Blumstein et al. 1983, p. 93), is nonetheless not racially neutral.

INTERACTION EFFECTS

Although research continues to examine the effects of specific legal and extralegal factors on sentencing decisions, most contemporary research has demonstrated that the interaction between these variables produces the most significant differences. Thus, as discussed above, research has demonstrated racial and ethnic differences in sentencing outcomes; however, these disparities are magnified when other extralegal variables, such as age, gender, educational level, employment, and socioeconomic status are taken into account (Franklin and Fearn 2008; LaFrentz and Spohn 2006; Spohn and Holleran 2000; Ulmer and Johnson 2004). Collectively, the research supports the proposition that young, poor, African-American males are sentenced more harshly than any other group (Curry and Corral-Camacho 2008; Steffensmeier et al. 1998).

DISCRIMINATION AND CAPITAL PUNISHMENT

Capital punishment has figured prominently in studies of racial discrimination in sentencing. Marked racial differences in the application of the death penalty in the South provide the most obvious historical evidence of racial discrimination in sentencing. From 1930 to 1966, 72 percent of the prisoners executed in the South were African-American. This proportion is dramatically higher than the ratio of African-Americans in the overall population or the ratio of African-Americans convicted of capital offenses. The racial gap was even more pronounced in rape cases. Only the South executed rapists, and 90 percent of those executed for rape were African-American. Those most likely to be executed were African-Americans who had raped white women (Wolfgang and Riedel 1973). Recall from Chapter 15 that in the modern era, rape is no longer a death-eligible offense. But the evolution of capital punishment law has not eliminated racial disparities in death penalty cases.

OFFENDER–VICTIM DYAD

The executions in the South clearly show major racial differences. As indicated earlier, however, racial imbalances in outcomes do not necessarily prove discrimination. Interestingly, many studies found that the most obvious factor—race of the defendant—was not as important as the race of the offender in combination with the race of the victim. The offender–victim dyad, ordered according to the perceived seriousness of the offense, is

1. Black offender, white victim
2. White offender, white victim
3. Black offender, black victim
4. White offender, black victim

Research on the offender–victim dyad established that blacks killing or raping whites were the most likely to be executed; conversely, whites killing or raping blacks were least likely to receive the death penalty. These findings have been interpreted as indicating that severe punishments were motivated by a desire to protect the white social order. Some also argue that black lives were not valued as much as white lives. A variety of studies indicated that the use of the death penalty in the South was racially discriminatory (Baldus, Pulaski, and Woodworth 1983; Hindelang 1972; Ralph, Sorensen, and Marquart 1992). A different conclusion emerged for the North. Studies of the death penalty in Northern states found no evidence of racial discrimination (Kleck 1981).

EVIDENCE OF DISCRIMINATION SINCE *GREGG*

Major racial differences in execution rates, together with studies finding racial discrimination in the application of the death penalty, figured prominently in the opinions of several justices when the Supreme Court struck down state death penalty laws in 1972 (*Furman v. Georgia*). The Court later upheld guided discretion statutes designed to reduce or eliminate the arbitrariness with which the death penalty is imposed. Since *Gregg v. Georgia* in 1976, several studies have reported evidence of racial discrimination in the application of post-*Gregg* death penalty laws.

Research on the use of the death penalty post-*Gregg* continue to find that the race of the defendant is rarely associated with the imposition of a death sentence (Williams, Demuth, and Holcomb 2007). Rather, studies that find evidence of discrimination in the modern era report that black defendants who kill white victims are more likely to receive adverse treatment than those with similarly situated cases with non-black defendant–white victim cases (Paternoster and Brame 2008). Conclusions like this have emerged in states as diverse as Maryland, Florida, South Carolina, Georgia, and Colorado (Spohn 2009).

One stage in the process at which discrimination occurs, according to these studies, is the decision of the prosecutor to charge the defendant with a capital homicide (rather than a homicide that typically carries a life sentence) (Radelet and Pierce 1985; Sorensen and Wallace 1999; Weiss, Berk, and Lee 1996). In South Carolina, for example, the race of the victim was found to be a significant factor structuring the district attorney's decision to request capital punishment. For African-American offenders who killed white victims, the prosecutor was 40 times more likely to request the death penalty than in the case of African-American defendants accused of killing other African-Americans (Paternoster 1984). Similarly in Colorado prosecutors were more likely to seek the death penalty for homicides with white female victims (Hindson, Potter, and Radelet 2006).

These studies also find that jurors are more likely to choose a sentence of death rather than life imprisonment during the penalty phase of the trial. Indeed, when the U.S. General Accounting Office (1990, p. 6) reviewed the body of literature on racial discrimination in capital litigation in the post-*Gregg* era, it reported that in "82 percent of the studies, race of the victim was found to influence the likelihood of being charged with capital murder or receiving the death penalty, i.e., those who murdered whites were found to be more likely to be sentenced to death than those who murdered blacks." More recent studies have confirmed that this pattern has continued (Baldus and Woodworth 2003; Baldus et al. 2002; Jacobs and Kent 2007; Jacobs et al. 2007; Paternoster and Brame 2008).

Evidence of No Discrimination since *Gregg*

Findings that the application of the death penalty remain racially biased despite the apparent protections required by *Gregg* were challenged by a study of all death-eligible cases appealed to the Louisiana Supreme Court (Klemm 1986). The initial analysis revealed the impact of extralegal variables. The chance of receiving a death sentence steadily decreased as one moved down the scale of offender–victim dyads. These findings clearly paralleled earlier ones in other states. More sophisticated analysis, however, highlighted the importance of legal variables.

Unlike previous researchers, Klemm also examined how the crime was committed. The prior relationship of the offender to the victim emerged as an important factor. Primary homicides are crimes of passion involving persons who knew each other. Nonprimary homicides occur during the commission of another felony (most typically, armed robbery), and the victim is a total stranger. Those convicted of nonprimary homicides were more likely to receive a sentence of death, regardless of the race of the offender or the race of the victim. Thus, the chances

of receiving a death sentence were greater if the victim was a stranger.

Overall, the race of the victim had only an indirect effect in Louisiana. Likewise, a study of the use of the death penalty in Texas prior to Furman found some remarkable parallels to the findings from Louisiana. In particular, nonprimary homicides were more likely to result in the imposition of the death penalty (Ralph, Sorensen, and Marquart 1992).

The importance of examining not just the victim but the nature of the homicide as well emerges in recent research on victim gender. In murder cases, defendants who victimize women are punished more harshly. The three victimization factors were rape, forcing the victim to disrobe, and killing an unclothed victim (Williams, Demuth, and Holcomb 2007).

McCleskey v. Kemp Rejects Social Science Evidence

The Supreme Court squarely addressed the issue of racial discrimination in capital punishment in a controversial 1987 decision, *McCleskey v. Kemp*. At issue was a study in Georgia that the application of capital punishment was related to the offender–victim dyad. Defendants convicted of killing a white victim were four times more likely to receive a sentence of death than those found guilty of slaying an African-American victim. These racial differences remained even after controls for relevant factors such as prior record and type of homicide were introduced. The authors concluded that Georgia had a dual system of capital punishment, based on the race of the victim (Baldus, Pulaski, and Woodworth 1983).

By a 5-to-4 vote, the majority rejected claims that statistical studies indicated that the state's death penalty law was "wanton and freakish" in application. To Justice Lewis Powell, "Disparities are an inevitable part of our criminal justice system." The opinion argued that the statistics do not prove that race enters into any capital sentencing decisions or that race was a factor in McCleskey's case. To be clear, though, the Supreme Court emphasized that racial discrimination in the imposition of the death penalty violates the Fourteenth Amendment's guarantees of due process and equal protection. However, proof of such discrimination cannot rest on statistical evidence of racially disparate sentencing outcomes. Rather, a defendant must prove that a specific state actor (or group of actors) intentionally discriminated against him or her in the specific case—a task that is often virtually impossible (Paternoster and Brame 2008).

Overall, as the Court has become more supportive of the death penalty, it has become less inclined to consider social science evidence that might show patterns of racial discrimination (Acker 1993; Fradella 2004). Nonetheless, critics continue to point to patterns of discrimination in the application of the death penalty. These concerns motivated Justice Harry Blackmun to shift his position on the death penalty just before his retirement (Exhibit 16.2).

DISPARITIES AND SENTENCING

Unlike discrimination, which focuses on attributes of defendants, disparity centers on the process that sentences defendants. Thus, **disparity** refers to inconsistencies in sentencing resulting from the decision-making process. The most commonly cited types of sentencing disparity involve geography (variations across jurisdictions) and judicial backgrounds and attitudes (variations among judges within the same jurisdiction).

THE GEOGRAPHY OF JUSTICE

What counts against defendants is not only what they do but also where they do it. Significant variations in the sentencing patterns of judges in different judicial districts within the same political jurisdiction is referred to as the "*geography of justice*" or "*community effects*" (Fearn 2005). The frequency of fines, proba-

tion, or imprisonment varies from county to county. Similar differences occur among the states in convicts imprisoned per 100,000 people (Figure 16.1).

Geographical differences in justice are the product of a number of factors, including the amount of crime, the effectiveness of the police in apprehending offenders, and the types of screening used by the court. Also, some courts deal with more serious offenses, as well as with a greater number of defendants who have prior records. But even after controlling for such factors, it is apparent that important geographic differences remain (Kautt 2002; Gertz and Price 1985; Myers and Talarico 1987; Rengert 1989).

Overall, it appears that the South imposes harsher sentences than other regions. Executions, for example, are concentrated in this region. Similarly, urban courts make greater use of probation and shorter prison terms than their rural counterparts (Austin 1981). Such geographic patterns demonstrate that court officials, drawn as they are from the local communities, vary in their views of what offenses are the most serious as well as what penalty is appropriate (Myers and Talarico 1986b; Myers and Reid 1995). These geographic differences also extend to the federal courts, where the applications of the federal sentencing guidelines vary (Johnson, Ulmer and Kramer 2008; Tiede 2009).

JUDGES' BACKGROUNDS AND ATTITUDES

What counts against defendants is not only what they do and where they do it, but also which judge imposes

Exhibit 16.2
JUSTICE BLACKMUN'S DISSENT

From this day forward, I no longer shall tinker with the machinery of death. For more than 20 years I have endeavored—indeed, I have struggled, along with a majority of this Court—to develop procedural and substantive rules that would lend more than the mere appearance of fairness to the death penalty endeavor....

Rather than continue to coddle the Court's delusion that the desired level of fairness has been achieved and the need for regulation eviscerated, I feel morally and intellectually obligated simply to concede that the death penalty experiment has failed. It is virtually self-evident to me now that no combination of procedural rules or substantive

regulations ever can save the death penalty from its inherent constitutional deficiencies. The basic question—does the system accurately and consistently determine which defendants "deserve" to die?—cannot be answered in the affirmative....

The problem is that the inevitability of factual, legal and moral error gives us a system that we know must wrongly kill some defendants, a system that fails to deliver the fair, consistent and reliable sentences of death required by the Constitution.

—Justice Harry Blackmun dissenting in *Callins v. James*, 1994

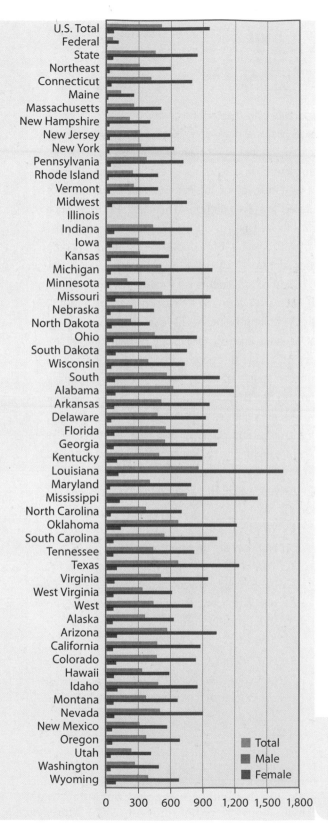

the sentence. Sentencing disparities among judges have fascinated social scientists for decades. A study of women's court in Chicago is typical of this interest. The proportion of shoplifting defendants placed on probation ranged from a low of 10 percent for one judge to a high of 62 percent for another (Cameron 1964). Similarly, downward departures in federal sentencing for certain types of offenders are routine in some districts and rare in others (Johnson, Ulmer, and Kramer 2008). Although such sentencing disparities are due, in part, to variations in the seriousness of the cases heard, differences in judges' backgrounds and attitudes are major contributing factors.

Judges come to the bench from a variety of backgrounds. We might reasonably expect these differences to be reflected in varying patterns of judicial behavior, and studies of judicial decision making support this proposition. U.S. district court judges appointed by Democratic presidents are more likely to decide for the defendant than those appointed by Republican presidents (Carp and Rowland 1983).

Variations in judges' backgrounds are associated with different perceptions of what crimes are serious as well as the relative weights to be assigned to conflicting sentencing goals. Several studies have directly examined judicial attitudes and sentences imposed (Gibson 1980; Green 1961). In Ontario, Canada, judges who stressed deterrence were more likely to favor prison sentences over other forms of sentencing. Conversely, judges who were more treatment-oriented were more likely to impose suspended sentences or relatively short jail sentences (Hogarth 1971).

Although the public views judges as either harsh or lenient sentencers, detailed studies indicate that the pattern is far more complex (Myers and Talarico 1987). It is an accepted fact that judges have different sentencing tendencies. Some have reputations for handing out stiff sentences. "Maximum Max" or "Mean Geraldine" are examples of the colorful labels used by members of the courtroom work group to characterize such judges. Others are known for lenient sentences. "Cut 'em Loose Bruce" is one

FIGURE 16.1   NUMBER OF PRISONERS IN STATE INSTITUTIONS PER 100,000 CIVILIAN POPULATION

*Data for Illinois unavailable.

Source: Heather West and William Sabol. *Prison Inmates at Midyear 2008*. Washington, DC: U.S. Department of Justice, Bureau of Justice Statistics 2009.

LAW AND POPULAR CULTURE

The Shawshank Redemption (1994)

Bank executive Andy Dufresne (Tim Robbins) is falsely convicted of shooting and killing his adulterous wife and her lover. Dufresne is to serve his two consecutive life sentences (one for each victim) in the maximum-security Shawshank Prison, where he soon meets Ellis Boyd "Red" Redding (Morgan Freeman), who has been denied parole after serving 20 years of his sentence. Red is the veteran convict who helps the new convicts adjust to the brutality of the guards and prisoners alike; he is also a smuggler who can get anyone just about anything. For Dufresne, the smuggled goods include a picture of actress Rita Hayworth and a geologist's rock hammer.

At the center of the drama is Mr. Samuel Norton (Bob Gunton), Bible-toting warden who lays down the cardinal rule: "No blasphemy. I'll not have the Lord's name taken in vain in my prison." But there is another side to the self-righteous warden—he runs several illegal businesses. Dufresne soon puts his business talents to work by keeping the warden's books (and documenting every detail of his corrupt enterprises).

Dufresne eventually escapes from prison using the rock hammer to tunnel his way out. He also smuggles out the warden's account records. He uses the passbooks to clean out the warden's secret bank accounts and mails the accumulated documentation to the local police. The police come to arrest the corrupt warden, who manages to escape justice by committing suicide.

Reflecting on prison movies *The Shawshank Redemption*, *Cool Hand Luke*, and *The Longest Yard*, Dr. Robert Freeman found himself cheering the inmates and detesting the sadistic guards, just as millions of other viewers have done. Unlike other viewers, he felt an element of disquiet as well—because (before embarking on a teaching career) he spent 20 years as an employee of the Pennsylvania Department of Corrections. Even though he had firsthand experience with the realities of prisons, Freeman found himself an avid consumer of the popular culture surrounding corrections.

Most of that culture is, of course, a negative one. In *Popular Culture and Corrections*, Freeman (2000) argues that prison movies have seven interwoven sets of negative imagery: systematic brutality in the service of inmate discipline; exploitation of inmates as a cheap source of labor; the degradation of female inmates; the condoning of homosexual rape; systematic racial prejudice; staff incompetence, corruption, and cruelty; and portrayal of guards as smug hacks who are indifferent to human suffering and obsessed with routine.

As you watch *The Shawshank Redemption*, ask yourself:

1. Which of the common themes are present and how are they portrayed?

2. Why is there an apparent disconnect in the public mind between negative images of prisons in the popular media and pressures to lock up more prisoners for longer periods of time?

3. How does this movie contribute to federal court decisions that require upgrading conditions of confinement in the nation's prisons?

name given such a judge by courthouse regulars. The sentences of most judges fall somewhere in between these extremes (Partridge and Eldridge 1974). Because they are less distinctive, these courtroom actors seldom get colorful nicknames. One study of judges in Pennsylvania underscores this point. After statistically controlling for a wide range of factors, minority judges were found to be a little more lenient in the sentences imposed, but interestingly, female judges were not (Johnson 2006). Moreover in jurisdictions that use sentencing guidelines, differences between judges are even less pronounced.

Overall variations between judges appear to have only a weak effect on sentencing outcomes (Steffensmeier and Hebert 1999).

Changing Sentencing Structures

During the late 1960s and early 1970s, an unusual (and temporary) political coalition developed between liberals and conservatives. Both sides found considerable fault in existing sentencing practices. Although their reasons reflected fundamentally different concerns, liberals and conservatives defined the problem in similar terms: The criminal laws permitted too much latitude in sentencing, providing judges with little or no guidance on how to determine the proper sentence for each individual case. This coalition therefore sought greater predictability in sentencing. The result was a fundamental change in how defendants are sentenced (see Chapter 15).

Law in Controversy: Reducing Judicial Discretion

Adherents of the due process model were concerned that excessive discretion resulted in a lack of fairness in sentencing. They perceived that criminal justice officials, ranging from police officers to parole boards, were making decisions in a discriminatory manner, especially on the basis of race. They were also concerned that judges' sentencing discretion resulted in sentencing disparities. Thus, the political left saw determinate sentences as a means of reducing individual discretion and thereby (presumably) reducing disparity and discrimination.

Adherents of the crime control model were far more concerned that excessive discretion resulted in a lack of effective crime control. They perceived that criminal justice officials were making decisions that produced undue leniency. Concern about disparity or discrimination was not part of the agenda. In particular, they viewed trial judges as all too ready to impose sentences well below the statutory maximum. They perceived that parole boards were too willing to release prisoners early; they were shocked that prisoners were back on the streets on parole well before the maximum sentence had expired. To conservatives, the essential problem was that sentencing was not reducing crime. In an effort to make sentencing more effective, a "justice" model

of sentencing came into increasing prominence. Wrongdoers should be punished on the principle of just deserts, which implies a certainty and uniformity of punishment (see Chapter 15).

Law on the Books: Determinate Sentencing Returns

In response to criticisms of the rehabilitation model, with its emphasis on indeterminate sentences and discretionary parole release, a number of states have adopted determinate or fixed sentencing laws (see Chapter 15). These sentencing laws are based on the assumption that judges should give offenders a specific amount of time to serve rather than a minimum and a maximum. The change to determinate sentencing is usually accompanied by a move to abolish release on parole as well. Under determinate sentencing, the prisoner is automatically released to community supervision at the end of the term. (See Exhibit 16.3 for a summary of key developments concerning sentencing.) It should be noted, though, that the statutory systems used in determinate sentencing states vary widely.

Law in Action: Diverse Impacts

Whether determinate sentencing laws are seen as successful depends somewhat on one's political vantage point. Some adherents hoped that these laws would increase the certainty of punishment; others feared that prison populations would swell. Several studies investigated the impact of determinate sentencing laws and found that the impacts were diverse. In one state, an offender's chance of receiving probation declined, but there was no change in another (Covey and Mande 1985; McCoy 1984). Likewise, in some states there was a projected 50 percent increase in the actual length of sentence for first offenders, yet in another jurisdiction only a modest increase was foreseen (Clarke 1984; Clear, Hewitt, and Regoli 1979). The lack of clear findings is not surprising. The American legal system consists of numerous independent units, and the laws in question vary in important ways.

Although the specific impacts of these laws varied from state to state, the overall pattern became quite clear—the overall prison populations increased. An early study in California (Casper, Brereton, and Neal 1982) reported a significant increase in the number of prisoners incarcerated there, a finding replicated

Exhibit 16.3

KEY DEVELOPMENTS IN SENTENCING

Determinate sentencing	Early 20th century	In most jurisdictions, the judge imposes a specific number of years of imprisonment.
Indeterminate sentencing	Through 1970s	Based on the rehabilitation model, many jurisdictions allow judges to impose a sentencing range. Corrections officials and parole boards decide the actual length of time served.
Mandatory minimums	1960s	Most jurisdictions require that a defendant serve a minimum prison sentence for selected offenses.
Maine	1976	First state in modern era to return to determinate sentencing.
California, Illinois, and Indiana	1977	Determinate sentencing laws enacted.
Minnesota	1980	First state to create a sentencing commission and adopt sentencing guidelines.
Sentencing Reform Act	1984	Federal sentencing guidelines adopted and parole abolished in federal courts, effective 1987.
McCleskey v. Kemp	1987	Court rejects use of statistical information to prove racial discrimination in the use of the death penalty.
Mistretta v. U.S.	1989	Federal sentencing guidelines and Sentencing Commission do not violate constitutional separation of powers.
Megan's Law	1994	Following the rape and murder of 7-year-old Megan Kanka, New Jersey passes law requiring convicted sex offenders to register with local police departments.
Polly's Law	1994	California passes three-strikes law, named after murder victim Polly Klaas.
"Three Strikes and You're Out"	1993–1995	Twenty-four states and the federal government pass three-strikes laws.
Truth in Sentencing Laws	1990s	First enacted in 1984, Truth in Sentencing Laws require offenders to serve a substantial portion of their prison sentence. Most often applied for violent offenses.
San Diego County v. Romero	1996	California Supreme Court holds that judges have discretion in counting prior convictions.

	Exhibit 16.3	
	CONTINUED	

Edwards v. U.S.	1997	Court refuses to hear challenge that federal sentencing laws dealing with crack are racially discriminatory.
Aimee's Law	1999	Proposed federal law named after murder victim Aimee Willard, a college athlete killed by a parolee. Law would encourage states to incarcerate individuals convicted of murder, rape, or child molestation.
Ewing v. California	2002	Three-strikes laws do not violate the Eighth Amendment prohibition against cruel and unusual punishment.
Connecticut v. Doe	2002	Affirmed Connecticut's "Megan's Law" requiring convicted sex offenders to register and have their names published in a registry.
Blakely v. Washington	2004	Under the Sixth Amendment, juries, not judges, have the power to make a finding of guilty beyond a reasonable doubt for facts used in state sentencing guidelines.
U.S. v. Booker	2005	The first part of the opinion struck down federal sentencing guidelines as unconstitutional for the reasons expressed in *Blakely v. Washington*. The second part of the opinion allows federal judges to continue to use federal sentencing guidelines as advisory.
Cunningham v. California	2007	California's sentencing guidelines are unconstitutional because juries, not judges, must decide whether facts are proven that justify enhancing a criminal sentence.
Rita v. United States	2007	Sentences that fall within the range established by the Federal Sentencing Guidelines may be presumed to be "reasonable," but appellate courts are not required to consider such sentences reasonable under the facts and circumstances of any particular case.
Gall v. United States	2007	In reviewing a sentence imposed by a U.S. District Judge that is more lenient than the guideline recommendations, the courts of appeal should be deferential and reverse only if the trial judge abused his or her discretion.
Kimbrough v. United States	2007	U.S. District Court Judges are not bound by federal sentencing guidelines that require offenses involving crack cocaine to be punished more harshly than offenses involving powder cocaine.

in other states as well (Carroll and Cornell 1985). By the mid-1990s the inescapable conclusion was that changes in sentencing structure begun in the late 1960s and early 1970s resulted in major increases in the prison population across the nation (Marvell and Moody 1996). As we discussed in Chapter 15, the increase in prison populations did not begin to level off until about 2005.

SENTENCING GUIDELINES

Early efforts to impose determinate sentencing suffered from a serious weakness: Legislative bodies had neither the time nor the skills to enact detailed sentencing rules. Therefore, since the 1980s, efforts to provide certainty and consistency in sentencing have taken a different form. Legislatures have created commissions to devise detailed sentencing rules, and the legislatures have then enacted these guidelines into law (Griset 1995).

STATE SENTENCING GUIDELINES

Statewide **sentencing guidelines** are mentioned most frequently as the procedures for ensuring fairness and appropriate severity in sentencing. They have been adopted in 21 states (Kauder and Ostrom 2008) and seriously considered in a few others (Reitz 2001). Sentencing guidelines direct the judge to specific actions that should be taken. The sample sentencing grid in Exhibit 16.4 illustrates how they operate. The far left column ranks the seriousness of the offense according to 10 categories. The top row provides a seven-category criminal history score for the defendant based on number of previous convictions, employment status, educational achievement, drug or alcohol abuse, and so on. Having determined the offense severity ranking and the criminal history score, the judge finds the recommended sentence in the cell where the applicable row and column meet. The cells below the bold black line call for sentences other than state imprisonment; these numbers specify months of supervision (that is, probation). The cells above the bold line contain the guideline sentence expressed in months of imprisonment. The single number is the recommended sentence. The range (shown below the single number) varies by plus or minus 5 to 8 percent from the guideline sentences and can be used for upward or downward adjustments.

State sentencing guidelines are best viewed as ranging along a continuum of more voluntary on one side and more mandatory on the other (Kauder and Ostrom 2008). Under voluntary sentencing guidelines, recommended sentencing ranges are derived by empirically analyzing the sanctions judges in the jurisdiction have usually imposed in various types of cases in the past. Thus, descriptive guidelines codify past sentencing practices as standards for future cases. Once adopted, these guidelines may voluntarily be used by judges but they are advisory only. Voluntary sentencing guidelines do not have the force of law, and noncompliance by a judge creates no right to sentencing appeal. As one would expect, not all judges actually use the guidelines when imposing sentences (Miethe and Moore 1989). Over the years some voluntary sentencing guidelines have fallen into such disuse that it is not always clear whether a particular state's guideline system is still operational (Kauder and Ostrom 2008).

Mandatory sentencing guidelines are used in a few states. The legislature delegates the authority for developing detailed sentencing criteria to a sentencing commission (Kramer, Lubitz, and Kempinen 1989). The resulting guidelines are prescriptive—that is, they express what sentence *should* be imposed, irrespective of existing practices. Once adopted, these guidelines must be followed by the sentencing judges. If a sentence is imposed outside the guidelines, the judge must provide reasons for the deviation. Both defendants and prosecutors have the right to have the judge's explanation reviewed by an appellate court. Mandatory guidelines have substantial legal authority. As you might expect, they achieve a much higher rate of judicial compliance and help reduce sentencing disparity.

Sentencing guidelines are complex in application (Kramer and Ulmer 2009). One major question asked by researchers and policy makers is whether sentencing guidelines do indeed result in fairer sentences. A three-state study concluded that in states that use sentencing guidelines, offenders are sentenced with more predictability, in a less discriminatory manner, and with increased transparency (Ostrom et al. 2008). Earlier studies reached similar conclusions. Racial, ethnic, and gender differences in sentencing generally decline (Kramer and Ulmer 1996; Parent et al. 1996). Disparity reductions, though, tend to erode somewhat over time. Studies in Minnesota (Koons-Witt 2002) and Ohio (Griffin and Wooldredge 2006) found only short-term reductions in gender-based dispositions in felony cases. Not surprisingly, mandatory guidelines are more likely to reduce sentencing disparity.

Exhibit 16.4

MINNESOTA SENTENCING GUIDELINES

Severity Level of Conviction Offense (Common offenses listed in italics)		Criminal history score						
		0	1	2	3	4	5	6 or more
Murder, 2nd Degree (intentional murder; drive-by-shootings)	XI	306 261-367	326 278-391	346 295-415	366 312-439	386 329-463	406 346-480 [2]	426 363-480 [2]
Murder, 3rd Degree Murder, 2nd Degree (unintentional murder)	X	150 128-180	165 141-198	180 153-216	195 166-234	210 179-252	225 192-270	240 204-288
Assault, 1st Degree Controlled Substance Crime, 1st Degree	IX	86 74-103	98 84-117	110 94-132	122 104-146	134 114-160	146 125-175	158 135-189
Aggravated Robbery, 1st Degree Controlled Substance Crime, 2nd Degree	VIII	48 41-57	58 50-69	68 58-81	78 67-93	88 75-105	98 84-117	108 92-129
Felony DWI	VII	36	42	48	54 46-64	60 51-72	66 57-79	72 62-84 [2]
Controlled Substance Crime, 3rd Degree	VI	21	27	33	39 34-46	45 39-54	51 44-61	57 49-68
Residential Burglary Simple Robbery	V	18	23	28	33 29-39	38 33-45	43 37-51	48 41-57
Nonresidential Burglary	IV	12 [1]	15	18	21	24 21-28	27 23-32	30 26-36
Theft Crimes (Over $5,000)	III	12 [1]	13	15	17	19 17-22	21 18-25	23 20-27
Theft Crimes ($5,000 or less) Check Forgery ($251-$2,500)	II	12 [1]	12 [1]	13	15	17	19	21 18-25
Sale of Simulated Controlled Substance	I	12 [1]	12 [1]	12 [1]	13	15	17	19 17-22

☐ Presumptive commitment to state imprisonment. First-degree murder has a mandatory life sentence and is excluded from the guidelines by law. See Guidelines Section II.E., Mandatory Sentences, for policy regarding those sentences controlled by law.

▨ Presumptive stayed sentence; at the discretion of the judge, up to a year in jail and/or other non-jail sanctions can be imposed as conditions of probation. However, certain offenses in this section of the grid always carry a presumptive commitment to state prison. See, Guidelines Sections II.C. Presumptive Sentence and II.E. Mandatory Sentences.

NOTE: The left-hand column ranks the seriousness of the offense according to 10 categories. The upper rows provide a seven-category criminal history score, calculated by summing the points allocated to such factors as the number of previous convictions, the total times incarcerated, whether the offender was on probation or parole, employment status or educational achievement, and the history of drug and/or alcohol abuse. After calculating the offense severity ranking and the criminal history score, the judge determines the recommended sentence by finding the cell of the sentencing grid in the applicable row and column. The cells below the bold line call for sentences other than imprisonment; these numbers specify months of supervision. The cells above the bold line contain the guideline sentence expressed in months of imprisonment. The single number is the recommended sentence. The range extends plus or minus 5 to 8 percent from the guideline sentence. By law, first-degree murder is excluded from the guidelines and continues to have a mandatory life sentence.

SOURCE: Minnesota Sentencing Guidelines Commission, 2008, p. 57.

Researchers have also asked if sentencing guideline laws are associated with increases in sentencing severity, whether intended or not. This has been the experience in Minnesota (Tonry 1987) and Pennsylvania (Kramer, Lubitz, and Kempinen 1989). The same holds true at the federal level.

Since 2000, the U.S. Supreme Court has raised serious doubts about the constitutionality of sentencing guidelines, holding that other than a prior conviction, any fact that increases the penalty for a crime beyond the statutory maximum must be tried before a jury (*Apprendi v. New Jersey* 2000). Based on this reasoning, in 2004 the Court struck down sentencing guidelines in the State of Washington, holding that the Sixth Amendment gives juries (and not judges) the power to make a finding of fact beyond a reasonable doubt (*Blakely v. Washington* 2004). The dissenters argued that the decision will serve only to increase judicial discretion and lead to less uniformity in sentencing, perhaps leading to increasing racial discrimination.

Some state supreme courts held that Blakely did not apply to their state sentencing schemes (Lankford 2006), only to be firmly rebuffed when the Supreme Court struck down the California sentencing laws, holding that the statute gave judges authority that the U.S. Constitution places with juries (*Cunningham v. California* 2007).

Federal Sentencing Guidelines

The legal and political factors leading to the creation of state sentencing guidelines likewise led to the creation of federal sentencing guidelines, which have become more visible and also more controversial than their state counterparts. In 1984, Congress created the U.S. Sentencing Commission (see Chapter 3) and charged it with developing guidelines for sentencing federal offenders. These standards became law in 1987. The Supreme Court upheld their legality in 1989 (*Mistretta v. United States*), only to rule them unconstitutional in 2005

The federal sentencing guidelines proved to be highly controversial (Stith and Cabranes 1998). Indeed, many federal judges, probation officers, defense attorneys, and even some prosecutors resent and resist the guidelines (Tiede 2009). According to Michael Tonry (1993), the federal sentencing guidelines "are a failure and should be radically revised or repealed." In support of this conclusion, he offers the following arguments: First, the guidelines are unduly harsh and as a result have produced a dramatic increase in the federal prison population. Second, the

guidelines have failed to achieve their primary goal of reducing unwarranted disparities in federal sentencing. Indeed, the guidelines contribute to unfairness in sentencing because they are rigid and complex.

In a complex ruling, the Supreme Court has greatly altered how federal guidelines are used (*U.S. v. Booker* 2005). The first part of the opinion struck down federal sentencing guidelines as unconstitutional for the same reasons used to declare state sentencing guidelines unconstitutional—Congress improperly allowed judges and not juries to make key factual decisions in sentencing. But the second part of the opinion allows federal judges to continue to use the guidelines as advisory, and appellate courts can review for reasonableness.

The impact of *Booker* on federal sentencing practices was not as dramatic as some hoped and others feared. At the District Court level, the rate of within-range sentences remained the same and average sentence lengths remained constant. There were more downward departures, but these were largely due to actions of U.S. attorneys and not the judges (Hofer 2007). The U.S. courts of appeals varied in their approaches: Some adopted a wait-and-see attitude, others held that *Blakely* did not apply to the federal sentencing guidelines, and still others held that the guidelines were unconstitutional (Hurwitz 2006). The Court revisited the issues, holding that sentences within the guidelines may be presumed "reasonable" but did not require appellate courts to do so (*Rita v. United States* 2007). Amid confusion about the impact of *Rita*, the Court again considered the issues, this time making it more difficult for appeals courts to reverse a trial judge who imposes a sentence more lenient than the guideline recommendations (*Gall v. United States* 2007). At the same time, the high court, by a vote of 7-to-2, held that trial judges may narrow the sentencing gap between crack cocaine and powder cocaine (*Kimbrough v. United States* 2007) (see Case Close-Up: *Kimbrough v. United States* and Federal Sentencing Guidelines in Crack Cocaine Cases). Although these decisions clearly restored some of the sentencing discretion taken away by the sentencing guidelines, they will likely result in only limited sentencing leniency. In all likelihood, specialists in sentencing law predict, federal judges will continue to use their sentencing power relatively sparingly (Liptak 2007). Moreover, in upcoming sessions, Congress might attempt to enact a new statutory sentencing scheme.

The short-term impact of *Booker* is unclear because the Court failed to state whether the decision

Kimbrough v. United States and Federal Sentencing Guidelines in Crack Cocaine Cases

According to his former lawyer, Derrick Kimbrough was leading a "pretty unremarkable" life until he fell into a drug habit. In his early 20s, Kimbrough enlisted in the Marines, fought in Operation Desert Storm, and received an honorable discharge. He then moved to Norfolk, Virginia, where he worked construction. Kimbrough's life took a decided turn for the worse when the Norfolk police spotted Kimbrough and another man sitting in a car in a drug-plagued neighborhood. The police questioned the two and then searched the car, with Kimbrough's consent. They found 56 grams, or about 2 ounces, of crack cocaine and 92 grams of powder cocaine, plus an illegal handgun (McGlone 2007a). Although the state charges were dropped, Kimbrough was indicted in U.S. District Court for the Eastern District of Virginia, where he pled guilty to the four counts in the indictment.

Based on the federal sentencing guidelines, the U.S. Attorney sought a prison term between 19 and 22 years, but U.S. District Judge Raymond Jackson balked. If Kimbrough had only been in possession of powder cocaine, he would have faced no more than a total of 8 years in prison, the judge noted. Jackson, a federal judge for nearly 14 years, and not noted for a history of being lenient according to the local paper, decided to take a stand. "The Justice Department has yet to recognize the disproportionate and unjust effect that crack cocaine guidelines have in sentencing." He added "I find it absolutely ridiculous that the Department of Justice demands the heart and lungs, feet and everything else in a case on these facts" (quoted in McGlone 2007b). Jackson concluded that the statutory minimum of 15 years was "clearly long enough."

The government appealed the downward departure as unreasonable and appealed to the Fourth Circuit of Appeals based in nearby Richmond, Virginia—a circuit that has the reputation of being one of the nation's most conservative judicial bodies when it comes to defendant's rights. In an unpublished opinion, the court vacated the sentence, writing that a sentence "outside the guidelines range is per se unreasonable when it is based on a disagreement with the sentencing disparity for crack and powder cocaine offenses."

During oral argument at the U.S. Supreme Court, several justices, both liberal and conservative, appeared to indicate a willingness to grant district judges the ability to deviate from sentencing guidelines. Weighty legal issues of defining abuse in judicial discretion (Chapter 17), though, did give way to humor. Justice Antonin Scalia, the anchor of the conservative wing, compared a drug dealer turned informant to Lex Luthor, the evildoer from the "Superman" comics, which brought a chuckle from the audience (McGlone 2007b).

Justice Ruth Bader Ginsburg authored the Supreme Court's majority opinion. She focused heavily on the contradictions in American drug policy. Working on the assumption that crack cocaine was more harmful than its powder form, the Anti-Drug Abuse Act of 1986 adopted a "100-to-1 ratio" that treated every gram of crack cocaine as the equivalent of 100 grams of powder cocaine. Although the intent of the law was to punish drug dealers more severely than drug users, the anomalous result of the 100-to-1 ratio was that retail crack dealers received longer sentences than the wholesale drug distributors who supplied the powder cocaine from which the crack is produced.

Extending its previous decision in *Booker* (2005), which held that federal sentencing guidelines were unconstitutional if mandatory, but judges could still refer to them as advisory, the Court held that the Fourth Circuit erred in vacating Kimbrough's sentence because district judges are not bound by the sentencing guidelines in crack cocaine cases. In dissent, Justices Clarence Thomas and Samuel Alito wrote little about the specific issue of crack cocaine. Instead, they repeated their opposition to the *Booker* opinion, expressing their continuing belief that the guidelines should have the force of law, rather than being merely advisory.

The public debate over crack cocaine versus powder cocaine has focused heavily on the issue of racial disparities (see Courts, Controversy, and Equal Justice: Should Federal Penalties for Crack Be Lowered to Remove Racial Disparities?). And, to be sure, concerns about race clearly underpin the *Kimbrough* case. Although Kimbrough is never identified as being African-American, a picture in the *Norfolk-Pilot* clearly leads to that conclusion. Moreover, an amicus brief filed by the NAACP Legal Defense Fund focuses on racial disparities in cocaine cases ("LDF Applauds Supreme Court…" 2007). The Court's opinion, however, mentions race only in passing. Without expressing a position, the Court's opinion cites a report of the U.S. Sentencing Commission that the crack/powder sentencing differential "fosters disrespect for and lack of confidence in the criminal justice system" because of a widely held perception that it promotes unwarranted disparity based on race.

The *Kimbrough* decision and other policy changes announced by the U.S. Sentencing Commission have greatly altered the debate over penalties for crack cocaine versus powder cocaine. But the debate is hardly over. After all, Derrick Kimbrough remains in prison serving a 15-year sentence for drug possession. Moreover, even though the U.S. Sentencing Commission has reduced the recommended punishment for possession of crack cocaine below its original levels (from the 100:1 ratio down to a low of 25:1), the disparate treatment of offenses involving crack versus powder cocaine still remains. The Obama administration believes that the disparity in sentencing between crack and powder cocaine is unwarranted and must be eliminated (Cose 2009). Thus, as with many other topics, politics, and not the law, may finally bring about a resolution of this divisive issue.

CASE CLOSEUP

was retroactive (potentially meaning that appellate courts must review past sentences). Likewise, the long-term impact of *Booker* is unclear because Congress might attempt to enact a new statutory sentencing scheme. Meanwhile, the Courts of Appeals are applying *Booker* in fundamentally different ways. Some have indicated that the guidelines are not enforceable, but others are enforcing them.

INCREASING THE SEVERITY OF THE PENALTY

For many years, the majority of Americans have believed that prison sentences are too lenient (Cullen, Fisher and Applegate 2000; Krisberg 1988; Rossi and Berk 1997), and elected officials often express these views (Thomson and Ragona 1987). Thus, when confronted with a crime problem, legislators responded by sounding a clarion call to get tough with criminals. Accordingly, criminal punishments grew harsher throughout the 1980s and 1990s. But the economic crisis in the late 2000s may have caused the American public to rethink its ever-more-punitive stance. Opinion research finds that the public "overwhelmingly favors spending more on policing, crime prevention programs for young people, and drug treatment for nonviolent offenders," while they oppose additional funding for prisons (Gottschalk 2009, p. 456; see also, Cohen, Rust, and Steen 2006). States have been experimenting with different sentencing formulas aimed at rehabilitation, especially for nonviolent offenders (Gottschalk 2009; King 2008). But there can be no doubt that the increased severity of criminal penalties over the past 30 years or so still causes the United States to incarcerate more people per capita than any other country in the world.

Increasing the severity of penalties is premised on the notion that they will deter criminals and reduce crime. These ideas are more often justified by philosophical claims than by valid scientific evidence. Indeed, researchers are skeptical that this type of deterrent effect actually exists.

LAW ON THE BOOKS: MANDATORY MINIMUM SENTENCES

Mandatory minimum sentencing laws are one method legislatures use to increase the severity of sentencing. These types of laws are typically enacted in response to allegations that lenient judges are allowing many serious offenders (particularly violent ones) to go free. (The "proof" of this proposition is often limited to one or two highly publicized cases.) Virtually all states have passed mandatory minimum sentencing laws.

Typically, **mandatory minimum sentencing** laws require that offenders convicted of certain offenses must be sentenced to a prison term of not less than a specified period of years, and nonprison sentences (such as probation) are expressly precluded. In short, a term of imprisonment is mandated regardless of the circumstances of the offense or the background of the individual.

In recent years, the most popular mandatory minimum laws have supposedly targeted violent offenders with previous felony convictions (see Courts, Controversy, and Reducing Crime: Are "Three Strikes and You're Out" Laws Fair?). Through the years, legislative bodies have also enacted mandatory minimums for crimes that are particularly unpopular at the moment, including convicted felons in possession of a firearm, repeat drunk drivers (Chapter 18), and those in possession of certain drugs (such as cocaine) with intent to sell. In addition, some states enacted so-called truth in sentencing laws, which require offenders to serve a substantial portion of their prison term (often 85 percent) before release (Ditton and Wilson 1999). Truth in sentencing laws were prompted by the 1994 Crime Act, a law that conditioned federal funds to help states expand their prisons to house violent offenders on their having such a law. But few states actually enacted such laws, and funding was discontinued in 2002 (Turner et al. 2006). As a result of skyrocketing prison costs, some states, most notably Iowa, have decreased the time inmates are required to serve to facilitate earlier release through parole (Public Safety Performance Project 2007).

LAW IN ACTION: NULLIFICATION BY DISCRETION

Mandatory minimum sentencing laws have proved popular because they promise certainty of punishment. "If Every Criminal Knew He Would Be Punished If Caught" is the title of an article by neoconservative James Q. Wilson (1973). But researchers caution that administering the law is seldom that automatic.

Sharp increases in formal penalties tend to be sidestepped by those who apply the law. At a variety of points in the application of legal sanctions—police arrest, prosecutorial discretion, jury conviction, and judicial sentencing—discretion may be exercised to offset the severity of the penalty (McCoy 1984; Stith 2008).

A reduction in the number of arrests is one type of discretionary reaction that may occur when the severity of the penalty is increased. This clearly occurred when Connecticut's governor tried to crack down on speeders by imposing a mandatory loss of the driver's license; arrests for speeding decreased after the severe penalties were announced, because the police and other legal officials perceived that the penalty was too severe for the offense (Campbell and Ross 1968).

An increase in prosecutorial discretion may also compensate for an increase in the harshness of sentencing. Prosecutors often respond to new legislative actions by reducing the number of charges for that category. In 1994, Oregon voters approved Measure 11, which imposed long mandatory prison terms for 16 designated violent and sex-related offenses. This measure had fewer negative system impacts than had been anticipated by many criminal justice administrators, largely because prosecutors exercised the discretion provided to them by the law. As a result, fewer mandatory-eligible cases were prosecuted. At the same time, more nonmandatory-sentence offenses were brought to court (Merritt, Fain, and Turner 2006). Thus, prosecutors may choose to file charges for an offense that does not carry the most severe penalties when they anticipate that judges and juries will be reluctant to convict.

A decrease in the number of convictions may also occur when legislators increase the severity of punishment. The most commonly cited example is capital punishment in late 18th- and early 19th-century England, when most felonies were punishable by death. Judges often strained to avoid convicting defendants by inventing legal technicalities (Hall 1952). Similarly, in New York State, after a tough drug law was passed, the number of convictions dropped.

After conviction, judges are reluctant to apply a severe penalty (Ross and Foley 1987). When Chicago traffic court judges sought to crack down on drunk drivers by voluntarily agreeing to impose a 7-day jail term, the penalty was rarely applied (Robertson, Rich, and Ross 1973).

Clearly, a relationship exists between punishment policy and the system that administers it. Through the discretionary actions of police, prosecutors, judges, and juries, harsh penalties are nullified. The more severe the penalty, the less likely it will be imposed when its severity exceeds what is viewed as appropriate. The final result is that more produces less. Stepping up the severity of the punishment does not increase the threat of punishment; it reduces it.

LAW IN CONTROVERSY: NEGATIVE SIDE EFFECTS

One reason legislators find raising penalties so attractive is that they appear to be fighting crime without having to increase appropriations. It is a policy apparently without costs; the public will be appeased without the painful necessity of voting for higher taxes. But a number of studies suggest that increasing the severity of the punishment produces negative side effects

Courts, Controversy, and Reducing Crime

Are "Three Strikes and You're Out" Laws Fair?

The kidnapping and murder of Polly Klaas focused the nation's attention on violent, predatory criminals. The man convicted of the crime, Richard Allen Davis, was an ex-con who had recently been released from prison on parole. The news coverage of the kidnapping and eventually the arrest fed the nation's fears that no one was safe, not even those who lived in a tranquil small town like Petaluma, California. At fault were not only societal outcasts like Richard Allen Davis, but also a criminal justice system that was a failure (Surette 1996).

Faced with an unsettled public, elected officials sought to reassure them by taking dramatic action. Thus, the murder of Polly Klaas became the reference event for passing "three strikes and you're out" legislation.

The basic arguments advanced by proponents of the three-strikes concept parallel the crime control model. Incapacitating chronic offenders who have demonstrated by their acts that they are both dangerous and unwilling to reform will protect the public. Moreover, repeat offenders will be deterred because they will be off the streets.

Critics counter that substantial increases in the use of imprisonment over the past decade have had little if any effect on violent crime rates. Life terms for three-time losers will require the allotment of expensive prison cells to offenders who are well past the peak age of criminal conduct. These adherents of the due process model argue that spending the same amount of money in other areas would produce a much greater reduction in crime than three-strikes laws (Greenwood et al. 1996).

Court arguments aside, public support for three-strikes laws was overwhelming, and in quick order elected officials in 24 states and the federal government enacted new laws using the "three-strikes" moniker. What was left largely unspoken during the debate was that for many years most states have had provisions in their laws for enhanced sentencing of repeat offenders (Clark, Austin, and Henry 1998). Thus, outside of California, three-strikes provisions rarely applied. These laws have had minimal impacts because they were drafted to apply to only the most violent repeat

(referred to by economists as *"hidden costs"* and by others as *"unanticipated consequences"*)—that is, harsher laws have impacts, but often not the ones intended.

One negative side effect of increasing the severity of punishments centers on the greater time, effort, and money courts must expend. Faced with severe sanctions, defendants demand more trials, which consume more court time. A backlog of cases results, delays increase, and the certainty and speed of conviction decline.

Critics are also concerned that mandatory minimum sentencing legislation results in a rigid and inflexible overreaction to problems of judicial discretion. Requiring every single defendant convicted under the same statute to serve the identical sentence threatens to create a system so automatic that it may operate in practice like a poorly programmed robot. In the words of U.S. District Court Judge Vincent Broderick, "The most frustrating aspect of mandatory

minimum prison sentences is that they require routinely imposing long prison terms based on a single circumstance, when other circumstances in the case cry out for a significantly different result. The same sentence is mandated for offenders with very different criminal backgrounds and whose roles differ widely one from another" (Vincent and Hofer 1994).

CONCLUSION

Richard Allen Davis was convicted of first-degree murder and sentenced to death. But as mentioned in Chapter 9, he used the sentencing hearing to make yet another dramatic statement, accusing the father of sexual misconduct with his daughter.

Whether the "three strikes and you're out" laws passed in the aftermath of the Polly Klaas kidnapping and murder will have a lasting impact is open to

offenders, the very defendants already covered by habitual offender laws and also the very offenders who fare the worst under existing normal penalties (Clark, Austin, and Henry 1997).

California's law potentially has greater impact because it was more loosely drafted. Because any felony can be a third strike, life sentences can be imposed for relatively nonviolent crimes. Thus, the California law applies to criminals with a record of one or more violent or serious felonies. After one such crime ("strike"), the sentence for any new felony is doubled. After two strikes, a new felony requires a term of 25 years to life (Criminal Justice Consortium 1997).

Three-strikes laws are the most recent example of spasmodic attempts by the public, and the politicians they elect, to respond in an extreme manner to what is perceived as skyrocketing crime rates and an unduly lenient criminal justice system. These outbursts are followed by adaptation by members of the courtroom work group (Feeley and Kamin 1996; Harris and Jesilow 2000). Adaptive behavior is readily apparent in the California Supreme Court's decision holding that judges do not have to impose life sentences on repeat criminals if they think the punishment is too harsh (*San Diego County v. Romero* 1996). Later, the court held that juvenile convictions likewise need not be counted (*San Diego County v. Garcia* 1999). In essence, the California high court held that the law went too far and judges should use discretion.

California experienced a major increase in its prison population and the economic consequences of the three-strikes policy came home to roost when the state experienced major financial problems. The Democratic governor was removed from office and replaced by former movie actor Arnold Schwarzenegger, a Republican. In his efforts to restore financial stability to the state, he has called for reducing the prison population.

What do you think? Are three-strikes laws an appropriate and effective response to violent crimes by predators? Or do you think that these laws are overreactions? Given that adaptation by the courtroom work group seems inevitable, why do legislatures periodically pass such laws?

question. The essential difficulty is that the criminals who figure prominently in the media bear little resemblance to the ones who appear before U.S. judges every day. Although the replica of Lady Justice outside the courthouse contemplates justice in the abstract, judges inside the courthouse must pass judgment on real-life defendants, not the stereotypical villains who dominate the rhetoric of elected officials. In deciding whether to send an offender to prison or grant him or her probation, the scales of justice require the judge (and other members of the courtroom work group) to weigh the normal penalty for the offense, the seriousness of the crime, and the defendant's prior record and social stability. The resulting decisions have become the focus of heated public debate.

To some, American courthouses do not mete out fair and impartial justice. These critics find that the blindfold is improperly pierced by sentences that are discriminatory, disparate, or both. To others, American courthouses hand out sentences that are too lenient. These critics argue that wielding the sword of justice will protect the public from crime.

These dual concerns have prompted numerous changes since the mid-1970s. Determinate sentencing laws, mandatory minimum sentencing provisions, and sentencing guidelines are the most prominent changes undertaken. Sentencing is likely to remain on the nation's political agenda. All too often, members of the public, as well as elected officials, have ignored an important reality: Prison populations are swelling. The United States sends more people to prison than any other Western nation, and the rate of incarceration is growing steadily. The result is severe prison overcrowding, compounded by federal court orders requiring major improvements in prison conditions. Limitations on the capacity and quality of prisons create a political dilemma. Although citizens and public officials want to send even more offenders to prison for longer periods of time, they are unwilling to spend large sums of tax dollars to build the needed facilities. Sentencing is thus likely to remain an important public policy issue for the foreseeable future. Alas, in the end, Lady Justice appears to cost more than the public is able or willing to spend.

CHAPTER REVIEW

1. Define the concept of normal crimes and indicate the two most important factors in determining normal penalties.

The concept of normal crimes refers to the group norms about the typical manner in which crimes are committed and the typical characteristics of defendants who commit those crimes. The seriousness of the offense and the prior record of the defendant are the most important factors in determining normal penalties.

2. Distinguish between the concepts of discrimination and disparity.

The concepts of discrimination and disparity highlight unwarranted variations in sentencing but point to different types of factors. Discrimination refers to illegitimate influences on the sentencing process related to the characteristics of the defendant being sentenced. By contrast, disparities refers to inconsistencies resulting from the decision-making process.

3. Describe the three competing explanations of why women are sentenced more leniently than men and indicate which one has the most support in the literature.

The three most common explanations for why women are sentenced more leniently than men are: (1) chivalry or paternalistic treatment, (2) evil women, and (3) equal treatment. The equal treatment explanation is now generally accepted in the literature because it examines the severity of the crime committed.

4. Explain how scholars approach the issue of racial discrimination differently than the general public and the implications these differing approaches have for the conclusions reached.

Evidence of racial imbalance in prison populations is not evidence of racial discrimination in the sentencing process. When studies analyze sentences in terms of the severity of the crime and the defendant's prior record, they generally conclude that sentencing is not characterized by a widespread pattern of discrimination.

5. Indicate why the offender–victim dyad is important in studies of racial discrimination in capital punishment.

The offender–victim dyad refers to the race of the defendant and the race of the victim. Studies have consistently found that the race of the defendant plays little if any role in the decision to apply the death penalty but that murders committed against whites are most likely to result in a sentence of death.

6. List the two major factors related to disparities and sentencing.

The two major factors involved in sentencing disparities are the geography of justice and judges' backgrounds and attitudes.

7. Recognize the main objective of changes in sentencing structure beginning in the late 1960s and the major consequences of these changes.

The main objective of changes in sentencing structure beginning in the late 1960s was a reduction in judicial discretion in sentencing. The major consequence of these changes has been a major increase in the number of persons in prison in the United States.

8. Outline how the U.S. Supreme Court has limited state sentencing guidelines.

Beginning in 2000 the U.S. Supreme Court has raised serious constitutional doubts about the constitutionality of state sentencing guidelines. In particular the Court has held that juries and not judges have the authority to determine important facts (other than prior record) that determine sentencing.

9. **Identify the most recent changes in how the U.S. Supreme Court has responded to federal sentencing guidelines.**

In *U.S. v. Booker* (2005), the nation's highest court held that the federal sentencing guidelines are unconstitutional but judges may use them as advisory. In later cases, the Court held that judges may indeed sentence defendants more leniently than the guidelines prescribe, particularly in crack-cocaine cases.

10. **Explain the law in action perspective on researching the impact of mandatory minimum sentences.**

A law on the books approach to mandatory minimum sentences stresses certainty of punishment, whereas a law in action approach stresses nullification by discretion. Researchers find that at a number of stages in the process, including police arrest, prosecutorial charging, trial convictions, and judicial sentencing, discretionary changes occur in the process that nullify the impact of these laws.

CRITICAL THINKING QUESTIONS

1. Within the courtroom work group, which actor is the most influential in sentencing decisions? Why? How might influence vary from one courtroom to the next?

2. In what ways do the crime control model and the due process model differ over the issues of disparity and discrimination in sentencing?

3. In what ways do sentencing guidelines reflect normal penalties? In what ways do they differ?

4. To what extent can slight variations in the defendant's background produce markedly different sentences? In Exhibit 16.4, calculate the recommended sentence for a defendant convicted of second-degree assault. How much does the sentence change if the criminal history score is a 2 or a 3? Do you think this is too much variation to be determined by a mathematical calculation?

5. How have public demands to "get tough with crooks" changed the sentencing process in the past two decades? Why do courtroom work groups resist such efforts and often subvert them?

KEY TERMS

discrimination 415
disparity 422
mandatory minimum
  sentencing 432

normal penalties 412
pre-sentence investigation
  (PSI) 409
sentencing guidelines 428

WEB RESOURCES

Go to the America's Courts and the Criminal Justice System companion website at

www.cengage.com/criminaljustice/neubauer

where you will find more resources to help you study.
Resources include web exercises, quizzing, and flash cards.

FOR FURTHER READING

Alozie, Nicholas, and C. Wayne Johnson. "Probing the Limits of the Female Advantage in Criminal Processing: Pretrial Diversion of Drug Offenders in an Urban County." *Justice System Journal* 21: 239–259, 2000.

Austin, James, and John Irwin. *It's About Time: America's Imprisonment Binge*. 3rd ed. Belmont, CA: Wadsworth, 2001.

Bosworth, Mary, and Jeanne Flavin (eds.). *Race, Gender, and Punishment: From Colonialism to the War on Terror*. Piscataway, NJ: Rutgers University Press, 2007.

Cole, David. *No Equal Justice*. New York: New Press, 1999.

Engen, Rodney, Randy Gainey, R. Crutchfield, and J. Weiss. "Discretion and Disparity under Guidelines: The Role of Departures and Structured Sentencing Alternatives." *Criminology* 41: 99–130, 2003.

Ewald, Alec, and Marnie Smith. "Collateral Consequences of Criminal Convictions in American Courts: The View from the State Bench." *Justice System Journal* 29: 145–164, 2008.

Finn, Peter, and Sarah Kuck. *Stress Among Probation and Parole Officers and What Can Be Done About It*. Washington, DC: National Institute of Justice, 2005.

Foglia, Wanda. "They Know Not What They Do: Unguided and Misguided Discretion in Pennsylvania Capital Cases." *Justice Quarterly* 20: 103–107, 2003.

Gabbidon, Shaun, and Helen Green. *Race and Crime*. Thousand Oaks, CA: Sage, 2009.

Grana, Sheryl. *Women and (In)Justice*. Boston: Allyn and Bacon, 2002.

Hartley, Richard, Sean Maddan, and Cassia Spohn. "Prosecutorial Discretion: An Examination of Substantial Assistance Departure in Federal Crack-Cocaine and Powder-Cocaine Cases." *Justice Quarterly* 24: 381–406, 2007.

Johnson, Robert. *Hard Time: Understanding and Reforming Prison*. 3rd ed. Belmont, CA: Wadsworth, 2002.

Keen, Bradley, and David Jacobs. "Racial Threat, Partisan Politics, and Racial Disparities in Prison Admissions Panel Analysis." *Criminology* 47: 209–238, 2009.

Kramer, John, and Jeffrey Ulmer. *Sentencing Guidelines: Lessons from Pennsylvania*. Boulder, CO: Lynne Rienner, 2009.

Lynch, Michael, E. Brit Patterson, and Kristina Childs (eds.). *Racial Divide: Racial and Ethnic Bias in the Criminal Justice System*. Monsey, NY: Criminal Justice Press, 2008.

Mann, Coramae Richey, and Marjorie Zatz. *Images of Color, Images of Crime*. Los Angeles: Roxbury, 1998.

Marquart, James, Sheldon Edland-Olson, and Jonathan Sorensen. *The Rope, the Chair, and the Needle: Capital Punishment in Texas, 1923–1990*. Austin: University of Texas Press, 1994.

Myers, Martha. *Race, Labor and Punishment in the New South*. Columbus: Ohio State University Press, 1998.

Pager, Devah. *Marked: Race, Crime, and Finding Work in an Era of Mass Incarceration*. Chicago: University of Chicago Press, 2007.

Pollock, Jocelyn. *Women, Prison, and Crime*. 2nd ed. Belmont, CA: Wadsworth, 2002.

Sharp, Susan, Meghan McGhee, Trina Hope and Randall Coyne. "Predictors of Support of Legislation Banning Juvenile Executions in Oklahoma: An Examination by Race and Sex." *Justice Quarterly* 24: 133–155, 2007.

Tarver, Marsha, Steve Walker, and Harvey Wallace. *Multicultural Issues in the Criminal Justice System*. Boston: Allyn and Bacon, 2002.

Tonry, Michael. "Crime and Human Rights—How Political Paranoia, Protestant Fundamentalism, and Constitutional Obsolescence Combined to Devastate Black America." *Criminology* 46: 1–34, 2008.

Vandiver, Margaret. *Lethal Punishment: Lynchings and Legal Executions in the South*. New Brunswick, NJ: Rutgers University Press, 2006.

APPELLATE
COURTS

With the addition of the Supreme Court's newest member, the high court sits for a class photo in 2009. Front row (from left to right): Anthony Kennedy, John Paul Stevens, John Roberts, Antonin Scalia, and Clarence Thomas. Back row: Samuel Alito, Jr., Ruth Bader Ginsburg, Stephen Breyer, and Sonia Sotomayor.

Chapter Outline

LEARNING OBJECTIVES

After reading this chapter, you should be able to:

1. Explain how appeals and appellate processes differ from trials and trial processes.

2. **Describe the two primary functions of appeals.**

3. Explain how Double Jeopardy limits appeals by the prosecution in criminal cases.

4. **Define the contemporaneous objection rule and explain its impact on appeals.**

5. Differentiate between mandatory and discretionary appellate jurisdiction.

6. **Identify the different appellate standards of review and evaluate their impact on the criminal appeals.**

7. Describe the six customary phases in the appeals process.

8. **Compare and contrast plain error, reversible error, and harmless error.**

9. Analyze the reasons why most criminal appeals result in convictions being affirmed.

10. **Compare and contrast appeals and postconviction review processes.**

11. Identify the leading causes of wrongful convictions.

12. **Analyze how state courts of last resort and the U.S. Supreme Court exercise their discretion to set justice policy.**

For 20 years, Paul House sat on death row proclaiming his innocence. A Tennessee jury had found him guilty for murder and sentenced him to death on the basis of forensic evidence—primarily bloodstains and semen. His case had already been reviewed by numerous courts, but along the way, he and his lawyers had failed to raise key points in their earlier court papers. But then new evidence, some of it based on DNA testing, cast doubt on the jury's verdict.

Should House be entitled to yet another hearing in federal court? Proponents of the crime control model argue that *House* is a textbook example of endless appeals, and therefore he should not be allowed yet one more review. Supporters of the due process model, on the other hand, counter that basic fairness is far more important than failure to comply with a narrow technical requirement.

House v. Bell highlights the importance of appellate court decisions. To be sure, appellate courts decide far fewer cases than the trial courts. Nonetheless, the relatively small numbers of cases decided by the appellate courts are critically important for the entire judicial process. Appellate courts subject the trial court's action to a second look, examining not a raw dispute in the course of being presented, but rather a controversy already decided.

This second look provides a degree of detachment, by a group of judges who can examine the process to see if mistakes were made. Appellate courts are important for a second reason: Through written opinions, appellate judges engage in significant policymaking.

Ultimately, the decisions of a group of judges not only determine the results of specific cases (the fate of individual defendants like Paul House) but also, and more important, they shape the law by providing the reasons for the decisions reached. *House v. Bell* also symbolizes how a relative handful of death penalty decisions receives a disproportionate share of appellate court time and attention.

NATURE OF THE APPELLATE PROCESS

One of the few aspects of the American judicial process about which consensus exists is that every loser in a trial court should have the right to appeal to a higher court. Yet, the appeals process is widely misunderstood. An appeal is not a retrial of the case, nor is it ordinarily a reexamination of factual issues decided by a trial court. Appellate courts hear no new testimony and consider no new evidence. Rather, they focus on how decisions were made in the trial court, basing their review on the appellate court record. Thus, an appellate court's function is primarily to review the questions of law presented in a case. Appellate courts were created in part because of the belief that several heads are better than one when examining such legal questions. In essence, the decisions of a single judge on matters of the law are subjected to review by a panel of judges who are removed from the heat engendered by the trial and are consequently in a position to take a more objective view of the legal questions raised. They operate as multimember or collegial bodies,

with decisions made by a group of judges. In the courts of last resort, all judges typically participate in all cases. On intermediate appellate courts, decisions are typically made using rotating three-judge panels, but in important cases, all judges may participate (this is termed an **en banc** hearing).

In unraveling the complexities of the review process, it is helpful to begin by asking why appellate courts exist and why dissatisfied litigants are permitted to appeal.

THE PURPOSES OF APPEAL

The most obvious function of appellate courts is **error correction**. During trial, a significant portion of the decision making is "spur of the moment." As one trial judge phrased it, "We're where the action is. We often have to 'shoot from the hip' and hope you're doing the right thing. You can't ruminate forever every time you have to make a ruling. We'd be spending months on each case if we ever did that" (quoted in Carp and Stidham 1990, p. 256). Fortunately, judges' quickly made decisions are often surprisingly accurate, although sometimes, mistakes do occur (Guthrie, Rachlinski, and Wistrich 2007).

As reviewing bodies, appellate courts oversee the work of the lower courts, ensuring that the law was correctly interpreted. Thus, the error-correction function of appellate review protects against arbitrary, capricious, or mistaken legal decisions by a trial court judge.

The other primary function of appellate courts is **policy formulation**. The lawmaking function focuses on situations in which appellate courts fill in the gaps in existing law, clarify old doctrines, extend existing precedent to new situations, and on occasion even overrule previous decisions. Thus, through policy formulation, appellate courts shape the law in response to changing conditions in society. Stated another way, error correction is concerned primarily with the effect of the judicial process on individual litigants, whereas policy formulation involves the impact of the appellate court decision on other cases (see Cooper and Berman 2000).

LIMITATIONS ON THE RIGHT TO APPELLATE REVIEW

A basic principle of American law is that the losing party has the **right to one appeal**. So long as the person seeking to appeal the decision of a lower court follows the rules for perfecting an appeal (such as filing a timely notice of appeal and meeting all appellate court deadlines), that initial appeal is guaranteed as a right. However, once a criminal defendant has been convicted at trial, the legal shield of innocence is gone. The individual is no longer considered innocent until proven guilty but rather now stands, in the eyes of the law, guilty. This has important implications for bail. Guilty defendants no longer have a right to bail; courts may set a bail amount (typically in higher amounts than prior to trial), but many defendants wait out their appeal in prison.

Although American law recognizes the right to one appeal, the right to appellate review is subject to several important limits and exceptions. Appeals, for example, may be filed only by parties who have lost in the lower court. In *Kepner v. United States* (1904), the U.S. Supreme Court held that the prosecution is not permitted to appeal an acquittal. This is because the Fifth Amendment guarantees, "Nor shall any person be subject for the same offense to be twice put in jeopardy of life or limb." This provision protects citizens from **double jeopardy** (a second prosecution of the same person for the same crime by the same sovereign after the first trial). Thus, once a "not guilty" verdict is returned, jeopardy is said to attach, and the prosecutor cannot appeal the acquittal, even if the original trial was littered with serious mistakes (*Sanabria v. United States* 1978). Prosecutors may, however, appeal questions of law that would not result in a defendant being put in jeopardy again. For example, if a judge made a serious error in an evidentiary ruling, the prosecution could appeal so that there would be appellate precedent on the books; therefore, that trial court judges would know not to make a similar mistake again in the future. Alternatively, if a defendant was never really in jeopardy because a trial was conducted fraudulently (for example, if the defendant bribed the judge or a juror), then double jeopardy will not prohibit a prosecutor from appeals for a new trial (*Aleman v. Judges of the Criminal Division, Circuit Court of Cook County, IL* 1998).

Appeals are also discretionary; that is, the losing party is not required to seek appellate court review. The lone exception involves capital punishment cases. When a jury imposes a sentence of death, the case must be appealed regardless of the defendant's wishes. Typically, this automatic review is heard directly by the state supreme court, thus bypassing any intermediate courts of appeals. The mandatory appeal requirements in capital punishment cases aside, in all other cases, civil and criminal, appeals are discretionary.

When cases may be appealed is limited. As a general rule, the losing party may appeal only from a final judgment of the lower court. In this context, a judgment is considered final when a final decision has been reached in the lower court. In very limited situations, however, litigants may appeal certain types of **interlocutory** (nonfinal) orders. Prosecutors may file an interlocutory appeal on certain pretrial rulings that substantially hinder the state's ability to proceed to trial. For example, if the trial court suppresses a defendant's confession or excludes physical evidence because of an illegal search and seizure, the prosecution may file an interlocutory appeal arguing that the judge's ruling was in error.

Appeals are also confined to issues properly raised in the trial court. Recall from Chapter 14 that during trial attorneys must make timely objections to the judge's rulings on points of law, or the objection will be deemed waived. This is called the **contemporaneous objection rule.** Thus, an attorney making an objection and the trial judge overruling it constitutes a disagreement over a point of law, properly preserving the issue for appeal.

Appeals in criminal cases have also historically been limited in the United States to legal rulings that led to a conviction. That is, a defendant was not able to appeal the sentence imposed as being too harsh, nor could the prosecutor appeal a sentence as being too lenient. This restriction, however, has changed slowly over time. Several states now allow defendants to appeal the sentence imposed by the trial judge. Defendants are also permitted to appeal illegally imposed sentences, such as sentences that fall outside a statutorily authorized sentencing range. And, under the U.S. Supreme Court's rulings in *Apprendi v. New Jersey* (2000) and *Black v. California* (2007), defendants may appeal sentences if penalty enhancements (other than those based on prior convictions) were applied by a judge without the facts underlying such aggravating factors having been proved to a jury beyond a reasonable doubt.

Finally, the right to appeal is limited to a single appeal, within which all appealable issues have to be raised. Appeals from U.S. district courts and most appeals from state courts of general jurisdiction are heard by intermediate courts of appeals. In the less-populous states, which do not have intermediate appellate bodies, the initial appeal is filed with the court of last resort (see Chapter 4). These courts have **mandatory appellate jurisdiction,** which means they must hear all properly filed appeals. But after the first reviewing body has reached a decision, the right to one appeal has been exhausted. The party that loses the appeal may request that a higher court review the case again, but such appeals are discretionary; the higher court does not have to hear the appeal. The U.S. Supreme Court and most state supreme courts have largely **discretionary appellate jurisdiction,** which means that they can pick and choose which cases they will hear. The overwhelming number of appeals is decided by intermediate courts of appeals; only a small fraction of appeals is heard by state courts of last resort and even fewer will be decided by the U.S. Supreme Court. Exhibit 17.1 shows the appellate court structure of the states.

APPELLATE STANDARDS OF REVIEW

Appeals courts approach appellate decision making in different ways, depending on the types of questions presented for review on appeal. Sometimes appellate courts are very deferential to what happened in lower courts, while other times they give no deference at all. How much deference (or conversely, scrutiny) an appellate court will afford to the decisions of a judge, jury, or administrative agency in an appeal is referred to as the **standard of review**. The most frequently used standards of review in criminal cases are presented in Exhibit 17.2.

Given these standards of review, criminal appeals rarely involve questions of fact decided by a judge or jury. Because they have not been directly exposed to the evidence, appellate courts are reluctant to second-guess findings of fact made in lower courts.

> Factual findings, whether by the trial court judge or the jury, are rarely a basis for reversal. . . . Absent certain types of error, it is improper for the reviewing court to substitute its judgment for that of the jury; having guilt or innocence decided by the community is a central tenet of the American legal system. The rationale for the principle that it is the exclusive province of the fact-finder to determine credibility is that the fact-finder had the opportunity to see the witness(es) testify at trial, and is therefore in a much better position to determine credibility issues. Equally cogent is the idea of judicial economy—that the already overburdened judicial system simply cannot afford to retry every case on appeal. (TerBeek 2007, p. 36)

In contrast to the highly referential appellate review of factual issues, questions of law are reviewed without deference on appeal. Questions of law (or mixed questions of fact and law) that are commonly raised on appeal include defects in jury selection, improper admission of evidence during the trial, and mistaken interpretations of the law. The appellant may also claim constitutional violations, including illegal search and seizure or improper questioning of the defendant by the police (see Chapter 12). Finally, some defendants who have pled guilty may seek to set aside the guilty plea because of ineffective assistance of counsel or because the plea was not voluntary.

Exhibit 17.1

STATE APPELLATE COURT STRUCTURE

COURT OF LAST RESORT ONLY	COURT OF LAST RESORT AND ONE INTERMEDIATE APPELLATE COURT		ONE COURT OF LAST RESORT AND TWO INTERMEDIATE APPELLATE COURTS	TWO COURTS OF LAST RESORT AND ONE INTERMEDIATE APPELLATE COURT
Delaware	Alaska	Massachusetts	Alabama	Oklahoma[a]
District of Columbia	Arizona	Michigan	New York	Texas
Maine	Arkansas	Minnesota	Pennsylvania	
Montana	California	Mississippi	Tennessee	
Nevada	Colorado	Missouri		
New Hampshire	Connecticut	Nebraska		
Rhode Island	Florida	New Jersey		
South Dakota	Georgia	New Mexico		
Vermont	Hawaii[a]	North Carolina		
West Virginia	Idaho[a]	North Dakota[a]		
Wyoming	Illinois	Ohio		
	Indiana	Oregon		
	Iowa[a]	South Carolina[a]		
	Kansas	Utah		
	Kentucky	Virginia		
	Louisiana	Washington		
	Maryland	Wisconsin		

[a] Court of last resort assigns cases to intermediate appellate court.

SOURCE: David Rottman, Carol Flango, Melissa Cantrell, Randall Hansen, and Neil La Fountain, *State Court Organization 1998*. Williamsburg, VA: National Center for State Courts, 2000.

Exhibit 17.2

STANDARD OF APPELLATE REVIEW IN CRIMINAL CASES (FROM LEAST DEFERENTIAL TO MOST DEFERENTIAL)

TYPE OF QUESTION PRESENTED	STANDARD OF REVIEW	LEVEL OF DEFERENCE	TEST	EXAMPLE
Questions of law	De novo (anew)	None	Plenary review of a legal issue for a second time with no deference to prior decision	Whether a judge erred in interpreting a statute Whether hearsay evidence was properly admitted or excluded
Mixed questions of law and fact	Mixture of de novo and clear error	Moderate	Underlying factual findings are given substantial deference (reviewed for clear error), but the legal consequences of those facts are reviewed de novo	Whether a suspect was subjected to "custodial interrogation" Whether a defendant knowingly, intelligently, and voluntarily waived a constitutional right
Questions of fact decided by a judge	Clear error	High	Trial court's factual findings are to be upheld unless they are so clearly erroneous that they have no support in the record	Whether a criminal defendant is competent to stand trial Whether a criminal defendant is guilty beyond a reasonable doubt (in a bench trial)
Questions of fact decided by a jury	Reasonableness/ substantial evidence	High	Jury's decision is upheld if it is reasonable in light of the evidence in the record; support for the jury's conclusion is adequate	Whether a criminal defendant is guilty beyond a reasonable doubt Whether a defendant has proven his/her insanity by clear and convincing evidence

Exhibit 17.2
CONTINUED

TYPE OF QUESTION PRESENTED	STANDARD OF REVIEW	LEVEL OF DEFERENCE	TEST	EXAMPLE
Discretionary decisions by a judge	Abuse of discretion	Very high	Trial court's decision will be upheld unless arbitrary, capricious, or manifestly unfair in light of any reasonable justification under the circumstances	Whether a judge abused his/her discretion when denying a continuance, limiting the scope of cross-examination, or refusing to dismiss a juror for cause

APPELLATE COURT PROCEDURES

Appellate court procedures reflect numerous variations among the nation's 51 legal systems. Nonetheless, each judicial system uses essentially the same six steps to start an appeal from a trial court judgment. Exhibit 17.3 summarizes the appeals process.

NOTICE OF APPEAL

An appeal does not follow automatically from an adverse trial court judgment. Rather, the **appellant** (the losing party in the lower court) must take affirmative action to set an appeal in motion. The first step consists of filing a **notice of appeal** with the trial court. As illustrated by Exhibit 17.4, a notice of appeal is short and simple. However, to trigger one's right to an appeal, the appellant must file a notice of appeal in a timely manner. The rules of appellate procedure in a particular jurisdiction fix the precise period—usually 10, 30, or 60 days.

Keep in mind that the filing of a notice of appeal initiates the appellate process for the first appeal—the appeal that is guaranteed as a right. In contrast, the party that loses a first appeal generally does not have a right to any subsequent appeals. Rather, the loser of a first appeal must usually seek permission to initiate any subsequent discretionary appeals. To do so, they do not file another notice of appeal. Rather, as described in Chapter 3, they file a petition for a **writ of certiorari**. From that point forward, the party seeking another appeal is usually known as the **petitioner** since they are filing a petition seeking another round of appellate review.

APPELLATE COURT RECORD

After the notice of appeal has been filed, the next step is preparing and transmitting the record. The **appellate court record** consists of the materials that advance to the appellate court. Many of these items—papers and exhibits—are already in the case file. A major item not in the clerk's office is the transcript of the testimony given at the trial. To include this in the record, the court reporter prepares a typewritten copy and files it with the court.

APPELLATE BRIEFS

The third step in the appeal process consists of writing briefs. An **appellate brief** is a written argument

Exhibit 17.3

STEPS OF CRIMINAL PROCEDURE: APPEAL AND POSTCONVICTION REMEDIES

	LAW ON THE BOOKS	**LAW IN ACTION**
Appeal	Legal challenge to a decision by a lower court	Virtually certain if the defendant is convicted at trial
Mandatory	Appellate court must hear the case.	Many appeals are "routine," which means they have little likelihood of succeeding.
Discretionary	Appellate court may accept or reject.	Appellate courts hear a very small percentage of discretionary appeal cases.
Notice of appeal	Written statement notifying the court that the defendant plans to appeal	Standards for indigent defenders mandate that an appeal must be filed.
Appellate court record	The transcript of the trial along with relevant court documents	Some appellate courts prefer a focused record of contested matters, whereas others want the entire record.
Appellate brief	Written statement submitted by the attorney arguing a case in court	Defense lawyers make numerous arguments in hopes that one will be successful.
Oral argument	Lawyers for both sides argue their cases before appellate court justices, who have the opportunity to question lawyers.	Judges often complain that they learn little during oral argument. To expedite decision making, some courts limit oral argument to select cases.
Written opinion	Reasons given by appellate courts for the results they have reached	Only appellate court opinions are considered precedent.
Disposition		
Affirmed	Appellate court decision that agrees with the lower court decision	Seven out of eight criminal appeals are affirmed.
Remanded	Case is sent back to the lower court for a hearing on a specific issue.	Often an indication that the appellate court is troubled by the judge's action but doe not wish to reverse.
Reversed	The lower court decision is set aside, and further proceedings may be held.	Defendants are very often remanded and reconvicted following retrial.

Exhibit 17.4
SAMPLE NOTICE OF APPEAL

Notice of Appeal to a Court of Appeals from a Judgment or Order of a District Court
United States District Court for the Southern District of New York

File Number _____

United States of America, Plaintiff |

v. | Notice of Appeal

[Name], Defendant |

_____ |

Notice is hereby given that [insert name], the Defendant in the above named case, hereby appeals to the United States Court of Appeals for the Second Circuit from the final judgment entered in this action on the _____ day of _____, 20__.

_____

Attorney for Defendant

Address:_____

---

that sets forth the party's view of the facts of the case, the issues raised on appeal, and the precedents supporting their position. First, the appellant's opening brief is filed, which lists alleged errors on questions of law that were made at trial. Next, the winning party in the lower court (termed the **appellee** during the initial appeal and the **respondent** in any subsequent, discretionary appeals, since they are responding to a petition for discretionary review) files a response brief setting forth arguments as to why the original decision of the lower court was legally correct and should stand. The appellant then has the option of filing a reply brief. Briefs are arguably the most important part of the appellate process because roughly three-quarters of all appeals are decided by appeals courts based on the briefs without the benefit of oral argument.

ORAL ARGUMENT

Oral argument provides an opportunity for face-to-face contact between the appellate judges and lawyers. The lawyers for both parties are allotted a limited time to argue their side of the case before the appellate court panel. The appellant's oral argument, for example, briefly discusses the facts on which the cause of action is based, traces the history of the case through the lower courts, and presents legal arguments as to why the decision of the trial court was erroneous. In this phase, judges typically ask lawyers questions about particular issues in the case.

Many judges view oral arguments as not particularly helpful in deciding routine cases (Hellman 2006; Wasby 1982). Thus, some courts have eliminated oral argument altogether in straightforward cases. By ruling solely on the basis of the appellate court record and the briefs, judges can decide cases more quickly. In some states, however, the litigants are entitled to oral arguments before an appeals court either if requested in a timely manner by one of the parties or by rule in certain types of cases (Binford et al. 2007).

WRITTEN OPINION

After the case has been argued, the court recesses to engage in group deliberations. Decisions are made in private conference, with one judge in the majority assigned the task of writing the opinion, which summarizes the facts of the case and discusses the legal issues raised on appeal. If the case is an easy one, the **opinion** of the court may be short, perhaps no more than a page or two. But if the legal issues are important or complex, the court's opinion may run dozens of pages. The decisions of appellate courts are compiled and published in books of reported court decisions, which can be found in law libraries. Attorneys and judges use these reported decisions as authorities for arguing and deciding future cases that raise issues similar to those already decided.

Judges who disagree with the majority often write **dissenting opinions**, explaining why they believe their fellow judges reached the wrong conclusions. In some cases, judges who agree with the case outcome on appeal might elect to write a **concurring opinion**. Judges who write concurring opinions may do so to emphasize particular points, or they may express disagreement with a portion of the rationale expressed in the majority decision. In courts of last resort where multiple appellate judges review a case, sometimes so many judges write concurring opinions that a true majority cannot be reached. For example, assume that six justices on the U.S. Supreme Court believe that a defendant petitioning to have his conviction reversed should win. Of those six votes, three justices sign a concurring opinion expressing their reasoning, and three others sign a separate concurring opinion expressing different reasons why they think the conviction should be overturned (leaving three justices in the dissent). In such cases with no majority decision, the decision is called a **plurality opinion**.

Opinion preparation consumes more of appellate judges' time than any other activity, and for this reason the opinion-writing process is a prime candidate for increasing the efficiency of appellate courts. Some appellate courts are therefore deciding some cases by summary affirmation, in which the court affirms the decision of the lower court without providing a written opinion and often without granting oral argument (Binsford et al. 2007; Neubauer 1985).

Many courts are reluctant to take the drastic step of not writing opinions, even in selected cases. Therefore, a more common practice is curtailing opinion publication; the litigants are given written reasons for the decision reached, but the opinion is not published. Unpublished opinions are used in error-correction cases when the court is applying existing law (Songer 1990). They save considerable judicial time because unpublished opinions need not be as polished as published opinions. Because unpublished opinions have limited precedential authority since they merely apply existing law, a number of courts prohibited citation to unpublished cases as precedent for many years. But, in 2006, the Judicial Conference of the United States banned this practice in the federal courts when it enacted a new rule that allows all cases to be cited for persuasive precedential authority. While roughly half of the states do not allow citation to unpublished cases, the modern trend is clearly away from such bans and toward the new federal rule that allows citation to all available precedent regardless of whether or not the opinion was formally published (Payne 2008).

DISPOSITION

The court's opinion ends with a disposition of the case. The appellate court may **affirm** (uphold) the judgment of the lower court. Or the court may **modify** the lower court ruling by changing it in part but not totally reversing it. Alternatively, the previous decision may be **reversed** (set aside) with no further court action required. A disposition of **reversed and remanded** means that the decision of the lower court is overturned and the case is sent back to the lower court for further proceedings, which may include holding a hearing or conducting a new trial. Often the defendant is tried a second time, but not always. Finally, the case may be **remanded** to the lower court with instructions for further proceedings. What the ultimate disposition of a case will be on appeal will turn on whether a majority (or plurality) of the appellate judges hearing the case find a reversible error under the applicable standard of review.

REVERSIBLE VS. HARMLESS ERROR

Appellate courts modify, reverse, remand, or reverse and remand only if they find **error**—that is, a mistake made during the trial. If the **error** is substantial, it is called **reversible error** by the higher court. If the error is minor, it is called **harmless error**. This distinction means that an appellate court may find error, but may nonetheless affirm the lower court decision anyway if the mistake was not significant enough to have had a prejudicial effect on the ultimate outcome of the case.

Recall that the contemporaneous objection rule bars an appellate court from considering any claim on appeal to which a timely objection was not made. However, one exception to this rule is for mistakes that constitute **plain error**. Plain errors are defects seriously affecting substantial rights that are so prejudicial to a jury's deliberations "as to undermine the fundamental fairness of the trial and bring about a miscarriage of justice" (*United States v. Polowichak* 1986, p. 416).

On the other hand, even when an appellant preserves a claim by timely objection and the appellate court finds that the trial court erred, the appellate court may still affirm the conviction if it finds that the error was harmless. This **harmless error rule** avoids the "setting aside of convictions for small errors or defects that have little, if any, likelihood of having changed the result of the trial" (*Chapman v. California* 1967). If the error was of constitutional dimensions, the appellate court must determine "beyond a reasonable doubt that the error complained of did not contribute to the verdict obtained" (p. 23). If the error was not of constitutional dimensions, the appellate court must determine with "fair assurance after pondering all that happened without stripping the erroneous action from the whole that the judgment was not substantially swayed by the error" (*Kotteakos v. United States* 1946, p. 765).

Most types of error are subject to harmless error analysis, including classic trial errors involving the erroneous admission of evidence (*Arizona v. Fulminante* 1991). Some types of error, however, involve rights so basic to a fair trial that they can never be considered harmless, such as conflicts of interest in representation (*Holloway v. Arkansas* 1978); denial of the right to an impartial judge (*Chapman v. California* 1967); racial, ethnic, or sex discrimination in grand jury or petit jury selection (*Vasquez v. Hillery* 1986; *Batson v. Kentucky* 1986; *J.E.B. v. Alabama ex rel. T.B.* 1994); and a failure to inquire whether a defendant's guilty plea is voluntary (*United States v. Gonzalez* 1987).

RISING CASELOADS AND EXPEDITED APPEALS

In recent years, traditional appellate court procedures have been modified because of exponential increases in appellate court filings. Appellate court caseloads have been increasing more rapidly than those of the trial courts. By way of illustration, appeals filed in the U.S. courts of appeals increased by a whopping 705 percent from 1961 through 1983, and then increased another 131% from 1983 through 2005, a year in which a record high of more than 68,400 cases were filed in federal appellate courts. While that caseload dropped slightly in 2006 and 2007, the federal appellate courts still heard nearly 60,000 cases in those years (Administrative Office of the U.S. Courts 2008).

Appeals in state courts have likewise grown rapidly. Today, the National Center for State Courts (2008) reports that state appellate courts hear about 290,000 appeals every year. To accommodate the steadily rising volume of appeals, reviewing bodies now often use expedited processing for some cases, such as shortening the period for submitting briefs, waiving the submission of formal briefs, denying extensions of time, and eliminating oral argument. (Binford et al. 2007).

CRIMINAL APPEALS

The bulk of trial court filings are never appealed because the case is settled without a trial—civil cases are negotiated and criminal cases are plea-bargained. As a result, only a small percentage of state trial court cases are reviewed by higher courts. The majority of appeals involve civil cases, but the number of criminal appeals has increased dramatically since the 1960s.

LAW ON THE BOOKS: EXPANDED OPPORTUNITY TO APPEAL CRIMINAL CONVICTIONS

For decades, most defendants found guilty by judge or jury did not appeal because they could not afford the expense. This pattern changed significantly in the early 1960s. A series of important Warren Court decisions held that economically impoverished defendants cannot be barred from effective appellate review. Indigent defendants, therefore, are entitled to a free trial court transcript (*Griffin v. Illinois* 1956) and a court-appointed lawyer (*Douglas v. California* 1963). Indigents, however, are not normally provided free legal service to pursue discretionary appeals (*Ross v. Moffitt* 1974).

As a result of these rulings, it is now rare for a convicted defendant not to appeal from a trial verdict of guilty. Indeed, indigent defendants have everything to gain and nothing to lose by filing an appeal. For example, if the appeal is successful but the defendant is reconvicted following a new trial, the sentencing judge cannot increase the sentence out of vindictiveness (*North Carolina v. Pearce* 1969; *Texas v. McCullough* 1986). See Exhibit 17.5 for a summary of key developments concerning appeals.

The Warren Court decisions expanding the opportunity for indigent defendants to appeal produced an exponential increase in the number of criminal appeals filed. Whereas criminal appeals composed only 10 to 15 percent of total appeals before 1963, they constitute approximately 40 percent of total appellate volume today (National Center for State Courts 2008).

LAW IN ACTION: DEFENDANTS RARELY WIN ON APPEAL

For many years, criminal appeals were drawn from a fairly narrow stratum of the most serious criminal convictions in the trial courts (Davies 1982). For example, more than half the criminal appeals contested convictions for crimes of violence (primarily homicides and armed robberies). Moreover, these appeals cases often involved substantial sentences (Chapper and Hanson 1990). In short, criminal appeals were fairly atypical of crimes prosecuted in the trial courts. However, over the past 20 years or so, penalties for all sorts of crimes have increased,

especially for drug offenses, as penal social control has been increasingly used to incapacitate criminal offenders (Tonry 2004). This has led to a broader range of criminal cases being appealed, as illustrated by Exhibit 17.6, which shows a recent distribution of the types of criminal cases appealed in the federal system.

Criminal appeals are generally routine because they seldom raise meritorious issues (Primus 2007; Wold and Caldeira 1980). Current standards of effective assistance of counsel often force lawyers to appeal, no matter how slight the odds of appellate court reversal. As a result, a significant number of criminal appeals lack substantial merit. According

Exhibit 17.5
KEY DEVELOPMENTS CONCERNING APPEAL

U.S. Constitution, Article I	1789	The Privilege of the Writ of Habeas Corpus shall not be suspended unless when in Cases of Rebellion or Invasion the public Safety may require it.
Fifth Amendment	1791	Prohibits double jeopardy
Griffin v. Illinois	1956	Indigents are entitled to a free trial court transcript.
Douglas v. California	1963	Indigents are entitled to a court-appointed attorney during first appeal.
Fay v. Noia	1963	Warren Court decision greatly expanded the right of state prisoners to file habeas corpus petitions in federal court.
North Carolina v. Pearce	1969	If the appeal is successful, the sentencing judge cannot increase the sentence if the defendant is later reconvicted.
Ross v. Moffitt	1974	Indigent defendants are not entitled to a court-appointed lawyer for discretionary appeals.
Stone v. Powell	1976	Burger Court decision held that federal courts cannot consider Fourth Amendment search-and-seizure questions in habeas corpus proceedings.
Coleman v. Thompson	1992	Death row inmate whose lawyers filed papers late has no further right to federal court review.
Antiterrorism and Effective Death Penalty Act	1996	State inmates are typically limited to only one review of their prisoner petition in federal courts.

Exhibit 17.5

CONTINUED

Felker v. Turpin	1996	Upheld the Antiterrorism and Effective Death Penalty Act.
Roe v. Flores-Ortega	2000	A lawyer's failure to file an appeal does not necessarily violate the right to counsel.
Williams v. Taylor	2000	Under the Antiterrorism and Effective Death Penalty Act, a federal judge can reject an inmate's claim only if the state court used an unreasonable interpretation of federal law.
Edwards v. Carpenter	2000	Limited state prisoner access to federal courts based on claims that their lawyers gave them inadequate help.
House v. Bell	2006	The Tennessee death row inmate is entitled to a federal habeas corpus hearing and can use DNA evidence to try to show his innocence.
District Attorney's Office for the Third Judicial District v. Osborne	2009	A criminal convict does not have any federal constitutional due process right to obtain post-conviction access to the state's evidence for DNA testing.

Exhibit 17.6

DISTRIBUTION OF TYPES OF CRIMINAL APPEALS IN THE FEDERAL APPELLATE COURTS, 2007

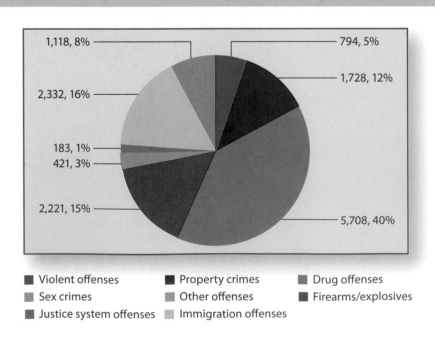

- ■ Violent offenses
- ■ Property crimes
- ■ Drug offenses
- ■ Sex crimes
- ■ Other offenses
- ■ Firearms/explosives
- ■ Justice system offenses
- ■ Immigration offenses

to one intermediate appellate court judge, "If 90 percent of this stuff were in the United States Post Office, it would be classified as junk mail" (Wold 1978). Although this quote is more than 30 years old, the sentiment expressed appears to be valid today (see Miner 1999; Stogel 2002). Consider, for example, that of the 3,642 criminal appeals filed in the California Supreme Court in 2007, relief was granted in only 8 percent. The success rate was even lower for defendants appealing to the state's intermediate appeals court, which granted relief in only 6 percent of the 4,792 appeals filed by criminal defendants that year.

Why do criminal appeals rarely succeed? The answer is twofold. First, as illustrated in Exhibit 17.2, the appellate standards of review applicable to most decision-making during criminal trials are highly deferential to trial court outcomes (Primus 2007). Thus, the rules of appeals are designed not to disturb the results of a criminal trial unless a serious, reversible error has occurred. Second, appellate courts often find that no reversible error was committed during the trial court proceedings. That is due, in large part, to the harmless error doctrine. Accordingly, the vast majority of criminal appeals affirm the conviction.

Roughly speaking, defendants win on appeal less than 10 percent of cases. A closer look, though, indicates that an appellate court reversal often produces only minor victories for many criminal defendants. For example, some "reversals" produce a modification but do not otherwise disturb the conviction or even order a new trial (Burke-Robertson 2008; Neubauer 1992). Moreover, if the appellate court reverses and remands the case to the lower court for a new trial, many defendants will be convicted a second time. In fact, the few studies that have examined retrials following successful appeals found that roughly half resulted in reconviction (Neubauer 1991, 1992; Roper and Melone 1981).

The types of cases in which reversals occur are also interesting. Neubauer (1991) found that defendants convicted of nonviolent offenses and who received a relatively lenient sentence were the most likely to win on appeal; conversely, defendants convicted of violent offenses and sentenced to lengthy prison terms were the least likely to win on appeal. He concluded that this pattern of winners and losers is far from random. Rather, the appellate court justices strained to find ways to affirm convictions for crimes such as murder and armed robbery when the defendant had a long criminal record. For an interesting exception to these usual patterns, read the

"Law and Popular Culture" box on *Reversal of Fortune: Inside the Von Bulow Case.*

POSTCONVICTION REVIEW

After the appellate process has been exhausted, state as well as federal prisoners may challenge their convictions in federal courts on certain limited grounds. These postconviction remedies are termed **collateral attacks**, because they are attempts to avoid the effects of a court decision by bringing a different court proceeding. Although they are filed by prisoners who have been convicted of a criminal offense, they are technically civil matters. Thus, they are usually filed against a prison warden or the chief administrator of a state's department of corrections. The Case Close-Up: *House v. Bell* and Federal Court Scrutiny of State Death Row Inmates illustrates this point. When Paul House appealed, the case title was *House v. State of Tennessee.* But after the right to appeal had been exhausted, he later filed a habeas petition in federal court, and the case was captioned *House v. Bell.* The warden, Ricky Bell, is considered a nominal respondent because no actions on his part are at issue. Bell is merely a stand-in; the defendant contends he is being illegally detained because of the actions of the trial judge.

HOW POSTCONVICTION REMEDIES DIFFER FROM APPEALS

Postconviction remedies differ from appeals in several ways that have important implications for the criminal justice system. First, they may be filed only by those actually in custody. Second, they may raise only constitutional defects, not technical ones. Third, they may be somewhat broader than appeals, which are usually limited to objections made by the defense during the trial absent plain error. Postconviction petitions can bring up issues not raised during trial, as well as assert constitutional protections that have developed since the original trial under certain circumstances. Finally, many state court systems allow unlimited postconviction remedies; thus, a prisoner could file numerous petitions in state court as well as seeking postconviction relief in the various levels of the federal court system.

House v. Bell illustrates these factors. House was eligible to file because he was in prison. Second, his postconviction relief petitions raised issues that had not been properly preserved at trial or on direct appeal. Finally, the petition had been filed in two state courts

LAW AND POPULAR CULTURE

REVERSAL OF FORTUNE: INSIDE THE VON BULOW CASE (1990)

While movies and television shows about the criminal justice system abound, very few mainstream media efforts depict the appellate process. The 1990 movie *Reversal of Fortune* is one of the few exceptions. The film, directed by Barbet Schroeder, is adapted from the nonfiction book by the same title written by Harvard University law professor Alan Dershowitz (Random House 1986). Both the book and the movie tell the story, from Dershowitz's perspective (played by Ron Silver), of how he won a reversal on appeal for his client, Claus Von Bulow, masterfully played by Jeremy Irons (in fact, he won an Oscar for his performance). Von Bulow had been convicted (twice) of the attempted murder of his socialite wife, Martha "Sunny" Von Bulow (played by Glenn Close). He was accused of having injected her with insulin, causing her to go into a persistent vegetative state from which she never awoke (she died in December of 2008). The movie focuses on the research Dershowitz and his team of law students conducted to convince the Rhode Island Supreme Court that the jury's decision was unreasonable and clearly erroneous in light of the evidence. The movie is exceptional not only because of the first-rate acting and story, but also because of its brilliant study of the law. Few films capture the complexities of how circumstantial evidence is used to build a criminal case the way this one does. Moreover, one would be hard pressed to find another film that focuses on the appeals process with such intensity. Finally, *Reversal of Fortune* stands out because it is a depiction of a real-life case, not a fictional one. Since so few real-life cases are overturned on appeal based on the facts (rather than the law), the story is both unique and compelling. After watching the movie, answer the following questions.

1. Do you think that Claus von Bulow was innocent or guilty? Explain your answer.
2. What were your perceptions of the criminal defense team led by Alan Dershowitz?
3. Do you think most criminal appeals are handled the same way that Von Bulow's was? Why or why not?
4. How did the court proceedings depicted in the movie differ from what you normally see in television and cinema?

and the U.S. District Court for the Eastern District of Tennessee, had been reviewed by the Sixth Circuit Court of Appeals, and was now being considered by yet another federal court—the U.S. Supreme Court.

The most common type of postconviction relief is **habeas corpus** (Latin for "you have the body"). Protected by the U.S. Constitution, it is a judicial order to someone holding a person to bring that person immediately before the court. Article I provides that "the Privilege of the Writ of Habeas Corpus shall not be suspended unless when in Cases of Rebellion or Invasion the public Safety may require it." This provision traces its roots to 17th-century England, when the king's officers often detained citizens without ever filing charges. The writ of habeas corpus has been described as the "great writ," because it prevents the government from jailing citizens without ever filing charges. Many totalitarian regimes have no such protections; even some Western democracies allow the police or prosecutors to detain a person suspected of a crime for up to a year without formally accusing the person of any wrongdoing. Note that a state prisoner who challenges the conditions of confinement or attempts to obtain damages for violations of constitutional rights should seek relief by means of a civil action under 42 U.S.C.A. § 198, not by filing a petition for a writ of habeas corpus.

Originally, habeas corpus was regarded as an extraordinary means to determine the legality of detention prior to trial. But the great writ of liberty has undergone considerable transformation in recent decades. See Courts, Controversy,

House v. Bell and Federal Court Scrutiny of State Death Row Inmates

Carolyn Muncey disappeared from her rural Tennessee home on Saturday night, July 13, 1984. The next day, two local residents found her body concealed amid brush and tree branches roughly 100 yards from her house. The police later arrested Paul House, a convicted sex offender, who lived in the area. During House's 1985 capital murder trial, several witnesses testified about Mrs. Muncey's disappearance and discovery, but no one could directly link House to the murder. Central to the state's case was what FBI testing showed (or seemed to show). Lab experts testified that the semen found on her nightgown and panties was consistent with House's blood type, and that small bloodstains on House's blue jeans were consistent with Carolyn Muncey's blood type. The jury convicted House and sentenced him to death.

On appeal, the Tennessee Supreme Court concluded the evidence was circumstantial but "quite strong." The U.S. Supreme Court refused to grant cert, thus ending House's appeals. His lawyers then filed successive writs of habeas corpus in both state and federal courts. At a key point in these protracted legal proceedings, House procedurally defaulted, that is, he failed to properly preserve issues for habeas corpus review. He now faced a very high legal hurdle—to proceed further, he had to prove actual innocence before a federal court would grant his habeas corpus petition seeking a new trial (*Schlup v. Delo* 1995).

Since House's 1985 conviction, DNA evidence has increasingly been introduced during trial (Chapter 14) and also used to overturn convictions on appeal and/or during postconviction relief (see the discussion in this chapter). No such testing had been done for the original trial because DNA testing did not exist then. But was it relevant in House's case? A majority of the Supreme Court said yes.

Justice Kennedy, the swing vote on the Roberts Court, wrote the opinion of the court stressing that DNA testing showed that the semen found on Mrs. Muncey did not come from the defendant. Similarly, the testimony based on bloodstains was suspect because of poor evidence control by the state crime lab—the samples were not properly preserved and were possibly contaminated during testing. The court's opinion also emphasized that not only did the new evidence tend to undermine the state's claim of guilt, but it also seemed to point to a different suspect—Carolyn Muncey's husband. The court concluded that "this is the rare case where—had the jury heard all the conflicting testimony—it is more likely than not that no reasonable jury viewing the record as a whole would lack reasonable doubt."

Chief Justice Roberts concurred in the judgment in part and dissented in part. He was joined by the other two conservatives, but Justice Alito did not participate because the case was argued before he was confirmed. The dissenters were unconvinced that the newly discovered DNA evidence was as important as the majority concluded, arguing "the case against House remains substantially unaltered from the case presented to the jury." As a result, Roberts wrote, "I do not find it probable that no reasonable juror would vote to convict him." In short, the threshold for federal review of state court convictions in matters like this should remain high.

In the end, the Court sided with House, but the holding is a narrow one. Future appellants will continue to face a high hurdle in convincing a reviewing court that they are actually innocent and therefore are entitled to federal court relief when they procedurally default in state court. Perhaps what is most important about this case is that for the first time the Supreme Court dealt with postconviction appeals based on DNA testing. For this reason, death penalty opponents view the case as a major victory. Peter Neufeld, co-director of the Innocence Project, concluded that *House* "recognizes that scientific advances have transformed our criminal justice system and must be weighed heavily in determining whether innocent people have been wrongly convicted" (quoted in Mauro 2006).

CASE CLOSEUP

Courts, Controversy, and the Administration of Justice

Should Federal Courthouse Doors Be Closed to State Prisoners?

The right of convicted offenders to seek review through habeas corpus proceedings has sparked a heated debate. Some people would keep the doors of the federal courts wide open to state prisoners; others would slam the doors firmly shut in most cases.

Some proposals to restrict habeas corpus relief are based on problems of judicial administration. Postconviction petitions contribute to the heavy case-load of the federal courts, are sometimes frivolous, and undermine the value of a final determination of guilt.

But most restrictive efforts are anticrime proposals. Typical is the letter President Reagan wrote to Congress urging passage of remedial legislation: "As a result of judicial expansion of the habeas corpus remedy, state prisoners are now free to re-litigate their convictions and sentences endlessly in the lower federal courts" (quoted in Remington 1988). Conservatives stress that a criminal trial is a procedure that determines the defendant's guilt or innocence, not a game in which the accused may elude justice for any imperfection (Fein 1994).

Writs of habeas corpus play a particularly important role in capital punishment cases. After exhausting appellate remedies, defendants engage in lengthy challenges to the sentence of death by filing multiple writs of habeas corpus in various state and federal courts. Chief Justice William Rehnquist criticized his colleagues for providing capital offenders with "numerous procedural protections unheard of for other crimes" and "for allowing endlessly drawn out legal proceedings" (*Coleman v. Balkcom*, 1981, pp. 958, 960, Rehnquist, J., dissenting).

Others counter that the death penalty is qualitatively different from other types of sanctions, so multiple scrutiny of such cases is more than justified. The argument for keeping the federal courthouse doors open was forcefully stated by Justice John Paul Stevens, who noted that federal habeas proceedings reveal deficiencies in 60 to 70 percent of the capital cases (*Murray v. Giarratano* 1989). Advocates of this policy also argue that not only should there be no rush to judgment, but also that death row inmates should have access to legal assistance,

and the Administration of Justice: Should Federal Courthouse Doors Be Closed to State Prisoners?

Expansion under the Warren Court

In three 1963 decisions, the Warren Court greatly expanded the application of habeas corpus, making it much easier for state prisoners to seek judicial relief in the federal courts (*Fay v. Noia* 1963; *Townsend v. Sain* 1963; *Sanders v. U.S.* 1963). These decisions opened the floodgate for federal review. The annual number of habeas corpus petitions jumped from 2,000 in 1960 to more than 68,000 in 1996.

How often prisoners actually win depends on the period being considered. In 1970, more than 12,000 petitions were granted—an indication that state courts were slowly adopting the new proce-

dural requirements of the Warren Court revolution in criminal justice. By the 1980s, however, prisoners were rarely successful; fewer than 2 percent gained release.

Contraction under the Burger and Rehnquist Courts

Warren Court decisions expanding habeas corpus relief have been steadily cut back in recent years by a more conservative Supreme Court. The Burger Court restricted the grounds for prisoner petitions, ruling that if state courts provide a fair hearing, federal courts cannot consider Fourth Amendment search-and-seizure questions in habeas corpus proceedings (*Stone v. Powell* 1976). The Rehnquist Court repeatedly tightened restrictions on prisoner

yet often do not. The majority of postconviction cases are pro se—the prisoner is appearing on his or her own behalf. Recall from Chapter 7 that the Court has held that defendants have no right to counsel after the first appeal has been exhausted. Many death row defendants must rely on overworked volunteer attorneys (Applebome 1992).

Since the passage of the Antiterrorism and Effective Death Penalty Act, the number of habeas corpus petitions filed in federal court has increased, rising to 31,556 in 2000 (Scalia 2002). Moreover, the law took effect just as national attention began to focus on innocents on death row. Thus, some now question whether the law went too far in denying federal court access to inmates—particularly death row inmates—who may be innocent (see Courts, Controversy, and the Administration of Justice: Innocent on Death Row?).

Justices of the U.S. Supreme Court have expressed increasing concern that the lower federal courts have become too cursory in reviewing death penalty appeals (Greenhouse 2004). Writing for the majority, Justice Kennedy said that while Congress

has instructed the federal courts to accord greater deference to state-court decisions, "deference does not imply abandonment or abdication of judicial review" (*Miller-El v. Dretke* 2005). In particular, the Court has often been critical of the Fifth Circuit court of Appeals for being too willing to uphold death penalty cases. Overall, the court has shown a willingness in recent years to reverse death penalty cases on the basis of ineffective assistance of counsel (Chapter 7), failure of prosecutors to disclose exculpatory evidence to the defense (Chapter 12), bias in jury selection (Chapter 14), and DNA evidence (this chapter).

What do you think? Should the federal courthouse doors be reopened to state prisoners, particularly those on death row, to ensure that justice is not short-circuited? Or should the federal courthouse doors remain as they are now, with only one federal review (unless the case presents an extraordinary issue)? Asked another way, where should the line be drawn between the interests of justice (ensuring that only the truly guilty are executed) and the need for finality (many of the habeas petitions raise issues that are very unlikely to succeed)?

petitions (*Butler v. McKeller* 1990; *Saffle v. Parks* 1990; *McClesky v. Zant* 1991; *Keeney v. Tamayo-Reyes* 1992).

CONGRESS GREATLY RESTRICTS FEDERAL HABEAS

For more than two decades Congress considered proposed changes in habeas corpus proceedings (Smith 1995). This inconclusive debate was shattered by the Oklahoma City bombing in 1995. Victims were anxious to channel their grief into tangible reform, and one avenue was habeas corpus reform (Gest 1996). Thus, as the 1996 elections loomed, Congress passed the Antiterrorism and Effective Death Penalty Act. In terms of habeas corpus actions filed in federal courts, the act does the following:

- Creates 1-year deadlines for filing habeas petitions
- Limits successive petitions
- Restricts the review of petitions by state prisoners if the claim was adjudicated on the merits in state courts
- Requires a "certificate of appealability" before a habeas petition may be appealed to a federal court of appeals
- Provides that decisions of a federal appellate panel are not appealable by writ of certiorari to the Supreme Court

Moving with unusual speed, the Supreme Court agreed to hear a challenge to the new law within 2 months of passage. A unanimous Court held that the law was constitutional in *Felker v. Turpin* (1996).

Wrongful Convictions

In spite of the many procedural protections afforded to the criminally accused prior to and during trial, it is clear that some defendants are wrongfully convicted of crimes they did not actually commit. It is impossible to get an accurate count of the number of innocent people who are wrongfully convicted each year. Using different methods (each with their own flaws), estimates of the rate of wrongful convictions range between a low of 0.5 percent and a high of 15 percent, with between 1 percent and 3 percent being the estimate with the most empirical support (Zalman, Smith, and Kiger 2008).

What causes people to be wrongfully convicted?

Although some miscarriages result from corrupt and criminal behavior, like perjury by perpetrators or by forensic examiners, most flow from human error. . . . [M]istaken eyewitness identification [i]s the most frequent cause. Other common errors include flawed and suggestive lineup techniques, perjury (by perpetrators, witnesses, jailhouse informants, and police), overzealous police and prosecutors who develop "tunnel vision," highly potent psychological interrogation techniques that lead some innocent suspects to falsely confess, prosecutorial misconduct (including the failure to disclose exculpatory evidence), inadequate defense lawyering (by incompetent or overworked attorneys), subjective investigative techniques (e.g., fingerprints, microscopic hair comparison) that are taken to be scientific and unerring, substandard forensic laboratories, and the like. (Zalman, Smith, and Kiger 2008, p. 73)

One might think that the appeals and postconviction review processes would routinely correct situations in which a defendant was wrongfully convicted, but that is clearly not the case. Up until the mid-1990s, public perception was that criminal defendants had gained too many rights during the Warren era, and, as a result, far too many criminal defendants escaped criminal punishment on technicalities (Uphoff 2006). Such perceptions led many—including judges and several Supreme Court justices—to deny that wrongful convictions were a major problem (see *Herrera v. Collins* 1993). Moreover, such sentiments caused legislators to sharply curtail "the avenues available to convicted defendants to challenge their convictions, including appellate review after a certain period (Rosen 2006, pp. 238–239). And the Antiterrorism and Effective Death Penalty Act's curtailment of habeas corpus review further complicated defendants' pursuit of judicial remedies for alleged wrongful convictions.

Since the mid-1990s, though, over 200 death row inmates have been exonerated by DNA evidence, largely due to the efforts of the Innocence Project, the Death Penalty Information Center, and similar organizations (Zalman, Smith, and Kiger 2008). As a result of these exonerations—and media portrayals of them—nearly 40 states have changed their laws to allow for appellate or postconviction review on the grounds of actual innocence, especially when supported by new DNA evidence (Zalman 2006). The federal government similarly enacted the Innocence Protection Act of 2004, which expands judicial review of convictions on the basis of evidence that tends to exonerate.

It is important to note, though, that the courts can do only so much to combat wrongful convictions. After all, courts make decisions based on the evidence presented. Neither participants in a trial nor judges in an appellate court may be aware of problems with faulty evidence. Thus, the most significant ways to combat wrongful convictions lie with reforms of other areas in the criminal justice system. These include changing the ways in which pretrial identifications are conducted to minimize the risk of misidentification; taping of interrogations of criminal suspects to help reduce the incidence of false confessions; and improving the collection, handling, preservation, and analysis of forensic evidence (Uphoff 2006; Rosen 2006).

State Courts of Last Resort

No typical state court of last resort exists. While some are referred to as state supreme courts, some go by other names, such as the *state court of appeals, supreme judicial court, court of criminal appeals,* or *supreme court of appeals.* More important, the role that state high courts play is affected by the control these judicial bodies exercise over their dockets. Perhaps just as important is the exact wording of the state constitution. But these legal factors only partially explain the policymaking role of state supreme courts. Perhaps nowhere is this more obvious than in death penalty appeals.

Law on the Books: State High Courts and Discretionary Dockets

In states that have not created intermediate courts of appeals, the responsibility for appellate review falls directly on the state supreme court. In such circumstances, the state's highest court finds itself relegated to dealing with a succession of relatively minor disputes, devoting its energies to error correction rather than to more time-consuming efforts to shape the law of the state.

By contrast, in the District of Columbia and in the 40 states that have created intermediate courts of appeals, it is the lower appellate courts that are primarily concerned with error correction. This leaves the state's highest court free to devote more attention to cases that raise important policy questions (Scott 2006; Tarr and Porter 1988). This high level of discretion not only yields low caseloads, but also transforms the nature of the judicial process. The high court is no longer merely reacting to disputes brought to it by disgruntled litigants; that is the job of the intermediate court of appeals. Rather, the high court exercises its considerable discretion to carefully select disputes in which it chooses to participate, usually for reasons of advancing public policy. In sum, the architecture of the system tells the judges of the top court to be creative (Carrington, Meador, and Rosenberg 1976; Scott 2006).

Law in Action: State High Courts as Policymakers

In recent years, state supreme courts have become important policymakers in a number of contentious areas, such as tort reform, same-sex marriages, and parental rights in divorce cases. No wonder that elections for state high court judgeships have become nastier, noisier, and costlier (Neubauer and Meinhold 2007).

Applications of U.S. Supreme Court decisions is one way that state supreme courts participate in policymaking. Although in theory federal law is supreme over conflicting state law, in practice state supreme courts do not invariably follow authoritative pronouncements of the nation's highest court (Bloom 2008; Tarr 1982). For example, noncompliance was pronounced in race relations cases, with southern state supreme courts often aiding and abetting their states' massive resistance to desegregation (Garrow 2008; Tarr and Porter 1988). Noncompliance has also occurred in a variety of states in areas such as the constitutionality of executing juveniles (*State ex rel Simmons v. Roper* 2003); the constitutionality of executing a rapist (*State v. Kennedy* 2007); the scope of Fourth Amendment search-and-seizure requirements (*State v. Kimbro* 1985; see also Comparato and McClurg 2007); the role the doctrine of proportionality plays in limiting criminal sentencing (*Andrade v. Attorney General of State of California* 2001); school districts' responses to school prayer decisions (*Murray v. Curlett* 1962; see also Abel and Hacker 2006), and how warning requirements for interrogation announced in *Miranda* would be applied (*Alvord v. State* 1975; see also Epstein, Cameron, Segal, and Westerland 2006; Gruhl 1981).

Interpretation of state constitutional provisions is another way that state supreme courts act as important government policymakers. The phrase **new judicial federalism** refers to the movement in the state supreme courts to reinvigorate state constitutions as sources of individual rights over and above the rights granted by the federal Constitution. New judicial federalism occurred partially as a response to the Burger Court's unwillingness to continue the Warren Court's understanding of civil liberties (Friedman 2000; Galie 1987). Just as important, though, new judicial federalism reflects the growing understanding that the federal Constitution establishes minimum guarantees of individual rights rather than maximum protections (Emmert and Traut 1992; Friedman 2000). In some instances, for example, state supreme courts have interpreted provisions regarding criminal procedures in the state's bill of rights more expansively than the equivalent sections of the U.S. Bill of Rights. Researchers have identified hundreds of state high-court decisions that interpret state charters as more rights-generous than their federal counterpart (Bloom and Massey 2008; Fino 1987). For example, reasoning that garbage was abandoned property, the U.S. Supreme Court ruled in *California v. Greenwood* (1988), that the Fourth Amendment to the U.S. Constitution does not require law enforcement to obtain a search warrant before searching someone's garbage. The high courts of New Jersey and Washington state, however, held that search warrants were required for police to search garbage in those states because their state constitutions afforded more privacy rights than the Fourth Amendment (*State v. Hempele* 1990; *State v. Boland* 1990).

COURTS, CONTROVERSY, AND THE ADMINISTRATION OF JUSTICE

Innocent on Death Row?

For 6 weeks, Ron Williamson sat in his cell next to the Oklahoma electric chair screaming, "I am an innocent man!" Just 5 days before his scheduled execution, his public defender persuaded a U.S. district judge that his state trial had serious constitutional flaws. Before the former professional baseball player was retried, however, the Innocence Project at the Benjamin Cardozo Law School arranged for new DNA testing. The results conclusively showed that Williamson was indeed innocent of the rape and murder of Debra Sue Carter.

In *Actual Innocence,* Barry Scheck, Peter Neufeld, and Jim Dwyer (2000) used the Williamson case and others to argue that many convicts are wrongly on death row. According to their most recent count, 183 death row prisoners in 32 states have been exonerated (Innocence Project 2006). Similarly, an influential article, "A Broken System: Error Rates in Capital Cases," examined 5,760 capital verdicts imposed between 1973 and 1995 (Liebman, Fagan, and West 2000a). The authors reported that 68 percent of all verdicts fully reviewed were found to be so seriously flawed that they had to be scrapped and retried.

And where retrials were known, only 18 percent resulted in the reimposition of the death penalty (Liebman, Fagan, and West 2000b). Studies like these lead proponents of the due process model to argue that "for every seven people executed in this country since 1976, when the Supreme Court reinstated capital punishment, an eighth person—completely innocent—has been condemned to die and later exonerated" (American Civil Liberties Union 2000).

But not all are convinced that the capital appeals process is broken. Barry Latzer and James Cauthen (2000) argued that the statistical conclusions cited above are flawed. They distinguished between two types of errors: conviction errors and sentencing errors. Their analysis shows that conviction errors constitute only a small percentage of appellate court reversals in capital cases. It is sentencing errors, then, that dominate reversals and this is to be expected because capital cases receive much closer scrutiny than noncapital appeals. Overall, advocates of the crime control model argue that the process is working—the few wrong trial court verdicts are indeed identified and corrected on appeal.

LAW IN CONTROVERSY: STATE HIGH COURTS AND DEATH PENALTY CASES

State courts of last resort reveal pronounced differences in their handling of death penalty cases. For example, before New Jersey abolished the death penalty in 2007, the state had not executed anyone since 1963, partially because the New Jersey Supreme Court had invalidated 27 of the 28 death sentences it had reviewed (Bienen 2008). At the other extreme, the high courts of Texas and Virginia routinely uphold the imposition of death sentences (Smith 2008). Consider, for example, that the Texas Court of Criminal Appeals upheld a death sentence for a criminal defendant whose lawyer slept through major portions of the trial, ruling that such behavior did not rise to the level of ineffective assistance of counsel (*Ex parte McFarland* 2005). Other states fit somewhere in between. Illinois and the Carolinas, for example, have thrown out roughly half of the sentences of death they reviewed while upholding the other half (Liebman 2000). (See Courts, Controversy, and the Administration of Justice: Innocent on Death Row?)

Differences in how state courts of last resort respond to death penalty appeals is not random. Justices on high courts in states with competitive judicial elections are more likely to uphold death sentences (Brace and Hall 1997; Brooks and Raphael 2003). In particular, liberal justices facing reelection with possibly close margins of victory are more likely to conceal their opposition to the death penalty; they cast votes reflecting their constituents' opinions.

In recent years, the debate over innocents on death row has focused on DNA testing (see Chapter 14). To be sure, some who have been freed from death row or life imprisonment were later found to be innocent because of witnesses who lied at trial. But some, like Williamson, have been freed after reexamination of trial evidence using advanced DNA-testing techniques that were not available during the original trial. Barry Scheck argues that all convicts on death row should be legally entitled to have the original evidence retested. Recently, the Supreme Court has for the first time recognized the use of DNA evidence in postconviction review of death penalty cases (see Case Close-Up: *House v. Bell* and Federal Court Scrutiny of State Death Row Inmates on page 439). Moreover, a few states have enacted legislation giving convicted death row inmates access to postconviction DNA testing. Conservatives quickly counter that calls for retesting are yet another delaying tactic for defendants who were convicted on the basis of overwhelming physical and testimonial evidence.

To date, there has been no conclusive proof that an innocent person has been executed since the death penalty was reinstated in 1976. But the possibility exists, and recently attention has focused on Ruben Cantu, who was convicted in 1985 of capital murder in San Antonio, Texas, largely on the testimony of an eyewitness. Cantu protested his innocence but was executed in 1992. Now the crime's lone witness has recanted, and a co-defendant said police pressured him to name Cantu (Olsen 2006). Another possibility is Cameron Willingham, convicted in Texas of killing two women in a house fire and executed in 2004 (Blumenthal 2006). Conclusive evidence that Cantu, or another person, was executed but innocent will likely greatly alter the debate over the death penalty.

What do you think? Does the number of innocent persons released from death row or life imprisonment indicate that the capital appeals process is broken or that it is actually working as it should? Do you think that all convicts on death row should have the right to have physical evidence retested using more-advanced DNA techniques, or should such requests be granted only upon a strong showing that the suspect might indeed be innocent?

The U.S. Supreme Court and Criminal Justice Policy

"I'll appeal all the way to the Supreme Court" is a familiar phrase. Alas, it is not very realistic. The jurisdiction of the U.S. Supreme Court is almost exclusively discretionary; that is, it can pick and choose the cases it wishes to decide. Most of the time it decides not to decide. Of the roughly 92 million lawsuits filed in the United States every year, only about 7,000 will ever be appealed to the nation's highest court; and from this small number, the justices will select a mere handful, about 90 in recent years. Of these, most are civil cases, as the Supreme Court tends to review only between 20 and 35 criminal cases each year.

Informally, scholars refer to Court eras according to the chief justice. Thus, the Warren Court refers to the period from 1953 to 1969, when Earl Warren (a former Republican governor of California appointed by President Eisenhower) was chief justice. Because the associate justices change, however, these references provide only informal guides to the dominant thinking of the court. Nonetheless, an examination of the Warren Court, Burger Court, Rehnquist Court, and now the Roberts Court offers a useful summary of major differences in the direction of criminal justice policy.

The Warren Court (1953–1969)

Although it is now more than 30 years since Chief Justice Earl Warren stepped down, the **Warren Court** (1953–1969) commands our attention because in the areas of civil liberties and civil rights it remains the benchmark against which subsequent periods of the Supreme Court will be measured. The Warren Court revolutionized constitutional law and American society as well, giving to minorities victories they had not been able to obtain from reluctant legislatures and recalcitrant executives. Thus, the Warren Court revolution reflected a distinct departure from earlier Courts, which were often characterized as conservative.

The Warren Court first captured national attention with its highly controversial 1954 decision invalidating racial segregation in the public schools (*Brown v. Board of Education* 1954). In addition, the Court first confronted the difficult problem of defining obscenity and considerably narrowed the grounds for prosecution of obscene material (*Roth v. U.S.* 1957). What produced the greatest controversy, however, was the adoption of a series of broad rules protecting criminal defendants.

During the 1960s, the Supreme Court for the first time attempted to exercise strong policy control over the administration of criminal justice. The nation's highest court began to apply to state courts some of the more specific requirements of the Bill of Rights. Earlier opinions enunciating vague standards of "due process" were replaced by decisions specifying precise rules. The Bill of Rights was seemingly transformed from a collection of general constitutional principles into a code of criminal procedure. These sweeping changes in constitutional interpretation have been called the "due process revolution."

Listing the significant Warren Court criminal justice decisions virtually constitutes a review of the major chapters of this book. The right to counsel was expanded (*Gideon v. Wainwright* 1963, discussed in Chapter 7); limits were placed on prosecutorial power (Chapter 6); courts were compelled to bring defendants before a judge without unnecessary delay (Chapter 10); restrictions were placed on police searches (*Mapp v. Ohio* 1961, Chapter 12); limits on police interrogations were mandated (*Miranda v. Arizona* 1966, Chapter 12); jury selection was significantly changed to ensure equality and fairness (Chapter 14); the death penalty was declared unconstitutional (Chapters 15 and 16); the ability of the guilty to appeal their convictions was made easier (this chapter); and the right of convicts to file habeas corpus petitions was also greatly expanded (also this chapter).

If nothing else, the Warren Court put the issues of criminal justice on its docket and eventually on the nation's agenda as well. The Warren Court revolution in areas as diverse as segregation, pornography, school prayer, and reapportionment greatly changed American society. But many of these changes were far from popular. The Supreme Court's attempt to nationalize, rationalize, and constitutionalize the criminal justice system came at a time of increasing crime in the streets, riots in big cities, political violence protesting the Vietnam War, and most tragically of all, assassinations of American leaders. To the public, there appeared to be a connection between the new trends of what was seen as judicial permissiveness and the breakdown of law and order. Supreme Court justices were accused of "coddling criminals" and "handcuffing the police." This controversy became the focus of national debate.

THE BURGER COURT (1969–1986)

During the 1968 presidential campaign, Republican candidate Richard Nixon made the Warren Court's decisions on criminal procedure a major issue. He promised to appoint "strict constructionists" to the Court, and after his election he made good on this promise. With his four appointments, Nixon achieved remarkable success in remodeling the Court. After Warren Burger, Harry Blackmun, Lewis Powell, and William Rehnquist took the bench, support for civil liberties quickly began to diminish (Segal and Spaeth 1989).

The Nixon Court was named after the new Chief Justice, Warren Burger. Although on balance the **Burger Court** (1969–1986) was more conservative than its predecessor, there was no constitutional counterrevolution, only modest adjustment. The withdrawal from Warren Court decisions was most apparent in criminal justice. *Miranda* was weakened but not overturned. Similarly, despite clamor by conservatives, *Mapp* was not overruled, although the Court began creating "good faith" exceptions to the exclusionary rule (see Chapter 12). To be sure, the death penalty was reinstated, but overall the Burger Court did not cut back on Warren Court criminal procedure rulings as much as had been expected.

Just as important, the Burger Court began to tackle new sets of issues not previously treated. In sex discrimination, women were not given as complete protection as had been given to racial minorities, but the tone was moderate to liberal, not conservative (Wasby 1993). Plea bargaining was openly discussed, and rather than abolishing it (as some conservatives urged), the Burger Court sought to regularize its practice (see Chapter 13). And in one of the most controversial decisions ever issued, the Burger Court struck down a variety of requirements that interfered with a woman's right to obtain an abortion (*Roe v. Wade* 1973).

Amid this diversity, it is hard to capture the essence of the Burger Court. Indeed, it is probably best characterized by the headline "Pragmatism, Compromise Marks Courts: Tricky Track Record Harder to Categorize than Pundits Predicted" (Wasby 1993, p. 17). Overall, the Burger Court was composed of seven justices appointed by Republican presidents. Yet President Reagan sought to remake this Republican body in his even more conservative image.

THE REHNQUIST COURT (1986–2005)

Presidents Ronald Reagan and George H. W. Bush continued the Republican policy of appointing conservatives to the court. The **Rehnquist Court** (1986–2005) officially began when William Rehnquist was elevated from associate justice to chief justice. Unofficially, it can be dated from the 1988 appointment of Anthony Kennedy, who provided a conservative vote far more dependably than did his predecessor Lewis Powell. Thus, it was during the 1988 term that the Rehnquist Court seemed to come of conservative age by cutting back abortion rights, condoning mandatory drug testing, and permitting capital punishment for juveniles and retarded persons convicted of murder. And as we have emphasized in this chapter, it virtually eliminated the right of convicts to seek habeas corpus relief.

But other Rehnquist Court decisions cannot be so easily categorized as conservative; for example, the high court upheld flag burning and unanimously ruled that mistaken jury instructions can never be considered harmless error. And most interesting, the Court announced a new constitutional right grounded in the Eighth Amendment's prohibitions against excessive fines; these limits place brakes on the government's aggressive use of its authority under the drug forfeiture laws (see Chapter 3). The Court's conservative justices have been criticized for their activist inclination to disregard precedent (Smith and Hensley 1993). For example, the 1991 decision permitting victim impact testimony in capital sentencing hearings (*Payne v. Tennessee,* discussed in Chapter 9) directly overturned precedents that were merely 2 and 4 years old (*Booth v. Maryland* 1987; *South Carolina v. Gathers* 1989).

Little doubt exists that the Rehnquist Court was more conservative on many issues than its predecessors. Perhaps Law Professor Yale Kamisar said it best in his comment that the Rehnquist Court gave "weight to the needs, convenience, and practical problems of law enforcement" (quoted in Wicker 1991). Overall, the Court was increasingly pragmatic but still very conservative.

The retirement of Byron White gave President Clinton the opportunity to become the first Democratic president in 26 years to make an appointment to the high court. He chose Ruth Bader Ginsburg. With his second appointment, he elevated Stephen Breyer to the high court (Exhibit 17.7). Both have been moderates who on some cases forge an alliance with the centrist justices.

Decisions reflect shifting alliances of the justices. Firmly on the right were Antonin Scalia, Clarence Thomas, and William Rehnquist, with Anthony Kennedy often joining them. Arrayed more to the left were John Paul Stevens, Ruth Bader Ginsburg, Stephen Breyer, and David Souter. It was Sandra Day O'Connor who often held the balance of power. These shifting alliances were reflected in two controversial 2003 decisions in which the court declared unconstitutional a state law prohibiting intimate sexual conduct between persons of the same sex (*Lawrence v. Texas*) and upheld some types of diversity programs in university admissions (*Grutter v. Bollinger*).

For 11 years the same nine justices sat on the Supreme Court, but this changed quickly in the summer of 2005. First, Sandra Day O'Connor announced her retirement, followed 2 months later by the death of the chief justice. Amid considerable public attention, President George W. Bush now had his long-anticipated opportunity to try to move the Court further to the right (Neubauer and Meinhold 2006).

THE ROBERTS COURT (2005–)

The **Roberts Court** (2005–) began on the first Monday in October 2005, when John Roberts officially assumed his duties as the nation's 17th chief justice. In selecting Roberts, President George W. Bush clearly stated his desire to make the Court more conservative. Although some Democrats viewed Roberts as too conservative, he was confirmed. But all eyes were on the next nominee. Bush eventually nominated Samuel Alito to replace O'Connor. Alito, who served on the Third Circuit Court of Appeals, appeared to be even more conservative in his views

Exhibit 17.7						
SUPREME COURT JUSTICES IN ORDER OF SENIORITY						
NAME	YEAR OF BIRTH	HOME STATE	RELIGION	YEAR OF APPOINTMENT	APPOINTED BY	SENATE VOTE
John Roberts	1955	Indiana	Catholic	2005	George W. Bush	78–22
John Paul Stevens	1920	Illinois	Protestant	1975	Gerald Ford	98–0
Antonin Scalia	1936	New York	Catholic	1986	Ronald Reagan	98–0
Anthony Kennedy	1936	California	Catholic	1988	Ronald Reagan	97–0
Clarence Thomas	1948	Georgia	Catholic	1991	George H. W. Bush	52–48
Ruth Bader Ginsburg	1933	New York	Jewish	1993	Bill Clinton	96–3
Stephen Breyer	1938	Massachusetts	Jewish	1994	Bill Clinton	87–9
Samuel Alito, Jr.	1950	New Jersey	Catholic	2006	George W. Bush	58–42
Sonia Sotomayor	1954	New York	Catholic	2009	Barack Obama	68–31

and decisions than Roberts. Although some Democrats talked about filibustering his nomination, Alito was eventually confirmed by the Senate by a relatively narrow margin of 58 to 42.

The Roberts Court appears to be slightly more conservative than the Rehnquist Court, but how much more conservative still remains to be seen. While some predicted that the addition of Justice Alito would lead conservatives to the "promised land," "empirical scrutiny of the Court's voting patterns reveals no significant distinctions between the Rehnquist and Roberts Courts" thus far; rather, the Court appears to be in a state of "relative continuity" rather than dramatic change (Epstein, Martin, Quinn, and Segal 2007, pp. 651–652). The difference, however, is that Justice Kennedy has replaced Justice Sandra Day O'Connor as the Court's key swing vote. For example, Justice Kennedy was the key fifth vote in *Boumediene v. Bush* (2008). This important case held that the "enemy combatants" being held as prisoners by the U.S. government at the U.S. Naval Station at Guantanamo Bay, Cuba, on suspicion of involvement in terrorist activities had the right to challenge their detention in civilian courts in habeas corpus proceedings even though Congress had enacted laws to prevent the prisoners from doing so. The

Court ruled that Congress acted unconstitutionally when they enacted the laws that attempted to suspend the writ of habeas corpus for enemy combatants. The Court also ruled that the detainees had the right to be informed about the specific grounds for their being kept in custody. Conversely, Justice Kennedy sided with the four conservative justices in *Hudson v. Michigan* (2006) when the Court ruled that the exclusionary rule was not an appropriate remedy for violations of the requirement that police officers knock and announce their presence before executing a search warrant (see Chapter 12).

In some closely watched death penalty cases, Justice Kennedy has sided with both ideological sides of the Court. On the so-called liberal side, Kennedy wrote the majority opinion that allowed a Tennessee death row inmate to use DNA evidence in a federal habeas corpus hearing (see Case Close-Up: *House v. Bell* and Federal Court Scrutiny of State Death Row Inmates on page 457). He also joined with the "liberal" branch of the Court in invalidating the use of capital punishment against a child rapist (*Kennedy v. Louisiana* 2008). Yet, he sided with conservatives in several other death penalty cases. With Justice Kennedy writing for the majority in *Ayers v. Belmontes* (2006), the Court ruled that juries need not consider forward-looking mitigating circumstances during death-sentence deliberations. Justice Kennedy also provided the key votes in: *Schriro v. Landrigan* (2007), which upheld a death sentence over an ineffective assistance of counsel claim; *Uttecht v. Brown* (2006), which upheld a trial court's dismissal of three because they were opposed to the death penalty over an objection that such dismissals violated the right to an impartial jury guaranteed by the Sixth and Fourteenth Amendments; and *James v. United States* (2007), which held that an attempted burglary qualified a "violent felony" for triggering a 15-year mandatory sentence under the federal Armed Career Criminal Act. The future direction of the Court will depend on the political balance between the President and the U.S. Senate. With the election of democrat Barack Obama and a solidly democratic U.S. Senate, it is likely that the people named to fill vacancies on the Supreme Court will be more liberal than Justices Roberts and Alito.. For example, Justice Sonia Sotomayor replaced retiring Justice David Souter in 2009. Although she is widely expected to vote with the Court's more liberal block, her presence on the Court is not expected to change the balance between liberals and conservatives. However, the balance on the Court may change if President Obama has the opportunity to replace a justice who was more conservative than David Souter.

THE SUPREME COURT IN BROAD PERSPECTIVE

Newspaper coverage of the Supreme Court tends to resemble the play-by-play commentary of an athletic event, with each decision in the term described as a "victory" or "defeat" for conservatives or liberals. Unfortunately, what gets lost in this commentary is the broader perspective.

Overall, the decisions of the Supreme Court swing back and forth much like a pendulum. Far from being random, however, these swings reflect major political movements in the nation. Most directly, this occurs because of the swing of electoral politics; presidential appointments control the composition of the bench and may temper the speed, if not shift the direction, of the Court. More indirectly, public opinion also affects the justices' lives and may serve to curb them when they threaten to go too far or too fast in their rulings. "But changes in the direction of the Court are ultimately moderated by its functioning as a collegial body, in which all nine justices share power and compete for influence" (O'Brien 1988, p. 13; see also Devins 2008). The Court thus generally shifts direction gradually, incorporating and accommodating the views of new appointees. Ultimately, these long-term trends, more than individual decisions, have the most influence.

CONCLUSION

"This is not a case of conclusive exoneration," wrote Justice Kennedy. Paul House was entitled to another hearing in federal district court, but with no guarantee as to the outcome of that hearing. Meanwhile, House remains on Tennessee's death row. Whether this decision will offer much hope to other inmates sitting on death row remains to be seen. But *House v. Bell* only adds a new chapter to the long-running debate over federal review of state court convictions, particularly federal court review of state death penalty cases. To some, allowing multiple reviews only introduces unnecessary complexities into the process, thus eroding the deterrent value of punishment. To others, though, allowing multiple reviews properly introduces multiple perspectives, thus ensuring that justice is done.

The right to one appeal is being increasingly used. Appellate court caseloads have grown dramatically in recent years. The explosive growth in appellate court caseloads not only reflects the greater willingness of litigants to ask reviewing bodies to correct errors but also represents the greater role appellate courts play in policymaking. U.S. Supreme Court decisions have important impacts on the criminal justice system. But the nine justices are often as divided over the correct answer to a legal problem as is society. Thus, predicting specific case outcomes is difficult; indeed, the conservative Rehnquist Court did not always rule in a predictably conservative manner, and it remains to be seen whether the Roberts Court will consistently rule as conservatively as predicted.

CHAPTER REVIEW

1. **Explain how appeals and appellate processes differ from trials and trial processes.**

Unlike trial courts, appeals courts do not hear evidence at trials. Thus, witnesses do not provide testimony at appeals. Rather, lawyers for both sides appear before a panel of judges to argue about the law applicable to the case.

2. **Describe the two primary functions of appeals.**

The two primary functions of appeals are error correction and policy formation.

3. **Explain how Double Jeopardy limits appeals by the prosecution in criminal cases.**

Although the prosecution can file an appeal over a question of law, the Double Jeopardy Clause of the Fifth Amendment to the U.S. Constitution prevents the prosecution from seeking to have a "not guilty" verdict overturned on appeal.

4. **Define the contemporaneous objection rule and explain its impact on appeals.**

When lawyers think an error is being made at trial, they must object in order to give the trial court judge the opportunity to correct the error. If the attorneys fail to object, then their objection is deemed waived and, therefore, cannot form the basis of a legal argument on appeal.

5. **Differentiate between mandatory and discretionary appellate jurisdiction.**

Mandatory appellate jurisdiction concerns the cases that an appeals court must hear. Discretionary appellate jurisdiction concerns the cases that an appeals court may elect to hear, but is not required to adjudicate.

6. **Identify the different appellate standards of review and evaluate their impact on the criminal appeals.**

Questions of law are reviewed de novo, questions of fact are reviewed for clear error, and discretionary rulings by judges are reviewed for an abuse of discretion. The de novo standard allows an appellate court to consider any legal question without regard or deference to the decision made by a lower court. The other standards of review require appellate courts to give deference to the decisions of a trial court.

7. **Describe the six customary phases in the appeals process.**

Appeals are started by the appellant filing a notice of appeal. The parties then designate the record on appeal and the trial court transmits the designated materials to an appellate court. The parties then brief their cases. The appeals court may then opt to hear oral arguments. The decision of the appellate court is memorialized in a written opinion that concludes with an order disposing of the case.

8. **Compare and contrast plain error, reversible error, and harmless error.**

Plain errors are severe defects in trial proceedings that require reversal of a conviction and remand for a new trial in order to avoid a miscarriage of justice. All other errors are subject to the harmless error rule. If the mistakes are minor such that they probably did not affect the outcome of the case, they are deemed "harmless" and, therefore, do not consistent grounds for the reversal of a conviction on appeal. In contrast, if the errors likely contributed to a defendant being convicted, then they are deemed prejudicial and, therefore, require that a conviction be reversed.

9. Analyze the reasons why most criminal appeals result in convictions being affirmed.

Most criminal cases are affirmed on appeal because of the harmless error rule and the standards of review applied by appellate courts.

10. Compare and contrast appeals and postconviction review processes.

So long as criminal defendants file a notice of appeal within the specified time limits, they are guaranteed the right to have an appellate court directly examine their convictions for all types of alleged errors. Postconviction reviews, however, collaterally attack convictions in civil court. The grounds for such postconviction reviews are usually much more narrow than the grounds that can form the basis of a direct appeal.

11. Identify the leading causes of wrongful convictions.

The leading causes of wrongful convictions include mistaken identifications, unvalidated or improper forensic science, false confessions, government misconduct, unreliable informants, and bad lawyering.

12. Analyze how state courts of last resort and the U.S. Supreme Court exercise their discretion to set justice policy.

High courts of last resort help to set justice policy through their exercise of their discretionary appellate jurisdiction. They accept only cases that present significant public policy questions while rejecting petitions that merely allege the need for error correction.

CRITICAL THINKING QUESTIONS

1. In the public's mind, at least, appeals drag on endlessly and result in a lack of finality in the process. Do you think this is a significant problem, or is it merely one of appearance?

2. How does the appeal-and-review process in a capital murder case differ from the appeal-and-review process in a serious felony?

3. Why are most findings of guilt at the trial level not appealed? In what ways are appellate cases unrepresentative of trial court cases?

4. Based on material in this chapter and earlier ones, what have been the significant differences in decisions among the Warren Court, the Burger Court, the Rehnquist Court, and now the Roberts Court? In particular, consider Court decisions related to right to counsel (Chapter 7), bail (Chapter 11), right to trial (Chapter 14), the death penalty (Chapter 15), and habeas corpus.

KEY TERMS

affirm 451

appellant 448

appellate brief 448

appellate court record 448

appellee 450

Burger Court 464

collateral attacks 455

concurring opinion 451

contemporaneous objection
   rule 445

discretionary appellate
   jurisdiction 445

dissenting opinion 451

double jeopardy 444

en banc 443

WEB RESOURCES

Go to the America's Courts and the Criminal Justice System companion website at

www.cengage.com/criminaljustice/neubauer

where you will find more resources to help you study.
Resources include web exercises, quizzing, and flash cards.

FOR FURTHER READING

Baumgartner, Frank, Suzanne De Boef, and Amber Boydstun. *The Decline of the Death Penalty and the Discovery of Innocence*. New York: Cambridge University Press. 2007.

Bierman, Luke. "Three Views of State Intermediate Appellate Courts: Introduction." *Justice System Journal* 26: 93–97, 2005.

Binford, W. Warren H., Preston C. Greene, Maria C. Schmidlkofer, Robert M. Wilsey, and Hillary A. Taylor. "Seeking Best Practices Among Intermediate Courts of Appeal: A Nascent Journey." *Journal of Appellate Practice and Process* 9: 37–119, 2007.

Bonneau, Chris. "Vacancies on the Bench: Open-Seat Elections for State Supreme Courts." *Justice System Journal* 27: 143–159, 2006.

Diascro, Jennifer Segal. "The Legacy of Chief Justice Rehnquist: A View from the Small Screen." *Judicature* 92: 106–117, 2008.

Eakins, Keith. "Agenda Setting in an Elected Supreme Court: The Case of Ohio." *Justice System Journal* 27: 160–179, 2006.

Eggers, David, and Lola Vollen, eds. *Serving Justice: America's Wrongfully Convicted and Exonerated.* San Francisco: McSweeney's, 2006.

Gould, Jon. "After Further Review: A New Wave of Innocence Commissions." *Judicature* 88: 126–130, 2004.

Matthew, Jonathan. *Inside Appellate Courts: The Impact of Court Organization on Judicial Decision Making in the United States Courts of Appeals.* Ann Arbor: University of Michigan Press, 2002.

Maveety, Nancy. *Queens' Court: Judicial Power in the Rehnquist Era*. Lawrence: University of Kansas Press, 2009.

Merriner, James. *The Man who Emptied Death Row: Governor Ryan and the Politics of Crime.* Carbondale: Southern Illinois University Press, 2008.

O'Brien, David. *Storm Center: The Supreme Court in American Politics.* 6th ed. New York: Norton, 2003.

Perry, Barbara. "The 'Bush Twins?' Roberts, Alito, and the Conservative Agenda." *Judicature* 92: 302-311, 2009.

Perry, Barbara. *The Priestly Tribe: The Supreme Court's Image in the American Mind.* Westport, CT: Praeger, 1999.

Scott, Kevin M. "Understanding Judicial Hierarchy: Reversals and the Behavior of Intermediate Appellate Judges." *Law and Society Review* 40: 163–191, 2006.

Turow, Scott. *Reversible Error.* New York: Warner Books, 2002.

Unnever, James. "Executing the Innocent and Support for Capital Punishment: Implications for Public Policy." *Criminology and Public Policy* 4: 3–38, 2005.

Williams, Jimmy. "Type of Counsel and the Outcome of Criminal Appeals: A Research Note." *American Journal of Criminal Justice* 19: 275–285, 1995.

Zalman, Marvin, Brad Smith, and Angie Kiger. "Officials' Estimates of the Incidence of 'Actual Innocence' Convictions." *Justice Quarterly* 25: 72–100, 2008.

18

THE LOWER COURTS

A lawyer questions a suspect on the witness stand. Individually, the cases heard in the lower courts may be minor. But collectively, such cases are important because traffic offenses and misdemeanors are the types of cases that bring typical citizens to court. How these courts handle drunk driving and domestic violence cases, for example, has a major impact on societal functioning and, therefore, are often the subject of intense public debate.

Chapter Outline

Learning Objectives

After reading this chapter, you should be able to:

1. Identify the three types of cases that the lower courts hear.

2. List the four problems confronting the lower courts in the United States.

3. Discuss the similarities and differences between justice of the peace courts and municipal courts.

4. Explain why the Supreme Court's opinion in *North v. Russell* is important.

5. Describe the sentencing process in the municipal courts.

6. Analyze the political and social factors affecting drunk-driving-law enforcement in the United States.

7. Name the two major efforts toward court-community collaboration.

"Drunk Driver Kills Mother of Two"
"Motorist Arrested for Fifth Drunk Driving
Offense"
Headlines like these have become all too familiar to
readers of local papers. In the most recent year for
which data is available, 12,998 people died in alcohol-
impaired crashes involving a drunk driver (32 percent

of the 41,059 total traffic fatalities) (National Highway
Traffic Safety Administration 2008). Moreover, the
police make more arrests—more than 1.4 million
annually—for drunk driving than for any other
crime. Public concern over drunk driving has focused
attention on the otherwise virtually invisible activities
of the nation's lower (and often forgotten) courts.

Every year, the lower courts process tens of millions of Americans accused of disturbing the peace,
shoplifting, being drunk in public, or driving too fast.
Individually, these cases may appear to be minor—
almost petty—but collectively, the work of the lower
courts is quite important. How the lower courts
handle these types of cases figures prominently in
discussions of important problem areas like domestic violence (Chapter 9) and drunk driving (this
chapter). How the lower courts handle these millions of offenses also plays a role in one of the most
provocative and controversial theories of modern
policing—broken windows. Moreover, these minor
offenses are front and center in discussions of community—community courts in this case.

Although the collective work of the lower courts is
important, appellate courts rarely scrutinize their activities, preferring instead to concentrate on the more
intellectually challenging legal issues raised by murderers and drug dealers who have been found guilty
in the major trial courts. One of the rare times that the
U.S. Supreme Court has considered a case from the
lower courts is profiled in the Case Close-Up in this
chapter. Allegations of drunk driving are common;
Supreme Court scrutiny of such matters are not.

This chapter discusses the rapid, rough justice
dispensed by the lower courts. We begin with an
examination of the scope of the lower courts and
then consider their problems. As we shall see, lower
courts exhibit immense variation; big-city courts
function very differently from their counterparts in
rural areas. Therefore, we consider the different issues presented in rural justice of the peace courts as
opposed to the big-city municipal courts. Finally, we
examine alternative dispute resolution (ADR), which
is designed to reduce the caseloads of the courts by
providing nonadversarial alternatives to traditional
courtroom procedures.

SCOPE OF THE LOWER COURTS

At the first level of state courts are **trial courts of
limited jurisdiction**, sometimes referred to as
inferior courts or, more simply, **lower courts**.
Although these minor courts stand at the bottom of
the judicial hierarchy, the base is much larger than
the typical pyramid diagram suggests. Indeed, when
we count up the number of courts, judges, and cases
filed in courts all across the nation, the numbers are
dominated by the nation's lowest judiciary. Nearly
18,500 lower court judges constitute 61.5 percent of
all state court judgeships in the nation (LaFountain
et al. 2008). The number of cases in courts of limited
jurisdiction is almost five times that of the courts
of general jurisdiction. Even if considering only the
nontraffic cases, the courts of limited jurisdiction
still process twice as many cases as do the courts of
general jurisdiction (p. 13). The precise jurisdiction
of lower courts varies from place to place. In some
states, major trial courts in rural areas hear traffic
cases and the like because there are few lower courts.
Moreover, in 10 states and the District of Columbia,
the lower courts have been consolidated with the
major trial courts; as a result, statistical comparisons
between these jurisdictions and the other 40 states
are difficult at best (Langton 2007). Nonetheless,
the workload of the lower courts can usefully be examined in terms of felony criminal cases, nonfelony
criminal cases, and civil cases.

FELONY CRIMINAL CASES

Lower-court jurisdiction typically includes the preliminary stages of felony cases (see Chapter 4). Thus,
after an arrest, a judge in a trial court of limited

jurisdiction will hold the initial appearance, appoint counsel for indigent defendants, and conduct the preliminary hearing, if applicable. Later, the case is transferred to a trial court of general jurisdiction for trial (or plea) and sentencing. Note also, from Exhibit 18.1, that lower-court judges typically sign search warrants—a decision that may prove crucial for decisions in the major trial court.

NONFELONY CRIMINAL CASES

Typically, criminal cases are divided into felony and misdemeanor, a distinction that fits nicely with the work of the trial courts of general jurisdiction. But for the lower courts, a broader concept of nonfelony cases is better. Nonfelony includes not only misdemeanors, but also ordinance violations and traffic cases.

A **misdemeanor** is a crime punishable by a fine, imprisonment (usually in a local jail, for a period of less than 1 year), or both. Misdemeanors are enacted by state legislative bodies and cover the entire state.

Ordinances, on the other hand, are laws passed by a local governing body such as a city council. They are similar in effect to a legislative statute, but they apply only to the locality, and any fine that is assessed for violations goes to the local government, not to the state. It is typical for ordinances to prohibit the same types of conduct (for example, disorderly conduct, public drunkenness) as state misdemeanors. Ordinance violations are technically noncriminal, which means that they are easier to prosecute. At times, police prefer to arrest a suspect for an ordinance violation because it presents fewer legal obstacles to gaining a conviction.

Traffic offenses refer to a group of offenses involving self-propelled motor vehicles. These violations range from parking violations to improper equipment. Speeding is the most common traffic offense, along with driving without a license and driving while a license is suspended or revoked. Traffic offenses are typically punishable by a small fine. But because the volume of these cases is quite

Exhibit 18.1
STEPS OF CRIMINAL PROCEDURE IN LOWER COURTS FOR NONFELONY CASES

	LAW ON THE BOOKS	LAW IN ACTION
Crime	*Misdemeanor:* Crime punishable by fine or local jail for less than 1 year. *Ordinance violation:* Law passed by local government similar to a misdemeanor. *Traffic offense:* Relating to motor vehicles.	With the exception of drunk driving and domestic violence, the criminal law has changed little in the past decades.
Arrest	*Arrest:* Taking of a person into custody for the purpose of charging him or her with a crime. *Citation:* Written order issued by a law enforcement officer notifying a defendant to appear in court. *Complaint:* Sworn statement by victim alleging that a specific person has committed a specified crime.	Drunkenness and other liquor law: 1,223,000. Disorderly conduct: 709,000. Driving under the influence: 1,427,000. Weapons: 189,000. Vandalism: 291,500.
Initial appearance	Suspects are told the charges pending; lower-court judges can take a plea in nonfelony cases.	Often held within 24 hours of arrest. Two out of three defendants plead guilty during the first appearance.

Exhibit 18.1

CONTINUED

	LAW ON THE BOOKS	LAW IN ACTION
Bail	Money posted for bail or for a citation may be forfeited as an alternative to appearance in court.	Many suspects plead guilty immediately, so bail release does not come into play.
Preliminary hearing	Preliminary hearings are not applicable in nonfelony cases.	
Charging	Charges are filed by police (based on an arrest or citation) or directly by the victim (complaint).	Prosecutor and judge typically proceed on the basis of the police arrest.
Grand jury	Grand juries are not applicable to nonfelony cases.	
Arraignment	Arraignments in trial courts of general jurisdiction are not applicable in nonfelony cases.	
Evidence	Lower-court judges have the authority to sign search warrants.	Search warrants are very rare in nonfelony cases.
Plea negotiations	Misdemeanor defendants sentenced to jail have a right to counsel (*Argersinger v. Hamlin*).	Few defendants have an attorney, so defendants must negotiate on their own.
Trial	Defendants have a constitutional right to a trial by jury only if the offense is punishable by imprisonment for more than 6 months (*Baldwin v. New York*).	Trials are rare indeed. Defendants charged with drunk driving may demand a trial, particularly if they have a previous drunk-driving conviction.
Sentencing	Defendants may not be jailed because they are unable to pay a fine (*Tate v. Short*).	Fines predominate. Jail sentences (short) sometimes imposed.
Appeal	Appeals from lower courts are heard by trial court of general jurisdiction or intermediate court of appeals.	Very few defendants appeal. Appeals may occur after drunk-driving convictions.

SOURCE: Bureau of Justice Statistics. 2009. Sourcebook of Criminal Justice Statistics, 2007. Washington, DC: Author. Available online at http://www.albany.edu/sourcebook/pdf/t412007.pdf

large, traffic tickets can be big moneymakers for local governments.

For a time the number of traffic cases heard in the lower courts was declining, but no longer. The most recent statistics for the past decade indicate that the volume of traffic cases increased 13 percent (National Center for State Courts 2008). To put these numbers into perspective, consider that in the state of Texas, nearly 10 million traffic violations are processed yearly. In terms of population, New Jersey leads the nation with 66,793 traffic cases per 100,000 people. Overall, traffic violations constitute nearly 60 percent of lower-court caseloads. The most watched aspects of traffic cases are prosecutions for drunk driving.

CIVIL CASES

On the civil side, the lower courts decide disputes under a set dollar amount, often referred to as small claims. **Small claims courts** handle cases involving maximum amounts that range from a low of $1,500 in some states to a high of $25,000 in others (NOLO 2009). The trend is clearly in an upward direction. The largest number of cases falling under these dollar amounts are debt collection, primarily involving nonpayment for goods purchased or services rendered. Another major category includes landlord–tenant disputes—mostly claims by landlords against tenants concerning past-due rent, evictions, and property damage. A smaller number of small claims cases involve alleged property damage, largely stemming from automobile accidents.

In most states, streamlined procedures have been adopted to provide quick, inexpensive processing by dispensing with strict rules of evidence and the right to trial by jury. Accordingly, small claims cases are less formal and less protracted than other civil cases. Yet, they comprise roughly 45 percent of the civil cases filed each year in the nation's state courts (LaFountain et al. 2008).

PROBLEMS OF THE LOWER COURTS

It is the quantity of cases (the caseload) that makes the trial courts of general jurisdiction so qualitatively important. Individually, the cases may be minor, but collectively they are of critical importance because these are the matters that bring typical citizens to court. Jury duty aside, an appearance in lower court is, for many citizens, their only direct encounter with the judiciary, and these encounters in turn shape citizens' perceptions of the quality of justice meted out by all courts, whether state or federal, trial or appellate.

For decades, reformers have criticized the lower courts, highlighting a variety of problems. Only a shadow of the adversary model of criminal justice can be found in these courts. Few defendants are represented by an attorney. Trials are rare. Informality, rather than the rules of courtroom procedure, predominates. Jail sentences are imposed, sometimes with lightning speed. In short, practices that would be condemned if they occurred in higher courts are commonplace in the lower courts. Is this justice? The President's Commission on Law Enforcement and Administration of Justice (1967, p. 128) found the conditions of the lower courts disquieting.

> The commission has been shocked by what it has seen in some lower courts. It has seen cramped and noisy courtrooms, undignified and perfunctory procedures, and badly trained personnel. It has seen dedicated people who are frustrated by huge caseloads, by the lack of opportunity to examine cases carefully, and by the impossibility of devising constructive solutions to the problems of offenders. It has seen assembly-line justice.

To identify the most pressing problems of the trial courts of limited jurisdiction, the American Judicature Society surveyed six states: Colorado, Illinois, Louisiana, New Hampshire, New Jersey, and Texas. They found the problems confronting the lower courts to be as varied as the courts themselves (Ashman 1975). Since this study, many states, but not all, have made marked improvements to their lower courts (Waldron 2008). For example, a more recent study of almost 2,000 part-time lower-court judges in the state of New York concluded that:

> people have often been denied fundamental legal rights. Defendants have been jailed illegally. Others have been subjected to racial and sexual bigotry so explicit it seems to come from some other place and time. People have been denied the right to a trial, an impartial judge and the presumption of innocence. (Glaberson 2006)

Courts, Controversy, and Traffic Fines

Do Traffic Fines Improve Safety or Merely Raise Revenue?

Traffic fines and fees are a multi-billion dollar business in the United States, but exactly how big is hard to determine. Since no official figures are compiled, one can only provide rough estimates. For the most recent year for which data are available (see Table 18.1), 55.6 million traffic cases were filed in the nation's courts. If we estimate that each ticket totals $150, then the yearly revenue stream is a little over $8.3 billion, big dollars indeed. (If we add in the dollars generated by filing fees in civil cases and fines collected in misdemeanor and ordinance violation cases, then the cash flow of the lower courts is even greater.)

Where does this money go? The answer is complicated because the money a driver pays for a typical traffic ticket includes both fines and fees. Revenue generated from fines goes to the government that has created the court, either the city, the county, or the state. Typically, this revenue stream is then used to pay the expenses of the court itself (judges, clerks, and the like) as well as the prosecutor's office and the public defender, but not necessarily. In some jurisdictions, the government makes a considerable profit from court-imposed fines. Over the years, cities have become known as speed traps. Although this appears to be less true today, there are still some small towns that finance

a considerable part of their expenses, including the police department, from tickets issued to out-of-town motorists. In Oklahoma, for example, 15 small towns with populations of fewer than 2,000 people reported more revenue from traffic fines and fees than from sales taxes (Killman 2006).

Revenue generated from court-imposed fees, on the other hand, goes to the court itself. In some jurisdictions, these fees are used to support important court matters, such as expenses of the public defender's office and reimbursing jurors. These revenues may also be dedicated to programs we have discussed throughout this book including drug courts (Chapter 4), crime victims fund (Chapter 9), domestic violence facilities (Chapter 9), ADR programs (this chapter), and drunk driving prevention (this chapter).

When governments, whether state or local, are faced with a budget crisis, one place they often look for additional revenue without having to take the unpopular step of raising taxes is to increase fines and fees on traffic offenses. Florida, for example, facing a major budget shortfall, increased traffic fines by a projected $63 million a year, sparing further budget cuts for courts, prosecutors, and public defenders (Dunkelberger 2009). At the local level, El Paso County, Colorado, is reaping 147%

Research over the years has focused on four problem areas: inadequate financing, inadequate facilities, lax procedures, and unbalanced caseloads.

INADEQUATE FINANCING

In general, lower courts are funded locally. Sparsely populated counties and small municipalities often lack funds to staff and equip their courts adequately. Even when funds are available, there is no guarantee that local governments will spend money on the lower courts. In many cities, these courts are expected to produce revenue for local governments. Indeed, some lower courts generate revenues much greater than their operating expenses, yet they still

lack adequate courtrooms and other facilities. The remainder of the funds go to pay for city services. (See Controversy: Do Traffic Fines Improve Safety or Merely Raise Revenue?)

INADEQUATE FACILITIES

Lower-court courtrooms are often crowded and noisy, with 100 or more people forced to spend hours waiting for their minute before the judge. Some are makeshift, hastily created in the side of a store or the back of a garage. In the state of New York, "Some of the courtrooms are not even courtrooms: tiny offices or basement rooms without a judge's bench or jury box" (Glaberson 2006). Such

more from moving violations than the year before thanks to an increase in traffic fines voted by the state legislature (Zubeck 2009). Legislatures in over 40 states are likewise looking to solve some of their fiscal crisis in a similar manner (Schwartz 2009).

Modern technology is making it even easier for local governments to generate more revenue through traffic enforcement. Across the nation, cities are installing cameras at traffic lights that take pictures of cars that run red lights. The result is often a significant increase in the citations generated by the computer and fines billed. In suburban New Orleans, for example, traffic cameras generated over 140,000 tickets and $11 million in fines. If supporters say traffic cameras increase safety, critics say the red-light system is all about seeing green (Waller 2008). The use of traffic cameras to collect fines has been being challenged in court (Roesler 2009). One such lawsuit alleged that using photographic evidence to nab speeders and red-light runners violates basic constitutional rights to due process, including the rights to be presumed innocent, to have a hearing before an impartial judicial official, and to have the opportunity to challenge the evidence. But the Ohio Supreme Court unanimously ruled that there were no constitutional violations because these infractions are civil and not criminal (*Mendenhall v. Akron* 2008).

If legal challenges to increasing traffic fines are rarely successful, political action occasionally is. In an effort to raise money for road projects, without having to raise taxes, the State of Virginia imposed fees ranging from $750 to $3,000 for those caught driving 20 miles above the speed limit or engaging in other forms of reckless driving (Urbina 2008). These enhanced fees proved so unpopular—more than 175,000 residents signed an online petition for its repeal—that even its Senate sponsor voted for repeal, saying it was "one of the greatest mistakes that I've made as a legislator," but the mistake was made in earnest (Davis 2008).

Efforts to generate more money from traffic enforcement by writing more tickets and increasing the fines and fees for each violation has limits, however. As the amount of fines and fees go up, more motorists are unable to pay, particularly during a recession. And as more motorists don't pay, the amount of money collected also declines. Hardest hit are low-income drivers who are most in need of a car to earn a living. To some, governments will soon face a "tipping point" at which more produces less revenue (Bousquet 2009).

What do you think? Is the primary purpose of traffic tickets increasing safety on the highway or raising revenue for government?

courtroom conditions lack dignity and leave a bad impression, suggesting that the judiciary is more interested in collecting the fine for speeding than in bothering to do justice. Such inadequate facilities are detrimental to the attitudes of the defendant, prosecutor, judge, and all others involved in the justice process.

LAX COURT PROCEDURES

Besides singling out inadequate facilities, critics of lower courts often cite lax procedures in the day-to-day administration of these courts. Many trial courts of limited jurisdiction do not have written rules for the conduct of cases. Conventional bookkeeping

methods are often ignored. How much fine money was collected and how it was spent is often impossible to determine. You can find some information in the city budget but not in the court records; this frustrates any attempts to assess the effectiveness of these courts.

UNBALANCED CASELOADS

Many lower courts are characterized by moderate to heavy caseloads, but others appear to have little to do. Because of unbalanced caseloads, some courts have huge backlogs for which they are unequipped. But because these courts are locally controlled, there is no way to equalize the workload.

TABLE 18.1

VOLUME OF CASES FILED IN LOWER COURTS AND MAJOR TRIAL COURTS IN A YEAR (IN MILLIONS)

CASE TYPE	JURISDICTION				
	UNIFIED	GENERAL	UNIFIED + GENERAL	LIMITED	TOTAL
Traffic	12.3	1.8	14.1	41.5	55.6
Criminal	3.3	3.2	6.5	15.0	21.6
Civil	3.0	4.6	7.6	9.7	17.3
Domestic relations	1.0	3.2	4.2	1.6	5.8
Juvenile	.4	1.0	1.4	.7	2.1
All cases	20.0	13.8	33.9	68.6	102.4

SOURCE: National Center for State Courts, *Examining the Work of State Courts, 2007.* Williamsburg, VA: National Center for State Courts, 2008.

Unbalanced caseloads are the clearest indication that any generalizations about the problems of the lower courts must be coupled with the observation that the nation's lowest tribunals are tremendously varied. From state to state, between one county and its neighboring county, and even within a city, wide discrepancies exist in the quality of justice rendered. There is no easy way to determine what is wrong (or even what is right) about these courts. Because of the wide disparity, it is best to examine rural justice of the peace courts separately from urban municipal courts. Although they share many problems, they are also sufficiently different to warrant separate treatment.

RURAL JUSTICE

More than 45 million Americans get their justice off the main road. Although the United States is increasingly a nation where most people live in big cities and surrounding suburbs, roughly 17 percent of the population still live and work in small towns and rural areas (U.S. Department of Agriculture 2009). For them, the law is meted out in rural courthouses that are more numerous than usually imagined: The legal system in the United States is county-based, and approximately 80 percent of the

counties are rural. Trial courts of general jurisdiction in rural areas are typically grouped in circuits or district, which means that the judges must drive from courthouse to courthouse on a regular basis. According to the Supreme Court of Nevada (Sweet and Dobbins 2005), judges in rural areas spend 22% of their time—one workday a week—traveling from one county seat to another. The trial courts of limited jurisdiction in rural areas are often presided over by non-attorney judges and part-time prosecutors.

Overall, the issues facing rural courts are qualitatively different from those faced by urban courts (Baehler and Mahoney 2005). Compared to their big-city counterparts, rural courts exhibit three special features: lower caseload, lack of resources, and greater familiarity (Bartol 1996; see also, McKeon and Rice 2009).

LOWER CASELOADS

Caseloads in rural courts are lighter than those in suburban or urban courts. An analysis of the FBI's *Uniform Crime Reports* shows that the rate of crime is much higher in urban than in rural areas. This is particularly true of violent offenses, which are more than four times more likely in urban as opposed to rural areas (Lee 2008; Thompson 1996; Weisheit, Falcone,

LAW AND POPULAR CULTURE

The Conspicuous Absence of the Lower Courts on Television and in Film

Unlike nearly all of the other chapters of this book, this chapter's exploration of "Law and Popular Culture" does not rely on a particular movie or television show. We tried to find a suitable example, but could not think of one. Perhaps the dearth of options is not surprising since proceedings in the lower court are rarely riveting. Indeed, as you learned in this chapter, the assembly-line the operation of the lower courts is mundane, especially compared with the juicy felony cases handled in television shows like *Raising the Bar* and the various iterations of *Law and Order*. The same is true for major motion pictures. Consider, for example, the American Bar Association's list of "The 25 Greatest Legal Movies" of all time (Brust 2008). A review of the list reveals that 18 of the movies deal with criminal cases, all of

which are serious felonies. Not a single film on the list depicts the operations of the lower trial courts.

At one time, however, there was a situation comedy on television that took place in a lower trial court. The show, *Night Court*, ran from 1984 to 1992. A poll of lawyers by the American Bar Association ranked the show in the top ten law-based television shows of all time (Ward 2009). But unlike all of the other law-based shows on the top-ten list that focused on cases in major trial courts (like *L.A. Law*, *The Practice*, and *Perry Mason*), *Night Court* centered around after-hours sessions in a misdemeanor court in New York City. Presided over by Judge Harry Stone (played by comedian Harry Anderson), the show "featured a lecherous prosecutor, a no-nonsense court clerk, a droll set of

Ranking and Movie Title	Crime or Legal Cause of Action
1. *To Kill a Mockingbird* (1962)	rape
2. *12 Angry Men* (1957)	homicide
3. *My Cousin Vinny* (1992)	homicide
4. *Anatomy of a Murder* (1959)	homicide
5. *Inherit the Wind* (1960)	violation of the Butler Act (which criminalized teaching about evolution)
6. *Witness for the Prosecution* (1957)	homicide
7. *Breaker Morant* (1980)	war crimes
8. *Philadelphia* (1993)	civil rights discrimination
9. *Erin Brockovich* (2000)	civil lawsuit for injuries caused by illegal dumping of toxic chemicals
10. *The Verdict* (1982)	civil lawsuit for medical malpractice
11. *Presumed Innocent* (1990)	homicide
12. *Judgment at Nuremberg* (1961)	war crimes
13. *A Man for All Seasons* (1966)	capital treason
14. *A Few Good Men* (1992)	homicide
15. *Chicago* (2002)	homicide
16. *Kramer vs. Kramer* (1979)	divorce and child custody
17. *The Paper Chase* (1973)	life as a first-year law student at Harvard University
18. *Reversal of Fortune* (1990)	attempted homicide
19. *Compulsion* (1959)	homicide
20. *And Justice for All* (1979)	rape
21. *In the Name of the Father* (1993)	terrorist bombing
22. *A Civil Action* (1998)	civil lawsuit for injuries caused by illegal dumping of toxic chemicals
23. *Young Mr. Lincoln* (1939)	homicide
24. *Amistad* (1997)	the kidnapping of slaves from Africa and their mutiny against their kidnappers
25. *Miracle on 34th Street* (1947)	the civil commitment of an alleged mentally-ill person who claims to be Santa Claus

The Conspicuous Absence of the Lower Courts on Television and in Film

bailiffs and a string of cover-girl public defenders. Full of pratfalls and seriously good intentions, the show managed to humanize the one place where most people meet up with the law (Ward para. 1). Although the show centered on comedic moments caused by eccentric offenders (many of whom were arrested on charges related to public drunkenness, disorderly conduct, prostitution, and other nuisance offenses), that is what made the show somewhat realistic. Indeed, because *Night Court* emphasized non-glamorous, non-violent petty crimes, it may just be the most realistic law-based television show of all time. Consider, for example, this excerpt from an article about the operation of the lower courts in a leading law journal:

> Those who have never seen the lower criminal courts (particularly in urban areas) in operation would likely be shocked at what they saw. Of course there is a judge, a jury box, and attorneys. But in most respects it does not comport with any image one might have of this country's court system, unless one is a devotee of Dickens' novels or television's *Night Court*. In the first place, these courts are generally teeming with people. Filled courtrooms, people standing in the hallways, and a constant stream of people walking in, and out and back in, over and over again is typical. Nearly twenty cases are disposed of for every one that progresses to Superior Court. Attorneys blithely walk up to the clerk to discuss some matter while a case is being heard, and bargain with the prosecutor on their own case while a defense attorney is addressing the court on another. And for the defender, the flow of cases is endless; a limitless stream of files. A dozen or so clean, raw files appear on their desks in

the morning, at most containing a police report and the defendant's application for indigent defense. Into court they come, stack of files in hand, yelling to determine if their clients have even shown up. "Is there a Mr. Firmen here? Is Ms. Nonce in court?" On some days, half of the defendants do not respond to their calls, and bench warrants are subsequently issued. This is not uncommon. These are the lower courts. (Mitchell 1994, pp. 12-39-1241)

1. Why do you think there are so few depictions of the operations of the lower trial courts in popular culture media? Explain your reasoning.

2. Why do you think comedy was a successful mechanism for *Night Court* to highlight a lower trial court? Do you think a drama devoted to judges making probable cause determinations at initial appearances, setting bail, and adjudicating misdemeanors and traffic disputes would enjoy the same type of success that kept *Night Court* on the air for eight years? Why?

3. In contrast to movies and prime-time television, there have been (and still are) many daytime, reality-based television shows that take place in "courts" that adjudicate civil small claims. Starting with *Divorce Court* and *The People's Court* and ranging to a number of shows entitled "Judge _____" (e.g., *Judge Judy, Judge Alex, Judge Joe Brown, Judge Hatchett, Judge Mathis*), these shows fill the daytime airwaves. What do you suppose is responsible for the popularity of these shows? Why do you think all of them focus on small claims or other civil matters rather than criminal misdemeanors?

and Wells 2006). But this does not mean that rural citizens do not experience crime. Over the past decades, rural crimes have increased at the same rate as big-city crimes. And some types of crime—drunk driving

and fraud, for example—are more prevalent in rural areas. Moreover, illegal drug use is increasingly common in rural areas, so much so that that the "scourge of social and criminal problems associated with the methamphetamine epidemic" is stressing rural courts (White 2008). Treating drug addiction is more difficult in rural areas because of the lack of public transportation, the shortage of treatment facilities, and the additional resources necessary to treat the medical conditions of addicts (Cooper 2003).

Law enforcement officials also recognize that rural areas may be attractive because their settings are fairly insulated from government and citizen monitoring. Rural settings present unique problems for domestic violence cases (Pruitt 2008). These areas also tend to harbor hate groups, militia, and others who bill themselves as antigovernment. Over the years, the United States has experienced a series of unrelated standoffs between law enforcement and private citizens in Ruby Ridge (1992), Waco (1993), and the Republic of Texas (1997), several of which ended with violent confrontations.

LACK OF RESOURCES

Although rural courts have lower caseloads, this does not mean that they do not face problems processing the workload. Rural courts receive less federal money and have a lower local tax base than larger counties (McDonald, Wood, and Pflug 1996; McKeon and Rice 2009). According to Don Cullen (2000), a former court administrator in rural Nebraska, in many rural counties, local (and not state) funding is the main source of revenue, which means the funding of local courts is closely tied to the success of the annual crop. As a consequence, court facilities are often outmoded and salaries are low.

Lack of resources is a particular problem in criminal cases in which defendants are indigent (Chapter 7). Because few attorneys practice law in rural areas, the defense pool is limited. These built-in limitations have been compounded in recent years by cutbacks in federal funding. Rural areas have been hardest hit by drastic reductions in publicly funded legal services for the poor, resulting in ever less access to justice for nonurban residents (Kerrigan 2008).

FAMILIARITY

Justice in rural areas involves fewer agencies and also fewer personnel than in urban or suburban systems. Whereas big-city courts are characterized by the interface of numerous bureaucracies, in rural areas contacts are invariably one-on-one (Weisheit, Falcone, and Wells 2006). The active bar consists of a dozen or fewer members, including the prosecutor, the judge, and the lawyer who represents the local government. Often, there are five or fewer sheriff's deputies and a single probation officer, each of whom is known to the judge. The clerk's office typically consists of two or three long-term employees. In short, "fewer than 30 people routinely work together, a group about the size of a small family reunion" (Fahnestock 1991, p. 14).

Not only is the number of actors in rural courts small, but their interactions are frequent and long term. By and large, justice is administered by those who grew up in the community, and they are bound together by long-standing social and family networks. As a result, rural courts place greater emphasis on informal mechanisms of social control, whereas urban courts are more legalistic and formal (Weisheit, Falcone and Wells, 2006).

ASSESSING RURAL JUSTICE

The most commonly mentioned aspect of rural justice is comity. Generally, it speaks of a friendly social atmosphere and group harmony. But in this context, it also can mean "You scratch my back, and I'll scratch yours." It's not always a conscious thing. The judge and the prosecutor are friends. Sometimes they're related. Thus, some point to a lack of an independent judiciary and a weak adversarial process in many parts of rural America. The danger is that community knowledge is substituted for the Constitution. Some specific types of injustices include capricious arrests, unduly high bonds, rubber-stamping prosecutorial decisions, and pressuring defendants into pleading guilty (Glaberson 2006; Sitomer 1985; Waldron 2008).

To Albert Barney, longtime chief justice of Vermont's Supreme Court, local mores and loyalty tend to work against an effective justice system in small towns. In Barney's words, "It's all in the name of protecting the community" (Sitomer 1985). Consequently, the process is sometimes more convenient than constitutional, more community-oriented than concerned with individual rights. In many places, lack of funds, lack of expertise, inadequate knowledge about proper procedures, and even unfamiliarity with constitutional mandates have often resulted in an uneven, unequal, unresponsive judicial process. Defendants who are not part of the community (either socially or geographically) may be at a disadvantage. They want to preserve the peace and their community's traditional values; however, doing so sometimes comes at the expense of minorities, the poor, and those considered "outsiders" (Sitomer 1985; see also, Pruitt 2006).

Citizens of small towns and rural areas beg to differ with their often urban-based critics. They are fearful of trying to impose urban solutions on rural problems. In the context of rural America, discussions of court reform typically center on the justice of the peace.

JUSTICE OF THE PEACE COURTS

In rural areas, the lower courts are collectively called **justice of the peace courts**. The officeholder is usually referred to simply as a **JP**. This system of local justice traces its origins to 14th-century England, when towns were small and isolated. The JP system developed as a way to dispense simple and speedy justice for minor civil and criminal cases. The emphasis was decidedly on the ability of local landowners, who served as part-time JPs, to decide disputes on the basis of their knowledge of the local community.

The small-town flavor of the JP system persists today (even in large urban places such as Harris County, Texas, which includes Houston, and Maricopa County, Arizona, which includes Phoenix). In the past, the vast majority of JPs were part-time nonlawyers who conducted court at their regular place of business—the back of the undertaker's parlor, the front counter of the general store, or next to the grease rack in the garage. Today, however, JPs tend to be more professional and hold court in a courthouse or another government building. Yet, many JPs are not trained lawyers and, as a result, they often fail to abide by the rules that are supposed to bind them (Mansfield 1999).

Many JPs were locally elected officials or mayors of small towns who served ex officio. A common list of qualifications includes the following for the state of Texas:

- U.S. citizenship.
- At least 18 years of age on the first day of the term or date of appointment.
- Not mentally incompetent by a final judgment of a court.
- Not finally convicted of a felony.
- Continual Texas resident for 12 months; precinct resident for 6 months.
- Have no conviction for giving or offering a bribe to procure election or appointment.

(The Office of Justice of the Peace in Texas 2009)

Critics argue that the JP system has outlived its purpose. It may have met the needs of the small, isolated towns of a century ago, but it is out of step with the modern era. Some lower courts administer fair and evenhanded justice, but all too many do not. Efforts at improving the quality of justice dispensed by the rural lower courts focus on abolishing the JP courts and upgrading the quality of the personnel.

ABOLITION OF THE **JP** SYSTEM

The ultimate goal of judicial reformers is to abolish the JP system altogether. A major defect is that JP courts are not part of the state judiciary; they are controlled only by the local government bodies that create them and fund them. Only recently have judicial conduct commissions (see Chapter 8) been granted the authority to discipline or remove local judges who abuse their offices.

Nor are the activities of the lower courts subject to appellate scrutiny. Rarely are trial courts of limited jurisdiction courts of record; no stenographic record is kept of the witnesses' testimony or the judges' rulings. When a defendant appeals, the appeal is heard by a trial court of general jurisdiction. This court must conduct an entirely new trial, taking the testimony of the same witnesses and hearing the same attorneys' arguments as the lower court did. This is called a "**trial de novo.**"

Today, many of the JPs have been replaced with magistrates. Magistrates assume the same kinds of responsibilities as traditional JPs but do not use that title. Magistrates are more likely to be appointed than elected and tend to have better training than JPs. For example, North Carolina has phased out its JPs and replaced them with magistrates who are required to have more education and are appointed by the district court (Neubauer and Meinhold 2010).

Some reformers would unify state courts into a three-tier system, consisting of a single trial court, an intermediate appellate court, and a supreme court (see Chapter 4). This reform would abolish the office of justice of the peace, require all judges to be lawyers, and eliminate the trial de novo system. The biggest change occurred in California, which began phasing out its JPs after a landmark 1974 decision in which the Supreme Court of California unanimously held that it was a violation of federal due process to allow a nonlawyer to preside over a criminal trial that could result in incarceration of the defendant (*Gordon v. Justice Court* 1974). The remaining justice courts (as well as municipal courts) were eliminated by the passage of Proposition 220 in June 1998, which merged all lower courts within the state judicial branch into the superior courts (the courts of general jurisdiction). Under current California law, all California judges must be licensed attorneys. Notably, the U.S. Supreme Court disagreed with California's analysis of the Fourteenth Amendment in the landmark case of *North v. Russell* (1976).

One major obstacle to abolition is the powerful influence of nonlawyer judges, who do not want their jobs abolished. Another is some people's belief that JPs are easily accessible, whereas more formal courts are miles away. For example, JPs are readily available to sign arrest warrants for the police or to try a motorist accused of driving too fast. JP courts are often viewed as people's courts, forums where people without much money can go to resolve their problems without the necessity of having a lawyer.

UPGRADING THE QUALITY OF THE PERSONNEL

Historically, the low pay and equally low status of the JP did not attracted highly qualified personnel. One survey showed that between a third and a half of California's lower-court judges were not even high-school graduates (Ashman and Chapin 1976). Perhaps most shocking of all, the assistant attorney general of Mississippi estimated that "33 percent of the justices of the peace are limited in educational background to the extent that they are not capable of learning the necessary elements of law" (*North v. Russell* 1976). Although some states have moved to upgrade the quality of the personnel, others have not. In the state of New York, 75 percent of the JPs are not lawyers, and over the past three decades over 1,100 have been reprimanded by the Commission on Judicial Conduct. Some are not even high-school graduates. The problems that arise are perhaps best summed up in a quote from a JP who, after threatening to jail a women because her dog was running loose, said: "I just follow my own common sense. And the hell with the law" (Glaberson 2006). And the problems persist. A rural judge has been cited for levying over $11,000 in illegal fines and at least created the appearance he was doing so to provide additional revenue for the city (Gorman 2009).

High on the judicial reformers' list of priorities has been upgrading the quality of lower-court judges, and they have made major strides. Many states have instituted training programs for lay judges. For example, Texas requires all newly selected JPs to attend a training seminar and provides ample opportunities for continuing judicial education. Indeed, most states now require judges of limited jurisdiction courts to have graduated from law school and passed the state bar. In 1987, only 44 percent of these courts required judges to be licensed attorneys, but today the comparable number is 52 percent (Langton 2007). But to many reformers, the ultimate goal remains the elimination of nonlawyer judges (see Case Close-Up: *North v. Russell* and Nonlawyer Judges).

North v. Russell **and Nonlawyer Judges**

The Lynch City Police Court meets every Thursday night, Judge C. B. Russell presiding. Like many others born and raised in the small towns of Kentucky's coal-mining region, Russell dropped out of high school and worked in the coal mines. Later, he was elected judge. During one session, Judge Russell found Lonnie North guilty of drunk driving and sentenced him to 30 days in jail. But Kentucky law allows only a fine for Lonnie North's charge. It seems that the nonlawyer judge had exceeded his legal authority.

On appeal, North's lawyers argued that defendants cannot receive due process of law when the judge is not a lawyer. Chief Justice Warren Burger's majority opinion disagreed, arguing that rural courts, with nonlawyer judges, were convenient to the citizens, providing simple and speedy justice. But critics wonder whether convenient and speedy equate all too often to rough justice.

Judge C. B. Russell made a number of legal errors in the Lynch City Police Court the night he sentenced Lonnie North to jail for drunk driving. Judge Russell refused the defendant's request for a jury trial, did not inform him of his right to a court-appointed lawyer, and failed to advise him of his right to an appeal. Perhaps most glaring of all, Judge Russell listened only to the arresting officer's story and did not allow the defendant to tell his version of events.

The facts of *North v. Russell* (1976) highlight the long-standing issue confronting the American judiciary: Should lower court judges be attorneys? Although judges in the major trial and appellate courts

North v. Russell **and Nonlawyer Judges (continued)**

are required to be lawyers, many states impose no such requirement for lower-court judges. A disproportionate number of these part-time, nonlawyer judges are located in New York and Texas.

The U.S. Supreme Court considered the question of nonlawyer judges in *North v. Russell*. Chief Justice Warren Burger's majority opinion argued that nonlawyer judges do not violate the due process clause of the Fourteenth Amendment, nor do they deny equal protection. He described the JP system as courts of convenience for citizens in small towns and spoke favorably of the fact that "the inferior courts are simple and speedy." Burger argued that any defects in the proceedings (which were numerous in this case) could be corrected by the availability of defense attorneys, the right to a jury trial, and a trial de novo. Significantly, though, these were the specific legal matters that Judge Russell failed to inform defendant North about.

In a dissenting opinion, Justice Potter Stewart stated the case for requiring judges to be lawyers. He found it constitutionally intolerable that nonlawyer judges can sentence defendants to jail. He further noted that a defendant's right to a lawyer is eroded if the judge is not capable of understanding a lawyer's argument on the law. Indeed, a later study found that lay judges in New York tended to be slightly more favorable toward police officers and prosecutors than were legally trained officials (Ryan and Guterman 1977).

Many states are have eliminated nonlawyer judges. The California Supreme Court has ruled that the existence of nonlawyer magistrates violates the state's constitution. Moreover, when states adopt court reorganization, they invariably abolish the nonlawyer JP, although incumbents typically are retained.

Does the elimination of nonlawyer judges alter the decisions reached? After Iowa amended its constitution to require lower-court judges trained in the law, small claims proceedings became more formal, which frightened away the individual civil plaintiffs. Moreover, decisions in small claims increasingly benefited the merchants (Green, Russell, and Schmidhauser 1975). A handful of other studies, however, have found few, if any, differences between the behavior of lay and lawyer judges (Provine 1981). A survey in New York concluded that nonlawyer judges are as competent as lawyer judges in carrying out judicial duties in courts of limited jurisdiction (Provine 1986).

CASE CLOSEUP

MUNICIPAL COURTS

The urban counterparts of the justice of the peace courts are **municipal courts.** Decades ago, the increasing volume of cases in the big cities overwhelmed the ability of the rurally conceived JP system to dispense justice. The forerunner of the municipal court was the police magistrate, who had strong ties to local police departments. Municipal courts were also shaped by political machines, which viewed the lower courts as opportunities for patronage. Party bosses controlled the selection of judges. Similarly, the positions of bailiff and clerk were reserved for the party faithful. It is not surprising that municipal courts were often tainted by corruption. Charges would be dropped, or files would mysteriously disappear, in return for political favors or cash. No wonder the judicial reformers of the 1920s and 1930s sought to clean up the courts by removing them from politics (see Chapter 4).

THE ASSEMBLY LINE

The overriding reality of municipal courts in the nation's big cities: the press of cases. The major concern is moving cases; any "obstacles" to speedy disposition—constitutional rights, lawyers, trials—are neutralized. In a process some have labeled an assembly line, shortcuts are routinely taken to keep the docket moving. Thus, the municipal courts more closely resemble a bureaucracy geared to mass processing of cases than an adjudicative body providing consideration for each case.

The emphasis on moving cases begins when the defendant is arraigned. Instead of addressing defendants individually—a time-consuming process—municipal court judges often open court by advising defendants of their constitutional rights as a group. Notification of rights is treated by the court as a clerical detail to be dispensed with before the taking of guilty pleas can begin.

Defense attorneys constitute another potential obstacle to the speedy disposition of cases. Although defendants have a theoretical right to be represented by an attorney, in practice the presence of an attorney in the lower courts is rare except for drunk driving prosecutions, for which defendants face potentially severe penalties. The general absence of defense attorneys reinforces the informality of the lower courts and the lack of attention to legal rules and procedures.

What of those too poor to hire a lawyer? In *Argersinger v. Hamlin* (1972), the Supreme Court ruled that "absent a knowing and intelligent waiver, no person may be imprisoned for any offense, whether classified as petty, misdemeanor, or felony unless he was represented by counsel." Thus, an indigent defendant may be fined without having a lawyer, but a judge considering imposing a jail term must give the impoverished defendant the opportunity to have a court-appointed counsel at state expense. Compliance, however, has generally been token in nature, meaning that the legal right to counsel in lower courts remains an empty right for many defendants. (See Exhibit 18.2 for key developments in the law concerning the lower courts.)

In municipal courts, the defendant's initial appearance is usually the final one. Most people charged with a traffic violation or minor misdemeanor plead guilty immediately. The quick plea represents the fatalistic view of most defendants: "I did it—let's get it over with." Realistically, a defendant charged with crimes such as public drunkenness and disorderly conduct probably cannot raise a valid legal defense. What has struck all observers of the lower courts is the speed with which the pleas are processed.

Few trials are held in the lower courts. A defendant has a right to a jury trial only if the offense can be punished by imprisonment for more than 6 months (*Baldwin v. New York* 1970). The absence of attorneys and the minor nature of the offenses combine to make requests for jury trials rare. If there is a trial, it is a bench trial often conducted in an informal manner.

THE COURTROOM WORK GROUP

It is no accident that most defendants waive their rights to counsel and trial before quickly entering a plea of guilty. The courtroom work group tries to

---

Exhibit 18.2

KEY DEVELOPMENTS CONCERNING THE LOWER COURTS

Tumey v. Ohio	1927	Paying a justice of the peace a fee only if the defendant is found guilty denies a defendant the right to trial before an impartial judge.
Baldwin v. New York	1970	Defendants have a constitutional right to a trial by jury only if the offense is punishable by imprisonment for more than 6 months.
Tate v. Short	1971	Defendants may not be jailed because they are unable to pay a fine.
Argersinger v. Hamlin	1972	Misdemeanor defendants sentenced to jail have a right to counsel.
North v. Russell	1976	Nonlawyer judges do not violate the rights to due process or equal protection of the U.S. Constitution.

encourage such behavior by controlling the flow of defendants. Some courts manipulate bail to pressure defendants into an immediate disposition. During arraignment, each defendant is informed of the right to a full hearing with a court-appointed attorney. But, if the hearing cannot be held for 2 or 3 weeks, during which time the defendant will have to be in jail, it is not surprising that the majority of defendants choose to waive their right to counsel in favor of a speedy disposition.

Above all, the routines of the lower courts may be threatened by uncooperative defendants. Judges and prosecutors dislike defendants who "talk too much." Those accused who unreasonably take up too much of the court's time can expect sanctions. Consider the case of a young middle-class white man who made a detailed inquiry into his rights and then gave a relatively lengthy account (roughly 2 minutes) of his alleged offense of vagrancy. Although the defendant was polite, the judge interrupted him with "That will be all, Mr. Jones" and ordered him to jail. Other defendants who "talked too much" received sentences that were longer than normal (Mileski 1971; see also, Mack and Anleu 2007).

SENTENCING

In a sense, municipal courts are not trial courts, because few defendants contest their guilt. In actuality, a municipal court is a sentencing institution. The courtroom encounter is geared to making rapid decisions about which sentence to impose. The punishments imposed by lower-court judges include many of those found in the major trial courts—fines, probation, and jail. In the misdemeanor courts, however, judges can choose alternative sanctions, including community service, victim restitution, placement in substance-abuse treatment programs, mandatory counseling, and required attendance in education programs (driver clinics, for example) (Meyer and Jesilow 1997). Despite the diversity of potential sanctions, fines play a predominant role. Few misdemeanor defendants are sentenced to jail.

The sentencing process in the lower courts involves elements of both routinization and individualization. Lower-court judges define their role as "doing justice"; rather than merely being bound by rules of law, judges use their discretion to achieve what they believe to be a fair and just result (Meyer and Jesilow 1997). In attempting to achieve justice, lower-court judges use readily identifiable characteristics to sort defendants into categories. In the lower courts, sentencing involves a process of quickly determining group averages. The result is a high degree of uniformity; by and large, a defendant gets the same sentence as all others in the same category. To the casual observer, the process appears to be an assembly line, but sentences can also be fitted to the specific defendant. During plea negotiations, there is some individual attention to cases. Despite sentencing consistencies, exceptions are made (Ragona and Ryan 1983). The most important factors in both the routinization and the individualization of sentencing in the lower courts are the nature of the event and the defendant's criminal record.

A key factor in sentencing is the defendant's prior criminal record. First offenders rarely receive a jail term. Indeed, for petty offenses, first offenders may be released without any penalty whatsoever. Repeaters are given more severe sanctions. For example, the jailing of defendants for public intoxication increases strikingly as prior arrests become more numerous and more recent. The importance of a prior criminal record in sentencing partially explains an otherwise unaccountable pattern: Serious misdemeanants are fined, while minor misdemeanants are jailed. The explanation is that few of the serious misdemeanor defendants had prior records, whereas more of the minor misdemeanor defendants did (Mileski 1971).

A study of drunk driving dispositions in Sacramento, California, highlights the importance of prior record and the nature of the event (Kingsnorth, Barnes, and Coonley 1990). For defendants with no prior convictions, the likelihood of a charge reduction to reckless driving increased three to four times. Similarly, the probability of receiving a jail sentence increased dramatically for those with a prior record. The nature of the event (measured by the level of blood alcohol) also played a role. A low level of blood alcohol was of primary importance in the decision to reduce charges from drunk driving to reckless driving. Similarly, defendants with a high level of alcohol in their systems were much more likely not only to receive a jail sentence but also a lengthy jail term. These two factors, of course, operate together. Defendants with no priors and low levels of blood alcohol fared much better than those with prior convictions and high levels of alcohol in their system. Studies like this one, however, rarely enter the public discourse. (See Courts, Controversy, and Reducing Crime: Should Drunk Driving Prosecutions Be Increased?)

BROKEN WINDOWS THEORY AND THE LOWER COURTS

Broken windows is one of the most hotly debated policing theories in the nation. First developed by James Q. Wilson and George Kelling (1982) it has been championed by a number of police departments in cities across the nation, including Los Angeles and New York (Gau and Pratt 2008). Broken windows theory focuses on social disorder and argues that when police pay attention to minor offenses, such as panhandling, graffiti, prostitution, and loitering, more serious crimes will decrease as a consequence. Today, broken windows theory is referred to as "order-maintenance policing" and associated with "zero tolerance" policing policies. The theory holds that if you fix the broken windows (minor social disorder) you will reduce serious crimes. To its critics, the broken windows theory defines social disorder way too broadly (Kubrin 2008) and does not reduce crime. Whatever the merits of the theory, police departments that adopt this approach will generate more arrests for minor crimes, producing greater workload. Two classic studies, combined with contemporary research, suggest that increasing arrests for minor disorder will be treated differently by different courts.

To Malcolm Feeley (1979), *the process is the punishment*. This finding is based on several years of studying the lower court in New Haven, Connecticut, firsthand. The main punishment of defendants occurs during the processing of cases, not after a finding of guilt. Feeley contends that the pretrial process imposes a series of punishments ("price tags") on the accused. These price tags often include staying in jail (briefly), paying a bail agent, and losing time from work and perhaps wages because of repeated court appearances. These costs far outweigh any punishment imposed after the defendant pleads guilty. These price tags also affect the roughly 40 percent of the defendants eventually found not guilty. In short, the pretrial process itself is the primary punishment, according to Feeley.

To John Paul Ryan, *the outcome is the punishment*. This contrasting finding is based on statistical analysis of actual court sentences in Columbus, Ohio. Unlike those in New Haven, lower-court judges in

Columbus routinely impose fines on convicted defendants. Often these fines are substantial. Further, 35 percent of the guilty in Columbus are sentenced to jail—six times as many as in New Haven. Finally, defendants in traffic cases often have their driver's licenses suspended, are ordered to attend drunk driver schools, or both. In short, Columbus defendants are more likely to be fined, to pay heavier fines, to go to jail, and to be required to participate in some sort of treatment program than their counterparts in New Haven.

A study of the race/ethnicity disparity in misdemeanor marijuana arrests in New York City seems to suggest that the process is indeed the punishment. As part of its strategy of aggressively addressing minor social disorder, the New York Police Department has vigorously enforced the prohibition on smoking marijuana in public. Indeed, 15 percent of all arrests by the NYPD are for this offense. But what happens after the arrest? The arrestees spend 16 to 36 hours in custody before appearing in court, where 99.7 percent receive the minimum sentence of zero days imprisonment. In short, these suspects do their jail time up front, which is consistent with Feeley's study. The authors of the study are clearly concerned that the enforcement of the misdemeanor marijuana law falls most heavily on Hispanic defendants (Golub, Johnson, and Dunlap 2007). And some debate whether this practice actually reduces crime (Harcourt and Ludwig 2007). The study of New York seems to suggest that order-maintenance policing will have its greatest impact in cities where there is minimal disorder and, therefore, court officials treat that disorder seriously; in contrast, such policing efforts may have less impact in cities in which disorder is so common that court officials focus on more serious offenses out of practical necessity.

COURT–COMMUNITY COLLABORATION

Since the 1960s, court reform efforts have consolidated the diverse minor courts into more centralized units. These reforms have had unintended consequences, however. Court activities have been consolidated and streamlined for good reasons, but in the process, some of the qualities of locally dispensed justice have been lost. As a result, court reformers continuously seek ways to reestablish court–community cooperation.

COURTS, CONTROVERSY, AND REDUCING CRIME

Should Drunk Driving Prosecutions Be Increased?

Drinking and driving has been a problem since the invention of the automobile, but did not gain recognition as a prominent social concern until the 1980s (Applegate et al. 1996). The group most responsible for focusing public attention on drunk driving is Mothers Against Drunk Driving (MADD). Depending on the state, drunk driving is termed "driving under the influence" (DUI) or "driving while intoxicated" (DWI).

MADD is not neo-Prohibitionist, recognizing that trying to eliminate alcohol would hamper the organization's ability to recruit members. Rather, MADD is victim-oriented, with many leaders having themselves experienced a family death due to drunk driving. They are closely related to the victims' rights movement (see Chapter 9). Publicly they are recognized as the leading proponents of increasing the criminal penalties for drunk driving. The almost sole emphasis on enforcement and punishment differs from other approaches, which stress prevention of early alcohol use and treatment of alcohol dependence as better approaches to prevent drug- and alcohol-related crashed (Hingson, Heeren, and Edwards 2008).

For almost three decades, legislatures—under considerable pressure from MADD and other groups like it—have passed a variety of "get tough with drunk drivers" laws, including

● Increasing the drinking age to 21
● Lowering from .15 to .08 the blood alcohol content (BAC) level at which a person is presumed legally intoxicated
● Increasing jail penalties for DWI, particularly for repeat offenders

● Mandating that drivers who refuse to take a breathalyzer test will automatically lose their driver's license.

But somehow the get-tough laws recently passed never seem to be harsh enough, so in subsequent years legislatures are called upon to crack down even harder on drunk drivers. And when the threats of even more arrests and harsher punishments don't seem to be working, the agenda is shifted to technology—mandating that even first offenders be required to install a device that tests drivers and shuts down the car if it detects alcohol (MADD 2009; Wald 2006). Evolving legislative agendas are crucial for organizations like MADD because they need to constantly motivate their constituents lest the organization lose momentum and also lose members.

To sociologist Joseph Gusfield, groups like MADD engage in symbolic politics, portraying drunk drivers as villains. The difficulty with this approach is that DWI arrestees reflect a range of social backgrounds, including ordinary citizens and at times even prominent members of the community. Moreover, the range of behavior varies greatly from a person barely at .08 and having caused no accident to those measuring near .30 (comatose for most people) who have killed several people. This analysis of MADD is reinforced by the organization's recent efforts to even discuss lowering the legal drinking age. MADD has long cast underage drinking in black-and–white terms, whereas many college officials see it as impossible gray. Raising the legal drinking age has not stopped student drinking, only displacing it, driving such activity off

The central target of these community justice efforts is minor disputes between parties in ongoing relationships (domestic partners, neighbors, consumers–merchants, landlords–tenants, employees–employers). Examples include unruly children who annoy neighbors, dogs who defecate on the wrong lawns, owners who neglect their property, and acquaintances who dispute small debts. It is not clear what role the criminal justice system can play in resolving such private disputes. Yet private disagreements between friends, neighbors, or significant others are the steady diet of the police and the lower courts. A

campus and behind doors, making it even more difficult to deal with (Hoover 2008).

The absence of criminal stereotypes is compounded by the pervasive role of alcoholic beverages in American social and economic life. As a result, there is considerable societal ambivalence toward drinking and driving (Homel 1988). Society is quick to condemn drunk drivers involved in serious accidents, but those who drive after a few drinks often evoke the attitude of "There but for the grace of God go I" (Gusfield 1981).

The contradictions in societal attitudes toward drinking and driving (which is different from drunk driving) explain why the enforcement of drunk driving laws is riddled with loopholes. These contradictions help us understand why actual enforcement of drunk driving laws blunts the cutting edge of the harsh penalties. Law on the books treats driving and drinking as a serious problem, but law in action sees drunk driving not as a criminal offense but as a traffic violation. The end product is not a series of absolutes propounded by MADD but a negotiated reality (Homel 1988). With the imposition of tougher laws:

- Police do not necessarily make more arrests. Faced with serious crime problems, big-city police forces assign higher priority to violent offenders than to drunk drivers (Mastrofski and Ritti 1996).
- Prosecutors are pressured to plea-bargain. Given that local jails are already overcrowded and most defendants are not as villainous as public images suggest, pleas to lesser charges such as reckless driving are often arranged.
- Juries are reluctant to convict. As discussed in Chapter 14, if jurors think the penalty is too harsh for the crime, they are less likely to convict.

- As more people go to jail for longer following DUI convictions, the prisons become overcrowded, which necessitates shortening actual sentences (Vermont Center for Justice Research 1995).
- Those who lose their license may continue to drive, and those previously convicted may continue to drive drunk. Indeed, one survey found that more than half the persons in local jails charged with DWI had prior sentences for DWI offenses (Cohen 1992).

Overall, studies of drunk driving laws tend to be skeptical of a deterrent effect of get-tough legislation (Fradella 2000). Typically, new, tougher laws are ushered in with announcements of a major crackdown followed by increased arrests for DWI. But over time, levels of drinking and driving return to previous levels as the perceived certainty of punishment declines with experience (Homel 1988; Ross 1992). For example, one study found "no evidence that lowering the BAC to .08 reduced fatality rates but other approaches like seat belt laws have been effective (Freeman 2007).

What works and what doesn't in reducing drunk driving fatalities is now being applied to a major new highway safety threat—texting while driving (Lowy 2009).

What do you think? Should there be tougher punishments for drunk driving, or are current punishment levels about right? Should more efforts be made to arrest and prosecute drunk drivers, or is the current level of effort about right? Overall, how do punishment and enforcement levels of drunk driving compare with other social problems, such as domestic violence and drug abuse?

---

trial would only obscure the underlying issues because the problem is either irrelevant or immaterial to the legal action. In such interpersonal disputes, the person who files a complaint may be as "guilty" as the defendant. Many of these private disputes are essentially civil matters, yet criminal justice agencies

must deal with them to head off the commission of a more serious crime—murder or battery, for example. In addressing problems such as these, mediation programs seek solutions not in terms of a formal finding by a judge but through compromise and bargaining. The goal is to seek long-term solutions in hopes the disputants will not return. The two most commonly mentioned types of programs are alternative dispute resolution and community courts.

ALTERNATIVE DISPUTE RESOLUTION

Efforts at court–community collaboration are but one example of a broader movement termed **alternative dispute resolution (ADR),** which seeks to settle disputes by less adversarial means than traditional legal processes (Goldberg et al. 2007; Nolan-Haley 2008). Many ADR programs function as alternatives to going to court. Others involve efforts to settle court cases after they have been filed but before they are tried by a judge. ADR efforts most often focus on civil matters, but nonserious criminal matters may also be included.

Alternatives to the formal judicial processes, of course, are hardly new. Juvenile courts, small claims courts, and family courts are a few examples of long-standing activities that were established because it was felt they would be more effective than traditional court operations. Today, drug courts and community courts have joined the list (see Chapter 4). In recent years, however, there has been a new wave of concern about court congestion and cost, and a new set of alternatives has appeared in response. Indeed, the rapid growth of ADR programs has produced a second-generation wave of reforms aimed at improving the qualifications of those who serve in these programs (Brown 2005; Pou 2005).

COMMUNITY COURTS

Courts across the nation are searching for ways to reach out in order to be more responsive to the needs of specific communities within their geographical jurisdiction. The phrase "justice community" refers to the range of organizations and people within any specific locale who have a stake in the justice system. It includes judges, court personnel, district attorneys, public defenders, private attorneys, probation departments, law enforcement personnel, community organizers, business groups, and others (Borys, Banks, and Parker 1999; Williams 2007).

Often these outreach efforts lead to an emphasis on mediation of minor disputes. There are important organizational differences, though, between court-based mediation and community courts.

Community courts, or community mediation programs, as they have sometimes been called, are government sponsored (by either court or prosecutor) and as

a result, these programs receive the bulk of their cases as referrals from criminal justice agencies. The dominant goal is to improve the justice system by removing minor cases from the court. In their view, cases such as simple assault, petty theft, and criminal trespass are prime candidates for mediation and not formal processing in the lower courts.

Initially, what today are called "community courts" were termed "criminal justice-based mediation programs," also known as "multidoor courthouses" or "neighborhood justice centers." Many of these dispute-resolution programs began with a primary emphasis on misdemeanor criminal cases and later added civil matters from the local small claims court and other sources. In a sense, they convert criminal matters to civil ones by treating the cases as matters for discussion between the individual disputants and not for processing between the state and the defendant.

The best-known community court in the nation is the Midtown Community Court in New York City. The Midtown experience was born of a profound frustration with quality-of-life crime in the neighborhood, particularly prostitution, graffiti, illegal vending, vandalism, and low-level drug offenses (Center for Court Innovation 2009). Offenders are sentenced to make restitution to the community through work projects in the neighborhood: removing graffiti, cleaning subway stations, and sorting cans and bottles for recycling. But at the same time the court attempts to link offenders with drug treatment, health care, education, and other social services. Perhaps one of the most distinctive features is that the courthouse includes an entire floor of office space for social workers to assist offenders referred by the judge in the courtroom a few floors below. Thus, instead of sending an offender to a distant bureaucracy, the courthouse now incorporates helping institutions within its midst. The Midtown Community Court is serving as a prototype for other jurisdictions as well (Clear and Cadora 2003).

CONCLUSION

North v. Russell is a reminder that one out of four Americans gets their justice off the main road. Here, they often find that justice is dispensed by part-time, nonlawyer justices of the peace who may or may not have much training in the law. Moreover, the justice officials are not only few in number but also are bound by long-term social relationships. Thus, compared to their big-city brethren, citizens in rural courthouses experience justice that is convenient and informal, but critics wonder if a little more of the Constitution might better serve outsiders.

The problems of the lower courts in urban areas are fundamentally different from those of rural courts. Courthouse officials are numerous and often knowledgeable about their tasks. Moreover, although the relationships are cordial, it is obvious that the courtroom is merely a place where representatives of many bureaucracies meet to do their work. Thus, compared to their brethren in more rural settings, citizens in municipal court experience justice that is quick and in many ways certain; sentences are arrived at by applying the group average. Critics argue that the process all too often resembles an assembly line geared to rapid dispositions, and the process is the punishment.

Whether lower courts are found in small towns or big cities, they share an important denominator: For most Americans, their only firsthand experience with real courtroom justice (as opposed to the courthouse justice they see on TV or read about in newspapers) will be the brief encounter before a lower-court judge. The lower courts come into contact with more citizens every year than virtually any other government institution. All too often, the average citizen comes away from such encounters with a poor impression, pondering whether the judge was really interested in justice or was merely in a hurry to feed the cash register.

The cases processed by the lower courts are indeed minor and have often been referred to as petty. The legal problems of drunks and drunk drivers, vagrants and vagabonds, used to be dismissed as of no interest, something for beat cops and low-level judges to deal with, but certainly not important enough for the real criminal justice system to be concerned about. Until fairly recently, judicial reformers boldly suggested that these cases should not even be in court. No longer. These cases are increasingly important to the public and, therefore, are now important to criminal justice officials as well. As discussed in Chapter 9, spousal abuse is the subject of serious debate, and no elected official dares dismiss these events as petty. The same holds true for drunk driving, which has catapulted to center stage in national attention. Moreover, some scholars and police officials see confronting minor crimes as an important way to reduce crime, arguing that cracking down on drunks and punks, thereby allowing good citizens to reclaim their community, will reduce major crimes.

CHAPTER REVIEW

1. Identify the three types of cases that the lower courts hear.

The lower courts hear the preliminary stages of felony cases, dispose of nonfelony criminal cases (which include misdemeanors, ordinances, and traffic offenses) and handle civil cases, primarily small claims cases.

2. List the four problems confronting the lower courts in the United States.

The four major problems confronting the lower courts are inadequate financing, inadequate facilities, lax court procedures, and unbalanced caseloads.

3. Discuss the similarities and differences between justice of the peace courts and municipal courts.

Both justice of the peace (JP) courts and municipal courts are considered lower courts. They differ primarily in terms of caseloads. The rurally based JP courts have relatively low caseloads, whereas the urban-based municipal courts have very large caseloads.

4. Explain why the Supreme Court's opinion in *North v. Russell* is important.

North v. Russell is important because it is one of the few times that the U.S. Supreme Court has ruled on procedures in the lower courts. The Court held that the Fourteenth Amendment to the Constitution does not require lower-court judges to be lawyers, but many states had adopted the opposite policy.

5. Describe the sentencing process in the municipal courts.

Sentencing in municipal courts involves elements of routinization and individualization. *Routinization* refers to the going rate for the given offense. *Individualization* occurs when the courtroom work group needs to adjust this going rate to an unusual aspect of the specific case.

6. Analyze the political and social factors affecting drunk-driving law enforcement in the United States.

The group most responsible for changing drunk-driving law enforcement in the United States is Mother's Against Drunk Driving (MADD), which favors lowering the legal blood alcohol content and imposing severe penalties on those convicted.

These laws are rarely fully enforced, however, because consumption of alcohol is relatively common in the United States and criminal justice officials often focus resources on more serious offenses.

7. Name the two major efforts toward court-community collaboration.

Alternative Dispute Resolution (ADR) is a major example of court-community efforts; it seeks to settle disputes without going to court. Community courts seek ways to be more responsive to specific communities and convert minor criminal offenses into civil matters.

CRITICAL THINKING QUESTIONS

1. The justice of the peace system provides quick and convenient access to the courts, but does it cheapen the notion of justice? Or are the critics off-base, seemingly suggesting that every speeding motorist deserves a high-priced lawyer to defend his or her actions?

2. To some, the shorthand used in the lower courts best achieves justice because sentences tend to be uniform. To others, relying on group averages violates a defendant's right to have his or her case considered on its own merits. What do you think?

3. Are the lower courts really courts? With few defense attorneys and even fewer trials, maybe we should label activities in lower courts as hearings, not trials. What are your views on this?

4. Each legislative session, laws are passed getting tougher with drunk drivers. How long do you think this trend will continue?

5. The municipal court studied by Meyer and Jesilow (1997) processed relatively few traditional misdemeanors—assaults and thefts, for example. Instead, much of the court's time was taken up with people who had committed many "victimless crimes," such as vagrancy, public drunkenness, drug use, and prostitution. Do these cases belong in the courts? Would society be better served by handling many of these types of cases in social institutions?

KEY TERMS

alternative dispute resolution (ADR)   492
inferior court   474
justice of the peace (JP)   484
lower court   474
misdemeanor   475
municipal court   486
ordinance   475
small claims court   477
traffic offenses   475
trial courts of limited jurisdiction   474

WEB RESOURCES

Go to the America's Courts and the Criminal Justice System companion website at

www.cengage.com/criminaljustice/neubauer

where you will find more resources to help you study.
Resources include web exercises, quizzing, and flash cards.

FOR FURTHER READING

Chermak, Steven, Edmund McGarrell, and Alexander Weiss. "Citizens' Perceptions of Aggressive Traffic Enforcement Strategies." *Justice Quarterly* 18: 365–391, 2001.

Clear, Todd, and Eric Cadora. *Community Justice.* Belmont, CA: Wadsworth, 2003.

Crow, Matthew, Richard Hough, Jason Mosley, John Smykla, and Kimberly Tatum. "Drunk and Alone in a K-Mart Parking Lot: The Pedagogy of Simulations and Contemporary Attitudes toward Drinking and Driving." *Journal of Criminal Justice Education* 19: 417–431, 2008.

Fell, James, Deborah Fisher, Robert Voas, Kenneth Blackman, and Scott Tippetts. "The Impact of Underage Drinking Laws on Alcohol-Related Fatal Crashes of Young Drivers." *Alcoholism, Clinical, and Experimental Research.* 33: 1208–1219, 2009.

Hedeen, Timothy. "Coercion and Self-Determination in Court-Connected Mediation: All Mediations Are Voluntary, But Some Are More Voluntary Than Others." *Justice System Journal* 26: 273–291, 2005.

Katz, Charles, Vincent Webb, and David Schaefer. "An Assessment of the Impact of Quality-of-Life Policing on Crime and Disorder." *Justice Quarterly* 18: 825–876, 2001.

Kelling, George, and Catherine Coles. *Fixing Broken Windows: Restoring Order and Reducing Crime in Our Communities.* New York: Martin Kessler, 1997.

Newaz, Daphne. "The Impaired Dual System Framework of United States Drunk-Driving Law: How International Perspectives Can Yield More Sober Results." *Houston Journal of International Law* 28: 531–573, 2006.

Richardson, Lilliard, and David Houston. "Federalism and Safety on America's Highways." *Publius* 39: 117–138, 2009.

Scott, Michael, Nina Emerson, Louis Antonacci, and Joel Plant. *Drunk Driving: Problem-Oriented Guides for Police Problem-Specific Guides Series Guide No. 36.* Washington, DC: U.S. Department of Justice, Office of Community Oriented Policing, 2006.

Warren, Patricia, Donald Tomaskovic-Devey, William Smith, Matthew Zingraff, and Marcinda Mason. "Driving While Black: Bias Process and Racial Disparity in Police Stops." *Criminology* 44: 709–738, 2006.

Wissler, Roselle, and Bob Dauber. "Leading Horses to Water: The Impact of an ADR 'Confer and Report' Rule." *Justice System Journal* 26: 253–272, 2005.

19 JUVENILE COURTS

© Shelley Gazin/CORBIS

A lawyer meets with her young client in a juvenile detention facility. The bleakness of the wire divider suggests not just a physical separation (perhaps he is a violent offender), but also a societal separation. Juvenile courts were created about 100 years ago to separate youthful from adult offenders, but some argue that the current juvenile justice system does not deal effectively with contemporary problems.

Chapter Outline

LEARNING OBJECTIVES

After reading this chapter, you should be able to:

1. Describe the child-saving movement and its relationship to the doctrine of *parens patriae*.

2. List the five ways in which juvenile courts differ from adult courts.

3. Discuss how states vary in terms of when a juvenile may be transferred to adult court for prosecution.

4. Contrast the three major types of cases that are heard in juvenile court.

5. Identify and briefly describe the single most important Supreme Court case with respect to juvenile justice.

6. Explain the difference between a juvenile case that is petitioned and one that is nonpetitioned.

7. Compare and contrast how adherents of the crime control model and proponents of the due process model of criminal justice see the future of juvenile courts.

GERALD GAULT was charged with making a lewd phone call. If he had been an adult, the maximum sentence was on the lenient side—a fine of $50 and 2 months in jail. But because he was 15 years old, the sentence was potentially much stiffer—up to 6 years in the state industrial school. These substantive differences mirrored important procedural contrasts as well. If he had been an adult, Gerald Gault would have had the right to confront the witness making the accusation and also the right to have a lawyer present. But because he was a juvenile, none of these basic legal protections applied.

In re Gault highlights the duality of juvenile court, which is part court of law and part social welfare agency. It sometimes operates formally, but more often its procedures are informal. These contrasts produce a series of contradictions, which are highlighted in the words of a former judge of the Denver Juvenile Court:

> It is law, and it is social work; it is control, and it is help; it is the good parent and, also, the stern parent; it is both formal and informal. It is concerned not only with the delinquent, but also with the battered child, the runaway, and many others. . . . The juvenile court has been all things to all people. (Rubin 1989, pp. 79–80)

The historic mandate of juvenile court was to rescue children from a criminal life by providing the care and protection normally afforded by the natural parents. Thus, helping a child was far more important than protecting constitutional rights. But in certain instances, helpful benevolence has been replaced by harsh punishments.

In deciding *In re Gault*, the Supreme Court confronted the difficult task of determining the relationship between the social welfare functions of juvenile court and basic due process so important to the American court system. The best starting point in unraveling these dualities is an examination of the past 100 years of juvenile court.

JUVENILE COURTS 100 YEARS AGO

Juvenile courts are a distinctly 20th-century development. The major economic and social changes of the late 19th century prompted a rethinking of the role of youth. The result was the creation of specialized courts to deal with what were thought to be distinctly youth-oriented problems. Many of the issues that arose 100 years ago remain with us today, shaping the thinking that will affect juvenile courts for the next 100 years.

INDUSTRIALIZATION, CITIES, AND CRIME

By the last third of the 19th century, the United States was well on its way to becoming the world's greatest industrial nation. What had once been a nation of small farmers was rapidly becoming a nation of city dwellers. The factories were located in the cities, and the workers for these factories were partially drawn from those who wished to escape the hard work of farming. But most of the new jobs were filled by immigrants from foreign lands who sought freedom from political oppression or economic want in their home countries. The result was a tremendous growth in cities. Indeed, the population of the nation almost doubled, growing from 40 million in 1870 to 76 million in 1900.

America's emerging big cities were truly diverse. The residents spoke different languages, ate strange foods, dressed differently, and worshiped in a variety of churches. The white Anglo-Saxon Protestants who controlled the institutions of the United States at the time did not extend a cordial welcome to these new immigrants. On the contrary, the immigrant urban masses were associated with the poverty, social disorder, and crime of the emerging big cities. Protecting society from the "dangerous poor" became a pressing social concern.

Then, as now, there was confusion over what was poverty and what was crime.

THE CHILD SAVERS AND THE PROGRESSIVE MOVEMENT

Beginning around 1890, members of the Progressive movement advocated a variety of political, economic, and social reforms. They were genuinely concerned about the economic disparities, social disorders, and excesses of industrialization, particularly as they affected children.

Progressives denounced the evils of child labor and pushed for legislation banning the practice. They were likewise appalled by the violent and exploitive conditions of reform schools. The fact that orphans were thrown into reform schools for the uncontrollable circumstance of having no parents shocked the Progressives' moral values. Taking up the plight of the children of the urban immigrant poor, they argued that these children were not bad, but were corrupted by the environment in which they grew up.

The Progressives' concern for the plight of the urban masses was also motivated by self-interest. They were largely middle class, and their position in society was threatened by the growth of a competing urban class composed of the poor and the working poor. These Anglo-Saxon Protestants found the culture of the Southern European Catholics shocking. Anthony Platt's (1969) classic study, *The Child Savers*, notes the types of behavior the Progressives sought to punish—drinking, fighting, begging, frequenting dance halls, staying out late at night, and sexual license. Within a generation, many of the social forces unleashed by the Progressive movement would lead to Prohibition, which was directed squarely at the growing political power of big-city Catholic immigrants, whose power base was the neighborhood tavern.

Thus, from its origins, the juvenile court movement reflected class distinctions: The children of the poor were processed through the system, but those of the more well-to-do were handled informally. These class differences would mark juvenile court activities throughout the century.

Then, as now, there was confusion over what was genuine social concern and what was self-serving class interest.

PARENS PATRIAE

The Progressives' efforts to save the children of the urban masses reflected a major shift in thinking about children. Historically, children had been viewed as miniature adults. Children under the age of 7 were presumed to be incapable of criminal intent and were therefore exempt from prosecution. Those 8 and older were considered adults in the eyes of the law, prosecuted as adults, convicted as adults, and served their sentences in the same prison cells as adults.

By the end of the 19th century, the notion of children as miniature adults was giving way to a very different conceptualization—children as persons with less than fully developed moral and cognitive capacities. This shift in thinking was reflected in the emerging legal doctrine of *parens patriae* (state as parent). No longer were parents considered to have sole and exclusive legal responsibility over their children. If the parents failed in their responsibility to raise a child properly, the state could intervene to protect children's welfare. This doctrine also meant that in extreme circumstances parents' rights over their children could be terminated altogether.

Then, as now, there was confusion over the right of parents to raise their children in their own image and the need of the state to limit social disorder.

How Juvenile Courts Differ from Adult Courts

The juvenile court is a continuing legacy of the Progressive movement. Not content to tinker with existing procedures, the Progressives insisted on a radical departure from past practices. Adopting the legal doctrine of *parens patriae* resulted in juvenile judicial proceedings that differed greatly from those used in adult courts.

The unique legal dimensions of **juvenile court** are reflected in the legal terms used. Whereas adults are arrested, tried, and sentenced to prison, juveniles are summoned, have a hearing, and are committed to residential placement. Juvenile courts differ from adult courts in five important ways: They emphasize helping the child, they are informal, they are based on civil law, they are secret, and they rarely involve a jury.

Emphasis on Helping the Child

Prosecution of adults at the turn of the 20th century sought to achieve punishment. By contrast, the newly created juvenile courts emphasized helping the child. Benevolence and rehabilitation, not punishment, were of paramount importance.

The doctrine of *parens patriae* became the underlying philosophy of juvenile court; the state should deal with a child who broke the law much as a wise parent would deal with a wayward child. The Progressives sought to use the power of the state to save children from a life of crime. Juvenile courts would provide flexible procedures for the treatment of the underlying social problems that were seen as the basis of juvenile crime. Guidance would be the norm.

Informal Proceedings

Criminal prosecutions involving adults are formal and adversarial in nature. By contrast, juvenile court proceedings emphasize informality. Although key elements of due process have been integrated into juvenile court in recent years, juvenile proceedings nonetheless retain their informal nature. As a result, rules of evidence and rules of procedure, so important in adult criminal courts, have little relevance in juvenile proceedings.

Flowing from the premise that juvenile courts are meant to help the child, the creators of juvenile court viewed procedural safeguards not only as unnecessary, but also as harmful. The concern was that a legal technicality might allow a child to avoid getting help (Sanborn 1993). In essence, the substance of the decision (helping the child) was more important than the procedures used to reach that decision.

Proceedings Based on Civil Law

Prosecutions of adults are based on the criminal law (see Chapter 2). By contrast, juvenile court proceedings are based on the civil law (see Chapter 2). This is why the legal terminology used in adult and juvenile courts differs so greatly. The terms *summons* and *commitment*, for example, are borrowed directly from civil practice.

Using civil rather than criminal law reinforced the key notion that juvenile courts were intended to rehabilitate, not punish. It is for this reason, for example, that a child's juvenile court record is not admissible in adult court. Regardless of the frequency or severity of the offenses committed by a juvenile, once he or she becomes an adult in the eyes of the criminal law, the person starts over with no prior record.

Over the years, the Supreme Court, state courts, and legislatures have added some procedural due process features of adult courts to juvenile proceedings. And, over the years, both punishment and protection of the community have joined rehabilitation as objectives of juvenile delinquency proceedings. Thus, today it is probably best to view juvenile proceedings as quasi-criminal—a blend of civil and criminal law quite different from the original ideals of the early juvenile courts (Moriearty 2008).

SECRET PROCEEDINGS

Criminal proceedings involving adults are open to the public (except grand jury proceedings, and, on the rarest of rare occasions, jury selection in ultra-sensitive cases). By contrast, juvenile court proceedings have historically been secret. This means that crime victims who are interested in what happens in their case, or ordinary citizens who are simply curious about what goes on in the courthouse, may freely attend sessions involving adults but not those involving juveniles. In most jurisdictions, it is illegal for law enforcement personnel or juvenile court officials to release the names of juveniles to the media. Moreover, even if the media are able to find out the names, journalistic ethics prohibit that information from being printed or broadcast.

The secrecy of juvenile proceedings is changing in some jurisdictions. Currently, 14 states open delinquency hearings to the general public, and 21 others have passed statutes that open such hearings for certain types of cases. However, judges often retain the authority to close hearings at their discretion (Snyder and Sickmund 2006).

To its supporters, the secrecy of juvenile court proceedings is essential in meeting the key goal of working with children in trouble to prevent future criminal behavior. To critics, this secrecy merely reinforces the informality of the process and prevents much-needed public scrutiny.

ABSENCE OF JURY TRIALS

Adults accused of violating the criminal law have the right to a trial by a jury of their peers. By contrast, juveniles have no such constitutional right. To be sure, a few states have created, often by statute, an extremely limited right to a trial by jury in some matters concerning juveniles. Nonetheless, the central point is clear: Whereas the possibility of a jury trial structures the disposition of adult offenders, the likelihood of a jury trial almost never enters into the discussion in juvenile court.

The absence of jury trials reinforces the informal nature of the proceedings. It also strengthens the control of juvenile court personnel—both judges

and probation officers. In adult courts, the views of ordinary citizens may prove to differ from those of judge or prosecutor, but there is no such possibility in juvenile court.

THE ORGANIZATION OF JUVENILE COURTS

Today, all states have juvenile courts, but their organizational relationship to other judicial bodies varies greatly. In some ways the term *juvenile court* is a misnomer. Only a few states have created juvenile courts that are completely separate from other judicial bodies.

As Chapter 4 emphasized, important variations exist in state court organization. Nowhere is this diversity more apparent than in the organization of juvenile courts. Along a continuum from the most to the least distinctive, juvenile courts are organized in one of three ways: a separate court, part of family court, or a unit of the trial court.

JUVENILE COURT AS A SEPARATE COURT

In a few jurisdictions, juvenile court is completely separate from other judicial bodies. This is the case in the states of Connecticut, Rhode Island, and Utah. A juvenile court as a separate statewide entity means that it has its own administration, judges, probation officers, clerks of court, and other employees. Stated another way, matters concerning juveniles are its exclusive jurisdiction. A few large cities, such as Boston and Denver, also separate juvenile courts from other judicial bodies.

JUVENILE COURT AS PART OF FAMILY COURT

A second organizational arrangement is for juvenile court to be a part of family court, which has broad responsibility over family matters. One major type of case is divorce and related issues, including child custody, child support, alimony, and property settlement. In addition, jurisdiction of family courts encompasses paternity matters and adoption of children. Most important for our purposes, family-court jurisdiction also typically includes matters concerning juveniles (delinquency, status offenses, and child-victim cases).

Six states and the District of Columbia have authorized family courts on a statewide basis. In

Delaware, New York, Rhode Island, and South Carolina, family courts are separately organized. In the District of Columbia, Hawaii, and New Jersey, family courts are a separate division of the trial court of general jurisdiction.

JUVENILE COURT AS A UNIT OF TRIAL COURT

The third place that juvenile courts are housed organizationally is as part of a trial court. Typically, juvenile court is part of the jurisdiction of the major trial court, but on occasion it is in the minor trial court.

Beyond the legal considerations of jurisdiction, the question of where matters concerning juveniles are heard is largely a function of case volume. In rural areas with few cases, they most often are a type of case on the judge's calendar much like tort and contract. But most areas have sufficient cases to justify one or more judges who devote themselves full-time to matters concerning juveniles. This specialization is dictated partly by case volume, but also by the requirement that juvenile proceedings be conducted in secret. Administratively, therefore, a separate section of court (sometimes in a different courthouse) makes it easier to keep juvenile proceedings closed to the public.

LAW IN ACTION: THE IMPACT OF STRUCTURE

Since juvenile courts were first established, there has been a debate over the appropriate place in the judicial hierarchy for this new judicial body. Where a state ended up placing its juvenile court was largely determined by broader debates over court organization.

Court reformers recommend that juvenile court be part of family court. But whether this structural arrangement results in "better" justice is, at best, hard to document. There is some evidence, for example, that the more the judge is a juvenile court specialist, the more likely the judge will handle cases informally rather than conduct a full hearing (Sosin 1978). Similarly, specialists are less likely to find a youth to be a delinquent (Johnson and Secret 1995). The structural differences, however, appear to be far less important than the social environment in which the juvenile court operates; juvenile courts in big cities march to a different drummer than those in rural or suburban areas (Sanborn 1994).

JUVENILE COURT JURISDICTION: AGE

For adults, court jurisdiction is largely determined by the nature of the criminal offense. For **juveniles**, on the other hand, jurisdiction is normally determined by their age. Different states provide complex sets of criteria relating to the **upper age of jurisdiction**, when a child becomes an adult (at least in the eyes of the criminal law), as well as the **lower age of jurisdiction**, when a juvenile may be prosecuted as an adult in court (see Figure 19.1).

NO CONSENSUS ON AGE OF JUVENILES

Most states consider children to be juveniles until they reach their 18th birthday. However, 18 hardly constitutes a consensus among the states. Three states establish the upper age of juvenile court jurisdiction at 15, eight others at age 16, and the remaining states at 17 (see Figure 19.1).

The adjoining states of New York and Pennsylvania illustrate this complex national pattern. In New York, a 16-year-old is considered an adult and is prosecuted in the adult criminal justice system. But move across the border, and Pennsylvania treats that same 16-year-old as a juvenile to be processed in the juvenile court system. This difference in laws of jurisdictions sometimes no more than a few feet apart illustrates the tremendous diversity of American law, which is highlighted in Chapter 4.

TRANSFER TO ADULT COURT

Although a fairly uniform upper age limit for juveniles has been established in the United States, there is far less uniformity involving lower age limits (see Figure 19.2). Juveniles charged with serious offenses, or who have a history of repeated offenses, may be tried as adults. **Transfer to criminal court** (alternatively referred to as certification or waiver) refers to the process whereby the jurisdiction over a juvenile delinquent is moved to adult court. Many states have no lower age for transfer. For those stating a lower age limit, 14 to 16 is the most common.

The procedures surrounding the decision to transfer juveniles to adult court also vary. In some jurisdictions, the juvenile court judge makes the decision, but in the majority, the prosecutor has the discretionary authority to decide which juveniles

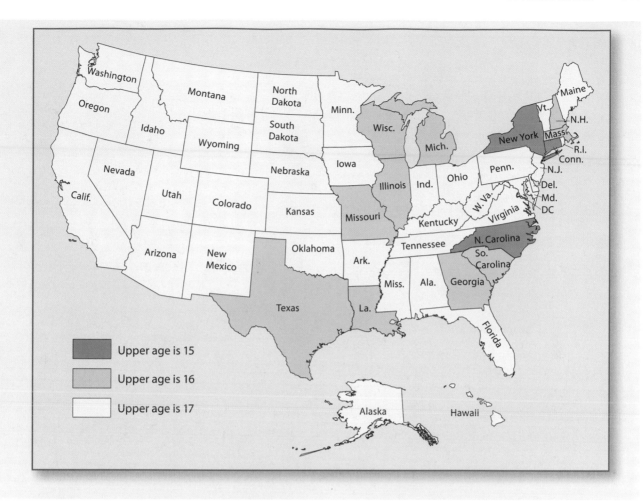

FIGURE 19.1 UPPER AGE OF JUVENILE COURT JURISDICTION IN STATES

Source: Adapted from the National Center for Juvenile Justice's State Juvenile Justice Profiles website, available at http://www.ncjj.org/stateprofiles/overviews/upperage.asp. (Accessed July 3, 2009.)

above the lower age will be tried as adults (Harris 2007).

Every year, only a very small proportion of juveniles are transferred to adult court. Those transferred are generally violent felony offenders accused of murder, robbery, or felony. The number of juveniles transferred to criminal court peaked in 1994 at 13,000 cases but since then has declined significantly to about 6,900 cases a year. The decrease in violent crime by juveniles has driven much of this decline (Adams and Addie 2009). A disproportionate number of juveniles transferred to adult criminal court are male African-Americans (Snyder and Sickmund 2006). Figures like these lead youth advocacy groups like Building Blocks for Youth (2009) to conclude that young people of color are overrepresented and that states have not done enough to address racial disparities.

How juvenile transfer laws actually operate is complex. For example, transferred juveniles, particularly those convicted of violent offenses, typically receive longer sentences than those sentenced in the juvenile court for similar crimes. However, they may be released on bail for a considerable period of time while they await trial in the criminal court (Meyers 2005; Redding 2008; Steiner 2009).

The Office of Juvenile Justice and Delinquency Prevention evaluated changes in Wisconsin, New Mexico, and Minnesota (Torbet et al. 2000). The final report highlights the following lessons learned:

• A disconnect exists between legislative intent and the actual implementation of new laws.

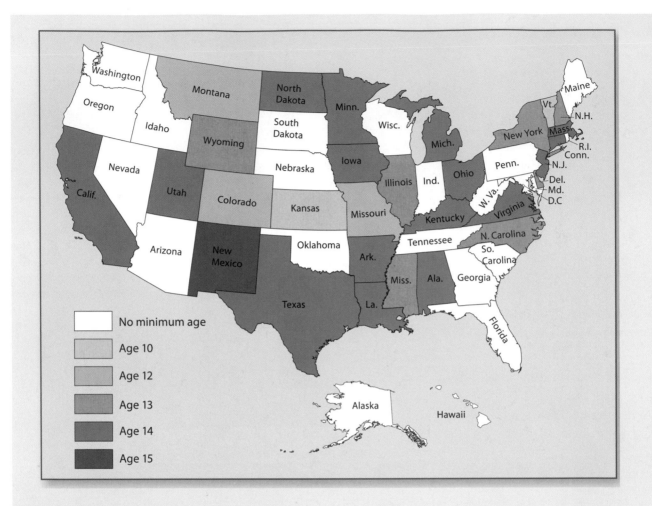

FIGURE 19.2 YOUNGEST AGE AT WHICH JUVENILE MAY BE TRANSFERRED TO CRIMINAL COURT BY JUDICIAL WAIVER

Source: Adapted from the National Center for Juvenile Justice's State Juvenile Justice Profiles website, available at http://www.ncjj.org/stateprofiles/overviews/transfer5t.asp. (Accessed July 3, 2009.)

- The new sentencing laws encourage plea bargaining.
- Judicial and prosecutorial discretion expand.
- Local application of new laws varies widely.
- New sentencing laws have a disproportionate impact on minorities.

Stated another way, alterations of laws on the books do not necessarily produce the intended changes in law in action.

Public pressure to try juveniles as adults is spawned by concerns over violent juvenile crimes. Reality, though, does not match the expectations of elected officials or the public. (See Courts, Controversy, and Reducing Crime: Should Juveniles Be Tried As Adults?)

JUVENILE COURT JURISDICTION: SUBJECT MATTER

Of the children brought before juvenile court because of their age, there is enormous variation in the types of cases. Felons and misdemeanants, petty offenders and truants are all under the jurisdiction of the juvenile court because of their age. And to complicate matters even further, some juveniles are before the court because of neglect or abuse by their parents.

Juvenile court matters fall into three major categories: delinquency, status offenses, and child-victim.

Juvenile Delinquency

Delinquency is a violation of a criminal law that would be a crime if the act were committed by an adult. Common examples include theft, burglary, sale or possession of drugs, and criminal damage to property. Thus, in a juvenile delinquency matter, there is no age difference in the substance of the criminal law, but the procedures are considerably different.

A juvenile delinquent may be placed on probation or committed to a juvenile institution. The period of confinement may exceed that of an adult. These criminal-type juvenile cases constitute 64 percent of all matters concerning juveniles.

Status Offenses

Status offenses involve acts that are illegal only for juveniles. Common examples include running away from home, truancy, possession of alcohol, incorrigibility/ungovernability, and curfew violations. Each year, juvenile courts handle almost 100,000 such cases. Traditionally, juveniles found to be status offenders could be sent to the same juvenile correctional institutions as those found to be delinquent, but this is changing. In recent years, some states have decriminalized some of these behaviors; offenders are now treated as dependent children, and child protective service agencies are given the primary responsibility for addressing the problem.

Child-Victim

Juvenile courts also deal with **child-victim** petitions involving neglect or dependency. Thus, the child is before the court through no fault of his or her own. Common examples include battered children, children abandoned by their parents, and children who are not receiving proper education or medical care. Neglected or dependent children cannot be sentenced to juvenile institutions. Rather, the court has a broad mandate to order social services, foster home or group home care, or medical or mental health services (DiPietro 2008).

Clearly, neglected or dependent children present strikingly different issues from those who are before

the court because of their own actions. Child-victim cases are also the ones that evoke considerable public emotion over the child's condition. Because of the complexities inherent in the distinctive nature of these cases, space does not permit further discussion.

Law in Action: One-Pot Jurisdiction

The broad subject-matter jurisdiction of juvenile courts complicates the task of addressing the problems facing juvenile justice. At any given time in juvenile court, the judge, prosecutor, probation officer, and police officer are simultaneously dealing with a wide variety of problems. This has been called the "**one-pot**" jurisdictional approach, in which youths who commit serious crimes, status offenders, and deprived children are put into the same "pot" (Springer 1986).

Consider the following three hypothetical cases, all of which would meet a given state's age criteria:

- A juvenile who has burglarized a liquor store
- A juvenile who has been stopped by the police for possessing liquor
- A juvenile whose parents drink so heavily that they have given up any efforts to raise their child

The first is a delinquent, the second a status offender, and the third a child-victim. Yet, all three kinds of kids were thought to be the products or victims of bad family and social environments; consequently, it was thought that they should be subject, as the wards of the court, to the same kind of solicitous, helpful care (Springer 1986, pp. 62–63).

It is this broad diversity of juvenile problems that members of the courtroom work group must confront in trying to dispense juvenile court's version of justice.

Due Process in Juvenile Courts

Juvenile court statutes set forth two standards for deciding the appropriate disposition for a child: the best interests of the child and the best interests of the community. Because the concept of the juvenile court was to aid—not punish—children, the due process guarantees of the adult criminal court were absent.

Courts, Controversy, and Reducing Crime

Public concerns about juvenile crime, particularly violent crimes committed by juveniles are often fueled by headlines about juveniles committing brazen or senseless crimes. And at one time the crime statistics seemed to bear out this public concern. Beginning in the mid-1980s the juvenile crime rate increased, with juvenile arrests more than doubling in the span of a decade or so (Cannon 1997). What attracted the most public attention is the increase in violent juvenile crime, which shot up 93 percent (compared with a 22 percent increase in property crimes).

To some observers, a juvenile crime wave was on the horizon. Newspaper headlines proclaimed, "Youth Violence Explosion Likely to Worsen" (Bass 1995) and "Violent Children Straining Limit of Justice System" (Hallinan 1993). These concerns were bolstered by the realization that the juvenile population would increase from 27 million to 39 million by 2010.

But these dire predictions failed to materialize. Beginning in 1995, arrests for violent juvenile crimes declined significantly ("Statistical Briefing Book" 2009). Thus, what some had predicted to be a juvenile crime wave now appears to have been only a ripple.

The commonly held belief that juvenile delinquents are becoming younger as a group and committing more serious crimes at earlier ages than in the past does not hold up to scrutiny. The Office of Juvenile Justice and Delinquency Prevention (1996) compared the characteristics of young offenders arrested in the 1990s with those arrested in 1980 and concluded that serious and violent juvenile offenders were not significantly younger than those of 10 or 15 years earlier.

But downward trends in juvenile crime have apparently had little impact on the public dialogue. The U.S. Congress and numerous states have

---

Procedures were more administrative than adversarial, stressing the informal, private, and noncombative handling of cases. It is for this reason that juvenile cases are often captioned *In re*, a Latin phrase meaning "in the matter of." But at what point do juveniles obtain benefits from the special procedures applicable to them that offset the disadvantage of denial of due process?

Key Court Decisions

The nature of the juvenile court process remained unchanged until the 1960s. When the Warren Court began to scrutinize procedures in adult criminal courts, its attention turned also to juvenile courts. In a groundbreaking decision, the Supreme Court held in *In re Gault* (1967) that the due process clause of the Fourteenth Amendment applied to juvenile court proceedings. The court emphasized that "under our Constitution the condition of being a boy does not justify a kangaroo court." The opinion specified that juveniles have: (1) the right to notice, (2) the right

to counsel, (3) the right to confront witnesses, and (4) privilege against self-incrimination. (See Case Close-Up: *In re Gault* and Due Process in Juvenile Courts.) Three years later, the Court ruled that when a juvenile is charged with an act that would be a crime if committed by an adult, then every element of that criminal act must be proved beyond a reasonable doubt (*In re Winship* 1970).

The *Gault* and *Winship* decisions point to the constant tension within the juvenile court system between those who think that children should be given all the due process guarantees accorded adults and those who reason that children must be handled in a less adversarial, more treatment-oriented manner so that legal procedures will not interfere with efforts to secure the justice that is in the children's best interests.

Gault and *Winship* signaled that the juvenile court must become a real court and its procedures must be regularized in accordance with constitutional requirements. Juvenile courts, however, afford far fewer due process rights than their adult

responded to public perceptions that violent juvenile crime is a growing menace. The typical legislative response has been to make it easier to transfer juveniles. Since the 1990s, for example, 40 states and the District of Columbia have changed their transfer statutes to make it easier to waive juveniles to adult courts (Snyder and Sickmund 2006). Some of these efforts involve lowering the age of transfer. Others involve increasing the list of crimes for which juveniles may be transferred. Others seek to mandate transfers in certain situations. Today, at least 24 states have laws that automatically send violent kids to adult courts, and several others are considering enacting such laws.

But do these laws work? A review of the major studies on this topic concludes that the answer is no. In terms of specific deterrence (deterring the specific person from committing another crime), several major studies find higher recidivism rates among juveniles convicted for violent offenses in criminal court when compared with similar offenders tried in juvenile court. The limited literature on general deterrence (deterring others from committing crime) is somewhat inconsistent but tentatively suggests that transfer laws do not deter crime (Redding 2008).

What do you think? Should juveniles be prosecuted as adults? If you answer yes, under what conditions should juveniles be prosecuted as adults, and for what crimes? In what ways are your standards similar to or different from existing practices? If you answer no, what would you suggest to strengthen rehabilitative efforts in juvenile court? In what ways are your recommendations similar to or different from existing practices? In forming your answer, also consider the following question: Do you think that the recent decrease in juvenile crime, particularly violent crime, is temporary or long term?

counterparts. Following the two landmark cases, however, the more conservative Burger and Rehnquist Courts were less enthusiastic about extending due process (see Exhibit 19.1). Juvenile delinquents, for example, have no constitutional right to a trial by jury (*McKeiver v. Pennsylvania* 1971), and preventive detention is allowed (*Schall v. Martin* 1984).

IMPORTANT CONGRESSIONAL ACTS

Congress has also imposed key mandates on the juvenile justice process. The Juvenile Justice and Delinquency Prevention Act of 1974 mandated deinstitutionalization of status offenders by stating that juveniles not charged with acts that would be crimes for adults shall not be jailed. Similarly, the law specifies that juveniles charged with criminal acts shall not be detained in any institution in which they have contact with adult inmates (Snyder and Sickmund 2006). There is little doubt that this law has fundamentally changed the way our nation deals with troubled youth.

Congressional mandates, coupled with *Gault* and other Supreme Court rulings, have had a marked effect on juvenile-court procedures. "Today's juvenile court is constantly discarding many of its traditional and fundamental characteristics, and it is adopting many of the features customarily associated with criminal court" (Sanborn 1993; see also, Moriearty 2008). Indeed, as juvenile courts have become more formal institutions of law, the benevolent *parens patriae* character that distinguished it from the adult criminal system has eroded. In recognition of this fact, the highest court in the state of Kansas took a radical step in 2008 by declaring that the rationale upon which the U.S. Supreme Court's decision in *McKeiver* was premised (namely benevolence, parental concern, rehabilitation, and sympathy) was no longer valid. Thus, the Kansas Supreme Court ruled that juveniles have a constitutional right to a trial by jury not only under their own state constitution, but also under the Sixth and Fourteenth Amendments to the U.S. Constitution (*In re L.M.* 2008). It remains to be seen whether other states

In re Gault and Due Process in Juvenile Courts

The sheriff of Gila County, Arizona, took 15-year-old Gerald Francis Gault into custody for making a lewd phone call to a neighbor. As to what was actually said, the Supreme Court would only say, "It will suffice for purposes of this opinion to say that the remarks or questions put to her were of the irritatingly offensive, adolescent, sex variety."

Gault was transported to the Children's Detention Home, and no effort was made to contact his parents. Over the next couple of weeks, several brief hearings were held, but no record exists of what happened. What is known, though, is that there is some dispute whether Gerald Gault actually made the phone call. According to one version, he dialed the number, but his friend did the talking. Whatever may have transpired, the hearing would not be able to determine, because the witness was never present.

After another brief hearing, Gerald was found to be a juvenile delinquent and committed to the State Industrial School "for the period of his minority [that is, until 21] unless sooner discharged by due process of law." This harsh sentence was probably influenced by the fact that at the time he was on 6 months' probation as a result of having been in the company of another boy who had stolen a woman's purse.

It was the lack of procedural regularity in cases like this one that concerned the American Civil Liberties Union (ACLU) (Manfredi 1998). Through a series of complex maneuvers, the ACLU was able to get the case before the Arizona Supreme Court and then the U.S. Supreme Court.

In deciding *Gault*, the Court was essentially writing on a blank slate concerning juveniles. A year earlier, the Court had ever so tentatively imposed some due process requirements for juveniles accused of serious felonies (*Kent v. United States* 1966). But now the Court was ready to confront head-on the basic question about juvenile courts: Does the Bill of Rights apply to juveniles, or are children's best interests protected by informal and paternalistic hearings? Justice Abe Fortas's opinion underscored the lack of procedural regularity, stressing that "Due process of law is the primary and indispensable foundation of individual freedom."

At the same time, the opinion in *Gault* supports the purposes of the juvenile court: A juvenile court proceeding is one "in which a fatherly judge touched the heart and conscience of the erring youth by talking over his problems, by paternal advice and admonition" to save him from a downward career. The goodwill and compassion of the juvenile court will not, however, be diminished by due process of law. In one bold stroke, *In re Gault* carved out the following four new constitutional rights in juvenile proceedings:

- Juveniles have the right to timely notice of charges. In the future, parents must be informed that their child has been taken into custody, and written charges must be filed.

- Juveniles have the right to counsel. Following *Gideon*, the Court held that juveniles, like adults, have the right to have an attorney present during the proceedings, and if they are indigent, to have a lawyer appointed.

- Juveniles have the right against self-incrimination. *Miranda*, decided by the Court just a year before, greatly extended the right for adults, and many of the same strictures were now extended to juveniles.

- Juveniles have the right to confront and cross-examine complainants and other witnesses.

The Court's opinion in *Gault* was supported by seven justices and partially by an eighth. Only Justice Potter Stewart dissented outright. He viewed the decision as "a long step backwards into the 19th century." The danger he saw was that abolishing the flexibility and informality of the juvenile courts would cause children to be treated as adults in courts.

CASE CLOSEUP

or the U.S. Supreme Court follow Kansas's lead, or whether the *In re L.M.* decision will be invalidated. Regardless of which path is ultimately taken, it is clear that the juvenile court system in the United States has changed dramatically in philosophy and operation from its original form.

Exhibit 19.1

KEY DEVELOPMENTS CONCERNING JUVENILE COURTS

Ex parte Crouse	1839	Philadelphia Supreme Court uses term *parens patriae*.
Illinois Juvenile Court Act	1899	First juvenile court created in Cook County, Illinois.
Juvenile Court Act	1938	Federal government adopts principles of juvenile court movement.
Wyoming	1945	Last state to create a juvenile court.
Kent v. U.S.	1966	Court establishes conditions of waiver to criminal court.
In re Gault	1967	Juveniles are entitled to due process guarantees.
In re Winship	1970	Proof must be established "beyond a reasonable doubt" in classifying juveniles as delinquent.
McKeiver v. Pennsylvania	1971	Juvenile delinquents are not entitled to a jury trial.
Juvenile Justice and Delinquency Prevention Act	1974	Mandates deinstitutionalization of status offenders.
Schall v. Martin	1984	Court departs from trend of increasing juvenile rights, upholding the general notion of *parens patriae*.
Thompson v. Oklahoma	1988	Execution of a person under the age of 16 at the time of his or her crime is unconstitutional.
Stanford v. Kentucky	1989	It is not unconstitutional to apply the death penalty to persons who were convicted of murder when they were 17.
Roper v. Simmons	2005	The Eighth amendment forbids the imposition of the death penalty on offenders who were under the age of 18 when their crimes were committed (reversing *Thompson v. Oklahoma* and *Stanford v. Kentucky*).

COURTROOM WORK GROUP

At first glance, members of juvenile courtroom work groups are similar to those found in adult courts—prosecutors bring charges, defense attorneys attempt to get the best deal possible for their clients, and judges decide matters that others have not successfully negotiated. These parallels, though, can be deceiving because the tasks of juvenile and adult courts are not the same. More so than courts dealing with adults accused of violating the law, juvenile courts grant judges and other officials unusually wide latitude in making discretionary decisions intended to "individualize justice." Moreover, although the Supreme Court has imposed minimal due process requirements, juvenile courts remain judicial bodies where informal processing still dominates.

Shared norms are the hallmark of courtroom work groups, Chapter 5 argued. In assessing the worth of a case, members of the juvenile court work group incorporate many of the same factors as those in adult courts—the severity of the offense and the prior record of the offender. The juvenile-court tradition of individualized treatment, though, encourages the consideration of another important factor—the characteristics of the family. The control the parent or parents have over the youth is a major consideration in deciding the disposition of the case (Fader et al. 2001). Similarly, members of the juvenile-court work group also consider family structure. Youths whose families are perceived to be dysfunctional were much more likely to receive an out-of-home placement than youths whose families were not perceived to be dysfunctional (Rodriguez, Smith, and Zatz 2009).

The legally trained members of the courtroom work group rely heavily on professional judgments of nonlawyers in assessing both the background of the youth and the characteristics of the family. This affects the juvenile court work group in a critical way. Whereas in adult court the skills of lawyers are of fundamental importance, in juvenile court they are secondary. Judges, lawyers, and defense attorneys have been trained to interpret and apply the law, but these skills provide little help in making the key decisions in juvenile court cases. Instead, social workers, psychologists, and counselors have been trained to assess the child's problem and devise a treatment plan.

JUDGES

Judges are the central authority in the juvenile court system. More so than their counterparts in criminal court, they have wide discretion over detention, the adjudicatory hearing, disposition, and other matters. Depending on the size of the court and the rotation system, an individual judge may spend only a little time or a great deal of time in juvenile court.

In many jurisdictions, assignment to the juvenile court is not a highly sought-after appointment. Although some judges like the challenges of juvenile court, to others it is a dead-end assignment. Judges who specialize in juvenile-court matters are often those who enjoy the challenges of working with people rather than those who are intrigued by nuances of legal interpretations. But even judges

deeply committed to the juvenile system may seek rotation to other sections to advance their judicial careers (Krisberg and Austin 1993).

HEARING OFFICERS

In many jurisdictions, judges are assisted by *hearing officers* (sometimes known as *referees*, *masters*, or *commissioners*). Typically, hearing officers are attorneys appointed by the court to serve on a full- or part-time basis to hear a range of juvenile-court matters. These hearing officers enter findings and recommendations that require confirmation by the judge to become an order.

PROSECUTORS

Over the past several decades, the power and influence of the prosecutor have grown in U.S. courthouses (see Chapter 6). Rising crime rates, coupled with Supreme Court decisions requiring more due process, have contributed to the growing role of the prosecutor in juvenile courts (Kupchik 2006; Shine and Price 1992).

Prosecutors now dominate the intake processing stage in most jurisdictions. At times, intake officers make the initial decision and the prosecutor later reviews that determination. But increasingly, prosecutors are the chief decision makers (with input from others, of course). Similarly, prosecutors, more so than judges, are typically the ones who negotiate the disposition of all but the most serious juvenile delinquency cases.

Although the role of the prosecutor's office has increased in juvenile court, an assignment to a section of juvenile court is not a sought-after promotion. On the contrary, it is the newly hired assistant DAs fresh out of law school who tend to be assigned to juvenile court. Thus, much like judges, assistant DAs typically hope for a promotion to a felony unit, where they can practice "real law," trying and convicting "real criminals" (Kupchik 2006).

DEFENSE ATTORNEYS

In re Gault (1967) held that juveniles were entitled to representation by defense counsel in delinquency proceedings. Yet, defense attorneys play a secondary role in the juvenile court (Burruss and Kempf-Leonard 2002). Studies reveal great disparities in the number of juveniles who are

LAW AND POPULAR CULTURE

The Client (1994)

It is interesting to speculate why there are so few movies about juvenile court. Perhaps the lack of public access to juvenile proceedings has discouraged writers from probing the human stories buried in the system. Or perhaps stories about cops catching kid crooks does not seem very interesting—a plot line works best when a smart detective is outwitting a sophisticated criminal, not chasing down a young punk. A notable exception that explores the world of juveniles and the law is *The Client*, based on a John Grisham novel of the same name.

The legal thriller begins with eleven-year-old Mark Sway and his younger brother Ricky sneaking into the woods to smoke cigarettes. Between puffs a big black car pulls up driven by W. Jerome "Romey" Clifford, a New Orleans lawyer whose only client is mobster Barry "The Blade" Muldanno. Romey is defending his client in the murder of a prominent state senator and has been told where the body is buried. Romey is now convinced the "The Blade" wants him dead, but prefers to take his own life first. Mark Sway prevents the suicide, Romey shares the secret and then commits suicide anyway.

Mark Sway calls the police and the suicide is now front page news. Everyone assumes that Sway knows more than he is telling (his lies are most unconvincing). Soon he is being questioned by the Memphis Police Department, the FBI, and U.S. Attorney Roy Foltrigg (Tommy Lee Jones). Foltrigg is known as the "Reverend" for his knowledge of the bible and his preaching style in the courtroom. Sway runs away from his questioners and hires a lawyer, Reggie Love (Susan Sarandon). Meanwhile the mob is busily hunting for Sway, intent on preventing him from sharing the secret. According to the plot line, there can be no trial without the body (which is, of course, pure hokum). Everyone wants Sway to talk and he is placed in juvenile lock-up (partly to protect him and partly to pressure him to talk). Sway runs away (yet again), this time to New Orleans with Reggie Love to search for the body.

The Client offers insights into the premise of the juvenile court system in the United States—children are persons with less than fully developed moral and cognitive capacities. Mark Sway fits these categories well. He is angry, hurt, and scared, unable to sort out what is in his own best interest. He lies to everyone, including his mother, his lawyer, the police, and federal authorities. (It is worth noting that the police and Reverend Bob are also liars, but at least their lying is instrumental, not pathological.) Mark Sway continues his denials, even when telling the truth might be the best course of action. Against this background of a confused and vulnerable juvenile, his lawyer provides the nurturing role envisioned in juvenile court; her character combines the roles of lawyer, judge, mom, and social worker.

The Client also provides a perspective on the legal protections (or lack thereof) for juveniles. Mark Sway is alternatively an important witness in a murder prosecution (he knows where the body is buried) and a possible law violator (to the U.S. Attorney, his lies amount to obstruction of justice). Throughout the movie, law enforcement authorities trample his rights by interrogating him without his mother present, questioning him without his lawyer in attendance, and failing to give him his *Miranda* rights. Moreover Mark is held in an adult jail in clear violation of federal law that requires juveniles to be separated by sight and sound from adult offenders.

The Client is set against the often harsh realities surrounding juvenile justice. The boys live in a low-rent trailer park. Their mother is single and seemingly more focused on keeping her minimum wage job than helping her younger son who is hospitalized with post traumatic stress disorder. Moreover, several of the principals have been scarred by divorce, neglect, lack of parenting, physical abuse, alcoholism,

CONTINUED

The Client (1994)

and drug addiction. These social realities are reinforced by the physical realities of the justice system—the movie projects a very grim image of the jail and jailers who run it.

Despite the harsh realities he faces, the movie has a happy ending for the fictional Mark Sway, but the same cannot be said for Brad Renfro, who played the role. After starring in *The Client*, Renfro carved out a niche in Hollywood, playing inarticulate, vulnerable, alienated youths. At the same time, he was an admitted heroin and methadone user who sometimes frequented skid row. At age 25, Renfro was found dead in his apartment and in the dry words of the Los Angeles Police Department, "foul play was not

suspected" (Seitz 2008). In the end, it is hard to say if in playing the role of Mark Sway, Renfro was imitating art, or art was imitating his life.

After watching this movie, be prepared to answer the following questions:

1. How would Mark Sway's legal situation been different if he had been an adult and not a juvenile? Would his situation been better or worse?

2. In what ways are the courtroom scenes more like an adult court than a juvenile court?

3. Who is more ethically challenged in the movie, the U.S. attorney or the defense lawyer?

---

actually represented by a lawyer, ranging from a low of 15 percent to a high of 95 percent (Guevara, Herz, and Spohn 2008). Contrary to what some may intuitively believe, studies reveal that youths represented by counsel actually receive a harsher disposition than those who appear in court without an attorney (Guevara, Herz, and Spohn 2008), a fact that might explain why so many juveniles waive their right to counsel, thereby keeping proceedings more informal. Yet, being unrepresented by counsel may compromise the due process rights guaranteed by *Gault* (Puritz et al. 1995; Young 2000). The American Bar Association has been working with other advocacy groups to ensure that juvenile offenders are competently represented by attorneys with "particularized training in youth development and juvenile law" and who are assisted by interdisciplinary support services (Shepherd 2003, p. 27).

Lack of representation by a lawyer partially reflects the nature of the caseload—many of the cases are minor. As we saw with adults in misdemeanor court, few have lawyers because the penalties are so light. The same holds true for juveniles—most cases will receive some form of probation, supervision, and/or restitution irrespective of whether a lawyer is, or is not, present.

The role of the defense attorney is further limited by the informality of juvenile courts. In contrast to adult court, juvenile court proceedings place little emphasis on the privilege against self-incrimination. From the initial police contact (and often arrest) through the intake proceedings, juveniles are urged to tell the truth. It should be no surprise, therefore, to learn that fewer than 10 percent of juveniles assert their right to remain silent (Grisso 1981).

Defense attorneys, when they are present at all, become involved after their client has cooperated with police and prosecutor, and perhaps the probation officer and judge as well. For the cases in which there is only weak evidence, the defense strategy is to seek a dismissal. For the vast majority of cases in which there is strong evidence, defense attorneys negotiate, based on the norms of the work group, the best possible deal for their client. Since most of the cases are, by adult standards, relatively minor, the dispositions reached tend to be on the lenient side—primarily probation, restitution, and community service.

PROBATION OFFICERS

From the beginning, probation and **probation officers** were a key part of juvenile court. In fact, probation in adult court traces its heritage to these developments. Juvenile probation takes several forms. In some states, probation officers are part of the judicial branch (either locally or statewide); in other jurisdictions, they are part of the executive branch (either locally or statewide).

As in adult court, probation officers in juvenile court conduct background reports and supervise those placed on probation. What is strikingly different, though, is the stage at which they become involved. In adult courts, probation officers are brought into the process after the defendant has entered a plea of guilty or been found guilty. In juvenile courts, they become involved at the early stages of the process. Thus, the probation officer, not a judge or prosecutor, is often the first court official to have contact with the child. Indeed, it is often the probation officer who recommends an informal disposition to the case. Moreover, in more serious cases, the probation officer's recommendation, along with the social worker's, most often becomes the order of the court.

Steps of the Juvenile Court Process

From the perspective of law on the books, the steps of the juvenile court process resemble those for adult courts. Although the terminology is slightly different, juveniles accused of violating the law appear to be treated the same as adults in the same situation (see Exhibit 19.2).

From the perspective of law in action, however, the steps of the juvenile court process are strikingly different from their adult counterparts. More than mere differences in terminology, what makes the processing of juveniles so distinctive is the heavy emphasis on informal decision making. The vast majority of decisions are reached not by lawyers and defendants standing before a judge in open court but rather by a juvenile, a parent, and a probation officer sitting around a desk discussing what will happen next.

Delinquency (Crime)

How many crimes are committed by juveniles (as opposed to adults) is impossible to determine with any great precision. As discussed in Chapter 10, the FBI's Uniform Crime Reports are based on crimes reported to the police, and most crime victims have no way of knowing the age of the person responsible. Juvenile crime increased steadily beginning

in 1985, but this increase declined dramatically after 1995. Two important features related to juvenile crime are worth noting:

- Crimes against juveniles are less likely to be reported to the police.
- Juveniles are 2.5 times as likely as adults to be victims of serious violent crime (Snyder and Sickmund 2006).

Summons (Arrest)

A **summons** is a legal document requiring an individual (in this case, a juvenile) to appear in court at a certain time and on a certain date. Although the summons is the official term used in juvenile court, it is informally referred to as an arrest. In the latest year for which data are available (Puzzanchera 2009), law enforcement agencies in the United States made an estimated 2.18 million arrests of persons under 18. Overall, juveniles were involved in 16 percent of all violent crime index arrests and 26 percent of all property crime index arrests. Juvenile arrest statistics include two noteworthy features:

- Almost 29 percent of juvenile arrests were of females, and the female proportion of arrests has grown in recent years (Shaffner 2006; Zahn et al. 2008).
- Juvenile arrests disproportionately involve minorities.

Intake (Initial Hearing)

Delinquency cases begin with a **referral**. Arrests by law enforcement personnel are by far the biggest source of these referrals—82 percent in a typical year. Referrals, though, may originate from several other sources; for example, some juvenile court cases stem from petitions filed by teachers, neighbors, merchants, or even parents unable to control their children. But mainly they follow after a juvenile has been arrested by the police.

These arrests and other referrals produce 1.6 million juvenile court delinquency cases every year. Best estimates indicate that 61 percent of juvenile filings involve delinquency, with the remainder evenly split between status offenses and child-victim cases.

Juvenile court cases have leveled off in recent years after a period of marked growth. Yet, juvenile courts still handle nearly four times as many cases today as in 1960.

Exhibit 19.2

STEPS OF THE JUVENILE COURT PROCESS

	LAW ON THE BOOKS	**LAW IN ACTION**
Adult	Juvenile	
Crime	*Delinquency*: Acts or conduct in violation of criminal laws.	Juveniles are more likely than adults to be victims of violent crime.
	Status offense: Behavior that is considered an offense only when committed by a juvenile.	Poor, young, minority males are disproportionately at risk of being victims of violent crime.
Arrest	*Summons:* A legal document ordering an individual to appear in court at a certain time on a certain date.	Some 2.18 million juveniles are arrested yearly. Juveniles are arrested primarily for property offenses.
Initial appearance	*Initial hearing:* An often informal hearing during which an intake decision is made.	There are 1.6 million juvenile cases a year. Sixty-five percent of juvenile filings involve delinquency.
Bail	*Detention:* Holding a youth in custody before case disposition.	There are 100,000 offenders in public and private juvenile detention facilities.
Charging	*Intake decision:* The decision made by juvenile court that results in the case being handled either informally at the intake level or more formally and scheduled for an adjudicatory hearing.	Intake decisions are often informal. Courtroom work group norms govern decision making.
	Nonpetitioned: Cases handled informally by duly authorized court personnel.	Forty-five percent of juvenile delinquency cases are handled informally (nonpetitioned).
	Petition: A document filed in juvenile court alleging that a juvenile is delinquent or a status offender and asking that the court assume jurisdiction over the juvenile.	Fifty-five percent of juvenile delinquency court cases are handled formally. Older juveniles with more serious charges are more likely to be handled formally.
Preliminary hearing	*Conference:* Proceeding during which the suspect is informed of rights and a disposition decision may be reached.	In the vast majority of petitioned cases, the juvenile admits guilt during the conference.

Exhibit 19.2
CONTINUED

	LAW ON THE BOOKS	LAW IN ACTION
Grand jury	Not applicable.	Few juvenile cases are transferred to adult court.
Arraignment	Occurs during the conference.	Fifty-five percent of juvenile delinquency cases are handled formally (petitioned).
Evidence	Juveniles have the same constitutional protections as adults with regard to interrogation and unreasonable search and seizure.	Police gathering of evidence is very rarely contested.
Plea bargaining	*Plea bargaining:* Formal and informal discussions resulting in juvenile's admitting guilt.	Even more than in adult court, dispositions in juvenile court are the product of negotiations.
Trial	*Adjudicatory hearing:* Hearing to determine whether a youth is guilty or not guilty.	Adjudicatory hearings are more informal than adult trials.
Sentencing	*Disposition:* A court decision on what will happen to a youth who has not been found innocent.	The disposition is often referred to as a treatment plan.
	Placement: Cases in which juveniles are placed in a residential facility or otherwise removed from their homes.	More than 144,000 juveniles are placed in residential facilities each year.
	Probation: Cases in which youths are placed under informal/voluntary or formal/court-ordered supervision.	More than 385,000 youths each year receive court supervision.
	Dismissal: Cases dismissed (including those warned, counseled, and released) with no further disposition anticipated.	Even case dismissals may include a treatment plan or restitution.
	Other: Miscellaneous dispositions including fines, restitution, and community service.	Teen courts are a modern version of other dispositions.
Appeal	*Appeal:* Request that a higher court review the decision of the lower court.	Appeals are very rare in juvenile proceedings

Soon after referral to juvenile court, an **initial hearing** (sometimes called a *"preliminary inquiry"*) is held. As with much of the terminology of juvenile court, *hearing* is often a misnomer. A hearing implies a formal setting in front of a judge, but more typically it is an informal exchange among the police officer, probation officer, child, and parent.

DETENTION HEARING

Police make the first **detention** decision shortly after taking the juvenile into custody. Typically, the police release the youth to the custody of his or her parents (or guardians). If the crime is serious, however, the police may detain the youth in a police lockup or local jail. In an earlier era, juveniles were held in the same facilities as adult offenders, but no longer. Federal law mandates that juveniles be held in facilities separated by sight and sound from detention facilities for adults. In many communities the number of cells is limited, so even serious violators may be returned to the streets.

A second detention decision may occur after the juvenile has been referred to the juvenile court. Intake personnel review the case and determine whether the youth should be released to parents or detained. Juveniles may be detained if they are thought to be dangerous to themselves or others if released. Statutes in most states now mandate that, if the juvenile is to be detained, a detention hearing must be held before a judge or other hearing officer within 24 to 72 hours of arrest.

In a typical year, one out of five juveniles is detained prior to the adjudicatory hearing (Snyder and Sickmund 2006). On any given day, 100,000 youths are held in public and private juvenile detention facilities (Sickmund, Sladky, and Kang 2008).

PETITION

During the initial hearing, a decision is made not only about detention but also about whether the case will be handled formally (petition) or informally (nonpetitioned). This decision is most often referred to as the **intake decision** (the juvenile equivalent of the charging decision for adults accused of violating the criminal law).

As Figure 19.3 shows, 42 percent of delinquency cases are handled informally (termed **nonpetitioned**). An informal process is used when the decision makers (police, probation officers, intake workers, and prosecutors) believe that accountability and rehabilitation can be achieved without the use of formal court intervention. Informal sanctions are voluntary. At times, they involve no more than a warning and counseling, but more often they consist of voluntary probation, restitution, and community service.

Juvenile cases that are handled formally are referred to as **petition** cases (or petitioned). Figure 19.3 indicates that 58 percent of cases each year receive such treatment. Intake officers are more likely to petition if

- Juveniles are older and have longer court histories
- The delinquency is serious (involves violence, for example)

Seventy percent of all formally processed delinquency cases result in a finding of delinquency. The sanction may be probation, with the juvenile released into the custody of a parent or guardian and ordered to undergo some form of training, education, or counseling. But in 23 percent of adjudicated cases, the juvenile is ordered by the court to residential placement, such as training school, camp, ranch, or group home. Every year, about 144,000 juveniles are committed to long-term facilities (primarily training schools).

CONFERENCE

The **conference** is roughly equivalent to a preliminary hearing in an adult proceeding. The more minor the transgression, the more likely the conference will be held at the same time as the initial hearing and the detention hearing. In more serious matters, particularly if the decision has been made to file a petition, the conference is more likely to be held in closed court.

During the conference, the judge informs the respondent of the charges in the petition. The person is also informed of constitutional protections, including the right to counsel, the right to free counsel, the right to subpoena witnesses for the defense, and the opportunity to cross-examine prosecution witnesses.

Vast numbers of juveniles admit to their offense during the conference, waiving the right to counsel and the right to trial. Others request counsel, adjourn to the hallway of the courthouse, and after 5 or 10 minutes with an attorney come back before the judge and admit their offense (Rubin 1989).

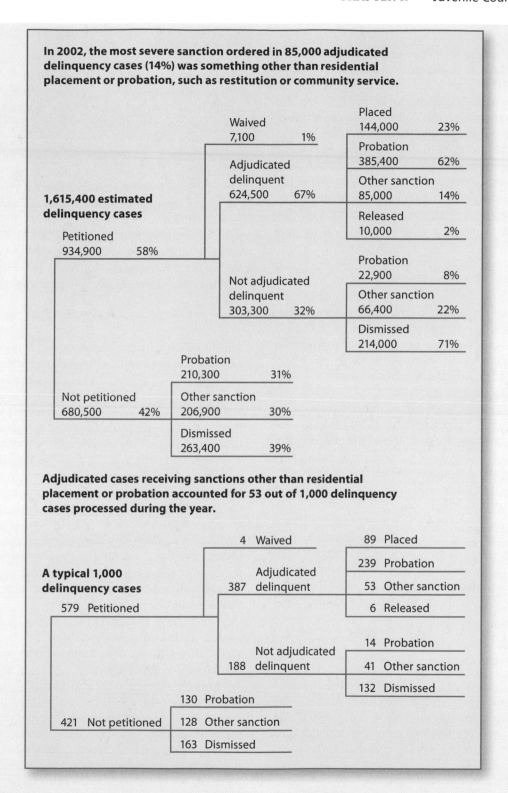

In 2002, the most severe sanction ordered in 85,000 adjudicated delinquency cases (14%) was something other than residential placement or probation, such as restitution or community service.

1,615,400 estimated delinquency cases

Petitioned 934,900   58%

Waived 7,100   1%

Adjudicated delinquent 624,500   67%

Placed 144,000   23%
Probation 385,400   62%
Other sanction 85,000   14%
Released 10,000   2%

Not adjudicated delinquent 303,300   32%

Probation 22,900   8%
Other sanction 66,400   22%
Dismissed 214,000   71%

Not petitioned 680,500   42%

Probation 210,300   31%
Other sanction 206,900   30%
Dismissed 263,400   39%

Adjudicated cases receiving sanctions other than residential placement or probation accounted for 53 out of 1,000 delinquency cases processed during the year.

A typical 1,000 delinquency cases

579 Petitioned

4 Waived

387 Adjudicated delinquent

89 Placed
239 Probation
53 Other sanction
6 Released

188 Not adjudicated delinquent

14 Probation
41 Other sanction
132 Dismissed

421 Not petitioned

130 Probation
128 Other sanction
163 Dismissed

FIGURE 19.3 JUVENILE COURT PROCESSING OF DELINQUENCY CASES

Source: Howard Snyder and Melissa Sickmund. *Juvenile Offenders and Victims: 2006 National Report.* Washington, DC: U.S. Department of Justice, Office of Justice Programs, Office of Juvenile Justice and Delinquency Prevention, 2006.

EVIDENCE: GATHERING AND SUPPRESSING

Challenges to how the police gathered evidence play a very minor role in juvenile cases. The presumption is that the child is in trouble (with the juvenile delinquency charge an indicator of that trouble). This presumption makes it difficult to challenge evidence gathering—the judge might conclude that there is insufficient evidence to find the child a delinquent, but still enough to conclude that the child is in need of supervision. Moreover, the informal nature of the entire proceeding discourages legal challenges. The general absence of defense attorneys likewise discourages raising issues associated with *Mapp* and *Miranda*.

PLEA BARGAINING

The informality of juvenile court makes it somewhat difficult to focus on plea bargaining as a distinct phase, because often it is not. Rather, the discretion that runs throughout the juvenile court process is really plea bargaining by a different name (Dougherty 1988; Kupchik 2006).

Efforts to negotiate the matter typically begin during the intake process. Parent, child, and probation officer discuss the matter and often arrive at a solution satisfactory to all parties. Thus, the 42 percent of juvenile delinquency cases that are nonpetitioned clearly represent what in adult court would be labeled as plea bargaining.

Efforts to negotiate a settlement continue after a petition is filed. As Figure 19.3 underscores, 32 percent of petitioned cases are in the "nonadjudicated" category. As we shall discuss shortly, even the adjudicatory hearing resembles an informal exchange of settlement possibilities more than a formal, combative trial.

ADJUDICATORY HEARING

The **adjudicatory hearing** is equivalent to the trial in adult court. The purpose is to determine whether the allegations contained in the petition are supported by a "preponderance of the evidence" (for status offenses) or "beyond a legal doubt" (for juvenile delinquency).

One of the key changes growing out of the due process revolution associated with *In re Gault* is that juveniles have the right to present evidence in favor, which includes cross-examining the government's witnesses and subpoenaing defense witnesses.

The juvenile also maintains the privilege against self-incrimination.

Statistics provided by the Office of Juvenile Justice and Delinquency Prevention indicate that 67 percent of petitioned cases are **adjudicated**. This seems like a high "trial" rate, but a closer look indicates that this is not the case. Adjudicatory hearings are much less formal than adult trials. This is due in part to the lack of juries (except in a few exceptional cases in a handful of states). The rules of evidence (see Chapter 14) are designed to keep certain information from lay jurors lest they place undue emphasis on some information. But since there are usually no juries, these rules have considerably less applicability. Of course, if the holding of *In re L.M.* (2008) is adopted beyond the state of Kansas, the formality of juvenile proceedings across the county will grow exponentially.

DISPOSITION

The more serious the crime and/or the longer the juvenile has been in trouble with the law, the more likely it is that a formal probation report will be prepared. Like its adult counterpart, the probation report (sometimes called the predisposition report) is prepared by the probation officer; it is based on interviews with the juvenile, the parents, school officials, and others. The report chronicles the juvenile's prior history with the court and also may estimate the economic harm suffered by the victim. Finally, the report makes a **disposition** recommendation.

The most common disposition is a **dismissal**. Cases dismissed (including those warned, counseled, and released), with no further disposition anticipated, are most likely to occur among cases that are handled informally.

The second most common disposition is **probation**. Probation cases are those in which youths were placed under informal/voluntary or formal/court-ordered supervision.

Another common disposition is **placement**. Placement cases are those in which youth are placed in a residential facility for delinquents or status offenders, or otherwise removed from their homes and placed elsewhere. Consistent with the nonpunishment orientation of the juvenile process, juveniles are not sentenced to prison, but rather are placed in residential treatment facilities called training institutes and the like.

Finally, a significant number of dispositions that do not fall under the previous three categories are referred to simply as **other dispositions.** These include fines, restitution, community service, and referrals outside the court for services with minimal or no further court involvement anticipated.

In making disposition decisions, juvenile-court judges focus primarily on offense characteristics and are influenced only marginally by the offender's social characteristics. These findings are more consistent with the view that juvenile courts are becoming more like adult criminal courts than with the view that individualized justice is the goal (Applegate et al. 2000).

Juvenile courts in urban areas tend to send proportionally fewer delinquents to state detention facilities than do courts serving less populous areas (Rubin 1989). Officials in rural areas are sometimes quicker to "pull the string" and send less serious delinquency cases to state placement—partially because they have fewer institutional resources to deal with these youths, but also because the equivalent event is viewed as more harmful in small towns than in big cities.

APPEAL

Juveniles have a right to appeal in nearly all states. The opinion in *Gault* discussed the importance of appeals for due process rights, but declined to make it a constitutional requirement. Prompted, however, by the possibility that the Supreme Court might indeed make it a constitutional right, state legislatures have passed laws granting juveniles the right to appeal. Thus, today the common practice is to give juveniles the same rights to appeal that apply to adults. By statute, juveniles also have the right to a transcript and a right to counsel for the first appeal.

The right to appeal is primarily limited to juveniles (and their parents). The state may appeal only in limited circumstances, and this right is seldom exercised.

JUVENILE COURTS: THE NEXT 100 YEARS

Juvenile courts, which were once virtually invisible judicial bodies, have in recent years become a major focus in the debate over crime. Amidst the

constantly evolving war on crime (Chapter 1), there are cross-cutting pressures to change the nature of juvenile court justice. Indeed, some critics argue that this grand experiment has been a failure and should be scrapped.

A little over a century after the founding of juvenile courts, it is appropriate to ask, what will juvenile courts be like 100 years from now? The debate over the future reflects basic disagreements along the lines of the crime control versus due process models.

CRIME CONTROL MODEL: MORE ADULT PENALTIES

The crime control model begins with the premise that crime is the product of moral breakdown. This is clearly the theme sounded by Darlene Kennedy (1997) of the National Center for Public Policy Research. "Let's hold juveniles responsible for their crimes," she argued, blaming undue leniency of juvenile court for violent juvenile crimes. "The solution is greater deterrence through expected punishments. Children who commit crimes should be punished like adults."

One version of more adult penalties for juvenile offenders involves increasing the number of transfers to adult court. According to the National District Attorney's Association (2007): "Very few juveniles are prosecuted and sentenced as adults in America... In those cases where adult court prosecution does occur, the simple fact of the matter is that adult court prosecution is clearly warranted. ..."

Some go so far as to argue that it is time to abolish juvenile court altogether. As far back as 1990, Marvin Wolfgang argued that: "The dual system of juvenile and criminal justice that prevents the sharing of information and permits a serious, chronic violent juvenile to become a virgin offender after his 19th birthday is a strange cultural invention" (quoted in Bureau of Justice Statistics 1990, p. 18). This line of thought led Peter Reinharz, chief of New York City's juvenile prosecution unit, to argue, "It's time to sell everything off and start over" (quoted in Butterfield 1997). Chronic overcrowding of juvenile justice facilities is one problem often mentioned, but it is unclear how merely shuffling the overcrowding problems of juvenile facilities to already overcrowded adult courts and adult prisons will alleviate the problem. Public opinion, however, supports the continued operation of a separate juvenile justice system in the United States, although there are disagreements about the details of its operation ranging from the age at which juveniles should be treated as adults to the appropriateness of harsh punishments over more rehabilitative efforts (Mears et al. 2007).

In short, a sharp increase in the public's fear of juvenile crime, particularly gangs, drugs, and violence, has added impetus to a get-tough attitude toward juvenile criminals.

DUE PROCESS MODEL: MORE YOUTH CRIME PREVENTION

The due process model starts with the premise that crime is a reflection of social problems. Punishment alone, therefore, is not necessarily the answer and might even be counterproductive. Placing juveniles in the same prisons as adults, for example, might simply make the youths more-hardened and more-accomplished crooks.

Amid numerous voices arguing that the juvenile court created 100 years ago is now outmoded, some respond that the nation should return to those roots. The Progressive movement was concerned about mistreatment of juveniles at the turn of the last century, and we should have the same concern today, argue groups like the American Civil Liberties Union. The core of the argument is that crime prevention works. Instead of pouring increasing amounts of public dollars into prisons (both adult and juvenile), we need to put more into education and prevention.

In "A Call to Action for Juvenile Justice" the American Civil Liberties Union (2008) outlined three priorities for the juvenile court system. Priority one is to keep children out of the criminal justice system. In particular, end the disparity in punitive sentences given to youths of color. Priority two is protect the rights of incarcerated children. Ensuring access to counsel and the courts is very important. Priority three is reintegrating children into communities. All too often juvenile adjudications can follow children for decades, hampering their ability to find employment.

CONCLUSION

The charge against Gerald Gault—making a lewd telephone call—seems tame compared with today's concerns about preteens committing violent crimes. Nonetheless, this irritating but hardly life-threatening behavior was to usher in a new era. Whereas the Progressives saw procedural rights as an impediment to helping children in need, a later generation viewed due process as providing an important safety net against high-handed behavior by government officials.

Court decisions like *In re Gault* and changing patterns of youthful behavior—to say nothing of the types of crimes committed by youths today—could not have been foreseen by the Progressive movement. Whether the founders of juvenile court would recognize their innovation 100 years later is debatable. Initially, juvenile court was supposed to make decisions based on the "best interests" of the child. Today, a get-tough attitude has come to dominate discussions of juvenile court. Holding the youth accountable to community standards now plays a major role in the dispositions reached.

The future of juvenile courts is rapidly unfolding. To some observers, juvenile courts need to provide more adult-like due process. To others, juvenile courts need to provide more adult-like sentences. Still others would stress the need for new and creative ways of dealing with contemporary problems of American youth. The Progressive movement, after all, responded to changing conditions in society produced by the Industrial Revolution. To many, the current challenge is to respond to the changing conditions of society produced by the information age.

CHAPTER REVIEW

1. **Describe the child-saving movement and its relationship to the doctrine of *parens patriae*.**

Under the legal doctrine of *parens patriae* (state as parent) the government can intervene to protect the child if the parents are failing in their responsibilities. The child-saving movement, which began around 1890, believed that juvenile offenders required treatment, not punishment.

2. List the five ways in which juvenile courts differ from adult courts.

Juvenile courts emphasize helping the child, the proceedings are informal, the process is based on civil law, the proceedings are secret, and jury trials are not allowed.

3. Discuss how states vary in terms of when a juvenile may be transferred to adult court for prosecution.

Most states consider children to be juveniles until they reach their 18th birthday but set this upper age as low as 15. Juveniles accused of serious offenses, or who have a history of repeated offenses, may be tried as adults. Some states set no lower age for transfer while others set the lower limit at 14 or 16.

4. Contrast the three major types of cases that are heard in juvenile court.

In juvenile delinquency cases, the child is charged with a violation of the criminal law that is not based on age. In status offenses, the child is charged with an activity that is illegal only for juveniles. In child-victim cases, the child has committed no crime but the parents are accused of neglect or the like.

5. Identify and briefly describe the single most important Supreme Court case with respect to juvenile justice.

The Supreme Court decided *In re Gault* in 1967. Gault was arrested for making an obscene phone call, but his parents were not notified of his arrest or told of the court hearing. The Supreme Court held that juveniles are entitled to many of the same due process rights of adults, including the right to notice, the right to counsel, the right to confront witnesses, and the privilege against self-incrimination.

6. Explain the difference between a juvenile case that is petitioned and one that is nonpetitioned.

In juvenile court, charging occurs during the intake decision. Less serious cases are nonpetitioned and handled informally. Petition cases are handled formally and often result in a finding of juvenile delinquency.

7. Compare and contrast how adherents of the crime control model and proponents of the due process model of criminal justice see the future of juvenile courts.

Adherents of the criminal control model of criminal justice stress that juveniles should face more adult-like penalties and that the juvenile courts should either be abolished or more juveniles transferred to adult court for prosecution. Proponents of the due process model of criminal justice stress that juveniles need more crime prevention programs and juvenile courts should be less punishment-oriented.

CRITICAL THINKING QUESTIONS

1. In what ways do juvenile courts differ from courts that process adults accused of violating the criminal law? In what ways are juvenile courts similar?

2. What are the key features of the juvenile courts in your state? How are they organized, what is the upper age limit, and what is the lower age limit?

3. What advantages do you see in adding due process rights to juvenile court? What disadvantages do you see? To what extent are discussions over this matter influenced by atypical cases?

4. Compare the courtroom work group of adult court and juvenile court. Which actors are the same? Which actors are different? Do the members of the courtroom work group function the same way in juvenile court as in adult court?

5. Compare the steps of the adult court process with the steps of juvenile court. In what ways are they similar? In what ways are they different?

6. What do you think juvenile courts will look like 100 years from now? Will they incorporate more adult due process? Will they stress more adult penalties? Or will they develop more innovative helping programs?

KEY TERMS

adjudicated 518	intake decision 516	probation 518
adjudicatory hearing 518	juvenile 502	probation officer 512
child-victim 505	juvenile court 500	referral 513
conference 516	lower age of jurisdiction 502	status offense 505
delinquency 505	nonpetitioned case 516	summons 513
detention 516	other dispositions 519	transfer to criminal court 502
dismissal 518	parens patriae 500	upper age of jurisdiction 502
disposition 518	petition 516	
initial hearing 516	placement 518	

WEB RESOURCES

Go to the America's Courts and the Criminal Justice System companion website at

www.cengage.com/criminaljustice/neubauer

where you will find more resources to help you study.
Resources include web exercises, quizzing, and flash cards.

FOR FURTHER READING

Armstrong, Gaylene, and Nancy Rodriguez. "Effects of Individual and Context Characteristics on Pre-adjudciation Detention of Juvenile Delinquents." *Justice Quarterly* 22: 521–538, 2005.

Chesney-Lind, Meda, and Randall Shelden. *Girls, Delinquency, and Juvenile Justice*. 3rd ed. Belmont, CA: Wadsworth, 2004.

Feld, Barry. *Bad Kids: Race and the Transformation of the Juvenile Court*. New York: Oxford University Press, 1999.

Flynn, Nicole, Roma Hanks, and Lindsey Gurley. "Stirred, Shaken, or Blended: Gender Differences in Processing and Treatment of Juvenile

Offenders." *Women and Criminal Justice* 18 (4): 17–36, 2008.

Gaarder, Emily, and Joanne Belknap. "Tenuous Borders: Girls Transferred to Adult Court." *Criminology* 40: 481–518, 2002.

Gaarder, Emily, Nancy Rodriguez, and Marjorie Zatz. "Criers, Liars, and Manipulators: Probation Officers' Views of Girls." *Justice Quarterly* 21: 548–563, 2004.

Getis, Victoria. *The Juvenile Court and the Progressives*. Champaign: University of Illinois Press, 2000.

Goodkind, Sara Amy. *From Delinquent Daughters to Independent Mothers: Gendered Expectations in*

Juvenile Justice and Alternative Programs for Girls. Ann Arbor, MI: Proquest/UMI, 2006.

Greenwood, Peter. *Changing Lives: Delinquency Prevention as Crime-Control Policy.* Chicago: University of Chicago Press, 2006.

Griffin, Patrick. *Trying and Sentencing Juveniles as Adults: An Analysis of State Transfer and Blended Sentencing Laws.* Pittsburg: National Center for Juvenile Justice, 2003.

Kupchik, Aaron. *Judging Juveniles: Prosecuting Adolescents in Adult and Juvenile Courts.* New York: NYU Press, 2006.

Nagin, Daniel, Alex Piquero, Elizabeth Scott, and Laurence Steinberg. "Public Preferences for Rehabilitation versus Incarceration of Juvenile Offenders: Evidence from a Contingent Valuation Survey." *Criminology and Public Policy* 5: 627–653, 2006.

Shaffner, Laurie. *Girls in Trouble with the Law.* Piscataway, NJ: Rutgers University Press, 2006.

Siegel, Larry, and Brandon Welsh. *Juvenile Delinquency: Theory, Practice, and Law.* 10th ed. Belmont, CA: Wadsworth, 2009.

Tannenhaus, David. *Juvenile Justice in the Making.* New York: Oxford University Press, 2004.

APPENDIX A
CRIMINAL COURT LANDMARKS

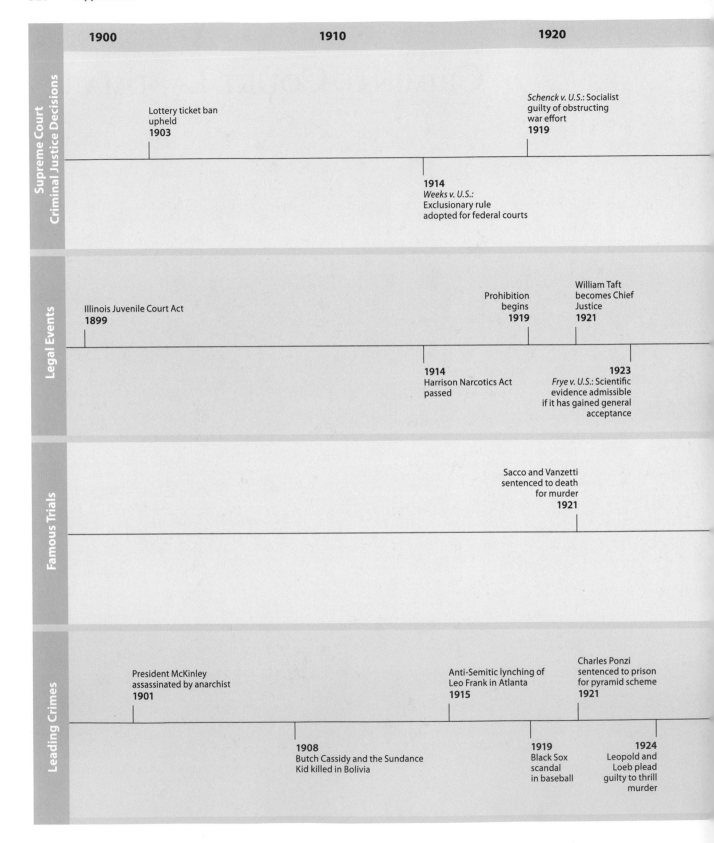

1900   **1910**   **1920**

Supreme Court Criminal Justice Decisions

Lottery ticket ban
upheld
1903

Schenck v. U.S.: Socialist
guilty of obstructing
war effort
1919

1914
Weeks v. U.S.:
Exclusionary rule
adopted for federal courts

Legal Events

Illinois Juvenile Court Act
1899

Prohibition
begins
1919

William Taft
becomes Chief
Justice
1921

1914
Harrison Narcotics Act
passed

1923
Frye v. U.S.: Scientific
evidence admissible
if it has gained general
acceptance

Famous Trials

Sacco and Vanzetti
sentenced to death
for murder
1921

Leading Crimes

President McKinley
assassinated by anarchist
1901

Anti-Semitic lynching of
Leo Frank in Atlanta
1915

Charles Ponzi
sentenced to prison
for pyramid scheme
1921

1908
Butch Cassidy and the Sundance
Kid killed in Bolivia

1919
Black Sox
scandal
in baseball

1924
Leopold and
Loeb plead
guilty to thrill
murder

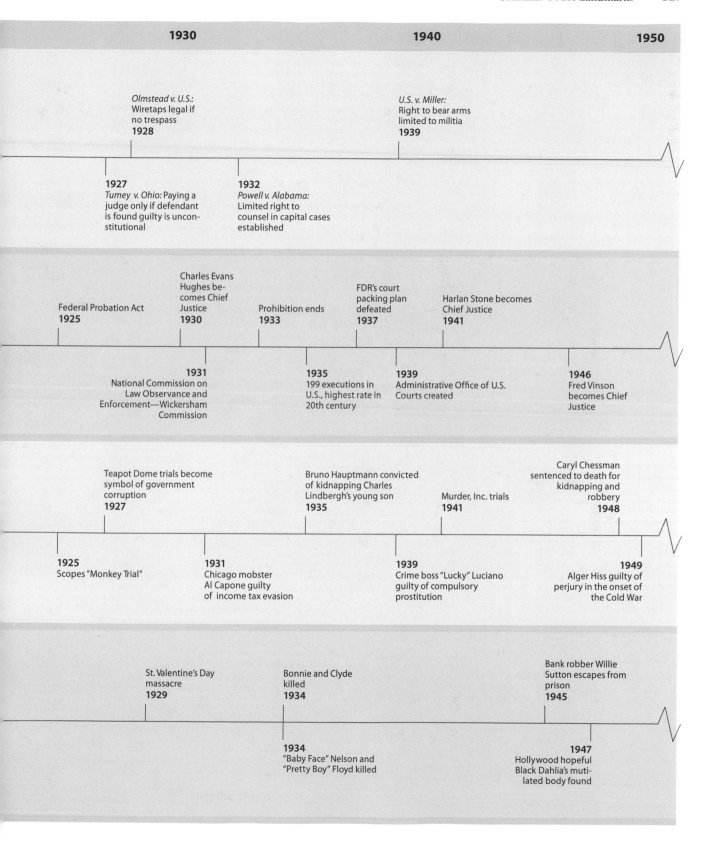

1930   **1940**   **1950**

Olmstead v. U.S.:
Wiretaps legal if
no trespass
1928

U.S. v. Miller:
Right to bear arms
limited to militia
1939

1927
Tumey v. Ohio: Paying a
judge only if defendant
is found guilty is uncon-
stitutional

1932
Powell v. Alabama:
Limited right to
counsel in capital cases
established

Charles Evans
Hughes be-
comes Chief
Justice
1930

FDR's court
packing plan
defeated
1937

Harlan Stone becomes
Chief Justice
1941

Federal Probation Act
1925

Prohibition ends
1933

1931
National Commission on
Law Observance and
Enforcement—Wickersham
Commission

1935
199 executions in
U.S., highest rate in
20th century

1939
Administrative Office of U.S.
Courts created

1946
Fred Vinson
becomes Chief
Justice

Teapot Dome trials become
symbol of government
corruption
1927

Bruno Hauptmann convicted
of kidnapping Charles
Lindbergh's young son
1935

Murder, Inc. trials
1941

Caryl Chessman
sentenced to death for
kidnapping and
robbery
1948

1925
Scopes "Monkey Trial"

1931
Chicago mobster
Al Capone guilty
of income tax evasion

1939
Crime boss "Lucky" Luciano
guilty of compulsory
prostitution

1949
Alger Hiss guilty of
perjury in the onset of
the Cold War

St. Valentine's Day
massacre
1929

Bonnie and Clyde
killed
1934

Bank robber Willie
Sutton escapes from
prison
1945

1934
"Baby Face" Nelson and
"Pretty Boy" Floyd killed

1947
Hollywood hopeful
Black Dahlia's muti-
lated body found

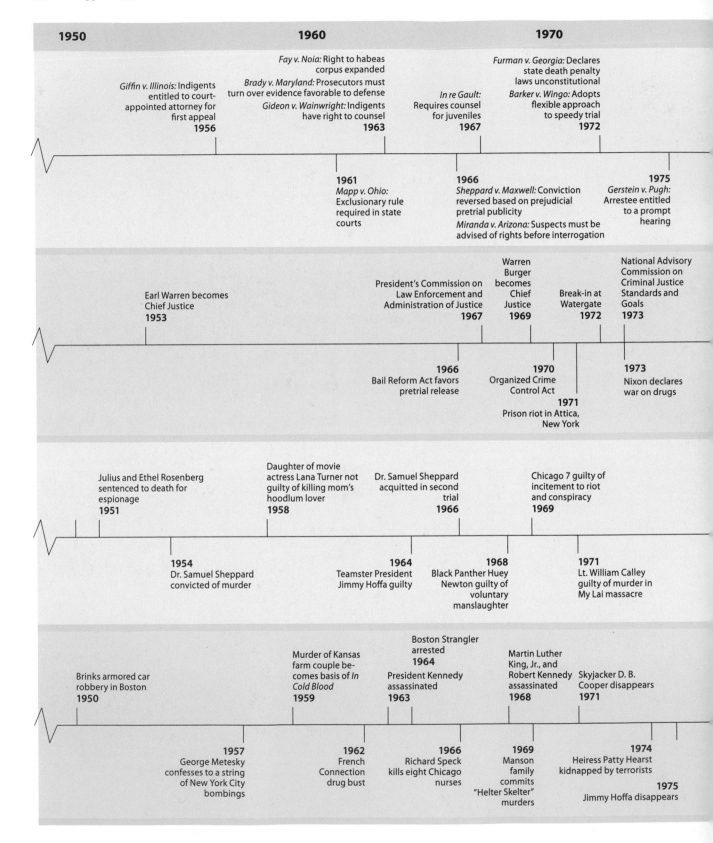

1950

1960

1970

Giffin v. Illinois: Indigents entitled to court-appointed attorney for first appeal
1956

Fay v. Noia: Right to habeas corpus expanded
Brady v. Maryland: Prosecutors must turn over evidence favorable to defense
Gideon v. Wainwright: Indigents have right to counsel
1963

In re Gault: Requires counsel for juveniles
1967

Furman v. Georgia: Declares state death penalty laws unconstitutional
Barker v. Wingo: Adopts flexible approach to speedy trial
1972

1961
Mapp v. Ohio: Exclusionary rule required in state courts

1966
Sheppard v. Maxwell: Conviction reversed based on prejudicial pretrial publicity
Miranda v. Arizona: Suspects must be advised of rights before interrogation

1975
Gerstein v. Pugh: Arrestee entitled to a prompt hearing

Earl Warren becomes Chief Justice
1953

President's Commission on Law Enforcement and Administration of Justice
1967

Warren Burger becomes Chief Justice
1969

Break-in at Watergate
1972

National Advisory Commission on Criminal Justice Standards and Goals
1973

1966
Bail Reform Act favors pretrial release

1970
Organized Crime Control Act

1971
Prison riot in Attica, New York

1973
Nixon declares war on drugs

Julius and Ethel Rosenberg sentenced to death for espionage
1951

Daughter of movie actress Lana Turner not guilty of killing mom's hoodlum lover
1958

Dr. Samuel Sheppard acquitted in second trial
1966

Chicago 7 guilty of incitement to riot and conspiracy
1969

1954
Dr. Samuel Sheppard convicted of murder

1964
Teamster President Jimmy Hoffa guilty

1968
Black Panther Huey Newton guilty of voluntary manslaughter

1971
Lt. William Calley guilty of murder in My Lai massacre

Boston Strangler arrested
1964

Brinks armored car robbery in Boston
1950

Murder of Kansas farm couple becomes basis of *In Cold Blood*
1959

President Kennedy assassinated
1963

Martin Luther King, Jr., and Robert Kennedy assassinated
1968

Skyjacker D. B. Cooper disappears
1971

1957
George Metesky confesses to a string of New York City bombings

1962
French Connection drug bust

1966
Richard Speck kills eight Chicago nurses

1969
Manson family commits "Helter Skelter" murders

1974
Heiress Patty Hearst kidnapped by terrorists

1975
Jimmy Hoffa disappears

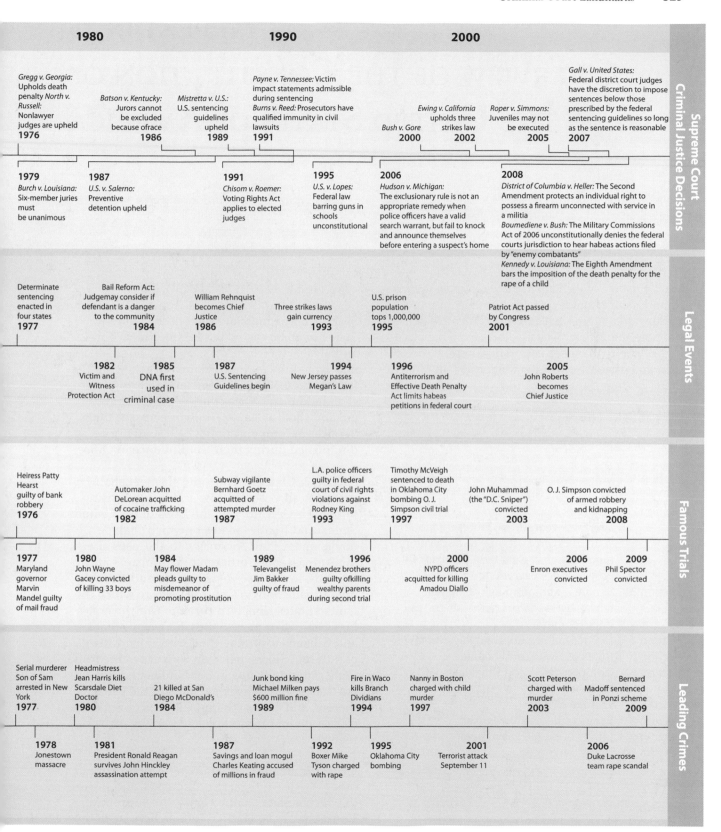

1980 **1990** **2000**

Supreme Court Criminal Justice Decisions

Gregg v. Georgia: Upholds death penalty *North v. Russell:* Nonlawyer judges are upheld
1976

Batson v. Kentucky: Jurors cannot be excluded because of race
1986

Mistretta v. U.S.: U.S. sentencing guidelines upheld
1989

Payne v. Tennessee: Victim impact statements admissible during sentencing
Burns v. Reed: Prosecutors have qualified immunity in civil lawsuits
1991

Ewing v. California upholds three strikes law
2002

Bush v. Gore
2000

Roper v. Simmons: Juveniles may not be executed
2005

Gall v. United States: Federal district court judges have the discretion to impose sentences below those prescribed by the federal sentencing guidelines so long as the sentence is reasonable
2007

1979
Burch v. Louisiana: Six-member juries must be unanimous

1987
U.S. v. Salerno: Preventive detention upheld

1991
Chisom v. Roemer: Voting Rights Act applies to elected judges

1995
U.S. v. Lopes: Federal law barring guns in schools unconstitutional

2006
Hudson v. Michigan: The exclusionary rule is not an appropriate remedy when police officers have a valid search warrant, but fail to knock and announce themselves before entering a suspect's home

2008
District of Columbia v. Heller: The Second Amendment protects an individual right to possess a firearm unconnected with service in a militia
Boumediene v. Bush: The Military Commissions Act of 2006 unconstitutionally denies the federal courts jurisdiction to hear habeas actions filed by "enemy combatants"
Kennedy v. Louisiana: The Eighth Amendment bars the imposition of the death penalty for the rape of a child

Legal Events

Determinate sentencing enacted in four states
1977

Bail Reform Act: Judge may consider if defendant is a danger to the community
1984

William Rehnquist becomes Chief Justice
1986

Three strikes laws gain currency
1993

U.S. prison population tops 1,000,000
1995

Patriot Act passed by Congress
2001

1982
Victim and Witness Protection Act

1985
DNA first used in criminal case

1987
U.S. Sentencing Guidelines begin

1994
New Jersey passes Megan's Law

1996
Antiterrorism and Effective Death Penalty Act limits habeas petitions in federal court

2005
John Roberts becomes Chief Justice

Famous Trials

Heiress Patty Hearst guilty of bank robbery
1976

Automaker John DeLorean acquitted of cocaine trafficking
1982

Subway vigilante Bernhard Goetz acquitted of attempted murder
1987

L.A. police officers guilty in federal court of civil rights violations against Rodney King
1993

Timothy McVeigh sentenced to death in Oklahoma City bombing O. J. Simpson civil trial
1997

John Muhammad (the "D.C. Sniper") convicted
2003

O. J. Simpson convicted of armed robbery and kidnapping
2008

1977
Maryland governor Marvin Mandel guilty of mail fraud

1980
John Wayne Gacey convicted of killing 33 boys

1984
May flower Madam pleads guilty to misdemeanor of promoting prostitution

1989
Televangelist Jim Bakker guilty of fraud

1996
Menendez brothers guilty of killing wealthy parents during second trial

2000
NYPD officers acquitted for killing Amadou Diallo

2006
Enron executives convicted

2009
Phil Spector convicted

Leading Crimes

Serial murderer Son of Sam arrested in New York
1977

Headmistress Jean Harris kills Scarsdale Diet Doctor
1980

21 killed at San Diego McDonald's
1984

Junk bond king Michael Milken pays $600 million fine
1989

Fire in Waco kills Branch Dividians
1994

Nanny in Boston charged with child murder
1997

Scott Peterson charged with murder
2003

Bernard Madoff sentenced in Ponzi scheme
2009

1978
Jonestown massacre

1981
President Ronald Reagan survives John Hinckley assassination attempt

1987
Savings and loan mogul Charles Keating accused of millions in fraud

1992
Boxer Mike Tyson charged with rape

1995
Oklahoma City bombing

2001
Terrorist attack September 11

2006
Duke Lacrosse team rape scandal

APPENDIX B
OVERVIEW OF THE CONSTITUTION OF THE UNITED STATES OF AMERICA

Note: Portions in **bold type** are especially important to criminal courts and judicial processes.

PREAMBLE

We the people of the United States, in order to form a more perfect union, establish justice, insure domestic tranquility, provide for the common defense, promote the general welfare, and secure the blessings of liberty to ourselves and our posterity, do ordain and establish this Constitution for the United States of America.

ARTICLE I—THE LEGISLATIVE BRANCH

Section 1   Vests legislative power in a bicameral (two-part) Congress

Section 2   House of Representatives—minimum age 25; 2-year terms; representation by state to be proportional to population; members elect their own Speaker; sole power of impeachment

Section 3   Senate—minimum age 30; 6-year terms; two senators per state; tries all impeachments

Section 4   Elections of Senators and Representatives

Section 5   Rules of House and Senate

Section 6   Compensation and Privileges of Members

Section 7   Passage of Bills

Section 8   Scope of Legislative Power

Section 9   Limits on Legislative Power

Section 10   Limits on States

ARTICLE II—THE PRESIDENCY

Section 1   Election, Installation, Removal

Section 2   Presidential Power

Section 3   State of the Union, Receive Ambassadors, Laws Faithfully Executed, Commission Officers

Section 4   Impeachment

ARTICLE III—THE JUDICIARY

Section 1. The judicial Power of the United States, shall be vested in one supreme Court, and in such inferior Courts as the Congress may from time to time ordain and establish. The Judges, both of the supreme and inferior Courts, shall hold their Offices during good Behavior, and shall, at stated Times, receive for their Services a Compensation which shall not be diminished during their Continuance in Office.

Section 2. Clause 1: The judicial Power shall extend to all Cases, in Law and Equity, arising under this Constitution, the Laws of the United States, and Treaties made, or which shall be made, under their Authority; to all Cases affecting Ambassadors, other public Ministers and Consuls; to all Cases of admiralty and maritime Jurisdiction; to Controversies to which the United States shall be a Party; to Controversies between two or more States; between a State and Citizens of another State; between Citizens of different States; between Citizens of the same State claiming Lands under Grants of different States, and between a State, or the Citizens thereof, and foreign States, Citizens or Subjects. (This section was modified, in part, by Amendment XI.)

Clause 2: In all Cases affecting Ambassadors, other public Ministers and Consuls, and those in which a State shall be Party, the supreme Court shall have original Jurisdiction. In all the other Cases before mentioned, the supreme

Court shall have appellate Jurisdiction, both as to Law and Fact, with such Exceptions, and under such Regulations as the Congress shall make.

Clause 3:   The Trial of all Crimes, except in Cases of Impeachment, shall be by Jury; and such Trial shall be held in the State where the said Crimes shall have been committed; but when not committed within any State, the Trial shall be at such Place or Places as the Congress may by Law have directed.

Section 3. Treason against the United States, shall consist only in levying War against them, or in adhering to their Enemies, giving them Aid and Comfort. No Person shall be convicted of Treason unless on the Testimony of two Witnesses to the same overt Act, or on Confession in open Court.

The Congress shall have power to declare the Punishment of Treason, but no Attainder of Treason shall work Corruption of Blood,[1] or Forfeiture except during the Life of the Person attainted.

ARTICLE IV—THE STATES

Section 1.   **Full Faith and Credit**
Section 2.   **Privileges and Immunities,**
                Extradition, Fugitive Slaves
Section 3.   **Admission of States**
Section 4.   **Guarantees to States**

ARTICLE V—THE AMENDMENT PROCESS

ARTICLE VI—LEGAL STATUS OF THE CONSTITUTION

Clause 1:   All Debts contracted and Engagements entered into, before the Adoption of this Constitution, shall be as valid against the United States under this Constitution, as under the Confederation.

Clause 2:   This Constitution, and the Laws of the United States which shall be made in Pursuance thereof; and all Treaties made, or which shall be made, under the Authority of the United States, shall be the supreme Law of the Land; and the Judges in every State shall be bound thereby, any Thing in the Constitution or Laws of any State to the Contrary notwithstanding.

Clause 3: The Senators and Representatives before mentioned, and the Members of the several State Legislatures, and all executive and judicial Officers, both of the United States and of the several States, shall be bound by Oath or Affirmation, to support this Constitution; but no religious Test shall ever be required as a Qualification to any Office or public Trust under the United States.

ARTICLE VII—RATIFICATION

AMENDMENT I

"Congress shall make no law respecting an establishment of religion, or prohibiting the free exercise thereof; or abridging the freedom of speech, or of the press; or the right of the people peaceably to assemble, and to petition the Government for a redress of grievances" (1791).

AMENDMENT II

"A well regulated Militia, being necessary to the security of a free State, the right of the people to keep and bear Arms, shall not be infringed" (1791).

AMENDMENT III

"No Soldier shall, in time of peace be quartered in any house, without the consent of the Owner, nor in time of war, but in a manner to be prescribed by law" (1791).

AMENDMENT IV

"The right of the people to be secure in their persons, houses, papers, and effects, against unreasonable searches and seizures, shall not be violated, and no Warrants shall issue, but upon probable cause,

---

[1]The corruption of blood would forbid the accused's family from inheriting his property.

supported by Oath or affirmation, and particularly describing the place to be searched, and the persons or things to be seized"(1791).

AMENDMENT V

"No person shall be held to answer for a capital, or otherwise infamous crime, unless on a presentment or indictment of a Grand Jury, except in cases arising in the land or naval forces, or in the Militia, when in actual service in time of War or public danger; nor shall any person be subject for the same offense to be twice put in jeopardy of life or limb; nor shall be compelled in any criminal case to be a witness against himself, nor be deprived of life, liberty, or property, without due process of law; nor shall private property be taken for public use, without just compensation" (1791).

AMENDMENT VI

"In all criminal prosecutions, the accused shall enjoy the right to a speedy and public trial, by an impartial jury of the State and district wherein the crime shall have been committed, which district shall have been previously ascertained by law, and to be informed of the nature and cause of the accusation; to be confronted with the witnesses against him; to have compulsory process for obtaining witnesses in his favor, and to have the Assistance of Counsel for his defence" (1791).

AMENDMENT VII

"In Suits at common law, where the value in controversy shall exceed twenty dollars, the right of trial by jury shall be preserved, and no fact tried by a jury, shall be otherwise re-examined in any Court of the United States, than according to the rules of the common law"(1791).

AMENDMENT VIII

"Excessive bail shall not be required, nor excessive fines imposed, nor cruel and unusual punishments inflicted"(1791).

AMENDMENT IX

"The enumeration in the Constitution, of certain rights, shall not be construed to deny or disparage others retained by the people"(1791).

AMENDMENT X

"The powers not delegated to the United States by the Constitution, nor prohibited by it to the States, are reserved to the States respectively, or to the people"(1791).

AMENDMENT XI

"The Judicial power of the United States shall not be construed to extend to any suit in law or equity, commenced or prosecuted against one of the United States by Citizens of another State, or by Citizens or Subjects of any Foreign State"(1795).

AMENDMENT XII

Election of President and Vice-President (1804).

AMENDMENT XIII

Abolition of Slavery (1865).

AMENDMENT XIV

Section 1. All persons born or naturalized in the United States, and subject to the jurisdiction thereof, are citizens of the United States and of the State wherein they reside. No State shall make or enforce any law which shall abridge the privileges or immunities of citizens of the United States; nor shall any State deprive any person of life, liberty, or property, without due process of law; nor deny to any person within its jurisdiction the equal protection of the laws.

Section 5. The Congress shall have power to enforce, by appropriate legislation, the provisions of this article (1868).

AMENDMENT XV

Rights Not to Be Denied on Account of Race (1870).

AMENDMENT XVI

Income Tax (1913).

AMENDMENT XVII

Election of Senators (1913).

AMENDMENT XVIII

Prohibition (1919).

AMENDMENT XIX

Women's Right to Vote (1920).

AMENDMENT XX

Presidential Term and Succession (1933).

AMENDMENT XXI

Repeal of Prohibition (1933).

AMENDMENT XXII

Two Term Limit on President (1951).

AMENDMENT XXIII

Presidential Vote in D.C. (1961).

AMENDMENT XXIV

Poll Tax (1964).

AMENDMENT XXV

Presidential Succession (1967).

AMENDMENT XXVI

Right to Vote at Age 18 (1971).

AMENDMENT XXVII

Compensation of Members of Congress (1992).

CONSTITUTION OF THE UNITED STATES

We the People of the United States, in Order to form a more perfect Union, establish Justice, insure domestic Tranquility, provide for the common defence, promote the general Welfare, and secure the Blessings of Liberty to ourselves and our Posterity, do ordain and establish this Constitution for the United States of America.

ARTICLE I

Section 1. All legislative Powers herein granted shall be vested in a Congress of the United States, which shall consist of a Senate and House of Representatives.

Section 2. The House of Representatives shall be composed of Members chosen every second Year by the People of the several States, and the Electors in each State shall have the Qualifications requisite for Electors of the most numerous Branch of the State Legislature.

No Person shall be a Representative who shall not have attained to the age of twenty five Years, and been seven Years a Citizen of the United States, and who shall not, when elected, be an Inhabitant of that State in which he shall be chosen.

Representatives and direct Taxes shall be apportioned among the several States which may be included within this Union, according to their respective Numbers, which shall be determined by adding to the whole Number of free Persons, including those bound to Service for a Term of Years, and excluding Indians not taxed, three fifths of all other Persons. The actual Enumeration shall be made within three Years after the first Meeting of the Congress of the United States, and within every subsequent Term of ten Years, in such Manner as they shall by Law direct. The Number of Representatives shall not exceed one for every thirty Thousand, but each State shall have at Least one Representative; and until such enumeration shall be made, the State of New Hampshire shall be entitled to chuse three, Massachusetts eight, Rhode-Island and Providence Plantations one, Connecticut five, New-York six, New Jersey four, Pennsylvania eight, Delaware one, Maryland six, Virginia ten, North Carolina five, South Carolina five, and Georgia three.

When vacancies happen in the Representation from any State, the Executive Authority thereof shall issue Writs of Election to fill such Vacancies.

The House of Representatives shall chuse their Speaker and other Officers; and shall have the sole Power of Impeachment.

Section 3. The Senate of the United States shall be composed of two Senators from each State, chosen by the Legislature thereof, for six Years; and each Senator shall have one Vote.

Immediately after they shall be assembled in Consequence of the first Election, they shall be divided as equally as may be into three Classes. The Seats of the Senators of the first Class shall be vacated at the Expiration of the second Year, of the second Class at the Expiration of the fourth Year, and the third Class at the Expiration of the sixth Year, so that one third may be chosen every second Year; and if Vacancies happen by Resignation, or otherwise, during the Recess of the Legislature of any State, the Executive thereof may make temporary Appointments until the next Meeting of the Legislature, which shall then fill such Vacancies.

No Person shall be a Senator who shall not have attained to the Age of thirty Years, and been nine Years a Citizen of the United States and who shall not, when elected, be an Inhabitant of that State for which he shall be chosen.

The Vice President of the United States shall be President of the Senate, but shall have no Vote, unless they be equally divided.

The Senate shall chuse their other Officers, and also a President pro tempore, in the Absence of the Vice President, or when he shall exercise the Office of President of the United States.

The Senate shall have the sole Power to try all Impeachments. When sitting for that Purpose, they shall be on Oath or Affirmation. When the President of the United States is tried, the Chief Justice shall preside: And no Person shall be convicted without the Concurrence of two thirds of the Members present.

Judgment in Cases of Impeachment shall not extend further than to removal from Office, and disqualification to hold and enjoy any Office of Honor, Trust or Profit under the United States: but the Party convicted shall nevertheless be liable and subject to Indictment, Trial, Judgment and Punishment, according to Law.

Section 4. The Times, Places and Manner of holding Elections for Senators and Representatives, shall be prescribed in each State by the Legislature thereof; but the Congress may at any time by Law make or alter such Regulations, except as to the Places of chusing Senators.

The Congress shall assemble at least once in every Year, and such Meeting shall be on the first Monday in December, unless they shall by Law appoint a different Day.

Section 5. Each House shall be the Judge of the Elections, Returns and Qualifications of its own Members, and a Majority of each shall constitute a Quorum to do Business; but a smaller Number may adjourn from day to day, and may be authorized to compel the Attendance of absent Members, in such Manner, and under such Penalties as each House may provide.

Each House may determine the Rules of its Proceedings, punish its Members for disorderly Behaviour, and, with the Concurrence of two thirds, expel a Member.

Each House shall keep a Journal of its Proceedings, and from time to time publish the same, excepting such Parts as may in their Judgment require Secrecy; and the Yeas and Nays of the Members of either House on any question shall, at the Desire of one fifth of those Present, be entered on the Journal.

Neither House, during the Session of Congress, shall, without the Consent of the other, adjourn for more than three days, nor to any other Place than that in which the two Houses shall be sitting.

Section 6. The Senators and Representatives shall receive a Compensation for their Services, to be ascertained by Law, and paid out of the Treasury of the United States. They shall in all Cases, except Treason, Felony and Breach of the Peace, be privileged from Arrest during their Attendance at the Session of their respective Houses, and in going to and returning from the same; and for any Speech or Debate in either House, they shall not be questioned in any other Place.

No Senator or Representative shall, during the Time for which he was elected, be appointed to any civil Office under the Authority of the United States, which shall have been created, or the Emoluments whereof shall have been encreased during such time: and no Person holding any Office under the United States, shall be a Member of either House during his Continuance in Office.

Section 7. All Bills for raising Revenue shall originate in the House of Representatives; but the Senate may propose or concur with Amendments as on other Bills.

Every Bill which shall have passed the House of Representatives and the Senate, shall, before it become a Law, be presented to the President of the United States; if he approve he shall sign it, but if not he shall return it, with his Objections to that House in which it shall have originated, who shall enter the Objections at large on their Journal, and proceed to reconsider it. If after such Reconsideration two thirds of that House shall agree to pass the Bill, it shall be sent, together with the Objections, to the other House, by which it shall likewise be reconsidered, and if approved by two thirds of that House, it shall become a Law. But in all such Cases the Votes of both Houses shall be determined by Yeas and Nays, and the Names of the Persons voting for and against the Bill shall be entered on the Journal of each House respectively. If any Bill shall not be returned by the President within ten Days (Sundays excepted) after it shall have been presented to him, the Same shall be a Law, in like Manner as if he had signed it, unless the Congress by their Adjournment prevent its Return, in which Case it shall not be a Law.

Every Order, Resolution, or Vote to which the Concurrence of the Senate and House of Representatives may be necessary (except on a question of Adjournment) shall be presented to the President of the United States; and before the Same shall take Effect, shall be approved by him, or being disapproved by him, shall be repassed by two thirds of the Senate and House of Representatives, according to the Rules and Limitations prescribed in the Case of a Bill.

Section 8. The Congress shall have Power To lay and collect Taxes, Duties, Imposts and Excises, to pay the Debts and provide for the common Defence and general Welfare of the United States; but all Duties, Imposts and Excises shall be uniform throughout the United States;

To borrow Money on the credit of the United States;

To regulate Commerce with foreign Nations, and among the several States, and with the Indian Tribes;

To establish an uniform Rule of Naturalization, and uniform Laws on the subject of Bankruptcies throughout the United States;

To coin Money, regulate the Value thereof, and of foreign Coin, and fix the Standard of Weights and Measures;

To provide for the Punishment of counterfeiting the Securities and current Coin of the United States;

To establish Post Offices and post Roads;

To promote the Progress of Science and useful Arts, by securing for limited Times to Authors and Inventors the exclusive Right to their respective Writings and Discoveries;

To constitute Tribunals inferior to the Supreme Court;

To define and punish Piracies and Felonies committed on the high Seas, and Offences against the Law of Nations;

To declare War, grant Letters of Marque and Reprisal, and make Rules concerning Captures on Land and Water;

To raise and support Armies, but no Appropriation of Money to that Use shall be for a longer Term than two Years;

To provide and maintain a Navy;

To make Rules for the Government and Regulation of the land and naval Forces;

To provide for calling forth the Militia to execute the Laws of the Union, suppress Insurrections and repel Invasions;

To provide for organizing, arming, and disciplining, the Militia, and for governing such Part of them as may be employed in the Service of the United States, reserving to the States respectively, the Appointment of the Officers, and the Authority of training the Militia according to the discipline prescribed by Congress;

To exercise exclusive Legislation in all Cases whatsoever, over such District (not exceeding ten Miles square) as may, by Cession of particular States, and the Acceptance of Congress, become the Seat of the Government of the United States, and to exercise like Authority over all Places purchased by the Consent of the Legislature of the State in which the Same shall be, for the Erection of Forts, Magazines, Arsenals, dock-Yards, and other needful Buildings;—And

To make all Laws which shall be necessary and proper for carrying into Execution the foregoing Powers, and all other Powers vested by this Constitution in the Government of the United States, or in any Department or Officer thereof.

Section 9. The Migration or Importation of such Persons as any of the States now existing shall think proper to admit, shall not be prohibited by the Congress prior to the Year one thousand eight hundred and eight, but a Tax or duty may be imposed on such Importation, not exceeding ten dollars for each Person.

The Privilege of the Writ of Habeas Corpus shall not be suspended, unless when in Cases of Rebellion or Invasion the public Safety may require it.

No Bill of Attainder or ex post facto Law shall be passed.

No Capitation, or other direct, Tax shall be laid, unless in Proportion to the Census or Enumeration herein before directed to be taken.

No Tax or Duty shall be laid on Articles exported from any State.

No Preference shall be given by any Regulation of Commerce or Revenue to the Ports of one State over those of another: nor shall Vessels bound to, or from, one State, be obliged to enter, clear or pay Duties in another.

No Money shall be drawn from the Treasury, but in Consequence of Appropriations made by Law; and a regular Statement and Account of Receipts and Expenditures of all public Money shall be published from time to time.

No Title of Nobility shall be granted by the United States: And no Person holding any Office of Profit or Trust under them, shall, without the Consent of the Congress, accept of any present, Emolument, Office, or Title, of any kind whatever, from any King, Prince, or foreign State.

Section 10. No State shall enter into any Treaty, Alliance, or Confederation; grant Letters of Marque and Reprisal; coin Money; emit Bills of Credit; make any Thing but gold and silver Coin a Tender in Payment of Debts; pass any Bill of Attainder, ex post facto Law, or Law impairing the Obligation of Contracts, or grant any Title of Nobility.

No State shall, without the Consent of the Congress, lay any Imposts or Duties on Imports or Exports, except what may be absolutely necessary for executing it's inspection Laws: and the net Produce of all Duties and Imposts, laid by any State on Imports or Exports, shall be for the Use of the Treasury of the United States; and all such Laws shall be subject to the Revision and Controul of the Congress.

No State shall, without the Consent of Congress, lay any Duty of Tonnage, keep Troops, or Ships of War in time of Peace, enter into any Agreement or Compact with another State, or with a foreign Power, or engage in War, unless actually invaded, or in such imminent Danger as will not admit of delay.

ARTICLE II

Section 1. The executive Power shall be vested in a President of the United States of America. He shall hold his Office during the Term of four Years, and, together with the Vice President, chosen for the same Term, be elected, as follows:

Each State shall appoint, in such Manner as the Legislature thereof may direct, a Number of Electors, equal to the whole Number of Senators and Representatives to which the State may be entitled in the Congress: but no Senator or Representative, or Person holding an Office of Trust or Profit under the United States, shall be appointed an Elector.

The Electors shall meet in their respective States, and vote by Ballot for two Persons, of whom one at least shall not be an Inhabitant of the same State with themselves. And they shall make a List of all the Persons voted for, and of the Number of Votes for each; which List they shall sign and certify, and transmit sealed to the Seat of the Government of the United States, directed to the President of the Senate. The President of the Senate shall, in the Presence of the Senate and House of Representatives, open all the Certificates, and the Votes shall then be counted. The Person having the greatest Number of Votes shall be the President, if such Number be a Majority of the whole Number of Electors appointed; and if there be more than one who have such Majority, and have an equal Number of Votes, then the House of Representatives shall immediately chuse by Ballot one of them for President; and if no Person have a Majority, then from the five highest on the List the said House shall in like Manner chuse the President. But in chusing the President, the Votes shall be taken by States, the Representation from each State having one Vote; A quorum for this Purpose shall consist of a Member or Members from two thirds of the States, and a Majority of all the States shall be necessary

to a Choice. In every Case, after the Choice of the President, the Person having the greatest Number of Votes of the Electors shall be the Vice President. But if there should remain two or more who have equal Votes, the Senate shall chuse from them by Ballot the Vice President.

The Congress may determine the Time of chusing the Electors, and the Day on which they shall give their Votes; which Day shall be the same throughout the United States.

No Person except a natural born Citizen, or a Citizen of the United States, at the time of the Adoption of this Constitution, shall be eligible to the Office of President; neither shall any Person be eligible to that Office who shall not have attained to the Age of thirty five Years, and been fourteen Years a Resident within the United States.

In Case of the Removal of the President from Office, or of his Death, Resignation, or Inability to discharge the Powers and Duties of the said Office, the Same shall devolve on the Vice President, and the Congress may by Law provide for the Case of Removal, Death, Resignation or Inability, both of the President and Vice President, declaring what Officer shall then act as President, and such Officer shall act accordingly, until the Disability be removed, or a President shall be elected.

The President shall, at stated Times, receive for his Services, a Compensation, which shall neither be encreased nor diminished during the Period for which he shall have been elected, and he shall not receive within that Period any other Emolument from the United States, or any of them.

Before he enter on the Execution of his Office, he shall take the following Oath or Affirmation:—"I do solemnly swear (or affirm) that I will faithfully execute the Office of President of the United States, and will to the best of my Ability, preserve, protect and defend the Constitution of the United States."

Section 2. The President shall be Commander in Chief of the Army and Navy of the United States, and of the Militia of the several States, when called into the actual Service of the United States; he may require the Opinion, in writing, of the principal Officer in each of the executive Departments, upon any Subject relating to the Duties of their respective Offices, and he shall have Power to grant Reprieves and Pardons for Offences against the United States, except in Cases of Impeachment.

He shall have Power, by and with the Advice and Consent of the Senate, to make Treaties, provided two thirds of the Senators present concur;

and he shall nominate, and by and with the Advice and Consent of the Senate, shall appoint Ambassadors, other public Ministers and Consuls, Judges of the supreme Court, and all other Officers of the United States, whose Appointments are not herein otherwise provided for, and which shall be established by Law: but the Congress may by Law vest the Appointment of such inferior Officers, as they think proper, in the President alone, in the Courts of Law, or in the Heads of Departments.

The President shall have Power to fill up all Vacancies that may happen during the Recess of the Senate, by granting Commissions which shall expire at the End of their next Session.

Section 3. He shall from time to time give to the Congress Information of the State of the Union, and recommend to their Consideration such Measures as he shall judge necessary and expedient; he may, on extraordinary Occasions, convene both Houses, or either of them, and in Case of Disagreement between them, with Respect to the Time of Adjournment, he may adjourn them to such Time as he shall think proper; he shall receive Ambassadors and other public Ministers; he shall take Care that the Laws be faithfully executed, and shall Commission all the Officers of the United States.

Section 4. The President, Vice President and all civil Officers of the United States, shall be removed from Office on Impeachment for, and Conviction of, Treason, Bribery, or other high Crimes and Misdemeanors.

ARTICLE III

Section 1. The judicial Power of the United States, shall be vested in one supreme Court, and in such inferior Courts as the Congress may from time to time ordain and establish. The Judges, both of the supreme and inferior Courts, shall hold their Offices during good Behaviour, and shall, at stated Times, receive for their Services, a Compensation, which shall not be diminished during their Continuance in Office.

Section 2. The judicial Power shall extend to all Cases, in Law and Equity, arising under this Constitution, the Laws of the United States, and Treaties made, or which shall be made, under their Authority;—to all Cases affecting Ambassadors, other public Ministers and Consuls;—to all Cases of admiralty and maritime Jurisdiction;—to Controversies to which the United States shall be a Party;—to Controversies

between two or more States;—between a State and Citizens of another State;—between Citizens of different States;—between Citizens of the same State claiming Lands under Grants of different States, and between a State, or the Citizens thereof, and foreign States, Citizens or Subjects.

In all Cases affecting Ambassadors, other public Ministers and Consuls, and those in which a State shall be Party, the supreme Court shall have original Jurisdiction. In all the other Cases before mentioned, the supreme Court shall have appellate Jurisdiction, both as to Law and Fact, with such Exceptions, and under such Regulations as the Congress shall make.

The Trial of all Crimes, except in Cases of Impeachment, shall be by Jury; and such Trial shall be held in the State where the said Crimes shall have been committed; but when not committed within any State, the Trial shall be at such Place or Places as the Congress may by Law have directed.

Section 3. Treason against the United States, shall consist only in levying War against them, or in adhering to their Enemies, giving them Aid and Comfort. No Person shall be convicted of Treason unless on the Testimony of two Witnesses to the same overt Act, or on Confession in open Court.

The Congress shall have Power to declare the Punishment of Treason, but no Attainder of Treason shall work Corruption of Blood, or Forfeiture except during the Life of the Person attainted.

ARTICLE IV

Section 1. Full Faith and Credit shall be given in each State to the public Acts, Records, and judicial Proceedings of every other State. And the Congress may by general Laws prescribe the Manner in which such Acts, Records, and Proceedings shall be proved, and the Effect thereof.

Section 2. The Citizens of each State shall be entitled to all Privileges and Immunities of Citizens in the several States.

A Person charged in any State with Treason, Felony, or other Crime, who shall flee from Justice, and be found in another State, shall on Demand of the executive Authority of the State from which he fled, be delivered up, to be removed to the State having Jurisdiction of the Crime.

No Person held to Service or Labour in one State, under the Laws thereof, escaping into another, shall, in Consequence of any Law or Regulation therein, be discharged from such Service or Labour, but shall be delivered up on Claim of the Party to whom such Service or Labour may be due.

Section 3. New States may be admitted by the Congress into this Union; but no new States shall be formed or erected within the Jurisdiction of any other State; nor any State be formed by the Junction of two or more States, or Parts of States, without the Consent of the Legislatures of the States concerned as well as of the Congress.

The Congress shall have Power to dispose of and make all needful Rules and Regulations respecting the Territory or other Property belonging to the United States; and nothing in this Constitution shall be so construed as to Prejudice any Claims of the United States, or of any particular State.

Section 4. The United States shall guarantee to every State in this Union a Republican Form of Government, and shall protect each of them against Invasion; and on Application of the Legislature, or of the Executive (when the Legislature cannot be convened) against domestic Violence.

ARTICLE V

The Congress, whenever two thirds of both Houses shall deem it necessary, shall propose Amendments to this Constitution, or, on the Application of the Legislatures of two thirds of the several States, shall call a Convention for proposing Amendments, which, in either Case, shall be valid to all Intents and Purposes, as Part of this Constitution, when ratified by the Legislatures of three fourths of the several States, or by Conventions in three fourths thereof, as the one or the other Mode of Ratification may be proposed by the Congress; Provided that no Amendment which may be made prior to the Year One thousand eight hundred and eight shall in any Manner affect the first and fourth Clauses in the Ninth Section of the first Article; and that no State, without its Consent, shall be deprived of its equal Suffrage in the Senate.

ARTICLE VI

All Debts contracted and Engagements entered into, before the Adoption of this Constitution, shall be as valid against the United States under this Constitution, as under the Confederation.

This Constitution, and the Laws of the United States which shall be made in Pursuance thereof; and all Treaties made, or which shall be made, under the Authority of the United States, shall be the supreme Law of the Land; and the Judges in every State shall be bound thereby, any Thing in the Constitution or Laws of any State to the Contrary notwithstanding.

The Senators and Representatives before mentioned, and the Members of the several State Legislatures, and all executive and judicial Officers, both of the United States and of the several States, shall be bound by Oath or Affirmation, to support this Constitution; but no religious Test shall ever be required as a Qualification to any Office or public Trust under the United States.

ARTICLE VII

The Ratification of the Conventions of nine States, shall be sufficient for the Establishment of this Constitution between the States so ratifying the Same.

Done in Convention by the Unanimous Consent of the States present the Seventeenth Day of September in the Year of our Lord one thousand seven hundred and Eighty seven and of the Independence of the United States of America the Twelfth

In witness whereof, We have hereunto subscribed our Names,

George Washington—President and deputy from Virginia
New Hampshire: John Langdon, Nicholas Gilman
Massachusetts: Nathaniel Gorham, Rufus King
Connecticut: William Samuel Johnson, Roger Sherman
New York: Alexander Hamilton
New Jersey: William Livingston, David Brearly, William Paterson, Jonathan Dayton
Pennsylvania: Benjamin Franklin, Thomas Mifflin, Robert Morris, George Clymer, Thomas FitzSimons, Jared Ingersoll, James Wilson, Gouverneur Morris
Delaware: George Read, Gunning Bedford, Jr., John Dickinson, Richard Bassett, Jacob Broom
Maryland: James McHenry, Daniel of Saint Thomas Jenifer, Daniel Carroll
Virginia: John Blair, James Madison, Jr.
North Carolina: William Blount, Richard Dobbs Spaight, Hugh Williamson

South Carolina: John Rutledge, Charles Cotesworth Pinckney, Charles Pinckney, Pierce Butler
Georgia: William Few, Abraham Baldwin

AMENDMENT I

Congress shall make no law respecting an establishment of religion, or prohibiting the free exercise thereof; or abridging the freedom of speech, or of the press; or the right of the people peaceably to assemble, and to petition the Government for a redress of grievances.

AMENDMENT II

A well regulated Militia, being necessary to the security of a free State, the right of the people to keep and bear Arms, shall not be infringed.

AMENDMENT III

No Soldier shall, in time of peace be quartered in any house, without the consent of the Owner, nor in time of war, but in a manner to be prescribed by law.

AMENDMENT IV

The right of the people to be secure in their persons, houses, papers, and effects, against unreasonable searches and seizures, shall not be violated, and no Warrants shall issue, but upon probable cause, supported by Oath or affirmation, and particularly describing the place to be searched, and the persons or things to be seized.

AMENDMENT V

No person shall be held to answer for a capital, or otherwise infamous crime, unless on a presentment or indictment of a Grand Jury, except in cases arising in the land or naval forces, or in the Militia, when in actual service in time of War or public danger; nor shall any person be subject for the same offence to be twice put in jeopardy of life or limb; nor shall

be compelled in any criminal case to be a witness against himself, nor be deprived of life, liberty, or property, without due process of law; nor shall private property be taken for public use, without just compensation.

AMENDMENT VI

In all criminal prosecutions, the accused shall enjoy the right to a speedy and public trial, by an impartial jury of the State and district wherein the crime shall have been committed, which district shall have been previously ascertained by law, and to be informed of the nature and cause of the accusation; to be confronted with the witnesses against him; to have compulsory process for obtaining witnesses in his favor, and to have the Assistance of Counsel for his defence.

AMENDMENT VII

In Suits at common law, where the value in controversy shall exceed twenty dollars, the right of trial by jury shall be preserved, and no fact tried by a jury, shall be otherwise re-examined in any Court of the United States, than according to the rules of the common law.

AMENDMENT VIII

Excessive bail shall not be required, nor excessive fines imposed, nor cruel and unusual punishments inflicted.

AMENDMENT IX

The enumeration in the Constitution, of certain rights, shall not be construed to deny or disparage others retained by the people.

AMENDMENT X

The powers not delegated to the United States by the Constitution, nor prohibited by it to the States, are reserved to the States respectively, or to the people.

AMENDMENT XI

The Judicial power of the United States shall not be construed to extend to any suit in law or equity, commenced or prosecuted against one of the United States by Citizens of another State, or by Citizens or Subjects of any Foreign State.

AMENDMENT XII

The Electors shall meet in their respective states, and vote by ballot for President and Vice-President, one of whom, at least, shall not be an inhabitant of the same state with themselves; they shall name in their ballots the person voted for as President, and in distinct ballots the person voted for as Vice-President, and they shall make distinct lists of all persons voted for as President, and of all persons voted for as Vice-President, and of the number of votes for each, which lists they shall sign and certify, and transmit sealed to the seat of the government of the United States, directed to the President of the Senate;—The President of the Senate shall, in the presence of the Senate and House of Representatives, open all the certificates and the votes shall then be counted;—The person having the greatest number of votes for President, shall be the President, if such number be a majority of the whole number of Electors appointed; and if no person have such majority, then from the persons having the highest numbers not exceeding three on the list of those voted for as President, the House of Representatives shall choose immediately, by ballot, the President. But in choosing the President, the votes shall be taken by states, the representation from each state having one vote; a quorum for this purpose shall consist of a member or members from two-thirds of the states, and a majority of all the states shall be necessary to a choice. And if the House of Representatives shall not choose a President whenever the right of choice shall devolve upon them, before the fourth day of March next following, then the Vice-President shall act as President, as in the case of the death or other constitutional disability of the President. The person having the greatest number of votes as Vice-President, shall be the Vice-President, if such number be a majority of the whole number of Electors appointed, and if no person have a majority, then from the two highest numbers on the list, the Senate shall choose the Vice-President; a quorum for the purpose shall consist of two-thirds of the whole number of Senators, and a majority of the whole number shall be necessary to a choice. But no person constitutionally ineligible to the office of President shall be eligible to that of Vice-President of the United States.

AMENDMENT XIII

Neither slavery nor involuntary servitude, except as a punishment for crime whereof the party shall have been duly convicted, shall exist within the United States, or any place subject to their jurisdiction.

Congress shall have power to enforce this article by appropriate legislation.

AMENDMENT XIV

Section 1. All persons born or naturalized in the United States, and subject to the jurisdiction thereof, are citizens of the United States and of the State wherein they reside. No State shall make or enforce any law which shall abridge the privileges or immunities of citizens of the United States; nor shall any State deprive any person of life, liberty, or property, without due process of law; nor deny to any person within its jurisdiction the equal protection of the laws.

Section 2. Representatives shall be apportioned among the several States according to their respective numbers, counting the whole number of persons in each State, excluding Indians not taxed. But when the right to vote at any election for the choice of electors for President and Vice President of the United States, Representatives in Congress, the Executive and Judicial officers of a State, or the members of the Legislature thereof, is denied to any of the male inhabitants of such State, being twenty-one years of age, and citizens of the United States, or in any way abridged, except for participation in rebellion, or other crime, the basis of representation therein shall be reduced in the proportion which the number of such male citizens shall bear to the whole number of male citizens twenty-one years of age in such State.

Section 3. No person shall be a Senator or Representative in Congress, or elector of President and Vice President, or hold any office, civil or military, under the United States, or under any State, who, having previously taken an oath, as a member of Congress, or as an officer of the United States, or as a member of any State legislature, or as an executive or judicial officer of any State, to support the Constitution of the United States, shall have engaged in insurrection or rebellion against the same, or given aid or comfort to the enemies thereof. But Congress may by a vote of two-thirds of each House, remove such disability.

Section 4. The validity of the public debt of the United States, authorized by law, including debts incurred for payment of pensions and bounties for services in suppressing insurrection or rebellion, shall not be questioned. But neither the United States nor any State shall assume or pay any debt or obligation incurred in aid of insurrection or rebellion against the United States, or any claim for the loss or emancipation of any slave; but all such debts, obligations and claims shall be held illegal and void.

Section 5. The Congress shall have power to enforce, by appropriate legislation, the provisions of this article.

AMENDMENT XV

The right of citizens of the United States to vote shall not be denied or abridged by the United States or by any State on account of race, color, or previous condition of servitude.

The Congress shall have power to enforce this article by appropriate legislation.

AMENDMENT XVI

The Congress shall have power to lay and collect taxes on incomes, from whatever source derived, without apportionment among the several States, and without regard to any census or enumeration.

AMENDMENT XVII

The Senate of the United States shall be composed of two Senators from each State, elected by the people thereof, for six years; and each Senator shall have one vote. The electors in each State shall have the qualifications requisite for electors of the most numerous branch of the State legislatures.

When vacancies happen in the representation of any State in the Senate, the executive authority of such State shall issue writs of election to fill such vacancies: Provided, That the legislature of any State may empower the executive thereof to make temporary appointments until the people fill the vacancies by election as the legislature may direct.

This amendment shall not be so construed as to affect the election or term of any Senator chosen before it becomes valid as part of the Constitution.

AMENDMENT XVIII

Section 1. After one year from the ratification of this article the manufacture, sale, or transportation of intoxicating liquors within, the importation thereof into, or the exportation thereof from the United States and all territory subject to the jurisdiction thereof for beverage purposes is hereby prohibited.

Section 2. The Congress and the several States shall have concurrent power to enforce this article by appropriate legislation.

Section 3. This article shall be inoperative unless it shall have been ratified as an amendment to the Constitution by the legislatures of the several States, as provided in the Constitution, within seven years from the date of the submission hereof to the States by the Congress.

AMENDMENT XIX

The right of citizens of the United States to vote shall not be denied or abridged by the United States or by any State on account of sex.

Congress shall have power to enforce this article by appropriate legislation.

AMENDMENT XX

Section 1. The terms of the President and Vice President shall end at noon on the 20th day of January, and the terms of Senators and Representatives at noon on the 3d day of January, of the years in which such terms would have ended if this article had not been ratified; and the terms of their successors shall then begin.

Section 2. The Congress shall assemble at least once in every year, and such meeting shall begin at noon on the 3d day of January, unless they shall by law appoint a different day.

Section 3. If, at the time fixed for the beginning of the term of the President, the President elect shall have died, the Vice President elect shall become President. If a President shall not have been chosen before the time fixed for the beginning of his term, or if the President elect shall have failed to qualify, then the Vice President elect shall act as President until a President shall have qualified; and the Congress may by law provide for the case wherein neither a President elect nor a Vice President elect shall have qualified, declaring who shall then act as President, or the manner in which one who is to act shall be selected, and such person shall act accordingly until a President or Vice President shall have qualified.

Section 4. The Congress may by law provide for the case of the death of any of the persons from whom the House of Representatives may choose a President whenever the right of choice shall have devolved upon them, and for the case of the death of any of the persons from whom the Senate may choose a Vice President whenever the right of choice shall have devolved upon them.

Section 5. Sections 1 and 2 shall take effect on the 15th day of October following the ratification of this article.

Section 6. This article shall be inoperative unless it shall have been ratified as an amendment to the Constitution by the legislatures of three-fourths of the several States within seven years from the date of its submission.

Amendment XXI

Section 1. The eighteenth article of amendment to the Constitution of the United States is hereby repealed.

Section 2. The transportation or importation into any State, Territory, or possession of the United States for delivery or use therein of intoxicating liquors, in violation of the laws thereof, is hereby prohibited.

Section 3. This article shall be inoperative unless it shall have been ratified as an amendment to the Constitution by conventions in the several States, as provided in the Constitution, within seven years from the date of the submission hereof to the States by the Congress.

Amendment XXII

Section 1. No person shall be elected to the office of the President more than twice, and no person who has held the office of President, or acted as President, for more than two years of a term to which some other person was elected President shall be elected to the office of the President more than once. But this article shall not apply to any person holding the office of President when this article was proposed by the Congress, and shall not prevent any person who may be holding the office of President, or acting as President, during the term within which this article becomes operative from holding the office of President or acting as President during the remainder of such term.

Section 2. This article shall be inoperative unless it shall have been ratified as an amendment to the Constitution by the legislatures of three-fourths of the several states within seven years from the date of its submission to the states by the Congress.

Amendment XXIII

Section 1. The District constituting the seat of government of the United States shall appoint in such manner as the Congress may direct: A number of electors of President and Vice President equal to the whole number of Senators and Representatives in Congress to which the District would be entitled if it were a state, but in no event more than the least populous state; they shall be in addition to those appointed by the states, but they shall be considered, for the purposes of the election of President and Vice President, to be electors appointed by a state; and they shall meet in the District and perform such duties as provided by the twelfth article of amendment.

Section 2. The Congress shall have power to enforce this article by appropriate legislation.

Amendment XXIV

Section 1. The right of citizens of the United States to vote in any primary or other election for President or Vice President, for electors for President or Vice President, or for Senator or Representative in Congress, shall not be denied or abridged by the United States or any state by reason of failure to pay any poll tax or other tax.

Section 2. The Congress shall have power to enforce this article by appropriate legislation.

AMENDMENT XXV

Section 1. In case of the removal of the President from office or of his death or resignation, the Vice President shall become President.

Section 2. Whenever there is a vacancy in the office of the Vice President, the President shall nominate a Vice President who shall take office upon confirmation by a majority vote of both Houses of Congress.

Section 3. Whenever the President transmits to the President pro tempore of the Senate and the Speaker of the House of Representatives his written declaration that he is unable to discharge the powers and duties of his office, and until he transmits to them a written declaration to the contrary, such powers and duties shall be discharged by the Vice President as Acting President.

Section 4. Whenever the Vice President and a majority of either the principal officers of the executive departments or of such other body as Congress may by law provide, transmit to the President pro tempore of the Senate and the Speaker of the House of Representatives their written declaration that the President is unable to discharge the powers and duties of his office, the Vice President shall immediately assume the powers and duties of the office as Acting President.

Thereafter, when the President transmits to the President pro tempore of the Senate and the Speaker of the House of Representatives his written declaration that no inability exists, he shall resume the powers and duties of his office unless the Vice President and a majority of either the principal officers of the executive department or of such other body as Congress may by law provide, transmit within four days to the President pro tempore of the Senate and the Speaker of the House of Representatives their written declaration that the President is unable to discharge the powers and duties of his office. Thereupon Congress shall decide the issue, assembling within forty-eight hours for that purpose if not in session. If the Congress, within twenty-one days after receipt of the latter written declaration, or, if Congress is not in session, within twenty-one days after Congress is required to assemble, determines by two-thirds vote of both Houses that the President is unable to discharge the powers and duties of his office, the Vice President shall continue to discharge the same as Acting President; otherwise, the President shall resume the powers and duties of his office.

AMENDMENT XXVI

Section 1. The right of citizens of the United States, who are 18 years of age or older, to vote, shall not be denied or abridged by the United States or any state on account of age.

Section 2: The Congress shall have the power to enforce this article by appropriate legislation.

AMENDMENT XXVII

No law varying the compensation for the services of the Senators and Representatives shall take effect until an election of Representatives shall have intervened.

Adjudication is the formal process by which legal disputes are judicially resolved in courts of law. Adjudication involves numerous processes, some of which are procedural in nature and some of which are mental insofar as they involve decision-making. Collectively, the mental components of adjudication are commonly referred to as **legal reasoning**.

Legal reasoning is a complicated process. In its most broad sense, it represents the ways in which judges (and sometimes jurors) make decisions in legal cases. Those decisions tend to involve three distinct types of rational thought processes: analogical, inductive, and deductive reasoning. But, to be sure, legal reasoning is not limited to the use of these logical forms of reasoning. Legal reasoning is more complicated than using logic to resolve factual disputes under the law. It also must take into account other elements of persuasion, such as current events and contemporary morals and values (Carter & Burke, 2007).

TYPES OF LOGICAL REASONING

REASONING BY ANALOGY

Reasoning by analogy, or **analogical reasoning**, is a type of inductive reasoning that involves comparing and contrasting things to find key similarities. An analogy is usually expressed in the form of one thing being like another (*X* is like *Y*; *A* is similar to *B*). You are probably most familiar with analogies used on standardized exams that test vocabulary. Here is a simple example:

Dolphin is to ocean as . . .
    A. Ant is to jungle   B. Salami is to lunch
    C. Camel is to desert D. Pencil is to lead

The correct answer would be "C"—camel is to desert. This is because a dolphin lives in the ocean like a camel lives in the desert. Ants may be found in jungles, but also live in many other places. Salami does not "live" anywhere; it may be eaten for lunch,

but it may be eaten for other meals as well. And pencils may contain lead, but pencils to do not "live" in lead. In this example, where the dolphin lives is what makes it most similar to the camel living in the desert. Selecting where the animal lives is the logical connection from which we draw the analogy. It is important to note, though, that there are other similarities upon which we could base a logical connection. For example, a dolphin and camel are both animals, while an ant is an insect, salami is a type of food, and a pencil is an inanimate object.

Let's try a slightly more complex analogy. Is an apple more like an orange or a banana? While all three are fruit, there are a number of characteristics upon which these fruits may be compared and contrasted.

Using the information in Table D.1, we find that apples and oranges are alike on only two of our selected dimensions: neither has edible seeds and both are round. Similarly, we find that apples and bananas are alike in only one way under our selected criteria for comparison: neither fruit is a member of the citrus family. Since apples and oranges are alike in two ways while apples and bananas are alike in only one, it would be a valid conclusion to say that apples are more like oranges than bananas. But what is critical to the analogy here is that we have selected six characteristics for comparison, one of which—color when ripe—is of no help whatsoever in comparing apples to the other two fruits. This illustrates one of the major shortcomings of analogical reasoning. It is dependent upon the criteria used for comparison.

Let's now apply this analogy in a legal framework. Supposed that a state prohibited the importation of "oranges and similar fruits," but allowed "bananas and similar fruits" to be imported into the state. Can apples be imported into this state? If you use shape as the basis for comparison, apples may not be imported. But if you use the criterion of whether the fruit belongs to the citrus family, then apples may be imported into the state. Both outcomes would be equally valid from the standpoint of logic. But only one outcome is likely to be correct

TABLE D.1

AN EXAMPLE OF REASONING BY ANALOGY

Characteristics for Comparison	Apple	Orange	Banana
Edible Seeds	No	No	Yes
Shape	Round	Round	Oblong
Edible Skin	Yes	No	No
Peelable Without a Knife	No	Yes	Yes
Citrus Family	No	Yes	No
Color When Ripe	Variable (Red, Orange, Yellow, Green)	Orange	Yellow

SOURCE: Martin, E.C. (n.d.). *Thinking like a lawyer.* http://www.samford.edu/schools/netlaw/dh2/logic

under the law. Given the ambiguity in the statutory law of this state, it would likely fall on the courts to figure out whether apples could be legally imported into the state. To make that determination, the courts would consider the arguments by analogy offered by the lawyers in the case and try to make as logical a ruling as possible.

In summary, analogical reasoning allows us to make comparisons. The validity of those comparisons depends upon the criteria or characteristics selected as the basis for the comparisons. In the end, though, analogical reasoning does not allow us to declare any general conclusions that may be used to support other arguments. That is where inductive and deductive reasoning comes into play.

INDUCTIVE REASONING

Inductive reasoning is the process of forming a generalization from a list of similar examples. The generalization is called a "conjecture."

The process of inductive reasoning begins by assembling a series of examples from a necessarily limited number of observations (because it is not possible to observe every example on the planet). This process uses analogical reasoning in order to group similar examples together. For example, suppose you observed the following types of fruit: apples, oranges, grapes, plums, tangerines, grapefruits, cranberries, cherries, coconuts, and lemons. From this limited set of examples, what generalization might you make about fruit? If you said, "all fruit are round," that would be an excellent conjecture based on the limited number of examples you had available to you. However, as you know, not all fruit are, in fact, round. Bananas, for example,

are oblong. So, your conjecture, although logical in light of your list of examples, would not be valid. This example illustrates the importance of having a sufficient number of examples that are drawn from a representative sample—something that is key to the scientific method. Determining whether the sample is representative is dependent, in part, on there being a sufficient number of examples that are comparable. Whether the examples are sufficiently alike as to warrant a logical comparison is dependent upon the criteria used to compare them. As discussed above, that comparison process involves analogical reasoning.

What color are swans? For thousands of years, all examples of swans in Europe led people to conclude that all swans were white. But they learned that all swans were not white when black swans were discovered in Australia in the late 1600s (Taleb 2007). These Australian counter-examples demonstrated that the conjecture "all swans are white" was not true. But it took going to a distant continent after centuries of first-hand observations to invalidate a conjecture that was assumed to be valid for centuries.

Let's examine an inductive argument as applied to legal reasoning. Suppose that you examined the facts and outcomes of a series of 20 murder cases from a single state in a given year (State *A*). In each case, the defendant intentionally killed the victim without the victim having done anything to provoke the killing. And, in each case of the 20 cases, the defendant was convicted. From this limited set of 20 examples, a good conjecture would be: "All people who intentionally kill another human being without any provocation will be convicted of murder."

Suppose you then studied 80 more murder cases—20 from each of four other states (States *B*, *C*,

D, and *E*) that occurred in the same year from which you drew your sample of 20 cases in State *A*. In all 80 of these cases, the defendant intentionally killed the victim without the victim having done anything to provoke the killing. Again, in each case of these 80 cases, the defendant was convicted. When added to the 20 murder cases from State *A*, you would be justified in having more confidence in your conjecture at this point because you not only examined more examples, but you diversified the representativeness of your sample by studying cases from four additional states. At this point, your conjecture could be called a **legal precept**—a generalized legal conclusion drawn from a reasonably representative list of examples. But your legal precept could not yet be considered a **rule of law** because it has not yet been established over time in a sufficient number of cases. For that to occur, you would need to examine many more murder cases from more states from a variety of years. See Exhibit D.1 for an illustration of the process of inductive reasoning as it applies within a legal framework.

Suppose, for example, that you studied a random sample of 200 cases drawn from 20 different states over a 50-year period of time. In all 200 cases, the defendant intentionally killed the victim without the

---

Exhibit D.1

FLOWCHART OF INDUCTIVE REASONING IN THE LAW

Inductive Reasoning

Observations
The observations must be made from representative examples. The representativeness of the examples is judged by using *analogical reasoning*. The strength of the analogy is based on the number of instances, the variety of instances, the number of similarities, the number of differences, the relevance of the observations, and the modesty of the conclusion.

↓

Pattern
Continuing to use analogical reasoning, similarities among and differences between the examples are noted until a pattern is discerned.

↓

Tentative Hypothesis/Conjecture
A logical generalization called a *conjecture* is made that links the similarities together. In legal reasoning, this conjecture is called a *legal precept*.

↓

Theory
Over time, as more and more representative observations are added, the tentative hypothesis/conjecture is refined into a theory. In legal reasoning, this process of refinement allows a legal precept to evolve into a *rule of law*. The rule of law can then serve as the major premise of a deductive argument.

victim having done anything to provoke the killing. Again, in each case of these 200 cases, the defendant was convicted (either by a jury or through a guilty plea). At this point, you may feel comfortable saying that your legal precept is a rule of law because the conjecture you made from your study of more than 200 cases was formed from a large number of examples drawn from a cross-section of states over a long period of time. In spite of these facts, though, you would be mistaken if you were to conclude that: "All people who kill another human being without any provocation will be convicted of murder."

Assume that you continued to gather data by looking at more cases in more states from different years. In one of the cases in State J, the defendant intentionally killed the victim without the victim having done anything to provoke the killing. However, the defendant in that case was not convicted because he was determined to be legally insane. Your conjecture/legal precept is now invalidated by this single counter-example. Therefore, the alleged "rule of law" must also be invalid as currently phrased. As you do more research, you find more cases in which mentally ill people were not convicted of murder for the intentional killing of another human being, some of which involved acquittals on the basis of insanity, others of which involved convictions of less serious forms of homicide after a determination of diminished capacity. You would have to refine your legal precept to take into account these examples. You might do so by forming the following inductive conjecture/legal precept: "All people who intentionally kill another human being without any provocation or legally recognized excuse will be convicted of murder."

DEDUCTIVE REASONING

In contrast to inductive reasoning, which goes from specific examples to a generalization, **deductive reasoning** goes from a generalization to a specific conclusion. The most simple and logically sound deductive argument takes the form of a "deductive syllogism." The syllogism allows us to compare the logical relationship between two arguments if arranged in a particular form. This form is as follows:

Major Premise	A generalized statement formed through induction.
Minor Premise	A statement capturing the essence of a particular example that relates

to the generalization in the major premise.

Conclusion	A statement that is logically consistent with both the major and minor premises.

Here is a classic example of a deductive syllogism:

Major Premise	All men are mortal.
Minor Premise	Socrates is a man.
Conclusion	Socrates is mortal.

The form of the deductive syllogism is key to the validity of its conclusion. There are a number of rules that must be met in order for a deductive syllogism to be validly formed[1] that are beyond the scope of this appendix. For our purposes, it is sufficient to say that a properly formed deductive syllogism guarantees the accuracy of the conclusion, assuming the truth of its premises. Recall, for example, the belief regarding the color of swans.

Major Premise	All swans are white.
Minor Premise	Daphne is a swan.
Conclusion	Daphne is white.

If, however, Daphne was one of the black swans discovered in Australia, then the logical form of the deductive syllogism is useless in providing a valid conclusion because one of the premises is false.

Let's apply the deductive syllogism to a legal example. Recall from the section above on inductive reasoning the generalization that we formed after examining murder cases in many states across a number of years. We eventually refined our inductive conjecture into a rule of law. That rule of law would serve as the major premise in a deductive syllogism.

---

[1]*E.g.*, there must be three and only three terms; at least one of the terms must be distributed using a universal term (like "all" or "none"); the conclusion cannot contain any term that is not distributed by a universal statement in one of the premises; if a negative universal term (like "none") is used to distribute one premise, then the other premise cannot also be phrased using a negative distributor; if either premise is negative, the conclusion must also be negative; and a syllogism with two universal premises cannot have a particular conclusion. For more information, see Martin. (n.d.)

Major Premise	All people who intentionally kill another human being without any provocation or legally recognized excuse will be convicted of murder.
Minor Premise	John intentionally killed another human being without any provocation or legally recognized excuse.
Conclusion	John will be convicted of murder.

There are two limitations to using deductive reasoning in the law that should be obvious at this point. First, as mentioned above, the conclusion will be invalid if either one of the premises is invalid. Thus, if it is not true that all people who intentionally kill other human beings without any provocation or legally recognized excuse will be convicted of murder, then we cannot know whether or not John will be convicted. Similarly, if John did not kill without provocation or legally recognized excuse, again we cannot form a valid conclusion about the outcome of his trial using the form of the deductive syllogism.

Second, the law rarely presents situations that can be reduced to the form of a pure deductive syllogism. There are clearly rules of law, but most of those rules have exceptions and some of those exceptions have even more specialized exceptions. Thus, it becomes quite difficult to form universal legal statements that can serve as the major premise of a deductive argument. Take, for example, the major premise concerning murder liability that we have been using in this appendix. "A person who intentionally kills another human being without any provocation or legally recognized excuse will be convicted of murder." This statement is fairly close to being an accurate statement of the law. But the problem is that we cannot say that all such people "will be convicted." Some people will be acquitted due to lack of evidence; others may be acquitted due to the sympathies of the jury; others may never even be caught and put on trial. Simply put, legal syllogisms are rarely, if ever, based upon absolute truths. Legal reasoning, therefore, is more complicated than the rules of logic.

LOGIC AS PART OF LEGAL REASONING

Analogical, inductive, and deductive reasoning all play important roles in the process of legal reasoning. But, as stated above, legal reasoning involves more than these forms of logic. The process of legal reasoning rests upon an important principle in law known as **stare decisis**—Latin for "to stand by decided matters." This principle stands for the proposition that prior cases should serve as **precedent** for deciding future cases that are factually and legal similar. This is especially important in the hierarchy of court structure. A decision of a higher court serves as binding precedent on a lower court within a particular jurisdiction. Thus, for example, a decision of the Supreme Court of Texas is binding on the lower appellate and trial courts of that state. That decision, however, is not binding on the courts of any other state. In our federal system, the decisions of the U.S. Supreme Court are binding on all lower courts, both state and federal, when it comes to interpretations of federal law (especially constitutional law). But state courts are free to interpret their state laws differently so long as they do not infringe upon the minimal baselines of federal constitutional protections as interpreted by the U.S. Supreme Court.

Given the roles of precedent and the principle of *stare decisis*, legal reasoning in the U.S. common law tradition brings a certain amount of stability to the law. It helps us to organize cases, using analogical reasoning, into legal precepts because we assume that the result in prior similar cases should guide the result in future similar cases. Moreover, the stability of law that *stare decisis* facilitates allows us to refine legal precepts over time into rules of law. These rules of law may then be deductively applied in new cases to produce reasonably predictable outcomes. The results in these cases then are added to the body of precedent to serve as even more examples to which analogies may be made in subsequent cases. This circular process is graphically represented in Figure D.1.

While stability in law is one of the benefits of reasoning from precedent within the principle of *stare decisis*, that stability can also have a downside. Because lower courts are bound to follow the precedents of higher courts, "bad precedent" must be overruled by the court that established it. It usually takes many years before courts recognize that one of its decisions was poor (or wrong) and, therefore, should not be retained as valid precedent. Part of what transpires over those years may be shifts in social conscience. After all, social norms evolve with time. For example, it took the Supreme Court nearly 60 years to overrule its decision in *Plessy v. Ferguson* (1896), which upheld the racial segregation on the "separate but equal" principle. By the time the Court

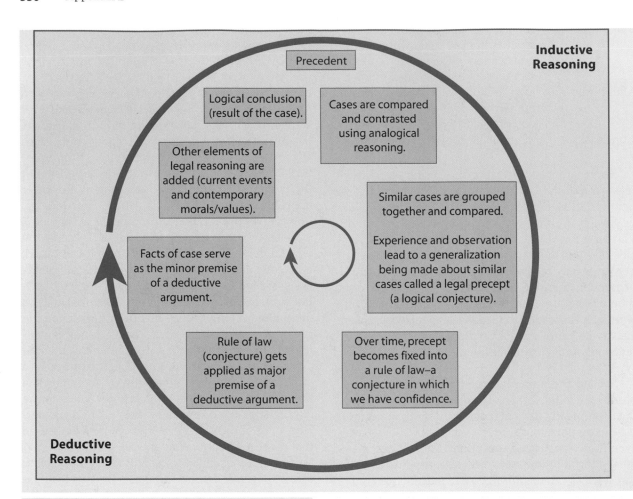

Precedent

Logical conclusion (result of the case).

Cases are compared and contrasted using analogical reasoning.

Other elements of legal reasoning are added (current events and contemporary morals/values).

Similar cases are grouped together and compared.

Experience and observation lead to a generalization being made about similar cases called a legal precept (a logical conjecture).

Facts of case serve as the minor premise of a deductive argument.

Rule of law (conjecture) gets applied as major premise of a deductive argument.

Over time, precept becomes fixed into a rule of law–a conjecture in which we have confidence.

Inductive Reasoning

Deductive Reasoning

FIGURE D.1   THE CIRCULAR PROCESS OF LEGAL REASONING

declared the "separate but equal" unconstitutional in *Brown v. Board of Education of Topeka* (1954), much had changed about the ways race was perceived in the United States.

Similarly, in 2003, the Supreme Court invalidated the nation's sodomy laws (i.e., laws criminalizing consensual oral or anal sex) on due process grounds when it decided *Lawrence v. Texas*. But only 17 years earlier, the Court had upheld the constitutionality of sodomy laws over a due process challenge in *Bowers v. Hardwick* (1986). Certainly, social mores and values had changed over those 17 years, especially with regard to views on homosexuality. That shift in social thought certainly had an impact on the Court's reasoning in *Lawrence* (see Fradella 2003).

Sometimes the passage of time is not enough; perhaps there needs to be a change in the judicial

composition of court such that new judicial officials bring a different philosophy of decision making to subsequent cases. Consider, for example, that several of the justices who had voted to uphold sodomy laws in *Bowers* had left the Supreme Court by the time *Lawrence* was decided and were replaced by justices who saw things differently, perhaps due in part, to different judicial philosophies (see below).

These examples illustrate that although the principle of stare decisis brings stability to the law, it does not necessarily mean that the law is stagnant. Other factors such as current events and evolving social norms and values also play an important role in legal reasoning (Carter & Burke 2007). This brings a certain amount of uncertainty to the law. You can never be quite sure how a court will rule in a case—especially when the case involves a complex question of constitutional law. This uncertainty is especially prominent when cases go to high courts, like the U.S. Supreme Court, since it is not bound by its own precedents. In light of such uncertainty, the politics of judicial decision making is frequently an issue when governors and the president select judges or justices.

JURISPRUDENCE AND LEGAL REASONING

There are many different theories of jurisprudence that collectively form the philosophy of law (see Table D.2).

A judge's belief in one of these schools of jurisprudential thought over another may have a significant effect on the outcome of case. But as Table D.2 should make clear, other factors clearly enter into the decision-making process. Carter and Burke (2007) posit that the decision in a given case is a product of a judge's views on (1) the law governing a particular type of dispute (L); (2) the relevant facts of a case (F); (3) current events (E); and (4) widely shared contemporary morals and values (V).

$$L + F + E + V \rightarrow D$$

While these four factors clearly form the basis for most legal reasoning as illustrated in Table D.2, it is important to keep in mind that the particular

TABLE D.2
MAJOR SCHOOLS OF JURISPRUDENTIAL THOUGHT

School	Summary of Major Beliefs	Descriptors	Equation Analogy
Natural Law	Human/Positive law (L) ought to reflect the law of nature or "nature law," which some would consider to be "God's Law." Decisions (D) should be a function (f) of moral principles (M) that are universally applied to promote human life, knowledge, community, friendship, and faith. Ambiguities in law must be resolved to harmonize positive law with natural law.	Static Infallible Humanistic	$f M(L + F) = D$
Legal Formalism	Judges apply the relevant positive law (L) to the pertinent facts of a case (F) and arrive at *the* correct legal decision (D). Normative or policy considerations are irrelevant. Thus, judges should be guided by the plain meaning of the words in a law, not by their interpretation of what the law should be. Ambiguities in the law should be resolved in accordance with the original meaning of the words and, if known, the intent of those who wrote the words.	Static Fallible Logical	$L + F = D$
Legal Realism	Law (L) is indeterminate. Law cannot be applied to the facts of a case (F) to reach a result without judges drawing on other extralegal considerations (ELC), especially the judge's personal experiences. ELC may go unstated in a legal opinion, but most often manifest themselves as part of the process of analogical reasoning process when judges decide which cases present the best "fit" to be followed as precedent.	Flexible Fallible Somewhat Idiosyncratic	$L + F + ELC = D$
Legal Process	Procedural consistency must guide legal reasoning. Decisions are a function (f) of applying positive law (L) to the facts of a case in accordance with certain neutral principles (NP) that restrain the discretion of any individual judge such as deference to legislative and/or executive intent, or widely shared ethical principles of societal goals as expressed in the plain language of positive law. Ambiguities in law should be interpreted in light of which neutral principle (NP) is consistently applied in such cases.	Somewhat Flexible Fallible Consistent	$f [NP(L + F)] \rightarrow D$

School	Summary of Major Beliefs	Descriptors	Equation Analogy
Law and Economics	Legal decisions (D) should be a function (f) of laissez faire economic principles (EP) being applied to the facts of the case (F) and the governing law. Ambiguities in law should be resolved to promote economic efficiency and maximize wealth.	Somewhat Flexible Fallible Consistent	$f[EP(L + F)] \rightarrow D$
Rights-Based Jurisprudence	Legal decisions (D) should be a function (f) of interpreting the facts of a case (F) and the applicable law (L) in ways that produce just outcomes and fair public policies. Ambiguities in law should be resolved to maximize individual rights and liberties (R) while simultaneously promoting social justice (J) and equality (E).	Highly Flexible Fallible Pragmatic and Humanistic	$f[(R+J+E)(L + F)] \rightarrow D$
Critical Legal Studies and Postmodern Jurisprudence	Law (L) represents a political and hegemonic device (i.e., it perpetuates the status quo) that is used promote social stratification in a manner that, overall, benefits certain groups of people over others. Indeed, judges interpret both the facts of a case (F) and the law as a function (f) of their indoctrination into ideologies that promotion deeply ingrained structural inequalities (SI) in society on the basis of socio-economic status, race (critical race theory), sex (feminist jurisprudence), and sexual identify (queer legal theory).	Somewhat Static Flawed Hegemonic and Illegitimate	$f[SI(L + F)] \rightarrow D$

judicial philosophy (P) of any judge can significantly influence his or her interpretation of any other variable. One judge might find a particular fact to be *the* legally operative fact in the case, while another judge may view that same fact as being less important. And, as presented in Table D.2, judges also clearly differ with respect to how to interpret the law, especially ambiguities in the law. And, finally, most of us recognize that current events and contemporary morals and values are all subject to different interpretations. Accordingly, judicial philosophy that judges bring with them to the bench clearly will have some effect on how they legally reason through a particular case. Collectively, these principles of legal reasoning may be represented by the equation:

$$f[P(L) + P(F) + P(E) + P(V)] \rightarrow D$$

Finally, how the judge perceives his or her own role also plays an important role in the legal reasoning process. While perceptions of the judicial role are related, to a certain degree, to a certain jurisprudential schools of thought, they are distinct, as we shall now explore.

JUDICIAL PHILOSOPHIES AND LEGAL REASONING

One of the most salient philosophical distinctions in legal reasoning stems from how a judge perceives his or her own role. Some judges believe that they should avoid making law through the common law process, and instead restrict themselves to narrow questions of law presented in the cases they adjudicate. This philosophy, most frequently associated with socially conservative judges, is referred to as **judicial restraint** (Carter & Burke 2007). Those who subscribe to judicial restraint generally believe that judges ought to focus on the original intent of a constitution or a statute. In doing so, they tend to strictly construe a legal provision by focusing on the actual meaning of the words used in a constitution or statute. Judges who subscribe to this point of view tend to be uncomfortable with the courts being used as agents of social change. Instead, they prefer for changes in the law to occur as a result of legislative actions.

In contrast, other judges see their roles as facilitating social change. They feel that they should make new laws in accordance with the changing needs of society. This philosophy, most commonly associated with liberal or moderate judges, is often referred to as **judicial activism**. Judges who subscribe to this perspective tend to view the language of constitutions and statutes as lenses through which interpretations can be made. To them, the law is as an evolving framework for courts to solve social problems that the other branches of government have neglected or refused to address.

It should be noted that the differences between the philosophies of judicial restraint and judicial activism might produce some false dichotomies, especially with respect to liberals and conservatives. Indeed, in their book *Battle Supreme*, Neubauer and Meinhold (2005) say that perceptions of judicial activism depends on whose ox is being gored.

> Historically, conservatives have tended to interpret legal doctrines quite flexibly, or actively, when it suited their purposes—for example, to extend more power to the executive branch, the police, and employers. Liberals have tended to read the Constitution quite strictly, or with restraint, when an amendment in is line with their beliefs—for example, the First Amendment stipulation that Congress make no law restricting freedom of speech. (Friedrichs, 2006, p. 58)

Consider, for example the Supreme Court's decision in *District of Columbia v. Heller* (2008). In that case, four conservative justices (Scalia, Roberts, Thomas, and Alito) were joined by one moderate justice (Kennedy) when they ruled that the Second Amendment to the U.S. Constitution grants an individual person the right to possess and use a firearm for lawful purposes, such as self-defense within the home. The Second Amendment provides: "A well regulated Militia, being necessary to the security of a free State, the right of the people to keep and bear Arms, shall not be infringed." They gave the Second Amendment an expansive (liberal?) reading when they decided that the introductory phrase regarding a militia was nothing more than a "prefatory clause" that in no way limited the "operative clause" of the Amendment—the one concerning the right to bear arms. In contrast, four liberal to moderate justices (Stevens, Breyer, Ginsburg, and Souter) dissented in the case by giving the Second Amendment a narrow, strict constructionist (conservative?) reading. They asserted the language used in the text of prefatory clause to the Amendment, as well as the original intent of the Framers, evidenced that the Amendment provided for the right of military and police use of firearms, not any right of private citizens to have and use such weapons. Since the outcome of the case was not in accordance with usual liberal/ conservative principles of judicial decision making, that tells us something about the role of judicial philosophy in the constitutional adjudication process. In short, legal reasoning is more complex than a reductionist label. Rather, it is a function of judicial philosophies, jurisprudential theories, current events, morals, and values as they collectively apply to the facts of a particular case and the interpretation of laws which, all too frequently, leave room for disagreement as to their meaning.

Box D-1

AN EXERCISE IN LEGAL REASONING

Assume that you and your friend Tom are in a bar together. Tom makes eye contact with an attractive young woman who, unbeknownst to him, is Scott's girlfriend. Scott, a very jealous person, sees this and immediately comes over to Tom and hits him over the head with a beer bottle without saying a word. As a result, Tom sustains a concussion and needs ten stitches to repair his injuries. And, for the first time in his life, Tom also starts to suffer severe headaches as a result of the injuries inflicted by Scott. Both you and Tom want

Scott brought to justice. In light of your knowledge of criminal justice, Tom asks you what you think will happen to Scott. To answer Tom, you decide to go to a law library in search of some answers.

First, you would need to determine which body of precedent to consult in order to find guiding legal precepts and binding rules of law. In doing so, you would disregard contract disputes, child custody cases, cases involving the probate of wills, and so on. Instead, you would be looking for criminal law cases.

Box D-1

CONTINUED

Thus, the type of legal dispute would be the organizing characteristic upon which we separate cases using analogical reasoning.

Once you identified criminal law as the subfield you needed to research, you would then need to engage in more analogical reasoning to find cases most similar to Tom's. Accordingly, you would not likely concern yourself with reading cases concerning homicides, thefts, or sexual assaults. Rather, you would look for cases involving the crime of battery—cases in which the victim sustained physical injuries without being killed.

Once you found a group of cases concerning battery, you would want to locate the ones with facts that are most similar to Tom's case. Again, this process would use analogical reasoning. Ideally, you would hope to find a case in which someone had been hit over the head with a beer bottle while in a bar. If you found such a case, you would be excited because the facts of that case would be nearly identical to yours. Unfortunately, you are unable to find such a case. However, you do find several cases that you think will help you answer Tom's questions.

Case 1:   During an argument, the defendant hit the victim over the head with a tire iron, causing the victim to sustain permanent brain damage. The incident took place in an auto repair shop. That defendant was convicted of aggravated battery and sentenced to 8 years in prison.

Case 2:   During an argument, the defendant used a chainsaw to sever the arm of the victim. The incident took place in the street in a residential neighborhood. The defendant was convicted of mayhem and sentenced to 12 years in prison.

Case 3:   After walking into his own bedroom to find a friend of his in bed with his wife, the defendant shot both his wife and his friend. Both victims lived, but required surgery to save their lives. The defendant was acquitted of attempted voluntary manslaughter, but was convicted of two counts of aggravated

battery with a deadly weapon. He was sentenced to 5 years in prison.

Case 4:   During an argument that occurred in a bar, the defendant punched the victim in the face, breaking his nose. The defendant was convicted of battery and sentenced to 6 months in jail.

Case 5:   The defendant slapped the victim across the face during an argument that occurred in a university dining hall. The defendant was suspended from school and was also criminally convicted of battery for which the defendant was placed on 6 months of probation.

- Which case is most like the one involving Tom and Scott? Why?
- Which case is most unlike the one involving Tom and Scott? Why?
- After reviewing these and other cases, you feel confident that Scott committed either a battery or an aggravated battery.
- Which crime do you think Scott committed? Explain your answer. What types of reasoning did you use to arrive at this answer?

You then look up the statute in your state governing the crimes of battery and aggravated battery. You find that simple battery is punishable by a term of probation to a maximum of 12 months in jail. The crime of aggravated battery, however, is punishable by a term of 5 to 10 years in prison.

- Based upon the case law and statutory research you did as summarized above, what do you think is the most likely outcome of the criminal case against Scott? Will he be convicted of a crime? If so, which one? What do you think the most likely sentence will be?
- As you no doubt surmised, you had to consider other factors in addition to the technical definition of the crimes of battery and aggravated battery in order to make a prediction about the likely outcome of Scott's case and the sentence he is likely to receive. What were those factors?

GLOSSARY

A

acquittal The decision of the judge or jury that the defendant is not guilty.

adjudicated Judicial determination (judgment) that a youth is a delinquent or status offender.

adjudicatory hearing Court hearing to determine whether a youth is guilty or not guilty.

administrative regulations Rules and regulations adopted by administrative agencies that have the force of law.

adversary system A proceeding in which the opposing sides have the opportunity to present their evidence and arguments.

aerial search A search conducted from an aircraft, usually a helicopter or a small, low-flying plane.

affidavit A written statement of facts, the truth of which the signer swears under oath.

affirm In an appellate court, to reach a decision that agrees with the result reached in the case by the lower court.

affirmative defense A defense in which the defendant bears the burden of production and/or persuasion to prove that extenuating or mitigating circumstances, such as insanity, self-defense, or entrapment, should result in a not guilty verdict.

alibi defense A defense alleging that the defendant was elsewhere at the time of the crime he or she is charged with.

Allocute/allocution hearing (1) The statement made by a defendant at the time he or she admits to the commission of a crime as a condition of the court accepting a guilty plea. (2) The statement made by a defendant at his/her sentencing hearing.

alternate jurors Jurors chosen in excess of the minimum number needed, in case one or more jurors is unable to serve for the entire trial.

alternative dispute resolution (ADR) Less adversarial means of settling disputes that may or may not involve a court.

American Bar Association (ABA) The largest voluntary organization of lawyers in the United States.

Anglo-American law The American legal system. See *common law*.

appellant (petitioner) The party, usually the losing one, that seeks to overturn the decision of a lower court by appealing to a higher court.

appellate brief A formal document submitted to an appellate court setting forth the legal arguments in support of a party's case on appeal. When a brief is filed in support of a motion at the trial court level, it is sometimes referred to as a "memorandum of points and authorities."

appellate court A court that hears appeals from trial courts on points of law.

appellate court record Papers, documents, and exhibits, as well as the transcript of the trial, that are submitted to the appellate court for review.

appellate jurisdiction The authority of a court to hear, determine, and render judgment in an action on appeal from an inferior court.

appellee (respondent) A party, usually the winning party, against whom a case is appealed.

arraignment The stage of the criminal process in which the defendant is formally told the charges and allowed to enter a plea.

arrest The act of depriving a person of his or her liberty, most frequently accomplished by physically taking the arrestee into police custody for a suspected violation of criminal law.

arrest warrant A document issued by a judicial officer authorizing the arrest of a specific person.

Article I Section of the U.S. Constitution concerning the legislative branch of the national government.

Article III Section of the U.S. Constitution concerning the judicial branch of the national government.

assembly-line justice The operation of any segment of the criminal justice system in which excessive workload results in decisions being made with such speed and impersonality that defendants are treated as objects to be processed rather than as individuals.

assigned counsel system Arrangement that provides attorneys for persons who are accused of crimes and are unable to hire their own lawyers. The judge assigns a member of the bar to provide counsel to a particular defendant.

attempt An act done with the specific intent to commit a crime, an overt act toward its commission, the failure to complete the crime, and the apparent possibility of committing it.

attendant (accompanying) circumstances Conditions surrounding a criminal act—for example, the amount of money stolen in a theft.

B

bail The security (money or bail bond) given as a guarantee that a released prisoner will appear at trial.

bail agent (bail bondsperson) A person whose business it is to effect release on bail for persons held in custody by pledging to pay a sum of money if a defendant fails to appear in court as required.

bankruptcy judge Judicial officer who presides over the legal procedure under federal law by which a person is relieved of all debts after placing all property under the court's authority. An organization may be reorganized or terminated by the court in order to pay off creditors.

bench trial Trial before a judge without a jury.

bench warrant (capias) An order issued by the court itself, or from the bench, for the arrest of a person; it is not based, as is an arrest warrant, on a probable cause showing that a person has committed a crime, but only on the person's failure to appear in court as directed.

best-evidence rule Rule requiring that someone coming into court must bring the best available original evidence to prove the questions involved in the case.

beyond a reasonable doubt Proof that leaves jurors firmly convinced of the defendant's guilt in a criminal case.

Bill of Rights The first ten amendments to the U.S. Constitution, guaranteeing certain rights and liberties to the people.

bind over If at the preliminary hearing the judge believes that sufficient probable cause exists to hold a criminal defendant, the accused is said to be bound over for trial.

Bivens **actions** The class of civil lawsuits that may be filed against federal officials for an alleged deprivation of one's constitutional rights.

boot camp A physically rigorous, disciplined, and demanding regimen emphasizing conditioning, education, and job training, typically designed for young offenders.

Boykin **form** Document intended to show that the defendant entered a guilty plea voluntarily and intelligently, understanding the charges and consequences of conviction (*Boykin v. Alabama* 1969).

brief A written statement submitted by the attorney arguing a case in court. It states the facts of the case, presents legal arguments in support of the moving party, and cites applicable law.

burden of persuasion The level or quantum of evidence necessary to convince a judge or jury of the existence of some fact in dispute. In a criminal case, the prosecution bears the burden of persuasion to prove each and every element of a crime beyond a reasonable doubt.

burden of production The responsibility of a party in a legal action to introduce sufficient evidence in support of an assertion such that a factual decision needs to be made at a trial or hearing to determine the truth of the assertion, as opposed to having a court summarily reject the assertion on the grounds of insufficient proof.

burden of proof The requirement to introduce evidence to prove an alleged fact or set of facts. See *burden of persuasion* and *burden of production*.

Burger Court The Supreme Court under the leadership of Chief Justice Warren Burger (1969–1986).

C

capital offense Any crime punishable by death.

capital punishment Use of the death penalty as the punishment for the commission of a particular crime.

career criminals Those people who commit a sequence of delinquent and criminal acts across the lifespan from childhood through adolescence and into adulthood.

cash bond Requirement that money be posted to secure pretrial release.

celerity of punishment The swiftness with which punishment is imposed on a criminal offender. Celerity is a central component of deterrence theory such that the more swift the punishment, the more the threatened punishment should deter the violation of law.

centralized administration The state supreme court, working through court administrators, provides leadership for the state court system.

centralized judicial budgeting The state judicial administrator (who reports to the state supreme court) has the authority to prepare a single budget for the entire state judiciary and send it directly to the legislature.

centralized rule making The power of the state supreme court to adopt uniform rules to be followed by all courts in the state.

certainty of punishment A core concept of deterrence theory which posits that the more certain it is that an offender will be caught, convicted, and punished, the less likely would-be offenders are to violate the law.

challenge for cause Method for excusing a potential juror because of specific reasons such as bias or prejudgment; can be granted only by the judge.

chambers The private office of a judge.

change of venue The removal of a case from one jurisdiction to another. It is usually granted if the court believes that, due to prejudice, a defendant cannot receive a fair trial in the area where the crime occurred.

charge bargaining In return for the defendant's plea of guilty, the prosecutor allows the defendant to plead guilty to a less serious charge than the one originally filed.

charging conference Meeting attended by judge, prosecutor, and defense attorney during which the judge's instructions to the jury are discussed.

charging document An information, indictment, or complaint that states the formal criminal charge against a named defendant.

child-victim Juvenile court case involving a child who has been neglected and/or abused by the parents.

circumstantial evidence An indirect method of proving the material facts of a case; testimony that is not based on the witness's personal observation of the material events.

civil law Law governing private parties; other than criminal law.

civil protection order Court order requiring a person to stay away from another person.

clerk of court An elected or appointed court officer responsible for maintaining the written records of the court and for supervising or performing the clerical tasks necessary to conduct judicial business.

closing argument Statement made by an attorney at the end of the presentation of evidence in which the attorney summarizes the case for the jury.

collateral attack An attempt to overturn the outcome of a court case by challenging it in a different proceeding or court.

common law Law developed in England by judges who made legal decisions in the absence of written law. Such decisions served as precedents and became "common" to all of England. Common law is judge made, it uses precedent, and it is found in multiple sources.

community service Compensation for injury to society, by the performance of service in the community.

complaint In civil law, the first paper filed in a lawsuit. In criminal law, a charge signed by the victim that a person named has committed a specified offense.

concurring opinion A written opinion in which a judge agrees with the outcome of a case on appeal, but wishes to emphasize different points or rationales than those used by the judges who sign on to the majority decision.

conditions of confinement lawsuit Lawsuit brought by a prisoner contesting prison conditions.

conference Juvenile court proceeding roughly equivalent to a preliminary hearing, in which the suspect is informed of his or her rights and a disposition decision may be reached.

confrontation A process by which a witness "confronts" a suspect in a lineup, a photo array, or even in person (i.e., a show-up) for the purpose of attempting to identify a suspect.

consent search A person, place, or movables may be lawfully searched by an officer of the law if the owner gives free and voluntary consent.

constitution The fundamental rules that determine how those who govern are selected, the procedures by which they operate, and the limits to their powers.

constitutional courts Federal courts created by Congress by virtue of its power under Article III of the Constitution to create courts inferior to the Supreme Court.

contemporaneous objection rule The requirement that an objection be made at a hearing or trial at the time of the alleged error in order for the mistake to qualify as the basis for an appeal.

contempt of court The failure or refusal to obey a court order; may be punished by a fine or imprisonment.

contract A legally enforceable agreement between two or more parties.

contract system Method of providing counsel for indigents under which the government contracts with a law firm to represent all indigents for the year in return for a set fee.

corpus delicti The body or substance of a crime, composed of two elements—the act and the criminal agency producing it.

count bargaining The defendant pleads guilty to some, but not all, of the counts contained in the charging document, which reduces the potential sentence.

courtroom work group The regular participants in the day-to-day activities of a particular courtroom; judge, prosecutor, and defense attorney interacting on the basis of shared norms.

courts of appeals Intermediate appellate courts in the federal judicial system.

crime control model A perspective on the criminal justice process based on the proposition that the most important function of criminal justice is the repression of crime, focusing on efficiency as a principal measure.

criminal justice system Agencies and institutions directly involved in the implementation of public policy concerning crime, mainly the law enforcement agencies, courts, and corrections.

criminal law Laws passed by government that define and prohibit antisocial behavior.

cross-examination At trial, the questions of one attorney put to a witness called by the opposing attorney.

cruel and unusual punishment Governmental punishment that is prohibited by the Eighth Amendment.

D

death-qualified juries Juries that sit in judgment of a defendant in a capital trial and are comprised of members (selected through the voir dire process) who are not morally opposed to voting to impose the death penalty.

death penalty Capital punishment, or executions by the state for purposes of social defense.

declaratory judgment Judicial pronouncement declaring the legal rights of parties involved in an actual case or controversy.

defendant The person or party against whom a lawsuit or prosecution is brought.

delay Postponement or adjournment of proceedings in a case; lag in case-processing time.

delinquency An act committed by a juvenile that would require an adult to be prosecuted in a criminal court. Because the act is committed by a juvenile, it falls within the jurisdiction of the juvenile court. Delinquent acts include crimes against persons or property, drug offenses, and crimes against public order.

demonstrative evidence Evidence created for demonstration purposes at trial, such as photos, maps, computer simulations, etc.

derivative evidence Secondary evidence derived from primary evidence obtained as a result of an illegal search or seizure.

detention Holding a youth in custody before case disposition.

determinate sentence A term of imprisonment, imposed by a judge, that has a specific number of years.

deterrence theory The view that certain, severe, and swift punishment will discourage others from similar illegal acts.

direct evidence Evidence derived from one or more of the five senses.

direct restitution The defendant pays money directly to the victim of the crime.

discovery Pretrial procedure in which parties to a lawsuit ask for and receive information such as testimony, records, or other evidence from each other.

discretion The lawful ability of an agent of government to exercise choice in making a decision.

discretionary appellate jurisdiction Jurisdiction that a court may accept or reject in particular cases. The Supreme Court has discretionary jurisdiction over most cases that come to it.

discrimination Illegitimate influences in the sentencing process based on the characteristics of the defendants.

dismissal Cases terminated (including those warned, counseled, and released) with no further disposition anticipated.

disparity Unequal sentences resulting from the sentencing process itself.

disposition A court decision on what will happen to a youth who has not been found innocent.

dissenting opinion An opinion written by a judge of an appellate court in which the judge states the reasons for disagreeing with the majority decision.

district courts U.S. trial courts established in the respective judicial districts into which the whole United States is divided. These courts are established for the purpose of hearing and deciding cases in limited districts to which their jurisdiction is confined.

diversity of citizenship When parties on the opposite sides of a federal lawsuit come from different states, the jurisdiction of the U.S. district courts can be invoked if the case involves a controversy concerning $75,000 or more in value.

domestic relations Relating to the home; the law of divorce, custody, support, adoption, and so on.

double jeopardy Fifth Amendment prohibition against a second prosecution after a first trial for the same offense.

drug courts Specialty courts with jurisdiction over cases involving illegal substances. Drug courts typically stress treatment rather than punishment.

dual court system A court system consisting of a separate judicial structure for each state in addition to a national structure. Each case is tried in a court of the same jurisdiction as that of the law or laws involved.

due process model A philosophy of criminal justice based on the assumption that an individual is innocent until proven guilty and has a right to protection from arbitrary power of the state.

due process of law A right guaranteed in the Fifth and Fourteenth Amendments of the U.S. Constitution and generally understood to mean the due course of legal proceedings according to the rules and forms established for the protection of private rights.

duress Unlawful pressure on a person to do what he or she would not otherwise have done.

E

elements of a crime Five principles of a crime that are critical to the statutory definition of crimes: guilty act, guilty intent, relationship between guilty act and guilty intent, attendant circumstances, and results.

en banc French term referring to the session of an appellate court in which all the judges of the court participate, as opposed to a session presided over by three judges.

entrapment The act of a government official or agent inducing a person to commit a crime that the person would not have committed without the inducement.

error A mistake made by a judge in the procedures used at trial, or in making legal rulings during the trial, that allows one side in a lawsuit to ask a higher court to review the case.

error correction Appellate courts seek to correct legal errors made in lower courts.

estate The interest a person has in property; a person's right or title to property.

evidence Any kind of proof offered to establish the existence or nonexistence of a fact in dispute—for example, testimony, writings, other material objects, demonstrations.

evidence-based corrections The use of rehabilitative programs, practices, and techniques in correctional settings that have been empirically evaluated and determined to be effective interventions.

exclusionary rule A rule created by judicial decisions holding that evidence obtained through violations of the constitutional rights of the criminal defendant must be excluded from the trial.

exculpatory evidence Evidence that casts doubt on the guilt of a criminally accused person.

expiation Atoning for sin through deserved suffering.

extradition Legal process whereby officials of one state surrender an alleged criminal offender to officials of the state in which the crime is alleged to have been committed.

F

federal question Case that contains a major issue involving the U.S. Constitution or U.S. laws or treaties.

felony The more serious of the two basic types of criminal behavior, usually bearing a possible penalty of one year or more in prison.

fine A sum of money to be paid to the state by a convicted person as punishment for an offense.

fruit of the poisonous tree The doctrine that evidence discovered due to information found through unconstitutional police behaviors (in interrogations or searches) may not be introduced by the prosecution in its case-in-chief.

Furman v. Georgia Supreme Court ruling that statutes leaving arbitrary and discriminatory discretion to juries in imposing death sentences are in violation of the Eighth Amendment.

fusion of the guilty act and guilty intent Criminal law generally requires that the guilty intent (mens rea) and the guilty act (actus reus) occur together. See *elements of a crime.*

G

gag order A judge's order that lawyers and witnesses not discuss the trial with outsiders.

general deterrence The theory which posits that rational, self-interested people will be deterred from committing crimes by the threat of certain, severe, and swift punishment.

geographical jurisdiction Geographical area over which courts can hear and decide disputes.

good time A reduction of the time served in prison as a reward for not violating prison rules.

grand jury A group of citizens who decide whether persons accused of crimes should be indicted (true bill) or not (no true bill).

Gregg v. Georgia Supreme Court ruling that (1) the death penalty is not, in itself, cruel and unusual punishment, and (2) a two-part proceeding—one for the determination of innocence or guilt and the other for determination of the sentence—is constitutional and meets the objections noted in *Furman v. Georgia*

gubernatorial appointment Method of judicial selection in which the governor appoints a person to a judicial vacancy without an election.

guilty act (actus reus) Requirement that, for an act to be considered criminal, the individual must have committed an overt act that resulted in criminal harm. See *elements of a crime.*

guilty intent (mens rea) Mental state required for a crime.

H

habeas corpus Latin phrase meaning "you have the body"; a writ inquiring of an official who has custody of a person whether that person is being lawfully imprisoned or detained.

harmless error An error made at trial that is insufficient grounds for reversing a judgment.

hearsay An out-of-court assertion or statement, made by someone other than the testifying witness, which is offered to prove the truth of testimony. Hearsay evidence is excluded from trials unless it falls within one of the recognized exceptions and does not otherwise violate the Sixth Amendment's Confrontation Clause.

hedonistic calculus A principle of utilitarian philosophy which posits that humans seek pleasure and avoid pain. This principle plays an important role in deterrence theory insofar as rational thinkers will seek to avoid the pain that criminal punishment will inflict upon them by avoiding lawbreaking behaviors if and only if the pain of punishment outweighs the pleasure that would be gained through the commission of crime.

hierarchical jurisdiction Refers to differences in the functions of courts and involves original as opposed to appellate jurisdiction.

hung jury A jury that is unable to reach a verdict.

I

illegal search and seizure An act in violation of the Fourth Amendment of the U.S. Constitution.

immaterial Evidence that neither proves nor disproves the issue of a trial.

immunity A grant of exemption from prosecution in return for evidence or testimony.

impeach To question the truthfulness of a witness's testimony.

impeachment Official accusation against a public official brought by a legislative body seeking his or her removal.

imprisonment Placing a person in a prison, jail, or similar correctional facility as punishment for committing a crime.

inference A logical conclusion that the trier-of-fact may make in light of the evidence.

in rem Against a thing; a legal proceeding instituted to obtain decrees or judgments against property.

incapacitation Sentencing philosophy that stresses crime prevention through isolating wrongdoers from society.

incorporation The theory that the Bill of Rights has been incorporated or absorbed into the due process clause of the Fourteenth Amendment, thereby making it applicable to the states.

indeterminate sentence A sentence that has both a minimum and a maximum term of imprisonment, the actual length to be determined by a parole board.

index crimes The specific crimes used by the FBI when reporting the incidence of crime in the United States in the *Uniform Crime Reports.*

indictment A formal accusation of a criminal offense made against a person by a grand jury.

indigents Defendants who are too poor to pay a lawyer and therefore are entitled to a lawyer for free.

inferior court (lower court) Term for a trial court of limited jurisdiction; also may refer to any court lower in the judicial hierarchy.

information A formal accusation charging someone with the commission of a crime, signed by a prosecuting attorney, which has the effect of bringing the person to trial.

inheritance Property received from a dead person, either by effect of intestacy or through a will.

initial appearance Shortly after arrest, the suspect is brought before a judicial official who informs the person of the reason for the arrest and makes an initial determination about whether there was probable cause for the arrest. In some jurisdictions, a preliminary determination regarding bail may also be made.

initial hearing In juvenile court, an often informal hearing during which an intake decision is made.

injunction A court order directing someone to do something or to refrain from doing something.

intake decision The decision made by a juvenile court that results in the case being handled either informally at the intake level or more formally by petition and scheduled for an adjudicatory or transfer hearing.

intensive supervision probation (ISP) Probation granted under conditions of strict reporting to a probation officer with a limited caseload.

interlocutory Provisional; temporary; while a lawsuit is still going on.

intermediate courts of appeals (ICAs) Judicial bodies falling between the highest, or supreme, tribunal and the trial court; created to relieve the jurisdiction's highest court of hearing a large number of cases.

intermediate sanctions Variety of sanctions that lie somewhere between prison and probation.

irrelevant Testimony that has no bearing on the issue of a trial.

J

judge-made law The common law as developed in form and content by judges or judicial decisions.

judgment The official decision of a court concerning a legal matter.

judicial conduct commission An official body whose function is to investigate allegations of misconduct by judges.

judicial election Method of judicial selection in which the voters choose judicial candidates in a partisan or nonpartisan election.

judicial independence Normative value that stresses a judge should be free from outside pressure in making a decision.

jurisdiction The power of a court to hear and adjudicate a case.

jury consultants Professionals who assist lawyers in selecting juries through the use of behavioral scientific principles and techniques.

jury deliberations The action of a jury in determining the guilt or innocence, or the sentence, of a defendant.

jury instructions Directions given by a judge to the members of the jury informing them of the law applicable to the case.

jury nullification Idea that juries have the right to refuse to apply the law in criminal cases despite facts that leave no reasonable doubt that the law was violated.

just deserts Punishment for criminal wrongdoing should be proportionate to the severity of the offense.

justice of the peace (JP) A low-level judge, sometimes without legal training, typically found in rural areas of some states, empowered to try petty civil and criminal cases and to conduct the preliminary stages of felony cases.

juvenile Youth at or below the upper age of juvenile court jurisdiction.

juvenile court Any court that has jurisdiction over matters involving juveniles.

juvenile delinquency An act committed by a juvenile for which an adult could be prosecuted in a criminal court.

L

law Body of rules enacted by public officials in a legitimate manner and backed by the force of the state.

legal defense Legally recognized justification for illegal actions, or acceptance that individuals were not legally responsible for their actions.

legal ethics Codes of conduct governing how lawyers practice law and how judges administer justice.

legislative courts Judicial bodies created by Congress under Article I (legislative article) and not Article III (judicial article).

lex talionis Latin for "the law of retaliation," it is the philosophical principle that punishments should be equal to the harm caused by the commission of a crime as embodied in the phrase, "an eye for an eye; a tooth for a tooth; an arm for an arm; a life for a life."

local prosecutors General term for lawyers who represent local governments (cities and counties, for example) in the lower courts; often called *city attorneys* or *solicitors*.

lower age of jurisdiction Minimum age at which a youth may be transferred to adult court.

M

mandamus petitions A type of lawsuit in which a plaintiff seeks a court order commanding someone to perform an act or duty imposed by law as an obligation.

mandatory appellate jurisdiction Jurisdiction that a court must accept. Cases falling under a court's mandatory jurisdiction must be decided officially on their merits, though a court may avoid giving them full consideration.

mandatory minimum sentencing Minimum required penalty specified for a certain crime.

master jury list A list of potential jurors in a court's district, from which a representative cross section of the community in which a crime allegedly was committed can be selected for a trial. It is usually compiled from multiple sources, such as voter registration lists, driver's license lists, utility customer lists, and telephone directories. Also called *jury wheel* or *master wheel*.

misdemeanor Lesser of the two basic types of crime, usually punishable by no more than one year in jail.

Missouri Bar Plan The name given to a method of judicial selection combining merit selection and popular control in retention elections.

mistrial Invalid trial.

monetary damage Compensatory damages—payment for actual losses suffered by a plaintiff. Punitive damages—money awarded by a court to a person who has been harmed in a malicious or willful way.

motions to vacate sentences Filings by prisoners who seek to have their sentences set aside or changed on the grounds that the sentence was imposed in violation of the Constitution or laws of the United States.

motor vehicle searches The warrantless search of a motor vehicle when there is probable cause to believe that the vehicle contains contraband or evidence of a crime.

municipal court A trial court of limited jurisdiction created by a local unit of government.

municipal ordinance Law passed by a local unit of government.

N

new judicial federalism Movement in state supreme courts to reinvigorate states' constitutions as sources of individual rights over and above the rights granted by the U.S. Constitution.

no true bill The decision of a grand jury not to indict a person for a crime.

nolle prosequi The ending of a criminal case because the prosecutor decides or agrees to stop prosecuting. When this happens, the case is "nollied," "nolled," or "nol. prossed."

nolo contendere Latin phrase meaning "I will not contest it." A plea of "no contest" in a criminal case means that the defendant does not directly admit guilt but submits to sentencing or other punishment.

nonpetitioned case A case handled informally by duly authorized court personnel.

normal crime Categorization of crime based on the typical manner in which it is committed, the type of defendant who typically commits it, and the typical penalty to be applied.

normal penalties Norms for proper sentencing based on the crime committed and the defendant's prior record.

notice of appeal Written document filed with the clerk of court stating that the defendant in the criminal case plans to appeal.

O

objection The act of taking exception to a statement or procedure during a trial.

officer of the court Lawyers are officers of the court and, as such, must obey court rules, be truthful in court, and generally serve the needs of justice.

open fields The doctrine that allows law enforcement to search open lands without a warrant.

opening statement Address made by attorneys for both parties at the beginning of a trial in which they outline for the jury what they intend to prove in their case.

opinion The reasons given for the decision reached by an appellate court.

oral argument The part of the appellate court decision-making process in which lawyers for both parties plead their case in person before the court.

ordinance A law enacted by a local government body for the regulation of some activity within the community.

original jurisdiction Jurisdiction in the first instance; commonly used to refer to trial jurisdiction as opposed to appellate jurisdiction. Appellate courts, however, have limited original jurisdiction.

other dispositions Miscellaneous dispositions, including fines, restitution, community service, and referrals outside the court for services, with minimal or no further court involvement anticipated.

P

pardon An act of executive clemency that has the effect of releasing an inmate from prison and/or removing certain legal disabilities from persons convicted of crimes.

parens patriae The state as parent; the state as guardian and protector of all citizens (such as juveniles) who are unable to protect themselves.

parole Early release from prison on the condition of good behavior.

parole board An administrative body whose members are chosen by the governor to review the cases of prisoners eligible for release on parole. The board has the authority to release such persons and to return them to prison for violating the conditions of parole.

peremptory challenge Method for excusing a potential juror without cause, so long as the reasons for doing so are not based on racial or gender discrimination.

personal injury Negligence lawsuits, often involving automobile accidents.

personal jurisdiction The power of a court over a particular person or legal entity (such as a partnership or corporation).

petit jury A trial jury as distinguished from a grand jury.

petition A document filed in juvenile court alleging that a juvenile is a delinquent or a status offender and asking that the court assume jurisdiction over the juvenile or that an alleged

delinquent be transferred to criminal court for prosecution as an adult.

petitioner The party filing a petition in a court of law. It is most commonly used to refer to the parting seeking discretionary appellate review through the filing a petition for a writ of certiorari.

petty offense A minor criminal offense that does not entitle the defendant to a trial by jury.

placement Cases in which youths are placed in a residential facility or otherwise removed from their homes and placed elsewhere.

plain error An exception to the contemporary objection rule in which a highly prejudicial error substantially affects the rights of the accused such that a failure to correct the error on appeal, even if an objection was not made at the hearing or trial at the time of the alleged error, would result in a miscarriage of justice.

plain view If police happen to come across something while acting within their lawful duty, that item may be used as evidence in a criminal trial, even if the police did not have a search warrant.

plaintiff The person or party who initiates a lawsuit.

plea bargaining The process by which a defendant pleads guilty to a criminal charge with the expectation of receiving some benefit from the state.

plea on the nose The defendant pleads guilty to the charges contained in the indictment or bill of information.

plurality opinion A decision, usually of an appellate court, in which no single opinion received the support of a majority of the court.

policy formulation Function of appellate courts to make new law and adjust existing law to changing circumstances.

post-verdict motions Various motions made by the defense after a jury conviction in hopes of gaining a new trial.

precedent A case previously decided that serves as a legal guide for the resolution of subsequent cases.

prejudicial pretrial publicity Prejudicial information, often inadmissible at trial, that is circulated by the news media before a trial and that reduces the defendant's chances of a trial before an impartial jury.

preliminary hearing A pretrial hearing to determine whether there is probable cause to bind a defendant over for felony trial.

preponderance of the evidence In civil law, the standard of proof required to prevail at trial. To win, the plaintiff must show that the greater weight, or preponderance, of the evidence supports his or her version of the facts.

pre-sentence investigation Investigation by a probation department into circumstances surrounding a crime in order to help judges make appropriate sentencing decisions.

presumption A conclusion that the law requires the trier-of-fact to accept as true.

presumption of innocence Assumption that whenever a person is charged with a crime, he or she is innocent until proved guilty. The defendant is presumed to be innocent, and the burden is on the state to prove guilt beyond a reasonable doubt.

presumption of sanity The rebuttable assumption that a criminal defendant was legally sane at the time of the commission of the crime(s) for which the defendant is charged. To overcome this presumption, most U.S. jurisdictions require the defense to prove that the defendant was insane by clear and convincing evidence.

preventive detention Holding a defendant in custody pending trial in the belief that he or she is likely to commit further criminal acts or flee the jurisdiction.

prisoner petition Civil lawsuit filed by a prisoner alleging violations of his or her rights during trial or while in prison.

privileged communication A recognized right to keep certain communications confidential or private.

pro se Acting as one's own attorney in court. Representing oneself.

probable cause Standard used to determine whether a crime has been committed and whether there is sufficient evidence to believe a specific individual committed it.

probation Punishment for a crime that allows the offender to remain in the community without incarceration but subject to certain conditions.

probation officer Employee of probation agency, responsible for supervision of convicted offenders who have been released to the community under certain conditions of good behavior.

procedural law Law that outlines the legal processes to be followed in starting, conducting, and finishing a lawsuit.

property Legal right to use or dispose of particular things or subjects.

property bond Use of property as collateral for pretrial release.

prosecutor A public official who represents the state in a criminal action.

public defender An attorney employed by the government to represent indigent defendants.

R

real evidence Objects, such as fingerprints, seen by the jury.

reasonable doubt The state of mind of jurors when they are not firmly convinced of a defendant's guilt because they think there is a real possibility that he or she is not guilty.

reasonable, articulable suspicion The reasons a law enforcement officer is able to articulate for being suspicious of criminal activity. It is the level of proof necessary to conduct a brief, limited investigative detention (also known as a *Terry stop*).

rebuttal The introduction of contradictory evidence.

referral A request by a law enforcement agency, governmental agency, parent, or individual that a juvenile court take jurisdiction of a youth. A referral initiates court processing.

rehabilitation The notion that punishment is intended to restore offenders to a constructive role in society; based on the assumption that criminal behavior is a treatable disorder caused by social or psychological ailments.

Rehnquist Court The Supreme Court under the leadership of Chief Justice William Rehnquist (1986–2005).

release on recognizance (ROR) The release of an accused person from jail on his or her own obligation rather than on a monetary bond.

remand In an appellate court, to send a case back to the court from which it came for further action.

remedy Vindication of a claim of right; a legal procedure by which a right is enforced or the violation of a right is prevented or compensated.

removal To dismiss a person from holding office.

respondent The party responding to a petition. It is most commonly used to refer to the party responding to the filing of a petition for a writ of certiorari.

restitution To restore or to make good on something—for example, to return or pay for a stolen item.

result A consequence; an outcome.

retribution A concept that implies the payment of a debt to society and thus the expiration of one's offense.

reverse In an appellate court, to reach a decision that disagrees with the result reached in the case by the lower court.

reversed and remanded Decision of an appellate court that the guilty verdict of the lower court be set aside and the case be retried.

reversible error An error made at trial serious enough to warrant a new trial.

right to counsel Right of the accused to the services of a lawyer paid for by the government, established by the Sixth Amendment and extended by the Warren Court (*Gideon v. Wainwright*) to indigent defendants in felony cases.

right to one appeal U.S. law generally grants the loser in trial court the right to a single appeal, which the upper court must hear.

Roberts Court The Supreme Court under the leadership of Chief Justice John Roberts (2005–).

routine administration A matter that presents the court with no disputes over law or fact.

rule of four The rule that four of the nine justices on the U.S. Supreme Court must vote in favor of granting a petition for a writ of certiorari in order for the Court to actually issue the writ, thereby accepting discretionary jurisdiction over an appeal.

S

scientific jury selection The use of social scientific techniques and expertise to select venirepersons to serve as petit jurors who are likely to be favorably disposed to one's side of a case.

search incident to arrest The ability of law enforcement to conduct a warrantless search of a person and the area around the arrestee's immediate control when making a lawful arrest.

search warrant A written order, issued by judicial authority, directing a law enforcement officer to search for personal property and, if found, to bring it before the court.

Section 1983 The shorthand way of referring to 42 U.S.C. § 1983, a statute which allows a person to sue someone acting under color of state law for an alleged deprivation of constitutional rights.

selective incapacitation Sentencing philosophy that stresses targeting dangerous offenders for lengthy prison sentences.

self-defense The right to use physical force against another person who is committing a felony, threatening the use of physical force, or using physical force.

self-incrimination Forcing a suspect to provide evidence against him- or herself; prohibited by the Fifth Amendment.

sentence bargaining The defendant pleads guilty knowing the sentence that will be imposed; the sentence in the sentence bargain is less than the maximum.

sentencing guidelines Recommended sentences based on the severity of the crime and the defendant's prior record in an attempt to ensure fair and consistent sentencing.

sequester To isolate members of a jury from the community until they have reached a final verdict.

severity of punishment A key component of deterrence theory concerned with how severe a criminal sentence may be. The theory posits that the more severe the punishment, the less likely people are to violate the law.

shock incarceration A short period of incarceration (the "shock"), followed by a sentence reduction.

simplified court structure A simple, uniform court structure for the entire state.

small claims court A lower-level court whose jurisdiction is limited to a specific dollar amount—for example, damages not exceeding $1,500.

solicitor general Third-ranking official in the U.S. Department of Justice who conducts and supervises government litigation before the Supreme Court.

specific deterrence The notion that the experience of criminal punishment should be unpleasant enough to deter an offender from committing future criminal acts.

standard of review The amount of deference an appellate court gives to the determinations made by a lower court.

stare decisis Latin phrase meaning "let the decision stand." The doctrine that principles of law established in earlier judicial decisions should be accepted as authoritative in similar subsequent cases.

state attorney general The chief legal officer of a state, representing that state in civil and, under certain circumstances, criminal cases.

state supreme court General term for the highest court in a state.

statewide financing Courts financed by the state government as opposed to local government.

status offense Behavior that is considered an offense only when committed by a juvenile—for example, running away from home.

statute A written law enacted by a legislature.

statutory exemptions Rules adopted by legislatures exempting certain types of persons or occupations from jury duty.

subject matter jurisdiction Types of cases courts have been authorized to hear and decide.

subpoena (power) An order from a court directing a person to appear before the court and to give testimony about a cause of action pending before it.

substantive law Law that deals with the content or substance of the law—for example, the legal grounds for divorce.

summons A legal document ordering an individual to appear in court at a certain time on a certain date.

Supreme Court The nation's highest court, composed of nine justices nominated by the president and confirmed by the Senate.

suppression motion Request that a court of law prohibit specific statements, documents, or objects from being introduced into evidence in a trial.

symbolic restitution The defendant performs community service.

T

testimony The giving of evidence by a witness under oath.

therapeutic jurisprudence Judicial bodies such as drug courts that stress helping defendants in trouble through nonadversarial proceedings.

tort A private or civil wrong, not arising as the result of a breach of contract, in which the defendant's actions cause injury to the plaintiff or to property.

traffic offenses A group of offenses, including infractions and minor misdemeanors, relating to the operation of self-propelled motor vehicles.

transactional immunity Absolute protection against prosecution for any event or transaction about which a witness is compelled to give testimony or furnish evidence.

transfer to criminal court A case is moved to a criminal court because of a waiver or transfer hearing in the juvenile court.

trial court Judicial body with primarily original jurisdiction in civil or criminal cases. Juries are used, and evidence is presented.

trial court of general jurisdiction A trial court responsible for major criminal and civil cases.

trial court of limited jurisdiction A lower-level state court, such as a justice of the peace court, whose jurisdiction is limited to minor civil disputes or misdemeanors.

true bill A bill of indictment by a grand jury.

trustworthiness Basic criterion for the admissibility of evidence, which seeks to ensure that only the most reliable and credible facts, statements, and testimony are presented to the fact-finder.

Type I offenses Serious crimes of homicide, rape, arson, aggravated assault, robbery, burglary, auto theft, and larceny, according to the FBI's *Uniform Crime Reports*; also called *index crimes*.

U

U.S. attorney general Head of the Department of Justice; nominated by the president and confirmed by the Senate.

U.S. attorneys Officials responsible for the prosecution of crimes that violate the laws of the United States; appointed by the president and assigned to a U.S. district court.

U.S. magistrate judges Judicial officers appointed by the U.S. district courts to perform the duties formerly performed by U.S. commissioners and to assist the court by serving as special masters in civil actions, conducting pretrial or discovery proceedings, and conducting preliminary review of applications for post-trial relief made by individuals convicted of criminal offenses.

unified court system A simplified state trial court structure with rule making centered in the supreme court, system governance authority vested in the chief justice of the supreme court, and state funding of the judicial system under a statewide judicial budget.

unreasonable search and seizure The Fourth Amendment provides for protection against unreasonable searches and seizures, or the illegal gathering of evidence, but was not very effective until the adoption of the exclusionary rule, barring the use of evidence so obtained (*Mapp v. Ohio* 1961).

upper age of jurisdiction The oldest age at which a juvenile court has original jurisdiction over an individual for behavior that violates the law.

use immunity A witness may not be prosecuted based on grand jury testimony he or she provides but may be prosecuted based on evidence acquired independently from that testimony.

V

venire A group of citizens from which members of the jury are chosen.

venue The geographic location of a trial, which is determined by constitutional or statutory provisions.

verdict The decision of a trial court.

voir dire French legal phrase meaning "to speak the truth." The process by which prospective jurors are questioned to determine whether there is cause to excuse them from the jury.

W

warrantless search Search without a search warrant.

Warren Court The Supreme Court under the leadership of Chief Justice Earl Warren (1953–1969).

writ of certiorari Order issued by an appellate court for the purpose of obtaining from a lower court the record of its proceedings in a particular case.

writ of certiorari, petition for The petition a party files asking an appellate court to exercise its discretionary appellate jurisdiction to review a case.

REFERENCES

Abel, C.F., and Hans. J. Hacker. 2006. "Local Compliance with Supreme Court Decisions: Making Space for Religious Expression in Public Schools." *Journal of Church and State* 48: 355–378.

Aberbach, Joel D., and Mark A. Peterson. 2006. *The Executive Branch.* New York: Oxford University Press.

Acker, James. 1993. "A Different Agenda: The Supreme Court, Empirical Research Evidence, and Capital Punishment Decisions, 1986–1989." *Law and Society Review* 27: 65–86.

Adams, Benjamin and Sean Addie. 2009. "Delinquency Cases Waived to Criminal Court, 2005." Washington, D.C.: Office of Justice Programs, U.S. Department of Justice.

Adams, Kenneth. 1983. "The Effect of Evidentiary Factors on Charge Reduction." *Journal of Criminal Justice* 11: 525–538.

Adler, Peter, Karen Lovass, and Neal Milner. 1988. "The Ideologies of Mediation: The Movement's Own Story." *Law and Policy* 10: 317–339.

Administrative Office of the U.S. Courts. 2008. *Federal Judicial Caseload Statistics: 2008.* Washington, DC: Author.

"After Death Threats, O'Connor Responds to GOP Attacks on Judges." 2009. Available online at http://www.perrspectives.com/blog/archives/001415.htm

Alarid, Leanne, James Marquart, Velmer Burton, Francis Cullen, and Steven Cuvelier. 1996. "Women's Roles in Serious Offenses: A Study of Adult Felons." *Justice Quarterly* 13: 431–454.

Albonetti, Celesta A. 1987. "Prosecutorial Discretion: The Effects of Uncertainty." *Law & Society Review* 21: 291–313.

Albonetti, Celesta. 1997. "Sentencing Under the Federal Sentencing Guideline: Effects of Defendant Characteristics, Guilty Pleas, and Departures on Sentence Outcomes for Drug Offenses, 1991–1992." *Law and Society* Review 31: 789–822.

Alexander, S. L. 1991. "Cameras in the Courtroom: A Case Study." *Judicature* 74: 307–313.

Alexander, S. L. 1996. "The Impact of *California v. Simpson* on Cameras in the Courtroom." *Judicature* 79: 169–175.

Alexander-Bloch, Benjamin. 2007. "Justice Can Be Lost in Translation." *Times-Picayune,* December 2.

Alfini, James, and Patricia Passuth. 1981. "Case Processing in State Misdemeanor Courts: The Effect of Defense Attorney Presence." *Justice System Journal* 6: 100–116.

Allen, G. Frederick, and Harvey Treger. 1994. "Fines and Restitution Orders: Probationers' Perceptions." *Federal Probation* 58: 34–38.

Alpert, Geoffrey, and Thomas Petersen. 1985. "The Grand Jury Report: A Magic Lantern or an Agent of Social Control?" *Justice Quarterly* 2: 23–50.

Alschuler, Albert. 1968. "The Prosecutor's Role in Plea Bargaining." *University of Chicago Law Review* 36: 50–112.

Alschuler, Albert. 1975. "The Defense Attorney's Role in Plea Bargaining." *Yale Law Journal* 84: 1179–1314.

Alschuler, Albert. 1979. "Plea Bargaining and Its History." *Law and Society Review* 13: 211–246.

American Bar Association Commission on Minimum Standards for Criminal Justice. 1968. *Standards Relating to Speedy Trial.* Chicago: American Bar Association.

American Bar Association. 1988. *Criminal Justice in Crisis.* Chicago: Author.

American Bar Association. 2004. *Gideon's Broken Promise: America's Continuing Quest for Equal Justice.* Chicago: Author.

American Bar Association. 2006. *Model Rules of Professional Conduct Center for Professional Responsibility.* Chicago: Author.

American Bar Association. 2009. National Database on Judicial Diversity in State Courts. Chicago, IL: Author. Available online at http://www.abanet.org/judind/diversity/national.html

American Civil Liberties Union. 1996. *ACLU Fact Sheet on Juvenile Crime.* Available online at http://www.aclu.org/congress/juvenile.htm

American Civil Liberties Union. 2000. "Act Now to Stop the Execution of the Innocent." Available online at http://www.aclu.org/deathpenalty

American Civil Liberties Union. 2008. "A Call to Action for Juvenile Justice." Available online at http://www.aclu.org/images/asset_upload_file183_37705.pdf June 29, 2009.

American Judicature Society. 2009. *Judicial Selection in the States: Appellate and General Jurisdiction Courts:*

Initial Selection, Retention, and Term Length. Des Moines, IA: Author. Available online at http://www.judicialselection.us/uploads/documents/Selection_Retention_Term_1196092850316.pdf

Anderson, Elijah. 1999. *Code of the Street: Decency, Violence, and the Moral Life of the Inner City.* New York: Norton.

Antonio, Michael, and Nicole Arone. 2005. "Damned If They Do, Damned If They Don't: Jurors' Reaction to Defendant Testimony or Silence During a Capital Trial." *Judicature* 89: 60–66.

Aos, Steve, Marna Miller, and Elizabeth Drake. 2006. Evidence-Based Adult Corrections Programs: *What Works and What Does Not.* Olympia: Washington State Institute for Public Policy.

Applebome, Peter. 1992. "Indigent Defendants, Overworked Lawyers." *New York Times*, September 18.

Applegate, Brandon, Francis Cullen, Bruce Link, Pamela Richards, and Lonn Lanza-Kaduce. 1996. "Determinants of Public Punitiveness toward Drunk Driving: A Factorial Survey Approach." *Justice Quarterly* 13: 57–79.

Applegate, Brandon, Michael Turner, Joseph Sanborn, Edward Latessa, and Melissa Moon. 2000. "Individualization, Criminalization, or Problem Resolution: A Factorial Survey of Juvenile Court Judges' Decisions to Incarcerate Youthful Felony Offenders." *Justice Quarterly* 17: 309–332.

Aquinas, Thomas. c. 1273. *Summa Theologica.* Fathers of the English Dominican Province (transl.). Notre Dame, IN: Christian Classics.

Ares, Charles, Ann Rankin, and Herbert Sturz. 1963. "The Manhattan Bail Project: An Interim Report on the Use of Pretrial Parole." *New York University Law Review* 38: 67–92.

Arrestee Drug Abuse Monitoring Program. 2003. *Preliminary Data on Drug Use and Related Matters among Adult Arrestees and Juvenile Detainees 2002.* Washington, DC: National Institute of Justice. Available online at http://www.adam-nij.net

Ashman, Allan, and Pat Chapin. 1976. "Is the Bell Tolling for Nonlawyer Judges?" *Judicature* 59: 417–421.

Ashman, Allan. 1975. *Courts of Limited Jurisdiction: A National Survey.* Chicago: American Judicature Society.

Aspin, Larry, William Hall, Jean Bax, and Celeste Montoya. 2000. "Thirty Years of Judicial Retention Elections: An Update." *Social Science Journal* 37: 1.

Associated Press. 2009. "Broken Bonds: Jail Policies Perturb Bail Bondsmen." *Greeley Tribune*, May 25.

Attorney General's Task Force on Violent Crime. 1981. *Final Report.* Washington, DC: U.S. Department of Justice.

Auerhahn, Kathleen. 1999. "Selective Incapacitation and the Problem of Prediction." *Criminology* 37: 703–734.

Auerhahn, Kathleen. 2006. "Selective Incapacitation and the Problem of Prediction." *Criminology* 37: 703–734.

Auerhahn, Kathleen. 2007. "Do You Know Who Your Probations Are? Using Simulation Modeling to Estimate the Composition of California's Felony Probation Population, 1980–2000." *Justice Quarterly* 24: 27–47.

Augustine. c. 1426. *The City of God.* R.W. Dyson (transl.) Cambridge, United Kingdom: Cambridge University Press, 1998.

Austin, James, and Patricia L. Hardyman. 2004. "The Risks and Needs of the Returning Prisoner Population." *Review of Policy Research* 21: 13–29.

Austin, Thomas. 1981. "The Influence of Court Location on Types of Criminal Sentences: The Rural–Urban Factor." *Journal of Criminal Justice* 9: 305–316.

Baar, Carl. 1980. "The Scope and Limits of Court Reform." *Justice System Journal* 5: 274–290.

Backstrand, John, Don Gibbons, and Joseph Jones. 1992. "Who Is in Jail? An Examination of the Rabble Hypothesis." *Crime and Delinquency* 38: 219–229.

Baehler, Aimee, and Barry Mahoney. 2005. "Strengthening Rural Courts." Denver, CO, Justice Management Institute. Available online at http://www.jmijustice.org/Data/DocumentLibrary/Documents/1159370501.66/JMI%20SJI%20Strengthening%20Rural%20Courts%20June%202005.pdf

Baker, Liva. 1983. *Miranda: Crime, Law and Politics.* New York: Atheneum.

Baker, Mark. 1999. *D.A: Prosecutors in Their Own Words.* New York: Simon and Shuster.

Baker, Newman. 1933. "The Prosecutor: Initiation of Prosecution." *Journal of Criminal Law, Criminology and Police Science* 23: 770–796.

Baker. Shannon M., Michael S. Vaughn, and Volkan Topalli. 2008. "A Review of the Powers of Bail Bond Agents and Bounty Hunters: Exploring Legalities and Illegalities of Quasi-Criminal Justice Officials." *Aggression and Violent Behavior* 13: 124–130.

Baldus, David C., and George Woodworth. 2003. "Race Discrimination in the Administration of the Death Penalty: An Overview of the Empirical Evidence with Special Emphasis on the Post-1990 Research." *Criminal Law Bulletin* 39: 194–226.

Baldus, David C., George A. Woodworth, Catherine M. Grosso, and Aaron M. Christ. 2002. "Arbitrariness and Discrimination in the Administration of the Death Penalty: A Legal and Empirical Analysis of the Nebraska Experience (1973–1999)." *Nebraska Law Review* 81: 486–754.

Baldus, David, Charles Pulaski, and George Woodworth. 1983. "Comparative Review of Death Sentences: An Empirical Study of the Georgia Experience." *Journal of Criminal Law and Criminology* 74: 661–753.

Banks, Cyndi. 2009. *Criminal Justice Ethics: Theory and Practice.* Thousand Oaks, CA: Sage.

Banks, Duren, and Denise Gottfredson. 2004. "Participation in Drug Treatment Court and Time to Rearrest." *Justice Quarterly* 21: 637–658.

Barnes, Brooks. 2009. "*American Violet* to Premier in Texas Town Where Story Occurred." *The Carpetbagger: The Hollywood Blog of the New York Times* (March 12), available online at http://carpetbagger.blogs.nytimes.com/2009/03/12/american-violet-to-premier-in-texas-town-where-story-occurred/#more-3725

Barnes, Robert. 2007. "Judicial Races Now Rife with Politics." *Washington Post*, October 28.

Barrineau, H. E. 1994. *Civil Liability in Criminal Justice.* Cincinnati: Anderson.

Bartol, Anne. 1996. "Structures and Roles of Rural Courts." In *Rural Criminal Justice: Conditions, Constraints, and Challenges*, edited by Thomas McDonald, Robert Wood, and Melissa Pflug, pp. 79–92. Salem, WI: Sheffield.

Bass, Alison. 1995. "Youth Violence Explosion Likely to Worsen." *Times-Picayune*, July 2, p. A14.

Baum, Lawrence. 1991. "Specializing the Federal Courts: Neutral Reforms or Efforts to Shape Judicial Policy?" *Judicature* 74: 217–224.

Baumer, Eric, Steven Messner, and Richard Felson. 2000. "The Role of Victim Characteristics in the Disposition of Murder Cases." *Justice Quarterly* 17: 281–308.

Bazelon, Lara A. 2009. "Putting the Mice in Charge of the Cheese: Why Federal Judges Cannot Always Be Trusted to Police Themselves and What Congress Can Do About It." *Kentucky Law Journal* 97: 439–503.

Beccaria, Cesare. 1764. "On Crimes and Punishments." In Aaron Thomas (ed. and transl.) *On Crimes and Punishments and Other Writings.* Toronto, ON: University of Toronto Press, 2008.

Beerhalter, Susan, and James Gainey. 1974. *Minnesota District Court Survey.* Denver: National Center for State Courts.

Begue, Yvette, and Candace Goldstein. 1987. "How Judges Get into Trouble." *Judges Journal* 26: 8.

Belenko, Steven, Iona Mara-Drita, and Jerome McElroy. 1992. "Drug Tests and the Prediction of Pretrial Misconduct: Findings and Policy Issues." *Crime and Delinquency* 38: 557–582.

Belknap, Joanne. 2007. *The Invisible Woman: Gender, Crime, and Justice.* 2nd ed. Belmont, CA: Wadsworth.

Bell, Griffin. 1993. "Appointing United States Attorneys." *Journal of Law and Politics* 9: 247–256.

Bell, Laura Cohen. 2002. *Warring Factions: Interest Groups, Money, and the New Politics of Senate Confirmation.* Columbus: Ohio State University Press.

Benner, Laurence A., and Charles T. Samarkos. 2000. "Searching for Narcotics in San Diego: Preliminary Findings from the San Diego Search Warrant Project." *California Western Law Review* 36: 221–266.

Bentham, Jeremy. 1830. "Principles of Penal Law: Rationale of Punishment. In *The Works of Jeremy Bentham*, Vol. 1, edited by John Bowring, pp. 365–398. Edinburgh, Scotland: W. Tait, 1843.

Berg, Kenneth. 1985. "The Bail Reform Act of 1984." *Emory Law Journal* 34: 687–740.

Berkson, Larry, and Susan Carbon. 1978. *Court Unification: History, Politics, and Implementation.* Washington, DC: National Institute of Law Enforcement and Criminal Justice.

Bertram, Eva, et al. 1996. *Drug War Politics: The Price of Denial.* Berkeley: University of California Press.

Bibas, Stephanos. 2004. "Plea Bargaining Outside the Shadow of Trial." *Harvard Law Review*, 117: 2463–2547.

Bienen, L. B. 2008. "Anomalies: Ritual and Language in Lethal Injection Regulations." *Fordham Urban Law Journal* 35: 857–881.

Binder, Sarah, and Forest Maltzman. 2004. "The Limits of Senatorial Courtesy." *Legislative Studies Quarterly* 29: 5–22.

Binford, W. W. H., P. C. Greene, M. C. Schmidlkofer, R. M. Wilsey, and H. A. Taylor. 2007. "Seeking Best *Practices* among Intermediate Courts Of Appeal: A Nascent Journey." *Journal of Appellate Practice and Process*, 9: 37–119.

Bing, Stephen, and Stephen Rosenfeld. 1974. "The Quality of Justice in the Lower Criminal Courts of Metropolitan Boston." In *Rough Justice: Perspectives on Lower Criminal Courts*, edited by John Robertson, pp. 259–285. Boston: Little, Brown.

Binnall, James M. 2008. "EG1900 . . . The Number They Gave Me When They Revoked My Citizenship: Perverse Consequences of Ex-Felon Civic Exile." *Willamette Law Review* 44: 667–697.

Bisceglia, Joseph. 2007. "CSI, Judge Judy and Civic Education." *Illinois Bar Journal* 95: 508.

Biskupic, Joan. 1993. "Congress Cool to Proposals to Ease Load on Courts." *Congressional Quarterly* (April 7): 1073–1075.

Blackwell, Brenda Sims, David Holleran, and Mary A. Finn. 2008. "The Impact of the Pennsylvania Sentencing Guidelines on Sex Differences in Sentencing." *Journal of Contemporary Criminal Justice* 24: 399–418.

Blankenship, Michael, James Luginbuhl, Francis Cullen, and William Redick. 1997. "Juror Comprehension of Sentencing Instructions: A Test of Tennessee's Death Penalty Process." *Justice Quarterly* 14: 325–357.

Blecker, Robert. 2006. "A Poster Child for Us." *Judicature* 89: 297–301.

Blokland, Argan A. J., and Paul Nieuwbeerta. 2007. "Selectively Incapacitating Frequent Offenders: Costs and Benefits of Various Penal Scenarios." *Journal of Quantitative Criminology* 23: 327–353.

Bloom, F. M. 2008. "State Courts Unbound." *Cornell Law Review* 93: 501–554.

Bloom, R. M., and H. Massey. 2008. "Accounting for Federalism in State Courts: Exclusion of Evidence Obtained Lawfully by Federal Agents." *University of Colorado Law Review* 79: 381–420.

Blumberg, Abraham. 1967a. *Criminal Justice*. Chicago: Quadrangle Books.

Blumberg, Abraham. 1967b. "The Practice of Law as a Confidence Game." *Law and Society Review* 1: 15–39.

Blumberg, Abraham. 1970. *Criminal Justice*. New York: Quadrangle Books.

Blumenthal, Ralph. 2006. "Faulty Testimony Sent 2 to Death Row, Panel Finds." *New York Times*, May 3.

Blumstein, Alfred, Jacqueline Cohen, Susan Martin, and Michael Tonry, eds. 1983. *Research on Sentencing: The Search for Reform*. Washington, DC: National Academy Press.

Boland, Barbara, and Brian Forst. 1985. "Prosecutors Don't Always Aim to Pleas." *Federal Probation* 49: 10–15.

Boland, Barbara, Elizabeth Brady, Herbert Tyson, and John Bassler. 1982. *The Prosecution of Felony Arrests*. Washington, DC: Institute for Law and Social Research.

Boland, Barbara, Paul Mahanna, and Ronald Sones. 1992. *The Prosecution of Felony Arrests, 1988*. Washington, DC: U.S. Department of Justice, Bureau of Justice Statistics.

Boland, Barbara. 1996. "What Is Community Prosecution?" *National Institute of Justice Journal* 231: 35–40.

Bonneau, Chris, and Melinda Gann Hall. 2003. "Predicting Challengers in State Supreme Court Elections: Context and Politics of Institutional Design." *Political Research Quarterly* 56: 337–349.

Bonneau, Chris. 2001. "The Composition of State Supreme Courts." *Judicature* 85: 26–31.

Bonneau, Chris. 2007. "The Effects of Campaign Spending in State Supreme Court Elections." *Political Research Quarterly* 60: 489.

Bonnie, Richard, Norman Poythress, Steven Hoge, John Monahan, and Marlene Eisenberg. 1996. "Decision-Making in Criminal Defense: An Empirical Study of Insanity Pleas and the Impact of Doubted Client Competence." *Journal of Criminal Law and Criminology* 87: 48–77.

Borenstein, Isaac and Erin J. Anderson. 2009. "Judicial Participation in Plea Negotiations: The Elephant in Chambers." *Suffolk Journal of Trial and Appellate Advocacy* 14: 1–34.

Borgida, Eugene, and Susan T. Fiske. 2008. *Beyond Common Sense: Psychological Science in the Courtroom*. Oxford: Wiley-Blackwell.

Boritch, Helen. 1992. "Gender and Criminal Court Outcomes: An Historical Analysis." *Criminology* 30: 293–317.

Borys, Bryan, Cynthia Banks, and Darrel Parker. 1999. "Enlisting the Justice Community in Court Improvement." *Judicature* 82: 176–185.

Bourgois, Philippe. 2003. *In Search of Respect: Selling Crack in El Barrio*. 2nd ed. New York: Cambridge University Press.

Bousquet, Steve. 2009. "Traffic Fines Are Going up in Florida." *Herald/Times*, January 9.

Bowes, Mark. 2009. "Localities Recoup Incarceration Costs." *Richmond Times-Dispatch*, January 12.

Brace, Paul, and Brent D. Boyea. 2007. "Judicial Selection Methods and Capital Punishment in the American States." *In Running for Judge: The Rising Political, Financial, and Legal Stakes of Judicial Elections*, edited by Matthew Justin Streb, pp. 186–203. New York: New York University Press.

Brace, Paul, and Melinda Gann Hall. 1997. "The Interplay of Preferences, Case Facts, Context, and Rules in the Politics of Judicial Choice." *Journal of Politics* 59: 1206–1241.

Bradley, Craig. 2006. "The Right Decision on the Juvenile Death Penalty." *Judicature* 89: 302–303.

Brennan, Pauline K., and Cassia Spohn. 2008. "Race/Ethnicity and Sentencing Outcomes among Drug Offenders in North Carolina." *Journal of Contemporary Criminal Justice* 24: 371–398.

Brennan, William. 1963. "The Criminal Prosecution: Sporting Event or Quest for Truth?" *Washington University Law Quarterly* 279–294.

Brenner, Susan. 1998. "Is the Grand Jury Worth Keeping?" *Judicature* 81: 190–199.

Brereton, David, and Jonathan Casper. 1981–1982. "Does It Pay to Plead Guilty? Differential

Sentencing and the Functioning of Criminal Courts." *Law and Society Review* 16: 45–70.

Breyer, Stephen, et al. 2006. Implementation of the Judicial Conduct and Disability Act of 1980: A Report to the Chief Justice." Washington, DC: The Judicial Conduct and Disability Act Study Committee. Available online at http://www.supremecourtus.gov/publicinfo/breyercommitteereport.pdf

Bright, Stephen. 1997. "Political Attacks on the Judiciary." *Judicature* 80: 165–173.

Britto, Sarah, Tycy Hughes, Kurt Saltzman, and Colin Stroh. 2007. "Does 'Special' Mean Young, White and Female? Deconstructing the Meaning of 'Special' in *Law & Order: Special Victims Unit*." *Journal of Criminal Justice and Popular Culture* 14(1): 39–57.

Broccolina, Frank, and Richard Zorza. "En$uring Access to Ju$tice in Tough Economic Times." *Judicature* 92:3 (November–December 2008): 124–128.

Brody, David C. 2008. "The Use of Judicial Performance Evaluation to Enhance Judicial Accountability, Judicial Independence, and Public Trust." *Denver University Law Review* 86: 115–156.

Broeder, D. W. 1959. "The University of Chicago Jury Project." *Nebraska Law Review* 38: 744–760.

Bronstein, Julie. 1981. *Survey of State Mandatory Judicial Education Requirements*. Washington, DC: American University.

Brooks, Daniel. 1985. "Penalizing Judges Who Appeal Disciplinary Sanctions: The Unconstitutionality of 'Upping the Ante.'" *Judicature* 69: 95–102.

Brooks, Richard R. W. and Stephen Raphael. 2003. "Life Terms or Death Sentences: The Uneasy Relationship between Judicial Elections and Capital Punishment." *Journal of Criminal Law and Criminology* 92: 609–640.

Brooks, Thom. 2004. "A Defence of Jury Nullification." *Res Publica* 10: 401–423.

Brown, Darryl. 1997. "Jury Nullification within the Rule of Law." *Minnesota Law Review* 81: 1149–1200.

Brown, Gina. 2005. "A Community of Court ADR Programs: How Court-Based ADR Programs Help Each Other Survive and Thrive." *Justice System Journal* 26: 327–341.

Brown, Mary, and Steven Bunnell. 2006. "Negotiated Justice: Prosecutorial Perspectives on Federal Plea Bargaining in the District of Columbia." *American Criminal Law Review* 43: 1063.

Brust, Richard. 2008 (August). "The 25 Greatest Legal Movies." *ABA Journal* 94: 38–47.

Buchanan, John. 1989. "Police–Prosecutor Teams: Innovations in Several Jurisdictions." *NIJ Reports* 214: 2–8.

Buchman, Jeremy. 2004. "The Legal Model and *Daubert*'s Effect on Trial Judges' Decisions to Admit Scientific Testimony." Paper presented at the annual meeting of the Midwest Political Science Association, Chicago.

Building Blocks for Youth. 2009. "Resources for Disproportionate Minority Confinement/Overrepresentation of Youth of Color." Available online at http://www.buildingblocksforyouth.org/issues/dmc (Accessed June 28, 2009.)

Burbank, Stephen. 1987. "Politics and Progress in Implementing the Federal Judicial Discipline Act." *Judicature* 71: 13–28.

Bureau of Justice Statistics. 1988a. *Criminal Defense for the Poor, 1986*. Washington, DC: U.S. Department of Justice.

Bureau of Justice Statistics. 1988c. *Report to the Nation on Crime and Justice: The Data*. 2nd ed. Washington, DC: U.S. Department of Justice.

Bureau of Justice Statistics. 1990. *Juvenile and Adult Records: One System, One Record?* Washington, DC: U.S. Department of Justice.

Bureau of Justice Statistics. 1995. *Violence against Women: Estimates from the Redesigned Survey*. Washington, DC: U.S. Department of Justice.

Bureau of Justice Statistics. 1996. *How to Use Structured Fines (Day Fines) as an Intermediate Sanction*. Washington, DC: U.S. Government Printing Office.

Bureau of Justice Statistics. 1997. *Correctional Populations in the United States, 1995*. Washington, DC: U.S. Department of Justice.

Bureau of Justice Statistics. 2002. "Criminal Victimization 2001: Changes 2000–2001 with Trends." Available online at http://www.ojp.usdoj.gov/bjs/abstract/cv01.htm

Bureau of Justice Statistics. 2003a. *Intimate Partner Violence, 1993–2001*. Washington, DC: U.S. Department of Justice, Bureau of Justice Statistics.

Bureau of Justice Statistics. 2006. "Criminal Victimization in the United States; Rape/Sexual Assault Tables, 1996–2005." Available online at http://www.ojp.usdoj.gov/bjs/abstract/cvus/number_of_incidents745.htm

Bureau of Justice Statistics. 2007. "Criminal Offender Statistics". Available online at http://www.ojp.usdoj.gov/bjs/crimoff.htm#lifetime

Bureau of Justice Statistics. 2009. "Expenditure and Employment Statistics." Available online at http://www.ojp.usdoj.gov/bjs/eande.htm

Bureau of Justice Statistics. 2009a. "Jail Statistics." Available online at http://www.ojp.usdoj.gov/bjs/jails.htm

Bureau of Justice Statistics. 2009b. "Prison Statistics." Available online at http://www.ojp.usdoj.gov/bjs/prisons.htm

Bureau of Justice Statistics. 2009c. "Probation and Parole Statistics." Available online at http://www.ojp.usdoj.gov/bjs/pandp.htm

Burke-Robertson, C. 2008. "Judging Jury Verdicts." *Tulane Law Review* 83: 157–218.

Burrell, Diane. 1997. "Financial Analysis of Traffic Court Collections in Ada County, Idaho." *Justice System Journal* 19: 101–116.

Burruss, George, and Kimberly Kempf-Leonard. 2002. "The Questionable Advantage of Defense Counsel in Juvenile Court." *Justice Quarterly* 19: 37–68.

Butler, Brooke. 2007. "Death Qualification and Prejudice: The Effect of Implicit Racism, Sexism, and Homophobia on Capital Defendants' Right to Due Process." *Behavioral Sciences and the Law* 25: 857–867.

Butler, Brooke, and Gary Moran. 2007a. "The Impact of Death Qualification, Belief in a Just World, Legal Authoritarianism, and Locus of Control on Venirepersons' Evaluations of Aggravating and Mitigating Circumstances in Capital Trials." *Behavioral Sciences and the Law* 25: 57–68.

Butler, Brooke, and Gary Moran. 2007b. "The Role of Death Qualification and Need for Cognition in Venirepersons' Evaluations of Expert Scientific Testimony in Capital Trials." *Behavioral Sciences and the Law* 25: 561–571.

Butler, Paul. 1995. "Racially Based Jury Nullification: Black Power in the Criminal Justice System." *Yale Law Journal* 105: 677–725.

Butterfield, Fox. 1997. "Justice Besieged: With Juvenile Courts in Chaos, Critics Propose Their Demise." *New York Times*, July 21.

Butts, Jeffrey, and Janeen Buck. 2000. "Teen Courts: A Focus on Research." *Juvenile Justice Bulletin*. Washington, DC: U.S. Department of Justice.

Buzawa, Eve, and Carl Buzawa. 1996. *Domestic Violence: The Criminal Justice Response*. 2nd ed. Thousand Oaks, CA: Sage.

Byrd, Harry. 1976. "Has Life Tenure Outlived Its Time?" *Judicature* 59: 266–277.

Byrne, James, Arthur Lurigio, and Christopher Baird. 1989. "The Effectiveness of the New Intensive Supervision Programs." *Research in Corrections* 2: 1–15.

Call, Jack, David England, and Susette Talarico. 1983. "Abolition of Plea Bargaining in the Coast Guard." *Journal of Criminal Justice* 11: 351–358.

Cameron, Mary. 1964. *The Booster and the Snitch*. Glencoe, IL: Free Press.

Campbell, Curtis, Candace McCoy, and Chimezie Osigweh. 1990. "The Influence of Probation Recommendations on Sentencing Decisions and Their Predictive Accuracy." *Federal Probation* 54: 13–21.

Campbell, Donald, and H. Laurence Ross. 1968. "The Connecticut Crackdown on Speeding: Time-Series Data in Quasi-Experimental Analysis." *Law and Society Review* 3: 33–54.

Campbell, Linda. 1990. "Court Urged to Protect Prosecutors." *Chicago Tribune*, November 29.

Campbell, Linda. 1991. "High Court Reduces Prosecutor Immunity." *Chicago Tribune*, May 31.

Campbell, William. 1973. "Eliminate the Grand Jury." *Journal of Criminal Law and Criminology* 64: 174–182.

Cannavale, F., and W. Falcon. 1976. *Witness Cooperation*. Lexington, MA: D. C. Heath.

Cannon, Angie. 1996. "Bill Spells Out Rights of Victims." *Times-Picayune*, April 23.

Cannon, Angie. 1997. "Violent Teen Crime Rate Drops Two Years in a Row." *Times-Picayune*, October 3.

Capers, I. Bennett. 2009. "Legal Outsiders in American Film: Notes on Minority Report." *Suffolk University Law Review* 42: 795–807.

Caplan, Lincoln. 1988. *The Tenth Justice: The Solicitor General and the Rule of Law*. New York: Vintage.

Caputo, Gail. 1999. *Evaluation of CAES CSP Program*. New York: Vera Institute of Justice.

Carbon, Susan. 1984. "Women in the Judiciary." *Judicature* 65: 285.

Carelli, Richard. 1996. "Independent Judiciary Vital, Rehnquist Says." *Times-Picayune*, April 27.

Caringella, Susan. 2008. *Addressing Rape Reform in Law and Practice*. New York: Columbia University Press.

Carlsmith, Kevin, John Darley, and Paul Robinson. 2002. "Why Do We Punish? Deterrence and Just Deserts as Motives for Punishment." *Journal of Personality and Social Psychology* 83: 284–299.

Carns, Teresa White, and John Kruse. 1992. "Alaska's Ban on Plea Bargaining Reevaluated." *Judicature* 75: 310–317.

Carp, Robert, and C. K. Rowland. 1983. *Policymaking and Politics in the Federal District Courts*. Knoxville: University of Tennessee Press.

Carp, Robert, and Ronald Stidham. 1990. *Judicial Process in America*. Washington, DC: Congressional Quarterly Press.

Carp, Robert. 1975. "The Behavior of Grand Juries: Acquiescence or Justice?" *Social Science Quarterly* 55(4): 855–870.

Carrington, Paul, Daniel Meador, and Maurice Rosenberg. 1976. *Justice on Appeal*. St. Paul, MN: West.

Carroll, Leo, and Claire Cornell. 1985. "Racial Composition, Sentencing Reforms, and Rates of Incarceration, 1970–1980." *Justice Quarterly* 2: 473–490.

Carroll, Susan. 2008. "A System's Fatal Flaws." *Houston Chronicle*, November 16.

Carter, L. H. & Burke, T. F. 2007. *Reason in Law* (7th ed.) Upper Saddle River, NJ: Pearson/Longman.

Carter, Lief. 1974. *The Limits of Order*. Lexington, MA: D. C. Heath.

Carter, Robert, and Leslie Wilkins. 1967. "Some Factors in Sentencing Policy." *Journal of Criminal Law, Criminology and Police Science* 58: 503–514.

Casey, Pamela, and David Rottman. 2004. *Problem-Solving Courts: Models and Trends*. Williamsburg, VA: National Center for State Courts.

Casper, Jonathan, David Brereton, and David Neal. 1982. *The Implementation of the California Determinate Sentencing Law*. Washington, DC: U.S. Department of Justice.

Casper, Jonathan. 1972. *American Criminal Justice: The Defendant's Perspective*. Englewood Cliffs, NJ: Prentice Hall.

Cassella, Stefan. 1996. "Third-Party Rights in Criminal Forfeiture Cases." *Criminal Law Bulletin* 32: 499–537.

Catalano, Shannan. 2009. "Intimate Partner Violence in the United States." Washington, D.C.: U.S. Department of Justice, Bureau of Justice Statistics. Available online at http://www.ojp.usdoj.gov/bjs/intimate/ipv.htm (Accessed June 8, 2009.)

Cauchon, Dennis. 1999. "Indigents' Lawyers: Low Pay Hurts Justice?" *USA Today*, February 3.

Cauthen, James, and Barry Latzer. 2008. "Why So Long? Explaining Processing Time in Capital Appeals." *Justice System Journal* 29: 298–312.

CBS News. 2004. "Scott Practiced Testifying." www.cbsnews.com (October 22.)

Center for Court Innovation. 2009. "Manhattan Community Court." Available online at http://www.courtinnovation.org

Chaiken, Marcia, and Jan Chaiken. 1990. *Redefining the Career Criminal: Priority Prosecution of High-Rate Dangerous Offenders*. Washington, DC: U.S. Department of Justice.

Champion, Dean J. 2007. *Sentencing: A Reference Handbook*. Santa Barbara, CA: ABC-CLIO.

Chapper, Joy, and Roger Hanson. 1990. "Understanding Reversible Error in Criminal Appeals." *State Court Journal* 14: 16–24.

Chesney-Lind, Meda, and Lisa Pasko. 2004. *The Female Offender: Girls, Women and Crime*. 2nd ed. Thousand Oaks, CA: Sage.

Chicago Tribune. 2000. "Paying for Justice." January 16.

Chilton, Bradley. 1991. *Prisons under the Gavel: The Federal Takeover of Georgia Prisons*. Columbus: Ohio State University Press.

Chiricos, Theodore, and William Bales. 1991. "Unemployment and Punishment: An Empirical Assessment." *Criminology* 29: 701–724.

Choi, Stephen J., G. Mitu Gulati, and Eric A. Posner. (In press). Professionals or politicians: The uncertain empirical case for an elected rather than appointed judiciary. *Journal of Law, Economics, and Organization*.

Church, Thomas, Alan Carlson, Jo-Lynne Lee, and Teresa Tan. 1978. *Justice Delayed: The Pace of Litigation in Urban Trial Courts*. Williamsburg, VA: National Center for State Courts.

Church, Thomas, and Virginia McConnell. 1978. *Pretrial Delay: A Review and Bibliography*. Williamsburg, VA: National Center for State Courts.

Church, Thomas. 1976. "Plea Bargains, Concessions and the Courts: Analysis of a Quasi-Experiment." *Law and Society Review* 10: 377–389.

Church, Thomas. 1982. "The 'Old' and the 'New' Conventional Wisdom of Court Delay." *Justice System Journal* 7: 395–412.

Church, Thomas. 1985. "Examining Local Legal Culture." *American Bar Foundation Research Journal* 449–518.

Clark, John, and D. Alan Henry. 2003. *Pretrial Services Programming at the Start of the 21st Century: A Survey of Pretrial Services Programs*. Washington, DC: Pretrial Services Resource Center.

Clark, John, James Austin, and D. Alan Henry. 1997. *"Three Strikes and You're Out": A Review of State Legislation*. Washington, DC: National Institute of Justice.

Clark, John, James Austin, and D. Alan Henry. 1998. "'Three Strikes and You're Out': Are Repeat Offender Laws Having Their Anticipated Effects?" *Judicature* 81: 144–154.

Clark, Tom. 2005. "A Note on the Moore Case and Judicial Administration." *The Justice System Journal* 26: 355–361.

Clarke, Stevens. 1984. "North Carolina's Determinate Sentencing Legislation." *Judicature* 68: 140–152.

Clear, Todd, and Eric Cadora. 2003. *Community Justice*. Belmont, CA: Wadsworth.

Clear, Todd, George Cole, and Michael Reisig. 2009. *American Corrections*. 8th ed. Belmont, CA: Wadsworth.

Clear, Todd, John Hewitt, and Robert Regoli. 1979. "Discretion and the Determinate Sentence: Its Distribution, Control and Effect on Time Served." *Crime and Delinquency* 24: 428–445.

Clear, Todd. 2007. *Imprisoning Communities: How Mass Incarceration Makes Disadvantaged Neighborhoods Worse.* New York: Oxford University Press.

Clynch, Edward, and David Neubauer. 1981. "Trial Courts as Organizations: A Critique and Synthesis." *Law and Policy Quarterly* 3: 69–94.

Cohen, Mark A., Roland T. Rust, and Sara Steen. 2006. "Prevention, Crime Control or Cash? Public Preferences Towards Criminal Justice Spending Priorities." *Justice Quarterly* 23: 317–335.

Cohen, Robyn. 1992. *Drunk Driving: 1989 Survey of Inmates of Local Jails.* Washington, DC: Bureau of Justice Statistics.

Cohen, Thomas, and Brian Reaves. 2006. *Felony Defendants in Large Urban Counties, 2002.* Washington, DC: Bureau of Justice Statistics.

Cohen, Thomas, and Brian Reaves. 2007. *Pretrial Release of Felony Defendants in State Courts.* Washington, DC: Bureau of Justice Statistics.

Cohn, Adam. 2005. "Want Social Condemnation with Your Justice? Tune in Judge Judy." *New York Times,* October 9.

Cole, George, Barry Mahoney, Marlene Thornton, and Roger Hanson. 1988. "The Use of Fines by Trial Court Judges." *Judicature* 71: 325–333.

Cole, George. 1970. "The Decision to Prosecute." *Law and Society Review* 4: 313–343.

Cole, George. 1992. "Using Civil and Administrative Remedies to Collect Fines and Fees." *State Court Journal* 16: 4–10.

Cole, Simon A., Max Welling, Rachel Dioso-Villa, and Robert Carpenter. 2008. "Beyond the Individuality of Fingerprints: A Measure of Simulated Computer Latent Print Source Attribution Accuracy." *Law, Probability, and Risk* 7: 165–189.

Coles, Catherine, and George Kelling. 1999. "Prevention through Community Prosecution." *The Public Interest* 36: 69.

Coles, Catherine, and Ronald Earle. 1996. "The Evolution of Problem-Oriented Prosecution." Paper presented at the annual meeting of the American Criminological Association, Chicago.

Collins, Reed. 2007. "Strolling While Poor: How *Broken-Windows* Policing Created a New Crime in Baltimore." *Georgetown Journal on Poverty Law and Policy* 14: 419–439.

"Community Prosecution." 2008. Cambridge, MA: Program in Criminal Justice Policy and Management, Kennedy School of Government, Harvard University. http://www.hks.harvard.edu/criminaljustice/research/community_prosecution.htm

Comparato, S. A., and S. D. McClurg. 2007. "A Neoinstitutional Explanation of State Supreme Court Responses in Search and Seizure Cases." *American Politics Research* 35(5): 726–754.

Comptroller General of the United States. 1979. *Impact of the Exclusionary Rule on Federal Criminal Prosecutions.* Washington, DC: General Accounting Office.

Congressional Quarterly. 1996. "House Republicans Advance Six Anti-Crime Bills." *1995 Congressional Quarterly Almanac.* Washington, DC: Author.

Connick, Elizabeth, and Robert Davis. 1983. "Examining the Problems of Witness Intimidation." *Judicature* 66: 438–447.

Coontz, Phyllis. 2000. "Gender and Judicial Decisions: Do Female Judges Decide Cases Differently than Male Judges?" *Gender Issues* 18: 59–73.

Cooper, Caroline. 2003 "Rural Drug Courts." Washington, DC: American University, Bureau of Justice Assistance Drug Court Clearinghouse. Available online at http://www1.spa.american.edu/justice/documents/2014.pdf

Cooper, J. O., and D. A. Berman. 2000. "Passive Virtues and Casual Vices on the Federal Courts of Appeals." *Brooklyn Law Review* 66: 712–754.

Corley, Charles, Timothy Bynum, and Madeline Wordes. 1995. "Conceptions of Family and Juvenile Court Process: A Qualitative Assessment." *Justice System Journal* 18: 157–172.

Corman, Hope, and Naci Mocan. 2005. "Carrots, Sticks, and Broken Windows." *The Journal of Law and Economics,* 48: 235–266.

Cose, Ellis. 2009. "Closing the Gap: Obama Could Fix Cocaine Sentencing." *Newsweek,* July 20.

Covarrubias, Rebecca J. 2009. "Lives in Defense Counsel's Hands: The Problems and Responsibilities of Defense Counsel Representing Mentally Ill or Mentally Retarded Capital Defendants." *Scholar* 11: 413–468.

Covey, Herbert, and Mary Mande. 1985. "Determinate Sentencing in Colorado." *Justice Quarterly* 2: 259–270.

Covey, R. D. 2008. Fixed justice: Reforming plea bargaining with plea-based ceilings. *Tulane Law Review,* 82: 1237–1290.

Covey, Russell D. 2008. "Fixed Justice: Reforming Plea Bargaining with Plea-Based Ceilings." *Tulane Law Review* 82: 1237–1290.

Covey, Russell D. 2009. "Signaling and Plea Bargaining's Innocence Problem." *Washington and Lee Law Review* 66: 73–130.

Covey, Russell. 2007. Reconsidering the Relationship between Cognitive Psychology and Plea Bargaining." *Marquette Law Review* 91: 213–247.

Cox, Gail. 1993. "Hellish Clients, Big Trouble." *National Law Journal* 15: 1.

Coyle, Marcia. 2009. "Written, Verbal Threats to Federal Judges Jump." *The National Law Journal.* Available online at http://www.law.com/jsp/nlj/PubArticleNLJ.jsp?id=1202429189887

Crew, B. Keith. 1991. "Sex Differences in Criminal Sentencing: Chivalry or Patriarchy?" *Justice Quarterly* 8: 59–84.

Criminal Justice Consortium. 1998. "Count of Prisoners Sentenced for Third and Second Strike Cases." Oakland, CA: California Department of Corrections.

Crouch, Ben, and James Marquart. 1990. "Resolving the Paradox of Reform: Litigation, Prisoner Violence, and Perceptions of Risk." *Justice Quarterly* 7: 103–123.

Crow, Matthew S. 2008. "The Complexities of Prior Record, Race, Ethnicity, and Policy Interactive Effects in Sentencing." *Criminal Justice Review* 33: 502–523.

Crow, Matthew S., and Katherine A. Johnson. 2008. "Race, Ethnicity, and Habitual-Offender Sentencing: A Multilevel Analysis of Individual Contextual Threat." *Criminal Justice Policy Review* 19: 63–83.

Cullen, Don. 2000. "Rural Courts: What Makes Them Unique?" Williamsburg: National Center for State Courts. Available online at http://contentdm.ncsconline.org/cgi-bin/showfile.exe?CISOROOT=/spcts&CISOPTR=148

Cullen, Francis T. 2005. "The Twelve People Who Saved Rehabilitation: How the Science of Criminology Made a Difference." *Criminology* 43: 1–42.

Cullen, Francis T., John Paul Wright, and Kristie R. Blevins. 2006. *Taking Stock: The Status of Criminological Theory.* Edison, NJ: Transaction.

Cullen, Francis T., Kristie R. Blevins, and Jennifer S. Trager. 2005. "The Rise and Fall of Boot Camp: A Case Study in Common-Sense Corrections." *Journal of Offender Rehabilitation* 40: 53–70.

Cullen, Francis, Bonnie Fisher and Brandon Applegate. 2000. "Public Opinion about Punishment and Corrections." *Crime and Justice* 27: 1–79.

Cunningham, Mark D., Thomas J. Reidy, and Jon R. Sorensen. 2008. "Assertions of 'Future Dangerousness' at Federal Capital Sentencing: Rates and Correlates of Subsequent Prison Misconduct and Violence." *Law and Human Behavior* 32: 46–63.

Currie, Elliot. 1985. *Confronting Crime: An American Challenge.* New York: Pantheon.

Currie, Elliot. 1989. "Confronting Crime: Looking toward the Twenty-First Century." *Justice Quarterly* 6: 5–15.

Currie, Elliott. 1993. *Reckoning: Drugs, the Cities, and the American Future.* New York: Hill and Wang.

Curry, Theodore R., and Guadalupe Corral-Camacho. 2008. "Sentencing Young Minority Males for Drug Offenses: Testing for Conditional Effects Between Race/Ethnicity, Gender and Age during the U.S. War on Drugs." *Punishment and Society* 10: 253–276.

D'Alessio, Stewart, and Lisa Stolzenberg. 2009. "Racial Animosity and Interracial Crime." *Criminology* 47: 269–296.

Daly, Kathleen. 1994. *Gender, Crime, and Punishment.* New Haven, CT: Yale University Press.

Dantzker, M.L. 2005. *Understanding Today's Police.* Monsey, NY: Criminal Justice Press.

Davey, Monica. 2006. "Missouri Says It Can't Hire Doctor for Executions." *New York Times*, July 15.

David, James R. 1980. *The Sentencing Dispositions of New York City Lower Court Criminal Judges.* Ph.D. Dissertation, New York University.

Davies, Thomas. 1982. "Affirmed: A Study of Criminal Appeals and Decision-Making Norms in a California Court of Appeal." *American Bar Foundation Research Journal* 543–648.

Davies, Thomas. 1983. "A Hard Look at What We Know (and Still Need to Learn) about the 'Costs' of the Exclusionary Rule: The NIJ Study and Other Studies of 'Lost Arrests.'" *American Bar Foundation Research Journal* 611–690.

Davis, Angela. 2007. *Arbitrary Justice: The Power of the American Prosecutor.* New York: Oxford University Press.

Davis, Chelyen. 2008. "With Senate Vote, Repeal of Virginia's Abusive-Driver Fees Headed to Governor." *Free Lance-Star*, March 9.

Davis, Robert, and Tanya Bannister. 1995. "Improving Collection of Court-Ordered Restitution." *Judicature* 79: 30–33.

Davis, Robert, Barbara Smith, and Susan Hillenbrand. 1992. "Restitution: The Victim's Viewpoint." *Justice System Journal* 15: 746–758.

Davis, Robert, Nicole Henderson, and Caitilin Rabbitt. 2002. *Effects of State Victim Rights Legislation on Local Criminal Justice Systems.* New York: Vera Institute of Justice.

Davis, Robert. 1983. "Victim/Witness Noncooperation: A Second Look at a Persistent Phenomenon." *Journal of Criminal Justice* 11: 287–299.

Davis, Samuel. 1984. *Rights of Juveniles.* 2nd ed. New York: Clark Boardman.

Davis, Sue. 1993. "The Voice of Sandra Day O'Connor." *Judicature* 77: 134–139.

Dawson, Myrna, and Ronit Dinovitzer. 2001. "Victim Cooperation and the Prosecution of Domestic Violence in a Specialized Court." *Justice Quarterly* 18: 593–649.

Death Penalty Information Center. 2009. "Prominent Conservative Calls for Death Penalty Moratorium." Available online at http://www.deathpenaltyinfo.org/new-voices-prominent-conservative-calls-death-penalty-moratorium (Accessed July 10, 2009.)

Dedel, Kelly. 2006. *Witness Intimidation*. Washington, DC: U.S. Department of Justice, Office of Community Oriented Policing Services.

DeFrances, Carol, and Kevin Strom. 1997. "Juveniles Prosecuted in State Criminal Courts." Washington, DC: Bureau of Justice Statistics.

DeFrances, Carol, and Marika Litras. 2000. *Indigent Defense Services in Large Counties, 1999*. Washington, DC: Bureau of Justice Statistics.

DeFrances, Carol, Steven Smith, and Louise van der Does. 1996. "Prosecutors in State Courts, 1994." *Bulletin*. Washington, DC: Bureau of Justice Statistics.

DeFrances, Carol. 2001. "State-Funded Indigent Defense Services, 1999." *Special Report*. Bureau of Justice Statistics.

DeLisi, Matt and Peter Conis. 2010. *American Corrections*. Sudbury, MA: Jones and Bartlett.

DeLisi, Matt. 2001. "Extreme Career Criminals." *American Journal of Criminal Justice* 25: 239–252.

DeLisi, Matt. 2005. *Career Criminals in Society*. Thousand Oaks, CA: Sage.

Delsohn, Gary. 2003a. *The Prosecutors: Kidnap, Rape, Murder, Justice: One Year behind the Scenes in a Big-City DA's Office*. New York: Plume.

Delsohn, Gary. 2003b. *The Prosecutors: A Year in the Life a District Attorney's Office*. New York: Dutton/Penguin.

Dempsey, John. 2003. "Wolf Pack Leads Cable with 'Law and Order.'" *Variety*, October 6, p. 26.

Demuth, Stephen. 2003. "Racial and Ethnic Differences in Pretrial Release Decisions and Outcomes: A Comparison of Hispanic, Black, and White Felony Arrestees." *Criminology* 41: 873–907.

Deutsch, Linda. 2004. "Two-Tiered Justice Favors Famous." Associated Press, July 25.

Devins, N. 2008. "Ideological Cohesion and Precedent (Or Why the Court Only Cares about Precedent When Most Justices Agree with Each Other)." *North Carolina Law Review* 86: 1399–1442.

Dewan Shaila and Brenda Goodman. 2007. "Capital Cases Stall as Costs Grow Daunting." *New York Times*, November 4.

Diamond, Shari Seidman, Mary R. Rose, and Beth Murphy. 2006. "Revisiting the Unanimity Requirement: The Behavior of the Non-Unanimous Civil Jury, 100. *Northwestern University Law Review* 100: 201–230.

Diamond, Shari Seidman. 2006. "Beyond Fantasy and Nightmare: A Portrait of the Jury." *Buffalo Law Review* 54: 717–763.

Diamond, Shari Seidman. 2007. "Dispensing with Deception, Curing with Care." *Judicature* 91: 20–25.

DiIulio, John, ed. 1990. *Courts, Corrections, and the Constitution: The Impact of Judicial Intervention on Prisons and Jails*. New York: Oxford University Press.

Dill, Forrest. 1975. "Discretion, Exchange and Social Control: Bail Bondsmen in Criminal Courts." *Law and Society Review* 9: 639–674.

DiPietro, Susanne. 2008. "From the Benches and Trenches: Evaluating the Court Process for Alaska's Children in Need of Aid." *Justice System Journal* 29: 187–208.

Ditton, Paula, and Doris Wilson. 1999. *Truth in Sentencing in State Prisons*. Washington, DC: Bureau of Justice Statistics.

Dorfman, David N. 1999. "Proving the Lie: Litigating Police Credibility." *American Journal of Criminal Law* 26: 455–503.

Dougherty, Joyce. 1988. "Negotiating Justice in the Juvenile Justice System: A Comparison of Adult Plea Bargaining and Juvenile Intake." *Federal Probation* 52: 72–80.

Douglas, James, and Helen Stockstill. 2008. "Starving the Death Penalty: Do Financial Considerations Limit Its Use?" *Justice System Journal* 29: 326–337.

Douglas, James, and Roger Hartley. 2004. "Sustaining Drug Courts in Arizona and South Carolina: An Experience in Hodgepodge Budgeting." *Justice System Journal* 25: 75–87.

Dubois, Philip. 1980. *From Ballot to Bench: Judicial Elections and the Quest for Accountability*. Austin: University of Texas Press.

Dubois, Philip. 1984. "Voting Cues in Nonpartisan Trial Court Elections: A Multivariate Assessment." *Law and Society Review* 18: 395–436.

Dunkelberger, Lloyd. 2009. "Fast Lane Offers Financial Fast Fix." *Sarasota Herald Tribune*, January 10.

Dunn, B. Michael. 2007. "'Must Find the Defendant Guilty' Jury Instructions Violate the Sixth Amendment." *Judicature* 91: 12–19.

Durose, Matthew, *State Court Sentencing of Convicted Felons, 2004*. Washington, DC: U.S. Department of Justice, Bureau of Justice Statistics, 2007.

Dyke, Andrew. 2007. "Electoral Cycles in the Administration of Criminal Justice." *Public Choice* 133: 417–437.

Dzienkowski, John, and Amon Burton. 2006. *Ethical Dilemmas in the Practice of Law*. St. Paul, MN: Thomson/West.

Easton, Stephen D., and Kaitlin A. Bridges. 2008. "Peeking behind the Wizard's Curtain: Expert Discovery and Disclosure in Criminal Cases." *American Journal of Trial Advocacy* 32: 1–56.

Eckholm, Erik. 2008. "Public Defenders' Offices Refuse to Take New Cases." *New York Times,* November 9.

Editorial. 2008. "Overcrowded Jails a Poor Investment." *Lexington Herald-Leader,* January 20.

Eisenberg, Theodore, Paula Hannaford-Agor, Valarie Hans, Nicole Mott, G. Thomas Munsterman, Stewart Schwab, and Martin Wells. 2004. "Judge-Jury Agreement in Criminal Cases: A Partial Replication of Kalven and Zeisel's *The American Jury.*" *Journal of Empirical Legal Studies* 2: 171–207.

Eisenstein, James, and Herbert Jacob. 1977. *Felony Justice: An Organizational Analysis of Criminal Courts.* Boston: Little, Brown.

Eisenstein, James, Roy Flemming, and Peter Nardulli. 1988. *The Contours of Justice: Communities and Their Courts.* Boston: Little, Brown.

Eisenstein, James. 1978. *Counsel for the United States: U.S. Attorneys in the Political and Legal System.* Baltimore: Johns Hopkins University Press.

Elias, Robert. 1986. *The Politics of Victimization: Victims, Victimology and Human Rights.* New York: Oxford University Press.

Elias, Robert. 1993. *Victims Still: The Political Manipulation of Crime Victims.* Thousand Oaks, CA: Sage.

Elliott-Engel, Amaris. 2008. "Judge Charged with Misconduct after YouTube Video Shows Him Soliciting Campaign Funds." *The Legal Intelligencer,* June 20.

Emmelman, Debra S. 2002. "Trial by Plea Bargain: Case Settlement as a Product of Recursive Decision-Making." In *Qualitative Approaches to Criminal Justice,* edited by Mark Pogrebin, pp. 219–236. Thousand Oaks, CA: Sage.

Emmelman, Debra. 1996. "Trial by Plea Bargain: Case Settlement as a Product of Recursive Decision making." *Law and Society Review* 30: 335–360.

Emmert, Craig, and Carol Ann Traut. 1992. "State Supreme Courts, State Constitutions, and Judicial Policymaking." *Justice System Journal* 16: 37–48.

Emmert, Craig, and Henry Glick. 1987. "Selection Systems and Judicial Characteristics: The Recruitment of State Supreme Court Judges." *Judicature* 70: 228–235.

Engstrom, Richard. 1971. "Political Ambitions and the Prosecutorial Office." *Journal of Politics* 33: 190.

Engstrom, Richard. 1989. "When Blacks Run for Judge: Racial Divisions in the Candidate Preferences of Louisiana Voters." *Judicature* 73: 87–89.

Epstein, L., A. D. Martin, K. M. Quinn, and J. A. Segal. 2008. "The Bush Imprint on the Supreme Court: Why Conservatives Should Continue to Yearn and Liberals Should Not Fear." *Tulsa Law Review* 43: 651–671.

Epstein, Lee, Charles M., Cameron, Jeffrey Segal, and Chad Westerland. 2006. "Lower Court Defiance of (Compliance with) the U.S. Supreme Court." Available at SSRN: http://ssrn.com/abstract=929018

Epstein, Lee, Jack Knight, and Olga Shvetsova. 2002. "Selecting Selecting Systems." In Stephen B. Burbank & Barry Friedman, eds. *Judicial Independence at the Crossroads: An Interdisciplinary Approach.* Philadelphia: American Academy of Political and Social Science/Sage Publications.

Erez, Edna, and Julian Roberts. 2007. "Victim Participation in the Criminal Justice Systems." In *Victims of Crime,* edited by Robert Carl Davis, Arthur J. Lurigio, and Susan Herman. Thousand Oaks, CA: Sage.

Erez, Edna. 1992. "Dangerous Men, Evil Women: Gender and Parole Decision-Making." *Justice Quarterly* 9: 105–126.

Fabian, John M. 2006. "State Supreme Court Responses to *Atkins v. Virginia*: Adaptive Functioning Assessment in Light of Purposeful Planning, Premeditation, and the Behavioral Context of the Homicide." *Journal of Forensic Psychology Practice* 6: 1–25.

Fader, Jamie, Philip Harris, Peter Jones, and Mary Poulin. 2001. "Factors Involved in Decisions on Commitment to Delinquency Programs for First-Time Juvenile Offenders." *Justice Quarterly* 18: 323–341.

Fagan, Jeffrey. 1996. *The Criminalization of Domestic Violence: Promises and Limits.* Washington, DC: National Institute of Justice.

Fahnestock, Kathryn. 1991. "The Loneliness of Command: One Perspective on Judicial Isolation." *Judges' Journal* 30: 13–19.

Farrington, David P. 2006. "Family Background and Psychopathy." In *Handbook of Psychopathy,* edited by C. J. Patrick, pp. 229–250. New York: Guilford.

Fearn, Noelle. 2005. "A Multilevel Analysis of Community Effects on Criminal Sentencing." *Justice Quarterly* 22: 452–486.

Federal Bureau of Investigation. 2008. *Crime in the United States: 2007.* Washington, D.C.: Author.

Federal Bureau of Investigation. 2008. *Integrated Automated Fingerprint Identification System.* Available online at http://www.fbi.gov/hq/cjisd/iafis.htm

Federal Bureau of Investigation. 2008. *Uniform Crime Reports for the United States—2007*. Washington, DC: U.S. Government Printing Office.

Federal Judicial Center. 2009. *Judges of the United States*. Available online at http://www.fjc.gov/public/home.nsf/hisj

Feeley, Malcolm, and Edward Rubin. 1998. *Judicial Policy Making and the Modern State: How the Courts Reformed America's Prisons*. New York: Cambridge University Press.

Feeley, Malcolm, and Sam Kamin. 1996. "The Effect of 'Three Strikes and You're Out' on the Courts: Looking Back to See the Future." In *Three Strikes and You're Out: Vengeance as Public Policy*, edited by David Shichor and Dale Sechrest. Thousand Oaks, CA: Sage.

Feeley, Malcolm. 1979. *The Process Is the Punishment: Handling Cases in a Lower Criminal Court*. New York: Russell Sage Foundation.

Feeney, Floyd, Forrest Dill, and Adrianne Weir. 1983. *Arrests without Conviction: How Often They Occur and Why*. Washington, DC: U.S. Department of Justice, National Institute of Justice.

Feige, David. 2006. *Indefensible: One Lawyer's Journey into the Inferno of American Justice*. New York: Little, Brown.

Fein, Bruce. 1994. "Don't Play Criminals' Game." *USA Today*, April 15, p. 11.

Feinblatt, John, and Greg Berman. 1997. *Responding to the Community: Principles for Planning and Creating a Community Court*. Washington, DC: U.S. Department of Justice, Bureau of Justice Assistance.

Ferdico, John, Henry F. Fradella, and Christopher Totten. 2008. *Criminal Procedure for the Criminal Justice Professional*, 10th ed. Belmont, CA: Wadsworth.

Finn, Peter, and Beverley Lee. 1988. *Establishing and Expanding Victim–Witness Assistance Programs*. Washington, DC: National Institute of Justice.

Fino, Susan. 1987. *The Role of State Supreme Courts in the New Judicial Federalism*. Westport, CT: Greenwood.

Fisher, George. 2003. *Plea Bargaining's Triumph: A History of Plea Bargaining in America*. Stanford: Stanford University Press.

Fisher, Jim. 2008. *Forensics Under Fire: Are Bad Science and Dueling Experts Corrupting Criminal Justice?* New Brunswick, NJ: Rutgers University Press.

Fitzpatrick, Collins. 1988. "Misconduct and Disability of Federal Judges: The Unreported Informal Responses." *Judicature* 71: 282–283.

Flanders, Steven. 1977. *Case Management and Court Management in United States District Courts*. Washington, DC: Federal Judicial Center.

Flanders, Steven. 1991. "Court Administration and Diverse Judiciaries: Complementarities and Conflicts." *Justice System Journal* 15: 640–651.

Flango, Victor Eugene, and Craig Ducat. 1979. "What Differences Does Method of Judicial Selection Make? Selection Procedures in State Courts of Last Resort." *Justice System Journal* 5: 25–44.

Flango, Victor. 1994. "Court Unification and Quality of State Courts." *Justice System Journal* 16: 33–56.

Flemming, Roy, Peter Nardulli, and James Eisenstein. 1987. "The Timing of Justice in Felony Trial Courts." *Law and Policy* 9: 179–206.

Flemming, Roy, Peter Nardulli, and James Eisenstein. 1992. *The Craft of Justice: Politics and Work in Criminal Court Communities*. Philadelphia: University of Pennsylvania Press.

Flemming, Roy. 1982. *Punishment before Trial: An Organizational Perspective on Felony Bail Process*. New York: Longman.

Flemming, Roy. 1986a. "Client Games: Defense Attorney Perspectives on Their Relations with Criminal Clients." *American Bar Foundation Research Journal* 253–277.

Flemming, Roy. 1986b. "Elements of the Defense Attorney's Craft: An Adaptive Expectations Model of the Preliminary Hearing Decision." *Law and Policy* 8: 33–57.

Flemming, Roy. 1989. "If You Pay the Piper, Do You Call the Tune? Public Defenders in America's Criminal Courts." *Law and Social Inquiry* 14: 393–405.

Flemming, Roy. 1990. "The Political Styles and Organizational Strategies of American Prosecutors: Examples from Nine Courthouse Communities." *Law and Policy* 12: 25.

Ford, Marilyn. 1986. "The Role of Extralegal Factors in Jury Verdicts." *Justice System Journal* 11: 16–39.

Forst, Brian, J. Lucianovic, and S. Cox. 1977. *What Happens after Arrest? A Court Perspective of Police Operations in the District of Columbia*. Washington, DC: Law Enforcement Assistance Administration.

Fortune, William, and Penny White. 2008. "Judicial Campaign Oversight Committees' Complaint Handling in the 2006 Elections: Survey and Recommendations." *Judicature* 91: 232–237.

Fox, James Alan, and Marianne W. Zawitz. 2007. *Homicide Trends in the United States*. Washington, D.C.: Bureau of Justice Statistics. Available online at http://www.ojp.gov/bjs/pub/pdf/htius.pdf

Fradella, Henry F. 2003. *Lawrence v. Texas*: Genuine or illusory progress for gay rights in America? *Criminal Law Bulletin*, 39: 597–607.

Fradella, Henry F. 1999. "In Search of Meritorious Claims: A Study of the Processing of Prisoner

Civil Rights Cases in a Federal District Court." *Justice Systems Journal* 21: 23–55.

Fradella, Henry F. 2000. "Minimum Mandatory Sentences: Arizona's Ineffective Tool for the Social Control of DUI." *Criminal Justice Policy Review* 11: 113–135.

Fradella, Henry F. 2004. "A Content Analysis of Federal Judicial Views of the Social Science 'Researcher's Black Arts.'" *Rutgers Law Journal* 35: 103–170.

Fradella, Henry F. 2007. *Mental Illness and Criminal Defenses of Excuse in Contemporary American Law.* Bethesda, MD: Academica Press.

Frank, Mitchell J., and Dawn Broschard. 2006. "The Silent Criminal Defendant and the Presumption of Innocence: In The Hands of Real Jurors, Is Either of Them Safe?" *Lewis and Clark Law Review* 10: 237–285.

Franklin, Cortney A., and Noelle E. Fearn. 2008. "Gender, Race, and Formal Court Decision-making Outcomes: Chivalry/Paternalism, Conflict Theory or Gender Conflict?" *Journal of Criminal Justice* 36: 279–290.

Frase, Richard S. 2005. "Punishment Purposes." *Stanford Law Review* 58: 67–83.

Freeman, Donald. 2007. "Drunk Driving Legislation and Traffic Fatalities: New Evidence on BAC 08 Laws." *Contemporary Economic Policy* 25: 293–310.

Freeman, Robert. 2000. *Popular Culture and Corrections.* Lanham, MD: American Correctional Association.

Friedenthal, Jack H., Mary Kay Kane, and Arthur R. Miller. 2005. *Civil Procedure, Hornbook Series.* 4th ed. Eagan, MN: West.

Friedman, Barry. 1998. "Attacks on Judges: Why They Fail." *Judicature* 81: 150–156.

Friedman, L. 2000. "The Constitutional Value of Dialogue and the New Judicial Federalism." *Hastings Constitutional Law Quarterly* 28: 93–144.

Friedman, Lawrence, and Robert Percival. 1976. "A Tale of Two Courts: Litigation in Alameda and San Benito Counties." *Law and Society Review* 10: 267–302.

Friedman, Lawrence. 1979. "Plea Bargaining in Historical Perspective." *Law and Society Review* 13: 247–259.

Friedman, Lawrence. 1984. *American Law: An Introduction.* New York: Norton.

Friedrichs, David. 2006. *Law in our Lives: An Introduction* (2nd ed.). Los Angeles, CA: Roxbury Publishing Co.

Friedrichs, David. 2009. *Trusted Criminals: White Collar Crime in Contemporary Society.* Belmont, CA: Wadsworth.

Fukurai, Hiroshi, Edgar Butler, and Richard Krooth. 1991. "Cross-Sectional Jury Representation or Systematic Jury Representation? Simple Random and Cluster Sampling Strategies in Jury Selection." *Journal of Criminal Justice* 19: 31–48.

Fulkerson, Andrew, and Michael Suttmoeller. 2008. "Current Issues Involving Lethal Injection." *Criminal Justice Studies* 21: 271–282.

Fyfe, James. 1982. "In Search of the 'Bad Faith' Search." *Criminal Law Bulletin* 18: 260–265.

Gabel, Jessica D., and Margaret D. Wilkinson. 2008. "'Good' Science Gone Bad: How the Criminal Justice System Can Redress the Impact of Flawed Forensics." *Hastings Law Journal* 59: 1001–1030.

Galanter, Marc. 1988. "The Life and Times of the Big Six: or, The Federal Courts since the Good Old Days." Working Paper 9:2. Madison: University of Wisconsin, Institute for Legal Studies.

Galaway, Burt, and Joe Hudson, eds. 1996. *Restorative Justice: International Perspectives.* Monsey, NY: Criminal Justice Press.

Galaway, Burt. 1988. "Restitution as Innovation or Unfilled Promise?" *Federal Probation* 52: 3–14.

Galiber, Joseph, Barry Latzer, Mark Dwyer, Jack Litman, H. Richard Uviller, and G. Roger McDonald. 1993. "Law, Justice, and Jury Nullification: A Debate." *Criminal Law Bulletin* 29: 40–69.

Galie, Peter. 1987. "State Supreme Courts, Judicial Federalism and the Other Constitutions." *Judicature* 71: 100–110.

Gallas, Geoff. 1976. "The Conventional Wisdom of State Court Administration: A Critical Assessment and an Alternative Approach." *Justice System Journal* 2: 35.

Gardiner, John. 1986. "Preventing Judicial Misconduct: Defining the Role of Conduct Organizations." *Judicature* 70: 113–121.

Garner, Joel. 1987. "Delay Reduction in the Federal Courts: Rule 50(b) and the Federal Speedy Trial Act of 1974." *Journal of Quantitative Criminology* 3: 229–250.

Garrett, Brandon L. 2008. "Judging Innocence." *Columbia Law Review* 108: 55–142.

Garrow, D. J. 2008. Bad Behavior Makes Big Law: Southern Malfeasance and the Expansion of Federal Judicial Power, 1954-1968. *Saint John's Law Review* 82: 1–38.

Garvey, Stephen P., Paula Hannaford-Agor, Valerie P. Hans, Nicole L. Mott, G. Thomas Munsterman, and Martin T. Wells. 2004. "Juror First Votes in Criminal Trials in Four Major Metropolitan Jurisdictions." *Journal of Empirical Legal Studies* 1: 371–398.

Gastil, John, Laura W. Black, E. Pierre Deess, and Jay Leighter. 2008. "From Group Member to Democratic Citizen: How Deliberating with Fellow

Jurors Reshapes Civic Attitudes." *Human Communication Research* 34: 137–169.

Gau, Jacinta, and Travis Pratt. 2008. "Broken Windows or Window Dressing? Citizens (In)Ability to Tell the Difference between Disorder and Crime." *Criminology and Public Policy* 7: 163–194.

Geller, Adam. 2005. "Martha Stewart Says Prison Changed Her." Associated Press, March 7.

Georgetown Law Journal. 2007. "The Judicial Nomination Process Over Time: Some Historic Background." *Georgetown Law Journal* 95: 1028–1039.

Gershman, Bennett. 1993. "Defending the Poor." *Trial* 29: 47–51.

Gertz, Marc, and Albert Price. 1985. "Variables Influencing Sentencing Severity: Intercourt Differences in Connecticut." *Journal of Criminal Justice* 13: 131–139.

Gertz, Marc. 1977. "Influence in Court Systems: The Clerk as Interface." *Justice System Journal* 3: 30–37.

Gest, Ted. 1996. "The Law That Grief Built." *U.S. News and World Report*, April 29, p. 58.

Giannelli, Paul C. 2007. "Wrongful Convictions and Forensic Science: The Need to Regulate Crime Labs." *North Carolina Law Review* 86: 163–235.

Gibson, James. 1978. "Race as a Determinant of Criminal Sentences: A Methodological Critique and a Case Study." *Law and Society Review* 12: 455–478.

Gibson, James. 1980. "Environmental Restraints on the Behavior of Judges: A Representational Model of Judicial Decision Making." *Law and Society Review* 14: 343–370.

Giffuni, Matthew. 1995. "Civil Forfeiture and the Excessive Fines Clause Following *Austin v. United States*." *Criminal Law Bulletin* 31: 502–533.

Gilboy, Janet. 1984. "Prosecutors' Discretionary Use of the Grand Jury to Initiate or to Reinitiate Prosecution." *American Bar Foundation Research Journal* 1–81.

Gillespie, Robert. 1988–1989. "Criminal Fines: Do They Pay?" *Justice System Journal* 13: 365–378.

Ginsburg, Ruth Bader. 1993. "Remarks for California Women Lawyers." *Pepperdine Law Review* 22: 1–5.

Givelber, Daniel, and Amy Farrell. 2008. "Judges and Juries: The Defense Case and Differences in Acquittal Rates." *Law and Social Inquiry* 33: 31–52.

Glaberson, William. 2003. "Family Seeks Longer Term for Stabbing in Crown Hts." *New York Times*, August 2.

Glaberson, William. 2006. "In Tiny Courts of N.Y., Abuses of Law and Power." *New York Times*, September 25.

Glater, Jonathan, and Ken Belson. 2005. "In White-Collar Crimes, Few Smoking Guns." *New York Times*, March 12.

Glick, Henry, and Kenneth Vines. 1973. *State Court Systems*. Englewood Cliffs, NJ: Prentice Hall.

Goehner, Amy, Lina Lofaro, and Kate Novack. 2004. "Where *CSI* Meets Real Law and Order." *Time*, November 8, p. 69.

Goerdt, John. 1992. *Small Claims and Traffic Courts: Case Management Procedures, Case Characteristics, and Outcomes in 12 Urban Jurisdictions*. Williamsburg, VA: National Center for State Courts.

Goldberg, Deborah, Craig Holman, and Samantha Sanchez. 2002. "The New Politics of Judicial Elections." Available online at http://www.justiceatstake.org/files/JASMoneyReport.pdf

Goldberg, Stephen, Frank Sander, Nancy Rogers, and Sarah Cole. 2007. *Dispute Resolution: Negotiation, Mediation, and other Processes*. 5th ed. New York: Aspen.

Goldfarb, Ronald. 1965. *Ransom: A Critique of the American Bail System*. New York: Harper and Row.

Goldkamp, John, and Doris Weiland. 1993. "Assessing the Impact of Dade County's Felony Drug Court." *National Institute of Justice Research in Brief*. Washington, DC: U.S. Department of Justice.

Goldkamp, John, and Peter Jones. 1992. "Pre-Trial Drug-Testing Experiments in Milwaukee and Prince George's County: The Context of Implementation." *Journal of Research in Crime and Delinquency* 29: 430–465.

Goldkamp, John, Cheryl Irons-Guynn, and Doris Weiland. 2002. *Community Prosecution Strategies: Measuring Impact*. Washington, DC: Bureau of Justice Assistance.

Goldkamp, John, Doris Weiland, and Cheryl Irons-Guynn. 2001. *Developing an Evaluation Plan for Community Courts: Assessing the Hartford Community Court Model*. Washington, DC: Bureau of Justice Assistance.

Goldkamp, John. 1980. "The Effects of Detention on Judicial Decisions: A Closer Look." *Justice System Journal* 5: 234–257.

Goldkamp, John. 2002. "The Importance of Drug Courts: Lessons from Measuring Impact." Paper presented at the American Society of Criminology, Chicago.

Goldman, Sheldon, and Elliot Slotnick. 1999. "Clinton's Second Term Judiciary: Picking Judges under Fire." *Judicature* 82: 264–285.

Goldman, Sheldon, and Matthew Saronson. 1994. "Clinton's Nontraditional Judges: Creating a More Representative Bench." *Judicature* 78: 68–73.

Goldman, Sheldon, Elliot Slotnick, Gerard Gryski, and Sara Schiavoni. 2007. "Picking Judges in a Time of Turmoil: W. Bush's Judiciary during the 109th Congress. *Judicature* 90: 252.

Goldman, Sheldon. 1997. *Picking Federal Judges: Lower Court Selection from Roosevelt through Reagan*. New Haven, CT: Yale University Press.

Goldschmidt, Jona, David Olson, and Margaret Ekman. 2009. "The Relationship between Method of Judicial Selection and Judicial Misconduct." *Widener Law Journal* 18: 455–481.

Golub, Andrew, Bruce Johnson, and Eloise Dunlap. 2007. "The Race/Ethnicity Disparity in Misdemeanor Marijuana Arrests in New York City." *Criminology and Public Policy* 6: 131–164.

"Go Directly to Jail: White Collar Sentencing after the Sarbanes–Oxley Act. 2009. *Harvard Law Review* 122: 1728.

Goodman-Delahunty, Jane, Lynee Forster Lee, and Robert ForsterLee. 2007. "Dealing with Guilty Offenders." In *Psychology and the Law: An Empirical Perspective*, edited by Neil Brewer and Kipling Williams. New York: Guilford.

Gordon, Corey, and William Brill. 1996. *The Expanding Role of Crime Prevention through Environmental Design in Premises Liability*. Washington, DC: National Institute of Justice.

Gorman, Sean. 2009. "Bedford Judge Admonished for Doling Out Excessive Traffic Fines." *LoHud.com* (New York's Lower Hudson Valley), July 30.

Gottfredson, Denise, Stacy Najaka, and Brook Kearley. 2003. "Effectiveness of Drug Treatment Courts: Evidence from a Randomized Trial." *Criminology and Public Policy* 2: 171–196.

Gottfredson, Michael. 1974. "Empirical Analysis of Pretrial Release Decisions." *Journal of Criminal Justice* 2: 287.

Gottschalk, Marie. 2009. "The Long Reach of the Carceral State: The Politics of Crime, Mass Imprisonment, and Penal Reform in the United States and Abroad." *Law and Social Inquiry* 34: 439–472.

Gottsfield, Robert L., and Marianne Alcorn. 2009. "The Capital Case Crisis in Maricopa County: What (Little) We Can Do About It." *Arizona Attorney* 45: 22–30.

Gould, Jon, and Stephen Mastrofski. 2004. "Suspect Searches: Assessing Police Behavior under the U.S. Constitution." *Criminology and Public Policy* 3: 315–362.

Gould, Jon. 2008. "Justice Delayed or Justice Denied? A Contemporary Review of Capital Habeas Corpus." *Justice System Journal* 29: 273–287.

Gourevitch, Philip. 2001. "The Crime Lover." *The New Yorker*, February 19, pp. 160–173.

Gover, Angela, John MacDonald, and Geoffrey Alpert. 2003. "Combating Domestic Violence: Findings from an Evaluation of a Local Domestic Violence Court." *Criminology and Public Policy* 3: 109–132.

Graham, Barbara Luck. 1990. "Do Judicial Selection Systems Matter? A Study of Black Representation on State Courts." *American Politics Quarterly* 18: 316–336.

Gray, Cynthia. 2003. "State Supreme Courts Play Key Role in Judicial Discipline." *Judicature* 86: 267–268.

Green, Edward. 1961. *Judicial Attitudes in Sentencing*. New York: St. Martin's Press.

Green, Justin, Ross Russell, and John Schmidhauser. 1975. "Iowa's Magistrate System: The Aftermath of Reform." *Judicature* 58: 380–389.

Greenhouse, Linda. 2004. "Death Sentence Overturned in Texas." *New York Times*, February 25.

Greenwood, Peter, C. Peter Rydell, Allan Abrahamse, Jonathan Caulkins, James Chiesa, Karyn Model, and Stephen Klein. 1996. "Estimated Benefits and Costs of California's New Mandatory Sentencing Law." In *Three Strikes and You're Out: Vengeance as Public Policy*, edited by David Shichor and Dale Sechrest. Thousand Oaks, CA: Sage.

Griffin, Timothy, and John Wooldredge. 2006. "Sex-Based Disparities in Felony Dispositions before versus after Sentencing Reform in Ohio." *Criminology* 44: 893–923.

Griset, Pamala. 1995. "Determinate Sentencing and Agenda Building: A Case Study of the Failure of a Reform." *Journal of Criminal Justice* 23: 349–362.

Grisham, John. 2008. *The Appeal*. New York: Doubleday.

Grisso, Thomas. 1981. *Juveniles' Waiver of Rights*. New York: Plenum.

Gruhl, John. 1981. "State Supreme Courts and the U.S. Supreme Court's Post-*Miranda* Rulings." *Journal of Criminal Law and Criminology* 72: 886–913.

Gryski, Gerard S., Eleanor C. Main, and William J. Dixon. 1986 "Models of State High Court Decision Making in Sex Discrimination Cases." *Journal of Politics* 48: 143–155.

Guevara, Lori, Denis Herz, and Cassia Spohn. 2008. "Race, Gender, and Legal Counsel: Differential Outcomes in Two Juvenile Courts." *Youth Violence and Juvenile Justice* 6: 83–104.

Gusfield, Joseph. 1981. *The Culture of Public Problems: Drinking-Driving and the Symbolic Order*. Chicago: University of Chicago Press.

Guthrie, C., J.J. Rachlinski, and A.J. Wistrich. 2007. "Blinking on the Bench: How Judges Decide Cases." *Cornell Law Review* 93: 1–43.

Guzik, Keith. 2007. "The Forces of Conviction: The Power and Practice of Mandatory Prosecution Upon Misdemeanor Domestic Battery Suspects." *Law and Social Inquiry* 32: 41–74.

Haapanen, Rudy. 1989. *Selective Incapacitation and the Serious Offender: A Longitudinal Study of Criminal Career Patterns*. New York: Springer-Verlag.

Hagan, John, John Hewitt, and Duane Alwin. 1979. "Ceremonial Justice: Crime and Punishment in a Loosely Coupled System." *Social Forces* 58: 506–527.

Hagan, John. 1974. "Extra-Legal Attributes and Criminal Sentencing: An Assessment of a Sociological Viewpoint." *Law and Society Review* 8: 357–381.

Hagan, John. 1977. "Criminal Justice in Rural and Urban Communities: A Study of the Bureaucratization of Justice." *Social Forces* 55: 597–612.

Hagan, John. 1983. *Victims before the Law: The Organizational Domination of Criminal Law*. Toronto: Butterworth's.

Hagstrom, Anna M. 2009. "*Atkins v. Virginia*: An Empty Holding Devoid of Justice for the Mentally Retarded." *Law and Inequality: A Journal of Theory and Practice* 27: 241–276.

Hakim, Simon, George Rengert, and Yochanan Shachmurove. 1996. "Estimation of Net Social Benefits of Electronic Security." *Justice Quarterly* 13: 153–170.

Hall, Jerome. 1952. *Theft, Law and Society*. Indianapolis: Bobbs-Merrill.

Haller, Mark. 1979. "Plea Bargaining: The Nineteenth-Century Context." *Law and Society Review* 13: 273–280.

Hallinan, Joe. 1993. "Violent Children Straining Limit of Justice System." *Times-Picayune*, October 31, p. A24.

Haney, Craig. 1984. "On the Selection of Capital Juries: The Biasing Effects of the Death-Qualification Process." *Law and Human Behavior* 8: 121–132.

Haney, Craig. 2005. Death by Design: Capital Punishment as a Social Psychological System. New York: Oxford University Press.

Hannaford, Paula L. 2001. "Safeguarding Juror Privacy: A New Framework for Court Policies and Procedures." *Judicature* 85: 18–25.

Hannaford, Paula, Valerie Hans, and G. Thomas Munsterman. 1999. "How Much Justice Hangs in the Balance? A New Look at Hung Jury Rates." *Judicature* 83: 59–67.

Hannaford-Agor, Paula L., Valerie P. Hans, Nicole L. Mott, and G. Thomas Munsterman. 2002. *Are Hung Juries a Problem?* Washington: The National Center for State Courts.

Hanson, Roger, and Henry Daley. 1995. *Challenging the Conditions of Prisons and Jails*. Washington, DC: U.S. Department of Justice, Bureau of Justice Statistics.

Hanson, Roger, William Hewitt, and Brian Ostrom. 1992. "Are the Critics of Indigent Defense Counsel Correct?" *State Court Journal* (Summer): 20–29.

Harcourt, Bernard, and Jens Ludwig. 2007. "Reefer Madness: Broken Windows Policing and Misdemeanor Marijuana Arrests in New York City, 1989-2000." *Criminology and Public Policy* 6: 165–182.

Harlow, Caroline. 1999. *Prior Abuse Reported by Inmates and Probationers*. NCJ 172879. Washington, DC: U.S. Department of Justice, Office of Justice Programs.

Harrell, Adele, Ojmarrh Mitchell, Alexa Hirst, Douglas Marlowe, and Jeffrey Merrill. 2002. "Breaking the Cycle of Drugs and Crime: Findings from the Birmingham BTC Demonstration." *Criminology and Public Policy* 1: 189–216.

Harrell, Adele, Shannon Cavanagh, and John Roman. 2000. "Evaluation of the D.C. Superior Court Drug Intervention Programs." Washington, DC: National Institute of Justice.

Harris, Alexes. 2007. "Diverting and Abdicating Judicial Discretion: Cultural, Political, and Procedural Dynamics in California Juvenile Justice." *Law and Society Review* 41: 387–427.

Harris, John, and Paul Jesilow. 2000. "It's Not the Old Ball Game: Three Strikes and the Courtroom Workgroup." *Justice Quarterly* 17: 185–204.

Hashimoto, Erica. 2008. "Toward Ethical Plea Bargaining." *Cardozo Law Review* 30: 949–963.

Hastie, Reid, Steven Penrod, and Nancy Pennington. 1984. *Inside the Jury*. Cambridge, MA: Harvard University Press.

Hastings, Deborah. 2009. "Money May Decide Execution Debate." Associated Press, March 8.

Haynie, Dana, Harald Weiss, and Alex Piquero. 2008. "Race, the Economic Maturity Gap, and Criminal Offending in Young Childhood." *Justice Quarterly* 25: 595–622.

Healey, Kerry. 1995. *Victim and Witness Intimidation: New Developments and Emerging Responses*. Washington, DC: National Institute of Justice.

Heflin, Howell. 1987. "The Impeachment Process: Modernizing an Archaic System." *Judicature* 71: 123–125.

Heinz, Anne, Herbert Jacob, and Robert Lineberry, eds. 1983. *Crime in City Politics*. New York: Longman.

Heinz, John, and Edward Laumann. 1982. *Chicago Lawyers: The Social Structure of the Bar*. New York: Russell Sage Foundation.

Helland, Eric, and Alexander Tabarrok. 2002. "The Effect of Electoral Institutions on Tort Awards." *American Law and Economics Review* 4: 341–370.

Helland, Eric, and Alexander Tabarrok. 2004. "The Fugitive: Evidence on Public Versus Private Law Enforcement from Bail Jumping." *Journal of Law and Economics* 47: 93–122.

Heller, Kevin Jon. 2006. "The Cognitive Psychology of Circumstantial Evidence." *Michigan Law Review* 105: 241–305.

Hellman, A.D. 2006. "The View from the Trenches: A Report on the Breakout Sessions at the 2005 National Conference on Appellate Justice." *Journal of Appellate Practice and Process* 8(1): 141–205.

Hemmens, Craig, Kristin Strom, and Elicia Schlegel. 1997. "Gender Bias in the Courts: A Review of the Literature." Paper presented at the Academy of Criminal Justice Sciences, Louisville, KY.

Henry, D. Alan, and John Clark. 1999. "Pretrial Drug Testing: An Overview of Issues and Practices." *Bulletin*, Bureau of Justice Assistance (NCJ 176341).

Herman, Susan N., and Erwin Chemerinsky. 2006. *The Right to a Speedy and Public Trial: A Reference Guide to the United States Constitution.* Westport, CT: Greenwood.

Herz, Denise. 2000. "Drugs in the Heartland: Methamphetamine Use in Rural Nebraska." Washington, DC: National Institute of Justice.

Heumann, Milton, and Colin Loftin. 1979. "Mandatory Sentencing and the Abolition of Plea Bargaining: The Michigan Felony Firearm Statute." *Law and Society Review* 13: 393–430.

Heumann, Milton. 1975. "A Note on Plea Bargaining and Case Pressure." *Law and Society Review* 9: 515–528.

Heumann, Milton. 1978. *Plea Bargaining: The Experience of Prosecutors, Judges, and Defense Attorneys.* Chicago: University of Chicago Press.

Hillsman, Sally, and Barry Mahoney. 1988. "Collecting and Enforcing Criminal Fines: A Review of Court Processes, Practices, and Problems." *Justice System Journal* 13: 17–36.

Hindelang, Michael. 1972. "Equality under the Law." In *Race, Crime and Justice*, edited by Charles Reasons and Jack Kuykendall, pp. 312–323. Pacific Palisades, CA: Goodyear.

Hindson, Stephanie, Hillary Potter, and Michael Radelet. 2006. "Race, Gender, Region, and Death Sentencing in Colorado, 1980-1999." *Colorado Law Review* 77: 549–574.

Hingson, Ralph, Timothy Heeren, and Erika Edwards. 2008. "Age at Drinking Onset, Alcohol Dependence, and Their Relation to Drug Use and Dependence, Driving under the Influence of Drugs, and Motor-Vehicle Crash Involvement Because of Drugs." *Journal of Studies on Alcohol and Drugs* 69: 192–201.

Hirschel, David, Eve Buzawa, April Pattavina, and Don Faggiani. 2007. "Domestic Violence and Mandatory Arrest Laws: To What Extent Do They Influence Police Arrest Decisions?" *Journal of Criminal Law and Criminology* 98: 255.

Hirschel, J. David, Ira Hutchison, Charles Dean, and Anne-Marie Mills. 1992. "Review Essay on the Law Enforcement Response to Spouse Abuse: Past, Present and Future." *Justice Quarterly* 9: 247–284.

Hirschkorn, Phil. 2006. "9/11 Victims Share Heartache with Moussaoui Jury." CNN website, http://www.cnn.com/2006/LAW/04/07/moussaoui.victims/ index.html

Hodges, Sam. 1997. "Should Federal Punishments for Crack, Powder Be Closer?" *Mobile Register*, June 22, p. A20.

Hofer, Paul. 2007. "*United States v. Booker* as a Natural Experiment: Using Empirical Research to Inform the Federal Sentencing Debate." *Criminology and Public Policy* 6: 433–460.

Hoffman, Richard. 1991. "Beyond the Team: Renegotiating the Judge–Administrator Partnership." *Justice System Journal* 15: 652–666.

Hogarth, John. 1971. *Sentencing as a Human Process.* Toronto: University of Toronto Press.

Holbrook, R. Andrew, and Timothy Hill. 2005. "Agenda-Setting and Priming in Prime Time Television: Crime Dramas as Political Cues." *Political Communication* 22: 277–295.

Holland, Gina. 2006. "High Court Rules for Death Penalty." *Times-Picayune*, June 27.

Holleran, David, Dawn Beichner, and Cassia Spohn. 2009. "Examining Charging Agreement between Police and Prosecutors in Rape Cases." *Crime and Delinquency* doi:10.1177. In press.

Holmes, Lisa M., and Jolly A. Emrey. 2006. "Court Diversification: Staffing the State Courts of Last Resort through Interim Appointments." *Justice Systems Journal* 27: 1–12.

Holmes, Lisa, and Elisha Savchak. 2003. "Judicial Appointment Politics in the 107th Congress." *Judicature* 86: 240–250.

Holmes, Malcolm, Howard Daudistel, and William Taggart. 1992. "Plea Bargaining and State District Court Caseloads: An Interrupted Time Series Analysis." *Law and Society Review* 26: 139–160.

Holmes, Oliver Wendell, Jr. 1881. *The Common Law.* Boston: Little, Brown.

Holmes, Oliver Wendell. 1920. *Collected Legal Papers.* Boston: Harcourt.

Holmstrom, Lynda, and Ana Burgess. 1983. *The Victim of Rape: Institutional Reactions.* New Brunswick, NJ: Transaction Publishers.

Homel, Ross. 1988. *Policing and Punishing the Drinking Driver: A Study of General and Specific Deterrence.* New York: Springer-Verlag.

Hoover, Eric. 2008. "For MADD, the Legal Drinking Age Is Not for Debate." *The Chronicle of Higher Education* 55(11).

Horney, Julie, and Cassia Spohn. 1996. "The Influence of Blame and Believability Factors on the Processing of Simple versus Aggravated Rape Cases." *Criminology* 34: 135–162.

Horowitz, Irwin A., Norbert L. Kerr, Ernest S. Park, and Christine Gockel. 2006. "Chaos in the Courtroom Reconsidered: Emotional Bias and Juror Nullification." *Law and Human Behavior* 30: 163–181.

Houck, Max M. 2006. "CSI: Reality." *Scientific American* 295: 84–89.

Hsu, Spencer. 2009. "U.S. to Expand Immigration Checks to all Local Jails." *Washington Post*, May 19.

Hubler, Shawn. 2005. "Spectacle Supplants Law as Focus of Jackson Trial." *Los Angeles Times*, June 13.

Hunter, Arthur. 2006. "Judges Are Like Referees, Guarding Citizen Rights." *Times-Picayune*, July 20.

Hurwitz, Mark S. and Dew Noble Lanier. 2003. "Explaining Judicial Diversity: The Differential Ability of Women and Minorities to Attain Seats on State Supreme and Appellate Courts." *State Politics and Policy Quarterly*, 3: 329–352.

Hurwitz, Mark. 2006. "Much Ado About Sentencing: The Influence of *Apprendi, Blakely*, and *Booker* in the U.S. Courts of Appeals." *Justice System Journal* 27: 81–94.

Hurwitz, Mark. 2008. "Give Him a Fair Trial, Then Hang Him: The Supreme Court's Modern Death Penalty Jurisprudence." *Justice System Journal* 29: 243–256.

Innocence Project, The. "Know the Cases: Search the Profiles." http://www.innocenceproject.org/know/Search-Profiles.php

Innocence Project. 2006. Available online at http://www.innocenceproject.org

"Issues in Judicial Independence and Accountability." 2004. *Judicature* 88: 114–121.

Iwata, Edward. 2003. "Has Hunt for Corporate Criminals Gone Too Far?" *USA Today*, July 22.

Jablon, Robert. June 20, 2003. "Bounty Hunters Assail Duane 'Dog' Chapman." Associated Press. Available online at http://www.beaumontenterprise.com/news/bounty_hunters_assail_duane__dog__chapman_07-05-2008_16_42_14.html

Jackson, Donald. 1974. *Judges*. New York: Atheneum.

Jackson, Patrick. 1987. "The Impact of Pretrial Preventive Detention." *Justice System Journal* 12: 305–334.

Jacob, Herbert. 1966. "Judicial Insulation: Elections, Direct Participation, and Public Attention to the Courts in Wisconsin." *Wisconsin Law Review* 812.

Jacob, Herbert. 1984. *Justice in America*. 4th ed. Boston: Little, Brown.

Jacob, Herbert. 1991. "Decision Making in Trial Courts." In *The American Courts: A Critical Assessment*, edited by John Gates and Charles Johnson, pp. 211–233. Washington, DC: CQ Press.

Jacob, Herbert. 1997. "Governance by Trial Court Judges." *Law and Science Review* 31: 3–37.

Jacobs, Andrew. 2007. "Newark Battles Murder and its Accomplice, Silence." *New York Times*, May 29.

Jacobs, David, and Stephanie Kent. 2007. "The Determinants of Execution Since 1951: How Politics, Protests, Public Opinion and Social Divisions Shape Capital Punishment." *Social Problems* 54: 297–318.

Jacobs, David, Zhenchao Qian, Jason Carmichael, and Stephanie Kent. 2007. "Who Survives on Death Row? An Individual and Contextual Analysis." *American Sociological Review* 72: 610–362.

Jacobson, Michael. 2005. *Downsizing Prisons: How to Reduce Crime and End Mass Incarceration*. New York: NYU Press.

Jacoby, Joan, Leonard Mellon, Edward Ratledge, and Stanley Turner. 1982. *Prosecutorial Decisionmaking: A National Study*. Washington, DC: U.S. Department of Justice, National Institute of Justice.

Jacoby, Joan. 1980. *The American Prosecutor: A Search for Identity*. Lexington, MA: D. C. Heath.

Jacoby, Joan. 1995. "Pushing the Envelope: Leadership in Prosecution." *Justice System Journal* 17: 291–308.

Jefferson, David. 2005. "America's Most Dangerous Drug." *Newsweek*, August 8, pp. 40–48.

Jehle, Jörg-Martin, and Marianne Wade. 2006. *Coping with Overloaded Criminal Justice Systems*. New York: Springer.

Jencks, Christopher, and Paul Peterson, eds. 1991. *The Urban Underclass*. Washington, DC: Brookings Institution.

Johnson, Brian D. 2006. "The Multilevel Context of Criminal Sentencing: Integrating Judge- and County-Level Influences." *Criminology* 44: 259–298.

Johnson, Brian, Jeffrey Ulmer, and John Kramer. 2008. "The Social Context of Guidelines Circumvention: The Case of Federal District Courts." *Criminology* 46: 737–783.

Johnson, James, and Philip Secret. 1995. "The Effects of Court Structure on Juvenile Court Decisonmaking." *Journal of Criminal Justice* 23: 63–82.

Johnson, Kevin, and Gary Fields. 1996. "Juvenile Crime 'Wave' May Be Just a Ripple." *USA Today*, December 13, p. 3.

Jonakait, Randolph N. 2006. *The American Jury System*. New Haven: Yale University Press.

Jones, David. 1994. "Prosecutorial Tenure in Wisconsin." Paper presented at the Midwest Criminal Justice Association Meeting, Chicago.

Jones, David. 2001. "Toward a Prosecutorial 'Civil Service': A Wisconsin Case Study." Paper presented at the annual meeting of the American Society of Criminology, Atlanta.

Justice at Stake. 2009. "Bybee Invited to Testify by Leahy." April 30. Available online at http://www.gavelgrab.org/?cat=8

Justice at Stake. 2009. "Caperton v. Massey Resource Page." Available online at http://www.justiceatstake.org/node/106

Kairys, David, Joseph Kadane, and John Lehorsky. 1977. "Jury Representativeness: A Mandate for Multiple Source Lists." *California Law Review* 65: 776–827.

Kalt, Brian C. 2003. "The Exclusion of Felons from Jury Service." *American University Law Review* 53: 65–189.

Kalven, Harry, and Hans Zeisel. 1966. *The American Jury*. Boston: Little, Brown.

Kamisar, Yale. 1978. "Is the Exclusionary Rule an 'Illogical' or 'Unnatural' Interpretation of the Fourth Amendment?" *Judicature* 78: 83–84.

Kant, Immanuel. 1790. *The Science of Right*. (W. Hastie, trans.). Available online at http://philosophy.eserver.org/kant/science-of-right.txt

Kanter, Lois H. 2005. "Invisible Clients: Exploring Our Failure to Provide Civil Legal Services to Rape Victims." *Suffolk University Law Review* 38: 253–289.

Kaplan, John. 1973. *Criminal Justice: Introductory Cases and Materials*. Mineola, NY: Foundation Press.

Kappeler, Victor, Michael Vaughn, and Rolando Del Carmen. 1991. "Death in Detention: An Analysis of Police Liability for Negligent Failure to Prevent Suicide." *Journal of Criminal Justice* 19: 381–393.

Karmen, Andrew. 2010. *Crime Victims: An Introduction to Victimology*. 7th ed. Belmont, CA: Wadsworth.

Karnow, Curtis E.A. 2008. "Setting Bail for Public Safety." *Berkeley Journal of Criminal Law* 13: 1–30.

Kasunic, David. 1983. "One Day/One Trial: A Major Improvement in the Jury System." *Judicature* 67: 78–86.

Katz, Charles M., and Cassia C. Spohn. 1995. "The Effect of Race and Gender on Bail Outcomes: A Test of an Interactive Model." *American Journal of Criminal Justice* 19: 161–184.

Kauder, Neal, and Brian Ostrom. 2008. *State Sentencing Guidelines: Profiles and Continuum*. Williamsburg, VA: National Center for State Courts.

Kautt, Paula. 2002. "Location, Location, Location: Interdistrict and Intercircuit Variations in Sentencing Outcomes for Federal Drug-Trafficking Offenses." *Justice Quarterly* 19: 633–669.

Keel, Timothy G., John P. Jarvis, and Yvonne E. Muirhead. 2009. "An Exploratory Analysis of Factors Affecting Homicide Investigations: Examining the Dynamics of Murder Clearance Rates." *Homicide Studies* 13: 50–68.

Keen, Bradley, and David Jacobs. 2009. "Racial Threat, Partisan Politics, and Racial Disparities in Prison Admissions: A Panel Analysis." *Criminology* 47: 209–238.

Kennedy, Darlene. 1997. "Let's Hold Juveniles Responsible for Their Crimes." National Center for Public Policy Research. Available online at http://www.nationalcenter.inter.net/NPA166.html

Kerrigan, Tim. 2008. "No Money? No Problem. Legal Aid Lawyers Find Innovative Ways to Serve the Rural Poor." *Public Interest Law Reporter* 13: 133–139.

Killman, Curtis. 2006. "Pushing the Limits: Towns Cash in on Traffic Fines." *Tulsa World*, August 6.

Kimora. 2008. "The Emerging Paradigm in Probation and Parole in the United States." *Journal of Offender Rehabilitation* 46: 1–11.

King, Nancy J., David A. Soulé, Sara Steen, and Robert R. Weidner. 2005. "When Process Affects Punishment: Differences in Sentences after Guilty Plea, Bench Trial, and Jury Trial in Five Guidelines States." *Columbia Law Review* 105: 959–1009.

King, Ryan S. 2008. *The State of Sentencing 2007: Developments in Policy and Practice*. Washington, DC: The Sentencing Project.

Kingsnorth, Rodney, and Louis Rizzo. 1979. "Decision-Making in the Criminal Courts: Continuities and Discontinuities." *Criminology* 17: 3–14.

Kingsnorth, Rodney, Carole Barnes, and Paul Coonley. 1990. "Driving under the Influence: The Role of Legal and Extralegal Factors in Court Processing and Sentencing Practices." Unpublished manuscript, Department of Sociology, California State University, Sacramento.

Kleck, Gary. 1981. "Racial Discrimination in Criminal Sentencing: A Critical Evaluation of the Evidence with Additional Data on the Death Penalty." *American Sociological Review* 46: 783–805.

Klein, Stephen, Joan Petersilia, and Susan Turner. 1990. "Race and Imprisonment Decisions in California." *Science* 247: 812–816.

Klemm, Margaret. 1986. "The Determinants of Capital Sentencing in Louisiana, 1979–1984." Unpublished doctoral dissertation, University of New Orleans.

Knudten, Richard, Anthony Meader, Mary Knudten, and William Doerner. 1976. "The Victim in the Administration of Criminal Justice: Problems and Perceptions." In *Criminal Justice and the Victim*, edited by William McDonald, pp. 115–146. Newbury Park, CA: Sage.

Koons-Witt, Barbara. 2002. "The Effect of Gender on the Decision to Incarcerate before and after the Introduction of Sentencing Guidelines." *Criminology* 40: 297–328.

Korecki, Natasha. 2008. "Feds: Cook County Jail Has Violated Inmates' Rights." *Chicago Sun-Times*, July 17.

Kovach, Gretel. 2009. "Mixed Opinions of a Judge Accused of Misconduct." *New York Times*, March 8.

Kramer, John, and Darrell Steffensmeier. 1993. "Race and Imprisonment Decisions." *Sociological Quarterly* 34: 357–376.

Kramer, John, and Jeffrey Ulmer. 1996. "Sentencing Disparity and Departures from Guidelines." *Justice Quarterly* 13: 81–106.

Kramer, John, and Jeffrey Ulmer. 2009. *Sentencing Guidelines: Lessons from Pennsylvania*. Boulder, CO: Lynne Rienner.

Kramer, John, Robin Lubitz, and Cynthia Kempinen. 1989. "Sentencing Guidelines: A Quantitative Comparison of Sentencing Politics in Minnesota, Pennsylvania, and Washington." *Justice Quarterly* 6: 565–587.

Kramer, Larry. 1990. "Diversity Jurisdiction." *Brigham Young University Law Review* 3–66.

Krantz, Sheldon, Charles Smith, David Rossman, Paul Froyd, and Janis Hoffman. 1976. *Right to Counsel in Criminal Cases: The Mandate of Argersinger v. Hamlin*. Cambridge, MA: Ballinger.

Krisberg, Barry, and James Austin. 1993. *Reinventing Juvenile Justice*. Newbury Park, CA: Sage.

Krisberg, Barry. 1988. "Public Attitudes about Criminal Sanctions." *Criminologist* 13: 1–21.

Krupa, Michelle. 2006. "Ex-judge is given term of 51 months." *Times-Picayune*, February 9.

Kubrin, Chris. 2008. "Making Order of Disorder: A Call for Conceptual Clarity." *Criminology and Public Policy* 7: 203–214.

Kupchik, Aaron. 2006. *Judging Juveniles: Prosecuting Adolescents in Adult and Juvenile Courts*. New York: New York University Press.

Kurlychek, Megan, and Cynthia Kempinen. 2006. "Beyond Boot Camp: The Impact of Aftercare on Offender Reentry." *Criminology and Public Policy* 2: 363–388.

Kyckelhahn, Tracey, and Thomas H. Cohen. 2008. *Felony Defendants in Large Urban Counties, 2004*. Washington, D.C.: Bureau of Justice Statistics.

Labriola, Melissa, Michael Rempel, and Robert Davis. 2008. "Do Batterer Programs Reduce Recidivism? Results from a Randomized Trial in the Bronx." *Justice Quarterly* 25: 251–282.

Lacks, Robyn Diehl. 2007. "The "Real" *CSI*: Designing and Teaching a Violent Crime Scene Class in an Undergraduate Setting." *Journal of Criminal Justice Education* 18: 2.

LaFave, Wayne. 1965. *Arrest: The Decision to Take a Suspect into Custody*. Boston: Little, Brown.

LaFrenz, C.D., and Cassia Spohn. 2006. "Who is Punished More Harshly in Federal Court? The Interaction of Race/Ethnicity, Gender, Age, and Employment Status in the Sentencing of Drug Offenders." *Justice Research and Policy* 8: 25–56.

Lamber, Julia, and Mary Luskin. 1992. "Court Reform: A View from the Bottom." *Judicature* 75: 295–299.

Landsberg, Brian. 1993. "The Role of Civil Service Attorneys and Political Appointees in Making Policy in the Civil Rights Division of the U.S. Department of Justice." *Journal of Law and Politics* 9: 275–289.

Landsman, Stephan. 2005. "In Defense of the Jury of 12 and the Unanimous Decision Rule." *Judicature* 88: 301–305.

Langton, Lynn. 2007. *State Court Organization*, 1987-2004. Washington, DC: U.S. Department of Justice, Bureau of Justice Statistics.

Lankford, Jefferson. 2006. "The Effect of *Blakely v. Washington* on State Sentencing." *Justice System Journal* 27: 96–104.

Lasley, James. 2003. "The Effect of Intensive Bail Supervision on Repeat Domestic Violence Offenders." *Policy Studies Journal* 31: 187–209.

Latzer, Barry, and James Cauthen. 2000. "Capital Appeals Revisited." *Judicature* 84: 64–71.

Lavoie, Denise. 2008. "Successful Schemers Know How to Charm Their Victims." *Times-Picayune*, December 20.

LaWall, Barbara. 2001. "Should Plea Bargaining Be Banned in Pima County?" Pima County (Arizona) Attorney's Office. Available online at http://www.pcao.co.pima.az.us/Newsletters/Summer%202001.pdf

Lawson, Harry, and Dennis Howard. 1991. "Development of the Profession of Court Management: A History with Commentary." *Justice System Journal* 15: 580–605.

"LDF Applauds Supreme Court Decision in *Kimbrough v. United States*." 2007. *US Newswire*, December 10.

Lee, Matthew. 2008. "Civic Community in the Hinterland: Toward a Theory of Rural Social Structure and Violence." *Criminology* 46: 447–463.

Lee, Monica. 1992. "Indigent Defense: Determination of Indigency in the Nation's State Courts." *State Court Journal* (Spring): 16–23.

Lefcourt, Gerald. 1998. "Curbing the Abuse of the Grand Jury." *Judicature* 81: 196–197.

Leinwand, Donna. 2007. "Lawmakers Consider Lessening Crack Penalties." *USA Today,* March 12.

Leo, Richard. 1996a. "Inside the Interrogation Room." *Journal of Criminal Law and Criminology* 86: 266–303.

Leo, Richard. 1996b. "The Impact of *Miranda* Revisited." *Journal of Criminal Law and Criminology* 86: 621–692.

Levine, James. 1983. "Using Jury Verdict Forecasts in Criminal Defense Strategy." *Judicature* 66: 448–461.

Levine, James. 1996. "The Impact of Sequestration on Juries." *Judicature* 79: 266–272.

Levitt, Steven. 2006. "The Case of the Critics Who Missed the Point: A Reply to Webster et al." *Criminology and Public Policy* 5: 449–460.

Levy, Leonard. 1996. *A License to Steal: Forfeiture of Property.* Chapel Hill: University of North Carolina Press.

Lewis, Anthony. 1972. *Clarence Earl Gideon and the Supreme Court.* New York: Random House.

Lewis, Neil A. June 3, 2009. "Debate on Whether Female Judges Decide Differently Arises Anew." *New York Times,* A16.

Lewis, Neil. 2006. "Moussaoui Given Life Term by Jury over Link to 9/11." *New York Times,* May 4.

Lichtenstein, Michael. 1984. "Public Defenders: Dimensions of Cooperation." *Justice System Journal* 9: 102–110.

Lieberman, Joel D., and Bruce Dennis Sales. 2006. *Scientific Jury Selection.* Washington, DC: American Psychological Association.

Lieberman, Joel D., Terance D. Miethe, Courtney A. Carrell, and Daniel A. Krauss. 2008. "Gold versus Platinum: Do Jurors Recognize the Superiority and Limitations of DNA Evidence Compared to Other Types of Forensic Evidence?" *Psychology, Public Policy, and Law* 14: 27–62.

Liebman, J.S. 2000. "The Overproduction of Death." *Columbia Law Review* 100: 2030–2156.

Liebman, James, Jeffrey Fagan, and Valerie West. 2000a. "A Broken System: Error Rates in Capital Cases, 1973–1999." *Texas Law Review* 73: 1862.

Liebman, James, Jeffrey Fagan, and Valerie West. 2000b. "Death Matters: A Reply to Professors Latzer and Cauthen." *Judicature* 84: 72–77.

Lininger, Tim. 2008. "Is It Wrong to Sue for Rape?" *Duke Law Journal* 57: 1557–1640.

Liptak, Adam. 2003. "County Says It's Too Poor to Defend the Poor." *New York Times,* April 15.

Liptak, Adam. 2005. "New Trial for a Mother Who Drowned 5 Children." *New York Times,* January 7.

Liptak, Adam. 2007. "Given the Latitude to Show Leniency, Judges May Not." *New York Times,* December 11.

Listwan, Shelley, Cheryl Johnson, Francis Cullen, and Edward Latessa. 2008. "Cracks in the Penal Harm Movement: Evidence from the Field." *Criminology and Public Policy* 7: 423–465.

Listwan, Shelley, Francis T. Cullen, and Edward Latessa. 2006. "How to Prevent Prison Re-entry Programs from Failing: Insights from Evidence-Based Corrections." *Federal Probation* 70: 19–25.

Litman, Harry, and Mark Greenberg. 1996. "Dual Prosecutions: A Model for Concurrent Federal Jurisdiction." *Annals of the American Academy of Political and Social Science* 543: 72–86.

Litras, Marika, and John R. Golmant. 2006. "A Comparative Study of Juror Utilization in U.S. District Courts." *Journal of Empirical Legal Studies* 3: 99–120.

Lochner, Todd. 2002. "Strategic Behavior and Prosecutorial Agenda Setting in United States Attorneys' Offices: The Role of U.S. Attorneys and Their Assistants." *Justice System Journal* 23: 271–294.

Losh, Susan C., and Robert G. Boatright. 2002. "Life-Cycle Factors, Status, and Civil Engagement: Issues of Age and Attitudes toward Jury Service." *Justice System Journal* 23: 221–234.

Lowy, Joan. 2009. "Summit to Focus on Driver Phone Use." *Times-Picayune,* August 5.

Lubasch, Arnold. 1986. "Reputed Mob Leader among 15 Indicted on Racketeering Counts." *New York Times,* March 21.

Lucas, Ann. 2008. "Women and the (U.S.) War on Drugs." Paper presented at the annual meeting of The Law and Society Association, Hilton Bonaventure, Montreal, Quebec, Canada, May 27.

Lurigio, Arthur, David Olson, and Jessica Snowden. 2009. "The Effects of Setting, Analyses and Probation Status." *Corrections Compendium* 34: 1–16.

Lushing, Peter. 1992. "The Fall and Rise of the Criminal Contingent Fee." *Journal of Criminal Law and Criminology* 82: 498–568.

Lynch, David R., and T. David Evans. 2002. "Attributes of Highly Effective Criminal Defense Negotiators." *Journal of Criminal Justice* 30: 387–396.

Lynch, Michael. 2007. *Big Prisons, Big Dreams: Crime and the Failure of America's Penal System.* Piscataway, NJ: Rutgers University Press.

Mack, Kathy, and Sharyn Roach Anleu. 2007. "'Getting Through the List': Judgecraft and Legitimacy in the Lower Courts." *Social Legal Studies* 16: 341–361.

MacKenzie, Doris L. 2006. *What Works in Corrections: Reducing the Criminal Activities of Offenders and Delinquents.* New York: Cambridge University Press.

MADD. 2009. "Mandatory Ignition Interlocks for all Convicted DUI Offenders." Available online at https://secure2.convio.net/madd/site/Advocacy?JServSessionIdr004=08v7ubeh61.app7a&pagename=homepage&id=477 (Accessed July 27, 2009.)

Mahoney, Barry, with Alexander Aikman, Pamela Casey, Victor Flango, Geoff Gallas, Thomas Henderson, Jeanne Ito, David Steelman, and Steven Weller. 1988. *Changing Times in Trial Courts.* Williamsburg, VA: National Center for State Courts.

Manfredi, Christopher. 1998. *The Supreme Court and Juvenile Justice.* Lawrence: University Press of Kansas.

Mansfield, Cathy Lesser. 1999. "Disorder in the Court: Rethinking the Role of Non-Lawyer Judges in Limited Jurisdiction Court Civil Cases." *New Mexico Law Review* 29: 119–174.

Marby, Marcus, and Evan Thomas. 1992. "Crime: A Conspiracy of Silences." *Time,* May 18, p. 37.

Maremont, Mark, and Chad Bray. 2005. "Tyco Trial Jurors Say Defendants Weren't Credible." *Wall Street Journal,* June 20.

Martin, E.C. (n.d.), *Thinking Like a Lawyer.* Retrieved July 6, 2008 from Samford University's website http://www.samford.edu/schools/netlaw/dh2/logic

Martin, Elaine. 1993. "Women on the Bench: A Different Voice?" *Judicature* 77: 126–128.

Martinez, Ramiro. 2007. "Incorporating Latinos and Immigrants into Policing Research." *Criminology and Public Policy* 6: 57–64.

Martinson, Robert. 1974. "What Works? Questions and Answers about Prison Reform." *Public Interest* 35: 22–54.

Marvell, Thomas, and Carlisle Moody. 1996. "Determinate Sentencing and Abolishing Parole: The Long-Term Impacts on Prisons and Crime." *Criminology* 34: 107–128.

Marvell, Thomas, and Mary Luskin. 1991. "The Impact of Speedy Trial Laws in Connecticut and North Carolina." *Justice System Journal* 14: 343–357.

Mastrofski, Stephen, and R. Richard Ritti. 1996. "Police Training and the Effects of Organization on Drunk Driving Enforcement." *Justice Quarterly* 13: 291–320.

Mather, Lynn. 1974a. "Some Determinants of the Method of Case Disposition: Decision-Making by Public Defenders in Los Angeles." *Law and Society Review* 8: 187–216.

Mather, Lynn. 1974b. "The Outsider in the Courtroom: An Alternative Role for the Defense." In *The Potential for Reform of Criminal Justice,* edited by Herbert Jacob. Newbury Park, CA: Sage.

Mather, Lynn. 1979. *Plea Bargaining or Trial?* Lexington, MA: D. C. Heath.

Matza, David. 1964. *Delinquency and Drift.* New York: Wiley.

Mauro, Tony. 1996. "Appeals Judge Steps Down after Dole Attacks." *USA Today,* June 5.

Mauro, Tony. 2006. "Court Backs Death Row Inmates." *Legal Times,* June 19.

Maxwell, Christopher, Joel Garner, and Jeffrey Fagan. 2002. "The Preventive Effects of Arrest on Intimate Partner Violence: Research, Policy, and Theory." *Criminology and Public Policy* 2: 51–80.

Mayer, Martin. 2007. *The Judges.* New York: Macmillan.

Maynard, Douglas. 1988. "Narratives and Narrative Structure in Plea Bargaining." *Law and Society Review* 22: 449–481.

Mays, G. Larry, and William Taggart. 1986. "Court Clerks, Court Administrators, and Judges: Conflict in Managing the Courts." *Journal of Criminal Justice* 14: 1–7.

McCampbell, Robert. 1995. "Parallel Civil and Criminal Proceedings: Six Legal Pitfalls." *Criminal Law Bulletin* 31: 483–501.

McCord, David. 2005. "Juries Should Not Be Required to Have 12 Members or to Render Unanimous Verdicts." *Judicature* 88: 301–305.

McCormack, Robert. 1991. "Compensating Victims of Violent Crime." *Justice Quarterly* 8: 329–346.

McCormick, John. 1999. "Coming Two Days Shy of Martyrdom." *Newsweek,* February 15.

McCoy, Candace. 1984. "Determinate Sentencing, Plea Bargaining Bans, and Hydraulic Discretion in California." *Justice System Journal* 9: 256–275.

McCoy, Candace. 1993. *Politics and Plea Bargaining: Victim's Rights in California.* Philadelphia: University of Pennsylvania Press.

McCoy, Candace. 2003. "Bargaining under the Hammer: The Trial Penalty in the USA," in Douglas Koski (ed.), *The Criminal Jury Trial in America.* Raleigh: Carolina Academic Press.

McDonald, Douglas, and Kenneth Carlson. 1993. *Sentencing in the Federal Courts: Does Race Matter? The Transition to Sentencing Guidelines, 1986–1990.* Washington, DC: Bureau of Justice Statistics.

McDonald, Thomas, Robert Wood, and Melissa Pflug, eds. 1996. *Rural Criminal Justice: Conditions, Constraints, and Challenges.* Salem, WI: Sheffield.

McDonald, William, ed. 1976. *Criminal Justice and the Victim.* Newbury Park, CA: Sage.

McDonald, William. 1979. "The Prosecutor's Domain." In *The Prosecutor*, edited by William McDonald. Newbury Park, CA: Sage.

McDonough, Molly. 2008. "Judge Dismisses Nifong from Duke Player's Civil Suit, For Now." *ABA Journal*, January 30.

McGarrell, Edmund, and Natalie Kroovand Hipple. 2008. "Family Group Conferencing and Re-Offending among First-Time Juvenile Offenders: The Indianapolis Experiment." *Justice Quarterly* 24: 221–246.

McGillis, Daniel. 1997. *Community Mediation Programs: Developments and Challenges*. Washington, DC: U.S. Department of Justice, National Institute of Justice.

McGlone, Tim. 2007a. "Judge's Stand on Norfolk Man's Sentencing Heads to Supreme Court." *The Virginian-Pilot*, September 29.

McGlone, Tim. 2007b. "Supreme Court Hears Case on Norfolk Drug Sentencing." *The Virginian-Pilot*, October 3.

McIntyre, Donald, and David Lippman. 1970. "Prosecutors and Disposition of Felony Cases." *American Bar Association Journal* 56: 154–1159.

McIntyre, Donald. 1968. "A Study of Judicial Dominance of the Charging Decision." *Journal of Criminal Law, Criminology and Police Science* 59: 463–490.

McIntyre, Lisa. 1987. *The Public Defender: The Practice of Law in the Shadows of Repute*. Chicago: University of Chicago Press.

McKeon, John C., and David G. Rice. 2009. "Administering Justice in Montana's Rural Courts." *Montana Law Review* 70: 201–220.

McQuiston, J. T. 1995. "In the Bizarre L.I.R.R. Trial, Equally Bizarre Confrontations." *New York Times*, February 5.

Mears, Daniel P., Carter Hay, Marc Gertz, and Christina Mancini. 2007. "Public Opinion and the Foundation of the Juvenile Court." *Criminology* 45: 223–257.

Mears, Daniel, Zia Wang, Carter Hay, and William Bales. 2008. "Social Ecology and Recidivism: Implications for Prisoner Reentry." *Criminology* 46: 301–348.

Meier, Kenneth. 1994. *The Politics of Sin: Drugs, Alcohol, and Public Policy*. Armonk, NY: M. E. Sharpe.

Meinhold, Stephen, and Steven Shull. 1993. "Policy Congruence between the President and the Solicitor General." Paper presented at the annual meeting of the Midwest Political Science Association, Chicago.

Merritt, Nancy, Terry Fain, and Susan Turner. 2006. "Oregon's Get Tough Sentencing Reform: A Lesson in Justice System Adaptation." *Criminology and Public Policy* 5: 5–36.

Meyer, Jon'a, and Paul Jesilow. 1997. *Doing Justice in the People's Court: Sentencing by Municipal Court Judges*. Albany: State University of New York Press.

Meyers, David. 2005. *Boys among Men: Trying and Sentencing Juveniles as Adults*. Westport, CT: Praeger.

Miethe, Terance, and Charles Moore. 1989. "Sentencing Guidelines: Their Effect in Minnesota." Washington, DC: U.S. Department of Justice, Bureau of Justice Statistics.

Mileski, Maureen. 1971. "Courtroom Encounters: An Observation Study of a Lower Criminal Court." *Law and Society Review* 5: 473–538.

Miller, Benjamin. 1991. "Assessing the Functions of Judicial Conduct Organizations." *Judicature* 75: 16–19.

Miller, Frank. 1969. *Prosecution: The Decision to Charge a Suspect with a Crime*. Boston: Little, Brown.

Miller, Herbert, William McDonald, and James Cramer. 1978. *Plea Bargaining in the United States*. Washington, DC: National Institute of Law Enforcement and Criminal Justice.

Miller, Marc L., and Ronald Wright. 2008. "The Black Box." *Iowa Law Review* 94: 125–196.

Miller, Susan L. and Shana L. Maier. 2008. "Moving Beyond Numbers: What Female Judges Say about Different Judicial Voices." *Journal of Women, Politics & Policy* 29: 527–559.

Mills, Carol, and Wayne Bohannon. 1980. "Jury Characteristics: To What Extent Are They Related to Jury Verdicts?" *Judicature* 64: 22–31.

Miner, R. 1999. "Professional Responsibility in Appellate Practice: A View from the Bench." *Pace Law Review* 19: 323–344.

Minton, Todd D., and William J. Sabol. 2009. *Jail Inmates at Midyear 2008*. Washington, DC: Bureau of Justice Statistics.

Misner, Robert. 1996. "Recasting Prosecutorial Discretion." *Journal of Criminal Law and Criminology* 86: 717–758.

Mitchell, John B. 1994. "Redefining the Sixth Amendment." *Southern California Law Review* 67: 1215–1319.

Mitchell, Josh. 2008. "Victims Fund Assists Felons." *Baltimore Sun*, March 16.

Mitchell, Ojmarrh. 2005. "A Meta-Analysis of Race and Sentencing Research: Explaining the Inconsistencies." *Journal of Quantitative Criminology* 21: 439–466.

Mitchell, Tara L., Ryann M. Haw, Jeffrey E. Pfeifer, and Christian A. Meissner. 2005. "Racial Bias in Mock Juror Decision-Making: A Meta-Analytic

Review of Defendant Treatment." *Law and Human Behavior* 29: 621–637.

Molesworth, Claire L. 2008. "Knowledge versus Acknowledgment: Rethinking the *Alford* Plea in Sexual Assault Cases." *Seattle Journal for Social Justice* 6: 907–942.

Moley, Raymond. 1928. "The Vanishing Jury." *Southern California Law Review* 2: 97.

Moore, Kathleen Dean. 1989. *Pardons: Justice, Mercy and the Public Interest.* New York: Oxford University Press.

Moore, Mark, Susan Estrich, Daniel McGillis, and William Spelman. 1984. *Dangerous Offenders: The Elusive Target of Justice.* Cambridge, MA: Harvard University Press.

Moran, Gary, and Brian Cutler. 1991. "The Prejudicial Impact of Pretrial Publicity." *Journal of Applied Social Psychology* 21: 345–367.

Moran, Gary, and John C. Comfort. 1986. "Neither 'Tentative' nor 'Fragmentary': Verdict Preference of Impaneled Felony Jurors as a Function of Attitude toward Capital Punishment." *Journal of Applied Psychology* 71: 146–155.

Morgan, Kathryn, and Brent Smith. 2005. "Victims, Punishment, and Parole: The Effects of Victim Participation on Parole Hearings." *Criminology and Public Policy* 4: 333–360.

Moriarty, Jane Campbell. 2007. "'Misconvictions,' Science, and the Ministers of Justice." *Nebraska Law Review* 86: 1–42

Moriearty, Perry L. 2008. "Combating the Color-Coded Confinement of Kids: An Equal Protection Remedy." *New York University Review of Law and Social Change* 32: 285–343.

Morris, Norval, and Michael Tonry. 1990. *Between Prison and Probation: Intermediate Punishments in a Rational Sentencing System.* New York: Oxford University Press.

Mosteller, Robert P. 2002. "Discovery in Criminal Cases." *Encyclopedia of Crime and Justice.* Farmington Hills, MI: Gale/Cengage.

Mushlin, Michael B. 2007. "Bound and Gagged: The Peculiar Predicament of Professional Jurors." *Yale Law and Policy Review* 25: 239–287.

Mushlin, Michael, and Naomi Galtz. 2009. "Getting Real about Race and Prisoner Rights." *Fordham Urban Law Journal* 36: 27–53.

Myers, Laura, and Sue Titus Reid. 1995. "The Importance of County Context in the Measurement of Sentencing Disparity: The Search for Routinization." *Journal of Criminal Justice* 23: 233–241.

Myers, Martha, and John Hagan. 1979. "Private and Public Trouble: Prosecutors and the Allocation of Court Resources." *Social Problems* 26: 439–451.

Myers, Martha, and Susette Talarico. 1986a. "The Social Contexts of Racial Discrimination in Sentencing." *Social Problems* 33: 237–251.

Myers, Martha, and Susette Talarico. 1986b. "Urban Justice, Rural Injustice? Urbanization and Its Effect on Sentencing." *Criminology* 24: 367–391.

Myers, Martha, and Susette Talarico. 1987. *The Social Contexts of Criminal Sentencing.* New York: Springer-Verlag.

Nader, Laura. 1992. "Trading Justice for Harmony." *National Institute for Dispute Resolution Forum* (Winter): 12–14.

Nagel, Ilene. 1983. "The Legal/Extra-Legal Controversy: Judicial Decisions in Pretrial Release." *Law and Society Review* 17: 481–515.

Nagin, Daniel. 1998. "Criminal Deterrence Research at the Outset of the Twenty-First Century." In *Crime and Justice: A Review of Research.* Vol. 23. Edited by Michael Tonry. Chicago: University of Chicago Press.

Nardulli, Peter, Roy Flemming, and James Eisenstein. 1984. "Unraveling the Complexities of Decision Making in Face-to-Face Groups: A Contextual Analysis of Plea-Bargained Sentences." *American Political Science Review* 78: 912–928.

Nardulli, Peter. 1978. *The Courtroom Elite: An Organizational Perspective on Criminal Justice.* Cambridge, MA: Ballinger.

Nardulli, Peter. 1979. "The Caseload Controversy and the Study of Criminal Courts." *Journal of Criminal Law and Criminology* 70: 89–101.

Nardulli, Peter. 1983. "The Societal Cost of the Exclusionary Rule: An Empirical Assessment." *American Bar Foundation Research Journal* 585–609.

Nardulli, Peter. 1986. "'Insider' Justice: Defense Attorneys and the Handling of Felony Cases." *Journal of Criminal Law and Criminology* 77: 379–417.

National Advisory Commission on Criminal Justice Standards and Goals. 1973. *Report on Courts.* Washington, DC: U.S. Government Printing Office.

National Association of Criminal Defense Lawyers. 2000. "Citizens Grand Jury Bill of Rights." Available online at http://www.criminaljustice.org

National Association of Women Judges. 2009. *Representation of United States State Court Women Judges.* Available online at http://www.nawj.org/us_state_court_statistics_2009.asp

National Center for State Courts, 2008. *Examining the Work of State Courts,* 2007. Williamsburg, VA: Author.

National Center for State Courts. 2003. "A Profile of Hung Juries." *Caseload Highlights* 9: 1.

National Center for State Courts. 2008. *Court Statistics Project.* Williamsburg, VA. Available online at http://www.ncsconline.org/D_Research/csp/CSP_Main_Page.html

National Center for State Courts. 2008. *Survey of Judicial Salaries* (Vol. 30). Williamsburg, VA: Author.

National Center for Victims of Crime. 2002. *Civil Legal Remedies for Victims of Crime*. Washington, DC: U.S. Department of Justice, Office for Victims of Crime.

National Center for Victims of Crime. 2009. "Issues: Victims' Bill of Rights." Available online at http://www.ncvc.org

National District Attorney's Association. 2007. "Statement in Response to the Proposed Resolution Concerning Sentence Mitigation for Youthful Offenders." Available online at http://www.ndaa.org (Accessed July 3, 2009.)

National Drug Court Institute. 2009. "Drug Courts: A National Phenomenon." Available online at http://www.ndci.org/courtfacts.htm

National Governors Association. 2009. "Prisoner Reentry Policy." Available online at http://www.nga.org/portal/site/nga/menuitem.1f41d49be2d3d33eacdcbeeb501010a0/?vgnextoid=6c239286d9de1010VgnVCM1000001a01010aRCRD (Accessed July 6, 2009.)

National Highway Traffic Safety Administration 2008. *2007 Traffic Safety Annual Assessment—Alcohol-Impaired Driving Fatalities*. Washington, DC: author. Available online at http://www-nrd.nhtsa.dot.gov/Pubs/811016.pdf

National Institute of Justice. 1982. *Exemplary Projects: Focus for 1982—Projects to Combat Violent Crime*. Washington, DC: U.S. Department of Justice.

Neubauer, David W., and Stephen S. Meinhold. 2010. *Judicial Process: Law, Courts, and Politics in the United States*. 5th ed. Belmont, CA: Wadsworth.

Neubauer, David, and Stephen Meinhold. 2006. *Battle Supreme: The Confirmation of Chief Justice John Roberts and the future of the Supreme Court*. Belmont, CA: Wadsworth.

Neubauer, David, and Stephen Meinhold. 2007. *Judicial Process: Law, Courts, and Politics in the United States*. 4th ed. Belmont, CA: Wadsworth.

Neubauer, David, Marcia Lipetz, Mary Luskin, and John Paul Ryan. 1981. *Managing the Pace of Justice: An Evaluation of LEAA's Court Delay Reduction Programs*. Washington, DC: U.S. Government Printing Office.

Neubauer, David. 1974a. "After the Arrest: The Charging Decision in Prairie City." *Law and Society Review* 8: 495–517.

Neubauer, David. 1974b. *Criminal Justice in Middle America*. Morristown, NJ: General Learning Press.

Neubauer, David. 1983. "Improving the Analysis and Presentation of Data on Case Processing Time." *Journal of Criminal Law and Criminology* 74: 1589–1607.

Neubauer, David. 1985. "Published Opinions versus Summary Affirmations: Criminal Appeals in Louisiana." *Justice System Journal* 10: 173–189.

Neubauer, David. 1991. "Winners and Losers before the Louisiana Supreme Court: The Case of Criminal Appeals." *Justice Quarterly* 8: 85–106.

Neubauer, David. 1992. "A Polychotomous Measure of Appellate Court Outcomes: The Case of Criminal Appeals." *Justice System Journal* 16: 75–87.

Neubauer, David. 1996. "A Tale of Two Cities: A Comparison of Orleans and Jefferson Parish, Louisiana." Paper presented at the annual meeting of the Academy of Criminal Justice Sciences, Louisville, KY.

Neubauer, David. 2001. *Debating Crime: Rhetoric and Reality*. Belmont, CA: Wadsworth.

Neufeld, Peter J. 2005. "The (Near) Irrelevance of *Daubert* to Criminal Justice and Some Suggestions for Reform." *American Journal of Public Health* 95: S107–S113.

Newman, Andy. 2003. "Investigation of Judge Touched Off Wider Inquiry." *New York Times*, April 25.

Nimmer, Raymond, and Patricia Krauthaus. 1977. "Plea Bargaining Reform in Two Cities." *Justice System Journal* 3: 6–21.

Nimmer, Raymond. 1978. *The Nature of System Change: Reform Impact in the Criminal Courts*. Chicago: American Bar Foundation.

Nobiling, Tracy, Cassia Spohn, and Miriam DeLone. 1998. "A Tale of Two Counties: Unemployment and Sentence Severity." *Justice Quarterly* 15: 459–485.

Nolan, Christian. 2009. "Paying a Price for Dishonest Bail Bondsmen." *Connecticut Law Tribune*, June 1.

Nolan-Haley, Jacqueline. 2008. *Alternative Dispute Resolution in a Nutshell*. St. Paul: West.

NOLO. 2009. "How Much Can I Sue for in Small Claims Court?" Available online at http://www.nolo.com (Accessed July 22, 2009.)

Norman, Michael D., and Robert C. Wadman. 2000. "Utah Presentence Investigation Reports: User Group Perceptions of Quality and Effectiveness." *Federal Probation* 64: 7–12.

Norris, Floyd. 2005. "Chief Executive Was Paid Millions, and He Never Noticed the Fraud?" *New York Times*, January 7.

Norton, Lee. 1983. "Witness Involvement in the Criminal Justice System and Intention to Cooperate in Future Prosecutions." *Journal of Criminal Justice* 11: 143–152.

Nugent, Hugh, and Thomas McEwen. 1988. *Prosecutor's National Assessment of Needs*. Washington, DC: U.S. Department of Justice, National Institute of Justice.

O'Brien, David. 1988. "The Supreme Court: From Warren to Burger to Rehnquist." *PS* 20: 13.

O'Neill, Michael Edmund. 2003. "When Prosecutors Don't: Trends in Federal Prosecutorial Declinations." *Notre Dame Law Review* 79: 221–290.

Oaks, Dallin. 1970. "Studying the Exclusionary Rule in Search and Seizure." *University of Chicago Law Review* 37: 665–753.

O'Connor, Sandra Day. 2003. *The Majesty of the Law: Reflections of a Supreme Court Justice*. New York: Random House.

Office for Victims of Crime. 1998. *From Pain to Power: Crime Victims Take Action*. Washington, DC: U.S. Department of Justice.

Office of Juvenile Justice and Delinquency Prevention. 1996. *Female Offenders in the Juvenile Justice System*. Washington, DC: U.S. Department of Justice.

Office of National Drug Control Policy. 2009. *ADAM II 2008 Annual Report*. Washington, DC: Executive Office of the President.

Official Teen Court Homepage. 1998. Available online at http://library.advanced.org/264

Ogloff, James R.P., and V. Gordon Rose. 2007. "The Comprehension of Judicial Instructions." In Neil Brewer and Kipling D. Williams. *Psychology and Law: An Empirical Perspective*. New York: The Guildford Press.

Olsen, Lise. 2006. "The Cantu Case: Death and Doubt." *Houston Chronicle*, July 24.

Olson, Trisha. 2006–2007. "The Medieval Blood Sanction and the Divine Beneficence of Pain: 1100–1450." *Journal of Law and Religion* 22: 63–129.

Oran, Daniel. 2000. *Law Dictionary for Nonlawyers*. 3rd ed. St. Paul, MN: West.

Ostrom, Brian J., Neal B. Kauder and Robert C. LaFountain. 2001. *Examining the Work of State Courts, 2001: A National Perspective from the Court Statistics Project*. Washington: National Center for State Courts.

Ostrom, Brian, and Roger Hanson. 2000. *Efficiency and Timeliness, and Quality: A New Perspective from Nine State Criminal Trial Courts*. Washington, DC: National Institute of Justice.

Ostrom, Brian, Charles Ostrom, Jr., Roger Hanson, and Matthew Kleiman. 2007. *Trial Courts as Organizations*. Philadelphia, Temple University Press.

Ostrom, Brian, Charles Ostrom, Roger Hanson, and Matthew Kleinman. 2008. *Assessing Consistency and Fairness in Sentencing: A Comparative Study in three States*. Williamsburg, VA: National Center for State Courts.

Pabst, William. 1973. "What Do Six-Member Juries Really Save?" *Judicature* 57: 6–11.

Packer, Herbert. 1968. *The Limits of the Criminal Sanction*. Palo Alto, CA: Stanford University Press.

Padawer-Singer, Alice, and Alice Barton. 1975. "The Impact of Pretrial Publicity on Jurors' Verdicts." In *The Jury System in America: A Critical Overview*, edited by Rita James Simon. Beverly Hills, CA: Sage.

Padgett, John. 1990. "Plea Bargaining and Prohibition in the Federal Courts, 1908–1934." *Law and Society Review* 24: 413–450.

Palmer, Barbara. 2001. "Women in the American Judiciary: Their Influence and Impact." *Women and Politics* 23: 89.

Parent, Dale, Barbara Auerbach, and Kenneth Carlson. 1992. *Compensating Crime Victims: A Summary of Policies and Practices*. Washington, DC: U.S. Department of Justice, National Institute of Justice.

Parent, Dale, Terence Dunworth, Douglas McDonald, and William Rhodes. 1996. *The Impact of Sentencing Guidelines*. Washington, DC: National Institute of Justice.

Parent, Dale. 2003. *Correctional Boot Camps: Lessons from a Decade of Research*. Washington, DC: U.S. Department of Justice.

Partridge, Anthony, and William Eldridge. 1974. *The Second Circuit Sentencing Study: A Report to the Judges of the Second Circuit*. Washington, DC: Federal Judicial Center.

Paternoster, Raymond, and Robert Brame. 2008. "Reassessing Race Disparities in Maryland Capital Cases." *Criminology* 46: 971–1007.

Paternoster, Raymond. 1984. "Prosecutorial Discretion in Requesting the Death Penalty: A Case of Victim-Based Racial Discrimination." *Law and Society Review* 18: 437–478.

Payne, Shenoa L. 2008. "The Ethical Conundrums of Unpublished Opinions." *Willamette Law Review* 44: 723–760.

Perkins, Craig, James Stephan, and Allen Beck. 1995. *Jail and Jail Inmates 1993–1994*. Washington, DC: Bureau of Justice Statistics.

Perkins, David, and Jay Jamieson. 1995. "Judicial Probable Cause Determinations after *County of Riverside v. McLaughlin*." *Criminal Law Bulletin* 31: 534–546.

Perlin, Michael. L. 1997. "The Borderline Which Separated You from Me: The Insanity Defense, the Authoritarian Spirit, the Fear of Faking, and the Culture of Punishment." *Iowa Law Review* 82: 1375–1426.

Perlstein, Michael. 1990. "DA's Office Suffers as Prosecutors Flee to Better Pay, Hours." *Times-Picayune*, July 22, p. B1.

Perry, Steven. 2006. "Prosecutors in State Courts, 2005." Washington, DC: Bureau of Justice Statistics, National Institute of Justice.

Peters, C. Scott. 2008. "Campaigning for State Supreme Court, 2006." *The Justice System Journal* 29: 166–186.

Peterson, Richard. 2004. "Manhattan's Specialized Domestic Violence Court." Research Brief No. 7. New York: New York City Criminal Justice Agency.

Petrello, Randi. June 26, 2009. "'Dog' Chapman Hit with $1.8M IRS Tax Lien." *Pacific Business News*. Available online at http://www.bizjournals.com/pacific/stories/2009/06/22/daily58.html

Phillips, Mary. 2007. "Bail, Detention and Nonfelony Case Outcomes." *Research Brief # 14*. New York: New York City Criminal Justice Agency.

Phillips, Mary. 2008. "Bail, Detention and Felony Case Outcomes." *Research Brief # 18*. New York: New York City Criminal Justice Agency.

Phillips, Thomas R. 2009. "The Merits of Merit Selection." *Harvard Journal of Law and Public Policy* 32: 67–96.

Piccarreta, Michael, and Jefferson Keenan. 1995. "Dual Sovereigns, Successive Prosecutions, and Politically Correct Verdicts." *Criminal Law Bulletin* 31: 291–304.

Piehl, Anne Morrison, and Shawn D. Bushway. 2007. "Measuring and Explaining Charge Bargaining." *Journal of Quantitative Criminology* 23: 105–125.

Pinello, Daniel. 1995. *The Impact of Judicial-Selection Method of State-Supreme-Court Policy: Innovation, Reaction and Atrophy*. Westport, CT: Greenwood Press.

Platt, Anthony, and Randi Pollock. 1974. "Channeling Lawyers: The Careers of Public Defenders." In *The Potential for Reform of Criminal Justice*, edited by Herbert Jacob. Newbury Park, CA: Sage.

Platt, Anthony. 1969. *The Child Savers: The Invention of Delinquency*. Chicago: University of Chicago Press.

Podgor, Ellen. 2007. "The Challenge of White Collar Sentencing." *Journal of Criminal Law and Criminology*. 97: 731.

Podlas, Kimberlianne. 2002. "Should We Blame Judge Judy? The Messages TV Courtrooms Send Viewers." *Judicature* 86: 38–43.

Pollock Joycelyn M., and Sareta M. Davis. 2005. "The Continuing Myth of the Violent Female Offender." *Criminal Justice Review* 30: 5–29.

Pollock, Joycelyn M. 2010. *Ethical Dilemmas and Decisions in Criminal Justice*, 6th ed. Belmont, CA: Wadsworth.

Pou, Charles. 2005. "Scissors Cut Paper: A 'Guildhall' Helps Maryland's Mediators Sharpen Their Skills." *Justice System Journal* 26: 307–325.

President's Commission on Law Enforcement and Administration of Justice. 1967. *Task Force Report: The Courts*. Washington, DC: U.S. Government Printing Office.

Pretrial Services Resource Center. 1999. *Integrating Drug Testing into a Pretrial Service System: 1999 Update*. Washington, DC: U.S. Department of Justice, Bureau of Justice Assistance.

Priehs, Richard. 1999. "Appointed Counsel for Indigent Criminal Appellants: Does Compensation Influence Effort?" *Justice System Journal* 21: 57–79.

Primus, E.B. 2007. "Structural Reform in Criminal Defense: Relocating Ineffective Assistance of Counsel Claims." *Cornell Law Review* 92: 679–732.

Propp, Wren. 2003. "Court Suspends Mora Magistrate." *Albuquerque Journal*, April 10.

Prosser, Mary. 2006. "Reforming Criminal Discovery: Why Old Objections Must Yield to New Realities." *Wisconsin Law Review* 2006: 541–614.

Provine, Doris Marie. 1981. "Persistent Anomaly: The Lay Judge in the American Legal System." *Justice System Journal* 6: 28–43.

Provine, Doris Marie. 1986. *Judging Credentials: Nonlawyer Judges and the Politics of Professionalism*. Chicago: University of Chicago Press.

Pruitt, Lisa R. 2006. "Rural Rhetoric." *Connecticut Law Review* 39: 159–240.

Pruitt, Lisa R. 2008. "Gender, Geography, and Rural Justice." *Berkeley Journal of Gender, Law & Justice* 23: 338–391.

Public Safety Performance Project. 2007. *Public Safety, Public Spending: Forecasting America's Prison Population 2007-2011*. Washington, D.C.: The Pew Charitable Trust.

"Publicly Censured." 2003 (June 3) *Tennessee Bar Journal* 39. Available online at http://www.tba.org/Journal_TBArchives/jun03/TBJ-jun03-news.html

Puritz, Patricia, S. Burrell, R. Schwartz, M. Soler, and L. Warboys. 1995. *A Call for Justice: An Assessment of Access to Counsel and Quality of Representation in Delinquency Proceedings*. Washington, DC: American Bar Association.

Puzzanchera, Charles. 2009. *Juvenile Arrests 2007*. Washington, DC: Office of Justice Programs, U.S. Department of Justice.

Radelet, Michael, and Glenn Pierce. 1985. "Race and Prosecutorial Discretion in Homicide Cases." *Law and Society Review* 19: 587–621.

Raftery, William. 2006. "The Legislatures, the Ballot Boxes and the Courts." *Court Review* 4: 102–107.

Ragland, James. 2009. "*American Violet* Tells Story of Ill-Fated Hearne Drug Raids." *Dallas Morning News* (March 13), available online at http://www.dallasnews.com/sharedcontent/dws/dn/localnews/columnists/jragland/stories/031409dnmetragland.33ada80.html

Ragona, Anthony, and John Paul Ryan. 1983. "Misdemeanor Courts and the Choice of Sanctions: A Comparative View." *Justice System Journal* 8: 199–221.

Ralph, Paige, Jonathan Sorensen, and James Marquart. 1992. "A Comparison of Death-Sentenced and Incarcerated Murderers in Pre-*Furman* Texas." *Justice Quarterly* 9: 185–209.

Rand, Michael. 2008. *Criminal Victimization*. 2007. Washington, DC: U.S. Department of Justice, Bureau of Justice Statistics.

Randall, Ronald, and James A. Woods. 2008. "Racial Representativeness of Juries: An Analysis of Source List and Administrative Effects on the Jury Pool." *Justice System Journal* 29: 71–82.

Rapaport, Elizabeth. 1991. "The Death Penalty and Gender Discrimination." *Law and Society Review* 25: 367–384.

Raymond, Paul. 1992. "The Impact of a Televised Trial on Individuals' Information and Attitudes." *Judicature* 75: 204–209.

Re, Richard M. 2007. "Re-Justifying the Fair Cross-Section Requirement: Equal Representation and Enfranchisement in the American Criminal Jury." *Yale Law Journal* 116: 1568–1614.

Reaves, Brian, and Jacob Perez. 1994. *Pretrial Release of Felony Defendants, 1992*. Washington, DC: U.S. Department of Justice, Bureau of Justice Statistics.

Reaves, Brian. 2001. *Felony Defendants in Large Urban Counties, 1998*. Washington, DC: Bureau of Justice Statistics.

Redding, Richard. 2008. "Juvenile Transfer Laws: An Effective Deterrent to Delinquency?" Washington, DC: Office of Justice Programs, U.S. Department of Justice.

Reid, Traciel. 1999. "The Politicization of Retention Elections: Lessons from the Defeat of Justices Lanphier and White." *Judicature* 83: 68–77.

Reiman, Jeffrey. 2007. *The Rich Get Richer and the Poor Get Prison: Ideology, Class, and Criminal Justice*. 8th ed. Boston: Pearson/Allyn & Bacon.

Reinkensmeyer, Marcus. 1991. "Compensation of Court Managers: Current Salaries and Related Factors." *Judicature* 75: 154–162.

Reitz, Kevin. 2001. "The Status of Sentencing Guidelines Reforms in the United States." In *Penal Reform in Overcrowded Times*, edited by Michael Tonry. New York: Oxford University Press.

Remington, Frank. 1988. "Post-Conviction Review: What State Trial Courts Can Do to Reduce Problems." *Judicature* 72: 53–57.

Rengert, George. 1989. "Spatial Justice and Criminal Victimization." *Justice Quarterly* 6: 543–564.

Report of the Federal Courts Study Committee. 1990.

Resick, Patricia. 1984. "The Trauma of Rape and the Criminal Justice System." *Justice System Journal* 9: 52–61.

Reskin, Barbara, and Christine Visher. 1986. "The Impacts of Evidence and Extralegal Factors in Jurors' Decisions." *Law and Society Review* 20: 423–439.

Resnik, Judith. 2006. "Whither and Whether Adjudication?" *Boston University Law Review* 86: 1101–1154.

Rhodes, William, Raymond Hyatt, and Paul Scheiman. 1996. "Research in Brief: Predicting Pretrial Misconduct with Drug Tests of Arrestees." Washington, DC: National Institute of Justice.

Rhodes, William. 1978. *Plea Bargaining: Who Gains? Who Loses?* Washington, DC: Institute for Law and Social Research.

Ribovich, Donald J., and Anthony Martino. 2007. "Technology, Crime Control, and the Private Sector in the 21st Century." *In New Technology of Crime, Law and Social Control*, edited by James Michael Byrne and Donald J. Ribovich, pp. 49–79. Monsey, NY: Criminal Justice Press.

Richardson, Richard, and Kenneth Vines. 1970. *The Politics of Federal Courts*. Boston: Little, Brown.

Risinger, D. Michael, Mark P. Denbeaux, and Michael J. Saks. 1989. "Exorcism of Ignorance as a Proxy for Rational Knowledge: The Lessons of Handwriting Identification 'Expertise.'" *University of Pennsylvania Law Review*: 731–788.

Roberts, Paul Craig, and Lawrence M. Stratton. 2008. *The Tyranny of Good Intentions: How Prosecutors and Law Enforcement Are Trampling the Constitution in the Name of Justice*. New York: Three Rivers Press/Random House.

Robertson, Leon, Robert Rich, and H. Laurence Ross. 1973. "Jail Sentences for Driving While Intoxicated in Chicago: A Judicial Action That Failed." *Law and Society Review* 8: 55–68.

Robinson, Gwen. 2008. "Late-Modern Rehabilitation: The Evolution of a Penal Strategy." *Punishment and Society* 10: 429–445.

Robinson, Mike. 1996. "Abrasive, Erratic Judge Sidelined." *Times-Picayune*, October 12.

Rodriguez, Nancy, Hilary Smith, and Marjorie Zatz. 2009. "'Youth Is Enmeshed in a Highly Dysfunctional Family System': Exploring the Relationship among Dysfunctional Families, Parental Incarceration, and Juvenile Court Decision Making." *Criminology* 47: 177–206.

Roesler, Richard. 2009. "Drivers Sue 19 Cities over Traffic Camera Fines." *Spokesman-Review*, June 24.

Roper, Robert, and Albert Melone. 1981. "Does Procedural Due Process Make a Difference? A Study of Second Trials." *Judicature* 65: 136–141.

Roper, Robert. 1979. "Jury Size: Impact on Verdict's Correctness." *American Politics Quarterly* 7: 438–452.

Rosen, Ellen. 1987. "The Nation's Judges: No Unanimous Opinion." *Court Review* 24: 5.

Rosen, R. A. 2006. "Reflections on Innocence." *Wisconsin Law Review* 2006: 237–290.

Rosencrance, John. 2004. "Maintaining the Myth of Individualized Justice: Probation Presentence Reports." In George Cole, Mark Gertz and Amy Bunger (eds.) *The Criminal Justice System: Politics and Policies.* 9th ed. Belmont, CA: Wadsworth.

Rosenthal, John. 2002. "Therapeutic Jurisprudence and Drug Treatment Courts: Integrating Law and Science." In *Drug Courts in Theory and Practice*, edited by James Nolan. Hawthorne, NY: Walter de Gruyter.

Rosett, Arthur, and Donald Cressey. 1976. *Justice by Consent: Plea Bargaining in the American Courthouse.* Philadelphia: J. B. Lippincott.

Rosoff, Stephen, Henry Pontell, and Robert Tillman. 2007. *Profit without Honor: White-Collar Crime and the Looting of America.* 4th ed. Upper Saddle River, NJ: Prentice Hall.

Ross, Darrell. 2002. *Civil Liability in Criminal Justice.* 3rd ed. Cincinnati: Anderson.

Ross, H. Laurence, and James Foley. 1987. "Judicial Disobedience of the Mandate to Imprison Drunk Drivers." *Law and Society Review* 21: 315–323.

Ross, H. Laurence. 1992. "The Law and Drunk Driving." *Law and Society Review* 26: 219–230.

Rossi, Peter, and Richard Berk. 1997. *Public Opinion on Sentencing Federal Crimes.* Washington, DC: United States Sentencing Commission.

Roth, Jeffrey, and Paul Wice. 1980. *Pretrial Release and Misconduct in the District of Columbia.* Washington DC: Institute for Law and Social Research.

Rothwax, Harold J. 1996. *Guilty: The Collapse of Criminal Justice.* New York: Random House.

Rottman, David, and Pamela Casey. 1999. "Therapeutic Jurisprudence and the Emergence of Problem-Solving Courts." *National Institute of Justice Journal* (July): 12–19.

Rowe, David C., and David P. Farrington. 1997. "The Familial Transmission of Criminal Convictions." *Criminology* 35: 177–201.

Rubenstein, Michael, and Teresa White. 1979. "Plea Bargaining: Can Alaska Live without It?" *Judicature* 62: 266–279.

Rubin, Alvin. 1976. "How We Can Improve Judicial Treatment of Individual Cases without Sacrificing Individual Rights: The Problems of the Criminal Law." *Federal Rules of Decisions* 70: 176.

Rubin, H. Ted. 1989. "The Juvenile Court Landscape." In *Juvenile Justice: Policies, Programs and Services*, edited by Albert Roberts. Chicago: Richard Irwin.

Ruckman, P. S. 1997. "Executive Clemency in the United States: Origins, Development, and Analysis (1900–1993)." *Presidential Studies Quarterly* 27: 251–271.

Rush, Christina, and Jeremy Robertson. 1987. "Presentence Reports: The Utility of Information to the Sentencing Decision." *Law and Human Behavior* 11: 147–155.

Ryan, Joan. 2002. "Do We Count Strikes or Justice?" *San Francisco Chronicle*, November 5.

Ryan, John Paul, and James Alfini. 1979. "Trial Judges' Participation in Plea Bargaining: An Empirical Perspective." *Law and Society Review* 13: 479–507.

Ryan, John Paul, and James Guterman. 1977. "Lawyers versus Non-Lawyer Town Justices." *Judicature* 60: 272–280.

Ryan, John Paul, Marcia Lipetz, Mary Luskin, and David Neubauer. 1981. "Analyzing Court Delay-Reduction Programs: Why Do Some Succeed?" *Judicature* 65: 58–75.

Ryan, John Paul. 1980–1981. "Adjudication and Sentencing in a Misdemeanor Court: The Outcome Is the Punishment." *Law & Society Review* 15: 79–108.

Saari, David. 1982. *American Court Management: Theories and Practice.* Westport, CT: Quorum Books.

Saks, Michael J., and Jonathan J. Koehler. 2005. "The Coming Paradigm Shift in Forensic Identification Science." *Science* 309: 892–895.

Saks, Michael J., and Mollie Weighner Marti. 1997. "A Meta-analysis of the Effects of Jury Size." *Law and Human Behavior* 21: 451–467.

Saks, Michael. 1996. "The Smaller the Jury, the Greater the Unpredictability." *Judicature* 79: 263–265.

Sanborn, Joseph. 1986. "A Historical Sketch of Plea Bargaining." *Justice Quarterly* 3: 111–138.

Sanborn, Joseph. 1993. "The Right to a Public Jury Trial: A Need for Today's Juvenile Court." *Judicature* 76: 230–238.

Sanborn, Joseph. 1994. "The Juvenile, the Court, or the Community: Whose Best Interests Are Currently Being Promoted in Juvenile Court?" *Justice System Journal* 17: 249–266.

Sarat, Austin, and Conor Clarke. 2008. "Beyond Discretion: Prosecution, the Logic of Sovereignty, and the Limits of Law." *Law and Social Inquiry* 33: 387–416.

Sarat, Austin, and William Felstiner. 1995. *Divorce Lawyers and Their Clients: Power and Meaning in the Legal Process.* New York: Oxford University Press.

Savage, David, and Maura Dolan. 2004. "New Media Struggle to Keep Ground Rules from Changing." *Los Angeles Times*, August 2.

Scalia, John. 2002. "Prisoner Petitions Filed in U.S. District Courts, 2000, with Trends 1980–2000." Washington, DC: Bureau of Justice Statistics.

Scardino, Albert. 1989. "Steinberg Live: Courtroom TV Is a Fixture, Even as New York Is Deciding." *New York Times*, January 22, p. E7.

Scheck, Barry, Peter Neufeld, and Jim Dwyer. 2000. *Actual Innocence: Five Days to Execution and Other Dispatches from the Wrongfully Convicted*. New York: Doubleday.

Scheingold, Stuart, Toska Olson, and Jana Pershing. 1994. "Sexual Violence, Victim Advocacy, and Republican Criminology: Washington State's Community Protection Act." *Law and Society Review* 28: 729–763.

Schelling, Thomas. 1960. *The Strategy of Conflict*. Cambridge, MA: Harvard University Press.

Scherer, Nancy, Brandon Bartels, and Amy Steigerwalt. 2008. "Sounding the Fire Alarm: The Role of Interest Groups in the Lower Federal Court Confirmation Process." *The Journal of Politics* 70: 1026–1039.

Scherer, Nancy. 2005. *Scoring Points: Politicians, Political Activists and the Lower Federal Court Appointment Process*. Stanford, CA: Stanford University Press.

Schlanger, Margo. 2003. "Inmate Litigation." *Harvard Law Review* 116: 1555–1706.

Schlesinger, Traci. 2005. "Racial and Ethnic Disparity in Pretrial Criminal Processing." *Justice Quarterly* 22: 170–192.

Schmidt, Janell, and Lawrence Sherman. 1993. "Does Arrest Deter Domestic Violence?" *American Behavioral Scientist* 36: 601–615.

Schmitt, Ben. 2006. "Embattled Judge, Facing Suspension, Calls It Quits." *Detroit Free Press*, June 1.

Schotland, Roy. 1998. "Comment." *Law and Contemporary Problems* 61: 149–150.

Schulhofer, Stephen. 1984. "Is Plea Bargaining Inevitable?" *Harvard Law Review* 97: 1037–1107.

Schultz, David. 2000. "No Joy in Mudville Tonight: The Impact of 'Three Strike' Laws . . . " *Cornell Journal of Law and Public Policy* 9: 557.

Schwartz, Emma. 2007. "A Debt Hard to Collect: Only 7 Percent of Restitution Orders Get Paid." *U.S. News & World Report*, December 24, 143: 29.

Schwartz, John. 2009. "Pinched Courts Push to Collect Fees and Fines." *New York Times*, April 7.

Schwartz, Victor E., Mark A. Behrens, and Cary Silverman. 2003. *The Jury Patriotism Act: Making Jury Service More Appealing and Rewarding to Citizens*. Washington, DC: American Legislative Exchange Council.

Schwarzer, William, and Russell Wheeler. 1994. *On the Federalization of the Administration of Civil and Criminal Justice*. Washington, DC: Federal Judicial Center.

Scott, K. M. 2006. "Understanding Judicial Hierarchy: Reversals and the Behavior of Intermediate Appellate Judges." *Law and Society Review* 40: 163–191.

Scruggs, Anna, Jean-Claude Mazzola, and Mary Zaug. 1995. "Recent Voting Rights Act Challenges to Judicial Elections." *Judicature* 79: 34–41.

Segal, Jeffrey, and Harold Spaeth. 1989. "Decisional Trends on the Warren and Burger Courts: Results from the Supreme Court Data Base Project." *Judicature* 73: 103–107.

Segal, Jennifer. 2000. "Judicial Decision Making and the Impact of Election Year Rhetoric." *Judicature* 84: 26–33.

Seitz, Matt. 2008. "Brad Renfro, Former Child Movie Actor, Dies at 25." *New York Times*, January 16.

Serrano, Richard. 2006. "With Case Closed, Moussaoui Silenced." *Times-Picayune*, May 5.

Shaffner, Laurie. 2006. *Girls in Trouble with the Law*. Piscataway, NJ: Rutgers University Press.

Sheindlin, Judy. 2001. *You Can't Judge a Book by Its Cover: Cool Rules for School*. New York. Harper Collins.

Shepherd, Robert E., Jr. 2003. "Still Seeking the Promise of Gault: Juveniles and the Right to Counsel." *Criminal Justice* 18: 22–27.

Sherwin, Richard. 2002. *When Law Goes Pop: The Vanishing Line between Law and Popular Culture*. Chicago: University of Chicago Press.

Shiff, Allison, and David Wexler. 1996. "Teen Court: A Therapeutic Jurisprudence Perspective." *Criminal Law Bulletin* 32: 342–365.

Shine, J., and D. Price. 1992. "Prosecutors and Juvenile Justice: New Roles and Perspectives." In *Juvenile Justice and Public Policy: Toward a National Agenda*, edited by Ira Schwartz. New York: Lexington Books.

Shinnar, Shlomo, and Reuel Shinnar. 1975. "The Effects of the Criminal Justice System on the Control of Crime: A Quantitative Approach." *Law and Society Review* 9: 581–611.

Shoham, S. Giora, Ori Beck, and Martin Kett. 2007. *International Handbook of Penology and Criminal Justice*. Boca Raton, FL: CRC Press.

Sickmund, Melissa, T. J. Sladky, and Wei Kang, "Census of Juveniles in Residential Placement Databook." Washington, DC: U.S. Department of

Justice, Office of Juvenile Justice and Delinquency Prevention. Available online at http://www.ojjdp.ncjrs.org/ojstatbb/cjrp (Accessed June 29, 2009.)

Siddiqi, Qudsia. 2004. "CJA's New Release-Recommendation System." *Research Brief Number 5*. New York: New York City Criminal Justice Agency.

Siddiqi, Qudsia. 2005. "Pretrial Re-Arrest among New York City Defendants." *Research Brief Number 8*. New York: New York City Criminal Justice Agency.

Siemaszko, Corky. 2005. "Report: Bryant Settled Civil Suit with Colorado Woman." *New York Daily News*, March 1.

Silbey, Susan. 1981. "Making Sense of the Lower Courts." *Justice System Journal* 6: 13–27.

Silverstein, Lee. 1965. *Defense of the Poor*. Chicago: American Bar Foundation.

Sims, Barbara, Berwood Yost, and Christina Abbott. 2005. "Use and Nonuse of Victim Services Programs: Implications from a Statewide Survey of Crime Victims." *Criminology and Public Policy* 4: 361–384.

Sinclair, J. Walter, Mark A. Behrens, and Cary Silverman. 2003. "Making Jury Duty a Little Friendlier." *Advocate* 46: 23–26.

Singer, Simon. 1993. "The Automatic Waiver of Juveniles and Substantive Justice." *Crime and Delinquency* 39: 253–261.

Sisk, Gregory C., Michael F. Noone, John Montague Steadman, Urban A. Lester. 2006. *Litigation with the Federal Government*. 4th ed. Chicago: ALI-ABA.

Sitomer, Curtis. 1985. "Rural Justice Affects Many, but May Serve Few." *Christian Science Monitor*, May 28, p. 23.

Skogan, Wesley, and Mary Ann Wycoff. 1987. "Some Unexpected Effects of a Police Service for Victims." *Crime and Delinquency* 33: 490–501.

Skolnick, Jerome. 1967. "Social Control in the Adversary System." *Journal of Conflict Resolution* 11: 52–70.

Skolnick, Jerome. 1993. *Justice without Trial*. 3rd ed. New York: Macmillan.

Slobogin, Christopher. 1998. *Criminal Procedure: Regulation of Police Investigation*, Charlottesville, VA: Lexis.

Slocum, R.W. 2009. "The Dilemma of the Vengeful Client: A Prescriptive Framework for Cooling the Flames of Anger." *Marquette Law Review*, 92: 481–549.

Smith, Alisa, and Michael J. Saks. 2008. "The Case for Overturning *Williams v. Florida* and The Six-Person Jury: History, Law, and Empirical Evidence." *Florida Law Review* 60: 441–470.

Smith, Brent, and C. Ronald Huff. 1992. "From Victim to Political Activist: An Empirical Examination of a Statewide Victims' Rights Movement." *Journal of Criminal Justice* 20: 201–215.

Smith, Christopher, and Thomas Hensley. 1993. "Assessing the Conservatism of the Rehnquist Court." *Judicature* 77: 83–89.

Smith, Christopher. 1995. "Federal Habeas Corpus Reform: The State's Perspective." *Justice System Journal* 18: 1–11.

Smith, Douglas. 1986. "The Plea Bargaining Controversy." *Journal of Criminal Law and Criminology* 77: 949–957.

Smith, Nancy, and Julie Garmel. 1992. "Judicial Election and Selection Procedures Challenged under the Voting Rights Act." *Judicature* 76: 154–155.

Smith, S. F. 2008. "The Supreme Court and the Politics of Death." *Virginia Law Review* 94: 283–383.

Smith, Steven, and Carol DeFrances. 1996. *Indigent Defense*. Washington, DC: Bureau of Justice Statistics.

Smitts, Todd. 2004. "Plot Summary for *Boston Legal*." *Internet Movie Database*. Available online at http://www.imdb.com/title/tt0402711/plotsummary

Snell, Tracy. 2008. "Capital Punishment, 2007, Statistical Tables." Washington, DC: U.S. Department of Justice, Bureau of Justice Statistics. Available online at http://www.ojp.usdoj.gov/bjs/pub/html/cp/2007/cp07st.htm (Accessed July 8, 2009.)

Snyder, Elizabeth. 1989. "Toward an Integrative Theory on Courtroom Decision Making: Observations on Bail Setting and Sentencing." Paper presented at the annual meeting of the Midwest Political Science Association, Chicago.

Snyder, Howard, and Melissa Sickmund. 2006. *Juvenile Offenders and Victims: 2006 National Report*. Washington, DC: Office of Juvenile Justice and Delinquency Prevention.

Snyder, Howard. 2000. *Juvenile Arrests, 1999*. Washington, DC: Office of Juvenile Justice and Delinquency Prevention.

Sobel, Russell S., and Joshua C. Hall. 2007. "The Effect of Judicial Selection Processes on Judicial Quality: The Role of Partisan Politics." *Cato Journal* 27: 69–82.

Solberg, Rorie Spill. 2005. "Diversity and George W. Bush's Judicial Appointments: Serving Two Masters." *Judicature* 88: 276–283.

Songer, Donald. 1990. "Criteria for Publication of Opinions in the U.S. Courts of Appeals: Formal Rules versus Empirical Reality." *Judicature* 73: 307–313.

Sorensen, Jon, and Donald Wallace. 1999. "Prosecutorial Discretion in Seeking Death: An Analysis of

Racial Disparity in the Pretrial Stages of Case Processing in a Midwestern County." *Justice Quarterly* 16: 559–578.

Sosin, M. 1978. "*Parens Patriae* and Dispositions in Juvenile Courts." Madison, WI: Institute for Research on Poverty.

Spangenberg Group. 2000. *Contracting for Indigent Defense Services: A Special Report*. Washington, DC: Bureau of Justice Statistics.

Spangenberg, Robert, Richard Wilson, Patricia Smith, and Beverly Lee. 1986. *Containing the Cost of Indigent Defense Programs: Eligibility Screening and Cost Recovery Procedures*. Washington, DC: U.S. Department of Justice, National Institute of Justice.

Spelman, William. 2000. "What Recent Studies Do (and Don't) Tell Us about Imprisonment and Crime. *Crime and Justice* 27: 419–494.

Spelman, William. 2009. "Crime, Cash, and Limited Options: Explaining the Prison Boom." *Criminology and Public Policy* 8: 29–77.

Spiecker Shelley C., and Debra L. Worthington. 2003. "The Influence of Opening Statement/Closing Argument Organizational Strategy on Juror Verdict and Damage Awards." *Law and Human Behavior* 27: 437–456.

Spill, Rorie, and Kathleen Bratton. 2001. "Clinton and Diversification of the Federal Judiciary." *Judicature* 84: 256–261.

Spohn, Cassia C. 2008. *How Do Judges Decide?* Thousand Oaks, CA: Sage.

Spohn, Cassia, and David Holleran. 2000. "The Imprisonment Penalty Paid by Young, Unemployed Black and Hispanic Male Offenders." *Criminology* 38: 281–307.

Spohn, Cassia, and Jeffrey Spears. 1996. "The Effect of Offender and Victim Characteristics on Sexual Assault Case Processing Decisions." *Justice Quarterly* 13: 649–679.

Spohn, Cassia, and Jerry Cederblom. 1991. "Race and Disparities in Sentencing: A Test of the Liberation Hypothesis." *Justice Quarterly* 8: 305–328.

Spohn, Cassia, and Miriam DeLone. 2000. "When Does Race Matter? An Analysis of the Conditions under Which Race Affects Sentence Severity." *Sociology of Crime, Law and Deviance* 2: 3–37.

Spohn, Cassia. 2008. "Editorial Introduction: Coordinated Community Response to Intimate Partner Violence." *Criminology and Public Policy* 7: 489–493.

Spohn, Cassia. 2009. *How Do Judges Decide?* Thousand Oaks, CA: Sage.

Springer, Charles. 1986. *Justice for Juveniles*. Washington, DC: Office of Juvenile Justice and Delinquency Prevention.

Springer, J. Fred. 1983. "Burglary and Robbery Plea Bargaining in California: An Organizational Perspective." *Justice System Journal* 8: 157–185.

Stanko, Elizabeth. 1981. "The Arrest versus the Case." *Urban Life* 9: 295–414.

Stanko, Elizabeth. 1981–1982. "The Impact of Victim Assessment on Prosecutors' Screening Decisions: The Case of the New York County District Attorney's Office." *Law and Society Review* 16: 225–239.

Statistical Briefing Book. 2009. "Juvenile Arrests Rates for All Crimes, 1980-2007." Washington, DC: Office of Juvenile Justice and Delinquency Prevention. Available online at http://ojjdp.ncjrs.gov/ojstatbb/default.asp (Accessed July 3, 2009.)

Steele, Walter, and Elizabeth Thornburg. 1991. "Jury Instructions: A Persistent Failure to Communicate." *Judicature* 74: 249–254.

Steffensmeier, Darrell, and Chris Hebert. 1999. "Women and Men Policymakers: Does the Judge's Gender Affect the Sentencing of Criminal Defendants?" *Social Forces* 77: 1163.

Steffensmeier, Darrell, Jeffrey Ulmer, and John Kramer. 1998. "The Interaction of Race, Gender, and Age in Criminal Sentencing: The Punishment Cost of Being Young, Black, and Male." *Criminology* 36: 763–798.

Steffensmeier, Darrell, John Kramer, and Cathy Streifel. 1993. "Gender and Imprisonment Decisions." *Criminology* 31: 411–446.

Steinberger, Barbara. 1985. "*Alford* Doctrine Popular in State's Courts." *New Haven Register*, June 9.

Steiner, Benjamin. 2009. "The Effects of Juvenile Transfer to Criminal Courts on Incarceration Decisions." *Justice Quarterly* 26: 77–106.

Steketee, Gail, and Anne Austin. 1989. "Rape Victims and the Justice System: Utilization and Impact." *Social Service Review* 63: 285–303.

Stern, Andrew. 2000. "Illinois Governor Halts Executions Pending Review." Reuters, January 23.

Sternlight, Jean R., and Jennifer Robbennolt. 2008. "Good Lawyers Should Be Good Psychologists: Insights for Interviewing and Counseling Clients." *Ohio State Journal on Dispute Resolution* 23: 437–548.

Stidham, Ronald, and Robert Carp. 1997. "Judges' Gender and Federal District Court Decisions." Paper presented at the Southwestern Political Science Association, New Orleans.

Stith, Kate, and Jose Cabranes. 1998. *Fear of Judging: Sentencing Guidelines in the Federal Courts*. Chicago: University of Chicago Press.

Stith, Kate. 2008. "The Arc of the Pendulum: Judges, Prosecutors, and the Exercise of Discretion." *Yale Law Journal* 117: 1420–1496.

Stogel, C. 2002. "Note, *Smith v. Robbins*: Appointed Criminal Appellate Counsel Should Watch for the *Wende* in their Hair." *Southwestern University Law Review* 31: 281–304.

Stott, E. Keith. 1982. "The Judicial Executive: Toward Greater Congruence in an Emerging Profession." *Justice System Journal* 7: 152–179.

Stout, David. 2007. "Crack Sentences Will Get Review." *New York Times*, December 12.

Straus, Sarena. 2006. *Bronx D.A.: True Stories from the Sex Crimes and Domestic Violence Unit*. Fort Lee, NJ: Barricade Books.

Strawn, David, and Raymond Buchanan. 1976. "Jury Confusion: A Threat to Justice." *Judicature* 59: 478–483.

Streb, Matthew J. 2007. *Running for Judge: The Rising Political, Financial, and Legal Stakes of Judicial Elections*. New York: New York University Press.

Streb, Matthew, Brian Frederick, and Casey Lafrance. 2007. "Contestation, Competition, and Potential for Accountability in Intermediate Appellate Court Elections." *Judicature* 91: 71–78.

Studebaker, Christina A., and Steven D. Penrod. 2007. "Pretrial Publicity and Its Influence on Juror Decision Making." In Neil Brewer and Kipling D. Williams. *Psychology and Law: An Empirical Perspective*. New York: The Guildford Press.

Sudnow, David. 1965. "Normal Crimes: Sociological Features of the Penal Codes in a Public Defender Office." *Social Problems* 12: 254–264.

Sullivan, Thomas. 2004. "Police Experiences with Recording Custodial Interrogations." *Judicature* 38: 132–136.

Surette, Ray. 1996. "News from Nowhere, Policy to Follow: Media and the Social Construction of 'Three Strikes and You're Out.'" In *Three Strikes and You're Out: Vengeance as Public Policy*, edited by David Shichor and Dale Sechrest. Thousand Oaks, CA: Sage.

Sweet, R.L., and Robert Dobbins. 2005. "Miles Driven by Rural District Court Judges in Nevada, Fiscal Years 2000-04." Carson City, NV: Supreme Court of Nevada, Administrative Office of the Courts.

Taggart, William. 1989. "Redefining the Power of the Federal Judiciary: The Impact of Court-Ordered Prison Reform on State Expenditures for Corrections." *Law and Society Review* 23: 241–272.

Taleb, Nassim Nicholas. 2007. *The Black Swan: The Impact of the Highly Improbable*. New York, NY: Random House.

Tarr, G. Alan, and Mary Cornelia Porter. 1988. *State Supreme Courts in State and Nation*. New Haven, CT: Yale University Press.

Tarr, G. Alan. 1982. "State Supreme Courts and the U.S. Supreme Court: The Problem of Compliance." In *State Supreme Courts: Policymakers in the Federal System*, edited by Mary Cornelia Porter and G. Alan Tarr. Westport, CT: Greenwood.

Taslitz, Andrew E. 2007. "Bullshitting the People: The Criminal Procedure Implications of a Scatological Term." *Texas Tech Law Review* 39: 1383–1435.

Taylor, Clifford W. 2009. "Merit Selection: Choosing Judges Based on their Politics under the Veil of a Disarming Name." *Harvard Journal of Law and Public Policy* 32: 97–101.

TerBeek, Calvin. 2007. "A Call for Precedential Heads: Why the Supreme Court's Eyewitness Identification Jurisprudence Is Anachronistic and Out-of-Step with the Empirical Reality." *Law and Psychology Review* 31: 21–51.

Thaler, Paul. 1994. *The Watchful Eye: American Justice in the Age of the Television Trial*. Westport, CT: Praeger.

The Office of Justice of the Peace in Texas. 2009. Brazos County, Texas. Available online at http://www.co.brazos.tx.us (Accessed July 23, 2009.)

Thomas, Wayne H., Jr. 1976. *Bail Reform in America*. Berkeley, CA: University of California Press.

Thomas, Wayne. 1970. *The Current State of Bail Reform: Bail Projects*. Davis, CA: Center on the Administration of Justice.

Thompson, Kevin. 1996. "The Nature and Scope of Rural Crime." In *Rural Criminal Justice: Conditions, Constraints, and Challenges*, edited by Thomas McDonald, Robert Wood, and Melissa Pflug, pp. 3–18. Salem, WI: Sheffield.

Thompson, William C. 2006. "Tarnish on the 'Gold Standard': Recent Problems in Forensic DNA Testing." *The Champion* 30: 10–16.

Thomson, Douglas, and Anthony Ragona. 1987. "Popular Moderation versus Governmental Authoritarianism: An Interactionist View of Public Sentiments toward Criminal Sanctions." *Crime and Delinquency* 33: 337–357.

Tiede, Lydia. 2009. "The Impact of the Federal Sentencing Guidelines and Reform: A Comparative Analysis." *Justice System Journal* 30: 34–49.

Tobolowsky, Peggy. 1993. "Restitution in the Federal Criminal Justice System." *Judicature* 77: 90–95.

Toborg, Mary, and John Bellassai. 1986. *Public Danger as a Factor in Pre-Trial Release*. Washington, DC: Toborg Associations, Inc., in cooperation with the National Association of Pre-Trial Service Agencies.

Toborg, Mary. 1983. "Bail Bondsmen and Criminal Courts." *Justice System Journal* 8: 141–156.

Tonry, Michael. H. 1987. *Sentencing Reform Impacts*. Washington, DC: U.S. Government Printing Office.

Tonry, Michael. H. 1993. "The Failure of the U.S. Sentencing Commission's Guidelines." *Crime and Delinquency* 39: 131–149.

Tonry, Michael. H. 2004. "Thinking about Crime: Sense and Sensibility in American Penal Culture." New York: Oxford University Press.

Torbet, Patricia, Patrick Griffin, Hunter Hurst, and Lynn MacKenzie. 2000. *Juveniles Facing Criminal Sanctions: Three States That Changed the Rules.* Washington, DC: U.S. Department of Justice, Office of Juvenile Justice and Delinquency Prevention.

Torres, Sam, and Elizabeth Piper Deschenes. 1997. "Changing the System and Making It Work: The Process of Implementing Drug Courts in Los Angeles County." *Justice System Journal* 19: 267–290.

Toutant, Charles. 2006. "Censure, Transfer in Store for Judge Who Drove Drunk." *New Jersey Law Journal*, July 24.

Tracy, Paul E., Marvin E. Wolfgang, & Robert M. Figlio. 1990. *Delinquency Careers in Two Birth Cohorts.* New York: Plenum.

Travis, Jeremy. 2005. *But They All Come Back: Facing the Challenges of Prisoner Reentry.* Washington, DC: Urban Institute Press.

Turner, Susan, and Judith Greene. 1999. "The FARE Probation Experiment: Implementation and Outcomes of Day Fines for Felony Offenders in Maricopa County." *Justice System Journal* 21: 1–21.

Turner, Susan, Peter W. Greenwood, Terry Fain, and James R. Chiesa. 2006. "An Evaluation of the Federal Government's Violent Offender Incarceration and Truth-in-Sentencing Incentive Grants." *Prison Journal* 86: 364–385.

Tyler, Tom R. 2006. "Viewing *CSI* and the Threshold of Guilt: Managing Truth and Justice in Reality and Fiction." *Yale Law Journal* 115: 1050–1085.

U.S. Census Bureau. 2009. "Census Bureau Estimates Nearly Half of Children Under Age 5 Are Minorities." Washington, DC: Author.

U.S. Department of Agriculture. 2009. "Measuring Rurality: New Definitions in 2003." Available online at http://www.ers.usda.gov/briefing/rurality/NewDefinitions (Accessed July 27, 2009.)

U.S. General Accounting Office. 1990. "Death Penalty Sentencing: Research Indicated a Pattern of Racial Disparities." Gaithersburg, MD: Author. Available online at http://archive.gao.gov/t2pbat11/140845.pdf

U.S. Senate Judiciary Committee. 1993. *The Response to Rape: Detours on the Road to Equal Justice.* Washington, DC: Author.

U.S. Sentencing Commission. 2003. *Federal Sentencing Statistics by State, District and Circuit.* Available online at http://www.ussc.gov/JUDPACK/JP2001.htm

Uchida, Craig, and Timothy Bynum. 1991. "Search Warrants, Motions to Suppress and 'Lost Cases': The Effects of the Exclusionary Rule in Seven Jurisdictions." *Journal of Criminal Law and Criminology* 81: 1034–1066.

Uhlman, Thomas, and Darlene Walker. 1980. "'He Takes Some of My Time: I Take Some of His': An Analysis of Judicial Sentencing Patterns in Jury Cases." *Law and Society Review* 14: 323–342.

Ulmer, Jeffery and Brian D. Johnson. 2004. "Sentencing in Context: A Multilevel Analysis." *Criminology* 42: 137–177.

Ulmer, Jeffrey, and Mindy Bradley. 2006. "Variations in Trial Penalties among Serious Violent Offenses." *Criminology* 44: 631–658.

Ulmer, Jeffrey. 1997. *Social Worlds of Sentencing: Court Communities under Sentencing Guidelines.* Albany: State University of New York Press.

United Press International. 2009. "Crack Sentencing Guidelines in Dispute." *UPI NewsTrack*, January 1.

Unnever, James. 2008. "Two Worlds Far Apart: Black-White Differences in Beliefs about Why African-American Men Are Disproportionately Imprisoned." *Criminology* 46: 511–538.

Uphoff, R. 2006. "Convicting the Innocent: Aberration or Systemic Problem?" *Wisconsin Law Review* 2006: 739–842.

Urbina, Ian. 2008. "Virginia Nears an About-Face on Costly Driver Penalties." *New York Times*, January 25.

Utz, Pamela. 1979. "Two Models of Prosecutorial Professionalism." In *The Prosecutor*, edited by William McDonald. Newbury Park, CA: Sage.

Van Duizend, Richard, L. Paul Sutton, and Charlotte Carter. 1984. *The Search Warrant Process.* Williamsburg, VA: National Center for State Courts.

van Dyke, Jon. 1977. *Jury Selection Procedures: Our Uncertain Commitment to Representative Panels.* Cambridge, MA: Ballinger.

Van Ness, Daniel, and Karen Heetderks Strong. 2006. *Restoring Justice.* 3rd ed. Cincinnati: Anderson.

Vaughn, Michael G., and Matt DeLisi. 2008. "Were Wolfgang's Chronic Offenders Psychopaths? On the Convergent Validity between Psychopathy and Career Criminality." *Journal of Criminal Justice* 36: 33–42.

Vaughn, Michael. 1996. "Prison Civil Liability for Inmate-against-Inmate Assault and Breakdown/Disorganization Theory." *Journal of Criminal Justice* 24: 139–152.

Vera Institute of Justice. 1977. *Felony Arrests: Their Prosecution and Disposition in New York City's Courts.* New York: Author.

Vera Institute of Justice. 1981. *Felony Arrests: Their Prosecution and Disposition in New York City's Courts*. Rev. ed. New York: Longman.

Vermont Center for Justice Research. 1995. "DUI Adjudication and BAC Level: An Assessment." *Data-Line: The Justice Research Bulletin* 4 (May).

Viano, Emilio. 1987. "Victim's Rights and the Constitution: Reflections on a Bicentennial." *Crime and Delinquency* 33: 438–451.

Vincent, Barbara, and Paul Hofer. 1994. *The Consequences of Mandatory Minimum Prison Terms: A Summary of Recent Findings*. Washington, DC: Federal Judicial Center.

Visher, Christy, Adele Harrell, Lisa Newmark, and Jennifer Yahner. 2008. "Reducing Intimate Partner Violence: An Evaluation of a Comprehensive Justice System-Community Collaboration." *Criminology and Public Policy* 7: 495–524.

Visher, Christy. 1987. "Incapacitation and Crime Control: Does a 'Lock 'Em Up' Strategy Reduce Crime?" *Justice Quarterly* 4: 513–544.

Visher, Christy. 1992. *Pretrial Drug Testing*. Washington, DC: U.S. Department of Justice, National Institute of Justice.

von Hirsch, Andrew. 1986. *Doing Justice*. 2nd ed. New York: Hill and Wang.

Voss, Jansen. 2005. "The Science of Persuasion: An Exploration of Advocacy and the Science Behind the art of Persuasion in the Courtroom." *Law and Psychology Review* 29: 301–327.

Wald, Matthew. 2006. "A New Strategy to Discourage Driving Drunk." *New York Times*, November 19.

Waldron, Jeremy. 2008. "Lucky in Your Judge." *Theoretical Inquiries in Law* 9: 185–216.

Walker, Samuel, Cassia Spohn, and Miriam DeLone. 2007. *The Color of Justice: Race, Ethnicity, and Crime in America*. 4th ed. Belmont, CA: Wadsworth.

Walker, Samuel. 1989. *Sense and Nonsense about Crime: A Policy Guide*. 2nd ed. Pacific Grove, CA: Brooks/Cole.

Walker, Samuel. 2006. *Sense and Nonsense about Crime and Drugs: A Policy Guide*. 6th ed. Belmont, CA: Wadsworth.

Waller, Mark. 2008. "Officials Say Jefferson's Traffic Cameras Increase Safety, but Critics Say the Red-Light System Is All about Seeing Green." *Times-Picayune*, December 10.

Wallman, Joel. 2005. "Unpacking Recidivism." *Criminology and Public Policy* 4: 479–484.

Walsh, Anthony. 1985. "The Role of the Probation Officer in the Sentencing Process." *Criminal Justice and Behavior* 12: 289–303.

Ward, Stephanie Francis. 2009 (August). "The 25 Greatest Legal TV Shows." *ABA Journal* 95: 34–44.

Warden, Alissa Pollitz. 2008. "Courts and Communities: Toward a Theoretical Synthesis." In *Criminal Justice Theory*, edited by David Duffee and Edward R. Maguire, New York: Routledge.

Wardlaw, Jack. 1997. "Foster Backs Police Changes." *Times-Picayune*, May 2.

Warren, Roger K. 2009. "Evidence-Based Sentencing: The Application of Principles of Evidence-Based Practice to State Sentencing Practice and Policy." *University of San Francisco Law Review* 43: 585–634.

Wasby, Stephen. 1982. "The Functions and Importance of Appellate Oral Argument: Some Views of Lawyers and Federal Judges." *Judicature* 65: 340–353.

Wasby, Stephen. 1993. *The Supreme Court in the Federal Judicial System*. 4th ed. Chicago: Nelson-Hall.

Washburn, K. K. 2008. "Restoring the Grand Jury." *Fordham Law Review* 76: 2333–2388.

Watkins, Matthew. 2009. "Screening Stirs Community." (March 17). Available online at http://www.theeagle.com/local/Screening-stirs-community

Watson, Richard, and Ronald Downing. 1969. *The Politics of the Bench and Bar: Judicial Selection under the Missouri Nonpartisan Court Plan*. New York: Wiley.

Webster, Barbara. 1988. *Victim Assistance Programs Report Increased Workloads*. Washington, DC: National Institute of Justice.

Webster, Cheryl, Anthony Doob, and Franklin Zimring. 2006. "Proposition 8 and Crime Rates in California: The Case of the Disappearing Deterrent." *Criminology and Public Policy* 5: 417–448.

Weed, Frank. 1995. *Certainty of Justice: Reform in the Crime Victim Movement*. New York: Aldine de Gruyter.

Weisheit, Ralph, and Sue Mahan. 1988. *Women, Crime and Criminal Justice*. Cincinnati: Anderson.

Weisheit, Ralph, David Falcone, and L. Edward Wells. 2006. *Crime and Policing in Rural and Small-Town America*. Long Grove, IL: Waveland Press.

Weisheit, Ralph, Edward Wells, and David Falcone. 1995. *Crime and Policing in Rural and Small-Town America: An Overview of the Issues*. Washington, DC: National Institute of Justice.

Weiss, Michael. 2005. *Public Defenders: Pragmatic and Political Motivations to Represent the Indigent*. New York: LFB Scholarly Publishing.

Weiss, Robert, Richard Berk, and Catherine Lee. 1996. "Assessing the Capriciousness of Death Penalty Charging." *Law and Society Review* 30: 607–638.

Welch, Susan, and Cassia Spohn. 1986. "Evaluating the Impact of Prior Record on Judges' Sentencing Decisions: A Seven-City Comparison." *Justice Quarterly* 3: 389–408.

Welch, Susan, Cassia Spohn, and John Gruhl. 1985. "Convicting and Sentencing Differences among Black, Hispanic and White Males in Six Localities." *Justice Quarterly* 2: 67–80.

West, Heather, and William Sabol. 2008. *Prisoners in 2007*. Washington, DC: U.S. Department of Justice, Bureau of Justice Statistics.

Wexler, David B., and Bruce J. Winick, eds. 1996. *Law in a Therapeutic Key: Developments in Therapeutic Jurisprudence*. Durham, NC: Carolina Academic Press.

Wheelock, Darren. 2005. "Collateral Consequences and Racial Inequality: Felon Status Restrictions as a System of Disadvantage." *Journal of Contemporary Criminal Justice* 21: 82–90.

White, John Valery. 2008. "A Time for Change." *Nevada Lawyer* 16: 38.

Wice, Paul. 1974. *Freedom for Sale*. Lexington, MA: D. C. Heath.

Wice, Paul. 1978. *Criminal Lawyers: An Endangered Species*. Newbury Park, CA: Sage.

Wice, Paul. 1985. *Chaos in the Courthouse: The Inner Workings of the Urban Criminal Courts*. New York: Praeger.

Wice, Paul. 1991. *Judges and Lawyers: The Human Side of Justice*. New York: HarperCollins.

Wice, Paul. 2005. *Public Defenders and the American Justice System*. Westport, CT: Praeger

Wicker, Tom. 1991. "Dee Brown and You." *New York Times*, May 15, p. A15.

Wilkey, Malcolm. 1978. "The Exclusionary Rule: Why Suppress Valid Evidence?" *Judicature* 62: 214–232.

Williams, Frank V. 2007. "Reinventing the Courts: The Frontiers of Judicial Activism in the State Courts." *Campbell Law Review* 29: 591–735.

Williams, Jimmy. 1995. "Type of Counsel and the Outcome of Criminal Appeals: A Research Note." *American Journal of Criminal Justice* 19: 275–285.

Williams, Marian, Stephen Demuth, and Jefferson Holcomb. 2007. "Understanding the Influence of Victim Gender in Death Penalty Cases: The Importance of Victim Race, Sex-Related Victimization, and Jury Decision Making." *Criminology* 45: 865–891.

Willing, Richard. 2003. "Judges Go Softer on Sentences More Often." *USA Today*, August 28, p. 1.

Wilmot, Keith Alan, and Cassia Spohn. 2004. "Prosecutorial Discretion and Real-Offense Sentencing: An Analysis of Relevant Conduct under the Federal Sentencing Guidelines." *Criminal Justice Policy Review* 15: 324–343.

Wilson, James Q. 1973. "If Every Criminal Knew He Would Be Punished if Caught." *New York Times Magazine*, January 28.

Wilson, James Q. 1983. *Thinking about Crime: A Policy Guide*. 2nd ed. New York: Basic Books.

Wilson, James Q., and George Kelling. 1982. "Broken Windows." Atlantic Monthly, March: 29–38.

Wilson, James. 2005. "Bad Behavior or Bad Policy? An Examination of Tennessee Release Cohorts, 1993–2001." *Criminology and Public Policy* 4: 485–518.

Wiseman, Jacqueline. 1970. *Stations of the Lost: The Treatment of Skid Row Alcoholics*. Englewood Cliffs, NJ: Prentice Hall.

Wiseman, Jacqueline. 1976. "Drunk Court: The Adult Parallel to Juvenile Court." In *The Criminal Justice Process: A Reader*, edited by William Sanders and Howard Daudistel, pp. 233–252. New York: Praeger.

Wiseman, Samuel. 2009. "Discrimination, Coercion, and the Bail Reform Act of 1984: The Loss of the Core Constitutional Protections of the Excessive Bail Clause." *Fordham Urban Law Journal* 36: 121.

Wold, John, and Greg Caldeira. 1980. "Perceptions of 'Routine' Decision-Making in Five California Courts of Appeal." *Polity* 13: 334–347.

Wold, John. 1978. "Going through the Motions: The Monotony of Appellate Court Decisionmaking." *Judicature* 62: 58–65.

Wolfgang, Marvin E., Robert M. Figlio, and Thorsten Sellin. 1972. *Delinquency in a Birth Cohort*. Chicago: University of Chicago Press.

Wolfgang, Marvin, and Marc Riedel. 1973. "Race, Judicial Discretion, and the Death Penalty." *Annals of the American Academy of Political and Social Science* 407: 119–133.

Wolfram, Charles. 1986. *Modern Legal Ethics*. St. Paul, MN: Thomson/West.

Worden, Alissa Pollitz, and Robert Worden. 1989. "Local Politics and the Provision of Indigent Defense Counsel." *Law and Policy* 11: 401–424.

Worden, Alissa Pollitz. 1990. "Policymaking by Prosecutors: The Uses of Discretion in Regulating Plea Bargaining." *Judicature* 73: 335–340.

Worden, Alissa Pollitz. 1991. "Privatizing Due Process: Issues in the Comparison of Assigned Counsel, Public Defender, and Contracted Indigent Defense Systems." *Justice System Journal* 14: 390–418.

Worden, Alissa Pollitz. 1993. "Counsel for the Poor: An Evaluation of Contracting for Indigent Criminal Defense." *Justice Quarterly* 10: 613–637.

Worrall, John L., Jay W. Ross, and Eric S. McCord. 2006. "Modeling Prosecutors' Charging Decisions in Domestic Violence Cases." *Crime & Delinquency* 52: 472–503.

Worrall, John, and M. Elaine Nugent-Borakove (eds.). 2008. *The Changing Role of the American Prosecutor*. Albany, NY: SUNY Press.

Worrall, John, and Tomislav Kovandzic. 2008. "Is Policing for Profit? Answers from Asset Forfeiture." *Criminology and Public Policy* 2: 219–244.

Wright, Ronald, and Marc Miller. 2002. "The Screening/ Bargaining Tradeoff." *Stanford Law Review* 55: 29–118.

Young, Malcolm. 2000. "Providing Effective Representation for Youth Prosecuted as Adults." Washington, DC: U.S. Department of Justice, Bureau of Justice Assistance Bulletin.

Zahn, Margaret, Stephanie Hawkins, Janet Chiancone, and Ariel Whitworth. 2008. *The Girls Study Group—Charting the Way to Delinquency Prevention for Girls*. Washington, DC: Office of Justice Programs, U.S. Department of Justice.

Zalman, M. 2006. "Criminal Justice System Reform and Wrongful Conviction: A Research Agenda." *Criminal Justice Policy Review* 17(4): 468–492.

Zalman, M., B. Smith, and A. Kiger. 2008. "Officials' Estimates of the Incidence of 'Actual Innocence' Convictions." *Justice Quarterly* 25(1): 72–100.

Zalman, Marvin, and Larry Siegel. 1997. *Criminal Procedure: Constitution and Society*. 2nd ed. Belmont, CA: Wadsworth.

Zatz, Marjorie. 1984. "Race, Ethnicity, and Determinate Sentencing: A New Dimension to an Old Controversy." *Criminology* 22: 147–171.

Zehner, Sharon. 1997. *Teen Court*. Available online at http://www.fbi.gov/leb/mar971.htm

Zeisel, Hans. 1979. "Bail Revisited." *American Bar Foundation Research Journal* 769–789.

Zeisel, Hans. 1982. "The Verdict of Five Out of Six Civil Jurors: Constitutional Problems." *American Bar Foundation Research Journal* 141–156.

Zimring, Franklin, Sheila O'Malley, and Joel Eigen. 1976. "Punishing Homicide in Philadelphia: Perspectives on the Death Penalty." *University of Chicago Law Review* 43: 227–252.

Zubeck, Pam. 2009. "El Paso County Reaps Bonanza in Traffic Fines." *Gazette*, July 20.

CASE INDEX

Italic page numbers indicate material in exhibits, figures, or tables

INDEX

Italic page numbers indicate material in exhibits, figures, or tables